ESTATE PLANNING

Eighth Edition

VOLUME I

A. James Casner
Late Austin Wakeman Scott Professor of Law, Emeritus
Harvard Law School

and

Jeffrey N. Pennell
Richard H. Clark Professor of Law
Emory University School of Law

.CCH
a Wolters Kluwer business

Editorial Staff

Editor . . . . Barbara L. Post, J.D.

Production . . . . Lou Dagostino, Jennifer Schencker

© 2012, 2011, 2009, 2007, 2006, 2005, 2004, 2003, 2002, 2001, 2000, 1999, 1995 by Jeffrey N. Pennell

ISBN: 978-0-8080-3031-7 (Set)
ISBN: 978-0-8080-3458-2 (Volume 1)
ISBN: 978-0-8080-3459-9 (Volume 2)
ISBN: 978-0-8080-3460-5 (Volume 3)

CCH
4025 W. Peterson Ave.
Chicago, IL 60646-6085
800 248 3248
CCHGroup.com

Printed in the United States of America

FSC
MIX
FSC® C103993

Summary of Contents

Volume 1

Contents
Preface
Abbreviations

Volume 2

Contents
Abbreviations

□

Contents

VOLUME 1

CHAPTER 1 Introduction

CHAPTER 2 Intestacy: Estate Plans by Operation of State Law

CHAPTER 3 Wills as Estate Planning Instruments

CHAPTER 4 Trusts as Estate Planning Instruments

CHAPTER 5 Income Taxation of Trusts, Estates, Grantors, and Beneficiaries

VOLUME 2

CHAPTER 8 Nonprobate Transfers: Life Insurance

CHAPTER 9 Nonprobate Transfers: Retirement Benefits

CHAPTER 10 Concurrent Interests

CHAPTER 11 Future Interests

Preface

Major demographic changes continue to affect estate planning and estate planners alike. One that is well known is the general aging of the population and, with it, a shift in focus from the last predominant generation of clients seeking estate planning—the G.I. generation—to their children in the baby boom generation. Especially as they inherit, approach retirement, and face their own mortality, Baby Boomers have become the largest cohort of estate planning consumers ever. And because their experiences, objectives, and perspectives differ from their parents, estate planners face new challenges as they reconsider whether traditional planning approaches are a proper fit for a different generation of clients.

Meanwhile, the cadre of experienced professionals who provide estate planning services is aging. Indeed, it is shrinking as Baby Boomer estate planners retire. Coupled with Congress' perpetual dance around issues that affect the sliver of the population that needs tax-driven estate planning, the profession is in a period of its own change and uncertainty.

The core of this treatise continues to reflect both substantive law changes and these sorts of demographic developments. It remains the encyclopedic exegesis of the law relating to estate planning that was begun by Professor Casner over 60 years ago and continues to encompass income and wealth transfer taxation and the laws of property, future interests, wills, and trusts.

Notwithstanding all this change, the fascinating reality is that the following few paragraphs from the Preface to the First Edition, written by Professor Casner in 1953, continue to remain true today:

> Estate planning has been a function of lawyers for centuries. Even under the feudal system in England, there were distinct advantages to be gained by careful advance planning for the devolution of a person's estate . . . . The nature and scope of these advantages have changed from time to time through the years, but . . . proper estate planning has always made a contribution to the financial welfare of a person's family and to the preservation of the family wealth.

> Estate planning is an inherently complex task because of the technicalities of the applicable law, the foresight required to provide for appropriate disposition of property under varying circumstances, and the extreme difficulty of drafting property arrangements so that the language employed carries the same connotations for all persons. The successful completion of this task . . . requires a background of study which enables the lawyer to visualize all the considerations which may be relevant. This book is designed to present for critical examination all these considerations and thereby to develop the framework within which the lawyer's process of thinking must operate . . . .

> An examination of the Table of Contents will reveal that this volume is designed to present for consecutive study and consideration the various types of arrangements with respect to the disposition of wealth which may be employed in an estate plan. The material included for discussion in each chapter has been selected because of its relevance in determining the circumstances under which the particular property arrangement should be used. Tax materials predominate when the choice is influenced largely by tax consequences, but this is by no means a book concerned solely with tax planning.

> Some of the material in the book is relevant only when substantial estates are involved. Most of it, however, deals with problems which may and do arise with respect to small

estates as well as large ones. In my opinion, estate planning should not be sharply divided into planning for small estates and planning for large estates. I believe, rather, that one who has a thorough comprehension of the problems involved in handling a very complicated estate will be best qualified to deal with the less complicated ones, for he or she will be in a position to select from his or her background of knowledge what is most suitable for the particular situation.

As the father of modern estate planning, Professor Casner's mature and now time-honored contributions had a major impact on the field of estate planning even as we know it today. His first edition drew traditional probate lawyers into an estate planning world in which tax laws have a major impact. Over time, however, he realized that some estate plans were focused so much on tax elements that the nontax and human issues sometimes were overlooked. And so, as is true about many important lessons that come to us later in life, Professor Casner also observed in the last edition that he wrote that our work "significantly influence[s] the lives of the beneficiaries. This human factor . . . is too frequently overlooked or given a subordinate position . . . . [A] plan that produces maximum tax avoidance is justified only if it also is a plan that is appropriate for the human beings who will be affected by it."

The property law origins of many estate planning techniques have returned to the fore as the wealth transfer tax laws wane in significance for a large percentage of the decedent population. This revision continues Professor Casner's emphasis on a proper balance between tax and nontax components of plans that most clients crave, ones that are reliable, understandable, and sensitive to family needs and personalities, rather than just fancy, convoluted, or gimmicky.

True to Professor Casner's tradition, the presumption throughout this work is that most clients are not interested in planning that shows only how brilliant the planner can be or that focuses principally on playing keep-away from the government, while ignoring the effect on the client's beneficiaries. It also reflects a prejudice against planning techniques that have a relative half-life that resembles bread or milk rather than diamonds or gold. Concepts and techniques that do not pass a smell test are not represented, notwithstanding that they may not yet have been invalidated by specific case law or legislation.

This revision remains conservative, it relies on time-tested techniques or those that are most likely to be, and it reflects an attitude that comes to most estate planners that the acquired ability to manipulate the tax laws is not the most important skill involved or sought in successful estate planning.

Jeffrey N. Pennell

Abbreviations

AOD	Action on Decision
AFR	Applicable federal rate
AMT	Alternative minimum tax
CCA	Chief Counsel advisory
CLAT	Charitable lead annuity trust
CLT	Charitable lead trust
CLUT	Charitable lead unitrust
CRAT	Charitable remainder annuity trust
CRT	Charitable remainder trust
CRUT	Charitable remainder unitrust
D	The first spouse to die
DNI	Distributable net income
DRD	Deductions in respect of a decedent
Ed/Med	Education and medical expense exclusion
ERISA	Employee retirement income security act
ESBT	Electing small business trust
ESOP	Employee stock option plan
ETIP	Estate tax inclusion period
FET	Federal estate tax
FIFO	First in, first out
FLP	Family limited partnership
FMV	Fair market value
FSA	Field service advice
GRAT	Grantor retained annuity trust
GRIT	Grantor retained income (or interest) trust
GRUT	Grantor retained unitrust
GST	Generation-skipping transfer tax
HEMS	Health, education, maintenance, and support
IDGT	Intentionally defective grantor trust
ILIT	Irrevocable life insurance trust
ILM	Internal Revenue Service legal memorandum
IRA	Individual retirement account
IRD	Income in respect of a decedent
ISO	Incentive stock option
LIFO	Last in, first out
LLC	Limited liability company

NICRUT	Net income charitable remainder unitrust
NIMCRUT	Net income with make-up charitable remainder unitrust
PLR	Private letter ruling
POD	Payable on death
QDOT	Qualified domestic trust
QFOBI	Qualified family owned business interest
QPRT	Qualified personal residence trust
QSST	Qualified subchapter S trust
QTIP	Qualified terminable interest property
RMD	Required minimum
S	The surviving spouse
SCIN	Self-cancelling installment note
SEP	Simplified employee pension
SNT	Special (or supplemental) needs trust
TAM	Technical advice memorandum
TOD	Transfer on death
UGMA	Uniform gifts to minors act
UNI	Undistributed net income
UPC	Uniform probate code
USDA	Uniform simultaneous death act
USRAP	Uniform statutory rule against perpetuities
UTC	Uniform trust code
UTMA	Uniform transfers to minors act
WIFO	Worst in, first out

This modern result favors a disappointed beneficiary's tort or contract[17] action to redress an attorney's estate planning mistakes and today the privity defense is a distinct and declining minority rule in the estate planning context.[18] Among the factors noted, the two common sticking points in proving a malpractice case are whether it is certain that the plaintiff suffered an injury and whether imposition of liability imposes an undue burden on the attorney.

To illustrate, consider an allegation that the decedent intended to benefit the plaintiff in an amount greater than the will bequeaths. Typically the issue is (1) whether the plaintiff may introduce extrinsic evidence of the decedent's alleged intent and (2) whether the burden on the drafting attorney to disprove this alleged intent to avoid liability many years after the estate planning representation ended is too great. Some cases (such as mistakes in execution or the proper application of state law relating to the rights of a pretermitted heir) present much easier facts to address in this connection than others.[19] On the other

---

[17] The contract law third party beneficiary theory for recovery is derived from the entitlement of a third party to enforce a contract that was intended to deliver a material benefit to that person. See Restatement (Second) of Contracts § 304 (1981); Corbin, Contracts § § 44.1-44.8 (2007). If the parties to a contract (attorney and client in the estate planning context) intended to bestow a benefit on a third party (the beneficiary), the promise between them supports a duty to the intended third party beneficiary that permits a claim for recovery by that intended beneficiary. The primary purpose of a testator is to benefit the individuals named in the will. That intent can be effected only by giving the intended beneficiaries a cause of action in the event of the attorney's failure to perform properly under the legal services contract. The attorney normally is not exposed to extensive liability that would militate against application of this theory because the class of intended beneficiaries who become potential plaintiffs is reasonably limited under the terms of most estate plans.

[18] Cases that follow the modern trend in estate planning situations can be found in several dozen states; many are collected in Blair v. Ing, 21 P.3d 452 (Haw. 2001); Annot., What constitutes negligence sufficient to render attorney liable to person other than immediate client, 61 A.L.R.4th 464 (1988), Feinschreiber & Kent, Estate Tax Malpractice, 84 Tax Notes 909 (1999), and Note, Legal Malpractice for the Negligent Drafting of a Testamentary Instrument: Schreiner v. Scoville, 73 Iowa L. Rev. 1231 (1988).

[19] See, e.g., Guy v. Liederbach, 459 A.2d 744 (Pa. 1983) (plaintiff, as a named beneficiary and the designated personal representative, was directed by the defendant attorney to sign the will as a witness, which invalidated both the

hand, a case alleging that an attorney failed to follow a testator's instructions about inclusion or the amount of a bequest would pose a far more difficult situation.[20]

(Footnote Continued)

bequest and the appointment); Heyer v. Flaig, 449 P.2d 161 (Cal. 1969) (will that intended to benefit testator's two children negligently failed to preclude testator's post-execution spouse from claiming a statutory share); Stowe v. Smith, 441 A.2d 81 (Conn. 1981) (alleging that the decedent intended to provide for distribution of a trust to the plaintiff when the plaintiff reached the age of 50 and distribution to the plaintiff's descendants only if the plaintiff died prior thereto; the will called for distribution to those descendants on the earlier to occur of plaintiff's death or reaching the age of 50); Licata v. Spector, 225 A.2d 28 (Conn. 1966) (failure to procure the proper number of witnesses to the will); Teasdale v. Allen, 520 A.2d 295 (D.C. 1987) (attorney failed to coordinate D's desire that S (a fourth spouse) receive D's property if S survived but that grandchildren by another marriage receive the property if S did not or if they died in a common disaster; S died 62 days after D); Needham v. Hamilton, 459 A.2d 1060 (D.C. 1983) (omission of residuary clause from will that attorney redrafted to insert an additional bequest); McAbee v. Edwards, 340 So. 2d 1167 (Fla. Dist. Ct. App. 1976) (attorney failed to advise client that remarriage would require revisions to the will to preclude claims by a post-execution spouse); Walker v. Lawson, 514 N.E.2d 629 (Ind. Ct. App. 1987) (failure to consider or advise testator regarding S's statutory forced heir rights); Auric v. Continental Casualty Co., 331 N.W.2d 325 (Wis. 1983) (attorney restated decedent's will and in the process failed to have the new will properly executed).

[20] See, e.g., Ventura County Humane Society for the Prevention of Cruelty to Children and Animals v. Holloway, 115 Cal. Rptr. 464 (Cal. Dist. Ct. App. 1974) (bequest to "Society for the Prevention of Cruelty to Animals (Local or National)"; suit was rejected because there was no indication on the face of the will that the plaintiff was a "clearly designated" beneficiary); De Maris v. Asti, 426 So. 2d 1153 (Fla. Dist. Ct. App. 1983) (unusual case allowing a disappointed beneficiary to produce extrinsic evidence of the testator's alleged intent); Ogle v. Fuiten, 466 N.E.2d 224 (Ill. 1984) (although decedents' wills were clear, the plaintiffs were allowed to prove that the wills failed to effectuate the clear intent of the testators); Succession of Killingsworth, 292 So. 2d 536 (La. 1973) (invalid will allowed as better evidence of the testator's intent than hearsay evidence regarding oral expressions of intent, the court noting that inability to use evidence of a failed disposition might in many cases preclude holding a negligent attorney liable); Kirgan v. Parks, 478 A.2d 713 (Md. Ct. Spec. App. 1984) (decedent's will left plaintiff all "tangible personal property" (worth approximately $7,000) rather than the decedent's entire personal fortune, as the plaintiff expected; recognizing the trend to defeat privity as a defense, the court nevertheless held for the defendant attorney because there was no indication from the face of the will that the decedent intended other than what the plaintiff received).

§1.0

With respect to burdens, one of the most difficult questions to arise involves a firm with several advisors who do different work for the same client and whether the advisor who does the latest work may be chargeable with knowledge of the effect it may have on work previously done by another advisor in the firm.[21]

Perhaps the most daunting aspect of malpractice exposure for estate planners is that the statute of limitation may not *begin* to run until the plaintiff should have discovered the error, which in many cases is not until the estate planning client died.[22] In a few jurisdictions the statute of

---

[21] See, e.g., Stanland v. Brock, 747 P.2d 464 (Wash. 1987) (one attorney in a law firm drew a will that gave the testator's "real property" to specified beneficiaries, another attorney in that firm later drew a contract of sale of the testator's principal realty, and a controlling state law regarded the vendor's interest under that contract as personal property rather than real property, which raised problems regarding the beneficiaries' rights to "real property" under the will, so a settlement was reached between those beneficiaries; the intended beneficiaries of the realty then sued the attorneys for not anticipating this problem in drawing the will and for not informing the client that the realty contract would affect the will provision, which the court dismissed, holding that the attorney who drew the will could not reasonably anticipate that the realty would be sold—quaere that conclusion, that the attorney who drew the contract did not have knowledge of the client's will, and that it would be unreasonable to impute such knowledge to either). Cf. Simon v. Zipperstein, 512 N.E.2d 636 (Ohio 1987) (attorney prepared a prenuptial agreement that limited S to a specific amount, then drew a will for the client under which S received one-third of the estate; when S collected both under the prenuptial agreement and the will the client's child alleged negligence in failing to provide in the will for a setoff of what S received under the prenuptial agreement—unsuccessfully because of the Ohio privity defense). A related question answered in the negative in Leak-Gilbert v. Fahle, 55 P.3d 1054 (Okla. 2002) (attorney did not ascertain that client had other heirs that the client did not reveal and that the attorney therefore could not know to disinherit), was whether an attorney must confirm information given by the client or conduct an independent investigation to verify the validity and accuracy of that information, saying that it would impose an unnecessary and inappropriate burden on the attorney and subsequently increase fees borne by the client; the attorney also was not charged with knowledge of information in files stored in the attorney's possession, dating from when the attorney's sibling represented the same client and the client's predeceased spouse, because the attorney and the sibling never practiced law together.

[22] See, e.g., Heyer v. Flaig, 449 P.2d 161 (Cal. 1969) (the continuing nature of the attorney's malpractice and the fact that, until the testator's death, there were no beneficiaries who could allege a loss served to prevent the running of the

limitation is said to begin running when the attorney ceases to represent the client. In estate planning, this typically produces the same result because the representation normally ends only when the client dies.[23] And, contrary to the common assertion that some issues are not worth worrying about because, if they arise, it will be long after the *attorney* has died, it has been held that a claim for malpractice may survive the attorney's death.[24]

Finally, it bears noting that ethics and malpractice are not the same, and that theoretically a violation of the ethics rules is not tantamount to malpractice. Model Rules of Professional Conduct Scope Comment [20] states:

> Violation of a Rule should not give rise to a cause of action nor should it create any presumption in such a case that a legal duty has been breached. . . . The Rules are designed to provide guidance to lawyers and to provide a structure for regulating

---

(Footnote Continued)

statute of limitation before the testator's death); Millwright v. Romer, 322 N.W.2d 30, 32 A.L.R.4th 251 (Iowa 1982) (will drafted in 1944, client died in 1945, perpetuities violation determined in 1978, and suit brought in 1980; statute deemed to begin running in 1945 when the court assumed that the perpetuities violation could have been determined); Jaramillo v. Hood, 601 P.2d 66 (N.M. 1979) (statute of limitation barred suit because will was denied probate over six years after testator's death and malpractice action was brought almost three years after that denial); Auric v. Continental Casualty Co., 331 N.W.2d 325 (Wis. 1983) (will executed in 1973 and death in 1975; under six year statute of limitation the plaintiff's 1981 action was timely); and Annot., When statute of limitations begins to run on action against attorney for malpractice based upon negligence—view that statute begins to run from time client discovers, or should have discovered, negligent act or omission—application of rule to property, estate, corporate, and document cases, 15 A.L.R.6th 427 (2006).

[23] See, e.g., Newsom v. Boothe, 524 So. 2d 923 (La. Ct. App. 1988); Greene v. Greene, 436 N.E.2d 496 (N.Y. 1982); Keaton Co. v. Kolby, 271 N.E.2d 772 (Ohio 1971). In Hale v. Groce, 730 P.2d 576 (Or. Ct. App. 1986), the court held that the defendant attorney's participation in a reformation proceeding to correct the attorney's drafting error served as an estoppel to a statute of limitation defense to a subsequent malpractice case. See generally Adams & Abendroth, Malpractice Climate Heats Up for Estate Planners, 126 Trusts & Estates 41 (Apr. 1987); Avery, Is It Safe to Be an Estate Planner?, 16 Law Off. Econ. & Mgmt. 240 (1975); Gates, Lawyers' Malpractice: Some Recent Data About a Growing Problem, 37 Mercer L. Rev. 59 (1986).

[24] See McStowe v. Borenstein, 388 N.E.2d 674 (Mass. 1979).

§1.0

conduct through disciplinary agencies. They are not designed to be a basis for civil liability. Furthermore, the purpose of the Rules can be subverted when they are invoked by opposing parties as procedural weapons. The fact that a Rule is a just basis for a lawyer's self-assessment, or for sanctioning a lawyer under the administration of a disciplinary authority, does not imply that an antagonist in a collateral proceeding or transaction has standing to seek enforcement of the Rule . . . .[25]

Nevertheless, the same activity that constitutes an ethics violation also may constitute malpractice and there are cases that support attorney liability on the basis of an ethics violation.[26]

§ 1.1 WEALTH TRANSFER TAXES GENERALLY

The Internal Revenue Code imposes a wealth transfer tax on the gratuitous disposition of property located anywhere by United States citizens or residents and on the United States situs property of nonresi-

---

[25] 2008 Am. Bar Ass'n Model Rules of Professional Conduct; see also Restatement (Third) of the Law Governing Lawyers § 52(2)(a) (2000), stating that an ethics violation does not create a cause of action but may be considered on the question of lack of proper care.

[26] Thomason, How estate planners can cope with the increasing risk of malpractice claims, 12 Est. Plan. 130 (1985), states that "[c]ourts frequently cite and rely on [the ethics rules] to determine whether an attorney's conduct meets an acceptable standard of care in civil damage actions." (Citing no cases.) More accurate is the assessment that most courts have declined to hold that an ethics violation establishes civil liability. See Dahlquist, The Code of Professional Responsibility and Civil Damage Actions Against Attorneys, 9 Ohio N.U. L. Rev. 1 (1983). Nevertheless, several cases have stated that the ethics rules may define or provide evidence of the proper standard of conduct required of attorneys. See, e.g., Woodruff v. Tomlin, 616 F.2d 924 (6th Cir. 1979) (although the Code of Professional Responsibility did not define standards for civil liability, it constituted "some evidence" of the requisite standards imposed on attorneys); Beattie v. Firnschild, 394 N.W.2d 107 (Mich. Ct. App. 1986) (an ethics violation is "rebuttable evidence of malpractice"); Lipton v. Boesky, 313 N.W.2d 163 (Mich. Ct. App. 1981) (same); Sullivan v. Birmingham, 416 N.E.2d 528 (Mass. App. Ct. 1981) (violation of ethics rule that was intended to protect persons in the plaintiff's position may be evidence of the attorney's negligence); In re Taylor, 363 N.E.2d 845 (Ill. 1977) (the ethics rules are a "safe guide" of standards required of attorneys); and cf. Jenkins v. Wheeler, 316 S.E.2d 354, 61 A.L.R.4th 605 (N.C. Ct. App. 1984) (relying on ethics rules regarding conflicts of interest to establish duty that would give rise to attorney civil liability).

dent noncitizens. Most states and some cities also levy a tax on the transfer of property at death[1] and several also have a gift tax.[2] Taxes imposed at death may be "estate" taxes[3] (a single tax determined by the value of the estate of the decedent) or "inheritance" taxes[4] (separate taxes imposed on each benefit conferred on a devisee, legatee, or heir, the amount of each tax usually being determined by the value of the gift and the degree of consanguinity of the person who receives it).

Only Connecticut[5] still imposes a gift tax, notwithstanding the correlation between estate and gift taxes. The tendency would be to make inter vivos gifts if there is a heavy tax on transfers at death but no tax on transfers during life. The low number probably reflects the fact that state wealth transfer tax rates are de minimis and probably do not often influence the transfer planning of individual citizens. In addition, the federal gift tax adequately deters most gifts that otherwise would be

---

[1] **§ 1.1** See § 1.5. At one time every state imposed a state death tax that was keyed to the amount of the § 2011 state death tax credit, which was repealed in four steps, complete in 2005. See LaPiana, State Responses to the Repeal of the State Death Tax Credit, 37 U. Miami Inst. Est. Plan. ¶ 700 (2003). That credit effectively shifted revenue from the federal government to the taxing states. The labels "sponge" or "pick up" tax reflected that the states took the full amount they could collect without costing their citizens added taxes. Death taxes imposed by states are a concern only in those states that do not limit their tax to the amount of this credit. For a description of the credit (which is zero under current law), see § 1.3.3 nn.30 et seq. and accompanying text.

[2] For a listing, see §§ 1.1 n.5.

[3] As recently as 2001, only Ohio and Oklahoma imposed estate taxes exceeding the amount of the § 2011 state death tax credit (and Ohio repealed its tax effective after 2012). Following repeal of § 2011, many states "decoupled" their tax from the federal regime such that now it is impossible to predict or easily summarize the impact of state death taxes. And see § 2058, which is a federal deduction for state death taxes that are imposed after 2004. See Schoenblum, 2013 Multistate Guide to Estate Planning Table 14.02 (2012). Another comprehensive list is mcguirewoods.com/news-resources/publications/taxation/state_death_tax_chart.pdf.

[4] Indiana, Iowa, Kentucky, Maryland, Nebraska, New Jersey, Pennsylvania, and Tennessee still impose inheritance taxes. See Schoenblum, 2013 Multistate Guide to Estate Planning Table 14.01 (2012) and mcguirewoods.com/news-resources/publications/taxation/state_death_tax_chart.pdf.

[5] See Schoenblum, 2013 Multistate Guide to Estate Planning Table 14.04 (2012).

§ 1.1

made solely for tax minimization purposes. Further, most individuals are disinclined to make gifts regardless of clear tax advantages of transferring property during life rather than waiting until death.

Similarly, Chapter 13 of the Internal Revenue Code is designed to prevent individuals from planning their estates to avoid all wealth transfer tax in the estates of their children or more remote descendants through the use of trusts that bestow benefits but do not grant sufficient enjoyment or control to require FET inclusion. GST § 2604 was a credit for state GST and several states adopted their own sponge or pick up tax version of the GST.[6]

The federal gift tax also helps to preserve the integrity of the income tax system. The owner of income producing property is burdened with the income tax on the income it produces, and the gift tax impedes gratuitous transfers of property designed to shift that income tax liability among the property owner's beneficiaries. Considering the relatively low income tax rates and the compressed income tax brackets in which income is taxed, there is relatively little incentive for income shifting in the form of gifts or otherwise under current law.[7] Yet the one-year repeal of the FET and GST in 2010 was not matched with gift tax repeal for just this deterrence reason. The gift tax remained on the books continuously.

---

[6] Like state death taxes that took advantage of the § 2011 credit, these state taxes merely diverted a portion of the federal GST to the state and therefore cost their citizens nothing. As of 2009 Alabama, California, Colorado, Connecticut, Florida, Hawaii, Idaho, Illinois, Indiana, Iowa, Maryland, Massachusetts, Michigan, Missouri, Montana, Nebraska, Nevada, New York, North Carolina, Ohio, Rhode Island, South Carolina, Tennessee, Texas, Vermont, and Virginia were reported as having adopted such a tax and it was expected that most states would follow suit, as all states had in imposing a death tax taking advantage of the § 2011 credit. See Schoenblum, 2013 Multistate Guide to Estate Planning Table 14.03 (2012). Like § 2011, however, this § 2604 credit also was repealed in 2001. Unlike § 2011, repeal of § 2604 was effective all at once in 2005—it was not phased out.

[7] See § 1.6.2 n.6 and accompanying text regarding income shifting using trusts.

Payment of federal gift or estate tax is avoided to the extent the § 2010 unified credit is available to the donor or the decedent's estate.[8]

§ 1.2 THE FEDERAL GIFT TAX

The Internal Revenue Code imposes a graduated tax on taxable gifts. Primary liability to pay the gift tax is imposed on the donor under § 2502(c) but transferee liability is imposed on the donee under § 6901(a) to the extent the donor fails to pay the tax. Under § 6019 a gift tax return must be filed for any gift not excluded under § 2503(b) (the annual exclusion) or § 2503(e) (the ed/med exclusion),[1] or any gift not qualifying for the § 2522 gift tax charitable deduction or the § 2523 gift tax marital deduction. The due date under § 6075(b) for filing the gift tax return is April 15 following the close of the calendar year in which the gift was made (with an automatic extension to file if the taxpayer is granted an extension of time to file the taxpayer's income tax return) or the time for filing the donor's FET return if the donor dies during the calendar year in which the gift was made.

§ 1.2.1 Gift Defined

According to § 2512(b), a gift is any voluntary and complete transfer of property to the extent FMV of the property transferred exceeds the value of any consideration received in money or money's worth. That differential in value may not be taxable because it meets the business transaction exception established in Treas. Reg. § 25.2512-8 (meaning that the transaction is bona fide, at arm's length, and free from donative intent), or some other exception applies.[2] Thus, for example, outright gratuitous transfers of money, realty, tangibles, or intangibles normally

---

[8] This credit is available to offset the payment of gift tax inter vivos as well as FET at death. See § 1.2.8.

[1] **§ 1.2** See § 1.2.2.

[2] For example, the § 2503(b) annual exclusion or the § 2503(e) ed/med exclusion. See § 1.2.2. See also Kirschling v. United States, 746 F.2d 512 (9th Cir. 1984) (Indian General Allotment lands and proceeds from the sale or harvest thereof are exempt from gift tax, regardless of whether the transferee is a native American), citing Squire v. Capoeman, 351 U.S. 1 (1956) (native American exempt from capital gains tax on timber proceeds from allotted land because the allotment is free from *all* taxes).

§ 1.2

would be taxable gifts. Some taxable transfers are less obvious than these, however. Some transfers that look like gifts are not, while others that do not appear to be gifts are taxable transfers. In general, the test is whether an economic benefit has been transferred gratuitously, but this is only a rough description. Consider the following illustrations:

(1) P transferred $100,000 to a trustee in trust to pay the income to child C for life, remainder to C's descendants. P reserved a power to revoke the trust and therefore did not make a completed transfer for gift tax purposes. However, income distributed from the trust to C constitutes a gift, and a completed gift would occur if P released the power of revocation. This gift would consist of a transfer to C of the value of the life estate and a transfer to C's descendants of the value of the remainder interest, both valued when the power is relinquished, on the basis of C's actuarial life expectancy and an assumed rate of return on trust assets dictated by § 7520.

(2) X sold a house and lot to Y for 40% of its FMV. This is a gift to Y of 60% of the FMV unless X can establish that the sale was made in the ordinary course of business, in a transaction that was bona fide, at arm's length, and free from donative intent. This would be difficult to prove if Y is a natural object of X's bounty.

(3) A and B, sole owners of a corporation, each transferred stock they owned in the corporation to key employees whom they considered important to continued success of the corporation. A and B are not related, nor is any employee related to them. For income tax purposes the employees must include the FMV of the stock they received in income and their income tax basis in the stock is the same amount. A and B are treated as having made a capital contribution to the corporation, and the corporation is entitled to a deduction for compensation paid to the employees to the extent allowed by §§ 162 and 83(h). No gift has been made for gift tax purposes because these transfers were made for full and adequate consideration in money or money's worth.[3]

(4) Assume in the prior example that only A transferred stock to the unrelated key employees and that B did not make a matching contribution. A's transfer still constitutes a capital contribution to the corporation that generates an increase in basis for A's stock in the corporation. Because A alone made a transfer, however, A is deemed to have made an indirect gift to B of half the value contributed to the corporation.[4]

---

[3] See Rev. Rul. 80-196, 1980-2 C.B. 32.

[4] See Treas. Reg. § 25.2511-1(h)(1); Heringer v. Commissioner, 235 F.2d 149 (9th Cir. 1956); Tilton v. Commissioner, 88 T.C. 590 (1987); Ketteman Trust v. Commissioner, 86 T.C. 91 (1986); Estate of Hitchon v. Commissioner, 45 T.C. 96 (1965); PLR 9114023. This gift does not qualify for the annual exclusion because B does not have an immediate right to possession or enjoyment of the capital

　　　　(5) P gratuitously guaranteed loans made by Bank to P's children. According to PLR 9113009:

> The agreements . . . to guarantee payment of debts are valuable economic benefits conferred upon [the children] . . . . Consequently, when [the taxpayer] guaranteed payment of the loans, [the taxpayer] transferred a valuable property interest to [the children]. The promisor of a legally enforceable promise for less than adequate and full consideration makes a completed gift on the date the promise is binding and determinable in value rather than when the promised payment is actually made.

According to the Ruling, this gift was taxable immediately, with the gift amount being "the economic benefit conferred" by the guarantee. The government gave no indication of the gift tax value of the economic benefit bestowed. It might consist of the value of any reduction in interest rate attributable to the added security provided by the guarantee, the amount the borrower did not pay a third party for the guarantee, or the diminution in value of the guarantor's collateral, pledged to secure the guarantee. If the taxpayer subsequently is required to make good on the guarantee, an additional gift would be made to the extent the taxpayer could, but does not, seek reimbursement from the borrower.[5]

(Footnote Continued)

increase represented by A's transfer. A would be in a better position if there was no other shareholder, or if B made a matching proportionate transfer that would net out the gifts made by each. Indeed, the results would be more favorable if A made gifts to the employees out of affection or other nonbusiness related motives because, presumably, the gift tax annual exclusion would be applicable. As proposed, all A gains from this transfer is a basis increase for the value of the deemed capital contribution. See §7.1.1.1 n.26.

[5] It is notable that the benefit to the borrower from receiving a guarantee does not constitute an immediate cost to the taxpayer who provides the guarantee. The government previously has taken the position that the value of a gift is not what the donee receives but what the donor relinquishes. See TAM 8907002 (transfer of a small percentage of stock in a transaction that terminated the donor's control of a corporation is deemed to be a gift of the total control premium relinquished). In this case the government took the opposite position, stating that value to the donee measured the gift, which is a more traditional holding. See Pennell, Wealth Transfer Taxation: "Transfer" Defined, 128 Tax Notes 615 (2010); Pennell, Valuation Discord: An Exegesis of Wealth Transfer Tax Valuation Theory and Practice, 30 U. Miami Inst. Est. Plan. ¶ 903 (1996). It may be that either valuation is correct in appropriate situations, although it is difficult to see what property transfer has occurred in the guarantee situation to

§ 1.2.2 Annual Exclusion and Ed/Med Exclusion

Every year a taxpayer may give up to $10,000, indexed for inflation in $1,000 increments ($14,000 in 2013), to each of an unlimited number of different donees without incurring a gift tax or even being required to file a gift tax return. This § 2503(b) "annual exclusion" does not apply to future interests, such as a gift in trust to pay principal to the beneficiary at some future date. However, certain gifts to minors that are future interests are treated by § 2503(c) as gifts of a present interest that qualify for the annual exclusion if (1) the gift property and the income therefrom may be expended for the benefit of the donee before the donee attains age 21 and, (2) to the extent not so expended, the gift property and the income therefrom will pass to the donee when the donee attains age 21 or, (3) if the donee dies before attaining age 21, will be payable to the donee's estate or as the donee appoints under a general power of appointment.

In addition, § 2503(e) provides that amounts paid on behalf of an individual as tuition to an educational organization for "education or training" or to any "medical" care provider with respect to an individual also are not taxable. These ed/med exclusion payments may be made in addition to the per donee annual exclusion.[6]

§ 1.2.3 Charitable Deduction

Transfers to qualified charities are deductible under § 2522(a) regardless of amount (and the same is true for FET purposes under § 2055(a)) notwithstanding that the § 170 income tax charitable deduction is limited to certain percentages of the donor's contribution base.

(Footnote Continued)

which the gift tax should apply. By citing Dickman v. Commissioner, presumably the government's position is that there is an imputed gift to the borrower of the cost of the guarantee, which the borrower immediately returns to the taxpayer in exchange for the guarantee. See § 6.3.3.6. PLR 9409018 modified PLR 9113009 with respect to its marital deduction holdings; it expressly declined to express an opinion about any other aspect of the situation involved in that prior Ruling, leaving intact (it would appear) these prior ruminations about the gift tax consequences of gratuitous loan guarantees.

[6] See § 7.1.1.

Qualified charitable donees are described in §§ 2055 and 2522 and include community funds, religious, scientific, literary, and educational organizations. Gifts to organizations designed to promote good government or world peace or to attain other political, economic, or social ends may be deductible if no substantial part of the organization's activities is carrying on propaganda or otherwise attempting to influence legislation. Also qualified is any political subdivision, such as a city or town, a state, or even the United States. For example, Justice Oliver Wendell Holmes left the entire residue of his estate "to the United States of America." But a particular family in need is not a qualified charity because a general distinction is drawn between public and private charity.

It is customary for organizations to submit their charters and bylaws to the Treasury Department for a ruling that they are qualified charities, gifts to which are deductible for federal income, estate, and gift tax purposes. If such a determination has been obtained, an organization typically will make this known in its solicitation of funds, and it always makes sense to verify this fact before making a sizable charitable gift.

Split interest charitable gifts benefit charities and individuals, with the charity benefiting exclusively for a term and the remainder then passing to individuals, or vice versa. As discussed in more detail below,[7] very technical rules must be observed to obtain a charitable deduction for split interest charitable gifts.

§ 1.2.4 *Marital Deduction*

The gift tax marital deduction was enacted in 1948 (along with gift splitting[8] and joint income tax returns) to provide parity between the taxation of spouses in community property and noncommunity property states. Spouses in community property states automatically own equally most property acquired during their marriage, with no tax consequence regardless of which spouse generated the resources (such as income from employment) to acquire the asset. If a noncommunity property taxpayer produced property and gave the same 50% to his or her spouse, that sharing of wealth as if the marriage was an economic partnership was subject to the gift tax before § 2523 was adopted.

---

[7] See §§ 14.3.2 and 14.3.6.

[8] See § 1.2.5.

§ 1.2.4

The original marital deduction was limited to 50% of the value of a gift between spouses. Community property spouses who shared resources automatically under state law had no tax, but noncommunity property spouses who shared their resources incurred gift tax on half of what each gave to the other. Because that was not the degree of parity needed,[9] Congress now makes most interspousal transfers totally free of tax if the donee spouse receives a qualifying interest[10] and is a citizen of the United States.[11]

§ 1.2.5 Gift Splitting by Spouses

Also adopted in 1948 was the gift splitting authority now found in § 2513, which applies to gifts by a married donor to a third party. Because a gift by spouses of community property is a gift by each of half the value of the property, § 2513 grants spouses the ability to treat a gift of noncommunity property as made half by each as well.[12]

§ 1.2.6 Concurrent Interests

Joint ownership of property with the right of survivorship is quite common, particularly between spouses. A completed gift results from creation of a joint ownership to the extent the respective owners' contributions are not equal. However, any gift represented by unequal contributions is not complete and therefore is not taxable to the extent the joint owners' respective contributions are withdrawable without consent of the other joint owners. This normally occurs with respect to joint bank accounts, brokerage accounts, and jointly owned United States Savings Bonds. In addition, between spouses, even if the contribution constitutes

---

[9] Recognizing this disparity, the original gift tax marital deduction was allowed only to the extent the transfer was of property that was not "held as community property," meaning it was separate property that was not the result of a conversion from community property. This complexity was altered in 1976 and then eliminated from interspousal gifts of community property made after 1981.

[10] See §§ 13.5.2 and 13.5.6.

[11] Gifts to a noncitizen spouse cannot qualify for the gift tax marital deduction. See § 2523(i). However, § 2523(i)(2) increases ten-fold (to $143,000 in 2013, which is $100,000 indexed for inflation) the § 2503(b) gift tax annual exclusion for gifts to a noncitizen spouse, provided the interest transferred otherwise would qualify for the marital deduction. Treas. Reg. § 25.2523(i)-1(c).

[12] See § 7.1.3.

a completed gift, the unlimited gift tax marital deduction makes the transfer tax free if the donee spouse is a citizen of the United States.[13]

§ 1.2.7 Preventing Valuation Freezes

Certain transactions seek to minimize the value of transferred property in ways that Congress regards as improper. As discussed in detail below,[14] Chapter 14 of the Internal Revenue Code precludes a number of these devices. Two provisions in Chapter 14 are particularly relevant for gift tax purposes.

In § 2701 Congress precludes a form of planning that best is illustrated by a preferred stock freeze transaction. The typical approach involved a taxpayer who caused a controlled corporation to issue both preferred and common stock to the taxpayer (general and limited partnership interests would be utilized in a partnership context). The junior interest (the common stock or the limited partnership interest) was structured to represent as little value of the enterprise as possible for gift tax purposes and, conversely, the senior interest (the preferred stock or general partnership interest) was designed to absorb as much value as possible. Indeed, "bells and whistles" (such as puts, calls, rights to convert into other stock, and a preference as to earnings of the enterprise) often were granted to the senior interest to increase its relative value. The taxpayer then would make a gift of the junior interest at what was meant to be a de minimis gift tax value.

Although the retained senior interest was deemed to represent the bulk of the value of the enterprise by virtue of its various entitlements, that value never was fully realized because the bells and whistles would not be exercised and, frequently, the preferred dividends were not declared. Instead, future growth and some of the initial value allegedly

---

[13] In valuing a gift subject to tax under § 2523(i) for transfers to a spouse who is not a citizen of the United States, § 2523(i)(3) adopts "the principles of sections 2515 and 2515A (as such sections were in effect before their repeal by the Economic Recovery Tax Act of 1981) . . . except that the provisions of such section 2515 providing for an election shall not apply." Thus, automatic gift taxation will apply on the creation of such tenancies if one of the spouses is not a citizen of the United States and if their contributions to the concurrent ownership are not equal. See § 13.5.7.1 nn.295-299 and accompanying text.

[14] See §§ 7.2.2 (§ 2702) and 7.2.3 (§ 2701).

§ 1.2.7

reposed in the senior interest would enhance the value of the junior interest. The object was to minimize the value includible in the estate of the taxpayer while the junior interest holders would receive more value than was reported for gift tax purposes.

To preclude this form of planning, § 2701 specifies that the value of the senior interest retained by the taxpayer is ignored in determining the gift tax value of the junior interest that is transferred. In essence, unless one of numerous exceptions is met, a gift of the junior interest attracts gift tax as if that interest represented full ownership of the enterprise. In this manner the government is assured that the taxpayer will not avoid paying tax on any part of the value of the enterprise.

A second form of common planning involved temporal interests, such as a term of years and a remainder interest. For example, in a GRIT transaction a taxpayer would create a trust to pay income to the taxpayer for a term of years, with the remainder to a natural object of the taxpayer's bounty. For gift tax purposes, the taxable transfer was the value of the remainder interest because the income interest for the term of years was retained. With assumptions regarding interest rates often showing incredible value for even short-duration retained interests, the ability to reduce the value of the remainder interest gift was substantial, especially if the property transferred to the trust was stock in a family corporation that produced much less income than the valuation tables presumed. Congress adopted § 2702 to restore reality to the valuation process in determining the gift tax consequences of this transaction. The provision essentially ignores the value of the interest retained by the taxpayer in determining the value of the interest transferred upon creation of the trust. Thus, again subject to several exceptions, taxation at inception of the trust protects the government from unrealistic assumptions that permit value to escape tax.

As discussed in much greater detail below,[15] §§ 2701 through 2704 (constituting Chapter 14 of the Internal Revenue Code) address several other perceived valuation abuses and, in the aggregate, seek to restore balance to wealth transfer taxation through imposition of valuation rules (the other provisions deal generally with the effect on wealth transfer tax

---

[15] See §§ 7.2.3 (§ 2701), 7.2.2 (§ 2702), 15.3.1.2 (§ 2703), and 15.3.1.3 (§ 2704).

§ 1.2.7

value of buy-sell agreements or other restrictions on the sale or use of transferred property, and with lapsing rights or restrictions).

§ 1.2.8 The Unified Estate and Gift Taxes

The tax on transfers that are not deductible or excepted (for example, under the §§ 2503(b) and 2503(e) gift tax annual and ed/med exclusions) is computed under a unified rate system found in § 2001 and incorporated by reference by § 2502 for both estate and gift tax purposes, respectively. This approach reflects the progressive nature of the estate and gift taxes and the policy that similar amounts of wealth should incur similar tax liability regardless of whether the transferor conveys it during life, at death, or some of each.

Thus, gifts made during life are added to gifts made previously during life to determine the appropriate graduated tax rate to impose on the latest transfer. For example, because the gift tax rate on a gift of $150,000 is less than the rate on a gift of $250,000, it is necessary to consider the progressive rate that must be imposed if a gift of $150,000 is made after a prior gift of $100,000.

Similarly, all taxable transfers made during a transferor's life must be considered in determining the proper rate for taxing transfers at death. To illustrate, if Donor transferred $X in year 1 and another $Y in year 2 and died with $Z in year 3, the tax on the year 2 gift would be computed as the tax on $X plus $Y and, because the tax on $X already was incurred in year 1, only the increase in tax attributable to the year 2 gift of $Y would be imposed. Similarly, the FET would be computed as the tax on $X plus $Y plus $Z and, again reflecting that the tax on $X and $Y was incurred during life, only the increase in tax attributable to the $Z taxable at death would be imposed for FET purposes.

There is a quirk in this unified rate system, attributable to the fact that the estate and gift taxes were not unified until 1976 but the unified gift tax computation regime existed beginning in 1932. Thus, taxable gifts made prior to 1977 must be reflected in determining the applicable tax for taxable gifts made after 1976 but not for determining the FET for any decedent.[16]

---

[16] A knowledge of the law prior to 1977 may be necessary to determine the taxable gifts that must be reflected in computing the tax on taxable gifts made

To illustrate, assume that Donor made taxable gifts before 1977 totaling $150,000 and a taxable gift after 1976 of $100,000. The gift tax on the $100,000 gift would be computed by determining the gift tax under the unified rate schedule on a gift of $250,000 and then subtracting the gift tax under the same schedule on a gift of $150,000. The difference is the gift tax on the post-1976 taxable gift of $100,000. Donor's FET, however, would be determined without regard to the gift made before 1977 of $150,000. Thus, if Donor's taxable estate was $700,000 at death, it would be added to the taxable gift made after 1976 of $100,000 but not to the taxable gift made before 1977 of $150,000. The tax on only $800,000 would be computed, and the tax on that amount would be paid to the extent it exceeds the tax on the $100,000 taxable gift made after 1976.[17]

(Footnote Continued)

post-1976 because taxable gifts made before 1977 are determined on the basis of the gift tax as it existed at the time of the gift.

[17] See § 2001(b). In computing the gift tax on that $100,000 post-1976 gift for FET computation purposes, TAM 9642001 confirmed in the absence of regulations that the pre-1977 gifts would be considered as they were in computing that gift tax during the decedent's life. But they otherwise are not a part of the FET computation.

See also TAM 9718004 (gift tax on last of three gifts of fractional interests in realty, only the last of which incurred a gift tax greater than the unified credit, and none was valued with the appropriate fractional interest discount; claim for refund of gift tax paid on the final fractional gift was barred by § 2504(c) because gift tax was paid and, although the value of the two prior gifts was open to reassessment—§ 2504(c) as it applied prior to its amendment in 1997 did not preclude revaluation because no gift tax was paid on them—their value was not timely challenged because it affected only the final gift, as to which the statute was a bar).

For a discussion of the application of § § 2001(f) and 2504(c) and the government's ability to revalue gifts made during life for purposes of computing the FET at death, see § 1.3.3. Because the rate schedule in § 2001(c) has been changed many times, § § 2001(b)(2) and 2001(g) call for the determination of all these amounts of tax on the basis of the rate schedule in effect at the decedent's death rather than the actual tax incurred during life. The effect of this provision is to deny a credit against the tax at death based on higher rates applicable during life than those applicable at death, if the rates have declined, which is relevant since 2001 because the highest marginal wealth transfer tax rates have declined under § 2001. The converse is true if the rates increased, because the credit is based on what the tax would have been at death rather than the amount that actually was imposed and paid during life, and this could occur any time the rates rise or the exclusion amounts decline.

§ 1.2.8

The tax computed under the unified rate schedule need not be paid[18] until the aggregate tax incurred during life and at death exceeds the unified credit granted by §§ 2010 and 2505.[19] Because the tax is computed at the time of each gift and at death on the aggregate amount of wealth previously transferred and subject to the tax, the credit is reflected in each computation, notwithstanding that it effectively is exhausted seriatim on transfers made during life and then at death. The effect is to allow tax-free passage of only the aggregate amount of property that produces a tax equal to the unified credit, whenever transferred.

§ 1.3 THE FET

The FET is an obligation of the residue of the decedent's probate estate and must be paid by the "executor" of the estate,[1] which distinguishes the tax from an inheritance tax like that imposed by some states on recipients of the decedent's property.

The FET is imposed on a decedent's taxable estate, as defined in § 2051 of the Internal Revenue Code, and requires answers to three basic questions:

(1) What property is includible in the decedent's "gross estate"?

(2) From the "gross estate," what amounts are deductible in determining the "taxable estate"?

(3) How much tax is imposed on the taxable estate?

---

[18] Indeed, in Rev. Rul. 79-398, 1979-2 C.B. 338, the government stated that the tax cannot be paid until the unified credit has been exhausted, which was relevant at the time for gift tax statute of limitation purposes under §§ 2001(f) and 2504(c). See § 1.3.3 for the current situation regarding revaluation; the position taken in the Ruling still applies notwithstanding that this rationale for its existence changed in 1997.

[19] Prior to its repeal in 2002, the benefit of the unified credit was effectively exhausted by imposition of the § 2001(c)(2) surtax, although the computation regime was not altered and a technical flaw in legislation adopted in 1997 made the surtax not applicable to retract the benefit of the credit. In addition, the law remains that reduces the credit under § 2010(b) if gifts were made by the transferor after September 8, 1976, but before 1977.

[1] § 1.3 §§ 2002 and 2205. The term "executor" is defined in § 2203 as the fiduciary charged with administration of the decedent's estate or, if there is none, then any person in possession of the decedent's property.

§ 1.3.1 The Gross Estate

A decedent's gross estate includes "the value of all property to the extent of the interest therein of the decedent at the time of . . . death."[2] Property a person owns[3] at death is includible in the decedent's gross estate,[4] but many other types of property or entitlements are includible even though the decedent did not own them in a classic sense.

> The word "property" in the statute is not limited in its scope by concepts of property that existed when the estate tax was conceived . . . .The economy and many of the elements of life today are different than they were even a generation or less ago. The Congress in its wisdom decided to use a general word like property rather than trying to envision what the ingenuity of man would evolve as something substantial. The tax gatherer is directed to seek out the esoterics of ownership . . . .[5]

---

[2] § 2033. Whalen v. Department of the Treasury, 80-2 U.S. Tax Cas. (CCH) ¶ 13,375 (N.D. Ohio 1980), was an estate beneficiary's action for declaratory judgment brought to determine the assets to be included in the decedent's gross estate for FET purposes. Evidently the beneficiary disagreed with the executor of the decedent's estate regarding assets that should be included and sought to use this method to resolve that dispute. The court dismissed the action because it had no jurisdiction over the subject matter or the defendant, citing § 7421, which prohibits a suit to restrain the assessment or collection of any tax.

[3] Price v. United States, 470 F. Supp. 136 (N.D. Tex. 1979), aff'd, 610 F.2d 680 (9th Cir. 1980), involved spouses whose wills gave the survivor of them all the property of the first of them to die. The husband died shortly after the wife, whose will was not offered for probate. His estate alleged that her property therefore was not includible in his gross estate, which the court rejected because controlling local law regarded an unprobated but apparently valid will as effective to convey sufficient entitlement to probate property to require inclusion in the devisee's gross estate for FET purposes.

[4] A few notable exceptions exist by virtue of legislative grace. See, e.g., § 2103, which excludes property not situated in the United States that is owned at death by a nonresident noncitizen; Estate of Summers v. United States, 85-2 U.S. Tax Cas. (CCH) ¶ 13,646 (D. Or. 1985) (exclusion of certain Indian tribal property), and Squire v. Capoeman, 351 U.S. 1 (1956) (native American exempt from capital gains tax on timber proceeds from allotted land because the allotment is free from *all* taxes).

[5] First Victoria Nat'l Bank v. United States, 620 F.2d 1096, 1104 (5th Cir. 1980) ("rice history acreage" is "property" for FET purposes).

Congress intends to tax all transfers of economic benefit upon a decedent's death, regardless of the niceties of property law or the legal forms employed. Some property transfers are reached by special provisions, including some that prevent tax avoidance by reaching inter vivos transfers in which virtually no economic benefit is retained and transferred at death.

(1) Transfers Made Within Three Years of Death. Prior to 1977 the value of gifts made within three years of the decedent's death was includible in the gross estate if the transfer was made "in contemplation of death."[6] In 1976 Congress adopted a § 2035(a) automatic three year return rule, eliminating the contemplation of death requirement. In addition, Congress addressed a significant estate reduction opportunity by enacting § 2035(b), which requires inclusion of the amount of any gift tax paid by D on any gift made by D or by S within three years of death.[7] This "gross up" inclusion rule subjects the dollars used to pay the gift tax to the FET, which matches the result at death because the dollars used to pay the decedent's FET themselves are subject to the FET.

In 1981 Congress enacted § 2035(a)(2) to severely limit application of the three year return rule to transfers made within three years of death of property interests that, if retained until death, would cause inclusion in the gross estate under any of § 2036, § 2037, § 2038, or § 2042. This inclusion rule has an exclusion for transfers made for full and adequate consideration in money or money's worth.[8]

(2) Revocable Transfers. The value of property transferred by a decedent during life but subject to a power to alter, amend, revoke, or

---

[6] As compared to gifts made "in contemplation of death," a gift "causa mortis" is made in immediate expectation or fear of death. Gifts causa mortis are revocable and automatically are revoked if the donor recovers from the illness or otherwise survives the immediate risk of death. Gifts made in actual or presumed contemplation of death for purposes of § 2035 are not necessarily revocable gifts causa mortis.

[7] If a married donor made a gift to a third person that the donor's spouse consented to split under § 2513, no part of the gift tax paid by the nondonor spouse would be subject to § 2035(b) if the donor spouse died within three years of the gift. If, however, the nondonor spouse died within three years of that gift, any gift tax paid by the nondonor spouse would be brought back into the nondonor spouse's gross estate.

[8] § 2035(d).

§ 1.3.1

terminate enjoyment[9] is includible in the decedent's gross estate (except to the extent the transfer was for full and adequate consideration in money or money's worth). This § 2038(a)(1) inclusion is consistent with the gift tax rule that a revocable transfer is not a completed gift and therefore is not taxable for gift tax purposes. Death constitutes termination of the retained power, which completes the transfer for wealth transfer tax purposes.[10]

(3) Retained Life Estates. Even if a transfer is irrevocable and therefore subject to gift taxation, the transferor may be exposed to § 2036(a) FET inclusion of the value of the transferred property at death because the transferor retained enjoyment of the property for life, or retained a power to designate who will enjoy the property and did not relinquish that power prior to death. The transferor's retained enjoyment or control causes the transfer to be regarded as if no transfer was made.

Unlike the situation involving § 2038, in which the typical transfer during life is not complete and the gift tax is not imposed, a donor who retained only the right to receive income for life would incur gift tax on the value of the remainder interest transferred irrevocably. Inclusion of the full value of the transferred property in the transferor's gross estate at death is a second tax on the same interest (the remainder being the full value of the property once the life estate ends). Thus, an adjustment is provided under the flush language of § 2001(b) to ameliorate this double taxation of the same interest.

For purposes of these rules, § 2036(b) regards the transfer of stock in a controlled corporation as a § 2036(a)(1) transfer with retained enjoyment if the transferor retains the right to vote the stock.

(4) Transfers That Take Effect at Death. Unquestionably the strangest FET inclusion provision is § 2037. It is applicable only if (1) some beneficiary must survive the decedent as a condition to obtaining possession or enjoyment of property the decedent transferred during

---

[9] The power need not be retained by the decedent; it is sufficient if the power was bestowed by another party after the transfer.

[10] Release of the power within three years of death causes the same result as if the power was retained until death. See § § 2038(a)(1) (last clause) and 2035(a)(2).

§ 1.3.1

life, and (2) the decedent retained a reversion in the corpus[11] of that property that was worth at death more than 5% of the value of the property that would revert. To illustrate, a transferor would have to make a transfer such as "to A for life, then reversion to the transferor if living and, if not, to B if living," and even then the amount subject to § 2037 would be only the value of the transferred property reduced by the value of the life estate in A, which is not subject to the reversion.

A reversionary interest that does not meet these requirements still may be includible in the decedent's gross estate under § 2033, although only the value of the reversion would be subject to inclusion in that event rather than the full value of the property subject to the reversion.

Notwithstanding that § 2037 has been in the FET since its inception, for decades it has been a veritable backwater and all significant litigation involving its provisions is antiquated.[12] This provision largely is irrelevant because modern estate planning seldom would call for retention of anything closely resembling the reversion that would trigger § 2037.

(5) Annuities. The value of an annuity at the decedent's death is includible in the decedent's gross estate under § 2039(a) if the decedent was entitled to receive annuity payments for life (including if the decedent had not yet begun to receive such payments but, once they began, they were payable for life, such as under a retirement benefit plan), and if some other beneficiary is entitled to enjoyment of that annuity after the decedent's death (such as under a joint and survivor payout option). At one time § 2039 excluded the full value of most retirement benefit annuities but, in a series of amendments over a relatively short period in the early 1980s, Congress reversed that exclusion to now require full inclusion. Because most retirement benefit annuity payments also constitute IRD for purposes of § 691(a), these deferred compensation entitlements that survive a taxpayer's death constitute one of the most heavily taxed forms of wealth and require special attention in the planning process.

---

[11] Under § 2037(b) a reversion of income only is not sufficient to trigger application of this rule.

[12] For example, the principal § 2037 cases are Estate of Spiegel v. Commissioner, 335 U.S. 701 (1949); Commissioner v. Estate of Church, 335 U.S. 632 (1949); and Helvering v. Hallock, 309 U.S. 106 (1940).

§ 1.3.1

(6) Concurrent Interests. Property held in joint tenancy with the right of survivorship or as tenants by the entireties (i.e., concurrent interests with the right of survivorship) is subject to special inclusion rules under § 2040, applicable with respect to the estate of all but the last concurrent owner to die. The general inclusion rule applies a consideration furnished test that requires inclusion in the gross estate of a portion of the value of the concurrently owned property that corresponds to the portion of the consideration furnished by the decedent to acquire the property.

The presumption is that the decedent furnished the entire consideration, in which case the entire value is includible in the decedent's gross estate. However, any surviving concurrent owner may prove that the decedent did not provide all the consideration, in which case a lesser amount will be includible. No part of the value will be includible in the decedent's gross estate if it can be proved that the decedent furnished none of the consideration. If the concurrent owners acquired the property by gift from a third party, an equal portion of the value is includible (or such other portion specified by the donor if the gift specified that the owners would not share the property equally).

In 1976 Congress adopted the qualified joint interest rule in § 2040(b), applicable only to property acquired after 1976[13] and held exclusively by spouses who are citizens of the United States.[14] Only half the value of a qualified joint interest is includible in D's gross estate, regardless of the source of the consideration furnished to acquire the joint interest.

Concurrent ownership that lacks the right of survivorship, such as a tenancy in common or community property, is not subject to § 2040. Instead, only D's undivided interest in the property (e.g., half the value of community property) is includible in D's gross estate.

To illustrate the application of § 2040(a) with respect to concurrent interests with the right of survivorship among persons who are not spouses, assume Donor devised Blackacre to A and B as joint tenants with the right of survivorship and not as tenants in common. Half the value of Blackacre will be included in D's gross estate and S will become

---

[13] See Gallenstein v. United States, 975 F.2d 286 (6th Cir. 1992).

[14] See § 2056(b)(1)(B).

§ 1.3.1

the sole owner of Blackacre pursuant to the right of survivorship. When S dies the full value of Blackacre will be subject to inclusion again, meaning that 150% of the value of Blackacre will be subject to FET over both estates.

If D had purchased Blackacre and placed the title in the names of D and S as joint tenants with the right of survivorship and not as tenants in common, D would make a taxable gift to S of half the value of Blackacre and still would suffer inclusion of 100% of the value of Blackacre in D's gross estate because D furnished all the consideration for its acquisition. Any gift tax paid by D will be allowed under §2001(b)(2) as a credit against D's FET. And the gift made upon creation will be purged from D's adjusted taxable gifts by the flush language of §2001(b) if the tenancy was created after 1976. The net result will be inclusion of 200% of the value of Blackacre over both estates.

If, however, S was to die first, no part of the value of Blackacre would be includible in S's gross estate because D furnished all the consideration for its acquisition, and only 100% of the value of Blackacre will be subjected to FET over both estates. Recall, however, that half the value of Blackacre was subject to gift tax when D created the joint tenancy, so in the aggregate 150% of the value of the property was subject to wealth transfer tax.

If D and S had owned Blackacre as undivided tenants-in-common, 50% would be included in each estate and, if they provided their own consideration, then only 100% of the value would be subject to FET over both estates.

(7) Powers of Appointment. Powers of appointment are important estate planning tools that provide flexibility in trust dispositions. Under §2041 the holder of the power (the "donee" or "powerholder") is treated as owner of any property subject to a general power, meaning that the powerholder may appoint the property to the powerholder, to the powerholder's estate, or to creditors of either. Any other power of appointment is a nongeneral power, which usually is harmless for FET purposes.[15] It generally makes no difference whether the power is exer-

---

[15] Unless the power is exercised in a manner that triggers the arcane provisions of the so-called Delaware Tax Trap of §2041(a)(3), meaning that exercise is effective to extend the duration of a trust for Rule Against Perpetuities

cised. An exception exists if the general power was created before October 22, 1942, in which case it must be exercised to trigger inclusion of the appointive property.

(8) Life Insurance. Life insurance proceeds are includible in the insured decedent's gross estate if at death the decedent possessed any "incidents of ownership" in the policies[16] or if the proceeds are payable to the insured's estate.[17]

(9) Qualified Terminable Interest Property. Property that qualifies for a marital deduction in D's estate under §2056(b)(7) as QTIP is subject to inclusion in S's estate under §2044. This inclusion essentially is a payback for the grant of the marital deduction to D's estate. Qualification for the marital deduction, which requires a QTIP election in D's estate, causes the property subject to that election to be treated as if S had a sufficient ownership interest to cause FET inclusion, notwithstanding that S never owned the property and, in many cases, cannot govern its ultimate disposition.

§1.3.2 The Taxable Estate

The §2051 taxable estate upon which the decedent's FET is computed under §2001 is determined by subtracting the amount of five deductions from the decedent's §2031 gross estate.

(1) Expenses, Claims, Debts, and Taxes. Ordinary and necessary expenses of administering the decedent's estate (including fees paid to the personal representative and to advisors such as an attorney or accountant), claims against the estate and recourse indebtedness for which the decedent was personally liable during life (in either case to the extent supported by full and adequate consideration in money or money's worth), and taxes that were the decedent's liability during life (i.e., taxes other than wealth transfer taxes or any tax that accrues after death), are deductible under §2053 if paid within time constraints found in §§2053(b) and (c)(2).

(Footnote Continued)

purposes. As explained in much greater detail below, this provision has become a planning opportunity for GST purposes. See §11.4.5.4.3.

[16] §2042(2).

[17] §2042(1).

(2) Casualty or Theft Losses. Losses incurred during administration of the estate that are not compensated by insurance are deductible under § 2054. No deduction is allowable if the estate elects alternate valuation under § 2032 and the asset value on the alternate valuation date reflects the loss incurred.

(3) Charitable Deduction. The § 2055 FET charitable deduction is the same as the gift tax charitable deduction.[18]

(4) Marital Deduction. The § 2056 FET marital deduction is the same as the gift tax marital deduction,[19] with one significant difference. Although § 2056(d) denies the FET marital deduction if S is not a United States citizen, § 2056A allows the FET marital deduction if the QDOT requirements of that section are met. No similar entitlement was granted for gift tax purposes. Essentially a QDOT must meet the § 2056(b)(5) or (b)(7) qualification rules and requires that at least one trustee be a citizen of the United States or a domestic corporation and that this trustee has a power to withhold a tax imposed on distributions to S as beneficiary of the trust.[20]

(5) State Death Tax Deduction. The § 2058 deduction of estate, inheritance, legacy, or succession taxes paid to any of the 51 American jurisdictions at any time before four years after filing the FET return.

§ 1.3.3 Computing the FET

The FET is computed under the § 2001 unified rate schedule[21] and involves four basic steps:

(1) the § 2051 taxable estate (gross estate minus deductions) is added to the decedent's adjusted taxable gifts made post-1976 (to the extent those gifts are not included in the decedent's gross estate);

(2) a tentative FET is computed on this amount under the unified rate schedule;[22]

---

[18] See § 1.2.3.

[19] See § 1.2.4.

[20] See § 13.5.7.3.

[21] See § 1.2.8.

[22] A special rate table is provided by § 2201 to members of the Armed Forces who die as a result of action in a combat zone. A prior version applicable with respect to § 2011(d) is illustrated by Rev. Rul. 78-381, 1978-2 C.B. 347.

§ 1.3.3

(3) the tentative tax is reduced by the aggregate gift taxes payable with respect to gifts made by the decedent post-1976,[23] determined as if the rate schedule in effect at the decedent's death had been applicable at the time of all gifts;

(4) the §§ 2010 through 2014 credits (e.g., the unified, the state death tax, the previously taxed property, and the foreign death tax credits) then are applied against this FET liability to reduce the amount of tax actually payable.

As established by legislation adopted in 1997,[24] § 6501(c)(9) provides that a gift properly disclosed (adequate to apprise the government of the nature of the gift) is entitled to estate and gift tax statute of limitation protection under §§ 2504(c) and § 2001(f). This legislation effectively reversed the government's previous position that the value of a gift or the gift tax liability was not barred under § 6501 until assessment

---

[23] For this purpose, if the decedent made a § 2513 split gift after 1976, any gift tax paid by the consenting spouse is treated under § 2001(d) as payable by the decedent if the entire gift is included in the decedent's gross estate under any of §§ 2035 through 2038 or § 2042.

[24] With respect to pre-1998 law, see Treas. Reg. § 25.2504-2 (if no gift tax was paid on a return, the statute of limitation did not run for valuation purposes with respect to any gift reported thereon); Rev. Rul. 84-11, 1984-1 C.B. 201 (upon audit of 1982 gift tax return government revalued a gift made in 1977, determining that (1) the value of that gift should have been higher than reported, therefore (2) the gift taxes owed thereon should have been greater, thus exhausting a larger portion of the available unified credit for future gift tax purposes, and (3) by virtue of the increased gift tax value of the 1977 gift, the bracket in which the 1982 gift tax or the decedent's estate at death was to be assessed also was increased); and TAM 8447005 (gift tax valuations always were subject to redetermination at death, even if the donor did not offset inter vivos gift taxes with the unified credit).

of a tax[25] and, therefore, that the statute of limitation did not run until the unified credit had been exhausted and a gift tax paid.[26]

The trade under § 6501(c)(9) for statute of limitation protection is that the taxpayer must properly disclose a gift. Otherwise, without § 2504(c) or § 2001(f) protection the government may redetermine the value of a prior gift, the proper gift tax thereon, the amount of unified credit exhausted thereby, and the effect on the determination of the donor's subsequent gift and estate taxes, all at any time in the future, regardless of how old and cold the facts and basis for determination of these questions may have become in the interim.[27]

---

[25] With respect to that prior position, see, e.g., Reilly v. United States, 88-1 U.S. Tax Cas. (CCH) ¶ 13,752 (S.D. Ind. 1987) (taxpayer and taxpayer's spouse made split gifts, reporting no tax as due because of their gift tax annual exclusions; government revalued the gifted property and asserted a tax that exhausted part of the taxpayers' unified credits; the court dismissed taxpayers' action to reinstate their unified credits because no tax was assessed or collected until the unified credit was exceeded, stating that the only available relief was to challenge the revaluation when their unified credits are exhausted and a tax is first being paid). Also as adopted in 1997, § 7477 now gives taxpayers a forum in the Tax Court in a case such as *Reilly* involving a gift tax valuation controversy. Required is only that the taxpayer exhaust all administrative remedies before filing for a Tax Court determination. See also Evanson v. United States, 30 F.3d 960 (8th Cir. 1994) (increasing gift tax valuation from under $15,000 to over $135,000) and TAM 8743001 (as explained in more detail and with other examples in § 7.1.2 n.132, after FET statute of limitation period expired, government determined that a gift was made inter vivos, notwithstanding that the taxpayer's estate already had filed an FET return, used the full unified credit with respect to the tax liability assessed thereon, received a closing letter, made distributions, and the FET limitation period had expired; the government asserted a gift tax liability and determined that no statute of limitation would prevent the assessment of a gift tax liability because no gift tax return was filed and no gift tax was paid).

[26] See § 1.3.3 n.24 with respect to the requirement that the credit be exhausted and a tax paid.

[27] For example, if § 6501(c)(9) disclosure is lacking, § 2001(f) will not preclude the kind of revaluation results in Estate of Smith v. Commissioner, 94 T.C. 872 (1990), acq., 1990-2 C.B. 1, a reviewed opinion with nine judges concurring and eight dissenting (taxpayer made a gift and paid gift tax; before FET statute of limitation expired the government increased the value of the gift to compute the taxpayer's adjusted taxable gifts in determining the taxpayer's FET; because the § § 2001(b)(2) and 2001(g) credit against the tentative tax for gift taxes paid is not for the tax actually paid on the value originally reported but (melding the two provisions together—read together they still are substantively the same as the

§ 1.3.3

The 1997 legislation reflects a policy that the limitation period ought to run to protect the taxpayer from stale challenges if a gift tax return puts the government on notice and provides it with an opportunity to challenge the facts revealed therein. Adoption of § 2001(f) will not alter the result in any case in which no return is filed, however, or if a return provides less than "adequate disclosure."[28] Nor does it preclude consideration of qualification for the annual exclusion.[29]

(Footnote Continued)

law when *Smith* was decided) "the aggregate amount of tax which *would have been payable* under [the gift tax] with respect to gifts made by the decedent . . . if the rates of tax . . . in effect at the decedent's death . . . had been applicable at the time of such gifts" (emphasis added), the credit also was recomputed based on revaluation of the gift; the effect of higher valuation was to begin taxing the estate at a higher level in the FET rate tables); Estate of Lenheim v. Commissioner, 60 T.C.M. (CCH) 356 (1990) (same); and Stalcup v. United States, 91-2 U.S. Tax Cas. (CCH) ¶ 60,086 (W.D. Okla. 1991) (same). See also Estate of Prince v. Commissioner, 61 T.C.M. (CCH) 2594 (1991), aff'd sub nom., Levin v. Commissioner, 986 F.2d 91 (4th Cir. 1993) (§ 2001(b)(2) adjustment for gift tax paid was denied for the amount of gift tax that would have been payable if gifts had been taxed properly inter vivos because no gift tax would have been payable—the taxpayer's unified credit would have covered that liability; the effect was to improperly consume the unified credit at death as if the gift tax assessment was not time barred); TAM 9141008 (same).

[28] See § 7.2.4.5 n.322 with respect to the information that must be provided under the adequate disclosure requirements of Treas. Reg. § 301.6501(c)-1(f)(2). If it applies, § 2001(f) essentially codifies Boatman's First Nat'l Bank v. United States, 705 F. Supp. 1407 (W.D. Mo. 1988) (decedent died after the § 2504(c) gift tax limitation period had run; government's attempt to revalue the gift in computing FET was rejected because it indirectly would be imposing an additional tax on the gift in violation of the spirit of § 2504(c) if the government could increase the gift in determining the tentative FET and then reduce that tax by only the gift tax paid on the lower previously reported gift tax value; the court did not consider the § 2001(b)(2) credit issue properly resolved in *Smith, Lenheim*, and *Stalcup*).

[29] See, e.g., Estate of Robinson v. Commissioner, 101 T.C. 499, 517 (1993) (claimed annual exclusions denied for transfers to named individuals that purportedly were implied trusts for additional unnamed individuals, which then was reflected in the subsequent FET calculation that relied upon the concept of adjusted taxable gifts, stating that "the basis for tax liability in a prior barred period may be recomputed for the purpose of calculating the tax liability for an open period," allowing the government to determine whether annual exclusions were claimed improperly in a barred year).

§ 1.3.3

Until it was fully repealed in 2005 (and replaced with a § 2058 deduction), the § 2011 credit for state death tax usually[30] was available only for taxes actually paid[31] (and the credit claimed) within four years after filing the FET return. A similar limitation now is found in § 2058(b)(1). An estate that defers payment of the FET under § 6161 or § 6166 could qualify for an exception under § 2011(c)(2) (now see § 2058(b)(2)(B)), but an estate that deferred only the state death tax payment without also deferring the FET had to pay that state tax within the four year window or lose the credit for any state taxes paid too late.[32] A refund of FET could be obtained if state death tax was paid after filing the federal return and within the four year period, but under § 2011(c)[33]

---

[30] An exception under § 2011(c)(3) was applicable to a claim for refund based on a § 2011 credit that was filed within the § 6511 two year period after payment of the FET. Rev. Rul. 81-263, 1981-2 C.B. 169. Now see § 2058(b)(2)(C).

[31] Cf. Rev. Rul. 86-117, 1986-2 C.B. 157 (an estate incurred capital gain or loss when it used property in kind to pay a state inheritance tax liability, as if the property had been sold for its FMV and the proceeds used to pay the tax), in which the government stated that the estate would generate § 61(a)(12) discharge of indebtedness income if the FMV of property transferred to the state was less than the tax satisfied, and that any such deficiency in value would not qualify for the § 2011 credit, presumably because the amount deemed forgiven by the state would not actually be *paid* (even though the income tax treatment is as if the state gave the estate the differential—making it income for income tax purposes—and the estate used that excess amount to pay the full balance of the state tax bill).

[32] See, e.g., Estate of Spillar v. Commissioner, 50 T.C.M. (CCH) 1285 (1985) (credit cannot be claimed prior to actual payment of a state death tax payable in installments); Rev. Rul. 86-38, 1986-1 C.B. 296 (no exception to the four year rule is available if the entire FET is paid when the return is filed but state death tax is paid in installments; so only those installments paid to the state within four years after filing the FET return qualify); TAM 8947005 (estate obtained an extension to pay state death tax and claimed the entire state death tax credit that would be allowable after full payment, notwithstanding that it had paid only slightly less than one-fourth of its state death tax liability; only the state death tax actually paid by the due date, without extensions, for paying the state death tax (or by the filing of the federal return, if later) properly could be claimed as a § 2011 credit and, because too much credit was claimed, FET properly payable as of the due date for filing the federal return was underpaid, generating interest on that underpayment between the federal filing due date and the date when the state death tax actually was paid and the credit therefore became available).

[33] The provision in the last clause of the flush language of § 2011(c) was interpreted to mean that interest was not allowable *to the extent* a refund was

no interest was earned on that refund because the state death tax credit was not retroactive to the due date for filing the FET return.[34]

The §2013 previously taxed property credit minimizes the taxation of the same property in more than one estate within a short time. A 100% credit is allowed for the tax previously paid if the prior transferor and the current decedent died within two years of each other; the credit diminishes as the dates of death become more remote and several limitations may preclude the credit from being equal to the entire FET previously paid.

Unfortunately, there is no credit against double taxation in rapid succession if a donor gives property inter vivos to a donee who dies shortly thereafter, because there is no FET credit for gift tax previously paid. Nor is there a credit if the transferor incurs FET and the transferee incurs gift tax on an inter vivos transfer within 10 years after the transferor's death. Only if the transferee dies and the transferor thereafter dies within two years *and* the gifted property is somehow includible in the transferor's gross estate might a §2013 credit be allowable, to the transferee (whose FET return might need to be reopened).[35]

(Footnote Continued)

attributable to the §2011 state death tax credit. See, e.g., Morgan Guaranty Trust Co. v. United States, 277 F.2d 466 (2d Cir. 1960) (the estate was entitled to interest on the entire amount of a refund received because no added state taxes were paid and no part of the refund was based on the §2011 credit); Guaranty Trust Co. v. United States, 192 F.2d 164 (2d Cir. 1951); Edinburg v. United States, 617 F.2d 206 (Ct. Cl. 1980); Rev. Rul. 61-58, 1961-1 C.B. 414.

[34] Rev. Rul. 79-219, 1979-2 C.B. 401 (FET ultimately was reduced by allowance of §2011 state death tax credit but interest paid on the FET deficiency was not recoverable because interest is earned by a taxpayer only on an overpayment of any tax and the taxpayer did not overpay by remitting the federal tax due before the state tax credit was available).

[35] Estate of Owen v. Commissioner, 104 T.C. 498 (1995), illustrates another major flaw in the credits and unification in 1976. See §3.3.15.4 n.153.

Like the §2013 previously taxed property credit, the §2014 credit for property of a citizen or resident situated in a foreign country similarly precludes double taxation at death of the same property, but again there is no credit for foreign gift taxes. Any tax treaty with the foreign country should be examined because it may provide additional relief.

Perhaps the most telling distinction that reveals flaws in unification is the discussion in §6.2.3 with respect to valuation differences between the estate and gift taxes.

§1.3.3

It may help visualize the FET computation to review the following truncated pro forma illustration.

> To determine the decedent's *gross estate*, **add**:
>> §2033 Probate Estate
>> §2035 Transfers and Gift Taxes Paid Within Three Years of Death
>> §§2036 through 2038 Property Transferred Inter Vivos
>> §2039 Annuities
>> §2040 Concurrently Owned Property
>> §2041 General Power of Appointment Property
>> §2042 Life Insurance Proceeds
>> §2044 QTIP
>>
>> **= Total Value of Gross Estate**
>
> To determine the decedent's *taxable estate*, **subtract** from the Gross Estate:
>> §2053 Expenses, Debts, Claims, and Taxes
>> §2054 Losses
>> §2055 Charitable Deduction
>> §2056 Marital Deduction
>> §2058 State Death Tax Deduction
>>
>> **= Total Value of Taxable Estate**
>
> To determine the *total tax base* **add** to the Taxable Estate:
>> adjusted taxable gifts made post-1976 (excluding those
>>> included in the gross estate)
>>
>> **= Total Tax Base**
>
> **Compute** the tentative FET on the total tax base and then **subtract:**
>> any gift tax payable on adjusted taxable gifts made post-1976
>> all allowable credits
>>
>> **= Total FET payable**

§1.4 THE FEDERAL GST

Before 1976 significant abuse of the wealth transfer tax system was possible through the use of generation-skipping trusts. For example, a settlor could create a trust to last for a child's lifetime, remainder to more remote descendants, without causing estate or gift taxation to the child. In such a trust it was possible to grant the child interests including (1) the right to all income, (2) principal in the trustee's discretion, or subject to a power of withdrawal in the child if limited by either an ascertainable standard or a §2514(e) five-or-five limitation, (3) a nongeneral power of appointment, and (4) if properly done, even full powers as trustee, all without causing any change in the tax minimization or avoidance possibility of the trust. In states that have no effective Rule Against Perpetuities,[1] such trusts could be created for successive generations to last forever and, even in states with the Rule, properly drafted generation-skipping trusts could run for well over 100 years. All of this prompted testimony by the original author of this work regarding the proposed GST: "We haven't got an estate tax; what we have, you pay an estate tax if you want to; if you don't want to, you don't have to."

According to Congress, to make the system work, this perceived gap in the coverage of the transfer taxes had to be plugged. Although the tax on generation-skipping transfers (Chapter 13 of the Code) was the answer to this problem, there is tax-free generation skipping still available and, although the favorable status of the law prior to 1977 has been altered, generation skipping is not dead. Indeed, it may be more popular than before attention was drawn to it, especially because the tax excepts smaller estates from its reach and may encourage some trusts to run for the full period of the Rule Against Perpetuities. Moreover, the tax does not reach trusts that were irrevocable prior to September 26, 1985.[2] However, additions to such chronologically exempt trusts are not protected.

The tax requires that there be a generation-skipping trust or equivalent arrangement (including a legal life estate or, in some cases, life insurance beneficiary designations) that shifts enjoyment more than one generation below the transferor (such as to grandchildren or more remote beneficiaries, known as "skip persons"). The tax applies to taxable transfers, which come in three varieties: direct skips and taxable distributions entail transfers to skip persons, and taxable terminations constitute the expiration of all interests in nonskip persons. Particularly unusual about the GST is that it is imposed at a flat rate equal to the highest §2001 rate for wealth transfer tax purposes.

---

[1] §1.4 See §11.2 n.3.

[2] Or trusts created by will or by revocable document executed prior to October 22, 1986, if the settlor died prior to 1987, or if the settlor was incompetent on October 22, 1986, and at all times thereafter.

§1.4

Most importantly for most taxpayers, there is an exemption (it began at $1 million, was indexed for inflation and, beginning in 2004, now is tied to the FET basic exclusion amount). It is available in the form of an "inclusion ratio" regime that, if properly applied, may cause a trust to be totally tax free for its entire duration. A number of other minor exclusions are available, such as counterparts to the gift tax annual and ed/med exclusions, although their operation is not as simple as under the gift tax. A full exegesis of the GST appears below.[3]

§ 1.5 STATE WEALTH TRANSFER TAXES

Every state imposes a tax on the transfer of property at death, although there is great variation in the nature of those taxes.

The oldest variety is the inheritance tax, also known as legacy or succession taxes. These are separate taxes imposed on each benefit conferred on a recipient of property passing from a decedent, the amount of each tax usually being determined by the size of the gift and the degree of consanguinity of the person who receives it. Only a handful of states impose inheritance taxes,[1] and virtually none[2] had their own estate tax any longer. When the § 2011 state death tax credit was repealed, some states enacted or restored prior estate, inheritance, or other succession taxes, such that today the state death tax picture is very difficult to summarize.[3]

Prior to 2005 every state imposed a tax that was a percentage of the FET as reported on the FET return after application of the unified credit.[4] Even the states that imposed their own taxes of the other two varieties collected a pick up or sponge tax to garner the benefit of the then-existing § 2011 credit for state death taxes. Every state imposed an estate tax in the amount of the credit (and virtually all imposed only that

---

[3] See § 11.4.

[1] **§ 1.5** See § 1.1 n.4 and accompanying text.

[2] See § 1.1 n.3 and accompanying text.

[3] A chart showing state death taxes is available at mcguirewoods.com/news-resources/publications/taxation/state_death_tax_chart.pdf. There likely will continue to be Balkanization and difficulty in summarizing the various state provisions.

[4] See § 2011(f) and § 1.1 n.1 and accompanying text.

§ 1.5

amount), which effectively shifted revenue from the federal government to the taxing state without increasing the tax burden on the estate. Indeed, failure to do so merely allowed money that could be diverted to the state to go to the federal government without reducing the total death taxes payable by a decedent's estate or beneficiaries.

The § 2011 credit was repealed in 25% increments between 2002 and 2005, although some states base their tax on the credit as it existed in a prior year, meaning that some pick up taxes continue to apply notwithstanding full repeal of § 2011 after 2004. Although this third form of tax is computed after the federal unified credit is allowed, not all estates with zero FET escape state wealth transfer tax, because not all state tax laws grant a marital deduction in the same amount or for the same transfers as the federal law. As a result, state death tax may be incurred in estates that are tax free for FET purposes.

Many states adopted their own sponge or pick up tax version of the GST as well, in all cases equal to the § 2604 state GST credit,[5] but only New York appears to have imposed a GST in excess of that credit amount. The § 2604 credit also was repealed in 2001, effective in one step in 2005.

State death tax is payable to the state(s) in which the decedent was domiciled at death. A state may tax the personal estate of a decedent who was domiciled in the state at death and may tax real property and tangible personal property located in the state even if the owner was domiciled elsewhere. Because many wealthy decedents spent parts of the year in various states (snowbirds who went to the sunbelt during the winter or sunbelt residents who went north for the summer), several states may be entitled to tax and each will determine for itself whether the decedent was domiciled in that state or otherwise was subject to that state's taxing jurisdiction.

Occasionally multiple state taxation of the same property results. The most famous example of this may be the estate of John T. Dorrance, of Campbell's Soup fame, who died in 1930 with an estate of $115 million and residences in New Jersey and Pennsylvania. The New Jersey courts ruled that he was domiciled in New Jersey and owed New Jersey a tax of $17 million. The Pennsylvania courts ruled that he was domiciled in

---

[5] See § 1.1 n.6 and accompanying text.

Pennsylvania and owed Pennsylvania a tax of the same amount. Both taxes were collected, as was an FET.[6]

More extreme was the case of a Texas decedent whose estate was assessed by Texas, Florida, New York, and Massachusetts, all claiming the decedent as their domiciliary. Collectively they threatened to levy taxes in an amount exceeding the full value of the estate, which was so outrageous that it produced a good result in Texas v. Florida,[7] which limited the state excise to only one tax. And the estate of eccentric billionaire Howard Hughes was involved in three United States Supreme Court cases before it was established that a forum even existed to resolve conflicting state tax claims.[8] Although the problem generally still exists, many state statutes provide a mechanism to resolve conflicting state claims regarding domicile.

In 2012 only Connecticut[9] still imposed gift taxes. The low number probably reflects the fact that state wealth transfer tax rates are de minimis and probably do not often on their own alter the transfer planning of individual citizens. It may be that a state gift tax will not correlate with the federal gift tax, which could result in imposition of a state gift tax when there is no federal gift tax. Nevertheless, there is no credit against the federal gift tax for gift taxes paid to a state, so there is no incentive for states to enact a gift tax merely to take advantage of the kind of revenue sharing made implicit by § 2011.

§ 1.6 THE FEDERAL INCOME TAX ON INDIVIDUALS

The graduated federal tax on the net income of individuals raises questions concerning what is returnable as gross income, special treatment for capital gains and losses, items that are deductible from gross income to produce taxable income, computation of the tax, and payment

---

[6] See Worcester County Trust Co. v. Riley, 302 U.S. 292, 297 (1937), for a summary (a substantial part, but not all, of the state taxes was deductible from the FET as it existed at that time).

[7] 306 U.S. 398 (1939).

[8] See California v. Texas, 457 U.S. 164 (1982) (allowing one state to sue another to establish their respective rights to tax the decedent's estate), and cases cited therein.

[9] See § 1.1 n.5 and accompanying text.

§ 1.6

of the tax. The following discussion may be more helpful if the current Form 1040 U.S. Individual Income Tax Return is available, to illustrate how various items mentioned here fit into the tax computation.

§ 1.6.1 Identifying Income

Amounts earned as compensation for services and amounts earned through business dealings or by investment comprise the bulk of most individuals' gross income. Thus, items such as wages, royalties, profits from businesses such as sole proprietorships or partnerships, investment gains, interest, dividends, and rent all are income. So too are bonuses paid at year end or for special achievements, and gratuities received by people who provide services (such as food servers, valets, and taxi drivers). Although these may appear to be gifts (which are excluded from income under § 102), they are sufficiently related to employment to be regarded as another form of earnings.

So are voluntary payments made by an employer to the surviving family of a deceased employee.[1] But life insurance proceeds are excluded from gross income under § 101, as are totally gratuitous transfers made inter vivos or at death. However, the income generated by insurance proceeds or gifted property must be reported, as must distributions that constitute income (as distinguished from principal) of a trust created gratuitously.

Contest or lottery winnings, prizes and awards, and gambling winnings (to the extent they exceed documented losses for the year) are income, returnable at FMV because, although these also may resemble gifts, some participation usually is required of the winner. The chance of winning therefore is regarded as compensation for that participation. Indeed, Commissioner v. Groetzinger[2] held that an individual who gambles full time is engaged in a trade or business. Under § 74(b), however, prizes or awards that are transferred to a governmental unit or a qualified charitable organization are excluded from income (much like a

---

[1] **§ 1.6** See §§ 9.2 n.15 and 5.10.1, regarding the FET exclusion of voluntary payments and income taxation of IRD, respectively.

[2] 480 U.S. 23 (1987).

§ 1.6.1

qualified charitable donation would be deductible). Rev. Proc. 87-54[3] describes the method to take advantage of this exception.

An exclusion from gross income is provided by § 117 for qualified scholarship funds, and § 127 excludes certain amounts paid and expenses incurred by employers for educational assistance to employees. Alimony paid to a former spouse is income to the recipient under § 71 and is deductible by the payor under § 215, but otherwise § 1041 makes most property transfers between spouses or incident to a divorce tax free.

In addition, some compensation or investment returns are exempt from income taxation. An example is the § 104 exclusion of compensation received on account of personal physical injuries or physical sickness. Similarly, § 103 exempts interest on municipal bonds issued by states and various units of government, including school districts, cities, sanitary districts, and counties. These are in constant demand because, for an individual whose income is taxable at an average rate of (say) 25%, a tax exempt municipal bond with a 6% yield is as desirable as any investment producing a taxable yield of 8% (and may produce more spendable income if state income tax exemptions also apply).

§ 1.6.2 *Identifying the Proper Taxpayer*

Income not yet received and as to which a taxpayer is not (yet) entitled nevertheless may be includible in the taxpayer's gross income. Usually this is true if the taxpayer made an incomplete transfer of property. The reason for attributing income to that taxpayer is apparent if the income tax is imposed at graduated rates because the total income tax on two separate amounts of income is less than the tax on the aggregate of those amounts if they are includible on one return. The following cases are typical:

Assignment of Income: P earns $50,000 annually while P's child C earns only $5,000 annually. P assigns to C the right to receive $20,000 of P's income for the next year, expecting that P will report $30,000 of income and C will report $25,000 of income and, in the process, that they will pay less income tax in the aggregate than they would without this arrangement. This anticipatory assignment of income will not be

---

[3] 1987-2 C.B. 669.

respected. P must report and pay tax on the $20,000 of income assigned to C.

Revocable Trusts: D receives substantial earned income and owns 1,000 shares of dividend paying stock. D transfers the stock to a trustee in trust to pay the income to E for life and then to distribute the principal to E's descendants. If this trust was irrevocable D would pay a gift tax on the transfer and any stock dividends would be reportable by E as income. Instead, D retains a power to revoke the trust at any time. This will cause the income from the stock to be chargeable to D as a grantor trust taxable under § 676, even though the trust never is revoked and E in fact receives all the trust income.

Even if E would have paid income tax at the same rate that will be imposed on D, this tax result may be favorable because it appears that D's payment of the tax is an indirect benefit to E that is not subject to additional gift tax. The same result would obtain if D kept the stock, received the dividend income and paid income tax thereon, and gave E the after tax net income, but the trust approach is preferable if FET will be avoided at D's death. In this case § 2038(a)(1) would apply when D dies because of D's retained power to revoke, but other sources of grantor trust exposure can be employed that avoid that result.[4] In this case, D's power to revoke the trust means that for gift tax purposes no completed gift is made to E until each income payment to E occurs and, as long as D's power to revoke remains in existence, D will not incur a gift tax on the property transferred to the trustee.

Short-Term Trust: D, in the previous illustration, transfers the stock to a trustee to pay the income irrevocably to E for five years. The result to D is the same, now under § 673, which causes the settlor of a trust to be treated as the owner of any portion of a trust in which the settlor or the settlor's spouse has a reversionary interest if, as of inception of that portion of the trust, the value of the reversion exceeds 5% of the value of that portion. The settlor will not be treated as the owner solely by reason of the reversionary interest in that portion if (1) the beneficiary is a lineal descendant of the settlor, (2) the descendant holds all the present interests in that portion of the trust, and (3) the reversion takes effect only on the death of the beneficiary before attaining age 21.

---

[4] See § 5.11.10.

If E is under the age of 19 (or a full-time student under the age of 24), however, the "kiddie tax" in § 1(g) would assess the income tax on that income at the tax rate applicable to E's parents, which could mean that there is no income tax minimization even if the grantor trust rules are avoided. In addition, D will have made a completed gift for gift tax purposes of the value of the term interest in income given to E, although the value of D's reversion will be includible in D's gross estate under § 2033 for FET purposes.[5]

Irrevocable Trusts: Under Subchapter J of the Internal Revenue Code, trust income not taxed to a trust's settlor under the grantor trust rules of Subpart E is taxable to the trust's beneficiaries (1) to the extent it is distributed (or deemed distributed) to them or (2) it is required to be distributed to them (even if it is not). Otherwise it is taxed to the trust, which is a separate income tax paying entity.

Income reportable by the trustee is not likely to generate a smaller tax because the number of brackets in which the income can be taxed is limited under § 1(e) and each bracket is compressed in terms of the amount of income taxed at less than the maximum rate. Thus, most accumulated trust income will be taxed in the highest marginal bracket applicable at any time under the Internal Revenue Code. This bracket compression usually eliminates any incentive to accumulate trust income in hopes of causing less income taxation currently. As a consequence, little income tax planning involving trusts is common currently.[6]

§ 1.6.3 *Capital Gains and Losses*

If X bought stock for $60 per share and sold it for $70 per share, X would realize a capital gain of $10 per share. Correspondingly, if X sold the same stock for only $50 per share, a capital loss of $10 per share would be realized. However, if the stock appreciated on the market to $70 or depreciated to $50 but X did not sell it, no gain or loss would be

---

[5] Cf. Estate of Watson v. Commissioner, 94 T.C. 262 (1990) (reversion existed because the decedent failed to effectively convey the entire fee simple interest); Estate of Graham v. Commissioner, 46 T.C. 415 (1966) (contingent reversion in trust as to which income might return to the settlor in the future).

[6] See Pennell, Income Shifting After TRA'86, 46 N.Y.U. Inst. Fed. Tax'n 50-1 (1988).

realized for tax purposes because the income tax does not recognize "paper" profits or losses.

The Internal Revenue Code distinguishes long-term capital gains and losses (with respect to property held more than 12 months) and § 1(h) freezes the tax rate on most long-term capital gains at a rate (which may be as high as 28% or as low as zero, under § § 1(h) (1) (E) and (B), respectively, depending on the type of gain and the tax year involved) that may be less than the marginal tax rate on ordinary income applicable to the taxpayer for the year of sale. An individual taxpayer may have long-term and short-term transactions, some profitable and some unprofitable, over a series of years. Normally any excess of gains over losses must be returned as income, but an excess of losses over gains may be employed as a deduction from ordinary income only to the extent allowed by § 1211(b)(1), with any excess available in additional years as allowed by § 1212(b).

Gain or loss is a function of selling price (amount realized) and basis (cost, with certain adjustments). Usually the amount realized is easy to determine, but determining basis may present difficulties. For example, if X bought stock for $60 and sold it for $70, the cost basis would be $60 and the gain would be $10. But consider the following cases:

(1) D bought stock at $60 and later gave it to E when its FMV was $80. E sold the stock for $70. Under § 1015(a), E's basis for determining gain or loss is a carryover of D's basis of $60, adjusted to reflect any gift tax paid attributable to net appreciation in the value of the gift (for gifts made before 1977 the increase was in the amount of the full gift tax paid). This adjustment may not, however, increase E's basis above the $80 FMV of the property at the time of the gift. In determining any capital loss in E's hands the carryover basis cannot exceed the FMV at the time of the gift. This discrimination precludes D from giving a tax loss to E (if, for example, it would be more useful to E than to D). In this case E has a gain of $10 (adjusted basis equals $60—ignoring any § 1015(a) basis adjustment—and amount realized is $70, notwithstanding the $80 value for gift tax purposes). If the FMV at the time of D's gift had been $50, however, and E sold the stock for $40, there would be only a $10 loss because basis would be limited to the gift tax FMV. Further, if the value of the gift was $50 and E sold the stock for $55, there would be no gain and no loss because basis for determining gain would be the carryover basis of $60 and basis for determining loss would be limited to the $50 gift tax FMV.

(2) D bought stock for $60 and held it until death, bequeathing it to E. The stock was worth $80 at D's death and E sold it for $75. Under the

§ 1.6.3

§ 1014(b)(9) new-basis-at-death rule, E obtained a basis in the stock equal to its FMV for FET purposes in D's estate. Thus, the stock had a basis of $80 in E's hands and a loss of $5 is allowable as a result of E's sale of the stock for $75. The Internal Revenue Code does not limit E's basis under § 1014 as it does under § 1015 because it is assumed that D did not die to shift a tax loss to E.

In 1981 Congress enacted § 1014(e) to deny new basis at death if appreciated property was acquired by a decedent by gift within one year before death and that property passed from the decedent back to the donor or to the donor's spouse. This provision prevents a basis advantage from being obtained by a person who owns low basis property and gives it to a person who is about to die, who gives it back to the donor with a new basis equal to its FET value. Although this abuse was deemed to be a significant problem only if the gift augmented the donee's gross estate for FET purposes but no tax was payable (because the donee's unified credit is adequate, or because the donor and donee are spouses and the gifts out and back qualify for the marital deduction), § 1014(e) is not limited to these circumstances.[7]

An exclusion of gain from the sale of a principal personal residence by an individual is granted by § 121, not to exceed $250,000 of gain

---

[7] According to H.R. Rep. No. 201, 97th Cong., 1st Sess. 188-189 (1981), § 1014(e) is applicable if the property passes directly or indirectly back to the donor or the donor's spouse, stating that:

> The denial of a stepped-up basis applies where the donor receives the benefit of the appreciated property regardless of whether the bequest by the decedent to the donor is a specific bequest, a general bequest, a pecuniary bequest, or a residuary bequest. However, in the case of a pecuniary bequest, the donor will receive the benefit of the appreciated property only if the inclusion of the appreciated property in the estate of the decedent affected the amount that the donor receives under the pecuniary bequest.

Thus, if the property increases the decedent's gross estate and thus increases the amount of the decedent's formula marital deduction bequest to the donor, § 1014(e) will deny a new basis even if the property is not used to satisfy that marital bequest. And, although the quoted language refers to a pecuniary bequest, it is likely that a court will impose the same result if the marital deduction bequest from the decedent to the donor is a formula fractional bequest under which the numerator is larger due to inclusion of the § 1014(e) property in the decedent's gross estate. In either case, a specific bequest of the property away from the marital bequest should not avoid § 1014(e) if the formula bequest is increased by virtue of inclusion.

§ 1.6.3

($500,000 in the case of married taxpayers filing jointly) every two years.[8] Rev. Rul. 87-104[9] held that a taxpayer's marital status for purposes of a prior version of § 121 is determined on the date the residence is sold. Thus, if two people are contemplating marriage and each owns a residence, sales before the marriage would entitle each to the § 121 exclusion whereas only one exclusion would be available if they wait until after the marriage and then sell the two residences. Presumably the same result will continue to apply under the current version of § 121.

In the case considered by the Ruling, D sold a residence in January 1984, and married S in June of that year. The couple filed a joint return for 1984, which made the § 121 election for the sale of D's residence (although S did not join in the election because they were not married when the residence was sold). D died in 1986 and thereafter S sold a residence that S owned prior to the marriage, also making the § 121 election. The government held that S was not prevented from doing so by the fact that D had made a § 121 election on their joint return, because they were not married when either residence was sold.

In addition, PLR 8909020 held that, if property is owned jointly by spouses and only one spouse satisfied all the § 121(a) requirements, both spouses would be treated as satisfying the requirements if they file jointly. If, however, one spouse satisfies some but not all of the requirements, and the other spouse satisfies some but not all of the requirements, the Ruling held that the transfer would not qualify for § 121 nonrecognition of gain. It appears that § 121(b)(2)(C) alters this treatment by requiring *both* spouses to meet the use requirements and neither to be disqualified by the prior sale limitation.

§ 1.6.4 Reductions from Gross Income

Various items are subtracted from gross income to compute the amount (taxable income) against which the income tax rates are applied. The first is the § 151 "personal exemption," allowed for every taxpayer in the stated amount of $2,000, but indexed under § 151(d)(4) for inflation

---

[8] See § 121 with respect to qualified use requirements, and § 121(d) for special rules dealing with property of deceased or former spouses and stockholders in cooperative housing corporations. Joint returns filed with the estate of a deceased spouse for the year of death are discussed in § 15.7.1.

[9] 1987-2 C.B. 45.

(e.g., the figure was increased to $3,800 in 2012 and is adjusted annually). This entitlement may be subject to phase out if the taxpayer's adjusted gross income exceeds certain amounts specified in § 151 (d) (3) (C) that also are inflation adjusted, and themselves are subject to relief provisions that may sunset after 2012. Spouses who file a joint return are entitled to an exemption for each.

Additional exemptions are available to taxpayers who are over 65 or blind and for each dependent (1) whose gross income for the calendar year is less than the amount of the exemption, or (2) who is a child of the taxpayer and is under age 19 or is a student under age 24. As defined in § 152, dependents must receive over half of their support from and be related to the taxpayer in a prescribed way (e.g., descendant of the taxpayer's grandparents and certain in-laws and step relatives).

Among the myriad deductions that are allowable are § § 162 and 212 for business expenses and the costs of producing income, such as reasonable wages and salaries, cost of goods sold, depreciation, investment advisory fees, costs for licenses, and expenses to protect income producing property. Interest paid on a personal indebtedness is deductible under § 163, subject to numerous limitations and exceptions (e.g., most personal interest is disallowed under § 163 (h), although interest to acquire a personal residence is a notable exception to this disallowance rule). Certain taxes are deductible under § 164, such as real estate taxes for owned property and state income taxes. The deductibility of real estate taxes and mortgage interest, as compared to the absence of a deduction for rent, means that there are tax advantages to owning a home. Under § 216, tenant stockholders are able to deduct as interest and as real property taxes portions of amounts paid to a cooperative housing corporation, which puts them on a par with other home and condominium owners.

Charitable giving is encouraged by the § 170 deduction of up to 50% of the contribution base (only gifts to certain specified charitable organizations qualify for the 50% ceiling; gifts to other charitable organizations are limited by a 20% ceiling for gifts of capital gain property and a 30% limitation for contributions of other property). In addition, the AMT may apply to certain charitable contributions, all diminishing the tax incentives of charitable giving.

§ 1.6.4

Certain other deductions are authorized, such as medical expenses in excess of a certain percentage of income (with a limitation on the amount of medicine that can be taken into account), casualty losses to the extent the loss from each casualty exceeds a specified amount, and alimony paid. In addition, some deductions are tax preference items subject to the AMT found in § 55 et seq. All deductions are less valuable if the top income tax bracket is low, and § 68(a)(1) imposes a reduction on some allowable itemized deductions for high income taxpayers (e.g., there is an inflation adjusted figure that also is subject to relief provisions that may sunset after 2012), which negates some of the benefit of their deductions.

Finally, the § 63(c) standard deduction is a flat allowance taken in place of itemized deductions if it is greater. As of 2012 the standard deduction was $5,950 for single persons, $8,700 for heads of households, $11,900 for married taxpayers filing jointly and for surviving spouses, and $5,950 for married taxpayers filing separately, all indexed for inflation and all subject to certain limitations under § 63(c)(5) if the taxpayer is allowable as a dependent on another taxpayer's return. The so-called marriage penalty implicit in different (lower) figures for married filing separate returns and single individuals was corrected beginning in 2003.

§ 1.6.5 Computation of the Tax

No tax is due unless adjusted gross income exceeds the sum of the taxpayer's exemptions and available deductions. The tax computation is adequately illustrated on each return and its printed instructions. The most striking feature is the split income provision that permits spouses to file a joint return that effectively computes their tax on half their aggregate income and then doubles that amount. This effectively averages their income and produces a tax saving under the graduated rate schedule. Spouses who have substantially equal incomes derive little benefit from this provision,[10] which is a federal subsidy of marriage for

---

[10] Moreover, joint filing opens married taxpayers to special provisions that may not be desirable. For example, a portion of a married couple's overpayment of tax on their joint return can be seized by the government in payment of one spouse's prenuptial tax liability. The portion that represents the liable spouse's interest in the overpayment on the joint return is determined by subtracting the liable spouse's share of the joint tax liability from the liable spouse's contribution

most married couples. This marriage bonus was *not* altered by the marriage penalty relief legislation enacted in 2003. To offset somewhat the income splitting advantage bestowed on married couples who file joint returns, single individuals are subject to reduced rate schedules, as are heads of households. This changed only in the bottom bracket for income tax purposes. See § 1 (f) (8).

§ 1.6.6 Payment of the Tax

It has been a principle of income tax policy since 1943 that income tax must be paid as income is earned. Thus, employers generally must withhold and remit directly to the government a percentage of wages and salaries as a credit against the employee's income tax liability. Self-employed taxpayers must file a Declaration of Estimated Tax and pay estimated taxes. All taxpayers remit any balance due, or receive a refund of any overpayment, when their return is filed after the close of the tax year. Provisions permit amendment of an estimated tax return and penalties apply for certain underestimates or underwithholding.

§ 1.6.7 Concurrent Interests

Income from jointly owned property is taxable to the joint owners, each being taxable on the portion of the income to which he or she is entitled under local law. Interest on joint bank accounts and interest on jointly owned government bonds is taxable to the joint owners in the same proportion as each contributed to the cost of the joint arrangement if each can withdraw his or her contribution from the arrangement at any time.

(Footnote Continued)

toward the liability. If the joint return relates to community property, and if state law provides that community property is subject to the premarital or other separate debts of either spouse, the government may offset the entire amount otherwise refundable to the nonliable spouse against the separate tax liability of the liable spouse. See Rev. Rul. 85-70, 1985-1 C.B. 361, amplifying Rev. Rul. 74-611, 1974-2 C.B. 399, and Rev. Rul. 80-7, 1980-1 C.B. 296.

§ 1.7 THE FEDERAL INCOME TAX ON CORPORATIONS

Tax rates applicable to corporations have fluctuated relative to the rates applicable to individuals. When the individual rate exceeds the maximum rate applicable to corporations, taxpayers are inclined to retain income in a corporation (at the risk of encountering an accumulated earnings problem). When individual rates are lower than the maximum rate applicable to corporations, taxpayers are inclined to use S Corporations (taxable under Subchapter S of the Internal Revenue Code) and partnerships (which term, as used here, includes LLCs, all taxable under Subchapter K of the Code) rather than traditional corporations (taxable under Subchapter C of the Code), because S Corporations and partnerships act as conduits so that all tax attributes pass through to the shareholders or partners.

The choice of tax entity is significant as well because another major feature of the corporate income tax imposed under Subchapter C is double taxation. The federal government taxes profits of a C Corporation twice on their way to its stockholders. First it imposes an income tax on the profits at the corporate level, and then any dividends declared by the corporation from what remains again are taxed to the stockholders, traditionally at their graduated individual income tax rates, but currently qualified dividend income is taxed under § 1(h)(11) at net capital gain rates, which minimizes (but does not eliminate) the double tax penalty on dividend income of C corporations. Closely held corporations that elect to be treated as S Corporations, and partnerships, avoid double tax because the Code ignores the entity as a separate taxpayer, which avoids the tax at the corporate level.

Each time tax rates fluctuate these dynamics change, particularly if the corporate income tax rates are lower than those applicable to individuals, which causes taxpayers to prefer to retain income at the corporate level to avoid the passthrough that applies to S Corporations and partnerships.

§ 1.8 STATE INCOME TAXES

Most states impose a tax on income, although a few tax only intangibles (such as investments). Those that tax income also differ in terms of the varieties of income that are excepted, whether the rate is uniform or graduated, and whether state law follows certain federal income tax conventions (such as computing the state tax on the basis of the individual's taxable income reported on the federal Form 1040). State income tax rates are low in comparison to the federal levy, and some state tax rates vary from year to year according to the fiscal needs of the state.[1]

---

[1] **§ 1.8** The only states that appear *not* to have an income tax at all are Alaska, Florida, Nevada, South Dakota, Texas, Washington, and Wyoming. For information on rates and imposition in general, see Schoenblum, 2013 Multistate Guide to Estate Planning Table 12 (2012).

2

Intestacy: Estate Plans by Operation of State Law

§2.0 DEFAULT PLANNING

Every decedent who dies subject to state law anywhere in the United States has an estate plan, either of their own choice or, in default of effective affirmative planning, by operation of state law. To the extent a decedent dies without a valid will, that decedent's probate estate is subject to intestate succession.[1] Most state statutes of descent and distribution (intestacy) are derived from English common law and, based on this shared origin, the statutory pattern is similar in most states. Nevertheless, there are local peculiarities, and modern reforms have refined these laws. Thus, local variations must be studied to address specific questions regarding the estate plan created by operation of law applicable to any particular estate.

A statutory distribution regime cannot reflect the infinite variety of family situations. Decedents who do not have a personal estate plan tailored to their special family needs or peculiarities therefore are subject to the statutory cookie cutter rules that stamp every estate plan with the same pattern. This may be inappropriate because the standard intestate distribution regime may not be in harmony with the realities of modern families and society.

Intestate statutes can be improved and modernized,[2] but legislative action in this area is slow and cumbersome and most individuals avoid intestacy by executing a valid will. Thus, it is difficult to generate public demand for legislative change. Among the more undesirable features of intestacy is the fact that beneficiaries usually receive their entitlements outright, without regard to their legal competence or practical capacity to manage the property. Further, the share provided to a surviving spouse (S) often is inadequate to support S, inequitable in terms of aggregate contributions, and ineffective marital deduction planning for optimum tax minimization. In addition, intestacy precludes effective asset management to avoid the claims of a beneficiary's creditors or

---

[1] **§2.0** Typically these laws apply only with respect to the decedent's probate estate, which usually is not the total amount includible in the decedent's gross estate for FET purposes. See Chapter 11 §§ 2031-2046 of the Internal Revenue Code; only § 2033 deals directly with probate property subject to intestacy.

[2] See, e.g., the UPC approved by the National Conference of Commissioners on Uniform State Laws in August 1969 and revisions thereto promulgated in 1990 and 2008.

other predators, and prevents tax planning designed to avoid successive exposure to wealth transfer taxation.[3] Finally, in some cases natural objects of a decedent's bounty are individuals such as committed part-

---

[3] Although § 2013 provides a previously taxed property credit that is designed to mitigate the effect of the same property passing through two estates in relatively quick succession, it is a poor substitute for effective planning that requires an individual to survive a decedent for a specified period before becoming entitled to a bequest or to placing the bequest in a trust that provides enjoyment without subsequent exposure to tax in the beneficiary's estate. The 120 hour survivorship requirement in UPC § 2-104 is designed to address this concern in the event of relatively simultaneous deaths, but it also is no substitute for effective planning using trusts.

To appreciate the ineffectiveness of § 2013 to avoid double taxation, consider its limitations. First, it applies only if the recipient of property dies within ten years after the transferor (or within two years before the transferor, if the recipient received the property and died first, followed within two years by the transferor's death, with inclusion of the gifted property in the transferor's gross estate under one of the string provisions or what remains of the § 2035 three-year rule, which is not likely).

Second, the credit declines by 20% for every two year differential in the date of death of the transferor and the recipient. For example, if the recipient dies more than two but less than four years after the transferor, the credit is only 80% of the credit that would apply if their deaths had occurred within two years of each other. Similarly, deaths over eight but less than ten years apart would result in only a 20% entitlement to the credit.

Third, the recipient's personal representative must establish that property includible in the recipient's gross estate came from a transferor who died within the twelve year window.

Fourth, the recipient's personal representative must establish the value of the property in the recipient's gross estate. See Estate of Meyer v. Commissioner, 83 T.C. 350 (1984), aff'd, 778 F.2d 125 (2d Cir. 1985) (computation made all the more difficult because recipient's estate included property received from several transferors, for which Treas. Reg. § 20.2013-6 requires the credits to be computed separately).

Fifth, two limitations restrict the credit to ensure that the property is taxed at the higher rate as between the two estates. The first limitation, under § 2013(b), restricts the credit to the amount of tax incurred in the transferor's estate attributable to the previously taxed property and is computed after all credits and deductions are reflected. Thus, if the property was taxed in the transferor's estate at an average rate lower than the rate imposed in the recipient's estate, the credit cannot exceed the tax incurred on the property in the transferor's estate. In effect, the tax computed at the recipient's higher rate is imposed, but only the difference in tax between the two estates is collected at the recipient's death.

§ 2.0

ners, children-in-law, unadopted stepchildren, and friends or employees who are not included in any class of intestate beneficiaries.

Given these realities, it is unlikely that any person properly is advised to die intestate. Even if the individual fully understands and accepts the beneficiaries who will take and in what shares (per stirpes, per capita, or some other mode) under the various potential circumstances that may exist at death, administration of that person's estate may require that added planning be considered before concluding that intestacy is satisfactory in all respects. With the convenience of modern word processing, if all these factors are evaluated, it hardly makes sense not to produce a will or other dispositive device to implement the client's objectives.

(Footnote Continued)

The second limitation, under § 2013(c)(1), prevents the credit from exceeding the tax attributable to the previously taxed property in the recipient's estate. Thus, if the property was taxed in the transferor's estate at an average rate higher than the rate imposed in the recipient's estate, the credit cannot exceed the tax incurred on the property in the recipient's estate. In effect, the credit from the transferor's estate cannot be used to eliminate the tax on the property in the recipient's estate and then reduce the tax on other assets in the recipient's estate as well. See, e.g., Estate of La Sala v. Commissioner, 71 T.C. 752 (1979) (recipient's § 2013 credit was limited because the transferor's FET was reduced by the marital deduction, which reduced the § 2013 credit the transferor's estate was entitled to receive for the same property the transferor previously had received from a predeceased child). See § 13.2.5 for a more detailed examination of § 2013 in the most likely context of its application, involving transfers between spouses.

§ 2.0

§2.1 S's SHARE

§2.1.1 Intestate Share of S

A spouse's entitlement[1] of an intestate decedent's estate is dependent on state law, which is remarkably similar in most states.[2] Typically,
statutes of descent and distribution give S an outright interest, with only
its size varying from state to state or, within a given state, depending on
the existence and the degree of consanguinity of other surviving
relatives.

UPC §2-102 is instructive in this respect, granting S a base amount
in all events—which varies depending on the relation of other takers to
D or to S—plus a share of the balance of the estate ranging from half (if
either D or S is survived by descendants not common to the other) to all
of the estate (if no descendant or parent survives D or all descendants of
D and of S are common to both).

Intestate property passing to S outright by operation of law is
deemed to pass from D for FET marital deduction purposes[3] and should

---

[1] §2.1 Whether an individual qualifies as a surviving "spouse" depends on
state law and may turn on whether the decedent effectively married another
person, was precluded from being married to that person because either of them
already was married to still another person, was deemed married to that person
under a common law marriage or committed partner regime, or was divorced
from that spouse before death in a legally binding proceeding. For an interesting
combination of these issues, see In re Estate of Shufelt, 211 A.2d 173 (Vt. 1965)
(S procured a divorce in another jurisdiction that S successfully challenged as
invalid after D's death intestate, allowing S to take a spouse's intestate share;
court recognized that S had resumed marital relations with D after S was
released from prison following a bigamy conviction based on invalidity of the
divorce decree). See also §13.4.2.2.2.

[2] Most intestate statutes have a similar common law origin dating to the 1700s
and are little changed to this date. Significant differences include the concept of
fraud on the spouse's share, which is addressed differently in various jurisdictions, and the fact that an election to take a statutory share may be available if S
is not satisfied with D's will in a testamentary estate (except in most community
property jurisdictions, in which S already owns a share of the spouses' aggregate
wealth and therefore has no additional entitlement). See §3.4.

[3] See Treas. Reg. §20.2056(c)-1(a)(5).

be deductible in its entirety.[4] The only issue of any significance is the value of S's share, which can depend on the size of the estate and the proper fraction for S,[5] or more subtly on whether the fraction is computed before or after payment of funeral and administration expenses, claims and debts, and federal and local taxes.

The marital deduction is limited to the net value of the share passing to S,[6] which requires a determination of the proper allocation of estate obligations. If the portion passing to S is computed "net" of these amounts, a circular computation is required because the value of the marital deduction cannot be determined until the amount of all taxes is

---

[4] The § 2056(a) marital deduction is unlimited in amount, which may subject more property to tax in S's estate and may make disclaimer of a portion of the intestate share appropriate. See §§ 7.1.6, 13.1.4, and 13.2 for a discussion of disclaimers for postmortem planning purposes.

A different problem was presented in PLR 9101025, in which S attempted to increase the marital deduction from the amount of the statutory share. The beneficiaries agreed that $30,000 of cash would be distributed to S outright. The remaining entitlement (in this case, under a forced heir share election but with the same effect as if an intestate share was involved) would be satisfied in the form of a life estate in a trust funded with an amount that produced a discounted present value equal to the remaining entitlement. A marital deduction was requested for the full amount of that trust corpus, even though it represented more property than the amount of S's share. The government concluded that the "passing" requirement for marital deduction qualification was not met by the settlement agreement because what passed from D was an outright interest in a fraction of the net estate, not a trust interest with an actuarially determined value equal to the statutory entitlement. Thus, the deduction was limited to the amount of the statutory share proper. See § 13.4.2.3.2 regarding settlement of postmortem controversies and marital deduction qualification.

[5] For example, S's intestate share under Alabama Code § 43-8-70(a)(1) is based in part on the amount of S's separate estate. See Risher v. United States, 339 F. Supp. 484 (S.D. Ala. 1972), aff'd, 465 F.2d 1 (5th Cir. 1972) (adopted child was entitled to pretermitted heir share equal to amount the child would have taken if the decedent had died intestate, notwithstanding S was beneficiary of entire estate under D's will; S's separate estate would have prevented S from taking anything had D died intestate, so child's share was larger and amount passing to S that qualified for marital deduction was reduced); Taylor v. United States, 67-1 U.S. Tax Cas. (CCH) ¶ 12,439 (M.D. Ala. 1966), aff'd, 388 F.2d 849 (5th Cir. 1967) (S's separate property reduced value of S's share of D's estate; S's personalty was applied first in reduction of the distributive share in D's personalty and real property was applied to reduce S's share in D's realty).

[6] See Treas. Reg. § 20.2056(b)-4 and § 13.4.2.3.3.

§ 2.1.1

known, and the taxes cannot be determined until the value of the deductible portion is known.[7] Only if the portion is determined using a "gross" estate computation (before reduction for these amounts) is this circularity avoided, and then only if S's portion is exempt from contributing to these payments.

At one time statutes of descent for real property differed from statutes of distribution for personal property, but now both types of property pass to the same persons in the same proportions with only occasional procedural differences (for example, title to real property may pass directly to the heir, subject to administration by the personal representative and potential sale to satisfy debts or expenses, while both the title and possession of personal property passes through the personal representative). Otherwise, statutes of descent and distribution generally follow a pattern set by the common law in the 1700s and still do not reflect a sensitivity to FET deductions.

The preferable tax minimization result is a gross estate division that produces a larger share than most statutes provide for S and calls for payment of all charges from the nonmarital portion. A tension exists in this respect, however, because a net estate division generates a larger nonmarital portion, notwithstanding that more FET is incurred due to a smaller marital portion (in a net estate division the marital portion is reduced by the full amount of both the increased taxes and the larger nonmarital portion).

The law of most states produces a compromise result, calling for determination of S's statutory share after payment of funeral and administration expenses and after paying or providing for claims and debts, but before taxes. Unfortunately, no generally accepted result can be stated, and confusion is generated in numerous states because this issue cannot be resolved without consulting both the statute granting S's entitlement and that providing for tax apportionment. Often these provisions are

---

[7] Publication 904 (now declared obsolete and out of print but available at 1990 WL 599448) provides supplemental instructions to Form 706 to compute the FET if an interrelated marital or charitable deduction is involved. The gross versus net fraction issue is explored in a different context illustrating these concepts in § 13.7.7.2.

located in different sections or even in different chapters of the law.[8] And this chore becomes geometrically more difficult if D owned property in more than one jurisdiction.[9]

§2.1.2 Dower and Curtesy

In states that have not abolished dower or curtesy[10] or both, S is forced to elect between these rights and any statutory rights in D's real property. Because most states no longer recognize dower or curtesy,[11] S's statutory entitlement is either the intestate share under the statute of descent and distribution or the forced heir share available upon electing against D's estate.[12]

Common law dower was a widow's entitlement to a life estate in one-third of the real property of which the deceased husband was seized of

---

[8] See, e.g., Mass. Gen. L. ch. 190, §1 and ch. 65A, §5, which are representative. UPC §2-102 refers to the "balance" of the intestate estate and the tax apportionment rule is discovered only upon inspection of §3-9A-103(b)(2) (the Uniform Estate Tax Apportionment Act protection against apportionment to the extent the marital deduction applies, as integrated into the UPC).

[9] See, e.g., Rev. Rul. 77-345, 1977-2 C.B. 337 (decedent owned realty in another state; equitable apportionment applied only in the state of the decedent's domicile, so S's intestate share could not be determined until the FET was ascertained, which introduced the added problem of ascertaining and allocating state death taxes in the aggregate amount of the §2011 credit, all of which was computed with illustrations in the Ruling).

[10] See 1 American Law of Property §§5.1-5.74 (Casner ed. 1952).

[11] See, e.g., the 1990 version of UPC §2-112, which repeals dower and curtesy absolutely. Schoenblum, 2013 Multistate Guide to Estate Planning Table 6.01 (2012) lists the only states that still recognize dower or curtesy or both as Arkansas, Kentucky, Massachusetts, Michigan (dower only), New Jersey (only for pre-1980 realty), and Ohio (dower only).

Significant variations may exist among state laws that no longer grant these rights. For example, the Uniform Marital Property Act, enacted to date only in Wisconsin, replaces all state property rights of a surviving spouse with an entitlement similar to community property. See Bascom, Irreconcilable Differences: Income from Separate Property Under Divorce Law and Under Wisconsin Marital Property Act, 70 Marq. L. Rev. 41 (1986).

[12] For a discussion of the statutory election available if S is dissatisfied with D's estate plan, see §3.4.

an estate of inheritance at any time during their marriage.[13] The right that was inchoate prior to the husband's death became consummate when he died.[14] Among the limited number of states that still recognize dower at all, some have reduced it to an entitlement only in realty the husband owned at death,[15] and dower has replaced curtesy in virtually every state that still recognizes the concept, making dower apply to all surviving spouses and not just to widows.[16]

Generally an absolute divorce terminates inchoate dower but, like most matters of this nature, local law must be examined.[17] For example,

---

[13] S would not be entitled to dower in property in which D owned only a remainder interest at death and therefore was not yet seized at any time during life.

[14] See Rev. Rul. 58-13, 1958-1 C.B. 342, regarding the federal gift tax significance of inchoate dower.

[15] Mich. Comp. Laws § 558.1 appears to be the only dower statute that does not apply equally to either spouse. Because Michigan does not grant curtesy, this gender based discrimination is constitutionally suspect.

[16] See, e.g., Ky. Rev. Stat. § 392.020.

[17] Marital status may be at issue with respect to dower in other respects, and state law will determine whether individuals who cohabit without marriage acquire rights in the property of each other. For example, state law may regard them as common law spouses, or there may be an enforceable express or implied agreement between the parties regarding division of their accumulated wealth. See, e.g., Marvin v. Marvin, 557 P.2d 106 (Cal. 1976) (landmark "palimony" decision, not involving a decedent's estate); Carlson v. United States, 84-1 U.S. Tax Cas. (CCH) ¶ 13,570 (D. Minn. 1983) (couple, not married, worked and lived together; survivor received life insurance proceeds from policy decedent owned on decedent's life, which was includible in decedent's gross estate and deductible under § 2053 because their agreement to share assets constituted a bona fide agreement for a full and adequate consideration in money or money's worth); Green v. Commissioner, 846 F.2d 870 (2d Cir. 1988) (similar; survivor's recovery in action against decedent's estate for the value of services rendered was taxable as income not excluded under § 102 as money acquired by gift, bequest, devise, or inheritance); Tyranski v. Piggins, 205 N.W.2d 595 (Mich. 1973). See also Sullivan v. Rooney, 533 N.E.2d 1372 (Mass. 1989) (constructive trust established based on the defendant's assurances and promises regarding ownership of assets and the plaintiff's reasonable reliance thereon).

Metz v. United States, 91-1 U.S. Tax Cas. (CCH) ¶ 60,071 (10th Cir. 1991), aff'g 89-2 U.S. Tax Cas. (CCH) ¶ 13,822 (D. Kan. 1989), illustrates the dangers of an agreement to perform services in exchange for a testamentary bequest. The plaintiff agreed to move in with and care for the decedent until death, and the

in some states dower rights in land owned prior to divorce outlive the divorce if misconduct was involved and led to the divorce.[18] Moreover, even if it does not terminate the right to dower in certain land, divorce extinguishes the right to waive dower and take a statutory forced heir share.

Common law dower may preclude conveyance without consent of land subject to the inchoate right, and dower rights trump D's creditors, but seizure and sale may be permitted if the value of the dower right is set aside for S out of the sale proceeds.[19]

(Footnote Continued)

decedent complied with their agreement by bequeathing decedent's home to the plaintiff. The decedent's estate also owned stock in a closely held business and the estate properly elected § 6166 deferral of the FET attributable to the business. The balance of the taxes were paid immediately and the home was distributed outright to the plaintiff. When the business subsequently declared bankruptcy and ceased paying on its § 6166 liability, the government successfully imposed the balance of the tax due on the plaintiff as a transferee of the estate. The court determined that the plaintiff was an estate beneficiary, not a purchaser or creditor, noting that the plaintiff did not report the home as income from services rendered to the decedent (and without considering whether distribution of the home was the payment of a deductible claim against the estate).

The parties might have structured their agreement to avoid FET inclusion and the FET lien, but with other costs. For example, the decedent might have transferred the home when the plaintiff moved in to care for the decedent, or could have sold the home to the plaintiff on installments that would be paid or forgiven over time. And the plaintiff might have reported the home as income from services and filed a claim against the decedent's estate for compensation under the contract. Difficulties would arise, however, if the plaintiff was obliged under state law to support the decedent, if the value of the services rendered was not fair consideration for the property promised in return, if significant capital gain would be incurred on a sale during the decedent's life, or in the unlikely event that the plaintiff's income tax bracket exceeded the decedent's projected FET bracket. Moreover, unless properly handled, the decedent's transfer might be deemed a gift with a retained life estate, leading to § 2036(a)(1) inclusion in the decedent's gross estate at death.

In any event, the agreement should be memorialized in writing if the plaintiff hopes to establish rights thereunder after the decedent's death.

[18] See 1 American Law of Property § 5.36 (Casner ed. 1952).

[19] See United States v. Washington, 251 F. Supp. 359 (E.D. Va. 1966), aff'd, 402 F.2d 3 (4th Cir. 1968) (tax lien satisfied with proceeds from forced sale free and clear of dower rights); United States v. Briggs, 76-2 U.S. Tax Cas. (CCH) ¶ 9543 (E.D. Va. 1976) (inchoate dower right protected upon foreclosure sale to satisfy

Dower is deemed to pass from D to S for marital deduction purposes[20] and, even if it is a terminable interest, it may qualify for the FET marital deduction.[21] Many statutes also provide an election to take a lump sum payment equal in value to the dower life interest in one-third of the decedent's realty, which also will qualify for the marital deduction.[22]

Dower applies to all lands of which D was seized of an estate of inheritance at any time during marriage that issue of the marriage might inherit. Whereas S's statutory forced heir share applies only to property owned by D at death. By comparison dower may be worth more than a statutory share even though it is limited to only a life estate in one-third

---

(Footnote Continued)

federal tax lien by setting aside a portion of the sale proceeds to be paid to the federal government only if S did not survive the debtor); Rev. Rul. 79-399, 1979-2 C.B. 398 (federal tax lien is not superior to S's competing claim for dower, curtesy, or a statutory right if the marriage occurred before the federal tax lien arose and if, under state law, dower, curtesy, or the statutory right cannot be defeated by D or by D's creditors prior to death).

[20] See Treas. Reg. § 20.2056(c)-1(a)(3) and § 13.4.2.3.

[21] See § 13.4.3.3 et seq. for a discussion of the § 2056(b)(1) FET marital deduction nondeductible terminable interest rule. Among the exceptions to that rule that may permit dower to qualify for the marital deduction is the QTIP exception under § 2056(b)(7). See § 13.5.6 et seq. In addition, the full and adequate consideration exception in § 2056(b)(1)(A) may apply. For example, if the land in which dower is claimed was sold for FMV but subject to an unreleased dower entitlement, the value of the dower interest passing to S should qualify for the FET marital deduction to the extent that value was included in D's gross estate under § 2034.

[22] United States v. Crosby, 257 F.2d 515 (5th Cir. 1958); United States v. Traders' Nat'l Bank, 248 F.2d 667 (8th Cir. 1957); Hawaiian Trust Company v. United States, 412 F.2d 1313 (Ct. Cl. 1969) (the mere procedural requirement that S signify the election or file a claim does not make an interest meaningfully contingent and therefore will not preclude the marital deduction); Mauldin v. United States, 468 F. Supp. 422 (E.D. Ark. 1979); Rev. Rul. 72-7, 1972-1 C.B. 308 (formal judicial proceeding is not necessary for an estate to qualify for the marital deduction for amounts paid in lieu of dower if they are a bona fide compromise and do not exceed the commuted value of the dower interest that S would have received if commutation was pursued in a court proceeding), modified by Rev. Rul. 83-107, 1983-2 C.B. 159 (commuted value of dower interest may be determined in bona fide negotiations rather than judicial proceedings). See also Rev. Rul. 66-139, 1966-1 C.B. 225, and TAM 9246002.

of the lands. Furthermore, dower may have the premier entitlement whereas the statutory forced heir share normally applies only to amounts remaining after debts and taxes have been paid. Because each can qualify for the marital deduction and each is entitled to the §2013 previously taxed property credit,[23] the tax consequences of a choice may be insignificant because the value of either will increase S's net worth for taxation at death.

§2.2 RELATIVES' SHARES

Intestate property that does not pass to S is payable to lineal or collateral relatives in shares determined by the applicable statute of descent and distribution, considering any assignments or advancements that may be a charge against a recipient's share.[1]

---

[23] Treas. Reg. §20.2013-5(b), available if S dies within 10 years of D. Although the dower entitlement may be limited to a life estate only, it passes to S by operation of law and is a transfer from D for purposes of the credit. The §2013 credit appropriately is available because the life estate will increase S's net worth subject to inclusion in S's gross estate at death. See §13.2.5.6.

[1] **§2.2** See §2.3 regarding advancements. An intestate taker may have assigned the expectancy, in which case the assignee would take the assignor's entitlement (assuming assignments are respected under local law). Because the assignee acquires only the assignor's expectancy, which is worthless if the assignor is disinherited or predeceases the decedent, assignments are not common and may be discounted significantly to reflect this risk. Rev. Rul. 70-60, 1970-1 C.B. 11, held that any amount received as consideration for an assignment is includible in the assignor's gross income under §61(a). The one sentence Ruling offered no explanation for its conclusion and did not mention the exclusion from income under §102 for property acquired by gift, devise, bequest, or inheritance.

Presumably the government's conclusion reflects the uncertainty surrounding an expectancy. If the assignor predeceases the decedent or is disinherited, amounts received from the assignee are not a substitute for amounts that would have been received tax free under §102. To reflect this possibility, presumably the government must collect tax on amounts the assignor receives at the time of the assignment rather than attempting to collect a tax if the facts develop that the assignor was entitled to nothing.

In any assignment for value the assignee must consider the adjusted basis in the entitlement that is acquired, as well as capital gain or loss issues if the property received is not equal to the consideration paid. None of these issues was discussed in the Ruling.

UPC § 2-103(a) is a typical intestate distribution statute disposing of property not passing to S. It provides for relatives of D, first lineals and then collaterals, as follows:

(1) to D's descendants by representation;

(2) if there is no surviving descendant, to D's parents equally if both survive, or all to the surviving parent;

(3) if there is no surviving descendant or parent, to the descendants of D's parents or either of them by representation;

(4) if there is no surviving descendant, parent, or descendant of a parent, but D is survived by one or more grandparents or descendants of grandparents, half of the estate passes to D's paternal grandparents equally if both survive, or all to the surviving paternal grandparent, or to the descendants of D's paternal grandparents or either of them if both are deceased, the descendants taking by representation; the other half passes to D's maternal relatives in the same manner and, if there is no surviving grandparent or descendant of a grandparent on one side, the entire estate passes to D's relatives on the other side in the same manner.

§2.2.1 Representation by Lineals

In every situation local law must be examined to determine the manner of distribution and the method for sharing among lineals and collaterals. Although the traditional common law approach is a per stirpes distribution, the original version of UPC § 2-103(1) calls for a per capita division among representatives, and the 1990 version of UPC § 2-106 is a replacement that may be referred to as the "per capita at each generation" approach. It reads:

Section 2-106. Representation.

(b) If, under Section 2-103(a)(1), a decedent's intestate estate or a part thereof passes "by representation" to the decedent's descendants, the estate or part thereof is divided into as many equal shares as there are (i) surviving descendants in the generation nearest to the decedent which contains one or more surviving descendants and (ii) deceased descendants in the same generation who left surviving descendants, if any. Each surviving descendant in the nearest generation is allocated one share. The remaining shares, if any, are combined and then divided in the same manner among the surviving descendants of the deceased descendants as if the surviving descendants who were allocated a share and their surviving descendants had predeceased the decedent.

§2.2.1

A similar provision is found in UPC § 2-106(c) with respect to distributions to descendants of the parents or grandparents.

To illustrate a per stirpes distribution, if D was survived by two children and six grandchildren, three grandchildren of whom being children of a deceased child and the other three being children of the two living children, a per stirpes distribution would give each living child one-third and the last third (which would have gone to the deceased child if living) would go in equal shares to that child's three children. The other grandchildren, being representatives of living children who received their own shares, would receive nothing. The original UPC § 2-103(1) "per capita" division calls for distribution "to the issue of the decedent; if they are all of the same degree of kinship to the decedent they take equally, but if of unequal degree, then those of more remote degree take by representation." Its operation best can be explained by altering this example to assume all three children are deceased, one leaving three living children (grandchildren of the decedent), one leaving two living children, and one leaving one living child.

Under a per stirpes division these grandchildren would stand in the shoes of their deceased parents (D's children), so the three children of the first child would share a one-third share equally (one-ninth to each), the next two would share a one-third share (one-sixth each), and the last grandchild would receive the last undivided one-third of D's estate. In a per capita distribution the first division into shares is made at the highest generation at which a taker is living, which is the grandchild level here, with one share for each member of that generation who is alive or who is deceased with descendants who are living. In this case six equal shares would be created. If one grandchild was deceased, his or her one-sixth share would descend to his or her representatives, as in a traditional per stirpes distribution, and if that grandchild was deceased, survived by no living representatives, only five shares would be created at the grandchild level.

To illustrate the replacement per capita at each generation procedure in UPC § 2-106, assume again in this example that all three of D's children are deceased and, in addition, assume that two of the grandchildren also are deceased, each leaving surviving descendants (between them three great-grandchildren). Under this provision, again six equal shares would be created (one for each living grandchild and one for each deceased grandchild with descendants who are living) and the one-sixth shares created for living grandchildren would be distributed to them. The two shares created for deceased grandchildren would be combined and divided at the great-grandchild level to give equal shares to the three living great-grandchildren who represent the two deceased grandchildren. Thus, they would receive shares of one-ninth each, rather than distribution of one-sixth to the one child of a deceased grandchild and half of one-sixth to each of the two children of the other deceased grandchild. In this way all of D's similarly related descendants take equal shares, which was not true under the original UPC per capita approach.

The perceived advantage of the per stirpes system is that it does not reward a line of descent with more representatives. For example, if one deceased child was survived by only one descendant while another deceased child was represented by several, the per stirpes approach would provide two shares to be divided among the respective children's representatives separately. The per capita at each generation system would reward the second deceased child's representatives as a class with a greater than equal share of the total to be distributed.

§2.2.2 Representation by Collaterals

In some jurisdictions, if there is no living relative descended through grandparents, the next step is distribution to collaterals of any degree of relation, with those in the nearest degree taking equally to the exclusion of all others. The term "degree of relation" has different meanings under three alternative methods for counting. For example, under the more common "civil" law method, the relationship of the decedent to a collateral relative is ascertained by counting upwards from D to their common ancestor and downwards from the common ancestor to the relative, the total of the steps up and down being the degree of relationship between them. For example, if the relative is D's cousin, their common ancestor is at the grandparent generation, which is two steps up from D, and the cousin is another two steps down from there. Thus, a cousin is in the fourth degree of relationship (consanguinity) to D.[2]

---

[2] In re Estate of Schottenfels, 314 N.Y.S.2d 719 (Surr. Ct. 1970), involved first cousins of the decedent who were in line to take the decedent's estate. One of whom was a first cousin on both the paternal and the maternal sides. The court

By contrast, the "common" law (also called the "canon" law) method of computing degrees of consanguinity is established by taking the greater of the number of steps up or down. In either case, civil or common law states each may have a modification providing that, if two collaterals are in the same degree of consanguinity but they share common lineal ancestors with D who are of different degrees of relation to D, those who claim the closer lineal ancestor in common with D take to the exclusion of those whose common ancestor is more remote.[3] This modification is similar to the third method of computing collateral entitlement, the "parentelic" approach, by which D's intestate property passes to the living descendants of the nearest lineal ancestor of D of whom descendants are living.[4]

§2.2.3 Escheat

The intestate estate escheats to the state only if D is survived by no spouse and no relatives who are within the class defined by the statute of descent and distribution as possible recipients.[5] In that case, although this property is includible in D's gross estate for FET purposes,[6] it is not deductible as a charitable transfer because it does not involve a transfer

---

(Footnote Continued)

held this cousin was entitled to only one share, notwithstanding the dual relationship. To the same effect is the 1990 version of UPC §2-113: "An individual who is related to the decedent through two lines of relationship is entitled to only a single share based on the relationship that would entitle the individual to the larger share."

[3] To illustrate, under both the civil law and the common law computation regimes, nephews and nieces are in the same degree of consanguinity as uncles and aunts (third under the civil law, second under the common law). Because nephews and nieces share a common ancestor in the decedent's parents but uncles and aunts trace their common heritage through the decedent's grandparents, this modification would favor the nephews and nieces to the total exclusion of the uncles and aunts.

[4] Because this is an old and uncommon approach, it is likely that, if it is respected anywhere, the distribution to descendants will follow the traditional common law per stirpes approach, but that should be verified.

[5] See, e.g., the 1990 version of UPC §2-105.

[6] Treas. Reg. §20.0-2(a) provides that escheat is a transfer that causes the property to be included in the decedent's gross estate.

by D as interpreted by the government.[7] In some states D's property will pass to heirs of D's predeceased spouse before it will escheat to the state.[8] And, under federal law,[9] intestate property that otherwise would escheat to a state instead is payable to the United States if the decedent received Veterans Administration benefits.[10]

---

[7] Although § 2055(a)(1) authorizes a deduction for the value of transfers to a state, Treas. Reg. § 20.2055-1(a)(1) requires a transfer during the decedent's life or by will. Senft v. United States, 202 F. Supp. 838 (M.D. Pa. 1962), aff'd, 319 F.2d 642 (3d Cir. 1963) (Code and regulations in existence since 1921 with the operative verb being "transfer" to a state, which is not broad enough to encompass an escheat; it replaced the word "gift" to clarify that gifts made during a decedent's life could not be deducted under § 2055 unless they were includible in the gross estate), citing Marine Nat'l Bank v. Commissioner, 168 F.2d 400 (3d Cir. 1948) (because a charitable bequest was void under mortmain statute when decedent died within 30 days after execution of will, residuary legatees directed payment of the charitable bequests, which made the deduction theirs and not the estate's because the charities received the property through their agreement, not under the decedent's will).

[8] See, e.g., Kan. Stat. Ann. § 59-514.

[9] 38 U.S.C. § § 5502(e) and 8520(a), the latter providing that intestate property otherwise subject to escheat of a veteran who dies as a patient in a veterans hospital becomes the property of the United States as trustee for the General Post Fund held for the benefit of patients in veterans hospitals.

[10] Rev. Rul. 78-14, 1978-1 C.B. 281, allowed a § 2053(c)(1)(A) deduction for this amount, citing Rev. Rul. 76-542, 1976-2 C.B. 282, which held that the § 2053 deduction is available regardless of the decedent's incompetence, notwithstanding that Rev. Rul. 75-533, 1975-2 C.B. 359, justified the same deduction by an analogy to a voluntary pledge satisfied after death because 38 U.S.C. § 8520(b) regards acceptance of care in a veterans' hospital as an acceptance of the condition that the decedent's property pass to the United States.

In re Levy, 574 F.2d 128 (2d Cir.), aff'd sub nom., New York v. United States, 439 U.S. 920 (1978), and In re Estate of Novotny, 446 F. Supp. 1027 (S.D. N.Y. 1978), held that no state death tax may be imposed on the veteran's estate that escheats to the United States, which is contrary to the decision rendered by In re O'Brine's Estate, 322 N.Y.S.2d 441 (Surr. Ct. 1971), aff'd, 354 N.Y.S.2d 589 (Sup. Ct. 1974), aff'd, 332 N.E.2d 326 (N.Y. 1975).

§2.2.4 Questions of Status

Most jurisdictions regard relatives of the half blood as if they were whole blooded relatives[11] and adopteds as natural born,[12] but it is uncommon to regard stepchildren as if related by birth.[13] In each respect, local law must be inspected, particularly with respect to rights as affected by adoption, as to which a number of questions are in a state of transition. For example, given the incidence of divorce and remarriage, an increasing number of stepparent adoptions exist, with mixed results under state law.

§2.2.4.1 Adoption

The normal rule is that adoption cuts all ties between natural parents and the child who was adopted away.[14] It also cuts all ties between the child and those who claim through the natural parents.[15] This rule could have calamitous and unexpected consequences if, for example, the unmarried partner of a natural parent adopts the natural parent's child. Most state laws make an exception to prevent termination of the parent and child relation in a stepparent adoption in which one of the natural parents is married to the adopting parent. In these cases state law typically preserves the parent-child relation between the child and the stepparent's spouse who is the natural parent.[16] In some states the

---

[11] See the 1990 version of UPC §2-107.

[12] See the 2008 version of UPC §2-118.

[13] Most statutes of descent and distribution make no provision for inheritance by a stepchild of the decedent. But see Md. Code Ann. Est. & Trusts §3-104(e), which provides for inheritance by a stepchild of the decedent in the absence of other specified persons. For the perspective of an author who teaches in Maryland, see Gerzog, Families for Tax Purposes: What About the Steps, 42 J. L. Reform 805 (2009).

[14] Or, as illustrated by Rist v. Taylor, 955 P.2d 436 (Wyo. 1998), between a first adoptive parent and a child who was adopted away a second time.

[15] See, e.g., In re Estate of Fleming, 21 P.3d 281 (Wash. 2001) (the decedent's estate escheated because, even without adoption by a new parent, a court order terminating the rights of the decedent's natural parent anticipatory to adoption was adequate to preclude that natural parent from inheriting from the child, and to prevent the child's natural sibling from inheriting through the parent as a biological heir).

[16] See the 2008 version of UPC §2-119(b).

child may continue to inherit from and through the other natural parent following a stepparent adoption (in effect giving the child three "parents" in the form of both natural parents and the adopting stepparent), but there is much less uniformity on this issue.[17]

The 2008 version of UPC§2-119(a) cuts the natural parent and child relation with respect to the natural parent who is not married to the adopting stepparent, but only in one direction: the child still may inherit from and through both natural parents but the other natural parent and that parent's relatives lose all ties and rights with respect to the child. Harder cases yet involve the rights of natural grandparents, who have nothing to do with an adoption of their grandchild by a stepparent (who may be the spouse of their child's former spouse following a divorce or following their child's death) but may be cut off from their natural grandchild.[18]

---

[17] See, e.g., N.Y. Dom. Rel. L. § 117, which preserves the natural parent and child relation (notwithstanding a stepparent adoption) only with respect to the natural parent who is married to the adopting stepparent or insofar as the child is a beneficiary under an instrument executed by the other natural parent. But Raley v. Spikes, 614 So. 2d 1017 (Ala. 1993), allowed children who were adopted to inherit from the natural parent who was not married to the stepparent, applying the law of the decedent's domicile and not that of each state of adoption. And see Mahoney, Stepfamilies in the Law of Intestate Succession and Wills, 22 U.C. Davis L. Rev. 917 (1989); Jones, Stepparent Adoption and Inheritance: A Suggested Revision of the Uniform Probate Code Section 2-109, 8 W. New Eng. L. Rev. 53 (1986); Rein, Relatives by Blood, Adoption, and Association: Who Should Get What and Why, 37 Vand. L. Rev. 711 (1984); Note, Intestate Succession and Stepparent Adoptions, 1988 Wis. L. Rev. 321; Note, Intestate Succession Rights of Adopted Children: Should the Stepparent Exception be Extended?, 77 Cornell L. Rev. 1188 (1992).

[18] See Miller v. Walker, 514 S.E.2d 22 (Ga. 1999) (three of four grandchildren were adopted away from the settlor's child to avoid further child abuse and were deemed no longer included in the class of beneficiaries of a trust the settlor previously created to protect and provide for those grandchildren); Pyles v. Russell, 36 S.W.2d 365 (Ky. 2000) (two children were adopted by their paternal grandparents and the third by a maternal aunt, all following their natural parents' accidental death; a maternal grandparent's estate passed under state law that precluded inheritance through the natural parent, notwithstanding that the law governing their adoption preserved that natural line of inheritance; quaere whether the lawyer who assisted in the adoption could be guilty of malpractice for not considering the consequences of the adoption vis-à-vis natural ancestors' estates); In re Estates of Donnelly, 502 P.2d 1163 (Wash. 1972) (one natural

PLRs 9310005 and 9106034 involved the GST predeceased child exception. According to the government, the predeceased ancestor exception to what otherwise would be a taxable transfer, now found in § 2651(e)(1), reflects a policy that the GST need not apply if a transferor gives property directly to a grandchild only because the grandchild's parent, who was the transferor's child, is deceased. In such a case there is no intent to avoid the tax that would apply if the transfer was made to the child, who then transferred the property to the grandchild. The PLRs held that the exception is not lost if a grandchild is adopted by a stepparent who is the spouse of the grandchild's surviving natural parent who was the surviving spouse of the transferor's child. Because that policy is not affected by adoption of the grandchild by the new spouse of the grandchild's surviving parent, the Rulings correctly held that the exception is not lost, notwithstanding state law that regarded the legal relation between the deceased natural parent (and all lineal relatives of that deceased parent) and the grandchild as terminated by the stepparent's adoption.

Another topic of growing concern is adoption of an adult to alter inheritance from a person who is not the adopting party. Thus, for example, the 2008 version of UPC § 2-705(f) essentially provides that dispositive provisions[19] in an estate plan of a transferor who is *not* the

---

(Footnote Continued)

parent of the child in question died, the surviving natural parent remarried, and the stepparent adopted the child; when the deceased parent's parent died the adoption was deemed to have severed the relation of grandparent and grandchild, notwithstanding that the natural grandparent did not consent to and could not have prevented the adoption); Hall v. Vallandingham, 540 A.2d 1162 (Md. Ct. App. 1988); In re Estate of McQuesten, 578 A.2d 335 (N.H. 1990) (both consistent with *Donnelly*). But see In re Estate of Van Der Veen, 935 P.2d 1042 (Kan. 1997) (grandchild the decedent never knew about—because the grandchild was adopted away from the decedent's child—was entitled to take in the child's stead under the local slayer statute because the child killed the decedent and local law provided that "adoption shall not terminate the right . . . to inherit . . . through the birth parent").

[19] A similar statute involved in Fleet Nat'l Bank v. Hunt, 944 A.2d 846 (R.I. 2008), underscores the limitation to a dispositive provision in an estate plan. The *Fleet* court addressed adoption of adult step children, which the statute regarded as invalid for purposes of a trust remainder distribution provision. That caused the remainder provision to fail, meaning the remainder passed by intestacy and, under state law, the adult adoption *was* effective for that purpose. *Fleet* thus

adopting parent do not include an adopted individual as if naturally born as a child of the adopting parent "unless the adopted individual lived while a minor, either before or after the adoption, as a regular member of the household of the adopting parent."[20]

(Footnote Continued)

underscores the legislative objective to preclude strategic adoptions to alter entitlements under express provisions in wills, trusts, or other dispositive instruments, but it does not preclude establishment of the parent-child status otherwise, including for purposes of any inheritance that is a "default" distribution under intestacy.

A similar defect in legislation of this nature is illustrated by Kummer v. Donak, 715 S.E.2d 7 (Va. 2011), in which the adoptee was 53 when adopted by a relative by marriage, which (like any other adoption under Virginia law) severed her status as a child of her biological parents. An unintended consequence arose when the adoptee's biological sister died with no descendants and the adoptee's children, as biological niece and nephews, stood first in line to inherit their aunt's estate. But due to their mother's adoption away from the biological family they were denied that inheritance right. UPC §2-705(f) would not have cured this result because it only governs construction of dispositive provisions that would favor children of the adoptive parent and Kummer dealt with intestacy and did not involve property passing to children of the person who adopted the adult.

[20] Compare Solomon v. Central Trust Co., 584 N.E.2d 1185 (Ohio 1992) (adoption of adult child respected because the child lived with adopting parent as a minor; will interpreted to include adopted child because it did not affirmatively exclude adopteds), with In re Trust Created by Belgard, 829 P.2d 457 (Colo. Ct. App. 1991) (adoption of adult spouse by trust beneficiary not respected, notwithstanding language in trust treating adopteds as natural born). See also and compare Ehrenclou v. MacDonald, 12 Cal. Rptr. 3d 411 (Cal. Ct. App. 2004) (the document designated California law to govern a trust created for the settlor's adopted daughter for life, remainder to her children, but her adoption of two adults was disregarded because it was performed under Colorado Rev. Stat. §14-1-101(2), which regarded an adult adoption as creating heirs at law of the adopting party for purposes of inheritance from the adopting party only, and was not effective to make them children or for any other purpose), with In re Trust Created by Nixon, 763 N.W.2d 404 (Neb. 2009) (a valid California adult adoption was accorded full-faith-and-credit recognition in Nebraska, even though it would not have been valid if attempted in Nebraska). Commerce Bank v. Blasdel, 141 S.W.3d 434 (Mo. Ct. App. 2004), suggested that the modern mechanism to combat sham or adult adoptions is through a tortious interference with inheritance action. See §3.1.2 n.36. Arguing the relative merits of allowing an adult to adopt another adult (such as a spouse, lover, or stepchild) to permit the adopted person to inherit as a child, and citing much of the applicable law to date on the issue, see Cohen, Adult Adoption May Qualify One as a Beneficiary, 19 Est. Plan.

A third area of concern involves the concept of "equitable" or "virtual" adoption that permits inheritance by a child as if a promised or "virtual" adoption was a reality, notwithstanding that no legal adoption was accomplished. Based on equitable principles, some courts treat as done that which should have been done and estop denial that an adoption occurred if the purported parents failed through neglect or design to fulfill their agreement to adopt.[21] The concept, however, is a one way

---

(Footnote Continued)

88 (1992); Connelly, Wills and Trusts: Disqualifying Adopted Adult "Children," 78 Ill. B.J. 612 (1990).

[21] See Robinson, Untangling the "Loose Threads": Equitable Adoption, Equitable Legitimation, and Inheritance in Extralegal Family Arrangements, 48 Emory L.J. 943 (1999); Bell, Virtual Adoption: The Difficulty of Creating an Exception to the Statutory Scheme, 29 Stetson L. Rev. 415 (1999); Bailey, Adoption "By Estoppel," 36 Tex. L. Rev. 30 (1957); Lankford v. Wright, 489 S.E.2d 604 (N.C. 1997) (classic facts and good rendition of requirements and state of the law, stating that 38 states had considered the issue and 27 had adopted the concept; states that the concept is limited to cases of intestacy, although cases in other states prove this to be debatable); In re Estate of Prewitt, 498 P.2d 470 (Ariz. Ct. App. 1972) (natural mother consented to adoption and child was baptized and enrolled in school as child of purported adopting parents; child treated as adopted with all legal formalities for inheritance purposes); Estate of Radovich, 308 P.2d 14 (Cal. 1957) (equitable adoption applied to entitle child to an adopted child's inheritance tax exemption); Welch v. Wilson, 516 S.E.2d 35, 37 (W. Va. 1999) (applying equitable adoption and suggesting in dicta that "the same strict standard of proof does not apply to the determination of dependency under any State remedial statute conferring State government benefits which must be liberally construed to effect its purpose"); First Nat'l Bank v. Phillips, 344 S.E.2d 201 (W. Va. 1985) (permitting an equitably adopted child to inherit from another child of the equitably adopting parent).

But see In re Estate of Seader, 76 P.3d 1236 (Wyo. 2003) (recognizing equitable adoption but denying child status for antilapse purposes to a situation in which the decedent's equitably adopted daughter died two months before the decedent and her children sought to stand in her shoes to take the share she would have received if living; in the process the court stated that equitable adoption does not create an adoption but merely recognizes its existence for limited purposes, and suggested that it should not apply in testate situations such as this); McGarvey v. State, 533 A.2d 690 (Md. 1987) (denying equitable adoption to determine applicable inheritance tax rate for child placed by natural parents in custody of an aunt who intended to adopt the child but never got around to doing so; relationship of parent and child, child's status as sole legatee under the aunt's will, and court's recognition of equitable adoption still did not entitle the child to the status of a truly adopted child for inheritance tax rate purposes). See also

§2.2.4.1

street: the parents and those claiming through them cannot inherit from the child because there have been no acts, promises, or conduct by the child to raise an estoppel.[22]

(Footnote Continued)

O'Neal v. Wilkes, 439 S.E.2d 490 (Ga. 1994), which rejected equitable adoption because the decedent never had authority to adopt (the child never was supported or acknowledged by the natural father and was given up for adoption after the mother's death, by a relative who was not appointed as the child's guardian and therefore had no authority to agree to the adoption); as an equitable remedy following failure to perform a contract to adopt, the court held that equitable adoption could not apply if there was no valid underlying contract to adopt. A substantial dissent argued that equitable adoption is an equitable maxim that treats as done what should have been done and that it should have applied because the facts indicated that the child had been bounced from one caretaker to another, all without the formalities of legal custody, until finally settling with the decedent, who acted in all respects as a parent and openly treated the plaintiff as a child until dying intestate many years later. And see Lee v. Gurley, 389 S.E.2d 333 (Ga. 1990) (equitable adoption doctrine recognized but denied on facts presented); Wilks v. Langley, 451 S.W.2d 209 (Ark. 1970) (absent clear and convincing proof of a contract to adopt, child could not inherit even though purported parents raised the child as their own); Estate of Joseph, 949 P.2d 472 (Cal. 1998) (equitable adoption status denied because state law required that there was a legal impossibility to adopt that must exist at all times during the joint lives of the parent and child; in this case the impossibility was the natural parents' refusal to consent to adoption and that impediment ended when the child reached the age of majority, long before the foster parent's death); Miller v. Paczier, 591 So. 2d 321 (Fla. Dist. Ct. App. 1991) (rejecting alleged virtual adoption of an adult, stating that the doctrine only has applied if the subject of the alleged adoption was a minor).

[22] Heien v. Crabtree, 369 S.W.2d 28 (Tex. 1963); Prather v. District of Columbia, 393 F.2d 665 (D.C. Cir. 1968) (by refusing equitable adoption to purported adopting parents caused deceased child to die without heirs and resulted in escheat); Kupec v. Cooper, 593 So. 2d 1176 (Fla. Dist. Ct. App. 1992) (rejecting equitable adoption argument by other heirs in an attempt to preclude a natural child from inheriting from a natural parent); Estate of Riggs, 440 N.Y.S.2d 450 (Surr. Ct. 1981) (refusing to apply equitable adoption on behalf of individuals claiming through the purported parent who never formally adopted the decedent).

In addition, In re Estate of Jenkins, 904 P.2d 1316 (Colo. 1995) (recognizing the doctrine but rejecting its application), and Board of Education v. Browning, 635 A.2d 373 (Md. Ct. App. 1994), held that the concept of equitable adoption is limited to inheritance from the purported adopting parent and precluded inheritance through that parent from a stranger to the adoption (such as a sibling of

§2.2.4.2 Nonmarital Children

The extent to which inheritance by or from a nonmarital[23] child is restricted normally is specified by statute. And the United States Supreme Court has addressed a number of times the constitutionality of state laws that discriminate against nonmarital children. For example, in Labine v. Vincent,[24] the child was acknowledged by both parents but was denied the right under Louisiana law to inherit from the father. The Court allowed that statute to stand, expressing the view that rules regarded as appropriate to "establish, protect, and strengthen family life" and regulate property transfers should be left to the legislature.

Six years later the Court held in Trimble v. Gordon[25] that it is an unconstitutional denial of Equal Protection for a state to permit intestate inheritance by nonmarital children from mothers but not from purported fathers, notwithstanding alleged difficulties of proving paternity after the father's death. The Court found that the statute bore no rational relation to any proper state interest and that the promotion of family relationships is not a sufficient justification if it entails imposition of sanctions on offspring. Then, not a year thereafter, the Court held in Lalli v. Lalli[26] that it is permissible to limit inheritance by a nonmarital child from a purported father to cases in which a court of competent jurisdiction determined paternity during the father's life. As a result, state law must be

---

(Footnote Continued)

the parent), in *Browning* notwithstanding that it resulted in an escheat of the sibling's estate, which the court recognized that the law normally would eschew.

[23] At various times the terms "bastard," "illegitimate," and "out-of-wedlock" have been used to describe a child whose parents were not legally married at the child's birth. The term "nonmarital" is less pejorative and reflects the fact that a child is nonmarital through no fault of its own and perhaps through no fault of its parents, who may have been living together as husband and wife after the performance of a marriage ceremony that was regarded as invalid because the prior divorce of one of them is not recognized.

[24] 401 U.S. 532 (1971).

[25] 430 U.S. 762 (1977). Subsequently, Reed v. Campbell, 476 U.S. 852 (1986), held that *Trimble* protects the interest of a nonmarital child to an intestate share of the estate of the child's father, even though *Trimble* was decided after the father's death. As a consequence, a state law that prohibited a nonmarital child from inheriting from its father unless its parents had subsequently married was declared unconstitutional.

[26] 439 U.S. 259 (1978).

consulted to determine what is required to establish paternity, when the determination must be made to be valid, and then assess the constitutionality of the provision involved.[27]

A developing issue regarding proof of paternity is whether DNA testing, using tissue or blood samples, may be used by a nonmarital child to prove paternity after a purported father's death. Estate of Sanders[28] held that the California version of the Uniform Parentage Act required that paternity be established before D died, or that D acknowledged the child. Thus, a postmortem DNA test to determine paternity was impermissible. But other courts have permitted postmortem testing to determine paternity.[29]

In addition to establishing the right of a child to inherit from its alleged parents, the issue can arise whether others may inherit from or

---

[27] In re Estate of King, 837 P.2d 463 (Ok. 1992), held over a strong dissent that proof required of a nonmarital child could be the more difficult "clear and convincing" standard, rather than a mere "preponderance," without constitutional invalidity. But Talley v. Succession of Stuckey, 614 So. 2d 55 (La. 1993), rev'g 604 So. 2d 1375 (La. Ct. App. 1992), held unconstitutional a state statute that treated the birth of a child as a revocation of an existing will only if the child was not born out of wedlock, rejecting a dissenting argument that a rebuttable presumption by statute that the decedent would not want to provide for the afterborn nonmarital child would be appropriate and constitutional.

[28] 3 Cal. Rptr. 2d 536 (Ct. App. 1992).

[29] See, e.g., Sudwischer v. Estate of Hoffpauir, 589 So. 2d 474 (La.), modifying 577 So. 2d 1 (La. 1991), and noted in Cullens, Should the Legitimate Child be Forced to Pay for the Sins of Her Father?: *Sudwischer v. Estate of Hoffpauir,* 53 La. L. Rev. 1675 (1993) (ordering decedent's marital child to submit to blood tests to help establish by DNA linking decedent's paternity of alleged nonmarital child); In re Estate of Rogers, 583 A.2d 782 (N.J. Super. Ct. 1990) (DNA testing properly ordered under New Jersey version of Uniform Parentage Act); Batcheldor v. Boyd, 458 S.E.2d 1 (N.C. Ct. App. 1995) and 423 S.E.2d 810 (S.C. 1992) (DNA testing used first to rebut the presumption that the husband of the plaintiff's mother at the time the plaintiff was born was the plaintiff's father, and then to prove the paternity of the decedent, who married the plaintiff's mother after the plaintiff's birth); Alexander v. Alexander, 537 N.E.2d 1310, 1314 (Ohio Prob. Ct. 1988) (ordering decedent's body disinterred to permit DNA testing because "[t]he accuracy and infallibility of the DNA test are nothing short of remarkable. . . . . The problems of proof that have been the basis of denying inheritance rights to illegitimate children have been removed by the advent of this new genetic testing"); In re Estate of Greenwood, 587 A.2d 749 (Pa. Super. Ct. 1991) (allowing use of blood and tissue samples).

§2.2.4.2

through a nonmarital child. The 2008 version of UPC § 2-117 provides that marital status of a child's parents is irrelevant to the child's inheritance rights, but 2-115(4) specifies that the parents' rights to inherit from or through the child depend upon having openly treated the child as their child and not having refused to support the child. Similarly, state law may preclude relatives of the purported father from claiming inheritance from or through the child if paternity has not been established as required by statute.[30]

§ 2.2.4.3 The New Biology

An issue that has become increasingly common relates to the "new biology," by which a child can be conceived by means of artificial insemination using the egg or sperm of donors, who do not constitute parents simply by virtue of their biological contribution. Instead, other more important factors are involved.[31] Thus, the Uniform Parentage Act and, before it, the Uniform Status of Children of Assisted Conception Act both provide generally[32] that any child conceived following artificial insemination of a woman is the child of that woman regardless of the lack of a biological relation. Similarly, if the birth mother is married, her husband is presumed to be the father, regardless of a lack of biological connection, unless he can prove that he did not consent to the artificial insemination.[33]

---

[30] In re Estate of Ford, 552 So. 2d 1065 (Miss. 1989); Estate of Stern v. Stern, 311 S.E.2d 909 (N.C. Ct. App. 1984), aff'd, 322 S.E.2d 771 (N.C. 1984); King v. Commonwealth, 269 S.E.2d 793 (Va. 1980).

[31] See Uniform Parentage Act § 702, and Uniform Status of Children of Assisted Conception Act § 4(b).

[32] Absent a gestational agreement otherwise. See Uniform Parentage Act Article 8.

[33] See Uniform Parentage Act § 705. See also Restatement (Third) of Property (Wills and Other Donative Transfers) § 14.8, and § 2.5 comment *l* (1999), stating that

the traditional view is that a child who is conceived and born after the decedent's death cannot be an heir. This proposition, however, is open to reexamination with respect to a child produced from genetic material of the decedent by assisted reproductive technology. Most statutory codifications . . . are not inconsistent with such a reexamination because they do not preclude inheritance by a child conceived after the decedent's death.

This may prove to be true even if the insemination and subsequent birth both occur after the husband's death.[34] When heirship is established under these new-biology dictates, a child produced by artificial insemination is treated as a naturally conceived child of the husband and wife for all purposes. Indeed, the child may be regarded as a *marital* child, because the parents *were* married, albeit one parent is deceased when the child is born (although this depends on state law and may not be true if state law provides that marriage ends upon the death of either spouse).

Easy early cases that confronted the policies involved here were In re Estate of Kolacy[35] and Woodward v. Commissioner of Social Security.[36] Both cases began in federal court and were certified to state court for a determination of heirship under state law. Both involved young, intestate, leukemia victims who banked sperm before beginning chemotherapy that proved to be unsuccessful. The issue was the child's entitlement to federal survivor benefits under the Social Security Act, which the courts resolved based on heirship as determined under state law.[37] Both cases involved posthumously conceived children—twin girls in

---

(Footnote Continued)

> This Restatement takes the position that, to inherit from the decedent, a child produced from genetic material of the decedent by assisted reproductive technology must be born within a reasonable time after the decedent's death in circumstances indicating that the decedent would have approved of the child's right to inherit. If the ... procedure occurs after the husband's death, and if the child is born within a reasonable time after the husband's death, the child should be treated as the husband's child for purposes of inheritance *from* the husband. Once conceived, such a child is the husband's and wife's child for all purposes of inheritance by, from, or through an intestate decedent who dies thereafter (emphasis in original).

[34] See Uniform Parentage Act § 707.

[35] 753 A.2d 1257 (N.J. Super. 2000).

[36] 760 N.E.2d 257 (Mass. 2002).

[37] The federal statutory construct in 42 U.S.C. §§ 402 and 416 involves the following provisions, the last of which providing the state intestacy connection:

§ 402(d)(1)(C): an applicant is entitled to survivor benefits if the applicant is "a child (as defined in section 416(e)) [who] was dependent upon the [decedent] at the time of the [decedent's] death."

§ 416(e)(1): one of several enumerated categories of persons who are a "child," this states that "child" means "the child or legally adopted child of an individual."

§ 2.2.4.3

each case—the product of their mother S being inseminated using the banked sperm after D's death. Each court concluded that D was the legal, genetic, and biological father of children born to his surviving widow 18 and 24 months (respectively) after his death.

The *Kolacy* court found that D's premortem deposit of sperm for artificial insemination of S after D's not unexpected death was consistent with the policy underlying an inapposite state law providing that a child born as a result of the artificial insemination of a woman "with the consent of her husband . . . with semen donated by a man *not* her husband is treated in law as if [the husband] were the natural father of a child thereby conceived" (emphasis added, to underscore that the statute did not address the case of semen donated by the inseminated mother's husband, which the legislature apparently did not anticipate). In *Woodward* the court did not make a factual finding whether the requisite consent existed to (1) permit posthumous reproduction and (2) support any resulting child. But the court did determine that, if unspecified timing requirements also are met, the resulting child will be a legal heir notwithstanding the traditional common law rule that heirs are ascertained at D's death.

Originally contrary to both cases was Gillett-Netting v. Commissioner of Social Security,[38] which is distinguishable only because the man was older and the twins were one boy and one girl, but otherwise involved essentially the same facts and issue as both *Kolacy* and *Woodward*. The lower court held that heirs under state law must "survive" D and therefore had to be in existence at D's death, and rejected notions of D's intent because the intestate statute applies in the absence of a will, which is how decedents are expected to indicate their intent. On appeal the court relied on Arizona state law to the effect that all legitimate (marital) children are dependents and that the children involved in the

---

(Footnote Continued)

§ 416(h)(2)(A): "In determining whether an applicant is the child of [a decedent] for purposes of this subchapter, the Commissioner of Social Security shall apply such law as would be applied in determining the devolution of [the decedent's] intestate personal property . . . by the courts of the State in which [the decedent] was domiciled at the time of . . . death."

[38] 231 F. Supp. 2d 961 (D. Ariz. 2002), rev'd, 371 F.2d 593 (9th Cir. 2004).

§ 2.2.4.3

case were the undisputed biological children of the decedent, citing *Woodward*.[39]

The original holding in *Gillett-Netting* is basically the same as the final decision in Khabbaz v. Commissioner, Social Security Adm'n,[40] a fourth pea out of essentially the same pod. The court focused on language in the applicable state law that referred to "surviving issue" and concluded that "survive" implies remaining alive after another person's death. This child was not yet alive when D died and therefore could not meet the intended classification as a "surviving" heir. In the process the court dodged a social policy argument that D's DNA product should be included in the benefited class, saying that these policy issues are best left to the legislature to resolve.[41]

Following a very similar path under slightly different facts, Finley v. Commissioner, Social Security Adm'n[42] a fourth pea out of essentially the same pod. The court focused on language in the applicable state law that referred to "surviving issue" and concluded that "survive" implies remaining alive after another person's death. This child was not yet alive when D died and therefore could not meet the intended classification as a "surviving" heir. In the process the court dodged a social policy argument that D's DNA product should be included in the benefited class, saying that these policy issues are best left to the legislature to resolve.[43]

---

[39] Later cases reveal that this holding ignored 42 U.S.C. § 416(h)(2)(A) and essentially relied on only §§ 402(d)(1)(C), requiring dependency, and 416(e)(1), defining a child, which the court held was not disputed, in terms of the biology.

[40] 930 A.2d 1180 (N.H. 2007).

[41] Curiously, the *Kolacy* court specifically disregarded the state Attorney General's request that it not rule, recognizing that the state court's ruling might not bind a federal determination of heirship and that its ruling in this particular case would not "unfairly intrude on the rights of other persons or . . . cause serious problems in terms of the orderly administration of estates." The court regarded its ruling as helpful until such time as the legislature undertook "to deal consciously and in a well informed way with at least some of the issues presented by reproductive technology" in the kind of situation posed.

[42] 372 Ark. 103 (2008).

[43] See Bass, What If You Die, And Then Have Children, 145 Trusts and Estates 20 (April 2006); Bailey, An Analytical Framework for Resolving the Issues Raised by the Interaction Between Reproductive Technology and the Law of Inheritance, 47 DePaul L. Rev. 743, 783, 797 (1998) (suggesting that, in states

§ 2.2.4.3

Also rejecting claims to survivor benefits, Stephen v. Commissioner of Social Security[44] found the critical factual difference to be that D's sperm was harvested on the day after his unexpected death due to cardiac arrest. The court held that, under the applicable state (Florida) law, "a child conceived from the . . . sperm of a person . . . who died before the transfer of their . . . sperm . . . to a woman's body shall not be eligible for a claim against the decedent's estate unless the child has been provided for by the decedent's will,"[45] which clearly could not have occurred here because the sperm was not obtained, much less transferred, prior to D's death.[46]

Similar to *Finley*, D's sperm also was harvested postmortem in Vernoff v. Astrue,[47] which allowed the court to reject the claim to survivor benefits – in *Vernoff* because a posthumously conceived child could not be dependent on a decedent who died prior to the child's conception. Subsequently, Beeler v. Astrue[48] rejected the child's claim because state law in effect at the decedent's death required conception of the child during the decedent's lifetime, and Schafer v. Astrue[49] rejected the child's claim because state law in effect at the decedent's death required that the child be born within ten months after the decedent's

---

(Footnote Continued)

that presume paternity based on conception during the marriage, if a woman's egg is fertilized before the husband dies, a posthumous child will be his heir regardless of the interval between his death and the child's birth, and stating that inheritance based on conception prior to death was the law in 19 states at that time); and Shapo, Matters of Life and Death: Inheritance Consequences of Reproductive Technologies, 25 Hofstra L. Rev. 1091 (1997).

[44] 386 F. Supp. 2d 1257, 1260 (M.D. Fla. 2005).

[45] See Fla. Stat. § 742.17(4).

[46] Readers who wish to inquire how this postmortem medical procedure works may consult Andrews, The Sperminator, NY Times Magazine, Mar 28, 1999, 62-65. See also Goldfarb, Posthumous Conception and Inheritance Rights, 36 N.Y. State Bar Ass'n Trusts and Estates L. Section Newsletter 43 (Summer 2003); Scott, A Look at the Rights and Entitlements of Posthumously Conceived Children: No Surefire Way to Tame the Reproductive Wild West, 52 Emory L.J. 963 (2003).

[47] 568 F.3d 1102 (9th Cir. 2009).

[48] 651 F.3d 954 (8th Cir. 2011).

[49] 641 F.3d 49 (4th Cir. 2011).

§ 2.2.4.3

death and in *Schafer* the child was born almost seven years after the decedent died.

Both *Beeler* and *Schafer* are poignant because they were decided subsequent to, and they rejected, the approach dictated by the court of appeals in Capato v. Commissioner of Social Security.[50] As such, those three cases created a conflict between the circuits, which the U.S. Supreme Court resolved by reversing *Capato*. By that convoluted pathway, *Capato* thus became the lodestar in this context.

Unlike the test articulated by the Social Security Administration, which relies on the law that would determine devolution of D's intestate personal property in the state of D's domicile,[51] the appellate court in *Capato* applied a simplistic analysis in which "dependency" would play the critical role if the parties agreed that the applicant was the DNA offspring — an "undisputed biological child" — of the decedent.[52] That conclusion would have resulted in a remand to address the question whether the claimants could have been the decedent's dependents at his death, given that they were born after he died, but the Supreme Court's grant of certiorari and reversal of the appellate court's ruling instead made the dependency question irrelevant.

The unanimous Supreme Court opinion in *Capato* validates the government's state law intestacy approach as being consistent with Congress' intent that survivor benefits only assist children who lost their source of support due to the unanticipated death of a parent. According to the Court, if state intestacy law permits a child to inherit, "it may reasonably be thought that the child will more likely be dependent during the parent's life" – which is a funny construct in the case of a posthumously conceived child, who could not possibly have been the decedent's dependent during life. In a sense, the government's approach, blessed by *Capato*, avoids the dependency issue entirely.

---

[50] 631 F.3d 626 (3d Cir. 2011), rev'd sub nom, Astrue v. Capato, 132 S. Ct. 2021 (2012).

[51] See Program Operations Manual System (POMS) GN 00306.001(C)(1)(c), "to meet the definition of 'child' under the Act, an after-conceived child must be able to inherit under State law." This provision is available at secure.ssa.gov/poms.nsf/lnx/0200306001.

[52] See 42 U.S.C. §§ 416(e)(1) and 402(d)(1)(C).

§ 2.2.4.3

In doing so, however, *Capato* does little to alter the fact that the government's approach yields different results under different state laws, because intestacy statutes differ. In Capato, the Court relied on Florida law,[53] under which a posthumously conceived child can only inherit as provided in a decedent's will – not by intestacy. But the Court acknowledged that intestacy determined by statute in other states would provide an inheritance to posthumously conceived children who are born or conceived within statutorily specified time limits.[54] As such, the Court's conclusion simply blesses the SSA approach of looking to state intestacy law as a valid and controlling regulatory approach, but it fails to establish a uniform national rule.

Albeit that these cases have produced inconsistent results, the issue in each was relatively easy. The more challenging situation is one that the courts have just begun to address. If D leaves DNA in the freezer and that DNA is used postmortem with the requisite permission to produce a child, it seems relatively clear that D intended that child to be a beneficiary of D's estate. But what about relatives of the DNA provider? Assume, for example, that the provider's ancestor created a trust for the provider's benefit for life, remainder to the provider's descendants. Does the settlor intend to give anyone (the provider's surviving spouse or anyone else) a blank check to create more remainder beneficiaries? That question was answered in the affirmative by In re Martin B.[55]

The question whether a provider intends for a posthumously conceived child to be treated as their own is easier than the question whether an ancestor intends for someone else to be able to use the DNA to create more beneficiaries of the ancestor's trust. Indeed, if clients were asked the question, "would you want your daughter-in-law to be able to make herself pregnant with your son's frozen sperm, to create more beneficiaries of your trust," would their answers predictably be the same as if they were asked "do you want your son-in-law to be able to withdraw your daughter's frozen egg (or their frozen embryo) and find a surrogate mother to make more beneficiaries of your trust"? There is

---

[53] Fla. Stat. Ann. § 742.17(4), which applied because Florida was the state of the decedent's domicile at death.

[54] The Court listed intestacy provisions in California, Colorado, Iowa, Louisiana, North Dakota, and the UPC.

[55] 841 N.Y.S.2d 207 (Surr. Ct. 2007).

§ 2.2.4.3

likely no way to predict a typical client's reaction to either question, nor to predict whether any client's response would distinguish between a daughter-in-law using the son's sperm and bearing the child herself as opposed to a son-in-law finding a surrogate mother to carry the daughter's child.

The court in *Martin B* may have reflected the direction the law appeared to be developing at that time, treating the offspring as a child of the DNA provider and therefore as a descendant of any other ancestor, for all purposes. But the issue in *Martin B* is similar to the stranger-to-the-adoption rule,[56] as to which the law remains unsettled. Remember the common law rule that an individual who adopted a child was regarded as the child's parent for all purposes relating to the adopting parent's estate, but the child was not treated as a descendant of the adopting parent's ancestors. That rule then was changed by statute and adopteds were treated as natural born for all purposes. But more recently there has been a push back with respect to adult adoption and the stranger-to-the-adoption rule. The notion being that maybe an ancestor's intent is not the same if adoption is used to make an adult a beneficiary of an ancestor's estate plan, and thus adopted adults should not be treated as natural born. It may be that a similar iteration will occur in the posthumous conception context as well, by creating a stranger-to-the-freezer rule.

As all this shakes out, it may be wise for estate planners to draft for these issues, to articulate their clients' intent in each regard. Particularly because state law is in flux, because one-size-fits-all legislation may not reflect a client's intent, and because conflict of laws issues may inform a court's reliance on the law of a different state.

§2.3 ADVANCEMENTS

A decedent who made lifetime transfers to or for the benefit of an intestate heir may have intended some or all of them to be treated as an advancement of the recipient's intestate entitlement. Whether this intent will be effectuated if the decedent does not leave a valid will that implements this intent will depend upon whether an advancement statute is applicable. For example, although inter vivos transfers to children

---

[56] See §2.2.4.1 at text accompanying note 20.

§2.3

are presumed to be advancements,[1] state law advancement rules are not predictable if the donee is a more distant heir.

UPC § 2-109 incorporates desirable aspects that improve upon the advancement statute of many states, including the following features:

(1) Unlike many state laws, it operates even in partially intestate estates as well as to those with no valid will.

(2) Advancement treatment may apply to the intestate share of any heir, not just children or more remote lineal descendants.

(3) Any property, real or personal, may be the subject of an advancement.

(4) Like most advancement statutes, if the advancement exceeds the intestate share of the recipient, no provision requires the recipient to return the excess.

(5) The decedent's intent that the transfer be treated as an advancement must be expressed in a writing contemporaneous with the gift or acknowledged in writing as such by the recipient.[2]

(6) The value of the property on the first to occur of the date the heir came into possession or enjoyment, or the date of the decedent's death controls in determining the amount of the advancement, which implicitly indicates that nonprobate transfers that are effective only at death may be treated as advancements.

(7) The advancement is not charged against any representative of a recipient who predeceased the decedent unless the contemporaneous writing or acknowledgment provides otherwise.

It is preferable for the decedent to have a will that addresses the consequences of lifetime transfers on final distribution of the decedent's estate, and the law in most states is that advancements are charged against distributive shares only in totally intestate estates,[3] the presumption being that a will (even if it disposes of less than all of the decedent's estate) states any intent regarding advancements. Thus, if a will exists but it is silent, the majority rule is that inter vivos transfers cannot be

---

[1] § 2.3 Atkinson, The Law of Wills § 129 at 722 (2d ed. 1953).

[2] In many states transfers, especially of more than insignificant amounts to children, are presumed to be advancements unless the recipient can prove otherwise. See McGovern, Kurtz, & English, Wills, Trusts & Estates § 2.6 (4th ed. 2010).

[3] See Atkinson, The Law of Wills § 129 at 724 (2d ed. 1953). The 1990 version of UPC § 2-109 is unusual in this respect.

reflected in the final distribution.[4] In some jurisdictions this rule is relaxed with respect to transfers to a testamentary beneficiary *after* execution of a will, although the better treatment of those distributions is that they affect the will only if they constitute an ademption by satisfaction or an ademption by extinction.[5]

In some cases advancement treatment will be desirable even if the estate beneficiaries are not adverse. For example, S's intestate share may be larger if D's estate reflects advancements made to lineal descendants, which may increase the available FET marital deduction and reduce taxes.[6]

A tax apportionment problem may be raised by advancement treatment, if each recipient is required to contribute to the decedent's FET bill in proportion to the amount each receives relative to the total taxable estate. If the taxes are prorated on the basis of the net shares of each beneficiary, computed after reflecting advancements, the donee whose share is reduced will pay a smaller share of the tax than if the estate is divided after payment of the tax and advancements treatment then is applied against these shares. An advanced donee should contribute pro

---

[4] Atkinson, The Law of Wills § 129 at 723 (2d ed. 1953). In some states even a will cannot impose advancements treatment. For example, D may not be able to treat as advancements inter vivos transfers to an heir (such as S) who can claim a share of D's estate regardless of the terms of D's will.

[5] Atkinson, The Law of Wills § 129 at 723 (2d ed. 1953) and § § 133 and 134. N.Y. Est., Powers & Trusts L. § 2-1.5 combines into one statute rules treating lifetime distributions as advancements in intestacy and as ademptions under a will, with the requirement for each being a contemporaneous writing signed by the donor or by the donee evidencing the decedent's intent regarding the transfer.

[6] See, e.g., Brodrick v. Moore, 226 F.2d 105 (10th Cir. 1955) (S renounced D's will, which benefited D's child, and elected to take a statutory forced heir share of the estate as augmented by an advancement of property acquired by D in joint tenancy with the child; because this advancement property was counted against the child's distributive portion of the estate, S's relative share was much larger than without the advancement and the marital deduction available likewise was increased, all under facts indicating that the sole object of the renunciation and advancement treatment was to minimize taxes imposed on D's estate). This technique will not work unless state law considers advancements in determining S's entitlement. See, e.g., N.Y. Est. Powers & Trusts L. § 2-1.5(e), which precludes anything in the advancement statute from increasing or decreasing S's elective share.

rata to the tax payment relative to all property transferred inter vivos and at the decedent's death, as if the decedent's intent was that advancements be treated for all purposes as if the inter vivos transfers were received at death along with the balance of the decedent's estate, even though the property advanced was not includible in the decedent's gross estate.[7]

§2.4 FAMILY ALLOWANCES

D's intestate estate available for distribution is the amount remaining after all charges that must be paid, including any award under local law for S's support (or that of dependents). Similar to homestead, this topic is relevant in both testate and intestate estates, although state law may permit a decedent to specify that distributions under a will are in lieu of a family allowance. Thus, local law should be consulted to determine any local variations or exceptions.

The most important issue for estate planning purposes regarding family allowances is whether amounts allowed and paid for S's support during settlement of the estate qualify for the FET marital deduction. Because the allowance in many states terminates upon S's death or remarriage and terminates in all cases upon final settlement of the estate, the question is whether the allowance is a nondeductible terminable interest.

No nondeductible terminable interest problem exists if the allowance passes to S as an absolute, vested property right that does not terminate by reason of death or other contingency, meaning that any unpaid balance under an award survives as an asset of S's estate. Unfortunately, in many states these allowances terminate upon such contingencies as death or remarriage, making their deductibility ques-

---

[7] See, e.g., In re Estate of Necaise, 915 So. 2d 449 (Miss. 2005) (a satisfaction case involving the same issue, in which the decedent's will actually addressed and dictated a pro rata recovery from the donee). If made after 1976, the inter vivos transfers are includible in the decedent's adjusted taxable gifts base for FET computation purposes and, therefore, are a part of the overall tax determination. Nevertheless, the recipient benefits from the inter vivos transfer rather than having to wait until the decedent's death to enjoy the property, and may benefit if the value of the gift appreciated but is frozen at the time of the gift for purposes of this computation.

tionable.[1] However, the marital deduction is allowable even if the allowance is terminable to the extent S is the estate beneficiary, because the nondeductible terminable interest rule applies only if an interest passes to a third party after S's interest ends.[2] Thus, only to the extent the allowance terminates and the estate passes to someone other than S is the deduction in peril, and even then this issue is subject to some dispute.

The House of Representatives version of the Internal Revenue Code of 1954 contained a provision specifically stating that a support allowance paid to S within one year of D's death would qualify for the marital deduction.[3] The Senate version of the Bill excluded that provision and the Conference Committee report[4] stated that the provision was not necessary because many allowances would qualify for the marital deduction under existing law. The confusion that has developed over this issue indicates that this was not so clearly understood. Although the passing requirement for marital deduction purposes clearly is met with respect to these awards (even though they may require that the probate court make a determination and declare an award),[5] authorities are divided on the nondeductible terminable interest aspect.[6]

---

[1] §2.4 Rev. Rul. 83, 1953-1 C.B. 395.

[2] Treas. Reg. §20.2056(b)-1(g) Example (8). See §13.4.3.3.2 nn.101- 103 and accompanying text.

[3] H.R. 8300, 83d Cong., 2d Sess., §2056(b)(7) (1954).

[4] H.R. Rep. No. 2543, 83d Cong., 2d Sess. 75 (1954).

[5] See Treas. Reg. §20.2056(c)-2(a) (penultimate sentence).

[6] See Estate of Green v. United States, 441 F.2d 303 (6th Cir. 1971); Molner v. United States, 175 F. Supp. 271 (N.D. Ill. 1959); Miller v. United States, 74-2 U.S. Tax Cas. (CCH) ¶ 13,039 (N.D. Ohio 1974), all allowing the deduction, and United States v. Edmondson, 331 F.2d 676 (5th Cir. 1964); Hamilton Nat'l Bank v. United States, 353 F.2d 930 (6th Cir. 1965); Estate of Abely v. Commissioner, 60 T.C. 120 (1973), aff'd, 489 F.2d 1327 (1st Cir. 1974); Connecticut Nat'l Bank v. United States, 76-1 U.S. Tax Cas. (CCH) ¶ 13,132 (D. Conn. 1976); Wachovia Bank & Trust Co. v. United States, 234 F. Supp. 897 (M.D. N.C. 1964); Iowa-Des Moines Nat'l Bank v. United States, 306 F. Supp. 320 (S.D. Iowa 1969), all denying the deduction. Estate of Moss v. Commissioner, 43 T.C.M. (CCH) 582 (1982), allowed the deduction in part, reflecting the facts and result in Treas. Reg. §20.2056(b)-1(g) Example (8).

For example, Jackson v. United States[7] held that the character of an allowance must be judged as of D's death and the award is a nondeductible terminable interest for marital deduction purposes if S must live to a certain date to become indefeasibly entitled to an allowance. The deduction was denied because that allowance was contingent on S being alive and unmarried when the award was made. The Court found support for this result in the legislative history showing that amendments that would negate the nondeductible terminable interest rule with respect to such allowances have been rejected by the Senate.

Similarly, in Estate of Rubinow v. Commissioner[8] a lump sum allowance was granted by the probate court retroactive to D's death and was not terminable by S's death, remarriage, or otherwise. The court nevertheless denied the deduction because the probate court could refuse to grant the allowance and must determine the amount of any award, how it is to be paid, and whether it should vest retroactively and not terminate for other reasons, making it contingent on judicial action and the discretion of the judge.

The court in Estate of Snider v. Commissioner[9] noted that other cases involving similar payments have found the allowance to qualify, at least in part, although *Snider* involved an unusual twist. Represented by the court as a case of first impression, the statutory authority for the allowance specified that no allowance would be made if S had adequate separate property to provide for his or her maintenance. As a result of that restriction, the court held that S's entitlement was contingent upon there being inadequate assets to provide for his or her needs, which involved a determination by the local probate court some time after D's death. Consequently, the court found that S had no unconditional, indefeasibly vested entitlement at D's death, making any award a nondeductible terminable interest.

Entitlement to an allowance may be unconditional in other jurisdictions even though the amount of the award may require a postmortem determination, and this has not by itself scuttled deductibility of an award ultimately made. It is difficult to distinguish a statute that, in

---

[7] 376 U.S. 503 (1964).

[8] 75 T.C. 486 (1980), aff'd in an unpublished opinion (2d Cir. 1981).

[9] 84 T.C. 75 (1985).

§2.4

essence, seems to say that the award will be zero if S has no unmet needs because of the existence of S's own assets, and it may be that the decision in *Snider* improperly exalts form over substance.

In Estate of Watson v. Commissioner,[10] for example, the Tax Court held that an award sufficient to provide one year's support, with no reduction or termination if S died or remarried, qualified for the marital deduction. The requirement that an affirmative request be made, and that a Chancellor determine the amount of the award, did not constitute a condition or contingency that made the award a terminable interest.

And in Estate of Radel v. Commissioner,[11] S survived an intestate D and received a spousal allowance of $27,000, paid in monthly installments, for which a marital deduction was claimed. S also received, under state intestate succession law, one-third of the remaining estate, for which a marital deduction also was claimed. The government disallowed two-thirds of the $27,000 allowance amount as a nondeductible terminable interest, the theory being that S had received what amounted to an income interest in the entire estate for a period of time and two-thirds of the award constituted a nondeductible terminable interest because the estate terminated and passed to other parties to the extent of that two-thirds portion. Finding that, by statute, there was no condition precedent to receipt of the allowance and, more importantly, that there was no subsequent condition that could cut short the allowance (such as death or remarriage before full payment of the awarded allowance), the Tax Court held that the full amount was deductible, essentially following Estate of Green v. United States.[12]

In *Green* and *Radel* it seems clear that the allowance *is* a terminable interest, notwithstanding the lack of any statutory conditions subsequent that are tied to the death or remarriage of S. For example, in *Radel*, by statute, the allowance could be paid for only a maximum of 18 months, and in any case of this type the estate ultimately will terminate, even if no other limitation is invoked. Without expressly saying so, the court appeared to justify treatment of the entire allowance as deductible (albeit a seemingly terminable interest) as if it was a specific award being paid

---

[10] 94 T.C. 262 (1990).

[11] 88 T.C. 1143 (1987), acq. 1987-2 C.B. 1 (facts very similar to Treas. Reg. § 20.2056(b)-1(g) Example (8)).

[12] 441 F.2d 303 (6th Cir. 1971).

in installments with no contingencies that would terminate the payment. Under such a vision, the allowance is no different from any installment payout of a guaranteed obligation, and the decision is proper.

It is not clear, however, whether state law actually supports such a conclusion, and the opinion did not indicate whether this in fact was the rationale supporting the court's decision. *Radel* was followed, however, in TAM 9219001 for an award described as "up to $500 per month for up to 18 months," which indicates that the amount was not yet established and the installment payout of a guaranteed obligation theory potentially was not the proper explanation.

Involving a different tax issue, payment of a family allowance does not qualify under § 663(a)(1) as a specific bequest that avoids the income distribution rules of §§ 661 and § 662. As originally written, the regulations[13] excluded family allowances from the category of distributions that carried out income from an estate except to the extent they were payable out of and chargeable to income under a court order or decree or under local law. As a consequence, the government's position was that payment of an allowance was deductible by the estate only to the same extent. But the Tax Court[14] held that allowances paid from any source are amounts properly paid or required to be distributed and thus are deductible by the paying estate under § 661(a)(2).

Although the court did not rule on whether the payments were income to the recipient under § 662(a)(2), the regulations[15] now so provide and, as amended, now dictate that DNI is carried out and that the estate may deduct amounts paid or required to be paid during the taxable year pursuant to a court order or decree or under local law as an allowance or award for the support of a surviving spouse or dependents for a limited period during estate administration.[16] Distribution of such

---

[13] Treas. Reg. § 1.661(a)-2(e).

[14] Estate of McCoy v. Commissioner, 50 T.C. 562 (1968), acq., 1973-2 C.B. 2.

[15] Treas. Reg. §§ 1.662(a)-2(c) (last sentence) and 1.661(a)-3(b) (last clause).

[16] See Cameron v. Commissioner, 68 T.C. 744 (1977) (distributions to support minor children had priority over most estate charges and were unrelated to inheritance rights; court nevertheless rejected contention that the recipient was not a beneficiary within the meaning of § 643(c) and, therefore, the distributions carried out DNI); Cummings v. United States, 69-1 U.S. Tax Cas. (CCH) ¶ 9359 (C.D. Cal. 1969); Schaefer v. Commissioner, 46 T.C.M. (CCH) 986 (1983).

§2.4

allowances is not regarded as the payment of a debt or claim that would avoid the income carryout rules[17] that apply to beneficiaries of an estate or trust.[18] As a consequence, the income tax liability carried out to a recipient, which will reduce the net value of the allowance, ought to be considered when the amount of an allowance is determined.

Consistent with the income tax treatment of family allowances as distributions to a beneficiary rather than payment of a debt or claim, these awards constitute property transfers for § 2013 previously taxed property credit purposes if the distributee dies within 10 years of the decedent whose estate made the payment. Although state law may regard the allowance as a charge against the estate in the category of an administration expense or a debt, it nevertheless passes to the distributee by operation of law and it is a transfer from the decedent for purposes of the credit.[19]

Family allowances normally are claims against D's estate that take precedence over debts, legacies, and administration expenses. Consistent with the income and FET treatment as entitlements rather than claims, however, the distributee is regarded as a transferee of estate assets subject to § 6901 transferee liability.[20]

Because a family allowance can alter the taxation and disposition of a decedent's estate, a number of factors should be considered in deciding whether to claim an award. For example, if D's estate plan, S's

---

[17] United States v. James, 333 F.2d 748 (9th Cir. 1964); Rev. Rul. 75-124, 1975-1 C.B. 183.

[18] Ferguson, Freeland, & Ascher, Federal Income Taxation of Estates, Trusts, and Beneficiaries § 6.10 (2d ed. 1993), states that distribution of an entitlement is not an income carryout event if state law provides an absolute right to a fixed portion of an estate, not dependent upon a court's order or discretion, because the award vests in the recipient immediately at death and "never becomes part of the probate estate." Only dower distribution authorities are cited as support, however.

[19] Rev. Rul. 58-167, 1958-1 C.B. 340; PLR 5612071620A.

[20] See Davis v. Birdsong, 275 F.2d 113 (5th Cir. 1960). An exception may apply, however, if the property received by the distributee is exempt under state law from creditor claims, as was the case in Estate of Connell v. Commissioner, 63 T.C.M. (CCH) 3190 (1992) (Texas homestead property passed to S outside probate and was exempt from sale to satisfy creditors' claims, making it also exempt from transferee liability under § 6901).

intestate entitlement or elective share, and disclaimer planning fail to produce the desired marital deduction, an additional deduction may be available through an award entitlement.

More importantly, if the distributee is in need of immediate financial assistance, it may be easier and safer for the personal representative to provide funds in the form of a family allowance pursuant to a court order or decree than by a partial interim distribution of the estate made in the representative's discretion. In this respect, payment of estate debts before satisfying governmental obligations makes the personal representative personally liable, up to the full amount distributed, for any unpaid governmental claims.[21] Although "debt" includes a beneficiary's distributive share of an estate,[22] it does not include family allowances, which therefore can be paid without exposure to personal liability.[23]

Limited authority suggests that no gift or FET liability attends the expiration or lapse of a right to elect a family allowance, as for example if S allows the time to claim an award to expire or dies before that period expires.[24] Because family allowances are awarded in the probate court's

---

[21] 31 U.S.C. § 3713(b).

[22] Treas. Reg. § 20.2002-1.

[23] Schwartz v. Commissioner, 34 T.C.M. (CCH) 1146 (1975), rev'd on other grounds, 560 F.2d 311 (8th Cir. 1977) (family allowance paid pursuant to state court decree has priority over debts due the United States; personal representative incurred no personal liability for paying allowance before satisfying obligations to United States); Rev. Rul. 80-112, 1980-1 C.B. 306 (state law priority for satisfying claims of a decedent was administration expenses, funeral expenses, costs of last illness, family allowances, wages of household employees, and all other claims; administration expenses and the family allowance were not debts under state law—they were charges against the decedent's property to be deducted before paying debts—and had priority over federal tax claims for which the government had no lien).

[24] See Rev. Rul. 74-492, 1974-2 C.B. 298 (death before expiration of S's right to elect statutory forced heir share regarded as tantamount to a renunciation thereof "by operation of law," in the sense that failure to affirmatively request the entitlement meant that it did not exist). The Ruling predated adoption of the § 2518 disclaimer rules and may no longer be probative. It also may not be on point because of differences between the entitlement mechanism under state law to elect a statutory forced heir share as compared to a family allowance. And see Ames v. United States, 86-2 U.S. Tax Cas. (CCH) ¶ 13,694 (N.D. Ohio 1986) (S elected to take against D's will; FET marital deduction for family allowance, claimed in addition to amount deducted for statutory forced heir share, denied

§ 2.4

discretion in most states, and because S has no support needs or ability to request an award if S is deceased, the proper result should be that death precludes an entitlement rather than causing it to lapse.[25] Therefore, death before expiration of the time to claim an award should not generate an FET liability. Furthermore, presumably there is no need for support if S is alive but does not seek an award within the time required by state law. Thus, arguably the right to an award has no value—even if failure to seek an award is tantamount to lapse of an otherwise taxable power over the decedent's estate.

§2.5 HOMESTEAD

The intestate distribution picture is not complete without considering homestead rights.[1] Like family allowances, however, homestead rights may be significant in testate estates and with respect to inter vivos transfers as well.

The three significant estate planning questions raised by homestead are (1) whether a client should acquire an estate of homestead, (2) whether S's homestead entitlement will qualify for the FET marital deduction, and (3) whether any spouse who acquires an estate of homestead makes a gift to anyone for federal gift tax purposes? Each of these questions should be answered in the context of the particular homestead statute that is applicable because there is variation among state entitlements.

It is unlikely that encumbering alienability of residential property with homestead restrictions is desirable, except to the extent an exemption from attachment, levy on execution, and sale for the payment of debts is desirable. In this respect, it is notable that homestead property

---

(Footnote Continued)

because the statutory forced heir share was the maximum amount S could receive under state law).

[25] See Foiles v. Whittman, 233 P.3d 697 (Colo. 2010), comparing S's entitlement to an "exempt property allowance" to S's entitlement to a "family allowance" and noting that the statute did not require S to remain alive with respect to the exempt property allowance but it did with respect to the family allowance.

[1] §2.5 See 1 American Law of Property §§5.75-5.120 (Casner ed 1952).

is not immune from all liabilities.[2] Otherwise, any desire to protect a spouse or minor children can be effected in numerous other ways, including the use of trusts, making homestead undesirable because of its tax detriments.

As in the typical case, assume that the homestead estate protects S and minor children until the last to occur of (1) there being no living children under the age of 18 and (2) S dies or remarries. In addition, in many states the homestead estate terminates upon abandonment. If there are no minor children who may succeed to the estate when S dies, termination of the entitlement if all children are over 18 and S dies or remarries constitutes the estate granted to S as a terminable interest that does not qualify for the marital deduction.[3] The marital deduction is available only if there are no minor children and the homestead estate exists solely for the benefit of S who (or whose estate) will receive the

---

[2] See United States v. Rodgers, 461 U.S. 677 (1983) (district court could order sale of family home in which delinquent taxpayer held an interest when indebtedness was incurred; homestead rights could not bar the sale, but must be considered in distributing proceeds of sale); Harris v. United States, 764 F.2d 1126 (5th Cir. 1985); United States v. Molina, 584 F. Supp. 1011 (S.D. Tex. 1984), rev'd, 764 F.2d 1132 (5th Cir. 1985) (same, involving community property; value of the homestead right was the discounted value of the life estate, which the district court did not value properly using tables that account for the fact that the property is subject to concurrent use by two people); United States v. Bachman, 584 F. Supp. 1002 (S.D. Iowa 1984) (same); United States v. Hershberger, 338 F. Supp. 804 (D. Kan. 1972), aff'd, 475 F.2d 677 (10th Cir. 1973) (homestead interest not subject to levy for satisfaction of federal tax liability, stating that homestead laws that confer only future privileges and exemptions are subordinate to federal tax liens but homestead laws that expressly provide a present property interest and confer more than an exemption are superior to federal tax liens); United States v. Weitzner, 61-2 U.S. Tax Cas. (CCH) ¶ 9527 (S.D. Fla. 1961), aff'd, 309 F.2d 45 (5th Cir. 1962) (interests of widow and children of a decedent in homestead property were subject to a lien for the unpaid income taxes of the decedent that was perfected before the decedent died).

[3] See, e.g., Estate of Kyle v. Commissioner, 94 T.C. 829 (1990) (marital deduction denied for a Texas homestead interest and also for a lump sum distribution in lieu of the homestead interest because a postmortem exchange of property for an otherwise nondeductible interest will not purify the defective interest otherwise passing from D to S); Estate of Nelson v. Commissioner, 232 F.2d 720 (5th Cir. 1956) (Florida homestead is nondeductible terminable interest). See § 13.4.3.3.2 n.102.

property upon termination of the interest.[4] The marital deduction is not allowable even if local law allows S to petition for a lump sum payment in lieu of the homestead life interest.[5]

Regarding the gift tax consequences of creating a homestead interest, assume the worst case: property in which homestead rights exist cannot be conveyed to defeat the rights of S and minor children unless S joins in the deed, thereby releasing those rights. When the homestead estate is created there is no transfer from the owner to S or the children that constitutes a gift for federal gift tax purposes because their entitlement is similar to inchoate dower and the acquisition of real property in which a spouse has an inchoate dower right is not a taxable gift.[6]

---

[4] See § 2056(b)(1)(A).

[5] See United States v. Hiles, 318 F.2d 56 (5th Cir. 1963), rev'd, 198 F. Supp. 857 (S.D. Ala. 1961) (payment to S by order of court to eliminate homestead rights cannot qualify for the marital deduction because the homestead right vests when the owner dies and any payment is merely a substitute for the nondeductible terminable interest). Accord, Estate of Kyle v. Commissioner, 94 T.C. 829 (1990) (lump sum distribution in lieu of an otherwise nondeductible homestead interest also could not qualify for the marital deduction). And see the stipulation that the homestead interest did not qualify for the marital deduction in Florida Nat'l Bank v. United States, 313 F. Supp. 1072 (M.D. Fla. 1970), aff'd in part and rev'd in part, 443 F.2d 467 (5th Cir. 1971). But see Rev. Rul. 72-153, 1972-1 C.B. 309 (Washington Rev. Code § 11.52.010 provided that the court "shall award and set off to the surviving spouse, if any, property of the estate . . . not exceeding [$X in] value . . . at the time of death" if no homestead was claimed in the manner provided by law; stressing the word "shall," the government concluded that the payment vested immediately on death and qualified for the FET marital deduction unless the interest would not survive S's own death prior to obtaining a court order granting the payment).

[6] Rev. Rul. 58-13, 1958-1 C.B. 342 (husband gave real property to children, notwithstanding that wife refused to release inchoate dower therein; value of the property was not affected by this fact, which supports the conclusion that no transfer was made to the wife when the inchoate dower right was created). See also Hopkins v. Magruder, 122 F.2d 693 (4th Cir. 1941); Carlton v. Commissioner, 190 F.2d 183 (5th Cir. 1951); Estate of Bartman v. Commissioner, 10 T.C. 1073 (1948); and Thompson v. Commissioner, 37 B.T.A. 793 (1938).

Estate of Johnson v. Commissioner, 77 T.C. 120 (1981), rev'd, 718 F.2d 1303 (5th Cir. 1983), considered whether the value of a decedent's homestead property should be reduced for FET purposes, to reflect S's interest therein. The Tax Court held that it should, refusing to follow a contrary holding in Estate of Hinds v. Commissioner, 11 T.C. 314 (1948), aff'd on another issue, 180 F.2d 930 (5th

However, a gift would occur if a property owner, wishing to obtain S's consent to a conveyance of homestead property, shared the proceeds received for the transfer with S. Under § 2043(b), relinquishment of dower is not regarded as consideration in money or money's worth, and this same position applies for federal gift tax purposes.[7] This payment should, however, qualify for the § 2523 gift tax marital deduction.

(Footnote Continued)

Cir. 1950). The court found this situation analogous to valuation reductions to reflect restrictions on transferring corporate stock, blockage discounts in valuing large holdings of any asset, and valuation of minority interests. In reversing, the appellate court concluded that § 2034 applied to the homestead property that, in this state, replaced an early dower statute. See also TAM 8651001 (minor children's homestead rights do not reduce the FMV of homestead property for FET purposes, referring to *Johnson* and § 2034, which specifically includes in the gross estate dower or curtesy rights, or other interests created by statute in lieu thereof, stating that "homestead rights, being in the nature of a forced testamentary disposition, are no more subject to discounting than any other testamentary disposition"); Estate of Radel v. Commissioner, 88 T.C. 1143 (1987), acq., 1987-2 C.B. 1 (S disclaimed homestead interest, attempting to defeat it and thereby acquire a one-third intestate interest in fee in the property, arguing that a spouse who disclaims is treated as predeceased, causing children to take the interest they were entitled to receive by intestacy, which would not include the homestead property; the court instead held that the disclaimer caused the homestead property to pass entirely to the children and not to fall into the pool of intestate property). For comments on *Johnson*, see Estate of Carli v. Commissioner, 84 T.C. 649 (1985), and see § 15.4.2.1.

[7] Treas. Reg. § 25.2512-8; Merrill v. Fahs, 324 U.S. 308 (1945); and see Rev. Rul. 79-312, 1979-2 C.B. 29 (seller gave S half the proceeds of a sale of real property to induce S to sign the deed releasing inchoate dower rights; the sales proceeds includible in the seller's gross income for income tax purposes were determined without reduction by the payment, which also did not increase the seller's basis in the property sold, and no amount of the payment was includible in S's gross income because it was a gift by the seller for gift tax purposes). If the transfer was pursuant to a property settlement by which S released support rights, § 2516 would regard the transfer as being for full and adequate consideration in money or money's worth for gift tax purposes. See Rev. Rul. 68-379, 1968-2 C.B. 414.

§ 2.5

§2.6 DISQUALIFICATION FOR MISCONDUCT

An individual who caused the death of a decedent may be precluded from profiting in any manner[1] from the decedent's death, as an intestate heir, as the recipient of a family allowance, as the holder of a homestead protection, as a beneficiary under the decedent's will, the recipient of nonprobate property dispositions, or even as the surviving tenant in a joint tenancy. In this respect, however, state law must be inspected because slayer statutes are common but not consistent. UPC §2-803 is representative in some respects of the norm for such statutes, although it addresses issues that are left unresolved or that are handled differently in various states. Nevertheless, the primary elements of such statutes include the following.

To be disqualified under §2-803, and in most states, the slayer must be guilty of the felonious and intentional act of killing the decedent. In many jurisdictions an involuntary killing or an act committed while insane[2] or otherwise incapable of forming the requisite intent will not trigger application of the statute. In jurisdictions in which there are multiple gradations of murder and manslaughter, the statute must be inspected carefully to determine which crimes are addressed by the slayer bar.[3] Moreover, the question must be resolved whether a criminal

---

[1] **§2.6** A very unusual application of the general principle that slayers may not profit from their crimes was adjudicated by In re Estate of Macaro, 699 N.Y.S.2d 634 (Surr. 1999), in which the slayer killed the decedent's sibling and was precluded from inheriting as an heir of that decedent by standing in the shoes of the murdered sibling. And see Kelley v. New Hampshire, 196 A.2d 68 (N.H. 1963) (because the amount a slayer received from the decedent was less than what the slayer expended on the decedent's property, no prohibition—in the form of a constructive trust—was imposed because there was no profit from the crime).

[2] See, e.g., In re Estate of Wirth, 298 N.Y.S.2d 565 (Surr. Ct. 1969) (heir acquitted of decedent's murder by reason of insanity may take intestate share); Campbell v. Ray, 245 A.2d 761 (N.J. Surr. Ct. 1968) (insane S who killed D allowed to inherit D's estate and to take proceeds of life insurance).

[3] See In re Estate of Seipel, 329 N.E.2d 419 (Ill. App. Ct. 1975) (statute that did not apply to manslaughter subsequently was expanded to include any intentional and unjustifiable killing); Wadsworth v. Siek, 254 N.E.2d 738 (Ohio Prob. Ct. 1970) (statute in effect did not apply to manslaughter; D's will excluded slayer, who was allowed to take a statutory forced heir elective share; legislature subsequently changed the law to apply to voluntary manslaughter).

conviction is required or whether a civil determination of guilt is sufficient.[4]

UPC §2-803(g) recognizes that the "beyond reasonable doubt" standard applied in criminal cases may be too severe to preclude an individual from profiting from the wrong of killing the decedent. It permits a civil determination independent of a criminal prosecution to determine whether a "preponderance of the evidence" proves the slayer's guilt. A criminal conviction, however, is conclusive after all rights to appeal have been exhausted. In some jurisdictions the statute also leaves unresolved the issue whether inability to convict because the slayer has died (for example, in a murder/suicide situation) will preclude operation of the prohibition.[5]

State laws vary considerably in terms of the property to which they apply. More traditional prohibitions against the slayer profiting from the killing extend only to probate property, whether passing under a will or by intestacy. More modern statutes, like UPC §2-803(c), are made applicable to any property disposition, including the grant or exercise of a power of appointment and any nonprobate property such as joint tenancy with the right of survivorship, life insurance, or an inter vivos trust. Slayer statutes appear not to be affected by the pre-emption rule in ERISA §514(a)[6] that state law will not be respected to the extent it is inconsistent with federal law as regards qualified retirement benefit plans.[7]

---

[4] See, e.g., In re Estate of Josephson, 297 N.W.2d 444 (N.D. 1980) (minor child shot and killed adoptive parent; although too young to be convicted of the crime, the child could be barred from inheriting under a "feloniously and intentionally" killing the decedent standard).

[5] See Estate of Draper v. Commissioner, 64 T.C. 23 (1975), rev'd on other grounds, 536 F.2d 944 (1st Cir. 1976) (murder/suicide did not preclude slayer statute from applying; because slayer could not benefit under decedent's will, bequests in slayer's favor were not includible in slayer's gross estate and marital deduction was unavailable in the decedent's estate).

[6] 29 U.S.C. §1144(a).

[7] See Egelhoff v. Egelhoff, 532 U.S. 141 (2001) (dicta, the Court nevertheless stating that slayer statutes have been adopted by nearly every state and apply a well established and more or less uniform result, making their interference with the aims of ERISA debatable); parroting Mendez-Bellido v. Board of Trustees, 709 F. Supp. 329 (E.D. N.Y. 1989) (because state laws are relatively uniform in precluding a slayer from benefiting from the crime, federal pre-emption need not

Finally, state laws differ on the consequence of a finding that the slayer caused the decedent's death. UPC § 2-803(b) provides that the slayer forfeits all benefits and, for purposes of intestate distribution, is treated as having disclaimed all entitlement in the decedent's estate. This is slightly different from the more common treatment of the slayer as having predeceased the decedent, and would preclude the issue resolved in several similar cases[8] involving spouses, murder/suicide, and disposition of the slayer's estate. Because state law treats the slayer as predeceasing the victim, the victim's surviving heirs argued in each case that the victim inherited the slayer's property and, therefore, that they were entitled to it. No such argument would be possible if the state statute merely treated the slayer as disclaiming the victim's property. The courts nevertheless reach the same result that would obtain under a disclaimer statute by pointing out that the presumption that the slayer predeceased the victim is applicable only for purposes of disposing of the slain decedent's estate and not for other purposes, such as disposing of the slayer's estate.

Under many state laws and under UPC § 2-106, if only grandchildren survive a decedent they receive per capita shares of equal size rather than a distribution by right of representation that may differ in size if several grandchildren represent several children (for example, if Child A had two children and Child B had only one, the grandchildren would receive shares of one-third each if neither child was alive, one by virtue of a slayer statute presumption, whereas A's children would receive shares half the size of B's child if either A or B was alive but was deemed to have disclaimed a share that then passed by representation).

In addition, treatment as predeceased creates questions regarding disposition of property held as joint tenants with the right of survivorship or as tenants by the entireties. The intent of slayer statutes is to preclude the wrongdoer from profiting from the crime rather than to punish.

(Footnote Continued)

apply to protect against a patchwork set of results), followed in New Orleans Electrical Pension Fund v. DeRocha, 779 F. Supp. 845 (E.D. La. 1991); and New Orleans Electrical Pension Fund v. Newman, 784 F. Supp. 1233 (E.D. La. 1992). See § 3.1.3 n.69 and accompanying text regarding the pre-emption issue in the divorce context in which it arose in *Egelhoff*.

[8] See, e.g., In re Estate of Miller, 840 So. 2d 703 (Miss. 2003); Keith v. Johnson, 440 S.E.2d 230 (Ga. Ct. App. 1993).

Thus, the slayer's entitlement in the property should not be diminished. Among the alternatives found among various state laws is to treat the slayer and the decedent's interests as severed, allowing the decedent's portion to pass as if it was not held jointly with the slayer. Other statutes treat the slayer as entitled to a life estate in an equal share of the jointly owned property but then as if the slain tenant survived the slayer for ultimate disposition of the property. Severance may be preferable because it accelerates disposition of the property, and it is adopted by UPC §2-803(c)(2).

Another alternative is to treat the slayer as a constructive trustee for the benefit of the decedent's rightful heirs,[9] which creates the problem of what title is acquired by an innocent transferee from the slayer before the constructive trust is imposed. And some states may still regard the criminal conviction as adequate punishment for the killing and therefore refuse to apply the misconduct prohibition at all.[10]

Other forms of misconduct leading to an inheritance bar are not common, although abandonment, desertion, or abuse may work to that effect in some cases.[11]

§2.7 ADMINISTRATION OF A DECEDENT'S ESTATE

The process of administering an estate is roughly the same whether the decedent died with a will or intestate. This chapter is about intestacy

---

[9] See, e.g., Estate of Wolyniec v. Moe, 226 A.2d 743 (N.J. 1967) (daughter who murdered her father was pregnant; she was deemed constructive trustee of intestate property for benefit of decedent's unborn grandchild).

[10] See Anstine v. Hawkins, 447 P.2d 677 (Idaho 1968) (Idaho statutes did not exclude S, who was convicted of voluntary manslaughter, from inheriting from D).

[11] See, e.g., UPC §2-114(a)(2) and N.Y. Est. Powers & Trusts L. §4-1.4(a) (abandonment of a child precludes parent from inheriting from or through that child's estate); Calif. Prob. Code §259(a) (a very restricted version of elder abuse—requiring bad faith and either reckless, oppressive, fraudulent, or malicious conduct—may preclude an individual from serving as fiduciary or taking as a beneficiary of the abused decedent); and Rev. Code Wash. §11.84.010 et seq. (a more expansive version of elder abuse, providing that an "abuser"—defined as any person who participates in the willful and unlawful financial exploitation of a vulnerable adult—may not acquire property or receive any benefit from the death of that abused adult).

and it will become clear that a will can and should address significant postmortem administrative requirements in estates of any size or complexity.

§2.7.1 *Personal Representative Defined*

Administration of a decedent's estate is conducted by a personal representative, of which there are several varieties. An Executor is designated by the decedent's will, while an Administrator is court appointed[1] if the decedent died intestate or if the decedent's will did not make a valid designation of a person or entity that is willing and able to act. An Administrator cum testamento annexo, or c.t.a. (with the will annexed), means the decedent died testate, and an Administrator de bonis non, or d.b.n. (of goods not administered), means the personal representative was appointed as a successor to complete the job begun by another. An Administrator both c.t.a. and d.b.n. is a successor acting under a will.

A temporary or special administrator may be permitted to act if there may be a delay in appointing a personal representative, particularly if a testate decedent's will is contested.[2] And in some jurisdictions a Public Administrator is appointed if no other suitable person or entity is willing and able to administer the decedent's estate. The need for a public administrator is illustrated by two cases. In Kurn v. Moran,[3] the decedent's heirs were overseas and unable to administer the estate, but they wanted to resist a claim being made against the estate. In United States v. Mize,[4] the public administrator was appointed at the request of the Internal Revenue Service, which wanted to file a claim to assert an outstanding 18-year-old FET liability.

---

[1] **§2.7** Statutes establish the order in which interested parties are entitled to be appointed as administrator. See, e.g., UPC §3-203. Reed v. Reed, 404 U.S. 71 (1971), declared an Idaho statute unconstitutional because it established a priority based on gender in violation of the equal protection clause of the Fourteenth Amendment.

[2] See, e.g., UPC §§3-614–3-618.

[3] 207 N.E.2d 688 (Mass. 1965).

[4] 73-1 U.S. Tax Cas. (CCH) ¶ 12,923 (C.D. Cal. 1972).

§2.7.2 *Jurisdiction for Administration*

A decedent's movables typically are subject to devolution and administration under the law of the state of the decedent's domicile at death.[5] The decedent's immovable assets (realty) must be administered where located,[6] which may necessitate ancillary administration. Moreover, because a personal representative's authority to act is derived from the law of the state in which the personal representative is appointed, a domiciliary personal representative may have no authority to act elsewhere (such as to pursue claims of the decedent against debtors located in other states) unless by statute the other jurisdiction recognizes the domiciliary personal representative.[7] Thus, again an ancillary administration may be necessary.

At the very least an ancillary administration would require that the fact of the decedent's death be established and that the decedent's will, if there is one, be admitted in the ancillary jurisdiction. This may allow a challenge to the validity of the will notwithstanding its admission to probate in the domiciliary state. For example, when the decedent's will was offered for probate in O'Brien v. Costello[8] to govern the disposition of ancillary movables, the court allowed an heir to challenge the domicili-

---

[5] See Restatement (Second) of Conflict of Laws §260 (1971); Atherton v. FitzGibbon, 192 N.E.2d 731 (Mass. 1963) (Massachusetts domiciliary's will that directed probate and administration as if the decedent was a New York domiciliary was probated in Massachusetts because of the decedent's domicile and because most of the decedent's property was located in Massachusetts); In re Estate of Janney, 446 A.2d 1265 (Pa. 1982) (dispute resolved under Pennsylvania law because decedent's New Jersey realty was sold and the proceeds invested in Pennsylvania); In re Estate of Rougeron, 217 N.E.2d 639 (N.Y. 1966) (petitioner was not entitled to a share of a New York domiciliary's estate under New York law, which the court held to be applicable because the decedent's movables located in Switzerland were moved to New York before litigation was instituted to confirm the petitioner's entitlement under Swiss law). But see In re Estate of Renard, 439 N.E.2d 341 (N.Y. 1982) (French domiciliary decedent's will directing application of New York law respected by New York court with respect to New York movables, thereby preventing child's forced heir entitlement under French law).

[6] See Restatement (Second) of Conflict of Laws §236 (1971).

[7] See, e.g., UPC §4-205.

[8] 216 A.2d 694 (R.I. 1966).

ary court's decision[9] that the decedent's will was valid. The court held that the domiciliary court's determination was not binding, that the will must be proved in the ancillary state to dispose of the ancillary movables, and that full faith and credit of the domiciliary court's decree was subject to the ancillary court's determination of the domiciliary court's jurisdiction, allowing issues resolved by the domiciliary court to be relitigated in the ancillary court. In addition, under Treas. Reg. § 1.6012-3, the ancillary personal representative may be required to file income tax returns with respect to any income produced by those ancillary assets, notwithstanding that the domiciliary personal representative is filing returns for the balance of the decedent's estate.

§2.7.3 Informal Administration

Many states permit succession without formal administration of the decedent's estate, in some cases only if the estate is of a sufficiently small size, in some cases only if the decedent died with a will that authorized "independent" administration, and usually only if there is no objection by an heir, beneficiary, creditor, or other interested party.[10] In these and other respects, administration of a decedent's estate is a uniquely localized process with significant variations in local law and procedure between states and even between counties or other subdivisions within a state. As a consequence of all these factors, ancillary administration of property located in multiple locales becomes a matter of some significance and frequently it is advisable to plan an estate for administration in a particular jurisdiction and to avoid ancillary administrations by implementing nonprobate dispositions such as inter vivos gifts, joint tenancy with the right of survivorship, or an inter vivos funded trust.[11]

---

[9] Costello v. Conlon, 182 N.E.2d 532 (Mass. 1962).

[10] See, e.g., Article 3 of the UPC, which provides several forms of administration of a decedent's estate, including small estate provisions in §§ 3-1201—3-1204, "informal" administration in §§ 3-301—3-311, "succession without administration" in §§ 3-312—3-322, "supervised" administration (which may be instituted by petition of any interested party or by the personal representative under § 3-502) in Part 5, and "formal" testacy proceedings (meaning litigation to determine whether the decedent left a valid will and for appointment of a personal representative) in Part 4.

[11] See § 4.1.6.

In light of these factors, normally it is preferable that the client nominate the personal representative by a provision in the client's will, with instructions regarding appointment of any successor that may be necessary and with any special restrictions or grant of powers (such as authority to conduct independent administration if permitted by local law, waiving onerous bond[12] or surety requirements, or directing that the personal representative not participate in managing the client's closely held business after death).

Together the client and the estate planner best know the nature of the estate and any peculiarities or problems that may arise in its administration. Effective estate planning includes the intelligent designation of a personal representative that considers personalities, talents, cost, jurisdictional prerequisites, and any potential tax consequences. In addition, as discussed throughout this treatise, postmortem administration involves many tax and related elections and decisions that are better informed and performed if adequate thought has been devoted to the process and appropriate powers and other provisions have been provided in a proper estate plan, which probably will include a will.

§2.7.4 Proof of Death

In some cases there is no definitive proof that a person is deceased if, for example, the individual has not been seen or heard from for an extended period or is being maintained by extraordinary medical procedures with no independent signs of life. The lack of independent proof of death creates little problem if there has been a catastrophe and it simply is impossible to recover the body. There may be difficulty if the question is whether a person is deceased if the person is in a permanent vegetative state or is being maintained by artificial means and is located in a jurisdiction that does not provide a workable definition of death.[13] The issue of death is most troublesome if the individual simply vanished and is only presumed dead.[14]

---

[12] See, e.g., UPC § 3-603.

[13] Such as UPC § 1-107(1), which is designed to provide a time of death if there is cessation of circulatory and respiratory functions, or of brain activity.

[14] See, e.g., UPC § 1-107(5) (five years continuous absence generates presumption of death); similar statutes are found in most states, many with a presumption that arises after a seven year absence.

§2.7.4

In all cases, however, a person's estate is administered pursuant to authority flowing from the jurisdictional requirement that the individual is deceased. As a result acts of the personal representative may be void or voidable if the individual subsequently is found or is deemed to be alive. Many state statutes protect a personal representative and those dealing with or receiving distributions from the estate in such a case.[15] Often the same statutes apply if the personal representative administers the estate in the mistaken belief that the decedent died intestate and later a valid will is discovered, including a will under which some other personal representative should have been appointed.[16]

A legally appointed guardian of a taxpayer who has disappeared must file federal income tax returns for the missing taxpayer until the taxpayer is found or is declared to be deceased, and the missing taxpayer's spouse may file a joint return with the missing taxpayer.[17] In addition, an FET return for the estate of a missing taxpayer must be filed

---

[15] See, e.g., UPC § 3-714.

[16] See, e.g., UPC §§ 3-612, 3-714, 3-909, and 3-910. Statute of limitation problems may arise for federal tax purposes if a later will is discovered. See Walkden v. United States, 57-2 U.S. Tax Cas. (CCH) ¶ 11,732 (N.D. Ohio 1957), and 58-2 U.S. Tax Cas. (CCH) ¶ 11,802 (N.D. Ohio 1957), aff'd, 255 F.2d 681 (6th Cir. 1958) (after paying decedent's FET a later will was found that contained a charitable bequest that would qualify for the § 2055 charitable deduction, but litigation regarding that will delayed filing a refund claim; that refund claim was deemed barred because it was made more than three years after the date the later will was admitted to probate); PLR 8501005 (additional pages were found to a will after the time for making a § 2056(b)(7)(B)(v) QTIP marital deduction election; government denied estate's request for an extension of time to make that election); Palmer v. United States, 83-1 U.S. Tax Cas. (CCH) ¶ 13,515 (D. Minn. 1983) (the later of decedent's two wills was admitted to probate over one year after the decedent's FET return was filed, and litigation with respect to the wills was not finally resolved for six additional years, after which an amended FET return was filed and a refund was requested; although the opinion noted the policy argument that the statute of limitation for a refund should not begin to run until the subsequent will is admitted to probate, the estate still was too late to request a refund; a protective refund claim should have been made when the second will was admitted to probate).

[17] Rev. Rul. 55-387, 1955-1 C.B. 131, supplemented by Rev. Rul. 66-286, 1966-2 C.B. 485, which was clarified and modified by Rev. Rul. 80-347, 1980-2 C.B. 342. Cf. Estate of Peterson v. Commissioner, 45 T.C. 497 (1966) (petition filed by S on behalf of S and D's estate, relating to income tax return filed jointly with D during life, deemed valid because S's subsequent appointment as personal

within nine months after the taxpayer is presumed dead under state law, or after any property is transferred as if the taxpayer was deceased. A transfer of the taxpayer's property to a court appointed receiver is not a transfer that will trigger this filing requirement, but a transfer pursuant to a state court proceeding or by individuals treating the taxpayer's property as if it was their own is.[18] Similarly, the date of death for

---

(Footnote Continued)

representative related back to D's death and validated the previously filed petition).

Notwithstanding that an income tax return must be filed for the missing person, and that a personal representative appointed to represent the missing person has the authority (indeed, under Rev. Rul. 55-387, may have an obligation) to file that return, PLR 9530020 opined that the missing person's personal representative could not make the § 121 election to exclude capital gain incurred on an authorized sale of the missing person's personal residence. Because the individual had not been missing long enough to be declared deceased, and therefore § 1014 did not yet apply to grant a new basis in the individual's property, the personal representative's sale generated a capital gain that the government held only the individual could elect to exclude. Citing no directly relevant authority, the government suggested that absence of any indication of the missing person's intent to sell the property was the relevant impediment to making the § 121 election, distinguishing Rev. Rul. 82-1, 1982-1 C.B. 26 (executor allowed to make the election after the death of a property owner who made the sale before dying) because in that case the decedent's intent to sell was manifested. The personal representative should be permitted to make all elections the missing person could make if state law regards the personal representative as standing in the missing person's shoes, acting properly on the missing person's behalf, and if federal law requires the personal representative to file an income tax return on behalf of the missing person. The suggestion that there was no expressed intent on the part of the missing person to sell the property is a specious justification for denying the election, given the fact that § 121 imposes no intent requirement (indeed, prior to its amendment in 1997, § 121(d)(4) permitted the election in the case of an involuntary conversion). Indeed, today the existence of § 121(f) makes clear that § 121 treatment is the norm; electing *not* to exclude the gain is the option provided. See § 15.8.1 with respect to filing a joint return for the year of the decedent's death.

[18] Rev. Rul. 66-286, 1966-2 C.B. 485, clarified and modified by Rev. Rul. 80-347, 1980-2 C.B. 342. See Rev. Rul. 76-468, 1976-2 C.B. 202, clarified by Rev. Rul. 78-372, 1978-2 C.B. 93, regarding the tax treatment of members of the Armed Forces and civilian employees who are prisoners of war or who are missing in action.

§ 2.7.4

§ 1014(a) new basis at death purposes is that date established by the state of the decedent's last known domicile.[19]

§2.7.5 Personal Representative's Primary Duties

The personal representative's primary functions are to marshal and preserve estate assets (including prosecution of any claims of the estate against others); to pay debts, expenses, and other proper claims against the estate; and to distribute the balance of the estate to the proper beneficiaries under the decedent's will or according to state law.

Notice must be given to creditors to alert them to the decedent's death and the relatively short period within which to file a claim for payment or be barred.[20] Tulsa Professional Collection Services, Inc. v.

---

[19] Rev. Rul. 82-189, 1982-2 C.B. 189, and PLR 8215029 (no new basis allowed for property of taxpayer who disappeared while flying and had not been found because the statutory period for presumption of death had not yet elapsed).

[20] See, e.g., UPC § 3-801. On the issue of creditors with notice who fail to file formal claims, see, e.g., Stilwell v. Estate of Crosby, 519 So. 2d 68 (Fla. Dist. Ct. App. 1988) (co-personal representative of the estate did not file a claim and was barred from collecting); Union Nat'l Bank & Trust Co. v. Estate of Werning, 665 P.2d 192 (Kan. 1983) (conservator of decedent before death delayed filing claim for payment and similarly was barred). Illustrating that nonclaim statutes may have a much broader reach than meets the eye is Steen & Berg Co. v. Berg, 713 N.W.2d 87 (N.D. 2006). The dissent argued that nonclaim statutes address obligations that, if paid, would reduce the value of the estate and that its action to enforce a buy-sell agreement was akin to any reinvestment that substituted one asset (typically cash) for another (the subject of the buy-sell agreement). The plaintiff-buyer argued that its action was in the nature of a title dispute, not barred by the accelerated nonclaim statute. The court instead concluded that the nonclaim statute under the UPC as adopted in North Dakota (and elsewhere) applied.

A slightly different issue was resolved in the creditor's favor by In re Estate of Villines, 122 P.3d 466 (Ok. 2005) (failure to give notice of the personal representative's denial of a creditor's claim), there involving a claim that was filed before publication or notice being sent to creditors, which was relevant because the creditor was not informed of the time limit for challenging a rejection of their claim. The court held that state law requires that the creditor receive actual notice that a filed claim was rejected.

And see Kannady v. Ball, 234 P.3d 826 (Ks. Ct. App. 2010) (claim filed in an estate seeking payment from the decedent's motorist liability insurer), which clarified that the nonclaim limitation only restricts claims against estate assets

Pope[21] requires that known or reasonably ascertainable creditors of an estate receive actual and not just constructive notice of the decedent's death.[22] In re Estate of Weidman[23] held that *Tulsa* also requires actual notice to known and reasonably ascertainable heirs for purposes of

---

(Footnote Continued)

and does not alter the normal statute of limitation for claims filed in an estate but not seeking satisfaction from the estate itself.

[21] 485 U.S. 478 (1988).

[22] On the issue whether a creditor was known or reasonably ascertainable and therefore was entitled to actual notice, see, e.g., Jefferson Federal Savings & Loan Ass'n v. Clark, 540 So. 2d 61 (Ala. 1989); In re Estate of Kopely, 767 P.2d 1181 (Az. Ct. App. 1989); District of Columbia v. Gantt, 558 A.2d 1120 (D.C. 1989); North Shore Medical Center, Inc. v. Estate of Szilvassy, 526 So. 2d 744 (Fla. Dist. Ct. App. 1988); Public Health Trust v. Estate of Jara, 526 So. 2d 745 (Fla. Dist. Ct. App. 1988); Rose v. Kaszynski, 533 N.E.2d 73 (Ill. 1988); In re Estate of McDowell, 777 P.2d 826 (Kan. 1989); Stewart v. Farrel, 554 A.2d 1286 (N.H. 1989). For a detailed discussion of *Tulsa*, see Reutlinger, State Action, Due Process, and the New Nonclaim Statutes: Can No Notice Be Good Notice If Some Notice Is Not?, 24 Real Prop., Prob. & Trust J. 433 (1990). Farm Credit Bank v. Brown, 577 N.E.2d 906 (Ill. App. Ct. 1991), refused to apply *Tulsa* retroactively to upset the title to property that passed through probate before the Court's decision.

[23] 476 N.W.2d 357 (Iowa 1991).

§2.7.5

foreclosing a will contest action.[24] In re Estate of Stanford[25] even declared void all probate proceedings because the court lacked in personam jurisdiction because proper notice was not given to known heirs.

The personal representative will prepare and file the decedent's final income tax return and all income tax returns for the estate during administration.[26] In addition, the primary obligation to file the FET

---

[24] In re Estate of Van Praag, 684 N.E.2d 1080 (Ill. App. Ct. 1997), went so far as to find fiduciary duties to creditors in a case involving a personal representative that did not protect creditor rights as against the government's tax levy. *Weidman* held that the notice requirement would not apply retroactively because the period for filing a will contest action in that estate expired long before the decision in *Tulsa*. It also may have been relevant that the claimant was a child of the decedent who was well aware of the decedent's death and for whom formal notice was irrelevant. See Moore, Fairness and Finality: Notice to Beneficiaries Under Prior Wills, 29 Real Prop., Prob. & Trust J. 817 (1995) (arguing for an extension of *Tulsa* to mandate notice to beneficiaries under prior wills who may have a will contest cause of action if they were excluded from the decedent's final will), and Wells, Responding to the Call for Fairness and Finality: Would Notice to Beneficiaries under Prior Wills Produce Either?, 29 Real Prop., Prob. & Trust J. 849 (1995) (responding to Moore).

In re Estate of Estes, 718 P.2d 298 (Kan. 1986) (sole beneficiary disclaimed all benefits under will), involved a state statute providing that the decedent's heirs are entitled to notice that a will has been offered for probate. State disclaimer statutes generally provide that disclaimed property passes as if the disclaimant had predeceased the testator. But the fictional death produced by a beneficiary's disclaimer did not change the decedent's heirs for purposes of determining who was entitled to notice of the probate proceeding. Thus, the court held that the persons who would have been the decedent's heirs if the sole beneficiary had predeceased the testator were not entitled to notice of probate.

[25] 581 N.E.2d 842 (Ill. App. Ct. 1991).

[26] Although § 644 requires trusts to report income on a calendar year basis, an estate may file its income tax return on either a calendar or a fiscal year basis and § 645 may apply and permit a trust to be treated as part of the estate. In addition, § 6654(l)(2) excepts estates (and grantor trusts to which the deceased settlor's estate pours over) from the estimated tax payment requirements for the first two tax years after the decedent's death. See § 5.7 regarding the timing aspects of the income taxation of trusts and estates.

Estate of Lammerts v. Commissioner, 456 F.2d 681 (2d Cir. 1972), imposed on the personal representative the § 6651 penalty for failure to file an estate's income tax return (estate's attorney thought family accountant who prepared family income tax returns would prepare the estate income tax return, but the accountant thought the attorney employed to prepare the FET return would file

return and pay the entire FET imposed on the decedent's gross estate rests on the personal representative,[27] even if assets included in the gross estate are not in the personal representative's possession or control.[28]

An FET return must be filed if the gross estate exceeds the basic exclusion amount,[29] and *payment* of the tax is required nine months after the decedent's death.[30] Extensions of time to *file* the FET return (also due under § 6075(a) nine months after the decedent's death, unless a six month extension to file is granted under § 6081) do not extend the time to pay the tax.[31] A separate extension of the time to pay must be secured.[32]

(Footnote Continued)

all estate returns); May v. Commissioner, 65 T.C. 1114 (1976), held that, unlike interest, any § 6651 penalty is nondeductible for income tax purposes.

[27] Under § 2002 "[t]he tax imposed by this chapter shall be paid by the executor" and § 2203 provides that "[t]he term 'executor' wherever it is used . . . in connection with the estate tax . . . means the executor or administrator of the decedent . . . ." The return filing obligation is placed on the executor by § 6018(a)(1). For more on the tax payment obligation see § 3.2.3.

[28] Treas. Reg. § 20.2002-1. See § 3.3 (6th ed.).

[29] No tax is payable if an estate produces less tax than the available § 2010 unified credit. The unified credit is equal to the tax on a *taxable* estate of the basic exclusion amount, but note that the *gross* estate, not the taxable estate, is used as the filing threshold in § 6018(a)(1). Note also that the filing rules were not increased in 2010 to reflect Congress' adoption of portability of a predeceased spouse's unused exclusion amount.

[30] See § 6151(a). Rev. Rul. 66-85, 1966-1 C.B. 213, held that the date and time of death for FET purposes is determined as if the decedent died at the decedent's domicile, regardless of the date and time in the time zone in which the decedent died, based on a rationale that domicile determines the place and therefore should determine the time for filing the FET return. Thus, for example, if it was Monday evening at the decedent's domicile in the United States when the decedent died while visiting Europe, the date and time of death would be Monday, even if it already was Tuesday at the place of death. Rev. Rul. 74-424, 1974-2 C.B. 294, clarified that this domicile rule does not absolve the return filing requirement just because the decedent was a nonresident alien.

[31] Treas. Reg. §§ 20.6081-1(d); 20.6151-1(a). See § 3.3.18 (7th ed.).

[32] See § 6161(a)(2). See § 3.3.20 regarding extensions of time to pay.

§ 2.7.5

A fiduciary must give notice to the government of its appointment and again after being discharged.[33] The personal representative remains liable for tax matters until the proper § 6903 Notice of Fiduciary Relationship is filed with the government, although personal liability for payment of tax may be discharged under §§ 2204 (FET) and 6905 (income and gift tax) if proper applications are made.[34] The personal representative

---

[33] Form 56 is required under § 6903(a) and Treas. Reg. § 301.6903-1(a).

[34] The government must notify the personal representative of the amount of tax within nine months after the later of making application or filing the return. Payment of that amount discharges the personal representative of personal liability for any subsequently determined deficiency. This discharge may depend on the personal representative posting the requisite bond required in conjunction with any extension that is granted for payment of the tax. See §§ 3.3.2 n.21 and 3.3.20 n.283 and accompanying text.

The value of a closing letter is revealed by Singleton v. Commissioner, 71 T.C.M. (CCH) 3127 (1996), in which the court imposed personal liability on a personal representative who did not obtain a § 2204(a) discharge and who distributed estate assets before obtaining a closing letter, ultimately to discover that all the FET had not been paid. In the process the court held valid an extension of the statute of limitation executed by one coexecutor, notwithstanding state law holding that a coexecutor acting unilaterally cannot bind the estate. The only blessing in the opinion was the court's refusal to impose interest on the personal representative, rejecting the government's suggestion that the result for personal liability cases should mirror that in transferee liability situations because the transferee has the personal benefit of the tax dollars pending any delay in payment. This is not true in a case in which the personal representative faces personal liability because estate assets were distributed prematurely and without retention of sufficient assets to pay the FET liability.

Numerous cases hold that a closing letter will not preclude the government from assessing a timely filed deficiency. Thus, the result of the closing letter is to protect the personal representative from personal liability if estate assets have been distributed in reliance on the closing letter, causing the government to assert transferee liability against the estate's distributees (albeit that the personal representative may receive the deficiency notice as the estate's representative). Estate of Bommer v. Commissioner, 69 T.C.M. (CCH) 2541 (1995) (alleged deficiencies attributable to substantial undervaluation of closely held stock); Estate of Keeler v. Commissioner, 49 T.C.M. (CCH) 243 (1984), aff'd in an unpublished opinion (4th Cir. 1985) (estate filed two returns that were audited in different field offices and obtained closing letter from one without revealing that an audit was underway in the other); Von Hagke v. United States, 79-1 U.S. Tax Cas. (CCH) ¶ 13,290 (E.D. Wis. 1979) (estate assets were distributed after government issued FET closing letter in response to § 2204 request for prompt audit, acknowledging that FET return was correct; 18 months later but within

also may make a § 6501(d) request for prompt assessment of the decedent's gift and income tax liability to minimize the duration of the estate's exposure.

Form 56, Notice Concerning Fiduciary Relationship, incorporates the § 6036 notice requirements for qualification as an executor for tax purposes, and the government has promulgated procedures[35] to notify it of a change of address for notices or refunds of tax overpayments that must be sent to the taxpayer's last known address. Upon giving notice of its appointment, the personal representative assumes all rights, powers, privileges, and duties of the estate, obligating the government to deal directly with the fiduciary in all matters involving the fiduciary's activi-

(Footnote Continued)

statute of limitation for assessing deficiencies government reconsidered valuation of closely held stock); Schwager v. Commissioner, 64 T.C. 781 (1975) (deficiency relating to split dollar life insurance assessed after FET closing letter was issued); Estate of Meyer v. Commissioner, 58 T.C. 69 (1972) (closing letter issued after initial audit, followed by notice of deficiency based on revaluation of stock to match value in two other estates).

Closing letters make it clear that, although they are not § 7121 closing agreements, the government will not pursue additional tax liability unless the conditions of the then applicable Revenue Procedure relating to reopening a case are met. Case law also makes it clear that these procedures are merely directory, not mandatory, and are not binding on the government. See Rev. Proc. 2005-23, 2005-1 C.B. 1206, establishing that a case closed after examination in the office of a District Director may be reopened to make an adjustment that is unfavorable to the taxpayer only if (1) there is evidence of fraud, malfeasance, collusion, concealment, or a misrepresentation of material facts, (2) the closing letter involved a clearly defined substantial error based on an established government position existing at the time of closing, or (3) "other circumstances exist that indicate failure to reopen would be a serious administrative omission." Contacts to correct mathematical errors or to adjust discrepancies between returns are not considered reopening a return for these purposes.

According to *Bommer*, 69 T.C.M. at 2545, notwithstanding issuance of an FET closing letter, the government may reopen a case and determine a deficiency and the taxpayer may claim a refund if the parties have not executed a formal closing agreement. But see Eisenbrandt v. Commissioner, 622 F. Supp. 27 (N.D. Ill. 1985) (taxpayer's action for refund estopped because personal representative executed Form 890-AD and, notwithstanding that it also is not a formal closing agreement, the government acted to its detriment in reliance on the agreement by foregoing its rights to assess deficiencies or appeal Tax Court judgments). See § 15.4.2.2 regarding protective claims for refund.

[35] See Rev. Proc. 2010-16, 2010-1 C.B. 664.

§ 2.7.5

ties.[36] Although the fiduciary may be liable as a fiduciary even without filing the Notice,[37] the obligation to file the Notice is effected by the rule that communications from the government need not be directed to the fiduciary absent the Notice.[38] The government may withhold the fiduciary's release from personal liability until the Notice is filed.[39]

The Form 56 Notice routinely is ignored, with potential inconvenience or liability for negligent administration or for tax deficiencies. For example, there may be no proper party to represent a decedent's estate if the administration was closed and the personal representative was dismissed before the government asserts an income tax deficiency against the estate. The fiduciary would be the only proper party to the deficiency action if the personal representative failed to file the § 6903 notice that its representation of the estate ended. Thus, a devisee's response to the income tax action would be dismissed because the court would lack jurisdiction over the proper parties.[40] Only if a § 6903 notice is filed would

---

[36] See § 6903(a).

[37] Fidelity Trust Co. v. Commissioner, 141 F.2d 54 (3d Cir. 1944), aff'g 1 T.C. 1214 (1943). For an interesting twist, see Estate of Gudie v. Commissioner, 137 T.C. 165 (2011), in which an estate beneficiary filed the estate tax return and was in possession of estate property but refused to be appointed by the probate court as executor of the estate; the government's notice of deficiency was mailed to this beneficiary and was valid because the beneficiary was a § 2203 statutory executor and no notice of termination of fiduciary relationship had been filed, making the beneficiary a proper party for receipt of the deficiency notice.

[38] Treas. Reg. § 301.6903-1(c).

[39] Treas. Reg. § 301.6903-1(b).

[40] See Estate of Hughey v. Commissioner, 54 T.C.M. (CCH) 41 (1987) (sole heir and devisee argued that it was the § 2203 "executor" following distribution of estate assets, which the Tax Court rejected because § 2203 does not apply for income tax purposes; the estate lost its ability to contest the deficiency because the personal representative failed to amend or join the devisee's petition within the requisite 90-day period and did not ratify the devisee's actions). But see Estate of Galloway v. Commissioner, 103 T.C. 700, 704 (1994) (the government attempted to dismiss an income tax dispute because there was no personal representative of the decedent's estate and, therefore, no one was authorized to act on the estate's behalf), in which the court, referring to state law independent and simplified administration procedures, held that it could appoint a "special administrator" under authority of state law (Cal. Civ. Pro. Code § 377.33 in this case, which by its terms appeared to be limited to a court in which an action "under this article" is brought, allowing the court to appoint a special administra-

§ 6901 allow transferee liability on the devisee, which would give the devisee standing to contest the deficiency. Otherwise, the estate must be reopened to reappoint the personal representative as the only permissible party to contest the assessment. In the process the time to contest the deficiency might expire before all necessary actions can be taken.[41]

In addition, actions by one fiduciary may disadvantage the estate and all its beneficiaries. For example, in Eversole v. Commissioner,[42] a personal representative who was discharged by the local probate court nevertheless consented to an extension of the estate's statute of limitation, which bound the estate because no notice of termination of the fiduciary relationship had been given to the government. Krueger v. Commissioner[43] held that a determination entered on the personal representative's stipulations bound the estate and its transferees.

More dramatically, Ewart v. Commissioner[44] involved a waiver of restrictions on assessment and collection under § 6213(d), executed by only one of two personal representatives (two brothers, who also were the two estate beneficiaries). Only one signed returns and the nonsigner

---

(Footnote Continued)

tor to "ensure proper administration of justice"). The court determined that the government's motion should be denied under Tax Court Rule 1(b), which provides that the Tax Court Rules "shall be construed to secure the just, speedy, and inexpensive determination of every case." The court stated that: "We discern no reason why heirs of a decedent should be required to choose between costly probate proceedings or cumbersome joinder of all beneficiaries in order to maintain a proceeding in the Court."

[41] See Estate of Walker v. Commissioner, 90 T.C. 253 (1988) (income tax deficiency asserted after the estate was closed and distributed, with a three year statute of limitation imposed because the estate failed to file for prompt assessment under § 6501(d); the personal representative failed to file the § 6903 notice of termination of fiduciary relations on Form 56, so the deficiency was imposed on the estate—notwithstanding that it already had been distributed—and the personal representative was the only permissible party to contest the assessment—notwithstanding that the personal representative already had been discharged); Jakel v. Commissioner, 54 T.C.M. (CCH) 264 (1987) (the trustee of a trust to which a state court had assigned the decedent's cause of action was the wrong taxpayer, stating that only executors of the decedent's estate were allowed to litigate the claim).

[42] 46 T.C. 56 (1966).

[43] 48 T.C. 824 (1967).

[44] 85 T.C. 544 (1985), aff'd, 814 F.2d 321 (6th Cir. 1987).

§ 2.7.5

never complied with § 6903(b) by filing its notice of fiduciary relation. Estate assets were distributed and the brothers agreed that each would be liable for any taxes assessed with respect to any revaluation of assets that each received. The signatory brother received realty and sold it for an amount exceeding its reported FET value, which prompted the government correspondingly to revalue that property and assert a deficiency. Meanwhile, that brother declared bankruptcy and, when the government assessed the deficiency, that brother also executed a Form 890 waiver, upon which the government then proceeded in asserting liability against the nonsigning brother, both in his fiduciary and transferee capacities. The nonsigning brother's argument that the signatory brother, acting alone, could not effectively execute the waiver and bind the estate was rejected by the Tax Court, which relied on the fact that federal law creates a joint action requirement only in Treas. Reg. § 20.6018-2, which requires cofiduciaries to file a single return to prevent the filing of multiple returns by independently acting cofiduciaries. Otherwise, either fiduciary acting alone was capable of binding the estate and wreaking havoc.

Furthermore, a fiduciary could face personal liability for unpaid taxes. For example, in Garst Trust v. Commissioner,[45] the Tax Court prevented a beneficiary of a terminated trust from representing the trust and on its own motion dismissed the action for a deficiency against the trust proper because the trust had terminated and therefore could not be a proper party to the deficiency action. Instead, the proper party was the trustee who, again, had failed to file the § 6903 notice. That the beneficiary had signed an agreement with the trustee at the time of termination assuming all outstanding unresolved tax liabilities was deemed irrelevant because no proper action against any taxpayer had been brought. Presumably, if a judgment was entered against the trustee, the agreement then might allow it to proceed against the distributee under that agreement. Quaere, however, whether the fiduciary's actions, if they prevented the distributee from defending against the tax liability, also would estop the fiduciary from asserting its rights under the agreement. And the fiduciary may be left with no recourse if the beneficiary no longer is solvent.

---

[45] 53 T.C.M. (CCH) 506 (1987).

§2.7.5

The personal representative, if still acting, is the proper party to make a refund claim if taxes are overpaid for any reason.[46] But if the estate has been distributed and the personal representative discharged, the issue addressed by Rev. Rul. 73-366[47] is who can claim the refund. Three situations were posited: (1) a trust that terminated before it was discovered that the trustee overpaid the trust's income tax; (2) an estate that terminated before it was discovered that the executor overpaid the estate's income tax, with the overpayment having reduced specific legacies because there was no residuary estate; and (3) an estate that terminated the same as in (2) but the overpayment reduced the residuary estate. In the first two cases, the government held that the refund claim could be prosecuted as a single claim for all beneficiaries or as a separate claim by each beneficiary in respect to his or her portion of the overpayment. In the third case, the residuary beneficiary was regarded as the proper claimant.[48]

In all its functions, the personal representative, acting as a fiduciary, must comply with basic fiduciary duties, such as the duty of impartiality. In cases in which the personal representative is not disinterested, severe conflicts may arise with estate beneficiaries in settling tax or other controversies,[49] which should be anticipated and addressed by the decedent, who should select an appropriate personal representative.

---

[46] Martin v. United States, 86-1 U.S. Tax Cas. (CCH) ¶ 13,664 (N.D. Ind. 1986), aff'd, 833 F.2d 655 (7th Cir. 1987), held that a formal refund claim is required under § 7422(a) to give the court jurisdiction, and that a protest letter to the government did not adequately present a claim for administrative review. And see Hofheinz v. United States, 511 F.2d 661 (5th Cir. 1975) (suit by executor to recover FET overpayment; residuary legatee denied leave to intervene because the executor was capable of suing and there was no need for others to act on the estate's behalf).

[47] 1973-2 C.B. 408.

[48] See Green v. United States, 2010-2 U.S. Tax Cas. (CCH) ¶ 60,600 (N.D. Okla. 2010), however, in which one of several reasons relied upon to deny a refund claim was that the plaintiff was not the taxpayer who paid the tax. In that case Stepfather died, leaving his entire estate to Mother, who subsequently died, and her Daughter was the plaintiff prosecuting a refund claim on behalf of Stepfather's estate, of which she was not a beneficiary.

[49] See, e.g., Estate of Smith v. Commissioner, 77 T.C. 326 (1981) (S stood to benefit individually by high FET valuation that would produce a high income tax basis that would minimize capital gain on a subsequent sale; because this value

§2.7.6 Fees

Fees payable to a personal representative for administering the decedent's estate may be based on such factors as time spent, the difficulty of the administration, the amount involved, and whether any extraordinary tasks were assumed (such as liquidating a family business). The personal representative must consider and sometimes must deal with nonprobate assets (for example, to prepare the FET return or to coordinate the payment of taxes or other expenses). As such, the fee should not be based solely on the size of the probate estate and consideration should be given to the proper allocation or proration to any nonprobate assets as to which tax and other services are performed,[50] which may recommend execution of a will.

Some states specify the fees for personal representatives by statute, and a will (if one exists) may condition appointment of a personal representative on a fee agreement. But it is more common to find that fees are subject to approval by the probate court, subject only to a reasonableness standard.[51] Fees paid to an attorney assisting in administration of an estate should be based on the same general criteria and attorneys who also act as fiduciaries must consult state law to determine whether it is proper to charge two fees for acting in both capacities.[52]

(Footnote Continued)

would negatively impact other beneficiaries, S was removed as personal representative and a disinterested party was appointed to settle the estate's valuation dispute with the government, in which S was refused the right to intervene but was allowed to file an amicus curiae brief).

[50] See, e.g., Roe v. Estate of Farrell, 372 N.E.2d 662 (Ill. 1978); Cloutier v. LaVoie, 177 N.E.2d 584 (Mass. 1961); N.Y. Est., Powers & Trusts L. § 2-1.8(h).

[51] See, e.g., UPC § 3-719.

[52] See, e.g., Fla. Stat. § 733.617(6). This assumes that acting in both capacities is permissible, or that an individual may hire his or her law firm to represent the entity, which may not be the law in some jurisdictions. See McGovern, Kurtz, & English, Wills, Trusts & Estates § 12.6 (4th ed. 2010); Annot., Right of executor or administrator to extra compensation for legal services rendered by him, 65 A.L.R.2d 809 (1959); Calif. Prob. Code §§ 2645, 10804, and 15687 (in varying terms, each specifying that, without court approval, neither an attorney nor anyone related to the attorney nor any partnership or corporation in which the attorney is a partner, shareholder, or employee may receive fees for serving both as a fiduciary—guardian, conservator, personal representative, or trustee—and for providing legal services to the fiduciary; in some cases an exception is

Unless agreed to in advance by the decedent or the estate beneficiaries, attorney or personal representative fees based solely on the size of the estate may be inappropriately large in some cases and unfairly small in others. The amount involved may be a relevant factor in determining the amount of risk assumed and potentially the difficulty of the administration. Minimum fee schedules relating to lawyers' fees in various matters are subject to the Sherman Act.[53] Yet the use of fee schedules in some form still is relatively common.

To illustrate this, and the current state of the law, consider In re Estate of Platt,[54] which held that neither a personal representative nor an attorney assisting in the estate administration was entitled to fees based solely on a percentage of the value of the estate. The decedent's will named a corporate fiduciary and an attorney to serve jointly as personal representatives, but did not specify the fees they were to receive. Before administration began the residuary beneficiaries objected to their proposed fees and requested that both keep time records. The corporate fiduciary and the attorney later petitioned for fees exceeding their original proposal; the corporate fiduciary kept no time records and the attorney's time computed to an hourly rate of over $500 per hour. The trial court permitted both fees solely by reference to the size of the estate, but the supreme court reversed, stating that, although size of the

---

(Footnote Continued)

provided if the fiduciary is related to—or cohabiting with—the ward, conservatee, decedent, or settlor; any provision in a document to the contrary is void). It is not necessarily unethical, however. See ABA Standing Committee on Ethics and Professional Responsibility Informal Opinion 1338 (1975) (involving issue of appropriate fees for acting in both capacities); Jackson v. Conland, 420 A.2d 898 (Conn. 1979); but see Cal. Bus. and Prof. Code § 6103.6, which provides otherwise if the attorney knew or should have known of the facts leading to the violation of the Probate Code prohibitions.

A written agreement with respect to this issue would be wise, at the same time being mindful of the prohibition against solicitation in the designation of the attorney as fiduciary and the fact that in some jurisdictions the agreement also may be invalid. See Cal. Prob. Code § 15642(b)(6); N.Y. Surr. Ct. Proc. Act L. § 2307-a (fees limited to half absent required disclosure and testator's acknowledged written agreement regarding designation of attorney or an affiliate as executor).

[53] Goldfarb v. Virginia State Bar, 421 U.S. 773 (1975) (title examination fees deemed to be illegal price-fixing).

[54] 586 So.2d 328 (Fla. 1991).

§ 2.7.6

estate was one factor to be considered, reasonable compensation must be determined by a more objective standard.

In reviewing the corporate fiduciary's fees, the court stated that it could not justify a determination of reasonableness based solely on fees customarily charged in the community because that would permit corporate fiduciaries to determine what is reasonable, which instead should be established by courts or the legislature. Absent an agreement with the testator regarding compensation, the corporate fiduciary's published fee schedule was rejected as the sole factor for a proper fee determination. Notwithstanding the decision in *Platt*, Florida law[55] requires that any specific arrangement in a will regarding fees to be paid to a personal representative be given effect, and that arrangement could be based on a fee schedule. The difference from *Goldfarb* is that the fee agreement may and likely will differ from one personal representative to another and thus does not constitute price-fixing.

Absent such an agreement, immediately following *Platt*, fees in Florida were based on reasonable compensation, reflecting criteria such as the time and labor required, the novelty and difficulty of the issues raised and the skill required for their resolution, the fee customarily charged locally, and other less immediately relevant factors that essentially parroted the fee factors in Model Rules of Professional Conduct Rule 1.5(a) governing an attorney's fees.[56] However, *Platt* prompted a response that resulted in an amendment to Florida law,[57] which now provides that attorney fees are payable from estate assets without court order based on an agreement with the personal representative or, in the absence of a prior agreement, then based in part on the size of the estate to "compensate the attorney's responsibility" and in part on time spent, and a personal representative's fees are based solely on the size of the estate.[58] In each case, fees may be increased to reflect extraordinary

---

[55] Fla. Stat. § 733.617(4).

[56] See Phipps v. Estate of Burdine, 586 So. 2d 381 (Fla. Dist. Ct. App. 1991).

[57] Fla. Stat. § 733.6171.

[58] Fla. Stat. § 733.617(2). In addition to this statutory compensation based on the size of the estate, § 733.617(3) authorizes additional amounts to reflect extraordinary services and § 733.617(7) permits modification of the compensation produced under either provision to reflect criteria such as those listed in the text accompanying note 56. See Myer, Paying For Personal Representatives and

services rendered. Thus, the state of the law in Florida, one of the most active estate planning and probate jurisdictions, reveals a significant degree of change.[59]

As illustrated in *Platt*, special concerns with respect to fees arise in estate administration situations in which the fiduciary or the attorney charges a flat percentage fee. "Widespread public criticism of the cost of dying focuses in part on the belief that the estate lawyer receives an overly generous fee determined solely as a percentage of the estate's assets and far in excess of the value of the services performed."[60] The fee issue is among the most disturbing to estates attorneys, who are being attacked on two relatively unexpected fronts.

The first comes from the government because, like most administration expenses, fees paid to a personal representative and attorney for the estate are deductible for FET purposes. Treas. Reg. § 20.2053-1(d)(4)

(Footnote Continued)

Their Attorneys May Cost You an Arm and a Leg, 49 U. Miami L. Rev. 855 (1995).

[59] As an illustration of other seemingly legitimate factors to determine compensation, see Paone v. Gerrig, 291 N.E.2d 426 (Mass. 1973), which regarded the size of the estate, the marketable nature of the assets, the factual and legal questions involved in the administration of the estate, the time reasonably required for completing the work, the skill and ability employed, the amounts usually paid others for similar work, and the results accomplished all as relevant in judging the reasonableness of the fees of both the personal representative and the estate's attorney.

[60] Johnston, An Ethical Analysis of Common Estate Planning Practices—Is Good Business Bad Ethics, 45 Ohio St. L.J. 57, 102 (1984); Link et al., Developments Regarding the Professional Responsibility of the Estate Administration Lawyer: The Effect of the Model Rules of Professional Conduct, 26 Real Prop., Prob. & Trust J. 1 (1991). This issue has been of concern for decades, as illustrated by it being the subject of a portion of the Statement of Principles Regarding Probate Practice and Expenses, 8 Real Prop., Prob. & Trust J. 293, 294-296 (1973). Model Rule of Professional Conduct 1.5(a) requires a fee to be reasonable in relation to the work performed; only one of many listed factors is the custom in the community for charging fees, which along with the ambiguous factor referring to the "labor" involved usually are the only objective factors supporting the percentage fee approach. According to In re Estate of Weeks, 950 N.E.2d 280 (Ill. App. Ct. 2011), courts at one time "relied on an American Bar Association disciplinary rule, inflating the importance of usual and customary charges . . . as a factor to be considered in setting a fee, [but] more recent cases interpreting the meaning of 'reasonable compensation' . . . omit this factor."

§ 2.7.6

limits the deduction to amounts paid or reasonably expected to be paid, and fees not fixed by a decree of the proper court will be allowed only if the government is satisfied that they will be paid, that they are allowable under controlling local law, and that they are within the range of amounts usually allowed in the jurisdiction in estates of similar size and character. More importantly, the government sometimes denies § 2053(a)(2) deductibility of fees that are approved by local courts, thereby requiring a federal court to determine the deductibility of fees.

To illustrate, assume a personal representative petitions the local probate court for approval of its fees and the court consents, perhaps with the approval of the estate's beneficiaries. The issue is whether that approval is determinative of the reasonableness of the fees for purposes of claiming a § 2053 deduction. In TAM 8636100 the government opined that it is determinative under either of two circumstances: (1) the state court passed on all the facts and circumstances surrounding the fee request, and the determination was made in a genuinely adversarial proceeding involving those fees; or (2) the state court entered a consent decree that constitutes a bona fide settlement by the parties of a valid dispute or claim regarding fees. In other situations, the Memorandum said the court order will not necessarily bind the government, nor must the government accept a local court decree that is at variance with state law (for example, if the awarded fees exceed statutory fees, with no special justification for the excess).

In United States v. White[61] the lower court determined that the government, under what is now Treas. Reg. § 20.2053-1(b)(3), is bound to accept the state court determination of fees unless there is prima facie evidence of fraud, overreaching, or some other reason to believe that the state court did not pass on the factors upon which deductibility depends. Further, the court held that the burden is on the government, particularly if the state court determination took into account all of the factors the government would consider. No added requirement was imposed

---

[61] 853 F.2d 107 (2d Cir. 1988), rev'g 650 F. Supp. 904 (W.D. N.Y. 1987), cert. granted, 489 U.S. 1051 (1989), and later retracted, 493 U.S. 5 (1989) (upholding government's subpoena of attorney White's time records).

§ 2.7.6

that the determination be made in a genuinely adversarial proceeding nor that it be a bona fide settlement of a valid dispute regarding fees.[62]

In reversing, the Court of Appeals for the Second Circuit stated that:[63]

> We do not read [§ 2053(a)(2)] as giving state *trial* court decrees preclusive effect with regard to IRS investigations. To be sure, the plain language of § 2053(a)(2) indicates that the federal deductibility of estate administrative expenses is governed by state law. [But] ... the deductibility of such expenses nonetheless remains a federal question. The statute does not address the effect of state trial court approval of estate administrative expenses under federal law. In the absence of preclusive language in the statute, we are not persuaded that Congress unambiguously intended to make state trial court decrees determinative of the federal deductibility of such expenses to the exclusion of any federal inquiry ....
>
> We believe the holding in [*Commissioner v. Estate of*] *Bosch*[64] supports the view that the Surrogate's decree is not conclusive and binding on the IRS under *I.R.C.* § 2053(a)(2).... We conclude that, with regard to the federal deductibility of White's fees, the IRS is entitled to make an independent assessment of the validity of White's fees under applicable state law as determined by the state's highest court [and is not precluded] from investigating the deductibility of White's fees under state law.

According to the court, the government would be bound by state law factors that are to be applied in determining the allowability of fees, but would not be bound by a lower state court's application of those factors in a particular case.[65]

---

[62] See also First Nat'l Bank v. United States, 77-2 U.S. Tax Cas. (CCH) ¶ 13,207 (D. Nev. 1977) (government argument that reasonableness of attorney's fee cannot be determined without evidence of time spent was rejected, the court stating that a proper state court determination that the fee was allowable is binding on the government absent allegations of fraud or collusion).

[63] 853 F.2d at 113-114 (footnote added).

[64] 387 U.S. 456 (1967).

[65] See also Estate of Baird v. Commissioner, 73 T.C.M. (CCH) 1883 (1997) (a deduction of $368,000 was allowed in principle for attorney fees in a $17 million estate for 229 hours of work—which rose to 556 hours when the deduction was challenged and litigation ensued—established by a formula that was applied prior to any administration of the estate and that equated the attorney fee to each executor's fee, rejecting the government's argument that the fee was excessive

§ 2.7.6

Meanwhile, in Estate of DeWitt v. Commissioner[66] the government challenged the deductibility of certain expenses of administration that were allowed for state law purposes. In allowing most of the deductions on motion for summary judgment, the Tax Court stated:

> a court decree ordinarily controls the deductibility under the Federal estate tax [but] . . . the [taxpayer] . . . must show that all the facts necessary for deductibility under Federal estate tax were considered and found pursuant to the state court's inquiry.

> In most instances the interest of the federal government in protecting its revenues will coalesce with the interest of the state in protecting its citizens, and state law may be relied upon as a guide to what deductions may reasonably be permitted for federal estate tax purposes. In some cases, however, the state law on its face or in its application may not be responsive to the interests traditionally protected by the state . . . . [Thus,] we are not stating as a rule of law a Surrogate's Court decree establishes deductibility of administration expenses . . . .

(Footnote Continued)

per se because over $16 million of the estate was marketable assets that posed no significant administration issues), in which the court did not regard itself as bound by the state court's allowance of the fee (because the state court did not articulate why its order was consistent with state law) and conducted its own analysis, but nevertheless upheld the amount of the fee as reasonable, based primarily on consistency with local custom in determining fees and the court's conclusion that time spent is not the most important factor. Disallowed, however, were fees attributable to securing early payment of the executors' fees and fees attributable to the sale of a house because each was for the convenience of the executors and beneficiary rather than necessary for proper administration of the estate.

Moreover, *White* also held that a government summons to investigate the attorney's records is enforceable, to help make an independent determination of the allowability of those fees. The court concluded that the rule in current Treas. Reg. § 20.2053-1(b)(3) is not inconsistent with this reading of §2053(a)(2), allowing an inquiry into the question whether the proper factors were properly considered under state law. Thus, the government had a legitimate purpose in investigating the attorney's fees and the time records that were relevant to a determination of reasonableness. To the same effect see TAM 9246008. Today Treas. Reg. § 20.2053-1(b)(3) specifically addresses the preclusive impact of a lower court decree, requiring that the court had jurisdiction, that it reviewed the facts relating to the expenditure, and that approval of the item was consistent with local law.

[66] 54 T.C.M. (CCH) 759, 762 and n.4 (1987).

§2.7.6

Only those deductions not proven by the taxpayer were denied on the motion for summary judgment, although the taxpayer was given the opportunity to present evidence to support their deductibility.

The second unexpected challenge to fees in probate comes at the local level. Unlike the facts in *Platt* in which the beneficiaries objected to fees before administration began, local courts on their own motion are challenging fees charged even though the beneficiaries are willing to pay without objection. A written fee agreement for the amount charged is no guarantee that it will not be an ethical violation[67] or, it seems, that a court or the government will allow payment or deduction. Thus, even without answering the ethical question, it seems only prudent to suggest that

---

[67] Conn. Inf. Op. 87-10 involved an attorney who was personal representative of an estate and acted as a broker for the sale of estate realty. In discussing fees, the opinion stated that no additional fee as personal representative was permissible in this added role and that, as attorney, a reasonable fee request to the probate court must indicate the basis for the fee and the extent to which it was based on a sale of realty, indicating that a flat percentage fee for effecting a sale would be improper unless supported by other factors. Also included in the opinion was a strong caution, repeated twice, about potential conflicts of interest. See also Conn. Inf. Op. 88-5 regarding real estate brokerage services by an attorney, stating that a flat 2% fee for brokering and closing a sale might be excessive. In re Lake, 702 N.E.2d 1145 (Mass. 1998), sanctioned an attorney for acting as real estate broker, for a separate commission, without disclosure of the conflict of interest or an informed written consent; it probably did not help that the broker was not a member of the multiple listing service where the property was located and attempted to retain the right to a commission even after associating with a local broker who also would charge a commission. Similarly, upon motion of the State Attorney General, who acted on behalf of an out-of-state charity that was a residuary beneficiary, In re Estate of Weeks, 950 N.E.2d 280 (Ill. App. Ct. 2011), reduced the fees of an estate's attorney who also acted as real estate broker.

White v. McBride, 937 S.W.2d 796 (Tenn. 1996), concluded that a contingent fee agreement with S for services to assist in recovery of a statutory elective share clearly was so excessive as to violate the state disciplinary rules and therefore was unenforceable; the court then reversed an award of quantum meruit because paying any compensation would fail to promote ethical behavior by providing a safety net of a reasonable fee if the endeavor to collect an exorbitant fee fails.

§2.7.6

attorneys be able to justify their fees with other factors, such as those listed by the amended Florida law adopted in response to *Platt*:[68]

- The promptness, efficiency, and skill with which the administration was handled by the attorney.

- The responsibilities assumed by, and potential liabilities of, the attorney.

- The nature and value of the assets that are affected by the decedent's death.

- The benefits or detriments resulting to the estate or its beneficiaries from the attorney's services.

- The complexity or simplicity of the administration and the novelty of issues presented.

- The attorney's participation in tax planning for the estate and the estate's beneficiaries and tax return preparation or review and approval.

- The nature of the probate, nonprobate, and exempt assets, and the expenses of administration and liabilities of the decedent and the compensation paid to other professionals and fiduciaries.

- Any delay in payment of the compensation after the services were furnished.

- Any other relevant factors.

These factors are appropriate criteria to establish fees in any case and attorneys might be well advised to consider this listing in justifying their fees as reasonable in all events, because allowable fees are likely to be scrutinized carefully.[69]

---

[68] Fla. Stat. § 733.6171(5), which allows a court to reduce attorney fees upon petition of any interested person, in which case the court will determine the reasonableness of fees. See, e.g., Sitomer v. First of America Bank—Central, 667 So. 2d 456 (Fla. Ct. App. 1996) (reduction of statutory fee charged by attorney who acted as personal representative to less than 25% of the amount billed, to reflect that virtually no assets were subject to administration, most of the decedent's wealth being held in a living trust in another jurisdiction; the final award reflected an hourly charge for the reasonable amount of time estimated to be required and compensation for the added risk presented by the size of the trust).

[69] See, e.g., In re Estate of Weinstock, 351 N.E.2d 647 (N.Y. 1976); In re Estate of Thron, 530 N.Y.S.2d 951 (Surr. Ct. 1988), both involving appointment of two lawyers from the same firm as coexecutors. The court in *Thron* stated that "[t]he appointment of two or more members from the same law firm as co-executors in double commission cases, in almost every instance, can only be the product of gratitude, greed or ignorance." 530 N.Y.S.2d at 955. And see In re Stortecky, 650

If a personal representative or attorney intends to serve without compensation (for example, to avoid compensation income at the expense of the estate's deduction for estate or income tax purposes), this fact should be made known before the services are rendered. For example, Rev. Rul. 56-472[70] considered a personal representative's agreement to serve for an amount less than the statutory commission and held that the personal representative did not realize taxable income by the anticipatory waiver of a larger commission, nor did a gift occur for federal gift tax purposes.[71] But Rev. Rul. 64-225[72] held that a waiver of statutory principal commissions[73] after submitting intermediate accountings that contained a request for those commissions constituted a constructive receipt for income tax purposes and a taxable gift for gift tax purposes, distinguishing Rev. Rul. 56-472 because it involved a timely waiver.

Then Rev. Rul. 66-167[74] considered a taxpayer who served as sole personal representative of an estate that the taxpayer and a child shared equally. Within a reasonable time after the decedent's death the taxpayer decided to decline compensation as personal representative and filed annual and final accounts consistent with that conclusion. The Ruling held that income was not constructively received and no gift was made, stating that the crucial test is whether the personal representative's actions evidence an intent to render a gratuitous service, based on

---

(Footnote Continued)

N.E.2d 391 (N.Y. 1995) (Surrogate Court has power to inquire into propriety of accounts and reasonableness of fees of attorney acting also as executor, notwithstanding assent by beneficiaries).

[70] 1956-2 C.B. 21.

[71] See also Commissioner v. Mott, 85 F.2d 315 (6th Cir. 1936) (trustee refused compensation for services); but cf. Kenny v. Commissioner, 32 T.C. 748 (1959) (person nominated as one of several personal representatives declined to serve, in exchange for payment of the same amount as the compensation that would have been earned, which was held to be income and not a gift).

[72] 1964-2 C.B. 15.

[73] Prior to the waiver the fiduciary had taken the annual statutory commission on income, but not statutory commissions for receiving and distributing principal nor additional statutory principal commissions, which state law specifically provided was not to be construed as a waiver of those commissions.

[74] 1966-1 C.B. 20.

§2.7.6

whether the timing, purpose, and effect of the waiver make it serve any other important objective.

The Ruling held that an adequate manifestation of intent to serve gratuitously would include a formal written waiver within six months after the initial fiduciary appointment and delivered to any principal legatee, devisee, or intestate taker. Or by an "implied waiver" if the fiduciary never claims commissions when filing accountings and all other facts and circumstances are consistent with the intent to serve gratuitously. Claiming the commission as a deduction for income, estate, or inheritance tax purposes ordinarily would be considered inconsistent with an intention to serve gratuitously.[75]

A testamentary bequest to a personal representative in lieu of compensation is deductible for FET purposes and constitutes income to the personal representative provided that the services must be rendered

---

[75] But see Rev. Rul. 70-237, 1970-1 C.B. 13 (trustee of testamentary trust formally waived right to increase in statutory commissions but continued to receive commissions at the old rate without income or gift tax liability with respect to the waived amounts). The personal representative in Breidert v. Commissioner, 50 T.C. 844 (1968), was the decedent's child, whose waiver of commissions was not filed until the final account, although at no time did the estate have sufficient cash to pay fees and there were deemed to be no facts upon which to apply the constructive receipt doctrine. The court rejected the government's Rulings on this issue as presenting no clear or "precise" theory and, based on the evidence, concluded that the child never intended to receive compensation; the written waiver was regarded as a mere formalization of the child's intention formed at the beginning of the administration.

to earn the bequest[76] and the amount does not exceed the compensation allowable by the local law or practice.[77]

§2.8 POSTMORTEM ESTATE PLANNING

As discussed in place throughout this treatise, often it is essential that a properly drafted estate plan exist to give the personal representative suitable powers and discretion to administer the estate, to apportion various tax and other burdens, to grant liberal powers of sale and reinvestment, to provide ample authority to liquidate or to conduct the decedent's business or other affairs, and ultimately to distribute the estate, all as the personal representative deems appropriate. As a further indication of the need for such authority, the following discussion notes elements of postmortem planning that may arise in a given estate and as to which the personal representative appropriately should be given special instructions, powers, and protections.

Although it is possible to conduct an intestate administration and accomplish many of these tasks, they should be the subject of forethought and planning that is reflected in a properly drafted estate plan. In addition to the discussion of each of these concepts at appropriate locations in this treatise, several excellent sources[1] are devoted exclusively to the concept of postmortem estate planning, which indicates the magnitude and importance of this topic and the planning that may be necessary inter vivos in anticipation of it.

---

[76] United States v. Merriam, 263 U.S. 179 (1923). And see Frank v. United States, 260 F. Supp. 691 (S.D. N.Y. 1966) (payment equal to a personal representative's fee made to coexecutor by estate beneficiary from residuary share disallowed as a deduction under §2053 but constituted income to the recipient; prior to the decedent's death the coexecutor relinquished the right to the payment but the residuary beneficiary released the coexecutor from that promise and agreed to make the payment out of the beneficiary's residuary share if the coexecutor would continue to serve); Cohn v. Commissioner, 27 T.C.M. (CCH) 350 (1968), aff'd, 410 F.2d 399 (2d Cir. 1969) (subsequent to *Frank* the other coexecutor alleged that amounts received in excess of fee allowed by state court was a gift, which the court rejected because the dominant purpose of the payment was to compensate services).

[77] See Treas. Reg. §§20.2053-1(d)(4) and -3(b)(2).

[1] **§2.8** See Chapter 15 for resources.

§2.8.1 Collaboration with S

The personal representative should consult with S to determine whether to file a separate income tax return for D or elect under §6013(a)(3) to file a joint return with S for the decedent's final tax year (and, if D died before the prior year's return was filed, with respect to that outstanding return as well). Alternatively, the personal representative may elect under §6013(a)(3) to disaffirm a joint return previously filed with S.[2] The personal representative and S also should decide whether to consent under §2513(a) to split any gifts made by either D or S in years that have not yet been reported for gift tax purposes.[3]

Although the personal representative has no duty to counsel S with respect to postmortem elections available to S,[4] in many cases these will be collaborative decisions made for the overall benefit of D's entire surviving family. In some cases, S also may be deceased when these decisions are being made, meaning that the personal representative may be, or may be dealing with, the personal representative of S's estate. Examples of such decisions available to S are whether to claim a family allowance or S's share in lieu of any entitlement under D's estate plan, if any, and whether to challenge any nonprobate transfers made by D and as to which S's entitlement otherwise may not apply.[5]

---

[2] See §15.7.1 n.14.

[3] See §15.1 nn.8-10 and accompanying text.

[4] Nor does the attorney engaged by D's personal representative to assist in administration of D's estate owe duties to S (or any other family members, as beneficiaries or heirs of the estate). For an excellent illustration of the importance of an engagement letter making this clear, however, see Estate of Fitzgerald v. Linnus, 765 A.2d 251 (N.J. Super. 2001) (S and children unsuccessfully sued the attorney engaged by S as executor for failing to advise S individually to disclaim insurance proceeds passing outside probate), in which the facts could not have been more helpful to the attorney, who was specifically engaged by D (a CPA-attorney) and who was specifically limited to drafting documents rather than full fledged estate planning, because D intended to undertake the necessary estate planning (which D never did); the attorney also advised S to obtain independent financial counsel, and made it clear that the attorney's undertaking was to assist S in facilitating rapid distribution of estate benefits to S, rather than to assess the wisdom of that course or to evaluate postmortem tax planning options such as disclaimer (to say nothing of the planning that would have been appropriate before D died).

[5] See §3.4.

Additional collaborative planning may occur with respect to the marital deduction in D's estate and whether a larger or smaller deduction would be desirable and can be generated by postmortem planning, such as disclaimers by descendants that would result in more property passing to S. Alternatively, D (or S's personal representative if S died shortly after D) may wish to disclaim any part of D's estate passing to S, thereby reducing the FET that will apply over both estates. Or it may be desirable for the personal representative to make only a partial QTIP election under § 2056(b)(7)(B)(v).[6] It also may be appropriate to make the § 2056(b)(7)(C)(ii) election against automatic QTIP marital deduction treatment afforded to a spousal annuity under a qualified retirement plan includible in D's gross estate under § 2039.[7]

S also should consider whether to roll any lump sum distribution from a qualified plan over to a spousal IRA to defer the income tax liability until S must begin receiving distributions from that account.[8]

Further, if S is not a citizen of the United States, postmortem planning and an election under § 2056A(a)(3) will be required to comply with the QDOT requirements to avoid loss of the marital deduction under § 2056(d).[9]

And when the personal representative gets around to making distribution of any marital bequest or other entitlement from D's estate, complex "marital funding" decisions must be made regarding such things as realization of capital gain or loss, DNI carryout, acceleration of IRD, whether to distribute frozen or split interests, and other consequences.[10]

§2.8.2 Income Tax Planning

Numerous additional income tax issues confront the personal representative during estate administration. For example, the personal representative must decide:

---

[6] See § 13.5.6.4.

[7] See §§ 9.2 and 13.5.6.7.

[8] See § 9.3.5.

[9] See § 13.5.7.

[10] See § 13.7.

- whether expenses for the decedent's medical care that are paid by the estate within one year after the decedent's death should be claimed as an income tax deduction under §213(c) on the decedent's final income tax return or as a §2053(a)(3) FET deduction;[11]

- whether to claim certain expenses of administration as an FET deduction under §2053(a)(2) or as an estate income tax deduction by making the §642(g) election;[12]

- whether to utilize selling expenses to reduce the amount realized to determine gain or loss rather than as additional §2053(a)(2) administration expense deductions;[13]

- whether to deduct uncompensated casualty losses as §165 income tax deductions rather than either a §2054 FET deduction or a reduction in FET value under the §2032 alternate valuation rule;[14] and

- whether to make the §454 election to accrue or recognize interest on any United States savings bonds owned by the decedent at death.[15] Additional elections relate to the basis of partnership property under §754 and whether to revoke a §1362(a)(2) S Corporation election.[16]

The personal representative also must select a §441 tax year for the estate's income tax purposes, which need not be the calendar year and, under §443, may be a short year in the first year after the decedent's death if that would fragment income received shortly after death and reduce the overall income tax burden. And when the estate is ready to terminate, the personal representative also must consider the §642(h) limitation regarding unused losses and deductions[17] and select the most appropriate time for termination of the estate.

All of these decisions must consider the income tax consequences under §§661 and 662 of estate distributions,[18] the amount of DNI carried out of the estate under the §643(e) limitation when property is distributed in kind, whether to make the §643(e)(3) election to treat distributions as a gain or loss realization event and correspondingly alter the

---

[11] See §15.7.1 n.12.

[12] See §15.4.5.

[13] See §15.4.5.

[14] See §15.4.4.

[15] See §15.7.1.

[16] See §15.7.2.

[17] See §5.8.3.

[18] See generally Chapter 5 regarding income taxation of estate and trust distributions.

DNI carryout amount and basis to the distributee,[19] and the opportunity to make "trapping" distributions during interim years of estate administration.[20] And if the estate is not terminated within two tax years after the decedent's death, §6654(*l*)(2) requires the personal representative to pay estimated income tax, which may be avoidable if a long first tax year is elected rather than a short year to fragment estate income.[21]

§2.8.3 Wealth Transfer Tax Elections

Perhaps most relevant in larger estates, the personal representative also must make various wealth transfer tax elections, beginning with the §2032 election to value estate assets on the alternate valuation date, which is six months after the decedent's death or the date of an earlier disposition, if any, rather than the date of the decedent's death.[22] Implicit in this election is the additional decision whether to dispose of any assets within the six month alternate valuation period, if §2032 might be elected and it is desirable to freeze the value of those assets by a disposition before the six month period elapses.

Special use valuation under §2032A also may be available with respect to qualified real property used in a farm or ranch (or other agricultural property, under the §2032A(b)(2) definition) or in a closely held business.[23] And a reduction in estate value may be available if the decedent's personal representative is able to disclaim property received by the decedent within a short period prior to death.[24]

The personal representative of an estate that holds closely held business property must consider whether a §303 redemption to pay estate or GST taxes[25] or a §6166 election to defer estate or GST attributable to that property is available and would be desirable, along with the §6324A election to create a lien for §6166 deferred tax. And additional FET deferral requests may be available under §6161(a)(1) for up to six

---

[19] See §5.8.1 nn.9-11 and accompanying text.

[20] See §5.8.2.

[21] See §2.7.5 n.26 and accompanying text.

[22] See §15.3.2.

[23] See §15.3.3.

[24] See §7.1.6.

[25] See §15.7.3.

months or under § 6161(a)(2) for up to 10 years for reasonable cause, or under § 6163 with respect to the tax attributable to inclusion of future interests in the decedent's gross estate.[26] An extension under § 6081 to file the decedent's FET return also might become relevant.[27]

With respect to allocation of the GST exemption: the personal representative must decide whether to override the § 2632 automatic allocation rules by making an affirmative allocation under § 2631, whether to allocate exemption to transfers made during the decedent's life,[28] and whether to make the § 2652(a)(3) "reverse" QTIP election.[29]

§ 2.8.4 Compensatory (Equitable) Adjustments

Finally, the personal representative must decide whether to waive the right to receive compensation. It also must consider whether any of its actions during administration of the estate gives rise to the need to make "compensatory" or "equitable" adjustments to neutralize the consequences of elections made that, for example, reduce taxes at the inequitable expense of one or more beneficiaries.[30] As illustrated, these various alternatives make the chore of administration infinitely more difficult than the average client anticipates and they demand that special consideration be given to selection of the personal representative. They make intestacy a particularly undesirable result in most substantial and even many modest estates.

---

[26] See § 15.2 with respect to all deferrals generally.

[27] See § 3.3.20.

[28] See § 11.4.5.5 regarding exemption allocation generally.

[29] See § 11.4.3.2.

[30] See § 5.8.4.

$$\boxed{3}$$

Wills as Estate Planning Instruments

§3.0 INTRODUCTION

As illustrated in Chapter 2, the default estate plan provided by intestate succession seldom provides all the powers and dispositive flexibility needed for most estates. Alternate forms of property disposition are common, and the numerous nonprobate property dispositions (such as life insurance beneficiary and settlement designations, annuities, joint ownership with survivorship rights, funded inter vivos and Totten trusts, and POD or TOD accounts), minimize the need for a will. But seldom is it possible to dispose entirely of a decedent's total wealth without using a will. Instead, virtually all estates require a will as part of a comprehensive estate plan. Unless ancillary administration or other

§3.0

probate avoidance incentives compel the use of nonprobate devices, a will appropriately may be the only dispositive document[1] needed to effect a proper estate plan. The will may constitute the complete estate plan if the client retains complete ownership of property and makes no other inter vivos arrangements to control the devolution of wealth at death. More significantly, a complete estate plan cannot exist in any but the most unusual cases without a will.

Practically any estate planning problem may arise in the context of a will, including most issues addressed in this treatise. This chapter does not consider issues more appropriately developed elsewhere.[2] Instead, it explores only those issues that are reasonably unique to wills, including:

- a recommended approach to execute a will that is valid in all United States jurisdictions;

- issues relating to revocation of wills;

- provisions that are essential to most well drafted wills and those that more appropriately should appear in some document other than a will;

- issues unique to testamentary gifts and to contracts with respect to wills or gifts made by contractual wills; and

- the ability of disappointed heirs—such as a surviving spouse or a pretermitted child—to claim a share of an estate notwithstanding contrary dispositive provisions in an otherwise valid will.

In addition, discussed at the end of this chapter are documents that normally should be produced in conjunction with but separate from execution of a will, such as a durable power of attorney, a health care proxy, a living will, instructions for disposition of the decedent's body, and an organ donation agreement. These are an integral part of most estate planning engagements that result in the production of a will and

---

[1] **§3.0** Other documents may help deal with problems related to living, such as a durable power of attorney, a health care proxy, or a living will, and some documents may address immediate problems related to disposition of the decedent's body, such as an organ donation agreement or funeral instructions. With the exception of a durable power of attorney (which may authorize inter vivos gifting), these other documents do not address disposition of wealth. See §3.10 for a discussion of these documents.

[2] Topics related to issues that are unique to the use of wills but that are addressed elsewhere include choosing between a will and a revocable inter vivos trust as the principal estate planning document and whether to distribute property outright or in trust. See §§4.1 and 6.5.

often are included in the package of documents produced for a client who seeks "just a simple will."

§3.1 EXECUTION, CHALLENGE, AND REVOCATION

§3.1.1 Suggested Execution Procedure

State law formalities for execution of a will vary.[1] Some states permit holographs (wills written entirely in the testator's hand and signed but

---

[1] **§3.1** Comprehensive compilations of will execution requirements can be found in McGovern, Kurtz, & English, Wills, Trusts & Estates ch. 4 (4th ed. 2010); Restatement (Third) of Property (Wills and Other Donative Transfers) Statutory Note to §3.1, at 181-186 (1999); and Miller, Will Formality, Judicial Formalism, and Legislative Reform: An Examination of the New UPC "Harmless Error" Rule and the Movement Toward Amorphism, 43 U. Fla. L. Rev. 167 (Part One) and 599 (Part Two) (1991) (hereafter Miller, Amorphism).

Langbein, Substantial Compliance With the Wills Act, 88 Harv. L. Rev. 489 (1975); Langbein & Waggoner, Reformation of Wills on the Ground of Mistake: Change of Direction in American Law, 130 U. Pa. L. Rev. 521 (1982); Langbein, Excusing Harmless Errors in the Execution of Wills: A Report on Australia's Tranquil Revolution in Probate Law, 87 Colum. L. Rev. 1 (1987); Fellows, In Search of Donative Intent, 73 Iowa L. Rev. 611 (1988); and Miller, Amorphism, all address the concept that insubstantial noncompliance with will execution formalities that constitutes harmless error should not invalidate an otherwise valid will, which the 1990 version of UPC §2-503 embraces if the proponent of the will proves by clear and convincing evidence that the decedent intended the document to be the decedent's valid will. Compare In re Will of Ranney, 589 A.2d 1339 (N.J. 1991) (adopting substantial compliance doctrine; although execution was defective because witnesses signed self-proving affidavit and failed to execute attestation provision, the court granted relief because the decedent's intent was clear and there were no abuses sought to be prevented by strict adherence to execution formalities), with Dalk v. Allen, 774 So. 2d 787 (Fla. Dist. Ct. App. 2000) (in the confusion of eight different estate planning documents circulated for execution in a single proceeding the will was properly attested and notarized but not signed by the decedent; the court refused to overlook the error), and Norton v. Hinson, 989 S.W.2d 535 (Ark. 1999) (refusing to apply substantial compliance doctrine to overcome invalidity due to one witness being underage, under circumstances suggesting impropriety—the 99-year-old decedent's caregiver proposing a will benefiting the caregiver, witnessed by the caregiver's child and grandchild), and cf. Rioux v. Coulombe, 19 E.T.R.2d 201 (Super. Ct. Quebec 1996) (a signed and dated envelope marked "this is my will," containing a computer diskette that recorded testamentary directions was allowed as the

not witnessed) or nuncupative (oral) wills, which deviate from the most basic requirements that a will be written and signed. Calls continue to be made to authorize video wills (yesterday's technology) or computer wills. And the National Conference of Commissioners on Uniform State Laws approved in 1984 a Uniform Statutory Will Act that it withdrew from consideration in 1996 as "obsolete."[2] It provided a form of will designed to meet the needs of testators with uncomplicated estates. These concepts are not discussed here, however, because they are quirky, they are not accepted, and it is rare to utilize any of these devices in planned estates—there simply is no need for or groundswell in favor of them.

More important is to avoid the issue whether a will executed in one jurisdiction is valid with respect to property located in another. Safety lies in following an execution procedure that complies with the formalities of every state, regardless of where the testator is domiciled at

---

(Footnote Continued)

decedent's last will; it met the "essential requirements" of form because a signature on the envelope was adequate and it unequivocally and unquestionably contained the decedent's last wishes). Not so severe but raising similar questions, Taylor v. Holt, 134 S.W.3d 830 (Tenn. Ct. App. 2003), held that a computer generated signature on a computer generated will was the symbol intended by the testator to authenticate the writing and qualified as a valid signature for execution of the will. Nevada Revised Statute § 133.085 authorizes an "electronic" will but it there may yet be no software that complies with its requirements. Note also that, in New Jersey where the doctrine originally was created, In re Alleged Will of Ferree, 848 A.2d 81 (N.J. Super. 2004), refused to extend substantial compliance to a holograph, saying that unwitnessed wills already represent a relaxation of the traditional execution requisites (and in this case the surplusage theory deviation from historical requirements also was implicated), such that additional relaxation of the execution requisites was inappropriate.

[2] 8A U.L.A. 293 (2001) and 150 (Supp. 2010). Compare Cal. Prob. Code § 6200 et seq.; Me. Rev. Stat. Ann. Tit. 18-A, § 2-514; and Wis. Stat. § 853.55 et seq., which provide statutory wills consisting of a series of multiple choices or blanks, with the testator filling in the appropriate box or blank for each clause. The more likely trend or market demand is for computer software allowing a user personally to create a will and avoid using a skilled estate planner entirely. Some on-line will forms are available, and some are not very good, which may portend two future developments—more litigation over faulty execution of do-it-yourself documents, and more construction or reformation suits to mend badly drafted or defective wills.

§ 3.1.1

execution or at death or where property subject to the will is located.[3] Thus, the following recommended procedure represents a minimum execution approach.

- First, the testator should examine the entire will and understand all its substantive provisions.

Although most testators do not fully understand all the technical provisions of their wills, the law does not require as much. Still, the lawyer should ascertain that the testator appreciates the nature and extent of the property subject to the will, the individuals benefited by the will, the nature of the beneficiaries' enjoyment, and whether any "natural objects of the testator's bounty." are excluded.[4]

- The testator, three observers who will witness the will, the person conducting the execution, and a notary public (if required with respect to a self proving affidavit, and if the person conducting the execution does not

---

[3] By statute most states recognize as valid a will executed in compliance with the law in effect at the time of execution in the jurisdiction in which the will was executed or where the testator was domiciled, or in effect at the testator's death in the jurisdiction of the testator's domicile at death. See UPC §2-506. Thus, a will not validly executed under any law at the time of execution may be valid at the testator's death if the law of the testator's domicile at death changed in the interim and the requirements in effect at death were met at the time of execution. See, e.g., Hardy v. Ross, 371 S.W.2d 522 (Ark. 1963) (decedent executed will when only 18 years old but subsequently the minimum age to make a valid will was reduced from 21 to 18; court held the will was valid, applying law in effect when testator died). A comprehensive summary of state choice of law rules regarding valid execution is contained in Restatement (Third) of Property (Wills and Other Donative Transfers) Statutory Note to §3.1, at 179-181 (1999).

[4] A standard formulation of the capacity required to execute a valid will is that the testator must have the ability to understand the nature and extent of the testator's property, the persons who are the natural objects of the testator's bounty, and the disposition the testator is making of that property, as these elements interact. Ability to understand is the required showing, not actual comprehension, and knowledge of the natural objects is not belied by a failure to benefit those people (although a stronger showing of capacity may be required if natural objects are excluded). See Atkinson, The Law of Wills §51 (2d ed. 1953); McGovern, Kurtz, & English, Wills, Trusts & Estates §7.1 (4th ed. 2010); Shulman v. Shulman, 193 A.2d 525 (Conn. 1963) (rejecting requested instruction that the testator must know the contents of the instrument and comprehend its provisions; it is sufficient if the testator understands and approves the purport and effect of the will, even if the testator does not fully comprehend the technical legal terminology employed).

§3.1.1

meet this requirement) should be in a room from which all others are excluded and from which no one will depart until the execution is completed.

Although the last state (Vermont) to require three witnesses to a valid will finally fell back to the "standard" two required everywhere else, it is wise to use a third witness in any jurisdiction, to better ensure that sufficient witnesses can be produced after the testator's death if admission of the will is contested. It should be standard practice to select witnesses who are likely to survive the testator and whose lifestyle and age make it predictable that they can be found if the need arises.

Moreover, because a will may be wholly or partially invalid in some jurisdictions if a witness is (or is related to) a beneficiary under the will,[5] it is preferable to select persons who have no incentive to lie about the testator's capacity and the events that transpire, either to help or to hinder admission of the will. In most states beneficial interest no longer is an absolute bar to being a credible witness because most statutes merely purge any incentive to lie about the execution by limiting a witness' entitlement under the will to whatever the witness would receive if the will was not admitted to probate.[6] In some cases the purge statute preserves the witness' entire entitlement under the will because the interested witness is an heir who would receive at least as much by intestacy. Moreover, an interested witness' entitlement may be unaffected if there are enough disinterested witnesses to meet the statutory requirements.

If neither exception is applicable, however, events subsequent to execution cannot rehabilitate a witness' credibility. For example, an interested witness may not disclaim a testamentary bequest in an effort to validate the will because interested witness statutes look to the witnesses' credibility and capacity when the will was executed.[7] If the

---

[5] See Atkinson, The Law of Wills § 65; McGovern, Kurtz, & English, Wills, Trusts & Estates § 4.3 (4th ed. 2010).

[6] For a list of such state statutes see Restatement (Third) of Property (Wills and Other Donative Transfers) Statutory Note to § 3.1, at 186-188 (1999).

[7] See Atkinson, The Law of Wills § 65, at 311 (2d ed. 1953); McGovern, Kurtz, & English, Wills, Trusts & Estates § 4.3 (4th ed. 2010). For an interesting twist on this rule, see Berndtson v. Heuberger, 173 N.E.2d 460 (Ill. 1961) (witness' marriage to beneficiary after testator executed will but before testator died did not undermine validity of will because interest was tested at execution).

rule was otherwise, other beneficiaries would have an incentive to compensate an interested witness for disclaiming to validate the will, and the interested witness' credibility would be suspect because of this possibility.

UPC § 2-505(b) provides that "[t]he signing of a will by an interested witness does not invalidate the will or any provision of it,"[8] but a number of states have statutes to the opposite effect that go to the extreme of regarding even the spouse of a beneficiary as an interested witness.[9] Thus, because the objective is execution of a will in a manner that is

---

[8] Similarly, even in states with interested witness prohibitions, a witness to a codicil is not precluded from taking as a beneficiary under the will or under any other codicil. See, e.g., King v. Smith, 302 A.2d 144 (N.J. 1973).

Consider the following quandary. Testator T is unwilling to allow anyone to witness execution of T's will who is not a beneficiary thereunder. Can a valid will be executed in a state with an interested witness prohibition if T is unable to write out a holographic will?

The solution is to prepare two wills for T, one that omits beneficiaries X and Y even though T wants to benefit them. That will would be executed by T and witnessed by X and Y and it would be valid because X and Y are not interested witnesses with respect to it. Immediately thereafter T would sign a second will that includes X and Y as beneficiaries. It would be signed by witnesses A and B who were beneficiaries under the first will and who receive no more under the second will than they receive under the first. Thus, they technically are not interested witnesses under the second will because they take no more under the second will than they do without it. Therefore, the second will should be valid.

If it is this easy to avoid the interested witness prohibition, then arguably the UPC appropriately eliminates the prohibition altogether and merely allows interest to be considered in testing credibility of a witness' testimony regarding execution.

[9] See, e.g., Dorfman v. Allen, 434 N.E.2d 1012 (Mass. 1982) (will witnessed by child's spouse excluded another child of the testator; the disinherited child was successful in precluding the child married to the witness from receiving a share of the estate but was not successful in receiving that property by intestacy as hoped because the court held that the disqualified entitlement passed to descendants of the child who was married to the witness, as provided by the terms of the will as if that child predeceased the testator); Rosenbloom v. Kokofsky, 369 N.E.2d 1142 (Mass. 1977) (spouse of one child was a witness, causing that child to be excluded entirely, notwithstanding pleas to construe the statute as purging only the amount exceeding the child's intestate share).

In re Longworth, 222 A.2d 561 (Me. 1966), involved a pourover will witnessed by employees of the corporate trustee to which the estate was distributable. The prohibition did not apply because the corporate fiduciary does not take a

universally valid, witnesses should be avoided if they have any direct or indirect interest that may affect their credibility.[10]

(Footnote Continued)

beneficial interest. Quaere whether the same result would apply if a trust beneficiary was a witness to the same pourover will.

[10] In re Estate of George, 137 N.E.2d 555 (Ill. App. Ct. 1956), held that an attorney who witnessed execution of a will designating the attorney as counsel for administration of the estate could not be compensated for representing the estate because local law precluded a witness from receiving a financial benefit under the will. In re Estate of Small, 346 F. Supp. 600 (D. D.C. 1972), held that a will provision granting the maximum allowable compensation to the attorney who drafted the will and that named the attorney as personal representative was void under the interested witness statute because the attorney witnessed the will; the court concluded that it should determine an appropriate compensation for the executor on the basis of work performed. 755 Ill. Comp. Stat. 5/4-6(b) legislatively overruled *George*, and other cases hold that, even if an attorney is named in a will, the attorney is not an interested witness because designation of the attorney for the personal representative is not binding or because the attorney earns any fee and therefore is not a beneficiary. See also Wis. Stat. § 853.07(3)(a) and Annot., Competency, as witness attesting will, of attorney named therein as executor's attorney, 30 A.L.R.3d 1361 (1970).

Will provisions designating the drafting attorney to assist the estate administration are unenforceable because the personal representative cannot be forced to hire an attorney designated by the testator. See Williams v. Maulis, 672 N.W.2d 702 (S.D. 2003), explaining the rationale that a personal representative who will be liable for errors ought to be permitted to hire the lawyer who will help manage that risk. In re Estate of Devroy, 325 N.W.2d 345 (Wis. 1982), however, enforced a will provision that designated the attorney to assist the personal representative because it also specified that only someone who would accept that attorney designation could be appointed as personal representative; there was no evidence of solicitation for the job as attorney. La. Rev. Stat. Ann. § 9:2448 provides that a testator may by will designate an attorney to handle the legal matters of the estate and that such a designation is valid and binding on the personal representative, the heirs, and legatees.

Being named in a will as attorney to assist the administration is permissible ethically if the attorney did not instigate the designation. ABA Standing Comm. on Ethics and Prof. Resp. Inf. Dec. 602 (1963). And see Model Code EC 5-6, imposing requirements similar to those involving a gift to the attorney under EC 5-5. New York State Bar Ass'n Comm. on Prof. Ethics Op. 481 (1978) states that the attorney may suggest that the client name the attorney only if the circumstances

> support a firm conviction that the client would request his lawyer to serve in that capacity if he were aware of the lawyer's willingness to accept the responsibility. Not only should the lawyer have enjoyed a long standing

- The person supervising the execution should ask the testator "Is this your will, do you understand it, does it express your wishes regarding disposition of your property after your death, and do you request these observers to witness your execution of it?" The testator's affirmative response should be audible to the three observers.

Although some states require "publication" of the will, meaning a declaration that the document being signed is a will, most jurisdictions

<hr>

(Footnote Continued)

relationship with the client, but it must also appear that the client is experiencing difficulty in selecting other persons qualified and competent to serve as executor.

New York State Bar Ass'n Comm. on Prof. Ethics Op. 610 (1990) is consistent, although it quotes from the Surrogate's Court for Suffolk County a local rule that:

In all probate proceedings, where the purported will and/or codicil of the deceased nominates an attorney as a fiduciary or cofiduciary, there shall be annexed to the probate petition an affidavit of the testator setting forth the following:

1. that the testator was advised that the nominated attorney may be entitled to a legal fee, as well as to the fiduciary commissions authorized by statute;

2. where the attorney is nominated to serve as a cofiduciary, that the testator was apprised of the fact that multiple commissions may be due and payable out of the funds of the estate; and

3. the testator's reason for nominating the attorney to serve as fiduciary.

Failure to submit an affidavit of this nature may warrant the scheduling of a hearing in order to determine whether the appointment of the attorney as fiduciary was procured by the exercise of fraud and/or undue influence upon the decedent.

The hard part about these rules is proving there was no impropriety, especially recognizing that a letter from the client to that effect may be as suspicious as the designation itself.

Regular insertion of a provision designating the drafting attorney would be improper. See ABA Standing Comm. on Ethics and Prof. Resp. Inf. Dec. 602 (1963); State v. Gulbankian, 196 N.W.2d 733 (Wis. 1972) (facts revealed high probability of solicitation because attorneys—siblings—were named in some capacity, either as fiduciary or as attorney or as both, in a significant percentage of the wills they drafted for their clients).

In re Estate of Meskimen, 235 N.E.2d 619 (Ill. 1968), held that a will naming an attorney as beneficiary was not invalid, notwithstanding that it was witnessed by the attorney's secretary and two attorneys who shared offices with the attorney. See § 3.2.5.5 regarding the ethics of an attorney preparing a will for a client if the attorney or a member of the attorney's family is a beneficiary under the will.

§ 3.1.1

no longer require that the witnesses know what the testator is signing.[11] Absent fraud, undue influence, mistake or the like, there is a presumption that a testator of sound mind executes a will with knowledge that it is a will and of its contents.[12] Nevertheless, it is preferable to have the testator declare the document to be a will and indicate affirmatively that the testator knows its contents.

A formal request by the testator that each witness attest the execution responds to a requirement in some jurisdictions[13] that witnesses not act of their own accord, which may protect against attestation by a volunteer who is interested and whose participation therefore might disqualify the execution. Although little is required to constitute the requisite request, including mere acquiescence by the testator to the witness' participation under some circumstances,[14] open and direct compliance with this formality avoids disputes.

---

[11] Atkinson, The Law of Wills § 68 (2d ed. 1953); McGovern, Kurtz, & English, Wills, Trusts & Estates § 4.3 (4th ed. 2010). Compare UPC § 2-502(a) (no declaration required) with § 2-1003 (declaration required with respect to an "international will"), and see, e.g., Ark. Stat. Ann. § 28-25-103; N.Y. Est. Powers & Trusts L. § 3-2.1(a)(3) ("The testator shall, at some time during the . . . execution and attestation, declare to each of the attesting witnesses that the instrument . . . is his will)"; 84 Okla. Stat. § 55(3).

[12] The testator's knowledge of a will need not be gained from a personal reading of the document; it may be read or explained to the testator in preparation for execution. See, e.g., Padykula v. Luoni, 459 A.2d 965 (R.I. 1983), and In re Estate of Hauschild, 137 N.W.2d 875 (Neb. 1965) (presumption of knowing execution not overcome even though wills were in English and the testators could not read English); In re Estate of Cohen, 284 A.2d 754 (Pa. 1971) (attorney explanation of contents of will to testator is adequate); Dobija v. Hopey, 233 N.E.2d 920 (Mass. 1968) (properly executed will upheld against probate court's denial of probate, relying on lack of evidence to rebut general presumption that testator knew contents); but see Duchesneau v. Jaskoviak, 277 N.E.2d 507 (Mass. 1972) (evidence justified conclusion that testator did not know contents of will), and Lejeune v. Succession of Duplechin, 260 So. 2d 37 (La. Ct. App. 1972) (presumption overcome with respect to will written in English for testator who spoke only French).

[13] See Atkinson, The Law of Wills § 67 (2d ed. 1953); Ark. Code Ann. § 28-25-103(c); N.Y. Est. Powers & Trusts L. § 3-2.1(a)(4); 84 Okla. Stat. § 55(4); Wash. Rev. Code § 11.12.020(1).

[14] See Atkinson, The Law of Wills § 67, at 326.

§ 3.1.1

> • The observers should witness the testator date and then sign the testimonium, which should appear at the end of the will. In addition, it is desirable to have the testator initial or sign each prior page of the will.

Signing or initialing every page minimizes the risk of page substitutions[15] and, if this suggestion is followed, a provision in the testimonium appropriately might state that the testator has "signed this will consisting of [**] pages and, for purposes of identification, have placed my [initials/signature] at the foot of each preceding page."[16]

Great care is required if more than one will is being signed during a single ceremony because it is not unusual, particularly involving mirror image wills for spouses, for one testator to sign the other testator's will by mistake.[17]

---

[15] See, e.g., In re Estate of Leavey, 202 P.3d 99 (Ks. Ct. App. 2009), in which the drafting attorney indicated that initials of the testator and two witnesses were included to preclude substitutions. The attorney meant to be one of the two witnesses. Although the attorney initialed every page, the attorney failed to sign the attestation provision itself, resulting in failure of the will itself (Kansas is a UPC state but its Probate Code lacks the normal UPC § 2-503 substantial compliance provision).

[16] Some jurisdictions do not require a witnessed will to be dated, and some statutes permit the testator to sign without the witnesses being present and then to acknowledge the signature to the witnesses at a later time. See, e.g., UPC § 2-502(a). Some statutes also do not require signature at the physical end of the document, although in some of those jurisdictions a signature before the end may cause all provisions following the signature to be ignored. See McGovern, Kurtz, & English, Wills, Trusts & Estates § 4.2 (4th ed. 2010), and compare In re Estate of Weiss, 279 A.2d 189 (Pa. 1971) (will was invalid because it was signed vertically along the margin), with In re Estate of Stasis, 307 A.2d 241 (Pa. 1973) (handwritten will with writing on both sides of a single piece of paper left no room for the testator's signature where the writing ended so the testator turned the page upside down and signed, which the court treated as the sequential (although not the spatial) end, thereby meeting the statutory end-of-will requirement).

[17] Compare In re Snide, 418 N.E.2d 656 (N.Y. 1981) (will signed by wrong spouse admitted to probate; relief from statutory formalities was limited to situations involving mirror image wills simultaneously executed with no other statutory defect), with In re Estate of Pavlinko, 148 A.2d 528 (Pa. 1959) (mistaken execution not corrected, notwithstanding clear indication of testator's intent and lack of fraud, forgery, incompetence, or other reason to insist on strict application of execution formalities); and see Comment, Mistakenly Signed Reciprocal Wills: A Change in Tradition After *In re Snide*, 67 Iowa L. Rev. 205 (1981). For a

- The person conducting the execution should instruct the three observers that, "your signature as witness attests that (1) [the testator] declared to each of you that the document is [his/her] will, (2) [he/she] dated and signed the will in your presence, and (3) [he/she] asked you to witness the execution. You are attesting that you signed in the presence of [the testator] and the other witnesses, believing [the testator] to be of sound mind and memory." If the observers agree, then in the presence of the testator and of each other, they should witness the will by signing the attestation provision and writing their addresses for future identification.

Attestation creates a rebuttable presumption that the will was executed properly.[18] Consequently, this provision is very important, because the presumption of due execution from a complete attestation provision may entitle the will to probate[19] if a witness is unavailable or unable to testify or recollect,[20] or even if the witness later recants and testifies that certain requirements were not met.[21] Thus, the witnesses should sign

---

(Footnote Continued)

discussion of this type of relief for substantial compliance with the formalities for will execution, see the authorities cited in §3.1.1 n.1.

[18] Atkinson, The Law of Wills §73 (2d ed. 1953); McGovern, Kurtz, & English, Wills, Trusts & Estates §4.3 (4th ed. 2010).

[19] In re Estate of Politowicz, 304 A.2d 569 (N.J. 1973), involved a witness who signed in a room adjoining that in which the testator was located, at a table about six feet from the testator. Notwithstanding that there was an opening in the wall between the two rooms and despite the presumption of due execution created by the attestation provision, the trial court referred to a counter-presumption that attestation in a room other than that in which the testator was located is prima facie not in the testator's presence, which shifted the burden to the proponent of the will to show that the attestation was proper. The Superior Court reversed, holding that the presumption of due execution prevailed and that the burden was on the contestant to show that the attestation was not seen by the testator.

[20] A will without an attestation clause was denied probate in Young v. Young, 313 N.E.2d 593 (Ill. App. Ct. 1974), because 27 years after execution the witnesses could not remember whether the will properly was executed. An attestation clause would have created a presumption that the enumerated events did occur.

[21] See In re Estate of Johnson, 780 P.2d 692 (Okla. 1989) (testimony in a will contest proceeding indicated that not all witnesses were present when the testator executed the will, notwithstanding an attestation clause to the contrary; the court permitted testimony that contradicted that attestation with the recognition that a witness who signed that clause would be subject to impeachment when later asserting that it was not accurate and with the additional possibility of prosecution of the witness for perjury, either for lying to the notary when the will

this statement affirming that the various requisites essential to validity of the will actually occurred.

Many states do not require that the witnesses sign in the presence of each other,[22] and the testator may not be required to be present when the attesting witnesses sign the will. Nevertheless, even if the controlling statute does not require witnesses to sign the will when the testator signs, the will might not be valid if the witnesses sign after the testator dies.[23] So immediate execution by the witnesses is preferable to any

---

(Footnote Continued)

was self-proved or later when testifying in probate court); In re Estate of Birkeland, 519 P.2d 154 (Mont. 1974) (recitals in attestation clause overcome by testimony of attesting witnesses).

[22] See, e.g., UPC §2-502, which only requires that the will be signed by persons who "witnessed either the signing of the will . . . or the testator's acknowledgement of that signature or acknowledgement of the will."

[23] In re Estate of Mikeska, 362 N.W.2d 906 (Mich. Ct. App. 1985), held that witnesses must sign during the testator's life. Accord, In re Estate of Flicker, 339 N.W.2d 914 (Neb. 1983); In re Estate of Peters, 526 A.2d 1005 (N.J. 1987); Rogers v. Rogers, 691 P.2d 114 (Or. Ct. App. 1984); and Perry v. Adams, 827 P.2d 930 (Or. Ct. App. 1992) (an attorney malpractice case, stating that execution of a will does not occur when the testator signs but, rather, when all execution formalities have been satisfied, including signature by the witnesses, which necessarily must occur before the testator dies).

In re Estate of Royal, 813 P.2d 790 (Colo. Ct. App. 1991), aff'd, 826 P.2d 1236 (Colo. 1992), stated support for a proposition enunciated by *In re Estate of Peters* that witnesses be permitted to sign after the testator's death in "exceptional circumstances," such as the testator's death so quickly after the testator signed that the witnesses simply could not execute in time, but the Supreme Court rejected that extrapolation, stating that the will must be complete when the decedent dies, which the court took to mean that, although the witnesses need not sign when the testator executes the will, they must sign prior to the testator's death. Estate of Eugene v. Union Rescue Mission, 128 Cal. Rptr. 2d 622 (Ct. App. 2002), upheld a will that the testator's attorney witnessed but inadvertently failed to sign until after the testator's death (it was one of two reciprocal wills and the attorney signed the other at the time both were executed by their testators), the court holding that state law no longer established either a witness signature presence or timing requirement. *Eugene* was followed by Estate of Sauressig, 19 Cal. Rptr. 3d 262 (Ct. App. 2004), in which the notary to a will was regarded as one witness and the notary's spouse was regarded as the second, notwithstanding that the spouse (who witnessed the notarization but did not sign as a witness until after the decedent's death, when a challenge to the will was mounted by the public administrator) never was requested and did not intend to act as a witness.

§3.1.1

delay, and the presence of all together eliminates numerous additional problems that otherwise could lead to disqualification of the will.[24]

(Footnote Continued)

State law was modeled after UPC § 2-502, which requires a witness to sign within a reasonable time, which did not necessarily mean premortem. Subsequently, and over dissent, Estate of Saueressig, 136 P.3d 201, 204 (Cal. 2006) (this is the same case, notwithstanding the spelling difference), reversed, stating that "to allow the validity of a will to depend on the will or caprice of . . . a witness by allowing such a person to wait until after the testator's death to decide whether . . . to subscribe . . . to the will . . . would invite fraud and subvert the basic intent of will authentication requirements."

In Robinson v. Ward, 387 S.E.2d 735 (Va. 1990), the testator dictated a will to a friend, who was a beneficiary thereunder. After the testator's will was written and signed, and after a rescue squad member signed the will as a witness, the decedent slipped into a coma and subsequently died. Upon advice that the will required the signature of two witnesses, the friend signed the will as a witness. On contest of the will's execution the court ruled that the act of writing the friend's own name into the will as a beneficiary was adequate to subscribe as a witness for execution validity purposes. No indication was given whether the friend would be precluded from taking under the will as an interested witness. Similarly, In re Estate of Jung, 109 P.3d 102 (Ariz. 2005), and In re Estate of Miller, 149 P.3d 840 (Idaho 2006), both permitted signature within a reasonable time of the testator's execution, even if that occurred postmortem, but neither addressed the interested witness issue, perhaps because each case involved state law that followed the UPC, which does not necessarily invalidate a will witnessed by a beneficiary (in *Miller* the interested witness also transcribed the will, and the other witness to the execution was the notary, and none of these issues were addressed). See § 3.1.1 nn.5-10 and accompanying text.

[24] See generally McGovern, Kurtz, & English, Wills, Trusts & Estates § 4.3 (4th ed. 2010). E.g., In re Estate of McGurrin, 746 P.2d 85 (Idaho 1987), denied probate to a will because the testator only acknowledged the signature by telephone to the witnesses. The controlling statute did not require the witnesses to sign in the testator's presence but the court held that, if they do not, the testator must acknowledge in person the signature on the will. In re Estate of Bender, 295 N.Y.S.2d 177 (Surr. Ct. 1968), held a will invalid because the witnesses never saw the testator's signature because of the way the paper was folded and they also did not see the testator sign. Although the testator declared the document was a will, the testator never acknowledged the signature. Waldrep v. Goodwin, 195 S.E.2d 432 (Ga. 1973), acknowledged that the longstanding requirement that the testator must sign before the witnesses sign is not applied rigidly if the testator and the witnesses assembled and all signed as an integrated ceremony, regardless of the order in which they each executed their roles; the court stressed, however, the requirement that the testator must sign or acknowledge the signature in the presence of the witnesses. But In re Estate of Zeno, 672

Self-proving affidavits are authorized in many states and should be utilized to avoid the need to produce witnesses in an uncontested probate. UPC § 3-406(b) provides that compliance with execution requirements is conclusively presumed (subject only to proof of fraud or forgery) if the will is self-proved, and § 2-504(b) provides a suggested provision, which acts essentially like a deposition of the witnesses that makes their testimony unnecessary.[25] The operative language is:

(Footnote Continued)

N.W.2d 574 (Minn. Ct. App. 2004), held that a self-proved will is conclusively presumed to comply with the signature requirements for execution absent proof that fraud or forgery affected the testator's acknowledgment or the witness's affidavit, citing UPC § 2-504 to the effect that the signature requirements of a self-proved will may not be contested.

[25] See Mann, Self-Proving Affidavits and Formalism in Wills Adjudication, 63 Wash. U.L.Q. 39 (1985); Schneider, Self-Proved Wills—A Trap for the Unwary, 8 N. Ky. L. Rev. 539 (1981).

Scribner v. Gibbs, 953 N.E.2d 475 (Ind. Ct. App. 2011), disallowed a contestant's challenge based on inconsistencies between a self-proving affidavit and the witnesses' subsequent testimony because execution requirements are presumed by the self-proving affidavit to have been met and any uncertainty or lack of memory of a participant to the execution is not sufficient to overcome the presumption: "To hold otherwise would defeat the very purpose of having self-proving clauses and the presumption that they establish the validity of a will's execution . . . ." Estate of Peterson, 2006 WL 1529520 (unpub. Minn. Ct. App.), upheld the constitutionality of the UPC § 3-406(b) conclusive presumption that a will was validly executed if the will contains a self-proving affidavit, in that case notwithstanding clear evidence that execution was improper.

As shown by a number of cases, however, execution with a self-proving affidavit introduces an added opportunity for mistake. For example, In re Estate of Milward, 73 P.3d 155 (Kan. Ct. App. 2003), Hickox v. Wilson, 496 S.E.2d 711 (Ga. 1998), and In re Will of Carter, 565 A.2d 933 (Del. 1989), involved testators who signed the self-proving affidavit but not the testimonium in the will, and Hampton Roads Seventh-Day Adventist Church v. Stevens, 657 S.E.2d 80 (Va. 2008), In re Estate of Fordonski, 678 N.W.2d 413 (Iowa 2004), In re Estate of Dellinger, 793 N.E.2d 1041 (Ind. 2003), and In re Will of Ranney, 589 A.2d 1339 (N.J. 1991), involved defective execution because the witnesses signed the self-proving affidavit but failed to execute the attestation provision. Fortunately, each court admitted the wills to probate because the facts showed the decedents' intent and there was no indication of abuse sought to be prevented by strict adherence to execution formalities. See UPC § 2-504(c) codifying this result, providing that "[a] signature affixed to a self-proving affidavit attached to a will is considered a signature affixed to the will, if necessary to prove the will's due execution."

§3.1.1

> We . . . declare . . . that the testator signed and executed the instrument as the testator's last will and . . . signed willingly (or willingly directed another to sign . . . as [a] free and voluntary act for the purposes therein expressed, and that each of the witnesses, in the presence and hearing of the testator, signed the will as witness and that . . . the testator was at that time [18] years of age or older, of sound mind, and under no constraint or undue influence.

UPC § 2-504(a) provides that a will "may be simultaneously executed, attested, and made self proved, by acknowledgement thereof by the testator and affidavits of the witnesses, each made before an officer authorized to administer oaths" and provides a suggested form. Many state laws also provide suggested execution forms.

§ 3.1.2 Special Circumstances: Anticipating Challenge

Special circumstances may require deviations from the suggested execution procedure—for example, if the testator is unable to sign due to

---

(Footnote Continued)

In a growing number of cases the signature of a notary public in a self-proving affidavit served to validate an otherwise improperly executed will, even though the notary did not intend to be a witness to the testator's execution of the will (as opposed to the witnesses or testator's signatures). See, e.g., Land v. Burkhalter, 656 S.E.2d 834 (Ga. 2008); Estate of Teal, 135 S.W.3d 87 (Tex. Ct. App. 2002); In re Estate of Friedman, 6 P.3d 473 (Nev. 2000), citing In re Estate of Zelkovitz, 923 P.2d 740 (Wyo. 1996); In re Estate of Gerhardt, 763 A.2d 1289 (N.J. Super. 2000); In re Estate of Alfaro, 703 N.E.2d 620 (Ill. App. Ct. 1998); In re Estate of Price, 871 P.2d 1079 (Wash. Ct. App. 1994); Simpson v. Williamson, 611 So. 2d 544 (Fla. Dist. Ct. App. 1992); In re Estate of Martinez, 664 P.2d 1007 (N.M. Ct. App. 1983). In Estate of Sauressig, 19 Cal. Rptr. 3d 262 (Ct. App. 2004), rev'd on other grounds sub nom, Estate of Saueressig, 136 P.3d 201, 204 (Cal. 2006), the notary was asked to simply notarize the will (not for self-proving purposes) and was regarded (without challenge) as a witness for execution validity purposes. And In re Estate of Hall, 51 P.3d 1134 (Mont. 2002), held a joint will valid with just the signature of the testator's spouse (the other joint testator) and a notary, not as if the two satisfied the witness execution requirement but under the dispensing power rule of UPC § 2-503; it would appear that either theory would suffice, however.

The UPC was amended in 2008 to adopt new § 2-502(a)(3)(B), which eliminates the need for witnesses entirely if the will is "acknowledged by the testator before a notary public . . . ." In effect, a single notary public is a super-witness—the only witness needed.

physical impairment (including blindness)[26] or if a will contest seems likely on grounds of mental incapacity or undue influence.[27] Anyone may contest the will[28] if they would receive more from a testator's estate if an offered will was not admitted. Thus, the dispositive provisions may alert the estate planner to the potential for a challenge, even though it seems certain that the testator is competent and acting free from any undue influence. For example, contest may be predictable if the plan cuts out natural objects of the testator's bounty, provides for beneficiaries who have unconventional relationships with the testator or with whom the testator enjoyed an alternate lifestyle, favors a spouse to the exclusion of children by a prior marriage or favors some children over others, or if there are no close relatives who would be reluctant to besmirch the testator's name in a contest action.

---

[26] A careful check of applicable local law will reveal whether exceptions to normal execution requirements exist. For example, UPC § 2-502(a)(2) is common in permitting a proxy to sign if done in the presence and at the direction of the testator. And signature with assistance also may be permitted. See Atkinson, The Law of Wills § 64, at 297-298 (2d ed. 1953). In re Estate of Milleman, 203 A.2d 202 (Pa. 1964) (execution with the assistance of someone who held the testator's hand to help form the signature), took notice of the fact that the testator had trouble holding small objects and therefore had signed checks and other documents with assistance; the court held that, although the statute required that the testator request a proxy to sign and had made no request for the assistance offered, this requisite was not applicable because the testator validly signed the will personally, albeit with assistance.

[27] E.g., in Tarricone v. Cummings, 166 N.E.2d 737 (Mass. 1960), the will was entirely in the handwriting of the principal beneficiary and designated personal representative, which suggested a strong possibility of fraud or undue influence.

[28] Intestate takers who benefit if the will is not allowed have standing to contest admission of a will to probate, as may their creditors. See Marcus v. Pearce Woolen Mills, Inc., 233 N.E.2d 29 (Mass. 1968) (creditor attached decedent's property, alleging it was owned by a debtor who was the decedent's heir). An heir may have standing to contest a will even if there is a prior will that does not benefit the heir because that will also may not be valid, or it may not be offered for probate. See In re Estate of Powers, 106 N.W.2d 833 (Mich. 1961) (stating that Georgia, Kansas, and Kentucky were in accord but that Louisiana and Tennessee were contra); but see Maddox v. Mock, 220 N.E.2d 773 and 222 N.E.2d 396 (Ind. 1966), rev'g 196 N.E.2d 412 (Ind. Ct. App. 1964), which disagreed with *Powers*. In addition, the state has standing to contest a will if there are no heirs who would preclude an escheat if the estate was intestate. In re Estate of Moll, 495 P.2d 854 (Ariz. Ct. App. 1972).

§3.1.2

In circumstances such as these it may be advisable to include an in terrorem provision in the will[29] or to utilize a form of disposition that is

---

[29] The law in most jurisdictions is as codified in the 1990 version of UPC § 2-517 ("A provision in a will purporting to penalize an interested person for contesting the will . . . is unenforceable if probable cause exists for instituting proceedings"), but inclusion of such a provision may dissuade nonmeritorious challenges and would be valid in most states to that extent. See Restatement (Third) of Property (Wills and Other Donative Transfers) § 8.5 (2003). In re Estate of Shumway, 9 P.3d 1062 (Ariz. 2000), addressed the definition of "probable cause" and embraced Restatement (Second) of Property—Donative Transfers § 9.1 comment *j* (2003), referring to a "reasonable person, properly informed and advised . . . conclud[ing] that there is a substantial likelihood that the contest or attack will be successful." The court determined that, although good faith alone is not adequate, the circumstances surrounding drafting and execution of the will, the existence of a presumption of undue influence (in that case because the drafter was a beneficiary and stood in a confidential relation to the decedent), and an informed challenge to the decedent's capacity was adequate to constitute the required probable cause to preclude application of the in terrorem clause.

Tunstall v. Wells, 50 Cal. Rptr. 3d 468 (Cal. Ct. App. 2006), reflected the view at that time that in terrorem provisions may foster the favorable public policy of discouraging litigation. In *Tunstall* the unusual provision negated the bequests of *all* three members of a group if *any* of the three brought a contest action, which the court regarded as valid against the challenge that actions by one should not defeat the gifts to all. The court held that a decedent may wisely regard a group as acting in concert and appropriately generate pressure from other group members on any one who might seek to litigate. Such a clause also discourages the group from colluding to have one contest the will and be compensated by the others. Notable about California law at that time was that, in conjunction with the notion that no contest provisions were not disfavored, it also allowed "safe harbor" proceedings by which potential litigants could determine whether an action would trigger the forfeiture provision. The policy issue illustrated was that a forfeiture provision should not dissuade meritorious proceedings such as to construe ambiguous provisions, to review fiduciary performance, to enforce contracts relating to the terms of a will, or similar actions that should not trigger the provision. This process led to so many safe harbor proceedings that the California law subsequently was amended to remove its favor for in terrorem clauses. See Cal. Prob. Code § 21310 et seq.

Note that an in terrorem provision has no effect at all if the will is defeated, because the provision falls with the will itself. It also has no value if the contestant receives nothing under the will and therefore has nothing to lose if the provision is valid.

§ 3.1.2

less susceptible to challenge than a will.[30] To the extent a will is utilized, it also is wise to discuss the details of the will with the testator in the presence of witnesses, to establish to their satisfaction that the testator was mentally competent to execute the will and was disposing of the testator's property as provided in the will, free from undue influence.[31] It also might be desirable for the witnesses promptly to record their impressions of the discussion, to help substantiate their determination of the testator's mental competence and freedom from coercion. The testator also could execute a waiver of any patient or client privilege to permit an examining physician or the attorney to testify regarding capacity.[32]

---

[30] For reasons not altogether intuitive, it nevertheless appears demonstrably true that challenges to nonprobate dispositions are much less common and even less successful than will contests. Thus, for example, if a disposition seems likely to evoke a challenge to the testator's will, the estate planner might consider use of transfers such as a joint tenancy with the right of survivorship or a funded inter vivos trust, in each case creating the interest in the intended beneficiary while the testator is alive and giving more credibility to the notion that the testator was acting with the requisite knowledge, capacity, and free will to avoid challenge. Moreover, in most cases it is more difficult for a disappointed party to challenge a testator's transfers while the testator is alive and able to testify regarding the motives underlying a particular transfer. Indeed, the time to contest an inter vivos nonprobate transfer may expire before the testator does. See Savage v. Oliszczak, 928 N.E.2d 995 (Mass. Ct. App. 2010), involving an in terrorem clause in a trust that was triggered by contesting a will that poured over to the trust. The court held the provision to be invalid, saying that it would be "draconian" to involve a forfeiture clause in a separate document from the will being challenged. Note that there was no contest to the trust, and that the court exhibited the predictable reluctance to enforce in terrorem provisions of all stripes.

[31] Notwithstanding that this information normally is not required for valid execution. See §3.1.1 n.11. Genovese v. Genovese, 153 N.E.2d 662 (Mass. 1958), held that publication as a will was not necessary and that the witnesses need not form an opinion regarding the testator's mental capacity. The same court upheld validity of the will in O'Brien v. Wellesley College, 190 N.E.2d 879 (Mass. 1963), specifically referring to the fact that the attorney supervising execution suspected that a contest was likely and therefore read the entire will to the testator in the presence of the witnesses, asking after reading each provision whether it was as the testator desired.

[32] Atkinson, The Law of Wills § 100, at 535 (2d ed. 1953), reports that neither an attorney nor a physician privilege usually will be allowed, citing Wigmore on Evidence §§ 2314, 2315, and 2391. And those who represent the testator may be able to waive any privilege deemed to exist. See Lembke v. Unke, 171 N.W.2d

§3.1.2

In extreme cases in which contest is assured it might be desirable to make a recording of these discussions or a videotape of the execution ceremony. A videotape may not suffice as a will itself. But it may illustrate the testator's knowledge of the contents of the will and the decedent's competence to execute it, making the only issue regarding the tape the evidentiary question whether the videotape is admissible as evidence of capacity.[33] Several states permit premortem validation of a will,[34] which might be helpful if lack of capacity or other contest grounds

---

(Footnote Continued)

837 (N.D. 1969)). Nevertheless, the issue could be avoided with an inter vivos waiver of the privilege. Doherty v. Fairall, 413 F.2d 381 (D.C. Cir. 1969), held an attorney in contempt for refusing to produce prior wills of the testator in the context of a will contest, stating that communications between the decedent and the attorney regarding execution of a will or similar documents are not privileged.

[33] See Beyer, Videotaping the Will Execution Ceremony—Preventing Frustration of the Testator's Final Wishes, 15 St. Mary's L.J. 1 (1983); Beyer & Buckley, Videotape and the Probate Process: The Nexus Grows, 42 Okla. L. Rev. 43 (1989); Buckley & Buckley, Videotaping Wills: A New Frontier in Estate Planning, 11 Ohio N.U.L. Rev. 271 (1984); McGarry, Videotaped Wills: An Evidentiary Tool or a Written Will Substitute?, 77 Iowa L. Rev. 1187 (1992); Zickefoose, Videotaped Wills: Ready for Prime Time, 9 Prob. L.J. 139 (1989). Indiana Code § 29-1-5-3.2 provides that a videotape is admissible, but only as evidence of the proper execution of a will, the intent or mental state or capacity of the testator, and the authenticity of a will. See Buckley, The Case For The Videotaped Living Will, 2 Prob. & Prop. 30 (May/June 1988); Buckley, Indiana's New Videotaped Will Statute: Launching Probate Into the 21st Century, 20 Val. U.L. Rev. 83 (1985); Nash, A Videowill: Safe and Sure, 70 A.B.A.J. 87 (Oct. 1984). Videotape has fallen from favor generally and, although other media could serve the same purpose, calls for the use of these recordings also have withered.

[34] See Alaska Stat. § 13.12.530 et seq. (which, by § 13.12.540, appears to indicate that a nondomiciliary may petition for premortem validation, although it is not clear whether the determination will have any extra-jurisdictional impact on the probate of a will in any other jurisdiction); Ark. Code Ann. § 28-40-202; Nev. Rev. Stat. § 30.040; N.D. Cent. Code § 30.1-08.1-01; and Ohio Rev. Code Ann. § 2107.081. The concept is controversial, on which even the scholars are not in agreement. See Leopold & Byers, Ante-Mortem Probate: A Viable Alternative, 43 Ark. L. Rev. 131 (1990); Fink, Ante-Mortem Probate Revisited: Can an Idea Have a Life After Death?, 37 Ohio St. L.J. 264 (1976); Langbein, Living Probate: The Conservatorship Model, 77 Mich. L. Rev. 63 (1978); Alexander, The Conservatorship Model: A Modification, 77 Mich. L. Rev. 86 (1978); Alexander & Pearson, Alternative Models of Ante-Mortem Probate and Procedural Due Process Limita-

may be raised after the testator's death. And the extreme situation may dictate that the estate planner advise a medical examination of the testator prior to execution of the will.[35] Measures such as these ordinarily would signal doubt about the testator's capacity and therefore should be considered only in extraordinary circumstances.

A corresponding premortem cause of action for a contestant is the tort of intentional interference with the right to inherit, which may be litigated against a third party either before or after the testator's death.[36] There also is a less common cause of action for intentional interference with an inter vivos gift.[37] Yet another cause of action has been acknowl-

---

(Footnote Continued)

tions on Succession, 78 Mich. L. Rev. 89 (1979); Fellows, The Case Against Living Probate, 78 Mich. L. Rev. 1066 (1980).

[35] See Note, Psychiatric Assistance in the Determination of Testamentary Capacity, 66 Harv. L. Rev. 1116 (1953); Sharpe, Medication as a Threat to Testamentary Capacity, 35 N.C.L. Rev. 380 (1957).

[36] See generally Fried, The Disappointed Heir: Going Beyond the Probate Process to Remedy Wrongdoing or Rectify Mistake, 39 Real Prop., Prob. & Tr. J. 357 (2004); Johnson, Tortious Interference with Expectancy of Inheritance or Gift-Suggestions for Resort to the Tort, 39 Univ. Tol. L. Rev. 769 (2008); Klein, River Deep, Mountain High, Heir Disappointed: Tortious Interference with Expectation of Inheritance - A survey with Analysis of State Approaches in the Mountain States, 45 Idaho L. Rev. 1 (2008), A Disappointed Yankee in Connecticut (or Nearby) Probate Court: Tortious Interference With Expectations of Inheritance—A Survey With Analysis of State Approaches in the First, Second and Third Circuits, 66 U. Pitt. L. Rev. 235 (2004), The Disappointed Heir's Revenge, Southern Style: Tortious Interference with Expectation of Inheritance—A Survey with Analysis of State Approaches in the Fifth and Eleventh Circuits, 55 Baylor L. Rev. 79 (2003), and Revenge of the Disappointed Heir: Tortious Interference with Expectation of Inheritance—A Survey with Analysis of State Approaches in the Fourth Circuit, 104 W. Va. L. Rev. 259 (2002); Mignogna, On the Brink of Tortious Interference with Inheritance, 16 Prob. & Prop. 45 (March/April 2002); Moore, At the Frontier of Probate Litigation: Intentional Interference With the Right to Inherit, 7 Prob. & Prop. 6 (Nov./Dec. 1993); Note, Intentional Interference with Inheritance, 30 Real Prop., Prob. & Trust J. 325 (1995); Restatement (Second) of Torts § 774B (1979). With respect specifically to the postmortem action, see Annot., Action for tortious interference with bequest as precluded by will contest remedy, 18 A.L.R.5th 211 (1994).

[37] See In re Marshall, 275 B.R. 5 (Bankr. C.D. Cal. 2002), ultimately affirmed by 547 U.S. 293 (2006), which reversed 392 F.3d 1118 (9th Cir. 2004), which itself had reversed the lower court.

§3.1.2

edged to exist for intentional interference with economic relations, applicable in a will context.[38]

Courts split on whether to permit a tort action only to the extent probate relief would be inadequate (for example, to recover attorney fees or punitive damages).[39] Jurisdictions that require a plaintiff to proceed with any available will contest in probate typically preclude a subsequent tort action (as an invalid collateral attack) if the probate result is unfavorable.[40] In re Estate of Ellis[41] noted that Illinois would prevent a tort action if the plaintiff could have pursued a will contest and chose not to do so (or inappropriately allowed the contest action statute of limitation to expire). The *Ellis* court allowed the plaintiff to pursue the tort action because the defendant failed to notify the plaintiffs of the decedent's death or of the filing of the decedent's will for probate, which precluded a timely will contest action. A successful will contestant shares in the decedent's estate, whereas a successful tort action results in a judgment against the tortfeasor. For that reason the tort action was permissible in

---

[38] See Allen v. Hall, 974 P.2d 199 (Or. 1999).

[39] Or perhaps, as noted in Theriault v. Burnham, 2 A.3d 324 (Me. 2010), because the burden of proof may be higher in a will contest because the plaintiff seeks to defeat an entire will, whereas tortious interference seeks only monetary damages.

[40] See, e.g., Munn v. Briggs, 110 Cal. Rptr.3d 783 (Cal. Ct. App. 2010), and Morrison v. Morrison, 663 S.E.2d 714 (Ga. 2008); Wilson v. Fritschy, 55 P.3d 997 (N.M. Ct. App. 2002); Jackson v. Kelly, 44 S.W.3d 328 (Ark. 2001); Annot., Action for tortious interference with bequest as precluded by will contest remedy, 18 A.L.R.5th 211 (1994); Keith v. Dooley, 802 N.E.2d 54 (Ind. Ct. App. 2004), citing Minton v. Sackett, 671 N.E.2d 160 (Ind. Ct. App. 1996), held that a will contest precludes a tort action if the parties are identical and the outcomes of each essentially would be the same. And see Beren v. Ropfogel, 24 F.3d 1226 (10th Cir. 1994), rejecting the claim at the federal level as duplicative of the cause of action available under state law.

[41] 923 N.E.2d 237 (Ill. 2010), distinguished by Bjork v. O'Meara, 964 N.E.2d 694 (Ill. Ct. App. 2012) (although the tortious interference action involved a probate avoidance joint tenancy bank account, if the plaintiff had succeeded the property would have passed through probate and there was no reason why the plaintiff could not have brought the action within the accelerated contest action statute of limitation, which therefore was deemed to invalidate the action as untimely). See also DeWitt v. Duce, 408 So. 2d 216 (Fla. 1981); Schilling v. Herrara, 952 So. 2d 1231 (Fla. Ct. App. 2007); McMullin v. Borgers, 761 S.W.2d 718 (Mo. Ct. App. 1988).

Ellis, even though the contest action statute of limitation had expired. A short statute of limitation on challenges against a will is designed to accelerate distribution of probate estates. This need not preclude a tort action such as *Ellis*, because any recovery against the tortfeasor does not delay estate administration.

§3.1.3 Revocation

A will known to be in the testator's possession but that cannot be found at death is presumed to have been destroyed by the testator with the intention to revoke it.[42] As a result some drafters do not recommend that the testator keep the original. Others advise the testator to keep the executed original will in a safe place.[43] If the testator wishes to have a copy for easy reference, the better approach is to conform a photocopy of

---

[42] Atkinson, The Law of Wills §86, at 442 (2d ed. 1953); McGovern, Kurtz, & English, Wills, Trusts & Estates §5.2 (4th ed. 2010).

[43] The testator's safe deposit box may be appropriate if access normally is allowed immediately after the testator's death to locate a will. But an alternative may be preferable if state law restricts access to a box until the contents can be inventoried in the presence of a state revenue representative. For example, some jurisdictions allow deposit of the will with the local probate court, and many corporate fiduciaries will provide safe storage for any will that appoints the corporation as fiduciary under the will. Many estate planners provide safekeeping as a service to their clients, although doing so may expose the estate planner to liability if the will is lost or destroyed or otherwise is not produced after the testator dies. It also may entail more than a minor expense for fireproof and secure storage in an office or warehouse as the estate planner's will file grows.

In addition, State v. Gulbankian, 196 N.W.2d 733 (Wis. 1972), expressed disapproval of the practice of an attorney retaining original wills, although *Gulbankian* was an unusual case, the evidence indicating that the attorneys involved (siblings) caused a significant percentage of their clients to name one or the other or both of them as attorney for the estate or as a personal representative, or both, giving the impression of overreaching and solicitation.

Attorney retention of original wills is criticized by some on ethical grounds, as making it harder for a client to change lawyers during life and for the testator's survivors to hire another attorney after the testator's death. See ABA Standing Comm. on Ethics and Prof. Resp. Inf. Op. 981 (1967); Tex. Prof. Ethics Comm. Op. 280 (1964); Johnston, An Ethical Analysis of Common Estate Planning Practices—Is Good Business Bad Ethics?, 45 Ohio St. L.J. 57, 126 (1984). Nevertheless, Penn. Bar Ass'n Comm. on Legal Ethics and Prof. Resp. Formal Op. 2001-300 concludes that the practice is not unethical if the client affirmatively requests the attorney to provide custody and the attorney informs the client in

the will[44] rather than leaving the original in the testator's possession. The testator should be warned, however, that physical acts to anything other than the executed original will are of no effect[45] and that any desired alterations should be manifested by a codicil or, if necessary (and if respected by local law), by physical acts performed to the executed original.

Execution of duplicate original copies of a will seldom is a good idea. The notion that destruction or loss of one executed copy will permit probate of the other is contrary to the general rule, which is that the testator's acts performed to one executed original copy with the requisite intent are deemed an alteration or revocation of all the executed original copies.[46] The presumption that the testator destroyed the will with the intention to revoke it arises if all copies *in the testator's possession* cannot be found, regardless of whether another executed, unaltered, original copy is in the possession of someone other than the testator.[47] Thus,

(Footnote Continued)

writing that the client may retrieve the document at any time and that the personal representative is under no obligation to hire the attorney postmortem.

[44] Conforming a copy means that all material (including signatures and addresses of witnesses) written onto the originally executed will are typewritten onto a photocopy. This guarantees legibility and shows the totality of the executed will, without creating the impression that the copy is an original and minimizing the risk of an unintentional revocation of the copy in the mistaken belief that it is the original.

[45] See, e.g., In re Estate of Tolin, 622 So. 2d 988 (Fla. 1993) (destruction of photocopy ineffective to revoke original held by testator's attorney).

[46] See Annot., Sufficiency of evidence of nonrevocation of lost will not shown to have been inaccessible to testator—modern cases, 70 A.L.R.4th 323 (1989); Annot., Destruction or cancellation of one copy of will executed in duplicate, as revocation of other copy, 17 A.L.R.2d 805 (1951).

[47] Compare In re Estate of Millsap, 371 N.E.2d 185 (Ill. 1977) (general rule applied; copy of will not admissible if decedent's copy could not be found), with Etgen v. Corboy, 337 S.E.2d 286 (Va. 1985) (decedent possessed two duplicate originals, one that was found in a safety deposit box with no changes and another found with the testator's personal possessions and on which various interlineations had been made; the court ruled that neither document was presumptively the true will and remanded for proof of which represented the decedent's intent); and see In re Estate of Shaw, 572 P.2d 229 (Okla. 1977) (the only executed original copy in decedent's possession could not be found; the court improperly applied the rule illustrated by *Etgen*, which applies only if fewer than all copies in the testator's possession were destroyed or altered).

§3.1.3

having another executed original after the testator's death is no guarantee that the will was not revoked or altered by the testator and only raises the possibility of litigation if less than all executed original copies are found or if they are found in differing conditions after the testator's death.[48]

Most wills expressly revoke all prior wills and codicils, which is a wise clarification of the testator's intent. The law of most states only presumes that a will purporting to dispose of the testator's entire estate revokes all prior wills by inconsistency.[49] Contrariwise, many codicils purport to affirm and republish the wills they amend, along with any prior codicils to the will that are not inconsistent with the latest codicil. This approach can raise questions of intent.[50] For example, Wells Fargo Bank v. United States[51] involved a §2055(e)(3) reformation of a charitable trust. The issue was whether the decedent's will was a pre-1979 document. The will was executed in 1971 but a 1982 codicil purported to republish the will as amended by that codicil. Looking to state law, the court held that a codicil republishes a will only if it does not defeat the testator's "most probable intention." In this case regarding the will as a 1982 document would defeat intent because it would preclude reliance on the reformation procedure otherwise available only if the will was regarded as a pre-1979 document. The court accordingly held that the

---

[48] The danger of executing duplicate original wills is illustrated by In re Succession of Talbot, 516 So. 2d 431 (La. Ct. App. 1987), rev'd, 530 So. 2d 1132 (La. 1988), in which duplicate wills were executed and the testator destroyed the copy in the possession of the estate planner but did not destroy the copy in the testator's possession. The appellate court's conclusion that the will was not effectively revoked ultimately was reversed, but only after extensive litigation.

[49] See UPC §2-507(c); Atkinson, The Law of Wills §87 (2d ed. 1953).

[50] In re Estate of Velie, 183 N.E.2d 515 (Ill. 1962), held that, absent an explicit manifestation of intent, a codicil revokes previous codicils only to the extent inconsistent with them. Thus, although the codicil purported to republish the will, which purported to revoke all preexisting codicils, the codicil was not regarded as a revocation of a preexisting codicil to the will. In re Estate of Heilig, 506 P.2d 1147 (Kan. 1973), involved a 1969 codicil that expressly reaffirmed a 1966 codicil to the will but failed to mention a 1967 codicil to the same will. The court held that the 1967 codicil was not revoked by implication because it was not inconsistent with the 1969 codicil.

[51] 91-1 U.S. Tax Cas. (CCH) ¶ 60,067 (C.D. Cal. 1991), aff'd, 93-2 U.S. Tax Cas. (CCH) ¶ 60,144 (9th Cir. 1993).

§3.1.3

solely by subsequent instrument.[58] Indeed, because intent may be an issue even with a total revocation by some physical acts,[59] anything short of a total destruction or an express revocation by subsequent instrument may prove to be problematic.[60]

---

[58] See, e.g., In re Estate of Funk, 654 N.E.2d 1174 (Ind. Ct. App. 1995) (mutilation of will was deemed to have been done by testator but nevertheless was ineffective to work partial revocation because it did not affect essential elements of the will such as the signature and because Indiana does not recognize partial revocations by mutilation); In re Estate of Minsinger, 364 P.2d 615 (Or. 1961), which held that a partially obliterated will should be probated in its original form because partial revocation by physical act was not recognized under applicable Oregon law.

[59] E.g., in Payne v. Payne, 100 S.E.2d 450 (Ga. 1957), the testator threw the will into a fire with the intent to destroy and thereby revoke it, but the testator's spouse retrieved the will before it was burned. The court held that the will was not revoked because local law required that the intent to revoke be accompanied by actual destruction of the will. And Gannon v. MacDonald, 279 N.E.2d 668 (Mass. 1972), involved the presumption that, if a will known to exist cannot be found after death, it is presumed destroyed by the testator with the intent to revoke it. If the presumption is overcome, the will may be administered as a lost will, the contents of which being proved by secondary evidence such as an unexecuted or other copy of the will.

[60] Note that UPC § 2-507 does not allow revocation by just any subsequent instrument. To be a valid revocation, the subsequent instrument must be a will. See Brown v. Brown, 21 So. 3d 1 (Ala. Ct. Civ. App. 2009), and In re Estate of Gushwa, 197 P.3d 1 (N.M. 2008), both holding that an instrument that was intended to be effective immediately (and therefore was not testamentary) or that was not itself intended to be a will could not revoke a prior will, even if executed with the requisite formalities of a will. Indeed, *Brown* denied revocation because the subsequent instrument declared that it was "my intention and desire to die without a will," meaning that the instrument of revocation itself was not meant to be a will. In *Gushwa* the testator's written intent to revoke was on a photocopy of the will and not on the will itself, meaning that it could not constitute a valid revocation by physical act. And, because that writing was not meant to be a subsequent will, it also failed as a revocation by subsequent instrument. If the same writing had appeared on the face of the original will it would have been effective as a revocation by physical act. But it failed, even though it was executed with all the formalities to make it a valid will. All of which makes the requirement that the subsequent document be a will seems overly formalistic. Particularly given that UPC § 2-503 harmless error or substantial compliance doctrine seeks to effect a testator's intent, and also given that a negative will is allowed by UPC § 2-101(b)—being a document that seeks only to cause property to pass by intestacy, which seems quite similar to a document

A will also may be revoked in whole or in part by operation of law, most typically by the testator's divorce subsequent to execution. Under some traditional statutes it is common to find that any provision for the former spouse is treated as revoked. Even less refined statutes treat divorce as revoking the entire will.[61] More precise provisions treat the former spouse as having predeceased the testator or as having disclaimed all benefits under the will.[62]

The most current statutes also purport to apply to documents other than wills, which eliminates disputes that can produce convoluted rules

---

(Footnote Continued)

that does not intend to dispose of property as a will but only intends to revoke a prior will and allow property to pass by intestacy. Regarding the notion in *Gushwa* that the subsequent document was meant to be effective immediately and therefore was not testamentary, see In re Estate of Doepper, 2009 WL 491588 (unpub. Ariz. Ct. App. 2009), which rejected this notion saying that it would be true of every document that revokes a prior will. It also is reminiscent of the revival issue addressed by UPC § 2-509 as discussed at text accompanying note 55.

[61] See, e.g., Conn. Gen. Stat. § 45a-257.

[62] See the 1990 versions of UPC § § 2-802 and 2-804, which are among the most refined current provisions. Disclaimer treatment rather than regarding the spouse as predeceased may diminish the impact of the statute on other provisions of the document if the decedent anticipated a postmortem disclaimer (e.g., for marital deduction planning) but provided alternate dispositions that apply only if the spouse does not survive and did not anticipate that the spouse might be alive but treated as predeceased. Compare Bloom v. Selfon, 555 A.2d 75 (Pa. 1989); In re Estate of Graef, 368 N.W.2d 633 (Wis. 1985) (both involving gifts over to others if spouses predeceased the testator, both held to apply because divorce had the effect of revoking any provision in favor of a former spouse, which caused the former spouse to be treated as predeceased), with In re Estate of Nash, 220 S.W.3d 914 (Tex. 2007) (notwithstanding a state law requiring a will to "be read as if the former spouse failed to survive the testator," an alternative bequest to former spouse's child if spouse predeceased failed because the spouse did not in fact die first; the issue would have been avoided if the UPC provision discussed in § 3.1.3 n.74 had been the law).

As shown, potentially difficult interpretative questions arise if a gift over anticipates actual death of the former spouse. For example, a distribution when no child of the spouse is under the age of 30 might reflect the testator's affection for the spouse's children by a former marriage, with no expectation that the testator and the spouse might divorce and thereafter the spouse might procreate additional children who would be included in the class and delay distribution.

§ 3.1.3

to reach equitable results.[63] Revocable inter vivos trusts, retirement benefit and life insurance beneficiary designations,[64] joint tenancies, and other nonprobate assets all should be subject to the same treatment as

---

[63] For a notable example, see Miller v. First Nat'l Bank & Trust Co., 637 P.2d 75 (Okla. 1981) (pourover will improperly deemed to incorporate insurance trust by reference to preclude former spouse from receiving insurance proceeds payable to the trust after divorce). See also Lynn, Will Substitutes, Divorce, and Statutory Assistance for the Unthinking Donor, 71 Marq. L. Rev. 1 (1987).

[64] Manhattan Life Insurance Co. v. Evanek, 762 F.2d 319 (3d Cir. 1985), held that a surviving former spouse who was named as beneficiary under a life insurance policy was entitled to the proceeds, notwithstanding that a divorce decree incorporated a separation agreement that purported to terminate all claims and property interests of the former spouse in the insured's estate. State law provided that divorce revokes all provisions in a conveyance that were revocable by the conveyor at the time of death and that were to take effect at or after death in favor of or relating to a former spouse. Nevertheless, the court held that the former spouse was entitled to the insurance proceeds because the statute was not applicable to the revocable beneficiary designation of a life insurance policy that was not a testamentary "conveyance" within the meaning of the statute. The separation agreement was deemed too general to apply to insurance proceeds. Similarly, In re Estate of Williams, 2003 WL 1961805 (Tenn. Ct. App.), involved a former spouse named as an annuity beneficiary by the decedent, who drowned 54 days after their divorce and without changing that designation. Worse, the tax payment provision in the decedent's will directed payment of all taxes from the residue of the estate and the court rejected the estate's argument that state law treating all provisions in the will in favor of the former spouse should be applied to disregard that tax apportionment direction. That law referred to "any disposition . . . to the former spouse" and was deemed not to override the tax payment provision, which thus superseded an apportionment result that would have imposed taxes on the former spouse.

The 1990 version of UPC §2-804(b)(1) would have revoked that beneficiary designation. But even the UPC should be studied carefully to determine its limitations. For example, although not on point (because it involved a subsequent marriage), but nevertheless informative (because it involved a prenuptial agreement that limited the surviving spouse's entitlements), Perdue v. American Express Travel Related Services, 609 N.E.2d 1141 (Ind. Ct. App. 1993), held that life insurance payable to S (because D rented a car using an American Express card) was payable to S notwithstanding contrary provisions contained in a prenuptial agreement regarding all life insurance on D's life. UPC §2-804 would not provide otherwise because the policy in this case would not meet the definition of a "governing instrument" (it could not be changed by, nor was it executed by, D). See UPC §§2-804(a)(4) and (a)(6).

that under a will in the event of a divorce.[65] This treatment is not universally favorable, however, unless the estate planner properly antici- pates it. For example, Tennessee law applicable in TAM 9127005 pro- vided that a divorce or annulment that occurs after the execution of a revocable inter vivos trust revokes any provision in the trust in favor of the former spouse and any nomination of the former spouse as trustee, unless the trust was executed as a property settlement related to a divorce or annulment or the trust agreement expressly provides other- wise. Because it did not override the state statute, an inter vivos QTIP trust was deemed not deductible because the statute made the spouse's interest terminable.[66]

---

[65] Ohio Rev. Code Ann. § 1339.62 provides that, on divorce, revocable trust provisions conferring a power of appointment on the settlor's former spouse, or nominating the former spouse as trustee or trust advisor, are revoked and the settlor's former spouse is deemed to have predeceased the settlor. The 1990 version of UPC § 2-804(b)(1) would have the same effect with respect to powers of appointment, fiduciary nominations, or any other provision in a trust.

Under 15 Okla. Stat. § 178 all provisions in favor of a spouse made in death benefit contracts (which include life insurance contracts, annuities, retirement arrangements, compensation agreements, and inter vivos trusts) are revoked by a divorce or annulment. Provisions in favor of a former spouse are applied as though the former spouse predeceased the settlor or the party to the contract with the power to designate the beneficiary. These provisions reversed Pepper v. Peacher, 742 P.2d 21 (Okla. 1987), which allowed a former spouse to receive teachers' retirement fund benefits under a beneficiary designation not altered after divorce or remarriage of the decedent. Whirlpool Corp. v. Ritter, 929 F.2d 1318 (8th Cir. 1991), deemed the Oklahoma statute to be invalid as a violation of the contract clause of the United States Constitution to the extent the statute had a retrospective application to insurance in existence when the statute was enacted, notwithstanding the decedent was not divorced until after that date. In defense of the statute, its objective, and the similar result reached in the 1990 version of the UPC, the Joint Editorial Board of the UPC issued a resolution strongly disagreeing with the opinion in *Whirlpool,* as does Buchholz v. Storsve, 740 N.W.2d 107 (S.D. 2007), and In re Estate of DeWitt, 54 P.3d 849 (Colo. 2002); see also Lewis v. Lewis, 693 S.W.2d 672 (Tex. Civ. App. 1985), and Bersch v. Van Kleech, 334 N.W.2d 114 (Wis. 1983) (all involving life insurance). In re Estate of Dobert, 963 P.2d 327 (Ariz. Ct. App. 1998), involved virtually identical facts to *Ritter,* including the apparent slaying by the plaintiff and timing of enactment before the divorce but after acquisition of the policy and failure to change the beneficiary designation, but again the court upheld the state statute.

[66] The 1990 version of UPC § 2-804(b)(1) would have the same effect as the Tennessee statute.

§ 3.1.3

In addition, the reach of such statutes may be subject to some restrictions. For example, retroactive application of Ohio Rev. Code Ann. § 1339.63 to contracts of insurance existing before the statute's effective date was declared unconstitutional by Aetna Life Ins. Co. v. Schilling[67] as a violation of the Ohio Constitution,[68] which prohibits retroactive legislation or laws that impair the obligations of existing contracts. The insurance beneficiary designation provision in the 1990 version of § 2-804 of the UPC is virtually identical to the Ohio statute. Further, Egelhoff v. Egelhoff[69] held that any state laws like UPC § 2-804 that could impact qualified retirement benefits and employer sponsored life insurance are pre-empted by ERISA. The Court therefore concluded that divorce did *not* cause the former spouse to be treated as predeceased for purposes of taking under the beneficiary designation.

UPC § 2-804(h)(2) may be valid, however, notwithstanding *Egelhoff*.[70] It would permit the former spouse to take as the designated beneficiary but impose a constructive trust on the former spouse in favor of those beneficiaries who would take if the state law revocation provision was allowed to apply. It may be that any post-payment cause of action given to one set of individuals against the designated beneficiary is not inconsistent with the stated objectives of the ERISA pre-emption statute (to provide national uniformity and ease of administration).

Kennedy v. DuPont Sav. & Invest. Plan[71] supports the notion that the plan administrator may rely on the beneficiary designation and disregard any waiver or allocation of property rights in a divorce decree

---

[67] 616 N.E.2d 893 (Ohio 1993) (decedent died 20 days after effective date of statute and 13 years after divorce from spouse who was named before the divorce as beneficiary of employer funded group term life insurance).

[68] § 28 of Art. II.

[69] 532 U.S. 141 (2001), rev'g In re Estate of Egelhoff, 989 P.2d 80 (Wash. 1999). To the same effect involving an IRA, see Luszcz v. Lavoie, 787 So. 2d 245 (Fla. Dist. Ct. App. 2001). To the same effect, involving a life insurance beneficiary designation (which was deemed to be subject to ERISA because the insurance was part of an employee group benefit plan) see In re Estate of Sauers, 32 A.3d 1241 (Pa. 2011), rev'g 971 A.2d 1265 (Sup. Ct. Pa. 2009).

[70] As suggested in Gary, State Statute Does Not Revoke Beneficiary Designation After Divorce, 28 Estate Planning 376 (2001).

[71] 555 U.S. 285 (2009).

that is not a QDRO.[72] And the court's footnote 10 *suggests* (but expressly does not address) the second proposition, which Rowley v. Rowley[73] essentially held, that a surviving former spouse's designation as benefici- ary would be honored by the plan administrator (who need not look

---

[72] Stating expressly that plan administrators should not be required to inquire beyond plan documents and records to determine whether other documents, agreements, or orders alter the proper distribution of plan benefits.

[73] 677 N.W.2d 889 (Mich. Ct. App. 2004). Cf. Estate of Kensinger v. URL Pharma Inc., 674 F.3d 131 (3d Cir. 2012), and cases cited therein (holding that the plan administrator could rely on the beneficiary designation but that the decedent's estate could sue the former spouse to enforce the spouse's waiver of plan benefits as part of a divorce property settlement).

Contra is In re Estate of Sauers, 32 A.3d 1241 (Pa. 2011), rev'g 971 A.2d 1265 (Sup. Ct. Pa. 2009), which may have gone farther than the court intended (and did so with no discussion of the underlying issue) by holding that the lower court erred in "ordering Ex Spouse, the named and unmodified primary beneficiary of the ERISA-governed insurance policy, to surrender all entitlement and interests in the proceeds of that policy." The court could have held that the former spouse would take those proceeds as dictated by the beneficiary designation, which the plan administrator would honor, and then be compelled under state law to hold those proceeds and eventually remit them to the proper state law beneficiaries. Coming as the penultimate sentence of a lengthy decision that did not mention this constructive trust issue, the result may not be a rejection of it so much as a failure to consider this refinement. *Egelhoff* figures prominently in the *Sauer* decision but *Kennedy* is never mentioned.

Unfortunately, the result in Maretta v. Hillman, 722 S.E.2d 32 (Va. 2012), cannot be dismissed so easily, notwithstanding a substantial dissent and the court's recognition that its decision is contrary to the substantial weight of authority in other states. Declaring invalid a Virginia statute very much like UPC §2-804(h)(2), the court held that FEGLI (the Federal Employees' Group Life Insurance) was meant by Congress to belong to the designated beneficiary and that the provisions of state law that imposed a constructive trust therefore violated this Congressional intent and were invalid. The dissent noted that FEGLI lacked an anti-alienation provision and therefore was distinguishable from cases on which the court relied, and made it more like ERISA and, therefore, that *Egelhof* should apply and permit operation of the state law constructive trust provision. The majority relied on Wissner v. Wissner, 338 U.S. 655 (1950), and Ridgway v. Ridgway, 454 U.S. 46 (1981), both long predating the statutes in question, and both distinguishable due to the existence of anti-alienation provi- sions in those situations. See Hardy v. Hardy, 963 N.E.2d 470 (Ind. 2012), which is in accord with the dissent in *Maretta* and is consistent with the substantial weight of authority. Clearly the proper resolution of these differences is yet to be determined.

§3.1.3

beyond the beneficiary designation, which is consistent with the ERISA pre-emption doctrine that is designed to ease administration of the plan) but that the former spouse's waiver of rights pursuant to a divorce property settlement was sufficient to permit the decedent's estate or its beneficiaries to compel distribution of the proceeds from the former spouse as the designated beneficiary to those rightful takers.

Finally, a few modern statutes also address the effect of divorce on provisions for relatives of the former spouse,[74] but elsewhere this issue should be addressed in the document and at the time of a divorce or annulment. Because state laws vary, no estate planner should rely on the effect of any of these statutes if the proper result is for the prior will not to apply, which calls for affirmative planning even to die intestate, if that is desired.[75]

---

[74] In Clymer v. Mayo, 473 N.E.2d 1084 (Mass. 1985), the decedent's inter vivos trust provided for a former spouse. Although it was not expressly subject to the state law revoking testamentary provisions for a former spouse, it was deemed to be subject to the legislative intent underlying that statute, the court stating that the law imputes an intent to revoke provisions favoring a former spouse that should apply to a trust funded by a pourover will. But provisions under the trust for the former spouse's nieces and nephews were not deemed revoked by the divorce. The 1990 version of UPC §2-804(b)(1) would have revoked those provisions as well, which the facts in *Clymer* indicate might not have been the decedent's intent.

[75] See, e.g., Hinders v. Hinders, 828 So. 2d 1235 (Miss. 2002), refusing to deem divorce and a property settlement as a revocation in the absence of any state statute, and In re Estate of Garver, 343 A.2d 817 (N.J. 1975), in which the decedent obtained a divorce while a resident of a state in which divorce revokes the will, but moved to and died a resident of a state in which divorce does not automatically revoke the will. Although the court held the will was revoked when the divorce was granted by the law of the first state, this conflict of laws result was based in part on various special facts indicating the decedent's intent. A different result might obtain under different circumstances. For example, Collela v. Coutu, 603 S.E.2d 296 (Ga. 2004), involved a divorce when state law provided for total revocation of a will, but death when the law only provided that the former spouse shall be treated as predeceased, and the court applied the latter result. This conclusion would have frustrated any intent of the decedent to die intestate.

Some state statutes also revoke a will by operation of law if the testator marries after executing the will, unless the will was executed in contemplation of that marriage.[76] In some states marriage alone does not

[76] See, e.g., Ga. Code Ann. § 53-4-48; Mass. Gen. L. ch. 191, § 9; Annot., Sufficiency of provision for, or reference to, prospective spouse to avoid lapse or revocation of will by subsequent marriage, 38 A.L.R.4th 117 (1985).

Barlow v. Barlow, 124 N.E. 285 (Mass. 1919), held that a will that benefited the individual the testator subsequently married nevertheless was revoked by that marriage because the will did not clearly indicate that it was made in contemplation of the marriage. But D'Ambra v. Cole, 572 A.2d 268 (R.I. 1990), held that a will providing for the testator's future spouse was not revoked by their subsequent marriage because, notwithstanding the absence of an express statement to that effect, the testator executed the will in contemplation of the marriage. In re Estate of Keeven, 716 P.2d 1224 (Idaho 1986), involved D, who lived with S prior to their marriage and, during that cohabitation, made a will that included (the not-yet-spouse) S as a beneficiary (referred to as a "dear friend"). Because D did not change the will after they were married, S (the "friend") claimed a statutory share as an omitted spouse, which the court rejected. Kirksey v. Teachers' Retirement System, 302 S.E.2d 101 (Ga. 1983), involved a decedent who designated a parent as beneficiary of retirement system survivor benefits and later married but never changed the beneficiary designation. Because that beneficiary designation was not a will it was not revoked by the subsequent marriage. In a slightly similar vein, In re Estate of Prestie, 138 P.3d 520 (Nev. 2006) (involving spouses who married, divorced, and remarried each other, in which D's post-divorce will poured over to a trust and the trust was amended in contemplation of the remarriage to provide a limited benefit for S), concluded that an amendment to an inter vivos trust did not alter the pretermitted spouse result under a will that poured over to that trust, stating that the statute clearly required an indication of intent in the will to alter S's statutory protection.

In re Estate of Klein, 239 A.2d 464 (Pa. 1968), involved a will executed before D entered into a prenuptial agreement with D's prospective spouse. When D died S sought both the benefits under that will and those guaranteed in the prenuptial agreement, to which the court held that, because the will predated the agreement, the inference was that the agreement limited S's entitlement and the will provision should be charged against that amount. If the will had been executed after the prenuptial agreement, however, the court expressed the view that S could take under both unless the will expressed that it was in lieu of the rights created by the prenuptial agreement. Similarly, In re Estate of Dennis, 714 S.W.2d 661 (Mo. Ct. App. 1986), held that a prenuptial agreement constituted a sufficient indication that omission was intentional from a will executed prior to marriage to S.

In Nelson v. United States, 89-2 U.S. Tax Cas. (CCH) ¶ 13,823 (D. N.D. 1989), S was omitted entirely as a beneficiary under D's will, which was executed

§ 3.1.3

revoke a will but marriage plus birth of a child will.[77] And in a few jurisdictions the birth or adoption of a child may revoke a will as well.[78]

§3.2 COMMON WILL PROVISIONS

Although they are not unique to wills, the following discussion focuses on certain provisions that address dispositive or other substantive matters (rather than procedure or estate administration) and that commonly appear in wills for large and small estates alike. Other dispositive provisions, such as marital or charitable bequests and provisions relating to the payment of taxes or trusts for children, may be found in documents such as living trusts as well as in wills and are discussed elsewhere in this treatise.

§3.2.1 *Disposition of Decedent's Body*

Normally a will is not the appropriate document in which to provide directions regarding a funeral or disposition of the testator's body, including organ donation for medical research or transplant purposes. These arrangements normally are made before a will is found, produced for probate, or even read. Particularly with respect to organ donations, some other alternative must be utilized, usually as authorized under the version of the Uniform Anatomical Gifts Act that has been adopted by the state to provide simplified procedures for making the decedent's

---

(Footnote Continued)

prior to their marriage and gave all of D's property to nieces and nephews. A few months after D died the nieces and nephews entered into an agreement by which S was to receive 50% of the estate before taxes, and the nieces and nephews would receive the balance. Because S was entitled to the entire estate as an omitted spouse, the government successfully asserted that S made a gift subject to gift tax by agreeing with the nieces and nephews that they take a share of the estate. In re Estate of Stewart, 444 P.2d 337 (Cal. 1968), held, however, that the omitted spouse's entitlement was subject to D's contractual obligation to leave property to designated beneficiaries and that the property bequeathed subject to that enforceable agreement was not part of the estate against which S's entitlement was determined.

[77] See, e.g., Md. Code Ann. Est. & Trusts § 4-105(3).

[78] See Ga. Code Ann. § 53-4-48; Annot., Adoption of child as revoking will, 24 A.L.R.2d 1085 (1952); Annot., Statutory revocation of will by subsequent birth or adoption of child, 97 A.L.R.2d 1044 (1964).

body available promptly after death.[1] Although not a traditional part of the estate planning process, many estate planners provide the requisite information regarding organ donation as a service to their clients and to society.[2]

Directions regarding a funeral or memorial service also are best left with those individuals who will be responsible for making these arrangements after the decedent's death, rather than in a will. In some cases the client has made provisions before death and may own a preneed funeral contract to cover the cost. These arrangements should be reviewed and the relevant documents made available to the responsible individuals.[3] If the decedent did not leave effective instructions,[4] state law must be consulted to determine who is responsible for making these decisions. Normally a surviving spouse, if any, or next of kin is designated.

§3.2.2 Designation of Family

Many wills contain a provision that lists the names and birthdates (and sometimes even the Social Security numbers) of the testator's family (spouse, children, and occasionally grandchildren), as a discrete method of addressing several potentially troublesome issues. For example, in some states a child who is not specifically mentioned in a will is entitled to take a pretermitted heir share of the testator's estate, equal to what the child would have received in intestacy.[5] Designation in this list should preclude that entitlement if the intent either is to disinherit the child or, more likely, to include the child in a disposition to "children" as a class, without individual specification. Many careful drafters provide somewhere in the document that terms such as "child" include any born

---

[1] **§3.2** Every state has adopted one of the three versions of the Act. See 8A U.L.A. 34, 147, and 155 (Supp. 2010).

[2] For more information about the need for organ donations for lifesaving purposes and the procedures and lack of cost to the donor or the donor's family, or to obtain forms for organ donor execution, contact The Living Bank, P.O. Box 6725, Houston, TX 77265, or call (800) 528-2971.

[3] See §5.11.11 regarding the income tax consequences of preneed funeral contracts.

[4] Or, in the rare case in which the decedent's wishes are not enforceable, such as if the decedent directed that valuables be destroyed or interred or otherwise constitutes a request that violates public policy.

[5] See §3.5 for the discussion of pretermitted heirs.

§3.2.2

or adopted after execution of the will to address the pretermitted heir issue.

This provision also is an effective opportunity to designate the testator's intent regarding whether adopted individuals should be treated as natural born. For example, the testator may not approve of a child's adoption of step-children (from the prior marriage of the child's spouse), which could be addressed by this provision specifying that only natural born grandchildren will be regarded as descendants of the testator.

More importantly in some cases, inclusion of individuals "as if" they were members of a class such as children or descendants increasingly is important, as for example in the case of a natural born grandchild who was adopted by a step-parent and therefore no longer is regarded under local law as a descendant of the natural grandparents.[6] This provision also presents an effective opportunity under local law to disinherit heirs (such as nonmarital children) that the testator does not wish to benefit or acknowledge, relying instead on a clause that specifies that the list of family members is complete and that the testator intentionally does not provide for any other individual.

Finally, some documents use this provision to define terms such as "spouse" (for example, the person to whom the testator is married and from whom the testator is not legally separated or in the process of divorcing or being divorced at the date of death) or to establish a drafting short form designation for individuals to whom frequent reference is made in the document.

§3.2.3 *Payment of Debts, Expenses, and Taxes*

Many wills "speak" chronologically, in the sense that they direct events and distributions in the order in which they are to occur. Thus, for example, one of the earliest provisions found in most wills is a direction regarding payment of the testator's debts, expenses, and taxes. The panoply of issues attendant to this topic is so extensive that it is discussed separately in §3.3.

Even estates that are not large enough to generate a federal wealth transfer tax payment obligation may have outstanding income taxes that must be paid as a claim against the decedent's estate, and may incur

---

[6] See §2.2.4.1 for the discussion of laws regarding step-parent adoptions.

§3.2.3

income tax liabilities during the course of administration, either of which could be significant.[7] Various other state, local, or even foreign death taxes,[8] debts, expenses of a funeral, and costs to administer the estate also should be the subject of this provision.

If it is adequate in size and liquid in nature, the "normal" source for payment of these items is the residue of the decedent's estate,[9] particularly if other specific items are meant to be distributed without reduction by these obligations. But in some cases it is sensible to consider the equity of this allocation and whether there are other logical sources of funds, particularly to pay administration expenses such as tax return preparation costs that may relate to various assets includible in the federal gross estate but not includible in the testator's probate or residuary estate. For example, a substantial portion of the testator's estate may be in a funded inter vivos or QTIP trust and a substantial portion of the estate's administration expenses will be tax preparation fees generated with respect to that property. If so, liquidity and equity considerations may dictate that the trust provide for payment of all or a fair portion of

---

[7] Introduced in 1990 was H.R. 5501, a bill that would have adopted an Appreciation Estate Tax that essentially treats death as a gain or loss realization event for federal income tax purposes. Although this proposal was not adopted, it has been considered on numerous occasions and could become part of the estate planning landscape, particularly in light of the fact that Canada already has an appreciation estate tax, showing that it is a functional tax system.

Also worthy of consideration in a well crafted tax payment provision are the estimated income tax payment obligation (effectively imposed by § 6654(l) after the estate's second tax year) and the § 55 AMT liability that may be incurred by an estate.

[8] To the extent exceeding the § 2014 credit and to the extent not the subject of a treaty that protects against imposition of the foreign death tax.

[9] UPC § 6-102(b) is unusual as a state law that burdens nonprobate property with debts or other claims, but it does so only "to the extent the estate is insufficient to satisfy . . . claims and allowances," and it is consistent with the notion that primary liability normally is on the probate estate and, within it, on the residuary estate. Within the residue it also is normal to pay these items using principal, although in some circumstances the authority to pay using income earned during administration of the estate may prove desirable. See § § 3.3.7.3; 13.3.6.

§ 3.2.3

these items.[10] The same issue could arise involving jointly held property,[11] although it is not likely to arise with respect to all nonprobate property, examples being life insurance and retirement benefits in most cases.

Regardless of the source of funds designated for payment, the will also needs to consider the personal representative's potential liability to disaffected beneficiaries of probate and nonprobate property alike, attributable to the payment of debts, expenses, and taxes. For example, probate estate beneficiaries may have a cause of action against a personal representative who fails to assert a right of reimbursement against a taker of nonprobate property. Alternatively, nonprobate beneficiaries who bear a portion of the estate's tax liability under an apportionment or reimbursement regime have a legitimate interest in actions taken by the personal representative that affect their tax payment liability.[12] Neither

---

[10] Cf. In re Estate of Klarner, 113 P.3d 150 (2005), imposing both state and federal estate taxes on a QTIP marital trust, but not attorney fees incurred in litigation.

[11] See, e.g., In re Estate of Wegner, 237 P.3d 387 (Wash. Ct. App. 2010) (by statute "a beneficiary of a nonprobate asset . . . takes . . . subject to . . . the fair share of expenses of administration reasonably incurred . . . in the transfer of or administration of the asset"), Estate of Fender v. Fender, 422 N.E.2d 107 (Ill. 1981), and Roe v. Estate of Farrell, 372 N.E.2d 662 (Ill. 1978), involving apportionment of administration expenses to such nonprobate property.

[12] See In re Estate of Whitaker, 538 N.E.2d 174 (Ill. App. Ct. 1989) (fiduciary personally liable for misapportioning estate tax burden). See Riggs, "Florida Estate Tax Apportionment," 25 U. Fla. L. Rev. 719, 737-38 (1973) (questioning whether a personal representative owes a fiduciary duty to nonprobate beneficiaries due to the potential for shifting the tax burden to nonprobate beneficiaries); Stephens, Maxfield, Lind, Calfee, and Smith, Federal Estate and Gift Taxation ¶ 8.06, at 8-24 (8th ed. 2002) (stating that "[i]t seems unlikely that legal principles regarding fiduciary obligations have developed to the point of answering the attending dilemma in cases such as this where a fiduciary's action affects not only interests in the probate assets, but somewhat related interests outside the probate estate"). LaBarbera v. Director, Division of Taxation, 24 N.J. Tax. 377 (2009), determined that the remainder beneficiaries of a QTIP trust who had § 2207A liability for payment of the FET attributable to inclusion in S's estate (and by virtue of that federal obligation also had a corresponding state death tax apportionment liability) have standing to challenge the state tax director's determination of liability, rejecting the director's assertion that only the personal representative of S's estate was a proper party, stating that the personal representative "has little incentive to challenge [an] assessment because federal and New

set of beneficiaries should be overlooked in administration of the probate estate, and it is important to remember that the payment of debts, expenses, and taxes "is an area in which costly litigation and costly surprises are nearly always possible."[13]

A number of simple precautions should be observed in drafting a provision relating to the payment of debts and expenses. For example, unless exoneration of estate assets is wise for economic purposes, it often makes sense to specify that debts secured by estate assets shall not be paid and to override expressly any state law duty otherwise applicable to repay outstanding indebtedness, notwithstanding its magnitude (such as a purchase money mortgage secured by the testator's personal residence, representing a significant percentage of the home's FMV), interest rate (such as an older debt with a fixed low interest rate), or maturity.[14] Thought should be given to whether the testator wishes the

---

(Footnote Continued)

Jersey law give the estate the right to demand recovery of the taxes attributable to the QTIP property" from the remainder beneficiary. Further,

> [i]t is not difficult to imagine scenarios in which animosity exists between the administrator of a second spouse's estate and the children from the first marriage. It is possible that the administrator would pay and refuse to challenge a legally vulnerable estate tax assessment attributable to a QTIP trust merely because doing so would diminish the financial recovery of the residuary beneficiaries, the step-children of the second spouse.

See also Estate of Rosta, 444 N.E.2d 704 (Ill. App. Ct. 1982) (because other nonprobate beneficiaries were represented, however, doctrine of virtual representation was deemed to apply with respect to nonprobate beneficiaries not made parties to court actions affecting apportionment of taxes); and cf. Estate of Lyons, 425 N.E.2d 19 (Ill. App. Ct. 1981) (estate beneficiaries successfully challenged personal representative's apportionment of tax burden, which was deemed improper, notwithstanding that it was based on FET values of assets received); In re Estate of Guattery, 656 N.Y.S.2d 695 (1997) (beneficiary of Totten trust account not entitled under state law to accountings but was entitled to copy of federal and state estate tax returns with which to audit executor's performance as it affected those trusts' estate tax liability).

[13] Scoles, Estate Tax Apportionment in the Multi-State Estate, 5 U. Miami Inst. Est. Plan. ¶ 700, at 7-28 (1971).

[14] Although the 1990 version of UPC §2-607 directs against exoneration of encumbered property, §3-814 grants the personal representative authority to repay any part or all of the encumbrance "if it appears to be for the best interest of the estate." See §3.2.5 at text accompanying nn.44-50 regarding bequests of encumbered property.

§3.2.3

estate to pay all expenses and debts attributable to community property, notwithstanding that only half of the property is includible in the gross estate for FET purposes[15] and only half of the property is subject to the testator's power of testamentary disposition. Further, a direction to pay debts should not automatically impose the obligation to pay items that are not yet due, or not properly presented and therefore subject to challenge under a state nonclaim regime.[16] And specific reference to funeral expenses may be necessary if state law otherwise imposes those items on the individuals who are responsible for disposing of the testator's physical remains.[17]

§3.2.4 Personal Effects

It is wise to include a specific provision directing the disposition of a testator's tangible personal property, such as jewelry and personal or household effects, even if they are distributable to the same persons who will receive the residue of the testator's estate. One significant justification for this seemingly repetitive and potentially unnecessary drafting relates to the income taxation of estates. Under §§661 and 662, an estate that distributes any asset causes DNI available for the year of distribution to be carried out to the distributee,[18] even if the asset distributed is only an item of sentimental value.

If the entire estate could be distributed in the same tax year, the effect of this income allocation regime would be modest, in most cases, because the available income would be shared by all distributees in proportion to the relative value of their respective distributions[19] But often personal effects are distributed early in the administration of an

---

[15] And for that reason, only half of the expense is deductible for FET purposes. Rev. Rul. 78-242, 1978-1 C.B. 292. See §10.7.2 n.43.

[16] See, e.g., UPC §§3-801 and 3-803.

[17] See, e.g., Rev. Rul. 76-369, 1976-2 C.B. 281, which refers to state law in some jurisdictions that imposes the cost of the funeral on the decedent's survivors rather than on the estate. See §15.4.1 regarding the deductibility of funeral expenses in such jurisdictions.

[18] See §§5.1 and 5.4.1 regarding the income taxation of trusts and estates.

[19] As discussed in more detail in the materials regarding the income taxation of trusts and estates, under §643(e)(2) the pro ration of estate income actually is based on the lesser of the FMV or the income tax basis of property distributed in kind. See §§5.4.2, 5.8.1 and 5.8.2.

§3.2.4

estate, to minimize the cost to the estate of storage or safekeeping, to avoid the need to administer assets that have little monetary value (but potentially significant sentimental value), and often just to allow the personal representative to make the testator's residence salable. The personalty may be the only property distributed during the taxable year. Meaning that all DNI of that separate share of the estate[20] that is available for taxation to the estate or its beneficiaries could be carried out to the recipient.

If the property has sufficient monetary value, the effect could be more than just the aggravation of the personal representative having to prepare and present to the recipient a Form K-1 reporting that the item constitutes taxable income to the recipient in the amount of the lesser of the FMV of that property or its basis for income tax purposes.[21] Notwithstanding that the property is not marketable or that the recipient would not think of selling it to generate sufficient cash to pay the income tax carried out on that distribution. If there is a specific bequest of these assets, however, the exception in § 663(a)(1) for gifts of specific property distributed in less than three installments will pre-empt this unpleasantness and distribution will not be an income carry out event. Any estate DNI will remain to be taxed to the estate or to be carried out to distributees of other estate assets.

A second reason for such a provision is to address special administrative issues that relate to items of personal or household property. Unlike estate assets such as stocks and bonds, these assets require special protection and attention, typically they are not worthy investments, and the personal representative must be excused from normal duties regarding retention of wasting or non-income-producing assets. An effective personal effects provision will indicate whether the cost of storing, packing, shipping, and insuring these assets will be borne by their ultimate recipients or by the estate as a whole as an expense of administration. For example, in some cases these costs could exceed the FMV of the assets themselves and, if not paid from the residue of the estate, might cause the beneficiary to reject the items notwithstanding the testator's strong desire otherwise.

---

[20] See Treas. Reg. § 1.663(c)-4 and § § 5.4.3 and 5.4.4.

[21] See § 643(e)(2) for the limitation on the amount of DNI carried out on a distribution of property in kind.

§ 3.2.4

If items are separately insured (such as jewelry that may be covered by a homeowner's personal property insurance rider or an automobile or boat with its own casualty policy), this provision also appropriately may direct that the policy will pass with the insured item, to minimize the time, the trouble, and often the expense to the recipient to acquire new insurance (which may entail a new appraisal or inspection) rather than to continue coverage under an existing policy.

A third reason to include a special provision dealing with tangible personal property relates to family harmony. Making an equal division of most investments included in an estate is easy compared to the squabbles and hurt feelings that may attend to the division and distribution of personal effects that carry significance unrelated to their monetary value. Should jewelry, furs, and other items of personal adornment pass exclusively to members of the same sex as the testator on the theory that they alone will display or wear those items? Or should the testator recognize that, for example, a son might want to give a mother's jewelry to his wife or daughters and that, therefore, the testator's daughters should not be the exclusive recipients of these items? Should a child who gave an item to the testator be entitled to receive that item back from the estate, on the theory that the child potentially has a special attachment or pride flowing from its selection? These issues will vary from case to case and may involve significant emotional (and therefore potentially irrational) reactions that should be anticipated and addressed by the testator in the provision itself.

At the very least, the provision should anticipate that division among multiple recipients by agreement may prove impossible. Therefore, it should establish a mechanism for allocation, recognizing that no personal representative wants to be thrust between two antagonists fighting over the same item of sentimental value, for which no amount of cash or other property is adequate compensation. Thus, the provision might create some form of lottery, priority for selection, auction, or other regime to accommodate disputes. One frequently effective mechanism is simply to provide that, to the extent the beneficiaries cannot agree to a division within a specified period, disputed items will be sold and the proceeds added to the residue of the estate. Disputing beneficiaries seem to find ways to agree on the eve of a forced sale.

§3.2.4

Care in drafting personal effects provisions is required to preclude being over- or underinclusive. For example, a gift of all the testator's "personal property" would be problematic because it would raise the question whether "personal" meant all property the testator owned (personal to the testator), all property that was not real property, or just personal effects such as clothing, jewelry, furniture, and housewares. Even a gift of *tangible* personal property may be too broad. Although it would exclude most items of investment property, arguably it would include cash or other investment assets such as valuable collections. Indeed, if the testator is a collector (whether it be antiques, artwork, automobiles, Barbie dolls, firearms, porcelains, stamps and coins, or $1,000 bills), the estate planner must determine whether the collection is meant to pass under such a provision or should be disposed of either as an investment like other intangible property or as the subject of a separate dispositive provision.[21.1]

Moreover, some items of tangible personal property should not be included in the gift made by such a provision. Examples would be the household furniture and other effects in a personal residence (such as a vacation home) that is the subject of another specific gift under the will, items bequeathed under another clause of the will, or machinery such as farm implements of extraordinary value that should not be separated from a farm or other business that is part of the estate.

[21.1] In re Gourary, 932 N.Y.S.2d 881 (Surr. Ct. 2011), illustrates this principle. The second article in the decedent's will (the tangible personal property provision) left to his widow their cooperative apartment and "household furniture and furnishings, books, pictures, jewelry and other article of personal or household use" (note the typo – "article" in the singular – and the lack of a serial comma). The issue was whether this bequest carried a $5.2 million collection of pre-1800 books, prints, manuscripts, pamphlets, and other items relating to "festivals," much (but not all) of which was physically maintained in the dwelling. The issue arose because some items in the collection were books and pictures, and the spouse claimed the entire collection. The court decided that the provision meant to convey only the couple's home and the personal use articles contained in it, and not any part of the collection, saying that "it is difficult to believe that decedent intended to include . . . his life's avocation, in the pedestrian phrases 'books, pictures . . . and other items of personal or household use.'" Particularly because doing so significantly would have altered the one-third/two-thirds split of the decedent's estate between his son by a prior marriage and the surviving spouse.

§3.2.4

Finally, the testator should specify whether particular items should pass to particular individuals, whether any beneficiary should have a right of first refusal if assets must be sold to generate estate liquidity, and whether beneficiaries should be required to survive the testator by a certain period to avoid having to administer the same property in two estates if the testator and the recipient die in rapid succession. 30 days usually is more than adequate, but six months is the maximum limitation[22] if the beneficiary is S and the FET marital deduction should be claimed for the value of these items. Some forms leave property to the testator's descendants of whatever degree of consanguinity while others limit the class of beneficiaries to children only, which is an issue that ought to be considered with the testator. And in either case, if a minor beneficiary might be involved, a mechanism for an adult to act on behalf of that minor and to hold assets received should be established.

UPC § 2-513 addresses an issue of frequent occurrence involving personal effects provisions, authorizing disposition of "tangible personal property other than money" under a written list not executed with the formalities of a will. Because these dispositions often involve sentiment and personalities they seem to encourage multiple revisions by some testators, with the consequent potential for invalidity because of improper self-made alterations to the will. Rather than frustrate the testator's intent regarding the disposition of property that often has little relative monetary value, the UPC recognizes as valid a separate list of dispositions that may be prepared either before or after execution of the will.[23] It may be altered from time to time without complying with normal will or codicil execution formalities. In states that recognize this alternative the will provision might simply direct disposition of those items not

---

[22] See § 13.4.4.2 for a discussion of § 2056(b)(3).

[23] Indeed, the written list may survive revocation of one will and execution of another. See In re Estate of Wilkins, 48 P.3d 644 (Id. 2002). Moreover, the separate list may be another legal instrument, such as a trust that satisfies the writing or signature requirements. See In re Estate of Blodgett, 95 S.W.3d 79 (Mo. 2003) (also holding that the gift by trust of "all my personal property" satisfied the UPC requirement of a list that described both items and devisees with "reasonable certainty"). Curiously, according to In re Moor, 879 A.2d 648 (Del. Ch. 2005), although the list cannot dispose of money held by the decedent at death, it can direct sale of certain tangibles and distribution of those monetary proceeds.

§ 3.2.4

otherwise validly transferred under a list found within a specified period after the testator's death.

§3.2.5 Bequests

The law of wills provides answers to numerous questions that may arise with respect to dispositions that could be made under other instruments (such as a trust), but that the law applicable to those governing instruments does not address.[24] As a consequence, these concepts are discussed here, with the understanding that the planning and drafting lessons to be learned from them should be transported into other forms of planning. All relate generally to "bequests," which is the term used here to describe any gift, whether it be of cash (traditionally known as a legacy), of any personalty other than cash (the traditional definition of a bequest), or of realty (traditionally called a devise).

The most simple bequest is a gift of cash: a pecuniary amount determined by a formula or a fixed amount specified in the document. For example, the testator might give $X to each sibling who survives the testator by 30 days, $Y to each individual in the testator's employ at the testator's death, or $Z to charity. Other more sophisticated approaches might give "X% of my gross estate as finally determined for FET purposes" to charity, "the largest pecuniary amount that can pass free of GST to my grandchildren who survive me, assuming my personal representative allocates the full amount of my unused GST exemption to this gift,"[25] "the largest pecuniary amount that can pass free of estate tax" to beneficiaries other than S (such as a nonmarital trust) and the residue of the estate to S (or a marital deduction trust), or "the smallest pecuniary amount necessary to reduce my taxable estate as finally determined for FET purposes to the largest amount as to which the least FET will be payable" to S (or a marital deduction trust) and the residue to beneficiaries other than S.[26]

---

[24] Part 7 of Article II of the 1990 version of the UPC is the exception in this respect. It causes rules traditionally applicable only with respect to wills to apply to various other dispositive documents.

[25] See § 11.4.5.5 for a discussion of this concept.

[26] See § 13.2.7 for the discussion of concepts such as drafting these optimum marital deduction bequests and transfers that take advantage of the testator's unified credit.

§3.2.5

In their various forms, each of these gifts is a pecuniary bequest and they could bankrupt an estate and produce an abatement issue if the aggregate of such gifts is not scrutinized carefully during the planning stage.[27] Thus, attention should be devoted to whether the aggregate of the pecuniary bequests should be limited to a percentage of the testator's probate estate, gross estate, taxable estate, or some other definable amount.[28] In addition, coordination with any tax payment obligation addressed under the will[29] is required to establish whether the bequest should be reduced by any taxes attributable to it and, if computed by a formula, whether taxes attributable to the testator's estate will affect that computation.[30]

To illustrate, assume the testator wanted a beneficiary to receive a bequest of $50,000, defined as a fraction of the testator's estate so that fluctuations in the value of the estate would affect the amount the beneficiary ultimately received. In defining that fraction the numerator would be $50,000. The question is whether the denominator should be defined by the size of the estate before or after payment of taxes. Thus, assume the estate was $500,000 before payment of taxes and only

----

[27] See § 3.2.5 nn.48-50 and accompanying text for a discussion of abatement.

[28] The choice of limitation also should be considered carefully. For example, a percentage bequest to charity that produces a charitable deduction would reduce the testator's taxable estate, which would necessitate a circular computation if that was the control limitation. Moreover, tax elections (such as valuation dates and methods or whether to deduct certain expenses under § 2053 for estate tax purposes or to make the § 642(g) election to claim them for federal income tax purposes) also could affect either the gross estate or taxable estate amounts. If substantial wealth is passing outside of probate, use of the probate estate might be appropriate in some cases but it might create too small a limitation in others. And reliance on tax concepts gives Congress a blank check to alter the plan (or, as the one-year hiatus in estate tax and GST in 2010 revealed, the power to totally muck up the plan).

A pecuniary bequest might be subject to abatement to the extent it exceeds a specific percentage of the testator's probate, gross, or taxable estate. If so, it is not clear whether the bequest no longer qualifies as a bequest of a specific amount that avoids the DNI carry out rule under the § 663(a)(1) exception, either if an abatement occurs or the estate is sufficiently large that no limitation is imposed in fact.

[29] See § 3.3.

[30] See §§ 3.3.15.3 and 13.7.7.2 for a discussion of this issue in the context of marital deduction planning.

•

$400,000 after payment of tax, and then assume that the $400,000 estate remaining after payment of taxes doubles in value before the bequest is satisfied. The issue is whether the beneficiary should receive one eighth of $800,000 (50,000 over 400,000) or one tenth of $800,000 (50,000 over 500,000). That issue is independent of the question whether the bequest (whether it is $80,000 or $100,000) then should bear its proportionate share of the taxes incurred on the estate (although it will affect the computation of the pro rata portion of the taxes that the bequest should pay).

The bequest also should specify whether it is payable with interest if distribution is delayed beyond a specified period after death and, if so, at what rate. Absent a contrary designation in the will, the law of many states would impose interest at a statutory rate beginning at a defined date, typically one year after the date of death.[31] Alternatively, the bequest could be distributed with a pro rata portion of any income earned in the estate between the testator's death and distribution,[32] which may be the result imposed by state law if the bequest is to a trust created under the will and that testamentary trust requires the trustee to distribute all income earned beginning with the testator's death.[33] Resolution of these issues may affect the income tax consequences of the bequest to the beneficiary.[34]

---

[31] See 4 Scott, Fratcher, and Ascher, Scott and Ascher on Trusts § 20.3.2 (5th ed. 2007); Atkinson, The Law of Wills § 135, at 751 (2d ed. 1953).

[32] See § § 5.4.4 for a discussion of the different results that will flow from each of these alternatives for income tax purposes. The payment of interest or income may be important for GST purposes, under the applicable interest requirements of Treas. Reg. § 26.2654-1(a)(1)(ii). See § 11.4.5.5.4.

[33] E.g., pursuant to the all-income-annually requirements of § § 2056(b)(5) and 2056(b)(7)(B)(ii)(I) for marital deduction purposes. See § § 13.5.2.2 and 13.5.6.1.2, respectively.

[34] See Estate of Stern v. United States, 98-1 U.S. Tax Cas. (CCH) ¶ 60,299 (S.D. Ind. 1998) (§ 2053 deduction allowed for amount claimed as compensation for caregiver's services, in part because the amount was included in caregiver's income); Zaharoolis v. Commissioner, 35 T.C.M. (CCH) 338 (1976) (at testator's request, taxpayer moved in with and became housekeeper for testator, who failed to comply with agreement to leave entire estate to taxpayer in return; amount paid in compromise of taxpayer's claim against estate held taxable as income for services rendered and not exempt from tax under § 102 as an inheritance or bequest); Rev. Rul. 78-271, 1978-2 C.B. 239 (S rendered services to

Additional income tax consequences will flow from "funding" (satisfaction) of the bequest[35] and may arise if the bequest is a form of payment to the beneficiary for services rendered.[36] To illustrate in a

(Footnote Continued)

D's business, submitted a claim for those services to D's estate, and was paid; absent a bona fide agreement to compensate S, the services were deemed to have been gratuitously rendered to the business and the payments were held not deductible by the estate under § 2053); and see Metz v. United States, 933 F.2d 802 (10th Cir. 1991), aff'g 89-2 U.S. Tax Cas. (CCH) ¶ 13,822 (D. Kan. 1989) (before entire FET payable in installments under § 6166 was paid, the source from which payments were being made went bankrupt and the government sought to enforce § § 6321 and 6324 liens against realty specifically bequeathed to plaintiff pursuant to testator's promise based on plaintiff's agreement to live with and care for testator; plaintiff claimed equitable title to the property passed to the plaintiff before testator died, which would take it out of testator's gross estate to which the government's lien could attach, and claimed to be a purchaser of the property, which would divest any lien, but the court held that the government could enforce its lien against the property, in part because plaintiff did not report the property as income from services).

[35] If the bequest is satisfied by distribution of property in kind, § 643(e) will limit the amount of any DNI carried out by distribution to the lesser of FMV or basis of the assets distributed, unless the personal representative makes the § 643(e)(3) election to treat distribution as a gain or loss realization event, which would cause basis and FMV to be equal, which correspondingly could affect the amount of income carried out, all only if the § 663(a)(1) exception is not applicable. See § § 3.2.4 at text accompanying nn.19-21 and 5.4.4 regarding the income tax provisions, and § § 13.7.3.2.3, 13.7.4.1.2 and 13.7.8.1.3 regarding the specific application of these factors in the context of funding marital deduction bequests.

[36] See Estate of Stern v. United States, 98-1 U.S. Tax Cas. (CCH) ¶ 60,299 (S.D. Ind. 1998) (§ 2053 deduction allowed for amount claimed as compensation for caregiver's services, in part because the amount was included in caregiver's income); Zaharoolis v. Commissioner, 35 T.C.M. (CCH) 338 (1976) (at testator's request, taxpayer moved in with and became housekeeper for testator, who failed to comply with agreement to leave entire estate to taxpayer in return; amount paid in compromise of taxpayer's claim against estate held taxable as income for services rendered and not exempt from tax under § 102 as an inheritance or bequest); Rev. Rul. 78-271, 1978-2 C.B. 239 (S rendered services to D's business, submitted a claim for those services to D's estate, and was paid; absent a bona fide agreement to compensate S, the services were deemed to have been gratuitously rendered to the business and the payments were held not deductible by the estate under § 2053); and see Metz v. United States, 933 F.2d 802 (10th Cir. 1991), aff'g 89-2 U.S. Tax Cas. (CCH) ¶ 13,822 (D. Kan. 1989)

more dramatic manner, assume that D provided in a will that Beneficiary (B) may purchase property from D's estate at a sweetheart price—the discount being a form of compensation for premortem services. Assume that FMV for FET purposes is $100 (determined under § 2703 without regard to the option) and that the striking price is $80.

In PLR 200340019 the facts also posited that B actually purchased the asset from the estate for only $70. The government held that B's basis following the purchase was $90, being the amount paid ($70) plus the basis in the "option" (the government's term for the sweetheart price entitlement) used to purchase the asset ($20). Basis in the option is said to be equal to FMV of the option, which the Ruling opined was FMV of the property ($100) less the striking price ($80). So B has a basis of $90 in the property (assuming that it is still worth $100). If B sells for that FMV gain ordinarily would be $10.

Not stated by the Ruling is whether § 267 would apply to disallow the loss on sale by the estate, if § 267(b)(13) is applicable (sale by an estate to a beneficiary of the estate, not excepted as a sale in satisfaction of a pecuniary bequest), and therefore § 267(a)(1) would apply. For this purpose assume the loss to the estate was only $10, because the property was worth $80 only and the option was worth the other $20. If that is so, then B has the right under § 267(d) to offset any gain on a future sale with the loss disallowed to the estate (unless § 469(g)(1)(B) is applicable because the transaction involves a passive activity loss). In essence B's "real" basis effectively is $100 for future gain purposes and $90 if B sells at a loss. The fact that the estate had a basis of $100 in the property de hors the option does not mean that it suffered a loss of $30 that B could take in the future against gain, because of the $20 option that "soaks up" that initial differential of value.

(Footnote Continued)

(before entire FET payable in installments under § 6166 was paid, the source from which payments were being made went bankrupt and the government sought to enforce §§ 6321 and 6324 liens against realty specifically bequeathed to plaintiff pursuant to testator's promise based on plaintiff's agreement to live with and care for testator; plaintiff claimed equitable title to the property passed to the plaintiff before testator died, which would take it out of testator's gross estate to which the government's lien could attach, and claimed to be a purchaser of the property, which would divest any lien, but the court held that the government could enforce its lien against the property, in part because plaintiff did not report the property as income from services).

§ 3.2.5

If this is right, the net result is that the estate's sale for $70 generates no loss, neither to the estate nor to the beneficiary. The net result is that it precludes the sweetheart deal from generating an artificial loss (and maybe some real loss if the reason for allowing B to purchase at $70 instead of at the striking price of $80 was because the property had gone down in value). An added thought that makes this particularly relevant is that the property involved was a dwelling and B moved into it premortem to care for D and B's incompetent sibling. The will provided the striking price discount only "if at the time of my death [B] is guardian of the person and estate of" the sibling. Quaere whether the $20 sweetheart option is compensation income, and whether that should alter the analysis in any way.

Any attempt in a will to explain why a beneficiary received a bequest may generate a contention that the bequest is contingent, requiring the beneficiary to prove that the contingency was met and potentially leading to income tax consequences if the contingency involved the rendition of services to the testator.[37] If the testator is indebted to the beneficiary, the will should specify whether the bequest is in partial or total satisfaction of that debt[38] (and, conversely, if the beneficiary is indebted to the testator, the will should specify whether the debt owed to the testator is to be deducted from the amount of the bequest).[39]

---

[37] See In re Estate of Sommerville, 209 A.2d 299, 300 (Pa. 1965) (testator left residue of estate "in consideration of [beneficiary] undertaking to offer me the protection and comfort of her home and to arrange for the necessary funeral ceremonies after my decease"; the court nevertheless held that the gift was not conditional and that the will simply described the testator's motives underlying the unconditional bequest).

[38] See Lopez v. Lopez, 96 So. 2d 463 (Fla. 1957); Maney v. Maney, 164 N.E.2d 146 (Mass. 1960) (will did not provide that claims against estate would be set off against bequests to creditors who were beneficiaries; creditor beneficiaries' acceptance of bequests was not an election to forsake their claims).

[39] Offsetting was not required in Old Colony Trust Co. v. Underwood, 8 N.E.2d 792 (Mass. 1937) (debt owing to testator was barred by statute of limitation), or in Estate of Berk, 16 Cal. Rptr. 492 (Ct. App. 1961) (beneficiary was taking by representation a bequest to testator's debtor), but in Longy School of Music, Inc. v. Pickman, 183 N.E.2d 289 (Mass. 1962), the testator excused all the beneficiary's debts and directed the personal representative to pay all notes of the beneficiary bearing the testator's endorsement; one outstanding note was not endorsed but was secured by stock that was sold to pay the debt and the

Bequests payable to a minor beneficiary should be subject to a provision permitting the personal representative to hold the amount as a trustee or expend it on the minor's behalf or to make payment to the minor personally, to a guardian of or person in loco parentis to the minor, or to a custodian for the minor under the UTMA or UGMA, all to avoid the need to appoint a legal guardian of the minor's property to receive payment for the minor or, worse, to keep the funds under the supervision of a local court until the minor attains the age of majority. And if the beneficiary may be entitled to Supplemental Security Income or Medicaid, distribution might be directed to a third party SNT to avoid disqualification.

A specific bequest of particular property is especially common with respect to ownership interests in a family business or a residence (either the testator's principal residence or a vacation home, including any retained reversion in a grantor retained annuity trust or QPRT that does not expire before the testator's death).[40] Bequests of business interests typically are part of a plan to give control to a particular beneficiary, such as a child who is active in running the enterprise, or to equalize the treatment of children following an inter vivos gift to an active child.

Because issues of equality and control are of particular concern, accomplishment of the testator's goals may require the creation of multiple classes of interests, such as preferred and common stock, voting and nonvoting interests, or limited and general partnership interests. It also may entail considerations such as whether a beneficiary who is not active in the business should be subjected to the status of a minority owner or instead should be given the opportunity to receive other property from the estate[41] or to put the business interest to the

---

(Footnote Continued)

court held that the bequest should be reduced by the value of the stock sold to pay that note.

[40] See §7.2.2.7 regarding this form of planning.

[41] See, e.g., In re Estate of Snyder, 2 P.3d 238 (Mont. 2000) (the decedent's intent was to provide control of a family business to one child, consistent with an equal division of the estate between that and a second child), in which the court concluded that the decedent's bequest to one child of 51% of the stock in a business did not predict that the remaining 49% necessarily would be distributed to the other child, who would not thereby receive equal treatment in the overall division of the estate. Instead, the remaining 49% also was distributed to the one

enterprise, perhaps at a specified price, in exchange for a debt instrument payable by the enterprise. All these issues should be considered in this context, along with more obvious concerns about not causing disagreeable consequences with respect to tax opportunities under § § 303 and 6166.

A gift of residential realty[42] often should be accompanied by a gift of the furnishings and household effects in and around the property, which may require that any other disposition of personal and household effects be modified to preclude conflicting dispositions.[43] More importantly, insurance on the property should be included in a bequest of the property itself. The will should address the payment of costs to maintain, insure, and pay real estate taxes outstanding at death or incurred during administration of the estate. And the issue of exoneration of any mortgage indebtedness must be considered, whether the property is encumbered when the planning is being done or might be used as a source of funds through future borrowing.

Contrary to the law in most jurisdictions and regardless of a general provision in a will that directs payment of the testator's debts,[44] an

(Footnote Continued)

child and an equal amount of other property was distributed to the other child, accomplishing the decedent's dual objectives.

[42] Caution is in order in drafting such a disposition to be sure that the property is not described as the property the testator was living in at death, because illness and medical care decisions may force the testator to abandon the property prior to death, creating interpretation questions. In addition, a bequest of the property should address ademption issues if the testator's residence may be sold to finance health care payments or otherwise because the testator has quit the premises permanently prior to death. See § 3.2.5.2 (6th ed.).

[43] See, e.g., Hanson v. Estate of Bjerke, 95 P.3d 704 (Mont. 2004), in which a gift of "[a]ny article of personal property not designated by [a list of personal belongings and household effects] shall be determined to be a content of my house" was determined to convey paper currency and coins, regardless of whether they actually were found within the dwelling.

[44] See § 3.3. A difficult exoneration issue relates to realty passing outside probate, as illustrated by Goldstein v. Ancell, 258 A.2d 93 (Conn. 1969), which held that a surviving joint owner was entitled to exoneration of an indebtedness secured by a mortgage placed on the jointly held property by the testator before it was jointly owned. Exoneration was required even though this situation was regarded as comparable to a bequest of mortgaged realty, which would call for exoneration by the decedent's estate under Connecticut law. A nonexoneration

§ 3.2.5

absolute nonexoneration rule is adopted by the 1990 version of UPC § 2-607. The intent is to preclude disruption of the decedent's estate plan by exoneration under the traditional rule that outstanding debts should be repaid even if not yet due.[45] Insertion of a similar provision in the testator's will should be considered if the property is located in or the testator may die subject to the law of a state that adheres to the traditional common law exoneration rule. The estate plan should consider how the trustee will service the debt if exoneration is precluded and if the realty is distributed to a trust. The usual rule is that amortization of the principal portion of the debt should be a charge against trust corpus, not trust income, which may pose a problem if there is insufficient corpus liquidity to finance that portion of the debt service.[46] In addition, the will should specify whether the property passes subject to or free from the encumbrance if the testator makes a bequest in the form of granting an option to purchase encumbered realty at a stipulated striking price.[47]

(Footnote Continued)

directive in the testator's will was deemed ineffective with respect to nonprobate property. See also Estate of Leinbach v. Leinbach, 486 N.E.2d 2 (Ind. Ct. App. 1985) (exoneration required, notwithstanding statutory reversal of common law with respect to probate property; liability limited to testator's contractual obligation with respect to half the indebtedness); Pietro v. Leonetti, 283 N.E.2d 172, 174 (Ohio 1972) ("[a]mple authority exists to support our conclusion that the right of contribution exists where, upon the decease of one of two joint obligors on a mortgage note, and payment in full of that note is made by the remaining obligor, the estate of the deceased is liable to pay one-half of the obligation"); but see Bonner v. Arnold, 676 P.2d 290 (Or. 1984) (no contribution for payment of debt from deceased joint owner's estate).

[45] However, UPC § 3-814 grants the personal representative authority to repay any part or all of the encumbrance "if it appears to be for the best interest of the estate," although in doing so "the share of the distributee entitled to the encumbered assets" is not increased "unless the distributee is entitled to exoneration" by virtue of an affirmative direction to that effect in the testator's will.

[46] See New England Merchants Nat'l Bank v. Koufman, 295 N.E.2d 388 (Mass. 1973); Rev. Rul. 90-82, 1990-2 C.B. 44 (payment of entire principal and interest from trust income constituted an indirect income accumulation that, among other results, affected the trust's depreciation deduction under § 642(e) and Treas. Reg. §§ 1.167(h)-1(b) and 1.642(e)-1). See §§ 5.2.1 n.9 and 5.3.1 n.27 and accompanying text.

[47] The will may stipulate the purchase price, provide a formula for its determination, or specify that the striking price will be established by an appraisal, in

§ 3.2.5

Exoneration is one cause of abatement, which occurs when some benefit under a will must be reduced (abated) because another payment or bequest has priority under the will or applicable law.[48] Provisions

(Footnote Continued)

which case the price determined by the appraiser is conclusive even if the personal representative believes the price fixed is too low. See In re Estate of Meyers, 206 A.2d 37 (Pa. 1965) (will provided for selection of three appraisers who were to fix a fair and just value; absent fraud, accident, or mistake, their appraisal was binding).

[48] See, e.g., UPC § 3-902(a), which states the traditional rule that intestate property is used first to satisfy claims and other obligations under a will, followed by residuary bequests, general bequests, and finally specific bequests. See also Atkinson, The Law of Wills § 136 (2d ed. 1953); McGovern, Kurtz, & English, Wills, Trusts & Estates § 8.4 (4th ed. 2010).

Consider In re Estate of Goldman, 158 P.3d 892 (Az. Ct. App. 2007), which addressed a timing question of abatement law, whether to determine entitlement at death or later, when distribution is made. Imagine an estate in 2007, worth $1.9 million on the date of the decedent's death, that grew to $2.2 million before termination. The decedent's will calls for a formula credit shelter pecuniary bequest of the largest amount that will pass free of tax and leaves the residue of the estate to a marital deduction trust. At death in 2007 the applicable exclusion amount sheltered by the unified credit was $2.0 million dollars, which exceeded the FET value of this estate by $100,000. On distribution at the end of estate administration does the preresiduary credit shelter bequest receive a full $2.0 million, because growth during administration precluded abatement entirely, and the added $200,000 of growth would remain as marital deduction residue? Or did abatement occur at death, which would limit the preresiduary bequest to just $1.9 million? In holding for a date of distribution evaluation the court rejected the estate's argument that delay in administration should have no impact on the entitlement of estate beneficiaries. A rule otherwise (such as the court adopted) puts the personal representative in an untenable situation. Accelerate distribution and the pecuniary bequest abates to $1.9 million, the legatee takes the entire estate, and any subsequent appreciation therefore belongs entirely to the preresiduary legatee; delay distribution and the pecuniary legatee can be made whole but any excess value goes to the residuary beneficiaries.

Classic wisdom is that estate entitlements are determined at the decedent's date of death, meaning in this example that the preresiduary general bequest would be reduced by abatement to $1.9 million and, under classic estate administration rules, delayed distribution of the preresiduary general bequest would entitle that legatee to interest, typically determined at a statutory rate, usually after a statutory date (such as one year after the date of death). See § 3.2.5.3 (6th ed.). Additional growth during administration of the estate would belong entirely to the residue. If statutory interest did not consume the full $300,000 of growth in

calling for payment of debts, expenses, and taxes are another cause of abatement and may alter the order of abatement in the sense that they apportion liabilities that reduce various entitlements. Any will may specify a different priority than that established under local law if, for example, modest specific bequests to nonrelatives should abate to protect a residuary or general marital deduction bequest that otherwise has a lower priority.[49] In addition, if the decedent agreed to provide certain

---

(Footnote Continued)

the hypothetical the remainder would constitute a residue that essentially did not exist at the date of death.

The notion that a residue can exist at the date of distribution albeit none existed at death is disconcerting to some who understand classic abatement doctrine, because the priority of abatement holds that a residue abates before general bequests abate. Under that priority, at the date of death in this example there was no residue to receive the growth that occurred during administration. Indeed, some observers want to argue that the preresiduary general bequest in this case would morph into or became the residue when it was determined at the date of death that the preresiduary general bequest exceeded the full value of the estate at the date of death. That also is not correct, and the court did not hold that all the postmortem appreciation belonged to the general legatee. (The primary significance of alleging a metamorphosis is to avoid income tax gain or loss consequences that normally would apply in funding preresiduary entitlements, such as the $2.0 million bequest in the hypothetical. See § 13.7.3.2.1).

The existence of accessions law suggests error in *Goldman*. Described in § 13.2.5.3 (6th ed.), the basic rule is that growth—be it income, interest, dividends, stock-on-stock splits, the birth of offspring to a herd, or whatever—belongs to the beneficiary of a specific bequest as if that beneficiary became the owner of the income producing or growing asset at death. Similarly, interest payments on delayed distribution of general bequests reflects the same logic applied to the reality that a general bequest is not particularized—there are no specific assets to which the beneficiary is entitled—so it is not possible to track the actual income or growth (accessions) on assets postmortem as belonging to the general legatee. But the notion of an entitlement to interest is that the legatee became entitled to the bequest at death and interest is the closest way to allocate postmortem earnings to that legatee. The flip side of each form of entitlement at the moment of death is that, if the estate was inadequate at death, the entitlement itself failed—the general bequest abated—at the moment of death, and postmortem appreciation cannot reverse that abatement result.

[49] Normally specific bequests abate last if there are insufficient assets to satisfy all dispositions under the will. But Osborn v. Osborn, 334 S.W.2d 48 (Mo. 1960), concluded that S should receive the full amount of a general marital deduction bequest and that the estate should have the benefit of the maximum allowable marital deduction, causing specific bequests to abate to provide the

benefits under a will (such as pursuant to a prenuptial agreement, a property settlement incident to divorce, or a contract to provide services), the will should specify that these dispositions be favored even if other bequests must abate to provide the necessary funds.[50]

§ 3.2.5.1 Ademption by Satisfaction

Ademption by satisfaction frequently is known simply as satisfaction, to distinguish it from ademption by extinction, which frequently is referred to simply as ademption. Similar to the doctrine of advancements that applies to intestate estates,[51] ademption by satisfaction regards some inter vivos gifts by a testator after execution of a will as a replacement or satisfaction of that bequest in whole or in part. Made to or for the benefit of the beneficiary of a bequest under that will, satisfaction (like advancements)[52] involves the difficult issue of intent.

The law provides a presumption that an inter vivos gift is in satisfaction of a testamentary bequest if the testator stands in loco parentis to the beneficiary. This presumption is especially strong if the subject of the inter vivos gift is the same as that of the bequest, although some flexibility is necessary in this respect, for several reasons. The first is that the bequest will adeem by extinction[53] if a bequest is sufficiently specific and the property is unique. Ademption by extinction occurs if the property no longer is in the testator's estate at death, in this case because the testator gave it to the beneficiary. For example, extinction will apply if the will bequeaths Blackacre to Child but the testator deeded Blackacre to Child and Child's spouse before dying. For that reason, a historical notion of little currency was that ademption by satisfaction could apply only to bequests that are *not* specific. For

---

(Footnote Continued)

necessary funds. UPC § 3-902(b) would produce the same effect if by implication or express provision the intent to reduce taxes was the testator's clear priority and would be frustrated by the normal abatement rules.

[50] See In re Estate of Zeitchick, 231 A.2d 131 (Pa. 1967) (bequest to testator's spouse pursuant to prenuptial agreement took priority over bequest to testator's child).

[51] See § 2.3.

[52] See Atkinson, The Law of Wills § 133 (2d ed. 1953); McGovern, Kurtz, & English, Wills, Trusts & Estates § 2.6 (4th ed. 2010).

[53] See § 3.2.5.2.

§ 3.2.5.1

example, if the will makes a *general* bequest of 100 shares of stock in a publicly traded corporation to Child and the testator gave Child that number of those shares during life, the possibility remains for there to be an additional 100 shares available for transfer at death as well. In this case ademption by extinction would not apply, so satisfaction is most relevant.

A second reason for doubt about application of ademption by satisfaction only to gifts of property that is substantially similar to the subject matter of a testamentary bequest is related to the concept of ejusdem generis. This concept traditionally specified that a bequest of XYZ stock in a will could not be satisfied by an inter vivos gift of some other property. That concept is relaxed, however, if the testator's intent is clear that a gift of other property is meant to satisfy the testamentary bequest. This is easier to establish if the gifted property is sufficiently similar to or serves the same purpose as the testamentary bequest. Thus, for example, assume that the testator's intent in providing a testamentary bequest of cash to each of two grandchildren is to take advantage of the GST exemption. And then assume that the testator during life instead transferred property in kind with a value of half of the amount of the available exemption at that time to one of the grandchildren. If the testator's intent otherwise is clear, the difference in the nature of the gifted property should not preclude a finding that the inter vivos gift satisfied the grandchild's testamentary entitlement.

The doctrine of ademption by satisfaction is not applicable to gifts made prior to execution of a will. Instead, it is assumed that any testamentary bequest that is meant to reflect pre-execution gifts will so provide. Thus, a specific provision in the will is necessary if a testator wants gifts to similarly situated beneficiaries made at any time before execution of the will to count against their ultimate distributive shares.

A provision addressing the same question with respect to post execution gifts is desirable even if not absolutely necessary. Indeed, because proof of intent is difficult in any case, the existence and value of any gifts made before or after execution of the will that are meant to satisfy a bequest under the will should be documented by the testator as close as possible to the time of the gift. It is easy enough to suggest that gifts made before execution that are meant to count against a beneficiary's testamentary entitlement be reflected by the bequest itself, and that

§ 3.2.5.1

gifts made subsequent to execution that are meant to satisfy the testamentary bequest should be reflected by a codicil updating that provision. But it is unlikely that the testator will follow this advice with any but the most major gifts or transfers that significantly disturb an intended equality under the estate plan.

Fortunately, it is sufficient if a contemporaneous written declaration by the testator or acknowledgment by the donee reflects the intent that the gift be charged against the testamentary bequest. Thus, a declaration should be prepared, in which the testator also should indicate at what value the gifted property is chargeable against the bequest, whether it is to be charged with interest from the date of the gift, and whether it will have any effect on the rights of representatives of the beneficiary if the testator outlives the beneficiary.

Like its advancements counterpart in §2-109, the 1990 version of UPC §2-609 contains several provisions that improve upon the historical concept of ademption by satisfaction:

> (1) Gifts to a third party (such as a spouse of the testamentary beneficiary or a trust for the beneficiary) may constitute an ademption by satisfaction as if they were gifts directly to the beneficiary. The example given in the Comment to §2-609 is of a will that bequeaths $20,000 to a beneficiary by a testator who subsequently makes inter vivos gifts of $10,000 to each of the beneficiary and the beneficiary's spouse, taking advantage of the opportunity to provide the same monetary benefit tax free under the gift tax annual exclusion.

> (2) The value of the property on the later of the date the beneficiary came into possession or enjoyment or the date of the testator's death controls in determining the amount satisfied. This implicitly indicates that nonprobate transfers that are effective only at death may be treated as an ademption by satisfaction.

> (3) Unlike the advancement rule, an ademption by satisfaction to a donee who predeceased the testator is charged against the donee's representative who takes the testamentary bequest under any applicable antilapse statute.[54]

A tax apportionment problem may be raised by transfers during life that constitute an ademption by satisfaction of bequests under a will. Assume that each testamentary beneficiary is expected to contribute to

---

[54] See the 1990 version of UPC §2-609(c), referring to §§2-603 and 2-604, which deal with the concept of laps e, and see §3.2.5.4.

§3.2.5.1

the testator's FET bill in proportion to the amount each receives relative to the testator's total estate. Also assume that taxes are prorated on the basis of the net shares of each beneficiary, computed after reflecting inter vivos gifts that satisfy the beneficiaries' entitlements at death. The donees whose shares are reduced will pay a smaller share of the total tax burden.

This inequity is not entirely avoided even if those beneficiaries whose entitlements were anticipated by inter vivos gifts paid the gift tax on their gifts, because the net gift concept[55] reduces their tax obligation. First because the gift tax is computed tax exclusive, and further because a net gift is reduced for computation of the tax by the amount of the gift tax liability imposed on the donee. Thus, instead, equity is generated only if those beneficiaries contribute pro rata to the tax payment obligation relative to all property transferred inter vivos and at the testator's death, as if the testator's intent was that gifts be treated for all purposes as if they were received at death along with the balance of the testator's estate. Even if the gifted property is not in fact includible in the testator's gross estate at death.[56]

Ademption by satisfaction or advancement treatment is an important consideration when drafting group trusts. Imagine a single trust to be held for the benefit of all the settlor's children until no living child is under a specified age, at which time the trust is divided into separate shares for the respective children. Distributions made before division that are not equal among the beneficiaries may generate acrimony, particularly if the amount of the inequity is significant. In some cases the settlor wants the trust to operate as an extension of the settlor's own pocketbook, to provide funds in the same way the settlor would if alive, which in most respects is without concern about inequities. For example, one desirable feature of a group trust is to provide that no child's

---

[55] See §§ 3.3.15.4 and 7.2.5.

[56] See, e.g., In re Estate of Necaise, 915 So. 2d 449 (Miss. 2005) (a satisfaction case in which the decedent's will dictated a pro rata recovery from the donee). If made after 1976, the inter vivos transfers are includible in the testator's adjusted taxable gifts base for FET computation purposes and, therefore, are a part of the overall tax determination. Nevertheless, the donee still benefits from inter vivos transfers rather than having to wait until the testator's death to enjoy the property, and may benefit if the value of the gift appreciated but is frozen at the time of the gift for purposes of this computation.

§3.2.5.1

education expenses will be charged against that child's separate share, reflecting the fact that the settlor may have educated some children already (meaning that their expenses came from the "general fund") but others' education is not yet complete and would need to be funded after the settlor's death. Division of such a trust might be delayed until it is reasonably likely that each child's higher education is complete. Presumably these expenses should not be charged against any beneficiary's ultimate distributive share.

Alternatively, however, the settlor might authorize the trustee to make distributions for extraordinary items, such as to start a business, to purchase a home, or to pay for a wedding, and would want those transfers made prior to division of the trust into shares to be treated as an acceleration of that recipient's ultimate share. In those cases the value used in charging the accelerated transfer, the imposition of interest, and resolution of the question whether the acceleration counts against the recipient's representatives if division occurs after the recipient's death are all issues that should be addressed in the trust document. Considerable thought also must be devoted to the definition of expenditures that should be so treated.

§3.2.5.2 Ademption by Extinction

Ademption by extinction (frequently known simply as ademption), is related to ademption by satisfaction and creates additional drafting issues surrounding testamentary bequests. In its most simple application, ademption by extinction anticipates that the testator's will may make a bequest of property that no longer exists in the testator's estate at death. In its easiest application, that property was so unique that it cannot be replaced by the personal representative in an effort to comply with the terms of the will. Thus, for example, a specific bequest of a unique necklace that the estate no longer owns when the testator dies adeems by extinction. The circumstances surrounding the ademption may affect this result, however, because the beneficiary might claim that proceeds from a sale of the item, or casualty loss insurance proceeds paid in the wake of its theft, loss, or destruction, should be paid to the beneficiary to compensate for the ademption. These kinds of issues should be addressed in any specific bequest of property that might not exist in the estate at death.

§3.2.5.2

The historical application of the doctrine of ademption by extinction excluded general bequests, probably because the subject matter was not unique and therefore could be obtained by the personal representative after the testator's death to satisfy the bequest.[57] For example, if the testator bequeathed stock of a publicly traded corporation and did not own sufficient shares at death, it would be no problem for the personal representative to merely acquire additional shares (or transfer to the beneficiary the monetary value of the number of shares involved) if the estate otherwise was sufficient to finance that remedy. A different situation would exist, however, if the gift involved stock of a family corporation (although the doctrine might apply to such a specific bequest if it was possible to acquire more shares in that corporation).

Unpredictability in this area turns in part on classification of the bequest as specific or general, which in turn might depend on the uniqueness of the asset involved. One traditional method of avoiding ademption by extinction is to classify a bequest as demonstrative, meaning that it has characteristics of both general and specific bequests. For example, although it would be very rare in actual practice, if a bequest was of "$X to be satisfied first from my account at the ABC Bank," a court likely would hold that insufficiency in the account at ABC Bank (or even its nonexistence at death) would not adeem the bequest because any dollars can be used to satisfy any shortfall in the bequest.

Traditional application of the doctrine of ademption by extinction was significantly unforgiving. It largely was unconcerned with whether absence of the specific item from the estate reflected an affirmative intent on the testator's part to adeem the bequest or flowed unintentionally from a totally involuntary and perhaps unknown loss or destruction of the subject of the bequest. Based on a rationale that the testator would amend the will if the intent was to preserve the bequest, some inroads developed in the form of exceptions if, for example, the testator was unable to alter the will before death—because the testator was incompetent or died from the same cause that destroyed the asset. And the doctrine never applied if the item existed at death but was destroyed or otherwise was removed after the testator's death.

[57] See Atkinson, The Law of Wills § 134 (2d ed. 1953); McGovern, Kurtz, & English, Wills, Trusts & Estates § 8.2 (4th ed. 2010).

§ 3.2.5.2

The 1990 version of UPC § 2-606 constitutes a modern legislative modification of the doctrine of ademption by extinction that serves as a roadmap to drafting bequests that avoid harsh and unintentional consequences. Its various applications alert estate planners to the types of provisions that might be included with specific bequests that a testator does not wish to adeem even if there is a change to the estate after execution of the will.

Ademption is meant to be avoided to the fullest extent possible under § 2-606(a), which provides that the recipient of a specific bequest is entitled to any proceeds from the sale of the subject property, any condemnation award, any fire or casualty insurance proceeds, any property owned by the testator as a result of or in lieu of foreclosure of the subject property, and any property acquired by the testator to replace the subject property. Indeed, § 2-606(a)(6) is a pecuniary award equal to the value of otherwise adeemed property, applicable "to the extent it is established that ademption would be inconsistent with the testator's manifested plan of distribution or that . . . the testator did not intend ademption . . . ."

A good illustration of the principles of ademption not covered specifically by other rules, and therefore meant to be addressed by this provision, was presented by In re Estate of Thornton.[58] The decedent's will made a specific bequest of "the net proceeds from a present [medical] malpractice case." The decedent died before the action was completed, so the malpractice action was converted into a wrongful death action. The proceeds finally collected from that proceeding passed to the beneficiary to the extent they represented amounts that would have been recovered in the malpractice action had it been prosecuted to completion prior to the decedent's death. In this case the court relied on the theory that a bequest will not adeem if the change was merely in form and not in the substance of a bequest.

Examples of bequests that trigger the need to consider the possibility of an ademption by extinction include:

> • A gift of the testator's principal personal residence, which the testator might sell to acquire a new home with the proceeds, or which might be sold by the testator's family or personal representative after the testator is

---

[58] 481 N.W.2d 828 (Mich. Ct. App. 1992).

§ 3.2.5.2

too old or ill to continue living there[59] and the proceeds used to finance the

---

[59] Local law may specify that sale by a personal representative rather than by the testator (especially after the testator is no longer competent to alter the will) works no ademption and the proceeds therefore would pass to the beneficiary by virtue of local law. See Annot., Ademption or revocation of specific devise or bequest by guardian, committee, conservator, or trustee of mentally or physically incompetent testator, 84 A.L.R.4th 462 (1991). It would be wise not to rely on that result, however, because it might depend on the question of the testator's capacity at the time of sale or identification of the proceeds that might have been commingled in an account from which the testator's living expenses were paid. Compare Estate of Mason, 397 P.2d 1005 (Cal. 1965), in which the beneficiary was entitled to the full amount of the sale proceeds through contribution by other beneficiaries because the expenses of caring for the testator should not have been paid out of the proceeds prior to exhaustion of funds that passed to those other beneficiaries, with Mississippi Baptist Found., Inc. v. Estate of Matthews, 791 So. 2d 213 (Miss. 2001), in which a conservator continued the decedent's investment account that owned municipal bonds, the maturation proceeds of which were invested in an investment advisor's mutual funds, which was deemed not to pass as part of a bequest of stocks and bonds. The potential for an accounting nightmare in such a case could be avoided by a provision in the bequest specifying the effect of sale. And see the 1990 version of UPC §§ 2-606(b) and (d), which would negate the beneficiary's entitlement to the proceeds of sale in such a case if the testator's incapacity was adjudicated as terminated more than one year before death.

It also might not be wise to rely on state law under which it depends on who sold the property. For example, in Ohio at the time In re Estate of Hagel, 668 N.E.2d 474 (Ohio 1996), was decided, sales by a guardian were subject to a legislative exception to the ademption rule but not sales by an attorney in fact acting under a durable power of attorney. Thus, the powerholder sold the personal residence of an incompetent testator, not knowing that the powerholder was the beneficiary of a specific bequest of that property under the testator's will. This is the antithesis of an abuse situation (the powerholder not gaining any advantage by the premortem sale of property that otherwise would pass to the powerholder). Yet the court reversed a lower court determination to extend the exception applicable to a court supervised guardian (in which the potential for abuse or frustration of intent is less) and also failed to consider application of an exception to ademption if the testator was incompetent to alter the will to reflect the sale and preserve the benefit of the bequest. In a case with very similar facts, In re Estate of Anton, 731 N.W.2d 19, 25 (Iowa 2007), cited *Hagel* and In re Estate of Bauer, 700 N.W.2d 572 (Neb. 2005), but disagreed with both to rule that the devisee should receive the remaining proceeds from sale of the decedent's dwelling, stating that "there are only a few cases dealing with the question of whether acts of an agent pursuant to a durable power of attorney cause ademption of specific bequests [and they] have not reached uniform results."

§ 3.2.5.2

testator's living and health care expenses. The home also might be transferred to a QPRT in which the testator retained only the use or possession for a term of years, might be destroyed by fire or other casualty, or might be seized by creditors or the government, including in eminent domain. In these and similar events, the will should specify whether the designated beneficiary is meant to take the proceeds from a sale,[60] any replacement residence or reinvestment of the proceeds, any insurance proceeds, or any cause of action flowing from the loss or destruction.

- A bequest of any wasting asset such as bonds, notes, installment sale contracts, a life estate per autre vie or a term of years, copyrights, patents, royalty interests, leaseholds, and the like all presumably should address the

---

[60] See, e.g., In re Estate of Hume, 984 S.W.2d 602 (Tenn. 1999) (reversing holding that permitted proceeds from a foreclosure sale six weeks prior to decedent's death to pass to the specific devisee, rejecting the notion that ademption should not apply if action by a third party rather than by the decedent caused the ademption). If the property was subject to a contract for sale when the testator died, the additional question raised is whether the property subject to the contract passes pursuant to the bequest or only the contract or proceeds of the sale itself. This might in turn depend on whether the concept of equitable or constructive conversion was applicable. That question could be relevant if the contract was subject to cancellation and the beneficiary wanted to retain the property, or if classification of the property as realty subject to a contract of sale rather than personalty in the form of proceeds could alter the beneficiary to whom either the proceeds or income from the property or the proceeds would pass under the will.

For example, in Lievi v. Sheridan, 281 N.E.2d 870 (Mass. 1972), the court held that rent from the property during the period pending completion of the sale passed to the residuary takers rather than to the recipient of the specific bequest of the property. Presumably there would be no concern over identification of the proceeds themselves, although tracing can be a classic issue following a sale if the proceeds are meant to pass to the beneficiary in lieu of ademption. But see Kelley v. Neilson, 745 N.E.2d 952 (Mass. 2001) (a specific devise to one of the decedent's grandchildren, subject to a life estate in the decedent's child who was the grandchild's parent and who was living in half the property, was adeemed by a contract to sell the property to the decedent's other grandchild, executed by the decedent and scheduled to close before death but extended by the decedent's attorney in fact and not actually closed until after death), in which neither the clearly identified proceeds of sale nor the property subject to a sale contract were deemed to pass to the devisee. According to the court, the decedent did everything necessary to effect the sale prior to death (including execution of a quitclaim deed); although the doctrine of equitable conversion was not applicable, the court reached the same result by looking at the decedent's intent rather than merely applying the identity theory that normally is the law in the majority of jurisdictions.

§ 3.2.5.2

question whether the beneficiary is entitled to proceeds or payments made prior to the testator's death or during the period of administration of the estate.

• Far more likely to be sold and reinvested in many cases is publicly traded stock, a bequest of which can raise traditional ademption by extinction issues if the bequest is regarded as specific rather than general or residuary. In addition, stock or other ownership interests in a business that might be changed by incorporation, redemption, merger, or divestiture raises traditional ademption issues.[61] An illuminating example involved the antitrust litigation-generated divestiture of American Telephone & Telegraph (AT&T), which distributed stock in its regional Bell Telephone companies to holders of existing AT&T stock. If a bequest of the original AT&T stock did not carry with it the regional Bell shares, the beneficiary would receive a different investment than the one the testator held when the will was executed.[62] The bequest would not adeem if the traditional change in the form over substance defense applies. Thus, changes in the structure of the business raise interpretative questions that best are avoided by inclusion of an express provision indicating the testator's intent.

• Less common but more significant is the situation in a case like In re Estate of Donovan,[63] in which the decedent's will and pour over trust both addressed stock in the decedent's business but only the trust anticipated a sale of the stock and disposed of the proceeds to intended beneficiaries. The stock was sold inter vivos, the trust provision therefore did not apply (because the stock never was poured over into the trust), and the will did not address the ademption issue, meaning that the disappointed beneficiaries had to make several assertions, all of which failed. One was that the proceeds of the inter vivos sale should pass to the trust and then be disposed of as if the sale had occurred as anticipated, by the trustee. Another was that the trust was incorporated by reference into the will and that the trust provision therefore applied to the proceeds from the inter vivos sale. The court addressed this by concluding that, even if incorporation by reference applied (and it should not) the trust provision applied only if the decedent still owned the stock at death. It would have been easiest to

---

[61] See Annot., Ademption of legacy of business or interest therein, 65 A.L.R.3d 541 (1975); Annot., Change in stock or corporate structure, or split or substitution of corporation, as affecting bequest of stock, 46 A.L.R.3d 7 (1972).

[62] See, e.g., McPhee v. Estate of Bahret, 501 So. 2d 1319 (Fla. Dist. Ct. App. 1986), in which the facts were even more involved because the testator exercised an option to take only shares in Bell South in what amounted to a corporate authorized swap of the shares in the other regional companies for more stock in the one. The specific bequest of "all of my shares of AT&T" was deemed to carry with it the Bell South stock received in the divestiture and swap.

[63] 20 A.3d 989 (N.H. 2011).

§ 3.2.5.2

provide in the will and trust alike that the proceeds from sale of the stock would pass to the intended beneficiaries, regardless of who sold or when.

- A gift of personal property such as jewelry, an automobile, a boat, or other valuables in which a risk of loss, destruction, or theft exists should address the beneficiary's entitlement to proceeds from insurance as well as replacement property or sale proceeds.

In addition to these relatively common issues regarding ademption by extinction, specific bequests also produce related issues about the right to additional property that is related to the subject matter of the bequest, known as accessions.

§3.2.5.3 Accessions

The question that is addressed by the concept of accessions is whether the beneficiary of a bequest is entitled to any income or other entitlements flowing from the property that constitutes the bequest. For example, the recipient of a general bequest normally is entitled to interest at a statutory rate beginning one year after the testator's death.[64] The recipient of a specific bequest normally is regarded as the owner of the specifically bequeathed property as of the date of the testator's death, meaning that all income actually earned on that property during administration of the estate belongs to the beneficiary (even if possession of the underlying property and its income may be delayed during administration of the estate and may be subject to prior rights in the personal representative if the property is needed to pay the testator's debts, expenses, and taxes).[65] And although the residuary beneficiaries are not entitled to income per se, they effectively receive all earnings after the testator's death that exceed whatever must be paid to the recipients of specific or general bequests. These rules are straightforward and typically require no special drafting to work equitable or intended results.

The more important problems regarding accessions involve income or other entitlements earned and paid prior to the testator's death.

---

[64] See §3.2.5 n.31.

[65] Under Treas. Reg. §1.661(a)-2(e) (last sentence), if the title to realty passes immediately at death to the beneficiary thereof, income from that property properly is taxable to the beneficiary. Otherwise, income received by an estate pending distribution is taxable to the estate notwithstanding that the income passes with the underlying property and belongs to the beneficiary. See §5.3.1 n.6 and accompanying text.

Because the right to receive identifiable assets typically only exists with respect to specific bequests, this issue is not relevant with residuary or most general bequests. However, it is germane with respect to specific bequests and may apply to some general bequests as well.[66] Under the general rules, if an accession is paid before death and is separated from the underlying asset, that accession does not pass to the recipient of the underlying asset.[67]

To illustrate, if the testator made a specific bequest of Blackacre and that property generates rent between the date of execution of the will and the testator's death, the beneficiary who receives Blackacre does not receive rentals paid and separated from Blackacre before the testator's death. The beneficiary of a specific bequest of Blackacre would be entitled to rent when paid after the testator's death but if the rent is paid in the form of improvements made to the property, or it is a crop share and the testator died between planting and harvest, or if rents were in arrears and therefore had not yet been paid.

Similarly, if the beneficiary was to receive a bank account and interest was declared on the account prior to death, that interest would not pass with the account unless it was deposited to the account and was not withdrawn before the testator died. If the beneficiary was entitled to receive a coupon bond and the matured coupons were separated from the bond, even if not yet cashed, the interest represented by those coupons would not pass with the underlying bonds. But the beneficiary would receive both the bond and the mature coupons if those coupons still were attached to the bond at death. And if the beneficiary was entitled to receive stock that produced cash dividends declared[68] after execution of the will but before the testator's death, those dividends would not pass with the underlying shares, while dividends declared after death out of earnings generated before the testator's death would pass to the beneficiary of a specific bequest of that stock.

---

[66] Although the common law limited application of these rules to specifics only, the Comment to the 1990 version of UPC §2-605 clarifies that it does not discriminate between general and specific bequests.

[67] See Atkinson, The Law of Wills §135 (2d ed. 1953); McGovern, Kurtz, & English, Wills, Trusts & Estates §8.3 (4th ed. 2010).

[68] For these purposes the declaration date or, if later, the record date is regarded as the relevant date, not the date of actual payment.

§3.2.5.3

These rules work expected and normally appropriate results. On some occasions, however, a different result will be necessary to avoid hardship or unintentional deviations from the testator's intent. Two circumstances stand out in this respect, and state law in some jurisdictions has changed the traditional common law rules to accommodate the need for more appropriate results. The first involves crop share rentals on productive realty. Imagine, for example, that the testator incurred personal liability on money borrowed to finance seed, fertilizer, and fuel to plant, cultivate, and ultimately harvest a crop. But the property passes pursuant to a specific bequest to someone other than the residuary beneficiaries. It is possible that the normal accessions rule would result in the residue being obliged to repay the debt but not being entitled to the crop with which to do so, it having passed with the underlying property if the testator died before the crop was harvested. Alternatively, if the property is pledged as collateral and the testator has no personal liability on the debt, then the traditional rule giving the crop to the recipient of the property is appropriate and would need to be restored by the testator's will if state law has been altered to provide that the crop belongs in whole or in part to the estate and not to the beneficiary of a specific bequest of the underlying property. In each case the issue needs to be addressed to assure a proper matching of the liability and the income to repay it.

More likely of significance in most estates is the rule with respect to stock splits and dividends paid in kind. The traditional rule is that stock split shares pass with the underlying stock on which declared, the notion being that the bifurcation of one share into several is a mere change in form and, more importantly, that failure to pass the new shares with the underlying shares would dilute the ownership interest being given by the bequest. But the traditional rule does not pass stock-on-stock dividends with the underlying shares, notwithstanding that the failure to do so works the same dilution of the beneficiary's percentile ownership in the corporation. The supposed rationale for this disparity in treatment is that a cash dividend does not pass with the underlying stock and neither should a dividend of the same earnings payable in a different form.

The 1990 version of UPC § 2-605 provides that the beneficiary of a bequest of securities (either specific or general) will receive additional shares owned by the testator at death to the extent the testator acquired

§ 3.2.5.3

them as a result of any stock-on-stock dividend, stock split initiated by the issuing organization and paid in additional shares of that organization, shares of another organization acquired as a result of a merger, shares acquired in any reinvestment plan, or shares received in any consolidation, reorganization, or similar distribution by the issuing organization or any successor or related organization. In effect, a mere change in the form of investment, actions that do not alter the testator's percentile ownership of the organization, and distributions that were made at the corporation's behest all are reflected in the bequest and cause an accession to the underlying securities that passes to the designated beneficiary of the original bequest.

This provision addresses the accessions issue without determining whether a dividend is paid out of current earnings that could have been declared as a cash dividend (unless the dividend was a cash dividend that offered an option that was exercised by the testator to take additional shares instead). And this provision operates without regard for the number of shares held by the testator when the will was executed. It simply provides that all "securities of the same organization acquired by reason of action initiated by the organization . . . excluding any acquired by exercise of purchase options" pass to the beneficiary of the underlying securities. In states that have no similar rule, wills that make specific bequests of stock would be improved by addition of a similar provision.

A subtle change made in the 1990 version of the UPC is illustrated by In re Estate of Holmes.[69] Unlike its predecessor in §2-607 of the pre-1990 version, §2-605(a) in the 1990 version refers to changes "after the will was executed" and would have altered the result in *Holmes*, which involved the disposition of stock split shares allegedly passing under a specific bequest of "my 180 shares of [Corporation X] and my 124 shares of [Corporation Y]." The decedent owned twice the number of shares of each corporation both at the time of execution and at death because both stocks had split two-for-one prior to execution of the will. Because the version of the law applicable in this case, old §2-607, did not refer to changes made only after execution of the will,[70] the court

---

[69] 821 P.2d 300 (Colo. Ct. App. 1991).

[70] Notwithstanding the term "Change" in the title to the section, which the court interpreted to mean after execution of the will, this concept was not mirrored in the body of the provision and therefore was given no effect.

§3.2.5.3

awarded the stock split shares along with the underlying shares that passed to the specific legatees. Under new § 2-605 that result would not be reached, even though it unquestionably was the intent of the decedent that the beneficiaries in that case receive all the decedent's shares in the two corporations.

As illustrated by *Holmes* and numerous other cases,[71] a bequest that refers to a particular number of shares owned by the testator or made subject to the bequest often is an invitation for litigation and potential defeat of the testator's intent. It would be better in most cases to refer to all or a certain percentage of the stock held by the testator in a particular corporation or any successor or replacement thereof, rather than to the number of shares owned at the time of execution or the number (as

---

[71] See, e.g., Igoe v. Darby, 177 N.E.2d 676 (Mass. 1961) (testator bequeathed a specified number of shares of stock to three beneficiaries totaling exactly the number of shares owned at the time of execution; the stock was split before the testator died and the court determined that the beneficiaries were entitled to receive the added shares represented by the split); Bostwick v. Hurstel, 304 N.E.2d 186 (Mass. 1973) (applying same rule to a general bequest of a specified number of shares, notwithstanding the traditional rule that accessions apply only to specific bequests and further notwithstanding that between execution and death the testator sold all the stock owned in the corporation at execution and later reacquired it before dying); Watson v. Santalucia, 427 S.E.2d 466 (W. Va. 1993) (also rejecting the general versus specific bequest distinction and adopting the more sensible rule that the bequest will be interpreted as if no split had occurred unless a contrary intent appears; in this case that meant the beneficiaries of bequests of 100 shares each received the equivalent thereof at death, which was 400 shares each due to a four-for-one split between execution and death of the testator); Polson v. Craig, 570 S.E.2d 190 (S.C. Ct. App. 2002) (finding a bequest of "400 shares" of a publicly traded stock to be a specific bequest (not general), based on circumstances indicating that the decedent was conveying shares received subject to a precatory request from the decedent's own benefactor; the court concluded that a change in the corporation's name and splits in its stock did not alter the legatee's entitlement under UPC § 2-605(a) to the original shares, in whatever form and number they had morphed, grown, or divided into before the decedent's death); Knight v. Bardwell, 205 N.E.2d 249 (Ill. 1965) (following execution of the will containing a bequest of a designated number of shares of stock there were two stock splits, one before and one after execution of a codicil to the will that made reference to the same number of shares involved in the original bequest, notwithstanding the split that already occurred or the potential for additional splits; because the will referred to the number of shares "as constituted when my will and codicil become effective," the court held that neither split could be reflected in the bequest).

§ 3.2.5.3

opposed to the percentage) thereof that the testator wants the benefici-ary to receive. And, because the law in many states has not been altered to work appropriate results in all cases, the estate planner appropriately will consider how accessions earned before and after death should pass and then specifically so provide in the bequest.

§3.2.5.4 Lapse

At common law a bequest would fail if it was to a beneficiary who was deceased on the date the will was executed (a void bequest) or to a beneficiary who died after the will was executed but before the testator died (a lapsed bequest).[72] Unless pursuant to an obligation (such as a poorly considered property settlement agreement) or for tax purposes,[73] it seldom would make sense to add the bequest to the predeceased beneficiary's estate and require another administration of that property.[74]

---

[72] See Atkinson, The Law of Wills § 140 (2d ed. 1953); McGovern, Kurtz, & English, Wills, Trusts & Estates § 8.5 (4th ed. 2010).

[73] See, e.g., §§ 2503(c)(2)(B) and 2642(c), although both provisions' require-ment that property be made includible in a beneficiary's estate can be met with a general power of appointment; thus, distribution of the property to the benefici-ary's estate after the beneficiary's death is not necessary, although it too is a permissible means of complying with the inclusion requirement.

[74] A vested bequest would belong to the deceased beneficiary for property law purposes. See Harbour v. SunTrust Bank, 685 S.E.2d 838 (Va. 2009) (bequest to remainder beneficiaries who survived the settlor of an inter vivos trust, with distribution on the death of the survivor of D and S, was deemed to be vested at D's death notwithstanding that the remainder beneficiaries all predeceased S); In re Estate of Braman, 258 A.2d 492 (Pa. 1969) (holding that, because the bequest was not part of the beneficiary's estate at death, it could not pass under the predeceased beneficiary's will and, therefore, passed to the predeceased benefi-ciary's intestate takers); Cumming v. Cumming, 135 S.E.2d 402 (Ga. 1964) (D's mirror image will left everything to S if S survived D and, if not, to S's estate so that, on the death of the survivor, S's will disposed of their combined estates); Annot., Effect of residuary clause to pass property acquired by testator's estate after his death, 39 A.L.R.3d 1390 (1971). The value of the bequest would be includible in the predeceased beneficiary's gross estate for FET purposes under § 2033, notwithstanding that the beneficiary did not enjoy the use of the property. The value presumably would be quite low if that bequest could be revoked by the testator after the beneficiary's death, although it would not necessarily be zero if, for example, the testator was incompetent to change the will. There appears to be no law on the question whether the interest would qualify for deferral of tax under § 6163, but if the beneficiary died within two years before the testator a

So unless the testator's will provided otherwise, a bequest to a predeceased beneficiary was not regarded as a bequest to that beneficiary's
estate. The common law thus provided that a preresiduary disposition to
an individual would fail and the subject property would fall into and pass
with the residue, while a residuary bequest[75] would fail and, because
there is no residue of the residue, would pass by intestacy. Only if the
bequest was to a class, any member of which survived the testator,
would the gift not lapse and instead pass to the surviving class
members.[76]

These consequences can and often should be altered by the testator's will, and applicable legislation changes these results in many cases.
Because legislation that precludes lapse (antilapse statutes) often produces results that are contrary to the testator's intent, and because
antilapse statutes do not apply in all cases (for example, older versions

---

(Footnote Continued)

§ 2013 credit for any tax paid in the testator's estate might be available. See
§ § 3.3.20 and 2.0 n.3 regarding § § 6163 and 2013, respectively.

[75] Determining whether a bequest is a true residuary gift that will pick up
lapsed gifts and that will produce an intestacy if it lapses may be a problem, as
illustrated by Davis v. Anthony, 384 S.W.2d 60 (Tenn. 1964), in which D's will
gave 50% of "the rest and residue and remainder of my estate" to S and "the
remaining 50% of my estate" to designated persons. The gift to S lapsed and the
court concluded that the true residue was the gift of "the remaining" portion,
which picked up the lapsed gift to S.

[76] See § 11.1 with respect to class gifts. Easy illustrations of the issue whether
a class gift is involved are presented by In re Estate of Kuruzovich, 78 S.W.3d 226
(Mo. Ct. App. 2002) (residuary bequest to three individuals "share and share
alike" did not override antilapse statute), and Martin v. Summers, 655 N.E.2d 424
(Ohio Ct. App. 1995), in which D's estate was left "equally to [S] and to my
[child], share and share alike." The child predeceased the testator and the court
held that the antilapse statute applied because the term "equally, share and share
alike" indicated that, rather than a class gift, each of S and the child were to
receive half of the estate. Compare Polen v. Baker, 752 N.E.2d 258 (Ohio 2001)
(bequest to four named individuals—which therefore could not be a class gift—
"equally share and share alike, . . . or to the survivors thereof," which the court
regarded as indicative that survivorship was required, which prevented application of the state antilapse statute), citing and distinguishing *Martin* because
there were no words of survivorship in the earlier case. Over dissent and
referring to the significant split of authority nationwide regarding words of
survivorship, the court concluded that the decedent in *Polen* intended a per
capita and not a right of representation disposition.

§ 3.2.5.4

apply to lapse situations but not to void gifts, although the UPC and other more modern statutes no longer make this distinction), it is better in most situations to specify the desired alternative disposition if a beneficiary predeceases the testator (or is deemed to predecease by virtue of a disclaimer) and negate application of the statute.

Indeed, it may be appropriate to incorporate different results under different provisions of the will. For example, it might be inappropriate to allow representatives of a deceased child to take the share of personal effects the child would have received if living, but desirable to specify that those representatives stand in the child's place as beneficiary of a share of the residue.

State antilapse statutes make substantial changes in the common law result, applicable unless the testator manifests an intent that overrides the statute. A study of antilapse statutes, particularly the 1990 version of UPC §2-603(b)(3), illustrates that overriding application of the statute may be easier said than done, which makes drafting in anticipation of lapse a chore that should not be taken lightly. Antilapse statutes generally substitute descendants of the predeceased beneficiary as recipients of a lapsing bequest, rather than the traditional lapse result, with those representatives taking directly from the testator, not through the predeceased beneficiary's estate. Thus, creditors of the predeceased beneficiary have no claim on the property, and the property is not subject to the control of and is not taxable to the predeceased beneficiary.

The issue under many antilapse statutes is the breadth of their coverage, because not all predeceased beneficiaries are included under the statute's application.[77] In cases not covered by the statute, traditional

---

[77] Most antilapse statutes apply only if the predeceased beneficiary was within a certain defined class of beneficiaries. For example, many statutes apply only to relatives and do not include a bequest to a testator's spouse. See, e.g., the 1990 version of UPC §2-603(b), which is applicable only with respect to grandparents, descendants of grandparents, or step-children of the testator (or of a donor of a power of appointment that is being exercised). In Oliver v. Bank One, 573 N.E.2d 55 (Ohio 1991), the state antilapse statute applied only to gifts to "relatives" and was deemed not applicable to a gift to siblings of the decedent's spouse because they were related only by affinity (marriage) rather than by consanguinity (blood). A summary of state laws can be found in Restatement (Second) of Property—Donative Transfers Statutory Note to §18.6 (1985). See also Note,

lapse rules continue to apply, which often is undesirable. In addition, substantial uncertainty exists in many states regarding application of antilapse statutes to class gifts. At common law there was no lapse in a class gift if a class member died before the testator, because the surviving class members took the share the deceased class member would have received if living. So it is argued by some that antilapse statutes should not apply to class gifts unless the statute specifically refers to class gifts or there is a total lapse because all class members predecease the testator.

The 1990 version of UPC § 2-603(b)(2) makes the antilapse dictate applicable to any class gift other than a gift to descendants, issue, next of kin, heirs, relatives, family, or any other "class described by language of similar import," all of which providing their own version of protection against a class member already being deceased in their definition of how the class shares the gift (that is, per stirpes, per capita, per capita at each generation under the 1990 version of UPC § § 2-103(a)(1) and 2-106, and so on). The result is to send a deceased class member's share to that member's representatives, not to the other class members, which also may not be the testator's intent.

Further, some statutes prevent a lapsed gift of a part of the residue from falling through the residue into intestacy by giving the lapsed residuary share to the other residuary takers. Subject to application of the antilapse statute first, to send the share that a deceased residuary taker would have received if living to representatives of that taker, if any, the 1990 version of UPC § 2-603(b)(2) may have this effect if the residuary gift is a class gift, which is uncertain because the term "class gift" is not defined.[78]

(Footnote Continued)

Lapsing of Testamentary Gifts, Antilapse Statutes, and the Expansion of Uniform Probate Code Antilapse Protection, 36 Wm. & Mary L. Rev. 269, App. A at 322-333 (1994).

[78] See, e.g., In re Estate of Eickmeyer, 628 N.W.2d 246 (Neb. 2001), in which the decedent's estate was left 50% to A, 20% to B, and 30% "to X, Y, and Z, share and share alike." A, X, and Y all predeceased the decedent, only Y leaving a representative. Without commenting on whether the 30% to X, Y, and Z was a class gift, the court instead found that the estate should go to B, Z, and Y's representative, and found that the 30% to the group meant that each of X, Y, and Z was to get 10% apiece, meaning that the estate was effectively left 20% to B, 10% to Z, and 10% to Y's representative. The court simply reformed those percentages

An estate plan is not well drafted if the destination of a testamentary disposition must be determined under either the common law lapse rules or an antilapse statute because a beneficiary predeceased the testator. The will should designate the alternate disposition in a way that overcomes the otherwise governing effect of the common law or statutory rules. In this respect, state law should be inspected carefully because intuitive drafting may not be effective. For example, the 1990 version of UPC § 2-603(b)(3) provides that the use of words of survivorship alone is not sufficient to preclude application of the antilapse rule. Required is a statement that the descendants of the named beneficiary are not to take if the beneficiary is not alive, or an alternative disposition of the gift if it lapses. That is, it will not suffice to provide for "X if X survives me." Instead, the document would need to say "to X if X survives me, and if not to Y" or "to X and not to X's descendants." Another alternative noted in the Comment to § 2-603 is to specifically provide that the residue of the estate includes all lapsed or failed bequests, although this probably is not the most clear approach a drafter could employ.[79]

Moreover, an alternative devise is effective only if the alternative beneficiary is alive and otherwise entitled to take under the will. If not, the antilapse statute is not precluded from applying under the 1990 version of § 2-603(b)(4). Thus, for example, in a bequest "to X if X

(Footnote Continued)

to 50%, 25%, and 25% to dispose of the entire estate. It seems possible that the relative percentages should have been 20%, 15%, and 15% instead, which would have translated into a 40%, 30%, and 30% division. Whichever was the decedent's intent, the will drafting was not sufficiently clear to avoid litigation.

[79] Compare, e.g., Colombo v. Stevenson, 563 S.E.2d 591 (N.C. Ct. App. 2002), aff'd per curiam, 579 S.E.2d 269 (N.C. 2003) (holding that "boilerplate language" in the residuary clause sweeping into that bequest "all lapsed legacies and devises, or other gifts made by this will which fail for any reason" was adequate to indicate the testator's desire to override the antilapse statute; no mention was made of the proper application of the antilapse statute to the residuary gift itself, which also named the same predeceased beneficiary whose failed preresiduary gifts were regarded as falling into the residue rather than passing by the antilapse statute), citing but rejecting as contrary to the bulk of authority in other states Blevins v. Moran, 12 S.W.3d 698 (Ky. Ct. App. 2000) (such a residuary clause reference to lapsed bequests did not overcome the state antilapse statute—not the UPC—but rather was deemed to apply only if a bequest could not be saved from lapsing by the statutory substitute disposition).

§ 3.2.5.4

survives me, otherwise to Y," the descendants of X would take under the antilapse statute if both X and Y were not living (assuming that X is within the class of beneficiaries to whom the antilapse statute is applicable). Similarly, in a bequest of "$X to my children A and B or to the survivor of them," the Comment to §2-603 specifies that, if A predeceased the testator, then B would take to the exclusion of the representatives of A because it is clear that the testator meant this to be a substitutionary gift.[80] A safer bequest would be to clearly create a class gift by stating that the money goes "in equal shares to such members of the class of my children A and B as survive me" and then further to specify whether the representatives of either child who predeceases the testator will receive the share the child would have received if living.

A bequest also needs to address the possibility of deaths under circumstances such that the order of death cannot be determined (frequently referred to as "simultaneous," although they may not be and still the order of death might not be capable of proof). Unless the marital deduction is involved,[81] rather than require a beneficiary merely to survive the testator, normally it is preferable to require survivorship by a period such as 30 days to better ensure that property will not be probated twice if injuries suffered in a common disaster result in death of the testator and the beneficiary within a relatively short period.[82]

---

[80] See, e.g., In re Estate of Snapp, 233 S.W.3d 288 (Tenn. Ct. App. 2007) (gift "to my three sisters . . . [but] if any sister should predecease me, then . . . the surviving sister(s) shall take the deceased sister's share" was deemed to preclude application of the state antilapse statute, even though all three sisters predeceased the testator).

[81] See §13.4.2.2.1 regarding survivorship in the marital deduction context.

[82] See, e.g., Estate of Acord v. Commissioner, 93 T.C. 1 (1989), aff'd, 946 F.2d 1473 (9th Cir. 1991) (decedent's gross estate included property received from prior decedent who predeceased decedent by only 38 hours, as a result of injuries sustained in a common accident; prior decedent's alternative bequest if decedent died at the same time or under circumstances that made it doubtful as to which died first did not apply because none of those events occurred, and a state law survivorship requirement was overridden by decedent's alternative condition).

The 1990 version of UPC §2-702 imposes an automatic survival requirement of 120 hours (five days), which can create a lapse result if the beneficiary dies within that period. But five days may not be an adequate survivorship requirement in light of the ability of modern medicine to sustain human life and the inability of the legal system quickly to decide whether to terminate extraordinary

§3.2.5.4

Moreover, a major drafting issue may entail coordination of multiple wills and their presumptions of survivorship. For example, assume testators A and B each provide that the estate of the first of them will pass entirely to the survivor of them. And the survivor of them leaves a monetary bequest to X. If A and B die under circumstances such that the order of their deaths cannot be proven, USDA § 1, adopted in all but one state,[83] would presume each of A and B to be the survivor with respect to their own estates, meaning that X potentially takes the monetary bequest under both wills. This would be contrary to the clear intent revealed from reading both wills, which is that X is to take only one bequest. One answer for drafting purposes is to provide in each will that death under such circumstances will reduce the monetary bequest to X from each estate to half the amount specified. If preferable, A and B could designate that X will receive the bequest from whichever estate A and B agree

---

(Footnote Continued)

life support procedures. See, e.g., Janus v. Tarasewicz, 482 N.E.2d 418 (Ill. App. Ct. 1985) (beneficiary entitled, notwithstanding requirement to survive another person, because beneficiary was kept alive with life supports until after that person died).

Under § 2056(b)(3) the maximum period of survival that should be imposed if marital deduction planning is involved is six months, which should be more than adequate. Because the concept of deaths as a result of a "common disaster" is too amorphous, use of that standard is not recommended even though it is authorized by § 2056(b)(3) and therefore is the concept that most individuals have in mind when drafting these provisions. See § 13.4.2.2.1 regarding "common disaster" provisions.

[83] See 8A U.L.A. 122, 128 (Supp. 2010). Only Louisiana appears not to have adopted any version of the Act.

The Act provides in relevant part that (1) if there is no sufficient evidence that persons have died otherwise than simultaneously, each person is deemed to be the survivor as regards the disposition of that person's own property, (2) a beneficiary is deemed not to have survived if the beneficiary's right to receive a bequest is conditioned upon surviving another person and they die under circumstances such that there is no sufficient evidence that they died otherwise than simultaneously, (3) if there is no sufficient evidence that several beneficiaries have died otherwise than simultaneously and property is disposed of in a way that each beneficiary would be entitled to the property if the others were predeceased, the property is divided into equal shares and distributed as if each beneficiary was the survivor, and (4) all of these rules can be overcome by an appropriate provision in the dispositive document providing for distribution of the property in a different manner or providing a different presumption of survivorship.

§ 3.2.5.4

to designate in this circumstance. A third alternative would be for one of A or B to reverse the presumption of survivorship that would apply in their respective estates, causing that testator to be treated as having died first for purposes of applying the bequest to X.

The 1990 version of UPC § 2-706 applies the antilapse statute to nonprobate dispositions and § 2-707 applies it with respect to future interests, both in virtually the same manner as § 2-603 applies to gifts at a testator's death.[84] But in states that have not adopted the UPC or similar legislation, it is uncommon for an antilapse statute to apply to nonprobate or future interest dispositions, which is a defect that also should be addressed in the estate plan. In a few situations death of a designated beneficiary before the testator will cause the transferor's will to apply with respect to nonprobate property.[85] Otherwise, those ancillary aspects of the estate plan also require attention to the lapse problem.

In a few cases the testator wishes to prevent certain individuals who otherwise would receive the testator's estate from benefiting. Few jurisdictions authorize "negative" will provisions that direct to whom property shall *not* pass.[86] In most states this requires that the testator make an

---

[84] See Dukeminier, The Uniform Probate Code Upends the Law of Remainders, 94 Mich. L. Rev. 148 (1995), for a detailed discussion of § 2-707 and its effect on the law of future interests.

[85] For example, if a life insurance beneficiary designation fails because the designated beneficiary predeceases the insured, the policy may provide a default alternative making the proceeds payable to the policy owner (or the owner's estate). In re Estate of Ingram, 510 P.2d 597 (Kan. 1973), involved a declaration of trust for the settlor for life, remainder to a child who predeceased the settlor, which the court held revoked and terminated the trust, causing the trust corpus to pass under the residuary clause of the settlor's will. And in United States v. Williams, 160 F. Supp. 761 (D. N.J. 1958), the beneficiary of a bank account (Totten) trust predeceased the depositor, which the court held terminated the trust and precluded the government from seizing the trust property for income tax deficiencies assessed against the beneficiary.

[86] See, e.g., the 1990 version of UPC § 2-101(b), which allows negative wills, and compare In re Estate of Jetter, 570 N.W.2d 26 (S.D. 1997) (two brothers, neither ever married and both without descendants, each executed wills leaving their entire estate to the other, stating an affirmative intent to exclude all other heirs, both failing to make an alternative disposition in the event the testator was the survivor of the two and the state antilapse statute not being applicable because each predeceased beneficiary had no descendants; the issue was whether the survivor's estate should escheat by virtue of the affirmative disinher-

§ 3.2.5.4

effective will that affirmatively distributes the entire estate[87] to other takers and may require that an antilapse statute be overridden if a designated taker predeceases the testator.[88]

(Footnote Continued)

itance and the court determined that it should not, because the state law UPC § 2-101(b) negative will concept ought not to apply in the absence of other takers and the so-called English rule should limit escheat to estates in which there are no other heirs to be found; a compelling dissent argued that neither brother needed a will to accomplish what the court concluded because the other brother was the natural heir in the event of survival and the ultimate beneficiaries under the court's ruling were the natural secondary takers, meaning that the only reason for the negative wills was to prevent exactly the result the court ordered); In re Estate of Scott, 659 So. 2d 361 (Fla. Ct. App. 1995) (statement that the testator "specifically and intentionally make no provision" for the children of the testator's sibling, who was the sole beneficiary of a trust created by the testator's will, was not adequate to express an intention contrary to application of the state antilapse statute that otherwise would apply because the sibling predeceased the testator and the will designated no other beneficiaries); Lindsey v. Burkemper, 107 S.W.3d 354 (Mo. Ct. App. 2003) (notwithstanding garden variety provision disinheriting any heir not otherwise identified in the will, death of a named heir caused the antilapse statute to apply rather than intestacy, sending the testator's estate to that heir's representatives); In re Will of Darmstadter, 280 N.Y.S.2d 223 (Surr. Ct. 1967) (nieces and nephews were entitled to the decedent's property as a result of the lapse of a residuary gift notwithstanding that decedent's will provided that no provision was made, or intended to be made, for siblings or their heirs). N.Y. Est., Powers & Trusts L. § 1-2.19 now defines a will as including a document that directs how a decedent's property is not to pass.

[87] See, e.g., In re Estate of Dammann, 191 N.E.2d 452 (N.Y. 1963) (residue given to eight named beneficiaries, one of whom predeceased the testator; because the will stated a desire that no part of the estate go to any other person, the court held that the deceased beneficiary's share passed to the surviving residuary beneficiaries and not by intestacy or under an antilapse statute to the individuals the testator intended to exclude).

[88] See, e.g., In re Estate of Ulrickson, 290 N.W.2d 757 (Minn. 1980) (will bequeathed estate to two siblings and provided that, if either predeceased the testator, the survivor would take everything; antilapse statute applied because both predeceased the testator); and compare Bridges v. Taylor, 579 S.E.2d 740 (Ga. 2003) (residue to three relatives in specified percentages and conditioned on survivorship precluded application of antilapse statute; all three predeceased and property passed by intestacy); and In re Estate of Hillman, 363 N.W.2d 588 (Wis. Ct. App. 1985) (bequest to the testator's sibling if living, otherwise to the sibling's spouse; both predeceased the testator) in which the court refused to follow *Ulrickson*, instead holding that a substitute gift to the sibling's spouse

§ 3.2.5.4

If a bequest is made to two persons with the right of survivorship (as joint tenants or as tenants by the entirety) so that the survivor will take the entire title if both survive the testator and then one dies, a reasonable interpretation of the testator's intent would be that the survivor also should take the entire title if one predeceases the testator. The issue is whether designation in the will of such form of joint ownership is sufficient to overcome operation of an antilapse statute. Like many other aspects of drafting in anticipation of a beneficiary not surviving the testator, the will should specify the testator's intent because there is virtually no law on this issue.[89] In an overall assessment, survivorship always should be considered, every possible contingency should be reflected in the bequest, and the testator's intent for disposition of the property in light of each possibility should be stated so that nothing is left to chance or to the operation of an antilapse statute.

§3.2.5.5 Bequests to the Estate Planning Attorney

Few items in a will raise suspicions of overreaching or unprofessional solicitation faster than the drafting attorney's name (or that of a relative or colleague of the drafter) as the designated personal representative, trustee, or attorney for either. But even worse is the attorney named as the beneficiary of a bequest. The truth may be that the attorney rendered legal services to the testator over a significant number of years, became a close personal friend of the testator and the testator's family, served as a trusted business advisor, became a surrogate parent and later counselor to the testator's children, was a neighbor, golf or tennis partner, fellow charity board member, and all around good per-

---

(Footnote Continued)

prevented the antilapse statute from applying because spouses of relatives were not within the class of beneficiaries to whom the antilapse statute applied, even though the substitute gift itself could not take effect. The 1990 version of UPC § 2-603(c) would dictate the opposite result, giving the gift to the sibling's descendants and not to the spouse's estate or the spouse's descendants.

[89] In re Estate of Flynn, 329 N.Y.S.2d 249 (Surr. Ct. 1972), held that the antilapse statute was not applicable in a case in which the interest of one beneficiary failed under an interested witness statute, but the 1990 version of the UPC does not appear to address this issue, notwithstanding its substantial revisions to and expansion of the antilapse rules normally applicable.

son.[90] Still, warning lights should flash when a testator asks an attorney to draft a bequest to the attorney as a token of the testator's gratitude or affection and will not consider the attorney's ardent admonition to have another attorney draft or at least review the will to be certain that this is what the testator wants.

The Model Rules prohibit an attorney from preparing an instrument that provides a substantial gift to the lawyer or a person related to the lawyer.[91] Although there is some room to wiggle in the rule—centering around the definition of a "substantial" gift and when a client is sufficiently "related"—in the vast majority of situations in which this issue

---

[90] See In re Petition for Disciplinary Action against Prueter, 359 N.W.2d 613 (Minn. 1984) (attorney who revised will and trust of friend with whom attorney had strong personal and business relationship to provide attorney and attorney's spouse with half the friend's estate was held to have violated Code of Professional Responsibility).

[91] 2008 Am. Bar. Ass'n Model Rules of Professional Conduct Rule 1.8(c) states:

> A lawyer shall not . . . prepare on behalf of a client an instrument giving the lawyer or a person related to the lawyer any substantial gift unless the lawyer or other recipient of the gift is related to the client. For purposes of this paragraph, related persons include a spouse, child, grandchild, parent, grandparent or other relative or individual with whom the lawyer or the client maintains a close, familial relationship.

Restatement of the Law Governing Lawyers § 127(1) (2000) prohibits a lawyer from preparing the instrument effecting the gift unless the lawyer is a relative or natural object of the client's bounty *and* the gift is "not significantly disproportionate to those given other donees similarly related to the [client]." Restatement of the Law Governing Lawyers § 127(2) (2000) even prohibits a lawyer from *accepting* a gift from a client under a document drafted by someone else unless the gift is insubstantial, the attorney is a relative or natural object of the client's bounty, *or* the client was encouraged to and had a reasonable opportunity to seek independent representation, which is a more lenient standard than the Model Rule and is more akin to Model Code of Professional Responsibility Ethical Consideration 5-5. Cal. Prob. Code § 21350 provides that the bequest is invalid if the beneficiary is the person who drafted or transcribed the document or caused it to be drafted or transcribed, or if the beneficiary is related to that person or is a partner or shareholder of any partnership or corporation in which that person is a partner, shareholder, or employee, unless the beneficiary is related to or a cohabitant with the donor, the bequest was reviewed by an unrelated attorney who counseled the donor and provided a signed certificate that the transfer was "not the product of fraud, menace, duress, or undue influence," or a court makes the same determination.

§ 3.2.5.5

might arise it will be clear enough what the rules prohibit, allowing the responsible estate planner to reach a clear conclusion about whether to require separate representation if the client is insistent upon making a bequest to the attorney or a member of the attorney's family.[92]

---

[92] See, e.g., In re Randall, 640 F.2d 898 (8th Cir. 1981) (former president of American Bar Association disbarred for drawing will totally disinheriting the testator's only child and grandchildren and leaving the attorney the testator's entire $2 million estate); Florida Bar v. Anderson, 638 So. 2d 29 (Fla. 1994) (drafter suspended for 90 days despite finding that drafter intended devises to drafter and drafter's spouse to protect testator's beneficiary from creditors); Carter v. Williams, 431 S.E.2d 297 (Va. 1993) (attorney also named as executor drafted will leaving bulk of testator's estate to attorney's spouse, thereby disinheriting individual testator raised as a child who was sole beneficiary under testator's prior will); In re Estate of Tank, 503 N.Y.S.2d 495 (Surr. Ct. 1986) (court struck bequest of $5,000 to attorney who drafted the will disposing of an estate of $50,000, ostensibly as the decedent's gratitude to the attorney for serving the decedent, notwithstanding that attorney was a total stranger to the testator prior to the abbreviated will drafting representation). In Lawyer Disciplinary Board v. Ball, 633 S.E.2d 241 (W. Va. 2006), and Krischbaum v. Dillon, 567 N.E.2d 1291 (Ohio 1991), the courts established rebuttable presumptions of undue influence by any attorney who drafts a will benefiting the attorney or family members of the attorney unless the testator was related to the attorney; otherwise, the attorney must refuse to draft the provision (and should not recommend another attorney to draft it either) because mere encouragement by the attorney that the client seek independent representation is not sufficient to rebut the presumption); In re Filosa, 964 A.2d 1148 (R.I. 2009), (censure of attorney who "enjoyed a close personal relationship as good friends" with an elderly widow who had no living relatives; when attorney advised client that another lawyer must prepare the document, the client selected the attorney's law partner, which the court held was not adequate). Also consider Allstate Life Ins. Co. v. Estate of Reed, 619 F. Supp. 2d 262 (S.D. Miss. 2007), in which spouses—a retirement home operator and volunteer—befriended a resident who they referred to their own attorney to draft a bequest to the spouses, which proved to be invalid because of a nursing home prohibition; quaere why the drafting attorney did not perceive the conflict of interest and ethics concerns involved for the drafter.

There are tough cases involving suspension of attorneys like those in Disciplinary Counsel v. Kelleher, 807 N.E.2d 310 (Ohio 2004) (attorney drafted a living trust for a client who had been a close personal friend of the attorney's family for over four decades and that named the attorney as successor trustee and named the attorney's family as remainder beneficiaries) and In re Boulger, 637 N.W.2d 710 (N.D. 2001) (attorney was a life long friend of the decedent and only later the decedent's attorney as well, had represented the decedent's

If the drafting attorney is named as beneficiary, the bequest may be void[93] but, even if it is not, it may create a presumption of undue influence that could cause the entire will to fail,[94] exposing the attorney to an action for negligence and at least the obligation to pay the costs of establishing the validity of the will. At a minimum, a drafting attorney who also is a beneficiary

---

(Footnote Continued)

business for years, and was made a remote contingent beneficiary but did not actually receive any bequest). Each court held that the Rule is absolute and mandates application of a bright line that protects the public notwithstanding the absence of evidence of overreaching or undue influence. But see Vaupel v. Barr, 460 S.E.2d 431 (W. Va. 1995) (separate counsel drafted the decedent's will that named the decedent's long-standing attorney and the attorney's spouse (who was a distant relative of the decedent) as beneficiaries, to the exclusion of the decedent's child and grandchildren (who seldom visited the decedent and who the decedent indicated had sufficient resources to provide for themselves); attorney at law also was decedent's attorney in fact, which the court regarded as proof that the decedent held a special high regard for the attorney and not a reason to impose the burden to prove the validity of the will on the attorney against a charge of undue influence by one in a confidential or fiduciary relation to the decedent).

See generally deFuria, Testamentary Gifts From Client to the Attorney-Draftsman: From Probate Presumption to Ethical Prohibition, 66 Neb. L. Rev. 695 (1987); Johnston, An Ethical Analysis of Common Estate Planning Practices—Is Good Business Bad Ethics, 45 Ohio St. L.J. 57 (1984); and see Annot., Attorneys at law: disciplinary proceedings for drafting instrument such as will or trust under which attorney-drafter or member of attorney's family or law firm is beneficiary, grantee, legatee, or devisee, 80 A.L.R.5th 597 (2000).

[93] See, e.g., Shields v. Texas Scottish Rite Hospital for Crippled Children, 11 S.W.3d 457 (Tex. Ct. App. 2000) and In re Karabatian's Estate, 170 N.W.2d 166 (Mich. Ct. App. 1969) (attorneys violated ethics rules and bequests were void).

[94] See, e.g., Franciscan Sisters Health Care Corp. v. Dean, 448 N.E.2d 872 (Ill. 1983) (attorney who named self as a beneficiary must, as a matter of public policy, provide clear and convincing evidence to rebut the presumption of undue influence). In re Estate of Barclay, 523 P.2d 376 (Kan. 1974), considered whether the drafting attorney was the "principal beneficiary" for purposes of a state law rule that any will prepared by the "sole or principal beneficiary" and who was the "confidential agent or legal advisor" of the testator is invalid absent a showing that the testator read or knew the contents of the will and received independent advice regarding it. The attorney was the residuary beneficiary and would net about $56,000, but there were two specific bequests to other persons in excess of $100,000 each, which led the court to conclude that the attorney was not the principal beneficiary and that the will therefore was not invalid.

§ 3.2.5.5

must not . . . decide unilaterally whether the circumstances justify his accepting employment despite a conflict of interest. He may not proceed to represent his client without her free, intelligent and informed consent. He must make sure she knows and understands the conflict and the threat it poses to the attorney's objectivity, and any other considerations material to the client's decision whether to entrust her affairs to the attorney. He must also take suitable precautions to minimize the damages and disadvantages to the client of his double role, including the risk that the attorney's advice about the initial decision to proceed despite the conflict may be biased. And for his own protection he should be prepared to prove later what really happened.[95]

Naming the attorney as fiduciary or as attorney for the fiduciary presents different considerations. One is unauthorized solicitation of business, which may not be a problem if the fact that the testator is an existing client means that securing the designation is protected under Model Rule 7.3, which prohibits only certain contacts with prospective clients.[96] Probably the more important issue if the attorney is asked to serve as fiduciary is the potential for conflicts of interest if the attorney also represents beneficiaries of the estate, such as S or the testator's

---

[95] In re Barrick, 429 N.E.2d 842, 846 (Ill. 1981) (attorney drew will for testator that gave the attorney a lifetime annuity of the amount the attorney had been receiving from the testator as an annual retainer; the actuarial value of the annuity was less than 5% of the value of the estate and, on the facts presented, the court did not discipline the attorney).

[96] Solicitation may be a problem if a jurisdiction still adheres to the substance of Ethical Consideration 5-6 promulgated under the American Bar Association's Model Code of Professional Responsibility:

> EC 5-6—A lawyer should not consciously influence a client to name him as executor, trustee or lawyer in an instrument. In those cases where a client wishes to name his lawyer as such, care should be taken by the lawyer to avoid even the appearance of impropriety.

This dictate has no counterpart under the Model Rules of Professional Conduct that were promulgated by the American Bar Association to replace the older Model Code, although it may be that the concepts involved were meant to be subsumed in other less direct rules. See generally In re Estate of Weinstock, 351 N.E.2d 647 (N.Y. 1976) (striking down appointment of attorneys as personal representative for overreaching); State v. Gulbankian, 196 N.W.2d 733, 734 (Wis. 1972) (involving attorneys who, in "[o]nly one will drafted after 1957 failed to name a member of the Gulbankian family to some fiduciary capacity").

surviving children.[97] And the possibility also exists of the attorney being accused of violating the Model Rule 1.8 prohibition against activities that compromise the attorney's independent professional judgment in advising the client. According to one ethics opinion:[98]

---

[97] See, e.g., Williams v. Maulis, 62 N.W.2d 702 (S.D. 2003) (estate planning attorney for D and S also represented S as executor, while also representing D's surviving sibling in a sale of realty to the sibling postmortem, the court finding conflicts on several levels and notwithstanding that S became personally dissatisfied with the attorney and sought the advice of another estate planner). Among other things *Williams* reveals the value of an "exit" letter that determines when one representation has ended and makes more clear whether the current client or former client conflict of interest rules are applicable. In re Wyatt's Case, A.2d 396 (N.H. 2009), is a good illustration of how a representation may morph into a conflict of interest, perhaps with the attorney being unaware or perhaps not knowing how to make an appropriate exit. The attorney began representing the client as personal counsel, prepared a durable power of attorney, advised the client in negotiations with a parent who had cut off support to the client, then became attorney for the agent under the durable power, then consulted with the client's spouse and with a conservator who was needed for the client. At some point the attorney realized that the appointment of the conservator was contrary to the client's wishes and that a conflict existed, so the attorney withdrew from representing the client and continued to represent the conservator. At that point it should have been clear that the Rule 1.7 present- or Rule 1.9 former-client conflict rules were applicable *and* that the client was unable to consent to the mutual representation.

[98] Georgia Formal Advisory Op. 91-1. Cf. Savu v. SunTrust Bank, 688 S.E.2d 276 (Ga. Ct. App. 2008), which addressed a corporate executor's "standard practice of employing the attorney who drafted a will to provide legal services in administration of the estate" and stated that the practice "is supported by numerous practical considerations," such as attorney familiarity with the family and the estate and that the attorney "is presumably the attorney whom the testator would select. Therefore, this is a pervasive practice endorsed by a 'Statement of General Policies' adopted by the Trust Division of the American Bankers Association and the American Bar Association." And "it is not prohibited by any ethics rule in Georgia." The court agreed, however, "that the practice raises ethical concerns where it is part of a reciprocal arrangement through which the will draft[er] names the bank as estate executor, and the bank then names the will draft[er] as estate attorney at a higher fee than that obtainable through negotiation with other qualified lawyers." *Savu* did not involve such a breach of fiduciary duty, but there are cases in which a drafter is not competent by experience to advise a fiduciary at any fee, meaning that hiring the drafter at even a competitive fee may raise a fiduciary breach issue, not an attorney conflict

§ 3.2.5.5

> It is not ethically improper for a lawyer to be named executor or trustee in a will or trust he or she has prepared when the lawyer does not consciously influence the client in the decision to name him or her executor or trustee, so long as he or she obtains the client's written consent in some form or gives the client written notice in some form after a full disclosure of all the possible conflicts of interest. In addition, the total combined attorney's fee and executor or trustee fee or commission must be reasonable and procedures used in obtaining this fee should be in accord with [local] law.

According to the Opinion, full disclosure should include a discussion of all potential choices of fiduciary, their relative abilities, competence, integrity, and cost, the nature of the representation and fee if the attorney is named as fiduciary, the potential that the attorney would hire the attorney or the attorney's own firm for legal advice and the costs entailed in that engagement, and the advantages to the testator of seeking independent legal advice with respect to the designation.

An additional caution is that exculpatory language should not be included in the document naming the attorney as fiduciary unless it is the standard language customarily used in all documents drafted by that attorney naming other fiduciaries to similar roles. Further, to deal with concerns regarding conflicts of interest with other clients, the attorney should explain the potential problems that may arise and obtain the consent of the testator and each of those other clients.

Even if local rules do not require all of these disclosures and consents to be in writing, good practice and concerns about appearances (to say nothing of the ability to defend at a later date against charges of impropriety) dictate that the attorney be able to document that all appropriate measures were taken and that voluntary informed consents were obtained.[99]

Two final questions related to the drafting attorney as beneficiary are whether any bequest under the will that is not invalidated constitutes income to the attorney as deferred compensation for services rendered to the testator and whether the estate may deduct the payment under

(Footnote Continued)

of interest or ethics violation—which technicality may be lost on a court that is weighing the complaints of disappointed beneficiaries.

[99] Regarding the separate issue of the ethical propriety of drafting a document designating the attorney that the fiduciary will hire, see § 3.1.1 n.10.

§ 3.2.5.5

§ 2053. These questions need not involve bequests just to drafting attorneys. For example, in Jones v. Commissioner[100] the attorney did not prepare the codicil in which the bequest was made, was not present when it was executed, and no part of the bequest was held to be income to the attorney. The Tax Court concluded that the bequest was inspired by gratitude for services rendered and because of the attorney's interest, concern, friendship, and affection for the testator over many years. But Wolder v. Commissioner[101] involved an agreement between an attorney and the testator under which the attorney agreed to render legal services without charge and the testator agreed to make a specific provision for the attorney in the will, which gave the attorney cash and stock without reference to the agreement. Although a state court held that the attorney received a bequest and was not required to prove a claim as a creditor, this characterization did not control the tax question and the attorney was deemed to have received compensation for services rendered. The government conceded that, if the amounts paid to the attorney were includible in the attorney's gross income, then the estate was entitled to a § 2053 deduction for those payments.[102]

§3.2.6 Exercise of Powers of Appointment

Many powers of appointment authorize the powerholder (donee of the power) to exercise the power only by a provision in the powerholder's will, making exercise of powers of appointment a nearly uniquely testamentary undertaking. Well drafted powers preclude exercise of the power without making specific reference to it,[103] to preclude inadvertent or violative exercises. But many powers do not require as much to constitute an exercise, which raises the question whether a

---

[100] 23 T.C.M. (CCH) 235 (1964).

[101] 493 F.2d 608 (2d Cir. 1974), aff'g in part and rev'g in part 58 T.C. 974 (1972).

[102] And see Estate of Boyce v. Commissioner, 31 T.C.M. (CCH) 1017 (1972), aff'd, 493 F.2d 608 (2d Cir. 1974) (FET deduction limited to value of stock on date of decedent's death rather than value on date it was delivered to attorney as beneficiary).

[103] See § 12.4.4. For an illustration of a case in which the specific reference requirement precluded exercise see In re Estate of Burgess, 836 P.2d 1386 (Utah Ct. App. 1992) (involving a marital deduction general power of appointment trust with a remainder passing to the settlor's children by a prior marriage).

testator's will constitutes an effort to exercise powers of appointment that are available to the testator as powerholder. The intent to exercise available powers should, therefore, be addressed in drafting all wills and, on the chance that the testator is a powerholder but does not know it, a well drafted will anticipates this issue by an affirmative statement of intent in the residuary provision.

It probably is a fair guess that, if clients were asked whether it is their intent to exercise any powers of appointment that might be available to them, the nearly universal answer would be "you bet," the notion being that clients want to exert control over as much property as possible. Thus, it is not uncommon to find residuary provisions in wills that dispose of "the residue of my estate, including all property over which I may have power of appointment." Sometimes referred to as "blanket" exercise provisions, these residuary clauses are not wise, for several reasons:[104]

(1) The provision disposing of the appointive property in default of effective exercise of the power of appointment may (indeed, is likely to) transfer the property in the same manner to the same individuals to whom the testator would appoint it, making exercise unnecessary.

(2) Although it no longer is common to find powers of appointment created before October 22, 1942, if it was the case that the power being exercised by such a provision is a pre-1942 general power of appointment, exercise makes the power taxable under § 2041(a)(1) and subjects the appointive property to inclusion in the powerholder's estate, whereas failure to exercise the power would be a nontaxable event. Thus, lacking a major advantage to exercise, the tax burden incurred is unnecessary. It is fair to predict that pre-1942 powers are more likely to be unknown to the powerholder, which increases the likelihood that a blanket exercise of unknown powers will trigger an unnecessary tax.[105]

(3) Without inspection of the power to determine the class of permissible appointees, blind exercise of the power might be wholly or partially invalid because the residuary takers under the powerholder's blanket exer-

---

[104] For commentary on the dangers or disadvantages of inadvertent exercise, see Casner, Estate Planning—Powers of Appointment, 64 Harv. L. Rev. 185, 202 (1950); Fleming, Provisions for Trusts and Powers of Appointment, 1950 U. Ill. L.F. 341, 362; Lauritzen, Drafting Powers of Appointment Under the 1951 Act, 47 Nw. U.L. Rev. 314, 328 (1952); Sargent, Drafting of Wills and Estate Planning, 43 B.U.L. Rev. 179, 197 (1963).

[105] See § 12.4.4 regarding the disadvantages of a silent or blanket exercise of unknown powers to appoint.

cise residuary provision are not permissible appointees. This could create thorny administrative problems for the trustee of the trust granting the power and the personal representative of the powerholder's estate, under the doctrines of marshaling and capture.

(4) Similarly, exercise of the power is almost certain to violate the Rule Against Perpetuities applicable to the appointive property because, unless the exercise is outright, the perpetuities period applicable to the powerholder's own property is different than that applicable to the appointive property) and the powerholder's will (if it addresses the issue at all) almost certainly was drafted only with the period of the Rule beginning at the powerholder's death in mind. Thus, invalid exercise again is likely, with the same potential for administrative difficulties in sorting out the property subject to the power from the powerholder's own property when, perhaps long in the future, it is determined that the Rule Against Perpetuities was violated with respect only to the appointive property.

(5) Finally, if the power of appointment is a general power and the powerholder happens to be insolvent, exercise will subject the appointive property to claims of the powerholder's creditors whereas nonexercise might have left those assets immune to creditor claims.[106] This unwitting and unnecessary subjection to the claims of creditors is inappropriate if the same beneficiaries will benefit whether the power is exercised or the property passes under a default provision.

As a result of these disadvantages or dangers, many drafters specify the exact opposite of what their client's first reaction would be and specifically provide in the residuary provision that the intent is not to

---

[106] See 5 American Law of Property §23.16 (Casner ed. 1952); Restatement (Second) of Property—Donative Transfers §13.4 (1982); 3 Restatement of Property §§327, 329-331 (1940). In a turnabout that occurred after its Tentative Draft No. 5 in 2006, Restatement (Third) of Property (Wills and Other Donative Transfers) §22.3(b) (2011) now states a different rule, providing that all general powers are treated as exposing appointive property to an insolvent powerholder's creditors, regardless of exercise. As noted in Comment *c* to §22.3, this is a divergence from the common law rule, it "represents the current position" of the American Law Institute, and it matches a divergence previously made by Restatement (Third) of Trusts §56. Because of this evolution it may not be the result embraced in a particular jurisdiction, and the change may be limited to prospective application in a jurisdiction that chooses to follow this deviation from the traditional common law. Given the flux in the law that this development represents, nonexercise better preserves the possibility that creditors cannot reach the appointive assets, making nonexercise the better position from which to operate if the powerholder is insolvent.

§3.2.6

exercise powers of appointment that are not specifically mentioned.[107] These drafters do not leave the document silent about the testator's intent, notwithstanding that the express statement declining to exercise powers may generate questions from the client. This is because the law in a minority of states provides that a silent residuary provision constitutes an exercise of available powers of appointment unless the intent not to exercise can be proven.[108] That proof can be difficult.[109] Even if the law

---

[107] See § 12.4.4.

[108] The 1990 version of UPC § 2-608 represents the majority rule that exercise does not occur under a silent residuary provision in a will, and provides an exception only if the power is a general power of appointment that does not contain a default provision. Restatement (Third) of Property (Wills and Other Donative Transfers) § 19.4 (2011) mirrors the UPC and adds a refinement that exercise also occurs if the general power had a default provision but it is not effective. For a listing of minority states that regard a silent residuary provision as an exercise, however, see Restatement (Second) of Property—Donative Transfers Statutory Note to § 17.3 (1986). Various state law modifications can be found, making it difficult to overgeneralize about the rule. For example, Fiduciary Trust Co. v. First Nat'l Bank, 181 N.E.2d 6 (Mass. 1962), held that a silent residuary provision would exercise any general power but not a nongeneral power. See generally French, Exercise of Powers of Appointment: Should Intent to Exercise Be Inferred from a General Disposition of Property?, 1979 Duke L.J. 747; Rabin, Blind Exercises of Powers of Appointment, 51 Cornell L.J. 1 (1965); Annot., Effect of statute upon determination whether disposition of all or residue of testator's property, without referring to power of appointment, sufficiently manifests intention to exercise power, 16 A.L.R.3d 911 (1967); Annot., Disposition of all or residue of testator's property, without referring to power of appointment, as constituting sufficient manifestation of intention to exercise power, in absence of statute, 15 A.L.R.3d 346 (1967).

[109] For example, N.Y. Est. Powers & Trust L. § 10-6.1(a)(4) requires proof that the testator affirmatively intended not to exercise and, like most instances of proving a negative, this is far more difficult than placing the burden on the proponents of exercise to show an affirmative intent to exercise the power, as under Cal. Prob. Code § 641. See, e.g., Shriners Hospital for Crippled Children v. Citizens Nat'l Bank, 92 S.E.2d 503 (Va. 1956) (testator's knowledge of difference between appointive assets and testator's own property, together with scrupulous avoidance of reference to the former, deemed sufficient evidence of lack of intent to exercise power to overcome statutory presumption of exercise otherwise applicable), and compare In re Smith's Trust, 107 N.E.2d 92 (N.Y. 1952) (will executed five years before creation of power deemed to exercise power absent evidence that powerholder intended to not exercise; quaere how to prove an affirmative intent not to exercise a power that does not exist yet). The *Smith*

in the testator's state of domicile is clear that a silent residuary provision does not exercise powers, it may be that the law governing the instrument granting the power will control on this issue,[110] making the only sensible and safe approach the specific statement that exercise is not intended.

§3.2.7 Appointment of Guardians

If the client's family includes minor children, the will should contain special provisions granting authority to make distributions on behalf of those children rather than to them directly (a facility of payment provision, which should apply under a personal effects provision as well as to any intangibles being distributed), and appointment of guardians and waiver of any state law bond requirement. A will may be the only

---

(Footnote Continued)

result was avoided in the similar case of In re Estate of Hamilton, 593 N.Y.S.2d 372 (App. Div. 1993), because a specific reference requirement was deemed impossible to meet by a will executed by the powerholder 15 years prior to creation of the power, notwithstanding that the powerholder's will purported to exercise a similar power of appointment created under the donor's prior will.

[110] See, e.g., White v. United States, 680 F.2d 1156 (7th Cir. 1982), and Toledo Trust Co. v. Santa Barbara Foundation, 512 N.E.2d 664 (Ohio 1987), which represent the modern but distinctly minority trend to apply the law of the testator's domicile rather than the traditional conflict of laws rule, because the testator likely knew only the former and assumed it to be the applicable law with respect to all issues under a will executed in that state. In re Chappell, 883 N.Y.S.2d 857 (N.Y. Surr. Ct. 2009), is an excellent illustration of various issues relating to silent exercise and conflict of laws. The normal conflicts rule would have selected Connecticut law because both the settlor and the powerholder were domiciled in Connecticut. But the trust itself contained a governing law provision designating the law of New York, which was the situs of trust administration. Consistent with the court's holding that New York would "recognize the settlor's direction to apply New York law," a statutory choice of law rule found in New York E.P.T.L. §3-5.1(g)(1) specified that the law of the powerholder's domicile would govern, under which the powerholder did not effectively exercise the powers under the residuary clause of the powerholder's will, which was silent regarding exercise. Had the court applied New York E.P.T.L. §10-6.1(a) the silent residuary clause would have exercised the general power of appointment. The power was a pre-1942 general power, so exercise would have attracted FET inclusion under §2041(a)(1) and might have subjected the appointive property to claims of the powerholder's creditors. See §12.4.3.2 regarding spendthrift protection relative to general powers to appoint.

document recognized under state law to nominate guardians for the client's minor children. If so, a will may be necessary, notwithstanding that the clients have little current wealth and their dispositive plan is well served by the statute of descent and distribution. In some cases the testator will attempt to designate guardians even if not the second parent to die—if, for example, there has been a divorce and custody dispute—and the will might be drafted to provide incentives to the surviving parent not to object to that designation. But state law should be considered carefully before attempting to make a designation that will not be respected and the dispositive provisions should be drafted carefully to apply only if the guardian appointment is respected in such a case.

If guardians are likely to be involved because the testator's children are below the age of majority, additional thought also should be given to whether the document should create trusts that grant the trustee power to make distributions to the guardian. These might be on behalf of the minor or to provide resources to the guardian commensurate with the added burden imposed, such as to remodel or add on to an existing residence to make room for the children or to (help) purchase a new residence. Further, the estate planner may be in the best position to counsel the client about appropriate individuals to serve in this capacity, both with respect to the financial commitment involved and such criteria as the presence of other children in the home, the age differential involved (for example, it may not make sense for the client to designate the minor's grandparents if a significant generational gap is involved), whether only a married couple that is living together may serve, and whether the children should remain in the community in which the client lives. Many of these considerations may result in special directives in the will provision addressing distributions and the appointment and succession of guardians proper.

§3.2.8 Appointment of Personal Representative

A final topic that is unique to the drafting of wills is a designation of personal representatives. State law normally establishes a priority for granting letters of administration to the extent the will does not effectively designate a personal representative who is willing and able to act, and state law will grant certain powers to personal representatives in administration of an estate. If those powers are inadequate, the will appropriately might give the executor the same powers granted to the trustee of any testamentary trusts created by the will, to be exercised without giving bond or other surety and, if authorized under state law, to be exercised independent of court supervision. As with any fiduciary appointment, the estate planner should determine whether any special assets or needs of the beneficiaries dictate that the designated individual or entity have special powers or abilities. Careful thought also should be given to whether coexecutors should be designated if the testator's choice is unable to perform certain functions. The alternative that often is preferable is to authorize the personal representative to hire agents or other professionals to perform the functions for which the executor is not well suited or is not willing to accomplish. If coextensive appointments are preferred, the will should specify how fees will be awarded or shared and the extent to which any fiduciary is responsible for the mistakes of another.[111]

§3.3 TAX PAYMENT PROVISIONS

This section is lengthy because the obligation to pay taxes is a complex subject that demands as much separate consideration as any dispositive provision in a will. Federal, state, and even local wealth taxes, plus any income taxes incurred during estate administration, can consume over half of a decedent's wealth, making the provision directing payment of these liabilities as important as the balance of the estate plan. Yet many estate planners regard this provision as boilerplate and give little individuated attention to it. This section illustrates that this lack of attention is a prescription for error. To assist readers who come to this study with varying degrees of knowledge, this summary first presents the law regarding the time and source of payment, elaborating on the federal and state rules that apply in the absence of other controlling principles, such as contrary will or trust provisions. Readers who are familiar with these fundamentals may want to begin their study with the discussion of planning aspects of the apportionment rules in §3.3.14, and readers who must prepare tax payment provisions will find in §3.3.16 materials that relate to drafting considerations. Included in §3.3.17 is a sample tax payment provision.

---

[111] See §4.1.15 n.41 regarding cotrustee liability.

§3.3.1 Tax Payment Burden on the Residue

Under §2002,[1] the obligation to pay the entire FET imposed on a decedent's gross estate (probate and nonprobate property alike) rests on the decedent's personal representative, regardless of the fact that certain assets includible in the gross estate for FET purposes may not be in the possession or control of that fiduciary. This primary obligation is so extensive that any recipient of nonprobate property included in the gross estate who is compelled to pay a portion of the FET (for example, under the transferee liability rules of §6324(a) or §6901(a)), is entitled under §2205[2] to reimbursement from the personal representative.

By virtue of the §2203 definition of executor, only "if there is no executor or administrator appointed, qualified, and acting [does] any [other] person in actual or constructive possession of any property of the decedent" become initially liable for payment of the tax. And even then the person paying the tax is entitled to reimbursement from the residue of the decedent's estate. This federal burden on the residue reflects the traditional common law rule that has been altered in nearly every American jurisdiction. This federal burden means that a decedent's

---

[1] **§3.3** "The tax imposed by this chapter shall be paid by the executor." Executor is defined by §2203 to mean "the executor or administrator of the decedent, or, if there is no executor or administrator appointed, qualified, and acting within the United States, then any person in actual or constructive possession of any property of the decedent."

[2] Stating:

> If the tax or any part thereof is paid by, or collected out of, that part of the estate passing to or in the possession of any person other than the executor in his capacity as such, such person shall be entitled to reimbursement out of any part of the estate still undistributed or by a just and equitable contribution by the persons whose interest in the estate of the decedent would have been reduced if the tax had been paid before the distribution of the estate or whose interest is subject to equal or prior liability for the payment of taxes, debts or other charges against the estate, *it being the purpose and intent of this chapter that so far as is practicable and unless otherwise directed by the Will of the decedent the tax shall be paid out of the estate before its distribution.*

(Emphasis added.)

primary (residuary) beneficiaries often incur the unintended liability for all estate beneficiaries.[3]

To illustrate, consider an example.[4] The decedent created a revocable inter vivos trust to hold funds she inherited from her first husband. The trust would be distributed after her death to children of that first marriage. The residue of the decedent's probate estate benefits children by a second marriage. Mirroring both state and federal law, the decedent's will contains a traditional burden on the residue tax payment provision and waives all rights of reimbursement. The trust corpus thus passes to the children by the first marriage and the residue of the decedent's probate estate pays the taxes thereon.

The estate residuary beneficiaries (children of the decedent's second marriage) claim reimbursement for those taxes, notwithstanding that the tax payment provision in the will waived all rights of reimbursement. They argue that the federal right of reimbursement under

---

[3] "Many testators unwittingly provided for the members of their immediate family by leaving them the residuary estate. As a consequence, the burden of the unforeseen taxes often fell upon the . . . members nearest to the decedent." Scoles & Stephens, The Proposed Uniform Estate Tax Apportionment Act, 43 Minn. L. Rev. 907, 915 (1959).

[4] Cf. Collier v. First Nat'l Bank, 417 S.E.2d 653 (Ga. 1992). A similar inappropriate result was reached in Estate of Sheppard v. Schleis, 782 N.W.2d 85 (Wis. 2010), which held that no § 2207B right of reimbursement existed with respect to the FET attributable to includible POD and TOD accounts. Again decided in a burden-on-the-residue state and citing no authority, the court determined that these accounts were not includible in the Federal gross estate under § 2036 and, therefore, that there was no § 2207B right of reimbursement. The net result was that the named beneficiary of the accounts contributed nothing to the payment of taxes, which befell the residuary beneficiaries of the decedent's estate, with no apportionment or reimbursement rights. The result would differ under most state laws, which reverse the traditional burden-on-the-residue rule. But many tax payment provisions reverse state law and place the tax payment burden back on the residue of the estate. In those cases the issue might turn on whether that tax provision contained an effective waiver of the § 2207B right of reimbursement (*Sheppard* held that there is no right to waive) or apportioned the tax to the beneficiary who received the accounts (assuming that such an allocation would be respected under state law). Ultimately the question might turn on whether *Sheppard* was correct about these accounts not being subject to § 2036.

§ 3.3.1

§ 2207B[5] applies because its express provision specifies that it cannot be waived without making specific reference to it, which they claim is lacking in this case. The children of the first marriage rejoin that the § 2207B right of reimbursement is not available because it applies only if property is includible in the decedent's gross estate under § 2036. They allege that the inclusion provision is § 2038, not § 2036.[6] On that all-important issue there appears to be no definitive authority.[7] Thus, there

---

[5] See § 3.3.5 regarding the § 2207B right of reimbursement for FET attributable to inclusion of § 2036 property in the decedent's gross estate.

[6] The Georgia Supreme Court "resolved" the dispute by saying:

> [T]he [parties] argue that the trust assets are includable in the decedent's gross estate . . . under different sections of the Internal Revenue Code, each with different estate tax consequences.

> The question of whether the transfer of these assets from the decedent . . . casts tax liability on the estate or upon the trust must be answered under the Internal Revenue Code. As such, it is beyond the jurisdiction of this court.

417 S.E.2d at 655. In other words: the Georgia Supremes don't do taxes.

[7] The issue *was* addressed, but in a less than satisfactory manner, by In re Estate of Meyer, 702 N.E.2d 1078, 1081 n.3 (Ind. Ct. App. 1998), which stated that the trust beneficiaries' argument ("without citing to any authority") that the trust property was "more properly included" under § 2038 than § 2036 and, therefore, that the § 2207B reimbursement right did not exist, "is without merit because the two sections are not mutually exclusive." The court cited Treas. Reg. § 20.2031-1(a)(2) for the proposition that there is overlap among inclusion provisions such as § § 2036 and 2038 and that property may be includible under more than one. Note that this was a state court case.

A handful of authorities address whether § 2033 trumps other inclusion provisions, which is not the immediate issue. See, e.g., Rev. Rul. 75-553, 1975-2 C.B. 477, 478 (favoring § 2033 because "the trust corpus is payable to the decedent's estate and [therefore] is property of the decedent"; this caused the government to lose the opportunity to assert a lien against the trustee for transferee liability); PLR 8940003 (under similar facts the trust was subject to § 2033 inclusion instead of § 2036 and the government lost the opportunity to assert application of § 2035(a)(2) with respect to property distributed from the trust within three years of the decedent's death). Both authorities are directly adverse to the government's interest. TAMs 9015001 and 9139002 touched upon the issue because the decedent retained a § 2038 power to revoke an inter vivos trust. The taxpayer argued for § 2033 inclusion to supersede § 2038 inclusion and correspondingly preclude application of § 2035(a)(2) to a transfer from that portion of the trust within three years of the decedent's death. The government rejected that interpretation.

§3.3.1

is no reliable answer to the question whether §2207B applies in this case. Thus, the decedent's plan created a significant and presumably unintended inequity and significant resources may be wasted in litigation of an issue that could have been resolved by the decedent's will.

A client need not have an unusual dispositive plan to reveal that a burden on the residue approach is inappropriate or that tax payment provisions require deliberate consideration. For example, consider In re Estate of Maierhofer.[8] The testator intended to provide equal shares of the estate to two siblings, and bequeathed a specific property to one of them and then distributed the residue with an equalization provision designed to provide a larger share to the other sibling so that, in the end, each took equal value. The residue was insufficient to accomplish the equalization—even if the second sibling took the entire residue—in part because the will called for payment of FET, on both the preresiduary devise and the balance of the estate, all from the residue. The court rejected a pro rata apportionment scheme proposed by the second sibling because the clear language of the will directed payment of taxes from the residue, which put the burden disproportionately on the second sibling. One method to guarantee equality would have been to substitute for the preresiduary devise a simple equal division of the residue, with the one sibling's share to be funded first with the specified realty; because that property exceeded half the value of the estate, the one sibling could have been required to purchase the other's share or simply accept less than 100% ownership.

A second set of tax payment problems can be generated simply because a client is married. The unlimited marital deduction makes it possible to defer payment of all federal (and many state) wealth transfer tax until the death of S. The risk is bankrupting S's estate if the source for payment of the tax at that time is not properly specified or considered. Alternatively, state or federal tax incurred in D's estate necessarily

---

(Footnote Continued)

The conclusion that §2033 is the proper inclusion provision is fitting because §2033 is the all-purpose inclusion rule for property owned by a decedent at death; §§2036 and 2038 are inclusion provisions designed to cause inclusion of property that §2033 does not reach. Thus, as a matter of statutory construction, it ought to be that application of §2033 precedes all other inclusion provisions and, if it is adequate to cause inclusion, then no other provision is applicable.

[8] 767 N.E.2d 850 (Ill. App. Ct. 2002).

§3.3.1

will reduce the amount left to some beneficiary. If not carefully addressed, it may reduce the marital deduction and increase taxes unnecessarily.[9]

Similarly, postmortem planning that involves the marital deduction makes it necessary to consider the source for payment of taxes caused by a smaller marital deduction. For example, due to S's partial disclaimer of a marital deduction bequest, or a personal representative's decision to make only a partial QTIP election under § 2056(b)(7)(B)(v).

It also pays to consider the unexpected: an asset or disposition about which the decedent never told the estate planner and that impacts the marital deduction and therefore the tax liability in totally unexpected ways. A striking illustration of this (albeit not a common one) highlights the consequences of placing the burden of tax payment on the residue of an estate, without knowing all the facts (indeed, without *ever* being able to know *all* the facts). Imagine a decedent's shadow estate plan, disposing of unknown assets to unknown beneficiaries.[10] It might be an insurance policy payable to comply with some unrevealed promise or obligation (such as to support a nonmarital child or part of a business deal), property discovered in a safety deposit box with a handwritten note constituting a valid disposition to (or confirming a joint tenancy

---

[9] To illustrate, imagine a 2012 estate of $15 million, left half to D's child and the residue to S, with taxes being payable from the residue. The child's half—$7.5 million before tax—would generate tax that would reduce the residue and, with it, the marital deduction, resulting in more tax, a larger reduction of the residue (and thus another reduction of the marital deduction), with the end result being a marital deduction of $6,995,151 after reducing the pre-tax $7.5 million residue by taxes of $1,009,697 on a taxable estate of $8,004,849.

[10] See, e.g., In re Estate of Kuralt, 981 P.2d 771 (Mont. 1999), ultimately finding to be valid a holographic will of journalist Charles Kuralt—not the decedent's well-crafted and fully executed document that disposed of the bulk of the decedent's wealth to the decedent's family, but the one the decedent penned from a hospital room while dying, leaving property in Montana that the estate planner (indeed, the family) didn't know existed, to a beneficiary that neither the family nor the estate planner knew anything about. In re Estate of Kuralt, 68 P.3d 662 (Mont. 2003), confirmed that the decedent's tax clause directing payment without apportionment of all taxes from the residue of his estate meant that the preresiduary bequest of the Montana property passed free and clear and the taxes thereon ate into the marital bequest, causing a circular whirlpool tax calculation as described in note 20.

with) a third party,[11] or an asset transferred inter vivos but includible in the gross estate.[12] Thus, the asset increases the gross estate for tax purposes but, because of the beneficiary, cannot qualify for the marital deduction. Disaster awaits if these items exceed the applicable exclusion amount, resulting in taxes that the estate plan unexpectedly imposes on the residue that otherwise must qualify for the marital deduction and, because it does not, generates a tax that further eats into the property that qualifies for the marital deduction, which further increases the tax liability, which again consumes marital deduction property and further increases the tax, ad nauseam.

Finally, §2056(d) further illustrates the importance of tax payment planning in conjunction with marital deduction planning because it disallows the marital deduction if S is not a United States citizen, unless a QDOT is utilized. Unexpected discovery that S is not a citizen is yet another of those surprises that sometimes even the most careful estate planner cannot always avoid—because clients don't always reveal all the facts (even when they are asked) or they do things on the eve of dying without seeking counsel. All speaking to the wisdom of placing the tax burden on the residue of the estate rather than apportioning the tax to each beneficiary or asset unless specifically identified and exonerated from that liability.[13]

A third major tax payment concern relates to "phantom" assets that are includible in a decedent's gross estate but that are not available for payment of the tax attributable to them. With respect to these, a burden on the residue approach can diminish the probate estate and frustrate the decedent's estate planning objectives.

Several phantom asset examples arise under the special valuation rules of Chapter 14. For example, under §2703 the mere failure of a buy-

---

[11] See Estate of Dehgani-Fard, 46 Cal. Rptr. 3d 289 (Cal. Ct. App. 2006), discussed in §3.3.15.3 n.148.

[12] See, e.g., Estate of Lurie v. Commissioner, 425 F.3d 1021 (7th Cir. 2005), affirming a determination that the marital deduction for a residuary bequest was reduced by a tax payment burden on the residue provision that superseded state law that would have apportioned tax caused by inclusion of over $40 million of inter vivos trust corpus that was transferred by the decedent for the benefit of children, resulting ultimately in over $47 million of tax in what appeared to be a zero tax (optimum marital bequest) estate plan.

[13] Compare §B.6 of the sample tax payment provision in §3.3.17.

§3.3.1

sell agreement for valuation purposes could create a situation in which the subject property is sold for the contract price but the amount includible in the decedent's gross estate is larger, in some extreme cases leaving less property in the estate than the amount of tax attributable to the includible value. Less likely are unpaid suspense account dividends under § 2701(d), as to which it is not clear who benefits from the deemed transfer attributable to them. If § 2701 triggers an additional tax, payment of the tax from the residue may be inappropriate. Either the donee of the interests that trigger § 2701(d) or the entity that was obligated to pay the dividends should pay the tax attributable to the suspense account. A similar problem can arise under § 2704 because of a deemed transfer attributable to the lapse or imposition of a restriction, which may have no readily apparent transferee to whom the generated tax should be apportioned. The logical source for payment of the tax is the property as to which the restriction applies.

Another source of phantom asset taxation is either § 529(c)(4)(C) or § 2035(b), in each case attributable to assets no longer owned. The former applies if a taxpayer made a § 529(c)(2)(B) transfer of up to five times the gift tax annual exclusion and died within the five year period, causing a recapture of the tax benefit attributable to annual exclusions for years in which the taxpayer was not living.

To illustrate the latter case, consider the decedent whose estate was involved in PLR 9339010, who made substantial gifts and paid substantial gift tax within three years of death. This triggered application of the § 2035(b) gross-up rule, which caused inclusion of the gift tax in the decedent's gross estate. That inclusion produced an FET liability that substantially exceeded the amount of the decedent's probate estate. The government determined that "under State law, the federal estate taxes are to be apportioned" among the donees of the gifts.[14] This was not a

---

[14] Citing no authority for this result and making it impossible to verify the government's conclusion. A computer assisted search and discussions with commentators with extensive experience in this area were unsuccessful in determining that any state had a tax apportionment rule that is on point. See Armstrong v. Commissioner, 114 T.C. 94 (2000) (imposing § 6324(a)(2) liability on the transferees of the gifted property).

Cf. Bunting v. Bunting, 768 A.2d 989 (Conn. App. Ct. 2000), in which the decedent made a sizeable inter vivos gift to a child, as to which the gift tax was less than the available unified credit. At death that gift, added to the taxable

gift tax imposed by Chapter 12, as required for application of § 6324(b) gift tax transferee liability. Rather, it triggered FET transferee liability under § 6324(a)(2), which applies to any beneficiary who has on the date of the decedent's death property included in the gross estate under sections 2034 to 2042, inclusive.

This liability applies with respect to § 2035(b) by virtue of § 2035(c)(1)(C), which deems the gifted property to be includible in the gross estate notwithstanding the otherwise inapplicability of § 2035(a). Thus, the lien exists even though it is not accurate to consider the donees as receiving the property that produced the § 2035(b) FET (because the federal government received the gift tax upon which the FET was incurred). Notice that federal law protects the government with a lien against the donees, but it does nothing to establish the proper source for payment of tax as between the donees and the beneficiaries of the decedent's estate. Nor does it give the personal representative authority similar to the government's tax lien to enforce payment by the donees of the gifted property. In this respect, transferee liability is of little comfort to the personal representative.

(Footnote Continued)

estate, caused the remaining property to incur estate tax in excess of the unified credit. The decedent directed payment of all taxes from the residue of the estate, which was smaller than the combined state and federal taxes due at death. The court concluded that the decedent never anticipated that the inter vivos gift would cause taxes to be generated and therefore could not have intended for the tax payment provision to relieve the inter vivos donee of responsibility to pay estate taxes attributable to inclusion of the taxable gift in the adjusted taxable gifts base for estate tax computation purposes. Therefore, the court apportioned *estate* tax to the donee of that inter vivos gift. See § 3.3.16.6 n.207.

Ripley v. Commissioner, 105 T.C. 358 (1995), rev'd on other grounds, 103 F.3d 332 (4th Cir. 1996), held that a transferee's potential § 6324(b) liability does not reduce the gift tax value of a gift, because that value is determined under a willing-buyer, willing-seller analysis and a willing buyer for full and adequate consideration in money or money's worth would take free and clear of the lien (which instead would attach to the proceeds of sale in the hands of the donee). Because the transferee liability therefore does not encumber the gifted property, it was deemed not to affect the value of that property for gift tax purposes. *Armstrong* similarly rejected the estate's contention that the transferee's assumed liability constitutes § 2043 consideration furnished in a net gift. See § 7.2.5 n.341-342 and accompanying text.

§ 3.3.1

Of the limited sources for payment of the § 529(c)(4)(C) recapture tax or the FET § 2035(b) gross-up rule, it is equitable that the donees who received the gifted assets should pay the tax generated by the property they received, as presumably they would if the decedent had died with that property includible in the gross estate and left it to the donees at death.[15] But it might be necessary under state law to condition the gift itself with an agreement to pay any recapture or gross-up tax

---

[15] So held In re Application of Rhodes, 868 N.Y.S.2d 513 (Surr. Ct. 2008), in which the gift tax paid on transfers made within three years of the decedent's death generated an FET liability, which the court regarded as part of the decedent's "gross tax estate" for purposes of the state law apportionment statute, requiring the donees of the gifts to pay this FET liability. In re Estate of Kennedy, N.Y.L.J. Oct. 10, 2001, col. 6, generated the same result with the added justification that to do otherwise would reduce the marital deduction and generate more tax, all contrary to what the court presumed to be the decedent's intent. Estate of Morgens v. Commissioner, 678 F.3d 769 (9th Cir. 2012), raised the previously unanswered question (which note 6 of the opinion also declined to answer) whether the § 2207A reimbursement right would extend to the estate tax caused by § 2035(b) gross up rule inclusion caused by an inter vivos trigger of § 2519. Because the court's treatment of the § 2035(b) issue itself was as if the donor had paid the gift tax in the first instance, it is both logical and equitable that the § 2207A reimbursement right extend to the added estate tax caused by the gross up rule inclusion. Note, however, that CCA 201020009 (involving a very unusual situation) rejected the notion that the gift tax subject to gross-up inclusion under § 2035(b) is part of the gift itself, which makes an apportionment result difficult absent state law or a provision in the deed of gift.

Some practitioners are worried about the possibility that gifts made in 2011 and 2012 will be tax free due to the $5 million gift tax exclusion amount but will be subject to tax at death if Congress does not prevent reversion to a $1 million exclusion in 2013. Known by some as "clawback," the notion is that any portion of a lifetime transfer in excess of $1 million may be tax free when made but will be taxable at death. Congress did not intend such a result, and §§ 2001(b)(2) and (g) appear to preclude it, but planners who worry about the lack of clarity should consider adding a sentence to the tax payment provision of such a donor to clarify the taxpayer's intent regarding who should pay any increase in estate tax if clawback is a reality. Few taxpayers will transfer so much wealth inter vivos that the estate remaining at death will be inadequate to pay the estate tax incurred on a recaptured inter vivos gift, but the possibility exists that the nonmarital portion of an estate at death may be too small to provide a ready source for payment of tax attributable to the gift that is subjected to clawback. In which case payment from the marital deduction portion of the estate would result in reduction of the marital deduction itself, and that would generate more estate tax, which would again result in a reduction of the deduction, ad nauseam. A

incurred, to be certain that, should the need arise, the donees will be obliged and the estate will not be facing the phantom asset tax liability problem. Equity aside, it also may not be the decedent's intent for those donees to pay the tax. Without planning at the time of the gift, the situation after death could be impossible for the personal representative to resolve as a matter of state law. In that regard the decedent's tax apportionment provision should provide appropriate direction, because state law fails to address these issues.

A final concern about phantom assets and the taxes attributable to them involves retirement benefits that are includible in a decedent's gross estate under § 2039 but that cannot be accessed for payment of the tax attributable thereto. More severe yet is the unresolved question whether a participant's spouse has an ownership interest in a qualified plan, either by virtue of provisions guaranteeing a § 401(a)(11) spousal annuity to the nonparticipant spouse or under community property laws that deem the account to be owned by each spouse equally. If either source of inclusion exists and if the nonparticipant spouse dies first, it is extremely unlikely that the plan would permit the nonparticipant spouse to apportion FET against the plan while the participant still is alive. Indeed, even if it was the participant who died and inclusion clearly was dictated, it still might be impossible to reach plan assets to contribute to the payment of that tax.

TAM 8943006 and § 2056(b)(7)(C) confirm that a nonparticipant spouse's community property interest in a qualified plan is deemed to pass to the surviving participant spouse and to qualify for the marital deduction. But that result is not guaranteed if the nonparticipant's interest is not a function of community property laws. Here again are assets that are not available to pay any tax that may be attributable to them, creating the need to carefully consider the tax payment obligation of the participant and nonparticipant spouses. At the very least, a burden on the residue result may create problems and inequities (although it may be unavoidable in this particular situation).

(Footnote Continued)

better alternative might be an agreement at the time of the gift that the donees will pay any estate tax attributable to the gift.

§ 3.3.1

§ 3.3.2 Transferee Liability

If the tax is not paid when due liability may attach to *each* transferee or holder of property included in the gross estate to the *full* extent of the value of any property received[16] or held by the transferee. This transferee liability[17] is not for a transferee's pro rata share of the outstanding

---

[16] Or treated as received by the transferee, as illustrated by Upchurch v. Commissioner, 100 T.C.M. (CCH) 85 (2010), in which the transferees were claimants against an estate to whom nondeductible settlement payments were made, partially to the claimants personally and partially to their attorneys as contingent fees for services. Treating the payments to the attorneys as if they were made to the claimants and then by the claimants to the attorneys, the transferee liability imposed on the claimants was the aggregate amount paid in settlement of the claims.

[17] See §§ 6324(a)(2) (lien) and 6901(a)(1) and (h) (transferee liability).

Metz v. United States, 933 F.2d 802 (10th Cir. 1991), aff'g 89-2 U.S. Tax Cas. (CCH) ¶ 13,821 (D. Kan. 1989), involved FET that was being paid in installments under § 6166. Bankruptcy precluded payment of all installments and the government was allowed to enforce its §§ 6321 and 6324 liens against real property specifically devised to the plaintiff. The bequest satisfied the testator's promise to reward the plaintiff for living with the testator and caring for him until he died. The plaintiff unsuccessfully claimed that she obtained equitable title to the property before the testator died (meaning that it was not part of his gross estate to which the lien could attach) and that she was the purchaser of the property (which would divest the lien pursuant to § 6324(a)(2)).

Evelpis Properties v. United States, 97-1 U.S. Tax Cas. (CCH) ¶ 60,272 (S.D. Ohio 1997), enforced transferee liability against *bona fide purchasers* for value from the decedent's transferee, notwithstanding that the government's § 6324 lien *was not recorded* and had not been enforced for over seven years. The purchaser argued that the § 6324 lien was supplanted by a § 6324A lien, which must be recorded, because the decedent's FET was deferred under § 6166. The court rejected that claim as not supported by sufficient facts (there was no proof of a § 6324A(c) agreement). And there was no § 2204 discharge of the personal representative that would have released the § 6324 lien. The end result was that the purchaser had no reason to know that there was an unpaid FET liability for which the property nevertheless was subject to the government's unrecorded lien. First American Title Ins. Co. v. United States, 2005-1 U.S. Tax Cas. (CCH) ¶ 60,501 (W.D. Wash. 2005), aff'd, 520 F.3d 1051 (9th Cir. 2008), similarly illustrates this unexpected rule. An estate sold three houses to bona fide purchasers, who obtained title insurance from plaintiffs, who performed competent title searches and did not discover a government lien, because there was none at the time. Note that the government is not required to record its lien. Again, there was no § 2204 discharge of tax liability at the time of sale, and the unpaid tax

tax liability, and it is in addition to that normally imposed on the personal representative[18] and the 10 year lien that attaches to estate property[19] (and to any proceeds from the sale of assets included in the estate).[20] In either case, personal liability is discharged once the tax is paid or payment is adequately secured.[21]

(Footnote Continued)

arose after the sales, when the government successfully increased the value of a different asset included in the estate. The estate failed to pay the added tax, the government enforced its lien against the purchasers of the houses, the title insurers made the insureds whole, and sued unsuccessfully to recover the taxes assessed under § 6324. Accord, Municipal Trust & Savings Bank v. United States, 97-1 U.S. Tax Cas. (CCH) ¶ 60,275 (7th Cir. 1997), rev'g and rem'g an unreported opinion (C.D. Ill.); United States v. Vohland, 675 F.2d 1071 (9th Cir. 1982); Noble v. Soler, 98-2 U.S. Tax Cas. (CCH) ¶ 60,297 (S.D. Ohio 1997). See Manigault, Trusts & Estates Issues in the Context of Corporate Transactions, 45 U. Miami Inst. Est. Plan. ¶ 1700 (2011), and ECC 201129037.

[18] Effected through a lien under § 6321 (based on 31 U.S.C. § 192, which imposes personal liability on anyone who distributes estate property prior to satisfaction of all indebtedness to the United States). Any interest or penalties on the tax are treated as part of the tax liability for all these lien and liability purposes. See § § 6601(e)(1) and 6665(a), respectively. See generally Turner, Transfer tax liens and transferee and fiduciary liability, 28 Est. Plan. 147 (2001); Hochberg & Silbergleit, Recent cases narrow scope of executor's personal liability for estate taxes, 7 Est. Plan. 2 (1980); 4 Casey & Smith, Federal Tax Practice ch. 12.III (18th. ed. 1997); Annot., Construction and effect of 31 USC § 192 imposing personal liability on fiduciary for paying debts due by person or estate for whom he acts before paying debts due the United States, 41 A.L.R.2d 446 (1955).

[19] See § 6324(a)(1). Property used to pay allowable expenses of administration and charges against the estate is excepted from the lien.

[20] See § 6324(a)(2) and Treas. Reg. § 301.6324-1(a)(2)(iii).

[21] See § § 2204(a) (discharge of personal representative), 2204(b) (discharge of fiduciary other than personal representative), and 6325(c) (discharge of transferee liability). But see § 6324(a)(3) (lien remains with respect to estate assets after § 2204 discharge of fiduciary from personal liability, until tax is paid or adequately secured). There may be an additional discharge available under the analogous authority of Little v. Commissioner, 113 T.C. 474 (1999), an income tax fiduciary liability case under 31 U.S.C. § 3713(b) (which is the successor to § 192), in which reasonable and good faith reliance on a tax advisor who provided improper legal advice was adequate to protect the fiduciary, based on the authority of United States v. Boyle, as discussed in § 3.3.19. See also ECC 201212020, quoting *Little* for the added proposition that a fiduciary is liable only if it had notice of a United States claim before making a distribution.

§ 3.3.2

Courts disagree about whether the § 6324(a)(1) lien is a 10 year to judgment rule (that is, litigation to foreclose the lien must be *completed* within 10 years of the decedent's death) or only a 10 year statute of limitation. Beaty v. United States,[22] United States v. Harrell,[23] United States v. Warner,[24] and United States v. Saleh[25] hold that a foreclosure proceeding instituted before expiration of the 10 year period may be completed beyond the 10 year period. United States v. Cleavenger,[26] United States v. Potemken,[27] and United States v. Schneider[28] hold that the lien is a 10 year to judgment rule and that the government lost its

---

[22] 90-1 U.S. Tax Cas. (CCH) ¶ 60,004 (E.D. Tenn. 1989), rev'd on other grounds, 937 F.2d 288 (6th Cir. 1991) (wrongful levy action brought under § 7426 by plaintiffs who were record title holders of realty that was levied upon and seized by the government, which claimed the property pursuant to a § 6324 FET lien).

[23] 88-1 U.S. Tax Cas. (CCH) ¶ 13,746 (M.D. Fla. 1987).

[24] 85-2 U.S. Tax Cas. (CCH) ¶ 13,641 (S.D. N.Y. 1985).

[25] 514 F. Supp. 8 (D. N.J. 1980).

[26] 517 F.2d 230 (7th Cir. 1975).

[27] 87-1 U.S. Tax Cas. ¶ 13,716 (D. Md. 1987). Although *Potemken* subsequently was reversed and remanded, 841 F.2d 97 (4th Cir. 1988), the court on appeal agreed with the district court that the 10 year statute of limitation was not tolled by the government's filing of a complaint to foreclose the lien during the 10 year time period of § 6324(a)(1) and, therefore, upheld the determination that § 6324(a)(1) is a 10 year to final judgment rule. Notwithstanding that the case was not completed in time under this rule, however, the court nevertheless held that the complaint met the assessment and demand prerequisites for the § 6321 general lien. Thus, it remanded to the district court for proceedings consistent with the recognition of the § 6321 general lien that, unlike § 6324(a)(1), is available without reference to duration. The remand decision in the district court granted summary judgment for the government. 700 F. Supp. 279 (D. Md. 1988), aff'd sub nom. United States v. 3809 Crain Ltd. Partnership, 884 F.2d 138 (4th Cir. 1989). The court held that the tax lien had priority over a deed of trust held by a bank on estate property sold at foreclosure to a secured creditor, despite the fact that the secured creditor's claim was perfected before the tax lien was filed. The so-called protected security interest did not prevail because it did not qualify on the facts as a § 6323(a) "security interest" (consideration for the deed of trust was not money or money's worth to the estate) and therefore could not take priority over the government's general tax lien.

[28] 91-1 U.S. Tax Cas. (CCH) ¶ 60,068 (D. N.D. 1991).

right to assert its lien by failing to prosecute to completion a claim under the lien provision within the 10 year period.[29]

An additional question is whether § 6324(a)(2) transferee liability may apply if the government never made a § 6901 assessment against the estate or the transferee. The government argues that § 6901 is an alternative to § 6324, notwithstanding the fact that failure to assess the taxpayer denies that taxpayer's right to a Tax Court adjudication. In ruling against the government, *Schneider*[30] read § 6901(a) as mandating that any FET liability *must* be assessed under § 6901 ("the following liabilities shall . . . be assessed . . .") and the government simply cannot proceed with its transferee liability remedy under § 6324(a)(2) if it lacks the ability to do so because the statute of limitation bars assessment.[31] The court distin-

---

[29] United States v. Estate of Davenport, 159 F. Supp. 2d 1330 (N.D. Okla. 2001), rev'd in part but aff'd sub nom. on this issue, United States v. Botefuhr, 309 F.3d 1263 (10th Cir. 2002) (involving a § 6324(b) lien for gift tax asserted against the donees for 10 years from the date of the gift; being late does not preclude the government from collecting, within the statute of limitation, but causes it to be unsecured, because § 6324(b) draws a clear distinction between the special lien and the donee's personal liability for the donor's gift tax liability); New England Acceptance Corp. v. United States, 97-2 U.S. Tax Cas. (CCH) ¶ 60,290 (D. N.H. 1997) (involving a § 6324(b) lien for gift tax asserted after the donor's death); and United States v. Davis, 52 F.3d 781 (8th Cir. 1995), followed the *Cleavenger, Potemken,* and *Schneider* durational holdings (lien must be enforced by full execution on a judgment actually obtained within 10 years; merely filing notice of lien, seizure, or encumbrance within the durational period is inadequate) and rejected the *Beaty, Harrell, Warner,* and *Saleh* limitational approach (government must commence action within 10 years), based on the clear language of § 6324(a)(1) that there "shall be a lien . . . for 10 years . . ." and not that the government has 10 years within which to file its action. See also United States v. McLendon, 99-2 U.S. Tax Cas. (CCH) ¶ 60,355 (N.D. Tex. 1999) (holding that the lien expired 10 years from the decedent's death, but without analysis of the issue or citation of other authority); and United States v. Kulhanek, 755 F. Supp. 2d 659 (W.D. Penn 2010), distinguishing the *Cleavenger* line of cases because they involved § 6324(a)(1) liens and *Kulhanek* involved § 6324(a)(2) transferee liability.

[30] United States v. Schneider, 92-2 U.S. Tax Cas. (CCH) ¶ 60,119 (D. N.D. 1992).

[31] Accord, Gumm v. Commissioner, 93 T.C. 475 (1989) (§ 6901 transferee liability for FET), which stated that the procedural requirements of transferee liability that must be established by the government are (1) the alleged transferee received property of the transferor, (2) for less than full and adequate

§ 3.3.2

guished United States v. Russell,[32] which held that assessment under §6901 was not essential to §6324(a)(2) assessment against the transferee, because the transferee in *Russell* was the personal representative who failed to guarantee payment of the FET. The transferee in *Schneider* had no information about the estate's administration, the personal representative had been deemed guilty of negligence in failing to pay the FET, the transferee had no control over the estate administration, and the transferee already had paid that portion of the FET attributable to the portion of the estate the transferee received. Finally, the *Schneider* court noted that the upshot of the government's argument would be transferee liability for what it deemed to be at least 13 years after the FET return is filed with no prior notice to the transferee that personal liability still exists, which the court deemed "patently unfair and unjust."

Notwithstanding very similar facts and equities, United States v. Geniviva[33] rejected *Schneider,* instead holding that the government's inability to pursue transferee liability under §6901 is no bar to its assertion of its entirely separate transferee lien entitlement under

---

(Footnote Continued)

consideration, (3) within or after the period during which the transferor's tax liability accrued, (4) the transferor was insolvent prior to or because of the transfer, or the transfer was one of a series that resulted in the transferor's insolvency, (5) all reasonable efforts to collect from the transferor were made and further collection efforts would be futile, and (6) the value of the transferred property (which determines the limit of the transferee's liability).

[32] 461 F.2d 605 (10th Cir. 1972).

[33] 94-1 U.S. Tax Cas. (CCH) ¶ 60,156 (3d Cir. 1994) (one child acted as personal representative and failed for over four years to either file a return or pay the decedent's FET; when it became clear that the personal representative and the estate's attorney were judgment proof for mismanagement and fraud, the government sued two other children who received distributions without knowledge that the estate's liabilities had not been paid). See also United States v. Estate of Davenport, 159 F. Supp. 2d 1330 (N.D. Okla. 2001), aff'd in part, rev'd in part sub nom., United States v. Botefuhr, 309 F.3d 1263 (10th Cir. 2002) (holding simply that §6901 is not a prerequisite to enforcement against the donees); Bentley v. Commissioner, 73 T.C.M. (CCH) 2254 (1997) (government missed statute of limitation with respect to decedent's estate but was timely with its claim for transferee liability, which the court permitted notwithstanding that the estate never was adjudged liable); Magill v. Commissioner, 43 T.C.M. (CCH) 859 (1982), aff'd sub nom. Berliant v. Commissioner, 729 F.2d 496 (7th Cir. 1984).

§ 6324(a)(2). Thus, citing Leighton v. United States[34] and *Russell*, *Geniviva* noted the inequity in finding, after a long delay, that two innocent children were liable for taxes, interest, and penalties that would consume their entire distributions. Yet it specifically rejected *Schneider*.

Illinois Masonic Home v. Commissioner[35] held that transferee liability under § 6901 is not a separate liability but is a secondary method of enforcing the transferor's liability. Thus, preclusion of transferor liability by expiration of the limitation period also precludes transferee liability. Similarly, Estate of King v. Commissioner[36] held that transferee liability for the same tax is barred if the § 6501 statute of limitation bars the government from assessing an FET deficiency against a decedent's estate. And Baptiste v. Commissioner[37] concluded that, once the FET liability has been adjudicated with respect to the decedent's estate, the court's final determination on the merits is res judicata for transferee liability purposes; because the issues involved are the same and the transferee is in privity with the decedent's estate, the transferee is not entitled to relitigate finally resolved issues.

A subsequent decision in the same matter[38] divided the court. At issue was whether § 6324(a)(2) limits absolutely a transferee's liability to the date of death value of the property the transferee received from the transferor, which was the dissenting view, or whether it applies only with respect to the tax and interest imposed on the transferor, leaving no limit

---

[34] 289 U.S. 506 (1933).

[35] 93 T.C. 145 (1989) (statutory notices of transferee liability issued after limitation period barred government from proceeding against decedent's estate).

[36] 61 T.C.M. (CCH) 2334 (1991).

[37] 63 T.C.M. (CCH) 2649 and 2653 (1992) (identical companion cases).

[38] Baptiste v. Commissioner, 100 T.C. 252 (1993) (reviewed opinion), aff'd, 29 F.3d 1533 (11th Cir. 1994), and aff'd in part and rev'd in part, 29 F.3d 433 (8th Cir. 1994) (consolidated Tax Court cases involving two siblings appealed to different circuits); followed by United States v. MacIntyre, 2012 WL 2403491 (S.D. Tex. 2012) (involving gift tax liability but the same issue regarding interest on the donee's unpaid portion of the donor's gift tax liability). Saigh v. Commissioner, 89 T.C.M. (CCH) 750 (2005), involving a Florida executor of a New Jersey estate, which applied the (disfavorable to the taxpayer) precedent in the Eleventh Circuit because that was the court to which any appeal would be prosecuted. See § 7482(b)(1)(A), which bases venue for an appeal on the residence of the personal representative. Estate of Clack v. Commissioner, 106 T.C. 131 (1996).

§ 3.3.2

on the amount of interest that may be collected from a transferee who is dilatory in making the transferee liability payment. At issue was §6601(a) interest incurred on the transferee's §6324(a)(2) liability, which in the aggregate exceeded the value of the property the transferee received. The court rejected the notion that the entire §§6601(a) and 6324(a)(2) liability of the transferee was limited by §6324(a)(2), recognizing that the government is able to impose interest on a dilatory transferee.[39]

§3.3.3 Apportionment Options

Congress determined[40] that the FET should be a burden on the estate as a whole, not on the individual beneficiaries of the estate as is the case with most inheritance taxes. But Riggs v. Del Drago[41] held that state law or the terms of the decedent's estate plan may alter this apportionment of the FET in any manner. Thus, the estate plan may apportion the tax burden so that, for example, the effect of credits, deductions, and the inclusion of assets affects or benefits those beneficiaries who receive includible assets, generating credits or deductions, and so forth. With this freedom to apportion, up to six major apportionment decisions must be made, several with additional subissues that may be addressed under state law but that the estate plan also might alter.

§3.3.3.1 Inside Apportionment

Inside apportionment deals with the question whether taxes ought to be borne by all classes of dispositions within (inside) a probate estate. Like §2205, the firmly established common law rule is that taxes in the probate estate are a "burden on the residue," meaning that all taxes are paid out of the residuary estate before any taxes are allocated to or

---

[39] Poinier v. Commissioner, 858 F.2d 917 (3d Cir. 1988), rev'g in part 86 T.C. 478 (1986), was distinguished on the ground that it limited the transferee's liability for the transferor's tax and the transferor's interest on the transferor's tax but did not speak to the alleged limitation on the transferee's interest on the transferee's liability. In addition, it was noted that the prohibition relied upon in *Poinier* was repealed in 1982.

[40] See §2205.

[41] 317 U.S. 95 (1942).

payable from other dispositions, such as general, demonstrative, or specific dispositions under a will.[42] To the extent inside apportionment is dictated, every taker under a will bears a share of the taxes payable— typically proportionate to the value received by each and regardless of the priority or class of disposition involved—and regardless of whether the subject property is realty or personalty.[43]

§3.3.3.2 Outside Apportionment

Within testate and intestate estates alike, outside apportionment stands in juxtaposition to inside apportionment, involving the issue whether taxes on the total taxable estate for FET purposes ought to be apportioned among the takers of probate assets (either with or without inside apportionment) and the recipients of includible nonprobate assets. Thus, if nonprobate property is includible in the gross estate of a decedent, outside apportionment would dictate that the recipient of the nonprobate property pay that portion of the taxes imposed on the total estate attributable to that inclusion (computed in one of several methods discussed in more detail below). And the same state law rules that

---

[42] See Annot., Ultimate burden of estate tax in absence of statute, will, or other provision, 68 A.L.R.3d 714 (1976).

[43] The share will be based on a proportionate or some other ratio or determination. At one time the common law distinguished between personalty and realty within any class of disposition, favoring the realty by specifying that the personalty should be used first to pay debts, expenses, and taxes. Thus, for example, even in a burden on the residue apportionment, the takers of residuary personalty would be disappointed prior to the takers of residuary realty. This antiquated system has been rejected by virtually every state, notwithstanding that this rule was consistent with the common law abatement rules that favored realty.

In re Estate of Overturf, 819 N.E.2d 324 (Ill. Ct. App. 2004), was a throwback in this respect. The residuary estate was divided equally between two daughters but the FET burden was placed on only the personal property in the residuary estate, which proved to be inadequate. One daughter was disfavored in joint tenancy property owned with the decedent. She argued that the unfulfilled tax liability should be charged under state law outside apportionment proportionately to the two daughters, each paying different amounts relative to the amounts of joint tenancy property each received. The court instead imposed equal amounts of the tax against the remaining probate estate, which affected the two daughters equally and preserved the joint tenancy inequity.

§3.3.3.2

govern outside apportionment of the FET presumably ought to govern apportionment of any state estate tax as well.[44]

It is with respect to outside apportionment that most state apportionment statutes apply and as to which the limited federal apportionment rules exist. However, apportionment to some forms of nonprobate property is addressed far more clearly and appropriately than it is with respect to other forms.

§3.3.3.3 Equitable Apportionment

Equitable apportionment involves the question whether dispositions that generate a tax deduction should be freed from contribution toward payment of the total taxes imposed on the estate. That is, under equitable apportionment the deductible disposition alone benefits from the deduction, rather than the deduction benefiting all beneficiaries of the estate. The most common example of this is property passing to S that

---

[44] See, e.g., In re Estate of Klarner, 113 P.3d 150 (Colo. 2005), rev'g and rem'g 98 P.3d 892 (Colo. Ct. App. 2003), which held that a QTIP trust had to bear its share of both federal and state estate taxes, stating that the Colorado estate tax is generally parallel to and consistent with the FET and, to achieve the coordinating effect envisioned under the Colorado statute, the court concluded that the same standards apply for purposes of both federal and state estate taxes; Jones v. German, 576 S.E.2d 401 (N.C. Ct. App. 2003), reached a similar result on a goofy argument that D's tax payment provision apportioned taxes at S's death, which was consistent with any state apportionment statute that essentially allocates all tax to the recipient of includible property, so the result is consistent with a full apportionment policy; In re Marital Deduction Trust under Will of Adair, 695 A.2d 250 (N.J. 1997), dealing with the state pick up tax attributable to a QTIP trust that was includible in S's gross estate, as to which state law apportionment rules were deemed to apply; contra Hollis v. Forrester, 914 So. 2d 855 (Ala. 2005), aff'g 914 So. 2d 852 (Ala. Ct. App. 2004), dealing with state death tax attributable to a QTIP trust as to which the then-applicable state (nonapportionment) burden on the residue rule was applied; and cf. Cleveland v. Compass Bank, 652 So. 2d 1134 (Ala. 1994), and Branch Banking & Trust Co. v. Staples, 461 S.E.2d 921 (N.C. Ct. App. 1995), both involving FET attributable to inclusion of QTIP corpus in S's gross estate, which yielded a larger state death tax credit that correspondingly increased the state pick up tax equal to that credit, which the court did (not) apportion to the QTIP trust along with the FET itself depending on whether state law called for apportionment of the federal tax (*Branch Banking*) or imposed the burden on the residue (*Cleveland*), absent an effective provision in the decedent's estate plan.

qualifies for the marital deduction. The question can apply in an intestate estate in which S takes a statutory share of the estate, in a testate estate in which S rejects D's estate plan in favor of a statutory forced heir share, in a testate estate (or will substitute) involving apportionment as between S's bequest (whether as a part of the residue or some other part of the total estate), and in any estate, to the extent a prenuptial agreement or §2053 deductible property settlement agreement creates a claim against the estate (or a disposition under the will is in satisfaction of such a contractual claim against the estate). The issue in each case is whether distributions in satisfaction of the claim are subject to apportionment of taxes. Also the source of equitable apportionment is the §2055 charitable deduction and, although less obviously so, §2032A(c)(5) which poses similar issues relating to the reduction in tax attributable to special use valuation and the subsequent liability for recapture tax under either provision.[45]

§3.3.3.4 Apportionment of Rate Differentials

Closely related to equitable apportionment is whether to apportion state estate or inheritance tax rate differentials based on each beneficiary's share of the estate, reflecting that some states impose a tax that favors more closely related beneficiaries than strangers or distant relatives.[46]

§3.3.3.5 Apportionment of Credits

Similarly related is the question whether to apportion the benefit of credits available to the estate that are connected with separate identifiable properties passing to designated individuals.

---

[45] See §3.3.11.

[46] See, e.g., Pfeufer v. Cyphers, 919 A.2d 641 (Md. 2007), in which two children, a sibling, and a nonrelative split the estate remaining *after* payment of all state death tax. Notwithstanding that all of the tax was incurred by the share of the nonrelative (who was the only nonexempt beneficiary), the court regarded "boilerplate language" in the decedent's will as an indication of intent to treat all four beneficiaries as if they were similarly situated. This litigation reached the highest state court, which tends to put the lie to the court's expressed notion that the will provision was "clear."

§3.3.3.4

For example, subject to §§ 2015 and 2016, if some property incurs more foreign death tax than others, the apportionment issue is whether the beneficiaries thereof should receive the benefit of any § 2014 credit attributable to the tax incurred on their bequests.

The § 2012 credit for gift taxes paid on pre-1977 transfers of property subsequently included in the estate may be apportioned.

And the § 2013 credit for previously taxed property may be apportioned and can be a source of real inequity if not considered properly. To illustrate, assume that the decedent was the beneficiary of a generation-skipping trust created by a parent, with a § 2041 general power of appointment to avoid GST. If the parent and the decedent died within 10 years of each other, a § 2013 credit would be available to the decedent's estate. If § 2207 liability for the FET attributable to the trust is imposed on the remainder beneficiaries of the trust, they also should receive the benefit of that credit, but they do not under most state laws. The decedent could match the tax liability with the credit by waiving the § 2207 reimbursement entitlement or by apportioning the credit. The issue is whether the decedent's estate can afford to pay the § 2041 taxes on the trust. And in a more sophisticated plan in which the GST might be allowed to apply instead of § 2041, it would be unwise to have the two tax liabilities payable by different sources, one by the decedent's estate and the other by the trust.[47]

Finally, the § 2015 credit for deferred taxes attributable to future interests may be apportioned to the takers of those interests.

§ 3.3.3.6 Apportionment to Temporal Interests

Related to apportionment of the § 2015 credit, a final apportionment alternative relates to the proper method for apportioning taxes attributable to property that is split into temporal interests, such as a life estate, a term of years, or an annuity given to one individual and the remainder or reversion given to another.

---

[47] See § 11.4.5.4.3 for a more extensive discussion of this issue.

§3.3.3.7 Apportionment Among Multiple Entities

If several estate planning documents (such as a will and an inter vivos funded trust or an ILIT) are involved, these issues are compounded by the need to decide how tax payment obligations should be imposed on the multiple entities. For example, the tax payment provisions in each document could

- provide for payment of all taxes out of the probate estate (with or without inside apportionment);

- provide for payment of all taxes from the trust corpus (similarly with or without a form of inside apportionment among several shares created thereunder);

- provide for a ratable apportionment of taxes between the several entities (with or without apportionment under each as among the respective shares thereunder);

- provide that the trust shall contribute to the payment of taxes only to the extent the probate estate is insufficient to pay all the taxes imposed on the gross estate (or vice versa, and again with questions of apportionment under each disposition);

- provide that the trustee shall pay taxes only in the discretion of the trustee (under established guidelines, and with or without apportionment);

- provide that the trustee shall pay taxes to the extent the personal representative of the decedent's estate certifies the need therefor (again under guidelines and a specified apportionment regime);

- or simply permit the trustee to purchase assets from the estate to provide needed liquidity.

Not incidentally, these decisions must take into consideration the potential for conflicts of interest and the difficulty of exercising discretion if conflicting beneficial interests and different fiduciaries are involved.[48]

§3.3.4 Decedent's Choice

With respect to all apportionment issues, it is relatively clear (but not totally without doubt) that, should the decedent wish to do so, a clear

---

[48] See, e.g., In re Hanson Revocable Trust, 779 N.E.2d 1218 (Ind. Ct. App. 2002), in which a beneficiary as trustee had "an irreconcilable conflict of interest" in exercising discretion to pay FET with all the trust assets other than those passing to the trustee individually, including a share passing to a charity for which a charitable deduction was claimed, notwithstanding application of the concept of equitable apportionment.

testamentary provision may expressly specify the property and the dispositions that will bear the tax burden, permitting alteration of the customary burden on the residue rule or any statutory apportionment regime. By a clear provision in a testamentary disposition the decedent may exonerate nonprobate property from any otherwise applicable state law directive requiring outside apportionment. Although not nearly as clearly permissible, it is relatively well established that the decedent may impose the burden for tax payment on nonprobate assets through the use of a will provision, subject to certain exceptions in dealing with the proper method for drafting such a provision.[49]

In advising a client as to the best apportionment approach, a number of policies or considerations might be relevant and the client's wishes need to be ascertained. For example, with respect to inside apportionment, the common law abatement rules presume that a client favors the particular beneficiaries over the residuary takers, and failure to permit inside apportionment is consistent therewith. In reality, however, often the particular beneficiaries fit into one of the following categories: first is a marital deduction bequest that the client wants to maximize, in most cases resulting in no tax at the client's death, so apportionment is a moot issue. Even if it does not totally eliminate taxes, however, protection of the deduction is served by equitable apportionment. Second are those relatively minor dispositions that most individuals place in a separate article preceding the heart of the estate plan; with respect to these, the common law abatement and apportionment rules are likely to be directly contrary to the intent of the client in the sense that, if anyone should suffer for insufficient assets in the estate, it should be these takers.

With respect to outside apportionment, does the client wish to have the probate estate pay taxes generated by property over which the client has no control? This is particularly important with respect to § 2044 QTIPs, especially in the second marriage or related situations in which the trust property passes to beneficiaries for whom S has no affinity.

With respect to the issue of equitable apportionment involving the marital deduction (and, to a certain extent, involving the charitable

---

[49] See generally Annot., Construction and effect of will provisions expressly relating to the burden of estate or inheritance taxes, 69 A.L.R.3d 122 (1976), and § 3.3.9.

deduction as well), should the deductible share bear no tax because it generated no tax? With an "optimum" or unlimited marital deduction, any FET imposed on the estate would be generated by property that did not qualify for the deduction. Most individuals will embrace the notion that the marital deduction is designed for the benefit of S and, therefore, that S ought to be the sole beneficiary of the deduction. A similar argument could be made in favor of charity, perhaps with even greater merit, because it is unclear whether the marital deduction was intended as a benefit solely for S as opposed to a benefit to the estate in general.[50]

To the extent the purpose of the intestate or forced heir marital share is to protect S, it could be argued that this protection should be maximized by computing the marital share without diminution by taxes. And because the original purpose of the marital deduction was to provide equality between common law and community property spouses, arguably at least a portion of the marital share should be computed without reduction by taxes in a noncommunity property state (because S takes half the community estate tax free in a community property state). But perhaps the most persuasive argument in favor of equitable apportionment is that the deduction itself will be reduced under § 2056(b)(4)(A) if the marital share bears a portion of the taxes imposed on D's estate (because equitable apportionment does not apply). Indeed, the marital deduction will be reduced by the full amount of tax that could be paid, even if for some reason it is not.[51]

In some cases a reduction in the deduction correspondingly increases taxes that further serve to reduce the size of the marital share (because that share is a portion of the total estate available for distribution), which further increases taxes that again reduce the deduction, ad nauseam. For example, consider the following illustration of the compar-

---

[50] There is authority that supports each proposition on this particular issue; for examples of those holding that the deduction is meant to benefit the entire estate and not just S, see Robinson v. United States, 518 F.2d 1105 (9th Cir. 1975); In re Estate of Mosby, 554 P.2d 1341 (Mont. 1976); In re Estate of Marans, 390 P.2d 443 (Mont. 1964). With respect to the converse position, see Kahn, The Federal Estate Tax Burden Borne By A Dissenting Widow, 64 Mich. L. Rev. 1499 (1966); Note, Estate and Gift Tax: Federal Estate Tax—Burden on a Marital Share, 33 Okla. L. Rev. 384 (1980). The last sentences of §§ 2206 and 2207 appear to favor marital deduction dispositions by apportioning taxes away from the marital.

[51] See § 13.4.2.3.3 nn.63 and 66 and accompanying text.

§ 3.3.4

ative computations of S's one-third forced heir share or intestate entitlement in an estate of $9 million computed in 2012:

⅓ of 'GROSS' Estate (i.e., *before* taxes)		⅓ of 'NET' Estate (i.e., *after* taxes)
$9,000,000	Estate	$9,000,000
3,000,000	Marital	2,883,774
6,000,000	Taxable	6,116,226
(308,000)	Taxes	(348,679)
5,692,000	Residue	5,767,548

The final result is that a net estate division produces a marital share exactly half the size of the remaining residue, preserving the one-third entitlement dictated by the marital share provision, but the method of computation generates a smaller marital deduction (by $116,226) and more taxes (by $40,679); curiously, the residue is actually better off (by $75,548) because of it. The issue whether the marital share should be a fraction of the net estate (after taxes) or the gross estate (before taxes) is simply the equitable apportionment issue working to protect the marital share from bearing a portion of the taxes in the gross estate division but not in the net estate computation.[52]

To say that the issue is confused is an understatement. As an illustration, in Illinois it apparently makes a difference whether the computation is to determine S's intestate entitlement as opposed to S's statutory forced heir marital share if S rejects D's estate plan by electing against it.[53] Further, in considering the proper division involving an election against D's estate, a tax clause in D's will is irrelevant because, by virtue of the election, S is deemed to reject any and all provisions in the will for S's benefit, including the tax clause (the so-called doctrine of equitable election).[54] Similar disputes arise in applying the concept of

---

[52] See TAM 8640009 (gross estate division adopted) and § 13.7.7.2.

[53] See Note, In re Estate of Gowling and In re Estate of Grant: The Limits of Equitable Apportionment, 13 Loyola U. Chi. L.J. 309 (1982).

[54] See Merchants Nat'l Bank and Trust Co. v. United States, 246 F.2d 410 (7th Cir. 1957); Annot., Surviving spouse taking elective share as chargeable with estate or inheritance tax, 67 A.L.R.3d 199 at § 5 (1975). See § § 3.3.15.1 and 3.4.4.

§3.3.4

equitable apportionment to the charitable deduction under § 2055 and the question whether division ought to be before or after taxes.[55]

§ 3.3.5 Federal Tax Rules Applicable to FET Reimbursement

Together, §§ 2202 and 2205 establish the general rule that distinguishes the FET from an inheritance tax. The executor is expected to pay the tax, and any nonprobate beneficiary who pays any FET is entitled to reimbursement from the personal representative out of probate property, "it being the purpose and intent of this chapter that . . . unless otherwise directed by the will of the decedent the tax shall be paid out of the estate before its distribution." This is a federal burden on the residue rule, but it does not apply if state law provides to the contrary or the decedent's will directs otherwise. In essence it creates a default rule that gives the federal government a single person—the executor—to look to for payment.[56] Then it creates four federal statutory rules that permit reimbursement of the executor who paid the federal (but not any state) estate tax imposed on specific types of nonprobate property. Thus, the executor pays, and then is entitled to reimbursement from some (but not all) nonprobate beneficiaries.

---

[55] Under § 2055(c), any tax burden on a charitable bequest reduces the charitable deduction as § 2056(b)(4) reduces the marital deduction. See §§ 13.4.2.3.3 (marital deduction) and 14.1.4 n.65 (charitable deduction) and accompanying text, and see, e.g., YMCA v. Davis, 264 U.S. 47 (1924); Lynchburg College v. Central Fidelity Bank, 410 S.E.2d 617 (Va. 1991) (a tax payment provision that did not identify source of payment and specified only that "my just debts and all expenses of the administration of my estate, including such taxes as may be levied against my estate, [be] paid as soon after my death as practicable," constituted a direction to pay taxes from the residue and a negation of statutory apportionment otherwise applicable; although a charitable bequest in the residue was reduced, equitable apportionment and the charitable deduction were not mentioned in the opinion); PLR 8842011 (if state law requires allocation of state and federal estate taxes among residuary beneficiaries and the will does not provide otherwise, a residuary gift of a portion of the residue to charity must contribute to the FET payment, thereby reducing the amount of the charitable deduction).

[56] This statement is misleading to the extent that § 2203 defines "executor" as anyone in possession of estate property, but that definition is secondary to the primary rule, which looks to whomever is empowered to administer the estate.

The oldest reimbursement provision, found in § 2206, provides a right of reimbursement for taxes paid by the estate with respect to § 2042 inclusion of insurance proceeds payable to a third party. The personal representative is entitled to collect from every beneficiary of includible insurance proceeds the proportionate share of the total taxes paid by the estate that is attributable to that insurance. This right of reimbursement is not applicable with respect to annuities, however, even if the annuity is underwritten by an insurance company.[57] And reimbursement may not be asserted against the insurer, even if the proceeds have not yet been distributed to the designated beneficiary. Most cases hold that the personal representative must recover from the beneficiary instead.[58]

Although authorized under the introductory clause of § 2206, great care should be exercised to avoid inadvertent waiver of this right.[59] Particularly because § 2206 may be the only way to finance the taxes caused by inclusion in some estates. Thus, in planning with respect to any ILIT, the settlor as insured ought to either preserve § 2206 or include a contingent tax clause in the trust, dictating (at the least) payment of taxes to the extent the decedent insured's estate is insufficient.[60]

---

[57] See Annot., Construction and application of statutes apportioning or prorating estate taxes, 71 A.L.R.3d 247, 302–303 (1976).

[58] See Annot., Remedies and practice under estate tax apportionment statutes, 71 A.L.R.3d 371 at 409–410 (1976).

[59] In this regard, consider In re Estate of Kapala, 402 N.W.2d 150 (Minn. Ct. App. 1987), in which the decedent's closely held corporation owned insurance on the life of the decedent, naming the decedent's partner as the beneficiary to provide liquidity to perform under a buy-sell agreement when the decedent died. The insurance was includible under § 2042 and the court found that § 2206 reimbursement was not waived, notwithstanding that the buy-sell agreement provided that the surviving partner would receive all assets "free and clear of all claims of every kind." The court determined that waiver of § 2206 must appear in an instrument with testamentary intent, which it found the buy-sell agreement to lack. There may be precedential value in this element of the case for § 2703 purposes. Although note that *Kapala* is a state court dealing with a federal tax provision. See § 3.3.16.1.

[60] Care must be taken in drafting any contingent tax payment provision to preclude inclusion by virtue of that direction alone. For example, in TAM 8551001 the decedent was beneficiary of a standard nonmarital trust that contained a provision authorizing payment of FET caused by inclusion of that trust in the decedent's estate. Without the clause, no other inclusion section would have caused estate taxation of the trust in the decedent's estate, and the question

Also consider that the effect of waiving §2206 essentially is a bequest to the insurance beneficiary. For example, a decedent's waiver of the §2206 right of reimbursement constitutes a "bequest" from the decedent to the beneficiary of the proceeds of the policy, which "bequest" that beneficiary may disclaim.[61] Indeed, that disclaimer (meaning that the beneficiary will instead pay the tax) may increase the decedent's residuary estate, which may pass to S and qualify for the marital deduction.[62]

Added with the general power of appointment provisions in 1942, §2207 employs virtually identical language to §2206 to grant an identical right of reimbursement for taxes attributable to "property included in the gross estate under *section 2041*." The personal representative may re-

---

(Footnote Continued)

was whether the tax payment authority alone would cause inclusion. The TAM concluded that the authority to pay was subject to the precedent condition of inclusion, which did not occur before the decedent's death, meaning that the power to pay did not itself generate inclusion in the decedent's gross estate. Most useful was the government's willingness to consider the question of inclusion in the proper sequence, stating:

> The power authorized by the Trust Agreement to pay estate taxes . . . is only exercisable if [the trust] assets are includible in [the Decedent's] gross estate. Absent inclusion of [the trust] in the gross estate through the action of another Code section (i.e. 2033, 2035, 2036, 2037, 2038, etc.), *section 2041* by itself will not trigger inclusion.

[61] In re Estate of Fogleman, 3 P.3d 1172 (Ariz. Ct. App. 2000), and Rosen v. Wells Fargo Bank Texas, 114 S.W.3d 145 (Tex. Ct. App. 2003), each regarded a burden on the residue tax payment provision waiving apportionment to be a failed bequest because the estates were insolvent. In re Estate of Wu, 877 N.Y.S.2d 886 (Surr. Ct. 2009), is an unusual application of the same principle. The decedent's sibling was beneficiary of insurance on the decedent's life, and the decedent's will waived the §2206 right of reimbursement. The sibling was a witness to the decedent's will and the court held that an interested witness purge statute therefore was applicable, because the sibling received the benefit under the will of taking the life insurance proceeds free from the §2206 reimbursement obligation. The purge statute denied the sibling the benefit of that indirect bequest, by negating the decedent's waiver of the estate's right of reimbursement.

[62] See Estate of Boyd v. Commissioner, 819 F.2d 170 (7th Cir. 1987), and PLR 200127007 (waiver of the §2207A right of reimbursement is an interest in property that may be disclaimed to increase the marital deduction available to the rest of the estate).

§3.3.5

cover from "the person receiving such property by reason of the exercise, nonexercise or release of a power of appointment."

Added in 1981 with adoption of §2044 and the §2056(b)(7) QTIP marital deduction provision, §2207A grants a significantly different right of reimbursement. Applicable with respect to §2044 includible QTIPs for which the §2056(b)(7) marital deduction was allowed, this right of reimbursement differs because it is an incremental rather than a proportionate entitlement. Effectively prorating all deductions and credits proportionately among all takers, §§2206 and 2207 apply to bottom line taxes imposed on a decedent's estate with respect to those portions causing inclusion under §§2042 and 2041, respectively (and after considering the marital deduction). But §2207A permits recovery of the amount by which taxes were increased by inclusion of §2044 property, meaning the incremental taxes without benefit of deductions or credits available to the estate as a whole.[63]

Thus, spouses may agree that S will have the use of D's wealth for S's overlife, but that their respective shares will pass at S's death to their respective beneficiaries. This provision disrupts the intended equity of that plan by imposing a greater than pro rata share of S's taxes on D's QTIP. Only if S is willing to alter the incremental dictate of §2207A by a provision in S's will would this be avoided, and D cannot guarantee that S will do so. It may be that no modification is appropriate, however, because the inequity is balanced by the fact that S's unified credit reduces that tax imposed on all the beneficiaries interested in S's FET computation, including those who take the QTIP trust remainder as well as S's other beneficiaries, while D's unified credit benefited the beneficiaries of D's nonmarital trust entirely. Either way, this serious issue

---

[63] The difference between these reimbursement provisions is illustrated in *Sarosdy v. Johnson*, 894 S.W.2d 640 (Ky. Ct. App. 1994), in which a general power of appointment versus a QTIP marital trust was involved. The estate was entitled to only pro rata reimbursement under §2207 rather than incremental reimbursement under §2207A, meaning that FET attributable to inclusion of the marital trust was payable in part from the decedent's own property, which would have passed totally free of tax under the decedent's unified credit had the marital trust not been includible. It also is highlighted by the reversal of a lower court's pro rata reimbursement decision because the property involved was a QTIP, as determined by *In re Estate of Klarner*, 113 P.3d 150 (Colo. 2005), rev'g and rem'g 98 P.3d 892 (Colo. Ct. App. 2003).

§3.3.5

must be anticipated in drafting prenuptial agreements or coordinated estate plans that involve disparate beneficiaries of his and her plans, such as children by former marriages.

The § 2207A right of reimbursement extends to gift taxes incurred under § 2519, caused by inter vivos relinquishment of any portion of a qualified terminable interest. No similar right exists under either of the § 2206 or § 2207 reimbursement provisions if gift taxes are incurred on insurance proceeds or power of appointment property. It does not, however, allow recovery of gift taxes incurred under § 2511 (as, for example, if the beneficiary of a QTIP trust assigned a portion of the right to receive income and incurred gift tax on both the § 2511 gift of income and the § 2519 imputed transfer of the remainder interest in the entire trust). And § 2207A does not grant any right to recover the benefit of any unified credit "used" on such a lifetime transfer under either § 2511 or 2519. The effect is to "use" S's unified credit on the § 2511 transfer first, then on the § 2519 transfer.

Section 2207A(d) specifies that interest and penalties attributable to QTIP are subject to the incremental right of reimbursement. This also has no counterpart in § § 2206 and 2207.

According to Treas. Reg. § 20.2207A-1(a)(2), failure to assert the § 2207A right of reimbursement constitutes a gift from the beneficiaries of S's estate to the beneficiaries of the QTIP who benefit from that failure. Treas. Reg. § 20.2207A-1(a)(3) states that this gift can be avoided to the extent S's will expressly waives the right of reimbursement or the beneficiaries of the estate cannot otherwise compel recovery. This might encourage waiver of the right of reimbursement, but the magnitude of § 2044 inclusion in some estates causes the inability to assert the right of reimbursement to have calamitous consequences, as the following example indicates.

D was married three times. D was the beneficiary of a QTIP trust created by D's second spouse. It passed to the settlor's surviving children (those children were not D's children). D created a QTIP trust for D's surviving (third) spouse, and created a nonmarital trust to benefit D's children (from D's first marriage). Inclusion of the second spouse's QTIP trust in D's estate generated sufficient taxes to wipe out D's nonmarital trust and exhaust a portion of D's marital deduction trust, all results that D likely did not intend. Similar issues have been experienced

§ 3.3.5

in cases in which a decedent's nonmarital trust was consumed by state death taxes or expenses of administration. These also could be the subject of apportionment under the decedent's estate plan in an effort to more equitably share those burdens among varying and disparate beneficiaries of the estate.

As illustrated only obliquely by Treas. Reg. §25.2207A-1(f), the §2207A right of reimbursement for gift taxes does not extend to any tax imposed under §2511 on the gift of the income interest and §§25.2207A-1(c) and 25.2207A-1(d) effectively provide that the principles of equitable apportionment will apply in determining which recipients of property subject to §2044 or §2519 will bear the cost of reimbursement. For example, if S remarries and the property passes to S's surviving spouse or to a charity, in either case qualifying for a deduction and therefore causing no tax, the recipient would not be required to contribute to the §2207A reimbursement. This is a form of equitable apportionment at the federal level.

Back in 1984 a statement appeared in the very first *Prop*. Treas. Reg. §25.2207A-1(a) that a "delay" in enforcement of the right of reimbursement would be treated as an interest free loan. That notion was deleted when those regulations became final in 1994. Presumably this was because there was no way to determine what would constitute a delay. Things stood that way until early 2002 when the Treasury Department reissued the exact same proposed regulation first introduced in 1984. First it elaborated on the principle that the gift under §2519 is the value of the corpus less the amount of any §2207A reimbursement to which S is entitled. Then it reinstated the Treas. Reg. §25.2207A-1(a) proposition that S makes an added gift of the amount of the reimbursement if it is not collected, and the "delay" in enforcement element. It also recognized that the donee of property subject to the §2207A right of reimbursement receives less value than if the right of reimbursement did not exist. Therefore, the value of any §2519(a) gift to the donee is calculated as a net gift, reducing the FMV of the property subject to §2519(a) by the amount of the §2207A(b) reimbursement. That sensible provision, which was omitted from the 1994 final regulations, was restored in 2003 when Treas. Reg. §§25.2207A-1(b) and 25.2519-1(c)(4) became final.

The government worries about the tax consequences of S not requesting the §2207A(b) reimbursement but instead remitting other funds in payment of the gift tax under § 2519(a). The proper result—embraced by the regulations—is to regard S's waiver of or failure to assert the right of reimbursement as an additional gift, itself subject to tax. As a practical matter it would be easier to treat all gifts as occurring in the year of the original transfer that triggered § 2519(a), rather than requiring a net gift computation in that year and an additional gift tax determination in a subsequent year. Nevertheless, the regulation takes the more cumbersome but theoretically correct approach: the gift occurs when the right of recovery no longer is enforceable, and adds the notion that this lapse of the right of reimbursement "is treated as a gift even if recovery is impossible."

S can waive the § 2207A(b) right of reimbursement but the added gift occurs upon the *later* of the date of that waiver or the date on which the gift tax is paid. Treas. Reg. § 25.2207A-1(b)(2). Unless the gift tax is paid in the year of the § 2519 triggering event, that "later of" date will be the following year, when the gift tax return is filed, which does not effectively combine all the gift tax consequences in one year. Under this standard it does not appear to be possible for S to simply indicate on the gift tax return reporting the § 2519(a) transfer that the § 2207A(b) right of reimbursement will not be asserted and therefore that the gift is the full § 2519 amount unreduced by the § 2207A(b) right of reimbursement (effectively releasing the right of reimbursement and accelerating the year of the gift), unless the gift tax actually is paid (and the waiver occurs) all in the year of the § 2519 transfer itself.

A tax simplification change made it impossible to waive § 2207A without "specifically indicat[ing] an intent to waive" the reimbursement right, thereby avoiding inadvertent waivers of a variety that have produced notable problems.[64] That same change added the ability to waive the right by a provision in a decedent's revocable trust as well as in a decedent's will.[65] Neither of § 2206 nor § 2207 so permit.

Somewhat like a QTIP trust is the QDOT of § 2056A, applicable with respect to any decedent if S is not a citizen of the United States. FET is imposed by § 2056A(b) upon certain events, such as if the trust ceases to qualify as a QDOT or if distributions of corpus are made during S's

---

[64] See also § 3.3.16.1 regarding the *Gordon* case.

[65] See § 3.3.16.5 regarding *Estate of Roe* and use of the wrong instrument to waive reimbursement rights.

§ 3.3.5

overlife, and at S's death. By §2056A(b)(2) the tax is computed at D's rates and is imposed ab initio on the trustee under §2056A(b)(5). In this respect, §2056A differs from the treatment of a normal QTIP trust under §§2044, 2519, and 2207A because the tax is not computed at S's estate or gift tax rates and the provision that imposes the tax on the trust property cannot be waived or overridden by S's estate plan. Nevertheless, the fundamental apportionment aspect is that the tax is paid out of the QDOT property.

A fourth FET reimbursement provision appears in §2207B. It applies to taxes caused by inclusion of property under any part of §2036.[66] It calls for a pro rata right of reimbursement, like §§2206 and 2207, but includes penalties and interest attributable to the tax in the amount that is subject to reimbursement, like §2207A. Also like §2207A, the entitlement created by §2207B may be waived by the decedent's revocable inter vivos trust as well as by a will, subject to the same requirement that any waiver "specifically indicates an intent to waive" the reimbursement right (whatever that means).[67] The tax simplification proposal that added this requirement to §2207A was accompanied by legislative history that almost surely will become a part of any regulations that are issued, providing that a specific reference to QTIP, §2044 or §2207A will suffice. Presumably a similar reference to §2036 or §2207B would suffice for §2207B specific intent purposes, but the legislative history was silent on this issue. Moreover, notwithstanding the close similarity of these most recently enacted reimbursement rights, the government has not provided even as much guidance under §2207B in the form of regulations as it has under §2207A, so it is unknown whether failure to waive or assert the right of reimbursement will result in a gift of the type imposed under §2207A.

For reasons that probably are more historical than substantive, there is no comparable federal provision for recovery of taxes attributable to nonprobate assets includible under §§2035 and 2037 through

---

[66] Not just §2036(c), which was the Code provision that prompted addition of §2207B, which remains in the Code notwithstanding repeal of §2036(c) and replacement of it with Chapter 14.

[67] See §3.3.16.1 regarding the specific reference required for an effective waiver of the federal reimbursement rights.

§3.3.5

2040 and none with respect to the FET aspects of §§2701 through 2704.[68]

Each of §§2206 and 2207 provides that the federal right of reimbursement will not apply if the decedent directs otherwise in his or her will, and §§2207A and 2207B provide a similar result if the decedent's will *or trust* directs otherwise, but only if either document exhibits a specific intent to waive those rights. §§2207 (but not 2207A or 2207B)

---

[68] There has been longstanding interest in a proposal to enact a provision similar to §§2207A and 2207B for the taxes caused by inclusion of §2039 retirement benefits in a decedent's gross estate. It is sensible to seek such an addition because these benefits typically pass outside probate and often constitute a large share of the estate, risking bankruptcy of the probate estate in payment of FET absent a right of reimbursement. One underlying justification for §§2207 and 2207A is that the decedent did not create the interest that generated the FET liability under §2041 or §2044. The absence of this element in most situations involving inclusion under §§2035 and 2037 through 2040 is not a persuasive justification for the lack of a right of reimbursement, however, given the fact that §2206 usually applies to insurance proceeds as to which the decedent possessed incidents of ownership that caused inclusion in the gross estate, and §2207B applies to property transferred during life in a manner that triggers §2036.

There has been some suggestion that the Treasury Department regards each of §§2206 through 2207B as matters properly left to state property law. Thus, it is suggested that, because these sections are not related to the imposition or collection of taxes in the first instance, the Treasury Department has no interest in adding a Code provision relating to §2039 or other nonprobate assets. Addition of a provision comparable to §§2206 through 2207B is not high on any list of tax reform priority. This is particularly unfortunate, given the magnitude of some of these assets relative to a decedent's total estate and the assets otherwise available to pay taxes caused by their inclusion.

Martin v. United States, 923 F.2d 504 (7th Cir. 1991), is a good illustration of the need for additional reimbursement provisions. D made transfers before 1981 that were brought back into D's gross estate under §§2035 and 2036(a)(1). The FET generated by these inclusions exceeded D's residuary estate and assets otherwise passing to S that would have qualified for the marital deduction were required to pay the tax. Using an interrelated algebraic computation, the estate determined the amount of tax to be paid after reducing the marital deduction to reflect invasions of marital property to pay the FET. State law did not require nonprobate property to pay its share of taxes caused by its inclusion, federal law at the time did not contain the necessary reimbursement provisions, and the estate lacked sufficient insurance and other funds to provide for the tax payment liability.

§3.3.5

also contain a provision that "allocates" the marital deduction in an estate, first to insurance proceeds and then to power of appointment property. By the last sentence of §§ 2206 and 2207, the right of reimbursement is inapplicable to the extent S receives proceeds of insurance or property subject to a general power of appointment, in either case to the extent qualifying for the § 2056 marital deduction. As between the two provisions, § 2207 presumes that insurance proceeds first qualify for any available marital deduction, with § 2041 power of appointment property filling only any excess of the amount of the deduction over the amount of insurance proceeds passing to the spouse and qualifying for the deduction.

The effect of these presumptions is to reduce any otherwise applicable reimbursement right in an estate that qualifies for the marital deduction. In effect, these sections work as a form of equitable apportionment, denying apportionment through reimbursement against assets deemed to qualify for the deduction. Neither section has a similar provision with respect to the charitable deduction, and §§ 2207A and 2207B are devoid of a comparable provision altogether. Treas. Reg. § 20.2207A-1(a)(1) reflects the fact that an equitable apportionment rule is unnecessary because the § 2207A increment in tax attributable to an asset that qualifies for either a marital or a charitable deduction is zero, but this effect does not apply with respect to the pro rata right of reimbursement in § 2207B. In effect, then, §§ 2206, 2207, and 2207A effectively embrace equitable apportionment with respect to the marital deduction. Of those, only § 2207A does so with respect to the charitable deduction, and that only by virtue of the incremental reimbursement regime. Curiously, by express provision, § 2207B(d) provides specifically that no taxes will be apportioned under § 2207B to a qualified CRT, but it has no counterpart with respect to the marital deduction. As this paragraph illustrates, these federal rules are a mess.

All of §§ 2206, 2207, 2207A, and 2207B appear to deny reimbursement for taxes deferred under §§ 6161, 6163, and 6166 and not yet *paid*, which may be equitable (why should the recipient provide reimbursement before the FET is paid) and avoids administrative problems such as when a deferred payment would occur with respect to property subject to reimbursement (that is, would a pro ration or some other rule apply

§ 3.3.5

with respect to all deferral property), and the need to track down the beneficiary to enforce reimbursement many years in the future.

§3.3.6 Federal Rules Applicable to GST Apportionment

The GST contains its own reimbursement provision in §2603(a), which specifies that the distributee will pay the tax in a taxable distribution, the trustee will pay the tax in a taxable termination, and usually the transferor (or the transferor's estate) will pay the tax in a direct skip. More obtusely, §2603(b) does not conform to the legislative language in each of §§2207A and 2207B but instead provides that "unless otherwise directed pursuant to the governing instrument *by specific reference to the tax imposed by this chapter,* the tax imposed by this chapter on a generation-skipping transfer shall be charged to the property constituting such transfer" [emphasis added]. Collectively the two clauses in §2603(b) establish a single, easily stated rule: in essence, "the person with the generation-skipping property pays the tax out of that property." But like most simplifications, this statement is not entirely accurate.

For example, because the transferor (or the transferor's estate) pays the tax in the case of most direct skips, the picture is drawn of a transfer that triggers the tax, with the transferor holding out enough dollars to pay the tax thereon. Because the tax is computed "exclusive" of the dollars used to pay the tax, however, in reality the transferor makes the direct skip transfer and then comes up with additional dollars to pay the tax. So §2603(b) is a fiction in the case of a direct skip because the tax is not in fact paid from the property that constituted the transfer. Indeed, §2515 recognizes this, in the sense that it imposes a gift tax on the dollars used by the transferor to pay the direct skip tax, to ensure that these dollars do not also escape gift tax liability. A net gift (or some other form of apportionment) presumably will not avoid this gift tax consequence because §2515 speaks to taxes imposed on the donor, not just those paid by the donor.

There probably are two reasons why §2603 is drafted as it is. If the transferor does not produce the added dollars to pay the direct skip tax, then transferee liability and lien provisions (incorporated by reference in §2661) allow the government to proceed against the transferee who received the direct skip property. The transferor also is protected in the

§3.3.6

case of an inadvertent direct skip. For example, assume the transferor gives property to a child, who disclaims, causing a direct skip because the property passes to the child's descendants. If the transferor did not anticipate the GST, § 2603(b) comes to the rescue by imposing the tax on the transferred and then disclaimed property received by the child's descendants. In most other cases, however, § 2603(b) merely states what may seem obvious: that the trustee who holds the property following a taxable termination, or the distributee who just received a taxable distribution, should use the property to pay the tax imposed under § 2603(a).

A number of interpretative questions are likely to arise under these provisions. For example, as in §§ 2207A and 2207B, the unresolved question is what constitutes a sufficiently "specific reference to the tax imposed" by Chapter 13 to overcome § 2603(b). A general waiver of reimbursement rights should not suffice,[69] which (at least in many direct skip situations) probably is appropriate because some transfers will be inadvertent or unexpected and the transferor may not have considered the unexpected tax thereon when directing in a standard tax payment provision that all taxes be paid from the residue of the transferor's estate, "without reimbursement." To illustrate, if a decedent's will bequeaths $2 million to a grandchild as a direct skip transfer, the issue is whether the decedent really meant to leave $2 million *after* the GST is paid from other property in the decedent's estate, or whether $2 million is to be set aside to be used to pay the tax as directed by § 2603(b), with only the balance actually passing to the grandchild. Without more, the proper result is the latter, in which case the tax (assuming no exemption or exclusion applies) would be computed as

---

[69] See, e.g., Estate of Monroe v. Commissioner, 104 T.C. 352 (1995), rev'd and rem'd on other grounds, 124 F.3d 699 (5th Cir. 1997) (referring to "federal estate taxes . . . or other death taxes attributable to" certain bequests); In re Estate of Denman, 270 S.W.3d 639 (Tex. Ct. App. 2008) (referring to any "transfer, estate, inheritance, succession and other death taxes which shall become payable by reason of my death"); and In re Estate of Tubbs, 900 P.2d 865 (Kan. Ct. App. 1995) (referring to "all estate, inheritance and other death taxes"), each holding that garden-variety tax payment provisions, with no specification or explicit reference to GST or Chapter 13 of the Code, were not adequate to overcome the § 2603(b) regime.

§ 3.3.6

$$[\text{rate}] \times [\text{transfer (after tax)}] = [\text{tax}]$$
$$.35 \times \$2 \text{ million} \div 1.35 = \$518,518$$

and the grandchild would receive $2 million less this tax = $1,481,481.[70] If this is not the decedent's intent, then the document must clearly override § 2603(b), causing a greater amount to be subject to the tax ($2 million rather than the $1,481,481 in the prior example) and causing the tax thereon to be greater ($700,000 rather than $518,518). Fortunately, because the tax itself is not subject to the GST, there is no algebraic circularity caused by increasing the bequest and thereby increasing the tax. Nevertheless, the difference in result is dramatic and should not be left to postmortem determination of the decedent's intent.[71]

Another interpretative question is whether taxes imposed on a direct skip transfer are subtracted before determining the inclusion ratio, or whether the exemption is applied first, followed by a portion of the exemption being "wasted" by § 2603(b) taking a portion of the transferred property to pay the tax. The GST regulations do not address this question. Nevertheless, the answer should be that the inclusion ratio denominator ("the value of the property . . . involved in the direct skip") is the amount subject to the tax ($1,481,481 in the prior example), not the amount actually transferred but before payment of the tax.

---

[70] As illustrated in the Form 706 Estate and Generation-Skipping Tax return, another formula to make this computation in 2012 is

$$\text{Transfer (before tax)} \div 3.8571428$$

The denominator is simply 1 plus the tax rate, divided by the tax rate. As illustrated by TAM 9822001, if any interest is computed on the direct skip tax owed it would *not* be reflected in this calculation.

[71] A poignant illustration of this is provided by Estate of Green v. Commissioner, 86 T.C.M. (CCH) 758 (2003), which held that the decedent intended to exonerate direct skip bequests from the GST but did not effectively exonerate them from state or federal estate tax, causing the GST to be imposed on the other residuary beneficiary, which was a charity, causing a reduction in the FET charitable deduction that generated FET that was imposed on the direct skip beneficiaries under state law equitable apportionment, nevertheless resulting in more wealth passing to the direct skip beneficiaries than if § 2603(b) had applied, all in accordance with the decedent's apparent intent.

§ 3.3.6

Treas. Reg. §27.2642-1(c)(1) arguably states this result by reference to "the value of the property . . . transferred in a direct skip not in trust," which should be the reduced amount and not the $2 million in the example. However, §2642 is not clear on this point. Indeed, §2642(a)(2)(B)(ii) specifies that the denominator shall be reduced by any estate or death taxes actually recovered from the transferred property, but says nothing about GST, indicating perhaps that a contrary result was intended (assuming Congress and the legislative drafters even considered this issue).

Adding to the lack of clarity is the clear fact that, if a trust was only partially exempt and suffered a taxable termination or made a taxable distribution, payment of the GST using trust or distributed assets would use partially exempt dollars to pay the tax, thereby "wasting" exemption on the tax payment. A legitimate question is whether a direct skip should be treated any differently.

The simplistic answer is that direct skips should be treated differently because they are taxed "exclusive" of taxes imposed, unlike taxable terminations and taxable distributions. But the issue is not whether the GST is imposed on the dollars used to pay the direct skip tax. The issue is whether the exemption is wasted in paying the direct skip tax. Although these are not the same questions, a proper interpretation would be that the exemption should be applied to the amount of the direct skip, not to the full amount transferred before payment of the tax. This is consistent with the tax exclusive intent of Congress to favor the direct skip and is supportable (even though not explicitly stated) by the language of §2642.

Several other situations exist in which §2603 is not clear. Assume that T is the income beneficiary of a trust and assigns that income to T's grandchild. As a taxable gift and a direct skip, this is one of the rare cases in which §2603(a)(2) may apply ("a direct skip from a trust"), in which case the trust pays the tax, rather than §2603(a)(3), which dictates that the transferor pays the tax. Even if this is not the correct conclusion, the further question is how to apply §2603(b), which says that the direct skip tax should be paid from "the property constituting such transfer," which is an income interest. An analogy could be applied that T received the income and made a direct skipping gift, making §2603(a)(3) applicable and removing this from the "direct skip from a

§3.3.6

trust" category. But, realistically, this transfer comes directly out of the trust as income is paid to the grandchild, which presumably is just the type of situation anticipated by § 2603(a)(2).

In either case, the property constituting the transfer is an income interest. Because the GST cannot be paid as income is received and paid to the grandchild, and because the tax imposed likely would exceed the income available in the year of the assignment, presumably the tax would be paid from trust principal. As discussed below,[72] imposing the tax on trust principal here only appears to be the wrong result, notwithstanding that it seems to shift the tax liability from the income beneficiary to the remainder beneficiaries. It is not wrong in fact, because reducing the principal correspondingly reduces income subsequently earned thereon, thereby effectively amortizing the tax out of income. Thus, despite some lack of clarity in the rule, it should be that the trust will pay the tax from corpus.

This is particularly true because regarding this as a direct skip from T, not from the trust, followed by T paying the tax to avoid this income versus principal issue, would trigger § 2515 (gift tax imposed on dollars T uses to pay the tax). And all of these problems would arise if T failed to pay the tax and the government asserted liability against the property subject to the transfer. In any case, if the tax is paid out of the property subject to this direct skip transfer (whatever that means), the amount subject to tax is only the remaining balance.

As a second example, assume that a decedent names a grandchild as beneficiary of insurance on the decedent's life. The issue is whether the direct skip represented thereby at the decedent's death is "from a trust" for purposes of § 2603(a)(2), presumably meaning that the insurer would be treated like a trustee and would be primarily liable to pay the GST. Moreover, and in any event, must the tax be paid from the insurance proceeds under § 2603(b)? The "clean" result is to say that an insurance policy is not the same as a trust, thus making § 2603(a)(3) apply (the decedent's estate would pay the tax). Then § 2603(b) would act like § 2206, meaning the grandchild, as recipient of the insurance proceeds, would reimburse the decedent's estate for the taxes incurred on the direct skip transfer (unless the decedent's will expressly waived

---

[72] See § 3.3.10.

§ 3.3.6

this right of reimbursement). And the amount of the transfer for GST purposes should be the amount of the proceeds less the taxes incurred thereon.

Unfortunately, Treas. Reg. § 26.2662-1(c)(2)(iii) and Schedule R-1 of Form 706 adopt the position that, if the insurance proceeds exceed $250,000, the personal representative of the decedent insured's estate should report the transfer on Schedule R-1 (and send a notice thereof to the insurer), but the insurer should pay the tax. If the proceeds are $250,000 or less, however, the personal representative would report the transfer on Schedule R and pay the tax from the decedent insured's estate, and then seek reimbursement from the insurance company or the beneficiary. This rule exposes fiduciaries to potential liability if this distinction is overlooked and the fiduciary improperly pays—or fails to pay—the tax. That liability would be avoided if the insurance was treated like a trust, thus clearly imposing the tax payment liability on the insurer (as "trustee"). Perhaps the best result here is for the personal representative to request the insurer to pay and debate these issues only if the insurer refuses.

Finally, for § 2601 transition rule purposes, if the special election was made to treat pre-enactment direct skips to grandchildren as qualifying for the "Gallo" amendment (the $2 million per grandchild exclusion), then "unless the grandchild otherwise directs by will, the estate of such grandchild shall be entitled to recover from the person receiving the property on the death of the grandchild any increase in FET on the estate of the grandchild by reason of the preceding sentence." The special election has the effect of causing subject property to incur tax "as if [it had been paid] to the grandchild's estate," with tax liability being imposed under § 2033, as to which no federal right of reimbursement otherwise exists. This provision calls for an incremental reimbursement right, like § 2207A, but is not coordinated with § 2207A to specify which right "goes first." Thus, the question is whether the increment in tax caused by § 2044 property would be considered before, after, or in conjunction with the increase caused by inclusion of this grandchild exclusion property. Presumably a pro ration of the aggregate increase caused by both types of property is the proper result. The provision also does not appear to require the same "specific reference" dictated in

§ 3.3.6

§ 2603(b) to override its application. Quaere whether this was intentional or merely another legislative oversight.

§ 3.3.7 Summary of State Law: Silence Generates What Result?

The law governing this topic is an amalgam of federal rules that defer to state law in most respects (while granting certain rights or imposing selected responsibilities that may trump state law). There are numerous legitimate choices to be made in determining the proper apportionment result, and conflicting results are dictated by the law in various jurisdictions in which apportionment issues have been resolved.

The following exegesis reveals the state law result to the extent an estate plan does not address the tax apportionment issue. If the documents are silent, in some states the issues are (partially) resolved by statute. In a (declining) number of states only judicial authority exists. But in a few states, on some issues, common law presumptions apply by default because state law is entirely silent. And from state to state (and occasionally within a given state), some of the results stated herein are confused and inconsistent because the law is not uniform. All of which means that careful and comprehensive drafting to address all issues is a must.

Although the intent is the exact opposite, the federal rules under § § 2002 and 2205 are the starting point regarding state law apportionment. Those provisions establish the fundamental proposition that the FET is not apportioned at all. It is a "burden on the residue" of the estate, as was true under common law. But the Supreme Court established very early that federal law governs only to the extent state law regarding apportionment is not inconsistent.[73] Thus, to the extent state law differs, the state law is supreme in this arena, and any state may alter the federal presumption and control the apportionment result.

If there is an established state dictate, especially if mandated under a state apportionment statute, that rule usually will apply unless the decedent clearly directs otherwise in an appropriate manner, whether by

---

[73] Riggs v. Del Drago, 317 U.S. 95 (1942).

§ 3.3.7

will, trust, or other document.[74] The burden of proof normally is on those who challenge the state apportionment result in determining whether a decedent has provided otherwise with sufficient specificity and clarity. Thus, a direction to pay all taxes from the residue of a decedent's estate typically will cause taxes on nonprobate property to be paid from the residue in an apportionment state, although some cases show that a nonspecific direction is likely to cause litigation if it does not unambiguously identify and override state law.[75] So clarity is essential. Moreover, if not carefully drafted, a general tax payment direction in a will may be read to negate apportionment, if any, only within the probate estate, leaving any state outside apportionment statute to apply with respect to nonprobate assets.[76]

---

[74] As discussed in more detail below. See § 3.3.16.1. The same is true about an alteration by settlement agreement in the wake of estate litigation, as painfully illustrated by In re Estate of Brabson, 752 A.2d 761 (D.C. App. Ct. 2000) (it likely is a precursor to malpractice litigation if a court has occasion to remark, as this one did, that "[i]t may even be that ... former counsel did not detect the issue, and he evidently did not insist during negotiations that FET liability be allocated proportionately"), and less so but equally disappointingly in Houghland v. Lampton, 33 S.W.3d 536 (Ky. App. Ct. 2000) (family settlement of a prior estate led to a favored bequest in the decedent's will that could not be fully satisfied due to tax payment obligation, which was not apportioned in a manner that protected the favored bequest), in which will contest litigants eventually resolved their differences in negotiated compromises that failed to anticipate the tax payment consequences of their resolution, and therefore totally failed to articulate how taxes would be apportioned among their respective beneficial interests. The courts therefore defaulted to state law pro rata apportionment as if that was the dictated distribution under the decedents' articulated estate plans.

[75] Compare In re Estate of Kirby, 498 N.E.2d 64 (Ind. Ct. App. 1986) (will provision directing payment of all taxes was deemed to overcome statutory outside apportionment rule, notwithstanding lack of specific reference thereto), and Ferrone v. Soffes, 558 So. 2d 146 (Fla. Dist. Ct. App. 1990) (will provision directing payment of all taxes from residue was deemed inadequate to override statutory outside apportionment without specific reference).

[76] See Note, Proposal for Apportionment of the Federal Estate Tax, 30 Ind. L.J. 217 (1955); Annot., Construction, and application of "pay-all-taxes" provision in will, as including liability of nontestamentary property for inheritance and estate taxes, 56 A.L.R.5th 133 (1998); Annot., Construction and application of statutes apportioning or prorating estate taxes, 71 A.L.R.3d 247 (1976); Annot., Construction and effect of will provisions not expressly mentioning payment of death taxes but relied on as affecting the burden of estate or inheritance taxes, 70

Because any effort to summarize the law in the 50 states is subject to unavoidable inaccuracies, and because the Uniform Estate Tax Apportionment Act is regarded by over half of the states as the best form of statutory apportionment,[77] it is appropriate to consider its major provisions briefly herein. Problems with these provisions (and similar statutes or judicial rules that apply in most of the remaining states as well) are considered in more detail in later sections. Because the most recent version of the uniform act has not been widely adopted, this summary reflects the 1964 version and is followed by a list of changes made in 2003.

(Footnote Continued)

A.L.R.3d 630 (1976); Annot., Construction and effect of will provisions expressly relating to the burden of estate or inheritance taxes, 69 A.L.R.3d 122 (1976).

[77] At last count just Arizona, Georgia, Iowa, and Kansas continue to apply the common law rule. See, e.g., Ga. Code 53-4-63; Iowa Code § 633.449. Yet most estate plans still embrace the common law burden-on-the-residue approach. With respect to all the state tax apportionment laws in general consult American College of Trust and Estate Counsel Study 12, Apportionment of Death Taxes (2002).

As of 2010, 28 states had adopted either the original (1958 Act), the first revised (1964 Act), or the latest revised (2003) Uniform Estate Tax Apportionment Act (most with some local modifications, a few so extensive that the Commissioners on Uniform State Laws do not claim parentage notwithstanding the Uniform Act was the template for the state statute). See 8A U.L.A. 193 (Supp. 2010) (2003 Act), 8A U.L.A. 261 (2003) (1964 Act), 8A U.L.A. 281 (2003) (1958 Act), or the UPC, 8 (Part II) U.L.A. 284 (1998) (§ 3-916 is the older version) and 8 (Part II) U.L.A. 88 (Supp. 2010) (§ 3-9A-101 et seq. is the most current version), which contain substantially the same provisions as the Uniform Act. The following list may be helpful, but be mindful of local modifications. Alabama (2003 Act), Alaska (1958 Act; UPC), Arkansas (2003 Act), Colorado (2003 Act; UPC), Hawaii (1964 Act; UPC), Idaho (2003 Act; UPC), Maine (UPC), Maryland (1964 Act), Massachusetts (2003 Act; UPC), Michigan (1958 Act; UPC), Minnesota (1958 Act; UPC), Mississippi (1964 Act), Montana (1958 Act; UPC), Nebraska (UPC), New Hampshire (1964 Act), New Jersey (UPC), New Mexico (2003 Act; UPC), North Carolina (1964 Act), North Dakota (1964 Act; UPC), Oregon (1964 Act), Rhode Island (1964 Act), South Carolina (UPC), South Dakota (1958 Act; UPC), Texas (1964 Act), Utah (UPC), Vermont (1964 Act), Washington (2003 Act), and Wyoming (1958 Act). Arizona and Florida have otherwise adopted the UPC, but not specifically § 3-916. See law.upenn.edu/bll/ulc/ulc.htm#uetaa for the official Acts.

§ 3.3.7

The Uniform Act establishes rules of four major types:

A. Inside and Outside Apportionment. First, § 2 provides that all taxes imposed on an estate (which would include an inheritance tax if it was a charge against the estate as a whole, which normally is *not* the case with an inheritance tax as opposed to an estate tax) should be pro rated among all persons "interested in the decedent's gross estate for FET purposes." This is a total inside and outside apportionment rule, applying a straight pro rata allocation based on the size of each interested individual's entitlement as compared to the size of the total estate (as computed for federal or state estate tax purposes). The apportionable estate is defined in § 2(1) of the 2003 Act as "the value of the gross estate as finally determined for purposes of the FET to be apportioned, which is reduced by" (1) claims or expenses allowable as FET deductions; (2) the value of interests qualifying for the FET marital or charitable deductions (or that are otherwise deductible or exempt for FET purposes); and (3) the amount added to the gross estate because of a gift tax on transfers before death (see, e.g., § 2035(b)).[78]

Two special rules are designed to prevent unnecessary conflicts with federal law. One special rule, equitable apportionment, is found in § 5(e) and is illustrated by a simple example. Assume that a decedent's estate passes to S in a fashion that qualifies for the FET marital deduction but not (entirely) for the state wealth transfer tax marital deduction. Under § 5(e) of the Act, the apportionment rule is not to apply if apportionment of a state tax to the marital share would have the effect of reducing the FET marital deduction. Thus, § 5(e) preserves the marital deduction without reduction. A similar result would apply for charitable deduction purposes, if relevant. This most likely applies in those states that did not conform their law to the 1981 addition of the FET unlimited marital deduction and the § 2056(b)(7) QTIP exception to the nondeduct-

---

[78] As noted in the comments to § 2 of the 2003 Act, the apportionable estate may differ for different taxes because the property included and deductions allowed for determining the taxes may differ. The gross estate is defined in § 2(3) as all interests in property subject to the FET. Ratable/ratably is defined in § 2(5) as apportioned or allocated pro rata according to the relative value of the interests to which the term is applied. Pursuant to § 2(7) the value of an interest refers to FMV as finally determined for purposes of the FET to be apportioned, reduced by any outstanding debts secured by the interest without reduction for taxes or special valuation adjustments.

§ 3.3.7

ible terminable interest property rules.[79] It has special significance in states that have decoupled from the federal basic exclusion amount, but only if the state death tax is not equitably apportioned totally against the nonmarital portion of the estate.

The other special rule is in § 9, added in 1982, specifying that federal law will control if federal and state laws differ with respect to apportionment. The rationale for this provision was addition in 1981 of § 2207A, calling for incremental rather than pro rata reimbursement of taxes. The Act is simply specifying that the difference between § 2207A and state law will be resolved in favor of federal law. Thus avoiding an inconsistency that might generate issues of pre-emption.

A different rule of a special nature applies to temporal interests, deviating from the otherwise pervasive pro rata allocation of the tax burden. Under § § 5(b) and 6, the tax otherwise attributable to a life estate, term of years, or annuity is not apportioned thereto. Instead, the tax is payable from corpus. This result is dictated even if the remainder interest qualifies for a deduction (most commonly the charitable deduction in a qualified CRT). This allocation against the deductible remainder interest of taxes attributable to the temporal interest reduces the available deduction and applies notwithstanding the equitable apportionment dictates of § 5(e).

B. Alteration. The second major proposition established by the Uniform Act is how to alter allocations under the Act. Two methods are authorized. In unusual circumstances a court may alter the proportionate allocation of taxes, under the authority of § 3(b). And a decedent may waive or alter the dictates of the Act under the authority of § 2, but only (as is expressly underscored by the comments to § 2) by a provision in the decedent's will. Unfortunately, a specific reference to the apportionment rule being waived or altered is not required by the Act, meaning that broad, nonspecific will provisions can raise important interpretative questions under the Act.

The 2003 Act provides expanded alteration provisions. Except as specified in § 3(c) of the 2003 Act, § 3(a) of the 2003 Ac t provides that:

---

[79] For a detailed explanation of all the ramifications of § 5(e), consult Scoles & Stephens, The Proposed Uniform Estate Tax Apportionment Act, 43 Minn. L. Rev. 907, 928–931 (1959).

§ 3.3.7

(1) an express and unambiguous direction in the decedent's will controls FET apportionment; (2) to the extent any portion of the FET is not so apportioned by the decedent's will, an express and unambiguous direction in the decedent's revocable trust then controls apportionment;[80] and (3) to the extent any portion of the tax still remains unapportioned, then an express and unambiguous provision in any other dispositive instrument controls the apportionment of the taxes to that interest.[81] This might include a life insurance beneficiary designation that directs whether an interest in property disposed of by the instrument will be applied to the payment of FET attributable to that interest

In addition, §3(b) of the 2003 Act contains several rules that apply[82] if the decedent does not expressly and unambiguously direct to the contrary. For example, a provision may exonerate an interest from the payment of taxes that otherwise would be apportioned to the interest. Those taxes are apportioned by §3(b)(1) among other persons receiving interests under the instrument. If the taxes attributable to the exonerated interest exceed the value of those other interests, then the excess taxes are apportioned ratably among other persons receiving interests in the apportionable estate that have not been exonerated.

An apportionment provision may direct that FET be apportioned to an interest that qualifies for the marital or charitable deduction. The FET is apportioned by §3(b)(2) ratably among the holders of any portion of that interest that is not deductible. Only if that portion is insufficient are taxes apportioned to the deductible portion.

---

[80] If two or more revocable trusts contain conflicting directions, the provision in the most recent trust instrument prevails.

[81] The comments to §3 note that a direction will not control apportionment "unless it explicitly refers to the payment of an estate tax and is specific and unambiguous as to the direction it makes for that payment." The comments to §3 also note that, although there is a split in the courts on whether §§2206 through 2207B pre-empt state law apportionment provisions, the 2003 Act takes the position that there is no pre-emption and it apportions taxes without regard to these provisions.

[82] Subject to §3(c), which indicates that an apportionment provision is ineffective to the extent it increases the tax apportioned to a person who has an interest in the gross estate over which the decedent had no "power to transfer" immediately before executing the instrument containing the apportionment direction. A testamentary power of appointment is a "power to transfer" for this purpose.

§3.3.7

Finally, an apportionment provision may direct that FET be apportioned to a time-limited interest The tax is apportioned by § 3(b)(3) to principal, "regardless of the deductibility of some of the interests in that property" (subject to a special rule in § 3(b)(4) if a charity has an interest in the time-limited property that otherwise qualifies for an FET charitable deduction).

C. Entitlements. Third, the Uniform Act establishes the proper treatment of certain entitlements that affect the tax burden. For example, § 5(c) provides that federal credits under § § 2012 (credit for gift tax on pre-1977 transfers), 2013 (previously taxed property credit), and 2014 (foreign death tax credit) inure to the proportionate benefit of all beneficiaries interested in the entire gross estate, rather than to the benefit of any particular recipient of property (such as the taker of the property that was previously taxed or subjected to a foreign death tax). Only the § 2011 state death tax credit is apportioned to individual takers, and that credit was repealed effective in 2005. Quaere how § 2015 is meant to be reflected—it allocates any § 2011 or § 2014 credits related to a future interest qualifying for § 6163 deferral to that interest, which is inconsistent with the Act.

Alternatively, however, § § 5(a), (b), and (d) provide that individual takers of interests included in the gross estate benefit from exemptions, deductions, and credits that relate specifically to "the purposes of the gift," "the relationship of any person to the decedent," or the payment of any taxes attributable to the property. Thus, the charitable and marital deductions usually inure to the benefit of the recipient of property qualifying therefor, this being the rule of equitable apportionment (subject to the special rule noted above, applicable to temporal interests in property). Moreover, it appears that the credit for state death taxes inured to the benefit of any recipient who paid the tax that generated the § 2011 credit (prior to its repeal), notwithstanding the difference in treatment of the allocation of the foreign death tax credit under § 5(c). Presumably the § 2058 deduction for state death tax (which took the place of the § 2011 credit in 2005) also should benefit the individuals who bear that tax, as the § 2011 credit also was apportioned.[83]

---

[83] For estates in which the prior § 2039(c) or (e) $100,000 exemption for retirement benefits is still applicable it is questionable whether the language or

§ 3.3.7

The entitlement rule also provides that the recipient is entitled to an adjustment in the allocation of tax to reflect any reduced rate of tax for state or other tax purposes based on the relation of the recipient to the decedent (for example, if a state inheritance tax is paid out of the estate and applies a reduced rate of tax to more closely related individuals).[84]

Under the unified federal wealth transfer tax computation procedure, the §2001(b) credit for gift taxes paid on property transferred during life should inure to the benefit of the estate as a whole if the transferred property is included in the gross estate for FET purposes (e.g., under §§2035 through 2038, §2041, or §2042). The credit for gift tax paid also ought to inure to the benefit of the estate as a whole if the gift tax was paid by the decedent (including if the transfer was a net gift, with the donee's payment of gift tax treated as a part-sale, part-gift to the donee with the donor thereafter paying the tax). In essence the estate has simply prepaid its wealth transfer taxes by virtue of the prior but included gift. Further, although the Act does not direct itself thereto, it appears that the unified credit is a benefit to the entire estate for apportionment among all takers.

D. Enforcement. Finally, the Act establishes mechanisms for enforcement of outside apportionment by providing for the "collection" of apportioned taxes. For example, §4(a) is a right of setoff, allowing a

---

(Footnote Continued)

intent of this provision would allow the recipient of those death benefits to enjoy the exemption.

[84] Cf. In re Estate of Morris, 838 P.2d 402 (Mont. 1992) (estate distributable in two halves, one for relatives of decedent's predeceased spouse and one for decedent's relatives, under will that directed payment of all taxes from residue of estate before its division, which overcame state law and argument by decedent's relatives that estate should be divided before payment from each half of the taxes attributable to that half). For a strange application of the rule "giving" the benefit of a special tax rate to the beneficiary who "generated" it, see In re Estate of Garrison, 728 P.2d 535 (Or. App. Ct. 1986) (Oregon estate tax credit for a handicapped child inured solely to the child's benefit, not to the benefit of the entire estate, providing a larger effective share of the estate for the benefit of that child). Cf. Pfeufer v. Cyphers, 919 A.2d 641 (Md. 2007) (the benefit of a state inheritance tax exemption for relatives of the decedent as opposed to "strangers" was *not* apportioned to those relatives, the court holding that the decedent's intent was that all beneficiaries should share the residuary estate after payment of tax generated by the share of only one of them).

§3.3.7

personal representative to withhold property otherwise distributable to a beneficiary in that amount necessary to recoup the beneficiary's proportionate share of apportioned taxes. In addition, §4(a) gives a right of recovery against any beneficiary whose share of taxes exceeds the amount of property the personal representative may withhold (if any). A right to pursue enforcement of the §4(a) recovery in a foreign jurisdiction is granted by §8, which also grants a similar right to an out-of-state personal representative, by reciprocity. Finally, §7 recognizes that some beneficiaries of nonprobate assets will be immune to collection procedures. It specifies that the residue of the estate should pay any deficiency if a portion of tax cannot be recovered and, if the residue is exhausted, then the remaining beneficiaries will bear the balance of the deficiency in proportion to their existing tax allocations.

The Uniform Act itself applies to the estate of any decedent dying more than a specified period following enactment, regardless of the time of execution of that decedent's estate plan and the unexpected effect the Act may have on the pattern of tax payment therein.

A final issue under the Act relates to the fiduciary's right to collect taxes apportioned to interested parties and the effect of a failure or inability to do so. Under §7 there is no duty to institute legal proceedings against any person interested in the estate to collect taxes apportioned to that person, prior to expiration of a specified period after determination of the tax. Further, any fiduciary who institutes a timely action to recover taxes is exonerated from liability if ultimately unable to collect. Implicit in this provision is the common law requirement that the fiduciary must assert any right of recovery for the benefit of the estate. Just as the fiduciary must marshal all assets available to the estate, the "right" to apportion taxes and the "authority" to recover properly are viewed as requirements or duty.[85] This duty imposes an obligation that the fiduciary may be unable to satisfy with respect to assets located out of state, or taxable nonprobate assets received by a beneficiary who expends the property prior to a demand for apportionment or collection of the amount owed.

---

[85] See Merchants Nat'l Bank v. Merchants Nat'l Bank, 62 N.E.2d 831 (Mass. 1945); Annot., Remedies and practice under estate tax apportionment statutes, 71 A.L.R.3d 371 (1976).

§3.3.7

Assuming the fiduciary acted reasonably but was unable to collect, the burden then must fall somewhere, either on the estate or on other beneficiaries. If the burden fell on other takers, §2205 would give them a right of recovery exercisable against the residuary estate. Under §7 of the revised Act, the burden for those uncollected taxes is apportioned directly to the residue of the estate, presumably because this would be the end result in any event. Only if the residue is insufficient for payment is the uncollected amount reapportioned among the remaining persons originally subject to apportionment.

Under §7 of the original Act, those uncollected taxes are apportioned directly against the full class of individuals who must contribute in the first instance, permitting apportionment to apply immediately to uncollected taxes as well as to the original amount of tax initially determined. Many state statutes appear to be silent on these issues, presumably meaning that general fiduciary principles will apply to the necessity to enforce apportionment and to the inability to recover from any individual who fails to pay an apportioned amount.[86] In any event, it appears that the inability to collect under a permitted proration entitlement generates a §166(d)(1) bad debt deduction to the individuals or individual who ultimately suffers therefrom.[87]

Revisions. The Revised Uniform Estate Tax Apportionment Act was completed in 2003 to freshen up the 1969 version of the Act. Although the 2003 revision is totally rewritten, it bears many resemblances to the old. For comparison purposes the drafters provided a document that identifies the major substantive changes made from the 1969 Act. Consult www.law.upenn.edu/bll/ulc/ulc.htm#uetaa. The drafters listed seven notable alterations:

1. It adds apportionment of foreign death taxes and GST on a direct skip occurring at the decedent's death.

2. It alters the mechanism for allocation of taxes by eliminating from the denominator of the fraction for pro ration (a) any deductible claims and expenses against the estate (regardless of whether they are deducted) and (b) any §2035(b) gross-up tax amount. In each case the

---

[86] See Annot., Construction and application of statutes apportioning or prorating estate taxes, 71 A.L.R.3d 247 (1976).

[87] See Rev. Rul. 69-411, 1969-2 C.B. 177.

§3.3.7

effect is to increase the tax apportioned to every person to whom tax is apportioned in the estate.

3. It expands the prior rule to permit a decedent to override the statutory regime by a provision in a revocable trust or other dispositive instrument, rather than just by a will.

4. It creates a complex approach for apportionment of tax to temporal or other "insulated" property (meaning dispositions such that access to liquid funds is impossible or impracticable). Tax attributable to such dispositions is paid from other "uninsulated" property and those payments constitute "advancements" that give the beneficiaries who incur the tax a future right to reimbursement from the takers of insulated property, delayed until a subsequent distribution of an insulated disposition occurs. Effected through a fractional reimbursement entitlement that is illustrated in the comments to §6 of the 2003 Uniform Act, observers will do well to carefully and independently evaluate the complexity of the approach adopted.

5. It allocates the benefit of the §§2012 and 2014 gift tax and foreign death tax credits.

6. It allocates the benefits generated under §2057 (the since-repealed deduction for QFOBIs), §2032A (special use valuation), and §2031(c) (conservation easements).

7. It identifies the costs to defer tax under §§6161, 6163, and 6166 and apportions interest and penalties attributable to them.

The 2003 Act does not make a number of other important changes that drafters may want to address:

a. Apportionment of the FET generated by §2035(b) gross-up rule inclusion of gift tax paid within three years of death. Should the donee of the gift that generated the gift tax that was paid by the donor incur the added FET attributable to the gross-up rule, or does the donor who paid the gift tax intend that the donee take free and clear of *all* tax, including any unanticipated FET attributable to the gift tax payment? This is a very hard issue, on which a colloquy on the topic appears below to indicate how the drafters considered issues of this nature, making it easier to see how or why a drafter might deviate from the 2003 Uniform Act, or add to it.

§3.3.7

b. There are a number of interesting equitable apportionment or adjustment issues not anticipated by the 2003 Uniform Act. One illuminating example is the §691(c) income tax deduction for FET attributable to IRD. Who should benefit from that income tax deduction: the beneficiary against whom the FET was apportioned that generated the income tax deduction, or whomever is the income beneficiary whose income tax is reduced? Another illustration is the §2058 state death tax deduction: it is not so clear how §2(1)(B) of the new Uniform Act is meant to operate when it refers to "the value of any interest in property that ... qualifies for the marital or charitable deduction *or otherwise is deductible or exempt*" in this context. Does that provision accomplish the equitable apportionment result that should apply for those who pay state death tax that generates the §2058 deduction? Unlike the 1969 version, a third example is the apparent failure of the 2003 revision to apportion differences in state inheritance or other death tax rates that vary based on the relation of the beneficiary to the decedent.

c. The 2003 Uniform Act does not apportion the benefit of a number of credits more important than §§2012 and 2014, most significantly the §2013 previously taxed property credit. The drafting issue is whether the person who incurred the FET that generates the credit should get the benefit of that credit. By default the Act allocates the §§2010 unified credit and 2058 state death tax deduction to all beneficiaries of the estate and potentially either or both benefits also should be allocated more directly to one class of beneficiaries or another (such as the §2058 deduction benefiting the takers of property that incurred and paid the state death tax in question).

d. The 2003 Uniform Act also addresses recapture taxes in an oblique manner but fails to consider all the different forms of recapture tax that may impact a decedent's estate. One obvious and likely to be common illustration is the §529(c)(4)(C) recapture of accelerated annual exclusions made available to contributors to college education plans.

e. The 2003 Uniform Act continues the basic paradigm that taxes attributable to property that is broken into temporal interests (such as a life estate or annuity, and remainder) shall be paid from corpus. The mechanism embraced is complex and most especially produces untoward results in cases in which a lead annuity of a fixed dollar amount is

§3.3.7

involved. The issue is whether an adjustment provision could be formulated that would be more fair and easier to employ.

f. Waiver by a will, trust, or other dispositive document requires an "express" or "unambiguous" provision (see §3) but the comment to that rule refers to "explicit" and "specific" references (not to express or unambiguous references). Federal law §§ 2207A and 2207B require the decedent to "specifically indicate an intent" to alter their entitlements. It might be wise to mimic federal law so that standards adopted under those provisions may inform the result under state law.

g. The provisions that consider the GST could be more refined. For example, any tax on a direct skip that occurs at death is addressed by the Act as if direct skip tax always is something the decedent could have anticipated. In that regard direct skip GST caused by a child's disclaimer often is excluded from well drafted tax payment provisions because it is thought that the child's trust normally would incur the GST (usually when the child dies) and the child's disclaimer should not accelerate that tax *and* change the source for its payment. Direct skip tax incurred on a disclaimer by a skip person is another story, because that direct skip tax presumably *was* anticipated by the decedent.

Moreover, apportionment of FET to a QTIP marital trust includible in the decedent's gross estate under §2044, either under the §2207A reimbursement right or a comparable state law, appropriately might be allocated first against property with an inclusion ratio of one rather than against exempt property attributable to a reverse QTIP election with an inclusion ratio of less than one. The Uniform Act does not does protect the exemption by invading the nonexempt property first.

h. The 2003 Uniform Act does not appear to apportion fees and expenses that are incurred by a probate estate in its compliance with the tax law but that are attributable to nonprobate assets. For example, a large valuation expense might be incurred with respect to nonprobate assets includible in an estate but directly expensed to the personal representative who is filing the FET return. Should those nonprobate assets pay for that expense? Nothing in most state laws or in the 2003 Uniform Act makes such an allocation.

i. Finally, this state law does not address the conflict of laws issue that regularly will arise with respect to decedents with property located

§ 3.3.7

in multiple jurisdictions, potentially subject to the state apportionment rules of several.

Now, here is that colloquy between an observer/commentator (**O**) regarding the Act in an earlier draft, and a member of the drafting committee advisory board (**A**). In addition to helping drafters and litigators to better understand the intent of the Act, it shows a number of ways that others in the legislative process might view their role and the standards to be applied by any legislature in making certain determinations regarding apportionment:

O: I agree [with a letter written by yet another commentator] that the estate tax attributable to the gross-up rule of § 2035(b) ought to be allocated to the donee of the gift.

A: There was probably no doubt that donors of inter vivos gifts intended them to be free of tax. This is not an issue of conceptual purity, but of almost certain intent.

O: I would bet that no donor ever considered the § 2035(b) gross-up tax (unless some advisor put the question to them). I grant that donors almost without exception (that exception being a net gift, in which intent is quite clearly expressed) want their donees to take free of GIFT tax, but this IS different. It is a tax that I would guess the donor never intended or contemplated. And if the transfer was at death—which is what § 2035(b) is equating —the statute y'all are drafting assumes that the donor would want the donee to pay the tax on the transfer—your paradigm is full apportionment. So I question whether this is as clear a case of presumed intent as you represent.

A: We started out with the proposition that preresiduary legacies would be exempt from apportionment, on the theory that probable intent justified this. The inter vivos gift is an a fortiori case. The preresiduary result was changed because of disputes on limitations on exemptions and the interplay between reapportionment and the marital and charitable deductions; that, however, shouldn't get in the way of the clearer case.

O: Imagine a situation involving an inter vivos gift, not to spouse or charity, that produces gift tax paid within three years of death. The estate at death goes entirely to charity or surviving spouse and would be nontaxable due to those charitable and marital deductions. But you have estate tax attributable to the gross-up rule. Is it really the intent of the drafting committee that the deductions at death—that everyone thought would make the estate tax free—would be reduced because tax attributable to the inter vivos gifts would be paid from the estate in general? Your result will start a whirlpool calculation that would produce a

§ 3.3.7

relatively large and entirely unexpected tax liability at death. And, I suspect, not the intent of the decedent or the drafter at all.

Every time I confront a tax apportionment issue, the only results that seem to work when you play them out to the end are full apportionment—everyone pays their own way. The only quibble here is what that means, and I think still it is clear that if the donor wants to exempt someone from a tax liability it is best if the donor specifically identifies the gift or the person and says "don't make that person pay"—but otherwise any tax attributable to a transfer to that person comes from that person. Here you have what I think we can agree would be an "unanticipated" tax liability and the only way I know that will avoid second and third level problems is to say, sorry, the donee pays. Even if the donor paid the gift tax on the original gift, if the planner and the donor failed to anticipate and plan specifically for the gross-up tax, I think having the donee pay is the right and less likely destructive result.

After all, isn't your statute meant to provide rules for when people failed to think these issues through and draft an efficient and different result? I truly believe that when you pursue these kinds of questions the initial notion of what someone would intend (donee gets the gift, tax free, for example) nearly always proves to be too blunt or simplistic or could not anticipate the kinds of events that unfold and produce the kinds of litigation that we encounter.

A: I am not troubled by exoneration of preresiduary gifts even if the residuary is nontaxable. In fact, that is what most, if not all, wills I have seen provide. On that basis I feel very comfortable that we have captured probable intent. It is also considerably simpler in cases where the donee is not a beneficiary at death.

O: I suspect most of the burden on the residue logic of most drafters is a function of ease of administration. But I also think that most of the disasters that occur are a function of burden on the residue. I'm not smart enough to know where to draw the line between trying to avert disaster and facilitate administration, and I don't have any experience in knowing what most people intend—especially the vast majority of those who never thought to form an intent!

The hard issue to my mind is whether such a statute should try to predict intent or avert disaster. I'm of a mind that intent is easy enough to draft affirmatively, so state law should do what so many UPC provisions have—which is to anticipate problems and prevent them from becoming disasters.

§ 3.3.7

As the colloquy shows, the objective of the drafters of the new Uniform Act may differ from what a client has in mind to accomplish with laws in this area. It is important to consider first how the legislature approached its task (the objective of the legislation) and then to consider the types of rules or decisions embraced under that policy. Whatever the result, wise estate planners realize that state law probably does not do everything that a well crafted tax apportionment provision should accomplish, and likely will create their own set of provisions either to override or to supplement state law. Given the variety of state laws that may apply and the diversity of client investments and their locations, it seems likely also that a wise drafter will not rely on the application of just one state's rules.

§3.3.7.1 Equitable Apportionment

If the estate plan is silent on the issue, state law determines whether equitable apportionment is available to any portion of the estate that qualifies for a deduction in the wealth transfer tax computation. With respect to the computation of dispositions that qualify for the marital or charitable deductions, the vast majority of states embrace equitable apportionment. At least to a limited extent, however, a number of states do not embrace equitable apportionment.

Moreover, if the estate plan calls for a larger disposition than qualifies for a deduction, only the qualifying portion should be protected from apportionment as under prior law when the marital deduction was not an unlimited entitlement or, under present practice, if S makes a disclaimer or only a partial qualifying election is made under § 2056(b)(7)(B)(v). So state law must be ascertained. In addition, in most states the treatment of distributions in satisfaction of a contractual entitlement, such as under a prenuptial agreement, is not certain. These dispositions should be treated in the same fashion as a charitable or marital disposition to the extent they are deductible under § 2053 as a claim against the estate. In this respect, § 2043 makes certain property settlements at death deductible under § 2053 if incident to a divorce and otherwise meeting the requirements of § 2516. Otherwise, obligations incurred incident to divorce that are satisfied out of an estate at death but that are not deductible (along with pretermitted heir shares, which are not deductible), normally are ineligible for equitable apportionment.

§ 3.3.7.1

An analogous result may apply in a limited number of cases if claims satisfied at death arising from a prenuptial agreement are treated as claims against the estate similar to the claims of other creditors. Notwithstanding that they are not §2053 deductible like most creditors' claims, the recipient of property under the prenuptial agreement is entitled to priority in payment, along with all other creditors. And because creditors are unaffected by the amount of taxes (except to the extent the estate is bankrupt, so that not all otherwise entitled claimants are satisfied) the claimant in these cases effectively is granted equitable apportionment.[88]

§3.3.7.2 Apportionment of State or Foreign Taxes

Even in states that embrace full inside, outside, and equitable apportionment, state inheritance taxes that are imposed directly on individual recipients of a decedent's wealth usually are not subject to apportionment in a manner that equitably allocates or apportions the burden. Thus, the decedent's estate plan must direct the estate to pay those taxes and, by virtue of this direction, cause the taxes to become an item subject to apportionment. Moreover, foreign inheritance taxes also ought to be considered to the extent they will be relevant.[89]

§3.3.7.3 Apportionment of Fees and Expenses

The issue raised in this section is essentially the same as that discussed in great detail in the context of marital deduction planning, to which readers looking for guidance in their drafting and administration of estates should turn for a more detailed history.[90] Portions of that discussion are repeated here as relevant to the particular aspect of administration expense allocation, but the most complete study of the entire topic is found there.

Outside apportionment of fees and expenses of administration has been dictated in several cases, and this is a sensible extension of the

---

[88] See, e.g., In re Cordier's Estate, 145 N.Y.S.2d 855 (Surr. Ct. 1955).

[89] See In re Estate of Herz, 651 N.E.2d 1251 (N.Y. 1995) (German inheritance tax (Erbschaftsteuer), normally payable by estate beneficiary, was deemed to be imposed on residue of decedent's estate by tax payment provision directing payment of all "estate, inheritance, and other death taxes").

[90] See §13.3.6.

§3.3.7.2

general apportionment theme.[91] The effect of fees and expenses and their source of payment can be significant in the marital and charitable deduction arena and generated several seemingly contradictory opinions addressing the proper treatment of estate income generated after a decedent's death in determining these allowable deductions, ultimately resulting in a Supreme Court decision that resolved little, and finally regulations that abandoned the government's historic position and charted a new course.

To illustrate, in Estate of Horne v. Commissioner,[92] the decedent's estate paid fees to the decedent's personal representative, using income earned during the period of probate administration to avoid invading corpus of the estate's residue. The estate claimed a deduction for the payment of these fees under §212 for federal income tax purposes rather than claiming them as a §2053 expense of administration for FET purposes. The estate then claimed a charitable deduction for the full value of the residue of the estate, measured by the full amount left available for distribution—unreduced by the fees paid from postmortem estate income. The Commissioner reduced the charitable deduction by the full amount of those fees, claiming a deficiency for the FET on that amount, which the Tax Court upheld.

Essentially the question in *Horne* turned on the proper determination of the "residue" for state law purposes, and how much of it was both includible for FET purposes and then passed in a qualified manner to the charity for §2055 deduction purposes. Citing Alston v. United States,[93] the Tax Court determined that the estate was improperly trying to

---

[91] See Roe v. Estate of Farrell, 372 N.E.2d 662 (Ill. 1978), cited in Estate of Fender v. Fender, 422 N.E.2d 107 (Ill. App. Ct. 1981); Cloutier v. Lavoie, 177 N.E.2d 584 (Mass. 1961); In re Estate of McKitrick, 172 N.E.2d 197 (Ohio Prob. Ct. 1960); Industrial Trust Co. v. Budlong, 76 A.2d 600 (R.I. 1950). Cf. Hanson v. Hanson Revocable Trust, 855 N.E.2d 655 (Ind. Ct. App. 2006), which dealt with apportionment of expenses of administration within a trust and not an inside versus outside apportionment issue, but still it adhered to the principle that fees should be apportioned as were taxes. Contra is In re Estate of Klarner, 98 P.3d 892 (Colo. Ct. App. 2003), rev'd on other grounds, 113 P.3d 150 (Colo. 2005), rejecting apportionment of administration expenses to a QTIP trust without authority to do so under state law.

[92] 91 T.C. 100 (1988).

[93] 349 F.2d 87 (5th Cir. 1965).

§3.3.7.3

"deduct" postmortem income by paying fees from the income account to prevent reduction of the residue that otherwise would pass to the charity and would be deductible under §2055. The court reasoned that the estate would have been forced to pay the personal representative's fees from the residue proper if there had been no income in the estate sufficient to pay those fees. In that case there would have been less available for distribution to the charity, resulting in a reduced deduction. According to the Tax Court, the estate could not improve on this position by expending postmortem income. More importantly, state law required these expenses to be charged to corpus for fiduciary accounting purposes, meaning that the estate's payment from income was improper for state law purposes.

Estate of Richardson v. Commissioner[94] was quite the opposite. D's estate incurred interest on unpaid FET liabilities, which the estate paid and properly charged to income for fiduciary accounting purposes. The government attempted to reduce the estate's marital deduction by the amount of this charge, which the estate successfully resisted. As explained by the Tax Court, payment of this interest as an administration expense using postmortem income earned by the residue of the estate did not diminish the amount passing to S for marital deduction purposes. Nor was the estate trying to increase the size of the deduction based on income earned postmortem. Because payment of FET was delayed, the estate was able to earn income while incurring interest payable to the government. Neither the income earned nor the interest payable should alter the amount of marital deduction properly claimed for the corpus remaining after payment of all the debts, expenses, and taxes, and *Richardson* reached a proper result.

Estate of Street v. Commissioner[95] involved both interest on unpaid state and federal taxes and other administration expenses. These items were paid from postmortem estate income and claimed as a deduction on the estate's income tax return. Again the question was the effect of these payments on the marital deduction for the balance of the estate. In *Street* the terms of the decedent's will and state law both denied exercise of any power or authority that would have the effect of preventing qualification

---

[94] 89 T.C. 1193 (1987).

[95] 56 T.C.M. (CCH) 774 (1988), aff'd in part and rev'd in part, 974 F.2d 723 (6th Cir. 1992); on remand, 68 T.C.M. (CCH) 1213 (1994).

§3.3.7.3

for the marital deduction. But both state law and the document granted the personal representative discretion to allocate items of income or expense to either income or principal. According to the Tax Court, under state law expenses of the type involved in *Street* were a proper income expense for trust accounting purposes, which is how the personal representative charged these items for estate accounting purposes. Based on that finding, the Tax Court extended its prior ruling in *Richardson* to cover payment of both interest and expenses of administration.

On appeal, however, the court distinguished the payment of administration expenses on the ground that they were deemed to accrue at the decedent's death and, as such, must be deemed to reduce the estate at death for purposes of determining the amount available for the marital deduction. Citing Treas. Reg. § 20.2056(b)-4(a), the court held that administration expenses are different from interest paid postmortem on the basis of when each expenditure is deemed to accrue and concluded that income from the marital share that is used to pay the expenses that accrued at death should belong to the marital trust and, if diverted, must cause a reduction of the marital deduction. Nevertheless, at about the same time *Street* was decided on appeal, the Tax Court again held, in Estate of Young v. Commissioner,[96] that administration expenses paid with estate income do not reduce the amount of the marital deduction, essentially following the court's decision in *Street* prior to its reversal.

The Tax Court ultimately rendered two very strong opinions that more forcefully determined that the government was wrong entirely on this issue. Estate of Hubert v. Commissioner[97] rejected the distinction between expenses of administration and interest on deferred tax payments made by the appellate court in *Street*, a position affirmed in *Hubert* by the Supreme Court. The Tax Court reaffirmed its position in *Richardson* and, the very next day, again held that the marital and charitable deductions should not be reduced by the use of postmortem income to pay administration expenses as authorized by state law or the terms of

---

[96] 64 T.C.M. (CCH) 770 (1992).

[97] 101 T.C. 314 (1993) (a 14-to-2 reviewed opinion), aff'd, 63 F.3d 1083 (11th Cir. 1995), aff'd, 520 U.S. 93 (1997).

the document.[98] As subsequent events unfolded it is even more clear that the Tax Court's opinion in *Hubert* is the truly significant decision because it reflects the only clear and well reasoned analysis available.

The Tax Court's majority opinion determined that (1) use of estate income to pay administration expenses was authorized, (2) there is no merit to the distinction drawn by the appellate court in *Street* between administration expenses (such as fees paid to a personal representative or the estate's attorney) and interest on deferred tax payments, and (3) the marital deduction issue properly analyzed involves Treas. Reg. § 20.2056(b)-4(a), which is "merely a valuation provision which requires material limitations on the right to receive income to be taken into account when valuing the property interest passing to the surviving spouse." Although there was no similar discussion for charitable deduction purposes (and there is no corresponding regulation under § 2055),[99] presumably the court's analysis under both sections would be the same. As events since unfolded, the government eventually folded its tent on this issue, essentially abandoning the regulatory position. Still, important lessons remain to be learned.

For example, according to the Tax Court, estate income has no effect on the estate's FET liability: it is not includible in the estate, it does not in any way increase the marital or charitable share, and it does not result in double deductions. Thus, there is no impact on either deduction if amounts charged to income are no greater than proper under state law and the governing document. This logic now is essentially embraced (but not in the same words) by the government's regulations, all as explained in more detail in the marital deduction context.[100] The critical aspect for this analysis is that mere discretion in a personal representative to allocate expenses to estate income will not preclude qualification for the marital or charitable deduction. Instead, it is exercise of that discretion and how the deduction for administration expenses is claimed that are critical.

---

[98] Estate of Allen v. Commissioner, 101 T.C. 351 (1993). Nevertheless, one dissenting opinion in *Hubert* claimed that "[t]he Tax Court stands virtually alone on this issue."

[99] Cf. Treas. Reg. § 20.2055-3, dealing with the charitable deduction reduction under § 2055(c) for death taxes payable from the charitable bequest.

[100] See § 13.3.6.

§ 3.3.7.3

Thus, well-drafted tax clauses should give the personal representative discretion to pay administration expenses from income or principal of the nonmarital trust, and to authorize the use of estate income otherwise payable to S or charity to permit postmortem administration to accomplish effective tax planning. Although the more conservative approach may be to specify that the personal representative may not charge administration expenses to the marital or charitable portion of the estate, that degree of caution is not required.

It bears noting that the *Hubert* estate did not charge all its administration expenses to income, and it is questionable whether it would have won if it did. The estate attempted to ascertain how various on-going expenses (like executor fees for management of the estate during an extremely prolonged administration and attorney fees for multiple layers of litigation), would be pro rated between income and principal under normal principal and income accounting rules. These were not the normal one-time expenditures in the asset-marshaling and claim-paying administration of a typical estate. In the context presented, the estate attempted to determine, under state law, how properly to allocate extraordinary expenses of an on-going administration as opposed to the typical one-time expenses of many estate administration functions.

The lodestar that guided the *Hubert* estate's allocation was how the various costs would have been allocated had the estate terminated in a timely manner and the following trusts had been funded promptly and then the trusts had incurred these on-going expenses. The question was how normal fiduciary expenses would be allocated in a normal on-going administration of a marital trust that entitles S to net income as determined for state law fiduciary accounting purposes. In essence this is the same form of analysis required by the regulations, all reflecting a reasonable approach to the administrative allocation of various items of expense.

§3.3.7.4 Apportionment of Interest and Penalties

Many state statutes, including the original and revised Uniform Acts, dictate apportionment of interest and penalties assessed along with

§3.3.7.4

the underlying taxes imposed on an estate.[101] In addition, §§ 2207A(d) and 2207B(d) specifically dictate this result for federal tax purposes. Unfortunately, this is not a universal rule and, in some states, these added items are not chargeable in the same manner as the underlying tax.[102] As illustrated by Estate of Whittle v. Commissioner,[103] interest on FET is not the same as the tax itself and may be chargeable in a different manner unless the document or applicable state or federal law specifically provide for it.

§3.3.7.5 Apportionment of Credits

Consistent treatment also is lacking with respect to a number of other important issues that often are ignored or only partially addressed under state law. For example, only partially recognized under the Uniform Act and ignored by many states entirely is the effect of credits. All of which again confirms that reliance on state law is not a wise alternative to drafting a tax payment provision that addresses all appropriate issues.

§3.3.8 Computing Various Entitlements

An issue upon which estate planning documents must focus because many state laws are silent is the order in which shares, taxes, and allocations are to be determined. For example, the FET is computed after all deductions are reflected. But the question is whether a deductible bequest is computed before or after payment of those taxes. It is not always clear how computations interrelate for purposes of federal tax, state tax, marital deduction and "forced" shares, and division of the "residue." To illustrate, imagine an estate that is divided equally between a charity and a private beneficiary. The estate owns bonds with an accrued income tax liability. Should the division occur first, and then each beneficiary pays its own income tax? Or should the estate pay all the income tax first and divide what remains? The former approach will

---

[101] See Rev. Rul. 80-159, 1980-1 C.B. 206, and Estate of Simpson v. White, 67 Cal. Rptr. 2d 361 (1997).

[102] See, e.g., Estate of Richardson v. Commissioner, 89 T.C. 1193 (1987); Annot., Construction and application of statutes apportioning or prorating estate taxes, 71 A.L.R.3d 247 (1976).

[103] 97 T.C. 362 (1991), aff'd, 994 F.2d 379 (7th Cir. 1993).

divide the pre-tax larger amount and the charity's half will be larger and totally tax-exempt. But a tax payment provision may dictate the post-tax division, to the government's advantage and to the detriment of the charity.[104]

The question may arise whether state law provides that the FET (reflecting all credits) is to be paid from or charged against the available assets, then any division into shares made, followed by computation and payment of state death taxes based on the various shares. Or whether to compute and subtract the federal and state taxes based on the same amount in the estate, and then divide the balance as provided in the estate plan. A third alternative mechanism would be to divide the estate according to the decedent's estate plan, then compute and subtract the federal and state taxes based on the size of each separate share. Each alternative can produce different results and therefore must be made clear, especially if state law is not.

In deciding whether or how the estate plan should resolve these issues it should be recognized that different approaches may be dictated in different situations. For example, the third alternative basically describes the operation of equitable apportionment, by which a deductible share, such as a marital or charitable deduction bequest, is computed before taxes while the balance of the estate incurs and pays all of the taxes. As revealed by the issue of equitable apportionment, there is no uniformity of approach on these issues. State law must be consulted to determine the "standard" approach and then the estate plan should be drafted with any desired changes clearly specified (that is, the decedent can change equitable apportionment by changing the marital share from a gross to a net estate division).[105]

Also notice that, procedurally, the order of payment of the tax and the apportionment and collection thereof may differ between jurisdictions. In some states it may be necessary to pay all taxes before their allocation and collection, this being the procedure that §§ 2206, 2207, 2207A, and 2207B appear to anticipate (in terms of their being rights of reimbursement for taxes already paid). Other states (apparently including states that have adopted the Uniform Acts) permit apportionment

---

[104] See Estate of Dehgani-Fard, 46 Cal. Rptr. 3d 289 (Cal. Ct. App. 2006), discussed in § 3.3.15.3 n.148.

[105] See the illustration in § 3.4.4.

§ 3.3.8

prior to payment, presumably improving liquidity by allowing (or requiring) interested parties to contribute liquid assets rather than require sale of estate assets, followed by reimbursement. In reality, either approach may be impractical in a given situation, and the applicable procedure during administration should be considered and potentially provided for in the documents. Finally, given the potential for a conflict of laws, a wise drafter may want to specify the desired result rather than to rely on any state's law.

§3.3.9 *Apportionment to Nonprobate Assets*

It is not universally established that a decedent's will may apportion taxes to nonprobate assets in the absence of, or contrary to, state law. Clearly a decedent's will may negate a local law calling for apportionment of taxes, instead by directing payment of all taxes out of the probate estate (assuming the decedent's intent is clear). Relieving a nonprobate beneficiary of a tax burden is essentially a bequest to that beneficiary, which the decedent's will may make.[106] But if state law contains no apportionment authority, or if state law expressly directs against apportionment, the issue is whether a decedent may affirmatively direct, by a provision in a will, that taxes will be allocated to nonprobate assets.

This is a particularly acute issue if the nonprobate disposition is an irrevocable transfer as to which the decedent relinquished all rights of control and in which the decedent included no special tax payment directive. Moreover, if the direction is not valid under local law but the beneficiary nevertheless accedes and does contribute, the question answered in the negative by PLR 200027016—is a gift made when the taker of nonprobate property contributes to the tax payment as obligated under state law—may turn the other way if there is no state law power to

---

[106] An interesting application of this notion was addressed by In re Estate of Williams, 2003 WL 1961805 (Tenn. Ct. App.), in which annuities were payable to the decedent's ex-wife. The tax payment provision in the decedent's will was a burden on the residue dictate that the court held was *not* revoked by a state law provision revoking dispositions in favor of a former spouse by the divorce. Notwithstanding the dispositive benefit to the spouse, the court held that the tax payment provision was an indirect benefit that accrued to the former spouse and others and was not meant to be addressed by the revocation by operation of law provision of state law.

compel those nonprobate takers to contribute but they do so nevertheless.

If a decedent's transfer was incomplete for federal tax purposes (or otherwise was subject to inclusion), the suggestion is that there is a correspondingly sufficient nexus to permit the decedent to exert control by means of a testamentary apportionment provision. Thus, for example, with respect to §§ 2-35-2040 and 2701(d), as to which no federal reimbursement provision exists, the legal issue is whether a decedent's will may apportion a share of the total taxes to the assets subject thereto.

A similar but perhaps less severe issue is whether a decedent may direct a different form of apportionment than that permitted or directed under state law, again in situations in which a will otherwise would be regarded as ineffective to alter or amend an irrevocable nonprobate transfer.[107] Although the authorities in this respect are not uniform, the better supported position appears to be that a sufficient nexus to require inclusion for FET purposes is a sufficient nexus to permit the decedent to require apportionment or to direct a different form of apportionment than that specified under state law.[108] It might be argued that the maximum amount of tax that could be collected from such property under § 6324(a)(2) (an amount equal to the asset's FET value) should be the only limitation on the decedent's power to alter state or federal apportionment rules.

---

[107] For example, if Congress was to amend § 2042 to cause inclusion of insurance owned by and payable to an ILIT, § 2206 would allow reimbursement of the pro rata share of taxes attributable thereto. The question is whether a decedent's will could call for an incremental reimbursement, direct the trust to pay those taxes directly, or alter the statutory taxable estate pro ration to a gross estate calculation. See, e.g., In re Estate of Smith, 891 So. 2d 811 (Miss. 2005), answering the gross (state law) versus taxable or net (federal) superiority question in favor of federal law controlling over state law. And see the 2003 Revised Uniform Estate Tax Apportionment Act § 3(c), which precludes an increase above the statutory apportionment to nonprobate property as to which the "the beneficiary has no power to transfer."

[108] See, e.g., United States v. Goodson, 253 F.2d 900 (8th Cir. 1958); In re Will of King, 239 N.E.2d 875 (N.Y. 1968); but see Warfield v. Merchants Nat'l Bank, 147 N.E.2d 809 (Mass. 1958) (citing but refusing to follow *Goodson*).

§ 3.3.9

§3.3.10 *Apportionment to Temporal Interests*

The law is relatively clear regarding apportionment of taxes allocable to life estates and terms of years but significant variations exist relative to taxes attributable to an annuity, which should alert estate planners to the fact that controversy exists in this issue and that tax payment provisions should address it. Uniform Act §6 is representative of the law in most states, specifying that taxes attributable to a life estate or term of years are to be paid out of corpus, not charged against the temporal interest.[109] Although this rule appears inequitable on its face, it actually is sensible, given the fact that a reduction of corpus for the payment of taxes correspondingly reduces income to be earned thereon and effectively amortizes the tax allocable to the income interest. The rule also is administratively attractive because the present interest income beneficiary need not contribute toward payment of taxes that might exceed any income received at the time of tax payment.

With respect to annuities, however, a different situation is presented because the annuity may be a guaranteed amount, payable from corpus to the extent annual income is insufficient. Thus, a reduction of corpus in payment of taxes allocable to the annuity may not cause a reduction in the amount of the annuity. More importantly, many annuities precede a qualified charitable remainder in situations in which taxes attributable to the lead annuity are the only taxes attributable to the entire property (because the remainder qualifies for the charitable deduction). Payment from corpus is inequitable *and* it will reduce the charitable deduction under §2055(c).[110]

Based on the actuarial and valuation tables applicable at any given time, CRATs may be more attractive than CRUTs in terms of the deduction generated. Unlike the annuity (which is fixed in amount regardless of the income of the trust), the unitrust interest more closely resembles an income interest. In fact, it may be geared to the annual income earned by the trust, making the standard temporal interest

---

[109] See, e.g., Estate of Jack v. Commissioner, 8 T.C. 272 (1947) (involving a charitable remainder and reduction of the charitable deduction by virtue of the apportionment rule); National Newark & Essex Bank v. Hart, 309 A.2d 512 (Me. 1973); In re Williamson's Estate, 229 P.2d 312 (Wash. 1951).

[110] See, e.g., Estate of Leach v. Commissioner, 82 T.C. 952 (1984); Rev. Rul. 82-128, 1982-2 C.B. 71; In re Estate of Masten, 546 N.Y.S.2d 880 (App. Div. 1989).

allocation rule seem more equitable. Although it still does not protect the charitable deduction entirely, illustrated by TAM 9419006 is that a reduction of trust corpus correspondingly will reduce any future unitrust payments that are a percentage of the annually determined FMV of the trust. But the same cannot be said about the straight annuity trust. Nevertheless, and notwithstanding reasons suggesting that annuities deserve different treatment than other term interests, the law in most states follows the uniform law approach for all of these term interests in general, causing all taxes to be paid from corpus.

The comments to Uniform Act § 6 state that this result is mandated by the fact that no other practical solution exists, although at least one state (New York) has, by statute, dictated that the proper treatment is to pay taxes allocable to the annuity interest from corpus and then reissue the annuity to pay a smaller annual amount as a result thereof.[111] Even in New York, however, there is authority that the payor of the annuity is not liable for payment of the tax, meaning that the source of payment as well as the computation of the tax and annuity all must be evaluated.[112] There is some support for the proposition that the annuitant should be charged with the full amount of taxes allocable to the annuity, regardless of the fact that this individual may not have liquid assets with which to pay that portion of the taxes.[113] But this is not widely accepted and produces cash flow issues for the annuitant in many particular cases.

To address this, a final recommendation[114] is that taxes be paid from the underlying corpus but be recovered by an amortization assessment against the annuitant over the life of the annuity itself. This approach is justified on the grounds that the risk of an early termination of the

---

[111] See Annot., Construction and application of statutes apportioning or prorating estate taxes, 71 A.L.R.3d 247, at § 19(b) (1976); Annot., Liability of income beneficiary of trust for proportionate share of estate or inheritance tax in absence of specific direction in statute, will, or other instrument, 67 A.L.R.3d 273, at § 4(d) (1975).

[112] See In re Bissell's Will, 130 N.Y.S.2d 103 (App. Div. 1954), although this is related to the New York position with respect to the general rule regarding the liability of an insurer for payment of taxes allocable to proceeds held by the company. See § 3.3.5.

[113] See Carpenter v. Carpenter, 267 S.W.2d 632 (Mo. 1954).

[114] See Scoles & Stephens, The Proposed Uniform Estate Tax Apportionment Act, 43 Minn. L. Rev. 907, 928 (1959).

§ 3.3.10

annuity, prior to full collection of total taxes allocable thereto, is matched by the benefit to the remainder beneficiaries if the annuity does in fact terminate early. The Revised Uniform Act[115] advocates a complex approach that approximates such a system, requiring payment from available liquid ("uninsulated") funds and giving the beneficiaries thereof a right to recover from the annuitant when subsequent distributions of liquid ("insulated") funds occurs.

Apportionment of the tax burden with respect to annuities could be addressed in drafting an estate plan, even though the vast majority of plans do not. Prior to 1984 this may have been an acceptable default in drafting, but the apportionment issue relating to annuities is extraordinarily important because of the repeal of all § 2039 exclusions for retirement benefits. The issue can be avoided if the annuity qualifies for the normal FET marital deduction and state law recognizes equitable apportionment. Similarly, no serious issue is raised with respect to payments made in a lump sum, because the recipient has the funds to make immediate payment. Otherwise, this a significant issue because of the amount of wealth tied up in retirement benefit plans because federal law does not grant a right of reimbursement with respect to these payments.

A number of issues are created under the law relating to qualified retirement benefit plans if the standard rule for apportionment is not followed with respect to retirement benefit annuities. For example, apportionment against a § 401(a)(11) qualified survivor's annuity (to the extent the annuity does not qualify for the § 2056(b)(7) marital deduction, for example, because the automatic election is reversed), raises the question whether either the spirit or the letter of § 401(a)(11) is violated. More directly, with respect to any beneficiary, the issue is whether the plan permits or even addresses apportionment, and whether apportionment even is possible without authorization in the plan or under federal law. Certainly it would affect the plan's assumptions regarding time of payments and its determination of liquidity needs.

In addition, one unresolved issue is whether the antialienation or antiassignment rules preclude apportionment against the plan. In this respect Treas. Reg. § 1.401(a)-13(b)(2) provides that the plan shall not preclude enforcement of federal tax levies under § 6331 (which covers

---

[115] See § 3.3.7 at text following note 87.

§ 3.3.10

any tax) or collection on judgments from unpaid tax assessments, and § 1.401(a)-13(c)(2) provides that "[a]ny arrangement for the withholding of Federal, State or local tax from plan benefits" is not regarded as an "assignment or alienation."[116]

There has been some agitation to add to the Code a clone of § 2206, § 2207, § 2207A, or § 2207B to apply with respect to § 2039. But many difficult problems must be addressed in drafting such a law and the will drafting in response to it (if adopted). For example, should such a rule apportion both the underlying FET plus any income tax on plan distributions deemed to be made pursuant to the right of reimbursement? And if normal annuity apportionment rules do not apply, apportionment among various interests must address questions such as whether equitable apportionment should apply and what apportionment of credits is appropriate. It also may come up whether the decedent may waive (or alter) this right of reimbursement, because waiver (or alteration) might be deemed to constitute a prohibited contribution to the plan.[117] Administratively, it also would be important to know whether the plan administrator may rely without verification on the personal representative's certification of the amount of reimbursement due.

Without question, however, is the simple reality that clients must be mindful of tax payment when selecting death benefit payout options, to ensure that liquidity will exist if needed to pay any taxes due, considering each of the marital deduction, the guaranteed spousal annuity rules of § 401(a)(11), the income tax consequences of all this, and any chronologically or otherwise exempt amounts.

§ 3.3.11 Apportionment of §§ 2032A and 2057 Recapture Taxes

If an estate qualifies for § 2032A special use valuation (or qualified for the § 2057 QFOBI deduction prior to its repeal in 2004), state law ought to (but virtually always does not) provide two specific rules. In

---

[116] See Hyde v. United States, 93-2 U.S. Tax Cas. (CCH) ¶ 50,605 (D. Ariz. 1993) (enforcement of § 6331 levy against plan benefit of taxpayer's surviving spouse; as a community debt, the survivor's entire benefit was deemed subject to the government's levy).

[117] See Estate of Boyd v. Commissioner, 819 F.2d 170 (7th Cir. 1987), and § 3.3.5.

most cases the benefit of the reduction in value, and the corresponding reduction in tax, should inure to the benefit of the recipient of the qualifying property.[118] This is because, if any disqualifying sale or act causes recapture of the tax benefit, the recapture tax should be apportioned against the qualified property. By § 2032A(c)(5) (and § 2057(i)(3)(F) before repeal) the qualified heir is personally responsible for the additional tax on recapture, but may post a bond to be relieved of that liability and may be able to argue that the decedent's tax clause otherwise overrides this burden.

California's apportionment provision[119] addresses these issues in a manner that itself may produce inequities. As such, it may be instructive for drafters whose state law is silent or similarly problematic. The California statute may create an inequity if the reduction in tax due to § 2032A was, say, $97,500 but the qualified heir's pro rata share of the FET was only $76,500.[120] Here the entire liability apportioned to the

---

[118] See In re Estate of Nevius, 2007 WL 4577908 (unpub. Kan. Ct. App.), In re Estate of Eriksen, 716 N.W.2d 105 (Neb. 2006) (§ 2032A), and Estate of Farnam v. Commissioner, 130 T.C. 34 (2008) (§ 2057). The hard question is whether the beneficiary who receives the qualified property, and who may be burdened later with any recapture tax, should receive the tax benefit generated by that special property. The issue in *Eriksen* was whether the decedent's tax payment provision directed against statutory equitable apportionment, which the court apparently thought would apportion the tax savings attributable to either special use valuation or any deduction (only the latter of which was expressly mentioned in the statute). The *Nevius* court remanded to the trial court to apply the Kansas version of the Uniform Estate Tax Apportionment Act and direct the tax saving to two sons who made the qualified use election and away from one daughter who refused to encumber her land with the special use election, unless the trial court specifically found that the decedent intended for some other apportionment to apply.

A curious application of a theory similar to apportionment of the tax saved by virtue of a § 2032A valuation reduction was rejected by In re Estate of Siebrasse, 678 N.W.2d 822 (S.D. 2004), in which one child successfully challenged the FET valuation of property that passed to that one child, and claimed the benefit of the full tax reduction attributable to that success. The court rejected the claim to a greater share of the tax saving than the child's pro rata portion, based on the value of the entire estate. In essence the child's effort benefited the other estate beneficiaries pro rata.

[119] Cal. Prob. Code § 20114.

[120] See Klug, The Effect of Special Valuation on Estate Tax Apportionment: A Plea for Uniform Legislation, 1 Prob. & Prop. 6 (Mar./Apr. 1987).

§ 3.3.11

qualified heir would be offset by the apportioned benefit, and the excess $21,000 of tax benefit would be allocated to other estate beneficiaries (to avoid wasting it). If, however, a subsequent recapture event occurred, the qualified heir would be required to pay the full $97,500 of tax attributable thereto. Thus, the other takers would have shared in the benefit but would bear none of the recapture risk.

The full $97,500 of benefit might be allocated to the recipient of the qualified property if there was significant tax liability apportioned to that beneficiary (not all attributable to the qualified property) against which the benefit could be allocated, but this may not be the case. And allocation of the full benefit to all takers pro rata would be even more unfair (unless all takers were made responsible for the recapture tax, which would create administrative problem and reduce the incentive on the qualified heir to avoid a recapture event). Another alternative in administering the estate would be to make only a partial § 2032A special use valuation election, to reduce the tax by only the amount of benefit that the qualified heir could enjoy, to avoid improper dispersion of the benefit. (That alternative does not seem as adaptable to the § 2057 context.) In any case a side agreement might be executed whereby the other takers would agree to indemnify the recipient of the qualified property to the extent of the $21,000 excess tax liability.

Also a problem is the temporal interest rules. If the qualified property was placed into a trust and the life tenant was the party causing recapture, the corpus of the trust nevertheless would incur the tax, constituting another form of inequity.[121] As these issues reveal, drafters working with § 2032A must consider fashioning a result that is equitable and that reflects the decedent's intent, all in light of § 2032A(c)(5) and any relevant state law. For example, with respect to temporal interests, the document might provide that any recapture tax will be imposed entirely on the income beneficiary if recapture was caused by a cessation of qualified use, but that the tax will be imposed in a manner that properly amortizes it against the income and remainder interests if recapture occurs because the land or business interest was sold.

---

[121] But see Estate of Libeu, 253 Cal. Rptr. 456 (Ct. App. 1988) (both income and remainder beneficiaries were required to pay tax).

§ 3.3.11

§3.3.12 *Apportionment of Income Tax Burdens*

Estate plans don't always address the numerous issues that surround payment of wealth transfer taxes, but they even more frequently overlook the income tax problems that can arise in estate administration.[122] Tax payment provisions today probably should address several income tax issues.

§3.3.12.1 Inequitable Sharing of DNI

Although the separate share rule of §663(c) is applicable to estates with substantially independent and separately administered shares for individual beneficiaries,[123] a separate share may have multiple beneficiaries and distributions of otherwise equal portions of the estate among them can result in a sharing of estate DNI that is not what the decedent intended nor what the beneficiaries regard as equitable. The end result of such distributions can be a need to make an equitable adjustment, if the document does not waive the need therefor.[124] To avoid the problem entirely, the document may dictate that distributions be made in such a manner that no inequitable allocation of estate income will result.

For example, in Harkness v. United States[125] the estate plan called for an equal split of the decedent's estate, with FET and expenses being payable out of the estate prior to division but being charged entirely to one of the two halves. To maintain the equality dictated by this division,

---

[122] See Estate of Dehgani-Fard, 46 Cal. Rptr. 3d 289 (Cal. Ct. App. 2006), discussed in §3.3.15.3 n.148, which involved an estate division issue whether to pay income tax and divide the balance of the estate, or to divide the estate and pay the income tax thereafter. Involving a tax exempt beneficiary, the latter approach would have reduced the income tax liability because the charity's portion of estate income would have avoided income tax, while payment of income tax before division meant that a larger income tax was incurred, leaving less wealth for division among the beneficiaries, including the charity.

[123] See Treas. Reg. §1.663(c)-4, discussed in detail in §5.4.3.

[124] See In re Estate of Holloway, 323 N.Y.S.2d 534 (Surr. Ct. 1971), modified, 327 N.Y.S.2d 865 (Surr. Ct. 1972). And see Blattmachr, The Tax Effects of Equitable Adjustments: An Internal Revenue Code Odyssey, 18 U. Miami Inst. Est. Plan. ¶ 1400 (1984); Moore, Conflicting Interests in Post-Mortem Planning, 9 U. Miami Inst. Est. Plan. ¶ 1900 (1975). The subject of income tax inequities and compensatory adjustments is discussed in more detail in §§5.8.2 and 5.8.4.

[125] 469 F.2d 310 (Ct. Cl. 1972).

every time the personal representative paid any tax or expense, a distribution was made to the other taker in the same amount. Because the case arose before the separate share rule applied to estates, the equalizing distribution carried out DNI but the payments did not, thus causing income to be taxed disproportionately to the share that did not incur the taxes and expenses. An equalizing adjustment was required so as to apportion and tax DNI in the same equal proportions as the estate was to be divided.

Under the separate share rule the result would be the same as if the personal representative had been authorized to make equal distributions to the two shares, then the one share had used its distribution to pay the taxes and expenses, with each share receiving equal amounts of DNI. If the decedent's intent had been that DNI be shared in the same proportions as the shares resulting *after* payment of taxes and expenses, however, the result reached in *Harkness* prior to the adjustment would have been appropriate and the separate share rule would need to be considered in how division and payment were structured. Some planners will not embrace a solution that calls for payment after division because that approach may mean that less liquidity exists in the share from which payment is to be made and, for other reasons, this detriment otherwise cannot be avoided. Because it is not possible to predict the best result or the client's intent in all cases, issues such as these simply must be evaluated in the planning process and the document drafted accordingly.

§3.3.12.2 Tax on Appreciation at Death

The Canadian tax on appreciation at death is not regarded as an estate tax for purposes of the §2014 foreign death tax credit.[126] As a result, the typical tax clause may not speak to the source for payment if the tax on appreciation is not regarded as an estate tax for other purposes as well. In addition, allocation of the benefit of any deduction for this tax under §2053 ought to be considered, particularly if the tax on

---

[126] Estate of Ballard v. Commissioner, 85 T.C. 300 (1985); Rev. Rul. 82-82, 1982-1 C.B. 127; TAM 8203135 (however, these authorities permit a §2053(a)(3) deduction for the tax, as a claim against the estate, not precluded as an estate, succession, legacy, or inheritance tax that is not deductible by virtue of §2053(c)(1)(B)).

appreciation might be imposed on one beneficiary while the benefit of the deduction inured to another.

§3.3.12.3 Estimated Tax Burden

As between fiduciary accounting income and principal, presumably the portion of a trust or estate that produces an income tax liability that is subject to estimated tax payment should be charged with the payment of that tax. And it ought to be the case that a trust will not lose simple trust status if the trust uses fiduciary accounting income to pay estimated taxes incurred by income of the trust. It may seem that an income account of a simple trust cannot incur an income tax liability (because all the DNI should be carried out by the mandatory income distribution provision), but in reality the loss of deductions under §67(e) may produce unanticipated income tax consequences that the document should consider.

To illustrate, assume that an estate's fiduciary accounting income is $500,000 and deductions subject to §67(e) are $130,000. If the expenses were a proper charge against fiduciary accounting income, the amount available for distribution would be $370,000 and the corresponding distributions deduction would be $370,000. The §67(e) threshold amount is 2% of the remaining $130,000 of income, meaning that $2,600 of deductions would be lost, leaving deductions of $127,400 and taxable income of $2,000 after reflecting the $600 deduction under §642(b)(1). With a tax at, say, 36% (applicable, perhaps, because of other income properly allocable to corpus), the estate would owe $720 of tax attributable to fiduciary accounting income and an estimated tax return would be necessary unless one of the estimated tax exceptions applies. A similar scenario could apply to a trust, including a simple trust.

Notice that less than $370,000 of income would be available for distribution in this example if estate income was used to pay the estimated tax liability attributable to the income account. That would reduce the distributions deduction and increase the amount subject to the 2% threshold, increase the amount of taxable income attributable to the income account, and thereby increase the taxes incurred by the estate and properly allocated to the income account. The allocation of this income tax burden will be of some significance and presumably it should

§3.3.12.3

not be allocated to corpus if the estate ultimately passes to beneficiaries other than those receiving current income.

The problem posed here could be avoided if the deductible items were paid from corpus, so that a full $500,000 of income was available for distribution. If DNI was that large the income beneficiary would pay more income tax and this effectively would "give" the benefit of those deductions to the beneficiaries of estate corpus. Unless the document provided for such a result, however, the normal principal and income act rules probably would dictate the results illustrated in the example.

A similar computation and similar results could occur under the AMT, attributable to items paid from fiduciary accounting income for which no AMT deduction is available. An AMT could be generated and, if paid using income (under normal fiduciary accounting principles), additional income taxes similarly could be incurred due to a similar loss of the distributions deduction due to the use of income to pay the AMT liability.[127] Moreover, unlike FET (which normally will be paid, and a closing letter obtained, before final distribution of an estate), the income tax liabilities and potential payment responsibilities considered here could arise several years after an estate has been closed and distributed. In this respect, fiduciaries need to pay attention to filing the proper § 6903 notice of the termination of fiduciary responsibility[128] so that, if an income tax assessment is brought, it is asserted against the proper distributees rather than the fiduciary.

§3.3.13 Conflict of Laws and Enforcement Jurisdiction

Perhaps the most perplexing and least definite issues under the entire apportionment umbrella are whose law should govern apportionment questions in multiple state estates and how an apportionment rule in one state is to be enforced against property or beneficiaries in another state (especially if the law of that other state is at variance with the law of the state calling for apportionment). Conflict of laws issues often are the

---

[127] See Hall, The Application of the Alternative Minimum Tax to Estates and Trusts, 22 U. Miami Inst. Est. Plan. ¶ 900 (1988).

[128] See § 2.7.5.

most difficult and least predictable aspect of any controversy, and this certainly is true with respect to apportionment.[129]

Based on how it sees the equities of the controversy, an apportionment question may be one that a court will want to decide a certain way on the merits. In such a case the court may undertake to resolve the conflict of laws issue in a manner that allows the court to select the substantive law needed to render the decision it prefers. In the conflict of laws arena, looking for a state whose law supports the result a court may prefer frequently involves a choice of law decision that is not entirely copacetic under accepted conflict of laws principles. And it probably is fair also to note that courts are prone to adopt their own state's law if possible, meaning that forum shopping to bring a case in a state whose law is favorable is a wily litigation tactic.

§3.3.13.1 Policy Principles and Applicable Rules

As a policy matter, it probably is unassailable that the law should favor four essential conflict of laws objectives in this arena: (1) uniformity; (2) predictability; (3) equal treatment of all parts of an estate, regardless of their physical or legal location for conflict of law purposes, with application of the same rules with respect to testate and intestate assets; and (4) equal treatment of various legal issues, applying the same conflict of laws rules for apportionment as, for example, for testing the validity of a will.

As an example of how confused this area may become, however, consider the following rules, all of which potentially are applicable in a particular situation.[130]

- With respect to intestate property, the law of the state of the asset's situs may be applicable, meaning the law of the decedent's domicile with

---

[129] No reader should undertake to resolve the conflict of laws issue in a given situation by relying on the following overly generalized synopsis, without also consulting two extremely helpful summaries of the conflict of laws rules in this area: Scoles, Apportionment of Federal Estate Taxes and Conflict of Laws, 55 Colum. L. Rev. 261 (1955), and its sequel in Scoles, Estate Tax Apportionment in the Multi-State Estate, 5 U. Miami Inst. Est. Plan. ¶ 700 (1971). Also see Annot., What law governs apportionment of estate taxes among persons interested in estate, 16 A.L.R.2d 1282 (1951).

[130] See also § 3.4.5 regarding conflict of laws in spousal rights planning.

§3.3.13.1

respect to movables and the law of the actual situs of the asset with respect to immovables (land).

• Regarding testate property, classification of the issue for conflict of laws purposes will affect the choice of law rules applied.

• For example, in all likelihood the law of the decedent's domicile will govern the choice of law if the apportionment question is regarded as either a succession or a validity question. The law of the situs of the primary estate administration may be applicable if apportionment is regarded merely as an administrative question. If inter vivos nonprobate transfers are involved, either the law of the donor's domicile at the time of the transfer or the law of the situs of the transferred property at the time the conflicts issue is resolved may apply for choice of law purposes (and these could differ).

• Regarding apportionment and the use of trusts, the law of the situs of the trust for administration may govern for choice of law purposes.

• Finally, if appointive property is involved, the traditional conflict of laws rule applies the law of the state of the domicile of the person who created the power (its donor) on the fiction that appointment relates back to the donor's estate plan, with the powerholder merely acting as the donor's "agent" in exercising the power or otherwise with respect to the appointive assets. The conflict of laws rule that the law of the donor's domicile, rather than that of the powerholder's domicile, shall govern is one of the most troublesome and least expected conflict rules applicable in the estate planning arena. Indeed, one highly regarded commentator suggests that § 2207 was enacted in large part to minimize the difficult and unexpected effect of this conflict of laws rule.[131]

§3.3.13.2 Proper Resolution

The same commentator also argues that the proper resolution of a conflict of laws issue in the apportionment setting should follow a two step analysis. First, the law of the situs of property should apply to determine whose law will govern the choice of law question. Thus, if a trust is involved, the choice of law rules of the state of trust administration should govern with respect to the choice of law issue. With respect to transfers at death, situs law also should govern the choice of law, whether the assets are probate or nonprobate and regardless of whether administration is domiciliary or ancillary. Second, regardless of the state of situs, every state's choice of law rule should then dictate selection of the substantive apportionment rules of the decedent's domicile, on the

---

[131] See Scoles, Apportionment of Federal Estate Taxes and Conflict of Laws, 55 Colum. L. Rev. 261, 285 (1955).

simple theory that the decedent's intent should govern the apportionment issue and that the decedent likely relied on domiciliary law.

This suggestion is not, however, necessarily what the courts of a given jurisdiction will adopt.[132] As a consequence, probably the only way to ensure consistent apportionment results is to either designate the applicable law with respect to all assets, which cannot be done in many cases because there is no way to designate the governing law with respect to some assets, or provide for tax payment and apportionment that does not rely in any manner on state law. The best result may be a combination—using a tax payment provision that seeks to address all issues and therefore does not rely on state law, but also providing conflict of law provisions.

§3.3.13.3 Jurisdiction

The jurisdiction issue is whether a personal representative with a duty to apportion taxes can obtain jurisdiction over beneficiaries of nonprobate property located in other jurisdictions. Uniform Act §8 provides that an out-of-state personal representative may bring an action in the enacting state to obtain reimbursement from a nonprobate benefici-

---

[132] Compare Doetsch v. Doetsch, 312 F.2d 323 (7th Cir. 1963) (law of the decedent's domicile governed apportionment involving inter vivos trust), with Isaacson v. Boston Safe Deposit & Trust Co., 91 N.E.2d 334 (Mass. 1950) (law of situs of trust governed apportionment). And consider In re Estate of McGathy, 2011 WL 3300393 (unpub. Ariz. Ct. App.), in which the decedent was an Arizona domiciliary at death but a New York domiciliary when the will was prepared and executed; the trial court held that New York law should apply, without realizing that New York law directed that apportionment of estate tax is controlled by the law of the decedent's domicile at death, which caused Arizona law to apply. Note also that even the question of domicile may be subject to debate, as illustrated in Gellerstedt v. United Missouri Bank, 865 S.W.2d 707 (Mo. Ct. App. 1993) (while living in Kansas—a burden on the residue state—the decedent executed a will in 1971 that was silent on the tax apportionment issue, then was moved in 1979 to a nursing home in Missouri—an equitable apportionment state—where death occurred in 1988; without determining whether domicile changed or even undertaking a traditional conflict of laws analysis, the court held that domiciliary law would govern the tax apportionment issue and remanded for a resolution whether the decedent intended to change domicile, which necessarily would entail the issue whether the decedent possessed the capacity to form that intent, all many years after the move and not a few after death).

§3.3.13.3

ary located in the enacting state. The Act requires that the state of the decedent's domicile be a "reciprocity" state to qualify for this privilege, and reciprocity is not always clear in states that are silent on the issue of jurisdiction over nonprobate takers. Thus, absent a statutory right to bring an action, whether a personal representative will obtain jurisdiction over a recalcitrant nonprobate beneficiary is guesswork. An even less helpful provision in this regard is § 11 of the 2003 revision.

The Act (and other state laws as well) grants a right of setoff against the probate share of an individual, allowing the personal representative to withhold testate assets pending full contribution with respect to nonprobate assets that the individual also receives.

In many cases this is sufficient to cover the apportioned liability, because the beneficiary of nonprobate property also frequently receives sufficient probate property to cover the total allocated tax liability. This is, however, at best a partial solution if the nonprobate taker receives a small share of probate property and bears a heavy allocation attributable to receipt of substantial amounts of nonprobate property. It has been suggested that § 2205 grants a federal right of action to beneficiaries of an estate who suffer from an inability to apportion taxes against beneficiaries of probate property located in another state. This does not, however, assist in obtaining judgment against out-of-state takers of nonprobate property who fail to comply with an outside apportionment dictate of the law of the decedent's domicile.[133]

§3.3.14 Planning Aspects of the Apportionment Rules

The following material addresses three basic aspects of drafting tax payment provisions in light of the apportionment rules above. First, a number of glitches and disadvantages can be identified for avoidance in planning and drafting. Second, several uncertainties that may affect administration are isolated for consideration. Third, affirmative planning choices and their merits are explored.

---

[133] See Scoles, Estate Tax Apportionment in the Multi-State Estate, 5 U. Miami Inst. Est. Plan. ¶ 718.2 (1971).

§3.3.14.1 Problems to Avoid

State law may shift the tax payment liability to nonprobate takers. Their interests must be considered during estate administration to avoid unintentionally affecting their rights without their knowledge or consent.[134] Thus, a state court might decide that they are entitled to representation regarding administration decisions that affect them, and any failure to notify or join these beneficiaries may invalidate certain orders obtained or actions taken during estate administration.

One easy mechanism to avoid this concern (and the general lack of state law to dictate the requisite form of joinder or notice) is simply to direct that all taxes be paid out of the probate estate. If negation of apportionment under state law is not appropriate or desirable, however, state law might permit the decedent to indemnify the fiduciary from liability to nonprobate takers and direct that all decisions of the fiduciary in the ordinary course of probate administration shall be final, without notice or joinder. Presumably, on the same theory that a decedent in a nonapportionment state may allocate taxes to nonprobate assets (because a sufficient nexus exists to require inclusion of the asset in the first instance), it ought to be permissible to disadvantage or restrict the rights of nonprobate beneficiaries in this lesser fashion.

Under §§2206, 2207, 2207A, and 2207B the estate initially pays its federal tax liability and then is entitled to reimbursement. As a consequence, liquidity may not be where it is needed, and collection problems may arise or be exacerbated by the existence of multiple beneficiaries, all subject to these rights of reimbursement. In this respect, directing apportionment in the first instance rather than preserving these reimbursement rights may be more expeditious.

In addition, §2207A creates a significant and easily overlooked gift tax liability if taxes subject to reimbursement are not collected by or on behalf of the beneficiaries entitled to assert the right of reimbursement. During life, gift taxes attributable to relinquishment of any part of a QTIP life estate are subject to reimbursement and failure to collect them is regarded as an added gift by S, who relinquished the income interest. Similarly, at death, failure to collect the §2207A reimbursement of taxes caused by §2044 inclusion may result in a gift if beneficiaries of the

---

[134] See §3.2.3 n.12.

§3.3.14.1

§ 2044 property differ from recipients of S's estate.[135] This problem presumably is avoided if S's estate pours over into the QTIP trust (or passes as that trust does) so that the same beneficiaries are both benefited and hurt by the failure to assert the reimbursement right.

If a gift occurs due to a failure to either waive or assert a right of reimbursement, that gift will be the result of the personal representative's failure to act, while the gift (and therefore the tax to be paid thereon) is regarded as made by the beneficiaries affected by this action. It seems entirely possible that those beneficiaries will be unaware of the fiduciary having caused this gift, meaning that a return may not be filed and substantial interest and penalties may be imposed. A nonprofessional personal representative especially should be made aware of the gift tax exposure, perhaps by including a warning to the personal representative to this effect in both the QTIP trust and in S's estate plan. In addition, the unexpected § 2207A inequity attributable to QTIP being taxed at the highest FET rate applicable to S's estate must be considered, especially if that property passes to D's remainder beneficiaries and S's property passes to S's beneficiaries.[136]

Unfortunately, although it would eliminate all these problems, waiver of the right of reimbursement may leave taxes (caused by inclusion of a QTIP trust in S's estate) of such magnitude that probate assets are insufficient to pay those taxes. In such a case waiver alone is not a viable alternative. Nor would waiver be necessary if no gift would result (due to identity of the beneficiaries). In most cases, therefore, the better approach is to waive federal reimbursement rights but to preserve all state law apportionment rights, except with respect to specifically designated assets or classes of assets. This resolution only works well in most states because state law calls for apportionment.

§ 3.3.14.2 Temporal Interests

A third negative result of the apportionment rules in most states relates to the manner in which taxes attributed to annuities, life estates,

---

[135] See Treas. Reg. § 20.2207A-1(a)(2). One difference between the inter vivos and testamentary consequences of § 2207A is that the right of reimbursement at death may be waived, with a concomitant relief from this gift tax consequence. See Treas. Reg. § 20.2207A-l(a)(3).

[136] See § 3.3.5.

and terms certain are allocated.[137] Because paid out of principal in most cases, it is possible for the taxes on a lead beneficiary's interest to diminish the share of the remainder beneficiaries. Thus, for example, the income beneficiaries presumably would be protected if § 2207A applied to a QTIP trust that continued after S's death for the life of a secondary income beneficiary, remainder to a third party. A reduction in corpus would, however, reduce income therefrom and essentially amortize the tax burden.

The consequence of this apportionment rule is to reduce the size of the deduction if the lead interest is nondeductible but the remainder qualifies for either the marital or charitable deduction. This will increase taxes as a direct consequence and thereby further reduce the deductible amount, again increasing the taxes incurred, ad infinitum. By way of example, the remainder would qualify for the marital deduction if a trust required income to be paid to a parent for life, remainder to S. Similarly, qualified CRTs present the same problem. In such cases, the result is a conflict in states that embrace both equitable apportionment and the temporal interest apportionment rule allocating taxes attributable to a lead interest to the remainder. Usually that conflict is resolved in favor of forcing corpus to pay, with unfavorable results for deduction purposes.

Resolution of this problem would require taxes on the lead interest to be directly apportioned to the lead interest (rather than indirectly doing so by amortization), itself creating a problem of how those taxes are to be charged. For example, if the taxes are substantial, the lead interest beneficiary would need to be able to pay the cost of an immediate apportionment, which frequently is not possible. And it is no solution to allow the charge to corpus and argue that this necessarily reduces the income interest over time because the charge to corpus reduces the deduction. It might be possible to "borrow" from corpus the amount of taxes attributable to the lead interest, with repayment out of income earned over time or reduction of an annuity. However, in a qualified CRT, such a loan may constitute a prohibited form of self-dealing and reduction of the annuity would affect computation of the deduction.[138]

---

[137] See § 3.3.10.

[138] Directed at preventing reduction of the charitable deduction by virtue of the temporal interest apportionment rules, § 2207B(e) provides that no taxes will be apportioned under § 2207B to a qualified CRT.

§ 3.3.14.2

Alternatively, waiver of apportionment entirely may avoid the problem if another fund exists for tax payment purposes and imposition of the tax liability also will not reduce available deductions. The important point here is that these are significant issues that should not be left to chance or to uncertain state law.

§3.3.14.3 Retirement Benefits

Taxes attributable to retirement benefits includible in the estate under §2039 must be considered carefully in conjunction with beneficiary designations and the terms of the plan. The question is whether the beneficiary can afford to pay taxes imposed by apportionment if the settlement of the plan is not in a lump sum. If not, and if the plan does not permit apportionment against the plan itself, then the planner must consider some other beneficiary designation, or some other source for payment of the tax. All other things being equal, it probably is wiser to impose tax on the beneficiary, not on the plan, and then attempt to provide the beneficiary with the funds to pay that tax, thereby avoiding plan restrictions, §401(a)(11) concerns, and acceleration of income tax on the plan. The planner also must pay careful attention to whether the spousal annuity rules will prevent the type of payout otherwise desired. Most especially, the income tax consequences of the payout option selected, and of the tax apportionment selected, also should be considered.

§3.3.14.4 Administrative Uncertainties

As a practical matter, the estate plan must consider whether the breadth of nonprobate assets is such that apportionment would be difficult (if not impossible) to administer and, if so, whether the tax clause should waive apportionment or reimbursement (at least with respect to certain assets or classes of property). With all the various forms of nonprobate property and taxes that may be involved, however, it seems unlikely that blanket waiver of all apportionment or rights of reimbursement will be appropriate or feasible.

In some states it is uncertain how various computations and allocations are to be made and in what order, in which case the estate plan should establish the mechanism and dictate apportionment consistent therewith. In addition, during (and in anticipation of) estate administration, a number of uncertainties or problems may affect the personal representative and ought to be considered at the time the estate plan is prepared.

One is the effect that an audit will have on the determination of estate and inheritance taxes and the apportionment and collection thereof. Any previously determined allocation of taxes under an apportionment routine will be affected if values change, resulting in either a change in taxes payable or simply a readjustment in the relative size of various shares. This will be particularly true in a state that imposes different wealth transfer tax rates, based on degrees of consanguinity, if property subject to audit passed to beneficiaries in different degrees and the rate differential is apportioned under state law. The issue is whether it is prudent to distribute the bulk of an estate prior to final determination and collection of taxes. The planner should consider whether needs of the beneficiaries are such that a mechanism must be established for early distributions with allocation of taxes secured by a lien, bond, repayment agreement, or other method, or whether apportionment should be waived entirely, or waived only with respect to changes resulting from audit.

In addition, problems of collection and asserting jurisdiction over nonprobate takers should be considered before the death of a client, with measures taken premortem to alleviate potential problems by waiving apportionment or assuring an ancillary administration in the beneficiary's domiciliary state to obtain jurisdiction. Indeed, if multiple jurisdictions might be involved, conflict of laws issues should be anticipated, especially if a change of the client's domicile is likely or if a conflict of laws battle is anticipated because of the nature and location of nonprobate assets. This probably is the easiest potential problem to address, with the estate plan adopting either or both of two defensive procedures.

First, the estate plan may dictate the method of apportionment (if any) desired, thereby alleviating the vagaries of state law and uncertain application of any state's rules. Second, the estate plan may dictate the law that should apply, making certain that there is a substantial relation of the client's estate or estate plan to the jurisdiction whose law is selected and that the policies of the governing law state do not violate

§3.3.14.4

any strong conflicting policy of any state that might be deemed to have the most significant relationship to the client's estate.

§3.3.15 Planning Choices

This section explores various affirmative apportionment planning options or decisions. Readers with knowledge of the background law may only wish to review these issues in any particular estate planning engagement.

§3.3.15.1 Marital Deduction

Effective apportionment of taxes may restrict S's entitlement. For example, a client may select a QTIP trust format for marital deduction purposes because D wants to tie S's hands. The likelihood of S electing against the estate to take a statutory forced share outright is greater in such a case than if S was given more control, so D's choice of such a "handcuff" trust for S may indicate that minimization of a statutory forced heir share would be appropriate. This is not the place to discuss available methods to effectively reduce the size of a client's estate for forced share purposes,[139] but apportionment of taxes is a planning tool that *may* assist in accomplishing this objective.

In states that recognize equitable apportionment, S's share will be computed before determination of taxes and S's forced heir share will be larger because taxes are not charged against it. Although the concept of equitable election in most states will prevent a tax clause from working to S's benefit after electing against the estate, it may be possible in a tax clause to specify that equitable apportionment will *not* apply if S elects against the estate. Even if that provision is not valid, it probably cannot hurt to attempt to override a state law equitable apportionment result by specifying in D's tax clause that taxes shall be apportioned without regard to the marital deduction if S elects against D's estate plan.[140]

---

[139] See §4.3 and Pennell, Minimizing the Surviving Spouse's Elective Share, 32 U. Miami Inst. Est. Plan. ¶ 900 (1998).

[140] See §3.4.4 regarding the concepts of the forced share and equitable election.

§3.3.15.1

§3.3.15.2 Partial QTIP Elections and Disclaimers

Taxes generated by a partial QTIP election usually should be paid out of the nonelected portion of the marital deduction trust.[141] By proper accounting, this decision should not affect the amount includible at S's death, at least if equitable apportionment applies, because taxes would not be paid from the qualified portion in any event. Moreover, forcing payment of taxes from the nonelected portion of the QTIP trust has the advantage of preventing an alteration of D's estate planning equities if the QTIP and the nonmarital trusts benefit different remainder beneficiaries. Otherwise, payment from the nonmarital property of taxes incurred by virtue of a partial election would shift taxes from S's death (under §2044) imposed on the QTIP trust (under §2207A) to D's death, imposed on the nonmarital property (assuming that is how D's tax clause otherwise apportions all taxes).

---

[141] See PLR 8301050 and Comm. Rep., Death Tax Clauses in Wills and Trusts: Discussion and Sample Clauses, 19 Real Prop., Prob. & Trust J. 495, 509-510 (1984).

Care is required even in this simple respect. For example, the tax clause in D's estate plan in TAM 8922001 apportioned estate and inheritance taxes attributable to any portion of the gross estate as to which a QTIP election was not made, directing that those taxes be paid from the nonelected portion. But no provision addressed the apportionment of taxes attributable to the portion of the estate as to which the election *was* made.

The estate incurred state inheritance tax attributable to an elected trust, and state law provided that, absent a conflicting provision in the decedent's estate plan, those taxes were to be charged proportionately against the property that produced the tax. As a consequence, the QTIP trust was obliged to pay the inheritance tax attributable to it, which caused a §2056(b)(4) reduction of the FET marital deduction, which generated an FET that also was deemed payable from the trust, which also reduced the deduction and further increased the tax burden, and so on.

The TAM stated that it was fair for the inheritance tax burden to fall on the marital bequest that generated the tax and opined that other provisions in the estate plan indicated that D did not seek to maximize the marital deduction. Those provisions dealt with the personal representative's ability to make a partial QTIP election. The provisions probably were employed to permit postmortem planning that would produce the minimum taxes over the estates of both D and S. It also is likely that the drafter simply failed to anticipate the imposition of taxes with respect to that portion of the gross estate as to which the election was made.

§3.3.15.2

To work properly and without conflict with the government, the elected and nonelected portions of the marital trust appropriately may be segregated following election, making it easier to identify each and to justify the apportionment of taxes to the nonqualified portion without jeopardizing the marital deduction for the qualified portion. Further, PLR 8517036 illustrates that it is important to draft the provisions of the nonelected portion in such a way that making taxes payable from that portion will not affect deductibility of the elected portion.

In that Ruling, the effort was to qualify a nonmarital trust that contained a tax payment provision. Had the government allowed the 100% election sought by the estate, there would have been no taxes and the provision authorizing payment of taxes from that nonmarital trust would have had no effect. As it was, however, the government opined that § 2056(b)(4) required reduction of the otherwise allowable marital deduction by the full amount of taxes that *could* have been paid from that trust—in this case, as if no marital deduction had been elected.[142] In the context presented here, taxes should be payable from the nonelected portion only if there is a separate trust to which the nonelected property is added. And then draft in such a manner to clarify that no part of the otherwise qualifying marital property could be diverted to the payment of taxes.

A similar concern should apply if S disclaims part of the marital bequest, causing taxes to be incurred. These taxes should be payable from the disclaimed property and, if the disclaimer would send the property to grandchildren or more remote beneficiaries, incurring a direct skip GST, that tax also probably ought to be imposed on the disclaimed property.[143]

---

[142] But see TAM 8823001, in which an examiner argued that the marital deduction should be reduced by taxes that would be incurred and paid from the marital trust if the QTIP election was not made. The TAM concluded that the personal representative's discretion to make or withhold the election did not constitute the type of event or contingency that will disqualify or preclude the deduction under § 2056(b)(1) and the deduction was not reduced.

[143] Cf. TAM 8639002, which involved a different but related issue. Children of the decedent disclaimed a fraction of a nonmarital trust to produce a marital deduction sufficient to eliminate taxes in the decedent's estate. Because administration expenses were payable from the disclaimed property, § 2056(b)(4) reduced the marital deduction. Nevertheless, because the disclaimer was based on

§3.3.15.3 Order of Events

Some thought also ought to be given to the proper sequence for payment of taxes in relation to division of an estate into shares, such as under a fractional marital deduction entitlement or in conjunction with a partial QTIP election. For example, assume that D's estate plan or a partial election called for a marital deduction of a certain fraction of the estate (not necessarily that amount needed to reduce taxes to zero) and, because of other assets passing to S, the amount specified totals $1 million to be set aside (by fractional distribution or qualified election) for S's benefit.

Accepting that equitable apportionment dictates that no taxes be paid from the marital share, a question still remains regarding division and payment of taxes. In this case, assume that the estate was $4 million at death and that taxes imposed on the nonmarital estate (including nonprobate properties) total $1 million, leaving $3 million after payment of the tax. Of this, $1 million is to qualify for the marital deduction and the balance will fund a nonmarital trust. Before the time for final distribution of the estate (but after payment of the taxes), assume that the remaining $3 million increases fourfold in value to $12 million. At the time for final distribution of the spousal share (or segregation of elected and nonelected QTIP portions), is the proper fraction one-third of the $12 million, or one-fourth? (Note that, in all of this discussion, it is assumed that no other distributions are made that would require adjustment of the fraction. Although this is not realistic in practice, it makes the illustration easier.)

The one-third fraction is based on an assumption that the decedent was directing a fraction of the true or net residue, after payment of all taxes, with the fraction being $1 million/$3 million to generate the proper sized entitlement using date-of-death values. The one-fourth fraction is based on an assumption that the decedent was directing a fraction of the gross residue, before payment of all taxes, with equitable apportionment dictating that the $1 million of taxes be paid from the nonmarital share, making S entitled to $1 million/$4 million and the remaining three-fourths bear the taxes after division. Under either argu-

(Footnote Continued)

a formula, additional amounts were deemed disclaimed to generate a sufficient marital deduction, after reduction, to produce the desired result.

§3.3.15.3

ment, the marital entitlement would remain at $1 million (using date-of-death values), protecting qualification of the marital deduction.

The issue nevertheless is worthy of consideration, as shown by the difference in the various beneficiaries' entitlements. The one-fourth of gross estate fraction is best if D's intent is to freeze S's estate to the extent possible, or to maximize the amount of generation-skipping exemption allocated to a nonmarital trust. Most drafters probably call for the one-third division, however, either by inadvertence, for liquidity purposes, or because that result best protects S.

Notice that the issue is not determination of the size of the deduction, nor is it whether equitable apportionment should apply. The simple issue is whether taxes are paid first, followed by division, or whether division occurs first, followed by payment of the taxes out of the nonmarital fund. The estate plan (and, for that matter, any prenuptial agreement that dictates such a bequest) ought to be clear in defining terms such as the "residue" available for division or distribution and whether it is being referred to as that amount before or after payment of taxes.[144]

---

[144] See, e.g., Barley v. Albertini, 694 So. 2d 843 (Fla. Ct. App. 1997), in which the tax payment provision preceded all other provisions in the document and directed payment from the *"residuary* estate," along with the proviso that "in no event shall any portion of such taxes be apportioned or allocated to my spouse or any property passing to my spouse . . . which qualifies for the marital deduction." Two paragraphs below this the marital trust was described as "90% of the *remainder* of my estate . . . after the payment of . . . taxes . . . referred to above." The trial court held that taxes should be paid first and the marital trust created out of the remaining balance, meaning that 90% of the taxes effectively would be paid from the marital bequest. On appeal the court reversed and remanded because an ambiguity existed. Between the inconsistent statements in the two provisions—relating to nonapportionment to the spouse and division after payment—along with the different terms used in the two provisions, this conclusion appears to be an understatement. Estate of McCoy v. Commissioner, 97 T.C.M. (CCH) 1312 (2009), applied a state law equitable apportionment statute to protect the marital deduction in a plan that similarly did not clearly identify the "residue" from which taxes were payable and "the rest, residue and remainder" that qualified for the marital deduction; the court held that the ambiguity should be resolved in favor of equitable apportionment. See also § 13.7.7.2 regarding this general issue.

A similar problem involving the charitable deduction is illustrated by two conflicting cases. In Greene v. United States[145] D's placement of the tax burden on the residue of the estate created problems of interpretation of earlier provisions in the will giving 10% of the residuary estate to charity, half of "the rest, residue, and remainder" to S, and "the entire remainder of my estate (hereinafter referred to as the 'Residuary Estate')" to a trust. In this context, payment of taxes from the residue was deemed to be after division into the charitable and marital shares, causing the tax payment to come from the "residue of the residue" and, not coincidentally, preserving a larger marital and charitable deduction.

On the other hand, In re Estate of Bell[146] held that the Uniform Estate Tax Apportionment Act was superseded by a tax payment provision directing payment of all taxes from the residue of the decedent's estate. The residuary provision included two charitable bequests of a fraction of the residue. The charities argued that equitable apportionment should apply so that a gross residue division would be made and all taxes would be paid from the noncharitable portion of the residue. The court concluded that the tax payment direction overrode all portions of the Uniform Act, including equitable apportionment, and held that a net estate division was mandated by the chronological aspect of the will, directing payment of taxes and then division of the balance of the residue. The court did not even mention the effect of this conclusion on the §2055 charitable deduction, nor did it discuss equitable apportionment as a matter of policy that might guide its decision.[147] Consistent

---

[145] 447 F. Supp. 885 (N.D. Ill. 1978). See also In re Estate of Robinson, 720 So. 2d 540 (Fla. Ct. App. 1998) (reformation of tax payment direction to change from payment before division into marital and nonmarital bequests, to provide instead for division followed by payment from the nonmarital alone); American Cancer Soc'y v. Estate of Massell, 373 S.E.2d 741 (Ga. 1988) (decedent bequeathed portion of undefined "said estate" to charity; court determined that, notwithstanding tax payment provision calling for division of residue after payment of taxes, decedent did not intend to reduce the residue before division and adopted a gross estate division that effectively reflected equitable apportionment and preserved charitable deduction).

[146] 764 P.2d 689 (Wyo. 1988).

[147] See also In re Estate of Robbins, 544 N.Y.S.2d 427 (Surr. Ct. 1989), and In re Estate of Atkinson, 539 N.Y.S.2d 112 (App. Div. 1989).

On the marital deduction side of this issue, the decedent's tax clause in Estate of Ransburg v. United States, 765 F. Supp. 1388 (S.D. Ind. 1990), clarified,

§ 3.3.15.3

about both cases is the courts' application of a chronological interpretation, by which division and payment of taxes were deemed to occur in the order in which the respective provisions were found in the documents. That approach is not always best, nor do courts always follow it,

(Footnote Continued)

800 F. Supp. 716 (S.D. Ind. 1991), directed payment of "all estate, inheritance and succession or other taxes, whether state or federal, which may be assessed as a result of my death and without regard to whether . . . payable by my estate or by any beneficiary," but without indicating from what source payment was to be made. State law contained an equitable apportionment dictate that would cause each beneficiary to pay the tax attributable to his or her bequest, but that rule could be overcome if the will specifically directed otherwise or if payment of taxes was to be made from the residue of the estate.

The *Ransburg* estate passed half to S, one-sixth to a qualified charity, and one-third to D's children by a prior marriage. The government argued that the apportionment statute did not apply and that taxes to be paid from the residue would come "off the top" of the estate. Thus, the amount ultimately distributable to S and charity that qualified for the marital and charitable deductions should be reduced. In accepting this interpretation, the court noted that the will failed to direct the source of tax payment and, chronologically, placed the tax payment provision before the residue distribution provision. This made it appear that taxes were to be paid from the residue first, followed by distribution. As such, the court found that the tax clause negated the state equitable apportionment regime and resulted in a reduction of the amounts qualifying for each deduction.

Surprising about *Ransburg* was that state law allowed the equitable apportionment regime to be overcome by a simple direction to pay taxes from the residue of the estate. To the same effect are Leavenworth Nat'l Bank & Trust Co. v. United States, 1996 WL 225193 (D. Kan.) (direction to pay taxes from residue of estate "without the necessity of charging them against the interest of any beneficiary," followed by pour over of the residuary estate to an inter vivos trust, which distributed half to S, deemed to negate equitable apportionment because of the chronology and the documents in which the payment and the bequest appeared); In re Estate of Weinheimer, 2002 Mont. Dist. LEXIS 3329 (Mont. Dist. Ct.) (direction to pay taxes as if they were an expense of administration was deemed to create a net estate division, which reduced the "50% of the adjusted gross estate" marital deduction bequest); Banker v. Northside Bank & Trust Co., 1996 WL 107545 (Ohio Ct. App.) (division equally between S and child of a former marriage, with the chronological order in which the provisions appeared in the document—pay taxes first, then divide—deemed significant in determining that the marital share should be computed net of FET; state law equitable apportionment was deemed to be overcome by a statement in the tax payment provision that the fiduciary "shall not seek to recover . . . taxes from any Beneficiary").

§ 3.3.15.3

making proper anticipation of these issues essential in the initial drafting of the document and each of its provisions.

Estate of Dehgani-Fard[148] is different again but related, and reminiscent of the topic in § 3.3.12 addressing payment of income tax. It involved income tax attributable to substantial income items discovered 11 years postmortem. A charity was one of several residuary beneficiaries and the question was whether its share of the residue should be calculated before or after payment of income tax on those items. This is a different equitable apportionment concept than typically is encountered. But the common notion is that a charity's portion of *any* estate should be calculated pre-tax (income *or* the more common wealth transfer tax) to properly apportion the benefit of any charitable deduction (here an income tax deduction) to the charity. It is not necessarily the decedent's intent to allocate the benefit of a charitable deduction entirely to the charity, which is why litigation is required if the document is silent. The way to maximize any charitable benefit and reflect the charity's tax exempt status is to divide before tax and subject only the portion passing to noncharitable beneficiaries to the tax, with all the tax being paid from that nondeductible portion. That was the result reached in *Dehgani-Fard*, but it required litigation and reversal here of a lower court determination that violated "the equitable principle requiring that 'the burden of the tax accompanies the income and should be borne by the account into which the taxed item goes.'"

Another subtle application of the same type of problem is illustrated by TAM 9126005, which involved a will that directed payment of all state and federal taxes from the residue of the decedent's estate. State law was the Uniform Estate Tax Apportionment Act, which would apportion taxes among all beneficiaries, subject to equitable apportionment, but only to the extent the decedent did not provide otherwise. The will made several preresiduary bequests and left the residue 25% to an individual and 75% to a charity. Faced with the question of how much the charitable bequest should be reduced under § 2055(c) for taxes payable from the residue, the government applied Rev. Rul. 76-358[149] because the state law applicable in each situation was similar. The Ruling concluded that equitable apportionment within the residue was not altered by the tax payment

---

[148] 46 Cal. Rptr. 3d 289 (Cal. Ct. App. 2006).
[149] 1976-2 C.B. 291.

§ 3.3.15.3

provision directing all taxes to be paid from the residue, but the effect was not to impose all taxes on the noncharitable portion of the residue.

Instead, the tax on the preresiduary bequests was payable from the residue prior to its division, which effectively reduced the charitable bequest by 75% of the tax on the preresiduary bequests. Only taxes generated by the residue, all attributable to the noncharitable portion of the residue, were apportioned under state law entirely against that noncharitable portion. The Ruling stated that the question whether the tax payment provision was a direction against statutory apportionment of every dimension was very close, indicating the significance of careful consideration and drafting of tax payment provisions in general, and the result reveals the need for careful thought in conjunction with charitable planning in particular.

The tax payment provision did not waive all rights to apportionment or reimbursement, which distinguished it from many poorly considered tax payment provisions. It also seems unlikely that the decedent intended that the charitable beneficiary receive a portion of the residue before reduction for taxes attributable to the preresiduary bequests (that is, that the individual residuary beneficiary should pay all taxes), so the Ruling probably reached the right result. But the decedent's intent was not as clear as it might have been and the Ruling could have dictated an even greater diminution of the charitable deduction.[150]

---

[150] See also In re Menchofer Family Trust, 765 N.W.2d 607 (Iowa Ct. App. 2009), In re Walrod, 25 Misc. 3d 1205 (N.Y. Surr. Ct. 2009), In re Probate of the Will of Lee, 910 A.2d 634 (N.J. Super. Ct. 2006), and Shriners Hospital for Children v. Schaper, 215 S.W.3d 185 (Mo. Ct. App. 2006) (each involving preresiduary bequests to individuals and residuary bequests to charity and each holding that taxes, which were entirely attributable to the noncharitable bequests, burdened the charitable residue because the decedent intended the individuals to receive particular amounts or property unreduced by any impost such as debts, expenses, or taxes); TAM 9616001 (debts, expenses, and taxes attributable to preresiduary bequests were payable from residue and reduced amount charity received by virtue of partial disclaimer by decedent's sibling, but equitable apportionment applied within a residuary bequest split between the charity and the sibling and assessed all taxes incurred by the residue against the sibling's share). Proceeding of Feil, 894 N.Y.S.2d 837 (Surr. Ct. 2009), reached a similar result in an uncommon situation involving taxes incurred upon termination of a QTIP marital deduction trust, from which a large nondeductible bequest was paid pretax and the balance was placed in a zero-gift CLAT that was required

§ 3.3.15.3

§3.3.15.4 Use of Credits

Apportionment of the benefit of credits available to the estate under §§ 2010 through 2015 also should be considered. A client may wish to alter the general rule, which is that (excepting credits attributable to charges actually borne by the recipient of a particular asset) these credits work to the overall benefit of the estate, not to the benefit of any

---

(Footnote Continued)

to bear the entire tax burden, all determined by D under the QTIP trust, not by S, in whose estate the trust was includible.

Hale v. Moore, 289 S.W.3d 567 (Ky. Ct. App. 2008), Estate of Bradford v. Commissioner, 84 T.C.M. (CCH) 337 (2002), Estate of Fagan v. Commissioner, 77 T.C.M. (CCH) 1427 (1999), and Estate of McKay v. Commissioner, 68 T.C.M. (CCH) 279 (1994), all found that the decedents' tax payment provisions in each case negated state law equitable apportionment and caused taxes on the entire estate to be charged to the residue before its division between charitable and noncharitable beneficiaries. In *Bradford* the provision was an insufficiency tax clause in a trust and a linked will provision that waived all rights of apportionment; the *Fagan* flaw was payment from the residuary estate under a will, with proper apportionment language in a pourover trust that provided for charity; *McKay* provided "that all . . . taxes . . . attributable to my probate estate . . . shall be paid out of the residue of my estate . . . without adjustment among the residuary beneficiaries, and shall not be charged against or collected from any beneficiary of my probate estate." The result was a § 2055(c) reduction in the charitable deduction for that portion of the residue passing to charities (and an increase in taxes that again reduced the deduction, which further reduced the residue, ad infinitum).

To avoid a similar result, In re Estate of Kidman, 2009 Ind. App. LEXIS 1465 (Ind. Ct. App 2009), regarded a pour over will as incorporating a receptacle trust by reference, which allowed the tax payment provision in the will to govern over the will and trust combined, preserving a residuary bequest to charity. In the process, however, the opinion trammels various will drafting principles, including one that regards a pour-over trust as a valid separate and independent will substitute.

See also In re Succession of Haydel, 780 So. 2d 1168 (La. Ct. App. 2001), in which no drafting cure would avoid the unfortunate loss of marital deduction because taxes on preresiduary bequests were a charge to the residue, which was a 100% QTIP marital trust. Equitable apportionment might work in some cases to make a nondeductible portion of a residue incur all the taxes attributable to preresiduary bequests, but that result is not common and, in a QTIP context, there is no effective severance of the deductible interest from the remainder. Nor is there any way to alter the temporal interest rule to reapportion the tax and avoid this consequence. Rather, payment from the marital residue was simply the wrong choice *if* preservation of the marital deduction was paramount.

§ 3.3.15.4

particular beneficiary. Instead, a client may prefer that the recipient of property subjected to a foreign death tax be granted the benefit of the credit therefor.

Failure to consider the effect of credits under general allocation rules can work unexpected consequences. For example, consider the §2013 credit available to the estate of a beneficiary who dies within 10 years after the client. On the death of that beneficiary, taxes paid by the client's estate on property subsequently included in the beneficiary's estate qualify as a §2013 credit against the beneficiary's FET. That result is totally appropriate if the taxes paid by the client's estate that generated the credit were charged against that beneficiary. Otherwise the beneficiary's estate enjoys a credit generated by the payment of the client's FET by other individuals, which may be inappropriate. Thus, in certain circumstances it might be best to preserve apportionment so that each beneficiary is obliged to pay the tax on the property the beneficiary receives, thereby "paying" the price for any possible §2013 credit that ultimately may be generated.

In a similar vein, if inclusion in the beneficiary's estate is due to a §2041 general power to appoint the client's trust, it also makes sense to marry the §2013 credit with the §2207 liability of the recipient of the appointive property to pay the beneficiary's tax, which also may not occur without proper coordination.

The result of the normal sharing of credits could cut either way with respect to property transferred by inter vivos gift. If the gifted property subsequently is included in the client's estate under any of §§2035-2038, §2040, or §2042, the donee may be required by apportionment to bear a pro rata portion of FET allocable to the gifted property, which may be an amount well in excess of the actual gift taxes incurred by the decedent at the time the gift was made. This would be true particularly with respect to life insurance, with its low gift tax value but much greater FET inclusion. Apportionment to the beneficiary is especially appropriate with respect to insurance because the proceeds provide such a ready source of liquidity and the tax could be such a large liability.

Moreover, if a donee is not required to bear a portion of the FET caused by inclusion of gifted property in the donor's estate at death, the donee enjoys the benefit of credits that otherwise would be reserved to the estate as a whole. That is, a donee who is not also a beneficiary of the

§3.3.15.4

estate "enjoys" FET credits because the gifted property is included in the adjusted taxable gifts base for FET computation purposes but the donee is not required to contribute to the taxes caused by that inclusion.

Indeed, the gift may have "used" the unified credit long before the client's death. For example, In re Estate of Finke[151] involved nonprobate assets transferred within three years before the decedent's death but included in the estate for state (but not for federal) estate tax purposes. Because the unified credit precluded a gift tax on the inter vivos transfer, the court held that the unified credit was a "credit directly attributable to a particular . . . gift [which] shall inure to the benefit of the . . . donee" under state law.[152] With that entitlement, the court held that apportionment of tax to the inter vivos donees was precluded because the credit exceeded the state tax liability on the gift. In essence, therefore, those donees enjoyed the unified credit to the exclusion of other objects of the donor's bounty.

In some cases the client may wish to consider whether some form of adjustment should be dictated so that recipients of assets during life are not placed at an advantage over beneficiaries who receive shares of the estate at death. Waiver of apportionment may be the only way to ensure that all beneficiaries receive their shares tax free, but this form of equalizing various shares will work only if a fund will remain for payment of taxes after all equalizing bequests have been satisfied.[153]

---

[151] 508 N.E.2d 158 (Ohio 1987).

[152] Ohio Rev. Code Ann. § 2113.88.

[153] Estate of Owen v. Commissioner, 104 T.C. 498 (1995), also illustrates how lifetime gifts create subtle inequities. It involved inter vivos gifts that were not includible in the decedent's gross estate for FET purposes but, because they constituted adjusted taxable gifts, they increased the marginal bracket for computing the decedent's FET. In that sense, they were no different than if the gifted property still were owned at death. The gifted property *was*, however, includible in the decedent's tax base for *state* death tax purposes, which generated a state death tax that the estate wanted to claim for § 2011 state death tax credit purposes. The court, however, held that the estate was not entitled to that credit because the express language of § 2011(a) limited the credit to transfers that were includible in the decedent's gross estate for FET purposes.

Had the transfer not been made during life the property would have been includible in the gross estate and this problem would not have arisen. Indeed, if the value of the property did not change between the date of the gift and the date of the decedent's death the effect of inclusion at death for federal wealth transfer

§ 3.3.15.4

More importantly, use of the unified credit during life generates a larger benefit than use at death, meaning that the inter vivos donee is favored even if credits otherwise are shared by a waiver of apportionment provision. For example, a client who wanted beneficiaries A and B each to receive $1 million in value at the time of the client's death, could follow either of two approaches. One is to leave each $1 million at death. Alternatively, the client could presently transfer a remainder interest in property that will be worth $1 million at the client's death (avoiding § 2036(a)(1) inclusion at death by transferring the intervening life estate to another party). For gift tax purposes, the value of the transferred remainder would be the discounted present value of $1 million, and the gift tax on that discounted value would be less than the FET on $1 million at the client's death due to both the discounting and the tax exclusive nature of the gift tax. Even if each beneficiary was required to bear the proportionate taxes allocable to the interest each received, that would impose the tax on a gift of only the discounted value made during life rather than the tax on a full $1 million if made at death (or if the gifted property was included in the client's gross estate).

The client who wants to equalize the treatment of the beneficiaries by adjusting for use of the unified credit during life must allocate tax to beneficiaries in a manner that reflects the value of their respective entitlements—determined at the same time, not at the time the various transfers were made—and reflect the time use value of any monies the donee used to pay taxes on the gift prior to the client's death. Although a net gift approach would avoid some of the inequity considered here (because the donee looses the use of the donee's money), the tax bracket at which the tax would be imposed might be lower by virtue of the gift and discounting technique, and the tax exclusive gift tax compu-

(Footnote Continued)

tax computation purposes would have been unchanged. Which may explain in part why the estate argued (unsuccessfully) for FET inclusion: presumably FET inclusion would have generated the § 2011 credit and a new basis at death under § 1014, with no significant (if any) detriment (for example, any loss of § 2503 annual exclusion with respect to the gifts might have been de minimis in relative terms). Although the final result seems improper for tax policy purposes, and almost certainly was not anticipated by the decedent, it also appears to be the correct interpretation of § 2011 (which since was repealed). It also highlights that unification of the wealth transfer taxes still has not fully occurred and the consequent need to be vigilant about these gift tax issues.

§ 3.3.15.4

tation also would benefit the donee. Furthermore, the net gift approach is not available until the donor's unified credit is exhausted.[154]

The effects of inter vivos gifts on a tax apportionment regime are invidious and difficult to contemplate. This is illustrated by In re Estate of Coven,[155] which involved a situation that is not unusual. The decedent's will directed that FET on probate and nonprobate assets be paid out of the decedent's estate, subject to a pro rata apportionment of the estate's total tax liability among the various beneficiaries under the will. Included in the decedent's FET computation base were gifts made to a child inter vivos, and those gifts caused the balance of the decedent's estate to be taxed in a higher marginal FET bracket. As a consequence, another child argued that the donee child should bear a larger share of the overall taxes incurred and paid by the estate under the pro rata apportionment dictate of the will. The court rejected that argument because neither the will nor state law apportioned taxes against property transferred by gift during life. Further, the § 2035(b) gross-up rule may require additional inclusion of any gift taxes paid on the transfer even if the transferred property is not subject to inclusion.[156]

---

[154] Rev. Rul. 79-398, 1979-2 C.B. 338. Regarding net gifts in general see § 7.2.5. A closely related planning issue was raised by gifting done by the decedent whose estate was involved in PLR 9339010, who made substantial gifts and paid gift tax within three years of death, triggering application of the § 2035(b) gross-up rule. See § 3.3.1.

[155] 559 N.Y.S.2d 798 (Surr. Ct. 1990).

[156] Contra, Shepter v. Johns Hopkins University, 637 A.2d 1223 (Md. Ct. App. 1994) (taxes otherwise payable from the residue, which passed to a charity, were apportioned against the beneficiary of an inter vivos gift that constituted an adjusted taxable gift and boosted the FET marginal bracket but otherwise was not includible in the decedent's gross estate for FET purposes, stating that full apportionment as adopted in states that enacted the Uniform Estate Tax Apportionment Act should include donees of gifts that are included in the FET computation). In re Estate of Necaise, 915 So. 2d 449 (Miss. 2005), held that the decedent's will effectively imposed a similar result on the donee of an inter vivos gift that fully constituted that beneficiary's share of the decedent's total wealth, by allocating tax at death as if the inter vivos gift was included in the estate and then fully apportioning the FET liability. By ch. 55 of Acts 1995 the Maryland legislature effectively rejected the result in *Shepter*, stating that the reference in Md. Code Ann., Tax-General § 7-308(a)(4) to persons to whom FET may be apportioned does not include the recipient of an adjusted taxable gift from the

In this latter event, it is not established who should pay the FET attributable to the gift tax includible in the estate under § 2035(b). A convenient result, but one not dictated by state laws, would be to regard the gross-up tax as part of the gift[157] and regard the donee thereof as responsible for the FET attributable thereto. This result has the inconsistent consequence of treating the FET attributable to the gift tax being paid differently from the gift tax itself (if the donor paid the gift tax without charge to the donee). The estate planner needs to consider the client's intent with respect to this issue if significant inter vivos gifts are being considered and may occur within three years of the donor's death, particularly if there will be insufficient assets in the estate to pay the tax on the § 2035(b) gross-up tax amount without invading otherwise deductible bequests (such as a testamentary marital deduction gift in an estate that has totally utilized its unified credit during the client's life and, therefore, has no nonmarital assets with which to pay FET attributable to § 2035(b) inclusion).

On the other hand, apportionment of the § 2035(b)-generated tax to the donee may not be viable (without some testamentary enforcement mechanism), or appropriate.[158] By way of example, consider Parent P, who intended to bequeath the entire P family business to child A. When A's siblings B and C discovered P's intent (and raised a ruckus) P agreed to transfer $5 million to each of them inter vivos, in exchange for their written waiver of any estate entitlement and their agreement not to contest P's will. P's estate planner anticipated P's impending demise and amended the tax payment direction in P's estate plan to provide that any gift tax on the two $5 million gifts would reduce A's bequest if P died before the gift tax on these two transfers was paid. P lived long enough to pay the gift tax but died within three years. So the gross-up rule in § 2035(b) required inclusion of the gift tax dollars and the question was whether the FET attributable to inclusion of the gift tax dollars should be apportioned to B and C (because they received the gifts) or to A. The

---

(Footnote Continued)

decedent that is not includible for FET purposes, "notwithstanding any holding or dictum to the contrary in *Shepter v. Johns Hopkins University*."

[157] But cf. CCA 201020009, suggesting (in a very unusual situation) that a "transfer" for gift tax purposes requires "a gratuitous transfer in some manner from a donor to a donee" and payment of gift tax is not such.

[158] See § 3.3.1 n.15 and accompanying text.

§ 3.3.15.4

intent was that B and C receive their gifts totally free-and-clear, but state law embraced full apportionment and the result reached (by an arbitrator) was that B and C should pay the § 2035(b)-generated FET. Notwithstanding their anticipation and probably contrary to P's intent.

§ 3.3.15.5 Benefit of Rates

The client also should consider whether the effect of any differentials in the rate of state wealth transfer tax imposed on the estate (based on degrees of consanguinity of the various takers)[159] should be preserved to the benefit of the respective takers. A spouse typically enjoys this benefit automatically, through equitable apportionment (unless state law does not recognize that doctrine). The benefit of a lower rate for children or descendants as opposed to more distant relatives or strangers also is preserved under some states' laws, including under the Uniform Estate Tax Apportionment Act.

An easy, common example of a situation in which this might be relevant is a client with children and step-children whom the client wants to benefit equally. In some states the step-children would bear a larger share of the state wealth transfer tax burden if state law imposes a higher tax rate on step-children than it does on natural born or adopted children. A client also may wish to alter the normal apportionment rule if the computation necessary to allocate rate differentials is easy, or if the client does not wish to discriminate against the step-children. Indeed, even if preservation of this apportionment rule is the intent, it might be possible to do so in an easier and roughly comparable manner by adjusting the size of various shares or bequests (taking into consideration the effect of state taxes and the beneficiary's relation to the client) and override the state apportionment rule.

§ 3.3.15.6 Bad Debt Deductions

The immediately foregoing discussions underscore the fact that apportionment of taxes can work a "tax free" shift of wealth among various beneficiaries of a decedent's estate, and that one way to shift

---

[159] See, e.g., Ky. Rev. Stat. §§ 140.070 (differing rates based on the relationship of the beneficiary to the decedent) and 140.080 (differing exemption amounts based on the relationship of the beneficiary to the decedent).

wealth as part of postmortem planning is to apportion (or waive the apportionment of) taxes. In fact, it may be possible to generate an income tax deduction for a beneficiary who pays taxes properly allocable to another, if the individual liable for payment refuses to pay, creating a § 166(d)(1) bad debt deduction for the party who bears the added tax.[160]

§3.3.15.7 GST

GST is a major tax allocation concern. For example, allocation of the GST exemption may have inequitable tax consequences to otherwise equally situated beneficiaries due to the way the GST burden falls. Many estate plans anticipate this inequity by inclusion of a clause dictating that GST incurred on a taxable distribution shall be paid by the trust (rather than by the beneficiary upon whom that tax otherwise would fall), notwithstanding the fact that this tax payment is itself an added taxable distribution that is subject to GST under § 2621(b).[161] Because that additional distribution is deemed to occur on the last day of the year of the actual distribution, the total distribution for the year requires an interrelated or algebraic computation to determine the tax on the actual distribution, and then the tax on the deemed distribution in the amount of that tax, and on any additional deemed distribution to cover that tax, and so on, all in the year of the original distribution.[162]

In addition, the instructions to Form 706-B under the 1976 tax provided that, if the GST paid by a generation-skipping trust upon termination of an interest was paid from a portion of the trust not the subject of the termination, that tax payment would constitute an addi-

---

[160] See Rev. Rul. 69-411, 1969-2 C.B. 177. Income or gift tax consequences of such a refusal and payment should, however, be evaluated before attempting this ploy.

[161] See Treas. Reg. § 26.2612-1(c)(1).

[162] The algebraic formula to determine the total distribution, actual and deemed, against which the tax applies, is:

$$\text{total distribution} = \text{actual distribution} \div 1 - \text{rate of tax}$$

For example, if the actual distribution in 2012 was $100,000 and the tax rate was 35%, the trustee's payment of the tax on that $100,000 actual distribution would be another $53,846. As verification: total actual and deemed distributions of $153,846 × .35 tax yields $53,846 in tax that goes to the government and leaves $100,000 that went to the beneficiary.

tional taxable termination. Although that position is not explicitly stated on the current version of Form 706 Schedule R, it is a proper result and could be important in group trusts, which should ensure that taxes paid are allocated to the respective shares subject to tax (unless the § 2654(b) separate share rule applies and the terms of the document do this automatically).

In the case of QTIP includible in S's estate under § 2044, payment of tax (either directly or pursuant to § 2207A) may exhaust assets as to which a § 2652(a)(3) allocation of exemption had been made, essentially wasting a portion of that exemption.[163] Waiver of § 2207A is one answer to this wastage. Another is D's QTIP trust direction that all taxes on QTIP should be paid from any portion of the QTIP that was not made exempt by an allocation under § 2652(a)(3).[164] Neither approach should constitute a constructive addition to the trust for GST purposes[165] be-

---

[163] PLR 199927007 addressed the question of the source for payment of FET generated under § 2044 on the death of S, in whose estate both a vanilla QTIP and a reverse QTIP trust were includible. The Ruling is quite obtuse about whether the QTIP trust or S's estate plan provided any direction regarding the § 2207A right of reimbursement for taxes attributable to this inclusion. In this context the Ruling specified that the FET right of reimbursement would be satisfied from both QTIP trusts pro rata, meaning that exempt dollars in the reverse QTIP would be wasted on tax payment.

This is a bit surprising in light of Treas. Reg. § 26.2652-1(a)(5) Examples 7 & 8, which apply in the context of a failure to exercise the § 2207A right of reimbursement or S providing that these taxes will be paid from some other source. These examples provide that failing to exercise the reimbursement right or directing payment from another source is not tantamount to a constructive addition to the exempt reverse QTIP trust, notwithstanding that either act leaves the trust with more assets than if the reimbursement right was exercised. As the rationale expressed in those examples the regulations specify that making the reverse QTIP election is tantamount to the QTIP election never being made and S therefore not being treated as the transferor, which means that there is no right of reimbursement and therefore nothing to constitute an addition. For the instant Ruling then to provide that there is a right of reimbursement and that it must be satisfied pro rata from each QTIP trust seems inconsistent. It probably reflects the notion that pro rata payment from each portion is the default result that would apply under state law absent some other direction in the document.

[164] Note that S probably cannot make that direction, although there likely is no harm in trying.

[165] The express language of § 2652(a)(3) supports this result, specifying that, if the election under this section is made, then "for purposes of [Chapter 13, the

§ 3.3.15.7

cause, due to the reverse QTIP election, for GST purposes the property is treated as not includible in S's estate. As a result, §2207A also is deemed not to apply, meaning that there can be no constructive addition.[166] Thus, for GST purposes, the trust is regarded as nontaxable at S's death and there is no tax burden properly allocable to the trust, meaning that waiver of §2207A or any other apportionment provision is no "benefit" to the trust for purposes of the tainting addition question under Chapter 13.

Unfortunately, this rationale leaves it open for the government to allege that failure to assert the §2207A right of reimbursement in a vanilla QTIP trust *is* a constructive addition. This is relevant for purposes of determining the transferor of the §2207A reimbursement amount,[167] and the gift tax treatment may make the beneficiaries (who are deemed to make a gift by failing to assert the right of reimbursement) the transferors to that extent.[168] That treatment might be regarded as inconsistent with a transition date rule that regards failure to assert the §2207A right of reimbursement as not a constructive addition that would taint a chronologically exempt trust, although the logic of the two provisions is not the same because a reverse QTIP trust is treated as if

---

(Footnote Continued)

result is] as if the election to be treated as qualified terminable interest property had not been made" by the settlor of the trust. The nonaddition position is that, lacking a QTIP election, there would be no §2044 inclusion in S's estate, and no §2207A reimbursement.

[166] The express language of §2652(a)(3) supports this result, specifying that, if the election under this section is made, then "for purposes of [Chapter 13, the result is] as if the election to be treated as qualified terminable interest property had not been made" by the settlor of the trust. The nonaddition position is that, lacking a QTIP election, there would be no §2044 inclusion in S's estate, and no §2207A reimbursement.

[167] See Treas. Reg. §26.2652-2(d) Example 3.

[168] Treas. Reg. §20.2207A-1(a)(2). Cf. PLR 200127007, in which the government held that S's waiver of the §2207A right of reimbursement was an interest in property, which the remainder beneficiaries of the QTIP trust were permitted to disclaim (the effect of which was to increase a charitable bequest of S's residuary estate that otherwise would have been reduced to pay the taxes caused by FET inclusion under §2044.)

§3.3.15.7

the QTIP election never was made and this issue relates to that portion of a trust as to which the reverse election in fact was *not* made.[169]

A similar issue reflects the fact that GST is apportioned under §2603(b) to the property "constituting" the generation-skipping transfer. If a trust is partially exempt, use of general trust assets to pay taxes on a taxable termination wastes partially exempt assets in payment of GST. §2653(b)(1) provides that "[u]nder regulations prescribed by the Secretary . . . proper adjustment shall be made to the inclusion ratio with respect to such trust to take into account any tax under this chapter borne by such trust which is imposed by this chapter on the transfer . . . ." It is not clear what this means and the regulations provide no guidance. Because the inclusion ratio operates in a partially exempt trust to make part of every asset "exempt" and part taxable, it is not possible to apportion the tax within such a trust to only wholly taxable assets. Thus,

---

[169] See Treas. Reg. §26.2601-1(b)(1)(iii)(A).

When the Temporary regulation was made final the sentence establishing the §2207A result noted in text was deleted. PLR 9523024 correctly noted that then Temp. Treas. §26.2601-1(b)(1)(v)(C) specified that a constructive addition would occur if a chronologically exempt QTIP trust was relieved of any liability, such as the trust's §2207A responsibility to pay any estate tax caused by its inclusion in S's gross estate under §2044. Nevertheless, and without citing then Prop. Treas. Reg. §26.2652-1(a)(5) Example 7 with which it was and still is consistent, the Ruling held that no constructive addition was deemed to occur if the surviving spouse waived the §2207A right of reimbursement and provided for payment of those taxes from another source. To the same effect are PLRs 9602027 and 9535042. Notice that this situation differs from the case stated in text in that the right of reimbursement is not asserted, rather than being waived by S. The result reached in the Ruling regarding waiver of the reimbursement right made consistent the treatment of chronologically exempt trusts and reverse QTIP trusts, which comports with the rule finally stated in Treas. Reg. §26.2601-1(b)(1)(iii) that chronologically exempt QTIP trusts should be treated as if a §2652(a)(3) reverse election had been made.

Outside the reverse QTIP election situation, Estate of Boyd v. Commissioner, 819 F.2d 170 (8th Cir. 1987) (waiver of §2206 right of reimbursement deemed to be a form of "bequest" that the beneficiary of insurance proceeds could waive), also supports the result that waiver of any right of reimbursement is a form of bequest that could constitute a tainting addition to an otherwise exempt QTIP trust. And the government's rationale with respect to the reverse QTIP (that no reimbursement right exists because of the reverse QTIP election) makes it seem clear that this result will not obtain in cases in which the reimbursement right clearly exists.

§3.3.15.7

in a partially exempt trust, some of the exemption is wasted with respect to every dollar of trust property used to pay GST. The easy solution to this problem is to create two trusts, one that is totally exempt and one that is totally taxable, with all tax inclusion and apportionment being limited to the totally taxable trust.

Another solution is a "net gift" type of approach by which the beneficiary of a generation-skipping trust directs his or her estate to pay any GST incurred by reason of that beneficiary's death. Assuming this tax payment is a constructive addition by the beneficiary, the result is to preserve the partially exempt assets but effectively decrease the exempt portion by virtue of the constructive addition. Mathematically, however, this constructive addition result may be preferable to using partially exempt dollars to pay the tax directly, as illustrated by the following example. Assume the trust is $10 million and the applicable fraction is one-fourth, making $2.5 million of the trust "exempt." Because the exemption actually is built into the inclusion ratio, which reduces the tax rate, the effect is to reduce the tax rate to 75% of the 35% impost in 2012, meaning that a GST of $2,625,000 would be incurred at the beneficiary's death, leaving $7,375,000 in the trust, still one-fourth ($1,843,750) "exempt."[170] If, instead, the constructive addition approach was followed, a new fraction would be struck of $2,500,000/12,625,000 and the new fraction would produce an "exempt" portion of 19.80198% ($1,980,198 out of the actual fund of $10 million).

Finally, § 2612(a)(2) must be considered. Applicable in the context of a trust with several beneficiaries and staggered distributions, this provision specifies that distributions that are not attributable to the death of a lineal descendant of the transferor are taxed as taxable distributions, not taxable terminations of that beneficiary's interest in the trust. The effect for tax apportionment purposes is on the source of tax payment—the tax being imposed on the beneficiary instead of on the trust. In many cases this probably is the most equitable form of tax apportionment. If § 2612(a)(2) does not dictate taxable distribution results, however, because a partial termination occurs on the death of a lineal descendant of the transferor, then an inequity may arise because taxable termination treatment causes the tax liability to befall the trustee. Unless this tax is allocated to the portion that terminated (for example, as a charge against

---

[170] Unless the § 2653(b)(1) regulations provide otherwise.

§ 3.3.15.7

the distributable share), the effect is that all beneficiaries of the trust pay the tax on a termination that provides a partial distribution to only one of the trust's beneficiaries. This is inequitable and likely not the transferor's intent. Here an appropriate remedy could include dictating GST apportionment either to the trust in all events or to the distributees in all events, regardless of the operation of § 2612(a)(2).

§3.3.15.8 Section 303

The effect of apportionment under state law or by virtue of provisions in the estate plan should be considered in conjunction with § 303 if sale or exchange treatment on redemption of § 303 stock is to be obtained. This provision permits avoidance of dividend treatment upon a distribution of property to a shareholder by a corporation in redemption of all or part of any stock of the corporation that is included in a decedent's gross estate,[171] but only to the extent the distribution does not exceed the amount of the decedent's estate, inheritance, legacy, and succession taxes (including interest), and expenses allowable as deductions under § 2053. Proper allocation of those burdens is essential because this dividend avoidance benefit is available only to the extent the owner of the redeemed stock bears the burden of paying the FET and administration expenses.[172] A valuable method for raising cash to pay death costs may be utilized if the other requirements of § 303 are met.

To qualify for § 303 redemption treatment the FET value of the decedent's stock in the corporation must exceed 35% of the value of the

---

[171] Rev. Rul. 87-132, 1987-2 C.B. 82, allowed application of § 303 to a redemption of stock that was distributed to the estate as part of the same transaction. The corporation was owned equally by an estate and an individual who had no interest in the estate and the value of the stock held by the estate exceeded the amount specified in § 303(b)(2)(A). To maintain the equal division of voting power and to preserve continuity of management following the redemption the corporation first issued 10 shares of a new class of nonvoting common stock on each share of common stock outstanding. Immediately thereafter the estate's nonvoting common shares were redeemed. Because the nonvoting common stock was issued within the time limits prescribed by § 303(b)(1)(A) and did not exceed the amount permitted by § 303(a), the Ruling concluded that congressional intent was consistent with application of § 303 to this redemption, notwithstanding that the stock was issued as part of the same plan as the redemption.

[172] See § 303(b)(3) and Treas. Reg. § 1.303-2(f).

§ 3.3.15.8

decedent's gross estate,[173] reduced by the full amount of any allowable § 2053 or § 2054 deductions.[174] Stock in more than one corporation is aggregated to meet this test if the decedent's gross estate includes at least 20% of the value of all the outstanding stock in each corporation. And a spousal attribution rule exists with respect to stock held by D and S as community property or as joint tenants, tenants by the entirety, or tenants in common.[175]

Dividend treatment is avoided only with respect to amounts distributed by the corporation within 90 days after expiration of the three year § 6501(a) limitation period for assessment of an FET deficiency,[176] or until expiration of the deferral period if a § 6166 election has been made to pay FET in installments. A § 303 redemption and deferral under § 6166 may be combined,[177] but distributions more than four years after the

---

[173] Determined as if § 2035(a) required inclusion of all property transferred within three years of the decedent's death. See § 2035(c)(1)(A) and Rev. Rul. 84-76, 1984-1 C.B. 91 (stock must be owned at death to be redeemable under § 303, but stock and other property transferred within three years of the decedent's death is reflected in determining the 35% test). Thus, the client cannot transfer by gift nonqualifying property within three years of death in an effort to increase the percentage of the estate at death consisting of qualifying stock.

[174] See § 303(b)(2)(A). The 35% test is easier to meet because reduction is by *all* allowable deductions rather than just those actually claimed and allowed.

[175] See § 303(b)(2)(B). In Rev. Rul. 79-401, 1979-2 C.B. 128, the government illustrated why the nonelective nature of this aggregation rule is important because Treas. Reg. § 1.303-2(g)(1) requires that multiple redemptions of stock during the § 303(b)(1) period are applied against the total amount that qualifies for § 303 treatment in the order in which those redemptions occur, which could be important if the total redemptions exceed the § 303(a) amount and the dividend treatment with respect to each corporation differs.

[176] See § 303(b)(1). A petition properly filed in the Tax Court within this period extends the period until 60 days after the Tax Court's decision becomes final.

Under Rev. Rul. 65-289, 1965-2 C.B. 86, a note given by the corporation in redemption of stock constitutes a timely distribution if the redemption occurred within the requisite period, even though full payment of the note will not occur until well after the prescribed period. See also Rev. Rul. 67-425, 1967-2 C.B. 134.

[177] Under § 6166(g)(1)(B) a § 303 redemption is not a disqualifying disposition that triggers the acceleration provisions with respect to unpaid installments, provided that the estate pays an amount of tax equal to the money or other property received in the redemption not later than the first to occur of one year after the redemption or the first installment payment after the redemption.

§ 3.3.15.8

decedent's death are entitled to § 303 insulation from dividend treatment only to the extent of the lesser of taxes and expenses that remain unpaid immediately before the distribution or that actually are paid within one year after the distribution.

§3.3.15.9 Principal and Income Rules

Finally, in considering apportionment of the tax payment burden, an income and principal rule should be kept in mind. Typically estate income earned on assets that are expended for tax payment purposes remains income in the estate.[178] A will may, however, direct that this income be added to principal to help compensate for the diminution caused by the tax payment expenditure. Alternatively, the will could provide that the income also be used to pay taxes, in either event shifting a part of the burden of tax payment to the income beneficiaries.[179]

§3.3.16 Drafting Considerations

Because equity favors equality, if the provisions of an estate plan are ambiguous, the presumption favors apportionment of taxes to achieve equality, putting a heavy burden on drafting to alter that result. It also

---

[178] See, e.g., Uniform Principal and Income Act (1997 Act) §201(2)(A), 7A U.L.A. 471 (2006), and Revised Uniform Principal and Income Act (1962 Act) §5(b), 7A U.L.A. 570 (2006). An extreme example that illustrates this rule is Union Planters Nat'l Bank v. Dedman, 1998 WL 3342 (Tenn. Ct. App.), in which the tax payment provision placed the burden on the residue of the probate estate without apportionment and taxes attributable to nonprobate property exceeded the value of the estate as determined at the date of death. There was sufficient postmortem income and capital appreciation, however, to satisfy the tax payment obligation but the court held that postmortem income was payable to the residuary beneficiary under what it called the "Massachusetts" rule that the income beneficiaries enjoy the income from the entire residue and not just the income from whatever corpus remains after satisfaction of all payments from the residue. The result is counterintuitive in that it assumes there to be residuary income even though there is no residue, although it correctly reflects that, prior to payment of these estate charges, there is the possibility for investment returns to the estate that must be considered in drafting those provisions that dispose of the estate.

[179] And in the process raising the issue in *Street, Richardson, Hubert,* and *Allen.* See §3.3.7.3.

requires a clear indication of intent to deviate from state law, even if (for example) the old burden on the residue rule is applicable.

§3.3.16.1 Waiving Rights of Reimbursement

The federal rights of reimbursement and whether to preserve or waive them is so important an issue that it ought to come first in thinking about drafting. Each of §§ 2206, 2207, 2207A, 2207B and, in its special way, § 2603(b) create a right of reimbursement for taxes caused by an individual's death or a taxable transfer for GST purposes. Inadvertent waiver of these rights could be calamitous, given all the other property that might generate taxes and the possibility that there will be insufficient assets otherwise available to pay taxes under a burden on the residue apportionment rule. It is in reflection of this fact that the most recent of those rules, in §§ 2207A, 2207B, and 2603(b) all require a specific indication of intent to waive these rights of reimbursement.

Nevertheless, for liquidity purposes full apportionment is better than reimbursement because apportionment forces the recipient of property to make the initial payment while reimbursement requires the estate to pay initially and then seek a recovery of the expended assets.[180] Liquidity and the apportionment versus reimbursement issue is particularly important in a tax environment that includes Chapter 14 and state death taxes that could exceed the amount of a nonmarital trust, even in an otherwise nontaxable optimum marital deduction situation. If this occurs, marital deduction property may be needed to pay taxes, which will generate a loss of the marital deduction and a corresponding imposition of FET, with the need to further invade the marital property to pay those taxes, resulting in another loss of more deduction and, ultimately,

---

[180] Because of this format, there may be no entitlement to interest even if the beneficiary who must contribute under a reimbursement provision delays in making payment. See Morell Estate, 318 A.2d 727 (Pa. 1974) (because the primary duty to pay is on the personal representative, payment followed by reimbursement is not like a loan and amounts subject to reimbursement do not bear interest). See also In re Estate of Zambrano, 875 A.2d 307 (Pa. Super. Ct. 2005), citing *Morell* and noting that state law may dictate whether apportionment follows payment by the estate and whether it carries interest, the court stating that Pennsylvania law does not require payment first and that the document can specify whether interest should be incurred by a beneficiary who does not timely pay.

a whirlpool computation effect. Even equitable apportionment cannot protect against this result to the extent the marital bequest does not fully work to eliminate taxes.

On the generation-skipping side of this issue, Congress was well advised to presume against waiver of the reimbursement right by requiring a specific reference to the GST to negate § 2603(b). Without this requirement, inadvertent and serious consequences could attend an innocent provision included in a tax payment provision with no conscious intent to impose the GST on the decedent's estate.[181]

In addition, waiver of the § 2207A reimbursement right should be considered carefully. First because the § 2207A reimbursement right is for incremental tax, not pro rata, which may create a conflict with state law. And second because the regulations under § 2207A[182] provide that the simple failure to enforce the right of reimbursement is a gift (neither § 2206, § 2207, nor § 2207B so provide).[183] This liability often will be unexpected and the beneficiaries deemed to have made the gift likely will be without knowledge. It can be avoided if S as beneficiary of a QTIP trust waives the § 2207A right of reimbursement, making it is important that S have the flexibility to decide whether to preserve or waive this right of reimbursement. Thus, normally the QTIP trust should specify that taxes attributable to trust property will be paid from the trust before it is distributed, unless S's will overrides that direction by a provision making specific reference to the QTIP trust.

With respect to the requisite indication of intent required under § 2207A itself, consider In re Estate of Gordon, in which the decedent's tax clause read "I direct that all . . . taxes . . . imposed . . . by reason of my death with respect to any property includable in my estate . . . whether such property passes under or outside my will be paid out of my Residuary Estate . . . without apportionment."[184] A charitable residuary

---

[181] See § 3.3.6 for illustrative cases.

[182] Treas. Reg. § 20.2207A-1(a)(2).

[183] Although there is yet no authority for the proposition, it seems likely that the government will provide in regulations that failure to assert the § 2207B right of reimbursement also constitutes a gift, but that this consequence may be avoided by an effective waiver of the right itself—which will require a specific indication of intent to be effective.

[184] 510 N.Y.S.2d 815, 817 (Surr. Ct. 1986).

§ 3.3.16.1

bequest would have abated completely if the court had found that the §2207A reimbursement right had been waived by this provision. Instead the court found that this provision was not adequate and a subsequent amendment to §2207A now generates the same result nationwide, matching in principle a change to New York law[185] providing that a general direction in a will to pay all taxes imposed on account of the testator's death is not applicable to taxes imposed at S's death as beneficiary of a QTIP trust unless the will specifically provides otherwise.[186]

---

[185] N.Y. Est. Powers & Trusts Law §2-1.8(d-1) (1992). In TAM 9140005 the decedent's tax payment provision directed payment of all taxes caused by reason of the decedent's death "as if such taxes were my debts, without recovery of any part of such tax payments from anyone who receives any items included in such computation." In re Estate of Beebe, 702 N.Y.S.2d 683 (App. Div. 2000), involved a provision stating that "there . . . be no proration or apportionment" of taxes among the residuary beneficiaries, on whom the tax burden fell, notwithstanding that some were charitable beneficiaries to whom state law equitable apportionment otherwise would apply. In each case it was determined that the tax payment provision was sufficiently clear to overcome the equitable apportionment statute (N.Y. Est. Powers & Trusts Law §2-1.8(a)), which similarly requires a clear and unambiguous direction in the decedent's will. In re Estate of Kramer, 610 N.Y.S.2d 31 (App. Div. 1994), however, held that a direction to pay from the residue of the decedent's estate all estate taxes except those attributable to property includible in the decedent's gross estate under §§2035, 2039, and 2041 was not sufficient to overcome the statutory requirement for specific reference to waive the §2207A right of reimbursement. As a result, a decedent's daughter by a prior marriage was not burdened with taxes caused by inclusion of a QTIP marital deduction trust that passed to the children of the decedent's predeceased husband by his prior marriage. Also note that only the deceased beneficiary of the QTIP trust may waive the entitlement. The drafter of the QTIP trust itself may not alter this federal entitlement. In re Estate of Stark, 2011 WL 3687421 (unpub. N.J. Super. A.D.) (QTIP settlor purported to override §2207A reimbursement right if the surviving spouse died more than three years after the settlor).

[186] Other similar state statutes include Minn. Stat. Ann. §3-916(b)(2)(i) (requiring a specific indication of intent to overcome §2207A); N.C. Gen. Stat. §28A-27-2(b) (1994) (general direction to pay all taxes from decedent's estate without specifically stating otherwise does not waive reimbursement under §§2206, 2207, or 2207A); Ohio Rev. Code Ann. §2113.86(I) (1995) (requiring reference to either §2044 or its state law counterpart, or to QTIP); 20 Pa. Cons. Stat. §3701(2) (1995) (waiver must expressly refer to §2207A right of reimbursement).

§3.3.16.1

(Footnote Continued)

Other courts have reached the same nonwaiver conclusion without the benefit of a state statute, although the predictability of result in this respect is quite low. See, e.g., In re Maurice F. Jones Trust, 637 N.E.2d 1301 (Ind. Ct. App. 1994) (direction to pay all estate taxes assessed "by reason of my death . . . which I am legally obligated to pay at the time of my death . . . without apportionment" deemed ambiguous with respect to taxes caused by inclusion of QTIP trust corpus; extrinsic evidence was allowed to establish that the decedent did not intend to exonerate the remainder beneficiaries of the marital deduction trust who were relatives of the decedent's predeceased spouse and charities); Firstar Trust Co. v. First Nat'l Bank, 541 N.W.2d 467 (1995), aff'g in part and rev'g in part 525 N.W.2d 53 (Wis. Ct. App. 1994) (will directing payment of all taxes "payable by reason of my death" and that would have exhausted funds otherwise passing to charity was deemed insufficient to overcome § 2207A— although it *was* adequate to leave unchanged the state law burden on the residue for the Wisconsin estate tax attributable to the marital deduction trust). Consider also In re Marital Deduction Trust Under Will of Adair, 695 A.2d 250 (N.J. 1997), in which the court concluded that the decedent's tax payment provision was "generic, boilerplate" that did not "evince a clear and unequivocal intention" to direct against apportionment of the tax burden.

In Eisenbach v. Schneider, 166 P.3d 358 (Wash. Ct. App. 2007), the issue was whether the incremental reimbursement regime of § 2207A was superseded by the decedents' pro rata apportionment dictate. The trial court rejected the § 2207A specific reference requirement—not saying that it was met, but instead saying:

> To interpret Section 2207A to override the testators' intent because they failed to use magic words enacted after their testamentary documents had been drafted and signed would constitute a broad reach for a federal statute, especially where the federal government has nothing to gain from the interpretation.

Citing Riggs v. Del Drago, 317 U.S. 95 (1942), to the effect that state law trumps federal law on the question of tax apportionment, the court on appeal held that Congress' purpose when imposing the specific reference requirement was to prevent decedents from "inadvertently" waiving the federal right of reimbursement, and that there is no hint in the committee reports that "a clear statement of testamentary intent regarding the allocation of the tax burden is to be displaced by the provisions of [§ 2207A]." The court then distinguished all prior cases on the specific reference requirement because all contained "general pay-all-taxes clauses" and not a provision retaining apportionment (albeit in a different amount than the federal, incremental tax regime).

Showing that *Eisenbach* did not start a trend, however, and involving the more normal pay-all-taxes, waive-all-reimbursement-rights case, see In re Blauhorn Revocable Trust, 746 N.W.2d 136 (Neb. 2008), citing *Riggs* but nevertheless holding that "§ 2207A pre-empts any applicable state law to the extent

As a matter of routine, similar results should be expected under § 2207B[187] with respect to property that is includible in a decedent's gross estate under § 2036, although some refinement will be required by virtue of the fact that the specific reference requirement originally part of § 2207B was moderated to make it identical to that added to § 2207A in 1997. Case law informed by the different rules before these provisions were coordinated might produce different results.[188]

For comparison purposes, the following language was adequate to waive §§ 2206 and 2207 rights of reimbursement in a case involving no "special" remainder beneficiary: "All estate taxes payable by reason of my death shall be chargeable against and payable out of my residuary

---

(Footnote Continued)

that state law might purport to deal with the payment of *federal estate tax attributable to qualified terminable interest property*" and that the tax provision did not effectively waive § 2207A (emphasis in original).

[187] Compare TAMs 199918003 and 199915001 (typical pay-all-taxes-from-the-residue provisions with nonspecific waiver of reimbursement language were inadequate to override § 2207B, notwithstanding that, in the earlier case, the same language *was* sufficient to waive reimbursement rights under § 2206 with respect to an insurance trust that was includible by virtue of § 2035) with Myers v. Ellerbusch, 746 N.E.2d 408 (Ind. Ct. App. 2001) (corporate fiduciary's formbook tax payment direction to pay

> all estate and inheritance taxes assessed by reason of my death whether with respect to property passing under this Will or property passing otherwise than under the Will and whether such taxes be payable by my estate or by any recipient of any such property. I waive for my estate all rights of reimbursement for any payments made pursuant to this item

was deemed adequate to waive the § 2207B reimbursement right notwithstanding the lack of any reference to § 2036 includible property or to § 2207B). Shoemaker v. Gindlesberger, 887 N.E.2d 1167 (Ohio 2008), discussed in § 1.0 n.5, applied the privity defense to attorney malpractice, and arose because a retained life estate in property transferred inter vivos generated § 2036(a)(1) inclusion and the corresponding estate tax liability reduced the decedent's residuary estate. That would not have been an issue if the decedent's tax payment provision had either preserved or had unambiguously waived the § 2207B right of reimbursement.

[188] Decided without having to evaluate the § 2207B specific reference or specific indication of intent requirement, In re Estate of Meyer, 702 N.E.2d 1078 (Ind. Ct. App. 1998), makes note of this change in the law. Arzt v. Savarese, 36 F. Supp. 2d 653 (D. Del. 1999), held it to be determinative because both includible trusts long predated the December 17, 1987 effective date of § 2207B.

§ 3.3.16.1

estate without contribution by anyone."[189] The court reached this result notwithstanding the drafter's testimony that the decedent and the drafter were unaware of nonprobate assets and that the purpose of the provision was to avoid inside apportionment only. Similarly in contrast with *Gordon*, Estate of Vahlteich v. Commissioner[190] originally held that a residuary charitable bequest was reduced by a tax payment provision calling for payment of "all transfer, estate or inheritance taxes . . . without apportionment." Notwithstanding that state law called for outside apportionment unless the decedent referred specifically to the statute "or to qualified terminable interest property." Lacking the statutory requisite of a reference to either § 2044 or its state law counterpart, or to QTIP, the court on appeal concluded that the Tax Court's holding that the decedent's will waived the QTIP trust's § 2207A and state law equitable apportionment share of the FET liability of the decedent "is wrong in its reading of [Ohio Rev. Code Ann. § 2113.86(I)] and doubly wrong in not reflecting the proper policy of the State" to preclude inadvertent exoneration of the QTIP. Especially if the result is that residuary charitable beneficiaries receive less and taxes are increased unnecessarily. "This is simply counterintuitive on its face and counter to a presumption in Ohio law that a testator intends to maximize deductions and pass as much to chosen beneficiaries as possible."

A similar burden on the residue variety tax payment provision was involved in TAM 9434004. It waived all rights of reimbursement and was deemed to override state apportionment rules that would have pro rated the tax liability against includible nonprobate properties. After making several preresiduary bequests, the will divided what it referred to as the residue into a formula bequest that it described as "the exemption

---

[189] In re Estate of Bruce, 516 N.Y.S.2d 748 (App. Div. 1987). Consistent and easier yet to regard as correct is In re Estate of Coe Marital and Residuary Trusts, 593 N.W.2d 190 (Mich. Ct. App. 1999) (general power of appointment marital deduction trust includible in S's gross estate that otherwise was not taxable; will provision nevertheless brought the tax liability into the probate estate by directing the personal representative "not to seek reimbursement of taxes from, and not to apportion any taxes among any persons receiving property by reason of my death"). See Estate of Cohen v. Crown, discussed in § 3.3.16.6 n.207 by way of comparison in a case involving potential reduction of a charitable deduction.

[190] 67 T.C.M. (CCH) 2704 (1994), rev'd in an unpublished opinion, 95-2 U.S. Tax Cas. (CCH) ¶ 60,218 (6th Cir. 1995).

§ 3.3.16.1

equivalent of the maximum unified credit allowable in determining the FET on my gross estate" and left the residue of the residue to a marital deduction trust. The formula bequest made reference to the preresiduary bequests passing under the will that did not qualify for the marital deduction but did not indicate that it also should have been reduced by the includible nonprobate assets or inter vivos gifts that consumed a portion of the decedent's unified credit because they too did not qualify for the marital deduction. As a result, the formula bequest called for an amount that was larger than the amount that could be sheltered from tax payment by what remained of the decedent's unified credit and taxes were incurred that were payable from the marital deduction residue. This reduced the estate's marital deduction, which increased the tax liability that also was payable from the marital bequest, resulting in a circular whirlpool computation of the decedent's FET liability.[191]

With respect to Chapter 14, §2701(d) presents difficulty because it is not clear who benefits by virtue of the deemed transfer attributable to unpaid suspense account dividends. Therefore, if outside apportionment exists under state law it is unclear who should pay any tax incurred under that provision. The value of the unpaid dividends may be reflected in the value of the underlying stock and, to that extent, will not be subjected to a separate tax under §2701(d). Thus, this issue may resolve itself in all but the more unusual valuation situations. But if it does not, payment from the residue of the tax attributable to the suspense account

---

[191] In addition, because the inter vivos transfers, the nonprobate includible assets, and the improperly described formula bequest totaled more than the $600,000 exemption equivalent at that time, and the marital deduction did not eliminate taxes in this estate, the marginal estate tax bracket in which the estate was taxable was higher than the 37% marginal rate that normally was applicable in computing the "exemption equivalent" of the $192,800 unified credit that applied at that time. This created its own circular computation because, at a higher marginal rate, less than $600,000 of total taxable property generated the same $192,800 of tax liability ("exemption equivalent of the unified credit" applicable in that estate), which caused the formula bequest to be smaller, resulting in a greater residue of the residue qualifying for the marital deduction. This produced slightly less tax and therefore a slightly larger marital deduction as a result of its own secondary circular computation, and that again affected the exemption equivalent computation, setting off another round of interrelated computations.

§3.3.16.1

may be inappropriate. Consequently, thought should be given to whether the donee of junior equities or the entity that was obligated to pay the dividends should pay the tax attributable to this account. State law outside apportionment is unlikely to answer this question.

Under §2702, a QPRT, a qualified interest, or a joint purchase that is treated as a split interest trust all may trigger §2036(a)(1) inclusion if the decedent's interest does not terminate before death. In each case inclusion should cause §2207B or outside apportionment under state law to apply.[192] Meanwhile, §2703 raises the prospect of FET inclusion at a value that is higher than the striking price under a buy-sell agreement. Conceivably the buyer could be regarded as an estate beneficiary to whom taxes attributable to this value differential should be apportioned, although the absence of an agreement anticipating this result is sure to generate litigation.[193]

Finally, §2704 poses a problem similar to that under §2701(d) because the deemed transfer attributable to the lapse or imposition of a restriction has no readily apparent transferee to whom the generated tax should be apportioned. The logical source for payment of the tax is the property as to which the restriction applies.

---

[192] The statement in text could be exactly wrong, however, depending on a number of factors. Consider, for example, the tax apportionment complication raised by §2036(a)(1) inclusion of a QPRT in Del Broccolo v. Torres, 780 N.Y.S.2d 857 (S. Ct. 2004). Part of a wrongful death recovery was based on an otherwise avoidable estate tax, attributable to a QPRT that would have terminated naturally just eight months after the untimely tortious death.

[193] See, e.g., In re Estate of Kapala, 402 N.W.2d 150 (Minn. Ct. App. 1987) (insurance funded buy-sell agreement generated tax in the decedent's estate that was apportioned to the buyer, notwithstanding an argument that the buy-sell agreement established the total liability of the buyer and was silent on this issue), Estate of Benton, 215 N.W.2d 86 (Neb. 1974), and In re Estate of Galewitz, 160 N.Y.S.2d 564 (App. Div. 1957) (both similarly treating buyers as estate beneficiaries, liable for pro rata taxes attributable to the imputed benefit received); but see In re Estate of Saylors, 671 N.E.2d 905 (Ind. Ct. App. 1996) (buyers were not liable for the inheritance tax attributable to a farm valued at $281,000 but acquired under an option to purchase it for $1,000; the tax payment provision waived all apportionment and, even if apportionment had applied, the court regarded the estate as including the proceeds and not the farm).

§3.3.16.1

§3.3.16.2 Items to Consider

A good tax clause will address the following topics clearly, even if state law is clear on many of these concepts, because of the migratory nature of clients and the potential conflict of laws problems that could arise.

• Which taxes are being apportioned (estate, generation-skipping, Chapter 14, state, income, alternative minimum income, and appreciation estate taxes).

• Both inside and outside apportionment, or the waiver thereof, clearly should be covered; often only outside apportionment is contemplated and statutory inside apportionment across the entire estate is forgotten.

• Equitable apportionment should be considered; it usually will be the client's intent to embrace it, even if no other form of apportionment is desired.

• Any intent to preserve the effect of state wealth transfer tax computation differentials (if any exist).

• Any desire to allocate credits to recipients of assets to which they relate.

• Alteration of the apportionment rule relative to temporal interests, particularly in estates with annuity or installment payouts of retirement benefits.

• Whether interest and penalties should be treated in the same manner as the taxes to which they relate.

• If it is known that there will be deductible claims against the estate, such as pursuant to a prenuptial or separation agreement, and they are similar to or in lieu of bequests from the estate, the determination of the size of those dispositions and apportionment of taxes to them, frequently applying the same considerations applicable to other bequests. Especially sensitive, however, is whether the agreement permits apportionment and whether various issues noted here were considered in the preparation of that agreement.

• Whether it is appropriate to look to particular assets first for tax payment, or whether the decedent intended to preserve certain assets. A stated preference to protect certain assets probably should not be allowed to override other presumably more important apportionment principles. For example, in Estate of Reno v. Commissioner,[194] the preference for preservation of farm property was alleged to cause marital deduction property to be tapped for tax payment. If this had been correct, the tax payment provision

---

[194] 945 F.2d 733 (4th Cir. 1991), rev'g (en banc) 916 F.2d 955 (4th Cir. 1990), which aff'd 51 T.C.M. (CCH) 909 (1986).

would have negated the concept of equitable apportionment and generated a tax, because the marital deduction would have been reduced.

As a checklist of other commonly overlooked apportionment issues that are discussed herein but don't always arise, remember to consider:

- Fees and expenses.

- State taxes that don't conform to FET rules and that can produce disparities.

- Special use valuation and recapture under § 2032A.

- Future interests that invoke tax that may be deferred under § 6163.

- Deferral of tax under § 6166 and the question of who shall pay the deferred tax and interest thereon.

- With respect to any apportionment that is preserved, how enforcement will be effected and whether to include a power of setoff in the client's will for any dispositions of probate property to takers of nonprobate property that will bear a share of the tax burden.

§ 3.3.16.3 Pro Rata or Incremental Apportionment

Incremental apportionment (like reimbursement under § 2207A) may be desirable because the § § 2206, 2207, and 2207B entitlements to only a proportionate amount of all taxes in the estate may nearly bankrupt a small probate estate that is taxed along with massive amounts of nonprobate property (such as a huge § 2056(b)(5) power of appointment marital deduction trust). A change to incremental apportionment (deviating from the pro rata approach dictated by most state statutes and by § § 2206, 2207, and 2207B) probably is permissible. The tax payment provision simply should call for apportionment of the amount by which the decedent's taxes were increased by virtue of nonprobate assets being included in the estate. But if there are several nonprobate items as to which incremental apportionment is to apply, the tax provision must specify the manner in which they will be considered for allocation purposes.

For example, if there was a marital deduction trust and substantial retirement benefits causing inclusion, the planner should consider whether either should be deemed included before the other for computation of the taxes caused by inclusion of each. They could be aggregated and the total increase in tax caused by both then prorated between them, which might be appropriate if remainder beneficiaries of each differ and the incremental tax burden should be shared pro rata by all. A third alternative would be to apportion taxes to each nonprobate asset as if the subject asset was taxed last, thereby imposing on the aggregate of the nonprobate property a larger share of taxes than either a pro rata share or the aggregate incremental share of tax.[195]

In any event, if apportionment is preserved, the order for computation of any bequest or share of the estate and for payment of taxes should be specified if it is not clear under state law. It is surprising how seldom this is done, given the number of cases revealing that the proper method frequently is unclear. Thus, for example, it should be specified clearly whether a gross or a net estate division is desired in computing a marital deduction fractional share.

§ 3.3.16.4 Be Wary of Discretionary Reimbursement

Unless a fiduciary's overriding duty to maximize the estate is waived, a right to allocate taxes probably is a duty instead, meaning that it is not discretionary at all. So flexibility the drafter thought was provided may prove to be illusory. If the duty to maximize the estate is waived to avoid this duty, then it is wise to specify the factors to be considered by the fiduciary in deciding whether to seek reimbursement, in which case "discretion" may approach a mechanical application of the relevant factors. And if discretion is meant to be granted, the fiduciary should be informed clearly of the tax consequences of a failure to seek reimbursement (for example, under § 2207A) and the income tax consequences of exercising discretion. These are complex decisions and it may be wise to spell them out in a letter to be included with the estate plan if the estate planner may not be advising the administration. In addition, conflicts of interest that may affect the exercise of fiduciary discretion should be considered if the personal representative will be personally interested in the outcome of the discretionary apportionment.

---

[195] Cf. 2003 Revised Uniform Estate Tax Apportionment Act § 3(c) and the last paragraph of the Comment to it, suggesting that such a provision may not be valid under that state law.

§ 3.3.16.4

§ 3.3.16.5 Coordinate Multiple Tax Clauses

As frequently occurs, it is likely that several tax clauses will (or should) be involved if a client has a funded living trust and perhaps an ILIT, both in addition to a will directing disposition of the probate estate. Most decisions indicate that the provision in the will controls to the extent those clauses differ or are contradictory.[196] But some cases hold that the later in time controls, which may be a trust.[197] As among other documents, no clear order of priority exists. More importantly, the pre-2003 versions of the Uniform Acts and § § 2206 and 2207 all ostensibly require that waiver of apportionment or reimbursement be by a will

---

[196] But cases go the other way, particularly if that appears to be the more equitable result. See, e.g., Estate of Thornhill v. Bloom, 2010 WL 1222757 (unpub. Ind. Ct. App. 2010), which involved a will that contained a "burden on the residue" tax payment mandate ("all taxes . . . shall be paid") that waived "reimbursement from any person" (meaning that it reversed the state law apportionment regime) and a trust that merely granted the trustee authority to pay ("the Trustee may, in the Trustee's discretion, pay . . . the estate and inheritance Taxes . . . directly or, alternatively, in the sole discretion of the Trustee, distribute such sums to the Personal Representative as shall be necessary to pay all or any portion of such taxes") and said nothing about apportionment or reimbursement. The state law apportionment statute required that any rebuttal of the state presumption of apportionment must be directed by a provision in the decedent's will, and said nothing about provisions in a trust. The decedent's estate was inadequate to pay all the taxes incurred, the trust therefore made payments, and the court required apportionment of those payments among the trust beneficiaries. Notwithstanding the express provision overriding apportionment in the decedent's will. This bizarre result is equitable (because everyone pays their own share) but quaere whether it was the decedent's intent.

[197] See In re Estate of Meyer, 702 N.E.2d 1078 (Ind. Ct. App. 1998); In re Estate of Pickrell, 806 P.2d 1007 (Kan. 1991). In re Estate of Patouillet, 601 N.Y.S.2d 385 (Surr. Ct. 1993), involved a will executed before a funded living trust, which benefited different individuals and provided that the trustee was to pay the decedent's executor any amounts designated by the executor as necessary to pay the estate's taxes. The will, however, directed payment of all taxes attributable to nonprobate property and waived all apportionment rights. The court held that N.Y. Est. Powers & Trust Law § 2-1.8(d)(2) provided that the nontestamentary document that was executed later in time would control and, in this case, that meant the trust would contribute.

Multiple inconsistent tax clauses also can occur a single document. Consistent perhaps with a later-in-time principle regarding multiple documents, In re McDevitt, 889 N.Y.S.2d 506 (Surr. Ct. 2009), held that the provision appearing later in the document controlled.

§ 3.3.16.5

provision. Only the Revised Uniform Act and §§ 2207A, 2207B, and § 2603(b) allow waiver by the decedent's trust as well. Thus, although waiver of reimbursement by a provision in a trust or other document may not succeed if the will does not *also* waive the right, it probably can't hurt (unless there is an inconsistency) for each document to state the client's intent.

The significance of this is well illustrated by Estate of Roe,[198] in which the decedent's will provided that "I make no direction for the payment of . . . taxes assessed by reason of my death, as I have provided for their payment under a certain Agreement hereinafter mentioned." The trust called for tax payment and specified that "the Trustee shall not seek contribution from anyone for any portion of the taxes so paid." The court held that apportionment under state law would apply, notwithstanding this clear intent that the trust pay for all, because the will failed to waive application of the state apportionment statute.[199] The most notable aspect of *Roe* is that the tax clauses involved were verbatim from a major Chicago fiduciary's forms book. This problem exists in literally thousands of estate plans nationwide.[200]

---

[198] 426 N.W.2d 797, 798, 799 (Mich. Ct. App. 1988).

[199] The court noted that an argument might be made that the trust waived apportionment so no further allocation of the tax burden from the trustee to other recipients of taxable property would be required, even though the will failed to prevent apportionment to the trust. But even if successful, that argument would not be helpful if some of the tax paid by the trust was attributable to other nonprobate assets that were required under state law to pay their proportionate share of the tax burden directly.

[200] The problem arises most frequently in the context of tax apportionment provisions contained in pour over wills and revocable trusts. Estate of Fagan v. Commissioner, 77 T.C.M. (CCH) 1427 (1999), is illustrative. The decedent's pour over will and revocable inter vivos trust each contained a tax apportionment clause. The will directed that all taxes be paid from the residue without apportionment. The trust agreement directed the trustee to pay to the decedent's executor such amounts as the executor might request and to charge all transfer taxes to shares passing to the grantor's descendants and none to a charity's bequest. The estate tax return thus reflected a charitable disposition not reduced by taxes. The Tax Court agreed with the government's argument that the charitable disposition should be reduced by a proportionate share of the taxes, because the will overruled the default equitable apportionment state law rule requiring the executor to pay all taxes from the residuary estate, without

With respect to the other end of the spectrum, if there is a tax payment obligation in more than one document, and taxes may be paid by more than one entity, the estate plan must coordinate these documents to specify how the burden is computed for each and how aggregated apportionment will work.

It makes sense to include a safety valve tax clause in trusts (such as an ILIT or a GRAT) that are intended to escape inclusion if everything goes as planned. That provision might specify that the fiduciary may purchase assets from the grantor's estate or loan money to it, to provide liquidity, and taxes caused by inclusion of any part of the trust that is includible in the grantor's estate are payable from that portion. To succeed probably requires that the grantor's estate plan not waive apportionment with respect to the trust. Also, the trust document needs to

---

(Footnote Continued)

apportionment. The court agreed that the language in the trust relieving the charitable disposition from taxes had no effect.

Fagan is particularly unsatisfactory. The fact that the trustee did not itself pay the taxes should not preclude the trustee from calculating the beneficiaries' shares by reference to the tax apportionment language contained in the trust instrument. Nevertheless, the message of *Fagan* is clear that the apportionment language was in the wrong document.

Cf. Estate of McCoy v. Commissioner, 97 T.C.M. (CCH) 1312 (2009), in which the tax clauses in a pour over will and the receptacle trust were not properly coordinated but the court applied equitable apportionment to protect a marital deduction bequest from reduction. Estate of Miller v. Commissioner, 76 T.C.M. (CCH) 892 (1998), aff'd per curiam, 209 F.3d 720 (5th Cir. 2000), reached a similar conclusion for essentially the same reason. Compare Patterson v. United States, 181 F.3d 927 (8th Cir. 1999), in which the decedent's estate plan also consisted of a pour over will that directed the executor to pay all death taxes "out of the residue of [the estate]," adding that taxes also could be paid from the decedent's inter vivos trust in the trustee's discretion. The court held that its first objective was to determine the decedent's intent, that "[t]he will and the trust [agreement] must be considered and construed together to determine which document shall govern the apportionment of death taxes," and that "the documents unambiguously express the decedent's intent to give the trustee discretion to pay taxes from the trust estate" without causing a reduction in the decedent's marital deduction. Quoting from In re Estate of Pickrell, 806 P.2d 1007, 1011 (Kan. 1991). The court probably overstated the clarity of the decedent's tax apportionment directions, so the important point was the court's willingness to construe all of the estate planning instruments together to ascertain the decedent's intent and minimize unnecessary taxes.

§ 3.3.16.5

clearly provide that this provision operates only if, quite independently, the trust is found to be includible, so as not to generate inclusion in the first instance.[201]

Further, caution must be exercised with respect to ILITs because the last sentence of §2206 presumes that insurance included in a decedent's gross estate will be used first to qualify for any available marital deduction. This means that, if there is a contingent marital deduction provision in the ILIT, principles of equitable apportionment may apply to and override any tax payment provision in the trust.

§3.3.16.6 Clearly Specify Intent

The case reporters are full of decisions involving the meaning of provisions relating to tax apportionment. Notwithstanding state law, many estate plans waive all apportionment and impose all taxes as a burden on the residue, as provided under common law. Apportionment rules create a more equitable method for payment of taxes and may represent the average decedent's intent when thought is given to the issue, but they create problems of their own, particularly of an administrative and enforcement nature.

As a general rule, the intent for a will provision (or, if permitted by state or federal law, a provision in some other instrument) to override a state apportionment statute must be expressed in language that is "clear, definite and unambiguous."[202] Cases differ significantly, however, on the

---

[201] See, for example, TAM 9533001, in which an ILIT instrument provided that any insurance proceeds that proved to be includible in the insured settlor's gross estate were to be poured-back to the settlor's revocable inter vivos trust. Footnote 2 of the TAM stated the government's position that the possibility that the policy proceeds might be payable to the revocable trust was inadequate to make a transfer of policies to the irrevocable trust incomplete for gift tax purposes. On that finding a gift tax was owed, and under the facts of the TAM §2042 inclusion was not relevant; §2035(a)(2) inclusion was triggered instead. Nothing in the TAM indicated whether the government might assert that the pour-back provision itself might cause §2042(1) inclusion, which would trigger the pour-back provision, all in some circular cause and effect dance.

[202] See In re Mescall's Will, 281 N.Y.S.2d 394, 397 (Surr. Ct. 1967). Compare illustrative cases such as In re Estate of Erieg, 267 A.2d 841 (Pa. 1970) (a classic burden-on-the-residue provision that did not alter Pennsylvania statutory equitable apportionment, thus preserving the marital deduction); Estate of Shannon v.

degree of specificity required. As a planning matter, therefore, the intent concerning apportionment questions should be expressed in as clear and specific terms as possible and, if a state enacts new apportionment legislation, it may be advisable to revise the estate plan to clarify the testator's intent.[203]

A seemingly straightforward tax payment provision may present numerous interpretative questions. Consider, for example, a simple attempt to override a state apportionment statute—the task requires more than simply directing "payment of all debts, expenses, and taxes from

---

(Footnote Continued)

Commissioner, 60 T.C.M. (CCH) 1361 (1990) (similar general burden-on-the-residue language was insufficient to override statutory apportionment); and Estate of Brunetti v. Commissioner, 56 T.C.M. (CCH) 580 (1988) (similar lack of an unambiguous direction caused the California equitable apportionment statute to apply, preserving a charitable deduction); with In re Succession of Haydel, 780 So.2d 1168 (La. Ct. App. 2001) (a provision instructing that estate tax charges on particular legatees be deducted from the gross value of assets before determination of the "net children's estate" was deemed to override the Louisiana apportionment statute, causing taxes to be charged to a residual QTIP trust); and Estate of Ransburg v. United States, 765 F. Supp. 1388 (S.D. Ind. 1990) (a nonspecific direction to pay all taxes was deemed to overcome state law equitable apportionment). See also In re Hanson Revocable Trust, 779 N.E.2d 1218 (Ind. Ct. App. 2002) (despite language giving trustee "discretion" to pay taxes, and despite the Illinois burden-on-residue rule, the trust settlor's intent to apportion taxes to all trust assets was sufficiently clear to require the trustee to apportion taxes to real estate and thus preserve the shares of residuary beneficiaries); PLR 200206024 (provisions in the decedent's will and revocable trust were not sufficiently clear and unambiguous to override the Colorado statute apportioning taxes generated by residuary bequests among all nondeductible residuary beneficiaries).

[203] In re Estate of Long, 918 P.2d 975 (Wash. Ct. App. 1996), illustrates the point. Washington followed the common law burden-on-the-residue rule when Edward Long executed his will in 1981. Edward's will made specific bequests to his daughters and left the residuary estate to his wife. The will overrode the default state apportionment rule by directing that each beneficiary would bear a proportionate share of all estate taxes. Washington adopted the Uniform Act in 1986, which implemented equitable apportionment and allows testators to direct otherwise by will. Edward died in 1993 and his widow argued that Edward did not intend for her share of the estate to be burdened by a portion of the taxes (all of which were generated by the specific bequests). The court ruled against the widow, holding that the will was effective to override the state apportionment statute, notwithstanding that the will was written before the statute was enacted.

§ 3.3.16.6

the residue of my estate," or directing the personal representative to "pay all taxes imposed on my estate by reason of my death" or to "pay all taxes out of my residuary estate without apportionment." Among the questions raised by provisions such as these is whether they actually waive apportionment, or only direct payment of taxes, which after payment may be apportioned through the reimbursement right.[204] If the decedent's death triggers a taxable termination or direct skip for GST purposes, does the language in the will mean that the estate has as-

---

[204] For example, in Estate of Fine v. Commissioner, 90 T.C. 1068 (1988), D's will directed payment of taxes "without apportionment," which in all likelihood was meant to impose the tax burden on the residue without apportionment to or contribution from takers of includible nonprobate property. The court determined, however, that the effect was to override a state statute calling for equitable apportionment of all taxes to the nonmarital portion of the estate. As a result, the court held that D's estate available for division between S and others was the residue left after payment of taxes, rather than dividing the estate before such payment and charging the taxes to the nonmarital share. The net effect was to reduce the allowable marital deduction.

See also Estate of Bradford v. Commissioner, 84 T.C.M. (CCH) 337 (2002) (decedent's will and trust indicated that taxes were to be paid from the residue before funding a charitable share and overrode equitable apportionment, thus reducing charitable share and deduction); Estate of Miller v. Commissioner, 76 T.C.M. (CCH) 892 (1998) (tax payment provision directing residuary estate to bear the entire burden was adequate to override state law equitable and outside apportionment, notwithstanding reduction of marital deduction as a result); Estate of McKay v. Commissioner, 68 T.C.M. (CCH) 279 (1994) (notwithstanding that 75% of the residue passed to charities, decedent's will directing payment of all taxes imposed on the probate estate from the residue without apportionment among the residuary beneficiaries was sufficient to require reduction of charitable bequest and the corresponding charitable deduction). But in McKeon v. United States, 151 F.3d 1201 (9th Cir. 1998), and Estate of Brunetti v. Commissioner, 56 T.C.M. (CCH) 580 (1988), involving marital and charitable deductions, respectively, and similar tax payment provisions, the courts refused to accept the government's position that the deduction should be reduced, because the courts read the state law apportionment rules as being applicable unless clearly overruled, and found that sufficient ambiguity existed in each document to preclude a finding of a clear intent to abandon that otherwise favored result. The government itself reached the same result in PLR 200206024, finding that state law equitable apportionment applied to a burden on the residue direction, such that residuary charitable and marital bequests were not obliged to contribute to the tax payment obligation.

Estate of Swallen is to the same effect. See n.225 and accompanying text.

§3.3.16.6

sumed the burden for those taxes that normally are imposed on the generation-skipping trust or property?[205] Should the provision be interpreted to include any additional FET imposed under §2032A upon a recapture event with respect to any special use property?[206] Or the §529(c)(4)(C) recapture tax? Does the reference to "my estate" mean the gross estate, the taxable estate, or the probate estate?[207] You get the picture.

---

[205] Estate of Green v. Commissioner, 86 T.C.M. (CCH) 758 (2003), held that the decedent intended to exonerate direct skip bequests from the GST but did not effectively exonerate them from state or federal *estate* tax, causing the GST to be imposed on the other residuary beneficiary, which was a charity, causing a reduction in the estate tax charitable deduction that generated estate tax that was imposed on the direct skip beneficiaries under state law equitable apportionment, nevertheless resulting in more wealth passing to the direct skip beneficiaries than if §2603(b) had applied, all in accordance with the decedent's apparent intent.

[206] See §3.3.11 for discussions of apportionment of recapture taxes.

[207] See, e.g., Landmark Trust Co. v. Aitken, 587 N.E.2d 1076 (Ill. App. Ct. 1992), in which litigation was needed to ascertain the decedent's intent because the will simply directed payment of all taxes from the residue, which was insufficient, and it was not clear whether state common law equitable apportionment should apply with respect to the balance. The court determined that state law apportionment was negated entirely by the tax clause and that common law abatement principles were applicable to determine how the excess taxes were to be paid. The result was that general bequests abated while specific bequests were protected from paying their proportionate share of the excess taxes. On the other hand, In re Estate of Williams, 853 N.E.2d 79 (Ill. App. Ct. 2006), and Rosen v. Wells Fargo Bank Texas, 114 S.W.3d 145 (Tex. Ct. App. 2003), held that pay-from-the-residue provisions that failed (because the residue was insufficient) resulted in state law equitable apportionment being applicable, causing nonprobate taxable transfers to bear the excess tax burden rather than deductible bequests. Reynolds v. Reynolds, 2007 WL 1234525 (R.I. Super. Ct.), involved TOD and other nonprobate property and a will provision directing payment "as an expense of administration, all estate, legacy, succession and inheritance taxes," which the court held was not "a clear and unambiguous directive" adequate to override state outside apportionment under the Uniform Act. According to the court the direction was only regarded as directing against inside apportionment among probate assets. Similarly, Barlow v. Brubaker, 465 N.W.2d 276 (Iowa 1991), held that a tax payment provision directing payment from the residue without apportionment did not relieve the recipients of property transferred inter vivos—but included in the decedent's gross estate under §2035—from paying their proportionate share of the tax bill. The estate was insufficient

§3.3.16.6

to pay all taxes and the will specified that these inter vivos donees should receive nothing under the will because the decedent had provided for them otherwise. Relief from taxation would have amounted to a testamentary benefit contrary to the decedent's stated intent.

See also First Nat'l Bank v. McGill, 377 S.E.2d 464 (W. Va. 1988), and Bunting v. Bunting, 768 A.2d 989 (Conn. App. Ct. 2000), in which the decedent made a sizeable inter vivos gift to a child, as to which the gift tax was less than the available unified credit. At death that gift, added to the taxable estate, caused the remaining property to incur estate tax in excess of the unified credit. The issue was whether the decedent's direction to pay all taxes from the residue of the estate was meant to apply—given that the residue was less than the combined state and federal taxes due at death. The court concluded that the decedent never anticipated that the inter vivos gift would cause taxes to be generated and therefore could not have intended for the tax payment provision to relieve the inter vivos donee of responsibility to pay estate taxes attributable to inclusion of the taxable gift in the adjusted taxable gifts base for estate tax computation purposes. Therefore, the court apportioned *estate* tax to the donee of that inter vivos gift. In addition to being completely wrong in citing and relying on the § 2012 credit for gift tax paid on pre-1977 gifts (the gift in *Bunting* was made in 1988), the dissent argued that the court improperly admitted extrinsic evidence regarding the decedent's understanding of the tax law and the decedent's intent (and that of the drafter of the document). But courts are not alone in making demonstrable blunders in this arena. For a good collection of cases dealing with sloppy drafting, consult Annot., Construction and effect of will provisions not expressly mentioning payment of death taxes but relied on as affecting the burden of estate or inheritance taxes, 70 A.L.R.3d 630 (1976); Annot., Construction and effect of provisions in nontestamentary instrument relied upon as affecting the burden of estate or inheritance taxes, 70 A.L.R.3d 691 (1976); and Annot., Construction and effect of will provisions expressly relating to the burden of estate or inheritance taxes, 69 A.L.R.3d 122 (1976).

Williams rejected the suggestion that "pay [all estate, inheritance, transfer, and succession taxes] from the residue of my estate . . . without apportionment or reimbursement," clarified D's intent. The question was whether an all-income, general power of appointment marital deduction trust should pay the estate tax caused by its § 2041 inclusion in S's estate, or whether the residue of S's estate should pay, which would adeem a charitable residuary bequest. The majority concluded that the pay-all-taxes provision in S's will "merely shows an intent to prohibit the beneficiary of the residue from seeking apportionment from the beneficiaries of the probate and nonprobate assets," but that it did not address the question of what would happen if S's residuary estate was insufficient to pay all taxes. Illinois lacked a tax apportionment statute but Illinois case law has "consistently applied the doctrine of equitable apportionment . . . among recipients of probate and nonprobate assets," unless "the testator has expressed

Consider first the question of *which taxes* the tax payment provision was intended to address. Does a direction to pay "all taxes without apportionment" override state apportionment law—both *inside and outside*—with respect to both *state and federal* estate taxes? Should it be

---

(Footnote Continued)

a clear intention to the contrary." Here the court concluded that the pay-all-taxes and waive-all-reimbursement provision was insufficient to alter that apportionment result.

In Estate of Malik v. Lashkariya, 861 N.E.2d 272 (Ill. App. Ct. 2006), the will directed "all taxes shall be paid by my estate" and this *was* deemed adequate to alter apportionment and place the full burden on the residue of the probate estate—in that case involving over $500,000 of life insurance (includible under § 2042), another $230,000 of joint tenancy property (includible under § 2040), and undisclosed value in a retail business and other probate assets that were substantially reduced by the tax burden. *Williams* may have reached the right result—that the power of appointment trust pay the taxes caused by its inclusion—but it generated a strong dissent based on an accurate assessment that "the majority manufactures testamentary ambiguity out of dislike for . . . the results."

Oddly, neither opinion addressed the existence of the federal § 2207 right of reimbursement, much less the more targeted question whether the will provision was sufficient to waive its application. In *Malik* no mention was even made of § 2206, the federal right of reimbursement for taxes attributable to § 2042, which appeared to generate over 50% of the taxable estate. Leaving the reader to wonder whether the litigants in both cases did not brief the issue of tax apportionment versus reimbursement. Unresolved in *Williams* was the fact that the marital trust default beneficiaries were a charity and private individuals and the issue whether taxes apportioned to the trust would be equitably apportioned so as to impose the total burden on the noncharitable beneficiaries (equitable because their entitlements generated all the tax). A well drafted tax payment regime will address all of these questions.

About a shockingly similar provision in the will of one Elmer Cohen, deceased ("I direct my Personal Representatives to pay, without reimbursement or contribution, all estate [taxes], inheritance taxes, and succession duties assessed by reason of my death by the United States or any State thereof"), the Probate Division of the Circuit Court of St. Louis County, Missouri, No. 113549 (April 22, 1996), ruled that the will was "not ambiguous. Ambiguous means reasonably susceptible of more than one meaning. [This provision] is not susceptible of any meaning and cannot be construed." This portion of the holding was overruled on appeal, Estate of Cohen v. Crown, 954 S.W.2d 409 (Mo. Ct. App. 1997), the court refusing to conclude that there was no meaning in the provision but still concluding that it did not effectively waive the § 2206 right of reimbursement with respect to includible insurance proceeds and thereby protecting a charitable bequest that otherwise would have been reduced.

§ 3.3.16.6

construed to override the federal *GST* apportionment rules? Is the provision intended to address state *inheritance* taxes?

A recurring interpretative question—typically arising from careless drafting—concerns the meaning of a direction to pay "inheritance taxes." Should a direction to pay "any and all inheritance taxes" from a testator's estate be interpreted to cover FET? *In re Estate of Hoffman*[208] ruled that such a provision did not override the state apportionment statute with respect to any FET. In so ruling, the court emphasized the distinction between the terms "inheritance" and "estate." "The testatrix . . . directed the payment of 'any and all *inheritance* taxes.' An inheritance tax is not an estate tax; the former is a tax on the right of succession to property and the latter is a tax on the transmission of property."[209]

Not all courts recognize this distinction. In Thomas v. Fox,[210] for example, a direction for the executors to pay "all of my debts . . . and all inheritance taxes" was construed to include both state and federal taxes (and there is only an estate tax at the federal level). Similarly, Gratz v. Hamilton[211] held that a direction to charge "debts, including the inheritance taxes" to the residue of the estate included both federal estate and state inheritance taxes. Although lay persons may equate "estate" and "inheritance" taxes (and politicians do not help distinguish between them when they refer to the "death" tax), they are distinct concepts, and drafters should utilize precise language that adequately differentiates between the two.

If a will directs the personal representative to pay from the residue "all taxes imposed on my estate," should the term "estate" be construed to include only the assets subject to administration—the *probate* estate under the personal representative's control? Or should the term be construed to include all *gross* estate includible assets, those that generate taxes, including both probate property and nonprobate assets not under the personal representative's control? This question has plagued courts

---

[208] 160 A.2d 237 (Pa. 1960); see also In re Estate of Britt, 445 N.E.2d 367 (Ill. App. Ct. 1983).

[209] 160 A.2d at 239 (emphasis in original).

[210] 202 N.E.2d 812 (Mass. 1964).

[211] 309 S.W.2d 181 (Ky. 1958).

§ 3.3.16.6

for decades, and there seems to be no consensus as to its proper resolution.[212]

In cases involving statutes that direct outside apportionment, a proper consideration in answering this question is whether the decedent has overridden the statute with sufficient specificity. Consider, for example, Morgan Guaranty Trust Co. v. Huntington,[213] in which the decedent's will directed the executors to pay "from the capital of my residuary estate . . . any or all estate, transfer, succession or inheritance taxes which may be levied upon my estate or any part thereof."[214] The court held that this language should not be construed to include taxes attributable to nonprobate property.[215]

A similar issue concerns the meaning of the term "residue." If taxes are paid from the residue, should those taxes be prorated *within the residue* and, more importantly, should the principle of equitable appor-

---

[212] See, e.g., Commercial Trust Co. v. Thurber, 42 A.2d 571, 573 (N.J. 1945) (holding that the term "estate" does not include nonprobate assets, because "such property does not form part of decedent's *estate* at his death") (emphasis added); In re Atwater's Will, 132 N.Y.S.2d 2 (Surr. Ct. 1954) (holding that the term should mean the gross estate for tax purposes and, thus, should include nonprobate assets).

[213] 179 A.2d 604 (Conn. 1962).

[214] 179 A.2d at 607.

[215] See also In re Estate of Shoemaker, 917 P.2d 897 (Kan. Ct. App. 1996) (holding that a direction to pay "all federal estate and inheritance taxes . . . from the residue of my estate" was not sufficient to override a statutory outside apportionment scheme with respect to state inheritance taxes). In Patrick v. Patrick, 182 S.W.3d 433 (Tex. App. 2005), directing "all taxes . . . payable by reason of my death . . . shall be . . . paid out of my estate. No contribution for any of the above taxes upon the proceeds of any insurance policy on my life shall be made by the beneficiary (other than my estate) of any such insurance policy," the question was whether to apportion taxes attributable to an IRA to the beneficiaries thereof. The court held that state law apportionment to nonprobate assets like the IRA should apply and that the tax payment direction was not a burden on the residue provision overriding state law. The court's rationale was that the reference to taxes attributable to insurance would not have been relevant if a burden-on-the-residue had been the decedent's intent, but notice that use of the word "estate" is the uncertainty and the parenthetical appears to indicate that the decedent intended it to mean the probate estate. But see Peterson v. Mayse, 993 S.W.2d 217 (Tex. App. 1999) (holding that the will need not make specific reference to nonprobate property to override an outside apportionment statute).

§ 3.3.16.6

tionment apply within the residue?[216] In re Estate of Wilson[217] illustrates this question. The testator directed that all taxes "payable by reason of my death, shall be paid out of my residuary estate," 10% of which passed to charity and the other 90% of which passed to individual beneficiaries. The state apportionment statute provided for equitable apportionment, except to the extent that the decedent provided to the contrary. At issue was whether the will overrode the equitable apportionment statute, so as to require that the share passing to charity be calculated *after*, instead of *before*, subtracting FET. The court ruled that the charity's share should be 10% of the after-tax residue, holding that the language in the will was sufficient to override the equitable apportionment statute. Although the court was concerned only with the property law aspects of its decision, a collateral consequence of the decision would be to reduce the charitable deduction and thus increase the aggregate tax burden of the estate.

A third issue is illustrated by a typical residuary disposition: "After payment of the foregoing I give the residue of my estate X% to A, $Y to B, asset Z to C, and the balance of the residue to D." Here D receives the "residue-of-the-residue" and the question is whether a reference to "the residue of my estate" as the source for payment of taxes under a "burden on the residue" tax provision means the gross residue (with inside apportionment among A, B, C, and D) or the net residue-of-the-residue (meaning D's share suffers all of the tax payment, which preserves the gifts to A, B, and C unreduced by tax payment).[218]

---

[216] See § 3.3.15.3.

[217] 315 P.2d 451 (Cal. Dist. Ct. App. 1957).

[218] Compare In re Will of Sued, 33 Misc. 3d 1206 (Surr. Ct. N.Y. 2011) (Article Fourth disposed of "all the rest, residue, and remainder of my estate" and two paragraphs within Article Fourth contained a specific devise and a gift of "[a]ll the rest and remainder of my estate," which raised the question whether Article Fifth, calling for payment of taxes from the residuary estate, meant to refer to Article Fourth before or after disposition of the specific devise; noting that the word "residue" appeared only in the primary provision of Article Fourth and not in the paragraph devising "the rest and remainder" of that residue, the court called for payment of taxes from the gross residue and directed apportionment against the beneficiaries of the specific devise and the rest of the residue), with Estate of Russell v. Kinsler, 2008 WL 4291165 (unpub. Ind. Ct. App.) (a tax payment provision provided that "all . . . taxes . . . with respect to the assets distributed pursuant to this Paragraph E, to any beneficiary shall be charged to and paid by such beneficiary" and Paragraph E itself contained two dispositive

As *Morgan Guarantee* and *Wilson* demonstrate, the ultimate interpretative issue is whether language in an estate planning instrument is effective to override the state apportionment statute. Most litigation concerning this question has arisen in two principal contexts: (1) whether a direction to pay taxes from the residue overrides a statutory outside apportionment rule, and (2) whether a direction to pay taxes without apportionment overrides a statutory equitable apportionment rule.

In re Marital Deduction Trust Under Will of Adair[219] illustrates the former question. D died a resident of New Jersey, leaving a QTIP trust for S's benefit. When S died in Florida the trustee of the QTIP trust paid its share of S's FET (because the trust instrument directed its payment) but refused to pay the Florida estate tax attributable to the trust (the payment of which the QTIP instrument did not address). Under Florida law at that time the Florida estate tax was to be apportioned to the trust property unless S "otherwise directed by the governing instrument."[220] Florida law also provided that "an implicit direction against apportionment is not sufficient to avoid the apportionment under state . . . law unless the court also finds that the testator considered and made a deliberate and informed decision about the burden of taxation."[221] The New Jersey Superior Court entered summary judgment for the trustee after reviewing Florida law and the provisions of S's will and revocable trust. That decision was affirmed by the Appellate Division, holding that the documents "clearly and unequivocally" directed against apportionment.[222]

(Footnote Continued)

provisions, one giving "all real property" to X and the second directing that all remaining assets be sold and then principal and accumulated income be distributed in fractions among four couples and a charity; the court held that the realty disposition was a specific devise, distinguishable from the fractional division of the residue-of-the-residue, and that the specific was protected from payment of taxes, all of which were charged to the fractional division).

[219] 695 A.2d 250 (N.J. 1997).

[220] Quoting then Fla. Stat. Ann. § 733.817(1) (e), now § 733 .817(5).

[221] Then Fla. Stat. Ann. § 733.817(2) (d), now cf. § 733.81 7(5) (h)4.

[222] 695 A.2d at 252. The wife's will directed her personal representative to seek payment from the trustee of her revocable trust of:

such amount or amounts as my Personal Representative, in her judgment, may determine to be required for the payment of debts, funeral and

The New Jersey Supreme Court unanimously reversed. In ruling that S had *not* overridden the statutory outside apportionment rule, the Supreme Court discussed the effect of the will and trust provisions as follows:

> [N]either [the] will nor standby trust explicitly or implicitly "otherwise directed" against apportionment. [S's] will merely directed her personal representative to request payment from her standby trust of such an amount as the personal representative, "in her judgment, may determine to be *required* for the payment of debts, funeral and administrative expenses, . . . and Estate and like taxes payable by reason of my death." That provision does not direct her personal representative actually to pay any death taxes. In fact, the word "required," as used in [S's] will can only mean debts and death taxes that [S's] estate would be "legally obligated to pay." Thus, . . . an ambiguity exists in the will and extrinsic evidence should be considered to determine whether [S] intended to "otherwise direct" against apportionment.
>
> In her standby trust, [S] did not direct her trustee to pay the Florida estate taxes. The trustee was directed to pay to [S's] personal representative only such funds as she requests for the payment of taxes. There is no direction, however, for the trustee to pay any death taxes to the taxing authorities.
>
> The tax provisions in [S's] standby trust and will are generic, boilerplate provisions . . . . [T]he lack of an express or implied direction against apportionment precludes a finding that [S] "made a deliberate and informed decision about the burden

(Footnote Continued)

administration expenses, in connection with the administration of my Estate and Estate and like taxes payable by reason of my death.

The wife's revocable trust provided:

All estate, inheritance, succession and other death taxes, including any interest or penalties thereon, imposed or payable by reason of [the wife's] death with respect to all property comprising his [sic] gross estate for death tax purposes, whether or not such property passes hereunder, shall upon the written request of the Personal Representative of [the wife's] estate be paid to such Personal Representative . . . out of the principal of the trust estate. The Trustee shall not be responsible for the determination of such taxes, nor shall the Trustee be required to determine or inquire into the availability of funds for such purposes from [the wife's] probate estate.

§ 3.3.16.6

of taxation [as required by the New Jersey apportionment statute].[223]

Although S's will and trust arguably did include an implicit direction to pay taxes without outside apportionment,[224] the court concluded that S had not "considered and made a deliberate and informed decision about the burden of taxation." In reaching this conclusion, the court relied on a record "replete" with evidence of S's "bitter feelings" toward the remainder beneficiaries of the QTIP trust. According to the court, it would defy "logic and common sense" to require the beneficiaries of S's separate estate to pay the taxes. Even without such evidence, however, the court was appropriately skeptical in construing boilerplate language as a direction against outside apportionment, especially in a case involving a QTIP trust with remainder beneficiaries who were not natural objects of the income beneficiary's bounty.

Estate of Swallen v. Commissioner[225] illustrates the question whether a direction to pay all taxes without apportionment is sufficient to override a statutory equitable apportionment scheme. The resolution of this issue in many cases affects both the relative amounts received by the beneficiaries and the total aggregate tax burden. Courts are reluctant to find a direction against equitable apportionment if doing so would reduce an otherwise deductible disposition. The *Swallen* irrevocable

---

[223] Similar results were reached in Steinhof v. Murphy, 2007 WL 2360066 (trial order, R.I. Super.), aff'd, 991 A.2d 1028 (R.I. 2010) (concluding that a will provision directing outside apportionment was not altered by a "pay any deficiency" tax payment provision in the trust), and In re Estate of Brownlee, 654 N.W.2d 206 (S.D. 2002) (provisions in will and trust were unambiguous but totally inconsistent (both directing payment without reimbursement or apportionment), leaving the state law full apportionment rule to apply).

[224] Such a direction is implied, in particular, by language in the revocable trust requiring the trustee to pay upon request of the wife's personal representative "[a]ll estate, inheritance, succession and other death taxes . . . imposed or payable by reason of [the wife's] death with respect to all property comprising his [sic] gross estate for death tax purposes." Although this provision did not literally require the trustee to pay all such taxes (those taxes being payable only upon request by the personal representative), the expansive reference to all taxes "payable by reason of [the wife's] death" suggests that the wife indeed contemplated all such taxes being so paid. On the other hand, as observed by the Supreme Court, the fact that the provision misidentified the wife's gender also suggests that little thought was devoted to the use of this language.

[225] 98 F.3d 919 (6th Cir. 1996), rev'g 65 T.C.M. (CCH) 2332 (1993).

§ 3.3.16.6

inter vivos trust was includible in D's gross estate and, although held for the benefit of S, did not qualify for the marital deduction. The residue of the probate estate passed to S and did qualify for the marital deduction. The decedent's will included two provisions that together arguably charged all FET (including those taxes attributable to the inter vivos trust) to the residue of the estate: (1) a declaration that the "Executor . . . pay from the residue of my estate, or from funds available to [the] Executor from other sources, all inheritance, succession or estate taxes . . ." and (2) a statement that "I further direct that no tax or interest thereon paid by my Executor shall be charged by my Executor against the share of the principal or income of any surviving joint tenant, donee, legatee, devisee, insurance beneficiary, or trust beneficiary, so long as the funds or property in the hands of my Executor, or made available to my Executor, are sufficient to pay the same."

Notwithstanding these seemingly clear indications that all taxes should be charged to the residue, the court found that the decedent had not overridden the equitable apportionment statute. The court first observed that, in response to a clear policy favoring equitable apportionment, courts construing the state (Ohio) apportionment statute had stated that "a will must contain a specific and clear intent that estate taxes be paid in a manner contrary to the apportionment statute in order to avoid application of the statute."[226] Applying this principle, the court found that the will was not sufficiently clear to override the equitable apportionment statute. First because the tax payment provision "has a definite 'boilerplate' quality about it . . . rather than a thoughtful effort to specify the exact source of tax payments." Second, because it was ambiguous with respect to the exact source of funds to pay the estate's tax burden, referring to "funds available to my Executor from other sources" without specifying those other sources.[227]

---

[226] Citing In re Estate of Drosos, 575 N.E.2d 495 (Ohio Ct. App. 1989). PNC Bank v. Roy, 788 N.E.2d 650 (Ohio Ct. App. 2003), held that the Ohio equitable apportionment statute applied because the decedent's intent was too ambiguous.

[227] For a decision similarly finding will "boilerplate" insufficient to override an equitable apportionment statute, see Estate of Shannon v. Commissioner, 60 T.C.M. (CCH) 1361 (1990) (the will stating: "I direct that my representative . . . pay all my just debts, funeral expenses, expenses of administration, inheritance and estate taxes as soon after my death as may be convenient"). Not all courts agree with the *Shannon* result. Consider, for example, Lynchburg College v.

§ 3.3.16.6

The court continued to opine that the provision "seems to evince an intent to burden no one with taxes—a feat that many aspire to, but few achieve legally . . . This strongly suggests that rather than a clear and careful declaration of [the decedent's] intentions regarding her estate, this section is stock language . . . ."[228] The court further relied on language in the will suggesting a general intention to minimize taxes, although the court failed to note that the language appeared in an income tax provision, not in a provision concerning transfer taxes.

The *Swallen* court also was influenced by the inclination of Ohio courts to "resolve ambiguity in favor of maximizing a marital deduction on transfers of property to a surviving spouse."[229] The *Swallen* result seems appropriate because both the inter vivos trust and the residuary estate benefited S. Notwithstanding the tax payment provisions in the will, it stands to reason that D would have preferred to reduce the non-deductible disposition rather than the deductible disposition, with the result that more total funds were available for the benefit of family members and fewer taxes were paid to the government. On the other

---

(Footnote Continued)

Central Fidelity Bank, 410 S.E.2d 617 (Va. 1991), in which the court ruled that the following constituted a sufficiently clear direction against statutory apportionment: "I desire my just debts and all expenses of the administration of my estate, including such taxes as may be levied against my estate, paid as soon after my death as practicable." The court rejected an argument that this language addressed only the timing of the estate's tax payments ("as soon after my death as practicable"). Rather, the court concluded that this language indicated that the testator "intended all of the items [debts, expenses, and taxes] to be treated alike and to be paid in the same manner and from the same fund." Quoting Baylor v. Nat'l Bank of Commerce, 72 S.E.2d 282 (Va. 1952). Like debts and administration expenses paid from the residue, the decedent intended the same to apply for tax payments. The court also stated that "where . . . there is a general direction to pay all debts, expenses, and taxes, there is an implied direction that the taxes are to be paid from the fund which also bears the burden of debts and expenses," quoting Annot., Construction and effect of will provisions expressly relating to the burden of estate or inheritance taxes, 69 A.L.R.3d 122 (1976).

[228] 98 F.3d at 924-25.

[229] 98 F.3d at 925, citing Sawyer v. Sawyer, 374 N.E.2d 166 (Ohio Ct. App. 1977). This is not unique to Ohio jurisprudence. See, e.g., Seegel v. Miller, 820 N.E.2d 809 (Mass. 2005) (decedent's will and trust were reformed for consistency with the decedent's overall intent to maximize use of the marital deduction and to minimize estate taxes).

§3.3.16.6

hand, a less sympathetic court easily could have reached the contrary result by construing the will boilerplate as it was likely intended by the drafter—which was to direct payment of all taxes from the residue.[230]

Another important interpretative issue is illustrated by Stickley v. Stickley,[231] in which the decedent directed payment of all estate and inheritance taxes (as well as all administration expenses) from the residue of the estate, specifically waiving all rights of reimbursement. Unfortunately, the residuary estate was insufficient for this purpose, raising the question whether the shortfall should be paid as a general charge against the estate (thus abating certain preresiduary probate dispositions, but freeing nonprobate assets from contribution) or apportioned in accordance with the state apportionment statute (thus charging a portion of the excess to nonprobate assets). The court resolved the question by asking simply whether the decedent intended to override the apportionment statute:

> The Testator . . . directed that the estate taxes, debts, funeral expenses, and administration costs be treated in the same manner by specifying that they all be paid from the residuary estate. An insufficient residuary estate does not change that intent. When the Testator initially directed identical treatment of all these expenses, he successfully invoked the anti-apportionment statute . . . , and having done so, apportionment does not apply, absent some direction to that effect by the Testator.

In reaching this conclusion the court rejected an argument that the decedent failed to consider payment of taxes if the residue was insufficient. Thus, the argument went, the decedent should not be considered

---

[230] Consider, for example, In re Estate of Beebe, 702 N.Y.S.2d 683 (App. Div. 2000), in which the decedent left a third of her residuary estate to a church, a third to a college, and a third to be divided among several relatives. No FET was due, but the New York estate tax was approximately $17,000. The will contained a tax apportionment provision directing "all inheritance taxes, estate and succession taxes . . . [to] be charged against my residuary estate" and further directing that "there shall be no proration or apportionment of taxes." The court concluded that the will provision overrode the equitable apportionment statute: "had decedent's will merely provided that 'all . . . taxes . . . be charged against [her] residuary estate,' such language indeed would have been insufficient to avoid statutory apportionment." But, the court indicated, the additional language directing no proration or apportionment expressed the decedent's intent to override the statutory scheme.

[231] 497 S.E.2d 862 (Va. 1998).

§ 3.3.16.6

to have overridden the state apportionment statute with respect to that portion of the tax obligation—because the decedent did not consider the question, and therefore the decedent could not have intended to override the statute. This argument has an intuitive appeal, and it highlights the need to consider the decedent's intent in resolving apportionment questions. In *Stickley* the court should have compared the preresiduary and nonprobate dispositions (and considered the identity of the preresiduary and nonprobate beneficiaries) and, based on this comparison, determined which dispositions the decedent would have preferred to be charged with the excess taxes.[232]

§3.3.17 Sample Tax Clause

Because of the complexity of this matter, the following sample tax clause is offered for discussion purposes only. It is designed for use in a will and reflects thinking based on the material in this section. It is far more complex than the typical user would want to incorporate, on the theory that it is easier to delete provisions that are not needed and better to be comprehensive if the user may not want to tailor the provision for every situation. In that regard, provisions in halftone background are likely sources for deletion in vanilla situations.

Because this sample is more extensive than the typical drafter employs, and as a result it is a good bit longer, most drafters will not put this provision up front where most drafters install their tax payment provision (because they draft chronologically, placing provisions in the order in which they expect things to be done in the estate administration, and payment of debts, expenses, and taxes will come early). But a sentence can be placed in the front, directing compliance with the more robust direction found in the back of the document (along with the other

---

[232] See also Rosen v. Wells Fargo Bank Texas, 114 S.W.3d 145 (Tex. App. 2003) (which relied upon the decedent's intent to pay the least amount of transfer taxes possible in holding that the state's default apportionment statute applied to apportion taxes to the taxable nonprobate assets). But see Estate of Lurie v. Commissioner, 425 F.3d 1021 (7th Cir. 2005), affirming a determination that the marital deduction for a residuary bequest was reduced by a tax payment burden on the residue provision that superseded state law equitable apportionment, resulting in over $47 million of tax in what was intended to be a zero tax (optimum marital bequest) estate plan.

provisions that the client will regard as boilerplate, and probably never read), and then provide a more comprehensive direction.

This provision may apportion taxes to recipients the client would want to spare. The presumption is in favor of apportionment except to the extent a recipient is absolved. By way of example, many users are likely to delete paragraph B.1.b, requiring apportionment with respect to donees who received gifts during life, because the amounts involved are too small to be concerned with and the hassle of apportionment is too great. Note that paragraph B.6 is where specified beneficiaries or assets are exonerated to reflect such an intent.

Debts, Expenses, and Taxes: My personal representative shall pay from the income or principal of the residue of my estate all obligations of my estate, including expenses of my last illness and funeral, costs of administration (including ancillary), other legally enforceable charges and claims allowable against my estate, and (subject to apportionment as provided below) death taxes as defined next below. Payments may be deducted for income or other tax purposes in the discretion of my personal representative without regard to whether any other deduction otherwise allowable is reduced.

A. *Death Taxes Defined:* Death taxes means all estate, inheritance, succession, or transfer taxes and any income or similar taxes on appreciation (including interest, penalties, and any excise or supplemental taxes) imposed by the laws of any domestic or foreign taxing authority at the time of or by reason of my death, but shall not include:

1. Any additional estate tax incurred under § 2032A(c) or § 2057(i)(3)(F) of the Internal Revenue Code (or any similar or corresponding state tax law or any successor provision to any such law, all as amended prior to my death, hereafter collectively referred to as the Code) because of the disposition of or failure to use qualified real property or family-owned business interests; and

2. Generation-skipping transfer taxes imposed by Chapter 13 of the Code [, except to the extent attributable to a direct skip of which I am the transferor and that is not caused by a qualified disclaimer by a non-skip person (as those terms are defined in the Code), which shall be paid from the residue of my estate without apportionment or reimbursement notwithstanding the provisions of §§ 2603(a)(3) and 2603(b) of the Code or any other provision of this will].

B. *Apportionment:* Except as otherwise provided herein, it is my intent that each recipient of property that is includible in my estate for death tax purposes (whether passing under this will or otherwise) pay the proportionate death taxes attributable to the property (s)he receives, determined as follows:

1. The death tax attributable to:

a. Appreciation is the full amount of income or similar taxes incurred by reason of my death.

b. Adjusted taxable gifts as defined by § 2001(b)(1)(B) of the Code, any gift taxes includible in my gross estate by § 2035(b) of the Code, any recaptured inter vivos transfer subject to § 529(c)(4)(C) of the Code, or any comparable inclusion (hereafter collectively referred to as completed lifetime gifts) is the difference between (i) the total death taxes incurred by my estate, less those death taxes described in paragraph B.1.a. and (ii) the death taxes that would have been incurred if there were no completed lifetime gifts. For apportionment purposes, the recipient of property that produced gift tax includible by § 2035(b) of the Code shall be treated as having received the amount of that gift tax, and the recipients of completed lifetime gifts will pay the tax attributable thereto.

c. The death tax attributable to all other property is the difference between (i) the total death taxes paid by my estate and (ii) those death taxes described in paragraphs B.1.a. and B.1.b. that actually are collected by my personal representative.

2. *Multiple Recipients:* If there is more than one recipient of property separately described in paragraph B.1. each recipient shall pay a proportionate share of the death tax attributable to all of the property described in that separate paragraph based on the value of the property received by the recipient as finally determined in the death tax computation as compared to the same value of all property described in that separate paragraph that is not excluded from apportionment under paragraph B.6.

3. *Tax Benefits:* Credits, deductions, exclusions, exemptions, and similar benefits shall be reflected as follows:

a. In computing the death tax paid by my estate for purposes of paragraph B.1.b. and determining the proportionate share of such tax to be paid by any individual recipient, any gift tax allowed as a credit by § 2001(b)(2) of the Code that was paid by the recipient shall inure to the benefit of that recipient.

b. In computing the death tax paid by my estate for purposes of paragraph B.1.c. and determining the proportionate share of such tax to be paid by any individual recipient, the credit granted by § 2001(b)(2) of the Code for gift taxes that were not paid by any individual recipient, the unified credit granted by § 2010 of the Code, the credit for gift taxes granted by § 2012 of the Code, any credit for property previously taxed granted by § 2013 of the Code that is attributable to property that cannot be identified specifically as includible in my estate at death, and any other credit the benefit of which is not allocated by paragraph B.3.c. because it is not possible to identify the property passing to a recipient that produced the credit shall inure to the benefit of all recipients of property described in paragraph B.1.c.

c. The benefit of any other credit shall inure to the recipient of property that produced the credit (e.g. the recipient of property that generates a state death tax shall enjoy the benefit of [the credit granted by § 2011 of the Code or]the deduction granted by § 2058 of the Code with respect to payment of that tax, the recipient of property subject to foreign death tax shall enjoy the benefit of the credit granted by § 2014 of the Code with respect to the taxation of that property, and the recipient of specifically identifiable property that is includible in my estate and that previously was taxed shall enjoy the benefit of any credit granted by § 2013 of the Code with respect to that property).

d. The benefit of any reduction in tax attributable to an election under § 2032A of the Code shall inure to the qualified heir who receives the property that is the subject of the election.

e. The benefit of any reduction in tax attributable to property qualifying for the marital or charitable deduction shall inure to the recipient of that property. Any increase in death taxes attributable to a disclaimer of such property or a failure to elect to qualify any part of a bequest that otherwise could constitute QTIP property under § 2056(b)(7) of the Code shall be charged to the disclaimed or non-elected property without the benefit of any marital or charitable deduction otherwise available to my estate.

f. The benefit of any tax rate differential in computing death taxes attributable to the relation of the recipient to me shall inure to that beneficiary.

g. The benefit of any other entitlement directly attributable to identifiable property shall inure to the beneficiary who receives that property.

4. *Temporal Interests:* Death tax attributable to property held in temporal interests (e.g., a life estate, annuity, or term of years, followed by a remainder) shall be paid from corpus to the extent the effect thereof is to amortize the cost over the respective interests but otherwise shall be apportioned between the respective interests based on

§ 3.3.17

their respective values. Apportionment to a lead interest may entail a loan from principal or recomputation of an annuity or other guaranteed payment, but neither this paragraph nor any provision of state law shall apply to the extent the effect is to reduce a deduction otherwise allowable for any part of the property.

5. *QTIP Property:* Notwithstanding paragraph B.3.e., with respect to property includible in my estate under § 2044 of the Code, all taxes attributable to all § 2044 property shall be determined on a pro rata rather than the incremental basis provided by § 2207A of the Code and shall be apportioned to the § 2044 property with the highest inclusion ratio to the extent doing so will not constitute a constructive addition with respect to any § 2044 property with a lower inclusion ratio.

6. *Exoneration:* Notwithstanding any other provision of this will, the recipient of property described in this paragraph shall not be subject to apportionment and the taxes attributable to this property shall be paid by the remaining recipients of property includible in my estate according to the computation of attributable tax described in paragraphs B.1. and B.2.

a. To the extent apportionment of the attributable tax would violate federal law relating to retirement benefits and deferred compensation.

b. To the extent apportionment of the attributable tax would cause an acceleration of income taxation or to the extent the property otherwise would be eligible for exclusion from my estate by § 2039 (c) or § 2039 (e) of the Code pursuant to the transition rules in § § 525 (b) (2) through 525 (b) (4) of the Tax Reform Act of 1984 as amended.

c. Proceeds of life insurance that are exempt from inheritance or similar death taxes to the extent not subject to apportionment because paid to a beneficiary other than my personal representative.

d. Property not passing under this will to the extent the total tax attributable thereto is less than *% of the total death taxes described in paragraph A.

e. Property passing under * of this will (relating to personal property) to the extent the total tax attributable thereto is less than *% of the total death taxes described in paragraph A.

C. *Reimbursement:* Because it is my intent to apportion death taxes as described above, it is unnecessary to assert the rights to reimbursement provided by §§2206, 2207, 2207A, 2207B, and 2603 of the Code (and any similar provisions hereafter adopted) and, except to the extent inconsistent with the foregoing, I hereby waive those entitlements.

D. *Interest and Set Offs:* In the discretion of my personal representative death taxes attributable to property not passing under this will may be paid out of the residue of my estate prior to recovering the attributable tax from the recipient of that property.

1. Attributable tax that has not been paid by the recipient before my personal representative pays death taxes or that is not yet due because my personal representative made a valid deferral election under §6161, §6163, or §6166 of the Code shall bear interest equal to that imposed by the Code on my personal representative.

2. In the discretion of either my personal representative or a beneficiary under this will, as a form of payment by that beneficiary to my personal representative, any entitlement of a beneficiary under this will may be applied in payment of that beneficiary's share of the taxes and interest attributable to other property received by that beneficiary.

3. In its discretion my personal representative may distribute my estate in whole or in part prior to final audit and settlement of the tax liability of my estate, notwithstanding that attributable taxes may be altered thereafter.

4. My personal representative shall not be personally liable for withholding an insufficient amount as a set off against the liability of a recipient or for failing to recover attributable taxes or interest following reasonable efforts and shall not be required to litigate to enforce apportionment unless indemnified against the costs thereof.

E. *Adjustments:* My personal representative's selection of assets to be sold to pay death taxes, and the tax effects thereof, shall not be subject to question by any beneficiary. My personal representative is hereby indemnified against any liability it may incur to any recipient of property not passing under this will for the effect of any action taken in the computation or payment of death taxes that directly or indirectly affects any recipient's liability under this provision. Elections or allocations authorized under the Code may be made by my personal representative in its discretion without regard to or liability for the effect thereof on any beneficiary or any tax consequence thereof. No adjustment shall be made between income and principal, in the relative interests of the recipients, or in the amount or selection of assets allocated to any trust under this will to compensate for the effect of any such action or for the effect on the amount of any tax attributable to any recipient of property includible in my estate for death tax purposes.

F. *Conflict of Laws:* For all purposes of interpreting this provision and ascertaining the rights of any recipient of property includible in my estate for death tax purposes the law of the state of my domicile at death shall govern notwithstanding the nature or location of the property or the domicile of the recipient.

CAUTION

The foregoing form is drafted for use in a will. If adapted for use in a trust, remember also to include a provision in the client's will waiving all rights of reimbursement (see paragraph C) because only a will may waive the rights granted by §§ 2206 and 2207.

If multiple documents will be used for the estate plan, be certain that all tax clauses mesh in terms of calling for payment in a consistent manner and all from the proper sources in the same order or under the same conditions. A provision in a trust authorizing a loan to or purchase of assets from the settlor's estate may be as effective as a separate tax payment directive in the trust, especially if the trust corpus otherwise is not includible in the settlor's estate at death.

THE FOREGOING FORMS ARE NOT WARRANTED AS SUITABLE EXCEPT TO ILLUSTRATE CONCEPTS DISCUSSED IN THIS CHAPTER, AND MAY NOT BE APPROPRIATE FOR ANY GENERAL OR SPECIFIC USE. THE USER IS RESPONSIBLE FOR DETERMINING HOW THEY SHOULD BE ADAPTED TO ANY PARTICULAR SITUATION.

§ 3.3.18 Time of Payment

In addition to evaluating the source (and liquidity) of funds needed to pay the FET and any state death taxes, the time allowed to raise the necessary capital must be considered. Most important in this respect is the date the FET return is due and the tax must be paid, although it may be possible to defer either. Under § 6151(a), the tax must be paid when the return is required to be filed, which is nine months after the decedent's death,[233] unless an extension of the time for payment is secured.[234]

§3.3.19 Interest and Late Filing or Late Payment Penalties

An extension of the time for filing an FET return does not constitute an extension of the time for payment of the FET. A separate extension for each is required[235]—an extension of one does *not* extend the other.

---

[233] See § 6075(a). Under § 6081 one automatic six month extension to file the return is available upon request. Treas. Reg. § 20.6081-1(b). See § 3.3.20 n.264 and accompanying text. As dramatically illustrated by Dickow v. Commissioner, 740 F. Supp. 2d 231 (D. Mass. 2010), aff'd, 2011-2 U.S. Tax Cas. (CCH) ¶ 60,626 (1st Cir. 2011), however, the government cannot give more than one extension of the time to file, even though it can grant multiple extensions of the time to pay. Curiously enough, an executor who relied on erroneous advice regarding this rule was found to have acted reasonably and thus was not responsible for an accuracy-related penalty. See Estate of Lee v. Commissioner, 97 T.C.M. (CCH) 1435 (2009), following behind the taxpayer's loss on another issue, 94 T.C.M. (CCH) 604 (2007).

[234] See §§ 6161 (extension for reasonable cause), and 6163 (extension with respect to future interests), as discussed in § 3.3.20, and § 6166 (extension of tax attributable to qualifying business), as discussed in § 15.2.

[235] Treas. Reg. §§ 20.6081-1(d), 20.6151-1(a). See, e.g., Treas. Reg. § 20.6161-1(c)(3); Rev. Rul. 81-237, 1981-2 C.B. 245 (imposing the § 6651(a)(1) addition to tax because the executor was granted an extension of time to file and pay the FET but only paid the tax within the extension period and filed the return late, without reasonable cause; no addition to tax for late filing of the return could have been assessed if the executor had paid no less than the amount of tax shown on the return on or before the date prescribed for payment of the tax, even though the return was filed late, but payment after the date prescribed for payment meant that the filing penalty was assessed on the full FET due).

Baccei v. United States, 2008-2 U.S. Tax Cas. (CCH) ¶ 60,562 (N.D. Cal. 2008), aff'd, 632 F.3d 1140 (9th Cir. 2011), underscores that an extension of the time to file a tax return is not the same as an extension of the time to pay the tax due with that return. It was not a compelling case for relief, because the accountant who filed the Form 4768 requesting an extension of the time to file actually attached a letter asking for an extension of the time to pay the tax but failed to properly complete that portion of the Form 4768 requesting the extension of the time to pay. The letter also failed to articulate an adequate reason for seeking the extension, vastly underestimated the tax the estate was required to pay, and did not offer to pay what the estate could afford at the time, all of which

Nor does an extension of the time to pay exempt the taxpayer from the obligation to pay interest during the deferral period.[236]

  Interest on the outstanding tax due is computed under § 6621 at the same rate as that charged on any underpayment.[237] With an exception for § 6166, interest paid on deferred FET normally is a deductible expense for FET purposes[238] or instead may be deductible for income tax purposes if the requisite § 642(g) election is made.[239] Any amount claimed as

---

(Footnote Continued)

the court did not view as purely administrative error. The opinion underscores the notable lack of relief for such missteps.

[236] See § § 6601(a), 6601(b)(1), 6166(f), and Treas. Reg. § § 20.6161-1(c)(2), 20.6161-2(e), 20.6163-1(d), and 20.6166-1(f).

[237] See § 6621. Under § 6622 the interest compounds daily. See § 15.2.3 regarding the imposition of interest with respect to § 6166.

[238] Rev. Rul. 79-252, 1979-2 C.B. 333 (interest on any deficiency); Rev. Rul. 81-256, 1981-2 C.B. 183 (interest on state taxes deferred); Rev. Proc. 81-27, 1981-2 C.B. 548 (method for computation of the amount of deductible interest). See § 15.4.3.4. This deduction is denied, however, with respect to interest incurred on tax deferred under § 6166. See § 2053(c)(1)(D).

[239] The § 163 interest expense deduction is denied, however, with respect to interest incurred on tax deferred under § 6166. See § 163(k). In addition, § 163(h) disallows a deduction for personal interest, subject to several exceptions. For example, under § 163(h)(2)(E) this disallowance does not apply to interest payable under § 6601 on any unpaid portion of tax imposed by § 2001 for the period during which the payment is deferred under § 6163.

Oddly, deferral under § 6161 is not mentioned, either in § 163(h) or (k) or in any of the committee reports or the general explanation accompanying the Tax Reform Act of 1986 provision that created § 163(h). If Congress thought that § 163(h) applies to the payment of interest on a § 6161 extension because there is no express exception for § 6161 as there is for § 6163, then it is not clear why Congress thought it was necessary to enact § 163(k) to deny the interest expense deduction for § 6166. CCA 200836027 regards it "plain" that § 163(h) denies a deduction for interest incurred under § 6161, citing no authority and stating as its rationale that "[t]he plain language of the statute, along with Congress's prior inclusion and then exclusion of § 6166, indicates that no interest payable on the estate tax during a period of extension other than under § 6163, qualifies as deductible, non-personal interest." Note that § 163(k) may have been added (and the reference in § 163(h)(2)(E) was deleted) because of the addition of § 6601(j)(1)(B), which grants taxpayers a reduced interest rate that (at the time) reflected the 55% estate tax rate, all of which occurred in 1997. In essence, by imposing interest at 45% of the normal annual rate of interest, Congress "built in" the deduction (at what was then a 55% rate) and, on that basis, no longer needed

an FET deduction generates an interrelated FET recalculation, which will result in a reduction of the FET and previously accrued interest.[240] Alternatively, any amount claimed as an income tax deduction may generate ancillary income tax consequences, such as under § 67(e) and any AMT complications,[241] making it necessary to carefully project the consequences of the various alternatives.[242]

In addition to interest, a penalty may be imposed under § 6651(a) on the personal representative if the return is not filed or the tax is not paid when due, including extensions.[243] An exception to the penalties for late filing or late payment exists if reasonable cause exists for the delay and

---

(Footnote Continued)

to address the question elsewhere. Blattmachr & Boyle, Deducting Interest Paid on Estate Taxes, 20 Prob. Prac. Rep. 1 (Oct. 2008), argue that the interest qualifies as a § 212 deduction that therefore is allowable under § 163(h)(2)(A). Arguably it also is investment interest excepted under § 163(h)(2)(B) and deductible under § 163(d), al though PLR 9449011 disagreed with that notion as regards interest incurred on a bank loan to pay taxes, debts, and expenses without having to liquidate estate assets at depressed values.

See § 15.4.3.4 n.100. The Tax Court has jurisdiction under §§ 6512 and 7481 to reopen a case solely to reflect interest incurred that is properly deductible under § 2053, which allows the Tax Court to enter a final judgment in a case without retaining jurisdiction to make such an adjustment.

[240] Rev. Rul. 80-250, 1980-2 C.B. 278, 279. See also Rev. Proc. 81-27, 1981-2 C.B. 548, which establishes the procedure to follow when installment payments are recomputed because of a reduction in the FET caused by the payment of interest on the tax due.

[241] Ungerman Revocable Trust v. Commissioner, 89 T.C. 1131 (1987), involved interest deducted for fiduciary income tax purposes that was allowed by the court as a § 212 expense for administering income producing property, making it not subject to the AMT, overruling the government's argument that § 163 was the more specific provision and that it precluded § 212 deductibility, making this a § 55 AMT itemized deduction.

[242] See § 15.4.3.4 nn.101-108 and accompanying text regarding how to keep the § 6503(a)(1) statute of limitation from precluding the deduction of interest paid as it becomes due.

[243] Rev. Rul. 81-154, 1981-1 C.B. 470, and TAM 9051002 confirm that interest incurred on an FET liability is a charge for the use of money (rather than a penalty) that is deductible under § 2053(a)(2) as a necessary administration expense, but any penalty imposed under § 6651 for the failure to timely file or pay is not a necessary expense in the proper administration of the estate and therefore is not deductible even if the expense is allowed under state law.

§ 3.3.19

there was no willful neglect by the taxpayer. In this respect, Treas. Reg. § 301.6651-1(c) regards reasonable cause to exist if the personal representative exercised ordinary business care and prudence, which essentially presents a facts and circumstances test. But certain excuses for lateness routinely are rejected.

Certain administrative decisions or lapses do not constitute reasonable cause because the personal representative simply failed to be careful, complete, conservative, or watchful. For example, an extreme case was presented by Estate of Hartsell v. Commissioner,[244] in which the estate was granted two extensions of the time to pay but when asked for substantiation of its third request for extension based on reasonable cause the estate failed to respond and, upon investigation, the government determined that the executor had paid state estate taxes to four states before paying federal tax, had forgiven loans to himself and his son, had not remitted funds that *were* available, and did not pursue reasonable opportunities to sell estate assets or borrow against them, altogether illustrating a total lack of the ordinary business care and prudence that might constitute reasonable cause for being late in payment. Less dramatic illustrations can be seen in cases like reliance on incomplete or outdated valuation information and old property tax assessments, rather than a professional appraisal, which is not ordinary business care and prudence.[245] As a result, a failure to timely file because a personal representative believes the estate is too small is not based on reasonable cause. A failure to timely file would involve willful neglect if the personal representative took the risk that the return would be accepted without adjustment.[246] And ordinary business care requires an ongoing evaluation, and inability to assemble or value estate property

---

[244] 88 T.C.M. (CCH) 267 (2004).

[245] Charman v. Commissioner, 88-2 U.S. Tax Cas. (CCH) ¶ 13,780 (S.D. Cal. 1988) (§ 6651(a)(1) penalty for failure to timely file an FET return; personal representative alleged mistaken belief that gross estate was below the § 6018 minimum size for which a return was required).

[246] Estate of Werner v. Commissioner, 56 T.C.M. (CCH) 1206 (1989) (the personal representative believed that no tax was payable because all inventoried assets were bequeathed directly to charity; an audit revealed an inter vivos transfer with a retained life estate that was includible and not subject to testamentary charitable bequest, which resulted in a tax and, with it, a § 6651(a)(1) late filing penalty).

§ 3.3.19

does not constitute reasonable cause for an ongoing failure to amend a prior nonfiling decision.[247]

A second category of cases revolves around excusable reliance on the advice of others, typically an attorney or accountant, regarding return filing or tax payment obligations. Such reliance on erroneous advice of professionals raises issues such as whether the personal representative gave the advisor complete and accurate information, whether the personal representative exercised care in selecting the professional, or whether the question is one upon which lay persons can be expected to verify advice or otherwise protect themselves. For example, a taxpayer may establish reasonable cause for failing to file a timely return by proving reasonable reliance on the advice of an accountant or attorney and later discovery that the advice was wrong but reasonable cause requires a prudent selection and verification of professional advisors and their advice.[248] Moreover, reliance on an advisor to perform an act the personal representative could perform or verify is not reasonable cause. Thus, in Estate of Fleming v. Commissioner,[249] the personal representative made every effort to file on time, including delivering the completed return to an attorney to timely file, which the attorney simply failed to do. The fact that the attorney told the personal representative that the return had been filed was not deemed persuasive.

The Supreme Court's pronouncement on these issues in United States v. Boyle[250] is the lodestar on the issue whether a personal representative's reliance on an attorney or accountant's mistaken advice or outright negligence regarding timely filing of an FET return is reasonable cause to avoid payment of § 6651 penalties for late filing and failure to

---

[247] St. Clair v. United States, 93-1 U.S. Tax Cas. (CCH) ¶ 60,139 (D. Minn. 1993) (§§ 6651(a)(1) and (a)(2) late filing and late payment penalties were measured from the date a successor personal representative filed the estate's income tax return reporting dividends from stock that, upon discovery, revealed the need to file the FET return).

[248] Estate of Newton v. Commissioner, 59 T.C.M. (CCH) 469 (1990) (reasonable cause did not exist because the advice was an offhand observation by an attorney who admittedly did not work on FET matters and who admonished the personal representative to verify the attorney's comment that the return was due 18 months after death).

[249] 58 T.C.M. (CCH) 1034 (1989), aff'd, 974 F.2d 894 (7th Cir. 1992).

[250] 469 U.S. 241 (1985), rev'g 710 F.2d 1251 (7th Cir. 1983).

§ 3.3.19

timely pay any taxes due. The Supreme Court granted certiorari in *Boyle* to establish "as 'bright' a line as can be drawn"[251] regarding the question of what is reasonable cause for late filing and payment, and unanimously ruled that reliance on a tax advisor with respect to deadlines is not reasonable cause for failure to comply.[252]

Taxpayers bear the heavy burden of proving that the taxpayer exercised ordinary business care and prudence but was unable to timely file and pay. In *Boyle* the Court distinguished between those circumstances that are beyond the control of the taxpayer and those that are within the competence of an ordinarily prudent person. The Court held that "[t]he failure to make a timely filing . . . is not excused by . . . reliance on an agent, and such reliance is not 'reasonable cause' for a late filing,"[253] although reliance on a tax advisor is reasonable if the advisor is rendering "substantive" advice.[254] In the context of deadlines, the Court

---

[251] 469 U.S. at 248.

[252] Numerous cases have had occasion to follow *Boyle*, including a flurry of decisions relatively soon after the Court spoke, including Ballard v. Commissioner, 854 F.2d 185 (7th Cir. 1988), rev'g 53 T.C.M. (CCH) 323 (1987) (no penalty actually was assessed, however, because the court ultimately determined that no tax was due); Estate of Cox v. United States, 637 F. Supp. 1112 (S.D. Fla. 1986); Alton OB-GYN Ltd. v. United States, 86-1 U.S. Tax Cas. (CCH) ¶ 9364 (7th Cir. 1986) (reliance on trustee of qualified plan to file Form 5500-C was not reasonable); United States v. Blumberg, 86-1 U.S. Tax Cas. (CCH) ¶ 13,658 (C.D. Cal. 1985); Constantino v. United States, 85-2 U.S. Tax Cas. (CCH) ¶ 13,629 (N.D. Cal. 1985); Estate of Brandon v. Commissioner, 86 T.C. 327 (1986), rev'd on other grounds, 828 F.2d 493 (8th Cir. 1987); Estate of Draper v. Commissioner, 55 T.C.M. (CCH) 797 (1988); Estate of DiFiore v. Commissioner, 54 T.C.M. (CCH) 1168 (1987); Estate of Rothpletz v. Commissioner, 53 T.C.M. (CCH) 1214 (1987); and Estate of Raab v. Commissioner, 49 T.C.M. (CCH) 662 (1985). *DiFiore* and *Rothpletz* both had the effect of disqualifying an otherwise valid § 2032A special use valuation election, which the Tax Court refused to allow, notwithstanding reliance on the delinquent attorney.

[253] 469 U.S. at 252.

[254] See, e.g., Estate of Paxton v. Commissioner, 86 T.C. 785 (1986), and Estate of Buring v. Commissioner, 51 T.C.M. (CCH) 113 (1985), in which failure to file estate and gift tax returns, respectively, was deemed to be based on reasonable cause attributable to erroneous advice of an attorney or accountant regarding taxability of transfers made. And see Autin v. Commissioner, 102 T.C. 760 (1994) (reasonable cause for failure to file gift tax return based on erroneous advice of counsel that gift was made in a prior year). Cf. Estate of Liftin v. United States, 101 Fed. Cl. 604 (2011), denying the government's motion for summary judg-

held that "reliance cannot function as a substitute for compliance with an unambiguous statute" because an individual need not "be a tax expert to know that tax returns have fixed filing dates . . . . It requires no special training or effort to ascertain a deadline and make sure that it is met."[255]

A concurring opinion in *Boyle* argued in favor of an exception if the taxpayer was incompetent or infirm, either physically or mentally, and the majority opinion stated that "disability . . . could well be an acceptable excuse for a late filing."[256]

Brown v. United States[257] involved a personal representative who relied on the decedent's former attorney, a sole practitioner, to file the FET return. That attorney was hospitalized and underwent surgery two weeks before the FET return was due. Although he was released in time to timely file the return, the attorney required a lengthy recuperation period and filing did not occur until about three months after the due date. Under these circumstances, and relying on the door left open by the Supreme Court in *Boyle*, the court found that late filing by the estate was excusable. To do so, however, the court had to find that the personal representative was prevented from timely filing due to infirmity, not that the attorney was so prevented. The court made that determination because the personal representative was elderly, retired, not well educated, and was inexperienced in matters of fiduciary administration and taxation and could not be expected to hire replacement counsel as quickly as required to surmount the attorney's medical emergency. Although a younger, more experienced consumer of legal services might not be able to rely on this form of escape from the penalties for late filing, the court in *Brown* essentially took the exception left by *Boyle* and turned the attorney's infirmity into that of the personal representative.

(Footnote Continued)

ment because the estate made a sufficient showing that it may be possible to prove that it was reasonable to rely on the advice of counsel to file and pay late, to take advantage of the §2056A marital deduction planning discussed in §13.5.7.1 at note 300 et seq. and accompanying text.

[255] 469 U.S. at 251-252.

[256] 469 U.S. at 248 n.6.

[257] 630 F. Supp. 57 (M.D. Tenn. 1985).

Additional guidance is found in Estate of LaMeres v. Commissioner,[258] which provides a lengthy exegesis of precedent on the issue of reasonable reliance on advice of counsel. It divided these authorities into three categories for analysis: (1) those in which reliance was unreasonable because the taxpayer did not provide all information needed for the advisor to give proper advice or in which the taxpayer should have known that the advisor was not sufficiently expert to be reliable; (2) those in which the taxpayer improperly relied on advice that no penalty would be imposed because no tax was due;[259] and (3) those in which reliance was reasonable following full disclosure and good faith reliance on erroneous advice either regarding the taxability of a transaction or the time required to file, stating that the latter advice is reasonable cause for late filing only if reasonable under the circumstances, which was the issue to which *Boyle* was addressed. The opinion is a comprehensive collection and summary of the law.[260]

Several examples illustrate the third category in which reliance was not reasonable under the circumstances. Hopping v. United States[261] involved a taxpayer who received an extension to file the FET return and to pay the tax, filed another request and was granted another extension

---

[258] 98 T.C. 294 (1992) (personal representative's reliance on erroneous advice of counsel, that a second § 6081 six month extension to file the FET return was available, was reasonable and constituted reasonable cause for late filing to avoid the § 6651(a) late filing and late payment penalties); followed in Estate of Lee v. Commissioner, 97 T.C.M. (CCH) 1435 (2009) (accuracy related penalty did not apply because taxpayer's reliance on erroneous advice of counsel was reasonable). See § 3.3.18 n.233.

[259] Estate of Melville v. Commissioner, 66 T.C.M. (CCH) 1076 (1993), added a subcategory to this second category, being reliance on improper advice that, although a return is required and a tax is due, the government will not assert a penalty for late filing. This did not constitute reasonable reliance in *Melville* because the executor was an experienced trust officer who should have known that a pending will contest was not a sufficient justification for late filing. Estate of Cox v. United States, 637 F. Supp. 1112, 1115 (S.D. Fla. 1986), similarly held that "[a] professional executor should be held to a stricter standard."

[260] And see Estate of Sharp v. United States, 97-1 U.S. Tax Cas. (CCH) ¶ 60,268 (E.D. Tenn. 1997), which disallowed a late filing penalty and found reasonable reliance by the taxpayer on the advice of an accountant that the decedent's FET return was due on April 15 of the year following the decedent's death, as if it was an income tax return.

[261] 92-1 U.S. Tax Cas. (CCH) ¶ 60,098 (S.D. Ind. 1992).

§ 3.3.19

to pay but not to file the return and, notwithstanding all this relief, still failed to file or pay within the times specified. The taxpayer alleged that counsel advised that the estate could wait until litigation involving the estate was complete before filing the return and paying the tax, which the court flatly rejected as not reasonable cause, in large part because the government responded to the taxpayer's extension requests with specific instructions about when to file and to pay the tax. And Estate of Campbell v. Commissioner[262] imposed penalties for late filing and payment, rejecting as reasonable cause the taxpayer's reliance on the advice of counsel that the return should not be submitted lacking an appraiser's report, which was delayed.

§3.3.20 Extensions of Time to File or Make Payment

Extensions of time may defer the time to file the FET return or to pay the FET. A nearly automatic extension of a reasonable period to file the return, not to exceed six months (longer if the taxpayer is abroad),[263] historically was granted with such regularity upon request that the government by regulation now has determined to grant it as a matter of course in most every case, but only upon request.[264] A similar extension

---

[262] 62 T.C.M. (CCH) 1514 (1991).

[263] As illustrated by TAM 8116019, the personal representative (taxpayer) must be abroad on the original § 6075 filing date to qualify for a longer than six month extension of the filing date under § 6081. By analogy, the personal representative would need to be abroad when the tax payment otherwise is due under § 6151, not just at any time before the § 6161(a)(1) extension expires.

[264] See § 6081(a); Treas. Reg. § 20.6081-1(b). In normal cases the request must be made before the return itself is due. Treas. Reg. § 20.6081-1(c). The government has discretion, however, to grant an exception for good cause, and Estate of Proske v. United States, 2010-1 U.S. Tax Cas. (CCH) ¶ 60,594 (D. N.J. 2010), establishes that the government "has wide latitude in determining whether an extension is appropriate," but it must exercise that discretion "in a non-arbitrary manner" and it is an abuse of discretion to deny a request without recording a rational explanation based on the facts and circumstances of the particular situation.

The automatic extension is not available with respect to Forms 706-A, 706-D, 706-NA, or 706-QDT, but the discretionary extension remains available in those cases. See also T.D. 9407, 2008-2 C.B. 330, updating various regulations that relate to the automatic six-month extension of the time to file an income tax return and an extension of the time to file gift tax and GST returns that are due at the same time.

of up to 12 months to pay the tax also is available under § 6161(a)(1) upon a request that must show "reasonable cause," but it is not so readily granted.

Extensions of the time to pay are not automatic and may be denied even in circumstances in which the extension of the time to file is automatic. To obtain the extension to file, all the taxpayer must do is file the request before the return is due. To obtain an extension to pay requires more, and failure to request both can cause serious consequences.

It is a matter of some bewilderment that the taxpayer may be entitled to an *automatic* extension of the time to file a return but still be expected to pay the tax due on that yet-to-be-filed return, without an extension. "How can you know how much to pay if you haven't completed and filed the return?" is a respectable (and prescient) question. To which the answer is: guess. Pay an estimate, and if you're wrong on the low side, expect to pay interest and potentially a penalty.

An extension of up to 10 years to pay the tax also may be granted in the discretion of the Secretary upon a showing of "undue hardship" and, if later, any installment payment under the tax deferral provisions of § 6166 may be extended for up to 12 months after that installment is due.[265] Separate extensions to pay any assessed deficiency also are available upon a showing of undue hardship,[266] again in the discretion of the Secretary, but not to exceed four years. Thus, if an extension is thought to be needed, a longer deferral is available in the Secretary's discretion if the tax is reported as due rather than assessed as a deficiency.

The "reasonable cause" needed to justify an extension is illustrated under Treas. Reg. § 20.6161-1(a)(1) Examples (1)-(4) as including: an inability to marshal liquid assets because they are located in other jurisdictions or because litigation is required to collect them; an inability to borrow on better than disfavorable terms (in relation to returns

---

[265] See § 6161(a)(2). Although it would appear that the same "reasonable cause" standard is applicable, Treas. Reg. § 20.6161-1(a)(2) imposes an "undue hardship" standard for the longer extensions.

[266] See § 6161(b)(2). See Treas. Reg. § 20.6161-2(b). However, § 6161(b)(3) denies the extension for any deficiency that is attributable to negligence, intentional disregard of rules or regulations, or fraud with an intent to evade tax.

§ 3.3.20

otherwise available to the estate on its investments); and an insufficiency of funds to maintain the decedent's family, pay claims against the estate, and pay the FET, coupled with an inability to borrow at prevailing market rates.

"Undue hardship" is a higher standard, illustrated by Treas. Reg. § 20.6161-1(a)(2)(ii) Examples (1) and (2) involving a farm or closely held business that constitutes a significant portion of the estate (but not necessarily enough to qualify for deferral of the tax under § 6166), sufficient other funds are not readily available, and an extension of time is needed to raise the capital without having to sell the farm or business; or the only available sale to generate liquidity would be at a sacrifice price or in a depressed market.

Apparently regardless of the merits, the application for any of these extensions must be filed before the date otherwise applicable for payment of the tax or deficiency.[267]

In addition to such discretionary deferral, § 6163 permits automatic extension of the time for payment of that portion[268] of the FET attributable to inclusion in a decedent's gross estate of either a reversion or a remainder.[269] Under § 6163(a) the tax need not be paid until six months after termination of all preceding interests in the property and for reasonable cause may be extended under § 6163(b) for an added three years, presumably under the same standards applied for extensions for

---

[267] Treas. Reg. §§ 20.6161-1(b) and 20.6161-2(c).

[268] Determined under Treas. Reg. § 20.6163-1(c), this portion is the proportionate amount of FET attributable to the value of the future interest includible in the decedent's gross estate, with appropriate reflection for any debts, other encumbrances, or deductible losses attributable thereto, and reflecting any credits (such as under § 2015) or deductions identifiable with respect to the interest.

[269] Treas. Reg. § 20.6163-1(a) specifies that deferral is not available to future interests created by the decedent's own testamentary act, which is sensible because it precludes a decedent from postponing the incidence of FET by creating only future interests under the estate plan. Although the regulation refers to a testamentary act of the decedent, it does not refer only to interests created by the decedent's will, and reversions or other future interests includible in the decedent's gross estate that were created by the decedent by inter vivos transfer should be treated as testamentary acts for this purpose. See § 11.3 for a discussion of future interests includible in the gross estate.

§ 3.3.20

reasonable cause under § 6161.[270] This extension is not by its terms available for taxes attributable to an executory interest,[271] presumably because an executory interest may never become possessory. This may be sensible because the tax payment obligation could be extinguished entirely if deferral was permitted until termination of all preceding interests. But the same could be said about many contingent remainder interests. And executory interests, just like reversions and vested or contingent remainders, present the same lack of cash flow or inability to liquidate the interest to generate funds to pay the tax, which is the reason Congress provided relief under § 6163. Thus, arguably § 6163 should apply to all future interests, and not just to reversions and remainders.

Rev. Rul. 76-472[272] discussed valuation of a remainder interest (following a life estate), which was vested subject to partial divestment by the birth or adoption of more children by the life tenant (who was 53 years old). The Ruling stated that appropriate consideration should be given to all facts and circumstances that might decrease the value of the remainder, such as the possibility that an individual of that age would parent or adopt additional children. Although the Ruling suggested that either event is far less likely than "the certainty . . . that attends most other human affairs," developments in the new biology and the potential, for example, for a grandparent to adopt a grandchild makes both possibilities greater than likely was the case in 1976. Thus, any contingent future interest may present valuation difficulties that will affect (and presumably diminish) the amount includible and the tax attributable thereto.

Grimm v. Commissioner[273] addressed the government's ability to collect the tax attributable to a future interest as to which § 6163 deferral was not elected. The remainder beneficiary of a trust died before the life tenant and the government unsuccessfully attempted under the fiduciary

---

[270] See Joint Comm. on Taxation, General Explanation of the Tax Reform Act of 1976, H.R. Rep. No. 1380, 94th Cong., 2d Sess. 546, reprinted at 1976-2 C.B. 558.

[271] For example, "to A, but if A remarries, to B." B's interest is a shifting executory interest.

[272] 1976-2 C.B. 264.

[273] 43 T.C. 623 (1965).

§ 3.3.20

liability provisions of § 6903 to require the trustee to pay the FET attributable to inclusion of the future interest in the remainder benefici-ary's gross estate. The court rejected application of that section because the trustee was not acting for the remainder beneficiary as a fiduciary with respect to any property transferred by the remainder beneficiary. This meant that the government was left with an action against the transferee of the remainder beneficiary's estate to force liquidation of the remainder interest or to seek collection from any other property they received from the remainder beneficiary. Because future interests often are not marketable, both because there is no ready market in the United States and because spendthrift provisions often prohibit their sale, this leaves the government largely without recourse if the future interest beneficiary has little or no other wealth. It also protects the present interest beneficiary from diminution of their interest by reduction in the corpus of the trust to pay the future interest beneficiary's taxes.

A second automatic extension of time for payment is granted under § 6166 for that portion[274] of the tax attributable to inclusion of the value of a closely held business in a decedent's gross estate. Available only to the estate of a citizen or resident of the United States,[275] the FET subject to deferral may be paid in as many as 10 equal annual installments, with the first required no sooner than five years after the time otherwise specified for payment.[276] To qualify for this extension, more than 35% of the value of the decedent's "adjusted gross estate"[277] must consist of an interest in a closely held business.[278] The election to defer FET under § 6166 must be made before the decedent's FET return is due, including any exten-

---

[274] Defined in § 6166(a)(2), the portion is a pro rata amount based on a comparison of the § 6166(b)(5) "closely held business amount" to the § 6166(b)(6) "adjusted gross estate."

[275] See § 6166(a)(1).

[276] See § 6166(a)(3).

[277] Defined for this purpose in § 6166(b)(6) as the gross estate reduced by all amounts that are allowable as § 2053 or § 2054 deductions, even if not allowed because, for example, a § 642(g) election was made to claim those amounts as income tax deductions.

[278] Defined in § 6166(b)(1), substantial complexity surrounds this definition and the planning that is involved in making an estate qualify for deferral under it. This lengthy subject is explored in greater detail in § 15.2.

§ 3.3.20

sions otherwise allowed.[279] And an election to defer any deficiency assessed with respect to an estate that includes an interest in a closely held business that otherwise qualifies may be made within 60 days after notice and demand for payment of the deficiency.[280] The personal representative may elect to treat the timely filed § 6166 deferral election as a timely filed election for discretionary deferral for reasonable cause under § 6161 if the estate ultimately fails to qualify for § 6166 deferral.[281] Finally, unlike other extensions available to defer the payment of tax, the § 6166 deferral may be accelerated upon the occurrence of certain events, such as accumulation of estate income, failure to timely pay an installment, or certain changes in or dispositions of the qualifying business interest.[282]

Although § 2661 incorporates by reference the gift and estate tax deferral provisions for GST purposes, there is as yet no case law, rulings, regulations, or other elaboration available to provide meaning to that seemingly simple proposition.

Problematic about all the automatic and discretionary deferrals is that each requires the taxpayer to pay interest on the taxes deferred. In addition, although the fiduciary's personal liability for payment of the deferred tax under § 6321 may be supplanted by posting a bond under §§ 2204 and 6165, often the requirements for the bond are so onerous[283]

---

[279] See § 6166(d). Protective elections that are dependent upon final determination of the decedent's FET valuation are permitted under Treas. Reg. § 20.6166-1(d). See § 15.2 n.11.

[280] See § 6166(h). The election is not available, however, if the deficiency was attributable to negligence, intentional disregard of rules and regulations, or to fraud with intent to evade tax. § 6166(h)(1) (flush language).

[281] Treas. Reg. § 20.6161-1(b).

[282] See § 6166(g). This complex subject also is explored in greater detail in § 15.2.4.

[283] See Treas. Reg. §§ 20.2204-1(b) and 20.6165-1(a), calling for bonds not in excess of twice the tax deferred, and §§ 2204(c) and 6324A, which provide for a lien with respect to taxes payable in installments under § 6166. See § 6324A(d)(6), which provides that the government may not require the § 6165 bond if the taxpayer makes the appropriate § 6324A lien election, but consult PLR 200027046, stating that the government "can require a *section 6165* bond or accept a *section 6324A* lien agreement, [which] action is discretionary . . ." but cannot require the taxpayer to make the § 6324A election.

On the other hand, CCA 200747019 specifies that the government may not insist on a § 6165 bond and "does not have the authority to reject collateral

that this alternative seems unattractive. Thus, deferral may be costly, and the personal representative may have continuing liability if deferral is selected, making the concept of deferred payment of tax a troubling prospect for many estates because of the possibility that the value of estate property available for payment of the tax will decline during the deferral period to a point at which it no longer is adequate, or that sufficient appreciation will occur to present a serious capital gain tax liability when the property ultimately is sold to produce liquidity for tax payment. Because the §2032 alternate valuation date is at most only six months after the date of the decedent's death, any additional deferral creates potential liability to the personal representative.

Finally, to reflect the fact that the government is made to wait to be paid, §6503(d) provides that any extension of the time to pay the tax under these provisions suspends the statute of limitation for the period of the extension.

§3.3.21 Extensions of Time to Make Elections

Rev. Proc. 92-85[284] establishes the proper procedure and elaborates on the entitlement to request an extension of time under Treas. Reg. §301.9100 to make certain elections required under the Code or Regulations. It is an improvement over prior pronouncements because §9100 relief no longer is strictly limited to deadlines prescribed only by regulation, ruling, procedure, notice, or announcement (administrative pronouncements). Relief now is available with respect to elections that are

---

(Footnote Continued)

proffered by the estate" if the three requirements of §6324A are met (the collateral is expected to survive the deferral period, the collateral agreement is binding on all parties with an interest in the collateral, and the value of the collateral is sufficient to pay the deferred tax and interest payable over the first four years of the deferral period). See ILM 200803016, which is a specific application of those standards to an actual case. Also consider Estate of Roski v. Commissioner, 128 T.C. 113 (2007), which held that the government's policy to never waive the §6165 bond was an invalid administrative failure to exercise discretion that Congress granted to make individuated determinations. Notice 2007-90, 2007-46 I.R.B. 1003, provides interim guidance following *Roski*, pending further review and promulgation of standards to be applied, and Program Manager's Technical Advice (PMTA) 2009-046 provides a comprehensive summary of the government's procedures.

[284] 1992-2 C.B. 490.

required by statute to "be made by the due date of the taxpayer's return
. . . including extensions."

In addition, certain extensions now are automatic and do not require
the filing of a PLR request or payment of fees. These extensions are
available under Treas. Reg. § 301.9100-2(a) and § 4.01 of Rev. Proc. 92-85
if corrective action is taken within 12 months of a deadline for making an
election that was specified only by regulation or other administrative
pronouncement, or under Treas. Reg. § 301.9100-2(b) and § 4.02 of the
Procedure if corrective action is taken within six months of a deadline
that is pegged by statute to the due date of a return (including
extensions).

If these automatic extensions are not applicable or do not give the
relief required, then a request for extension under Treas. Reg.
§ 301.9100-3 and § 5.01 of Rev. Proc. 92-85 requires that the taxpayer
show that the taxpayer acted reasonably and in good faith and that the
requested relief will not prejudice the government's interests. Reasonable action is presumed if the request is made before the government
discovers the failure to timely elect, and prejudice is deemed to exist
only if granting the requested relief gives the taxpayer a lower tax
liability than if the election had been timely made. Treas. Reg.
§ 301.9100-3(c)(ii) and Procedure § 5.02(2) state that "ordinarily [the
government] will not grant relief when tax years . . . affected . . . are
closed by the statute of limitations," which is more likely to involve
income tax issues than those elections under the wealth transfer taxes.

As with avoiding penalties, there is a strong incentive under Rev.
Proc. 92-85 to review elections previously made, because different rules
apply if the government, rather than the taxpayer, discovers a defect.[285]

---

[285] PLRs 9335051, 9335050, and 9335049 all involved the since repealed supplemental FET on excess retirement accumulations imposed by § 4980A and an
election available in § 4980A(d)(5) to defer that tax. Although § 4980A(d)(5) did
not specify how this election was to be made, and no other administrative
pronouncement stated the time within which it must be made, the government
designated a schedule to the FET return Form 706 as the appropriate place to
make the election. The issue involved in these Rulings was: if the FET return as
filed originally did not make the election, could the estate file an amended return
to make that election?

The government's response to requests for § 9100 extensions to make the
election was the interesting aspect of the three nearly identical Rulings, because
it allowed the estates involved to make the election on amended returns but
essentially denied the availability of § 9100 relief. According to the government,

§ 3.3.21

Thus, if a defective election is discovered by the government before a relief request is made, Treas. Reg. §301.9100-3(b)(1) and Rev. Proc.

(Footnote Continued)

(1) because §6018(a)(4) (since repealed) required the Form 706 to be filed if §4980A otherwise would have applied, and (2) because §§6075, 6501, and 6511 prescribed the time within which that return must be filed, any assessment had to be made with respect to it, and any refund claimed, (3) "we will treat the three year [refund] period of section 6511(a) of the Code as the election period" and, on the basis thereof, (4) because "the section 4980A(d)(5) election period is prescribed by statute, relief under section 301.9100-1 of the regulations and Rev. Proc. 92-85 would not be available" to a taxpayer who failed to make the election on a timely basis. In these cases the amended returns making the elections were filed within the §6511(a) three year period; thus, they were timely and the government respected them for §4980A(d)(5) election purposes, without the need for a §9100 extension. But clearly the upshot of these Rulings is that further relief under §9100 would be denied to any taxpayer who failed to make the election on a proper amended return. PLR 9437041 reached the same effective result, the government stating that the time for filing an amended return had not expired and that this was the appropriate avenue rather than requesting §9100 relief.

The result reached probably is correct even though the government's explanation of its conclusion was not entirely accurate, and notwithstanding that it seems questionable whether the intent of Rev. Proc. 92-85 and §9100 is served by the backhanded determination that the time for filing the election is prescribed by statute and therefore is not subject to §9100 relief. Treas. Reg. §301.9100-2(b) and Rev. Proc. 92-85 §4.02 automatically permit corrective action to be taken within six months of a deadline that is pegged by statute to the due date of a return, which may mean that §9100 relief should not be denied in other cases involving this election (although it might have been denied properly in these cases, under facts that cannot be determined from the Rulings themselves). Furthermore, Treas. Reg. §301.9100-3(b) and Rev. Proc. 92-85 §5.01 state that, even if this automatic extension period is not available, a request for extension will be respected if the taxpayer acted reasonably and in good faith, provided that the requested relief will not prejudice the government's interests.

Presumably the reason these Rulings stated categorically that no §9100 relief could be obtained is attributable to Treas. Reg. §301.9100-3(c)(1)(ii) and Rev. Proc. 92-85 §5.02(2), which state that "ordinarily [the government] will not grant relief when tax years . . . affected . . . are closed by the statute of limitations." Although the Rulings did not elaborate sufficiently to verify this analysis, this provision might explain the government's focus on the §6511 refund period and its statement that, once that period has expired, no relief under §9100 is available. Whatever the rationale, the Rulings underscore the importance of timely postmortem action that follows diligent attention to a comprehensive checklist of estate administration actions and elections that are available.

§3.3.21

92-85 §5.01(2) get into specifics of what must be shown to prove reasonable action by the taxpayer, including reasonable reliance on a tax professional, and they then define reasonable reliance for this purpose in a manner that may become a standard for other tax purposes as well, such as to avoid the late filing or late payment penalties. Although this is pure speculation, it might be useful to consider that included in the list are:

> (a) the taxpayer inadvertently failed to make the election because of certain intervening events beyond the taxpayer's control or, because after exercising reasonable diligence (taking into account the taxpayer's experience and the complexity of the return or issue), the taxpayer was unaware of the necessity of the election;

> (b) the taxpayer reasonably relied on the written advice of the Service; or

> (c) the taxpayer reasonably relied on a qualified tax professional . . . [who] failed to make or advise the taxpayer to make the election.

Notice the requirement that instructions from the government be in writing, and note also the term "qualified" tax advisor. The Procedure also states that reasonable reliance does not exist if "the taxpayer knew or should have known the tax professional was not competent to render advice on the election [or] . . . was not aware of all relevant facts."

Finally, Treas. Reg. §301.9100-3(b)(3) and Rev. Proc. 92-85 §§5.01(4) and (5) state affirmatively that "[a] taxpayer will not be considered to have acted reasonably and in good faith . . . if . . . the taxpayer seeks to alter a return position for which an accuracy related penalty . . . could [be] imposed . . . [or] uses hindsight in requesting relief." As is the case under §6503(d), which suspends the statute of limitation for collecting any tax that is the subject of an extension of the time to pay the tax, Treas. Reg. §301.9100-3(d) and §8 of the Procedure establish the government's right to re-examine issues affected by an extension and the time within which to assess taxes based on an election that is allowed.

§3.3.22 Statutes of Limitation on Contesting Decedent's Tax Liability

Under §6511(a) a claim for refund of tax must be commenced within two years after the tax was paid or within three years after the return was filed, whichever is later. Thus, like § 6503(d) and the statute of limitation regarding payment, § 6511(a) effectively expands the statute of limitation with respect to a return if a filing extension was granted.[286]

Any taxpayer suit to enforce a refund[287] must be filed within the § 6532(a) two year period after a refund claim is disallowed.[288] Thus, for example, in Jones v. United States,[289] the government disallowed an FET marital deduction, believing that D was not married to S. A refund claim was disallowed under § 6511(a) because it came only after a local probate court found—four years later—that there was a common law marriage. In Snyder v. United States[290] the three year window for filing a claim after filing the return did not apply (because no return was filed) and some tax was paid more than two years before filing the claim and some tax was paid within the two year period. The court held that § 6511(b)(2)(B) limits recovery to only the portion paid during the two years immediately

---

[286] A number of exceptions to the three year statute may apply. For example, in Estate of Williamson v. Commissioner, 72 T.C.M. (CCH) 687 (1996), the taxpayer requested and the government granted an extension of the time to file the FET return. When the FET return ultimately was filed a copy of that extension request was included. The request revealed the assets involved and their values. The government missed the three year limitation period to assess a deficiency but, because the return did not otherwise itemize assets or values, the government asserted that the applicable statute of limitation was six years under § 6501(e) because there were substantial omissions from the return. Stating that the question was a matter of first impression, the Tax Court rejected the government's argument because the return with the extension request attached was adequate to put the government on notice regarding the nature and amount of the omitted items.

[287] Edinburg v. United States, 617 F.2d 206 (Ct. Cl. 1980), illustrates that § 6532(a)(1) applies equally to a suit instituted within two years after disallowance of a claim to recover interest paid on an amount claimed as well as to the amount itself.

[288] In addition, noted in Estate of Davenport v. United States, 736 F. Supp. 2d 1087 (E.D. Mich. 2010), and in Green v. United States, 2010-2 U.S. Tax Cas. (CCH) ¶ 60,600 (N.D. Okla. 2010), aff'd, 2011-2 U.S. Tax Cas. (CCH) ¶ 60,620 (10th Cir. 2011), is a jurisdictional prerequisite to a suit for a refund, that a claim for refund must be filed with the government and either denied or not acted upon for six months. Prior to either event the federal district courts have no § 7422(a) jurisdiction to hear such a suit.

[289] 89-2 U.S. Tax Cas. (CCH) ¶ 13,826 (D. S.C. 1989).

[290] 616 F.2d 1187 (10th Cir. 1980).

§ 3.3.22

preceding filing of the claim.[291] And Union Commerce Bank v. United States[292] shows that § 6532(a) operates in a similar manner if separate refund claims are disallowed but suit is commenced within two years after only the last of those determinations.

The absolute character of these limitations is illustrated by Fletcher v. United States,[293] in which a refund suit was disallowed, notwithstanding that it was determined—almost seven years after the decedent died

---

[291] And see Essex v. United States, 80-1 U.S. Tax Cas. (CCH) ¶ 13,342 (D. Neb. 1980) (refund claim filed within two years after paying deficiency but more than three years after the return was filed and more than two years after the tax shown on the return was paid; only the deficiency amount was recoverable); TAM 9535013 (taxpayer paid estimated tax when making a request to extend the time to file, and then delayed for over three years before filing the return and subsequently asking for a refund of the money originally paid; under § 6511(b)(2)(A) the government rejected the refund request because the payment of estimated tax was regarded as a payment and not a deposit, meaning that the three year statute of limitation applied from the date of the payment and had expired); Boensel v. United States, 2011-2 U. S. Tax Cas. (CCH) ¶ 50,560 (Ct. Fed. Cl. 2011) (taxpayer paid estimated tax but did not timely file a return or request to extend the time to file; when the return subsequently was filed over seven years later the taxpayer's refund request properly was denied because the remittance was regarded as a payment of estimated tax and not as a deposit, and the request for refund came more than three years after the date of that payment).

[292] 638 F.2d 962 (6th Cir. 1981), aff'g 463 F. Supp. 842 (N.D. Ohio 1979) (plaintiff's second refund claim sought $2,000 more than a first and, after both claims were disallowed, suit was timely filed only with respect to the second claim; only the additional $2,000 not barred by the statute of limitation from the first claim could be sought in the refund suit).

[293] 81-1 U.S. Tax Cas. (CCH) ¶ 13,385 (Ct. Cl. 1980). See also Webb v. United States, 66 F.3d 691 (4th Cir. 1995), rev'g 850 F. Supp. 489 (E.D. Va. 1994) (taxpayer whose attorney in fact made fraudulent transfers and paid gift tax thereon recovered the transferred funds after discovering the fraud and thereafter sought a refund of gift tax paid; equitable tolling was denied and the statute of limitation was applied as to the portion of tax paid more than two years before the refund action was filed); Southern California First Nat'l Bank v. United States, 298 F. Supp. 1249 (S.D. Calif. 1969) (similar; a protective refund claim should have been filed when the action challenging validity of gifts was commenced, which was more than eight months before expiration of refund limitation period); First Nat'l Bank v. United States, 226 F. Supp. 166 (S.D. Fla. 1963) (denying a gift tax refund action brought shortly after a state court invalidated

§ 3.3.22

and almost six years after the return was filed and the tax was paid—that an asset included in the decedent's gross estate was improperly acquired by and, therefore, did not belong to the decedent.

§ 3.3.23 Equitable Recoupment After the Limitation Period Expires

Equitable recoupment (and the related "duty of consistency") can be used in limited circumstances to mitigate the effect of the statute of limitation serving to bar a tax refund claim. These equitable doctrines have been applied in only a handful of cases and rulings, most notably

---

(Footnote Continued)

the gifts but more than three years after the gift tax return was filed and more than two years after the gift tax was paid).

On the income tax side of this issue see Brockamp v. United States, 519 U.S. 347 (1997), rev'g 67 F.3d 260 (9th Cir. 1995), rev'g an unpublished opinion (C.D. Cal.), unanimously reversing the appellate court's holding that in appropriate cases the statute of limitation may be equitably tolled in a tax refund suit. Involved in *Brockamp* was an allegedly senile taxpayer who, before death, paid income tax that was not owed to the government and that was not discovered until after the taxpayer's death. The appellate court stated that "it would be unconscionable to allow the government to retain money that it concedes it was not owed, and may have only received due to a 93 year-old man's senility," and concluded that, if "extraordinary circumstances beyond [the] plaintiff's control" make it impossible to file a tax refund claim on time, equitable tolling of the statute of limitation may apply. There was a triable issue of fact whether the taxpayer was senile when the overpayment was made and therefore whether the taxpayer's personal representative could pursue a refund after the taxpayer's death. The Supreme Court found that all other cases have properly rejected equitable tolling on administrative grounds, and concluded that the clear and explicit limitations of § 6511 suggest that Congress decided to impose an occasional unfairness in exchange for a more workable tax enforcement system that would not generate the administrative problem of evaluating every alleged equitable reason for deviating from the statute of limitation.

See also Kellogg-Citizens Nat'l Bank v. United States, 330 F.2d 635 (Ct. Cl. 1964) (deduction of income tax liability and attorney fees was precluded because income tax dispute was resolved after limitation period expired and no protective refund claim was filed), and Stein, Will Equitable Tolling of the Statute of Limitations Gain Wider Acceptance in Tax Cases?, 81 J. Tax'n 370 (1994), discussing earlier cases.

the Supreme Court's decision in United States v. Dalm,[294] and the application of each doctrine still is being tested.

Equitable recoupment may apply if a single transaction or taxable event is subjected to two taxes based on inconsistent theories, with the amount claimed in recoupment barred by limitation but the government's alleged deficiency not. *Dalm* illustrates the type of circumstance in which relief is claimed. The taxpayer was a former employee of the decedent and served as personal representative of the decedent's estate. In this capacity the taxpayer was paid a fee, which the taxpayer reported as income. The decedent's surviving brother also distributed to the taxpayer amounts totaling one-third of the decedent's estate, to "carry out the decedent's wishes." The taxpayer paid the brother's gift tax on these distributions, treating them as a net gift. Six years later the government determined that these distributions were income to the taxpayer, representing additional fees for serving as personal representative, and assessed an income tax deficiency. The taxpayer contested this asserted income tax liability in the Tax Court but ultimately settled the case and paid the income tax liability.

In the income tax case the taxpayer did not assert a claim for credit or refund of the gift tax already paid on the inconsistent gift tax allegation of the government. Instead, the taxpayer promptly filed a claim with the government for refund of the gift tax previously paid, which the government refused to honor because the gift tax statute of limitation had run. So the taxpayer filed an action in district court for equitable recoupment, which the district court dismissed for lack of jurisdiction. The court of appeals reversed, holding that equitable recoupment should be available in the taxpayer's case, notwithstanding that it was brought as an affirmative claim for a refund rather than asserted as a defensive offset in another case in which the taxpayer properly asserted jurisdiction. The Supreme Court reversed the court of appeals on the jurisdictional ground originally relied upon by the district court.

The taxpayer in *Dalm* correctly alleged that the government had argued inconsistent positions (income and gift tax) relative to the same transaction but failed to assert the equitable recoupment defense in the

---

[294] 494 U.S. 596 (1990), rev'g 867 F.2d 305 (6th Cir. 1989), rev'g 89-1 U.S. Tax Cas. (CCH) ¶ 13,807 (W.D. Mich. 1987).

§ 3.3.23

proper action. In reversing the district court's dismissal of the case, the court of appeals found merit in the taxpayer's claim because it was not until the income tax case was resolved that the taxpayer was able to seek a refund of the improper and inconsistently assessed gift tax. Notwithstanding the taxpayer's posture as plaintiff in the case, the appellate court regarded the equitable recoupment action as "in the nature of a defense" to the income tax case and held that it was not barred by the statute of limitation because it was timely filed in response to the government's income tax deficiency.

Thus, although the taxpayer could not have filed the equitable recoupment action as an affirmative gift tax refund claim after the gift tax statute of limitation had run, the appellate court held that the claim was timely because "there [was] a timely government claim of deficiency based on an inconsistent theory" of taxing the same transaction for income tax purposes. According to the court of appeals, if a single transaction is taxed twice under inconsistent legal theories and the government has collected the second tax in a timely action, the earlier tax may be offset against the later tax as a claim for refund, even if that claim is a separate legal proceeding that otherwise is time barred by the statute of limitation.

The Supreme Court rejected this logic and the taxpayer's argument that it should not matter whether the claim is asserted as an offset in the income tax case or as a separate claim for a refund of the gift tax improperly assessed and paid, stating that

> [a] distinction that has jurisdiction as its central concept is not meaningless . . . .
>
> [A] party litigating a tax claim in a *timely* proceeding may, in that proceeding, seek recoupment of a related, and inconsistent, but now time-barred tax claim relating to the same transaction . . . . To date, we have not allowed equitable recoupment to be the sole basis for jurisdiction.[295]

A vigorous dissent by Justice Stevens suggested that the taxpayer did not err in failing to assert equitable recoupment in the Tax Court proceeding involving the income tax because Rev. Rul. 71-56[296] states that equitable recoupment is not available in the Tax Court. As a result,

---

[295] 494 U.S. at 606, 608 (emphasis added).

[296] 1971-1 C.B. 404.

Justice Stevens argued that the taxpayer was justified in settling the income tax case and then suing for a refund of the gift tax in a separate proceeding. According to his dissent, the majority opinion in *Dalm* essentially foreclosed equitable recoupment except to those with enough wealth to pay the second asserted tax liability and sue for a refund in District Court or the Court of Federal Claims, in which an equitable recoupment claim properly is asserted.

In Estate of Mueller v. Commissioner[297] the Tax Court determined in a 13-to-5 reviewed decision that Rev. Rul. 71-56 is not correct. The Tax Court concluded that it has jurisdiction to apply the concept of equitable recoupment, notwithstanding the absence of express statutory authority and despite a long line of cases in which the Tax Court previously rejected the notion that it has jurisdiction to entertain that affirmative defense. The Tax Court concluded[298] that equitable recoupment does not require the court to exercise jurisdiction beyond the taxpayer's claim for a redetermination of its total tax deficiency and that the taxpayer is entitled to assert affirmative defenses to a government asserted deficiency. Therefore, the taxpayer was permitted to assert affirmative defenses, including equitable recoupment, notwithstanding that the taxpayer is the nominal plaintiff in the Tax Court. Thus, the court rejected the government's motion in *Mueller* to dismiss the taxpayer's amended petition to assert an income tax overpayment that was time barred as an affirmative defense against the government's asserted FET deficiency, all attributable to a valuation redetermination[299] that would increase the amount includible in the decedent's estate and, correspondingly, would increase the beneficiary's basis in that property.

If the equitable recoupment offset claim is raised properly in a timely suit for redetermination of the taxpayer's deficiency in a case otherwise subject to the Tax Court's jurisdiction, *Mueller* would have allowed taxpayers to litigate in one forum all aspects of a tax case. Rather than asserting some affirmative defenses to an alleged deficiency in the Tax Court and litigating separately in District Court or the Court of Federal Claims any right to a refund that is attributable to the Tax Court

---

[297] 101 T.C. 551 (1993).

[298] Based on a reference in *Dalm*, 494 U.S. at 611 n.8.

[299] See Estate of Mueller v. Commissioner, 63 T.C.M. (CCH) 3027 (1992).

§ 3.3.23

resolution (with the risk that the refund litigation may be time barred when the deficiency determination has been resolved).[300]

A dissent in *Mueller* concluded on a simple reading of the Code that Tax Court jurisdiction is limited to determining the correct amount of any deficiency asserted by the government and that the term "deficiency" as defined in § 6211 does not include ancillary rights not involved in the tax computation on the return involved in the government's claimed deficiency. Because the decedent's FET liability is separate from the income tax consequences of the decedent's beneficiaries, the dissent would have held that the Tax Court has no jurisdiction over the equitable recoupment claim of an income tax refund offset against an FET liability. That dissenting opinion appears to be a proper reading of the Code, and was affirmed by the court on appeal of the third Tax Court decision in *Mueller*, noted below. Notwithstanding that the majority opinion had the advantage of judicial economy and (dare it be said in a tax context) equity. As illustrated in *Dalm* itself, if not available as an affirmative defense in the case pending before the court, equitable recoupment may be unenforceable by the taxpayer elsewhere. Notwithstanding that it is proper due to inconsistent positions taken by the government. The Tax Court majority opinion freed the taxpayer from the tyranny of procedural impediments to establishing the proper overall tax liability without requiring piecemeal litigation.

---

[300] This result in *Mueller* subsequently was followed in Estate of Bartels v. Commissioner, 106 T.C. 430 (1996), involving a time barred FET overpayment asserted as an offset against a stipulated income tax liability. The government and taxpayer agreed that all factors affecting equitable recoupment were met and the sole issue was the court's jurisdiction, the government urging the court to overrule *Mueller*. Citing its "painstaking" review of the issue in *Mueller*, the Tax Court rejected this "invitation" and instead held that the issue was not jurisdictional at all, because the income tax case properly was before it. In affirming its prior determination that the court has authority to apply equitable recoupment, in this case against an income tax deficiency, the Tax Court also noted that § 6214(b) upon which the government relied does not refer to FET deficiencies and "therefore [does] not preclude us from allowing equitable recoupment of an estate tax overpayment against an income tax deficiency." On that point the Tax Court subsequently was reversed, as noted below.

Subsequently, Estate of Mueller v. Commissioner[301] came before the Tax Court again, following the court's earlier decision that the court had jurisdiction of both the government's timely filed FET deficiency and the taxpayer's otherwise time barred income tax refund. In this iteration the Tax Court held that equitable recoupment may apply the otherwise time-barred affirmative defense as an offset to the timely-asserted deficiency, but it cannot be used by the taxpayer to assert a time-barred claim to a refund. The simple facts in *Mueller* involved the government asserting a higher FET value for stock subsequently sold by the taxpayer at a gain that would have been less had the proper valuation informed the tax-payer's determination of basis under § 1014(b)(9). The asserted income tax overpayment was applied as an offset against the FET liability attributable to revaluation of the stock and the refund flowed from a subsequently discovered § 2013 previously taxed property credit that was available to the taxpayer and that eliminated all FET liability notwith-standing the stock revaluation. Having litigated the otherwise time-barred income tax issue, and not needing the offset it produced to eliminate the FET liability attributable to the stock revaluation, the taxpayer claimed a refund for income tax purposes. The Tax Court rejected this on the ground that equitable recoupment may permit a time-barred issue to be asserted as an affirmative defense to an asserted deficiency but may not operate to overcome the statute of limitation that otherwise would bar the income tax refund.

In its affirmation of this result the court on appeal let the Tax Court's decision stand that the taxpayer could not recover, but did so by holding that the earlier Tax Court opinion allowing the taxpayer to assert the equitable recoupment claim was in error. According to the court on appeal the Tax Court lacked jurisdiction over the income tax refund claim. On that basis, essentially this affirmation of the Tax Court's third *Mueller* decision was a reversal of the second. Notwithstanding that conclusion, the Tax Court yet again, in Estate of Orenstein v. Commis-sioner,[302] disagreed with the appellate court in *Mueller* and concluded

---

[301] 107 T.C. 189 (1996) (a 12-5 reviewed opinion), aff'd, 153 F.3d 302 (6th Cir. 1998).

[302] 79 T.C.M. (CCH) 1971 (2000) (decedent's income tax deficiency was determined postmortem, after the decedent's FET statute of limitation had expired; a § 2053(a)(3) protective claim to an estate tax deduction was not claimed for that income tax liability).

§ 3.3.23

that it had jurisdiction to permit a reduction in an income tax deficiency for FET that would have been saved if the income tax deficiency was allowed as a time barred FET deduction.

One dissenting opinion to the third Tax Court decision in *Mueller* argued that, once equitable recoupment has opened the statute of limitation door and a determination on the merits is authorized, a refund should be available if the government's asserted deficiency is less substantial than the taxpayer's asserted overpayment. The notion expressed was that equitable recoupment should permit a transactional review in which all the tax consequences of an interrelated transaction are open to revision. Under that vision, the §2013 credit would eliminate the government's asserted FET liability and the income tax overpayment would remain for taxpayer recovery.

The ultimate conclusion of a second dissenting opinion (which contained an exhaustive summary of the equitable recoupment doctrine itself) was that equitable recoupment is a joinder rule that allows consideration of all issues properly brought before the court, regardless of whether the final result of the litigation is a deficiency or refund. Otherwise, the dissent argued, the majority decision means that it might be impossible to know until the final Rule 155 calculation whether a taxpayer was in an overpayment or a deficiency position in a case involving multiple issues and, therefore, it would be impossible until the final adjudication to know whether equitable recoupment should be applicable in the first instance. In the wake of the final appellate resolution of the third *Mueller* decision in the Tax Court, neither dissenting position states a viable position. Between *Dalm* at the Supreme Court and *Mueller* on final appeal, it may be that equitable recoupment has been restored to a narrow and not particularly useful theory.

Equitable recoupment also was involved in Fairley v. United States.[303] After the FET statute of limitation had run, the decedent's estate filed an amended FET return, seeking a refund by deducting under §2053 an income tax liability assessed for tax years prior to the decedent's death. The amended FET return was rejected as untimely, so the decedent's personal representative next claimed this FET refund amount as a reduction of the income tax liability. In allowing a setoff of

---

[303] 90-1 U.S. Tax Cas. (CCH) ¶ 60,018 (8th Cir. 1990), rev'g 89-1 U.S. Tax Cas. (CCH) ¶ 9128 (E.D. Ark. 1988).

§ 3.3.23

this amount against the income tax deficiency, the lower court noted that the doctrine of equitable recoupment is designed "to avoid the bar of the statute of limitations, especially in cases such as this where the income tax deficiency was not assessed until after the opportunity to seek a refund of the estate [tax] was barred."[304] In reversing, the Court of Appeals for the Eighth Circuit relied on *Dalm* for the proposition that the taxpayer's remedy was to assert equitable recoupment in a timely filed defense to, or refund action arising from, the asserted income tax deficiency. Having failed to establish the appropriate jurisdictional predicate for relief, the court rejected the use of equitable recoupment as a means independently to obtain relief by seeking a time barred refund of the FET.[305]

In United States v. Commercial National Bank,[306] the taxpayer disputed the FET valuation of stock that was includible in a decedent's estate. In addition, shares of that stock were sold and a capital gains tax was paid on the basis of the original FET valuation. When a compromise of the FET case was reached, resulting in a higher valuation, the taxpayer requested a refund of income tax paid on the capital gain, reflecting the higher stepped up basis attributable to the settlement. Notwithstanding that the statute of limitation had run on that refund claim, the court permitted the taxpayer's claim but admonished taxpayers in general: "We strongly hope that taxpayers faced with similar situations will heed our now explicit warning to file conditional or protective claims or requests for an extension of time if the nature or amount of their refund likely will remain unsettled until after the limitations period has expired."[307] The court's advice would avoid the need to litigate these types of cases.[308]

---

[304] 89-1 U.S. Tax Cas. at 87,099.

[305] See also Schenectady Trust Co. v. United States, 88-1 U.S. Tax Cas. (CCH) ¶ 13,751 (N.D. N.Y. 1987); Estate of Schneider v. Commissioner, 93 T.C. 568 (1989). But see Estate of Orenstein v. Commissioner, 79 T.C.M. (CCH) 1971 (2000), which allowed just such a timely claimed reduction in an income tax deficiency for the FET that would be saved if a § 2053(a)(3) deduction for that income tax liability had not been time barred by the FET statute of limitation.

[306] 874 F.2d 1165 (7th Cir. 1989).

[307] 874 F.2d at 1176.

[308] See, e.g., Malcolm v. United States, 92-1 U.S. Tax Cas. (CCH) ¶ 60,097 (N.D. Cal. 1992) (§ 6511 barred § 2053 deduction for attorney's fees incurred in

§ 3.3.23

Litigation is not required to assert the doctrine, as recognized by the government in PLR 7839131, in which late gift tax returns were filed for a decedent after the FET limitation period had expired. Because gift tax and interest payable would have been deductible in determining the decedent's FET liability, the government allowed equitable recoupment of the FET overpayment against the gift tax deficiency.

Because equitable recoupment can be a two edged sword, taxpayers should be careful when considering whether to seek a refund on an issue that is related to one previously settled. For example, in Trust Services of

---

(Footnote Continued)

will contest settled after limitation period expired; executors failed to follow the court's advice in *Commercial National Bank*, which the *Malcolm* court cited with approval, that the taxpayer file a conditional or protective refund claim or a request for extension of the statute of limitation); Swietlik v. United States, 85-2 U.S. Tax Cas. (CCH) ¶ 13,622 (E.D. Wis. 1985), aff'd, 779 F.2d 1306 (7th Cir. 1985) (will contest was settled over four years after decedent died, resulting in attorney's fees that would be deductible for FET purposes; FET return was filed and tax paid nine months after decedent died, so attempt was made to obtain a refund of FET paid as if the deduction for attorney's fees had been taken) denied a refund claim, stating that § 6511(a) requires that a claim for refund must be filed within three years of the date the return was filed or within two years of payment of the tax, whichever is longer. Therefore, the plaintiff should have filed a protective claim because the will contest that led to the attorney's fees was known about within the § 6511 period.

Davis v. United States, 2012-1 U.S. Tax Cas. (CCH) ¶ 60,634 (N.D. Miss. 2011), aff'd per curium, 2012-2 U.S. Tax Cas. (CCH) ¶ 60,650 (unpub. 5th Cir. 2012), is another unfortunate illustration of the wisdom of the court's advice. The estate filed its Form 706 based on a mistaken belief that the decedent owned farm property in fee simple. Postmortem litigation established that the decedent owned only a vested remainder. The first determination on that issue in state court was well within the time to file an amended return, to reduce the value reported for estate tax purposes and claim a refund. But the estate delayed filing that claim until it lost a subsequent appeal and its petition to the state supreme court was denied. By then it was too late to make a timely claim for refund and the court, notwithstanding being "sympathetic to the plaintiff's plight," concluded that the law precluded the taxpayer's suit for refund. Noting that the original determination was made within the time for filing, the court stated that the estate could have filed an administrative claim to preserve its right to a refund when the litigation was finally resolved.

See § 15.4.2.2 with respect to filing protective claims for refunds based on Treas. Reg. § § 20.2053-1(d) and -4 and the deduction of fees and other administration expenses not yet paid when a decedent's FET return is filed.

§ 3.3.23

America, Inc. v. United States,[309] the decedent's estate filed an FET return, was audited, paid an agreed upon deficiency, and received a closing letter. The estate filed a refund claim 13 months later, which resulted in a District Court action in which the government asserted an offset against the claimed refund, based on several issues that were resolved when it issued the closing letter. Eventually the parties agreed that a refund was appropriate unless the court found for the government on its setoff defenses. Based on the closing letter, the District Court held that the government was estopped from raising those offsetting defenses. The Court of Appeals for the Ninth Circuit reversed because "the government cannot be estopped from reevaluating the tax consequences of the items on which the taxpayer's claim for refund is based."[310] Although the government could not raise those issues anew on its own motion, it could raise them as a direct defense to the same or a closely related issue that was raised by the taxpayer's action. In essence, the door was closed to the government until the taxpayer opened it. The government is not estopped once the taxpayer puts the issue on the table.[311]

---

[309] 885 F.2d 561 (9th Cir. 1989).

[310] 885 F.2d at 566. The court also stated that it did "not condone the government's behavior in this case. If the government does not view an FET closing letter as binding in a refund suit, it should say so in the letter." The government does not do so.

[311] See also Wilmington Trust Co. v. United States, 79-1 U.S. Tax Cas. (CCH) ¶ 13,283 (Ct. Cl. 1979) (notwithstanding that FET statute of limitation precluded government from assessing FET deficiency, government was allowed to reduce income tax refund by FET liability that arose because estate deducted income taxes that were the subject of the refund); Mann v. United States, 552 F. Supp. 1132 (N.D. Tex. 1982), aff'd, 731 F.2d 267 (5th Cir. 1984) (government precluded from reducing income tax refund by FET that, although barred by statute of limitation, would have been due if value of income tax refund had been included as asset for FET purposes, but only because FET liability and income tax refund were not subject of a single transaction or taxable event that was subjected to two taxes on inconsistent theories); TAM 8322001 (rejecting equitable recoupment claim that involved three taxpayers: Donor made gifts to Donee that Donor never reported for gift tax purposes; that property was includible in Donee's gross estate when Donee subsequently died, and passed to Donee's surviving Spouse; when Donor died a gift tax transferee liability was assessed against Spouse, who sought to reduce that tax liability by a claimed FET refund because, if the gift tax liability had been known when Donee's estate was administered, a § 2053 deduc-

§ 3.3.23

In the same vein, PLR 9033034 involved a § 2053 deduction claimed for fees the estate expected to pay the personal representative and its attorney. The fiduciary and the attorney agreed to a reduction in their fees long after the statute of limitation for that return had expired. The government agreed with the estate that it was too late to alter the FET return and that its deduction would not be reduced. Instead, the government opined that the reduction in fees constituted a § 61(a)(12) discharge of indebtedness that caused income to the estate, based on

> a longstanding doctrine known as the "duty of consistency." This rule is applicable when:
>
>> (1) the taxpayer has made a representation or reported an item for tax purposes in one year, and
>>
>> (2) the Commissioner has acquiesced in or relied on that fact for that year, and
>>
>> (3) the taxpayer desires to change the representation, previously made, in a later year after the statute of limitations on assessments bars adjustments for the initial tax year.

Having deducted the fees as if it had paid them already, the estate simply was not allowed in retrospect to act as if it really did not owe them to the fiduciary and the attorney. As a result, the estate incurred income that flowed out to its beneficiaries under § 662 for income tax purposes. This duty of consistency is of the same nature as equitable recoupment and constitutes the government's equity theory precluding taxpayers from advocating inconsistent positions. Application of the duty of consistency on the government's behalf is not at odds with the result in *Dalm,* which denied equitable recoupment relief purely on jurisdictional grounds and not because the theory lacks legitimacy.

An important limitation on the theory of equitable recoupment is illustrated by TAM 9036002, in which Husband and Wife made gifts of joint tenancy property within three years of Husband's death. Although each properly reported a gift of only half the property, Husband's estate

---

(Footnote Continued)

tion would have been available and Donee's FET would have been reduced; because FET statute of limitation had expired, Spouse claimed equitable recoupment against transferee gift tax liability, which the government rejected because gift tax and FET were not the result of inconsistent tax treatment of the same transaction); TAM 8441005 (equitable recoupment does not allow FET barred by statute of limitation to be applied against transferee liability for income tax).

included 100% of the value of the property for FET purposes, apparently under the pre-1982 version of § 2035. This error was not discovered until an audit was conducted of Wife's FET return, which was after the limitation period had expired for Husband's estate to claim a refund of the taxes it paid attributable to this error.[312] So Wife's estate asserted a right to apply those taxes improperly paid by Husband's estate against Wife's FET liability, thinking that Wife's FET liability was affected by inclusion in Wife's adjusted taxable gifts base of half of the gift and that this was inconsistent with Husband's FET treatment of the gift. Thus, under the doctrine of equitable recoupment, the Wife's estate claimed it was entitled to Husband's FET refund as an offset against its liability, notwithstanding that the time for Husband's estate to claim a refund had expired.

The TAM agreed that Husband's FET treatment was inconsistent with Wife's gift tax treatment and that these inconsistent tax results arose from the same transaction. It also agreed that equitable recoupment is a proper mechanism to apply a time barred refund against an asserted tax liability (or vice versa, if the government is asserting the theory to offset a time barred tax liability against a timely claim for refund), provided that (1) the overpaid tax liability and the asserted deficiency arose from the same transaction, and (2) the overpayment and deficiency involve the same taxpayer. Because the government was not subjecting Wife's estate to inconsistent tax liabilities, it deemed equitable recoupment to be unavailable because Wife "is requesting a refund of taxes correctly paid [by Wife] in order to obtain a refund of taxes incorrectly paid by [Husband's estate]. We do not believe that equitable recoupment was meant to apply in such a way." Despite the unfortunate mistake made by Husband's estate, it seems proper that one—albeit related—taxpayer not be permitted to assert a right to a refund that was not prosecuted by another taxpayer. The inherent fairness of this conclusion is illustrated by the fact that Wife's estate would have had no

---

[312] The TAM cited Rev. Rul. 81-227, 1981-2 C.B. 168, which dealt with a similar joint tenancy gift situation and reveals that the FET rule applicable when Husband died was inconsistent with the related gift tax results, so it is understandable that Husband's estate made the error.

§ 3.3.23

opportunity for equitable recoupment if Husband had died after Wife and made the same mistake.[313]

On the other hand, there may be a sufficient relation between taxpayers that, albeit they are separate and their liabilities are different, they are sufficiently linked to permit equitable recoupment. At least that was the holding in Estate of Branson v. Commissioner,[314] in which excessive capital gain income tax liability otherwise barred from refund by the statute of limitation was offset against an FET deficiency. Each tax liability flowed from a valuation increase for FET purposes that informed a higher basis and lower capital gain, so equitable recoupment was regarded as proper. The unusual aspect was that the decedent's estate realized the capital gain upon its sale of estate assets that were the subject of revaluation, but the tax was reported and paid by beneficiaries

[313] Parker v. United States, 110 F.3d 678 (9th Cir. 1997), confirms this analysis that spouses are two separate taxpayers and that equitable recoupment cannot net the tax liability of one against an overpayment by the other. The decedent's estate overpaid its FET because it failed to deduct the decedent's debt to a predeceased spouse (attributable to the decedent having embezzled from the spouse). One of the government's defenses to the claimed refund of overpaid tax was that the predeceased spouse had a cause of action against the decedent that should have been included in the spouse's estate and that, although the statute of limitation had expired with respect to the predeceased spouse's estate, the government could net the spouse's unenforceable liability against the claimed refund. The lower court embraced equitable recoupment because the same parties who sought the refund also enjoyed the benefit of undertaxation of the predeceased spouse's estate. In reversing, the court on appeal noted that equitable recoupment can apply only if a single taxable event or transaction is subject to two taxes based on inconsistent legal theories and that, if separate taxpayers are involved, equitable recoupment requires "a sufficient identity of interest" between them that the separate taxpayers should be treated as one. Although the same ultimate beneficiaries were involved in the two estates, the court then noted that the real taxpayers in interest were two separate estates and that there was no single transaction or taxable event, meaning that netting the overpayment of the one estate against the time-barred underpayment of the other was inappropriate. On the other hand, occasionally the government argues that separate taxpayers, including spouses and their estates, are sufficiently joined in interest that they cannot take inconsistent tax positions. See the discussion of this duty of consistency in § 13.5.6 at text accompanying nn.93–96.

[314] 113 T.C. 6 (1999) (a reviewed opinion with three judges dissenting), aff'd, 264 F.3d 904 (9th Cir. 2001). A companion case on the substantive valuation issue is Estate of Branson v. Commissioner, 78 T.C.M. (CCH) 78 (1999).

§ 3.3.23

of the estate to whom that liability was attributable because of estate distributions that carried it out to them. Nevertheless, because of that linkage, the income tax capital gain liability was properly regarded as the estate's. More importantly in the wake of the earlier reversal of the Tax Court in *Mueller III*, the courts in *Branson* adhered to the Tax Court's prior position that equitable recoupment has a proper jurisdictional predicate in the Tax Court.[315]

As articulated by the government's own lawyer in FSA 200118002 and reaffirmed in ILM 201033030, "[t]he doctrine of equitable recoupment may apply to lift the statutory bar by allowing a party to use a tax claim, barred by the statute of limitation, as a defense to the opposing party's timely tax claim . . . " but, as established by Supreme Court precedent, only if:

> (1) the refund or deficiency for which recoupment is sought by way of offset is barred by time; (2) the time-barred offset arises out of the same transaction, item, or taxable event as the overpayment or deficiency; (3) the transaction, item, or taxable event has been inconsistently subjected to two taxes; and (4) if the subject transaction, item, or taxable event involves two or more taxpayers, there is sufficient identity of interest between the taxpayers subject to the two taxes so that the taxpayers should be treated as one.

The agent requesting the FSA wanted to prevent an improper taxpayer advantage attributable to improper filing of post-1976 gift tax returns (the error involved a pre-1977 gift), as to which the statute of limitation was a bar, when the estate computed its FET (and the credit for gift tax "payable" in establishing the amount of FET that must be remitted) as if prior gifts all had been reported correctly. The gift and estate tax issues were different, albeit related and involving the same taxpayer. As a result, the estate, with its separate tax liability, was not inconsistently

---

[315] It is really only in that respect that *Branson* is an informative case, the underlying tax issue—higher FET valuation producing a higher income tax basis producing a lower capital gains tax being unremarkable—except, perhaps, in the court's statement that the link between §§ 2031 (valuation) and 1014 (basis) is a Congressional policy that FMV is meant to be "taxed only once." Thus, according to the court, if the FET applies, no income tax capital gain should ever be recognized on the same value. The "inconsistent" tax liability, therefore, was regarded as taxation of the same value as corpus under the FET and as capital gain under the income tax. See § 15.3 n.14 regarding the duty of consistency in connection with income tax basis and FET inclusion valuation.

§ 3.3.23

subjected to two taxes, and it therefore was not permissible for the government to assert the improper but time barred gift tax treatment when evaluating the proper but inconsistent FET calculation.

Finally, Chertkof v. United States[316] shows that an additional relief measure may be available under the mitigation provisions of §§ 1311-1314, even if equitable recoupment is not. The basis of stock sold by the estate in that case was its FET value, which was increased as a result of Tax Court decisions after an income tax refund of capital gains tax was barred by the statute of limitation. The government's inconsistent position regarding value and basis was deemed sufficient to entitle the estate to a § 1311(b)(1) equitable adjustment. As shown by Malm v. United States,[317] however, these mitigation provisions may be too narrow to provide effective relief. Saying that *Chertkof* was wrong to permit an income tax adjustment flowing from an increase in the FET value of stock includible in the decedent's estate, *Malm* concluded that "a decision in an estate tax matter cannot qualify as a 'determination' under § 1313(a)." Thus, it could not generate the claimed income tax adjustment. According to *Malm*, if the error involved income tax attributable to basis for income tax purposes, then the transaction that generated that error must also be an income tax matter, not (in this case) an FET valuation error.

§3.4 S's ELECTION AGAINST THE WILL

Excluding the community property jurisdictions,[1] in which spouses own equally property earned by either of them during their marriage,

---

[316] 676 F.2d 984 (4th Cir. 1982).

[317] 420 F. Supp. 2d 1040 (D. N.D. 2005).

[1] **§3.4** The community property states are Arizona, California, Idaho, Louisiana, Nevada, New Mexico, Texas, Washington, and (by adoption of the Uniform Marital Property Act) Wisconsin. In addition, Alaska has adopted a form of voluntary community property but otherwise is not a community property jurisdiction. See § 10.7.

only one United States jurisdiction[2] does not grant S the right to re-nounce D's will and claim a statutory share of D's estate.[3]

§3.4.1 Size of the Share

Substantial variations exist in the size of the statutory share received on election against D's will, relative to S's share in an intestate estate. For example, the UPC spousal entitlement ranges from only a

---

[2] Georgia. In other states the right may not exist under certain circumstances, such as those in Carr v. Carr, 576 A.2d 872 (N.J. 1990), in which spouses were separated and in the process of obtaining a divorce when the testator died, which terminated the divorce action. Under the New Jersey elective share statute, S is precluded from receiving a share of D's estate if they had ceased to cohabit because of circumstances that would support a divorce action, regardless of the party at fault. As a consequence, S was caught between the ability to obtain a share of the estate through election and a portion of their property through equitable distribution pursuant to divorce. That it was D's desertion of S that triggered the statutory bar to the elective share rights did not overcome this inconsistency. To address the inequity generated by this statutory black hole, the court imposed a constructive trust on D's property and remanded the case to determine what property should pass to S to reflect contributions to the marital estate.

In a similar circumstance, Casella v. Alden, 682 S.E.2d 455 (N.C. Ct. App. 2009), found that the spouses had reconciled just three weeks before D's death (they separated and divided most of their investment assets after fifty years of marriage, he took up with a new girlfriend, and then after eighteen months of separation and both spouses had filed for divorce he was diagnosed with terminal cancer; S returned to care for D in D's final weeks, which terminated D's equitable distribution action against S and allowed beneficiary designations in favor of S to remain intact).

[3] See, e.g., UPC §2-202. The typical right of election is not the same as legislation in other countries that assures a surviving family adequate maintenance out of the testator's property, declared by a court in its discretion to the extent the decedent's estate plan does not adequately so provide. Many state statutes authorize a court to grant allowances for support during administration, which address the same concern. But they are limited to a relatively short duration and are nothing like the power given courts in some foreign countries to provide for permanent family maintenance, notwithstanding the terms of a decedent's estate plan. See Laufer, Flexible Restraints on Testamentary Freedom—A Report on Decedents' Family Maintenance Legislation, 69 Harv. L. Rev. 277 (1955).

"supplemental amount"[4] if S was married to D for less than one year, to half of the "marital property portion of the augmented estate" for marriages of over 15 years,[5] which is larger than the share in many states (one third is very common) and which includes property normally not subject to S's right of election. If the intestate share is greater than the elective share (however it is computed), then merely leaving a will that S must renounce causes a reduction in S's entitlement in D's estate.[6]

§3.4.2 Planning in Anticipation of Election

Regardless of its size, S's elective share may impact D's estate plan because it operates like a creditor's claim, typically with a high priority for satisfaction, which leaves only the balance of D's estate to satisfy the estate plan as drafted. Significant abatement problems may be created by S's election, and issues regarding computation of the share must be anticipated by the estate planner. Various alternatives may be considered to minimize the size and impact of S's election against the will if an

---

[4] As defined in §2-202(b), each enacting state is expected to determine its own amount. In 2008 the drafters of the Code recommended $75,000.

[5] The accrual form of elective share implemented in the 1990 version of UPC §2-202 is a dramatic change from prior law. It reflects a quasi community property concept, without adoption of a community property regime. The notion is that a statutory elective share reflects an economic partnership. It accounts for the fact that, the longer duration of a marriage, the more property the spouses own that was acquired during that economic partnership and therefore ought to be subject to S's entitlement. For an extensive discussion of the merits of this approach, see Waggoner, The Uniform Probate Code's Elective Share: Time for a Reassessment, 37 U. Mich. J.L. Reform 1 (2003); Langbein & Waggoner, Redesigning the Spouse's Forced Share, 22 Real Prop., Prob. & Trust J. 303 (1987).

[6] See, e.g., Newman v. George, 755 P.2d 18 (Kan. 1988), in which state law permitted D to bequeath up to half of D's estate away from S, limiting S's statutory elective share entitlement to the other half of D's estate. But D died intestate and S was entitled to all of D's probate estate. The court invalidated D's funded inter vivos trust, treating D's entire estate as both probate and entirely intestate, which produced the anomalous result that S received the entire trust corpus whereas S would have received no more than half if D merely used a will instead of a trust to effect the entire estate plan. As revealed in Taliaferro v. Taliaferro, 843 P.2d 240 (Kan. 1992), this glitch in Kansas law was corrected by legislation in 1992, which limited S's entitlement to half under these circumstances.

election against the will is likely (because of the size or terms of D's bequest to S under the will).

Whether for meritorious or other reasons D wants to restrict S's rights, the issue presented to the estate planner is how and to what extent this minimization may be accomplished.[7] State law in this respect is not even close to uniform.[8] It is made all the more difficult to understand because courts utilize terminology like "fraud on the marital share" and "illusory transfer" inconsistently, often to invalidate transfers away from S and produce results that, at best, can be explained only as doing equity as the court views it, leaving the law in substantial disarray and planners with significant uncertainty.[9] One of several improvements of the UPC § 2-203 augmented estate concept over the law in most jurisdictions is its treatment of nonprobate transfers that, if recognized,

---

[7] Failure to advise the client on the potential for an election and on alternatives to anticipate that action may constitute malpractice. See Machulski v. Boudart, 2008 WL 836056 (unpub. Del. Super.) (denying attorney motion for summary judgment in a legal malpractice case, because certain of D's assets easily could have been placed beyond the reach of the elective share); Johnson v. Sandler, Balkin, Hellman & Weinstein, 958 S.W.2d 42 (Mo. Ct. App. 1998) (reversing summary judgment dismissing case against attorneys).

Also as shown by *Johnson*, although it is not always the case, planning by one spouse to disfranchise the other may indicate that a conflict of interest exists and that the same attorney may not represent both spouses for estate planning purposes without complying with the informed and voluntary consent provisions of Rule 1.7 of the Model Rules of Professional Conduct (or its counterpart under a particular state's rules governing the ethical conduct of attorneys). Unless the one spouse is willing to have the attorney make sufficient disclosure to obtain such a consent, the practical consequence normally would be the need to withdraw from representing the disfranchised spouse and, if the attorney previously represented that spouse, perhaps from representing either spouse due to the former client representation conflict parameters of Model Rule 1.9 (or its counterpart). See § 13.10 regarding the ethics of representing both spouses for estate planning purposes, and Pennell, Minimizing the Surviving Spouse's Elective Share, 32 U. Miami Inst. Est. Plan. ¶ 900 (1998), with respect to reasons for disinheritance and empirical information on the frequency of this planning.

[8] For a summary of state laws, see American College of Trust and Estate Counsel Study 10, Surviving Spouse's Rights to Share in Deceased Spouse's Estate (1994), and Schoenblum, 2013 Multistate Guide to Estate Planning Table 6.03 (2012).

[9] See, e.g., § 4.3 regarding the use of trusts designed to defeat the rights of a surviving spouse and the effects of challenges thereto.

§ 3.4.2

would disfranchise S. A summary of that provision is enlightening even with respect to the law in states that have not adopted the UPC because it focuses attention on the types of planning and issues that might be addressed by the estate planner.

The augmented estate consists of all property that must be considered in determining what D and S own and may divide between themselves, under an economic partnership view of marriage. Thus, the augmented estate includes the value of D's probate estate (after payment of certain expenses, allowances, and claims), D's "reclaimable estate" (as it was known in the 1990 version, now more generically called the decedent's nonprobate transfers to others), property to which S succeeds by reason of D's death (other than allowances, exempt property, or property already counted in the augmented estate), property owned by S at D's death, and S's nonprobate transfers to others.

The element most relevant to the ability to disfranchise S's statutory right of election is D's nonprobate transfers to others. These include:

- property that was subject to an inter vivos general power of appointment in D at any time within two years of D's death,[10]

- right of survivorship property owned jointly with anyone other than S at any time within two years of D's death,

- insurance on D's life payable to anyone other than S if D held any incidents of ownership in the policy within two years of D's death,[11]

---

[10] Bongaards v. Millen, 793 N.E.2d 335 (Mass. 2003), rejected application of a similar rule in Restatement (Third) of Property (Wills and Other Donative Transfers) §9.1(c) to property "owned in substance" by D as reaching property in a trust *not created by D* but over which D possessed at death a general power of appointment. The UPC provision appears to apply to such a trust, as §2-205(1)(A) reaches property subject to D's general presently exercisable power and is not limited to transfers by D, as opposed to transfers by third parties over which D was given broad dispositive powers.

[11] Inclusion of insurance payable to a third party in the augmented estate is a major change from the pre-1990 version of the UPC augmented estate concept, which inexplicably excluded this form of wealth and therefore allowed a major diversion of funds from S through investment of D's available funds in insurance premiums for policies payable to persons other than S. See, e.g., Rice v. Garrison, 898 P.2d 631 (Kan. 1995) (S denied recovery against insurance and pension benefits of intestate D; those nonprobate assets constituted the vast majority of D's wealth and designated D's former spouse as beneficiary; there was no argument that the beneficiary designation, which was made after D's divorce and

- property transferred to anyone other than a bona fide purchaser if at any time within two years of D's death D was entitled to the income from the transferred property or the income or principal was subject to a power exercisable for D's benefit,[12] or

- property gratuitously transferred within two years of D's death to the extent the value exceeded $12,000 per donee per year (originally meant to align with the gift tax annual exclusion, this figure is *not* indexed for inflation and no longer is identical to the annual exclusion amount).

S's nonprobate transfers to others are defined similarly.

Thus, in a UPC jurisdiction D cannot diminish S's statutory entitlement by transfers that are revocable until death,[13] by transfers in which D retained enjoyment until death, by the purchase of life insurance payable other than to S, or by gifts exceeding a de minimis amount that usually is the gift tax annual exclusion amount when the statute was adopted or last amended. Nor can D escape application of these rules by actions taken within two years prior to death. But S still may be disfranchised if D, prior to that two year window, is willing and able to make large transfers to third parties with no retained interests or powers.

Perhaps the most insightful aspects of the UPC approach are (1) the recognition that nonprobate property received by S from D should be counted against S's statutory entitlement. For example, S should not be allowed to benefit from nonprobate entitlements, such as a life estate in an inter vivos trust, while at the same time rejecting D's will and taking a

(Footnote Continued)

before D's remarriage to S, was a mistake deserving of correction, because evidence indicated that annual reports to D confirmed the beneficiary designation).

[12] Note that even a CRT for the decedent for life, remainder to charity (or a secondary life estate in S, then to charity) could be reached, notwithstanding the generally desirable motives behind such planning. Because S may be able to reach into such a trust, Rev. Proc. 2005-24 provided that the charitable status of the trust will not be recognized unless an effective waiver of S's right to reach the trust is executed. The revenue procedure subsequently was placed in hiatus and does not apply currently because the government is studying the issue further, as discussed in § 14.3.2 n.40.

[13] Compare the prior version of UPC § 2-202, as adjudicated by In re Estate of Chrisp, 759 N.W.2d 87 (Neb. 2009), which held that premarital transfers to a revocable inter vivos trust were beyond S's reach under the original version of the UPC, which the court said the Nebraska legislature intentionally chose not to alter when the UPC was revised in 1990.

§ 3.4.2

full, unreduced elective share of the probate estate.[14] Moreover, because an economic partnership is involved, (2) S's wealth should be counted just as is D's wealth in determining D and S's aggregate wealth, as to which S is entitled to a "partnership" interest. Both of these refinements are unknown to the law of most jurisdictions and make the augmented estate statutory share more like community property and, as a result, more equitable.

Because most state elective share rules do not approach the UPC augmented estate concept, issues arise whether, for example, nonprobate transfers can be reached by S, such as into a trust of which D is a beneficiary or trustee.[15] In addition, some jurisdictions are havens if D is seeking to disfranchise S's statutory entitlement. For example, because there is no statutory entitlement at all in Georgia, an individual who dies a Georgia domiciliary with property subject to the laws of Georgia effectively may disfranchise S. In addition, the community property states provide no share to S other than S's ownership interest in any of the couple's community property. Thus, a testator who dies in a community property state owning separate property also may escape any statutory election entitlement that is provided to S in states that do not embrace community property.[16]

---

[14] See §§3.6 n.4 and 13.6.1.2.1 n.12 and accompanying text with respect to qualification for the marital deduction in such a situation if the inter vivos trust provides that S's enjoyment will terminate and S will be treated as predeceased, as would be the case under the will, to the extent the forced heir share election is made by S, all to prevent S from "double dipping" in the form of receiving a share of the probate estate and retaining all nonprobate benefits as well. The UPC works in reverse, counting the trust entitlement against the elective share and thereby reducing what S otherwise will receive from the probate estate.

[15] See §4.3.

[16] Care is required, however, because several community property states recognize a concept of "quasi" community property, in which S is granted an entitlement like that in legitimate community property. Any property brought to these states that would have been community property had D lived in that state when it was acquired is afforded this treatment. Thus, for example, if an Oregon testator moved to California shortly before death, taking property owned by D but acquired while married to S, that separate property would be quasi community property and treated as if it was legitimate community property for purposes of determining S's rights.

§3.4.2

Finally, if D's object is not to disfranchise S but, rather, to control ultimate disposition of D's property (for example, because S has children by a prior marriage and D wants to guarantee that D's property will pass to D's children by a prior marriage), the object should be to find a way to provide for S in a manner that S will not challenge by making an election. In these cases the solution may be found in providing sufficient enjoyment to S that there is no incentive to make the election. By way of example, if D's concern is control after S's subsequent death, the vehicle of choice might be a QTIP marital deduction trust giving S lifetime enjoyment but little or no testamentary dispositive control. S may find this arrangement acceptable even if S is given no more than a nongeneral testamentary power of appointment that is narrowly circumscribed, especially if S is made trustee during S's overlife.

§3.4.3 Satisfying the Elective Share

An additional issue that is addressed well in the UPC but relatively poorly in many other jurisdictions is the manner in which the statutory elective share is satisfied. The current version of UPC §2-209 (enumerated as §2-207 prior to technical amendments that reorganized the Code in 1993) provides that S's elective entitlement is satisfied first by counting property included in the augmented estate that S already owns, property included in S's reclaimable estate, nonprobate property passing to S from D, and property passing to S under D's will.[17] The liability for

---

[17] Under the pre-1990 version of §2-209 a life estate in a trust benefiting S was valued arbitrarily at 50% of the FMV of the trust corpus for purposes of computing its offset of the elective share. No corresponding valuation presumption appears in the current version of §2-209, meaning that the parties must determine the appropriate reduction of S's entitlement based on commonly accepted valuation principles. By statute in some states the value of a life estate, such as in a QTIP marital deduction trust, also is counted against the statutory share and, in each of these cases, may be worth enough to fully satisfy the elective share. See statutes noted in Schoenblum, 2013 Multistate Guide to Estate Planning Table 6.03 Part 3 (2012). See also In re Estate of Myers, 594 N.W.2d 563 (Neb. 1999) (adopting valuation of S's life estate in trust using Treasury tables for purposes of satisfying UPC statutory share); Estate of Karnen, 607 N.W.2d 32 (S.D. 2000) (adopting valuation of S's life estates in trust using state unisex inheritance tax annuity tables for purposes of satisfying UPC statutory share); In re Estate of Finch, 389 S.E.2d 126 (N.C. Ct. App. 1990) (testamentary QTIP trust, established by formula as that amount needed to preclude S from being able to elect against

any deficiency between the value of these items and the value of the statutory share then is imposed pro rata on each taker of property included in D's probate estate and property counted as D's nonprobate transfers to others, with the option for nonprobate takers to contribute either a portion of the included property or other property of equal value (determined using the same value used to compute the augmented estate).

The relevant planning point is that D may bequeath less desirable assets to S in a UPC state and, to the extent of their value, preclude S from taking assets D wishes other beneficiaries to receive. In some jurisdictions, S may renounce D's will to claim a statutory elective share and is entitled to a fractional share of each item in the estate against which the fractional share is computed, in which case planning to engineer satisfaction of the elective share becomes difficult.[18]

In states in which property bequeathed to S does not first satisfy the elective share, any benefits must be disposed of that S would have received under the will but instead elected to reject. State law usually regards S as predeceased and the normal lapse rules[19] are applied. Because those results may be inappropriate, D's will should anticipate

---

(Footnote Continued)

D's estate plan, was adequate to preclude S's election). Quaere the value of an SNT created in an effort to preclude disqualification of S for Medicaid, and a state's effort to count the elective share (or that portion not satisfied by the trust) as an available resource that itself would disqualify S, all as discussed in § 3.4.7.

[18] See, e.g., Winters Nat'l Bank & Trust Co. v. Riffe, 206 N.E.2d 212 (Ohio 1965) (testator created a trust of specific stock for a friend and business associate and bequeathed the residue of the estate to a trust for S, who renounced the will and became entitled under state law to half of every asset in the estate, leaving the trust of the specific stock reduced by half; litigation was required to alter this result, the court directing that the specific stock be used only to the extent other property was not adequate to satisfy S's entitlement).

Sometimes engineering is for tax minimization purposes. See, e.g., Florida Nat'l Bank v. United States, 313 F. Supp. 1072 (M.D. Fla. 1970), aff'd in part and rev'd in part, 443 F.2d 467 (5th Cir. 1971) (government properly reduced estate's marital deduction to the statutory percentage of the total estate as valued for FET purposes and not the value of the specific items awarded in satisfaction of the elective share, which had appreciated on the applicable tax valuation date more than the balance of the estate and therefore exceeded that proportionate share of the total estate value).

[19] See § 3.2.5.4.

§ 3.4.3

this issue by defining the alternate disposition that should apply if S predeceases D or elects against D's will. This issue may be particularly relevant if, for example, descendants of S are not the descendants of D would receive benefits if S predeceased D and who D would prefer removed from the will entirely if S instead makes the statutory election.

Some state laws accomplish this objective, but caution is required. UPC §2-804(b) is the revocation-upon-divorce rule and it treats provisions for the former spouse's relatives as revoked as well, but there is no counterpart in the event S asserts the elective share. It might appear that there is no need for such a provision in a UPC state because those dispositions in favor of S are applied in satisfaction of S's entitlement. But a decedent might not want the spouse's family to benefit after the spouse's interest terminates in such a case. And other states may have adopted portions of the UPC but less than all, which could complicate these sorts of issues.

In addition, equity may direct that benefits S would have received under the will should be allocated to specific beneficiaries to compensate for their contribution to satisfaction of the elective share if the abatement rules do not work properly. For example, if S was income beneficiary of a trust that passes to designated remainder beneficiaries other than the residuary takers of D's will, the normal abatement rules might satisfy S's elective share from the residue of the probate estate and the normal lapse rules might accelerate the remainder in that trust. The trust beneficiaries would reap an unexpected windfall from the election and the estate residuary beneficiaries would pay for that. In that case the residuary beneficiaries appropriately might receive the value of the life estate that S renounced as compensation for their loss in satisfaction of the elective share. All of these issues are relevant in drafting a will in anticipation of abatement, with satisfaction of S's statutory share being just one source of that problem.

§3.4.4 Charges Against the Elective Share

In computing S's entitlement it is necessary to determine not only what is included in the estate but also all charges or other obligations that reduce the estate against which the statutory share is computed. This may prove relevant in the planning and drafting process because it may affect the likelihood of an election and influence how D's will allocates taxes and satisfies contractual obligations. It also may determine whether, for postmortem planning purposes, it is sensible for S to renounce the will in favor of the statutory elective share if, for example, that entitlement will generate a larger FET marital deduction and reduce taxes accordingly.[20]

To illustrate, In re Estate of Dunham[21] held that an estate's contractual testamentary obligations are inferior to S's right of election, which allowed S to defeat a specific bequest of stock in satisfaction of D's obligation. Although a court might dictate use of other assets first to satisfy the elective share, the result is that a specific bequest might abate to satisfy the elective share, even if that bequest is pursuant to an enforceable contract. Alternatively, however, Rubenstein v. Mueller[22]

---

[20] See Treas. Reg. § 20.2056(c)-2(c). The marital deduction is available and the passing requirement is met for whichever of the elective share or the testamentary entitlement that the spouse ultimately receives, but not for both.

In PLR 9524020 S elected against D's will in favor of a statutory share of D's estate and, exercising a state law right to select the assets in D's estate that would satisfy that elective share, designated a portion of qualified plan proceeds otherwise payable to D's estate as the designated beneficiary. In PLR 9626049 S and all descendants of D disclaimed a fraction of D's estate, causing an intestacy that S was entitled to receive, and D's personal representative funded that fractional entitlement with D's IRAs. In each case the government ruled these payments constituted distributions directly to S (not to the estate and then to S), thus permitting a tax free § 402(c)(9) rollover to an IRA created by S. No mention was made whether either situation was an event that would constitute a § 691(a)(2) IRD acceleration event. The earlier Ruling states that the rollover amount "is not taxable in the year of [the] rollover" and § 402(c)(9) itself speaks as if S was the participant. Unfortunately, that treatment is limited to "the preceding provisions of this subsection," which would not appear to protect against acceleration under § 691(a)(2). See §§ 5.10.5 and 9.3.5 with respect to this income tax realization on satisfaction of marital bequests with the right to receive IRD, and with respect to the tax free rollover of lump sum distributions.

[21] 320 N.Y.S.2d 951 (App. Div. 1971) (involving an obligation under a separation agreement incident to the testator's prior divorce).

[22] 225 N.E.2d 540 (N.Y. 1967) (involving testamentary disposition pursuant to joint and mutual will with D's predeceased former spouse). Gregory v. Estate of Gregory, 866 S.W.2d 379 (Ark. 1993), also denied S's claim to property covered by a contractual will with D's predeceased former spouse. The difference was that S was claiming a share of property that did not originate with D's predeceased former spouse, as in *Rubenstein*, but only was subject to the contractual will. The court nevertheless held that D's property was converted into a life

§ 3.4.4

held that property received by D subject to a binding contractual obligation to distribute it to designated beneficiaries at D's subsequent death was not part of D's estate for determining the amount of S's elective share. Unlike *Dunham*, the court held that receipt of property subject to a binding contractual obligation to dispose of it pursuant to agreement when D died meant that D effectively owned only a life interest in those assets that were subject to the contract (perhaps with a power to

---

(Footnote Continued)

estate with a power to consume by virtue of the predeceased former spouse's compliance with the contract.

To the contrary are a slew of cases, cited in Via v. Putnam, 656 So. 2d 460 (Fla. 1995), which relied upon Shimp v. Huff, 556 A.2d 252 (Md. 1989). These cases involve D's contractual obligation, typically D as the survivor under a joint and mutual will executed with a predeceased spouse, and the claim to a statutory share made by D's subsequent surviving spouse S. These cases consider the conflict between S's statutory entitlement in D's estate and the claims of beneficiaries under the contractual will—either as D's legatees if D complied with its provisions or as creditors entitled to damages if D breached the contractual will by providing for S (or perhaps for failing to protect against S's statutory entitlement).

Establishing the priority as between these antagonists requires a balancing of the public policy underlying S's statutory forced heir share, and the notion that D's estate is encumbered by the binding obligations imposed by the contractual will. *Shimp* concluded that D's contractual will obligation would be void as against public policy to the extent it anticipated priority over S. As a result, S's statutory entitlement was given priority over any claim based on the contractual will. Similar issues exist with respect to S's family allowance entitlement.

The resolution of these cases suggests that the contractual will is the flaw in the planning. It could require D to execute a spousal agreement that prevents S from taking a portion of D's estate (as augmented by the estate of D's predeceased spouse). See §3.4.6. Unfortunately, states following the *Shimp* approach probably would regard any rights generated by breach of the spousal agreement obligation as inferior to those of S. Thus, it seems clear that D's own property would be vulnerable to S's claims to the extent the spousal agreement obligation is not effectively fulfilled.

Overall, therefore, it appears that the only true protection is to insulate property received by D from D's predeceased spouse and thus preclude S from having any entitlement, by creating QTIP marital deduction and nonmarital trusts for D, never granting rights in that trust property that could be bequeathed by D or subjected to the claims of S. In this planning, however, caution should be exercised to give D enough control and enjoyment that there is no compulsion for D to elect against this plan and take a statutory forced heir share of D's predeceased spouse estate.

§3.4.4

consume the property during life) with no remainder against which S's right of election could operate.

In each case the moral is that the estate plan must reflect D's contractual obligations and anticipate the effect of S's election of the statutory share on the estate's ability to comply with the estate's obligations. Indeed, it may prove wise to make inter vivos transfers to satisfy those obligations rather than wait until death and generate these types of postmortem disputes.

A more common illustration of the same form of issue is the estate's obligation to pay FET and whether S's share is computed before or after that liability (and, if computed before, whether any part of the tax liability is payable from the elective share).[23] This issue, in turn, may affect the amount of any FET marital deduction available to D's estate with respect to the elective share, which itself may affect the amount of FET imposed on D's estate, which again could alter the size of the elective share and generate a circular, whirlpool computation.[24] To illustrate, assume D's gross estate is $9.3 million and that debts and expenses payable therefrom total $300,000. The issue is how much S would receive under a statutory elective share of one-third of the net estate after payment of all the testator's debts and expenses.

That fraction of the amount left after payment of debts and expenses ($9 million) would be $3 million, resulting in a taxable estate of $6 million (assuming that a marital deduction is not available for any part of the balance of the estate and that the elective share itself qualifies for the deduction).[25] Taxes would be $350,000 after application of the unified credit,[26] leaving a residue after tax of $5,650,000. Instead of two-thirds of the estate, this is only about 62.777% of the available estate, S's share

---

[23] See Kahn, The Federal Estate Tax Burden Borne by a Dissenting Widow, 64 Mich. L. Rev. 1499 (1966), cited in Reynolds v. Reynolds, 837 So. 2d 847 (Ala. Ct. Civ. App. 2002) in which S's statutory share (elected against a QTIP trust estate plan) was calculated before payment of tax, applying the equitable apportionment result.

[24] For the similar interrelated computation issues involved in determining the intestate share of a surviving spouse and the computation of any fractional or percentile share of an estate, see §§ 2.1.1 nn.6-7 and 3.2.5 at text accompanying n.30.

[25] See § 13.6.1.2.1 n.12 and accompanying text.

[26] Applying 2012 rates and credits.

§3.4.4

having been computed without bearing any portion of the taxes. Because it qualifies for the marital deduction and, therefore, generates no taxes, it may be thought to be equitable that no taxes are apportioned to the marital portion. This is the equitable apportionment result.[27]

The common law result would differ from this computation, however. A computation scheme that does not recognize equitable apportionment requires that the fraction be applied after taxes have been paid, which creates circularity problems because the size of the marital share cannot be computed until taxes on the estate are subtracted, but those taxes cannot be computed until the size of the marital share that will generate a deduction is known. The algebraic circularity can be avoided by computing the tax and subtracting it as if there was no elective share or marital deduction, determining the size of the elective share, then recomputing the tax with that sized deduction, subtracting a smaller tax and dividing the larger product, then redetermining the size of the share and making a new tax computation, ad nauseam. But the government has provided formulae for use in this and other interrelated computation situations.[28] The result of the computation in this case is an elective share of $2,883,774, with taxes computed on a taxable estate of $6,116,226, totaling $348,679 and leaving a residue of $5,767,548. The surviving spouse receives $116,226 less, taxes are $40,679 higher, and the balance of the estate is $75,548 greater, which is why beneficiaries other than the surviving spouse might argue for this approach even though the government receives more tax.

A tax payment provision in the testator's will, calling for payment of tax from the residue, will not affect the result of this issue because the taxes *are* being paid from the residue. The issue is whether the amount to be divided is the residue before or after payment of the taxes. Indeed, there are two "residues": a "gross net" residue, which is the amount available for division after payment of debts and expenses but before payment of taxes, and a "net net" residue, which is the amount available for division after payment of all of the debts, expenses, and taxes.

---

[27] See §3.3.4.

[28] See §3.3.4 n.52 and accompanying text, and Publication 904 (now declared obsolete and out of print but available at 1990 WL 599448). There also are computer programs that make this and other interrelated tax computations.

§3.4.4

Furthermore, if the concept of "equitable election"[29] is applicable in the jurisdiction, then reliance on the will to provide for the payment of taxes is meaningless to this issue and the only real inquiry is which residue is meant by the provision calling for division. For example, In re Barnhart's Estate[30] involved a will that directed payment of all taxes imposed on any part of the testator's estate from the residuary estate without charge against the respective beneficiaries. S elected to take the statutory share and the personal representative computed that entitlement as half the gross estate before FET. The government took exception to this, claiming that the share should be computed net of those taxes and that the marital deduction for that share therefore was smaller, resulting in more FET. The court held that the FET may constitute a lien against the gross estate but that it is not a debt or an administration expense within the meaning of state law defining the elective share as half the estate "remaining after the payment of debts and expenses of administration." Thus, the court concluded that the share should be computed before payment of the tax, as proposed by the personal representative.

To the opposite effect was Weeks v. Vandeveer,[31] which concluded that an elective share of the "net estate" must be computed after FET is paid and that the testator cannot increase or decrease that amount by a provision in the will because D should not be permitted to alter S's statutory share. Contrariwise again, however, are a variety of cases[32] in which the tax payment provisions operated to free an elective share from contributing to payment of taxes and the courts rejected a contention that equitable election meant that S's renunciation of the will barred S

---

[29] See § 3.6.

[30] 162 A.2d 168 (N.H. 1960).

[31] 233 N.E.2d 502 (Ohio 1968). Accord, In re Estate of Thompson, 512 N.W.2d 560 (Iowa 1994) (computation of elective share not affected by state law or document provision regarding payment of taxes; in any event, will provision could not benefit spouse due to equitable election).

[32] See, e.g., In re Estate of Neamand, 318 A.2d 730 (Pa. 1974); In re Estate of Williams, 2003 WL 1961805 (Tenn. Ct. App.), (a divorce case making the same argument about the tax payment provision in the decedent's will not benefiting the former spouse and the court similarly rejecting that equitable notion; see § 3.1.3 with respect to revocation by divorce).

§ 3.4.4

from enjoying the benefits of that tax payment provision.[33] Computing the share without reduction by FET is consistent with the equitable apportionment result reached in PLR 8337011, which reflected the Uniform Estate Tax Apportionment Act as enacted in Virginia.[34]

The general rule (and the apparent trend among modern court decisions) is that the tax payment provisions of D's will are not operative with respect to determining the apportionment of tax to S's elective share.[35] In re Estate of Shapiro is illustrative.[36] D's will included a tax payment provision that directed the payment of all taxes from the residuary estate as a cost of administration. The Minnesota tax apportionment statute, if it applied, would relieve S from any obligation to pay taxes, because the elective share qualified for the marital deduction. The court framed the issue as "whether the tax clause in a will can affect the amount of the statutory elective share" and ruled that it cannot. In determining the amount of the elective share the tax apportionment

---

[33] It took an amendment to local law to reverse that result in Pennsylvania. See Estate of Bertolet, 397 A.2d 776 (Pa. 1979).

[34] See § 3.3.7.1. The Comment to UPC § 2-204 makes it clear that computation without reduction of the residuary estate by payment of taxes is the result under the UPC augmented estate computation.

[35] See, e.g., DeShazo v. Smith, 2006-1 U.S. Tax Cas. (CCH) ¶ 60,524 (E.D. Va. 2006) (S may not benefit from tax payment provision that protected the marital bequest that S rejected by claiming the elective share instead); Rockler v. Sevareid, 691 A.2d 97, 100 (D.C. 1997) (when the right of election was exercised the tax payment provisions of the will became inapplicable as to S); In re Estate of Thompson, 512 N.W.2d 560, 564 (Iowa 1994) (S "cannot benefit from [the tax payment provisions of the will] because [S] has elected to take against the will. When a surviving spouse elects to take her statutory share instead of that provided by the will, she abandons all right to benefit from any provision of the will"); In re Estate of Shapiro, 362 N.W.2d 390 (Minn. 1985) (tax payment provisions of a will cannot alter the elective share amount to which S is entitled); Estate of Clark, 433 N.Y.S.2d 328 (Surr. Ct. 1980) (determination of elective share is controlled by state tax apportionment statute, notwithstanding contrary tax payment provisions of will). But see Commerce Union Bank v. Albert, 301 S.W.2d 352, 354 (Tenn. 1957), and In re Barnhart's Estate, 162 A.2d 168 (N.H. 1960) (stating that a widow's election does not render the tax payment language of a will inoperative). See Merchants Nat'l Bank and Trust Co. v. United States, 246 F.2d 410 (7th Cir. 1957); Annot., Surviving spouse taking elective share as chargeable with estate or inheritance tax, 67 A.L.R.3d 199, at § 5 (1975).

[36] 362 N.W.2d 390, 393 (Minn. 1985).

§ 3.4.4

statute applied to permit S's share to pass tax free. The court also noted that applying D's tax clause would have what it regarded as the inappropriate effect of causing the spouse to receive less than if D had died intestate. According to the court, construing the elective share statute as being controlled by the tax clause "would allow a testator to determine the amount of the statutory share, a result we cannot believe was intended by the legislature when it passed the apportionment statutes."[37]

Further illustration of state law conflict on this issue is the position in Illinois, which has no tax apportionment rule in this respect. For

---

[37] *Shapiro* reflects the sense of elective share policy that denies testamentary freedom to D. A contrary result would allow D to manipulate the elective share, which is what the denial of testamentary freedom represented by the right of election is designed to preclude. For example, if the elective share is deductible and D's tax clause was respected, D could reduce S's entitlement by modifying the state law equitable apportionment rule, as follows:

> Decedent D died with a will that totally disinherits D's surviving spouse S in favor of D's child C. As permitted by local law, D's will directed that all taxes payable by D's estate be apportioned among each person interested in the estate, without regard to whether any interest is deductible. S claimed an elective share, entitling S to one-third of D's estate. If the tax clause is respected S receives one-third of the total estate, reduced by one-third of the total estate tax—which is generated entirely by the other two-thirds of the estate. If the tax clause is disregarded, S will enjoy one-third unreduced by taxes, and C will receive the other two-thirds, reduced by all the tax on that portion.

Notice, however, that *Shapiro* does not always benefit S. Consider the following more unusual illustration:

> Testator T leaves T's entire estate to Charity C. T's will directs that all taxes are to be apportioned among the persons interested in T's estate, without regard to whether an interest is deductible. T is survived by a noncitizen spouse S, to whom dispositions are not generally eligible for the marital deduction (see § 2056(d)). If S claims an elective share of one-third of T's estate, and if the tax clause is given effect, S will receive one-third of the estate, reduced by one-third of the tax, and C will receive two-thirds of the estate, reduced by two-thirds of the tax. If the tax clause is disregarded, S will receive one-third of the estate, reduced by all the tax—as require by the equitable apportionment statute — and C will receive two-thirds of the estate, reduced by none of the tax.

As shown in this example, if T's tax payment direction is given effect, the size of the elective share depends in part on the identity of the other beneficiaries of the decedent's estate, and S is not always better protected by the *Shapiro* rule.

§3.4.4

example, Northern Trust Co. v. Wilson[38] and Farley v. United States[39] reached opposite results, *Northern Trust* having been decided before equitable apportionment was recognized in Roe v. Estate of Farrell,[40] which influenced the court in *Farley* to hold that the elective share should be computed before the estate is reduced by the payment of taxes. In re Estate of Comstock[41] and In re Estate of Gowling[42] reached the same result as *Farley*, but then In re Estate of Grant[43] reverted to the prior *Northern Trust* result of computing the elective share after taxes.

PLR 8141007 discussed the Illinois situation and concluded that, if the Illinois Supreme Court was presented with the issue, it would decide that S's statutory elective share need not be reduced by any FET, stating that, absent legislation or a prior Supreme Court determination, the marital deduction would be based on "the amount that the spouse could receive in a fair settlement" and that *Farley* demonstrated that a fair settlement would be computed before taxes. But the Illinois situation again was considered in PLR 8240014, in which D's residuary estate was divided equally between S and D's sister and the government concluded that this division should be made after reducing the residue by the FET incurred on the entire residue, notwithstanding that S's share produced none of the tax or that this result reduced the marital deduction and increased the resulting FET burden.

Even further interpretative and postmortem planning questions must be addressed with respect to computation of S's elective share. For example, if S's share on renunciation is determined on the basis of what remains in the probate estate after paying debts, expenses, and taxes, the question arises as to what taxes should be considered. If the doctrine

---

[38] 101 N.E.2d 604 (Ill. App. Ct. 1951).

[39] 581 F.2d 821 (Ct. Cl. 1978).

[40] 372 N.E.2d 662 (Ill. 1978).

[41] 397 N.E.2d 1240 (Ill. App. Ct. 1979).

[42] 396 N.E.2d 82 (Ill. App. Ct. 1979), aff'd, 411 N.E.2d 266 (Ill. 1980) (involving computation of a bequest under the testator's will, not a determination of the elective share amount).

[43] 396 N.E.2d 872 (Ill. App. Ct. 1979), aff'd, 415 N.E.2d 416 (Ill. 1980). Accord, In re Estate of Pericles, 641 N.E.2d 10 (Ill. App. Ct. 1994) (because S's entitlement was computed as a share only of D's Illinois property, however, only estate tax attributable to Illinois property was subtracted before that share was determined).

§3.4.4

of equitable election is applicable,[44] then a tax apportionment provision in the will is not effective and local law regarding payment of taxes should control, which may leave the burden on the residue for all taxes, for only the taxes generated by the probate estate alone,[45] or for only the taxes generated by the residue of the probate estate alone.[46] Alternatively, local law may apply the concept of equitable apportionment, relieving the marital share of all taxes because it does not generate tax due to the marital deduction.[47] These objectives may not be met even if the testator manifested an intent regarding the tax burden, and even if the will reflects an intent to minimize taxes, which further illustrates the significance of planning that minimizes the likelihood of an election by S.

Further complications also may arise in more complex FET computations. For example, In re Estate of Hardesty[48] involved the proper

---

[44] See § 3.6.

[45] See, e.g., In re Estate of Marans, 390 P.2d 443 (Mont. 1964) (elective share computed as a fraction of the estate after taxes attributable to the probate estate only, because otherwise the right of election would be nullified if substantial nonprobate property produced taxes payable out of the probate estate).

[46] Rockler v. Sevareid, 691 A.2d 97 (D.C. Ct. App. 1997), is to this effect, holding that the elective share in the District of Columbia is computed before tax due to equitable apportionment and that D's will, which imposed the tax liability on the residue without apportionment, was not effective to alter this because S's election had the effect of rejecting all provisions in the will that affected S's entitlement.

[47] For an interesting application of equitable apportionment, see Tarbox v. Palmer, 564 So. 2d 1106 (Fla. Dist. Ct. App. 1990), in which S elected to take a 30% statutory elective share outright rather than 100% of D's estate for life only. Because the life estate could have generated a marital deduction for 100% of D's estate through a QTIP election, estate taxes were increased by reduction of the available marital deduction caused by S's election. Those taxes still were charged against the nonmarital property under the state law concept of equitable apportionment, because what S did receive generated no tax and because, even after payment of taxes, D's other beneficiaries still were better off by virtue of S's election. In a similar vein, In re Estate of Palmer, 600 So. 2d 537 (Fla. Dist. Ct. App. 1992), awarded S a refund of taxes improperly charged against S's share of the estate, with interest payable from the date that share was payable under state law. See also Boulis v. Blackburn, 16 So. 3d 186 (Fla. Ct. App. 2009) distinguishing application of the same statute applied in *Tarbox* because S was not a citizen of the United States and the marital deduction therefore did not apply.

[48] 708 P.2d 596 (Okla. Ct. App. 1985). A similar but less cogent determination is In re Estate of Hjersted, 135 P.3d 216, and a related case at 135 P.3d 202 (Ks.

computation of S's statutory elective share in the context of gift taxes incurred by D during life but not paid prior to death. The taxes were generated by gifts that were made to donees other than S and the issue was whether the statutory share should be based on the estate as determined before or after payment of those outstanding gift taxes. To illustrate, assume D transferred $500,000 during life, incurring gift taxes of $100,000. At death, assume D possessed an added $1.5 million and that S's statutory share is half. S's forced share was computed on the basis of the estate as reduced by the outstanding gift taxes. Thus, in the illustration, S would receive half of the $1.4 million remaining after payment of the $100,000 in tax. Notwithstanding this aspect of its decision, the court adhered to the established Oklahoma position regarding equitable apportionment, imposing the obligation to pay the outstanding gift taxes against the shares of takers other than S. The effect was a smaller statutory share (by virtue of the outstanding taxes being regarded as a debt against the estate), resulting in a smaller marital deduction, resulting in higher FET, but with all the estate and gift taxes being paid out of the nonspousal share of the estate to avoid further reducing the marital deduction.

Particularly striking about the decision is that the gifts involved transfers that triggered application of §2036(a)(1), meaning that the value of the gifts was brought back into D's gross estate for FET purposes, with consequent wealth transfer taxation as if no transfers during life had been made. With a §2001(b) credit for gift taxes incurred, the gift taxes were like a down payment of the FET imposed on D's estate. Viewed in that light, those taxes could have been ignored in computing the size of the estate for purposes of determining S's statutory share, the same as they would have been if D had made no transfers during life. The conclusion reached is unfortunate because it essentially

---

(Footnote Continued)

Ct. App. 2006), involving creation of an FLP, followed by a gift made within two years of D's death, and an unpaid gift tax imposed on revaluation of that gift. Notwithstanding that the gift within such close proximity to death was invalid to diminish S's entitlement, and notwithstanding that gift tax is a functional prepayment of estate tax that otherwise would apply if a lifetime transfer was not made (which is the treatment generated by the proximate to death gift being ignored for elective share purposes), the court held that the gift tax was an outstanding obligation of the estate that should reduce the sum on which the elective share is calculated.

§3.4.4

reduced both S's entitlement and increased the taxes paid by the remaining beneficiaries of the estate. Other courts confronting this issue might find it advisable to rule that the gift taxes are neither a proper reduction of the estate for purposes of computing S's share nor a proper charge against the share ultimately computed.

Once the tax apportionment issue is resolved, there is a timing issue that can be addressed by D's will as well, as illustrated by Iandoli v. Iandoli.[49] Taxes were a charge against the nonmarital share of the estate under the state law principle of equitable apportionment. The dispute involved when apportionment should occur for purposes of dividing appreciation earned by the estate between death and final distribution. The court agreed with S that appreciation should be apportioned reflecting the relative size of each portion of the estate under a "changing fraction" method that charged each portion with payments made, as those payments were made. Thus, as soon as taxes were paid, the share of appreciation enjoyed by the portion of the estate charged with that payment was reduced.[50]

§3.4.5 Conflict of Laws

Given the differences that are encountered under the law of various states regarding the elective share (for example, its size, availability, abatement in satisfaction, or allocation of taxes to or away from it), it is inevitable that conflict of laws issues will arise regarding the determination of which state's law governs these kinds of questions. For example, D may own realty in a state other than D's domicile or the will might attempt to specify that the law of some other state should govern an aspect of the elective share entitlement or satisfaction that is not clear or desirable under domiciliary law.

---

[49] 547 So. 2d 664 (Fla. Dist. Ct. App. 1989).

[50] The beneficiaries responsible for payment of taxes argued for a "true residuary" method of apportionment that would delay reflection of the tax payment until final distribution of the estate, with appreciation being shared proportionate to the relative size of the shares of the estate before charging those taxes against some of those shares. For a discussion of different alternative methods of computation, see Covey, The Marital Deduction and Credit Shelter Dispositions and the Use of Formula Provisions 80 (1984); Cantrill, Fractional or Percentage Residuary Bequests: Allocation of Postmortem Income, Gain and Unrealized Appreciation, 10 Prob. Notes 322 (1985).

The traditional conflict of laws rule is that the law of the situs state governs all questions regarding testamentary disposition of realty, which means that real estate owned in an ancillary state is subject to the elective share rules of that jurisdiction.[51] This could mean that S may receive a full elective share under the law of the domiciliary state, perhaps computed under a scheme that increases the domiciliary entitlement by a portion of the value of property—including the ancillary realty—that passes outside the domiciliary probate estate (but without

---

[51] See, e.g., Pfau v. Moseley, 222 N.E.2d 639 (Ohio 1966), which contains a good illustration of the issues involved in the selection of governing law under the traditional rule found in Restatement (Second) of Conflict of Laws §§ 241 and 242 (1971) (existence and size of the elective share regarding immovables—realty—is determined by the law that would be chosen by the courts of the situs state, which normally would apply situs law). See, e.g., In re Estate of Pericles, 641 N.E.2d 10 (Ill. App. Ct. 1994) (Illinois decedent's Florida and Georgia realty not subject to S's Illinois elective share; making the conflict of laws issues more challenging was the fact that the parties were married in Georgia, S was a Georgia resident, and Georgia provides no elective share for a surviving spouse); In re Estate of Rhoades, 607 N.Y.S.2d 893 (Sup. Ct. 1994) (Florida decedent's New York realty escaped S's claim because Florida's statutory share did not consider out of state realty and because New York law did not grant a right of election to the surviving spouse of a nondomiciliary decedent; the court agreed with the plaintiff's conclusion that a New York decedent intent on disinheriting a surviving spouse with respect to New York property therefore can establish domicile in another state that does not consider out of state property in computing or satisfying the elective share and then execute a will in that other state that disinherits the spouse); and see In re Schwarzenberger, 626 N.Y.S.2d 229 (App. Div. 1995) (establishing D's clear intent to be a Florida domiciliary, disfranchising D's New York surviving spouse).

UPC § 2-202(d) (2008) alters the result stated in text by specifying that "[t]he right, if any, of the surviving spouse of a decedent who dies domiciled outside this State to take an elective share in property in this State is governed by the law of the decedent's domicile at death." That statute would make the planning in *Rhoades* effective because Florida did not grant a share in out-of-state property. If D in *Pericles* had been a Georgia resident it would have operated to disfranchise S everywhere, because Georgia provides no elective share to a surviving spouse.

Equitable conversion, generated by a testamentary provision directing sale of realty and distribution of the proceeds, probably would not alter these results. See, e.g., In re Seifert's Estate, 242 A.2d 64 (N.H. 1968) (equitable conversion did not cause rules relative to personalty to govern S's entitlement in realty D directed to be sold).

§ 3.4.5

charging that realty against S's domiciliary elective share entitlement). S also may receive a share of the ancillary realty under the laws of that state.

If the law in the various jurisdictions is not uniform, the lack of their integration could either over- or undersubscribe S's elective share rights, in addition to providing for elective shares of different portions of D's estate. For that reason alone, it may be wise to plan for any disparity of result by transferring ancillary realty by a form that is not subject to the law of the situs state. For example, by placing it in a revocable inter vivos trust that would not be regarded as situs realty for purposes of applying the situs state's elective share. Or by causing it to pass outside of probate (such as by placing it in joint tenancy with right of survivorship—including joint ownership with S) if that would eliminate elective share controversies under the law of both states.

More interesting and controversial issues arise if D seeks to specify by will that the law of another jurisdiction should govern the elective share. For example, In re Estate of Clark[52] involved a Virginia domiciliary whose will designated that New York law would govern all dispositions under the will. Most of D's wealth was securities on deposit in New York so there was some nexus to the law chosen, but Virginia law provided a more extensive elective share. The court embraced the conflict of laws rule that domiciliary law should govern on questions of testamentary freedom and applied the law of Virginia with respect to movables.[53]

The same result likely would obtain even if D selected the law of a state that grants no elective share to S and therefore has no legislative mandate that S receive any portion of D's estate. Based on notions of comity and the well accepted principle that it is the state of D's domicile that has the primary interest in S's entitlement. It could be argued, however, that the law of the state of S's domicile has an interest if the rationale for its elective share is to prevent S from being left destitute and therefore a charge on the state. But in a state that recognizes the

---

[52] 236 N.E.2d 152 (N.Y. 1968).

[53] A contrary result was reached in New York involving the legitime elective share of a child under the law of France; the facts are sufficiently distinguishable that it cannot be regarded as a repudiation of the result in *Clark*. See In re Estate of Renard, 417 N.Y.S.2d 155 (Surr. Ct. 1979), as discussed in § 3.5 n.16.

§ 3.4.5

elective share on the principle of marriage constituting an economic partnership, it is likely that the law of the domicile will govern with respect to movables. Indeed, it might be a better rule if the law of the domicile applied with respect to immovables as well, although such a deviation from traditional conflict of law principles is less likely.

§3.4.6 Spousal Agreements

In addition to moving property to another jurisdiction or becoming a domiciliary of another state to avoid S's elective share, D may minimize that entitlement by an agreement with S, executed before or after marriage. Although prenuptial agreements are more common, postnuptial agreements also can be valid under state law if supported by proper consideration, and no distinction is made here between the two.[54] For convenience, both are referred to merely as spousal agreements and, if the government's position with respect to the elective share and CRTs remains an issue, postnuptial agreements (waivers of the elective share as against any inter vivos CRT) may become very common, especially among the very wealthy who tend to be the settlors of such trusts.[55]

-----

[54] See the 2008 version of UPC §2-213 (enumerated as §2-204 prior to technical amendments that reorganized the Code in 1993 and §2-207 between 1993 and 2008), which makes no distinction; although it embraces the Uniform Premarital Agreement Act standards of enforceability, it is not limited only to premarital agreements. The spousal annuity requirements of §401(a)(11) cannot be waived by a prenuptial agreement so, in that respect, a distinction between prenuptial and postnuptial agreements is relevant. See Treas. Reg. §1.401(a)-20 Q&A 28; Hurwitz v. Sher, 982 F.2d 778 (2d Cir. 1992); Zinn v. Donaldson Co. Salaried Employees Retirement Savings Plan, 799 F. Supp. 69 (D. Minn. 1992); contra, In re Estate of Hopkins, 574 N.E.2d 230 (Ill. App. Ct. 1991). Indeed, §417(a)(4)(A) may operate to require renewal of a waiver within 90 days of the participant reaching the annuity starting date.

[55] See Rev. Proc. 2005-24, as discussed in §§3.4.2 n.12 and 14.3.2 n.40. Terminology can be a problem in this arena, as illustrated by just the following title: Smith, The Unique Agreements: Premarital and Marital Agreements, Their Impact Upon Estate Planning, and Proposed Solutions to Problems Arising at Death, 28 Idaho L. Rev. 833 (1992), in which postnuptial is replaced by "Marital," which is the author's antithesis to premarital, and "Unique" is said to be appropriate because the parties are not bargaining at arm's length, which is not universally true.

§3.4.6

Under the Uniform Premarital Agreement Act and the 2008 version of UPC § 2-213 S's waiver of the elective share is enforceable[56] unless S proves that execution of the agreement was not voluntary or that it was unconscionable when it was executed. Usually this means that before execution S was not provided with a "fair and reasonable disclosure of the property or financial obligations of the decedent," did not "voluntarily and expressly waive, in writing, any right to disclosure" of that information, and did not and reasonably could not have "an adequate knowledge" of that information.[57]

Absent a divorce and property settlement agreement meeting the requirements of § 2516, S's voluntary relinquishment of marital rights such as the elective share, in exchange for a predetermined testamentary transfer, fails to meet the requirements of § 2043(b). Thus, it does not constitute § 2053(c)(1)(A) full and adequate consideration in money or money's worth that would support a § 2053(a)(3) deduction for the value of S's claim under the agreement against D's estate.[58] Neverthe-

---

[56] See Springs & Bruce, Marital Agreements: Uses, Techniques, and Tax Ramifications in the Estate Planning Context, 21 U. Miami Inst. Est. Plan. ¶ 700 (1987); Davis, Till Death Do Us Part: Antenuptial Agreements Concerning Wills and Estates, 8 Prob. L.J. 301 (1988); Younger, Perspectives on Antenuptial Agreements, 40 Rutgers L. Rev. 1059 (1988); Melbinger & Melbinger, How to Allocate Pension Benefits in Prenuptial Agreements, 125 Trusts & Estates 26 (July 1988).

In re Estate of Johnson, 452 P.2d 286 (Kan. 1969), held that D's failure to comply with the spousal agreement did not give S the option to reject the agreement to instead elect against D's will to claim an entitlement larger than the share specified under the spousal agreement. In re Estate of Anderson, 552 N.E.2d 429 (Ill. App. Ct. 1990), involved a spousal agreement that failed to address S's rights to insurance provided by the federal government. S was the default beneficiary under the insurance contract and federal law alike, but D's executors successfully argued that the spousal agreement established S's entire entitlement; therefore, assets such as insurance proceeds not allocated to S were the estate's entitlement.

[57] See Ruzic v. Ruzic, 549 So. 2d 72 (Ala. 1989), holding that fair disclosure exists if the waiving party received adequate consideration or competent independent representation. The consideration in *Ruzic* was marriage, which was deemed adequate, and the waiving party instigated the agreement and sought the assistance of professional advisors in the process.

[58] See §§ 2043(b)(1) and 2053(e); Estate of Ellman v. Commissioner, 59 T.C. 367 (1972); Estate of Rubin v. Commissioner, 57 T.C. 817 (1972), aff'd, 478 F.2d

less, because even a prenuptial agreement is not enforceable until the parties marry,[59] property transferred in satisfaction of the obligations created by spousal agreements qualifies for the § § 2056 and 2523 estate and gift tax marital deductions.[60]

§3.4.7 Postmortem Planning

The foregoing discussion relates to planning aspects of the elective share as they relate to D, with little attention to the effects on S. From S's perspective, sometimes the elective share is used for postmortem planning to improve the overall consequences to a happily married couple with no antipathy or disappointment regarding D's will. For example, D's plan may favor S but it is flawed in a way that precludes qualification for the marital deduction. A rejection in favor of the elective share may cure the problem.

It also is possible that postmortem manipulations using the elective share may arise because beneficiaries or other parties with an interest in S's wealth wish to improve upon their interest in D's estate. This may be

(Footnote Continued)

1399 (3d Cir. 1973); Estate of Myers v. Commissioner, 27 T.C.M. (CCH) 975 (1968); Sutton v. Commissioner, 32 T.C.M. (CCH) 982 (1973), aff'd, 535 F.2d 254 (4th Cir. 1974) (all denying § 2053(a)(3) deduction for claim by S against estate to postmortem annuity payable pursuant to prenuptial agreement and, because predating the QTIP marital deduction, also denying § 2056 marital deduction). See also Treas. Reg. § 25.2512-8, holding that the waiver of marital rights also does not constitute consideration for gift tax purposes, again unless the requirements of § 2516 are met.

In Estate of Carli v. Commissioner, 84 T.C. 649 (1985), a § 2053(a)(3) deduction was allowed and § 2043 consideration was deemed to support the agreement because S relinquished rights (although not all to the testator) other than marital property rights under state law. For a full discussion of the § 2053(a)(3) deduction for claims against the testator's estate, see § 15.4.2.1.

[59] See Rev. Rul. 69-347, 1969-1 C.B. 227.

[60] See Estate of Cline v. Commissioner, 43 T.C.M. (CCH) 607 (1982); Rev. Rul. 68-271, 1968-1 C.B. 409 (spousal agreement required D's estate to distribute specified amount S; even absent bequest, the § 2056(e) (now § 2056(c)) passing requirement was deemed met with respect to transfers made pursuant to that obligation); Rev. Rul. 54-446, 1954-2 C.B. 303. An exception to this marital deduction entitlement could apply if the agreement calls for each spouse to execute a mutual will, which imposes an obligation on S that is deemed to disqualify the marital deduction. See § 3.7.1 nn.31-34 and accompanying text.

true even though S is not disaffected, often because S is incompetent or already has died.

Finally, D's plan may be overqualified for the marital deduction, but it is too late under state law[61] to disclaim the excessive amount or because a technical flaw precludes a §2518 qualified disclaimer that avoids gift taxes.[62] Renunciation of D's will may prove to be an effective salvation of a plan that otherwise is not objectionable if it is not too late to elect against D's will and take an elective share that is better suited to the overall object of minimizing FET in both estates.[63]

Oddly enough, notwithstanding that UPC §2-1105 permits a post-mortem disclaimer even if S died shortly after D, UPC §2-212(a) (previously §2-206 and, before 1993, §2-203) expressly limits the right of election to an inter vivos exercise, making it impossible to elect if S already is deceased. The rationale for this provision is that there is no need to protect S by providing a certain level of benefit if S already has died, which seems inconsistent with one rationale for the elective share itself, which is to recognize the economic partnership of marriage.

---

[61] For example, some state laws provide a shorter period within which to disclaim than §2518, and in some states it is too late to disclaim if S already has died. See, e.g., the pre-1990 version of UPC §2-801, which was changed in the 1990 version to remove the impediment to disclaimer after S has died. The 2008 version, §2-1105(b), along with the definition of "fiduciary" in §2-1102(4), provides the same authority, albeit not as obviously.

In Estate of Lamson v. Estate of Lamson, 662 A.2d 287 (N.H. 1995), spouses died within three months of each other and the government refused to accept a disclaimer made by S's personal representative with respect to an entitlement in D's estate until the authority to do so was established by the highest court of the state. The court ruled favorably to the estates, applying a standard that the disclaimer is authorized if it benefits either the estate of the disclaimant or the beneficiaries of that estate. This standard may not be the test under other state laws.

[62] For example, if S's acceptance of benefits under D's will precludes a qualified disclaimer but, under state law, does not disqualify a subsequent rejection of the will to elect the statutory share.

[63] Both Rev. Rul. 90-45, 1990-1 C.B. 175, and PLR 8817061 involved a combination of postmortem planning techniques by which S elected the statutory share and then disclaimed a portion of it to even further refine the amount qualifying for the marital deduction.

§3.4.7

State laws are not uniform regarding the right to elect after S becomes incompetent or dies. The UPC is not alone in regarding S's death as a termination of the opportunity to elect the statutory share,[64] but other states may permit a postmortem election. Curiously, however, more susceptible to litigation is the question whether the election is in the best interests of an incompetent S based purely on monetary grounds.[65] A number of cases have approved elections made on behalf of an incompetent S when the election was made and who died before it was approved, notwithstanding that death before the election was made would have extinguished the right to elect entirely.[66] Additional cases

---

[64] See, e.g., Payne v. Newton, 323 F.2d 621 (D.C. Cir. 1963); Sarbacher v. McNamara, 564 A.2d 701 (D.C. Ct. App. 1989); In re Estate of La Spina, 397 N.E.2d 1196 (Ohio 1979).

[65] See Barnabeo, The Incompetent Spouse's Election: A Pecuniary Approach, 18 U. Mich. J.L. Ref. 1061 (1985); In re Estate of Clarkson, 226 N.W.2d 334 (Neb. 1975) (the appropriate test normally ought to be monetary, although considerations of what the incompetent S would have done if competent may be entertained); In re Estate of Cromley, 440 N.E.2d 588 (Ohio 1981) (also following minority view that monetary considerations alone may support election on behalf of incompetent S); but see Kinnett v. Hood, 185 N.E.2d 888 (Ill. 1962) (rejecting renunciation by guardian of incompetent S, notwithstanding that elective share exceeded value to S under the will, because S was deemed amply provided for under the will and the only benefit derived by renunciation would inure to S's heirs); In re Estate of Dalton, 328 N.E.2d 257 (Ill. 1975); In re Guardianship of Scott, 658 P.2d 1150 (Okla. 1983).

[66] See, e.g., Spencer v. Williams, 569 A.2d 1194 (D.C. Ct. App. 1990) (election made by conservator before S died allowed, resulting in S receiving $160,000 outright rather than only a life estate in $200,000, because the court regarded S's best interest as equating with the most value to S and because countervailing notions that D's intent should be preserved are irrelevant); Williams v. Skeen, 401 S.E.2d 442 (W. Va. 1990) (although state law required S's personal representative "to preserve, protect, and manage" S's estate, the election on behalf of an incompetent S could not be made without the court's approval, even if it produced a larger monetary amount); on remand, In re Will of Sayre, 415 S.E.2d 263 (W. Va. 1992) (personal representative's election was effective even though it was not approved until after S's death); 1990 version of UPC § 2-206(a) (enumerated as § 2-203(a) prior to technical amendments that reorganized the Code in 1993) (election is valid if S is alive when election is made, not when it is approved); 2008 version of UPC § 2-212(a) (election valid only if petition is filed in court before S dies).

See also In re Estate of Cross, 664 N.E.2d 905 (Ohio 1996), which involved a probate court election on behalf of S that was reversed on appeal and then

§ 3.4.7

have approved elections on S's behalf by an authorized representative because S was unable to do so for reasons other than incapacity.[67]

Regarding a related issue to S of the income tax consequences of the election right, normal distributions of estate property generate a distributions deduction for the estate under §661 and carry DNI to the recipient under §662,[68] whereas satisfaction of a debt of the testator's estate normally is not an income taxable event.[69] Property distributed to S on renunciation of D's will is regarded by the government as a separate share of the estate,[70] similar to real property that passes under §102 to an heir or devisee free of income tax.[71] Only estate income earned on

(Footnote Continued)

restored by the Supreme Court, because S was living in a nursing home paid for by Medicaid and would have lost those benefits for failing to make the election. See §3.4.7.

[67] See In re Celenza's Estate, 162 A. 456 (Pa. 1932) (attorney in fact exercised election for S who resided in Italy, notwithstanding that statute required election to be in writing and signed by S); In re Skewrys' Will, 33 N.Y.S.2d 610 (Surr. Ct. 1942) (Polish Consul General acting under power of attorney could exercise right of election); In re Zalewski's Estate, 55 N.E.2d 184 (N.Y. 1944) (consular officers had power under treaty between United States and Poland to appear for nationals in estate matters to the same extent as if they had a power of attorney, which allowed consular officer to elect against D's will, notwithstanding there had been no authorization by or communication from S in Poland); but see In re Estate of Klekunas, 205 N.E.2d 497 (Ill. App. Ct. 1965) (rejecting attempt by consular officer to assert right of election available to S who resided in Lithuania because no power of attorney had been granted in fact or by treaty); Harmon v. Williams, 615 So. 2d 681 (Fla. 1993) (rejecting attempt by attorney at law to file election because the attorney did not act under a power of attorney in fact).

[68] Unless the specific bequest exception in §663(a)(1) is applicable. See §§5.4.1 and 5.4.4 regarding §§661 and 662.

[69] Except to the extent distribution of assets in kind is regarded as a sale or exchange generating gain or loss. See §§5.8.1 and 13.7.3.2.1.

[70] See Treas. Reg. §1.663(c)-4(b), specifically identifying an elective share as subject to separate share rule treatment, as discussed in more detail in §5.4.3.

[71] See Treas. Reg. §1.661(a)-2(e), applicable if title to realty passes under state law directly to the beneficiary (subject in some states to a power in the personal representative to administer the property and to sell it if necessary to pay estate debts).

If it is clear that distribution of the elective share normally does not carry out estate income to S, an interesting question nevertheless remains unanswered regarding the income tax consequences if S elects the statutory share but

elective share property between the testator's death and distribution is attributable to that share and taxable, first to the estate as received, and then as DNI that is taxable to S in the amount of the estate's distributions deduction when paid, all under the normal income carryout rules of §§ 661 and 662.[72]

To illustrate, decided prior to but consistent with this separate share rule approach, Deutsch v. Commissioner[73] concluded that an elective share entitlement that is not increased by income earned during admin-

---

(Footnote Continued)

disclaims all but a portion of it. Distribution of that amount may be sufficiently like a § 663(a)(1) specific bequest to remain tax free, but distribution of assets in kind in satisfaction of the elective share might constitute a gain or loss realization event (as it would if distribution was in satisfaction of a pecuniary marital bequest), or it might be regarded more like distribution of a fractional share of an estate (which is a nonrealization event). Because the federal income tax consequences are not clear if S cuts back on the elective share by disclaimer, planners should specify in the election and disclaimer how the share received by S should be computed. For example, it would be possible to disclaim an elective share in excess of a fractional amount, of which the numerator is the amount needed to produce a desired tax result and the denominator is the total elective share, and presumably generate the same tax consequences that would apply to satisfaction of a fractional marital entitlement if income tax applies to this situation at all. For a discussion of analogous concepts, see § 3.2.4 nn.15-17 dealing with intestate distributions; chapter 5 dealing with estate income tax in general; § 5.4.4 n.85 and accompanying text regarding this particular issue; and § 13.7.7 dealing with marital deduction fractional funding.

[72] Rev. Rul. 64-101, 1964-1 C.B. 77, modified by Rev. Rul. 71-167, 1971-1 C.B. 163, and applied retroactively by McKay v. United States, 74-2 U.S. Tax Cas. (CCH) ¶ 9536 (S.D. Fla. 1974), aff'd, 510 F.2d 579 (5th Cir. 1975). Both were declared obsolete by promulgation of the separate share regulations applicable to an estate. See §§ 5.2.2 and 5.4.1 regarding the estate distributions deduction and income carryout rules.

[73] 74 T.C.M. (CCH) 935 (1997). See contra, in an exceptionally poor analysis that cited none of the controlling precedent, Bingham v. United States, 983 F. Supp. 46 (D. Mass. 1997), aff'd, 160 F.3d 759 (1st Cir. 1998), applying the literal language of the normal § 662(a)(2) income carry out rules, with no mention of the distributions deduction issue under § 661(a)(2), the full amount distributed over several years to S in partial satisfaction of the elective share was deemed to carry out DNI to the extent thereof, because no other distributions were made that might have shared the DNI for those years. The court also denied § 663(a)(1) specific bequest treatment because the elective share distributions were not "under the terms of the governing instrument" as required by the Code.

§ 3.4.7

istration of the estate should not incur any liability for estate income. The distribution of the underlying entitlement (as opposed to any income earned on that share, if S is entitled thereto) properly is excluded from the income carryout and distributions deduction rules of §§ 662 and 661, respectively. Not as a specific bequest excluded under § 663(a)(1) but as a distribution that is "outside" the Subchapter J estate and as to which the normal distribution rules of Subchapter J are not applicable. The court's conclusion was based on a number of factors, the most telling of which were the similarities between statutory dower, as to which Rev. Rul. 64-101 held that the DNI carryout rules are not applicable, and the particular state's (Florida) elective share.[74]

According to the *Deutsch* court, the elective share also may be analogized to the Treas. Reg. § 1.661(a)-2(e) exclusion from the DNI carryout rules of any interest in real property that vests at death and passes under state law directly from the decedent to the entitled beneficiary, again without reliance on the specific bequest exclusion of § 663(a)(1). Just as that exclusion treats these realty interests as passing outside the Subchapter J estate itself (essentially like any nonprobate entitlement, as to which the distributions deduction and income carryout rules also do not apply), Rev. Rul. 64-101 held that statutory dower also was excluded from the parameters of Subchapter J. The Tax Court held that the same rationale should apply to the elective share because of its many similarities to dower.

Expressly excluded from the *Deutsch* opinion was any determination of whether or how the court's conclusion might differ if or to the extent the elective share is entitled to postmortem income, although footnote 21 of the opinion noted that dower that carries postmortem income would be subject to the Subchapter J income carryout and distribution deduction rules to the extent of that income only.[75]

---

[74] Among those similarities was the fact that both statutory dower and the elective share vest under state law at the decedent's death, neither dower nor the elective share is entitled to income earned or any portion of any appreciation generated between the date of the decedent's death and the date when distribution is ordered, and they each take precedence over distributions to all other estate beneficiaries (coming only after debts of the decedent and, in a sense, constituting a lower priority claim against the estate).

[75] Citing Rev. Rul. 71-167, 1971-1 C.B. 163, which was made obsolete by the separate share regulations applicable to estates.

§ 3.4.7

One portion of the *Deutsch* opinion may be questionable, however. A large component of the decedent's estate consisted of distributions from the decedent's IRAs, allocable to principal under state law but carrying IRD that was includible in the estate's DNI. The court concluded that none of this income was attributable to the elective share either, which may be improper under the same analogy to dower.

Dower or the elective share may be a fractional interest entitlement in each estate asset (which state law may permit the personal representative to satisfy with non pro rata distributions rather than a portion of every estate asset). If so, it might be appropriate to consider S as the owner of a fractional interest in the right to this IRD from the date of D's death, and with that entitlement also to regard S as subject to income tax thereon. This is underscored by the notion that, had the income represented by these assets not been recognized by the estate prior to distribution of the elective share (for example, if the payout under those IRAs was not in a lump sum), and if S had received any portion of those accounts as a part of the elective share distribution, any income thereafter received would constitute S's IRD.[76]

The Tax Court conclusion in *Deutsch* is administratively easy, in the sense that there is no tracing requirement to determine which assets S received and whether any IRD was received from them prior to distribution, and in the sense that the underlying elective share entitlement is regarded in its entirety as free from DNI carryout liability.

Finally, S may incur attorney fees and other costs in perfecting the elective share right on renunciation of D's will, but these costs are regarded as personal capital expenditures to acquire title to income

---

[76] Quaere whether this income tax exposure should vary depending on the time of receipt of the income from the IRAs—either before distribution to the spouse or after—and whether actual distribution of a right to receive this item of IRD would entitle the spouse under state law to additional assets to reflect a value that is reduced by the built-in income tax liability. For FET purposes that built-in income tax liability will not reduce the marital or charitable deduction, as discussed in §§ 13.7.3.2.4 n.80 and 14.1.4 n.71. Whether its value would reflect the liability for state law elective share computation and satisfaction purposes is a separate question.

§3.4.7

producing property and, therefore, are not deductible by S for income tax purposes.[77]

For most purposes S's decision not to elect against a testator's will is not tantamount to a transfer of the elective share in exchange for whatever benefits are provided by D's will. Thus, for example, S's creditors cannot reach S's interest in a testamentary spendthrift trust.[78] Nor is the decision not to elect regarded as a taxable gift, even if the elective share is more valuable than the benefits received under the will.[79] Moreover, a gift will not occur even if S renounces the testator's will to take a less valuable elective share, unless the election does not comply with the formal requirements for a qualified disclaimer under § 2518.

Note, however, that case law varies from state to state on the issue whether the elective share is an available asset for Medicaid qualification purposes. Tannler v. Wisconsin Dep't of Health and Social Services[80] held that failure of an institutionalized surviving spouse to assert a claim against the decedent's estate constituted a disqualifying divestment

---

[77] See Wilson v. Commissioner, 37 T.C. 230 (1961), aff'd per curiam, 313 F.2d 636 (5th Cir. 1963); Hartt v. United States, 65-2 U.S. Tax Cas. (CCH) ¶ 9547 (D. Wyo. 1965) (§ 212 deduction is available only for expenses incurred in the production or collection of income or for the management, conservation, or maintenance of property held for the production of income, and not for the acquisition of income producing property). See also Commissioner v. Butterworth, 290 U.S. 365 (1933) (denying amortization deduction claimed by S, who argued that life estate under D's will effectively was purchased by S's decision to forsake the elective share). The same issue comes up with respect to the costs of a will contest action and is addressed in § 3.8 n.7.

[78] See, e.g., American Security & Trust Co. v. Utley, 382 F.2d 451 (D.C. Cir. 1967), rev'g 258 F. Supp. 959 (D. D.C. 1966); 3 Scott, Fratcher, & Ascher, Scott and Ascher on Trusts § 15.4.4 (5th ed. 2007). See also Aragon v. Estate of Snyder, 715 A.2d 1045 (N.J. Super. Ct. Ch. Div. 1998), rejecting efforts of S's creditors to reach assets of D's estate by forcing S to make the forced heir share election. Additional cases to the same effect are collected in Annot., Creditor's right to prevent debtor's renunciation of benefit under will or debtor's election to take under will, 39 A.L.R.4th 633 (1985).

[79] Cf. Rev. Rul. 74-492, 1974-2 C.B. 299 (S's failure to elect statutory share before death is not taxable as the lapse of a general power of appointment; S does not own the elective share for tax purposes unless the election actually is made to take it).

[80] 564 N.W.2d 735 (Wis. 1997).

under 42 U.S.C. § 1396p(e)(1). Miller v. Department of Social and Reha-bilitation Services[81] held that S's consent to D's estate plan in lieu of the elective share essentially made S the settlor of a trust consisting of that entitlement and causing the trust to be a countable resource for Medi-caid eligibility disqualification. In re Estate of Dionisio[82] regarded S's anticipatory waiver of the elective share right as a disqualifying transfer for look back period calculation purposes. And In re Mattei[83] held that Medicaid countable resources included S's elective share. The court required appointment of a guardian to exercise the right to the extent necessary to support the spouse for the period of ineligibility attributable to the right of election.

Bezzini v. Department of Social Services[84] was different, treating the settlor of an inter vivos trust as having made a disqualifying transfer at death, when the disinheriting trust became irrevocable, rather than treating S's failure to elect a share of the estate as the disqualifying transfer, but the effect essentially was the same. Curiously, in the domiciliary state D's testamentary transfer would not have been a dis-qualifying transfer and S was unable to defeat the trust or reach trust assets for elective share purposes.[85]

Estate of Wyinegar[86] treated the elective share as countable notwith-standing that S had been counseled by the Department to convey assets to D while they both were alive, to qualify S for benefits. Similarly, Hinschberger v. Griggs County Social Services[87] and In re Flynn v. Bates[88] charged the elective share against S even though it was not asserted, but Bradley v. Hill[89] held that the unexercised right to elect the share would not count against S. And although New York law is clear

---

[81] 64 P.3d 395 (Kan. 2003).

[82] 665 N.Y.S.2d 904 (Sup. Ct. 1997).

[83] 647 N.Y.S.2d 415 (Sup. Ct. 1996).

[84] 715 A.2d 791 (Conn. App. Ct. 1998).

[85] See Skindzier v. Commissioner of Social Services, 784 A.2d 323 (Conn. 2001) (only trusts created other than by will are subject to the disqualifying transfer rules).

[86] 711 A.2d 492 (Pa. 1998).

[87] 499 N.W.2d 876 (N.D. 1993).

[88] 413 N.Y.S.2d 446 (1979).

[89] 457 S.W.2d 212 (Mo. Ct. App. 1970).

§ 3.4.7

that an incompetent S's failure to elect the statutory share will be reflected in a Medicaid disqualification determination, In re Street[90] rejected a request by the Department of Social Services to order S's guardian to make the election, holding that state law would not disqualify S or otherwise affect qualification for Medicaid benefits if the election was not made. Nor would S's care and treatment, lifestyle, and environment be improved or altered, and nothing in the record indicated that the election otherwise would benefit S or that the failure to elect would injure S.

On the other hand, In re Estate of Cross[91] involved a determination that, notwithstanding S's incapacity (and, indeed, death before prosecution of the appeal), the probate court was required to assert the elective share on S's behalf. Otherwise S would have been disqualified for Medicaid payment of nursing home costs for failing to utilize a resource in which S had a legal interest and the ability to use or dispose of it. Similarly, I.G. v. Department of Human Services[92] held that failure of an incompetent S to elect the statutory share constituted a disqualifying disposition under state regulations providing that "all . . . resources . . . the individual . . . is entitled to but does not receive because of . . . inaction . . ." constitute available assets and specifically identifying waiver of the "spousal elective share" as a disqualifying transfer.

As thus seen, the law regarding Medicaid qualification is in significant turmoil, although it is clear that, if elected, the share will count against eligibility. If it is undecided in a given jurisdiction whether the share will be charged as a countable asset even if not elected, the wise approach may be to forsake the election in hopes that the elective share entitlement will not be treated as owned property for qualification purposes, which would be consistent with the treatment for gift tax purposes. Better yet is premortem planning that causes the elective share to be regarded as worthless, so that any deemed transfer is valueless for Medicaid disqualification purposes.

---

[90] 616 N.Y.S.2d 455 (Surr. Ct. 1994).

[91] 664 N.E.2d 905 (Ohio 1996).

[92] 900 A.2d 840 (N.J. Super. Ct. App. Div. 2006).

§3.4.7

§3.5 OMITTED CHILD'S ELECTION AGAINST THE WILL

Except under the limited Louisiana concept of legitime that, like the elective share of a surviving spouse, precludes a testator from totally disinheriting certain children, the law elsewhere in the United States allows a testator to disinherit[1] children and their descendants if the will is drafted properly. However, absent a statutory provision such as the negative will authority granted by the 1990 version of Uniform Probate Code §2-101(b), the clarity of a testator's intent to disinherit an heir is irrelevant if property not effectively disposed of by the will passes by intestacy. Thus, a planner whose client wants to exclude a particular intestate taker must overcome application of any pretermitted heir statute *and* must make a complete disposition of the client's property.[2]

Statutes prevent inadvertent omission of natural objects of the testator's bounty (pretermitted heir statutes).[3] A complete disposition of the testator's estate is required, with an indication that omission of a particular individual was intentional, not the result of accident or mistake.[4] For

---

[1] **§3.5** See La. Const. art. XII, §5 with respect to legitime. Forced heirship for descendants is prevalent in civil law and Islamic law jurisdictions but not the common law.

A decedent may not be able to totally disfranchise a child to the extent local law permits the award of family allowances or recognizes homestead. See §2.4 and §2.5, respectively.

[2] See, e.g., In re Estate of Cancik, 476 N.E.2d 738, 739, 741 (Ill. 1985), which involved a will that stated: "I have intentionally omitted the names of any of my relatives from this my last will and testament for reasons I deem good and sufficient, with the exception of my aforesaid cousin." Because the will failed to dispose of all the testator's property, the court held that heirs in addition to the cousin shared in the remaining property, stating: "When a testator provides that certain indicated heirs are not to take from his estate and the will disposes of less than all of the estate, the provision excluding the heirs is without effect as to the property which is not disposed of by the will." See also §3.6 n.4 for a discussion of Waring v. Loring, 504 N.E.2d 644 (Mass. 1987), and In re Estate of Smith, 353 S.W.2d 721 (Mo. 1962). See also §3.2.5.4 n.86 and accompanying text, regarding negative wills.

[3] See, e.g., UPC §2-302, applicable with respect to children of the testator born or adopted after execution of the will and not mentioned or provided for therein.

[4] Estate of Smith, 507 P.2d 78 (Cal. 1973), required strong and convincing language on the face of the will to disinherit a child. A pretermitted heir who

example, an effective will provision that would preclude the claims of otherwise pretermitted children might read "I intend to provide by this will for all my children, including any hereafter born or adopted" or, coupled with a designation of family members,[5] "I intentionally make no

(Footnote Continued)

asserts a claim is not contesting the will (although omission of a natural object of the testator's bounty may lead to a contest based on a lack of capacity as well). Thus, an in terrorem provision in the document, specifying that any relative who challenged the will would receive only one dollar, was not effective to preclude the child from taking a portion of the testator's estate.

In re Estate of Cooke, 524 P.2d 176 (Idaho 1973), adopted the same standard that intent must appear on the face of the will, but many states permit the intention to omit to be established by extrinsic evidence. See, e.g., In re Estate of Blank, 219 N.W.2d 815 (N.D. 1974) (decided before state adoption of the UPC); Estate of Crump v. Freeman, 614 P.2d 1096 (Okla. 1980) (omission of one grandchild representing a deceased child deemed not intentional absent statements in the will because extrinsic evidence was not admissible, lacking ambiguity regarding intent as revealed in the document); but see In re Estate of Rogers Flowers, 848 P.2d 1146 (Okla. 1993) (adopted child subsequently returned to custody of state as a delinquent was entitled to pretermitted heir share because order terminating parental rights did not cut child off from parents; evidence of the order was only extrinsic evidence, making application of will ambiguous regarding testator's intent to disinherit the child).

[5] See §3.2.2. American Bar Association Standing Committee on Ethics & Professional Responsibility Formal Op. 05-434 (2004) specifies that no ethics violation occurs if an attorney assists a client in such a disinheritance, *even if* the attorney represents the prospective beneficiary, provided that there is no conflict of legal rights and duties between the two clients, the representations are unrelated, and the attorney is not providing advice about whether to disinherit the prospective beneficiary that may heighten the risk that the attorney may not exercise independent judgment because of a sense of duty or loyalty to the disinherited beneficiary. Further, the attorney may not proceed if the disinheritance violates some previous agreement or family planning in which the attorney was involved. The opinion does not mention, but it should be stressed, that the attorney may not reveal that the prospective beneficiary has been disinherited, and the attorney must not allow that knowledge to infect or alter any other representation, which may inform resignation because the attorney is uncertain about whether that is too difficult an obligation to uphold.

In the process of encouraging the testator to reveal the existence of family members who might be entitled to a share of the estate if not mentioned or otherwise effectively disinherited, the estate planner may acquire information (such as the existence of a nonmarital child) that the client has not revealed to other family members, which may emphasize the need for an agreement be-

provision for any child not specifically mentioned herein, including any hereafter born or adopted."[6] Otherwise, satisfaction of a pretermitted heir's claim may cause unexpected abatement problems and increase FET by diverting assets from a marital or charitable deduction bequest.

(Footnote Continued)

tween the client and that estate planner regarding secrets that are relevant to the client's spouse and underscore the need to address the potential for conflicts of interest early in the representation. See § 13.10 regarding ethics in estate planning and the joint representation of spouses.

[6] Notice that "child" or "children" is a better term to use in such a provision than "heir," as illustrated by In re Estate of Robbins, 756 A.2d 602 (N.H. 2000), in which a pretermitted "heir" provision in a will was regarded as ineffective with respect to one natural child and an adopted child, neither of whom was mentioned or provided for in the decedent's will. The court specifically stated that "use of a generic term such as 'heirs' was insufficient" to constitute the requisite indication of an intent to disinherit those children. According to the court the decedent should have referred more specifically to "children" or "issue."

Harris Trust & Savings Bank v. Donovan, 560 N.E.2d 1175 (Ill. App. Ct. 1990), rev'd, 582 N.E.2d 120 (Ill. 1991), involved a decedent's pourover will that named three lawful children as "my only children now living," notwithstanding a nonmarital child who had been filiated many years before. The decedent's will poured over to a trust that stated only lawful children were included as beneficiaries. The lower court held the nonmarital child was not adequately disinherited, in part because one other child specifically was mentioned as not to receive a share, indicating that the decedent knew how to disinherit, which was not the approach followed with respect to the nonmarital child. A more direct statement like that in text probably would have avoided this type of litigation. See generally Annot., Pretermitted heir statutes: what constitutes sufficient testamentary reference to, or evidence of contemplation of, heir to render statute inapplicable, 83 A.L.R.4th 779 (1991).

In Azcunce v. Estate of Azcunce, 586 So. 2d 1216 (Fla. Dist. Ct. App. 1991), an omitted child's claim to a share of the decedent's estate was foreclosed by the fact that a codicil to the decedent's will, executed after the child's birth, was deemed to republish the will that was executed prior to the child's birth. As a consequence the child was not an afterborn as required under state law. The result was particularly unsettling because testimony of the decedent's attorney revealed that yet another will had been prepared to include the omitted child but it was not executed before the decedent's untimely death (at age 38). In the companion case of Espinosa v. Sparber, Shevin, Shapo, Rosen & Heilbronner, 586 So. 2d 1221 (Fla. Dist. Ct. App. 1991), aff'd, 612 So. 2d 1378 (Fla. 1993), the court rejected the omitted child's claim against the drafting lawyer for malpractice in failing to provide for afterborn children in earlier drafts of the will, because the child and lawyer were not in privity of contract.

§ 3.5

Contrariwise, a pretermitted heir who chooses not to assert the claim should be afforded the same no-gift treatment as a surviving spouse who chooses not to claim an elective share.[7]

Some pretermitted heir statutes apply only with respect to children born or adopted[8] after execution of the will, reflecting a presumption that a testator will not forget a child who was alive when the will was executed. Some apply as well to a child the testator mistakenly thought was deceased.[9] Some are not applicable if D left substantially all of the estate to S, who is the other parent of the pretermitted heir,[10] reflecting a presumption that S will provide for those children. And disinheritance under a will may be respected if the testator provided for the pretermitted heir by nonprobate transfers (such as insurance, a trust, or an inter vivos gift) meant to be in lieu of testamentary dispositions, as shown by the testator's statements[11] or by reasonable inference.[12]

There is no concept applicable to pretermission similar to the augmented estate regime designed to protect a surviving spouse, and

---

[7] See § 3.4.7 n.79.

[8] In re Estate of Hamilton, 441 P.2d 768 (Wash. 1968) (testator's bequest of $1 to a step-child the testator adopted after execution of will did not preclude pretermitted heir entitlement); In re Will of Stier, 345 N.Y.S.2d 913 (Surr. Ct. 1973) (will gave testator's entire estate to surviving spouse, if any, otherwise to three step-children; subsequent adoption of one of the step-children permitted that child to take an intestate share on the testator's death because there was no evidence to indicate that the will was drafted in anticipation of the adoption); Estate of Turkington, 195 Cal. Rptr. 178 (1983) (testator bequeathed entire estate to two nieces the testator raised from childhood; after execution the testator adopted one of the nieces but did not change the will, which caused the adopted niece to receive the entire estate under the California pretermitted heir statute).

[9] See the 1990 version of UPC § 2-302(c). Compare the result under the prior version of this provision, § 2-302(a)(2), as applied in Gray v. Gray, 947 So. 2d 1045 (Ala. 2006), in which a devise in favor of the surviving parent was deemed to preclude pretermission, notwithstanding the parents' divorce, which negated that devise by operation of another state law.

[10] See, e.g., the 1990 version of UPC § 2-302(a)(1).

[11] An inter vivos gift meant to advance or satisfy the child's entitlement at death should be accompanied by a contemporaneous declaration of that intent to foreclose pretermitted heir status at death. See §§ 2.3 and 3.2.5.1, respectively regarding advancements and ademption by satisfaction.

[12] See, e.g., the 1990 version of UPC § 2-302(b)(2).

§ 3.5

pretermitted heir entitlement may not apply to nonprobate property. As a result, a pretermitted heir may receive little or nothing if there is little or no probate estate against which a pretermitted heir share may be asserted.[13] Moreover, a will provision disposing of property to "children" as a class will be deemed to include afterborn or afteradopted children and prevent pretermission in some states,[14] which indicates the wisdom of class gifts and group descriptions. In these and other respects, however, local law must be studied to know the breadth of any problems that may be created,[15] and conflict of laws issues should be addressed if, for example, the will is executed in one state but purports to dispose of property in another, subject to different pretermitted heir provisions.[16]

---

[13] See Kidwell v. Rhew, 268 S.W.3d 309 (Ark. 2007), Bell v. Estate of Bell, 181 P.3d 708 (N.M. Ct. App. 2008), Robbins v. Johnson, 780 A.2d 1282 (N.H. 2001), and In re Estate of Cayo, 342 N.W.2d 785 (Wis. Ct. App. 1983) (pretermitted heir statutes did not apply to the omission of children in revocable trusts), and Fiske v. Warner, 109 A.2d 37 (N.H. 1954) (a pretermitted heir cannot claim appointive assets not part of the testator's estate).

[14] See, e.g., the 1990 version of UPC § 2-302(a)(2), applicable if there were any children alive when the will was executed and granting the afterborn or after-adopted child the same entitlement as all the other children.

[15] For example:

- The constitutionality of statutes that fail to afford equal rights to nonmarital pretermitted heirs should not be relied upon since the decision in Trimble v. Gordon, 430 U.S. 762 (1977).

- See UPC §§ 2-117 through 2-119 (§ 2-114(a) in the 1990 version) and the Uniform Parentage Act, 9B U.L.A. 299 (2001), regarding the existence of a parent and child relation. Equitable legitimation may be applicable. See Prince v. Black, 344 S.E.2d 411 (Ga. 1986); Robinson, Untangling the "Loose Threads": Equitable Adoption, Equitable Legitimation, and Inheritance in Extralegal Family Arrangements, 48 Emory L.J. 943 (1999). The concept was rejected in Breedlove v. Estate of Breedlove, 586 So. 2d 466 (Fla. Dist. Ct. App. 1991).

- The effects of the new biology may be involved. See § 2.2.4.3.

[16] See, e.g., In re Estate of Wright, 637 A.2d 106 (Me. 1994) (involving legitime interest of children of a U.S. citizen but Swiss domiciliary who died in Maine with a will directing that Maine law would govern; court held that a Swiss court applying Swiss choice of law rules would honor the governing law provision, even with respect to French and Swiss property, notwithstanding that it would deny the legitime interest of the decedent's children); Royce v. Estate of Denby, 379 A.2d 1256 (N.H. 1977) (law of state in which testator was domiciled at execution of will applied, not law of state of domicile at testator's death, because

§ 3.5

§3.6 EQUITABLE ELECTION

Another will drafting approach that anticipates the possibility of a surviving spouse or potentially pretermitted heir's[1] election against the testator's estate plan is to take advantage of the doctrine of equitable election. Based on the principle that a testator has no right to bequeath property the testator does not own or have the power to appoint by will, the doctrine puts the rightful owner of property to an election: the owner can dispute a will that attempts to dispose of the owner's property by denying the testator's ability to transfer that property, or the owner can accept the will[2] and, in the process, concede its validity for all purposes—

(Footnote Continued)

testator was incompetent when removed from former state and because the will designated the law of the former state as applicable); Price v. Johnson, 428 P.2d 978 (N.M. 1967) (New Mexico law, which did not protect pretermitted heir, applied with respect to testator's Texas will disposing of New Mexico real estate); In re Estate of Renard, 417 N.Y.S.2d 155 (Surr. Ct. 1979) (involving legitime interest of French testator's surviving child (a resident of California) and a French will designating that New York law should apply; the New York court accepted the designation of New York law with respect to the testator's assets located in New York, denying the child's claimed share). *Renard* is representative of numerous New York decisions that reflect a basic tenet that inter vivos transfers of property that rely on or designate New York law will be respected in New York regardless of the transferors' domicile. See, e.g. In re Meyer, 876 N.Y.S.2d 7 (App. Div. 2009), and Wyatt v. Fulrath, 211 N.E.2d 637 (N.Y. 1965). A caveat to all planning involving nonresidents is the impact of applicable treaties or the Haig Convention on the law applicable to succession.

[1] §3.6 It is not entirely accurate to describe the doctrine of equitable election as a method to anticipate a pretermitted heir's claim to a share of the estate, but only because the effect of making a bequest under the will to a child or other potential claimant is to preclude pretermission because the testator did not omit them. The effect, however, is the same.

[2] The beneficiary's decision to accept the will and allow disposition of the beneficiary's property may be implied from the beneficiary's acceptance of benefits under the will without objection to its terms. See, e.g., Kentucky Trust Co. v. Kessel, 464 S.W.2d 275 (Ky. 1971), in which D owned real property as tenants by the entirety with S. The will created a trust of property, including this realty, to pay income and discretionary principal to S, who enjoyed those benefits until death. S's will made no mention of the entireties realty and the court concluded that S made the equitable election and thereby consented to D's disposition of that property after the life estate terminated. Thus, beneficiaries under S's will were not entitled to that property.

including to dispose of the owner's property. In the most important context of interspousal planning in anticipation of a statutory share election by a disappointed surviving spouse, the technique can be used to provide a sufficient testamentary entitlement to the surviving spouse that the spouse will be loathe to relinquish it in exchange for an elective share. Equitable election specifies that the spouse cannot have both.

In nonmarital situations the doctrine of equitable election may be a useful mechanism for a testator to dispose of property the testator wishes to control but does not own. The doctrine also might be used by a testator who wishes to make a bequest to a creditor in satisfaction of the testator's debt to that creditor, allowing the use of property the testator wishes the creditor to accept. Equitable election cases frequently are a result of simple mistake or inadvertence. For example, the testator or the estate planner thought property was owned by the testator in fee simple but it was held in joint tenancy with the right of survivorship; if the surviving co-owner stands to receive other property under the will, equitable election applies. The concept also can be used intentionally to engineer a result the testator otherwise had no right to accomplish. And it can be used to punish an individual who disrupts the testator's planning by denying all interests and benefits flowing to that individual under the will, including such indirect benefits as the effects of tax allocation, exoneration clauses, or appointment as personal representative or trustee.

To be effective, care is required to guarantee that an affirmative or intentional application of the doctrine cannot be questioned,[3] and to dispose of all the testator's property that otherwise might pass to the

---

[3] According to Atkinson, The Law of Wills § 138 (2d ed. 1953), there is a presumption against the will being interpreted to dispose of property not owned by the testator. See, e.g., Estate of Williamson v. Williamson, 657 N.E.2d 651 (Ill. App. Ct. 1995) (court unwilling to extend doctrine of equitable election to joint tenancy with the right of survivorship as to which decedent's ownership terminated at death, in part because the doctrine is of civil law origin and should not be extended to override the legislated law of joint tenancy, in part because it was not clear that the decedent intended to put the beneficiary to an election, and in part because the beneficiary was not attacking the validity of the will under which the beneficiary was taking; the result was to allow the beneficiary to take a portion of the estate as bequeathed, and to deny the effect of the will to dispose of the property that had been owned in joint tenancy with the decedent and as to which the beneficiary was the sole survivor).

§ 3.6

beneficiary by intestacy or outside probate, as to which the doctrine does not apply.[4] In addition, the will should specify the alternative disposition of all property bequeathed to the beneficiary under the will if the doctrine is triggered by the beneficiary's decision to relinquish all benefits under the will and retain or assert the beneficiary's other property rights.

(Footnote Continued)

Slightly different but of similar import is In re Estate of Hermann, 864 N.E.2d 334 (Ind. 2007), in which D's will provided that S "shall receive the home in which we are living at the time of my death as a part of [S's] one-half (1/2) of the residue of my estate." According to the court, this reflected D's intent that the residuary estate be divided equally between S and the plaintiff trustee and that D's residence be included in the calculation, notwithstanding that it was owned as tenants by the entireties and passed automatically to S at D's death. Rather than create an equitable election (as a purported disposition of the dwelling), the intent was deemed to merely consider the value of the dwelling in calculating S's distributive share, without regard to whether it passed to S under the will or otherwise.

[4] See, e.g., Waring v. Loring, 504 N.E.2d 644 (Mass. 1987), involving the intestate distribution of a trust remainder that D failed to convey effectively. The will provided that its provisions were "in lieu of dower and all . . . statutory rights" of S, and the issue was whether S was entitled to a share of the intestate remainder interest. The court rejected the contention that the will required S to elect to take under the will and relinquish all other rights in D's estate and instead held that it merely referred to the statutory elective rights available to a spouse and not to any other intestate entitlement that may come to the spouse. As a result, S was entitled to a share of the intestate property. The court conceded, however, that its decision was against the majority rule laid down by the few American courts that have considered the issue.

Bravo v. Sauter, 727 So. 2d 1103 (Fla. Ct. App. 1999), and Carnahan v. Stallman, 504 N.E.2d 1218 (Ohio Ct. App. 1986), both involved S as the income beneficiary of an inter vivos trust created by D. Those elections against D's will did not affect any rights under the trust, including the right to enjoy trust benefits in estate assets that poured over to the trust, because the doctrine of equitable election is limited to testamentary dispositions. To make equitable election applicable D should have created the trust by will, in which case the election would have precluded S from benefiting under the trust in addition to taking the elective share. Otherwise D should have provided by explicit provision in the trust that S would be treated as predeceased if S elected against D's will. Regarding the marital deduction aspects of such a condition, see § 13.6.1.2.1 n.12 and accompanying text.

§3.6.1 Tax Consequences of Election

For tax purposes a beneficiary's election to take property under the testator's will in exchange for relinquishing rights or property already owned is a transfer that occurs after the testator's death. As a result, the beneficiary's property is not includible in the testator's gross estate for FET purposes[5] and the beneficiary has made a transfer that may constitute a part-sale, part-gift transaction if the value received under the will is less than the value of the property or rights the beneficiary relinquished.[6] Thus, for example, if the beneficiary relinquished to the trust an asset worth $1 million in exchange for a life estate worth $750,000 in other trust property, the gift would be the excess $250,000. Moreover, if the beneficiary retained any interests in the beneficiary's own property relinquished to the trust, normally only the value of the interests not retained in the beneficiary's property would be subject to gift tax. Thus, there would be no gift at all in this example if the beneficiary retained an income interest in the $1 million asset and that interest was worth at least $250,000.

Unfortunately, the value of any interests retained by the beneficiary in the beneficiary's own property is disregarded for gift tax purposes[7] if

---

[5] See Rev. Rul. 67-383, 1967-2 C.B. 325 (community property forced election will disposing of both halves of spouses' community property did not cause inclusion of S's interest in D's gross estate). Although §2040(a) may apply with respect to joint tenancy or tenancy by the entirety property, this inclusion is not a function of equitable election.

[6] Treas. Reg. §§25.2511-1(h)(2) and (3). Sherman v. United States, 79-1 U.S. Tax Cas. (CCH) ¶ 13,288 (E.D. Va. 1979), held that no gift for gift tax purposes resulted from S's election to take a bequest under D's will and allowed D to dispose of their tenancy by the entirety property to their child because the court regarded the transfer as involuntary and therefore not subject to gift taxation. That result is not correct, because S could refuse all benefits under the will. See AOD 1979-160, which nevertheless recommended no appeal in *Sherman* because, on reconsideration, it appeared that no gift tax would be due because the consideration received by S was at least as valuable as the property relinquished.

[7] It is not clear from the express language of §2702 or its regulations whether this treatment applies with respect to anything but the gift tax consequences of a part-sale, part-gift transaction. The conservative response also appears to be the correct interpretation, that §2702 only applies for gift tax purposes and not for purposes of determining income tax consequences of the sale portion of the transaction. See §2702(a)(1), which reads "[s]olely for purposes of determining

§2702 is applicable, which will be the case if the beneficiary's property ultimately passes to members of the beneficiary's family and no exception is available. As defined in §2702(e) by reference to §2704(c)(2), "family" includes the beneficiary's spouse, lineal ancestors and descendants of the beneficiary or the beneficiary's spouse, siblings of the beneficiary, and spouses of any of these. As a consequence, §2702 is likely to apply in most equitable election situations. One exception to its application is if the transfer is not a completed gift because, for example, the beneficiary retains a sufficient power over the transferred property, but that result is not likely to be favorable.[8] Another exception would apply if the beneficiary's retained enjoyment constitutes a §2702(b) qualified interest, the value of which is not disregarded under §2702(a)(2)(A).[9]

In addition to potential gift tax consequences of an intentional equitable election plan, gain or loss on the sale portion of the transaction also may result, both to the testator's estate and to the beneficiary. Under the new basis-at-death rule in §1014(b)(9), the testator's estate has a basis equal to the FET value of property included in the testator's estate, but the amount realized could exceed this amount, resulting in the possibility that the estate or trust that is exchanging a term interest for the beneficiary's property will incur a capital gain or loss on the deemed sale.[10] Moreover, the beneficiary will incur gain or loss unless

---

(Footnote Continued)

whether a transfer of an interest . . . is a gift (and the value of such transfer) . . . ." Although not entirely clear, this interpretation that §2702 is not applicable for income tax purposes would maximize the value of the amount transferred by the beneficiary in exchange for benefits bestowed by the testator's will, which generates a larger amount realized for income tax part-sale purposes, which is likely to produce a greater income tax liability, and therefore is the government's likely argument (unless a loss is involved on the transaction).

[8] See §3.6.2 n.20 and accompanying text.

[9] See §7.2.2.2. Treas. Reg. §25.2702-2(d)(1) Example 3 illustrates that §2702 is not applicable with respect to an income interest in the decedent's property originally placed in trust, but this exception would not preclude application of §2702 with respect to the beneficiary's own property transferred to that trust and as to which the beneficiary retained an income interest.

[10] Price, Contemporary Estate Planning §9.31 (2010), reports that it is unclear whether §1001(e) may apply to this transaction. By its terms, §1001(e)(1) is applicable to a sale of any term interest such as a life estate or income interest in trust, and provides that basis is ignored for purposes of determining gain or loss

§3.6.1

(Footnote Continued)

on the sale portion. An exception to this treatment applies under § 1001(e)(3) if all interests in the trust are sold at the same time.

The full amount realized would be taxable as income if § 1001(e)(1) is applicable on the sale of an income interest. See, e.g., PLR 200231011 (commutation of a CRAT with the charitable remainder beneficiaries receiving outright distributions and the lead private interest being converted from an annuity into a unitrust interest, coupled with trustee discretion to distribute corpus and a testamentary general power to appoint the balance, was regarded as an exchange that caused gain realization under § 1001(e) because the lead interest was deemed to have zero basis; no indication was given regarding how that gain would be reported vis-à-vis the continuing unitrust distributions, nor whether the impact of realization was to convert ordinary income reportable in installments into capital gain reportable all at the time of the transaction); PLR 200210018 (income beneficiary's renunciation generated gift tax consequences that were structured as a net gift, with income tax sale or exchange treatment that raised the issue because the beneficiary was deemed by § 1001(e) to have no basis in the income interest; the income interest was deemed to be a capital asset under Estate of McAllister v. Commissioner, 157 F.2d 235 (2d Cir. 1946), acq. Rev. Rul. 72-243, 1972-1 C.B. 233); PLRs 200648016 and 200648017 (commutation of interests in chronologically exempt generation-skipping trusts, with capital gain or loss treatment), and § 5.9 n.10.13 and accompanying text for a similar transaction involving sale of both lead and remainder interests, and § 14.3.2.1 n.53 for rulings dealing with the commutation of lead interests in CRTs and potential application of the self-dealing rules.

In those latter cases it was a grantor's lead interest that was commuted. That transfer would be regarded as a bargain sale to charity if the grantor had never created the trust and instead transferred the underlying trust corpus to the charity for an amount less than the full FMV of that corpus—for example, for an amount equal to the value of the retained unitrust lead interest in these cases. In such a case the grantor's basis would be prorated to the sale and the gift portions, with a less than total capital gain result. Quaere why those two transactions should differ. See also PLRs 200230017 and 200027001 (sale of S's income interest in a QTIP trust). See § 6.4.1 n.6.

There appears to be no authority directly on point with respect to the potential application of § 1001(e) to these cases, and all examples in the regulations and all transactions upon which authority does exist involve sales of term interests by the beneficial owners thereof, leaving some doubt about whether § 1001(e) is meant to apply to a sale of an interest by a fiduciary entity itself. That doubt may be dispelled by the letter of conveyance accompanying Treasury Decision 7142, 1971-2 C.B. 295, which contained final regulations under § 1001(e) and stated that a request was made during the comment period relating to the regulations in proposed form to alter the regulations under § 1001(e) to make it clear that the sale deemed to occur under a "widow's

§ 3.6.1

the beneficiary's property being relinquished has a basis equal to FMV. That could be the case if the property involved is jointly owned, as frequently is the case in inadvertent applications of the doctrine, and 100% of its value was included in the testator's gross estate under § 2040(a), generating a new basis in 100% of the property, which would preclude gain or loss to the beneficiary as the surviving joint tenant. In addition, if the property is community property, the new basis-at-death rule in § 1014(b)(6) gives a new basis to both halves of the community property, notwithstanding inclusion of only the testator's half for FET purposes, which eliminates gain or loss to S as beneficiary in such a transaction.

A further consideration that must be addressed if the plan involves skip persons is the effect of equitable election for GST purposes. To the

---

(Footnote Continued)

election" will does not trigger this provision. The stated response was that the "Tax Legislative Counsel and the Chief Counsel considered . . . the suggestion . . . and rejected it on the ground that the rule requested . . . was too obvious, particularly in view of § 1.661(a)-2(f)(1), to warrant a specific statement." See 1971 TM LEXIS 38 (July 30, 1971). An additional statement relating to Treasury Decision 7142 also was made that, in the light of Gist v. United States, 423 F.2d 1118 (9th Cir. 1970), and Estate of Christ v. Commissioner, 54 T.C. 493 (1970), aff'd, 480 F.2d 171 (9th Cir. 1973), the question the government considered that might arise was "Could the estate be treated as having sold . . . the life estate for purposes of *section 1001(e)*? This possibility was regarded as too remote for treatment in these regulations." See 1971 TM LEXIS 118 (Apr. 19, 1971).

A reading of Treas. Reg. § 1.661(a)-2(f) does not reveal an obvious answer to this issue, but it seems reasonable to assume that the government's inaction and the Treasury Department's unwillingness to specify in regulations that § 1001(e) is applicable in the election situation are sufficient indications that the government does not believe they apply and, based on that assumption, to disregard § 1001(e) in reporting the tax consequences of the transaction. Attention to this issue should, however, be paid if future developments reveal that this speculation is incorrect because the fiduciary could incur a substantial gain on the transaction if it is applicable.

Even if it is applicable in general, one form of property that may be includible in the testator's estate and available for the equitable election transaction but as to which § 1001(e) would not apply is life insurance cash proceeds, which do not receive a new basis under § 1014 (because cash has no basis—or, if it is easier to think this way, the basis of cash always is equal to its face value). See Price, Contemporary Estate Planning § 9.37 (2010). By its terms, § 1001(e) is applicable only if basis is determined under any of § 1014, § 1015, or § 1041.

extent the testator's trust receives property from a beneficiary by gift, the trust has two different transferors, each potentially creating GST problems and each potentially needing to consider allocation of his or her exemption to the trust.[11] Under § 2654(b), a trust with different transferors is treated as two different trusts for exemption allocation purposes, so the beneficiary's contribution to the trust should be addressed separately from the testator's property. As to that property, however, retention of any interest in the beneficiary's property relinquished to the trust that would trigger application of the FET at the beneficiary's death[12] will invoke the ETIP rule of § 2642(f),[13] which would preclude allocation of the beneficiary's exemption to that deemed trust.

The gift tax valuation rules in § 2702 are not applicable for GST purposes,[14] so this complication may not arise if any gift on the beneficiary's relinquishment of property to the testator's trust is attributable only to the application of § 2702. Because this element of the law is not clear, the beneficiary would be well advised to allocate exemption to the trust by a formula described as that amount needed to produce an inclusion ratio of zero[15] if it is appropriate to allocate exemption to the trust to preclude imposition of a future GST.

§3.6.2 Forced Election Estate Plans

Spouses who each own property may be able to benefit from a form of planning that takes advantage of the doctrine of equitable election. Because it requires that each spouse have property with which to engage in the transaction, historically it has been more common in community property states because each spouse owns half of their community property.[16] Sometimes known as a forced election estate

---

[11] See § 11.4.5.5.

[12] Typically under § 2036(a)(1). See § 3.6.2 n.21-31 and accompanying text.

[13] See § 11.4.5.5.3. Estate tax inclusion is a possibility as discussed in the context of the *Gradow* transaction. See § 3.6.2 n.21-31 and accompanying text.

[14] See § 2701(a)(1) and Treas. Reg. § 25.2702-1(a).

[15] See § 11.4.5.5.

[16] For a thorough examination of revocable transfers of community property and the estate and gift tax consequences of placing community property in a revocable trust or a forced election estate plan, see Johanson, Revocable Trusts, Widow's Election Wills, and Community Property: The Tax Problems, 47 Tex. L.

plan, it also benefits from the basis rules applicable to community property includible in the estate of the first spouse to die.[17] But it can be useful in noncommunity property jurisdictions as well.[18]

Under the forced election plan D puts S to an election. If S wants to receive income from D's nonmarital deduction property (such as in a nonmarital or family trust),[19] S must agree to let D's estate plan dispose of S's share of their community property after S's death. If S agrees, the election is to receive a life estate in D's property in exchange for the remainder interest in S's property.[20] Essentially, this is the transaction

(Footnote Continued)

Rev. 1247 (1969); Johanson, Revocable Trusts and Community Property: The Substantive Problems, 47 Tex. L. Rev. 537 (1969); and Morrison, The Widow's Election: The Issue of Consideration, 44 Tex. L. Rev. 223 (1965).

[17] See § 1014(b)(6), which gives both halves of the community a new basis at the death of the first spouse to die, notwithstanding inclusion of only half the value of that property in that decedent's gross estate.

[18] Indeed, if D in a noncommunity property state owned the bulk of the spouses' property, it has been suggested that S could be allowed to engage in this planning if D's estate plan allowed S to utilize marital deduction property received from D, either by outright transfer to S or by permissible withdrawal from a marital deduction trust. See, e.g., Price, Contemporary Estate Planning § 9.25 (2010).

[19] This plan would consider only the income from D's property that is not meant to qualify for the marital deduction. The value of the interest the spouse was required to relinquish would reduce the marital deduction under § 2056(b)(4) if the right to receive income from a marital deduction trust was made conditional.

[20] Regarding the gift tax cost to S prior to adoption of § 2702, see Commissioner v. Chase Manhattan Bank, 259 F.2d 231 (5th Cir. 1958); Kaufman v. United States, 462 F.2d 439 (5th Cir. 1972); Estate of Vardell v. Commissioner, 307 F.2d 688 (5th Cir. 1962); Estate of Bressani v. Commissioner, 45 T.C. 373 (1966); Turman v. Commissioner, 35 T.C. 1123 (1961). Regarding the timing of the gift, compare Rev. Rul. 69-346, 1969-1 C.B. 227 (gift is complete when D dies), with Hambleton v. Commissioner, 60 T.C. 558 (1973) (gift not taxable until S died because, unlike most forced election estate plans, S's transfer was revocable until death), and Robinson v. Commissioner, 75 T.C. 346 (1980), aff'd, 675 F.2d 774 (5th Cir. 1982) (gift not taxable until S released retained power to appoint S's property contributed to the trust). Delaying gift taxation will increase the value of the remainder interest being transferred and decrease the income interest being received in consideration therefor, which will produce a larger gift in exchange for the delay, and decrease the consideration offset element that makes the transaction attractive. Indeed, Johanson, Revocable Trusts, Widow's

§ 3.6.2

that was involved in Gradow v. United States[21] and a digression into the facts and holding in *Gradow* is useful to illustrate and understand this planning.

D, the testator in *Gradow*, was the deceased spouse in a community property state. D's will undertook to dispose of both halves of community property owned by D with S. The will put S to the typical election. S could retain S's share of the community property or S's share of the community property would go into a trust under which S would receive all the income for life but D's plan would govern disposition of the remainder. As is typical in most community property forced election transactions, D funded that trust with D's share of the couple's community property, so the election effectively involved a trade of a life estate in D's share of the community property in exchange for the remainder interest in S's share of the community property (because S retained the income from S's share of their community property and relinquished only the right to dispose of the remainder therein).

Although *Gradow* involved community property and a forced election estate plan, the form of the transaction was not particularly relevant. *Gradow* is important because it speaks to any transfer of a remainder interest with a retained life estate in the subject property. In *Gradow*, as in many of these cases, the issue was the tax consequences to S, particularly inclusion of the transferred property in S's gross estate at death under §2036(a)(1), because S made a transfer with a retained life estate. And today it also may trigger application of §2702, because it entails a transfer of only the remainder interest.

The argument to avoid §2036 inclusion of S's share of the community property in S's gross estate at death is that S transferred that property for a full and adequate consideration in money or money's worth, thereby qualifying the transaction for the parenthetical exception

(Footnote Continued)

Election Wills, and Community Property: The Tax Problems, 47 Tex. L. Rev. 1247 (1969), argues that the consideration offset of §2043 is not available at all if the transfer is not complete at the time of the transfer. If §2702 is applicable in the valuation of the gift, the value of S's retained income interest will be disregarded and only the value of the income interest received will change. See §7.2.2 regarding §2702.

[21] 87-1 U.S. Tax Cas. (CCH) ¶ 13,711 (Ct. Cl. 1987), aff'd, 897 F.2d 516 (Fed. Cir. 1990).

to application of § 2036(a)(1). In *Gradow*, S's estate alleged that the life estate received in D's share of the community property was worth more than the remainder interest that S transferred in S's share of the community property.[22] The court rejected the full and adequate consideration argument, however, on the ground that, to avoid § 2036(a)(1), full and adequate consideration is measured by the full FMV of the subject property—the fee simple interest therein—not just by the value of the interest transferred—which was the remainder in *Gradow*.[23]

As phrased by the court, the issue was whether § 2036(a)(1) required that "the consideration be paid for the interest transferred, or for the interest which would otherwise be included in the gross estate."[24] In this respect, the court illustrated at the very outset that it had little appreciation for what was involved in the case because the interest transferred—the remainder interest—is the very interest that would be included in the gross estate if no transfer was made during life. This is true because, when the life estate has expired, it is the remainder interest that remains and that would be includible in S's gross estate were it not for the sale.[25]

The aspect that apparently confused the *Gradow* court is the fact that the remainder interest, viewed at D's death, "looked different" (because of S's outstanding intervening life estate) than a remainder interest as seen at the later death of S. Nevertheless, ignoring the intervening life estate, the remainder interest, viewed at S's death, is

---

[22] More sophisticated forced election plans are designed to work by a formula so that these two items are exactly equal in value.

[23] Under the law now in effect, this would be the result if § 2702 applied because the value of the retained life estate would be ignored under § 2702 in valuing S's gift. That was not the case when *Gradow* was decided, and other cases under current law may not trigger the application of § 2702. See § 7.2.2.8.

[24] 87-1 U.S. Tax Cas. at 87,931, quoting from United States v. Allen, 293 F.2d 916, 917 (10th Cir. 1961).

[25] Actually, any proceeds from the life estate that were not consumed with no remaining value at death would be included, but the court's concern was over what would be includible but for the sale. The court properly was concerned only with the remainder because the proceeds from the life estate would be included in all events. Although the court appeared to assume that the proceeds of the life estate would be entirely consumed by S before death (which may not be accurate), consumption would be the same whether the remainder was sold or retained until death, making that an irrelevant factor.

exactly the same interest as the remainder interest during life. More importantly, the value of the remainder interest at S's death is the amount that would be included in S's gross estate if no transfer was made during life.[26] Instead of recognizing this simple economic reality, the court stated that "[t]he only way to preserve the integrity of [§ 2036(a)(1)], then, is to view the consideration moving from the surviving spouse as that property which is taken out of the gross estate."[27] Obviously the court thought that there was some difference between the remainder interest at S's death (at that time being labeled a "fee" but still being the same "quantity" and "quality" of interest) and the remainder interest transferred during life.

In this respect, the court failed to recognize two very important concepts: (1) the retained life estate was irrelevant to the case; the income will be enjoyed (and includible) in S's gross estate whether the remainder is sold or retained;[28] and (2) the remainder that was sold during life (and replaced with consideration of an equal value) is the equivalent of the full fee interest at death. As a result, the court was bound to reach the wrong result. With a proper view of the case and the purpose of § 2036(a)(1), there would be tax avoidance in a case such as this only if the consideration for sale of the remainder interest was inadequate, measured against the value of the transferred remainder at the time of the transfer. The court did not appreciate this. Indeed, the court stated that[29]

> if plaintiff is correct that one should be able, under the "bona fide sale" exception to remove property from the gross estate by a sale of the remainder interest, the exception would swallow the rule. A young person could sell a remainder interest for a fraction of the property's worth, enjoy the property for life, and then pass it along without estate or gift tax consequences.

---

[26] Again, ignoring the income interest—whether consumed or preserved.

[27] 87-1 U.S. Tax Cas. (CCH) at 87,933.

[28] Inclusion results to the extent the income is not consumed or to the extent it is consumed for the acquisition of assets that remain in the estate, and the balance of the income that is consumed presumably preserves for inclusion other property that S would have consumed had there been no income interest from the subject property.

[29] 87-1 U.S. Tax Cas. (CCH) at 87,934.

§ 3.6.2

In seeing an abuse in this scenario, the court overlooked the fact that the consideration received for the sale of the remainder interest would grow and produce income over that once young person's life and would equal the value of a full fee interest at death in the property that was the subject of the original sale. Any other result would be attributable only to those inaccuracies that are inherent in the tables used to value remainder interests, which sometimes work for the government's benefit and sometimes benefit the taxpayer.

The proof of this, and the proof that the court did not understand the economics of the transaction, is found in comparing the transaction involved (sale of a remainder) with its cousin, the split purchase of property.[30] For example, if S sold the full fee interest in the community property and received cash, and then invested a portion of the cash in a life estate in similar property, the transaction would produce exactly the same results but would not run afoul of §2036(a)(1)—and rightly so, because there is no abuse. In *Gradow*, S effectively took the proceeds from sale of a full fee interest in S's share of the community property and invested a portion of the proceeds in the purchase of a life estate in that same property, which ought to be treated no differently.

Nevertheless, the *Gradow* court was not without impressive precedent in reaching its conclusion that §2036(a)(1) "is a reflection of Congress' judgment that transfers with retained life estates are generally testamentary transactions and should be treated as such for estate tax purposes" and that "[f]or the purposes of evaluating whether plaintiff's election constituted full and adequate consideration within the meaning of §2036(a), the consideration flowing from [the surviving spouse] consists of the property which would otherwise have been included in her gross estate by virtue of her retention of a life estate."[31] Taken in its historical context, what *Gradow* convincingly proves is that, until only very recently, most courts have failed to adequately evaluate the poten-

---

[30] The split purchase "cousin" of the sale of remainder interest transaction is subject to §2702(c)(2), just as Treas. Reg. §25.2702-4(d) Example 2 makes it clear that the government regards §2702(c)(1) as applicable to the *Gradow* form of transaction because it refers to the "transfer of an interest in property with respect to which there is 1 or more term interests." See §7.2.2.8.

[31] 87-1 U.S. Tax Cas. (CCH) at 87,935.

tial for abuse in this arena, and many have reached the wrong conclusion; only a very few have reached the correct result.[32]

---

[32] See Estate of D'Ambrosio v. Commissioner, 105 T.C. 252 (1995), rev'd, 101 F.3d 309 (3d Cir. 1996), and Wheeler v. United States, 77 A.F.T.R.2d 1405 (W.D. Tex. 1996), rev'd, 116 F.3d 749 (5th Cir. 1997), both of which involved the proper pre-§ 2702 treatment of sales of remainder interests. Both lower courts followed *Gradow* and both were reversed in the first opinions in recent times to appreciate and properly apply future interest and time value of money concepts. Like *Gradow* itself, both cases are of limited consequence because of the adoption in the Revenue Reconciliation Act of 1990 of § 2702, which appears to stop transactions like the sale of remainder interest. Nevertheless, the decisions are of some interest because each opinion may indicate that courts finally have begun to understand the issue involved. Prior to these two proper decisions there had been four similar cases in just two years that got it wrong, the others being the mindless decision in Pittman v. United States, 878 F. Supp. 833 (E.D. N.C. 1994), and (because the taxpayer failed in its burden of proof) in Parker v. United States, 894 F. Supp. 445 (N.D. Ga. 1995) (the court stating without specification that it had "some reservations about the correctness of *Gradow*"; the facts also indicated that the consideration allegedly received in *Parker* may have belonged to the taxpayer and therefore would not be consideration at all). *Parker* and *Pittman* both were cited in the lower court opinions in *Wheeler* (which was a Magistrate Judge's recommendation of distressingly poor quality), and Estate of Magnin v. Commissioner, 71 T.C.M. (CCH) 1856 (1996), rev'd and rem'd, 184 F.3d 1074 (9th Cir. 1999), on remand, 81 T.C.M. (CCH) 1126 (2001) (sale of remainder interest case in which the taxpayer sought to apply the § 2043 consideration offset rule).

In a painstaking analysis of the cases relied upon in *Gradow* that dissected the flaws in each or their improper application to the *Gradow* situation, the *D'Ambrosio* and *Magnin* opinions competently evaluated the situation and properly analyzed both the language of the Code and Regulations (which the *D'Ambrosio* court correctly detected the *Gradow* court had misstated by leaving out significant portions of § 2036(a)(1)). According to *D'Ambrosio*, "it is difficult to fathom either the tax court's or the Commissioner's concerns about the 'abusiveness' of this transaction." 101 F.3d at 316. See also Estate of McLendon v. Commissioner, 66 T.C.M. (CCH) 946, 972 n.24 (1993) (without deciding the issue, the opinion noted that the validity of *Gradow* is open to question), rev'd and rem'd, 96-1 U.S. Tax Cas. (CCH) ¶ 60,220 (5th Cir. 1995), an unpublished opinion, because the court found that the evidence did not support the Tax Court's determination that the asset involved was more than an assignee interest in a family partnership rather than the partnership interest itself, and because the Tax Court's determination with respect to the decedent's mortality was "ambiguous and ambivalent" and therefore required more precision. On remand, the Tax Court restated its determination that it was improper to value the remainder interest transferred by the decedent using standard mortality assumptions be-

Not to be overlooked is the important question why the forced election transaction is desirable if the value of the property transferred by S will be includible in S's gross estate under § 2036(a)(1) or if, under current law, § 2702 will be applicable to regard S as making a gift of the full value of S's community property interest. The answer is found in the fact that *Gradow* allowed S's estate a consideration offset under § 2043 for the value of the income interest received from D's share of the community property as consideration for the transfer of S's remainder interest.[33] Although this consideration offset was valued (as required under § 2043) at the time of the transaction (meaning that appreciation in

---

(Footnote Continued)

cause decedent's death was clearly imminent and the possibility of survival for a year or more was so remote as to be negligible, regardless of the standard used to establish those conclusions. 72 T.C.M. (CCH) 42 (1996), rev'd on other grounds, 135 F.3d 1017 (5th Cir. 1998). For a full discussion of *McLendon* see § 7.2.1.

[33] Only a few other cases grant the § 2043 offset in this context. They include Estate of Christ v. Commissioner, 480 F.2d 171 (9th Cir. 1973); In re Estate of Bomash v. Commissioner, 432 F.2d 308 (9th Cir. 1970); United States v. Gordon, 406 F.2d 332 (5th Cir. 1969); United States v. Past, 347 F.2d 7 (9th Cir. 1965); Estate of Vardell v. Commissioner, 307 F.2d 688 (5th Cir. 1962); Whiteley v. United States, 214 F. Supp. 489 (W.D. Wash. 1963); Estate of Simmie v. Commissioner, 69 T.C. 890 (1978); Estate of Steinman v. Commissioner, 69 T.C. 804 (1978); Estate of Bressani v. Commissioner, 45 T.C. 373 (1966); and Estate of Sparling v. Commissioner, 552 F.2d 1340 (9th Cir. 1977), which is consistent in that it denied a § 2013 previously taxed property credit to S's estate for the income interest received from D because it was acquired by purchase rather than by gift, bequest, or inheritance (its value being less than the consideration given by S in exchange for it).

In Estate of D'Ambrosio v. Commissioner, 105 T.C. 252 (1995), rev'd on other grounds, 101 F.3d 309 (3d Cir. 1996), the consideration offset for § 2043 purposes was in the amount of an annuity that was received in exchange for an unsuccessful transfer of a remainder interest, with the annuity value being determined at the time of the transfer (which was $1,324,014) rather than the amount the decedent actually received pursuant to that annuity before dying (which was $592,078). Thus, an asset that would have been includible in the decedent's estate at its full date of death value (which was $2,350,000) if nothing had been done during the decedent's life instead resulted in estate tax inclusion of approximately two-thirds of that amount (only $1,618,064). On reversal, the result was inclusion of only the amount of the annuity payments received and not the asset that was the subject of the sole remainder interest, making the result even more favorable than the taxpayer's "defeat" in the Tax Court.

the consideration was not excluded along with the underlying consideration itself), S's estate was reduced by the value of the income interest in
D's property, granted in exchange for S's election. Normally D would
give this interest to S anyway, meaning that the *Gradow* forced election
served to reduce S's gross estate by the amount of this income interest,
which would have been included in S's estate in any event and otherwise
would have generated no reduction in the amount includible in S's gross
estate.[34] Any gift tax paid on the original transfer constitutes a credit
against the FET at death.[35] And the amount of any gift deemed made
under the original transfer is purged from S's adjusted taxable gifts base
for computation of the FET in S's estate.[36] Thus, the only detriment to
this transaction is any income tax incurred on the transfer caused by the
election[37] and loss of the use of any gift tax paid at that time.[38]

---

[34] If a client previously sold a remainder interest, the client might consider
transferring the retained life estate to prevent the possibility of § 2036(a)(1)
inclusion. In this respect, however, the transfer of the retained life estate will
need to occur more than three years before death to avoid application of
§ 2035(a)(2), or it must be sold for a full and adequate consideration. Pursuant to
United States v. Allen, 293 F.2d 916 (10th Cir. 1961), this would require sale for
an amount equal to the full FMV that would be includible if the life estate was
retained until death. Because this would not be an economically sensible transaction, a transfer of the retained life estate in hopes of surviving for at least three
years to avoid the operation of § 2035(a)(2) probably is all the client can
accomplish as fallout protection in the aftermath of *Gradow*.

[35] See § 2001(b)(2).

[36] See the flush language in § 2001.

[37] At one time an added benefit of the transaction might offset this income tax
detriment, but that benefit no longer is available. Effective with respect to
interests acquired or created after July 27, 1989, § 167(e) denies an amortization
or depreciation deduction for the life interest involved in this transaction because
the remainder is held by a § 267(b)(6) related party (the trustee of the trust of
which S is the beneficiary). Under § 167(e)(3), however, basis in the life estate
will be reduced and basis in the remainder interest will be increased, in each
case by the amount that would be allowed as a deduction were it not for
§ 167(e)(1). Thus, the amortization deduction claimed by S (for the cost of the
income interest purchased in D's share of the community property under a
forced election plan) in Gist v. United States, 423 F.2d 1118 (9th Cir. 1970), and
Estate of Christ v. Commissioner, 480 F.2d 171 (9th Cir. 1973), no longer is
relevant, except for determining the basis of the remainder interest.

[38] The gift tax paid may be more than anticipated if § 2702 is applicable,
because the effect of that provision is to treat the full value of S's property

§ 3.6.2

§3.7 CONTRACTUAL WILLS

Testamentary decisions may be influenced by a contract relating to a will, whether it mandates that a testator execute a will that includes certain provisions or not revoke an existing will or certain provisions in it, or requires an individual to die intestate. Before considering the effect of such a contract, it is necessary to determine whether a contract exists. In this respect, the 1990 version of UPC § 2-514 specifies that:

> A contract to make a will or devise, or not to revoke a will or devise, or to die intestate, if executed after the effective date of this Article, may be established only by (i) provisions of a will stating material provisions of the contract, (ii) an express reference in a will to a contract and extrinsic evidence proving the terms of the contract, or (iii) a writing signed by the decedent evidencing the contract. The execution of a joint will or mutual wills does not create a presumption of a contract not to revoke the will or wills.

Thus, oral contracts are not respected and oral testimony seeking to establish a contract would not be permitted unless the will makes express reference to the contract. Although there is substantial variation in state laws on this topic, many state laws now require any alleged contract to be in writing.[1]

A common source of contracts relative to wills entails the performance of personal services for the testator. Both the UPC and most state laws would grant a recovery in quantum meruit or restitution to a person who rendered services to the testator or otherwise relied on an oral promise by the testator to provide certain benefits by will. But absent a written contract that establishes the terms of the agreement, a family member who agrees to care for an elderly relative with the expectation of receiving testamentary compensation may be denied recovery entirely on the ground that the service was obligatory under state law or was

(Footnote Continued)

transferred—not just the value of the remainder interest therein—as subject to gift tax. See § 7.2.2.

[1] **§ 3.7** See, e.g., Mass. Gen. L. ch. 259, § 5, which is representative of many other state statutes in providing that no contract relative to a will, codicil, bequest, or devise is enforceable unless it is in writing. In re Estate of Loflin, 81 P.3d 1112 (Colo. Ct. App. 2003), is representative of the conflict of laws rule that the law of the state where the will was executed determines whether a valid contractual obligation exists.

meant to be gratuitous and therefore does not constitute consideration to support any contract regarding those services.[2]

A contract relating to the disposition of property owned by a decedent is not the same as a contract to exercise a power of appointment, which is invalid and unenforceable if the power is not exercisable presently.[3] And a contract relating to a will is not the same as a will, nor is a contract relating to a will enforceable in a probate proceeding that seeks to dispose of a decedent's estate as agreed in the contract. Nevertheless, the existence of any contract and remedies for its breach provided under contract law, such as monetary damages or restitution for property conveyed in reliance on the contract, may exert a strong influence on an individual to comply with the contract.[4] Thus, these agreements straddle both contract law and the law of wills and can be a powerful element in the estate planning process.

Probably the most common form of allegedly contractual will is the joint and mutual will, which is a single document designed to serve as the will of two people (often but not necessarily spouses), under which

---

[2] See Field, Will Contracts for Personal Services and Real Property During the Lifetime of the Aging Devisor: Resolving the Continuing Dilemma, 11 Prob. L.J. 57 (1992). In Estate of White, 521 A.2d 1180 (Me. 1987), and Goodman v. Estate of Mayer, 1993 WL 171314 (unpub. Conn. Super. Ct.), the courts held that caretakers were not entitled to the precise property the caretakers expected to receive from their relatives' estates, although the courts recognized that their relatives received the benefit of valuable services and intended to compensate the caretakers. Although the courts awarded the caretakers the value of those services, this was less than what the caretakers expected to receive. And see Estate of Hann v. Hann, 614 N.E.2d 973 (Ind. Ct. App. 1993) (no implied contract to pay for services rendered by family members living with testator because presumption is that those services were rendered gratuitously).

[3] Restatement (Third) of Property (Wills and Other Donative Transfers) § 21.2 (2011). See, e.g., Carmichael v. Heggie, 506 S.E.2d 308 (S.C. Ct. App. 1998) (holder of general testamentary power of appointment could not exercise the power inter vivos, nor presently contract to exercise the power by will, but did convey the balance of the powerholder's life estate in the subject property to a child who agreed to provide care for the powerholder for life), relying on Restatement (Second) of Property—Donative Transfers § 16.2 (1986); 5 American Law of Property § 23.35 (Casner ed. 1952).

[4] For good synopses of the law and literature on contractual wills, see Atkinson, The Law of Wills § 48 (2d ed. 1953); McGovern, Kurtz, & English, Wills, Trusts & Estates § 4.9 (4th ed. 2010).

§ 3.7

the survivor receives the property of the first to die and their combined assets pass in a mutually agreed manner on the death of the survivor. The nature of these documents frequently leads to the allegation that an underlying contract precludes the survivor from altering or revoking the will. The last sentence of the 1990 version of UPC § 2-514 specifically provides that execution of a joint will or mutual wills does not create a presumption that any contract exists with respect to the wills.

Notwithstanding this helpful provision, the moral learned from cases that generate litigation involving joint or mutual wills is to make it clear—preferably from express terms in the will itself—whether a contract is intended, in any case in which the will might be alleged to be contractual, especially if the will is a joint will or one of several mutual wills. Even if state law specifies that any alleged contract must be in writing or must be referred to expressly in the allegedly contractual will.

The law of other jurisdictions often leaves open the question whether a joint or mutual will is accompanied by, and therefore is controlled by, a contract relating to the will, which is one of several reasons to eschew joint or mutual wills entirely. Indeed, contractual wills in general, and joint or mutual wills in particular, are such litigation breeders, particularly the latter if the survivor alters or revokes the will, that experienced estate planners seldom utilize contractual wills of any variety.[5]

For example, Schwartz v. Horn[6] involved mutual wills that recited that they could not be modified or altered without the written consent of the other testator. The issue was whether the surviving testator could make inter vivos gifts to beneficiaries other than those designated under

---

[5] See, e.g., Dobris, Do Contractual Will Arrangements Qualify for Qualified Terminable Interest Treatment Under ERTA?, 19 Real Prop., Prob.& Trust J. 625, at 625 (1984): "No attorney I know likes, or even uses, joint or mutual wills"; and Hess, The Federal Transfer Tax Consequences of Joint and Mutual Wills, 24 Real Prop., Prob. & Trust J. 469, at 469, 515 (1990): "The mention of joint and mutual wills to most experienced trusts and estates attorneys will likely evoke a sardonic smile and the comment that the subject can be covered in one word—'Don't!' . . . The practitioner should discourage the use of mutual wills for two reasons. First, use of a mutual will rarely is the simplest way of fulfilling a client's estate planning goals. Second, use of a mutual will increases the difficulties of assuring predictable transfer tax results."

[6] 290 N.E.2d 816 (N.Y. 1972).

the mutual will. In holding that the survivor could not, the court stressed the fact that the subject of the gift was referred to specifically in the survivor's mutual will. It held that the general rule—that inter vivos gifts could be made or that assets could be consumed for daily living expenses of the survivor—would not apply with respect to assets identified specifically, as opposed to a general agreement regarding the survivor's entire remaining estate.[7] Unusual about *Schwartz* was that the dispute was resolved while the surviving testator still was alive. This form of litigation usually occurs after the death of both testators under the joint or mutual will, which creates additional complications.

Hatbob v. Brown[8] is another relatively rare case in which breach of a contract to make or not to revoke a will was litigated while one of the testators still was alive. *Hatbob* involved spouses with children by former marriages, and the court determined that no contract existed, a finding facilitated by testimony of the surviving spouse and the attorney who drafted the spouses' mutual wills. A malpractice action against the drafting attorney also failed, but warns estate planners that an express statement that no contract exists appropriately might be inserted in a will if the provisions of several testators' wills might lead to an allegation that those wills are contractually circumscribed.

The same joint and mutual will was the subject of litigation twice in Klooz v. Cox[9] and In re Estate of Wade[10] because a contract not to revoke was found to exist in the prior case. The later case held that funds placed by the survivor in joint bank accounts should be returned to the survivor's estate at death because the contract prevented the survivor from making gifts. Oursler v. Armstrong[11] required protracted litigation to

---

[7] See Ernest v. Chumley, 936 N.E.2d 602 (Ill. App. Ct. 2010) (applying first a minority rule presuming the existence of a contract from the mere existence of mutual will provisions and then holding that an inter vivos transfer into was a violation of the contract); Self v. Slaughter, 16 So. 3d 781 (Ala. 2008) (creation of an inter vivos trust was a breach of a contract to devise because a surviving party's inter vivos transfers must be reasonable and not an effort to circumvent the contract).

[8] 575 A.2d 607 (Pa. Super. Ct. 1990).

[9] 496 P.2d 1350 (Kan. 1972).

[10] 449 P.2d 488 (Kan. 1969).

[11] 170 N.Y.S.2d 458 (Sup. Ct. 1958), aff'd, 186 N.Y.S.2d 829 (App. Div. 1959), appeal dismissed, 161 N.E.2d 754 (N.Y. 1959), rev'd, 179 N.E.2d 489 (N.Y. 1961).

§3.7

establish that spouses who contemporaneously executed wills that contained similar provisions with respect to disposition of their combined assets upon the death of the survivor did not intend to preclude the survivor from altering the survivor's will. Glass v. Battista,[12] decided under the same law, held that a joint will of spouses was contractual, notwithstanding that it contained no express contractual language as to its binding effect on the survivor. The *Glass* court held that a natural inference of contractuality flowed from the parties' relation and the use of plural pronouns in the joint will. Thus, the predictability of result under these documents is quite low, absent an express statement that establishes or negates the existence of a contract.

A different type of litigation may flow from a contract to provide services to the testator in exchange for testamentary benefits. Questions can arise regarding the quality of the care provided or the ability to terminate the arrangement if the testator marries or otherwise is taken in and provided for by another individual. Thus, one of the first lessons to learn in this area is that the contract itself is an essential segment of the plan and must be prepared as carefully as the wills contemplated in it. As a consequence, a more appropriate solution might be to employ a QTIP marital deduction trust in the most common example involving a married couple, if the spouses wish to deny control to S over D's property while providing S with enjoyment of that property for the balance of S's overlife. A trust should be no harder to draft than a proper contract relating to the survivor's will. The only difference in effect between the two approaches is any trustee fees that might be incurred, and those can be avoided by making S trustee (after all, the alternative is to leave the property to S outright and rely on a contract to establish the rules of the agreement).[13]

---

[12] 374 N.E.2d 116 (N.Y. 1978).

[13] Two disadvantages might exist with respect to such a plan. The first is that the QTIP trust does not lock S into a specified plan with respect to S's property. It only protects D's property from being diverted by S. The second relates to the right of reimbursement under § 2207A for the taxes caused by § 2044 inclusion of the QTIP trust in S's estate. It provides that the full amount by which S's taxes are increased by inclusion of the value of the trust's assets in S's gross estate is to be paid from the trust. This effectively causes the trust property to be burdened by tax computed at the highest marginal estate tax rates applicable to the combined property of S and the trust, rather than bearing only its pro rata

The relatively common assumption that a joint or mutual will is less expensive to create than would be separate wills (or trusts) for two individuals almost certainly is not true if the contract relating to the joint or mutual agreement is prepared properly. By way of example, consider again a contractual will in exchange for home care provided to an elderly testator. A proper contract relating to that arrangement would define the quality of care to be provided, the effect of wrongful behavior by the caregiver, the definition and effect of insufferable treatment of the caregiver by the testator, the effect of the testator having to abandon living at home and move to a facility providing services previously contracted for, and the ability of the testator or the caregiver to terminate the arrangement. None of this would admit to facile drafting or use of a standard form, given the myriad variations in the circumstances in which the services may arise.

In addition, probate administration of an estate under a joint or mutual will is not likely to generate cost savings. For example, spouses frequently provide that all of D's property will go to S and S's will bequeaths their combined assets to their intended beneficiaries. The same person also may be designated as personal representative of both estates.

In this context, In re Estate of Buccola[14] involved reciprocal wills of spouses who died within one year of each other. As dictated by their wills, the personal representative of D's estate transferred D's property to S's estate and then transferred S's assets to their intended beneficiaries, in the process claiming double commissions as personal representative of both estates. The court noted that D's estate could have been paid directly to the intended beneficiaries and that the personal representative should not receive double commissions by running the same assets through both estates (although the court recognized that D's assets should be valued when distributed from S's estate in calculating the commission payable to the personal representative of both estates).

(Footnote Continued)

share of S's taxes computed on all includible property. The solution to both problems is to execute a contract that obligates S to execute a will that disposes of S's property as agreed, and that waives the § 2207A right of reimbursement. This is a step that few estate planners choose to take because of the tax consequences of such a contract. See § 3.7.1.

[14] 507 N.Y.S.2d 363 (Surr. Ct. 1986).

§3.7

There would have been no dispute about double fees if S had not died before administration of D's estate was completed. Which illustrates that cost savings seldom are effected in the administration of joint or mutual wills unless the will is ignored until the survivor's death.

A related assumption is that it is cheaper to create a single joint will than it is to prepare separate wills for several testators. This also almost certainly is not true in light of the necessary care required in drafting that single document properly, along with the cost of preparing the separate contract relating to the agreement of the parties that is required in these cases. All as compared to the relatively inexpensive cost of producing mirror image wills using modern word processing equipment.

As just one illustration of the added thought that must be devoted to the drafting of joint or mutual wills, consider the question raised if an intended beneficiary under a joint or mutual will dies after one of the testators dies but before the death of the last testator. Some cases hold that an antilapse statute controls the destination of the deceased beneficiary's entitlement.[15] Others hold that the estate of the deceased beneficiary has a vested remainder interest in the property of the first testator to die and an enforceable right against the property of the survivor, so that the beneficiary's estate is entitled to the property.[16] A well drafted contractual will should address the possibility of lapse and survivorship until the time for distribution to the ultimate beneficiaries, the same as if the first testator to die had created a trust giving the surviving testator a life estate and a remainder to the designated beneficiaries. Reflecting this added degree of thought should be no more time efficient than drafting separate traditional documents for each testator, and is not likely to generate a real cost saving if the documents are prepared properly.[17]

---

[15] See, e.g., In re Estate of Arends, 311 N.W.2d 686 (Iowa Ct. App. 1981).

[16] See, e.g., Jones v. Jones, 692 S.W.2d 406 (Mo. Ct. App. 1985); In re Estate of Duncan, 638 P.2d 992 (Kan. Ct. App. 1982).

[17] Thoughtful drafting seems to be in peril with joint and mutual wills, as illustrated by Painter v. Coleman, 566 S.E.2d 588 (W. Va. 2002), in which spouses with reciprocal wills provided for the survivor or for a niece of each of them in the event of their simultaneous deaths. D died, S knew enough to have a new will executed but the drafter (an accountant) merely deleted the bequest to D and failed to consider the need to provide for those nieces *in all events*. The court ultimately found for the nieces (had it not the new will would have been a nullity,

The same issues also arise if two or more individuals create joint settlor or mutual trusts that operate like joint or mutual wills, with constraints on amendment or revocation. But in addition to questions regarding the existence, terms, and enforceability of any agreement between the settlors, tax issues that are relatively unique to this form of planning also can arise.

For example, joint settlors may transfer property owned as joint tenants to a joint settlor trust. Or they may partition the property and transfer the pieces to trusts created separately but that grant rights to and impose restrictions on each settlor. In each case the survivor may be deemed to have made a transfer with retained powers or interests in the trust created by the first to die, potentially causing inclusion in the survivor's gross estate under § § 2036 and 2038.

For example, Rev. Rul. 71-51[18] involved the FET consequences of a joint and mutual will that restricted S's disposition of joint tenancy property and life insurance proceeds. S was treated as having made a transfer with a § 2036(a)(1) retained life estate because S agreed to hold that property subject to a contractual obligation that restricted disposition of the property at S's death. The effect at S's death is the same if jointly held property is transferred before either joint tenant's death. Only the timing of the transfer differs.[19] The unanswerable question is

---

(Footnote Continued)

which the court refused to assume was S's intent) but only after protracted delay and litigation.

[18] 1971-1 C.B. 274.

[19] In Estate of Stewart v. Commissioner, 79 T.C. 1046 (1982), and Wilcoxen v. United States, 310 F. Supp. 1006 (D. Kan. 1969), a tenancy by the entirety and a joint tenancy, respectively, were deemed severed by execution of joint wills that were inconsistent with the surviving tenants' survivorship entitlements. In neither was the transfer with a retained life estate issue involved. *Stewart* determined that S did not make a gift to children who received a half interest when D died because that property, having been severed when the will was executed, was deemed to have passed to them from D. *Wilcoxen* held that the property could not qualify for the marital deduction because the property no longer constituted a tenancy by the entirety and did not grant sufficient entitlement to S. But both holdings would yield § 2036(a)(1) consequences because the spouses enjoyed life estates in the property after the severance events in each. But see PLR 8946029, which held that conversion of tenancy by the entirety into tenancy in common, followed by D creating a life estate for S in D's half, would

whether partition of jointly held property prior to either tenant's transfer into their respective separate trusts, or before execution of a joint will or trust, is sufficient to preclude a step transaction analysis if one tenant enjoys benefits in a trust funded with the other joint tenant's interest in the property.[20] In addition, unlike the case with a joint will in which no transfer is made until the death of one of the joint testators, a taxable gift may occur upon creation of a joint settlor trust if the consent of other joint settlors is required to revoke or amend the trust.[21] Moreover, these trusts are an even more unpredictable planning device than are contractual wills because state law applicable to joint or mutual trusts is less clear than is state law with respect to joint or mutual wills.[22]

(Footnote Continued)

not cause estate tax inclusion to S unless D's estate made a QTIP election with respect to that trust. One attraction of such division planning would be to generate fractional interest valuation discounts for both spouses.

[20] A different analysis that could avoid application of §§ 2036 and 2038 might be provided by a series of PLRs dealing with transfers with retained secondary life estates following inclusion in the estate of some other taxpayer. See §§ 7.1.4, 10.4, 13.2.5, and 13.5.6.5. Regarding these sorts of questions in general, see Hess, The Federal Transfer Tax Consequences of Joint and Mutual Wills, 24 Real Prop., Prob. & Trust J. 469 (1990).

[21] See Treas. Reg. § 25.2511-2(e).

[22] See Adams & Abendroth, The Joint Trust: Are You Saving Anything Other Than Paper?, 131 Trusts & Estates 39 (Aug. 1992), and Williams, The Benefits and Pitfalls of Joint Revocable Trusts, 131 Trusts & Estates 41 (Nov. 1992). To illustrate the uncertainties that can be involved if the document is not sufficiently prescient to address all important issues, it took litigation in Northern Trust Co. v. Tarre, 427 N.E.2d 1217 (Ill. 1981), just to determine that a surviving settlor of a joint settlor trust could amend the trust. Although the court drew on joint and mutual will precedent, it did not determine whether the law relating to joint or mutual wills would apply in all respects to joint or mutual revocable trusts.

On the other hand, the joint settlor trust may prove to be a panacea if the results described in § 13.5.6.5 involved in PLR 200101021 can be trusted. That Ruling had not been released when these earlier critiques were written and many critics of the joint settlor trust technique may moderate their resistance if the government's favorable conclusions become certain through litigation or reliable authority, such as a revenue ruling.

§3.7.1 Tax Consequences of Contractual Wills

Contractually mandated payments made by a decedent's estate may constitute income to the recipient and may entitle the estate to a § 2053 deduction.[23]

Regarding the § 2053 deductibility of payments made under a contractual will, assume that a joint and mutual will is supported by a contract that precludes the survivor from changing his or her will, but that the survivor makes a change that entitles the intended beneficiaries to enforce a claim in contract against the survivor's estate. Under § 2053 (c) (1) (A), to be deductible under § 2053 (a) (3), a claim must be based on an agreement contracted for "adequate and full consideration in money or money's worth," which case law regards as lacking if there was no arm's length bargain between the contracting parties.[24]

To illustrate the additional tax considerations that militate against the use of joint or mutual wills that impose obligations on the surviving testator, consider three cases involving the same state law and revealing that the estate and gift tax consequences of these instruments are unpredictable and again make this planning undesirable. Although this discussion refers to joint or mutual wills, joint settlor trusts may create the same issues.[25]

---

[23] With respect to the income tax consequence, see § 3.2.5.5.

[24] See, e.g., Bank of New York v. United States, 526 F.2d 1012 (3d Cir. 1975); Estate of Huntington v. Commissioner, 100 T.C. 313 (1993); Luce v. United States, 444 F. Supp. 347 (W.D. Mo. 1977). But see Childress v. United States, 77-1 U.S. Tax Cas. (CCH) ¶ 13,181 (N.D. Ala. 1977) (deduction allowed based on jury finding that bequest was in discharge of a contractual obligation supported by consideration in the form of the beneficiary's agreement to forsake a teaching career and work for the decedent). Transfers made in satisfaction of a contractual obligation that was part of a marital property settlement that complies with the requirements of § 2516 (a written agreement relative to marital property rights incident to a divorce within two years thereafter) are deemed to be made for full and adequate consideration in money or money's worth for § 2053 (a) (3) purposes by virtue of § 2043 (b) (2). See also Beecher v. United States, 280 F.2d 202 (3d Cir. 1960); Florida Nat'l Bank & Trust Co. v. United States, 182 F. Supp. 76 (S.D. Fla. 1960).

[25] Regarding the tax consequences of these instruments in general, see Hess, The Federal Transfer Tax Consequences of Joint and Mutual Wills, 24 Real Prop., Prob. & Trust J. 469 (1990).

Estate of Lidbury v. Commissioner[26] involved a joint will between spouses specifying that

> we, and each of us, do covenant and agree that upon the death of one of us, the survivor will not in any manner directly or indirectly dispose of his or her property to the end that the general plan of distribution, as provided herein, shall be altered and changed in any form whatsoever; and we and each of us do further covenant and agree that the survivor of us shall hold and manage the property which he or she may own outright and of which he or she may have the use, by reason of this, our Last Will and Testament, in a careful and prudent manner, so as not to dissipate any of said property.

As is common, the joint will was not probated on D's death because the bulk of the spouses' property was realty that the spouses owned in joint tenancy, as to which S became the sole owner by right of survivorship. The issue was whether S made a gift to the children who were named as takers under the joint will on D's death, in view of the fact that the joint will imposed a binding obligation on S when D died. If restrictions imposed by the contract reduced S's interest in property already owned, then a transfer occurred when the contract became enforceable at D's death, with attendant gift tax consequences.

The court analyzed various controlling cases relating to joint wills and held that no transfer taxable as a gift occurred when D died, because the contractual will merely created enforceable contract rights in the children but did not constitute a transfer of a present property interest to them. In affirming that conclusion on appeal, the court looked to see how much S was restricted in dealing with the joint tenancy property and held that no gift occurred when D died because the joint and mutual will required only that S manage the property carefully and devise whatever remained as agreed. It distinguished contrary tax cases involving similar situations because the joint and mutual will involved in those other cases imposed more severe restraints on S's ability to enjoy and control the property than those in *Lidbury*. Thus, the conclusion was that no gift tax should be imposed if S has sufficient power to consume the property and the contract only requires disposition of whatever remains at S's death.[27]

---

[26] 84 T.C. 146, 148 (1985), aff'd, 800 F.2d 649 (7th Cir. 1986).

[27] See also Estate of Emerson v. Commissioner, 67 T.C. 612 (1977); Hambleton v. Commissioner, 60 T.C. 558 (1973); Brown v. Commissioner, 52 T.C. 50 (1969); PLR 7944009; TAM 7910004.

§3.7.1

Estate of Grimes v. Commissioner,[28] decided after *Lidbury*, also involved spouses who executed a joint and mutual will providing that it could not be changed or revoked by either party without the written consent of the other and that joint tenancy property would be disposed of under the will at S's death. In this case the court held that S made a completed gift at D's death because all of the spouses' property was subject to the agreement and no power was reserved by S to control disposition of the property during S's overlife or at S's death. As a result, the court held that S transferred dominion and control over all property subject to the will when D died. Because S retained only lifetime enjoyment in that property, the gift made at D's death constituted a gift by S of a remainder interest in all property owned by S that was subject to the agreement. In some cases today that gift may be subject to unanticipated consequences under § 2702.

Because the *Grimes* gift was subject to S's retained lifetime enjoyment of the property, the court also concluded that this property was includible in S's gross estate under § 2036(a)(1). Consequently, the value of the inter vivos gift would be purged from S's adjusted taxable gifts base under the flush language of § 2001(b) and S's estate would receive a credit for any gift tax paid. But the overall effect of the joint and mutual will was full taxation of the FMV of that property at S's death. This meant that no valuation freeze occurred at D's death, and a portion of the total tax was prepaid at D's death, with a subsequent loss of the use of the tax dollars during the balance of S's overlife.

Lidbury and *Grimes* followed Pyle v. United States,[29] in which it was *conceded* that S made a gift of the remainder interest in S's estate and the only question was when that gift was complete. State law regarded the spouses' joint and mutual will as creating an obligation on S to conserve all property of both spouses for the benefit of the remainder beneficiaries. However, the will granted S a power to consume corpus for "health, support, comfort or maintenance," with the essential question being whether consumption was limited by an ascertainable standard. If it was, then the gift of the remainder constituted a complete transfer as of D's death, when the contractual nature of the will became irrevocable, because S's enjoyment was subject to definable constraints. The lower

---

[28] 54 T.C.M. (CCH) 1 (1987), aff'd, 851 F.2d 1005 (7th Cir. 1988).

[29] 766 F.2d 1141 (7th Cir. 1985), rev'g 581 F. Supp. 252 (C.D. Ill. 1984).

court found that the term "comfort" was not ascertainable[30] but was reversed, the court on appeal regarding the gift as measurable and complete when D died. That conclusion is enlightening because it indicates that state law variations and differences in the wording of various joint and mutual wills may produce unexpected results, ultimately making the tax consequences of these devices unpredictable.

The contractual obligation with respect to D's property also may cause loss of the FET marital deduction in D's estate. For example, in a second *Grimes* case[31] and in TAM 9023004, joint and mutual wills failed to meet the § 2056(b)(5) all income, general power of appointment marital deduction trust requirements. This was because, under state law, the power to deal with assets bequeathed subject to the will's provisions was too limited (in the TAM, notwithstanding that S was granted a life estate with full right to consume, gift, and otherwise dispose of D's property during S's overlife).[32] Unless S freely may consume D's property, the § 2056(b)(5) FET marital deduction will be unavailable.[33]

---

[30] This holding was consistent with Treas. Reg. § 20.2041-1(c)(2).

[31] Estate of Grimes v. Commissioner, 56 T.C.M. (CCH) 890 (1988), aff'd, 937 F.2d 316 (7th Cir. 1991) (involving the son of the decedent in the former *Grimes* case, who also lost the marital deduction under a similar joint and mutual will).

[32] Citing Estate of Field v. Commissioner, 40 T.C. 802 (1963), Estate of Vermilya v. Commissioner, 41 T.C. 226 (1963), and Stockdick v. Phinney, 65-2 U.S. Tax Cas. (CCH) ¶ 12,351 (S.D. Tex. 1965), the government concluded that state law regarded the interest in S as less than a full fee simple absolute and that this "defeasible or conditional fee" was not made deductible by the power to consume or dispose of the property because S was not free to appoint the property to S or S's estate. Similarly, the joint will in TAM 8105006 permitted amendment by S but only on the condition that any final distribution provide for their descendants per stirpes. Because S lacked absolute freedom of alienation, the government denied the marital deduction to D's estate. However, because S had some control over the property, the government held that no gift was made by S at D's death. TAM 8347002 recognized that the mere fact that wills are mutual is not sufficient to justify a conclusion that the wills are subject to a binding contract not to revoke and referred the question back to the District Office to determine whether there was such a contract.

[33] See Estate of Krampf v. Commissioner, 464 F.2d 1398 (3d Cir. 1972); Estate of Opal v. Commissioner, 450 F.2d 1085 (2d Cir. 1971); Estate of Goldstein v. United States, 72-1 U.S. Tax Cas. (CCH) ¶ 12,819 (D. Minn. 1971); Estate of Siegel v. Commissioner, 67 T.C. 662 (1977); Estate of Abruzzino v. Commissioner, 61 T.C. 306 (1973); TAM 7810001. But see PLR 9435014 (involving a joint

§ 3.7.1

Again clearly illustrated is that a better alternative is for D to bequeath his or her property into a QTIP trust for S, with no obligation imposed with respect to S's own property. This plan guarantees that D's property will pass to whomever D prefers while granting S enjoyment of the property and qualifying for the marital deduction to defer taxes until the death of S. But even a QTIP trust approach requires caution if the agreement obligates S not to alter S's estate plan, which may trigger application of § 2056(b)(4) to reduce the marital deduction by the value of that obligation.[34]

Similar estate and gift tax consequences may be incurred for state tax purposes as well.

In drafting contracts relating to wills, a final issue that should be addressed is the tax payment liability that may affect the beneficiary. Metz v. United States[35] illustrates the dangers of a contract to perform services in exchange for a testamentary bequest, and suggests that the government always is a potential (albeit silent) party to the contract even if all parties perform and act in good faith. The plaintiff agreed to move in with and care for the testator until death, and the testator complied with their agreement by bequeathing the testator's home to the plaintiff. Also included in the testator's estate was stock in a closely held business. Together the home and the stock generated over $1 million in FET. The estate properly elected § 6166 deferral of the FET attributable to the

---

(Footnote Continued)

and mutual will but state law and a document were deemed to permit sufficient consumption to satisfy the general power of appointment requirements and to qualify for the § 2056(b)(5) marital deduction).

[34] See Treas. Reg. § 20.2056(b)-4(b) Examples (1) and (3). See also § 3.6.2 regarding forced election estate plans. This reduction is relevant only to the extent the right to receive property is encumbered by S's obligation under that agreement. Thus, for example, property passing to S outside probate qualifies for the marital deduction without reduction in value even if there is a binding contractual will if passage of the nonprobate property is not contingent on S being bound by the contractual will. United States v. Ford, 377 F.2d 93 (8th Cir. 1967); Olson v. Reisimer, 271 F.2d 623 (7th Cir. 1959); Estate of Awtry v. Commissioner, 221 F.2d 749 (8th Cir. 1955); Rev. Rul. 71-51, 1971-1 C.B. 274; TAM 7810001.

[35] 933 F.2d 802 (10th Cir. 1991), aff'g 89-2 U.S. Tax Cas. (CCH) ¶ 13,822 (D. Kan. 1989).

§ 3.7.1

business, the balance of the taxes were paid immediately, and the home was distributed outright to the plaintiff.

About seven years after the testator's death the business declared bankruptcy and ceased paying on its § 6166 liability, so the government sought to collect the balance of the tax due from the plaintiff as a transferee of the estate. Noting that the plaintiff did not report the home as income from services rendered to the testator (and without considering whether distribution of the home was the payment of a § 2053(a)(3) deductible claim against the estate), the court determined that the plaintiff was an estate beneficiary, not a purchaser or creditor, and held that transferee liability for these unpaid taxes applied. The plaintiff's argument that equitable conversion made the plaintiff the home's owner prior to the testator's death was deemed not supportable under state law, and the testator's stated intent that the plaintiff receive the home free of FET was deemed irrelevant. The court regarded FET inclusion of the home in the testator's estate as proper and concluded that, as a consequence, an FET lien could attach to the home.

The testator and the plaintiff could have structured their agreement differently and avoided FET inclusion of the subject property, thereby eliminating exposure to the FET lien involved in *Metz*, but with other costs that may have been more significant. For example, the testator might have transferred the home when the plaintiff moved in to care for the testator or could have sold the home to the plaintiff on installments that would be paid or forgiven over time. And the plaintiff might have reported the home as income from services and filed a claim against the testator's estate for compensation under the contract. Difficulties would arise, however, if the plaintiff was obliged under state law to support the testator, if the value of the services rendered was not fair consideration for the property promised in return, if significant capital gain would be incurred on a sale during the testator's life, or if the plaintiff's income tax bracket exceeded the testator's projected FET bracket. And, unless properly handled, the testator's transfer might be deemed a gift with a retained life estate, leading to § 2036(a)(1) inclusion in the testator's estate at death.

As *Metz* illustrates, FET inclusion for any reason generates taxes that complicate the plan. The agreement should be memorialized in writing if the plaintiff hopes to establish rights thereunder after the

§ 3.7.1

testator's death. And that agreement should address the issue of tax payment obligations because, if the parties provide that no death taxes shall be borne by the property subject to the contract, a tax clause in the will that directs otherwise would be ineffective.[36] If the issue is not addressed in the agreement, the question might arise whether transferee liability such as in *Metz* reduces the value deemed received under the contract, entitling the recipient to additional compensation.

§3.8 POSTMORTEM MODIFICATION BY SETTLEMENT AGREEMENT

A will contest or other controversy involving a will may result in a court order or a settlement agreement that alters the ultimate disposition of the testator's estate. A number of issues should be considered in fashioning any such postmortem modification of the testator's estate plan.

First, the parties must guarantee that any order or agreement is binding on all potentially interested beneficiaries. This may require a court order that adopts the settlement agreement if unborn, unascertained, or minor beneficiaries are involved.[1]

Second, the Claflin doctrine[2] may preclude certain modifications if the effect is to terminate or abolish a trust and thereby leave unfulfilled a material and legitimate purpose of the testator. Limited case law has held

---

[36] See In re Estate of Guest, 183 N.E.2d 194 (Ill. App. Ct. 1962).

[1] **§3.8** See UPC §3-1101 for an example of legislation that grants courts authority to bind such beneficiaries through an order or approved settlement, "even though it may affect a trust or an inalienable interest."

[2] So named after Claflin v. Claflin, 20 N.E. 454 (Mass. 1889). See Restatement (Second) of Trusts §337(2) (1959); Restatement (Second) of Property—Donative Transfers §2.1 (1983); 5 Scott, Fratcher, & Ascher, Scott and Ascher on Trusts §34.1.6 (5th ed. 2008); McGovern, Kurtz, & English, Wills, Trusts & Estates §9.9 (4th ed. 2010). An exception to the principle that an unfulfilled purpose will preclude termination is recognized if the purpose is impossible to accomplish, or if continuance would be contrary to the testator's original intent. See 5 Scott, Fratcher, & Ascher, Scott and Ascher on Trusts §§33.2, 34.1 (5th ed. 2008); UTC §410(a), and UPC §3-1101. Restatement (Third) of Trusts §65 (2003) also alters the emphasis given to an unfulfilled purpose, allowing a court to reform a trust if the reasons supporting modification outweigh the settlor's original intent or underlying material unfulfilled purpose.

that modification of an estate plan prior to creation of a testamentary trust is permissible, notwithstanding that termination of the trust after its creation would be precluded.[3] It is difficult to accept this distinction if the justification supporting the Claflin doctrine is that the testator's unfulfilled purpose is superior to the beneficiaries' wishes and the only difference in fact is the timing of the action that generates the modification.[4] True to the Claflin doctrine, the most common unfulfilled purpose that precludes premature termination of a trust is a spendthrift provision that indicates the testator's intent to protect property from the beneficiary's creditors or other predators (or from the beneficiary's own improvidence). Seldom has a compromise that commutes and distributes the value of various beneficiaries' interests been permitted if the effect is to free property from the protection of a spendthrift provision.[5]

Third, the income tax consequences of a contest, compromise, and any recovery should be considered. Reasonable expenses incurred by the estate to defend against a challenge or to reach a compromise may be deductible for federal estate or estate income tax purposes,[6] although the contestant's expenses usually are not deductible because they consti-

---

[3] See Budin v. Levy, 180 N.E.2d 74 (Mass. 1962) (compromise that precluded creation of trust, in exchange for cash payment to residuary charitable beneficiary, was allowed because all interested parties were in agreement and the trust had not yet been established).

[4] See 5 Scott, Fratcher, & Ascher, Scott and Ascher on Trusts § 34.1.6 (5th ed. 2008).

[5] See 5 Scott, Fratcher, & Ascher, Scott and Ascher on Trusts § 34.1.2 (5th ed. 2008); St. Louis Union Trust Co. v. Conant, 499 S.W.2d 761 (Mo. 1973) (testator's child, who did not want beneficial interest tied up in trust, contested testator's will and, in compromise, was given portion of estate outright; lower court's approval of the agreement was reversed because testator's intent to protect the child's interest with a spendthrift provision could not be defeated in the guise of a will contest compromise). 5 Scott, Fratcher, & Ascher, Scott and Ascher on Trusts § 34.1 n.14 (5th ed. 2008), reports that Mo. Rev. Stat. § 456.590(2) may have abrogated the Claflin doctrine in Missouri. See Wiedenbeck, Missouri's Repeal of the Claflin Doctrine—New View of the Policy Against Perpetuities?, 50 Mo. L. Rev. 805 (1985). UTC § 411(c) reverses the spendthrift provision effect under the Claflin doctrine directly. With respect to trust reformation in general see § 4.1.1 n.12 et seq. and accompanying text.

[6] See § 15.5.3.3 n.86 and accompanying text regarding deductibility under § 2053 for FET purposes. Under § 642(g) the estate instead may elect to deduct the same allowable expenses for estate income tax purposes as a § 212(2)

tute costs to acquire property rather than to preserve or defend the title to property already owned.[7] Amounts received from the estate in compromise or adjudication of a contest are not income to the recipient,[8] nor do they add to the basis of the estate.[9] But distribution of those amounts will carry out DNI or generate gain or loss in the same manner as any other estate distributions.[10]

(Footnote Continued)

ordinary and necessary expense paid or incurred to conserve income producing property.

[7] See Treas. Reg. § 1.212-1(k) (expenses to defend, perfect, or assert rights to property of a decedent as heir or beneficiary are not deductible and instead must be capitalized by addition to basis); Burch v. United States, 698 F.2d 575 (2d Cir. 1983), aff'g in part and rev'g in part 81-2 U.S. Tax Cas. (CCH) ¶ 9767 (N.D. N.Y. 1981); McDonald v. Commissioner, 592 F.2d 635 (2d Cir. 1978), rev'g 36 T.C.M. (CCH) 852 (1977) (amounts paid to contestants by beneficiary in settlement of will contest are not deductible); Elrick v. Commissioner, 485 F.2d 1049 (D.C. Cir. 1973), rev'g 56 T.C. 903 (1971) (depreciation deduction also disallowed for litigation costs incurred in enforcing rights under a contract to make a will because the § 273 prohibition against depreciation of the basis of a life estate obtained by gift or inheritance is applicable if the interest is obtained in settlement of a will contest or other litigation to enforce what would have been a gift or inheritance); Merriman v. Commissioner, 55 F.2d 879 (1st Cir. 1931), aff'g 21 B.T.A. 67 (1930); Hartt v. United States, 65-2 U.S. Tax Cas. (CCH) ¶ 9547 (D. Wyo. 1965); Perret v. Commissioner, 55 T.C. 712 (1971); Stevens v. Commissioner, 78 T.C.M. (CCH) 230 (1999). This same issue can arise in the context of a surviving spouse asserting an elective share entitlement, and is discussed in § 3.4.7 n.77.

[8] Lyeth v. Hoey, 305 U.S. 188 (1938). However, income payments distributed as part of the agreed upon settlement will be taxable as if the recipient had been the direct beneficiary of that income interest. See, e.g., Edwards v. Commissioner, 37 T.C. 1107 (1962) (claim against decedent's estate released in exchange for payments to claimant by income beneficiary of decedent's trust; amounts received were taxable as income to the claimant and not to the income beneficiary of the trust).

[9] Lare v. Commissioner, 62 T.C. 739 (1974) (payment to contestants is not a capital expense that allows a basis increase to the estate's remaining property).

[10] See §§ 5.2.2, 5.4.1, and 5.8.1 regarding the income taxation of estate distributions. Protracted litigation involving these principles was required in Lemle v. United States, 75-1 U.S. Tax Cas. (CCH) ¶ 9355 (S.D. N.Y. 1975), 76-2 U.S. Tax Cas. (CCH) ¶ 9651 (S.D. N.Y. 1976), and 77-2 U.S. Tax Cas. (CCH) ¶ 9653 (S.D. N.Y. 1977), aff'd, 579 F.2d 185 (2d Cir. 1978) (income tax treatment could not be altered by settlement agreement's characterization after payments were made).

§ 3.8

Fourth, under the business transaction exception to the gift tax, transfers made pursuant to an arm's length compromise of a bona fide claim and not for donative reasons are regarded as involuntary and supported by full and adequate consideration in money or money's worth and therefore exempt from gift tax.[11] Nevertheless, the identity of the transferor (indeed, multiple transfers may be involved) should be considered if, for example, tax consequences will depend on the settlor of property to be held in trust (for example, for income tax grantor trust treatment, or for potential FET inclusion at the death of a transferor who retains an interest in or power over the trust).[12]

Fifth, the deductibility of amounts passing to S or to charity in settlement of a controversy involving the will should be considered. Regarding the marital deduction, payments made in a compromise context qualify for the marital deduction only to the extent the compromise is a "bona fide recognition of enforceable rights of the surviving spouse."[13] Although Rev. Rul. 83-107[14] states that a court order is not necessary to establish deductibility, payments pursuant to an agreement not to contest or probate a will are not necessarily regarded as a bona fide settlement of S's enforceable rights.

To illustrate, in TAM 9246002, S received cash from D's estate equal to the commuted value of S's statutory entitlement to a life estate in one-third of D's realty. Citing Rev. Rul. 83-107 and stating that local law granted the right to partition the property, force a sale thereof, and receive an amount from the proceeds equal to the commuted value, the government held that a settlement with the estate that produced a

---

[11] Treas. Reg. § 25.2512-8. See, e.g., Estate of Noland v. Commissioner, 47 T.C.M. (CCH) 1640 (1984), and cases cited therein. See also § 7.1.1.

[12] See, e.g., Bailey v. Ratterre, 144 F. Supp. 449 (N.D. N.Y. 1956), aff'd, 243 F.2d 454 (2d Cir. 1957) (S regarded as settlor of trust created for benefit of S's surviving child because evidence failed to show that the trust was a compromise of a challenge the child threatened to lodge against D's will; as settlor, S's retained power to amend the trust resulted in its inclusion in S's gross estate).

[13] Treas. Reg. § 20.2056(c)-2(d). For a discussion of the marital deduction flowing from a compromise of postmortem controversy involving D's estate, see § 13.4.2.3.2.

[14] 1983-2 C.B. 159, reconsidering the government's longstanding holding in Rev. Rul. 72-7, 1972-1 C.B. 308, relating to the deductibility of property received by S in settlement of claims against D's estate.

distribution of the same amount was effective for marital deduction purposes. An alternative would have been to make a QTIP election with respect to the property producing the life estate, if a larger deduction and larger amount taxable to S would be acceptable.

Estate of Brandon v. Commissioner[15] also is instructive, regarding the availability of the marital deduction for payments made to S based on enforceable state law rights. S elected against D's estate plan and, in negotiations with D's other beneficiaries, agreed to an admittedly bona fide settlement of the claim premised on state law dower rights. Shortly after reaching this settlement, however, the state supreme court determined that the dower statute was unconstitutional. As a result, the government disallowed the marital deduction based on the settlement, stating that the payment could not have been a bona fide settlement of enforceable rights. Because the Tax Court did not inquire whether the dower statute would be held constitutional by the state's highest court if the litigation went to that extent, the court held that the Tax Court improperly allowed the marital deduction, requiring that the Tax Court determine enforceability of the dower claim "under state law *at the time the settlement was reached*."[16] On remand,[17] the Tax Court found that, at the time of the settlement, the state statute was indeed unconstitutional and that no marital deduction should be allowed in excess of a small amount left to the surviving spouse under the decedent's will.

Similarly, amounts passing to charity in settlement of a controversy involving the testator's will may not qualify for the charitable deduction.[18] Often this is significant in the context of nonqualifying split interest

---

[15] 828 F.2d 493 (8th Cir. 1987), rev'g 86 T.C. 327 (1986).

[16] 828 F.2d at 499 (emphasis added). Surprising about this position is that the determination of deductibility was not made as of D's death, which is when most aspects of the marital deduction are tested. See Treas. Reg. § 20.2056(c)-3 (last sentence).

[17] 91 T.C. 829 (1988).

[18] See Treas. Reg. § 20.2055-2(d). Irving Trust Co. v. United States, 221 F.2d 303 (2d Cir. 1955), limited the charitable deduction to the value of property passing to charitable beneficiaries under a will, which reflected a reduction by the amount the charities paid various heirs in return for withdrawal of their objections to the will. Similarly, Wilcox v. United States, 185 F. Supp. 385 (N.D. Ohio 1960), reduced the allowable charitable deduction by an amount the charity paid from its own funds to settle a will contest.

§3.8

trusts that are reformed or eliminated entirely by a postmortem settlement. For example, in First National Bank v. United States,[19] D's estate plan created a split interest trust that granted S an impermissible income interest, which was eliminated when S elected against the estate plan. And in Oetting v. United States,[20] the decedent's estate plan created nonqualifying CRTs. To generate a charitable deduction and avoid a perceived fiduciary liability, the estate obtained a court order directing payment of a large portion of the estate directly to the charities. Both cases held that there was no reason to disallow the claimed deduction because there was no uncertainty regarding either the entitlement or amount to be received by the charities. Nor did the form of the ultimate payment to charity present any of the abuses to which the split interest charitable trust rules are addressed. Enacted in the wake of these cases, § 2055(e)(3) now provides a mechanism to reform nonqualifying split interest charitable trusts, but it is available only if reformation proceedings are instituted within 90 days after the due date for filing the FET return, including any extensions granted.

The government's position, as illustrated by TAM 9326003, is that reformation under § 2055(e)(3) is the exclusive mechanism to generate a charitable deduction in an estate that does not comply with the split interest rules of § 2055(e)(2), even if a court ordered modification directs outright distribution to a charity.[21] Thus, although it may appear that postmortem reformation or payments made in compromise of litigation involving a testator's nonqualifying will should generate a charitable deduction, not all postmortem changes will be respected under the requirements of § 2055(e)(3). For example, § 2055(e)(3)(C)(i) restricts reformation to transfers that would have qualified for the deduction were it not for a failure to comply with the technical split interest requirements, § 2055(e)(3)(C)(ii) limits permissible noncharitable interests to those expressed in terms of a specified dollar amount or percentage of FMV if the interest passes under a document executed after 1978, and the § 2055(e)(3)(C)(iii) exception applies only if the reformation is timely

---

[19] 727 F.2d 741 (8th Cir. 1984), aff'g 82-2 U.S. Tax Cas. (CCH) ¶ 13,478 (W.D. Ark. 1982).

[20] 712 F.2d 358 (8th Cir. 1983), rev'g and rem'g 544 F. Supp. 20 (E.D. Mo. 1982).

[21] For a full discussion of reformation under § 2055(e)(3), see § 14.3.7.1.

§ 3.8

commenced.[22] Further, § 2055 (e) (3) (E) caps the available reformed deduction at the amount that would be available if the split interest rules did not exist, and § 2055 (e) (3) (B) (i) provides that reformation is effective only if the reformed and the unreformed interests do not differ in value by more than 5%. Finally, in a qualified CRT, § 2055 (e) (3) (B) (ii) (I) requires that any reformed lead interest terminate at the same time as before reformation, with an exception allowing reduction of a greater than 20 year term to the maximum 20 year permissible period.

In this context, a disturbing dichotomy is presented by a series of § 2055 reformation and deduction cases[23] that regard the government's denial of the charitable deduction, the courts stating that, in enacting § 2055, Congress sought to encourage gifts to charity and that there were none of the abuses to which the split interest charitable trust rules were directed. Consequently, the courts saw no reason to deny a deduction for actual benefits passing to the respective charities.

Subsequently, in Rev. Rul. 89-31,[24] the government relaxed its rules to provide that, if a bona fide contest settlement results in there being no split interest trust to which § 2055 (e) (2) might apply, then § 2055 (e) (3) is not relevant:

---

[22] For example, in TAM 9326003 the decedent's plan did not comply with the split interest rules and the estate delayed too long to reform the trust before obtaining a local court order commuting the values of the private and charitable interests and ordering outright distribution of each, terminating the nonqualified disposition in search of a deduction. The government predictably held that reformation under § 2055 (e) (3) is the exclusive method for rectification of a nonqualifying disposition in such a situation and that the court ordered remedy was not adequate to generate the deduction. Contrariwise, however, PLRs 200227015 and 9326056 involved timely reformations under § 2055 (e) (3) (C). In the earlier Ruling the estate petitioned a local court to divide out sums needed to produce two annuities equal to 5% of the initial value of the trust and to distribute the balance of the corpus directly to charity, thus curing the defect under the original document that the annuities did not equal or exceed 5% of the initial FMV of the trust. In the more recent Ruling judicial reformation of a nonqualifying trust converted a life estate and a secondary monthly annuity into a sole and survivor annuity. The government respected the reformations and allowed the charitable deductions sought because all other requirements for compliance with the § 664 split interest rules were met and because these actions were taken within the requisite time allowed.

[23] See § 14.3.7.2.

[24] 1989-1 C.B. 277.

§ 3.8

> In situations involving settlements of bona fide will contests the Service will no longer challenge the deductibility of immediate payments to charities *solely* on the ground that they were made in lieu of a split interest that would not constitute an allowable deduction under *section 2055(e)(2)* of the Code. However, settlements of will contests will continue to be scrutinized in order to assure that the settlement in question is not an attempt to circumvent *section 2055(e)(2)* by instituting and settling a collusive contest.[25]

No indication was given of what constitutes a "collusive contest" or a "bona fide settlement," and it is notable that consistent treatment still is not available for § 2056 marital deduction purposes if a will contest is brought and settled to convert a nondeductible terminable interest into a deductible outright transfer.[26] Obviously, in postmortem actions in which deductions are sought, the current state of the law should be studied and the bona fides of the litigation and any compromise must be well established.

Finally, state inheritance tax consequences of a settlement must be considered. For example, In re Estate of Granger[27] involved a 1963 will that benefited only a Class A beneficiary, and a 1971 will under which the Class A beneficiary received only a life estate and the remainder passed to Class B and C beneficiaries. The court approved a settlement by which the 1963 will was admitted to probate, the 1971 will was denied probate, and an outright distribution was made to the Class B and C beneficiaries. Recognizing that the authorities were divided on the issue whether the inheritance tax should be assessed on the basis of the distribution called for under the will admitted to probate or on the basis of the settlement that was effected, the court embraced the former as the majority approach. It regarded this as justified by substantial logic and ease of administration. If another controversy involved facts that resulted in more tax being assessed under the will as written, a preferable result might be engineered if, for example, neither will was admitted to probate and the estate passed by intestacy, or if the latter will was admitted and the payments were made in the opposite direction. Thus, postmortem

---

[25] 1989-1 C.B. at 278 (emphasis added). This Ruling reversed Rev. Ruls. 77-491, 1977-2 C.B. 332, and 78-152, 1978-1 C.B. 296 (postmortem settlement distributions are nondeductible if not in compliance with § 2055(e)(3)).

[26] See Treas. Reg. § 20.2056(c)-2(d).

[27] 516 P.2d 505 (Wash. 1973).

modifications should not be blind to state tax issues such as these, in addition to all the federal tax consequences that may be involved.

§ 3.9 LIBELOUS WILLS

A testator who uses a will to comment on the character of disfavored survivors may create a cause of action for libel. For example, the will in Brown v. Du Frey[1] stated that the testator intentionally made no provision for a former spouse who allegedly abandoned and displayed neither affection nor regard for the testator. As it turned out, the former spouse divorced the testator 34 years earlier for adultery, and recovered damages from the testator's estate for damages attributable to the testamentary libel.[2] Because a will must be presented for probate and because the personal representative must administer the testator's estate according to the will, an action will not lie against the personal representative individually for publication of the libel in the course of probating a will that contains libelous statements.[3] But the estate's potential liability for testamentary libel may encourage the personal representative to consider a request that the probate court omit the libelous material from the public record or otherwise seal the will to minimize its dissemination and any consequent damage.[4]

---

[1] **§ 3.9** 134 N.E.2d 469 (N.Y. 1956).

[2] See also Kleinschmidt v. Matthieu, 266 P.2d 686 (Or. 1954) (grandchild accused by will of having squandered inter vivos gifts, taken sides in litigation against testator, being a "slacker," and having shirked duty during World War II), overruled by Binder v. Oregon Bank, 585 P.2d 655 (Or. 1978); Harris v. Nashville Trust Co., 162 S.W. 584 (Tenn. 1914); Reynolds, Defamation from the Grave: Testamentary Libel, 7 Cal. W.L. Rev. 91 (1970); Annot., Libel by will, 21 A.L.R.3d 754 (1968). But see Citizens' & Southern Nat'l Bank v. Hendricks, 168 S.E. 313 (Ga. 1933), rev'g 158 S.E. 915 (Ga. Ct. App. 1931); Carver v. Morrow, 48 S.E.2d 814 (S.C. 1948).

[3] Nolin v. Nolin, 215 N.E.2d 21 (Ill. App. Ct. 1966); Brown v. Mack, 56 N.Y.S.2d 910 (Sup. Ct. 1945); Nagle v. Nagle, 175 A. 487 (Pa. 1934), noted in 48 Harv. L. Rev. 1027 (1935).

[4] See Schell Estate, 20 Pa. D. & C. 2d 628 (Montgomery County 1960); In re Croker's Will, 105 N.Y.S.2d 190 (Surr. Ct. 1951); In re Palmer's Estate, 104 N.Y.S.2d 643 (Surr. Ct. 1951); In re Draske's Will, 290 N.Y.S. 581 (Surr. Ct. 1936); and In re Speiden's Estate, 221 N.Y.S. 223 (Surr. Ct. 1926). Atkinson, The Law of Wills § 95, at 497 (2d ed. 1953), states that, although the libelous material should

§3.10 LIVING WILLS, HEALTH CARE DIRECTIVES, ORGAN DONATION, AND DURABLE POWERS OF ATTORNEY FOR PROPERTY MANAGEMENT

An issue that many estate planners fail to address in routine representations (and that thereby is not confronted at all in many cases because other advisors do not fill the void) is what to recommend to clients who may become disabled or incapacitated before they die. Reflecting increased life expectancy and improved medical science, this is likely to occur in a substantial number of cases, and planning is necessary to anticipate property management and health care needs for the balance of the client's life, in addition to traditional planning of the client's estate after death. Thus, notwithstanding their traditional focus on planning for clients who are going to die, estate planners today frequently must create mechanisms that will assist clients who will live with diminished health and capacity, sometimes for a long time.

Before attention was drawn to these needs the common result was that a guardianship of the client's property[1] was created if the client became incapacitated prior to dying and if property management or health care decisions could not be undertaken in an informal manner. Guardianships are undesirable in many cases, however, because a stigma may attach to having a client judicially adjudicated as incompetent and because court costs, recurring guardian and attorney's fees, annual accountings, bonding requirements, and delay in seeking permission to conduct the client's affairs can be substantial burdens, made geometrically more complex if interstate or international complications exist.[2] Moreover, investment restrictions and limitations on amounts that

---

(Footnote Continued)

not be expunged from the will proper, it may be omitted from the public record if it has no bearing on the dispositive provisions, which frequently is true.

[1] §3.10 Or conservatorship, as it is called in some jurisdictions.

[2] See Hurme, Mobile Guardianships: Partial Solutions to Interstate and International Issues, 17 Prob. & Prop. 51 (2003) (containing useful charts of state laws regarding out of state and foreign guardians). Regarding the advantages and disadvantages of judicial versus clinical health care determinations, Meisel, The Right to Die ch. 6 (1989), identifies the advantages of a judicial end of life determination as elimination of liability for those who otherwise would make these decisions, protection against abuse or conflicts of interest (between family

may be expended on the ward's behalf without prior court approval often prove cumbersome.

A number of alternatives compare favorably to guardianships if court supervision protections are not necessary. Although normally used premortem, or before discovery and production of a will, these alternatives are discussed in this chapter on wills because typically they are implemented when the client's will is prepared. Included may be a living trust that is created currently and funded with property that requires management and should not pass through probate. Or a standby trust is created currently but not funded until incapacity or some other event. Also common is a durable power of attorney over the principal's affairs that grants the attorney in fact powers that lapse only at death and not on a prior incapacity (and that may be used to transfer assets into a funded or standby trust if the client becomes incapacitated). A living will may direct that life sustaining procedures be withheld or withdrawn in the event of a terminal illness or injury. And health care directives in the form of a durable power of attorney for health care may authorize another person to make decisions regarding health care (including the life or death decisions contemplated by a living will).

Also useful may be a guardianship designation (in case more supervised administration becomes necessary, or to pre-empt a third party's endeavor to seize control of the client's affairs by seeking appointment as guardian with powers to override all the client's prior planning),[3] along with a power to object to any third party's petition for the appointment of

(Footnote Continued)

members, between the patient or family members and their medical care providers, or between medical care providers), and the lack of an effective surrogate who can and will work with medical care providers in a clinical setting. The identified advantages of a clinical determination include simplicity, speed, convenience, lower cost, greater privacy, and the availability of more knowledgeable decision makers than in a judicial setting. This comparison could be applied almost without modification to determinations relating to property management in a guardianship or conservatorship setting.

[3] UPC § 5B-108 specifies that:

(a) In a power of attorney, a principal may nominate a [conservator or guardian] of the principal's estate or [guardian] of the principal's person for consideration by the court if protective proceedings for the principal's person or estate are begun after the principal executes the power of attorney. [Except for good cause or disqualification, the court shall make

a guardian. And an organ donor designation and funeral instructions are useful (both of which must be available before or immediately at the client's death if an indication of intent to donate organs and a statement of desires regarding disposition of the testator's remains is to be effective).[4] This segment addresses all of these ancillary issues[5] and documents except living or standby trusts, which are discussed separately.[6] These should be regarded with the same importance to effective estate planning as preparation of a will is regarded as an important mechanism to prevent the client from being subjected to the default estate plan represented by intestacy.[7]

(Footnote Continued)

its appointment in accordance with the principal's most recent nomination.]

(b) If, after a principal executes a power of attorney, a court appoints a [conservator or guardian] of the principal's estate or other fiduciary charged with the management of some or all of the principal's estate or other fiduciary charged with the management of some or all of the principal's property, the agent is accountable to the fiduciary as well as to the principal. [The power of attorney is not terminated and the agent's authority continues unless limited, suspended, or terminated by the court.]

[4] See § 3.2.1.

[5] Issues that may need attention might be covered in relevant state statutes dealing with wills or trusts, autopsies or coroners, anatomical gifts or organ donations, conservators or guardians, health care proxies or surrogates, living wills, natural death, or rights of the terminally ill. Thus, imaginative research may be necessary to locate all these relevant but ancillary laws and to confront and solve all the client's related problems.

[6] See Chapter 4.

[7] Lieberson, Advance Medical Directives § 9:14, at 140 (1992), estimates that only 10% of all Americans have signed a living will, speculating that feelings of immortality and youth, lack of available advisors or material regarding the benefits of an advance directive, notions about the lack of effect of such directives, and cost may explain this low number. Included in an appendix to that work is an extensive client questionnaire (called a Values History form) that is not copyrighted, which would permit the advisor to determine where to locate documents, what decisions should be left to which advisors, the client's feelings regarding death with dignity or other end of life decisions, whether organ donations are desired, and so forth.

§ 3.10

§3.10.1 Living Wills

Estate planners are familiar with traditional wills that dispose of a decedent's property (sometimes now called property wills to distinguish them from living wills), but many clients today are more concerned about living wills, which address health care decisions that must be made at the end of life. The National Conference of Commissioners on Uniform State Laws has approved a Uniform Rights of the Terminally Ill Act,[8] and most states have enacted some form of natural death act,[9] authorizing a client to provide instructions regarding termination of health care and related issues.

State living will laws can be quite inconsistent, however, making living wills less than desirable for a number of reasons.[10] For example, the most restrictive statutes may limit the use of a living will to decisions regarding treatment that is merely life prolonging for patients whose terminal condition is incurable and irreversible, whose death is imminent, who were aware of their diagnoses when their living wills were executed, and who currently are unable to participate in treatment decisions. Others relax some of these requirements, such as the need to be diagnosed as terminal when the living will was executed, meaning that the statutory opportunity is available to more individuals, but they may not be as well informed when their documents are signed.

In addition, no living will can anticipate every health care option or variation or even the end of life treatment decisions that ultimately will be presented. As a consequence, living wills are only a partial answer to

---

[8] See 9C U.L.A. 339 and 311 (2001) for the 1985 and 1989 versions, respectively. It likely will be superseded by those states that adopt the newer Uniform Health-Care Decisions Act, 9 Pt. IB U.L.A. 83 (2005).

[9] All states except Massachusetts and New York have some form of legislation that adopts a living will or natural death act. For a listing of relevant statutes, see Schoenblum, 2013 Multistate Guide to Estate Planning Table 10.01 (2012). Because the terms, execution requirements, and especially the circumstances in which they operate vary considerably, inspection of a particular state's law is imperative and may require that additional health care directives be utilized to address decisions that the client must make in circumstances in which a living will is not operative.

[10] See generally Schoenblum, 2013 Multistate Guide to Estate Planning Table 10.01 (2012); Collin, Planning and Drafting Durable Powers of Attorney for Health Care, 22 U. Miami Inst. Est. Plan. ¶ 504.2 (1988).

the problem of making health care decisions near the end of life. And execution, witness, and revocation[11] requirements vary, as does the fundamental question whether a statutorily prescribed form must be used and whether the authority granted under the living will is superior to the power of a court appointed health care surrogate or guardian of the person.

Some statutes omit some limitations entirely, while others formulate them in different ways. For example, unlike some statutes that require the patient to be terminally ill before decisions dictated by a living will are compelling, the Uniform Health-Care Decisions Act permits a surrogate to make end of life decisions if the patient is only "unconscious and, to a reasonable degree of medical certainty, . . . will not regain consciousness, or . . . the likely risks and burdens of treatment would outweigh the expected benefits."[12] As a result, universal application of a living will is a veritable impossibility,[13] living will statutes can have a very limited function or utility, and living wills appropriately need to be supplemented or supplanted entirely with extensive health care directives.

Standardized forms are available for living wills that are designed to comply with the laws of every state. The following declaration is recommended but not required by §2(c) of the 1989 version of the Uniform

---

[11] Potentially the most significant issue is how easy it should be to revoke a living will and whether the document itself may mandate requirements that are more severe than those otherwise applicable under state law. See Francis, The Evanescence of Living Wills, 24 Real Prop., Prob. & Trust J. 141, 152–155 (1989), describing that some states permit oral revocations (which could give a lone dissenter from a family's decision an effective veto based on a fabricated oral revocation), oral revocations only if witnessed by more than one person, or oral revocations only when communicated, such as to a health care provider. Many statutes fail to provide that divorce, filing for divorce, or estrangement may revoke a spouse's designation as agent, or that a living will can be revoked by a guardian or even by the simple act of a guardian being appointed.

[12] See Paragraph 6(a) of Part 2 of the Optional Form in Uniform Health-Care Decisions Act §4, 9 Pt. IB U.L.A. 102 (2005).

[13] See Francis, The Evanescence of Living Wills, 24 Real Prop., Prob. & Trust J. 141 (1989).

Rights of the Terminally Ill Act (which will be superseded by those states that adopt the newer Uniform Health Care Decisions Act):[14]

Declaration

If I should have an incurable and irreversible condition that, without the administration of life-sustaining treatment, will, in the opinion of my attending physician, cause my death within a relatively short time,[15] and I am no longer able to make decisions regarding my medical treatment, I appoint ____ or, if he or she is not reasonably available or is unwilling to serve, ____, to make decisions on my behalf regarding withholding or withdrawal of treatment that only prolongs the process of dying and is not necessary for my comfort or to alleviate pain, pursuant to the Uniform Rights of the Terminally Ill Act of this State.

[If the individual(s) I have so appointed is not reasonably available or is unwilling to serve, I direct my attending physician, pursuant to the Uniform Rights of the Terminally Ill Act of this State, to withhold or withdraw treatment that only prolongs the process of dying and is not necessary for my comfort or to alleviate pain.][16]

Some planners have the agent sign the document to indicate an awareness of the designation and willingness to serve. In some states the declarant must recite that the declaration is made freely and that the declarant is acting of sound mind. The Uniform Rights of the Terminally Ill Act requires that the witnesses declare that the execution was voluntary but nothing is said about capacity.

Although the Uniform Act does not specify who may be a witness or whether any persons are precluded, some state laws prohibit using witnesses who have real or potential conflicts of interest. As a result, it

---

[14] See generally English, The Uniform Health-Care Decisions Act and its Progress in the States, 15 Prob. & Prop. 19 (May/June 2001).

[15] According to Lieberson, Advance Medical Directives 54 n.9 (1992), this standard could be problematic because it would describe the administration of insulin to a diabetic or performance of dialysis for a patient suffering renal failure. While those patients are competent this concern is academic, but the Act anticipates patients who are unable to make decisions. Thus, in some circumstances, it might be appropriate to consider whether existing conditions mandate that a different or slightly modified standard be used.

[16] The bracketed language may be deleted or, after deleting the introductory phrase, may be used in lieu of everything following the sixth comma of the first paragraph.

may be unwise to allow as a witness the declarant's health care providers (such as an attending physician) or anyone in their employ, any owner or employee of a health care facility in which the declarant is a patient or resident, any claimant, spouse, relative by consanguinity or affinity, potential beneficiary of the declarant's estate, or any person who is financially responsible for the costs of the declarant's health care. Although only two witnesses are required in most states, it makes as much sense to use three in this case as it does in the execution of a will, to better assure the portability of the declaration. The Uniform HealthCare Decisions Act dispenses with virtually all these formalities.

A few states also may impose special execution requirements if the declarant is a resident in a nursing home or skilled nursing facility, in which case a state ombudsman or other state designated witness must sign. And some states may require notarization of the declaration. State law should be consulted to determine whether a statutory form must be used, and whether there are restrictions on when the declaration may be signed (for example, must the declarant already be diagnosed as suffering a terminable illness), the chronological limits on its validity, and the effect of inconsistent prior or subsequent declarations. Conflict of law issues also must be considered if the directive might be relied upon in multiple jurisdictions.[17]

---

[17] Restatement (Second) of Conflict of Laws § 291 (1971) provides that validity of an agency agreement is determined by the law of the state that has the most significant relation to the parties and the transaction with respect to the particular issue involved. Usually that is the jurisdiction in which the agency is executed. If an advance directive is characterized as a principal and agent arrangement, this provision should govern with respect to execution requirements. Uniform Rights of the Terminally Ill Act § 13 (1989), 9C U.L.A. 335 (2001), adopts the rule commonly applicable with respect to a will that an advance directive is valid if it is valid under the formalities of the state where it was executed or of the state in which the directive is being used. This "valid anywhere is valid everywhere" rule is like the same rule applied to the execution of a property will. Both are designed to promote validity, and it is likely that a court will favor this policy with respect to an advance directive.

Restatement (Second) of Conflict of Laws § 292 (1971) specifies that the validity of an agent's acts typically is determined by the law of the state in which the agent acts. Presumably this is the jurisdiction in which the principal is receiving medical care. A well drafted advance directive should include a choice of law provision, however, to attempt to preclude different results flowing from the fortuitousness of where a patient happens to receive medical care. That is, if

§ 3.10.1

The declaration or living will should be delivered to the declarant's health care providers, it should be made a part of the declarant's medical record, and it should confer immunity on health care professionals who comply with it. It should specify procedures to follow if a health care provider will not comply, such as directing transfer to a facility or provider who will comply, and it should reflect whether the declarant wishes that treatment should be withdrawn only under certain specified circumstances, any special wishes regarding the delivery of nourishment and hydration as opposed to other forms of care, and any moral or religious convictions that inform decisions made on the client's behalf.[18]

§3.10.2 Health Care Directives and Surrogate Decision Making

Numerous health care issues that may become important to a client cannot be anticipated with any degree of specificity or precision. For this reason, documents that address identifiable issues, such as a living will, may not be appropriate or sufficiently comprehensive. Indeed, because of state law restrictions on the application of a living will or natural death directive, a more expansive document may be needed just to deal with the limited issues that are the focus of those documents.[19] In this respect, garden-variety durable powers of attorney[20] have become very

---

(Footnote Continued)

an injury occurs on a bridge spanning a river that divides two states with very different laws, the effectiveness of the advance medical directive should not depend on the direction in which the ambulance travels. Unfortunately, even the protection of a governing law provision may not be enforceable if the law selected is deemed to violate a strong public policy of the state that would be the default state in the absence of a choice of law provision (such as the state of the patient's domicile at execution) and that state has a materially greater interest (such as the state in which care is being provided) than the state whose law was chosen with respect to the particular issue. Restatement (Second) of Conflict of Laws §187(2)(b) (1971).

[18] See Jordan, Durable Powers of Attorney and Health Care Directives §7:2 (4th ed. 2009).

[19] State law must be checked, however, to be certain that it does not preclude a particular form of directive. See, e.g., N.Y. Pub. Health Law §2981(5)(e), which prohibits the combination of a health care proxy with a power of attorney for financial or property management.

[20] See §3.10.4.

common, and every state permits some form of advance medical direc-tive.[21] Thus, it makes sense to utilize a durable power of attorney for health care[22] to provide directions regarding discrete health care issues (instructional advance directives) or to designate a surrogate or proxy to act on the principal's behalf with respect to issues that were not or could not be anticipated or as to which the advance directive cannot be sufficiently specific (proxy advance directives), or both.

Advance medical directives may relate to maintenance, diagnosis, or treatment of the principal's medical condition and may permit the agent to consent to, refuse to consent to, or withdraw consent relating either to overtreatment (such as heroic or extraordinary measures, which is the form of medical activity that many individuals want to prevent and that could be addressed in a living will if state law requirements are met) or undertreatment[23] (this less frequent concern might be addressed by a client who wants to direct the use of specific items of health care, such as the form or frequency of medication such as pain killers, or nutrition and hydration that might prolong life but not in an artificial manner).[24]

---

[21] For citations to various state statutory enactments involving advance medi-cal directives and living wills, consult Schoenblum, 2013 Multistate Guide to Estate Planning Table 10 (2012), and Jordan, Durable Powers of Attorney and Health Care Directives (4th ed. 2009). See also Rozovsky, Consent to Treatment, A Practical Guide (4th ed. 2009), and English, The UPC and the New Durable Powers, 27 Real Prop., Prob. & Trust J. 333 (1992).

Not covered in this discussion are the perfunctory advance directive disclo-sure requirements imposed by the Patient Self-Determination Act on health care providers who participate in Medicare or Medicaid. They apply when a patient is admitted to a health care facility and relate to the patient's right to make decisions regarding medical care and the provider's policies regarding advance directives. See 42 U.S.C. §§ 1395cc(a)(1)(Q), 1395cc(f), 1395mm(c)(8), 1396a(a)(57), 1396a(a)(58), and 1396a(w).

[22] See generally English, The UPC and the New Durable Powers, 27 Real Prop., Prob. & Trust J. 333 (1992).

[23] Referred to by Lieberson, Advance Medical Directives (1992), as a Direc-tion to Provide Maximum Care (DPMC).

[24] Nutrition and hydration might be regarded as care that is related only to the client's comfort and not to treatment for an ailment that may terminate the client's life. Therefore, it might not be regarded as artificially prolonging the dying process, which arguably could leave decisions regarding nutrition and hydration outside a state's statutory provisions regarding decisions near the end of life. Indeed, without specification, it might be contended that these decisions

In addition to authorizing the designated agent to act, the durable power of attorney for health care might authorize the designated agent to delegate certain decisions or responsibilities to other decision makers, if desired or appropriate, for selected matters or if the agent is unwilling or unable to act and a successor either is not named in the power of attorney or is not willing and able to act. In such cases it may be more favorable for the agent to designate someone else to serve, rather than relying on statutes that create a priority among family members or other surrogates.[25] Such consent statutes may create uncertainty regarding the priority among family members to make decisions on behalf of a principal, the potential for disagreement regarding issues about which the principal feels strongly,[26] or the inability to establish the principal's desires because the standard of proof is too high and the principal's expressions of intent are too vague or difficult to establish by proof.

In addition, the proper standard to be applied in the absence of an effective advance directive may be unclear or may require a balancing (such as a benefits and burdens test) that is too subjective to be

---

(Footnote Continued)

do not relate to treatment at all and therefore also are not contemplated by a generic health care power of attorney. See Jordan, Durable Powers of Attorney and Health Care Directives §3:20 (4th ed. 2009), and Meisel, The Right to Die 124–125 and §11.15 n.63 (1989).

     Lieberson, Advance Medical Directives 46, 73 (1992), suggests a distinction between procedures that merely postpone death and those that are employed in hopes of returning the patient to a meaningful existence, and states that a direction to forsake nutrition or hydration undoubtedly will be honored as an advance medical direction even if state law is silent on the issue. At the other extreme from decisions that prima facie are covered by a health care directive are some invasive forms of mental health care (such as convulsive treatment or psychosurgery) or decisions relating to reproduction (such as sterilization or abortion), that legislatively are excluded from the scope of a health care directive in some jurisdictions.

  [25] Under laws such as the Uniform Health-Care Decisions Act, 9 Pt. IB U.L.A. 83 (2005). This may be particularly relevant if applicable state law would not select the person the client most wants to exercise this control, such as a nonfamily member (including a same sex partner).

  [26] But see §5(h) of the Uniform Health-Care Decisions Act, 9 Pt. IB U.L.A. 111 (2005), which would permit a principal to make a negative appointment to preclude certain otherwise priority individuals from serving as surrogate, for example because the potential surrogate's views are incompatible with the principal's.

§3.10.2

predictable.[27] Indeed, it may not even be clear whether state law permits a surrogate to act on behalf of a principal who may not meet statutory threshold standards (for example, because the principal is not in danger of imminent death even though suffering from a terminal illness, is only comatose but not terminally ill, or is in a persistent vegetative state but is not suffering an incurable ailment that will result in death regardless of treatment). As a result, a durable power of attorney for health care that is tailored for the individual client may be necessary.[28]

At the very least, a durable power of attorney for health care should grant the ability to waive the physician-patient privilege so that necessary medical information may be given to the appropriate decision maker. In addition, to comply with the Health Insurance Portability and Accountability Act (HIPAA) regulations,[29] it is essential that disclosure of "individually identifiable health information" by a "covered entity" (any medical records holder) be addressed in durable powers, living trusts, living wills, and any other documents that anticipate that a client's capacity to act be a trigger for judgments that need to be made or for a succession of fiduciaries to occur. This particularly is important regarding a springing durable power of attorney that precludes the powerholder from becoming the client's agent until a determination of incapacity is made, because frequently that determination cannot occur without a sharing of medical information that is prohibited without the consent of the client or the client's personal representative, which the agent would become

---

[27] See, e.g., In re Estate of Greenspan, 558 N.E.2d 1194 (Ill. 1990), establishing a clear and convincing evidence of intent standard that necessitates an explicit expression of the client's intent or knowledge of the client's personal value system.

[28] For a summary of the law regarding medical decision making in the absence of statute, see Collin, Planning and Drafting Durable Powers of Attorney for Health Care, 22 U. Miami Inst. Est. Plan. ¶ 503 (1988), and Meisel, The Right to Die ch. 9 (1989), both explaining standards such as the patient's best interests, pure objective versus subjective testing, benefits versus burdens evaluations, quality of life determinations, substituted judgment, and so forth.

[29] HIPAA also is known as the Kennedy-Kassebaum Act. For extensive materials and useful links see www.hhs.gov/ocr/hipaa. The regulations are 45 CFR Parts 160 and 164. An excellent practical article on the subject is Evans, What Estate Lawyers Need to Know About HIPAA and "Protected Health Information," 18 Prob. & Prop. 20 (July/August 2004). Or perform an internet search on "protected health information."

§ 3.10.2

only if authorized to act (which cannot occur without the information that would inform the determination).

This circularity issue may inform abandonment of springing powers, because a fully authorized agent under a durable health care power is a "personal representative" to whom disclosure or access is provided (even with no special provision in the durable power) and as to whom this issue need not arise. The personal representative is treated as the client regarding the use and further disclosure of all health care information that relates to decisions made under the health care power.

It may be impossible to know how any agent exercising judgment on behalf of a principal might evaluate the principal's best interests. Thus, it may be advisable in drafting a durable power of attorney for health care to be specific about the range of permissible issues for the agent to address (such as whether to record a do-not-resuscitate direction), and to provide broad outcome oriented statements conveying the principal's general feelings about health care and treatment options, rather than trying to be specific about particular medical procedures that might be regarded by the principal as either too passive or too aggressive. Self-determination may be better served if the principal and the estate planner consider whether an advance directive in the form of a durable power of attorney for health care should cover termination of life decisions as well as routine health care matters, and how much specificity is appropriate with respect to either the general or specific beliefs and desires of the principal.

In addition, the durable power of attorney for health care might specify the principal's wishes regarding issues that are ancillary but related to direct medical care determinations, such as the location and level of personal care (ranging from home care, hospice, or residential care facilities to group care homes, nursing facilities, or full hospitalization), funeral and burial arrangements, anatomical gifts, and employment of skilled and semi-skilled medical personnel or companions.[30] At the very least, advance medical directives should not be limited to issues regarding end of life decisions. Quality of life considerations, the application of procedures that may extend life at a diminished level, and related

---

[30] See Jordan, Durable Powers of Attorney and Health Care Directives § 3:2 (4th ed. 2009).

§ 3.10.2

issues tailored to the particular principal's religious and other beliefs and emotions also should be addressed.

Further, to better ensure compliance with the principal's wishes, the durable power of attorney for health care should indemnify medical care personnel who rely on the agent's directions and absolve them from the need to verify whether the agent is acting within the authority of the power. Finally, the law in some jurisdictions may provide that appointment of a guardian automatically terminates a durable power of attorney and, in any event, a guardian would acquire the principal's power to revoke a durable power. Thus, well crafted durable powers of attorney for health care either preclude appointment of a guardian or designate the agent as the desired guardian.[31]

Again because of concerns about the portability of a durable power of attorney for health care and conflict of law resolutions, attention should be devoted to the formalities for execution.[32] At a minimum, execution formalities for both property and living wills should be followed, on the assumption that (1) each of them and a health care power of attorney will be signed at the same time (which may make it easier to demonstrate the client's capacity),[33] and (2) it is uncommon that formali-

---

[31] See UPC § 5B-108, § 3.10 n.3. But see In re Guardianship of Friend, 1993 WL 526643 (Ohio Ct. App.), in which the holder of a power of attorney, who also was named as residuary beneficiary and executor of principal's estate, was denied appointment as guardian of the principal's estate because the durable power failed to designate that the powerholder be named as guardian and because, as residuary beneficiary, the powerholder had a conflict of interest (because every dollar not spent on the principal would pass to the powerholder when the principal died). Conceivably, a court exercising its discretion to designate a guardian might refuse to appoint an individual designated to serve as guardian for the same reasons. UPC § 5B-108(a) does not require the court to appoint the person nominated in a durable power of attorney to serve as guardian if the court finds appointment to be inappropriate "for good cause shown or disqualification."

[32] See generally Schoenblum, 2013 Multistate Guide to Estate Planning Table 10 (2012); Jordan, Durable Powers of Attorney and Health Care Directives (4th ed. 2009) (a 50 state compendium), Meisel, The Right to Die § 11.9 (1989), and English, The UPC and the New Durable Powers, 27 Real Prop., Prob. & Trust J. 331, 369–372 (1992), regarding execution requirements.

[33] See Restatement (Third) of Agency § 3.04(1) (2006) (capacity to be a principal is that required to perform the delegated act or transaction itself); Uniform Health-Care Decisions Act § 1(3), 9 Pt. IB U.L.A. 89 (2005) (defines capacity to mean the "ability to understand the significant benefits, risks, and

---

§ 3.10.2

ties more stringent than the property will execution requirements are imposed. Living will formalities regarding prohibited witnesses and any requirement that the agent sign to indicate acceptance of office provide appropriate safeguards that also should not be difficult to meet, the theory being that living will or natural death statutes define the protections and abuses that might be of concern and, if the document fails as a durable power, it still might qualify as a living will if decisions of that nature become relevant.

Because they probably are harmless and may prove helpful, saving clauses or statements about the principal's overall intent regarding care, that the document supersede any prior direction, that it not be limited by state law statutes, and that it be effective where executed and in any other jurisdiction, also should be considered. However, inspection of state law is an absolute necessity because these documents tend to have a wide variety of execution requirements or prohibitions and the circumstances in which, or the issues upon which, they are allowed to operate.

There may be different execution requirements, limitations on who may serve as agent, or on the maximum duration a delegation is effective, and different agents may be empowered and will be using the documents with respect to different third parties. Thus, it makes sense to cause a durable power of attorney for property management and that for health care decisions and any freestanding living will all to be separate documents. At the same time, however, the estate planner must guarantee that they are sufficiently integrated that they do not conflict, appoint different agents with overlapping authority or, worst of all, give different indications of the principal's intent. And, because some states limit the effective duration of a durable power of attorney for health care or living will, these documents should be updated or at least republished periodically. Major events in the principal's family life might cause a change of mind about the values expressed in the durable power of attorney for health care, medical developments might cause a change of mind regarding health care decisions, and state law may change to

---

(Footnote Continued)

alternatives to proposed health care and to make and communicate a health-care decision").

§ 3.10.2

require execution of a living will after diagnosis of a terminal illness, making it wise to revisit these directives after such experiences.[34]

§3.10.3 Organ Donation

Every state has enacted a version of the Uniform Anatomical Gift Act[35] and organ donor cards and designations are commonplace. What is not common is for estate planners to assist their clients in assessing whether to execute an organ donation form or to grant their health care agent the authority to execute such a direction on their behalf. Given the desperate need for organ donors, it is appropriate for estate planners to suggest to their clients and for any agent acting under a durable power of attorney for health care to consider whether to consent to organ transplants following the principal's death. Also worthy of consideration is whether advance medical decisions at the end of life impact or are affected by that direction.

§3.10.4 Durable Powers of Attorney for Property Management

Every United States jurisdiction authorizes a power of attorney that is durable,[36] meaning that it is a special form of agency that does not

---

[34] For assistance in drafting a durable power of attorney for health care, see the sample with annotations in Collin, Planning and Drafting Durable Powers of Attorney for Health Care, 22 U. Miami Inst. Est. Plan. ¶ 505.5 (1988), drawn from a prior edition of the treatise with forms: Jordan, Durable Powers of Attorney and Health Care Directives (4th ed. 2009). As indicated in the instructions to the monograph produced by the American Bar Association Commission on Legal Problems of the Elderly, Health Care Powers of Attorney: An Introduction and Sample Form (1990), local variations play such a significant role in the preparation of durable powers for health care that the drafter should begin with a template that has been blessed by the local bar association or, if such a form is not available, to take a generic sample and carefully compare state law with the assumptions made in that document. Because of these local law variations, no model form is produced herein.

[35] See §3.2.1.

[36] See, e.g., UPC §5B-104: "A power of attorney . . . is durable unless it expressly provides that it is terminated by the incapacity of the principal." By UPC §5B-109(a) the principal may provide that the power is not effective upon execution but, instead "that it becomes effective at a future date or upon the occurrence of a future event or contingency"—commonly known as a springing

terminate on the principal's incapacity or the passage of time.[37] Even for clients with limited means, the durable power of attorney for property management (referred to herein simply as a durable power of attorney, as distinguished from a durable power of attorney for health care),[38] is an economical[39] alternative to a funded revocable trust, serving as a useful grant of authority to handle various matters and transactions on behalf of the principal. Frequently a durable power is used in conjunction with an unfunded or standby revocable trust rather than in lieu of inter vivos trust planning altogether. If the power is durable and not earlier revoked, the authority granted by the power can continue until the principal's death and may be used to transfer assets to the trust for proper management after the principal becomes incapacitated. It also may be useful even if the principal is not incapacitated but, by virtue of health problems or impaired judgment, finds it difficult to manage property effectively.

A durable power of attorney may not be the most convenient device for property management in larger situations, however, because powers

---

(Footnote Continued)

power of attorney (which may not be authorized in every jurisdiction that has not adopted the UPC or the freestanding Uniform Power of Attorney Act, 8B U.L.A. 33 (Supp. 2010) or its predecessor, the Uniform Durable Power of Attorney Act, 8A U.L.A. 233 (2003), which is Article V Part 5 of the UPC).

See generally Schoenblum, 2013 Multistate Guide to Estate Planning Table 10 (2012); Jordan, Durable Powers of Attorney and Health Care Directives (4th ed. 2009), Frolik & Brown, Advising the Elderly or Disabled Client (1992), and Hook, Durable Powers of Attorney, 859 Tax Mgmt. (BNA) Estates, Gifts, and Trusts Port. (2000), each being a comprehensive resource on the law relating to powers of attorney, with extensive citations to the various legislative enactments and providing sample forms. Jordan also provides an extensive computerized forms drafting system. See also Rozovsky, Consent to Treatment, A Practical Guide (4th ed. 2009), and English, The UPC and the New Durable Powers, 27 Real Prop., Prob. & Trust J. 333 (1992).

[37] UPC §5B-110(c) specifies expressly that "[u]nless the power of attorney otherwise provides, an agent's authority is exercisable . . . notwithstanding a lapse of time since the execution of the power of attorney."

[38] See §3.10.2.

[39] The Uniform Statutory Form Power of Attorney Act, 8B U.L.A. 191 (2001), provides a statutory laundry list of powers that may be withheld or granted by simple designation on a form, making it even easier to prepare and execute a durable power of attorney for clients of limited means or whose needs are relatively straightforward.

§3.10.4

of attorney often are questioned by third parties in ways that trusts are not. But the durable power is appropriate for modest estates or in situations in which extensive management will not be necessary due to the nature of the client's investments and family situation. Moreover, for clients with substantial wealth, or unusual assets or needs, the combination of a funded revocable trust and a durable power of attorney is a superior management device. Finally, if the advantages of a funded revocable trust are desired in a less than substantial situation, the Uniform Custodial Trust Act authorizes creation of a statutory trust in the nature of a UTMA account, with limited discretion and outright distribution following the settlor's death.[40] Coupled with a durable power of attorney, it too could provide all the property management needed.

§3.10.4.1 Problems with Durable Powers

Durable powers are not a total panacea, however, and a number of practical problems or issues must be considered in their preparation and use. For example, unlike a trust of any variety, the durable power of attorney cannot be made to survive the principal's death, meaning that some other form of asset transfer device must be used to complete the principal's estate plan.

Also unlike the principles governing trust administration, durable powers and the laws applicable to them are of recent vintage. There are unresolved questions regarding the permissible scope of authority and the principles of administration and fiduciary liability that apply to durable powers of attorney. Indeed, there is relative uncertainty whether the fiduciary principles of agency, trust, or guardianship law should apply to the agent under a durable power of attorney. By contrast, the law of trusts and trust administration is well established. Local trust codes and well drafted powers of administration granted by trust instruments routinely provide clear rules and flexible powers.

---

[40] See 7A Pt. I U.L.A. 103 (2002). The Uniform Trust may be a desirable alternative to a guardianship or conservatorship and may provide better acceptance from third parties than a durable power alone. And, unlike even a durable power of attorney, the trust survives the settlor's death for property distribution in lieu of probate. See Mezzullo & Roach, The Uniform Custodial Trust Act: An Alternative to Adult Guardianship, 24 U. Rich. L. Rev. 65 (1989), and Schilling, The Uniform Custodial Trust Act—One Alternative to Guardianship, 19 Prob. Notes 146 (1993).

§3.10.4.1

Finally, a trustee holds legal title to trust assets and has unquestioned authority to deal with them, but financial institutions, stock transfer agents, the government, and others occasionally still challenge or refuse to honor durable powers of attorney on grounds ranging from questions about revocation (indeed, revocation of a durable power and retraction of the authority to act on behalf of the principal is a serious issue, not to be overlooked in the preparation of the document) and notions regarding "staleness," or age of the power, to uncertainty about the scope of the authority granted by the power.

Some techniques can help minimize these concerns. For example, a durable power of attorney might provide that it must be recorded and that it can be revoked only by an instrument of revocation recorded in the same manner as the power itself, even though neither recordation of the power nor of the revocation is required by local law. Moreover, the power appropriately might indemnify or exonerate third parties from liability if the agent executes an affidavit affirming that the principal was competent when the power was executed, that the power has not terminated or been revoked, and that the transaction is authorized by the power.[41] Notwithstanding these protections, however, some third parties may take conservative and unyielding positions that limit the effectiveness of durable powers, meaning that the durable power of attorney cannot be relied upon as a client's primary property management authority. Some powers go so far as authorizing or even directing the agent to seek redress for any damages caused by a third party's refusal to recognize the agent's authority under the power.

---

[41] UPC § 5B-110(d) provides that "[t]ermination of an agent's authority or of a power of attorney is not effective as to the agent or another person that, without actual knowledge of the termination, acts in good faith under the power of attorney." Thus, the need for protection under the terms of the durable power is eliminated. But in states that do not have comparable rules it may be necessary for the document to provide the assurance that the UPC guarantees to third parties who rely in good faith on the power. For example, the power might specify something to the effect that revocation is not effective with respect to a third party until actual notice or knowledge thereof is received by that third party and that the principal and the principal's estate indemnifies any third party against liability for relying on the provisions of a power of attorney prior to such actual notice.

§ 3.10.4.1

§3.10.4.2 Springing Powers

Some powers of attorney become effective only when the principal is determined to be incapacitated. These powers "spring" into existence (or are delivered by the principal's attorney) when incapacity is certified, which may present the potentially vexing issues of how to determine incapacity, how to guarantee that necessary information is available to the person who will make that determination, how to assure third parties that the determination was made properly and thereby inspire their reliance on the agent's authority, and whether the power should retract if the principal regains capacity. Springing powers effectively give the person who determines incapacity a pre-emptive veto power over any action by the agent, which also may not be appropriate.

Some springing powers seek to minimize these problems by making their effectiveness conditional upon a designated event, or even expiration of a specified period of time. Notwithstanding the limitations of all these devices, some individuals are committed to the use of springing powers, either because granting the power of attorney is an emotional issue or because the principal is unwilling to admit the need for or actually to relinquish any immediate form of control. In these cases there is little that can be done to assuage these concerns short of using a springing power, except perhaps to have the principal or the attorney hold an immediately effective durable power but deliver it to the agent only when the need arises.

A third concern that sometimes is suggested as recommending the use of springing powers is that the agent is not trustworthy and therefore should not possess authority to act any earlier than absolutely necessary. Distrust is an odd element when dealing with a power of attorney because, while capable, the principal can negate or revoke undesirable acts performed by the agent and presumably does not need protection against overreaching or abuse. Indeed, it might be preferable to give the agent a "trial run" while the principal still can exercise some oversight ability, which speaks in favor of making the power effective immediately.

Once incapacity has occurred, however, the license to steal represented by even a springing power is unleashed. Thus, if distrust is a legitimate concern, rather than using a springing power, these cases would be addressed better with a joint power, a power that is subject to the veto of a protector of some sort, or stringent limitations on the authorities granted by the power (such as only to transfer assets to an unfunded standby trust). Requiring periodic accountings or, worse, prior court permission to act are not sensible, given that they effectively introduce the negative attributes of a guardianship that the power of attorney presumably was meant to avoid. If this degree of protection is desired, a fully funded living trust with complete trust law protections probably would be preferable.

§ 3.10.4.3 Gifting and Other Tax Concerns

A significant issue relating to the effectiveness of durable powers of attorney for property management relates to the authority of the agent to make gifts on behalf of the principal, including the power to engage in transactions such as creation of a GRAT or disclaiming gifts or bequests made to the principal. Arguing against this authority is that gifts reduce the principal's estate, which indirectly affects the principal's will, and the agent under a power of attorney may not modify the principal's will.[42] That gifting may reduce the principal's estate ultimately passing under the principal's will is potentially true, however, of almost any action taken by an agent (such as incurring health care costs that might dissipate the principal's estate, or selling assets that may constitute a specific bequest under the will), and these activities are not regarded as limited by notions of restraint regarding the principal's will.[43]

---

[42] Cf. Restatement (Third) of Agency § 3.04(3) (2006) (a principal may not authorize an agent to perform a nondelegable act, such as making, modification, or revocation of the principal's will). On the other hand, a durable power may grant the authority to execute or revoke trusts. See, e.g., In re Schlagel Trust, 51 P.3d 1094 (Colo. Ct. App. 2002) (trust created and subsequently revoked by the settlor's agent under a durable power; a subsequently enacted state law requires specific authority for the actions undertaken in this case under a power that permitted execution of a trust but that did not mention revocation). UTC § 602(e) provides that a trust "settlor's powers with respect to revocation, amendment, or distribution of trust property may be exercised by an agent under a power of attorney only to the extent expressly authorized by the terms of the trust *or the power*" (emphasis added).

[43] Indeed, the 1990 version of UPC § 2-606(b) is designed to prevent the agent's acts from causing an ademption of a specific bequest, which prima facie recognizes the agent's authority to act in ways that impact the principal's will. See § 3.2.5.2 and Jordan, Durable Powers of Attorney and Health Care Directives § 4:10 (4th ed. 2009). And compare UPC § 5B-217(c), authorizing the agent to

As illustrated by numerous cases, the ability to make gifts is a particularly useful provision if the principal's projected gross estate will exceed the amount protected from tax payment by the unified credit, and the government actively denies the authority of agents to make gifts, especially close to the principal's death, absent express authority in the power of attorney. For example, TAMs 8635007 and 8623004 involved revocable trusts that did not specifically authorize the trustees to make gifts of trust property. The settlors had created powers of attorney (durable and nondurable, respectively), but they too did not specifically authorize the agents to make gifts of the settlors' property. The agents nevertheless made transfers that the government held were includible in the settlors' gross estates for FET purposes because they were not authorized, the theory being that the settlors therefore possessed the right to recover those transferred amounts, which triggered inclusion under § 2038(a)(1).

In rejecting the agents' authority to make gifts, the government observed that a nonspecific authorization "to do anything the principal could" does not include the power to dissipate the principal's assets in any manner, including through making gifts. According to the TAMs, this especially is true if the power of attorney grants specific powers that do not include an express power to make gifts, which tends to show that the gifting power was not intended.[44]

Estate of Bronston v. Commissioner[45] involved a power of attorney that authorized the agent "to *grant*, bargain, sell, *convey*, or lease, or contract for the sale, conveyance, or lease of *any property now or in the future owned by me*." The only assets owned by the principal when the power of attorney was executed were passive investments and the

---

(Footnote Continued)

make gifts "consistent with the principal's objectives if actually known by the agent and, if unknown, as the agent determines is consistent with the principal's best interest based on all relevant factors"—which may include foreseeable needs, tax minimization, eligibility for entitlement benefits and "the principal's personal history of making . . . gifts."

[44] See generally Restatement (Second) of Agency § 37(2) (1958): "The specific authorization of particular acts tends to show that a more general authority is not intended." No corresponding provision appears in the Restatement (Third) of Agency.

[45] 56 T.C.M. (CCH) 550, 551 (1988) (emphasis in original).

§ 3.10.4.3

principal had a history of making gifts that qualified for the gift tax annual exclusion. The agent made annual exclusion gifts of the principal's property to each of six donees and, in answer to the question whether those gifts were authorized under the power of attorney, the Tax Court deemed the terms "grant" and "convey" broad enough to include appropriate gifts, stating that the principal's pattern of making similar gifts was relevant.

Estate of Casey v. Commissioner[46] involved a similar durable power that granted the agent the authority "to do and perform all things and acts relating to my property . . . which I might do," including to "convey . . . any and all of my property," and stating the principal's "intention . . . to give my attorney . . . full and complete power . . . to deal with any and all of my property . . . in his full and absolute discretion." Pursuant to this power, the agent made annual exclusion gifts that the government challenged as unauthorized. Because these gifts continued a program begun by the principal's predeceased spouse, and because the principal's annual income was adequate for the principal's support, the Tax Court again held that, under state law, the language of the power and the principal's circumstances would compel a state court to conclude that the gifts were within the scope of the power and disallowed the government's challenge.

Surprisingly, Estate of Pruitt v. Commissioner[47] and TAM 199944005 both reached similar, taxpayer-favorable results, under general powers of attorney with no specific authority to make gifts and with no state court order, based on findings that the gifts were limited relative to the size of the estate, the decedent was not economically disadvantaged by the gifts, and the gifts were consistent with the decedent's will and consistent with (indeed, some were smaller than) prior lifetime gifts made by the decedent personally.

The Tax Court was reversed on appeal in *Casey*,[48] finding as a matter of law that the Tax Court was in error about the ability under state law to

---

[46] 58 T.C.M. (CCH) 176 (1989), citing *Bronston* and Estate of Gagliardi v. Commissioner, 89 T.C. 1207 (1987).

[47] 80 T.C.M. (CCH) 348 (2000) (involving Oregon law).

[48] Estate of Casey v. Commissioner, 948 F.2d 895 (4th Cir. 1991). To the same effect are Townsend v. United States, 889 F. Supp. 369 (D. Neb. 1995) (annual exclusion gifts of almost $500,000 made under power of attorney that lacked

§ 3.10.4.3

make gifts under the power involved, causing doubt about the validity of *Bronston* as well. Subsequently, in TAM 9231003, which involved similar facts, the government stated that powers of attorney usually are "carefully drawn by skilled persons . . . and it is assumed that the document represents the entire understanding of the parties." Citing *Casey*, the government therefore held that the absence of specific authority to make gifts means that gifts are not authorized and therefore may be challenged by the principal. In this situation a local court purported to ratify the gifts in an action some six months after the principal's death, which the government agreed would bind the parties to the gift but could not retroactively complete the gifts for federal gift tax purposes. Interestingly, the TAM confirmed that "an annual exclusion . . . is allowable . . . against the total gifts affirmed" by that postmortem court order, which was obtained before the end of the calendar year in which the principal died.[49]

(Footnote Continued)

specific authority to make gifts), Estate of Collins v. United States, 94-1 U.S. Tax Cas. ¶ 60,162 (E.D. Mich. 1994) (court refused to imply a power to make gifts in a durable power of attorney), Estate of Gaynor v. Commissioner, 82 T.C.M. (CCH) 379 (2001) (attorney in fact cannot make gifts under Connecticut law absent express authority in the power), and Archbold v. Reifenrath, 744 N.W.2d 701 (Neb. 2008) (notwithstanding a grant "without limitation . . . exercisable in the absolute judgment and discretion of my Agent" the court held that the powerholder could not make substantially gratuitous transfers to the powerholder or to objects of the powerholder's bounty "absent an express provision [or] specific authorization" in the power). And cf. Estate of Smith v. United States, 97-2 U.S. Tax Cas. (CCH) ¶ 60,291 (D. Vt. 1997) (durable power holder donated conservation easement pursuant to a power to "convey"; the court denied the taxpayer's petition for summary judgment, stating that the power was ambiguous and that any "power to make a gift is . . . potentially hazardous to the principal's interests and therefore will not lightly be inferred from broad, all-encompassing grants of powers to the agent"). But see Estate of Ridenour v. Commissioner, 36 F.3d 332 (4th Cir. 1994) (gifts made were validated by state statute with retroactive application enacted after *Casey* was decided; in addition, unlike the power in *Casey*, which was limited to business transactions, the power in *Ridenour* was broad and the gifts continued a pattern of giving begun by the taxpayer).

[49] TAMs 9731003, 9634004, and 9347003 (court orders validating gifts made without express authority were not binding on the government), 9342003, and 9403004 (powers of attorney lacked specific authority to make gifts; transfers made by the agents to themselves and their families deemed invalid and there-

Collectively, these illustrations underscore the need, in drafting a durable power of attorney, to make specific reference to gratuitous transfers, preferably with an indication of the permissible parameters of that authority.[50] TAM 9513001 concluded that durable powers of attorney

---

(Footnote Continued)

fore subject to the principal's implicit state law power of revocation), and Estate of Swanson v. United States, 2001-1 U.S. Tax Cas. (CCH) ¶ 60,408 (Fed. Cir. 2001) (13 of 38 gifts by check were not presented prior to death and would have been invalid on that ground, as discussed in § 7.1.7; more importantly, all the gifts were made under a durable power of attorney that lacked specific authority, and a deemed "ratification" came before the fact and therefore was ineffective), each state the consistent conclusion that transferred property is includible in the principal's gross estate at death under § 2038(a)(1). See also PLRs 9509034 and 9410028. The 1995 Ruling was interesting in that it noted that inclusion generated a new basis for the gifted property, which is not such a bad result in some cases, although it denied a new basis with respect to those gifted assets that were sold by the donee after the gift and before the principal's death (as if the principal personally had sold those assets and owned the cash proceeds at death). See Treas. Reg. § 1.1014-1(a). And a gift tax refund flowing from invalidation of the gifts themselves also was deemed includible in the principal's estate under § 2033.

Distinguishable from the typical durable-power-of-attorney, late-in-life-gift situation are PLR 9839013, allowing gifts on behalf of an incompetent because state law had been amended to authorize that action, and Estate of Neff v. Commissioner, 73 T.C.M. (CCH) 2608 (1997), in which gifts made by the holder of a durable power of attorney within one month prior to the decedent's death were regarded as effective and qualified for the gift tax annual exclusion, notwithstanding the lack of specific authority under the durable power to make gratuitous transfers. Unusual was that the donor was competent and the evidence indicated both a direction to make the gifts and a ratification of them. In addition, the subject matter of the gifts was annuities that would have passed at the donor's death to the donees to whom the transfers were made inter vivos, meaning that the premortem transfers were merely an acceleration of transfers as to which the decedent had already indicated the donative intent by purchasing the annuities and naming the successor beneficiaries.

[50] Specificity is important for nontax reasons as well. See, e.g., Jones v. Brandt, 645 S.E.2d 312 (Va. 2007) (estate beneficiaries unsuccessfully challenged the durable power holder's designation of the principal's long-term companion as POD beneficiary of a certificate of deposit at the principal's direction and later with ratification by the principal); In re Estate of Kurrelmeyer, 895 A.2d 207 (Vt. 2006), in which the court finally determined that the powerholder had the authority to create a trust, but remanded to determine whether exercise of that authority was a breach of the powerholder's duty of loyalty under the durable

under the Uniform Durable Power of Attorney Act grant adequate authority, but §201 of the more recent Uniform Power of Attorney Act makes clear that gifting (and a variety of other acts) is permitted only if the power expressly grants that authority. Even in states that have adopted the earlier Durable Power Act, some estate planners prepare *two* durable powers of attorney, one a traditional power that details the authority of the agent to perform various enumerated acts,[51] and the other an unlimited durable power that, in its most significant part, provides:

> Each authorized agent of mine is hereby granted the power to represent me and perform any and all acts in my behalf in all matters and affairs (except those relating to my health care), without limitation of any kind (other than as provided below), including the power to make every decision and take every

---

(Footnote Continued)

power because the trust contained provisions that were more beneficial to the powerholder than would have applied under the principal's will with respect to the property transferred to the trust; and Mischke v. Mischke, 530 N.W.2d 235 (Neb. 1995) (inequitable transfer, to three siblings to exclusion of a fourth, found to be unauthorized because power of attorney did not specifically mention gratuitous transfers).

[51] The list of powers that might be included in a long form durable power of attorney is nearly limitless, depending on the scope of authority the principal intends to delegate, which indicates why it is so dangerous to attempt to itemize powers if the intent is to authorize the agent literally to stand in the principal's shoes. If, however, only limited functions are meant to be delegated, then it should be relatively easy for the drafter to itemize particular authorities. Numerous sources for model or form provisions exist to inform such drafting.

As a practical matter, if a particular activity is meant to be authorized and it requires acceptance of the power of attorney by a third party, such as an insurance company, stock transfer agent, title insurer, or financial institution, it makes sense to obtain those parties' preferred power of attorney form and execute it or model the power being drafted after that document.

Among the most comprehensive authorities available on the drafting of durable powers of attorney in general, see Jordan, Durable Powers of Attorney and Health Care Directives (4th ed. 2009), which includes a computer assisted forms drafting system. Another useful source for ideas about standard provisions to include in an all purpose power of attorney is §301 of the Uniform Power of Attorney Act, 8B U.L.A. 87 (Supp. 2010), or §§3 through 16 of the Uniform Statutory Form Power of Attorney Act, 8B U.L.A. 207-219 (2001), which describe what each short form power referred to in the Statutory Form Act is meant to entail and provide a useful template for drafting.

§3.10.4.3

action, even making gifts, for me that I could in my own behalf—
excluding only those rare things (if any) that applicable law does
not at the time of exercise permit any agent or attorney in fact to
do for or in behalf of a principal, no matter how all encompassing
nor how specific the authorization. I expressly grant to each
authorized agent the power to execute in my behalf, as I could
myself, any and all kinds of power of attorney documents that
name as my attorney in fact my authorized agent or any other
person to whom my authorized agent deems it appropriate to
delegate any powers set forth in such document. Any specific
listing of powers in such document not expressly excluded by
this document, including the power to make gifts, is expressly
authorized. Aside from that one express power, I list no examples of the powers hereby granted to my authorized agent because their very enumeration might appear to limit those
powers. I intend the powers hereby granted to each of my
authorized agents to be absolutely as broad as applicable law will
allow—in other words, an unlimited power.[52]

Such a power appropriately might specify the class of permissible donees (for example, descendants and spouses of descendants), limit the
amount of any single gift to the amount of the then applicable gift tax
annual exclusion, perhaps in addition to expenditures for tuition and
medical payments for members of the class of potential donees if that is
the principal's intent and the potential inequality of that authority is not a
concern. It also should protect against the agent possessing a general
power of appointment if the agent is within the class of permissible
donees.

Arguably this is not a problem if all acts of the agent are subject to
challenge by the principal, because §2041(b)(1)(C)(i) provides that a
power that can be exercised only in conjunction with the grantor of the
power is not a general power of appointment, but this defense is without
support and may be incorrect.[53] Even if the defense is correct, however,

---

[52] This "unlimited power" is a durable general power that gives the agent all
powers permitted by law—even the power to make gifts from the property of the
person. This provision is adapted from a form copyrighted (1992) by the late
Frederick R. Keydel, who specifically granted free use in the practice of law by
attorneys. This power of attorney is intended to be given effect on a full faith and
credit, comity basis to the greatest extent possible in all states and countries.

[53] That the principal may object to exercise of a power by challenging the
agent's acts may not be the same as making a power exercisable jointly or in
conjunction with the grantor, which is what §2041(b)(1)(C)(i) contemplates.

§3.10.4.3

care is required in the overall coordination of the various provisions of the power, because a power that exonerates the agent from liability to the principal inadvertently may generate an unexpected tax problem if, for example, the agent dies while acting in that capacity.

For example, the document from which the unlimited power of attorney is reproduced also specifies that the principal ratifies and confirms all acts done by any authorized agent or others properly appointed to act on the principal's behalf. It also provides that documents executed or delivered by an agent bind the principal and the principal's estate, heirs, successors, and assigns. It authorizes self dealing but requires receipt of full and adequate consideration and precludes actions that might trigger application of §2041 other than gifts or disclaimers that benefit the agent that do not exceed the gift tax marital deduction or any allowable gift tax exclusion.

Although that provision permits the agent to make transfers to the agent personally that constitute the power as a general power of appointment, those transfers cannot exceed the amount of the gift tax annual exclusion, which is a conscious limit on the agent's exposure to potential FET liability. Moreover, if the amount subject to the agent's total discretion exceeds 20 times the annual exclusion amount, the 5% arm of the §2514(e) exception will protect the agent from all gift tax consequences, leaving only FET inclusion of the annual exclusion amount if the agent dies while still acting. Avoidance of even that exposure would require that the agent's authority to make distributions to the agent be limited with a §2041(b)(1)(A) ascertainable standard or that some other party be granted the exclusive power to make distributions to the agent.[54]

(Footnote Continued)

See, e.g., Treas. Reg. §20.2041-3(c)(1). Furthermore, it is especially problematic to argue that a joint power exists if the principal is incompetent, particularly under a springing power in which the agent's authority did not exist until the principal in reality was unable to exercise the power to challenge the agent (although it is true that, in other respects, it is the existence of the power and not the ability to exercise it that is relevant).

[54] Beware, however, the use of reciprocal powers, by which one agent can make gifts to a second agent, who can make gifts to the first agent, because the government might argue that the reciprocal trust doctrine applies to ignore that artifice. See §§7.3.2 and 12.1 nn.14-17 and accompanying text, respectively, for a discussion of the reciprocal trust doctrine in the context of annual exclusion gifts and for §2041 purposes.

§3.10.4.3

Additional protection ought to be added to preclude the agent from making any distribution that would have the effect of discharging the agent's own legal obligation to support any other person, precluding the agent from satisfying any contractual obligations as well, preventing the agent from exercising any powers of appointment available to the principal that include the agent in the class of permissible appointees, precluding the agent from making any distributions that would decrease the powerholder or a beneficiary's entitlement to public benefits, and precluding the agent from exercising any incidents of ownership over insurance on the agent's life owned by the principal.[55] In short, all precautions that would be taken in naming an individual as trustee of the principal's living trust should be exercised in naming an agent under a durable power with respect to the principal's affairs.

In addition, tenure of the agent and the extent of the agent's discretion should be considered in the same manner as in designating an individual as trustee. For example, if the principal's spouse is named as agent, it may be appropriate to terminate the durable power if they become estranged, separated, or divorced. Family harmony should be considered if, for examles, one of several children is to be agent, and questions of control over various aspects of the principal's life and assets might be addressed by naming different agents for different functions. Thus, for example, a child who is running the family business might have power over activities relating to that endeavor, while another is charged with control over the management of other property, and perhaps a third might govern health care decisions.

Finally, several good lessons can be learned from TAM 9601002, in which the government might legitimately have questioned execution of a power of attorney granting the attorney in fact specific power to make annual exclusion gifts, or the method by which that authority was exercised (a withdrawal of $170,000 from a revocable inter vivos trust created by the decedent, followed by a transfer to an irrevocable inter vivos trust created by the attorney in fact that granted Crummey clause

---

[55] Regarding drafting in general that precludes the agent from possessing any authority that would cause inclusion in the agent's gross estate, see Pennell, Estate Planning: Drafting and Tax Considerations in Employing Individual Trustees, 60 N.C. L. Rev. 799 (1982), abridged and reprinted in 9 Est. Plan. 264 (1982), most of which is directly on point with respect to the appointment of any individual as a fiduciary or an agent, and see §§ 12.3.2.4 and 12.4.2.

§ 3.10.4.3

powers of withdrawal to permissible donees identified in the durable power; the TAM did not indicate the terms of the irrevocable trust if those powers of withdrawal were not exercised or whether the overall mechanism was consistent with the gifting authority granted by the durable power). It did not, however, and the flaw that scuttled the premortem planning was not inadequate authority in the durable power of attorney to make premortem gifts, as so often is the case.

Instead, the TAM focused on the fact that the revocable inter vivos trust instrument specified that the power of withdrawal reserved by the decedent as settlor "must be exercised solely by [the decedent] and may not be exercised by any other person, including any agent or conservator." Finding that this provision made a withdrawal on behalf of the decedent under the durable power of attorney invalid under the express terms of the trust, the TAM concluded (although in not so many words) that the withdrawn amounts were includible, asserting without elaboration that § 2038 was applicable. Presumably the theory was that the withdrawn amounts were subject to a power of recall, in that the trust had a cause of action against the attorney in fact for making an unauthorized withdrawal.

There was no discussion of the fact that the decedent was the trustee, that the power of attorney gave the attorney in fact the power to do all acts that the decedent could do and ratified any actions taken by the attorney in fact, and that a cause of action in this situation probably lay in the trust beneficiaries against the decedent as trustee for allowing the unauthorized withdrawal. Because of the ratification, there might be an argument that the decedent had no rights against the attorney in fact and therefore had a liability to the trust beneficiaries with no matching cause of action against the attorney in fact, which would reduce the decedent's gross estate by an amount equal to the value of the cause of action the government relied upon to cause inclusion under § 2038. The important point is that the durable power and the trust were not coordinated properly to guarantee the success of the premortem transfers designed to take advantage of the annual exclusion, illustrating that drafting the durable power is not the sole focus for effective planning in this arena.

§ 3.10.4.3

§3.10.4.4 Execution

Durable powers of attorney must comply with state law dictates, which vary at least as much as the state law requirements for execution of a living or a property will. Because it is difficult to know with certainty in which states a durable power might be employed (for example, to convey real property or reregister stocks with a transfer agent in another jurisdiction) or the law that will be applied,[56] it is advisable that a durable power be executed with at least the same formalities as a property will, using universal will execution formalities.[57] This will cause no significant added burdens if the durable power will be signed at the same time a property will is executed. In addition, because some states may impose greater requirements for execution of the durable power of attorney, it is necessary to inspect and comply with state law in the state of execution and advisable to comply with any special requirements in other jurisdictions in which the power likely will be employed. For example, if the power can be used to convey real estate, it would be prudent to execute the durable power in compliance with the deed execution and recording formalities of the state in which the land is located.

A generic execution provision appropriately would specify that the principal is of sound mind and legal capacity, understands the extent of the powers granted to the agent, signs willingly, and is free of duress or undue influence. In addition to the principal's signature, it would be wise to include the principal's social security number, the agent's signature,

---

[56] Restatement (Second) of Conflict of Laws § 291 (1971) provides that validity of the power itself is determined by the law of the state that has the most significant relation to the parties and the transaction with respect to the particular issue involved. Usually that is the jurisdiction in which the power is executed. But § 292 specifies that the validity of an agent's acts typically is determined by the law of the state in which the agent acts, which could be the locus of realty that is the subject of a transaction or the agent's domicile with respect to transactions involving intangibles. Because it could be questioned where an agent acts with respect to a particular transaction, the well drafted power of attorney should include a choice of law provision. Even the protection of a governing law provision may not be enforceable, however, if the law selected is deemed to violate a strong public policy of the state that would be the default state in the absence of a choice of law provision and that state has a materially greater interest than the state whose law was chosen with respect to the particular issue. Restatement (Second) of Conflict of Laws § 187(2)(b) (1971).

[57] See § 3.1.1.

and to then have both signatures guaranteed by a bank or trust company or a stock exchange member firm whose guarantee is known to transfer agents. Three witnesses should sign an affidavit like that found in a property will, recounting that everyone signed in the presence of all other signatories and that the witnesses signed at the principal's request, that each witness is of legal capacity, is not the principal's agent or otherwise disqualified by interest, but nevertheless that each witness is acquainted with the principal who, according to each witness, appeared to be of sound mind and legal capacity and was not acting under duress or undue influence. Although not necessarily required, notarization like a property will also is advisable.

In some cases, depending on the likely use of the power and the demands of third parties, it might be prudent to cause multiple original copies to be executed, or to specify that third parties will be held harmless if they rely on a photocopy. However, the use of photocopies makes it more difficult to revoke the power with the certainty that additional copies are not being used and relied upon by third parties, so some deliberation should be given to these factors. In some conspicuous place, such as where all these execution formalities are presented and therefore where a third party presumably will focus attention, the document also might authorize or even instruct the agent to seek judicial relief or damages if a third party refuses to honor the power of attorney. Finally, like a durable power of attorney for health care, the durable power should be updated or republished periodically if possible, particularly because some third parties tend to discount or refuse to honor powers of attorney that have become stale. This option no longer is available once the principal becomes incompetent, and many clients will not comply with a refresher recommendation anyway. So it probably will be more useful to specify in the enforceability provision that age of the power is not relevant to its validity and to underscore the agent's authority or direction to pursue legal enforceability if a third party refuses to honor the power on any grounds.

4

Trusts as Estate Planning Instruments

§4.0 INTRODUCTION

Trusts are marvelous devices that provide the mainstay for modern estate planning. As a legal entity, nothing serves as many functions for estate planners as trusts, because settlors literally may write their own rules. The trustee's duties and the beneficiaries' interests may effect any purpose that is neither illegal nor against public policy.

> The purposes for which we can create trusts are as unlimited as our imagination. There are no technical rules restricting their creation. . . . Through the trust it is possible to separate the benefits of ownership from the burdens of ownership. . . . Trusts enable us to create successive interests that would be difficult . . . to create with successive legal interests . . . [and] to protect the beneficiaries' enjoyment of their interests by making them inalienable and putting them beyond the reach of creditors.[1]

This chapter explores the benefits of trusts employed for estate planning purposes. In the process it compares the legal consequences of trusts to those of wills. A will almost always is a necessary component in an estate plan that disposes of all of an individual's wealth. Thus, this comparison does not anticipate a selection between alternatives. Rather, it provides a foundation to determine whether and to what extent trusts effectively may supplement wills for property disposition purposes. And it informs the planning process when both might be useful.

Although many trusts are created by wills (testamentary trusts), this comparison concentrates primarily on the advantages of trusts created during the settlor's life (inter vivos or living trusts) as a supplement to the package of estate planning documents that often includes a will, an advance directive for health care, a living will, an organ donor designation, and perhaps a durable power of attorney for property management. Thus, the legal consequences considered here relate principally to the period when the settlor is alive and thereafter before administration of the settlor's estate ends. Less attention is devoted in this chapter to the balance of the trust's existence-which could be for as long as the Rule permits.

---

[1] **§4.0** Scott, Fratcher, & Ascher, Scott and Ascher on Trusts § 1.1 at 4 (5th ed. 2006).

§4.0

§4.1 THE USE OF TRUSTS IN ESTATE PLANNING

Although estate planners often tend to think in tax terms, the nontax oriented reasons for using trusts probably are twice as numerous and, as periodic tax reforms continue to illustrate, the nontax reasons are the ones that most likely will endure.

Historically, trusts evolved to accomplish objectives that otherwise were impossible to achieve, such as circumvention of feudal duties or restraints on alienation. Their continued viability for related purposes today should not be overlooked. For example, as compared to the procedure that must be followed in altering a will, use of any trust format as the settlor's primary estate planning document (coupled with a pour over will) permits easier amendment of the plan during the settlor's continued life.

Restrictions imposed by state law on the freedom of testation[1] that apply only to probate assets may be circumvented by using a trust to avoid probate. Further, to the extent those restrictions are not limited by one state's laws to probate assets, they can be minimized by placing the property in a trust that is subject to more favorable laws of another state.[2] Clients who want interstate or transnational mobility in their affairs also may find trusts to be more transportable than other forms of property ownership.

Trusts also provide for voluntary property management with more flexibility than is available with other devices, such as durable powers of attorney that preserve the agent's powers beyond incompetence of the principal.[3] Indeed, due to their flexibility, trusts often prove to be the answer when more conventional business devices (for example, a bailment or escrow) prove too inflexible.

The beauty of trusts is that they permit the creation of unique relations and the ability to tailor the agreement to govern the engagement. A good example of this is tort litigation settlement trusts that allow the parties to lawsuits to settle on terms notwithstanding significant differences of opinion regarding such damage recovery elements as the

---

[1] **§4.1** For example, S's statutory entitlements. See §4.3.

[2] With respect to the conflict of law applications of this planning, see §4.3.2.

[3] See §3.10.4.

plaintiff's life expectancy or expected medical care costs. In such a case a defendant may agree to fund a trust with a certain amount of money to provide defined benefits for the balance of the plaintiff's life, with a reversion to the defendant at the plaintiff's death. If the funding proves to be excessive, as the defendant may assume, all the defendant has lost is use of the money, but the plaintiff is protected by a fund that potentially is large enough to take care of all anticipated needs, with a sufficient cushion for an optimistic life expectancy or a pessimistic medical cost prognosis.

§4.1.1 Flexibility and Dead Hand Control

More to the point for estate planning purposes, trusts also permit the imposition of either attractive or reprehensible (depending on who you represent) "dead hand" controls over the future use of property. Limited in most cases only by the rule against perpetuities, a settlor essentially may tie the hands of several generations of beneficiaries. The settlor can assure the accomplishment or avoidance of certain uses, or reward or punish certain conduct, all limited only by any prohibition against restrictions or conditions on use that violate public policy. For example, a total restriction on a beneficiary's first marriage might be invalid,[4] but a lesser restraint or a forfeiture of benefits upon a remarriage may be respected.[5] Coupled with judicious use of powers of appointment, trustee discretion, and trust protector provisions, flexibility to adapt uses to changing conditions also is attainable.

Although there are circumstances in which a settlor's unbending desires should be mandated in a trust that may last several generations, the key to most effective estate planning is providing flexibility to adapt to changing circumstances, whether those be family, tax, or other law or circumstantial developments. The most direct mechanism to provide for

---

[4] An excellent example of the conflict and differing opinions and policies involved is In re Estate of Feinberg, 919 N.E.2d 888 (Ill. 2009), rev'g 891 N.E.2d 549 (Ill. App. Ct. 2008), which ultimately ruled that a properly limited restraint (in that case to encourage grandchildren to marry within the Jewish faith) was valid, whereas an absolute prohibition against marriage (or, worse, a provision that encouraged divorce) might not be valid.

[5] See Restatement (Third) of Trusts § 29(c) and comment *j* thereto (2003), and Restatement (Second) of Property—Donative Transfers § 6.2 in particular and § § 5.1-10.2 (1983) with respect to restraints in general.

§ 4.1.1

change is a power to terminate, alter, or amend a trust, which can be reposed in almost anyone other than the settlor (and, if it is appropriate to avoid grantor trust income tax problems, other than the settlor's spouse). Thus, this power could be given to a committee, the fiduciary, or a trust protector. It also *could* be given to the trustee, although in some respects that defeats the "separation of powers" or check-and-balances nature of bifurcating this sort of authority. Whomever is the chosen holder of the authority to make changes, the issue then is to what extent and to reflect what kinds of circumstances the power should be granted, what to do with the trust property on a termination, and any tax exposure to the powerholder, especially if that person is a beneficiary.

A will (or testamentary trust) can be defeated in full only if all the beneficiaries agree not to probate the will in the first instance. But trusts can be made more finely adaptable with a number of surgical approaches. For example, common are "small trust" termination provisions, allowing the fiduciary to terminate a trust if the fees being incurred are excessive in relation to the income generated by the trust. Less common but more important in long term trusts are provisions permitting termination in the trustee's discretion, based on factors such as impossibility to accomplish the trust purposes (e.g., to prevent trust assets from being counted in the determination of a beneficiary's need for public benefits, or creditor protection through an off-shore trust rather than spendthrift trust provisions), accomplishment of trust purposes (e.g., providing education, or assuring support for an incapacitated beneficiary), or a change in the law or circumstances making the trust purpose no longer relevant (e.g., protection of assets from a since repealed wealth transfer tax).

An intermediate level of authority is what some planners refer to as a "decanting" power—the authority of a trustee to pour the contents of an existing trust into a new trust with slight variations[6] in terms or

---

[6] The constraint to "slight" changes is a function of the conceptual underpinning of decanting itself, which is that a trustee with the power to make corpus distributions outright to a beneficiary may instead make those distributions into another trust for the benefit of that beneficiary. Based on an analog to the exercise of a nongeneral power of appointment, which also permits appointment in further trust, as authorized by Restatement (Third) of Property (Wills and Other Donative Transfers) § 19.14 (2011), the notion is that the power does not

powers. This approach may be useful to change the situs (and thus the state income taxation) of a trust, moving it from a tax-expensive jurisdiction to a tax haven, or to obtain flexibility under governing laws that are more amenable to the trust. Without express authority under the terms of the original trust, or under state law,[7] any meaningful change in any beneficiary's interest may cause income and wealth transfer tax consequences, as if the beneficiary whose interest is diminished (but who did not object) made a gift when the right to challenge the change lapsed.[8] As a consequence, any available trust modification or reformation may be a preferable avenue for change.

The extent of any permissible change should be made clear, such as in terms of beneficiaries that may be added or affected (e.g., only the settlor's blood relatives and their spouses), powers of appointment that

---

(Footnote Continued)

allow the trustee to change the beneficiaries or their beneficial interests. Thus, the trust-to-trust conversion must protect the basic beneficial interests while improving trust administration or taxation.

Notice 2011-101, 2011-2 C.B. 932, requested comments regarding trust decanting if trust beneficial interests are affected. (Apparently the government is not focused on transfers that only change trust administration provisions or affect state taxation of the trust or its beneficiaries.) The Notice specifically invited comments regarding the relevance and effect of various facts and circumstances that may affect one or more federal tax consequences, including (1) trust beneficial interests in principal or income are added, deleted, or changed, (2) income tax grantor trust status is altered, (3) the trust term is extended, (4) the identity of the donor or transferor for gift or GST tax purposes is changed, and (5) whether the trust is GST chronologically exempt or has a zero inclusion ratio. These items highlight the government's concerns and the Notice specifies that no further PLRs will issue with respect to transfers that change beneficial interests or the applicable rule against perpetuities period, which means that taxpayers must fly blind during the current silent phase.

[7] As of 2012, the following state laws were known to allow decanting: Alaska Stat. § 13.36.157; Ariz. Rev. Stat. Ann. § 14-10819; 12 Del. Code § 3528; Fla. Stat. Ann. § 736.04117(1)(a); Indiana Code § 30-4-3-36; Mo. Rev. Stat. § 456.4-419; Nev. Rev. Stat. § 163.556; N.H. Rev. Stat. § 564-B:4-418; N.Y. E.P.T.L. § 10-6.6; N.C. Gen. Stat. § 36C-8-816.1; Ohio Rev. Code § 5808.18; S.D. Codified L. § 55-2-15; Tenn. Code Ann. § 35-15-816(b); Va. Code § 55-548.16:1.

[8] See Culp & Mellen, Trust Decanting: An Overview and Introduction to Creative Planning Opportunities, 45 Real Prop., Prob. & Trust J. 1 (2010); Halperin & O'Donnell, Modifying Irrevocable Trusts: State Law and Tax Considerations in Trust Decanting, 42 U. Miami Inst. Est. Plan. ¶ 1300 (2008).

§ 4.1.1

may be granted or withdrawn (e.g., for GST purposes), changes to accomplish or preclude certain consequences (e.g., causing grantor trust income tax exposure to the settlor of an inter vivos trust, eliminating or altering a source of wealth transfer taxation to a beneficiary or fiduciary, elimination of a spendthrift clause to permit beneficiaries to transfer their interests, or tinkering with a vesting provision to avoid violation of the Rule), to conform to new laws (e.g., increased federal security law reporting requirements), and provisions that under no circumstances may be altered (e.g., anything that would cause loss of the marital deduction or a zero inclusion ratio in an exempt generation-skipping trust, provisions relating to the identity and accountability of fiduciaries,[9] or the provision under which all these changes are authorized).

---

[9] The Uniform Trust Code imposes various mandatory restrictions and reporting requirements that may not be altered. In some cases, these provisions apply retroactively to pre-existing trusts, which are not excepted. See, e.g., UTC §§ 813(a) (duty to respond to beneficiary requests for information about a trust), 813(b)(3) (duty to notify trust beneficiaries of the existence of an irrevocable trust), and 1106(a). Zimmerman v. Zirpolo Trust, 2012 WL 346657 (Ohio Ct. App. 2012), applied the Ohio version of § 813(a) to a pre-enactment trust without even discussing the retroactive application of the mandate to provide information to a current beneficiary, in that case notwithstanding express language in the trust that "the Trustee shall . . . provide no information about the trust proceeds to the beneficiaries . . . until they are entitled to receive the proceeds."

As of late in 2010, nearly a dozen states—roughly half of the states that had adopted the UTC—had altered either § 813 disclosure rule, allowing a settlor to override these reporting or notice provisions. Presumably any other person with the power to alter the trust could override them, also. In Wilson v. Wilson, 690 S.E.2d 710 (N.C. Ct. App. 2010), both state law and the trust itself modified the mandate to provide information to beneficiaries or any court. The court held this modification to be invalid, saying that a "beneficiary is always entitled to such information as is reasonably necessary to . . . enforce . . . rights under the trust or to prevent or redress a breach of trust." Information that is "reasonably necessary to enable [beneficiaries] to enforce their rights under the trust" cannot be withheld and no state law or document may "override the duty of the trustee to act in good faith, nor can [either] obstruct the power of a court to" prevent or redress an abuse, or to enforce the trust. "Any other conclusion renders the trust unenforceable." And a trust simply cannot exist without the ability to enforce a trustee's fiduciary duties.

See 4.1.5 n.97 regarding a similar issue of enforceability and trust validity, presented by binding arbitration provisions that some drafters include in trusts and that state courts may find to be invalid because they similarly impede a beneficiary's right to enforce rights under the trust.

§ 4.1.1

In addition, procedures for exercise should be established (e.g., only independent fiduciaries may act, only with the approval of a court of competent jurisdiction, and only to accomplish a reduction of taxes or a furtherance of the settlor's objectives). State statutory or judicial authority to reform a trust-particularly the nonadministrative or nonministerial aspects-may be too restrictive. So this kind of provision should be considered for inclusion in any trust that will have an extended duration or in which other forms of providing flexibility (e.g., powers of appointment) will not be effective or appropriate. The key is that trusts permit this kind of engineering for future adaptations.[10]

Reformation is a growing but localized trend and the circumstances in which it typically is granted are somewhat monochromatic, with many cases making changes seeking to minimize or avoid the GST.[11] Most

---

[10] Restatement (Third) of Property (Wills and Other Donative Transfers) § 12.2 (2003) and UTC § § 410-417 are modeled after various cases or legislative provisions in numerous jurisdictions and would cement the state law authority to alter trust provisions. Most reformations do not run afoul of the Claflin doctrine discussed in § 3.8 n.2 and accompanying text, which precludes premature termination (prior to fulfillment of the settlor's objectives), although at the extreme edges reformation may present that issue. See, e.g., In re Estate of Somers, 89 P.3d 898 (Kan. 2004) (in the first state to adopt the UTC, the adopting state included a presumption that a spendthrift provision constitutes an unfulfilled purpose and, based thereon, termination but not modification was denied; UTC § 411(c) reverses that presumption, which likely will generate a different result in other adopting jurisdictions, although In re The Pike Family Trusts, 38 A.3d 329 (Me. 2012), recognized that—even lacking the traditional presumption—a court may conclude that a spendthrift provision is a material purpose of the settlor; in *Pike* the trustee simply failed to establish that case). Adoption of enabling legislation may be the future trend, so readers should investigate local law for favorable legislative developments.

Not incidentally, these authorities come on the heels of the almost total abandonment of the privity defense to malpractice liability of a drafting attorney, which makes reformation a useful protection against exposure. After all, mistakes do happen, and these days disappointed beneficiaries are not so reluctant to sue. With respect to malpractice in general see § 1.0 n.12 et seq. and accompanying text. It also follows behind the mass marketing of poorly drafted trusts by "trust mill" operators, with postmortem efforts to rectify the messes left behind. See generally Dobris, Changes in the Role and the Form of the Trust at the New Millennium, or, We don't Have to Think of England Anymore, 62 Albany L. Rev. 543, 565 (1998).

[11] See § 11.4.8 n.266.

§ 4.1.1

other cases still are directed at tax minimization.[12] Unusual about In re

---

[12] See, e.g., PLRs 200615025 (reformation of a defectively drafted provision via decanting—pouring one trust into another), 200043036 (government respected local court's correction of a document in which marital and nonmarital trust provisions inadvertently were transposed), and 9805025 (respecting a lower state court reformation to correct scrivener's error by converting general power of appointment in a nonmarital trust into a nongeneral power), Dwyer v. Dwyer, 898 N.E.2d 504 (Mass. 2008) (reformation to convert a general power of appointment into a nongeneral power, and to limit certain trustee powers); Grassian v. Grassian, 835 N.E.2d 607 (Mass. 2005) (reformation to adapt to changes in state death tax), and Wright v. Weber, 768 N.E.2d 545 (Mass. 2002) (granting an increase in what appeared to be a gift tax annual exclusion motivated withdrawal power, but refusing to include a hanging power variety of limitation); Walker v. Walker, 744 N.E.2d 60 (Mass. 2001) (same except highest state court in expedited proceeding granted the appropriate relief by reformation to add an ascertainable standard to limit the otherwise general power to appoint); Carlson v. Sweeney, Dabagia, Donoghue, Thorne, Janes & Pagos, 895 N.E.2d 1191 (Ind. 2008) (dicta in a legal malpractice case, the state's highest court affirming reformation of trust language to strictly ascertainable standards); Hillman v. Hillman, 744 N.E.2d 1078 (Mass. 2001) (reformation to preclude child's exercise of inter vivos power to appoint corpus to settlor's "issue" from including the child personally); Seegel v. Miller, 820 N.E.2d 809 (Mass. 2005) (reformation to embrace equitable apportionment that absolved a marital deduction bequest from a tax payment obligation and therefore avoided reduction of the deduction); Barker v. Barker, 853 N.E.2d 1057 (Mass. 2006) (reformation of tax payment provision to avoid § 2042(1) inclusion); In re Estate of Robinson, 720 So. 2d 540 (Fla. Ct. App. 1998) (reformation of tax payment direction to change from payment before division into marital and nonmarital bequests to provide instead for division followed by payment from the nonmarital alone); Fleet Nat'l Bank v. Wajda, 750 N.E.2d 923 (Mass. 2001) (reformation of tax payment direction to change to payment before creation of CRT); Fleet Bank v. Fleet Bank, 706 N.E.2d 627 (Mass. 1999) (pour over of nonmarital bequest into S's trust "as amended" reformed to limit changes to only those made prior to D's death, to prevent S from having a general power of appointment through that power to amend); Freedman v. Freedman, 834 N.E.2d 251 (Mass. 2005) (reformation to remove powers retained by the settlor in an effort to reduce exposure to § 2036(a)(2) inclusion); Bilafer v. Bilafer, 73 Cal. Rptr. 2d 880 (Cal. Ct. App. 2008) (notwithstanding the default rule in California, as noted in § 4.2.2 (6th ed.), the settlor's trust was expressly made irrevocable and the settlor retained no beneficial interest, but the court nevertheless affirmed the settlor's standing to petition to reform the trust to comport with the settlor's original intent and cure drafter's errors); McCance v. McCance, 868 N.E.2d 611 (Mass. 2007) (restoration of a power to assign the lead beneficiaries' interest to the remainder beneficiary in a CRUT); Ratchin v. Ratchin, 792 N.E.2d 116 (Mass. 2003) (accelerated distribu-

Kamp[13] was that reformation was conversion of an incompetent's mandatory income interest into a discretionary entitlement, to qualify the trust as a SNT, which the court stated was consistent with state law and policy, and in which the state enforcement authorities (like the Internal Revenue Service in federal tax matters) did not make an appearance. In re Rappaport[14] was similar and also reformed a mandatory income interest, creating instead a discretionary entitlement, notwithstanding an appearance by the state authority, which objected to the reformation. The court granted the motion stating that it was state policy "to encourage the creation of supplemental needs trusts to enhance the quality of a disabled individual's life without jeopardizing Medicaid eligibility." The Riddell[15] case also allowed consolidation and reformation of trusts to create a SNT for an incompetent remainder beneficiary under "equitable deviation" standards, saying that any economic loss to the state should not be factored into the court's determination.

The unresolved issue in the state court in many of these cases is whether the government will be bound. Commissioner v. Estate of Bosch[16] indicates that, short of adjudication by the highest court of the state, the federal government may not be bound, although retroactive

---

(Footnote Continued)

tion of a portion of a CRT to cause the balance of the trust to meet the 5% minimum annual annuity distribution requirement); Putnam v. Putnam, 682 N.E.2d 1351 (Mass. 1997) (reformation of CRUT to add a net income limitation; compare PLRs 200601024 and 200649027, both indicating courts made similar reformations but the latter denying tax recognition of the change because it was found that "the judicial reformation . . . was not due to a scrivener's error" but instead was based on changes in investment climate that frustrated the trust's original intended purpose); Dassori v. Patterson, 802 N.E.2d 553 (Mass. 2004), and Pond v. Pond, 678 N.E.2d 1321 (Mass. 1997) (reformations to garner marital deduction by creating a qualifying income interest for S); Florez v. Florez, 803 N.E.2d 323 (Mass. 2004) (reformation to prevent merger of two trusts to minimize GST, but denial of request to add a general power of appointment, presumably to attract a cheaper FET instead of GST); Van Riper v. Van Riper, 834 N.E.2d 239 (Mass. 2005) (reformation to a QPRT to provide a reversion to the settlor if death occurred within the reserved term); Simches v. Simches, 671 N.E.2d 1226 (Mass. 1996) (reformation of QPRT to avoid GST); and cases cited in each.

[13] 790 N.Y.S.2d 852 (Surr. Ct. 2005).

[14] 866 N.Y.S.2d 483, 487 (Surr. Ct. 2008).

[15] 157 P.3d 888 (Wash. Ct. App. 2007).

[16] 387 U.S. 456 (1967).

§ 4.1.1

reformations rather than mere interpretations favorable to the taxpayer may provide protection as if the trust never contained the undesirable provision. DiCarlo v. Mazzarella[17] is interesting in its recognition that failure to reform an improper income provision would cause a loss of the marital deduction, which would generate unnecessary estate taxes that would reduce the corpus available to provide income to care for S, which was D's primary intent. Essentially that same argument was embraced by the court in Estate of Ellingson v. Commissioner[18] to favorably interpret a marital deduction trust to qualify for the deduction under federal law.[19]

In re Trust D[20] is nearly unique in refusing to grant the taxpayer's requested reformation even though no beneficiary objected, based on the court's own determination that rights of beneficiaries were negatively affected. Kirchick v. Guerry[21] also refused to grant the taxpayer's relief because it was solely for tax avoidance purposes, even though the reformation would not have affected the rights of any of the parties. Also unusual about *Kirchick* was that the federal government actually appeared and filed a brief requesting that the court not act.[22] Breakiron v. Guidonis[23] similarly involved the very unusual appearance of the federal government and the court ruled in the taxpayer's favor notwithstanding the tax motives underlying the requested ruling.

If qualified individuals are expected to exercise powers to terminate, alter, or amend a trust, the document should provide standards or criteria that supply guidance in the exercise of discretion, along with exoneration and indemnification from liability to any disgruntled benefi-

---

[17] 717 N.E.2d 257 (Mass. 1999).

[18] 964 F.2d 959 (9th Cir. 1992).

[19] See § § 13.5.2.2 n.30 and n.82 and accompanying text.

[20] 234 P.3d 793 (Kan. 2010).

[21] 706 N.E.2d 702 (Mass. 1999) (seeking a determination of the date of creation of a trust for pre-1942 general power of appointment tax issues).

[22] PLR 200848009 is unusual in that the taxpayer obtained a local court's interpretation of a trust provision that clearly was wrong and that was totally tax motivated (regarding a formula pecuniary bequest to shelter the GST exemption as if it was a fractional division, to avoid gain on funding and to pick up a share of postmortem appreciation) and that the government properly refused to honor.

[23] 2010-2 U.S. Tax Cas. (CCH) ¶ 60,597 (D. Mass. 2010).

ciary, either because the individual did or chose not to act.[24] If a committee or protector is acting in this capacity, the fiduciary also should be protected from liability for following their dictates. The document also should establish that the holder of any power to terminate, alter, or amend may relinquish the power if appropriate or necessary, and a provision should provide for appointment of successors to ensure that someone is in a position to exercise the powers that exist.[25]

---

[24] See, e.g., McLean Revocable Trust v. Patrick Davis, P.C., 283 S.W.3d 786 (Mo. Ct. App. 2009), involving a trust protector's alleged liability for failing to exercise the authority to remove and replace trustees and protect the trust from maladministration. Conflict of interest concerns were lurking in the background for both legal ethics (the protector was an attorney who was involved in litigation that resulted in creation of the trust) and fiduciary liability purposes. The trust document provided that "[t]he Trust Protector's authority hereunder is conferred in a fiduciary capacity and shall be so exercised, but the Trust Protector shall not be liable for any action taken in good faith." The protector claimed that state law imposed no duties on a trust protector and that there was no duty to supervise the trustees, nor to monitor or direct them, and therefore no liability for any trustee malfeasance. According to the court, lacking any duties imposed by state law, the question would turn on whether the document generated any duties. Although the court did not opine as to what those duties might be, it did suggest that reference to "fiduciary capacity" implied "at least the basic duties of undivided loyalty and confidentiality . . . [and] the existence of at least some duty of care." UTC § 808(d) is similar, but state laws vary a good deal on the question. See, e.g., Alaska Stat. § 13.36.370(d), which provides that a trust protector is not a fiduciary unless the document provides otherwise, S.D. Codified L. § 55-1B-4 provides that a trust protector (acting as an investment advisor) is a fiduciary unless the document provides otherwise, and Mich. Comp. Laws Ann. § 700.7809(1)(a), N.H. Rev. Stat. Ann. § 564-B:12-1202 , and Va. Code § 55-548.08.E.1 all provide that the trust protector is a fiduciary, without exception.

The *McLean* opinion was confused regarding to whom any fiduciary duty of good faith was owed and who had standing to enforce the protector's liability. One option is to regard a trust protector's duties as flowing to the beneficiaries, but some drafters wish to relieve the protector of any such liability. In which case these issues need careful resolution. Drafters who use the trust protector concept need to define the role and better establish the liabilities that may be imposed. Particularly if the trust protector is *not* meant to be held to fiduciary standards, which is an option recognized by the comment to UTC § 808.

[25] For help in drafting provisions that permit the alteration of an existing document, see McBryde & Keydel, Back to the Future for the Estate Planner: Building Flexibility in Estate Planning Documents, 30 U. Miami Inst. Est. Plan. ¶ 1200 (1996), abridged and reprinted as Building Flexibility in Estate Planning

In addition to or instead of the dramatic power to terminate, alter, or amend an otherwise irrevocable trust, many lesser powers also may be appropriate in a given case. For example, authority to divide or consolidate trusts can be essential for effective, efficient, and equitable administration, as well as for tax purposes (e.g., allocation of GST exemption, partial QTIP elections, reverse QTIP elections, disclaimers, income tax avoidance of the §643(f) multiple trust rule or the §667(c) third trust rule, or to permit the S Corporation election with respect to shares held in trust). Consolidation may be relevant with respect to trusts created by different transferors for the same beneficiary and with the same trustee, as to which virtual identity of provisions might exist (and might be essential for consolidation) but as to which the applicable period of the Rule likely differs with respect to each. Thus, authority to round 'em up may require authority in a trustee to distribute trust assets to another trust, created specifically for this purpose, rather than to just consolidate assets from various trusts or shares. In this respect, the issue is the

---

(Footnote Continued)

Documents, 135 Trusts & Estates 56 (Jan. 1996). Regarding the function and role of trust protectors in particular see 3 Scott, Fratcher & Ascher, Scott and Ascher on Trusts § 16.7 (5th ed. 2007) (on powers to direct and control trustees); Bove, The Trust Protector: Friend or Fiduciary?, in Asset Protection Strategies, Wealth Preservation Planning with Domestic and Offshore Entities (Vol. II 2005); Bove, The Trust Protector: Trust(y) Watchdog or Expensive Exotic Pet?, 30 Est. Plan. 390 (2003) (discussing, among other important issues, whether the trust protector is a fiduciary with correspondent duties and liabilities, and the extent to which trust instrument language can alter those fundamental characteristics and implications); Bove, Asset Protection Strategies: Planning With Domestic and Offshore Entities (Vol. I 2002); Ruce, The Trustee and the Trust Protector: A Question of Fiduciary Power. Should a Trust Protector Be Held to a Fiduciary Standard?, 59 Drake L. Rev. 67 (2010), and authorities cited in each.

In addition to matters noted in text, drafting specifics noted by Bove include: (a) the positive and negative powers granted—such as to approve or veto trustee investments and distributions, or self-dealing or other otherwise prohibited activity, to add or remove beneficiaries or trustees, to amend or terminate the trust, or to change trust situs or governing law; (b) rights of the protector—such as to resign, to compensation, to recover costs, to hire counsel or agents, or to access trust records—and protections (if any) from liability; and (c) allocation of duties as between the trustee and the protector, the trustee's right to information from the protector, and the trustee's rights, duties, and liability if the protector performs improperly or improperly fails to perform within a designated period of time.

extent of the trustee's discretion in selecting appropriate vehicles for distribution or to create a new trust to be the recipient of a distribution from one or more other trusts. To this last extent the trustee would be able effectively to alter or amend the terms of any of the trusts that will make terminating distributions to the newly created trust and then go out of their own separate existence.

Matters such as control, consolidated administration, and risk management sometimes motivate families with multiple trusts (often with different family member settlors) and sufficient resources to create a captive trustee—a private trust company. The difficult aspect of this only begins when planners attempt to navigate the state and federal regulations that may govern the creation and operation of such an entity. More important often is the question whether tax consequences will be altered by family involvement in or control over the fiduciary. In an unusual approach the government issued Notice 2008-63,[26] which is labeled as a "proposed" revenue ruling, available for comment, much like regulations are issued in proposed form. It constitutes a "first draft" of guidance to taxpayers who wish to create a private or family controlled trust company.

Although not without a few flaws, which have delayed issuance of the ruling itself, the general drift of the guidance provided by the Notice is amenable to taxpayers who may avoid untoward income or wealth transfer tax consequences by following a number of easy prescriptions. Remember, however, that these notions may change when the promised revenue ruling finally is released, but for now, as examples, consider:

• A "discretionary distribution committee" (DDC) that controls all discretionary distributions of income or principal will insulate family members from liability if "no member of the DDC may participate in the activities of the DDC with regard to any trust of which that DDC member or his or her spouse is a grantor, or . . . , a beneficiary . . . [or] with respect to any . . . beneficiary to whom the DDC member or his or her spouse owes a legal obligation of support." This does not necessarily address distributions for the support of a beneficiary to whom the grantor (or the grantor's spouse) owes a legal obligation, which can be a common concern in any inter vivos trust and is not unique to the identity of DDC members or the trustee.

---

[26] 2008-2 C.B. 261.

§4.1.1

- "No Family member may enter into any reciprocal agreement, express or implied, regarding discretionary distributions from any trust for which [the private trust company] is serving as trustee" (although "reciprocal agreement" is not defined, presumably this constitutes a broad prescription against any "I'll-scratch-your-back-if-you-scratch-mine" style of vote-trading arrangement).

- Only officers and managers of the trust company may participate in personnel decisions (but family members may be officers and managers of the trust company without hazard).

- An independent "Amendment Committee," "a majority of whose members must always be individuals who are neither Family members nor persons related or subordinate . . . to any shareholder" of the private trust company, has the sole authority to make changes to the documents that govern the trust company. Requiring that the authority to change the governing documents be given to individuals who are not shareholders has been criticized as an unprecedented (and therefore potentially invalid) form of corporate governance.

These prescriptions create barriers to individual participation in tax sensitive endeavors. Compliance means that the private trust company itself will not

- cause FET inclusion exposure under §§ 2036, 2038, or 2041 to family members;

- prevent completed gift treatment for transfers to a trust administered by the private trust company;

- alter GST exemptions and inclusion ratios; or

- affect otherwise applicable grantor trust income tax treatment.

The Subchapter J income tax consequences to trust grantors are the most convoluted:

- § 675 exposure turns (as is usual) on how fiduciary powers actually are exercised;

- § 677(b) exposure turns on whether distributions are made for the support or maintenance of someone the grantor is obliged to support or maintain (misstated in the draft by reference to actual use to discharge a support obligation—which is not the metric used by the Code but is the short-handed reference made by the Treasury Regulations and by most casual students of Subchapter J); and

- adverse party treatment will not be provided by the trust company or the DDC.

Interestingly, use of "ascertainable" or "reasonably definite external" standards is neither required nor useful (although one comment to the Notice suggests that any distribution that is so limited is not discretionary and that the discretionary distribution committee rules therefore should not apply). Acting as an employee or director of the private trust company is benign, and "voting control of [the private trust company] has been made irrelevant as it applies to the power to make distributions from the Family trusts. . . . Thus, the ownership of voting stock should not be deemed to be 'significant' under section 672(c)" and, instead, is relevant only to the extent it gives control over discretionary distributions. Thus, §672(c) related or subordinate party treatment is avoided unless more than half the members of the DDC may be nonadverse parties who are related or subordinate to the grantor. In essence, membership on the DDC is the functional equivalent of service as fiduciary, so in virtually every respect looking at the DDC members is more important than looking at control of the private trust company proper.

The point here is that flexibility is important, particularly the longer an estate plan will last. Various mechanisms exist to provide it if a trust is the primary vehicle in the plan, including powers of appointment, flexible trust distribution provisions, and powers to terminate, alter, or amend trust provisions.[27] It ought to be possible in most cases to provide whatever degree of flexibility the settlor wants or feels comfortable providing.

§4.1.2 Bifurcated Enjoyment

Trusts permit a sharing or bifurcation of enjoyment in myriad contexts. For example, a group or "pot" trust for descendants provides flexibility and fairness, the way the settlor would use money if still alive, plus important GST minimization and deferral opportunities.[28] Distributions are made in the trustee's discretion among the class of beneficiaries, typically until all the settlor's children have received an education, followed by division of what remains into equal shares.

In a different setting, use of a trust to provide lifetime support of S while guaranteeing ultimate receipt of the remainder by children of a former marriage is an especially important consideration because all or a

---

[27] Depending on the settlor's confidence in the beneficiaries, the fiduciary, trust committees, or protectors, and on the drafter's ability.

[28] See §§11.4.1.2 and 11.4.2.

§4.1.2

substantial part of D's property may be made to qualify for the marital deduction without disinheriting the ultimate natural objects of D's bounty. Without the ability to control final distribution of this gift, D would be forced to choose between S and the children. The "handcuff" feature of a §2056(b)(7) QTIP trust permits lifetime enjoyment by S while assuring that designated remainder beneficiaries ultimately will receive the property.[29]

Bifurcation between present and future interest beneficiaries is not unique to trusts (a legal life estate and remainder disposition could be used instead). But trusts are more elegant, and the remainder beneficiaries enjoy better protections,[30] while the life tenant is freed from uncertainties that surround the permissible consumption or enjoyment of property subject to a legal life estate.

Other uses of trusts that involve dead hand control include providing support to a dependent beneficiary only until marriage, remarriage, or some other event that terminates the need for benefits; guaranteeing the support or education of various beneficiaries but providing for charity once those needs have been met; protecting a son- or daughter-in-law (the forgotten family members) after a child's death without diverting ultimate ownership from lineal descendants; permitting enjoyment by successive generations without fear of dissipation through profligacy, improvidence, or inexperience; creating incentives to encourage or discourage certain conduct; and providing benefits to individual beneficiaries whose financial peccadilloes or litigation exposure (such as the potential professional malpractice of a doctor or lawyer) make it likely

---

[29] See §§13.5.6 and 3.4.4 n.22, respectively, with respect to QTIP marital deduction trusts, and with respect to using trusts to avoid the claim of a surviving spouse.

[30] A striking (albeit not unique) illustration of this is Manson v. Shepherd, 116 Cal. Rptr. 3d 1 (Ca. App. Ct. 2010), in which S was trustee and income beneficiary of a trust, of which the primary asset was 100% of the stock of a company of which S also was President and Chair of the board of directors. The remainder beneficiaries were D's children by a former marriage. The company declared a partial liquidating distribution that S allocated 82% to the income account, which the court held should instead be allocated 100% to the trust corpus. A different trustee might have avoided the controversy entirely, but existence of the trust guaranteed that the children were protected in a way that likely would not have applied if D had given S a legal life estate (or any other disposition) in the stock.

§4.1.2

that outright ownership would expose the wealth to the claims of predators.[31]

§4.1.3 Property Management

Trusts also permit expert management-assuming a competent trustee (which need not mean a corporate fiduciary) is involved-and sometimes facilitate administration of property. To illustrate, consider the hassles of several beneficiaries' co-ownership of a life insurance policy or income producing property as joint tenants or as tenants in common, as opposed to a trustee's sole administration of that property on behalf of several trust beneficiaries. Fiduciary administration is especially useful in the context of a split purchase or ownership of property that normally would not be easy to administer if held in legal life estate and remainder form by two different parties. A good example might be commercial real estate that should be leased over a longer term than the present interest beneficiary's life expectancy, or mineral interests that may be leased over a similar extended period.

Trust administration also produces better management if the beneficiary either lacks the desire, experience, or ability to manage property, or is immature or improvident and cannot (yet) be trusted to manage property. At the other end of the spectrum, management of assets may be a relevant concern for elderly settlors beyond their most active years, as well as for their ultimate beneficiaries. An individual may reach a stage in life when day-to-day management of investment properties or business interests is more work or inconvenience than the individual wishes to assume, particularly involving record keeping and management decision making. Especially if the individual currently is utilizing some other form of asset management arrangement, such as an investment advisory or stock depository service. The same management benefits are available through the use of a durable power of attorney or a revocable living trust.

Thus, in a complex investment and economic environment, an individual with substantial assets may need management assistance available through either approach, but more so with a revocable living

---

[31] See McCue, Planning and Drafting to Influence Behavior, 34 U. Miami Inst. Est. Plan. ¶ 600 (2000) and § 4.1.4.

§ 4.1.3

trust that provides proper and professional asset management and application of funds for the individual's benefit. And, although durable powers of attorney can be useful in many cases, often third parties are not as willing to deal with a powerholder as they are with a trustee,[32] particularly if greater amounts of wealth are involved.

Individuals in need of professional assistance need not relinquish control of their property. Indeed, with a "springing" form of durable power of attorney the agent's powers may not become effective until certain conditions have occurred, such as the principal's incapacity,[33] and in a revocable living trust the settlor may act as trustee while able.[34]

Living trusts created for the settlor's own benefit may provide more certainty than durable powers of attorney (which themselves are more beneficial than a guardianship or other property management relationship)[35] and, unlike the durable power of attorney, trusts may continue after the settlor's death. And either arrangement can be amended, modified, or revoked at any time. Furthermore, trusts created for third

---

[32] See § 3.10.4.1.

[33] See § 3.10.4.2.

[34] See § 4.2.3.

[35] The state law ability of a guardian, conservator, or other personal representative to deal with the property of an incompetent ward usually is severely restricted, relative to the authority that may be granted to either a durable power holder or a trustee. State law will vary on questions such as the ability to exercise or relinquish powers of the ward, to alter the ward's existing estate plan, or to make gifts of the ward's property, usually determined under the state law substituted judgment doctrine. See, e.g., Millard v. United States, 84-2 U.S. Tax Cas. (CCH) ¶ 13,597 (S.D. Ill. 1984); Estate of Christiansen, 56 Cal. Rptr. 505 (1967); In re Labis, 714 A.2d 335 (N.J. Super. Ct. 1998); In re Shah, 733 N.E.2d 1093 (N.Y. 2000); In re John XX, 652 N.Y.S.2d 329 (App. Div. 1996); In re Trusteeship of Kenan, 138 S.E.2d 547 (N.C. 1964) (all authorizing actions designed to minimize taxes or qualify for state or federal benefits, based on factors such as the permanence of the ward's incapacity, wealth of the ward, relation of the objects of the planning to the ward, and other evidence of the ward's likely wishes if competent), but see Estate of Bettin v. Commissioner, 543 F.2d 1269 (9th Cir. 1976) (holding that approval of a court is required before any action may be undertaken). See generally Fliegelman & Fliegelman, Giving Guardians the Power to Do Medicaid Planning, 32 Wake Forest L. Rev. 341 (1997); Annot., Power of court or guardian to make noncharitable gifts or allowances out of funds of incompetent ward, 24 A.L.R.3d 863 (1969). See also § 3.10.4.3 regarding gifts made under the authority of a durable power of attorney.

parties simply provide more benefits and serve more needs with more flexibility than conservatorships or guardianships (which require court supervision and may limit the individuals who may be appointed),[36] or statutory arrangements (such as the UTMA[37] or its predecessor UGMA,[38] which cannot be tailored to fit specific needs and which terminate when the beneficiary reaches a designated age, usually 18 or 21).

If an individual is not yet ready to undertake the trust approach, it is possible to nominally fund a trust created currently and later transfer assets to the trust as the individual becomes more comfortable with it (or less capable of dealing with the property). In the process the trustee performs a trial run, allowing the settlor to assess the trustee's performance and to advise the trustee with respect to difficult administrative questions created by unusual assets. The key to this standby trust plan is for some other person to have a durable power of attorney[39] to transfer assets to the trust if the settlor becomes incompetent before the trust is fully funded. Because all actions pursuant to a power of attorney are subject to veto by the principal who granted the power, virtually anyone may be given this power without fear of giving them a general power of appointment for §2041 purposes and without the principal who grants the power fearing a loss of control or risk of being disfranchised by unauthorized acts (at least prior to becoming incapacitated, after which time any fiduciary, trustee or powerholder alike, must be trustworthy).[40]

---

[36] See, e.g., Fla. Stat. § 744.309(2) (nonresident may not serve unless related to ward. Compare UPC Art. V, which is substantially devoid of the types of restrictions normally found in state statutes.

[37] See 8C U.L.A. 1 (2001).

[38] See 8A U.L.A. 297 (2003).

[39] The power of attorney must be durable to prevent its lapse on the principal's incapacity. See § 3.10.4.

[40] Normally it would not be advisable for a trust to become irrevocable upon the settlor's incapacity because that might constitute a gift taxable event. Nor is it likely to be necessary, because state law probably precludes a personal representative (guardian or conservator) from acting on behalf of the settlor to exercise the settlor's retained power to revoke, unless the trust instrument grants that authority. 5 Scott, Fratcher, & Ascher, Scott and Ascher on Trusts §35.1 (5th ed. 2008). This also normally would not be desirable, because it would expose the settlor's well formulated plans to defeat at the hands of an appointed representa-

With respect to management of realty, a property owner may be liable for the cost to clean up polluted property, even if the owner had nothing to do with the contamination and knew nothing of it when the property was acquired.[41] Because this liability may extend to fiduciaries, many knowledgeable professionals refuse to accept property in an estate or trust unless an environmental audit has been conducted and a clean report has been received. If a landowner dies with probate realty and a will naming a professional personal representative, the lack of adequate notice and time to conduct the audit may cause the fiduciary to reject the appointment rather than be appointed and later learn it has a contaminated asset and liability on its hands. To ensure that property the decedent wants held in a fiduciary capacity will not produce such a response, it may be wise to create a living trust to hold the property and guarantee that a fiduciary is given adequate notice and an opportunity to inspect the property and will accept the appointment.[42]

Legislation adopted in 1996[43] exempts most garden-variety fiduciaries from most sources of personal liability for environmental torts attributable to assets held in a fiduciary capacity. The full quantum of assets of the fiduciary entity are subject to liability, but the fiduciary's liability is limited to those assets held in the fiduciary entity unless the fiduciary negligently caused or contributed to the environmental contamination.[44] Although the original property holder's entire estate may be

---

(Footnote Continued)

tive who was not selected by the settlor and who might act contrary to the settlor's wishes in that respect.

[41] See Comprehensive Environmental Response, Compensation and Liability Act of 1980 (CERCLA), 42 U.S.C. §§ 9601 et seq.

[42] But see § 4.1.11 regarding avoidance of CERCLA claims under a nonclaim statute available only by allowing the property to pass through probate.

[43] The Asset Conservation, Lender Liability, and Deposit Insurance Protection Act of 1996 added 42 U.S.C. § 9607(n); comparable provisions amended the Resource Conservation and Recovery Act, 42 U.S.C. §§ 6901-6992k, dealing with underground storage tanks and the handling, storage, and disposal of hazardous substances.

[44] Curiously, 42 U.S.C. § 9607(n)(3) precludes absolution of a fiduciary for its own negligence, and § 9607(n)(4)(I) provides that the fiduciary has no liability even if it declines to monitor or inspect the property. Not protected is a fiduciary acting with respect to an entity that was organized to engage in a trade or business for profit, not as part of an estate plan. 42 U.S.C. § 9607(n)(5)(A)(ii)(I).

§ 4.1.3

liable for the costs of any remediation, it may be that liability can be minimized with proper planning, such as by placing the potential risk property in a separate trust that would insulate other assets in the settlor's estate and that does not expose the fiduciary to personal liability. These precautions may be the only way to guard against a knowledgeable fiduciary's cautious rejection of a needed appointment.

§4.1.4 Asset Protection

A related but substantially more troublesome element of liability for toxic torts is the issue whether a landowner who is responsible for a CERCLA mandated clean up can insulate other assets from the risk of loss through seizure to pay for that compliance. And this raises the similar question whether any property owner may insulate assets from potential future liability to any claimant, such as trade or financial creditors or judgment holders from tort recoveries (such as from malpractice or hazardous business endeavors). Spendthrift trusts generally protect trust assets from the creditors of third party trust beneficiaries[45] and from other claimants.

With perhaps one controversial exception.[46] As America's premier trust law scholar of his time, Professor Scott advocated an involuntary tort creditors' exception to any spendthrift protection otherwise availa-

---

(Footnote Continued)

Nor is a fiduciary protected if the property was acquired in the fiduciary capacity for the "objective purpose" of avoiding liability. 42 U.S.C. §9607(n)(5)(A)(ii)(II). A fiduciary acting in a capacity other than as fiduciary or beneficiary and who benefits from the fiduciary entity or relationship also is not protected; there is no legislative history clarifying the meaning of this provision. 42 U.S.C. §9607(n)(7)(A). Finally, no protection is afforded to a fiduciary who also is a beneficiary of the same entity and who "receives benefits that exceed customary or reasonable compensation" as fiduciary. 42 U.S.C. §9607(n)(7)(B).

[45] See Restatement (Third) of Trusts §58 (2003) regarding traditional spendthrift protection. In most respects UTC §§502-503 address the same subject. Consult Newman, Spendthrift and Discretionary Trusts: Alive and Well Under the Uniform Trust Code, 40 Real Prop., Prob. & Tr. J. 567 (2005), for an extensive exegesis of the UTC and its minor differences from both the common law and the Restatement.

[46] See 3 Scott, Fratcher, & Ascher, Scott and Ascher on Trusts §15.5.5 (5th ed. 2007); Restatement (Second) of Trusts §151 et seq. (1959).

§4.1.4

ble. Sligh v. First Nat'l Bank[47] and In re Estate of Nagel[48] both allowed recovery of tort claim judgments against spendthrift trusts. But the Mississippi legislature codified a judicial spendthrift protection in Mississippi shortly after *Sligh* was decided,[49] prompting speculation that it reverses that decision (because it does not distinguish between types of creditors), and *Nagel* is not much of an inroad because the trust would not have been immune had the settlors lived until the judgment was presented. Both cases provide only a slight indication that there may be evolution in the range of spendthrift trust protection.[50]

There are few other state law exceptions to spendthrift protection, the one for government liens typically trumping spendthrift or forfeiture provisions. But CCA 200614006 makes it clear that the government itself does not think it's lien can accelerate a beneficiary's interest (rather, it only permits collection when it becomes payable). In that case the beneficiary's right to income could be levied upon but income could be collected only as it was payable).[51]

---

[47] 704 So. 2d 1020 (Miss. 1997) (plaintiff was severely and permanently injured by the habitually and criminally negligent beneficiary of a discretionary trust).

[48] 580 N.W.2d 810 (Iowa 1998) (tortfeasors were settlors of a revocable trust that became irrevocable when the settlors died during their tort that resulted in a judgment).

[49] Miss. Code Ann. § § 91-9-503 through -507 (1998).

[50] See Newman, The Rights of Creditors of Beneficiaries Under the Uniform Trust Code: An Examination of the Compromise, 69 Tenn. L. Rev. 771 at nn.148-167 and accompanying text (2002). Newman references Ga. Code Ann. § 53-12-28 and La. Rev. Stat. Ann. § 9:2005(3) as both permitting some tort claimants to reach beyond spendthrift restrictions. The Louisiana legislation was repealed in 2004 by La. Acts No. 521 § 2, and more recent litigation suggests that the movement is trending contrary to *Sligh*. See, e.g., Duvall v. McGee, 826 A.2d 416 (Md. Ct. App. 2003) (in an extensive evaluation of the public policy arguments, the court rejected an effort to satisfy a wrongful death tort judgment in violation of a spendthrift trust provision), and Scheffel v. Krueger, 782 A.2d 410 (N.H. 2001) (similarly rejecting a tort judgment for sexual assault of a minor).

[51] See, e.g., In re Estate of Gist, 763 N.W.2d 561 (Iowa 2009) (applicable to trusts addressed in Restatement (Third) of Trusts § § 50 and 60 (2003), being "discretionary support trusts with standards," the court held that the common law "necessity exception" still applied following Iowa's adoption of a new trust code); Bank One Ohio Trust Co. v. United States, 80 F.3d 173 (6th Cir. 1996) (government's levy and attachment could not be barred by forfeiture provision because the government already owned an interest in the property by virtue of

On the other hand, at least to the extent of any retained interest or power in a domestic trust, spendthrift provisions traditionally do *not* protect a settlor who is a beneficiary of the trust.[52] To protect a *settlor*

(Footnote Continued)

its lien); First Northwestern Trust Co. v. Internal Revenue Service, 622 F.2d 387, 390 (8th Cir. 1980) ("the income from a spendthrift trust is not immune from federal tax liens, notwithstanding any state laws or recognized exemption to the contrary . . . [even if] the elements of a spendthrift trust are combined with provisions granting discretionary powers of distribution to the trustee"); Magavern v. United States, 550 F.2d 797 (2d Cir. 1977) (state court decision that beneficiary had no attachable property interest was not controlling and government's levy was valid); LaSalle Nat'l Bank v. United States, 636 F. Supp. 874 (N.D. Ill. 1986) (a beneficiary's interest in a spendthrift trust is a sufficient right to property as to which the federal lien may attach notwithstanding a state spendthrift protection statute); United States v. Riggs Nat'l Bank, 636 F. Supp. 172 (D. D.C. 1986) (levy on delinquent taxpayer's trust income not defeated by forfeiture clause); United States v. Taylor, 254 F. Supp. 752, 755 (N.D. Cal. 1966) (lien could attach to support trust interest notwithstanding forfeiture provision; state law establishes whether a property interest exists but "state-created exemptions and limitations are inoperative to prevent the attachment of federal tax liens" to those property interests); but see In re Wilson, 92-2 U.S. Tax Cas. (CCH) ¶ 50,333 (N.D. Tex. 1992) (discretionary income interest in spendthrift trust was not a property right to which federal tax lien could attach and the government could not compel the trustee to make discretionary income distributions to the beneficiary for the government to attach unless it was proven that the trustee was guilty of fraud, misconduct, or a clear abuse of discretion).

[52] 3 Scott, Fratcher, & Ascher, Scott and Ascher on Trusts § 15.4 (5th ed. 2007); Restatement (Third) of Trusts § 58(2) (2003). A good illustration of a special case is Okla. Stat. tit. 31, § 10 et seq., which permits creation of a *revocable* asset protection trust for the benefit of select *third* parties (descendants and a spouse of the settlor, plus § 501(c)(3) exempt organizations) but not for the settlor's own benefit, subject to certain limitations (such as a $1 million initial value cap, the need to use an Oklahoma trustee, and to fund the trust exclusively with "Oklahoma assets," which apparently can include interests in an Oklahoma business entity created to hold non-Oklahoma assets). Hawaii Rev. Stat. tit. 30, ch. 554G originally was regarded as less useful because it did not permit entrustment of closely-held business interests or interests in FLPs or LLCs and imposed a 1% tax on creation of the trust – both of which provisions were eliminated in 2011; Tenn. Code Ann. § 35-15-505 also affords limited benefits, while Tenn. Code Ann. § 35-16-101 to -112 and the statutes of several other states go farther. See, e.g., Alaska Stat. § 34.40.110 and Del. Code Ann. tit. 12, § § 3570-3576, each of which provides the same asset protection benefits of a spendthrift clause for a third party with respect to a settlor's own interests in an *irrevocable* trust, provided that creation of the trust was not a fraudulent transfer

§ 4.1.4

from creditors probably requires that the trust be located beyond the jurisdiction of courts that would respect the creditor's claims.[53] Alterna-

or otherwise intended to hinder, delay, or defraud then existing creditors. Subsequently Nev. Rev. Stat. § 166.040, N.H. Rev. Stat. Ann. § 564-D, R.I. Gen. Laws § 18-9.2, S.D. Codified Laws ch. 55-16; Utah Code Ann. § 25-6-14, Va. Code Ann. § 55-545.05, and Wyo. Stat. § § 4-10-505, 4-10-510 et seq. all were enacted to provide similar benefits. Mo. Rev. Stat. § 456.5-505.3 affords similar benefits (and apparently existed long before Alaska and Delaware started the current trend). Allegedly Colo. Rev. Stat. § 38-10-111 affords creditor protection against any but existing creditors as well, but In re Cohen, 8 P.3d 429 (Colo. 1999) (dicta in a lawyer discipline case) casts doubt on that interpretation. These state legislatures continue to tweak these provisions, seeking asset protection superiority, but until case law tests these constructs it remains too early to determine whether creditors from other states with judgments against trusts in these states will be rebuffed by courts in enacting states or will be honored under the full faith and credit provisions of the United States Constitution.

[53] The linchpin to an asset protection case involving a domestic asset protection trust is likely to be operation of the full-faith-and-credit mandate of U.S. Const. art. IV, § 1. To date there is no authority directly on point that addresses the following scenario. Assume that Victim sues Tortfeasor and obtains a judgment in a majority jurisdiction that does not recognize self-settled spendthrift trusts. Instead, state law provides that assets held in a self-settled trust for the settlor's own benefit are fully subject to attachment in satisfaction of the settlor's legal obligations. The trust corpus originated in that jurisdiction, the tort occurred in that jurisdiction, and the litigation that yielded the judgment was prosecuted in that jurisdiction, but the trust is administered in a domestic asset protection state. So Victim seeks judicial enforcement of the judgment, based on a ruling by the court in Tortfeasor's home jurisdiction that the trust is not effective to shield those assets from Victim's judgment.

Will a court in the asset protection state refuse to honor the court order to satisfy Victim's judgment using those trust assets? Asset protection trust advocates suggest that the order is invalid because the court in Victim and Tortfeasor's home jurisdiction lacks jurisdiction over the trust. Certainly the case might differ if the tort, and the assets, and the parties, all were located in the asset protection state—it is one thing for that state's legislature to decree that tortfeasors may insulate their assets from liability to victims in that state. But here every connection except trust administration is in a jurisdiction that says such insulation is not available. The issue is whether courts in the asset protection state will reject the order from the state court where all those other contacts exist, and that believed it had jurisdiction to render the order mandating return of the assets to satisfy the judgment. Refusal to honor that court order may escalate into other states refusing to honor orders from courts in the asset protection jurisdiction, which is a battle that the courts may not willingly em-

§ 4.1.4

tively, the trust could be made irrevocable and the settlor could retain no enjoyment that can be attached,[54] but this would entail potential gift tax on creation of the trust[55] notwithstanding the settlor's retention of sufficient enjoyment or control to cause trust income to be taxable to the settlor[56] and inclusion of the FMV of the trust property in the settlor's gross estate at death.[57] Thus, from a practical perspective, protection

(Footnote Continued)

brace. Which means that it is one thing for the legislature to decree that their state is a haven, and a totally different thing for their courts to enforce that notion.

[54] 3 Scott, Fratcher, & Ascher, Scott and Ascher on Trusts § 15.4 (5th ed. 2007); Restatement (Third) of Trusts § 58 comment *e* (2003).

[55] Gift tax would be incurred if the settlor transferred the remainder interest at creation of the trust because the trust is irrevocable and the settlor retained only a life interest. See, e.g., Paolozzi v. Commissioner, 23 T.C. 182 (1954) (because trustees could pay settlor income in their absolute discretion for settlor's best interest, settlor's creditors had recourse to full amount of trust income and only FMV of remainder interest was a completed gift for gift tax purposes); TAM 8617006 (revocable trust established by spouses with community property to pay income to settlors for their respective lives became irrevocable at D's death, which constituted a gift at that time by S of remainder interest in S's share of their community property). See §§ 7.1.7 and 7.3.4.2. Under § 2702 the value of the gifted remainder may be deemed to be 100% of the FMV of the property placed in the trust, notwithstanding the retained enjoyment. See § 7.2.2.

[56] It is possible for the settlor to relinquish sufficient enjoyment to incur a gift tax and preclude creditor attachment but still retain enough enjoyment or control to be regarded as the trust's owner for income tax grantor trust purposes. See § 5.11. Indeed, some jurisdictions have enacted legislation to address the most common illustration of this, which is an inter vivos QTIP trust in which the settlor retains a secondary life estate if the primary life beneficiary—the settlor's spouse—dies first. While both spouses are alive such a trust is a grantor trust by virtue of § 677(a)(1) and the spousal unity rule of § 672(e). See, e.g., Ariz. Rev. Stat. § 14-10505.E(2); Del Code Ann. Tit. 12, § 3536(c)(2); Fla. Stat. § 736.0505(3); Wyo. Stat. § 4-10-506.

[57] It also is possible to transfer sufficient enjoyment to incur a gift tax and thwart creditors but still attract FET inclusion at death. But cf. Estate of German v. United States, 85-1 U.S. Tax Cas. (CCH) ¶ 13,610 (Ct. Cl. 1985) (adverse trustees of irrevocable living trust with discretion to distribute income to settlor; creation of trust was a completed gift taxable event and government's § 2036(a)(1) inclusion argument was not adequate to support its motion for summary judgment); Estate of Uhl v. Commissioner, 241 F.2d 867 (7th Cir. 1957) (payment of gift tax on creation was deemed adequate to preclude FET inclusion notwithstanding settlor's retained discretionary income interest); Rev. Rul.

§ 4.1.4

from improvidence probably is effective only (1) with respect to beneficiaries other than the settlor, (2) to the limited extent that the settlor wishes to put the trust property beyond the settlor's indiscreet adventures but not beyond the reach of the settlor's creditors, or (3) to the extent the settlor creates an effective asset protection trust, which may require an offshore entity.

Asset protection planning is desirable to individuals who fear political instability, economic uncertainty, liability flowing from the fact that theirs is a deep pocket that may attract vexatious litigation, or because they are engaged in financially hazardous ventures that expose them to potentially substantial future liability.[58] As a means of insulating a "nest egg" portion of their wealth[59] without making an irrevocable transfer that is subject to gift tax, the most frequently considered asset protection device is a foreign situs trust[60] that almost always is created in a

---

(Footnote Continued)

2004-64, 2004-2 C.B. 7 (the trustee's discretion in an IDGT to make distributions to reimburse the settlor's payment of income tax on trust income is not adequate to require § 2036(a)(1) inclusion if the settlor's creditors cannot attach the trust); and PLRs 200822008, 9332006 and 8037116. In most jurisdictions, because creditors of the settlor could reach trust assets under facts like those in *German*, § 2036(a)(1) inclusion would occur at the settlor's death, notwithstanding a completed gift at creation of the trust of at least the value of the remainder interest and perhaps of the entire trust. See, e.g., Estate of Skinner v. United States, 316 F.2d 517 (3d Cir. 1963); Estate of Paxton v. Commissioner, 86 T.C. 785 (1986); and see § 7.1.7.1.

[58] For example, corporate directors, professionals such as doctors, lawyers, accountants, engineers, and architects who are subject to potential malpractice liability exceeding their insurance coverage and who cannot protect themselves adequately with a limited liability venture, or individuals whose businesses entail significant risk, such as a hazardous chemical or waste disposal operation.

[59] I.e., no more than that amount as to which a transfer would not make the transferor insolvent as defined under state law. See § 4.1.4 n.62.

[60] For literature dealing with this form of planning (and some regarding their domestic trust counterparts) consult Asset Protection: Domestic and International Law and Tactics (Osborne, ed., 1995); Bailey, Asset Protection Trusts Protect the Assets But What About the Trustees, 21 Prob. & Prop. 58 (Jan./Feb. 2007); Boxx, Gray's Ghost-A Conversation About the Onshore Trust, 85 Iowa L. Rev. 1195 (2000); Bruce, Gray, & Luria, Exploring the Protection of Assets Trusts, 130 Trusts & Estates 32, 39 (Nov. & Dec. 1991); Danforth, Rethinking the Law of Creditors' Rights in Trusts, 53 Hastings L.J. 287 (2002); Eason, Home From the Islands: Domestic Asset Protection Trust Alternatives Impact Tradi-

jurisdiction that has enacted Statute of Elizabeth[61] override legislation, making it difficult or impossible for future creditors to reach assets that were not fraudulently transferred.[62]

As against both present and future creditors, §4(a)(2) of the Uniform Fraudulent Transfers Act[63] specifies that conveyances made without fair consideration are deemed to be fraudulent without regard to actual intent if the transferor is or is about to be engaged in activities for which the transferor's remaining property is "unreasonably small" in relation to that activity, or if existing debts or debts that are likely to be incurred after the transfer will exceed the transferor's ability to pay. Prima facie, under §4(a)(1) of the Act, a transfer is fraudulent if the transferor had actual intent to hinder, delay, or defraud any present or future creditor, and actual intent would be shown by any number of factors or circumstances surrounding the transfer, such as that the transfer was concealed, the transferor was being sued or being

(Footnote Continued)

tional Estate and Gift Tax Planning Considerations, 52 Fla. L. Rev. 41 (2000); Engle, Using Foreign Situs Trusts for Asset Protection Planning, 20 Est. Plan. 212 (1993); Gingiss, Putting a Stop to "Asset Protection" Trusts, 51 Baylor L. Rev. 987 (1999); Hirsch, Fear Not the Asset Protection Trust, 27 Cardozo L. Rev. 2685 (2006); Nenno & Sullivan, Domestic Asset Protection Trusts, 868 Tax Mgmt. (BNA) Estates, Gifts, and Trusts Port. (2010); Nenno, Choosing and Rechoosing the Jurisdiction for a Trust, 40 U. Miami Inst. Est. Plan. ¶ 400 (2006); Nenno, Planning with Domestic Asset Protection Trusts, 40 Real Prop., Prob. & Trust J. 263, 477 (Parts I and II) (2005); Osborne, New Age Estate Planning: Offshore Trusts, 27 U. Miami Inst. Est. Plan. ¶ 1700 (1993); Roth, Asset Protection Planning, at ali-aba.org/index.cfm?fuseaction=courses.course&course_code =CM066&contenttype=6 (Feb. 2007); Rothschild, Establishing and Drafting Offshore Trusts, 23 Est. Plan. 65 (1996); Sterk, Asset Protection Trusts: Trust Law's Race to the Bottom?, 85 Cornell L. Rev. 1035 (2000).

[61] Statute of 13 Elizabeth ch. 5 (1571), the precursor to modern fraudulent transfer and creditor protection legislation, was enacted to void any conveyance that was not upon consideration and bona fide, if it was "contrived . . . to delay, hinder or defraud Creditors or others of their just and lawful Actions, Suits, Debts, Accounts, Damages, Penalties . . . and Reliefs."

[62] Because any fraudulent transfer is voidable, a fraudulent transfer into a trust will not prevent creditors from defeating the trust to reach the transferred assets, notwithstanding the settlor's lack of retained interests or powers. 3 Scott, Fratcher, & Ascher, Scott and Ascher on Trusts § 15.4 (5th ed. 2007). This is true even in most Statute of Elizabeth override jurisdictions.

[63] 7A Pt. II U.L.A. 58 (2006).

§4.1.4

threatened with suit, the transfer was of "substantially all" of the transferor's assets, the transfer was for inadequate consideration, occurred close to when a substantial debt was incurred, the transferor retained possession, use, or benefit of the transferred property, or the transferor was insolvent following a conveyance (meaning that the sum of the transferor's debts exceeds the sum of the transferor's readily accessible assets or that the transferor cannot pay debts as they become due).

Bankruptcy Code (11 U.S.C.) § 548 is very similar to the Uniform Fraudulent Transfers Act in that it grants the trustee in bankruptcy power to set aside any transfer made within one year of filing a petition for bankruptcy if the transfer was made with actual intent to hinder, delay, or defraud any present or future creditor or it was made for less than FMV consideration and the transferor was insolvent following the conveyance, the transferor was or was about to be engaged in activities for which the transferor's remaining property was "an unreasonably small capital," or the transferor intended to incur debts beyond the transferor's ability to pay as they matured.[64] The addition of § 548(e) in 2005 gives the bankruptcy trustee ten years to avoid transfers to a "self-settled trust or similar device" if the debtor is a beneficiary and made the transfer with the same actual intent.[65]

---

[64] See, e.g., In re Schwarzkopf, 626 F.3d 1032 (9th Cir. 2010) (transfer while settlors were insolvent with respect to a prior creditor was deemed fraudulent and thus was invalidated in a subsequent bankruptcy proceeding, unrelated to the original creditor issue); In re McCoy, 2002 WL 1611588 (N.D. Ill. 2002) (granting a bankruptcy trustee access to a classic nonmarital trust created by the bankrupt's deceased spouse using assets the bankrupt transferred to the decedent 11 years before the spouse died, which was 9 years before the bankrupt filed for voluntary protection, all based on typical controls granted to the bankrupt as surviving spouse beneficiary and trustee of the nonmarital trust); In re Brooks, 217 Bankr. 98 (D. Conn. 1998) (making none of the fraud based determinations in finding that the assets of an offshore trust were part of the bankruptcy estate). Cf. In re Portnoy, 201 Bankr. 685 (S.D. N.Y. 1996) (summary judgment denial to debtor who created an offshore trust, arising in an action to deny bankruptcy discharge based on debtor's alleged efforts to conceal assets).

[65] In re Mortensen, 2011 WL 5025252 and 5025249 (Bkrptcy D. Ak. 2011), reached this conclusion with respect to creation of an Alaska asset protection trust by an Alaska domiciliary settlor. See generally Alces, The Law of Fraudulent Transactions ¶ 1.02[1][b] and ch. 5 (1989); Henkel & Turner, Asset Preservation Aspects of Domestic Estate Planning, 29 U. Miami Inst. Est. Plan. ¶ 602 (1995).

§ 4.1.4

If state law protections are inadequate,[66] the settlor may acquire a degree of protection against *future* potential creditor claims if a valid asset protection trust exists. The future creditor distinction is an important refinement.[67] Fraudulent conveyance laws distinguish between pre-

---

[66] Although many states protect a limited amount of assets, such as homestead, insurance, annuities, employee benefits, and tenancy by the entireties property against debts of only one spouse, the amounts that are immune to creditor claims may be inadequate or the forms of protected property may not be desirable or appropriate for the transferor.

[67] Note also that other legal theories may permit a creditor to defeat transfers into trust. Consider the following "alter ego" and "nominee" discussions from Dexia Credit Local v. Rogan, 2008 WL 4543013 (N.D. Ill. 2008) (citations omitted), which allowed creditors to attach trusts created for a debtor's children:

> . . . A trust may be considered to be the alter ego of a judgment debtor if the debtor used the trust's assets for his own benefit and exercised authority over the trust's assets. The factors considered include whether there was a close personal relationship between the transferor and the trust; the transferor received consideration for the transfer; the trust was created to shield the transferor's assets from creditors and the transfer was made in anticipation of incurring debts or in anticipation of collection activity; the transferor continued to enjoy the benefits of the property following transfer; the transferor contributed all or just part of the trust's assets; and there was commingling of management and record keeping of the assets of the transferor and the trust.

> . . .

> . . . A judgment creditor may levy upon property held in the name of someone other than the judgment debtor if the debtor engaged in a legal fiction by placing title to the property in the hands of someone else while, in actuality, retaining all or some of the benefits of ownership. In determining whether a person . . . is a nominee for a debtor, courts consider factors such as whether the person paid consideration for the property, whether the property was given to the person in anticipation of a suit or liability, whether the judgment debtor exercises control of the property after its transfer, whether there is a family or other close relationship between the debtor and the transferee, whether the debtor has the benefits of the property after the transfer, and whether the debtor maintains the property after the transfer.

In United States v. Evseroff, 2012-1 U.S. Tax Cas. (CCH) ¶ 50,328 (E.D. N.Y. 2012), the court allowed a future creditor (the United States, pursuing collection of a tax liability) to pierce a trust under three theories, two of which are relevant here. One was that the trust was the settlor's "nominee," which allows a creditor to access trust assets because they essentially are regarded as still owned by the settlor. The *Evseroff* court *also* found that the trust was the settlor's alter ego, due

§ 4.1.4

sent and subsequent creditors (being those to whom liability already exists or at least those to whom the transferor knew a future liability might run), as to whom fraudulent transfers may be set aside, and those "nameless, faceless" persons about whom the transferor had no awareness and no current dealings that might ripen into future liability (such as the next unknown client of a professional person or a tort claimant alleging liability from a yet unanticipated future harm), as to whom fraudulent conveyance limitations do not apply.[68]

Because of the ability of creditors to set aside transfers that are in actual or constructive fraud of their rights,[69] this form of planning is effective only against the potential future claimant who is not yet even a cloud on the horizon. "Asset protection planning is a vaccine and not a cure . . . . [It is] best implemented when the client is least inclined to do so; that is, when the client's legal seas are calm."[70] Indeed, experienced practitioners in this arena report that advisors and reputable trust companies will not assist a client who is looking to dodge existing creditors,

---

(Footnote Continued)

to the settlor's control over the trust itself, as opposed to the assets inside the trust, and this *too* allowed access to the trust assets, the court saying that:

> although the New York Court of Appeals has never held that the alter ego theory may be applied to reach assets held in a trust, . . . there is no policy reason why veil piercing would apply only to corporations but not to trusts. The policy behind corporate veil piercing is to prevent a debtor from using the corporate legal form to unjustly avoid liability. That policy applies equally to trusts.

[68] See Alces, The Law of Fraudulent Transactions ¶ 5.04 (1989).

[69] See § 4.1.4 n.62.

[70] Engle, Using Foreign Situs Trusts for Asset Protection Planning, 20 Est. Plan. 212, 217 (1993). One recommendation is to provide in the asset protection trust that all claims of present and existing future claimants be paid from the trust, making it clear that the protection sought by the trust is only with respect to those subsequent potential unknown claims as to which the present transfer is not an actual or constructive fraud.

§ 4.1.4

spousal[71] or child support obligations, tax liabilities,[72] or to engage in any form of criminal activity.[73]

This raises the question why an individual would engage in this form of planning, which can be expensive in terms of transaction costs to create the trust and transfer assets to it,[74] may entail annual reporting

---

[71] Indeed, to the extent asset protection planning removes property from S's reach the advisor may be committing an unintended breach of ethical duties to S, if S also is a client of the advisor for other purposes (such as for traditional estate planning). See § 3.4.2 n.7, and consider ABA Standing Committee on Ethics & Professional Responsibility Formal Op. 05-434, as discussed in § 3.5 n.5.

[72] See United States v. Evseroff, 2006 WL 2792750 (E.D. N.Y. 2006), vac'd and rem'd by 270 Fed. Appx. 75 (2d Cir. 2008), on remand, 2012-1 U.S. Tax Cas. (CCH) ¶ 50,328 (E.D. N.Y. 2012), which originally appeared to prove that a properly planned trust may preclude even the federal government from reaching trust assets in satisfaction of tax liabilities. The settlor retained sufficient nontrust assets to maintain the settlor's solvency, which established that creation of the trust was not a fraudulent transfer and therefore could not be defeated. On remand the court found that the trust could be reached on three different grounds—that the trust was the taxpayer's alter ego, nominee, and the transfer into the trust was a fraudulent conveyance—even if the tax liability did not arise until after the conveyance and even though the taxpayer technically was not insolvent. Compare, United States v. Townley, 181 Fed. Appx. 630 (unpub. 9th Cir. 2006) (in which taxes already were owed when the transfer into trust was made, making for a fraudulent transfer), and In re Middendorf, 381 B.R. 774 (Bkrptcy D. Kan. 2008) (in which the taxpayer pre-paid capital gains tax on gains realized before filing for bankruptcy protection, which was a non-dischargeable tax liability, and the court held that there is nothing improper about paying an estimated tax liability).

[73] See, e.g., 18 U.S.C. § 1032 (concealment of assets from Federal Deposit Insurance Corporation, Resolution Trust Corporation, or any conservator appointed by the Comptroller of the Currency, the Director of the Office of Thrift Supervision, or the National Credit Union Administration Board), and § § 1956 & 1957 (money laundering provisions, targeting financial transactions designed to conceal the location or control of proceeds of specified unlawful activity). See generally Bruce, Gray, & Luria, Exploring the Protection of Assets Trusts, 130 Trusts & Estates 32, 39 (Nov. & Dec. 1991).

[74] For example, the advisor must ascertain the most appropriate jurisdiction in which to create such a trust, hire local counsel to advise on the legal and tax aspects of the offshore location, and draft documents that probably are not cookie-cutter arrangements. In terms of the available havens, consult Klienfeld, Smith, & Langer, Practical International Estate Planning (4th ed. 2000); Osborne, New Age Estate Planning: Offshore Trusts, 27 U. Miami Est. Plan. Inst. ¶ 1700

§ 4.1.4

requirements,[75] and presents the potential for making an inadvertent fraudulent transfer.[76] Indeed, the risk of the advisor being liable for assisting in a fraudulent transfer will compel most advisors to seek verification of facts and representations made by the individual relating to solvency, with additional attendant costs.[77]

(Footnote Continued)

(1993); Schoenblum, Multistate and Multinational Estate Planning § 18.02 (2012), and consider aspects such as the political and economic stability of the jurisdiction, the local taxes, fees, and other costs for establishing such a trust, the prospects for future taxation of trust income or the underlying principal, tax treaties (which might mitigate any unexpected future tax law changes by making the tax a § 901 credit against any United States tax that otherwise would be imposed, making the tax issue a matter of paying whichever is the greater of the United States or the foreign jurisdiction tax rather than paying double taxes) and exchange controls, the general banking and business environment, and the legal, accounting, communication, and transportation facilities of the jurisdiction. The legal environment with respect to enforceability of foreign judgments against assets held in local trusts also must be analyzed.

[75] See § 4.1.4 n.82.

[76] Under Uniform Fraudulent Transfers Act § § 2 and 5, 7A Pt. II U.L.A. 37, 129 (2006), exempt assets are ignored in determining whether the transferor is insolvent under an assets-exceeding-debts test, but debts secured by those assets are not ignored. Thus, it is possible to have debts that count exceeding assets that count and technically be insolvent, making a transfer a fraud and exposing the transferor to avoidance and potentially subjecting the advisor to exposure for assisting in that fraudulent transaction.

[77] One noted New York practitioner who is proactive in speaking about and representing clients with respect to asset protection trust planning stated in a 1994 speech that "although a planner is unlikely to have violated any ethical rules if proper precautions were followed . . . , there is the possibility that a client may have misrepresented their liabilities or that an aggressive creditor may name the planner as a coconspirator in an attempt to gain some leverage in the litigation." This practitioner claims that protection can be improved by representing only clients that the advisor "knows" and then by requiring full disclosure from that client and by obtaining an affidavit from the client that there are no pending or threatened claims against the client, nor is the client presently under investigation of any nature, that the client is not involved in any administrative proceeding against the client, and that no situation has developed that will lead to any claims, investigation, or administrative proceeding. In addition, the client is asked to affirm that the client intends to remain solvent and able to pay anticipated liabilities as they come due after the transfers anticipated in the asset protection planning. Finally, the client is required to affirm that no transferred asset was derived from "specified unlawful activities" as defined in the Money Laundering

§ 4.1.4

The precise construct of such an asset protection trust arrangement will vary depending on the needs and desires of the transferor and the laws of the various jurisdictions involved, but the general format of offshore asset protection devices is something in the order of a revocable trust with at least one non-United States trustee and a custodian of trust assets who is located in a different non-United States jurisdiction. There may be cotrustees, who might be located in the United States (indeed, they might be relatives, friends, or advisors of the settlor), the custodian may be located in the United States so that physical transfer of trust assets is not required, and the custodian may employ nominee registrations that further the objective of keeping a low profile to the trust's existence. The trust may contain an Emergency Trustee provision or other duress and flee clauses that operate in case trouble looms in the United States, severing all connections that would support the jurisdiction of a United States court, such as in the event of a claim being filed against the settlor or the trust.

The trust also may have "protectors" (which may include the settlor) whose function is to "advise" but not instruct the trustee, so that their involvement does not constitute a formal fiduciary role that might subject the trust to the jurisdiction of courts where the protectors are located. In addition, the protectors may have a power to remove the trustee and replace it with another (for legitimate reasons or merely to give a degree of leverage to their advisory role), although typically this power will not be exercisable in cases of duress. The trustee or custodian also may be instructed to employ an investment advisor located in the United States but who will make all investments through an offshore order desk arrangement.

Consistent with the notion that not all the settlor's assets should be transferred to such a trust but, instead, only a nest egg, the only property made subject to the arrangement might be marketable intangibles (although realty located in the United States might be encumbered and the proceeds used to purchase additional intangible investments that also would be protected).

(Footnote Continued)

Control Act of 1986. As an added measure to protect the advisor, the practitioner recommends that advisors document all cases that failed to meet these legitimacy tests and that the advisor therefore refused to undertake.

§ 4.1.4

To the extent concerns over any release of information are important, various participants may be made privy to only some of the identities of the various actors involved and the identity and location of trust assets. Thus, for example, the settlor may know the protectors, the initial trustee, and the investment advisor, but not the identity of the emergency trustee, the custodian, or the nominee owner of trust assets. The investment advisor may know only the nominee and not the custodian, trustee, or location of trust assets, and so forth, giving less opportunity to a plaintiff in any deposition or discovery action to obtain all the facts needed to attempt to sue the trustee or attach trust assets. Although the existence of the trust itself would not be a secret (if it was, this secrecy might raise concerns about fraudulent transfers or contempt of court orders that require revelation of the arrangement), no single individual or institution would be privy to sufficient information to permit easy access to the trust.

To protect against an immediate gift tax on the transfer of assets to the trust the settlor may retain a nongeneral power to change trust beneficiaries,[78] insufficient to permit forced exercise in favor of creditors or other claimants but adequate to constitute the trust as a grantor trust for § 674(a) income tax purposes. In addition, § 679 imposes income tax grantor trust liability on a United States transferor to a foreign trust with any United States beneficiaries.[79] In either case, grantor trust treatment may be significant for income tax purposes, but it will not necessarily prevent the trust from being classified as a "foreign trust"[80] that is

---

[78] See PLR 9535008 (retained nongeneral inter vivos and testamentary power of appointment precluded gift tax on creation, notwithstanding that trustee could alter all terms of trust (subject to settlor's veto); distributions or amendments by trustee could cause gifts to be complete and tax to be incurred in the future). According to ILM 201208026, a retained testamentary (but not inter vivos) power to appoint would preclude gift tax on creation of only the remainder interest in the trust (measured using the settlor's life expectancy) and, in most cases, § 2702 would apply to ignore the remainder interest and treat creation of the trust as a taxable gift of the entire value of the trust corpus.

[79] And see § 672(f), which treats a beneficiary as the grantor of a trust created by a foreign person with property that the beneficiary gave to the foreign person.

[80] See § 7701(a)(31)(B): a foreign trust is defined as any trust that is not a domestic trust, as defined in § 7701(a)(30)(E), which requires that a United States court exercise primary supervision over the trust and United States trustees must control all substantial decisions of the trust. Since 1996 it no longer

subject to the flush language of § 1361(c)(2)(A) (denying qualified trust status to a foreign trust that owns S Corporation stock), and the special income tax discriminations[81] and reporting requirements[82] imposed on or with respect to foreign trusts.

In the final analysis the net result of an asset protection trust may be only a chicane rather than a total roadblock precluding a creditor's claim. This alone may be a sufficient impediment to recovery, in terms of the claimant's ability to locate assets and then the need to research foreign laws, hire local counsel, and prosecute an action overseas. A claimant may settle early and for a reduced amount, or abandon all hope altogether. On the other hand, the settlor of an offshore asset protection trust may be ordered to return the assets to the United States or stand in contempt of court,[83] notwithstanding that the typical asset protection trust provides that any retained power of revocation is not available in the event of duress (which would include an involuntary revocation pursuant to a court order) and therefore compliance would be impossible.

(Footnote Continued)

is relevant whether the recipient of income is a nonresident alien or whether the trust is comparable to a nonresident alien, and it no longer is determinative where the trust was created, situs of the trust assets, situs of the trust administration, or the residence and nationality of the settlor, the trustee, and the beneficiaries. Thus, with the simplicity of the § 7701(a)(30)(E) definition comes a greater likelihood of a trust being regarded as a foreign trust by such a simple matter as having a controlling foreign trustee.

[81] For example, under § 643(a)(6) capital gain is includible in DNI and may be taxed to the beneficiary on an accumulation distribution as ordinary income because the special status as capital gain is not preserved, and under §§ 667(a)(3) and 668 a special 6% interest charge is assessed on the throwback tax imposed on an accumulation distribution made from a foreign trust.

[82] See § 6048 and Notice 97-34, 1997-1 C.B. 422. Very stiff penalties also may apply under § 6677 for failure to comply.

[83] See, e.g., Federal Trade Commission v. AmeriDebt, 373 F. Supp. 2d 558 (D. Md. 2005) (stating that the plaintiff could move for contempt if the defendant failed to comply with a repatriation order, allowing that the defendant would be free to argue an impossibility defense); United States v. Grant, 2005 WL 2671479 (S.D. Fla. 2005) (magistrate's recommendation that the court order repatriation to satisfy a federal tax lien, making several potentially erroneous statements regarding trust law and fiduciary duties but nevertheless showing which way the winds blow in these matters). See also notes 92-94 and accompanying text.

§ 4.1.4

Normally impossibility would be an absolute defense to contempt,[84] but not if the impossibility is of the settlor's own creation. Thus, before a court orders a settlor to bring the trust assets back to the United States, it ought to consider the duress provision and the impossibility defense. A legitimate impossibility defense should be determinative at that stage, to preclude the order itself. If the court finds the defense to be meritless, however, the settlor's proper remedy is to appeal that order, not to stand in contempt of it.[85] This then raises an interesting dilemma, to which there appears to be no ready answer in the asset protection context.

If the settlor refuses to honor the court order to return the trust assets to the United States, again pleading the impossibility to comply and notwithstanding that the court already rejected that argument when it issued the order to return the trust assets, the issue is whether the impossibility defense is effective as against contempt. The traditional rule is that only evidence of something that has occurred since the order was entered, showing that there is a newly discovered inability to comply with the order, is relevant to the impossibility defense at the contempt stage. A newly arisen inability cannot be of the settlor's voluntary making.[86] Furthermore, the impossibility defense never is applicable if the contemnor "wrongfully" or "voluntarily" created the impossibility.[87] The problem is that most decisions involving the defense and its rejection entail actions that created the impossibility *after* the order was entered, and in the asset protection trust context the impossibility defense will turn on the settlor's actions that predated any court order to return trust assets.

---

[84] See United States v. Fleischman, 339 U.S. 349, 367 (1950) (Black, dissenting): "punishment [for contempt] is justifiable only when a person has failed to comply with an order . . . when he has the power himself to do what is ordered."

[85] United States v. Ryerson, 460 U.S. 752 (1983).

[86] See 17 Am. Jur. 2d Contempt § 141.

[87] See, e.g., Eulich v. United States, 2004 WL 1844821 (N.D. Tex. 2004) (taxpayer created the dilemma by selection of the jurisdiction in which a trust was created and therefore was precluded from benefiting from application of that jurisdiction's laws because the situation was self created); Cook County v. Fry Roofing Co., 319 N.E.2d 472 (Ill. 1974) (stating that it does not matter with what intent the contemnor did the act that created the impossibility if the contemnor voluntarily created the impossibility); Brown v. Cook, 260 P.2d 544 (Utah 1953); Society of the Divine Word v. Martin, 38 N.W.2d 619 (Iowa 1949).

§ 4.1.4

In the asset protection trust context involving transfers that predate liability or any court orders, intent appears to be relevant and the inquiry appears to turn on the settlor's motive in creating the impossibility.[88] The burden of proof is on the party seeking to impose a contempt order, to establish by more than a preponderance of evidence that the alleged contemnor acted in bad faith.[89] There are many cases involving actions in anticipation of particular decrees that were regarded as contumacious.[90] In the context of this discussion, the question is whether the act of establishing an asset protection trust with a duress provision in anticipation of a potential court order to return assets to the United States to satisfy a potential judgment is sufficient to establish the bad faith that would negate the impossibility defense in a contempt proceeding.

Some commentators suggest that holding a settlor in contempt in this or any other case would be tantamount to holding the settlor in debtors' prison, which is contrary to public policy.[91] Others might argue that the settlor personally was responsible for being placed in that prison and, unlike the debtors' prisons of old, holds the key to their release. The notion is that, notwithstanding the duress provision, if the settlor really wants to be free of contempt the settlor, trustee, and protectors will "find a way" to have the trust assets returned.

Perhaps the most poignant element regarding this debate is that, regardless of how these issues ultimately are resolved, it may be that the court issuing the contempt citation will require that the settlor await the judicial determination of good faith and the effect of the impossibility defense while sitting in jail for the contempt. Asset protection trust advocates often cite the fact that the device is merely a mechanism to

---

[88] McLean v. District Court, 97 P. 841 (Mont. 1908), is representative of cases in which the impossibility predated the court's order and was not deemed to be in bad faith, the defendant having received money pursuant to a judgment that the defendant immediately used to pay pre-existing creditors, after which the judgment was vacated and the defendant was ordered to return the money, which then was impossible due to the good faith payment of the creditors.

[89] See Federal Trade Commission v. Blaine, 308 F. Supp. 932 (N.D. Ga. 1970).

[90] See, e.g., American Fletcher Mortgage Co. v. Bass, 688 F.2d 513 (7th Cir. 1982); Ex Parte Coffelt, 389 S.W.2d 234 (Ark. 1965); Laing v. State, 137 S.E.2d 896 (Va. 1964); Hodous v. Hodous, 36 N.W.2d 554, 12 A.L.R.2d 1051 (N.D. 1949).

[91] See LoPucki, The Death of Liability, 106 Yale L.J. 1 (1996).

§ 4.1.4

slow down creditors. In this context, delay works to the distinct disadvantage of the settlor.

In effect this happened in Federal Trade Commission v. Affordable Media,[92] in which the lower court ordered the settlors of an irrevocable offshore trust to repatriate assets transferred to the trust, the trustee refused the request on the basis of a duress provision in the trust, and the court held the settlors in jail for civil contempt. According to the lower court the impossibility defense was unavailable because it was created by insertion of the duress provision in the trust and then by the settlors' revelation to the trustee that the attempt to recover the assets was pursuant to court order. Presumably the trustee would have complied if the request had been made without alerting the trustee to the facts that triggered that request. So it was the indication of the circumstances under which the request was being made that created the post-order impossibility, for which contempt could not be avoided under the impossibility defense.

The contemnor was released from jail after six months, pending appeal of the contempt order. It is not clear what happened after the contempt finding was affirmed. In a subsequent similar case the settlor of a Mauritius trust similarly was jailed for contempt for failure to comply with an order to repatriate assets.[93] Allegations that he was released after only two days were untrue. The contemnor was jailed for over six years and finally was released when the court concluded that there was no realistic potential that he would comply with the court's order.[94] It is not

---

[92] 179 F.3d 1228 (9th Cir. 1999) (arising from fraudulent trade practice litigation involving a telemarketing Ponzi scheme in which the court ordered the wrongdoer to return several million dollars of profits from a Cook Islands trust).

[93] In re Lawrence, 279 F.3d 1294 (11th Cir. 2002). See also Securities and Exchange Commission v. Solow, 682 F. Supp. 2d 1312 (S.D. Fla. 2010), In re Coker, 251 B.R. 902 (Bankr. M.D. Fla. 2000) and Securities and Exchange Comm'n v. Bilzerian, 112 F. Supp. 2d 12 (D. D.C. 2000) (all finding trust settlors in contempt for failure to comply with court orders to repatriate assets in offshore asset protection trusts). Consult www.trustsassetprotection.com for further information and updates on this developing area.

[94] Compare Rothschild & Rubin, Asset Protection After *Anderson*: Much Ado About Nothing?, 26 Est. Plan. 466, 474 n.32 (1999), asserting his release, with Lawrence v. Goldberg, 279 F.3d 1294 (11th Cir. 2002), and Lawrence v. United States Bankruptcy Court, 153 Fed. Appx. 552 (11th Cir. 2005), each showing that

clear that he now or ever will have access to the funds themselves. "Bring your toothbrush" not being what the typical trust settlor wants to hear, and even "just" half a year being longer than most estate planning clients are willing to spend in jail, each of these cases gives new significance to the contempt possibilities and puts asset protection planning in a harsh light.

§4.1.5 Avoiding Will Contests

The time to win a will contest is when the will is prepared,[95] and the most effective way to avoid a successful challenge to a decedent's estate plan is to use a living trust instead of a will as the principal estate planning document. Will contests invariably entail a postmortem critique of the testator's habits, reputation, foibles, lifestyle, and sometimes even lack of capacity or other deficiency that constitutes a legitimate will contest ground. Because one of the estate planner's duties is to insulate the testator's dispositive plan and reputation from challenge, a trust may be called for if a will contest is likely. Fortunately, those cases in which a will contest is predictable often are readily identifiable.

A significant percentage of all will contests arise in one of four fact settings. The most common involves a surviving spouse who is not a parent of D's surviving children, and it really doesn't matter which of S or the children the will favors. A second likely source of potential litigation exists if children are treated differently, whether they all have a common set of parents or they are descended from several different combinations of parents. A third dangerous situation exists if the decedent had no close relatives and the dispositive plan deviates from the intestate distribution among collateral relatives. In this case there may be parties with standing to contest the will who may be disappointed by the will's terms and are so distant in relation that they will have no reticence about contesting the will and possibly besmirching the decedent's reputation. Finally, contest is likely in the growing number of cases involving "alternate lifestyles." If a client wants to leave property to a lover (not a spouse)-whether of the same or a different sex-there are

---

(Footnote Continued)

he still was incarcerated. His release came in mid-December 2006. See In re Lawrence, No. 05-20485-CIV (S.D. Fla. Dec. 12, 2006).

[95] See Jaworski, The Will Contest, 10 Baylor L. Rev. 87 (1958).

§4.1.5

indications that juries, and courts reviewing evidence on appeal, are affected by their feelings about the morality or normalcy of the relationship.[96]

Potential contests may be deflected with an explanation of the decedent's dispositive plan, or by inclusion of an in terrorem clause,[97] by soliciting the opinions of a psychiatrist, or videotaping execution of the will. But a revocable trust is significantly less vulnerable to challenge than a will and usually is the contest avoidance technique of choice.

As a technical fact a revocable trust is as subject to challenge on grounds of lack of capacity or undue influence as a will[98] (indeed, a

---

[96] See Annot., Existence of illicit or unlawful relation between testator and beneficiary as evidence of undue influence, 76 A.L.R.3d 743 (1977).

[97] See § 3.1.2 n.29. Some trusts include binding arbitration provisions that similarly intend to preclude litigation and, like in terrorem clauses, their validity is questionable. See, e.g., Rachal v. Reitz, 347 S.W.3d 305 (Tex. Ct. App. 2011), one of only a small number of cases, all of first impression in their respective jurisdictions, all consistently ruling that a trust provision denying a beneficiary the right to litigate a grievance and instead mandating arbitration is not enforceable. Similar cases are Schoneberger v. Oelze, 96 P.3d 1078 (Az. Ct. App. 2004) (superseded by Ariz. Rev. Stat. Ann. § 14-10205), Diaz v. Bukey, 125 Cal. Rptr. 3d 610 (Cal. Ct. App. 2011), and cf. In re Calomiris, 894 A.2d 408 (D.C. 2006) (involving a will rather than a trust), each holding that binding arbitration provisions must be the product of an enforceable contract agreement between the parties, which cannot be established in the will or trust context, in part because there is no consideration and in part because the beneficiaries did not consent to such a provision. See also In re Chantarasmi, 938 N.Y.S.2d 762 (Surr. Ct. Westchester County 2012) (suggesting that an arbitration provision in a proposed trust would not be enforceable).

   ILM 201208026 concluded that the combination of a mandatory arbitration provision and an in terrorem clause caused beneficiaries of an inter vivos trust to lack any enforceable present interest in the trust, which led the government to opine that gifts to the trust could not qualify for the gift tax annual exclusion. Which means that these provisions may be both ineffective for their intended purpose and detrimental to the taxpayer's tax planning.

[98] 1 Scott, Fratcher, & Ascher, Scott and Ascher on Trusts § 4.6 (5th ed. 2006). But cf. Estate of Langston v. Williams, 57 So. 3d 618 (Miss. 2011), holding for the first time that a typical will contest presumption of undue influence flowing from a confidential relation would apply equally to nonprobate property transfers (in that case joint tenancy and a certificate of deposit), showing that the law has been very slow to mimic will contest doctrine with respect to nonprobate transfers.

§ 4.1.5

greater capacity may be required to validly execute a trust, being the capacity to make a deed or contract).[99] Yet the practical reality is that there are formidable obstacles to such a challenge. For example, potential heirs cannot challenge a revocable trust during the settlor's life, because the contestants are only heirs apparent or expectant and therefore lack standing.[100] Instead, concerned but disappointed potential heirs would need to have the settlor declared incompetent and a conservator appointed who could seek to revoke the trust, presumably requiring a showing that revocation is in the best interests of the settlor. All this presupposes that the potential heirs know that the trust has been created, which is not required. And even if potential heirs knew about the trust and were inclined to challenge it, they are unlikely to bring suit if the settlor is capable of amending the trust. It is one thing to contest a will when the testator cannot retaliate, but taking the settlor on during life presents an altogether different setting.

Moreover, after the settlor's death actual heirs may lack standing to challenge a trust on grounds of lack of capacity or undue influence. Typically only a decedent's duly appointed personal representative has standing to bring any action on behalf of the decedent or regarding the decedent's assets.[101] This obstacle might be avoided if the heirs could file a contest before the will is admitted to probate, and petition for the appointment of a Temporary Administrator of their choosing, who then would enforce the obligation to collect, marshal, and preserve all assets to which the decedent's estate may have a claim. The heirs might exert sufficient pressure to commence an investigation or an action with respect to the revocable trust, but this is not extremely likely either.

Even if heirs surmount the standing hurdle, enormous practical difficulties confront them in contesting a trust. A respectable trustee of a funded living trust usually is an excellent witness to establish that the settlor had capacity and was in control of his or her faculties and affairs during life. Furthermore, the settlor's continuing contacts with the trustee during life normally constitute a continuous validation of the capacity

---

[99] 1 Scott, Fratcher, & Ascher, Scott and Ascher on Trusts § 3.2 (5th ed. 2006).

[100] See, e.g., Davis v. Hunter, 323 F. Supp. 976 (D. Conn. 1970).

[101] See 1 Scott, Fratcher, & Ascher, Scott and Ascher on Trusts § 4.6 (5th ed. 2006) and 4 Scott, Fratcher, & Ascher, Scott and Ascher on Trusts § 24.4.1 (5th ed. 2007).

§ 4.1.5

to deal with the trust assets. Thus, the heirs must persuade a court to rule that the trust was void from the outset, and that every act taken by the trustee in the intervening years was without legal authority. It is uncommon for a court to open this can of worms. Thus, experience reveals that an attack on a trust after the settlor's death, when the trust already has operated during the settlor's life, is substantially less likely to succeed than an attack on a will. This makes trusts the will contest avoidance technique of choice.

§4.1.6 *Probate Avoidance*

The foremost factor recommending the use of living trusts or self-trusteed declarations of trust[102] to many people is avoidance of the need to probate trust assets. Probate estate assets are in suspended state until letters of administration are issued and a personal representative undertakes estate administration. And they must be transferred again, with another potential interruption when probate administration ends, even if the same fiduciary acts as personal representative of the estate and trustee of any following trust.

Conversely, assets held in a revocable living trust remain under the trustee's continuous administration from before the settlor's death through administration that may last for the lives of successive beneficiaries. A trustee will be careful regarding distributions that would leave the trust inadequately secured against obligations imposed on trust property, such as a portion of the settlor's estate tax liability. But most trust funds are available without interruption, for the needs of beneficiaries. And management of the decedent's assets does not suffer from bureaucratic or administrative delays or disruptions common to some probate administrations. This continuity may be of particular import if the settlor's estate consists of a family business that would suffer from interrupted management.

State law might limit the right of creditors to reach estate or trust assets after the settlor's death, but the clear trend is to provide the same access as would exist in a probate estate administration.[103] And revocable

---

102 See §4.2.3.

103 See 5 American Law of Property §23.18 (Casner ed. 1952); 3 Scott, Fratcher, & Ascher, Scott and Ascher on Trusts §15.4.2 (5th ed. 2007). In many cases the availability of state nonclaim protection against creditor claims is a

trusts often are used to avoid the costs and delays of probate in jurisdictions in which estates are subject to court supervised administration (dependent administration),[104] as well to avoid the public scrutiny of a decedent's assets and dispositive plan that is permitted in the public probate court process.[105]

Furthermore, many jurisdictions draw a distinction between "court" trusts and "noncourt" trusts, the former being created as a result of a court decree (for example, a testamentary trust), and the latter being created without any court action. Noncourt trusts arise solely by the settlor's execution of a trust instrument and conveyance of assets to the trustee. Unless state law permits the document to negate the requirement and the drafter of the trust instrument chooses to do so,[106] court

---

(Footnote Continued)

significant factor that dictates at least a modest probate estate and administration to generate a bar against late filing creditors. See § 2.7.5 n.20.

[104] See Dacey, How to Avoid Probate-Updated! (Crown 1980), R. Esperti & R. Peterson, The Living Trust Revolution: Why America Is Abandoning Wills and Probate (Viking 1992); and R. Esperti & R. Peterson, The Loving Trust: The Right Way To Provide For Yourself and Guarantee the Future of Your Loved Ones (Viking 1988). Although many advisors are critical of the probate avoidance craze, these have been very popular and highly marketed techniques. For reasons to favor probate and with respect to probate administration fees, see §§ 4.1.11 and 2.7.6, respectively.

[105] Public scrutiny of the decedent's living trust is not generated even if the probate estate pours over to the trust, unless the will makes the mistake of incorporating the trust by reference. Any required notice from the estate should be given to the trustee of the pour over trust, not its beneficiaries, thus obviating any indirect revelation of that aspect of the decedent's estate plan. See generally 1 Scott, Fratcher, & Ascher, Scott and Ascher on Trusts § 7.1.3 (5th ed. 2006), and see § 4.1.8.

[106] Statutes allowing the settlor to override the court's supervision may be limited. For example, Mass. Gen. L. ch. 206, § 24 permits the court to dispense with the appointment of a guardian ad litem in an accounting proceeding if a legally competent person entitled to notice of the proceeding has a general power to appoint the property or a power to appoint to a class of appointees larger than the class that would take in default of the exercise of the power. Or if the settlor dispensed with the requirement and there is no "good cause" shown for the court to disregard that dispensation. See Roche & Kehoe, New Uniform Practice XVIa and Allowance of Probate Accounts, 28 Boston B.J. 38-40 (1984), which explains how an account also may be allowed without a guardian ad litem if there is an overlapping cofiduciary.

§ 4.1.6

trusts usually are subject to stringent court accounting proceedings,[107] at which a guardian ad litem may be appointed to represent the interests of minor or contingent beneficiaries.[108] The accounting rules applicable to testamentary trusts can be avoided by utilizing a revocable living trust as the principal dispositive vehicle with a pour over will, along with life insurance beneficiary designations and retirement benefits made payable to the trustee of the revocable trust.[109]

Revocable living trusts are widely used in planning estates in jurisdictions that lack independent administration. As the principal document in the dispositive plan, containing tax payment and dispositive provisions, with the will serving an ancillary function by making a pour over gift of remaining assets into the revocable trust. But estate planners are not as concerned about avoiding probate in the growing number of states that offer independent administration (or the UPC unsupervised administration procedures), especially if the personal representative does not compute its fee as a percentage of the probate estate.

Nevertheless, avoiding *ancillary* administration of out-of-state assets may be appropriate, even if the decedent's home state is not a probate avoidance locale and even if other reasons exist to make probate advantageous. Seldom is it desirable to conduct probate and administration in every jurisdiction in which assets are located.[110] Some jurisdictions offer an ancillary administration that is simple and inexpensive, but real property located in most states may generate costs to clear title through ancillary proceedings that may be substantial in relation to the FMV of the property. This particularly is true because often knowing the law isn't sufficient to conduct an ancillary administration. Local practice may vary and require research for which the estate should not be requested to

---

[107] See 3 Scott, Fratcher, & Ascher, Scott and Ascher on Trusts § 17.4 (5th ed. 2007).

[108] See 4 Scott, Fratcher, & Ascher, Scott and Ascher on Trusts § 23.1 (5th ed. 2007).

[109] UPC § 2-511(b) is representative of most pour over statutes in providing that, absent a provision to the contrary in the settlor's will, testamentary additions to a revocable living trust do not make the trust a testamentary trust, which should preclude any argument that the pour over mandates court trust compliance. See § 4.1.8 nn.123-125 and accompanying text.

[110] See § 5.7 n.2, regarding ancillary administration and the need to consolidate for estate income tax filing purposes.

§ 4.1.6

pay. A revocable trust is one of several planning arrangements that can be used to avoid the delay and cost of these ancillary probate proceedings.

If the client is willing, making a gift of the property also can eliminate ancillary administration. Title is cleared while the client is alive by executing, delivering, and recording a deed.[111] But if the FMV of the property exceeds the § 2503(b) gift tax annual exclusion, a gift transfer will require the filing of a gift tax return[112] and payment of some gift tax may be required if the client's unified credit[113] is not sufficient to cover any gift tax incurred.[114] These consequences can be advantageous, but many clients resist both disclosure and payment of any tax inter vivos.

The revocable trust also may be appropriate for a mobile client, by centralizing management while the client retains control through a power to alter, amend, or revoke the trust. For example, mid-level executives who are moved from location to location as their employers move them up the management ladder, or the "snowbird" retired client who spends the summer up North and winters down South, both may find a trust to be useful for administration. And although many states replaced their inheritance taxes with estate taxes,[115] the growing number of states that have decoupled from the federal regime makes state death taxation a serious consideration. Utilization of a revocable trust can put intangible assets beyond the reach of the taxing authority of any state in

---

[111] If the client is not inclined to part with the property or place it in trust, another potential alternative to avoid ancillary administration if the property does not require active management is to transfer the property by a deed with a retained life estate. This transfer will have no FET advantages because the retained life estate will require § 2036(a)(1) inclusion in the decedent's gross estate, and may incur disastrous gift tax due to application of § 2702, but title will be cleared by the simple expedient of recording the deed, again avoiding ancillary administration at the client's death. See § 7.2.2, with respect to § 2702.

[112] § 6019(1).

[113] § 2505(a).

[114] There is some compensation, however, in addition to clearing title, because any post-gift income and appreciation in the property will escape FET, and gift taxation is cheaper than FET. See § 7.2.

[115] See § 1.1 nn.1, 3.

§ 4.1.6

which the settlor resides only temporarily, if that state's tax would be costly.[116]

Finally, clients who move to a noncommunity property jurisdiction may wish to segregate their community property. Settlement of community assets in a revocable trust situated in the community property state will tend to ensure that, upon the death of one of the spouses, the community character of the assets will be recognized and administration will not be thwarted by ignorance regarding community property. This may be of particular importance if the community assets have substantially appreciated in value, such that the new basis at death accorded to both halves of the community under § 1014(b)(6) will be important to the estate.[117]

§4.1.7 Statutory Entitlements

An additional factor that is worthy of separate discussion because of the emotional baggage it usually carries relates to the use of trusts to disinherit. Creditors of a decedent probably cannot be disfranchised by creation of a trust during the settlor's life,[118] but it may be possible to minimize or eliminate S's statutory forced heir entitlement or a descendant's civil law legitime entitlement to a portion of a settlor's wealth. This issue is relevant with respect to a decedent's share of community or separate property to the extent state law grants rights to a protected beneficiary, but only to the extent a living trust is immune to challenge. That topic is discussed separately because of its significance.[119]

§4.1.8 Pour Over from Wills to Trusts

Notwithstanding the utility of creating and funding revocable living trusts, seldom is a trust a total substitute for the use of a will. Usually at

---

[116] See, e.g., Blood v. Poindexter, 534 N.E.2d 768 (Ind. Tax Ct. 1989) (decedent avoided Indiana inheritance tax by transferring Indiana realty to Illinois trust, which effected a conversion of the property to intangible status for tax purposes).

[117] Compare Rev. Rul. 68-80, 1968-1 C.B. 348, in which community property assets, moved to another state and reinvested in another form, were ruled not entitled to the benefit of § 1014(b)(6).

[118] See Restatement (Third) of Trusts § 58(2) (2003).

[119] See § 4.3.

least a portion of the settlor's wealth is not transferred to the trust (or, having been placed in the trust, it got removed by inattention to proper accounting or other inadvertent acts during the balance of the settlor's life). Thus, a will usually is necessary to transfer assets not impressed with the trust, and often a will is desirable to glean advantages of probate administration.[120] In these cases a will typically "pours over" to the trust, which is meant to be the primary estate planning document. The will provides simple directions regarding disposition of a limited number of selected probate assets (such as personal effects), a tax payment provision and directions regarding whether the will or the trust governs tax payment to the extent they create inconsistent obligations,[121] and distribution of the inevitable residue of the testator's estate to the receptacle trust (created by the testator). Some wills pour over to a trust created by another settlor, such as the testator's predeceased spouse.

In an historical context it was not always clear that pour over wills were valid. Early in the development of this planning the prevailing legal concept underlying the delegation by will to a trust of dispositive control was the doctrine of incorporation by reference, by which a completely separate document is treated as if it is a part of a will. Incorporation by reference requires that the incorporated document be a separate instrument that was in existence when the will was executed, that it is adequately identified by the incorporating will, and that the incorporating will clearly expressed an intent to treat the incorporated document as a part of the will. Incorporation of a revocable living trust was respected under this doctrine only with respect to the trust terms as they existed when the will was executed. Subsequent amendments of the trust were ignored unless they were followed by re-execution of the will.[122]

The doctrine of independent legal significance was crafted because of the legal impediments to a successful and complete incorporation by reference, and to avoid creating by incorporation a testamentary or court

---

[120] See § 4.1.11.

[121] With respect to the need for coordination of tax payment in the context of multiple estate planning documents, see § 3.3.16.5.

[122] See generally 1 Scott, Fratcher, & Ascher, Scott and Ascher on Trusts § 7.1.1 (5th ed. 2006).

§ 4.1.8

trust governed by the will.[123] The doctrine permits a will to pour property over to a trust (typically a revocable living trust that was created by the testator as settlor), to be governed by the terms of the trust as amended from time to time, without the inconvenience or impossibility of re-execution of the will after each trust amendment.[124] Because the trust has its own independent legal significance, the doctrine permits it to be a beneficiary under the will and to serve in lieu of separate dispositive provisions in the will. All without being incorporated by reference as a part of the will or being subject to probate administration or court trust supervision.[125]

Under the law of many states a receptacle trust need not have its own separate valid existence prior to the pour over. Instead it may be validated in the first instance by the testator's bequest to it, if all other

---

[123] See Second Bank-State Street Trust Co. v. Pinion, 170 N.E.2d 350 (Mass. 1960) (breakthrough case recognizing the trust's independent significance and validating this approach).

[124] See 1 Scott, Fratcher, & Ascher, Scott and Ascher on Trusts § 7.1.2 (5th ed. 2006), and UPC § 2-511, 8 Pt. II U.L.A. 381 (1998), which is the freestanding Uniform Testamentary Additions to Trusts Act that is the law in the vast majority of states, even those that have not adopted the UPC. 8B U.L.A. 355 (2001).

Although a testator may pour over to a trust that remains revocable or amendable after the testator's death, and thereby permit additional changes to govern disposition of the poured over property, normally this would not be desirable because the poured over property would be subject to the trust settlor's power of revocation or amendment, which could generate undesirable FET inclusion in that settlor's gross estate under § 2041 as a general power of appointment.

[125] Occasionally a court holds that a pour over will incorporates the receptacle trust by reference, to accomplish a result that is clear with respect to a testamentary trust but not with respect to the receptacle trust. See, e.g., § 3.1.3 n.63, addressing the question whether a divorce that would revoke a bequest under a will also revokes a bequest under the receptacle trust. Other common circumstances in which this issue might arise include determining the rights of adopted or nonmarital relatives under a trust rather than a will, or application of the state antilapse statute. Many of these types of issues now are resolved by the 1990 version of UPC Article II, Part 7, which purports to apply all rules of construction to "governing instrument[s] of any type," probate and nonprobate alike, thus eliminating the need to misconstrue a pour over provision into an incorporation by reference.

§ 4.1.8

requisites for a valid trust have been met.[126] Many states also permit a pour over to a trust established after execution of the testator's will, including testamentary trusts created by the will of another person that was not executed until after execution of the testator's will, provided that the receptacle trust is in existence when the testator dies (meaning that the other testator must have predeceased the pour over testator).[127] Indeed, a pour over will does not necessarily fail even if the receptacle trust terminates or is revoked before the testator dies, unless the testator provides to the contrary.[128]

There also is authority providing that, if a pour over does fail, the testator's disposition will be effected by treating the will as an incorporation of the receptacle trust by reference.[129] Because not all state laws are as liberal as these, however, and because absence of the receptacle trust when the testator dies means that the pour over might fail for lack of a taker, the safest approach in all cases is to guarantee that the pour over is to a trust with at least a nominal trust corpus when the will is executed and that will remain in existence until the testator dies.

§4.1.9 Receptacle Trusts

Two final nontax reasons to create trusts during a settlor's life are to serve as a receptacle for benefits received in a divorce settlement or under a personal injury claim, and to receive and coordinate the disposition of the proceeds of life insurance policies and the death benefits under retirement benefit plans. The former may allow for expert management of funds the beneficiary otherwise could not administer. The latter permits more rapid collection of proceeds than if a testamentary

---

[126] See Uniform Testamentary Additions to Trusts Act and §2-511 of the UPC; Clymer v. Mayo, 473 N.E.2d 1084, 1090 (Mass. 1985): "We agree with the [lower] court's conclusion that 'the statute is not conditioned upon the existence of a trust but upon the existence of a trust *instrument.*'"

[127] See Uniform Testamentary Additions to Trusts Act and §2-511 of the UPC; 1 Scott, Fratcher, & Ascher, Scott and Ascher on Trusts §7.1.4 (5th ed. 2006).

[128] Uniform Testamentary Additions to Trusts Act and §2-511 of the UPC; 1 Scott, Fratcher, & Ascher, Scott and Ascher on Trusts §7.1.3 (5th ed. 2006); Marshall v. Northern Trust Co., 176 N.E.2d 807 (Ill. 1961) (pour over to testamentary trust created by will of testator's spouse, who revoked the will and died before the testator's death).

[129] See, e.g., Hageman v. Cleveland Trust Co., 343 N.E.2d 121 (Ohio 1976).

§4.1.9

trust was named (because there is no delay in having a will admitted to probate and the testamentary trustee qualified to act before collection can be undertaken). This allows more timely payment of estate taxes and accelerated administration and investment of these funds, which may represent the bulk of the decedent's wealth.[130]

§4.1.10 Tax Minimization

In addition to the numerous nontax reasons for using trusts, there are several common tax minimization reasons for their use. The most obvious is creation of an irrevocable living trust that will not be includ-

---

[130] In a few cases payment of retirement benefits and life insurance proceeds to a receptacle trust may reduce wealth transfer taxation, even though the trust was revocable until the settlor's death. For example, between 1983 and 1985 up to $100,000 of retirement death benefits payable in installments under various qualified plans was excluded from a decedent's gross estate for FET purposes, and before 1983 this exclusion was unlimited; these exclusions still apply if the employee separated from service before 1985 or 1983, respectively. See §9.2. Similarly, some state death taxes are not imposed on life insurance proceeds. See §8.3 n.6 and accompanying text.

Each exclusion is lost, however, to the extent payments are made to or for the benefit of the decedent's executor, making designation of a receptacle trust the effective choice to preserve these exclusions. In either situation, subjecting the excluded amounts to the executor's demand, such as to pay estate obligations, would be tantamount to making payment to the executor, so an added element to this exclusion-preservation planning is to tailor any tax or expense payment provision in the receptacle trust to limit use of these assets until all other assets have been exhausted. Cf. Old Colony Trust Co. v. Commissioner, 39 B.T.A. 871 (1939) (former federal exclusion of insurance proceeds not receivable by executor was preserved, notwithstanding receptacle trust that authorized trustee to pay debts of and taxes imposed on insured's estate, because there was no legally binding obligation on the trustee); Estate of Salsbury v. Commissioner, 34 T.C.M. (CCH) 1441 (1975) (qualified retirement plan benefit exclusion not lost notwithstanding trust permitted trustees to lend money to and purchase assets from decedent's estate to provide liquidity to meet estate obligations, again because there was no legally binding obligation). Even a mandate to use retirement benefits or insurance proceeds to pay estate obligations should not cause a loss of the exemption-as the equivalent of a payment to the executor-to the extent the obligations to which the mandate relates are not obligations of the executor (such as taxes attributable to nonprobate property that local law imposes on that nonprobate property).

ible in the settlor's gross estate at death.[131] Although no gift taxable transfer is made by the settlor of a *revocable* living trust (except to the extent distributions are made to third parties) until the settlor releases the power to revoke the trust, the settlor's transfer of assets to an immediately *irrevocable* trust will invoke an immediate gift tax, computed on the present FMV of the assets transferred. There are advantages of making current taxable gifts (rather than waiting to incur a subsequent gift or estate tax).[132] But taxpayers seldom embrace planning that causes an intentional acceleration of wealth transfer tax liability, even though it may reduce taxes and increase the overall net worth of the assets involved.

More complicated planning that combines bifurcated enjoyment with transfer tax minimization involves techniques that § 2702[133] may regulate (but does not eliminate), such GRATs, GRUTs, and QPRTs, all created during the settlor's life. Although gifts can be made without using a trust (even these specialized and highly regulated techniques), any reluctance regarding loss of control or about the donee's ability to manage the property can be minimized with appropriate use of trusts. In addition, compliance with highly complicated statutory requirements that must be met if tax objectives are to be gleaned generally is facilitated with a trust instrument rather than with some other form of deed or arrangement.

Trusts also present a number of income tax opportunities because they are respected as separate income tax paying entities with their own rate schedule, allowing a final bit of opportunism. Trusts have the unique advantage of allowing the settlor to control the income tax liability for trust income, by causing a trust or its beneficiary to be regarded as the owner of the trust income. Making the trust or the beneficiary pay tax on its income, or intentionally making the trust "defective"[134] for income tax

---

[131] The FMV of the property held in a revocable living trust at the death of the settlor will be includible in the settlor's gross estate as if no transfer into trust had been made during life. See § 2038(a)(1) and see § 7.3.3.

[132] See § 6.2.

[133] See § 7.2.2.

[134] For discussions of the many reasons why defective grantor trust planning is sensible and how to make a trust defective for grantor trust rule purposes see § § 5.11.9 and 5.11.10, respectively.

§ 4.1.10

grantor trust purposes (which allows the settlor to continue to incur income tax as if no trust was created), all depends on the relative income tax rates and any advantages of engineering the liability for income tax.[135]

Also made possible with trusts is the current enjoyment of a high level of benefits without causing state or federal estate or gift taxes to the beneficiary. For example, all without causing the beneficiary to be

---

[135] Trusts also may play a role in conjunction with tax free redemptions. Corporate redemption of all its stock owned by a shareholder is protected under § 302(b)(3) from dividend treatment but the § 318 stock attribution rules apply to determine whether all of a shareholder's stock is redeemed. For this purpose stock of a trust beneficiary is attributable to the trust and stock of an estate beneficiary is attributable to the estate and, if the trust is a beneficiary of the estate, stock of the trust beneficiary attributable to the trust can be attributed again to the estate. See §§ 318(a)(3) and 318(a)(5)(C), the latter of which precluding attribution from a beneficiary up to an entity and then down from the entity to another beneficiary under § 318(a)(2), but not precluding attribution from a beneficiary up to an entity and then up again to another entity under § 318(a)(3). Rev. Rul. 67-24, 1967-1 C.B. 75 (attribution from beneficiary to trust to estate notwithstanding that trust was created by will and estate had not yet been closed). Thus, if the trust or its beneficiary owns stock in the redeeming corporation, the estate's redemption would not be regarded as complete and dividend treatment would not be avoided.

In this respect, however, Treas. Reg. § 1.318-3(a) terminates attribution to an estate from a beneficiary when the beneficiary no longer has a claim against the estate because all estate property to which the beneficiary is entitled has been distributed and the estate has no more than a remote possibility of seeking recontribution from the beneficiary to satisfy estate claims or administration expenses. In Estate of Weiskopf v. Commissioner, 77 T.C. 135 (1981), attribution was precluded once distribution from an estate to a trust was complete and the trust already had provided all that it was required to contribute toward the estate's liabilities. So distribution by an estate followed by any redemption by the estate that depends on attribution not applying is viable if the trust and estate are separate and the trust no longer is an estate beneficiary. In this way, rather than make a shareholder a beneficiary of the decedent's estate, it might be effective to make that shareholder a beneficiary of a separate trust and the trust a beneficiary of the estate. Note, however, Rev. Rul. 60-18, 1960-1 C.B. 145, denying this opportunity to prevent attribution from the trust beneficiary to the estate if the trust is the residuary beneficiary of the estate (which frequently is the case with both testamentary trusts and trusts as beneficiaries of pour over wills) because the estate's liability to its residuary beneficiary does not end until the estate is closed. With respect to pour over wills, see § 4.1.8.

§ 4.1.10

deemed the owner of the trust property for wealth transfer tax purposes, a trust may provide for mandatory payment of all income, limited amounts of income in the trustee's discretion (permitting dissipation of the beneficiary's own resources before distribution of trust income), distribution of principal in the trustee's discretion, withdrawals by a beneficiary limited by an ascertainable standard[136] or a "five-or-five" restriction,[137] or distributions to third parties pursuant to nongeneral powers of appointment exercisable either inter vivos or at death. Indeed, if properly done,[138] a trust may even give a beneficiary full power over trust administration as trustee.

Trusts enjoy certain advantages over outright dispositions to younger generation beneficiaries even if the GST is applicable (and it may not apply even to a trust that could last for as long as permitted under the Rule and that benefits multiple generations of individuals, all to the extent the settlor's GST exemption is allocated properly to protect the trust against tax).[139] These advantages may include leveraging the exemption, making it possible to choose the least expensive form of tax, and the ability to defer or accelerate tax, all through expeditious use of nongeneral powers of appointment in trust.[140]

§4.1.11 Reasons to Favor Probate

Revocable living trusts are not always a panacea, and seldom exist without an accompanying pour over will. A number of factors may diminish the utility of revocable living trusts, and a significant number of reasons explain why knowledgeable estate planners nationwide wisely

---

[136] See § 12.3.2.4.

[137] See § 12.3.2.5.

[138] See Halbach, Tax-Sensitive Trusteeships, 63 Or. L. Rev. 381 (1984); Horn, Whom Do You Trust: Planning, Drafting and Administering Self and Beneficiary-Trusteed Trusts, 20 U. Miami Inst. Est. Plan. ¶ 500 (1986); Pennell, Estate Planning: Drafting and Tax Considerations in Employing Individual Trustees, 60 N.C. L. Rev. 799-820 (1982), abridged and reprinted in 9 Est. Plan. 264-272 (1982).

[139] See § 11.4.5.5.

[140] See §§ 11.4.5.4.3, 11.4.5.5.1, 11.4.5.5.4, and 11.4.14.

§4.1.11

embrace probate in appropriate circumstances to glean the many benefits that only probate can provide.[141]

Often the most important benefit is that probate allows a court
determination of the proper beneficiaries in "sticky" situations, such as
involving a potential conflict between several sets of descendants of a
decedent who had several spouses. Probate also provides nonclaim
statutory protections against "stale" claims of creditors,[142] which otherwise must be brought within a normal statute of limitation period that
may expire long after the client's death.[143]

Integration of the total estate plan is made easier in some cases by
directing all assets back to the probate estate to avoid the risk of
overfunding a marital deduction bequest or otherwise failing to coordinate the total dispositive pattern,[144] losing the availability of liquid assets
for tax payment or other purposes,[145] losing the ability to redeem without
dividend treatment stock in a close corporation equal in value to the
decedent's § 303(a)(1) death taxes and § 303(a)(2) funeral and adminis-

[141] See, e.g., Collier v. First Nat'l Bank, 417 S.E.2d 653 (Ga. 1992), and Estate
of Gillespie, 547 N.Y.S.2d 531 (Surr. Ct. 1989) (decedents' revocable living trusts
poured back to their probate estates to be distributed under the provisions of
trusts created under their wills).

[142] See § 2.7.5 n.20.

[143] A compelling illustration of the value of this protection is Witco Corp. v.
Beekhuis, 38 F.3d 682 (3d Cir. 1994), in which CERCLA environmental clean up
liability was precluded by a state probate law nonclaim statute. The decedent was
a potentially responsible party and the party that incurred those remediation
costs sued the decedent's estate for contribution, relying on the three year
statute of limitation under CERCLA, 42 U.S.C. § 9613(g)(3). The personal representative was granted summary judgment because the court determined that the
period for filing claims under the state law nonclaim statute had expired and that
the state nonclaim statute could coexist with the CERCLA statute of limitation.
Essential to the decision was that the plaintiff was aware of a potential contribution claim against the decedent and, under state law, could have filed its potential
claim in a timely manner in the decedent's probate proceeding. But compare
Bacigalupo v. United States, 399 F. Supp. 2d 835 (M.D. Tenn. 2005), which held
that a federal income tax liability of the taxpayer was not time barred because the
United States is not bound by a state statute of limitation, nor would it matter
how a nonclaim statute is characterized for that purpose under state law.

[144] See § 13.0.1.

[145] See § 3.3.16.

tration expenses,[146] and to preclude transferee liability on the trustee.[147] Furthermore, for postmortem planning purposes, disclaimers may be easier and more certain under state law if the disclaimed interest is a probate entitlement.[148]

By virtue of the historical development of certain laws that apply with respect to estates but not trusts, it remains true in many states that the effect of divorce on various dispositions is more clear in probate than it is for nonprobate dispositions. The same may be true regarding the rights of adopted or nonmarital descendants and children of the "new biology," the treatment of a slayer, and the effect of lapse, ademption, advancements, and tax apportionment rules, just to name a few.[149] Care is required in this domain, however, because sometimes these disparities are advantageous, in terms of avoiding certain state law restrictions that apply to estates but not to trusts. Thus, it is impossible to proclaim a best approach for all cases.

In the income tax arena, for a number of reasons, estates subject to probate may be slightly more desirable than living trusts that continue after the settlor's death.

- At one time all estates enjoyed an advantage over all trusts because income accumulated in and taxed to an estate was not subject to the throwback rules that applied only to trusts.[150] In 1997 Congress limited

---

[146] Under §303(b)(3) dividend treatment is avoided only to the extent the redeemed shareholder had the obligation to pay the decedent's taxes or expenses. Thus, this insulation from dividend treatment is lost if the trust owns the stock and the estate has the obligation, or vice versa.

[147] Although §6324(a)(2) imposes personal liability on a trustee to the extent of the FMV received or held by the trustee of property that was included in the decedent's gross estate under §§2034-2042, assets held by a trustee that the trust directs the trustee to pour back to the settlor's probate estate do not create personal liability exposure under §6324(a)(2) because those trust assets are includible in the settlor's gross estate under §2033 and not under any of §§2034-2042. Rev. Rul. 75-553, 1975-2 C.B. 477.

[148] See §10.5.3, regarding this with respect to disclaimers of joint tenancy property. The issue also can arise in determining the direction in which disclaimed property should pass if the intestate statute does not apply to a revocable living trust. UPC §2-1105 is unusual among state statutes in its application to testamentary and nontestamentary documents alike.

[149] See §4.2.1 n.8.

[150] See §5.6 n.4.

§4.1.11

throwback with respect to all trusts except those itemized in § 665(c)(2): trusts that are (or at one time were) foreign trusts, and pre-1984 multiple trusts that would be consolidated if they were not chronologically exempt from the application of § 643(f). In any event, compression of the federal income tax rates virtually eliminates any significant advantages of utilizing either an estate or a trust as a separate taxable entity.

- Trapping distributions[151] from an estate are not regarded as outside income to a recipient simple trust (such as a marital deduction trust created following the settlor's death), but that is not true with respect to trust distributions.[152] This means that the income distributed to a simple trust by an estate cannot be subject to the throwback rules when that income subsequently is distributed by the simple trust. But income distributed from a living trust to the same simple trust could be subject to throwback if the simple trust remains subject to throwback under § 665(c)(2). Because the repeal of throwback was not total, those revocable living trusts that distribute income to a trust that remains subject to throwback can generate a disadvantage relative to estate distributions to the same trust. Fortunately, this also should not be a frequent issue.

- The § 267 related party transfer rules that disallow losses generated by trust-to-beneficiary distributions do not apply to distributions in satisfaction of a pecuniary bequest (such as a formula marital deduction bequest) made by a decedent's estate,[153] and a similar disallowance rule is applicable to trusts but not to estates for passive activity loss purposes.[154]

- Depending on the reach of the separate share regulations,[155] to the extent an estate does not meet the test of having "substantially separate and independent shares of different beneficiaries" the estate may not be subject to the separate share rule of § 663(c). Thus, an estate may be free to shift taxable income among the estate's beneficiaries, creating the possibility of having income taxed to beneficiaries in lower tax brackets. By contrast, again depending on the terms of the trust, the separate share rule may prevent a trust from shifting taxable income to lower bracket taxpayers.[156]

---

[151] See § 5.8.2 n.17 and accompanying text.

[152] Treas. Reg. § 1.665(e)-1A(b).

[153] See § 267(b)(13), and Estate of Hanna v. Commissioner, 320 F.2d 54 (6th Cir. 1963) (rejecting government effort to attribute estate stock to beneficiaries and, on that basis, disallow losses on estate transfer to corporation as if it was the beneficiaries' transfer to the corporation).

[154] § 469(g)(1)(B). See § 5.8.3. n.33.

[155] Treas. Reg. § 1.663(c)-4(b).

[156] This estate advantage is made more attractive by the fact that the § 663(b) 65-day rule permits an executor or a trustee to elect to treat distributions to a beneficiary within 65 days after the close of a fiduciary's taxable year as though

- Estates are not required by § 644 to use a calendar year for tax reporting purposes, as must trusts that are recognized for income tax purposes.[157] Estates also are entitled to a two-taxable-year moratorium on compliance with the estimated tax rules, which is available to a trust under § 6654(*l*) only if the trust was entirely a grantor trust prior to the deceased settlor's death and it is the pour-over receptacle[158] of the residue of the settlor's estate. Although a revocable living trust may be entitled to the same treatment as the estate if both the executor and the trustee make the requisite § 645(a) election, this alternative is available only if the trust was treated as a § 676 grantor trust because it was revocable by the grantor during life, and this treatment (as if the trust was part of the estate) is available only for the § 645(b)(2) period (two years after the settlor's death if no FET return was required, or six months after "the date of the final determination of the liability for [estate] tax" if an FET return was required). The timing rules[159] for reporting income distributions make these rules important, and proper estate administration takes advantage of them to accelerate or defer a beneficiary's year for reporting that income, as appropriate.

Similarly, to the extent a § 645(a) election to treat a trust as part of the settlor's estate does not provide equivalence treatment, a number of other disparities also favor estates:

- The § 642(c) charitable set aside deduction is available only to estates. As a result, an executor need not worry about accelerated distribution of estate income to a charitable beneficiary to avoid income tax on it in the estate. Trust income destined for a charitable beneficiary must be paid currently to avoid income tax in the trust, which may create timing problems or involve risk if distribution is accelerated while litigation is pending that may alter the charity's entitlement.

- Estates enjoy a § 642(b) $600 deduction in lieu of the personal exemption, which (although not much) is twice as large as the largest

---

(Footnote Continued)

they had been distributed to the beneficiary in the prior year. In some cases, however, separate share treatment in an estate would be appropriate to maintain equality among the beneficiaries, so a fiduciary must be careful with respect to disparities created by varying distributions. Regarding the need to make an equitable adjustment in these cases, see § 5.8.4.

[157] Excepted from this rule are trusts that are wholly grantor trusts, because the trust's taxable year is ignored for income tax purposes and the tax timing abuse targeted by § 644 is irrelevant. Rev. Rul. 90-55, 1990-1 C.B. 161. See §§ 5.7 and 5.11.

[158] See § 5.7 at text accompanying n.6.

[159] See § 5.7 at text accompanying n.22.

§ 4.1.11

deduction available to any trust that is not a §642(b)(2)(C) qualified disability trust.

- Under §469(i)(4), $25,000 of passive real estate activity losses are allowed to estates for the first two taxable years after an active-participant-decedent's death; no similar benefit is available to trusts used as will substitutes.

- Under §6013, S and D's personal representative may elect to file a joint income tax return for D's final tax year. This election is not available to the trustee of a probate avoidance trust, even if the trust income was taxable to D during life under the grantor trust rules.[160]

- Under §1361, stock of an S Corporation may be held in an estate for the duration of reasonable estate administration; it may be held in a trust for only two years after the deceased shareholder's death unless the trust made the §645 election or it qualifies as an ESBT or as a QSST.[161]

A number of other important differences between living trusts and probate estates also favor estates for wealth transfer tax purposes.

- The existence of an "executor" is important for making elections under the §2056(b)(7)(B)(v) FET QTIP and the §2632 GST exemption allocation rules, and for purposes of the §2204 discharge of personal liability for FET, the §6905 discharge of personal liability for gift and income taxes of the decedent, and for the §6501(d) request for prompt assessment of FET.

- Pursuant to Treas. Reg. §20.2056(b)-5(f)(9), a delay in funding a marital deduction trust caused by problems of reasonable estate administration is forgiven under the all-income-annually rules applicable to the §§2056(b)(5) and 2056(b)(7) forms of marital deduction trust. The delay does not deprive the marital trust of the right to this income, and there will be an accounting for it when the trust finally is established. No similar relief is granted by the regulations to reasonable delays caused by trust administration, even though the same possibility for delay and ultimate accounting exist in the case of a marital deduction trust created under a revocable trust instrument after the settlor's death.

- A distinction exists between the treatment of decedents who utilize funded irrevocable living trusts and those who do not. According to a series of cases and rulings,[162] transfers made to third parties by irrevocable trusts within three years of the decedent's death may be subject to inclusion in the decedent's gross estate under §2035(a)(2) even though identical transfers from the decedent's personal estate during that period would be exempt

---

[160] See §5.7 n.22.

[161] See §4.1.13.

[162] See §7.3.7 nn.224-228 and accompanying text.

§4.1.11

from that rule. The § 2035(b) gross up rule precludes end of life transfers from generating an advantage attributable to the tax exclusive nature of the gift tax,[163] but gift tax valuation differentials[164] and the gift tax annual exclusion may be significant reasons for transfers proximate to death and dictate holding enough property out of any irrevocable living trust to finance those sorts of gifts. Fortunately, most living trusts are revocable and therefore constitute § 676 grantor trusts, as to which § 2035(e) provides an exception to this disparate treatment by regarding distributions from those revocable trusts as coming directly from the settlor and not subject to § 2035(a)(2).

• Expenses for administration of trust property after the settlor's death may be deductible under § 2053(b),[165] such as because the assets must be appraised for inclusion in the settlor's gross estate or sold to pay estate expenses or taxes properly imposed on the trust.[166] A slight and normally manageable disadvantage of trusts is that these expenses must be paid within the § 6501 statute of limitation period for assessment of FET in the settlor's estate (which usually is three years after filing the settlor's FET return).[167] More significant is the § 2053(c)(2) limitation, requiring that

---

[163] See § 6.2.1.

[164] See §§ 6.2.3 and 7.2.4.

[165] See § 15.4.3.5.

[166] See §§ 4.1.4 at text accompanying n.54 and 3.3.3.2 et seq., respectively, regarding creditor rights with respect to nonprobate property, and regarding apportionment of taxes and expenses against trust property.

[167] This period may be suspended under § 6503(a)(1) while litigation is pending and the Commissioner is prohibited from assessing any additional tax. According to Rev. Rul. 61-59, 1961-1 C.B. 418, additional expenses (such as attorney fees) incurred in conjunction with that litigation are deductible if paid within 60 days after the court's decision becomes final. Rev. Rul. 78-323, 1978-2 C.B. 240, clarified Rev. Rul. 61-59 "to remove the implication that the representative of the decedent's estate may recompute the estate tax liability . . . and file a claim for refund . . . ." The proper procedure under § 6215 is a prayer to reflect the deductible expenses in the court's final decision computing the decedent's FET liability. Gillum v. Commissioner, 49 T.C.M. (CCH) 240, 243 (1984), referred to both Rulings in a case in which the statutory notice of deficiency was issued to transferees after expiration of the § 6501(a) three year period but within the additional year allowed to assess transferees under § 6901(c). The court held that the transferees were not entitled to a deduction for any interest as an administration expense. Furthermore, the deduction for legal and accounting fees was limited to the amount paid prior to the three year period provided by § 6501(a), because "the plain language of section 6901(c) does not directly or by implication extend the period provided by section 6501(a). It merely provides a statutory period within which liability of an initial transferee can be assessed or a

§ 4.1.11

deductible amounts must be paid within the time for filing the FET return.[168] Applicable only to the extent those expenses exceed the FMV of property subject to claims against the decedent's probate estate,[169] neither timing limitation applies with respect to probate assets.

§4.1.12 Other Disadvantages of Revocable Living Trusts

Living trusts can create additional complications that may diminish their appeal, especially if a nonprofessional trustee is utilized. For example, to replicate the safekeeping of trust property that most professional fiduciaries offer may require a nonprofessional trustee to open one or more bank accounts, rent a safety deposit box, and perhaps hire a custodial accounting service. Moreover, the settlor must transfer legal title to trust assets to the trustee, securities must be reregistered and, if land is involved, deeds must be executed and recorded and homestead protection may be lost. All of these may attract nondeductible[170] state and local transfer taxes that would not apply at death, potentially could trigger a due-on-sale clause in a mortgage on nonresidential property or violate restrictions that may apply to restricted stock or stock options, cause the loss of nonassignable title insurance coverage,[171] and generate the legal and other costs of making effective conveyances under state law.

Furthermore, the trustee must maintain adequate records and keep trust assets and activities separate from the trustee's own assets and activities. This particularly is important if it is contemplated that a professional fiduciary will succeed a nonprofessional trustee at some future time, because a professional fiduciary typically will be more careful about reviewing its predecessor's conduct if it does not succeed

---

(Footnote Continued)

statutory notice issued." The property subject to FET in *Gillum* was not subject to claims.

[168] Normally this is nine months after the decedent's death, under § 6075(a).

[169] See § 15.4.3.5.

[170] Transfer taxes were repealed from federal law by Excise Tax Reduction Act of 1965 § 401, and are made a basis adjustment item (rather than a deduction) by § 164(a).

[171] See Rivin & Stikker, Title Insurance for Estate Planning Transfers, 12 Prob. & Prop. 15 (May/June 1998).

another professional fiduciary. Although professional trustees' fees are avoidable if the settlor or a family member is serving as trustee, often a custodial or investment advisory service fee will be only slightly less than a professional fiduciary's total fee, especially if the fiduciary would provide services (such as tax return preparation,[172] dividend and interest collection and investment, and automated inventory, valuation, and accounting services) for which other professional fees otherwise would be incurred.

In any event, all these legal fees and other costs attributable to creation, funding, and administration of funded revocable living trusts are in addition to the cost to prepare a will, which remains an essential aspect of the overall plan, and they are deductible for income tax purposes as § 212(2) expenses incurred in the management, conservation, or maintenance of income producing properties[173] only to the extent they exceed the 2% disallowance under § 67(e), applicable with respect to any expense the settlor would incur if no trust existed.[174]

Regardless of the § 67(e) issue, all of these costs may be regarded as just a prepayment rather than an added excise, to the extent they would be incurred at death as part of normal estate administration, but few people appreciate the opportunity to accelerate even unavoidable

---

[172] See Treas. Reg. §§ 1.671-4(a) and 1.6012-3(a)(9). A statement attached to a Form 1041 fiduciary income tax return must be filed if the settlor is not the trustee or a cotrustee, even though the federal income tax picture does not change in most cases during the settlor's life. The settlor will be treated as owner of the trust for income tax purposes because it is held for the settlor's benefit and because it is revocable. See §§ 677 and 676, respectively. Thus, all income, deductions, credits, and such of the trust will be attributable to the settlor, even if income is accumulated in the trust or paid to beneficiaries other than the settlor. See § 5.11.

[173] See, e.g., Estate of Kincaid v. Commissioner, 52 T.C.M. (CCH) 1003 (1986) (trust beneficiary's deduction for legal expenses incurred to prevent perceived abuses in trust administration that would be detrimental to the beneficiary's receipt of trust income allowed as § 212(2) expenses that relate to the management, conservation, or maintenance of property held for the production of income).

[174] See § 5.11 n.8 regarding the application of § 67(e) in the context of a grantor trust, which would apply in virtually any case involving a revocable inter vivos trust. See § 5.3.1 at text accompanying n.16 regarding application of § 67(e) in a nongrantor trust context.

§ 4.1.12

expenses early. And if the estate plan calls for distributions immediately after the settlor's death, these costs and any trustee's fee for termination of the revocable living trust may exceed the costs that would have been incurred in a normal probate of the settlor's entire estate.

§4.1.13 Subchapter S Election Concerns

Under § 1361(c)(2)(A)(i), a revocable trust is a permissible shareholder in an S Corporation because of grantor trust treatment,[175] typically under §§ 677 and 676. But § 1361(c)(2)(A)(ii) allows the Subchapter S election to continue for only two years after the settlor's death. If it is desired to have the election continue beyond the two year period, the stock must be distributed from the trust either into the settlor's estate or to a beneficiary, or the trust either must make a valid § 645 election or it must qualify either under § 1361(d)(3) as a QSST or under § 1361(e) as an ESBT.

A QSST may have only one current income beneficiary (who must be a United States citizen or resident), all trust income must be distributed currently to that beneficiary, the beneficiary's income interest may terminate no sooner than the beneficiary's death or termination of the trust, and while that beneficiary is alive trust principal may be distributable only to that beneficiary. A § 2056(b)(7) QTIP marital deduction trust is a good example of a QSST. An ESBT may have numerous individuals, estates, and certain charities as beneficiaries and there is no mandatory income distribution requirement, but all S Corporation income is taxed at the highest rates under the Code (even if distributed to the beneficiaries-because it is not includible in DNI and there is no distributions deduction with respect to it).[176]

---

[175] Absence of passthrough taxation explains why an IRA (either traditional or Roth) may not be a qualified S Corporation shareholder. See, e.g., Taproot Administrative Services Inc. v. Commissioner, 133 T.C. 202 (2009), aff'd, 679 F.3d 1109 (9th Cir. 2012); Treas. Reg. § 1.1361-1(h)(1)(vii) (last sentence); Rev. Rul. 92-73, 1992-2 C.B. 224.

[176] See Treas. Reg. § 1.641(c)-1, creating an S portion and a non-S portion for the trust, with the former being regarded as a separate taxpaying entity as to which no distributions are deemed made and all income, credits, deductions, and losses from the S Corporation are taxable separately. See generally § 15.7.2 regarding S Corporation taxation and postmortem estate planning.

§ 4.1.13

In some contexts, a QSST may not be favorable because a separate trust for each beneficiary would be required, no power to add nonqualifying beneficiaries may be included (other than by any § 1361(e)(2) unexercised power of appointment), and income could not be accumulated. An ESBT may be preferable in those cases, notwithstanding the high income tax impost. By way of comparison, however, an estate and a § 645 electing trust may be an S Corporation shareholder for as long as the estate properly is under administration, without compliance with any of these requirements.

§ 4.1.14 Joint Settlor Trusts

Trusts created by multiple settlors can create problems that may be better avoided than cured.[177] Seldom is it a sufficient reason for creation of a joint settlor trust that the property being contributed to it is concurrently owned (community property or tenancy in common, joint tenancy, or tenancy by the entireties), or the joint settlors are not spouses. Each is easy to address if the property is subject to partition, which actually may be beneficial if it generates fractional interest discounts for valuation purposes. Although partition is possible with respect to community property, it might be a mistake to do so because of the loss of the new basis in both halves of the community property provided by § 1014(b)(6) on D's death.

A better reason to consider a joint settlor trust may be illustrated by PLRs 200210051 and 200101021, in which spouses were able to employ joint settlor trusts to better plan to shelter their collective unified credits than through bifurcation of their assets and allocation of assets in hopes of guessing correctly which spouse will die first.[178]

---

[177] See § 3.7 n.22.

[178] See § 13.5.6.5. A refinement in PLRs 200604028 and 200403094 might be more attractive because it does not entail a joint trust and the control granted to D is limited to a formula driven general power to appoint the amount of D's unused exclusion. It is essential that S not be regarded as a transferor of any property in a trust meant to escape inclusion when S dies, which may be difficult to assure if joint tenancy or tenancy by the entireties property is contributed to the trust because there is no partition or separate identification of D's portion as there is with respect to community property at either spouse's death. This identification and inclusion problem explains why it may be risky to use joint settlor trusts with respect to co-owned property other than community property.

Otherwise a joint settlor revocable living trust, funded with community or other jointly owned property, may be sensible if other reasons support the selection of a revocable living trust for property management and disposition during the spouses' joint lives and thereafter during S's overlife. In community property situations a revocable living trust also may be useful to keep each spouse's separate property separate (such as separate property brought to a community property state from a noncommunity property jurisdiction, property inherited by one of the spouses, or property owned by either spouse before the marriage).

If the trust is to become irrevocable upon D's death, however, both spouses must join in creation of the trust because, otherwise, S loses a valuable property right. And in a community property jurisdiction, S might be able to defeat the trust on grounds that the trust constitutes a fraud on the community if it holds any community property.[179] In any case in which a trust becomes irrevocable during either settlor's life further care is required to ensure that a completed gift does not occur unintentionally, in this case consisting of S's property interests that were contributed to the trust. A power of withdrawal exercisable by S with respect to S's property interests would make irrevocability of the trust harmless, as would retention by S of a general or nongeneral power to appoint that property, exercisable inter vivos or only at death.[180] Alternatively, these concerns all can be avoided if S retains a power to revoke or amend any separate trust funded with S's property interests.

(Footnote Continued)

See Estate of Whiting v. Commissioner, 87 T.C.M. (CCH) 1097 (2004), and PLR 200311020, which involved joint settlor trusts as to which state court reformations were obtained, in *Whiting* to guarantee marital deduction qualification for amounts in excess of the basic exclusion amount, and in the Ruling to preclude the existence of prohibited interests or powers that might cause the nonmarital trust to be includible in S's estate. The government ruled that the taxpayer had no § 2036 exposure at S's death and did not release a general power of appointment on reformation, so § 2041 also would not apply with respect to the nonmarital trust.

[179] See Commissioner v. Chase Manhattan Bank, 259 F.2d 231 (5th Cir. 1958); Land v. Marshall, 426 S.W.2d 841 (Tex. 1968).

[180] See § 7.1.7.

§ 4.1.14

The point never to overlook is that there are two transferors, each of their respective property interests.[181] S should retain some power over S's property but not over D's property interests, to the extent the plan is to preclude estate taxation to S of any part of D's property in the joint trust.

§4.1.15 Trustee Selection

Selecting a trustee may be the most difficult issue that the settlor must address in creating a trust.[182] In some cases selection of the initial trustee is easy, but trustee succession is difficult. In that regard, the expected duration of the particular trust is a critical consideration. It may terminate on the death or remarriage of a surviving spouse or continue until some well defined moment (such as children completing their higher education, a return to the private sector by the settlor of a political blind trust, or cessation of some defined form of disability, turmoil, or hazard), or it might extend forever (in a perpetual GST exempt dynasty trust or a charitable trust). Finally, the chore is magnified if the trust uses cofiduciaries or bifurcates fiduciary functions among a formal trustee and a committee, trust advisor, trust protector, or distribution and investment directors.

The office of trustee entails various functions, each requiring particular talents and skills. For example, expert trust management usually requires substantial investment acumen (unless the trust is to retain designated assets and exonerates the trustee from traditional duties to diversify). There is an extensive array of choices for prudent investment of funds under management, leading some nonprofessional trustees to delegate this aspect to a professional investment manager. Yet it is not uncommon to discover that the investment manager's fee is nearly as

---

[181] This separate transferor treatment explains why division of the respective properties after D's death does not constitute a distribution that otherwise would accelerate the alternate valuation date under §2032(a)(1). Compare Rev. Rul. 78-431, 1978-2 C.B. 230 (division of community property), with Treas. Reg. §20.2032-1(c)(2)(ii) and Rev. Rul. 73-97, 1973-1 C.B. 404 (division of trust into separate shares for various beneficiaries).

[182] Just as naming guardians for a testator's minor children causes some testators more trouble than selecting the dispositive provisions of a will.

high as a professional trustee would charge to provide all services expected of a full-fledged trustee.

In addition to asset management, there are "back office" chores (such as fiduciary accounting and tax compliance), and distribution functions (such as exercising discretion to make distributions among a group of beneficiaries). Frequently the array of skills needed in a particular situation is more extensive than those brought to the task by any one individual, meaning that some functions must be delegated or a full-service entity such as a corporate trustee should be selected.

Whatever the initial selection, another difficult trustee selection aspect is removal or replacement. Nothing is more certain to protect beneficiaries from an incompetent, arrogant, or inattentive trustee than the threat of removal. Which makes a "revolving door" power[183] reposed in a beneficiary,[184] a trust protector, a trust advisor, or some other third party a critical form of "checks-and-balances" that maintains a degree of equilibrium in the trust relationship. In addition, every trust should anticipate trustees who fail to become or cease to act.

Thus, every trust should establish a method to designate successor trustees. Alternatives might include selection by the current beneficiaries, or delegation to the local probate judge, to the manager of the law firm that drafted the trust, or to a committee of individuals (for whom replacements also may be needed). This succession issue is even more difficult if the trust will extend for a long time, because any designation could fail as circumstances change (for example, if probate courts no longer exist, the law firm disappears, or no committee members remain).

---

[183] See §§ 7.3.3 and 12.0 n.20, discussing the tax consequences of a power to remove and replace trustees.

[184] Some trusts permit the current income beneficiaries to remove or replace (or both), but this will not be appropriate in some circumstances, either because the beneficiaries cannot easily be determined (for example, because the class of beneficiaries is too large or vague) or are not suitable (for example, due to incapacity, age, or lack of experience). See § 12.0 n.20 regarding the government's abandoned § 2041 power of appointment argument flowing from the alleged ability of a trust beneficiary to benefit from a power to remove and replace trustees.

§ 4.1.15

Various tax aspects of serving as trustee can be found in place throughout this work,[185] the most common issues being §2041 general power of appointment concerns if a beneficiary has (or is treated as having) the trustee's powers, and potential §678 income tax pseudo-grantor trust concerns. Those considerations need no rehearsal here. Moreover, careful drafting can protect against any untoward tax liabilities (for example, by using ascertainable or reasonably definite external standards and an Upjohn clause). *Anyone* can serve as trustee, including a beneficiary, if appropriate compromises are made in some cases to limit the trustee's powers to avoid undesirable tax consequences. The selection of trustee might be more constrained in a handful of more refined circumstances,[186] but the choice of trustee is virtually unrestricted in most garden-variety situations.

Some trusts employ cotrustees and restrict or delegate certain functions among them to avoid making these compromises. Others employee multiple trustees because certain trustees lack some of the skills that are needed. The notion is that cotrustees may bring a collection of skills to the endeavor that, in the aggregate, provides all the expertise needed. Given the nature of cotrustee liability,[187] however, it may be more desirable to name a single trustee and then "fill in" any gaps in their skills or authority by naming (or allowing the trustee to designate) others to serve as agents for the trustee.

For example, an individual trustee who is selected because of special knowledge of the settlor's family or business might hire a professional to provide back office administration, accounting, tax compliance, and investment advice. Alternatively, in such a case it might be wise to name a professional trustee to administer the trust and name the individ-

---

[185] Indeed, little has changed since publication of Pennell, Estate Planning: Drafting and Tax Considerations in Employing Individual Trustees, 60 U. N.C. L. Rev 799 (1982), abridged and reprinted in 9 Est. Planning 264 (1982).

[186] For example, the beneficiary should not be the trustee of a SNT, and the settlor should not be the trustee of a blind trust.

[187] Traditionally cotrustees were jointly and severally liable (unless the document provided otherwise). UTC §703 and Restatement (Third) of Trusts §81(2) (2007) modify this to provide that one trustee is not directly liable for actions taken by another trustee, but each must exercise reasonable care to prevent a cotrustee from committing, and to compel a cotrustee to redress, any serious breach of trust.

§4.1.15

ual as "distribution director" to make dispositive decisions. The trustee also might be relieved of any investment authority with respect to the family business, which would repose instead in a directed-investments advisor. The same may be advisable with respect to delegated authority to perform due diligence with respect to insurance policies held in an ILIT. With appropriate authority to delegate, and adequate exoneration for the trustee regarding these agents' authority, the limited function approach poses fewer risks to the various players than does cotrustee liability. It also might generate lower fees.[188]

Finally, trust law reforms relating to trust enforcement may ease concerns about the selection of trustees. The historic notion was that a trust was a relationship, not an entity, meaning that the trust itself could not sue or be sued.[189] Instead, the trustee was the appropriate litigant,[190] with the power to bind the trust if the trustee's actions were proper and the power to sue on behalf of the trust or to be sued and then be

---

[188] Given the current state of the law under §67(e), it also may alter the amount of the aggregate fees (a single professional's bundled fee or the fees paid to separate advisors) that is subject to the 2% loss of deductions. See §5.3.1.

[189] See, e.g., Restatement (Second) of Trusts §§261, 264 (1959). The rule was applied in an unusual manner in Stoltenberg v. Newman, 101 Cal. Rptr. 3d 606 (Ct. App. 2009), in which litigation against the trustee was time-barred by the state nonclaim statute because the trustee died, rather than the longer statute that would apply in litigation against an entity that continued beyond the death of any principal of the organization. And in Portico Management Group, LLC v. Harrison, 136 Cal. Rptr. 3d 151 (Cal. Ct. App. 2011), the court concluded that an arbitration award against a trust was "meaningless and unenforceable" because the trust is merely a relationship and does not hold title to any assets against which enforcement could be had.

Cf. the similar historical rule about an estate also not being a jural personality, which explains why the injured parties in Idoux v. Estate of Helou, 691 S.E;.2d 773 (Va. 2010), and Estate of James v. Peyton, 674 S.E.2d 864 (Va. 2009), were precluded from suing a deceased tortfeasor, because their pleadings named as defendant "the Estate of Tortfeasor, Individual as Administrator" instead of the mandated "Individual as Administrator of the Estate of Tortfeasor."

[190] Reflecting a change from the traditional rule, Gould v. Gould, 280 S.W.3d 137 (Mo. Ct. App. 2009), declined to rule that only a successor trustee may sue a predecessor—the court held that a disappointed beneficiary *also* has standing. King v. Johnston, 101 Cal. Rptr. 3d 269 (Ct. App. 2009), allowed a beneficiary to sue a third party who had participated with a predecessor trustee in a breach of trust and was not precluded from continuing in that litigation just because a successor trustee had been appointed.

§4.1.15

indemnified by the trust.[191] A modern trend recognizes the entity as a legitimate litigant,[192] making it easier and less threatening to name an appropriate trustee without considerations relating to the possibility or need for litigation.

In addition, trust enforcement also is undergoing modification, such that the beneficiaries are not the only parties entitled to sue to enforce trust terms.[193] As a result, others (such as a trust protector) may stand in the beneficiary's shoes, particularly if a beneficiary is not able to supervise a trustee or to enforce the trust. If a particular trustee fails to hew to the settlor's intent, the settlor[194] or a third party of the settlor's choosing also may be authorized to oversee and to enforce compliance—which is important in an environment in which beneficiaries or the trustee may seek court ordered trust reformations.

---

[191] A common law trustee was liable personally to third parties for contracts entered into or torts committed in the course of trust administration to the same extent as if the trustee had owned the trust property and acted individually, regardless of whether the trustee violated any fiduciary duties. The trustee may have been entitled to indemnification from the trust estate, but only if the contract was entered into in the course of trust administration or if the tort liability was incurred by the trustee without fault.

[192] See Restatement (Third) of Trusts, Chapter 21 and specifically § 106 (2012), and state laws such as UTC § 1010(b) and UPC § 7-306, which alter the common law rule unless the contract expressly so provides or the trustee did not reveal the representative capacity and identify the trust estate in the contract, or the trustee acted outside the course of trust administration or personally was at fault in committing the tort.

[193] But cf. Raines v. Synovus Trust Co., 41 So. 3d 70 (Ala. 2009), in which UTC § 603(a) was applied, to the effect that beneficiaries of a revocable trust could not sue the trustee for mismanagement while the settlor was still alive.

[194] Cf. Hardt v. Vitae Foundation, Inc., 302 S.W.3d 133 (Mo. Ct. App. 2009), in which estate executors selected charitable beneficiaries based on a grant proposal and sought relief on the grounds of misuse. The court dismissed, stating the traditional rule involving charitable gifts that only the State Attorney General has standing to enforce the terms of a charitable donation (and in this case the AG had not even been notified of the executors' allegations). The court noted that Missouri has adopted the UTC, which grants settlors of charitable trusts the right to enforce the trust but declined to extend that authority to other forms of disposition.

§ 4.1.15

§4.2 REVOCABLE TRUSTS

§4.2.1 Validity as a Testamentary Substitute

Most living trusts are fully revocable until the settlor dies.[1] A settlor's power to revoke could be made exercisable by the settlor only with the consent of an adverse party (such as a beneficiary) or a nonadverse party (such as the trustee or another contributor to the trust).[2] But usually there is no reason to make a trust revocable only with consent. Nontax reasons for restricting the settlor's ability to revoke unilaterally might include protecting against the settlor's improvidence, or because the trust was created as part of a property settlement incident to divorce. In addition, except in the case of a trustee's power to distribute trust principal to or for the benefit of the settlor (and thereby terminate the trust),[3] most living trusts are not revocable by someone other than the settlor during the settlor's life. As a result, it is common to refer to a revocable living trust as one that only the settlor may terminate, at will.

In this sense, a revocable living trust raises the issue whether it accomplishes anything during the settlor's life that makes it different from a will. In addition, revocable living trusts raise questions regarding the tax consequences of creation and administration of the trust during the settlor's life, about the general effect and integration of trusts as a component in the settlor's overall estate plan, and about the rights of third parties-such as creditors or a surviving spouse-who may have claims against the settlor.

Extensive litigation has rejected the proposition that revocable living trusts are invalid testamentary dispositions on the alleged grounds that they are intended to operate only from and after the settlor's death

---

[1] §4.2 Even some irrevocable trusts are subject to amendment or change because the settlor granted a power to a third party to alter the trust terms or to appoint the trust property. See §4.1.1, regarding flexibility to adapt a trust to changing circumstances.

[2] See 5 Scott, Fratcher, & Ascher, Scott and Ascher on Trusts §§35.1.3 to 35.1.5 (5th ed. 2008), with respect to revocations with consent.

[3] See 5 Scott, Fratcher, & Ascher, Scott and Ascher on Trusts §33.1.1 (5th ed. 2008).

and fail to comply with all the formalities required of a will. Wills are ambulatory (they have no legal effect while the testator is alive), but trusts created by a settlor inter vivos are legally operative immediately, regardless of the settlor's retained enjoyment of trust benefits or reserved control over the management or disposition of trust property. Even though most living trusts are revocable until death and distribute the settlor's property to third parties only after the settlor's death, it is well established today that revocable living trusts created by formal trust instruments are not testamentary or invalid merely because they do not comply with the formalities for execution of a will.[4] As stated in a leading case:[5]

> The distinguishing feature of a testamentary disposition is that it remains ambulatory until the death of the one who makes it. Until he dies, his title remains unimpaired and unaffected. A testamentary disposition becomes operative only upon and by reason of the death of the owner who makes it. It operates only upon what he leaves at his death. If the interest in question passes from the owner presently, while he remains alive, the transfer is inter vivos and not testamentary.
>
> . . . [T]hat the settlor sought to avoid making a will, or to "evade" or "circumvent" the statutory requirements for a will [is] . . . immaterial. The law prohibits only an unattested disposition that takes effect in a testamentary manner. If an owner of property can find a means of disposing of it inter vivos that will render a will unnecessary for the accomplishment of his practical purposes, he has a right to employ it. The fact that the motive of a transfer is to obtain the practical advantages of a will without making one is immaterial.

Thus, it is not sufficient to render a transfer in trust incomplete or testamentary and therefore subject to will execution formalities that the settlor retains a power in any form to amend or revoke the trust, to control investments or other aspects of trust administration, or even full powers as trustee.

There is some case law to the contrary, but invariably it arises when a court is looking to apply legal principles or statutory solutions to work equitable results that normally are available only to wills.[6] Thus, occa-

---

[4] See 1 Scott, Fratcher, & Ascher, Scott and Ascher on Trusts § 8.2.1 (5th ed. 2006), and cases cited therein.

[5] National Shawmut Bank v. Joy, 53 N.E.2d 113, 122 (Mass. 1944).

[6] See § 3.2.5.4, regarding antilapse statutes.

§ 4.2.1

sionally courts characterize trusts as testamentary to thereby make available a remedy normally applicable only under the law relating to wills.[7] This does not mean that revocable living trusts are testamentary, and the occurrence of these legal gymnastics is dwindling as more jurisdictions adopt legislation that introduces concepts first developed for the law of wills into the law governing other wealth transfer devices, most especially trusts.[8]

In garden variety situations that do not call for these equitable deviations, the consensus is that revocable living trusts are not testamentary and need not comply with the formalities of will execution. Nevertheless, some estate planners advise that execution of a revocable living trust comply with all the formalities required of a will, to avoid controversy or challenge, and at least one state has enacted legislation that appears to require such an execution to prevent the postmortem aspects of the trust from being disregarded.[9] This particularly is encouraged if the settlor also is the trustee and the sole beneficiary prior to death (a self-trusteed declaration of trust) because of the even greater appearance that nothing substantive has changed during the settlor's life notwithstanding creation of the trust.[10]

---

[7] See, e.g., Dollar Savings & Trust Co. v. Turner, 529 N.E.2d 1261 (Ohio 1988), which held that, if a will substitute is involved-such as a revocable trust-the controlling antilapse statute would apply and, because a trust beneficiary died before the settlor, the substitute takers named in the antilapse statute would receive the trust property the predeceased beneficiary would have received if that beneficiary had survived the settlor.

[8] See, e.g., the 1990 version of UPC Article II, Part 7, which applies to nontestamentary instruments such will concepts as survivorship requirements and presumptions, class gift construction rules, antilapse protections, and questions regarding status (such as adopted or nonmarital children). In what the court regarded as a case of first impression, Ruby v. Ruby, 2012 Il. App (1st) 103, 210 (withdrawn from WL at request of court), applied ademption by extinction to a trust and held that, in essence, the mere-change-in-form exception to ademption was applicable.

[9] Fla. Stat. § § 689.075 and 736.0403(2)(b). And see Zuckerman v. Alter, 615 So. 2d 661 (Fla. 1993), which predated modifications to the Florida statutes to make clear that will execution formalities are required for executions that occur in the state of Florida. Regarding valid will substitutes generally see Schoenblum, 2013 Multistate Guide to Estate Planning Table 5.01, Part 1 (2012).

[10] See § 4.2.3.

The conceivable danger of this added precaution is that a revocable living trust executed with all the formalities of a will may be deemed to *be* a will and hence a disposition that is subject to an unintended formal probate administration. This possibility should be avoidable by making it clear in the trust instrument that the settlor's intent is to not to create a will but, rather, to create a trust that is operative immediately. It also might be advisable to create an interest in someone other than the settlor that might provide enjoyment prior to the settlor's death, however slight or unlikely, thereby distinguishing the trust from a truly testamentary disposition.

§4.2.2 Is It Revocable?

Although this discussion assumes that the trust is revocable, the historical default rule in most jurisdictions was that a trust was not revocable unless the power to revoke specifically was retained. Usually silence meant that the trust was irrevocable.[11] Due entirely to adoption of the UTC, which reverses this rule,[12] the majority rule today is that *new* trusts are revocable unless expressly made irrevocable.[13] Savings account (Totten) trusts also are regarded as revocable, even in many states that embrace the traditional default rule that garden variety trusts are irrevocable unless provided otherwise.[14] In all of these cases a statement in the trust instrument that the trust is irrevocable will suffice to overcome state law, and some Totten trust cases hold that notification of the beneficiary or delivery of the passbook to the beneficiary also may

---

[11] 5 Scott, Fratcher, & Ascher, Scott and Ascher on Trusts §35.1 (5th ed. 2008).

[12] UTC §602(a).

[13] See also Alaska Stat. §13.36.338; Cal. Prob. Code §15400; Ind. Code §30-4-3-1.5(a); Iowa Code §633A.3102(1); Mont. Code Ann. §72-33-401; Okla. Stat. tit. 60, §175.41; Tex. Prop. Code Ann. §112.051. Restatement (Third) of Trusts §63(2) comment *c* (2003) states a presumption that a trust is revocable if the settlor reserves a beneficial interest in the trust but is presumed to be irrevocable if not.

[14] See 1 Scott, Fratcher, & Ascher, Scott and Ascher on Trusts §8.3.4 (5th ed. 2006), and 5 Scott, Fratcher, & Ascher, Scott and Ascher on Trusts §35.1 (5th ed. 2005).

suffice to make the trust irrevocable[15] (although other cases have found that neither notification nor delivery necessarily indicate irrevocability).[16]

Because state law is in a major state of (essentially) reversal, issues of interpretation are likely to arise unless the settlor expresses the intent to make a trust revocable or irrevocable. For example, the power to revoke may be implicit in other provisions that are explicit,[17] or it may be a specific retained power that imposes special requirements to constitute an effective revocation, in which case any attempted revocation must conform to those requirements.[18] By way of a simple but increasingly common example, if a power to revoke the trust is meant to be exercisable by the holder of the settlor's durable power of attorney, that fact ought to be articulated in both the trust and the durable power.[19]

---

[15] See 1 Scott, Fratcher, & Ascher, Scott and Ascher on Trusts § 8.3.1 nn.6 and 8 (5th ed. 2006).

[16] See 1 Scott, Fratcher, & Ascher, Scott and Ascher on Trusts § 8.3.1 nn.7 and 9 (5th ed. 2006). Indeed, Estate of Sulovich v. Commissioner, 587 F.2d 845 (6th Cir. 1978), rev'g 66 T.C. 250 (1976), held that delivery of passbooks and notice to the donees together did not make Totten trusts irrevocable because the account signature cards required the settlor's consent to any withdrawal by the holder of the passbook. Notwithstanding that the donee reported the trust income for income tax purposes, the trust account balances were deemed to be includible in the settlor's gross estate at death.

[17] See, e.g., Scott v. Dane, 196 N.E.2d 195 (Mass. 1964) (unrestricted power to amend includes power to revoke).

[18] See, e.g., Dallinger v. Abel, 557 N.E.2d 936 (Ill. App. Ct. 1990) (trust revocable only with consent of remainder beneficiaries not affected by attempted unilateral amendment); Trager v. Schwartz, 189 N.E.2d 509 (Mass. 1963) (requirement that revocation or amendment must be recorded to be effective did not specify who must record it or when; settlor breached promise to record an amendment and later attempted to disavow that amendment, which the court held was thwarted because the promisee subsequently effectively recorded the amendment); Kline v. Utah Dep't of Health, 776 P.2d 57 (Utah Ct. App. 1989) (trust revocable only until settlor died or became disabled could not be revoked by settlor's spouse pursuant to durable power of attorney; because the trust therefore was regarded as irrevocable, state could not deny Medicaid benefits to incompetent settlor on basis of trust assets being available to settlor).

[19] See, e.g., In re Lee, 982 P.2d 539 (Okla. Ct. App. 1999), holding that the general rule is that the powerholder may *not* exercise the settlor's power to revoke. See generally Radford, Bogert, & Bogert, The Law of Trusts and Trustees § 1000 n.42 and accompanying text (3d ed. 2006) (power to revoke does not pass to settlor's guardian).

§ 4.2.2

These elements are significant because revocability may alter the time when wealth transfer tax liability is incurred,[20] it may alter the income taxation of the trust,[21] it will affect control or access by the settlor, and it may impact the rights of the settlor's creditors or other claimants.[22] Thus, revocability should not be left to chance, conflict of law or governing law provisions, or default rules.[23]

In addition, proper drafting of a power to revoke demands careful attention. For example, many well drafted powers indicate that they are exercisable only by an instrument in writing *other than a will*, signed by the settlor and delivered to the trustee before the settlor's death.[24] This avoids the issue whether a settlor may revoke a trust by a provision in the settlor's will.[25] Alternatively, if revocation by a will provision is

---

[20] Other powers or interests also may affect the time when a transfer into trust is sufficiently complete to incur gift tax and may cause the transfer to be deemed sufficiently incomplete to require FET inclusion when the settlor dies. But a retained power to revoke absolutely will make a transfer into trust incomplete for gift tax purposes and require FET inclusion under § 2038(a)(1). See generally §§ 7.1.7 and 7.3.3, regarding the estate and gift tax treatment of transfers into trusts.

[21] See generally § 5.11.3, regarding the grantor trust income tax provisions.

[22] See §§ 4.1.4 and 7.1.7.1, and 4.3, respectively, regarding spendthrift trusts and spousal rights.

[23] See, e.g., Heintz v. Commissioner, 41 T.C.M. (CCH) 429 (1980) (notwithstanding taxpayers' representations of intent to the contrary, failure to explicitly override California's deemed power to revoke resulted in various transfers to savings account trusts being regarded as revocable for grantor trust income tax purposes).

[24] See, e.g., Cianciulli v. Smyth, 678 N.Y.S.2d 881 (Sup. Ct. 1998) (attempted revocation of Totten trust by withdrawal slip signed by the decedent premortem but not delivered to bank trustee until postmortem was not effective; a clear designation in the trust provisions regarding time of revocation would have avoided the litigation issue whether it was time of execution or time of receipt by the bank that mattered).

[25] Unless the trust expressly provides otherwise UTC § 602(c)(2)(A) permits a trust to be amended or revoked by a will provision that expressly refers to the trust or specifically devises property otherwise governed by the trust. See also Restatement (Third) of Property (Wills and Other Donative Transfers) § 7.2 comment *e* (2003) and Restatement (Third) of Trusts § 63 comment *h* (2003), all coordinated to avoid uncertain case law. See, e.g., In re Estate of Furst, 55 P.3d 664 (Wash. Ct. App. 2002) (even though will and trust were executed at the same time, replacement of the will to alter the fundamental division of the decedent's

authorized,[26] the power to revoke should specify whether a mere change of beneficiary by will provision also is permitted, and whether the trust may be altered or revoked by a will that predates the trust.

Inadvertent retention of a power to revoke usually is easy to cure by subsequent action by the settlor,[27] although incompetence or death prior to corrective action would result in unintended inclusion in the settlor's

---

(Footnote Continued)

estate did not serve to revoke the pour over trust, notwithstanding that the settlor also was trustee); In re Last Will and Testament of Tamplin, 48 P.3d 471 (Alaska 2002) (although Alaska Stat. § 13.36.340(a)(2) was not yet enacted, requiring a document other than a will to revoke an inter vivos trust, the court treated that rule as indicative of the proper result and held that the settlor's deathbed will was inadequate to specifically devise realty in revocation of the trust); In re Estate of Sanders, 929 P.2d 153 (Kan. 1996) (revocable inter vivos trust not revoked by provision in will that made no specific reference to the trust); In re Estate of Anderson, 217 N.E.2d 444 (Ill. App. Ct. 1966) (savings and loan trust accounts were revocable "in any manner," which the court held did not include by will because that would cast the validity of the trusts into doubt as testamentary dispositions that fail to comply with will execution formalities-notwithstanding that Restatement (Second) of Trusts § 57 comment *a* (1959) at that time specifically designated that a trust is not testamentary even if the settlor reserves a power to revoke it by will; to the same effect now see Restatement (Third) of Trusts § 25 comment *b* (2003)); Serpa v. North Ridge Bank, 547 So. 2d 199 (Fla. Dist. Ct. App. 1989) (residuary bequest in a settlor's will "including . . . bank accounts" deemed ineffective to revoke Totten trust accounts without a more specific indication of intent to revoke); Estate of Bol, 429 N.W.2d 467 (S.D. 1988) (extrinsic evidence used to support conclusion that nonspecific residuary clause in settlor's will revoked Totten trusts by implication). When decided *Serpa* was consistent with then UPC § 6-104(a), which required "clear and convincing evidence of a different intention at the time the account is created" and, lacking that evidence, § 6-104(e) provided that a will may not change the beneficiary designation in a Totten trust or POD account. The current version of UPC § 6-213 now specifies that these nonprobate documents "may not be altered by will" and no similar opportunity to prove a different intent by clear and convincing evidence is preserved. See also 1 Scott, Fratcher, & Ascher, Scott and Ascher on Trusts § 8.3.4 (5th ed. 2006), regarding the revocation of Totten trusts by will.

[26] See generally 1 Scott, Fratcher, & Ascher, Scott and Ascher on Trusts § 8.2.1 (5th ed. 2006).

[27] See, e.g., Estate of Varian v. Commissioner, 47 T.C. 34 (1966), aff'd, 396 F.2d 753 (9th Cir. 1968) (California trust, originally revocable because state law default rule was not overcome by express provision, became irrevocable 27 days after execution of the trust by settlor's execution of document stating intent that trust be irrevocable).

§4.2.2

gross estate at death. In any event, timing and therefore valuation differences will plague any situation requiring subsequent action. Failure to retain a power to revoke in those states that follow the traditional default irrevocability rule is a very different story, typically requiring a showing of fraud, duress, undue influence, or (in a few cases) simple mistake before revocation will be permitted.[28] The intent to make a trust irrevocable should be stated affirmatively and clearly, today even if silence would generate that result by default, merely to alert the settlor to this important decision and to preclude improper allegations that a trust intentionally made irrevocable was meant to be revocable.

§4.2.3 Declarations of Trust

The most controversy regarding a settlor's retention of control or benefits in a revocable living trust has centered around the self-trusteed declaration of trust. The settlor of which is trustee and beneficiary, typically with exclusive enjoyment and control until incompetence or death. Frequently these self-trusteed trusts are warranted for asset management purposes because the settlor's health is poor, there is concern that senility approaches, or for probate avoidance purposes,[29] but the client is unwilling to relinquish control presently. The trust allows the mechanics for independent administration to be created, with the settlor retaining control until a change in management becomes necessary.

Instead of waiting for disability or incapacity to become a problem, the trust is created and funded immediately so that, at the right time, the successor trustee simply steps forward and continues uninterrupted administration of the trust corpus. Although something akin to this might be accomplished through the use of a durable power of attorney, the transition would not be as smooth or rapid as with the declaration of trust.

Indeed, if a corporate fiduciary is successor trustee, the plan might even include placing assets in the corporate fiduciary's name under a custodianship arrangement, or naming the corporate fiduciary as a

---

[28] See 5 Scott, Fratcher, & Ascher, Scott and Ascher on Trusts § 35.1 (5th ed. 2008).

[29] See § 4.1, regarding various advantages and disadvantages of living trusts as compared to wills.

§ 4.2.3

cotrustee at the outset,[30] all to minimize transition problems. The trust could be drafted to sharply limit the powers and liabilities of the corporate fiduciary while the settlor is serving as cotrustee. In effect, the corporate fiduciary would have only record keeping and custodial duties while the settlor is serving as a trustee. In this way the transition would be even quicker and the corporate fiduciary's concerns about its duties with respect to accountings and responsibility for acts of the settlor as the predecessor trustee also would be reduced. Many corporate fiduciaries will negotiate a reduced fee to reflect the fact that they would serve only in a reduced custodial or investment advisory role during the settlor's trusteeship.

A second reason to use a self-trusteed declaration of trust is because the settlor may be the best trustee of certain assets that are located in jurisdictions in which ancillary administration is to be avoided through use of a living trust. In these cases the plan is useful even if no other reason for the use of a trust exists and is all the more appropriate because the settlor's ability to act as trustee is not in question. In either case, the primary advantage of the self-trusteed declaration of trust is that creation involves no taxable transfer for wealth transfer tax purposes,[31] and the trust is ignored for income tax purposes.[32] About the only tangible manifestation that anything different has happened with respect to the settlor's ownership of the trust property is a transfer of trust assets from the name of the settlor individually into the name of the settlor as trustee of the trust.

Even this extreme form of trust with retained enjoyment and control is deemed acceptable as against the charge that it is testamentary and therefore invalid for failure to comply with the statute of wills.[33] Any

---

[30] This approach avoids any merger issue, as discussed below, and is the mechanism of choice in many cases.

[31] See §§ 7.1.7 and 7.3.3.

[32] See § 5.11. The government does not require even the filing of an income tax return for the trust while the settlor is acting as trustee. Instead, the settlor reports all trust income, deductions, credits, and such as if the trust did not exist and the settlor still owned the trust property individually. Treas. Reg. §§ 1.671-4(b), 1.6012-3(a)(9).

[33] See Restatement (Third) of Trusts §§ 10(c) and 25(1) (2003); 1 Scott, Fratcher, & Ascher, Scott and Ascher on Trusts §§ 3.1.1, 8.2.2, 8.2.6 (5th ed. 2006).

§4.2.3

lesser degree of control or retained enjoyment also will survive challenge. The only potential danger of any concern is that the settlor's legal interest as trustee and equitable interest as beneficiary will merge, thereby causing termination of the trust. Merger is precluded, however, if at least one other person is given a beneficial interest (either present or future, vested or contingent), even if that interest is subject to revocation by the settlor.[34] Thus, the settlor may call for distribution of the trust at death in the same manner as would a testator who devises the residue of a probate estate. More commonly, the trust would continue after the settlor's death as it would under either a living trust or a testamentary plan.

Excepting that the trust has the settlor as its trustee, essentially it is the same as any other trust, only no transfer of assets, recordation, or consideration is required. Instead, the trust is valid if four essentials exist. First, there must be a sufficiently clear expression of intent to create the fiduciary relation. Almost any unambiguous indication will suffice. Second, the trust must have enforceable terms for an ascertainable beneficiary other than the settlor. This need not be a current beneficiary, but it must be a beneficiary with an interest that prevents merger and supports the existence of the trust.

Third, there must be an identifiable trust corpus. Lacking an actual delivery or transfer of assets, a segregation or identification of trust assets is essential to avoid the appearance that the trust is dry or testamentary (because otherwise it appears that nothing really happens until death). Funding the trust through identification of trust assets is guaranteed by reregistration of assets represented by an indispensable document (such as stock certificates, deeds, certificates of deposit, and bank account passbooks), execution of a bill of sale for other assets in

---

[34] See 2 Scott, Fratcher, & Ascher, Scott and Ascher on Trusts §§ 11.2, 11.3 (5th ed. 2006); Farkas v. Williams, 125 N.E.2d 600 (Ill. 1955) (landmark self-trusteed declaration of trust validation case); Will of Sachler, 548 N.Y.S.2d 866 (Surr. Ct. 1989); Contella v. Contella, 559 So. 2d 1217 (Fla. Dist. Ct. App. 1990).

Some jurisdictions have enacted statutes to confirm that merger will not occur if the settlor is the trustee and beneficiary, provided there is some other future interest beneficiary of the trust. See, e.g., Cal. Prob. Code § 15209 and Nev. Rev. Stat. § 163.007. Compare Mathias v. Fantine, 1990 WL 21446 (Ohio Ct. App.), which held that a self-trusteed declaration of trust was invalid under the doctrine of merger, *notwithstanding* the existence of remainder beneficiaries.

§ 4.2.3

favor of the trustee, maintenance of books of account that show trusteed ownership, creating trust margin and brokerage accounts, and rental of a separate trust safety deposit box.

Fourth, and perhaps most important and most difficult to maintain due to natural client proclivities, is the essential trust validity requirement of independent trust administration. The settlor must begin to act like a fiduciary and avoid acts that belie trust ownership, and fiduciary principles must be followed. For example, the settlor should render periodic accountings, conform investments to the requirements established by the trust document or local law, and avoid any conduct that bespeaks self-dealing. The estate planner should make the settlor aware of the need to act like a trustee if the trust is to be respected, and should consider whether the settlor is capable of compliance with fiduciary principles. It is advisable to avoid using a declaration of trust if the assessment is not favorable.

One special consideration must be reflected in using the self-trusteed declaration of trust because a sensitive issue is succession of trustees. This involves replacement of a settlor who, due to senility or other diminished capability, may not recognize the need to relinquish control.[35] Thus, before putting the plan into effect, it is imperative that the designated successor be contacted and be willing to act, and the requisite authorizations be executed to permit the settlor's physicians to release individually identifiable health information.

In addition, there must be a method for determining when succession is to occur. Death, resignation of the settlor as trustee, or incapacity of the settlor are normal triggering events for the successor to take over, with determination of incapacity being the touchy issue. It should not be done by the successor, who may be seen as having a conflict of interest. Moreover the successor may not be competent to judge, or it may be too time consuming to bring sufficient facts to the successor to permit it to judge the settlor's condition.

Instead, a common and effective procedure is for the settlor's spouse, adult child, durable health care power holder, physician, or any combination of them, to make the determination. Many physicians are reluctant to take on such a responsibility, particularly without adequate authorization to disclose protected health information. Thus, a physi-

---

[35] It also may require access to information otherwise protected from disclosure by the HIPAA regulations discussed in § 3.10.2.

§ 4.2.3

cian's opinion should be required only if there is a close and continuing relationship between the settlor and a family physician. Even then, the physician must be notified before the document incorporates this procedure and should agree to take on this responsibility. Appropriate authorization and documentation should be executed to address rules relating to privacy and disclosure of patient health records or other information. And the decision should be made conclusive on all concerned parties. Finally, the document should anticipate that the particular physician may not be available when the decision must be made, and address that issue by naming a substitute or by allowing the remaining evaluators of the settlor's capacity to act alone. These issues are illustrated by the following skeletal example.

Sample Declaration of Trust[36]

I, [Settlor], have transferred to myself as trustee the property listed in the attached schedule, and I declare that I hold that property and all investments and reinvestments thereof and

---

[36] Based on forms produced by The Northern Trust Company, which grants permission to attorneys to use any part or all of its forms in the preparation of wills and trusts for clients, all subject to a notice and disclaimer that "no form is a substitute for informed legal judgment. The attorney must make an independent determination as to whether a particular form . . . is generally appropriate for a client and, further, whether it must be modified to meet any special circumstances and objectives of the client." Note also that the preparation of forms by nonattorneys may constitute the unauthorized practice of law. See, e.g., In re Advisory Opinion, 613 So. 2d 426, 427, 428 (Fla. 1992) ("nonlawyer companies selling living trusts are engaging in the unlicensed practice of law and . . . the public is either actually being harmed or has the potential of being harmed by this practice . . . . '[A]ttorney review . . . does not . . . remove the activity from the unlicensed practice of law.'"). By stipulation the opinion "does not apply to the activities of corporate fiduciaries associated with financial trust departments or to the practice of public accountancy," but other jurisdictions are pursuing the unauthorized practice of law in the context of living trust "mills" without exception. See Cincinnati Bar Ass'n v. Mid-South Estate Planning LLC, 903 N.E.2d 295 (Ohio 2009), Cincinnati Bar Ass'n v. Kathman, 748 N.E.2d 1091 (Ohio 2001), and In re Mid-America Living Trust Assoc., Inc., 927 S.W.2d 855 (Mo. 1996) (involving ethics violations by attorneys assisting in this unauthorized practice), and abundant authorities cited in each; Ballsun, Summary Chart of Responses to Trust Mills, 21 Prob. Notes 330 (1996) and an updated version in Comm. Rep., State and Local Action Against Trust Mills: The Unauthorized Practice of Law, 27 ACTEC Notes 162 (2001); Lopata, Can States Juggle the Unauthorized and Multidisciplinary Practices of Law?: A Look at the States' Current Grapple with the Problems in the Context of Living Trusts, 50 Catholic U.L. Rev. 467 (2001).

§ 4.2.3

additions thereto (herein collectively referred to as the "trust estate") upon the following trusts:

FIRST: During my life the trustee shall pay the income from the trust estate in convenient installments to me or otherwise as I may from time to time direct in writing, and also such sums from principal as I may request at any time in writing.

If at any times I am unable to manage my affairs, the trustee may use such sums from the income and principal of the trust estate as the trustee deems necessary or advisable for my care, support, comfort, or any other purpose the trustee considers to be for my best interests, and for the health and maintenance in reasonable comfort of any person dependent upon me, adding to principal any income not so used.

For purposes of this declaration, I shall be considered to be unable to manage my affairs if I am under a legal disability or by reason of illness or mental or physical disability am unable to give prompt and intelligent consideration to financial matters. The determination of my inability shall be made by _____ and my physician, who I hereby authorize to disclose all needed information to determine my inability, or the survivor of them], and the trustee may rely upon written notice of that determination.

SECOND: Upon my death the trustee shall pay from the principal of the trust estate . . . . (tax payment provision).

THIRD: (Specific gifts that otherwise would be made under will).

FOURTH: (Marital and Residuary Dispositive Provisions).

FIFTH: (Administration Provisions-typical except for):

SECTION *: I may resign at any time by written notice to the successor trustee. After my resignation, death, or inability to manage my affairs, _____, of_____, shall be successor trustee.

Every successor trustee shall have all the powers given the originally named trustee. No successor trustee shall be personally liable for any act or omission of any predecessor. With my approval if I am living, otherwise with the approval of the beneficiary or a majority in interest of the beneficiaries then entitled to receive or have the benefit of the income from the trust, a successor trustee may accept the account rendered and the property received as a full and complete discharge to the predecessor trustee without incurring any liability for so doing, *except that a successor to me as trustee shall accept the assets delivered to the successor trustee as constituting all of the property to which the successor trustee is entitled and shall not inquire into my administration or accounting as trustee.*

SIXTH: The law of the state in which the trust property from time to time has its situs for administration shall govern the validity and interpretation of the provisions of this declaration.

SEVENTH: (Typical provision permitting additions to trust).

EIGHTH: (Revocability).

In Witness whereof I have signed this declaration this ___ day of _____.

_____
Individually and as trustee

§4.3 EFFECT OF ELECTIVE SHARE

Every American jurisdiction except Georgia has a regime designed to protect S in some respect against disinheritance, either with community property or an elective share statute.[1] Although they are designed to

---

[1] §4.3 See §3.4, regarding both community property and S's elective share entitlement to renounce a will and take a statutory portion of D's property. In a sense some community property states protect S in two ways, as illustrated by Cal. Prob. Code §21610, which grants a share equal to an intestate entitlement to S if S is omitted from a will that predated the marriage and that does not indicate that the omission was intentional. Estate of Allen, 16 Cal. Rptr. 2d 352 (Cal. Ct. App. 1993), rejected S's claim under this provision to a share of Totten trusts created by D before their marriage. The couple was married for less than one year and D's will (which also predated the marriage) simply failed to provide for S. Because Totten trusts are nonprobate property, the court determined that they could not be considered as part of the estate for computing S's intestate entitlement.

Of concern in any community property state is whether one spouse with rights as manager of the community may make a conveyance that deprives the other spouse of beneficial enjoyment of that property, particularly if the manager could not by will bind the other spouse in such a manner. See, e.g., Commissioner v. Chase Manhattan Bank, 259 F.2d 231 (5th Cir. 1958) (managing spouse's transfer to revocable living trust was binding on S, who was deemed to make a taxable gift of the value of the remainder interest following a life estate in S when the trust became irrevocable on the manager's death); Land v. Marshall, 426 S.W.2d 841 (Tex. 1968) (manager's transfer to revocable living trust without consent of other spouse was invalid because the trust was illusory due to excessive retention of control by manager).

protect S against disinheritance, elective share statutes are toothless to the extent D effectively can defeat S's entitlement by placing property outside the probate process.[2] For clients with wealth and sophisticated planning advice, the technique of choice for minimizing S's entitlement while retaining enjoyment and control during life has been the revocable living trust. Notwithstanding the rule in a majority of jurisdictions that assets settled in such a trust may be subject to S's elective share, a substantial minority of jurisdictions have held that trust assets may not be counted in determining the size of an elective share and may not be reached in satisfaction of an elective share.[3]

This discussion assumes that it is the planner's legitimate goal to protect trust assets from S's right of election. It does not presume whether a particular client is justified in seeking to minimize S's share and the tax and other reasons that might inform that judgment, or whether S's claim might be tainted by conduct or other factors that

[2] E.g., through inter vivos gifts (in trust or otherwise, with or without retained enjoyment for life), Totten trusts, joint tenancy, life insurance, employee benefit and other annuity beneficiary designations, POD or TOD accounts, and other forms of probate avoidance transfers. For example, In re Reifberg, 446 N.E.2d 424 (N.Y. 1983), involved a buy-sell agreement calling for purchase of D's closely held business stock, with payment to be made directly to D's children by a prior marriage. See § 3.4.2, regarding the augmented estate concept that is designed to minimize the ability to disfranchise S's entitlement.

[3] In addition to cases cited elsewhere in this discussion, see, e.g., Estate of Overmire v. American Nat'l Red Cross, 794 P.2d 518 (Wash. Ct. App. 1990) (D transferred all D's separate property to a revocable living trust in which D retained a life estate; S was entitled to income from a portion of the trust but petitioned for an award in lieu of homestead, to be charged against the trust because there was no probate or other property, which petition the court rejected because the trust was not part of D's probate estate and was not subject to S's claim); Richards v. Worthen Bank & Trust Co., 552 S.W.2d 228 (Ark. 1977); Cherniack v. Home Nat'l Bank & Trust Co., 198 A.2d 58 (Conn. 1964); Leazenby v. Clinton County Bank & Trust Co., 355 N.E.2d 861 (Ind. Ct. App. 1976); DeLeuil's Executors v. DeLeuil, 74 S.W.2d 474 (Ky. 1934); Brown v. Fidelity Trust Co., 94 A. 523 (Md. 1915); Rose v. Union Guardian Trust Co., 1 N.W.2d 458 (Mich. 1942); Smyth v. Cleveland Trust Co., 179 N.E.2d 60 (Ohio 1961). Most of the older jurisprudence on both sides of this issue is collected in Annot., Validity of inter vivos trust established by one spouse which impairs the other spouse's distributive share or other statutory rights in property, 39 A.L.R.3d 14 (1971).

§ 4.3

justified or validated D's planning.[4] The questions to be resolved in such planning are (1) what state's law will determine whether the trust is valid as against S's challenge, (2) under that law, what test will a court apply to determine whether the trust may prevail as against S's claim, and (3) under that test, what degree, if any, of control or enjoyment may D retain and still succeed? Thus, there are substantive law issues and conflict of laws aspects of this planning that must be anticipated.

§4.3.1 Various Tests Applied

A passion often permeates cases in this arena that informs the lack of precision in the tests and even the terms used in the cases that resolve these controversies. Further, the law itself is in a state of flux[5] and

---

[4] See Pennell, Minimizing the Surviving Spouse's Elective Share, 32 U. Miami Inst. Est. Plan. ¶ 900 (1998), with respect to reasons why D disinherits S and empirical research showing the high probability that it is the appropriate (and not unethical or immoral) plan in most cases. For example, women disinherit their surviving husbands almost twice as often as men disinherit surviving wives, and often because S has the larger estate, there was adequate nonprobate property passing to S, D felt S was in need of asset management in a trust, there were children by D's prior marriage, or because the spouses were in the process of divorce when D died. Disinheritance also might be appropriate and effective to qualify S for governmental benefits such as Medicaid.

A court may apply the same tests described in this segment in cases in which D owes child support that continues postmortem, in which event hardly any argument can be mustered that efforts to protect assets against that obligation are legitimate. See, e.g., L.W.K. v. E.R.C., 735 N.E.2d 359 (Mass. 2000) (finding a revocable inter vivos trust invalid as against the court ordered support claim of a minor nonmarital child; the court allowed access to a trust that might have withstood challenge against a surviving spouse's claim under the test described in § 4.3.1 at text accompanying n.22, notwithstanding that the court regarded that test as being the proper application in that case).

[5] See § 4.3.1 at text accompanying n.24. Meanwhile, the Kansas court, in Newman v. George, 755 P.2d 18 (Kan. 1988) (son of incompetent S's prior marriage had a guardian appointed to claim S's intestate share of D's intestate estate, notwithstanding that D had created a living trust to benefit D and S until the survivor's death, with remainder in equal shares to D's sister and S's sister, both of whom had cared for D and S; although the trust was not created to disfranchise S's share and was not abusive in any manner, the court allowed S to invalidate the trust and, because D died intestate, to take 100% of D's estate) produced an anomalous result (had D created a trust for S and an election had been made against that estate plan, S's statutory forced heir share would have

therefore constitutes a moving target. Thus, it is hard and may be impossible to reach any definitive determinations whether a particular trust will fail in light of a judicial challenge by S. In a very real sense, settlors pay their money and take their chances, hoping the equities favor their position and the courts see those equities in a favorable light.[6]

Two cases from the same jurisdiction illustrate the changing nature of the decisional law. Kerwin v. Donaghy[7] involves a second spouse and children by a former marriage who were equal one-fifth beneficiaries of trust established to minimize S's statutory share. Notwithstanding D's power to amend or revoke the trust, the court rejected S's attempt to invalidate the trust. Sullivan v. Burkin[8] involved the challenge of an estranged surviving spouse. In it the court announced that, for future purposes, the assets of a trust over which D retained an inter vivos or testamentary general power of appointment would be considered part of D's estate in computing S's statutory share. This is regardless of D's motive or intent and without consideration of whether the trust was colorable, fraudulent, or illusory.[9]

(Footnote Continued)

been limited to 50%) that resulted in legislative change and decisions in Taliaferro v. Taliaferro, 843 P.2d 240 (Kan. 1992), and Rice v. Garrison, 898 P.2d 631 (Kan. 1995), that disapproved the *Newman* result, showing again the lack of continuity in this area of the law. With respect to the power of a guardian to make an election against D's estate plan, see §3.4.7 at text accompanying nn.64-67.

[6] With respect to the equities of a given situation, it is notable that far fewer trusts are regarded as invalid if S is a surviving husband rather than a surviving wife. See, e.g., Estate of Allen v. First Presbyterian Church, 16 Cal. Rptr. 2d 352 (Cal. Ct. App. 1993); Briggs v. Wyoming Nat'l Bank, 836 P.2d 263 (Wyo. 1992); In re Estate of George, 265 P.3d 222 (Wyo. 2011); Hanke v. Hanke, 459 A.2d 246 (N.H. 1983); Johnson v. La Grange State Bank, 383 N.E.2d 185 (Ill. 1978) (two consolidated cases, each rejecting claims by surviving husbands); In re Kohut, 519 N.Y.S.2d 858 (App. Div. 1987); In re Estate of Soltis, 513 N.W.2d 148 (Mich. Ct. App. 1994) (a particularly interesting case because some of the trust property the surviving husband sought had been contributed by him to D's trust, in part to prevent his former wife from reaching that property and, in all likelihood, reducing the "equity" of his lament).

[7] 59 N.E.2d 299 (Mass. 1945).

[8] 460 N.E.2d 572 (Mass. 1984).

[9] The same result is advocated in Restatement (Third) of Property (Wills and Other Donative Transfers) §23.1 (2011).

§4.3.1

At approximately the same time these authorities were lining up in favor of S, Johnson v. La Grange State Bank[10] validated a trust and announced a new standard by which challenges by S would be nearly impossible to sustain. More recently, Karsenty v. Schoukroun[11] held that

> In Maryland, the completeness of the transfer and the extent of control retained by the transferor, the motive of the transferor, participation by the transferee in the alleged fraud and the degree to which the surviving spouse is stripped of his or her interest in the estate of the decedent have all been considered material, and no one test has been adopted to the exclusion of all other tests.

In essence, the Maryland court applied a balancing of the equities test that permits analysis of the relative merits of a spouse's claim, considers assets received by the spouse in other ways (which was the case in *Karsenty*), and judges factors such as other legitimate claims to the decedent's wealth (such as a disabled child or a dependent parent whom the decedent intended to support postmortem) and the needs and moral standing of the surviving spouse (for example, whether the surviving spouse was a long devoted Penelope or presented many challenges to the spouses' vows during their marriage).

What follows is an effort to summarize and give meaning to this issue, but it is subject to the emotion, imprecision, and consequent uncertainty that bedevils this area of the law and the jurisprudence it spawns.[12]

---

[10] 383 N.E.2d 185 (Ill. 1978).

[11] 959 A.2d 1147 (Md. 2008).

[12] For illustrations of decisions in which it simply is not clear what approach a court was following, see, e.g., Johnson v. Farmers & Merchants Bank, 379 S.E.2d 752 (W. Va. 1989) (trust found to involve impermissible retained control and indicative of a lack of good faith by D, the opinion referring to the trust as being illusory, testamentary, and fraudulent, but claimed to focus on the illusory trust doctrine); Seifert v. Southern Nat'l Bank, 409 S.E.2d 337 (S.C. 1991) (in a UPC jurisdiction but without reliance on the augmented probate estate concept of UPC §2-203 – because it was not adopted by the state legislature – the court nevertheless produced essentially the same result as augmentation because D retained "substantial control" over a revocable living trust, the court determining that D had such extensive powers over the trust that D essentially was in the same position as if the trust had not been created, which is a classic illusory trust approach); Sieh v. Sieh, 713 N.W.2d 194 (Iowa 2006) (saying that D "had full control of the assets of the inter vivos trust at the time of his death, including the

At least three tests are now in use in various jurisdictions to judge the validity of an inter vivos transfer into trust as against S's claim. They often go under different names and courts routinely toss around terms such as "fraudulent" or "colorable" that have no definitive meaning or that misdescribe the test actually being applied.[13] Consequently, it is wise not to focus on lingo and instead to consider particular facts and resolutions to judge what a court really did-as opposed to what it said it was doing.[14]

Of the three articulated tests in use, the least predictable and, if S presents an equitably compelling case, the most likely to permit S to

(Footnote Continued)

power to revoke the trust," but without articulating which test the court thought this mimicked). And compare In re Estate of George, 265 P.3d 222 (Wyo. 2011), and In re Estate of Soltis, 513 N.W.2d 148 (Mich. Ct. App. 1994), in which both courts regarded it as significant that their state legislatures also had adopted the UPC but without the augmented estate concept, and rejected S's effort to reach trust assets in satisfaction of the statutory share.

[13] See, e.g., Jarvis v. Jarvis, 824 P.2d 213 (Kan. Ct. App. 1991) (terms "fallacious, illusive, and deceiving" used in a decision that would have been the same under a retention of control test). In re Estate of Mocny, 630 N.E.2d 87, 90 (Ill. App. Ct. 1993), referred to "what has been misleadingly termed 'a fraud on a marital right.' Misleadingly, because fraud is not an element of this cause of action." And In re Revocable Trust of McDonald, 814 S.W.2d 939, 945 (Mo. Ct. App. 1991), made reference to the fact that the type of conveyance involved in these cases is, "unfortunately, commonly referred to as a conveyance 'in fraud of marital rights.' As so used, the term 'fraud' bears a meaning distinct from the meaning of that term when used in the conventional sense [and] has resulted in confusion."

[14] On this topic in general, little has changed since an excellent summary and explication was prepared by Pherigo, Estate Planning: Validity of Inter Vivos Transfers Which Reduce or Defeat the Surviving Spouse's Statutory Share in Decedent's Estate, 32 Okla. L. Rev. 837 (1979). Another useful resource is Kwestal & Seplowitz, Testamentary Substitutes-A Time for Statutory Clarification, 23 Real Prop., Prob. & Trust J. 467 (1988). And for the most comprehensive collection of case law see 1 Scott, Fratcher, & Ascher, Scott and Ascher on Trusts § 8.2.5 (5th ed. 2006). Older but still useful are MacDonald, Fraud on the Widow's Share (1960); Smith, The Present Status of "Illusory" Trusts-The Doctrine on Newman v. Dore Brought Down to Date, 44 Mich. L. Rev. 151 (1945); Note, Uniform Probate Code Section 2-202: A Proposal to Include Life Insurance Assets Within the Augmented Estate, 74 Cornell L. Rev. 511 (1989) (a change that was effected in the 1990 version of the UPC but that the insurance industry successfully has reversed or blocked in numerous adopting jurisdictions).

recover, is the variously named "intent," "motive," "fraudulent transfer," or "balancing the equities" test. Under it courts tend to consider D's apparent motive for creating the trust, as revealed by factors such as proximity of creation of the trust to D's death, length and "quality" of the marriage, extent of interests retained by D, size of the conveyance relative to what remains subject to the spousal share, S's relative wealth,[15] and S's moral or equitable standing relative to the takers favored by D.[16]

To illustrate the uncertainty of this test consider first Sullivan v. Burkin,[17] which was decided under a retained control test (D was the trustee and retained a general power of appointment) and not the intent test, but that nevertheless is revealing in this respect. The spouses had been separated for many years and a significant justification for the court's holding in favor of S was that S should not fare better in divorce than on termination of a marriage by death. The spouses must have reached some accommodation regarding their marriage and found greater value in remaining married than in being divorced, all without imposing contractual or other restrictions on each other and without attempting to guarantee or preserve property rights. That being the case, the court's focus on divorce rights seems anomalous.

---

[15] See, e.g., Davis v. KB & T Co., 309 S.E.2d 45 (W. Va. 1983) (applying a "flexible standard" to consider all "equities on each side," the court concluded that D's trust was bona fide and motivated by concern for health problems of both D and S, who had suffered a "mental collapse" and also possessed relatively significant independent wealth, including the family residence).

[16] See generally Hanke v. Hanke, 459 A.2d 246 (N.H. 1983) (rejecting S's challenge, apparently driven by tax factors because S was provided for in a trust that did not qualify for the marital deduction), and see Rice v. Garrison, 898 P.2d 631 (Kan. 1995), in which the court recounted irrelevant facts about the marriage of D and a former spouse-who was the designated beneficiary of D's employer-funded life insurance, notwithstanding D's remarriage-and precluded S from reaching the insurance proceeds by invalidating the beneficiary designation as would a court invalidate a trust; perhaps the court's object in revealing those facts was to bolster its conclusion that it could not have been inadvertent that D designated the former spouse and that it would not be appropriate for the court to override that designation in favor of S.

[17] 460 N.E.2d 572 (Mass. 1984).

§ 4.3.1

In all but its conclusion, Dumas v. Estate of Dumas[18] is almost indistinguishable from *Sullivan,* including the poor quality of the marriage and the fact that D was both trustee of the trust and retained a general power to appoint the trust assets. It probably turned on the fact that S had deserted D and filed for divorce a scant nine days before D's fatal heart attack. Had the spouse known that D was in extremis the divorce action might have been strategic, recognizing the difference in property division on divorce compared to what S stood to receive if the trust was upheld following D's death. As it was, however, the proximity of filing to D's death may just have sealed S's fate in terms of the poor equities it presented.

Friedberg v. Sunbank[19] does not reveal who was trustee of D's trust but flatly noted the court's dismay that the Florida legislature made it clear "that a divorced spouse is entitled . . . to reach assets held in a revocable, inter vivos trust but a loving, devoted spouse is not." Quaere whether the record supported the assumptions inherent in that conclusion. And in any event, consider the recognition by In re Estate of Chandler[20] that although

> dissipation of marital assets by one spouse in contemplation of divorce . . . is not . . . an acceptable practice . . . [j]udicial authority to distribute property . . . is expressly confined to those proceedings which culminate in a declaration of invalidity or a judgment of dissolution [and] . . . death of either party to a divorce action prior to final judgment deprives the . . . court of jurisdiction over all aspects of the marriage relationship.

Which is to say that, in many states, there is a well conceived and intentional disparity between rights in divorce and at death. In *Chandler* the court made special note of the fact that the parties addressed their respective entitlements in jointly held properties, reflecting their respective contributions to the economics of the marriage, and based its decision on that factor, which arguably is the manner in which these cases ought to be decided.

The more commonly articulated test is the "illusory trust" or "retention of control" approach, a middle ground that denies the efficacy of a

---

[18] 627 N.E.2d 978 (Ohio 1994).

[19] 648 So. 2d 204, 206 (Fla. Dist. Ct. App. 1994).

[20] 413 N.E.2d 486, 489 (Ill. App. Ct. 1980).

trust to cut S out if D retained so much control that no substantial or meaningful transfer occurred during D's life.[21] Most cases hold that retention of a life estate and power to revoke is permissible,[22] but also acting as trustee or otherwise retaining significantly more control would invalidate the trust as against S's challenge.[23]

The most recently formulated test permits exclusion of S if there was a "present donative intent" by which any interest (present or future) was created in beneficiaries other than D.[24] In essence, this is the same

---

[21] See, e.g., 1 Scott, Fratcher, & Ascher, Scott and Ascher on Trusts §8.2.5 n.25 (5th ed. 2006), and two of the more controversial recent cases that applied this approach: Sullivan v. Burkin, 460 N.E.2d 572 (Mass. 1984), and Seifert v. Southern Nat'l Bank, 409 S.E.2d 337 (S.C. 1991).

[22] See 1 Scott, Fratcher, & Ascher, Scott and Ascher on Trusts §8.2.5 nn.5 to 7 (5th ed. 2006), citing jurisdictions in which cases go both ways on the issue. See, e.g., Davis v. KB & T Co., 309 S.E.2d 752 (W. Va. 1983), and Johnson v. Farmers & Merchants Bank, 379 S.E.2d 752 (W. Va. 1989).

[23] Quaere how much or why more control needs to be retained than the power to revoke, yet courts tend to look for some indication that D did not really mean to accomplish a meaningful transfer prior to death, making the trust suspect from a purely will substitute perspective or, because that is not typically the source of the challenge, at least for purposes of disfranchising S's statutory share.

[24] See Johnson v. La Grange State Bank, 383 N.E.2d 185 (Ill. 1978), in which this test was formulated, and In re Estate of Puetz, 521 N.E.2d 1277 (Ill. App. Ct. 1988). 755 Ill. Comp. Stat. §25/1, originally adopted in 1977 as declaratory of existing law, reveals an antipathy toward actions to defeat inter vivos transfers to trust, providing that "[a]n otherwise valid transfer of property, in trust or otherwise, by a decedent during his or her lifetime, shall not, in the absence of an intent to defraud, be invalid, in whole or in part, on the ground that it is illusory because the decedent retained any power or right with respect to the property."

An intent to defeat S's statutory rights does not constitute an intent to defraud, which instead requires that D intended by secret or tacit understanding to retain complete and total ownership of the trust property. This is a very different standard than would apply under a traditional intent or motive analysis.

In the present context, intent to defraud . . . refers to a transfer that is illusory or colorable . . . one which takes back all that it gives . . . one which appears absolute on its face but due to some tacit or secret understanding . . . is in fact not a transfer because the parties intended that ownership be retained by the transferor. In either case, the question is really whether there was present donative intent, or instead the intent to retain complete ownership.

§4.3.1

test by which trusts are judged to be valid as against a charge that they are testamentary and invalid for failure to comply with Wills Act formalities.[25] As such it is extremely unlikely that S will succeed in overturning a trust for elective share purposes.

An individuated determination of the merits of any spouse's challenge is time consuming and somewhat unpredictable but, given the very low incidence of improper disinheritances,[26] this approach actually produces the most balanced or equitable results to all parties who claim a right to a decedent's largess. Saying that "the question to be determined in any case in which a surviving spouse seeks to invalidate an inter vivos transfer is whether the transfer was set up as a mere device or contrivance," *Karsenty*[27] is a comprehensive and balanced exegesis of the law applicable to this question. It is a must-read by any estate planner who seeks an objective analysis of the various competing interests at play in an elective share controversy, and it places Maryland along with Illinois and a handful of other states that make it clear that trusts created inter vivos will not necessarily be subject to defeat at the hands of a court acting on behalf of a surviving spouse.

§4.3.2 *Conflict of Laws*

In this and other circumstances, conflict of law principles can be an essential element in effective planning. For example, under each of the three common tests, different forms of interest and control may be retained by D, making it very important for the planner to invoke the most favorable test by knowing which state's law will govern the issue of validity.

(Footnote Continued)

In re Estate of Mocny, 630 N.E.2d 87, 92 (Ill. App. Ct. 1993), which also stated that, at least in Illinois, "[t]he paramount rule . . . grants an owner of property the absolute right to dispose of his property during his lifetime in any manner he sees fit . . . even with the expressed intent of minimizing or defeating the statutory marital interest of his or her spouse." 630 N.E.2d at 91. See also Payne v. River Forest State Bank & Trust Co., 401 N.E.2d 1229 (Ill. App. Ct. 1980).

[25] See §3.1.

[26] As revealed by the empirical evidence presented in Pennell, Minimizing the Surviving Spouse's Elective Share, 32 U. Miami Inst. Est. Plan. ¶ 900 (1998).

[27] 959 A.2d 1147 (Md. 2008).

In conflict of law controversies, two questions must be answered to determine the applicable law on the particular substantive issue involved. First, whose law governs the choice of law process? And second, under the choice of law rules of that state, which substantive law will be chosen to resolve the issue involved?[28]

In answering these questions in the context of the effect of a living trust and S's entitlement,[29] two additional questions may be relevant. One is what constitutes the trust corpus? Different conflict of law principles may apply to trusts of movables as compared to trusts of immovables (realty).[30]

The other is how should the underlying issue be characterized? The conflict of law principles tend to differ based on the substantive issue involved. For example, there are three general classifications of questions that may require court resolution in terms of general conflict of law rules that *might* apply to the fundamental issues involved in the living trust context (subject in almost all cases to the inevitable decisions that prove the exception to any "rule" in in this arena). These are trust

---

[28] In the context of this discussion, this dichotomy is best illustrated by Restatement (Second) of Conflict of Laws § 265 (1971), which provides that S's statutory entitlement "is determined by the law that would be applied by the courts of the state" of D's domicile, and those courts "would usually apply their own law" on the substantive issues involved. Which is to say that domicile choice of law rules apply to determine which state's substantive law will govern, and usually domiciliary choice of law rules would select domiciliary law on the substance of forced heir share questions.

With respect to conflict of law questions involving trusts in general, see all of Part 12 in 7 Scott, Fratcher, & Ascher, Scott and Ascher on Trusts (5th ed. 2010).

[29] With respect to conflict of laws and S's entitlement and election itself, see Annot., Conflict of laws regarding election for or against will, and effect in one jurisdiction of election in another, 69 A.L.R.3d 1081 (1976).

[30] Compare Restatement (Second) of Conflict of Laws § § 267-275 (movables) with § § 276-282 (immovables) (1971). Because of this dichotomy, it may not be possible to change the applicable law with respect to a trust funded with realty simply by moving the trust administration to another jurisdiction, the way it may be possible to alter the governing law with respect to movables settled in a trust administered in a state with favorable authority. Cf. In re Estate of Pericles, 641 N.E.2d 10 (Ill. App. Ct. 1994) (not involving a trust; Illinois decedent's realty in Georgia and Florida excluded from computation of elective share because laws of those jurisdictions were applicable with respect to those properties and did not grant S an entitlement).

§ 4.3.2

administration, trust validity, and trust construction questions. In addition, the underlying issue itself-the statutory forced heir share-might define the controversy,[31] all with potentially different consequences for conflict of law purposes.

Questions of trust administration usually turn on the law designated in the document, if that state has a substantial relation to the trust and its law with respect to the issue involved does not violate a strong public policy of the state with the most significant relation to the trust. Absent a valid designation, however, situs law most often prevails.[32] Trust validity issues usually turn on a general principle that "valid anywhere is valid everywhere," revealing a preference to find trusts to be valid, if possible. Nevertheless, in the face of spousal rights issues, a trust validity issue more likely will turn on the law of the decedent's domicile.[33] Cases that involve construction or interpretation issues often turn on the law of the decedent's domicile if the trust was testamentary, or on the law of the state in which a living trust was executed.[34]

To illustrate, S's challenge to a living trust may be classified according to the source of the claim that allegedly justifies invalidation of the trust (S's elective share entitlement) rather than by some alleged defect in or of the trust (for example, that D retained too much control-the trust

---

[31] See Restatement (Second) of Conflict of Laws § 265 (1971).

[32] Regarding questions of administration in general see Restatement (Second) of Conflict of Laws § § 267, 271, 272, and 279 (1971); Johnson v. La Grange State Bank, 383 N.E.2d 185 (Ill. 1978) (with no governing law provision, Illinois trust of Florida domiciliary was effective under situs law to disfranchise S, who was an Illinois resident); National Shawmut Bank v. Cumming, 91 N.E.2d 337 (Mass. 1950) (in spite of challenge by S, law of situs was designated by the settlor and was applied by a court in the situs state); Rose v. St. Louis Union Trust Co., 241 N.E.2d 16 (Ill. App. Ct. 1968) (Illinois decedent created Missouri trust as to which Illinois court applied Missouri law to find the trust invalid as against S's challenge). In re Estate of Renard, 417 N.Y.S.2d 155 (Surr. Ct. 1979) (involving a pretermitted child rather than a spouse and not involving a trust, but still turning principally on situs of the assets subject to administration).

[33] Regarding questions of validity in general see Restatement (Second) of Conflict of Laws § § 269, 270, and 278 (1971). In re Estate of Clark, 236 N.E.2d 152 (N.Y. 1968) (although recognizing that situs law should control for administration purposes, S's statutory election was determined under domiciliary law).

[34] Regarding questions of construction in general see Restatement (Second) of Conflict of Laws § § 268 and 277 (1971).

is illusory). In which case the primary substantive issue usually would turn on the law chosen according to the choice of law rules in the state of D's domicile, which usually would choose domicile law with respect to the substantive question whether the trust is invalid for purposes of disfranchising S.[35] Thus, for example, for an Illinois domiciliary Illinois law would apply for choice of law purposes and the Illinois choice of law principles likely would select Illinois law on the issue of S's entitlement and other ancillary questions.

On the other hand, the law of the state with which the trust has the most contacts usually would govern the choice of law process if the question was framed simply in terms of whether a living trust is valid as against a challenge that it should be ignored-because of its effects on S's rights, because it fails to comply with the statutory execution requisites of a will, or in any other respect. Under that governing law, the substantive law chosen typically would be whatever law was designated in the document, unless (1) that designation violated some strong public policy of the state with the most significant relation to the trust, or (2) the state whose law was selected has no substantial relation to the trust.[36]

---

[35] Restatement (Second) of Conflict of Laws § 265 (1971). See In re Estate of Clark, 236 N.E.2d 152 (N.Y. 1968) (situs court applying domiciliary law to invalidate trust for purposes of disfranchising S, notwithstanding governing law provision selecting law of the situs); but see Johnson v. La Grange State Bank, 383 N.E.2d 185 (Ill. 1978) (situs court applying situs law to validate trust for purposes of disfranchising S; because D was a domiciliary of Florida for only a short time before dying, and all other contacts were with situs state, the decision may be appropriate notwithstanding its deviation from traditional principles).

[36] See Restatement (Second) of Conflict of Laws §§ 269 and 270 (1971). The governing law provision was ignored and S's statutory share was protected in *Clark*, 236 N.E.2d 152 (N.Y. 1968), and the governing law provision was respected to protect S's statutory entitlement in Rose v. St. Louis Union Trust Co., 241 N.E.2d 16 (Ill. App. Ct. 1968) (domiciliary court applied governing law provision that selected situs law to invalidate trust as against challenge by S in D's domicile), but the governing law provision was respected to *reject* S's challenge in National Shawmut Bank v. Cumming, 91 N.E.2d 337 (Mass. 1950) (situs court respected selection of situs law to protect trust against challenge based on S's rights in D's domicile), and In re Estate of Renard, 417 N.Y.S.2d 155 (Surr. Ct. 1979) (not involving a trust; situs court respected selection of situs law to protect against challenge based on rights of pretermitted child in decedent's domicile).

§ 4.3.2

Thus, for example, a governing law provision in the trust probably would be respected if trust validity as a general matter is involved. But the designation probably would fail if the trust had no relation to or contacts with the state whose law was selected (none of the beneficiaries, trustee, or settlor is a domiciliary and none of the trust assets are situated there). In addition, notwithstanding a contact to the designated state, the governing law provision might be ignored if some other state is deemed to have the most significant relation to the trust on the particular issue involved (for example, S is a domiciliary), *if* the law designated regarded the trust as valid but the law of the state with the most significant interest in the issue regarded it as flawed.

In the planning stages it bears noting that, in selecting among conflicting laws, an unstated reality often appears to be that courts work backwards from the bottom line result they want to reach. Choice of law principles are the means employed to justify that end result.[37] Thus, if the equities tend to push a court to reach a particular resolution, it may appear that the law chosen under the particular choice of law rules applied is that which produces the preferred result. If there is no clear equity driving a court's selection, it also is predictable that a court will prefer to apply the law of its own state. It is convenient for the court to select the law with which it is most familiar if the result reached under its own local law is not distasteful.[38] This observation may make forum

---

[37] See, e.g., Johnson v. La Grange State Bank, 383 N.E.2d 185 (Ill. 1978) (notwithstanding that the lower court regarded the issue as a trust validity challenge and the decedent died a Florida domiciliary, the court selected the law of the trust situs on the substantive law issue and formulated a new test that validated the trust). See §4.3.1 at text accompanying n.24.

[38] Commerce Bank v. Bolander, 239 P.3d 83 (Kan. Ct. App. 2007), is an interesting study in this respect. The court addressed a conflict of laws issue that ultimately resulted in application of Kansas law based on a variety of factors that all properly dictated that result (a governing law provision specified Kansas law, the trust was created in Kansas with a Kansas trustee and successor trustee, it incorporated Kansas trustee powers, held Kansas realty, was the residuary beneficiary under a Kansas decedent's will, and the plaintiff was a Kansas bank). But the consequence was loss of exemption for an inherited IRA that would have been protected from the plaintiff's creditor claim had any of several other factors gone the other way (for example, designation of a trust as beneficiary of the IRA caused loss of an exemption that would have applied had the trust beneficiaries been named as the direct beneficiaries of the IRA, and Kansas law provided that a settlor's creditors did not lose their right to reach self-settled trust assets once

shopping important. For example, if the issue is likely to be couched as a trust administration question that tends to turn on the law of the trust's situs for administration, selection of a trustee with a situs in a state that applies rules that are favorable on the underlying issue makes sense, all other things being equal.[39]

Thus seen, the conflict of law issue in a typical elective share case may turn on factors such as whether the trust is funded with movables or immovables and whether the trust document contains an effective choice of law designation. Although many well drafted documents contain a governing law provision, parties and courts can disagree over both the substantial relation issue and which state has the most significant relation. Nevertheless, although there is no assurance of success, as a practical matter there is little to lose in designating the law of a state that is most likely to produce the desired result and manipulating factors such as trustee selection, situs of trust assets, and locus for execution in preparing trusts that present the best case for spousal disinheritance purposes.

§ 4.3.3 Totten Trusts

With respect to S's challenge, tentative or "Totten" trusts arguably present special equities not necessarily subject to rules governing gar-

---

(Footnote Continued)

the settlor died, which is not universally the case). It is impossible to discern from the opinion whether the court stretched to reach the creditor-favorable result, or was troubled by it, or whether the conflict of laws analysis might have gone the other way had the court wanted to reach the opposite result than it did.

[39] Cf. Norton v. Bridges, 712 F.2d 1156 (7th Cir. 1983) (situs was not clear because the trustee was an Illinois individual but the trust was "registered" in Wisconsin and the court determined that the individual trustee's acceptance of the trust was an acknowledgement that the trust was to be administered in Wisconsin). Care also is required that, in the effort to apply a favorable state law with respect to one aspect of the planning, a different unfavorable result is not generated, as for example by making it possible for more than one state to impose its income or death tax. See § 1.5. Or altering a court's jurisdiction to consider a particular controversy, as in Yueh Lan Wang v. New Mighty U.S. Trust, 841 F. Supp. 2d 198 (D. D.C. 2012) (in an elective share case, the issue whether the federal court had diversity of citizenship jurisdiction turned on citizenship of a trust, which bears the citizenship of both the trustee *and* the beneficiaries at the time of the suit).

§ 4.3.3

den-variety trusts in general.[40] Because these savings account deposit arrangements are such thin trusts, courts that would validate other trusts as against S's elective share challenge have regarded the tentative trust as invalid.[41] And courts that would permit S's challenge as against a revocable living trust also permit it as against tentative trusts.[42] Although the authorities are far from consistent, it seems prudent to suggest that,

---

[40] See Restatement (Third) of Trusts §26 comment *d* (2003) and 1 Scott, Fratcher, & Ascher, Scott and Ascher on Trusts §8.3.5 at 463 (5th ed. 2006), the latter of which, after recognizing the validity of the typical revocable living trust, asserts that, "[i]n the case of a tentative [Totten] trust, however, the depositor reserves such complete control that it would seem that, even though the trust is valid as against the depositor's personal representative, it should not be valid as against a surviving spouse."

[41] Compare, for example, Johnson v. La Grange State Bank, 383 N.E.2d 185 (Ill. 1978) (involving in one of the consolidated cases a fully revocable living trust as to which D was trustee and in the other of the consolidated cases a joint tenancy bank account, both of which were regarded as immune to challenge by S), with Montgomery v. Michaels, 301 N.E.2d 465 (Ill. 1973), In re Estate of Prusis, 434 N.E.2d 443 (Ill. App. Ct. 1982), and In re Estate of Mertes, 340 N.E.2d 25 (Ill. App. Ct. 1975) (all involving and invalidating Totten trusts as against S's challenge).

In re Estate of Jeruzal, 130 N.W.2d 473 (Minn. 1964), noted that there are three differing positions that various courts have taken on this issue, only one of which being an "invalidation" of the Totten trust. Some courts regard these tentative trusts as beyond S's reach, because they are not less valid than garden variety trusts and D was not the trustee. See, e.g., Dalia v. Lawrence, 627 A.2d 392 (Conn. 1993) (notwithstanding that D retained effective control until death, S's challenge was rejected on the ground that these are not probate assets and identity of the claimant should not matter if they are valid under state law in general). Most courts regard these trusts as includible for purposes of computing S's share but subject to invalidation only to the extent D's probate assets are inadequate to satisfy the entire elective share as inflated by this inclusion. Finally, citing dicta in Whittington v. Whittington, 106 A.2d 72 (Md. 1954), the court opined that some courts might subject these to the claim of a surviving spouse who otherwise would be impoverished.

[42] Cases are collected in 1 Scott, Fratcher, & Ascher, Scott and Ascher on Trusts §8.3.5 (5th ed. 2006), and Annot., Inclusion of funds in savings bank trust (Totten trust) in determining surviving spouse's interest in decedent's estate, 64 A.L.R.3d 187 (1975). See, e.g., Riggio v. Southwest Bank, 815 S.W.2d 51 (Mo. Ct. App. 1991) (Illinois residents with Missouri bank account trusts), which also specified that the governing law is that which would be applied by the state in which the deposit was made.

§4.3.3

if the object is to disfranchise S, more substantive nonprobate transfers be employed because they are more likely to withstand S's challenge.

§4.3.4 Planning to Overcome S's Challenge

If the foregoing discussion appears confusing and the authorities cited conflicting, the fault lies in the fact that courts often mouth a particular rule but do something different, and because there are no firm rules in the context of cases that present varying equities. Because the final result therefore cannot be predicted with much success, the planning process is fraught with uncertainty. In that respect, the issue is how to minimize the likelihood of S successfully defeating D's objectives. Several tactics offer some promise. They all require action that may be inconsistent with D's normal desires. They also raise the issue of how high a price D is willing to pay, particularly in terms of how much control or enjoyment D is willing to relinquish, to construct a plan that accomplishes uncertain results.

Unquestionably the most certain advice if D wants to minimize S's entitlement is to change domicile to a jurisdiction that does not support the elective share. Because domiciliary law typically governs S's entitlement, regardless of the location of D's property,[43] this one planning technique is most likely to generate the protection sought by D.[44] Among the viable jurisdictions for this purpose are Georgia (because there is no elective share) and any of the community property jurisdictions that do not embrace to the notion of "quasi-community property."[45] Unfortu-

---

[43] See, e.g., the 1990 version of UPC §2-202(d), which provides that "[t]he right, if any, of the surviving spouse of a decedent who dies domiciled outside this State to take an elective share in property in this State is governed by the law of the decedent's domicile at death." The corresponding provision in the 1969 version of the UPC is §2-201(b).

[44] See In re Schwarzenberger, 626 N.Y.S.2d 229 (1995), in which D successfully changed domicile from New York to Florida by purchasing a Florida residence, acquiring a Florida driver's license, registering to vote in Florida, and signing a Declaration of Domicile declaring Florida as D's domicile "to the exclusion of all others." In so doing D effectively prevented S from asserting a statutory forced heir share with respect to assets that remained subject to New York law.

[45] For example, Arizona, New Mexico, and Texas embrace quasi-community property for divorce only, but not at death. Nevada appears not to embrace quasi-

nately, a change of domicile is a major decision that many clients simply cannot or will not consider.

A second alternative is to settle D's wealth in a jurisdiction that provides legislative protections against S's challenge. Notably, under New York law,[46] the local law right of election "is not available to the spouse of a decedent who was not domiciled in this state at the time of death" unless D affirmatively elected to have the New York elective share provision apply. Thus, if D is or becomes domiciled elsewhere, D may own New York property and, if it is not subject to the law of D's new domicile (for example, because it is realty,[47] although local law may vary about the reach of the elective share statute), it also will not be subject to the law of New York.[48]

Other states with similar provisions include the UPC jurisdictions that provide that S's entitlement with respect to realty of a nonresident decedent is determined by the law of D's domicile and not the law of the situs of the property.[49] In addition, New York law raises another interesting issue with respect to United States savings bonds and Treasury bills, which are exempted from S's challenge because of a perceived constitu-

---

(Footnote Continued)

community property notions at all. But California, Idaho, Louisiana, Washington, and Wisconsin (using the term "deferred marital property") all appear to have quasi-community property at death. See § 10.7.1 n.14. Because this is a moving target and state laws can change, it makes sense to consider carefully all aspects of a potential move to any of the nine community property states.

[46] N.Y. Est. Powers & Trusts Law § 5-1.1-A(c)(6), applicable to decedents dying after 1992.

[47] See § 3.4.5.

[48] See In re Estate of Rhoades, 607 N.Y.S.2d 893, 894 (Sup. Ct. 1994) (D moved to Florida, leaving real property in New York that Florida law did not consider with respect to S's rights and that the New York court regarded as immune to the claim of an elective share), which affirmatively confirmed that if D wants to disinherit S D may simply become a domiciliary of other states and execute wills disinheriting S. "This result, however unfortunate, is precisely what New York State law allows."

[49] See Schoenblum, 2013 Multistate Guide to Estate Planning Table 6.03 Part 1 (2012), and American College of Trust and Estate Counsel Study 10, Surviving Spouse's Rights to Share in Deceased Spouse's Estate (2004).

tional mandate.[50] Although the state of D's domicile may not have similar legislation, the theory underlying New York's statute ought to apply everywhere (if it is valid at all), meaning that investment in Treasuries or savings bonds also could be effective to disfranchise S.

Other states exempt other specified forms of property, with variations among them that are impossible of summary. Half of the noncommunity property states appear to have no form of augmenting the probate estate against which the elective share is computed, meaning that virtually any form of nonprobate settlement potentially avoids S's claim.[51]

---

[50] The exclusion of United States savings bonds under N.Y. Est. Powers & Trusts Law §5-1.1(b)(2)(C) is based on the notion that to do otherwise would violate the United States Constitution. See Free v. Bland, 369 U.S. 663 (1962), and a document found in 31 C.F.R. §315.20 referred to as Treasury Direct by In re Estate of Scheiner, 535 N.Y.S.2d 920 (1988), which deemed this provision to apply to Treasury bills as well, in reliance on 31 C.F.R. §357, which treats Treasury bills and savings bonds alike. That provision specifies that "the Treasury will not recognize a judicial determination that gives effect to . . . a judicial determination that impairs the rights of survivorship conferred by these regulations upon a co-owner or a beneficiary."

[51] Schoenblum, 2013 Multistate Guide to Estate Planning Table 6.03 (2012), lists augmentation of some variety as applying in 21 of the 42 noncommunity property states: Alaska, Colorado, Delaware (relying on the FET gross estate), Florida, Hawaii, Kansas, Maine, Michigan, Minnesota, Montana, Nebraska, New Jersey, New York, North Carolina, North Dakota, Pennsylvania, South Dakota, Tennessee, Utah, Virginia, and West Virginia. American College of Trust and Estate Counsel Study 10, listed six states in 2004 that did not embrace augmentation but that now appear to have adopted augmentation of some form since publication of the Study: Delaware, Hawaii, Michigan, North Carolina, Pennsylvania, and Tennessee. A useful but older source for comparison is the Reporter's Statutory Note to Restatement (Second) of Property-Donative Transfers §13.7 (1985).

Notice that some states without augmentation (such as South Carolina and Wyoming) are UPC jurisdictions that intentionally did not embrace the augmented estate concept when they enacted the balance of the Code, which gives a pretty strong indication that augmentation should not be imposed by a court. See In re Solnik, 401 So. 2d 896 (Fla. Dist. Ct. App. 1981) (recognizing Florida's rejection of the augmented estate concept as allowing disinheritance of S, citing Fenn & Koren, The 1974 Florida Probate Code, 27 U. Fla. L. Rev. 1 (1974); another 20 years passed before Florida adopted legislation that now augments the probate estate); In re Estate of George, 265 P.3d 222 (Wyo. 2011), and In re Estate of Soltis, 513 N.W.2d 148 (Mich. Ct. App. 1994) (both courts regarded it as

The new UPC augmented probate estate concept has certain gaps in it that can be exploited, although there isn't much wiggle room left. For example, §2-205(1)(D) still does not reach the proceeds of insurance received by an ILIT as to which §2-205(2)(A) is not applicable and the two year gift rule in §2-205(3) also is not relevant. Transfers more than two years before death as to which D retained no strings also are excluded, but gifting that long before death is a high price to pay to disinherit S. Annual exclusion gifts also are not subject to the augmented estate, even if made on D's death bed; gifts that qualify for the ed/med exclusion of §2503(e), however, are not similarly exempted. Only a fractional share of jointly held property is brought back into D's augmented probate estate by §2-205(1)(B), apparently regardless of the source of consideration for its acquisition.

The pre-1990 version of the UPC augmented probate estate concept did not reach certain assets, most specifically §2-202(1) did not reach life insurance proceeds, retirement benefits, and certain annuities. Nor did it preclude dispositions within close proximity of death of interests that otherwise would be subject to the augmented estate if still held at death. Many of the existing UPC states have not changed their law to adopt the upgraded augmented probate estate concept, and some states that have embraced the new UPC did so without adopting the new and improved augmented probate estate rules.

A fourth affirmative and, in a majority of states, predictably success-ful planning recommendation is that D create a trust and retain less control or enjoyment than would trigger application of the illusory trust or retention of control test. Although it makes little sense, the majority of cases applying that test affirm that a revocable living trust as to which D retained no more than a life estate and power of revocation is not subject

---

(Footnote Continued)

significant that the legislature adopted the UPC without the augmented estate concept, and rejected S's effort to reach trust assets). In addition, several other states have an exception for any transfer that constitutes fraud on the spousal right, whatever that means under local jurisprudence. Included among that list would be District of Columbia, Illinois, Missouri, New Hampshire, Oklahoma, and Vermont. Again, be sure to verify these results because summaries of the law can be inaccurate when written or may change as the law develops over time.

§4.3.4

to challenge. Required is more control, typically in the form of D being the trustee or retaining some form of direction or veto power.[52]

Often the planning designed to disfranchise S is undertaken late in D's life (as revealed by numerous cases in which D died shortly after the trust was created). Thus, it makes sense to question whether D really needs to retain as much control as required to trigger this most prevalent test. Particularly if the trust may be revocable and avoid invalidation under this test, and assuming the trustee is chosen wisely, it hardly seems necessary for D to retain more control. Although this planning might not succeed in a state that applies the intent or motive test, it certainly will succeed under the present donative intent test and, all things considered, will maximize the possibility of success for clients who are unwilling to engage in a change of domicile or realignment of assets.

Even if state law will count nonprobate property in determining S's share, affirmative planning still may be advisable if state law counts D's dispositions first against S's elective share entitlement. Which is to say, if there are some assets that are more desirable than others, D effectively can require S to accept the less desirable assets in partial satisfaction of the elective share just by making a bequest of them to S.[53] In addition, if state law is not clear on the issue, an attempt can be made to minimize S's entitlement by directing that the elective share be computed after payment of wealth transfer taxes on D's estate, effectively overriding any equitable apportionment regime under state law.[54]

Finally, many living trusts provide for S but perhaps not in a manner that S will regard as an acceptable alternative to the elective share. In

---

[52] See §4.3.1 nn.22-23 and accompanying text.

[53] See, e.g., UPC §2-209(a)(1). In some jurisdictions this will include the discounted present value of a QTIP trust income interest, which could be quite substantial, depending on the interest rate and mortality assumptions that are applicable. See §3.4.3 n.17.

[54] See §3.4.4. As illustrated in Rockler v. Sevareid, 691 A.2d 97 (D.C. Ct. App. 1997), however, this effort may not be successful, the court holding that the elective share in the District of Columbia was computed before tax due to equitable apportionment and that the decedent's will, which imposed the tax liability on the residue without apportionment, was not effective to alter this because the spouse's election had the effect of rejecting all provision in the will that affected the spouse's entitlement.

§4.3.4

these cases it pays to consider whether it makes sense to draft in anticipation of the trust being regarded as ineffective to disfranchise S. Under the law of most states, S is not required to relinquish nonprobate benefits when an election is made against D's will.[55] Nor are nonprobate benefits typically counted in determining the share of D's property S receives pursuant to such an election.[56] "Double dipping"-by which the S receives an elective share plus enjoys benefits provided under a living trust or other nonprobate disposition-may not be the client's intent. In which case affirmative planning should condition the latter on S not asserting the former. This should not imperil any marital deduction that otherwise would be available with respect to the nonprobate property.[57] In addition, most state statutes that regard S as having predeceased D do not apply with respect to nonprobate transfers. Thus, the client may want to specify that S shall be treated as having predeceased if a forced share election is asserted.

§4.4 MEDICAID TRUST PLANNING

Trust planning that seeks to disguise assets of clients otherwise too wealthy to qualify for Medicaid benefits is largely ineffective. Medicaid

---

[55] See, e.g., Bravo v. Sauter, 727 So. 2d 1103 (Fla. Ct. App. 1999) (spouse who made election against estate plan entitled to retain life estate in inter vivos trust). State law must be evaluated carefully, however, as illustrated in Estate of Evers v. Commissioner, 57 T.C.M. (CCH) 718, 720 (1989) (Minnesota statute provided that a spouse electing to take against a will "also must elect to take against all conveyances within the scope of section 525.213 of which the spouse is a beneficiary," which encompasses conveyances to third parties and away from S; S's interest under the right of survivorship in a joint tenancy is not a conveyance away from S and thus was not one deemed described in § 525.213, although a revocable trust that included third parties as beneficiaries would seem to be included, presumably making an election against a will also an election against beneficial rights in a revocable trust).

[56] See § § 3.4.3 n.17 and 3.6 n.4 and accompanying text.

[57] See § 13.6.1.2 n.10.

Qualifying Trusts, SNTs, *Pollak* Trusts,[1,2] and other techniques have evolved and will not disqualify an applicant for Medicaid or Social Security Disability Income benefits. But they may be unacceptable to clients who wish to preserve significant wealth for private beneficiaries to enjoy after the applicant no longer is in need. This topic involves legal and procedural rules and practice that are a moving target, subject to substantial and potentially frequent change, and possible criminal penalties.[3] Readers must pay careful attention to legislative and regulative

---

[1] §4.4 Liberal use has been made with the author's permission of the more comprehensive article on this subject: Henkel, Medicaid Changes and Effective Planning for Your Client, 134 Trusts & Estates 26 (Dec. 1995). An extremely useful resource (notwithstanding its date) is Dobris, Medicaid Asset Planning by the Elderly: A Policy View, 24 Real Prop., Prob. & Trust J. 1 (1989).

[2] See Pollak v. Dep't of Health & Rehabilitative Services, 479 So. 2d 786 (Fla. Dist. Ct. App. 1991).

[3] Legislation adopted in 1996 (and amended in 1997 in a significant manner as discussed below) added 42 U.S.C. § 1320a-7b(a)(6), providing that it was a criminal act to "knowingly and willfully dispose[] of assets . . . in order . . . to become eligible for medical assistance . . . if disposing of the assets results in the imposition of a period of ineligibility . . . ." Although a number of interpretations of this provision were possible, it was thought that Congress' intent was to prevent intentional asset transfers followed by a strategic application for benefits during an ineligibility period, hoping that the spend down transfers would not be discovered. This "Granny goes to jail" provision was amended to become a "Granny's advisor goes to jail" provision because it was limited to anyone who "*for a fee* knowingly and willfully *counsels or assists* an individual to dispose of assets . . . in order for the individual to become eligible . . . " (emphasis added).

Prior to 2006 no period of ineligibility was imposed if application was not made within the look-back period. Planning that entailed asset transfers followed by a delay in making application for benefits until expiration of the appropriate three or five year (depending on the nature of the transfer) look-back period all changed under legislation adopted in 2006. With respect to the advisor penalty provisions, by virtue of the 1997 amendments, it appears that no sanctions will apply unless the counseling or assistance was knowing and willing and for a fee, in addition to the previously imposed requirement that it be with the purpose of becoming eligible for assistance, and a period of ineligibility actually is imposed.

New York State Bar Ass'n v. Reno, 999 F. Supp. 710 (N.D. N.Y. 1998), granted a preliminary injunction against enforcement of this provision in the context of allegations that the statute constitutes an unconstitutional infringement of free speech and is invalid due to vagueness regarding the required intent (in the context of transfers with multiple purposes). A subsequent action challenging the rule was rejected as not presenting a cognizable case or controversy,

developments and be aware that regional differences exist because some entitlement programs are administered at the state level. These state administered programs require careful review for local variations, as well as the underlying federal law.

Medicaid qualification looks at the combined assets of a married couple, making asset transfers to a spouse ineffective to qualify one spouse for coverage while preserving their collective assets for the use of the other spouse and ultimately for their intended beneficiaries. Wealth that exceeds established limits must be exhausted (spent down) before either spouse may apply for Medicaid, and unauthorized asset transfers made within a look-back period measured from a determination date may cause a period of ineligibility. The look-back determination date occurs when an individual is both institutionalized and has applied for Medicaid benefits.[4] The look-back period, originally 36 months for some transfers, now is 60 months in all cases.[5] Thus, nonexempt asset transfers made within five years of a determination date will be considered in the ineligibility period computation.

Care is required here, because many observers misperceive that the *penalty period* is 60 months. It is the *look-back period* that is 60 months. The period of ineligibility could be many months more or less than that. The period of ineligibility begins when the applicant otherwise would be eligible[6] and is calculated by dividing (1) the aggregate uncompensated asset transfers made during the 60 month look-back period by (2) the

---

(Footnote Continued)

absent objectively reasonable fear of prosecution, because the Attorney General had informed Congress of her unequivocal opinion that the statute was unconstitutional and had commanded U.S. attorneys not to investigate or prosecute alleged violations. See Magee v. United States 93 F. Supp. 2d 161 (D. R.I. 2000). Although there may be less risk involved in advising clients in this arena today, changes to the ineligibility rules reveal that the last word on these issues may not have been written, and cautious advisors may continue to steer a wide berth around the eligibility provisions.

[4] 42 U.S.C. § 1396p(c)(1)(B)(ii).

[5] 42 U.S.C. § 1396p(c)(1)(B)(i). If income or principal could be distributed *to the applicant* the trust would be a countable asset and it would preclude qualification for benefits. See § 4.4 at text accompanying n.10.

[6] 42 U.S.C. § 1396p(c)(1)(D)(ii). This means when the person is financially eligible and "would otherwise be receiving institutional level care . . . but for the application of the penalty period." Which is to say that the period of ineligibility

average monthly cost of private nursing facility services in the applicant's community at the time of the Medicaid application.[7] The number produced by that division is the number of months of ineligibility, and a large transfer divided by the average cost could result in a period of ineligibility of many years.

The key to avoiding a substantial ineligibility period is to make unauthorized transfers more than 60 months prior to the anticipated determination date and need for coverage. This requires some guess work as to how much wealth to retain on which to live during the 60 months following the last uncompensated transfer. There are exceptions to these rules for transfers to the recipient's spouse, minor or dependent children, and certain family members under certain circumstances,[8] and transfers that were meant to be for full FMV or that were not made with the intent to qualify for Medicaid.[9] None of these is likely to be of much use in the typical spend down asset transfer context.

In determining need, "self-settled" trusts created by or on behalf of a Medicaid applicant typically are regarded as countable assets to the extent distributions may be made to the applicant.[10] There are, however, three exceptions to this rule, known as the (d)(4)(A), (d)(4)(B), and (d)(4)(C) trusts-of which the first and last are regarded as generally useful. Some commentators distinguish by name between these, based on who creates them,[11] but the generally accepted terminology for each

(Footnote Continued)

does not start until the individual actually needs the care and has made application for benefits.

[7] 42 U.S.C. § 1396p(c)(1)(E). The average cost of private nursing services varies from one jurisdiction and time period to another.

The SSDI penalty period calculation is similarly computed by dividing the prohibited transfer amount by, in this case, the transferor's combined monthly federal (and any state) SSDI payment, but the penalty differs in that the period cannot exceed 36 months. 42 U.S.C. § 1382b(c)(1)(A)(iv)(II).

[8] 42 U.S.C. § 1396p(c)(2). The similar, corresponding SSDI exceptions are found in 42 U.S.C. § 1382b(c)(1)(C).

[9] 42 U.S.C. § 1396p(c)(2)(C).

[10] 42 U.S.C. § 1396p(d).

[11] A 42 U.S.C. § 1396p(d)(4)(A) trust may be created only for a disabled person who is under age 65 at the time of creation and funding, and only by that person's parents, grandparents, legal guardian, or a court. The (d)(4)(C) trust *also* allows trusts created or funded at any time by any of those parties *or* by the

§4.4

is "special" or "supplemental" needs trusts (both abbreviated SNT and called a "snit") without distinction.

So, for example, a (d)(4)(A) trust is distinguishable from a (d)(4)(C) trust primarily because the (d)(4)(A) trust remainder after a disabled settlor's lifetime enjoyment may provide for private beneficiaries. But first the trust must repay the state for Medicaid benefits provided to the disabled beneficiary during life. So only any excess funds remaining after that repayment may be distributed to beneficiaries of the trust settlor's choice. A (d)(4)(C) trust is essentially a pooled fund managed by a nonprofit association that *either* reimburses the state *or* may retain the funds remaining after the disabled settlor's death for the nonprofit's own qualified programs.

In any case these trusts permit safety net benefits for a disabled individual, without disqualification for Medicaid or SSDI. To qualify, these trust distributions cannot be in lieu of *basic* governmental support. Instead, these trusts provide for items *in excess of* basic entitlements-hence the terminology "supplemental" needs. These are "luxury" or added benefits. Trust drafters may hobble-but do not preclude-distributions for food, clothing, or shelter that would reduce or supplant benefits otherwise available. Indeed, the trust typically prohibits distributions that would decrease a beneficiary's entitlement to public benefits.

The primary problem with the self-settled version of these trusts is that some (perhaps all or most) of what remains after the recipient's death will not pass to private beneficiaries-either it is distributed to the

(Footnote Continued)

individual. See also 42 U.S.C. § 1382b(e) for the aligned SSDI version of these rules.

Some experts reference states in which the "pay-back" requirement in a (d)(4)(A) trust dictates the use of the word "special" in self-settled SNTs, and they use the word "supplemental" in third party SNTs in which there is no required payback for qualification. See Fleming & Davis, The Elder Law Answer Book § 8.3 (Supp. 2011), identifying states that detail variations in language that include "supplemental needs trusts." Another analysis focuses "special" on the protection of the SNT corpus for the beneficiary while public benefits are maintained, and focuses "supplemental" on the limitations on the trustee's discretion to make distributions. See Zimring, Morgan, & Frigon, Fundamentals of Special Needs Trusts § 1.02 (LexisNexis 2009), citing Social Security Administration Program Operations Manual System (POMS), secure.ssa.gov/apps10/SI 01120.200, SI 01120.200.B.13, and SI 01120.200.H.1.a.

state in repayment or it is kept by the nonprofit that administered the (d)(4)(C) trust. To this extent the wealth is not preserved for other private parties, making these trusts of limited utility to many clients. This is *not* true for a third party SNT (but beware of efforts to disguise the settlor or the source of the funds in such trusts).

Self-settled SNTs of any variety may be desirable because they provide a safety net for a disabled individual and because any repayment to the state in a (d)(4)(A) trust typically is a smaller amount than if the beneficiary had been totally under private care (because the state likely pays less for similar services) and is without interest (meaning that these essentially turn the state into an interest free lender of the cost of needed basic services).

The (d)(4)(B) variety of trust, often referred to as a *Miller* trust,[12] is not a SNT. Rather, it is used purely to avoid disqualification of a beneficiary in an "income cap" state that regards income in excess of specified amounts as a disqualification. These trusts may provide income that is not subject to the income cap calculation to the extent these court-created trusts pay income for nursing facility services or equivalent care. It is unlikely that this exception will provide much affirmative planning opportunity because of the manner in which these trusts are created, the limited use of the resource itself, and their modest function-to avoid the income cap limitation.

All of this is to be distinguished from a "third party" SNT, which is *not* a payback approach, it holds funds contributed by a settlor *other than* the beneficiary, and it can provide for multiple current and remainder beneficiaries, not all of whom are seeking to qualify for needs-based entitlements.

As thus seen, SNTs are a staple for needs-based entitlement benefit planning, and are not uncommon if significant wealth is transferred to a disabled plaintiff in a personal injury litigation damage recovery, regardless of the plaintiff's age. But they are not very common for garden variety estate planning purposes. As a result, the specialists who tend to

---

[12] After Miller v. Ibarra, 746 F. Supp. 19 (D. Colo. 1990), and the subject of Issue Memorandum Concerning Miller Trusts After OBRA 1993, Elder Law Advisory No. 38 (May 1994), describing a government position that is not found in 42 U.S.C. § 1396p(d). There is no corresponding *Miller* trust exception for SSDI purposes.

§ 4.4

use SNTs come from practice settings that don't necessarily share the same trust law experience, and their use of SNTs therefore is not always consistent with traditional trust law principles. This can create issues for fiduciaries who assume that documents using common trust terms have a similar meaning to those normally encountered, and the trusts themselves may create issues for drafters who are not familiar with the special SNT environment.

That there is such a disconnect among professionals who use SNTs is easy to illustrate by several telltales that appear in the vast majority of SNTs. For example, some SNT drafters refer to "administrative provisions," while trust and estate planners would typically refer to "administration provisions." Notwithstanding the nearly identical lingo, they would be addressing different matters. In model SNT forms these provisions often are orphan clauses that don't fit elsewhere in the document, such as the governing law, tie vote, and singular-means-plural (and vice-versa) provisions. Garden variety trust administration provisions deal with trustee succession, trustee powers, principal and income allocations, trust accounting, and similar trust operation dictates—which sometimes are missing entirely from SNT forms (perhaps because the drafter relied on default rules under state law).

In addition, state laws often inform SNT provisions that seem odd to garden variety trust drafters. Often these are informed by the need to satisfy or reflect local pronouncements regarding the use of SNTs to avoid disqualification for public benefits. Meaning that SNTs often reflect regional variations, notwithstanding that they have a common objective. Frequently this occurs without regard for any multistate elements of the trust or the possibility that the beneficiary may move to another jurisdiction. Garden variety trust drafters who attempt to use these SNT forms therefore need to know about local rulings on particular issues that inform these provisions, and need to know that they may vary in another county or a different state, often in unexpected ways.

A second observation is that some SNT forms have a grown-like-topsy character, with provisions in various segments of the trust that may address the same or similar concepts. They tend to confirm that the document was constructed by "accretion," as the drafter learned of issues that generated solutions that resolved or avoided a particular controversy. In some cases these additions create problems because they are inconsistent with other provisions in the document. Meanwhile, garden variety trust drafters are prone to add standard boilerplate provisions to SNTs with no appreciation for how they might disqualify a beneficiary for various entitlements.[13]

These realities make the practice in this arena complex and risky, especially for garden variety estate planners who assume that SNTs should be easy and familiar because trust drafting is part of their standard practice.

An especially critical distinction also must be remembered so as not to confuse a self-settled SNT with a third party SNT, as to which payback is not required. A garden variety estate planner easily could stumble by inadvertence into drafting one SNT on behalf of a client who actually needs the other, perhaps by adopting a form without careful consideration of the variety involved.

Fiduciaries who administer SNTs frequently confront two sources of conflict. One is the beneficiary's family, who may have the beneficiary's best interest at heart but who also may see a pot of money that their disabled relative may never personally enjoy. The other is the entitlements authorities, whose perceived duty is to protect a dwindling entitlement resource by forcing individual claimants to tap into their own funds before drawing on the public fisc.

Because SNTs are designed to prevent the trust corpus from being a countable resource that might disqualify the trust beneficiary for needs-based entitlements, the document must preclude the beneficiary (and any of the beneficiary's retinue) from having a "right" to receive any distributions from the trust. The beneficial interest must be totally discretionary. As a means of impressing everyone involved that the trust does not provide any enforceable entitlement, SNTs routinely specify that corpus distributions will be made only in the "sole and absolute discretion" of the fiduciary. Which is to say that no one—not the beneficiary, not any family member, and not the entitlements authorities—may force the trustee to make any amount available to anyone.

---

[13] One easy illustration is a facility of payment provision that could violate the sole benefit requirement in a self-settled SNT. For a collection of these sorts of issues see Pennell, Special Needs Trusts: Reflections on Common Boilerplate Provisions, 6 NAELA J. 89 (2010).

§4.4

The problem with this is that there is no such thing as a fiduciary's unfettered—sole and absolute—discretion. Because, if there was, then the trust would not be enforceable, and a trust that is not enforceable is not a trust at all. Indeed, the linchpin to being a viable trust is that the fiduciary must be subject to enforceable duties. Meaning that unfettered—sole and absolute—discretion is not real. "It is . . . a contradiction in terms, to permit the settlor to relieve a 'trustee' of all accountability. . . . Once it is determined that the authority over trust distributions is held in the role of trustee . . . , words such as 'absolute' or 'unlimited' or 'sole and uncontrolled' are not interpreted literally."[14] "The terms of the trust may enlarge the trustee's discretion by use of qualifying adjectives or phrases such as 'absolute,' 'sole,' 'uncontrolled,' or 'unlimited.' Such terms are not, however, interpreted literally; they do not confer on the trustee unlimited discretion."[15]

Authorities who administer entitlement programs tend not to be trust law specialists and may not appreciate this aspect of fiduciary law. As a result, it is not likely that drafters will deviate from the use of such language—although an easy alternative is to provide that a disinterested third party—such as a trust advisor, a trust protector, or a trust committee—has the responsibility to review a trustee's actions and the power to hold the trustee accountable. Indeed, SNTs make frequent use of these faux-fiduciaries for various functions that are not common in garden variety estate planning. Such as making determinations or recommendations regarding the beneficiary's needs or appropriate supplemental distributions, where and how the beneficiary should live, the best situs for the trust, governing law, and perhaps amending the trust to continue to comply with the changing entitlements landscape.

One common issue with SNTs that employ faux-fiduciaries is that the document may fail to address issues such as tie-votes or the removal and succession of advisors, protectors, or committee members. Indeed, some SNTs seem to be drafted with an expectation that the duration of

---

[14] See Restatement (Third) of Trusts § 50 comment *c* (2003).

[15] 3 Scott, Fratcher, & Ascher, Scott and Ascher on Trusts § § 13.2.3, 18.2 (5th ed. 2007), citing Uniform Trust Code § 814(a): "Notwithstanding the breadth of discretion granted to a trustee in the terms of the trust, including the use of such terms as 'absolute', 'sole', or 'uncontrolled', the trustee shall exercise a discretionary power in good faith and in accordance with the terms and purposes of the trust and the interests of the beneficiaries."

§ 4.4

the trust will be months rather than years or decades, even though the beneficiary may not have a shortened life expectancy.

Another aspect of typical SNTs is that they tend not to be drafted with an understanding of fiduciary income taxation and may not reflect an appreciation for subtle aspects of IRC Subchapter J. As a result, planning to convert these otherwise complex trusts into intentionally defective grantor trusts for income tax purposes has not been very common in the SNT context.[16] And SNTs that are defective grantor trusts may not reflect the same drafting approaches that garden variety trust drafters might select. This may reflect the drafter's perception of how best to coordinate with various entitlement rules, or it may reflect a different understanding of the grantor trust rules.

These illustrations merely underscore that practitioners who work with sample SNT documents must dedicate extra effort to learn and appreciate the local variations that drive SNT drafting and to tread lightly before making any changes to sample forms. And, because the administration of entitlement programs tends to vary by region, it also is critical to use forms that are suited to that locale, while maintaining the flexibility to move the trust or its beneficiary elsewhere.

---

[16] Issues relating to distributions from a SNT to pay the beneficiary's income tax can be avoided if the trust's income is taxable to a third party, such as the trust's grantor.

§ 4.4

5

Income Taxation of Trusts, Estates, Grantors, and Beneficiaries

§ 5.0 INTRODUCTION

This chapter addresses an area of the estate planning practice that largely is ignored by the government and that is not routinely covered in law school, even if the curriculum includes courses in trusts and estates, wealth transfer taxation, income taxation, or estate planning. As a consequence of nonenforcement and inattention, most estate planners also ignore the issues that arise or—worse—don't know enough to pay them no mind. These problems and the limited planning opportunities sometimes presented simply are invisible in most representations.

Unfortunately, this topic is important nevertheless. The manner in which documents are drafted and various obligations are imposed or discretions are granted influence how fiduciaries comply with the income tax rules that apply to fiduciary entities. Ultimately these rules

§ 5.0

impact the ultimate parties in interest, being the settlor of most inter vivos trusts and the beneficiaries of estates and all other trusts. So, having discussed estates, wills, and trusts, now we investigate the income taxation of fiduciary entities, their creators, and their beneficiaries.

Notwithstanding a number of elaborate proposals for change in this area of the tax law,[1] the most recent substantive legislative change that affected this topic was the 1984 compression of the income tax rates that apply to fiduciaries,[2] making trusts and estates the most heavily taxed entities under the Internal Revenue Code. The effect is to severely restrict the extent to which income taxes can be reduced through the use of these entities. Indeed, it encourages planning that permits or requires distribution of income to the extent it can be taxed at lower rates in the hands of the beneficiaries. It also favors planning that causes trust settlors to be treated as if the trust did not exist under the grantor trust provisions.

§5.1 GENERAL OVERVIEW

Subchapter J of Chapter 1 of the Internal Revenue Code[1] recognizes fiduciary entities as separate taxpayers,[2] subject to their own rate table in

---

[1] **§5.0** Including an American Law Institute project in 1984 (of which Professor Casner was the Reporter), an American College of Trust and Estate Counsel proposal in 1985 (of which Professor Pennell was the Reporter and that was the substance of the Tax Reform Bill of 1985 provisions that passed the House of Representatives but went no further), and the President's Tax Proposals for Fairness, Growth and Simplicity in 1985. See also Kamin, A Proposal for the Income Taxation of Trusts and Estates, Their Grantors, and Their Beneficiaries, 13 Am. J. Tax Policy 215 (1996).

[2] See §1(e) and compare the rates that apply to other taxpayers. Trusts and estates reach the maximum tax rate with an extraordinarily small amount of taxable income, which makes them virtually worthless for tax minimization purposes as separate tax paying entities. It was largely in recognition of this reality that the accumulation distribution and throwback rules were repealed in 1997 with respect to most trusts. See §5.6.

[1] **§5.1** See §§641 through 692, broken into two Parts—Part I being broken into five Subparts that address garden variety fiduciary income taxation, and Part II dealing with IRD. Tax lingo refers in general to Subchapter J as the income taxation of trusts and estates and to Subpart E of Part I as the special rules applicable to the taxation of trust settlors known as the grantor trust rules.

[2] See §641.

§1(e) and set of rules regarding allocation of income, deductions, and credits between the settlor or decedent, the entity, and its beneficiaries. Fiduciary entities are divided into two categories for income tax purposes to the extent a trust is not ignored under the grantor trust rules (and the settlor instead taxed as if the trust did not exist).[3] There are simple trusts[4] and complex trusts,[5] with estates always being taxed under the complex trust rules.[6]

As the following discussion reveals, the difference between the simple and the complex trust rules is almost entirely without significance. In virtually every respect the simple trust rules are merely a Readers' Digest condensed version of the complex trust rules, applicable only to trusts that do not present the circumstances that make the complex trust rules complicated. Thus, a student of this area could do just as well never studying the simple trust rules and reach the right results by applying only the complex trust provisions.

The basic premise of Subchapter J is that fiduciary entities are conduits to the extent income is distributed. Unlike passthrough taxation of S Corporations and partnerships, however, Subchapter J is not a comprehensive system by which the entity is transparent for all income tax purposes. Instead, Subchapter J taxes income to the entity to the extent it is not actually or deemed to be distributed currently.

To the very limited extent still applicable through the accumulation distribution and throwback rules,[7] income may be taxed to the beneficiaries at a later time, usually with a credit for any tax already paid on that income by the trust (throwback does not apply at all to estates). The throwback computation usually produced no additional tax because the credit for tax paid at the trust's rates almost always exceeded the tax liability visited on the beneficiaries when the income ultimately was distributed. It therefore was unnecessary in virtually all cases, attention seldom was devoted to this aspect of Subchapter J, and in 1997 it was repealed for most domestic trusts (although it remains applicable to

---

[3] See § 5.11 et seq.

[4] See Subpart B, § § 651 and 652.

[5] See § § 661-663 in Subpart C.

[6] See § 661(a)

[7] See § § 665-667 in Subpart D, which were made inapplicable to most domestic trusts in 1997.

foreign trusts). As a consequence, the key to understanding Subchapter J is the current tax aspects made operative through a deduction for distributions and a factor known as DNI.

An attenuated summary may be useful before looking at all of this in more detail. The first sanity-retaining notion to remember is that DNI is a pivotal but relatively insignificant concept. It is important to know that DNI basically is taxable income (computed pretty much the same way any other taxpayer computes taxable income) to which a number of adjustments are made.[8] Its role is limited to a definition, measurement, and characterization function. DNI determines the size of the distributions deduction and defines the amount and character of income that is taxed to the beneficiary.

The really operative aspect of Subchapter J is that distributions by a trust or an estate are deemed to be income to the beneficiary to the extent of DNI. Distributions usually carry out DNI to the extent any is available. The mechanism by which this occurs is a distributions deduction for the entity and a corresponding inclusion rule for the beneficiary.[9] Unless an exception exists, distributions from a fiduciary entity are deemed to be income taxable to the beneficiary until DNI is exhausted, after which they are deemed to be any accumulated income from a prior year—also subject to tax (if a trust is involved) under the throwback rules to the limited extent those rules still are operative. Finally, after that current DNI (and in a trust subject to throwback, after prior year UNI) is exhausted, distributions are tax free trust corpus.[10]

To the extent applicable, the grantor trust rules can trump all of this but, otherwise, that's all there is to it. Tax the beneficiary to the extent income is distributed, deem it distributed to the extent of most distributions made, and tax it to the entity to the extent income is accumulated (subject to what is left of the throwback rule.

---

[8] See § 643(a) and § 5.3.2.

[9] See §§ 651 and 661 (the deductions for simple and complex trusts) and §§ 652 and 662 (the inclusion rules for beneficiaries of simple and complex trusts).

[10] Made free of income tax by § 102, applicable to property received by gift, devise, bequest, or inheritance. The underlying corpus as opposed to income earned by it falls into this category, making the only difficult chore an identification of tax free corpus and the income generated by it prior to its distribution.

§5.2 SIMPLE AND COMPLEX TRUSTS DEFINED

Not every entity that calls itself a trust[1] or an estate[2] will be respected as such for Subchapter J purposes. For example, in some circumstances a trust will be regarded as an association taxable as a partnership or a corporation.[3] As articulated in PLR 8842043 (issued when the current regulatory standard was in place):

> . . . an arrangement will be treated as a trust . . . if . . . the purpose . . . is to vest in trustees responsibility for the protection of and conservation of property for beneficiaries who cannot

---

[1] **§5.2** E.g., notwithstanding that an insurance policy settlement option permitted proceeds to be held by the insurer "as trustee," the arrangement created a debtor-creditor relationship and not a trust as to which Subchapter J was applicable. Rev. Rul. 68-47, 1968-1 C.B. 300, which noted that the insurer typically pays a fixed rate of interest rather than income from investment of the proceeds, and the beneficiaries incur none of the risks or rewards normally attributable to trust investment performance. See also Rev. Rul. 76-486, 1976-2 C.B. 192, which involved an honorary trust (in this case, a trust for a dog) that the government respected as a taxpaying entity but as to which it could not apply the normal trust tax conventions, instead imposing tax on the entity notwithstanding distributions of income that normally would produce a distributions deduction and carry out DNI to the beneficiary (which, in this case, was the dog). See §14.3.2 n.28 regarding the state law validity of honorary trusts.

[2] E.g., a bankruptcy estate is not taxable under Subchapter J. See §§1398(c) and 1399.

[3] Compare Rev. Rul. 88-79, 1988-2 C.B. 361 (trust formed by associates to carry on a business properly was taxable under then existing Treas. Reg. §301.7701-2(a) as a partnership for federal income tax purposes because the trust was formed to buy, hold, and sell oil and gas royalty interests and lacked the corporate characteristics of continuity of life, free transferability of interests, and limited liability; the "check-the-box" version of this regulation for distinguishing between corporations and partnerships do not alter the trust versus association determination), with Elm Street Realty Trust v. Commissioner, 76 T.C. 803, acq., 1981-2 C.B. 1 (trust created by two business associates to operate investment realty), and Bedell v. Commissioner, 86 T.C. 1207 (1986) (testamentary trust created by the decedent to hold the assets of a business the decedent operated as a sole proprietorship). These trusts were not associations taxable under §7701 as corporations, in *Bedell* because the decedent created a unique family estate plan characterized by a dominant family objective, the beneficiaries neither created nor contributed to the trust, the beneficial interests in the trust were not transferable, and only a few of the beneficiaries participated in the trust affairs. In *Elm Street* the original associates no longer held interests in the trust.

§5.2

share in the discharge of this responsibility and, therefore, are not associates in a joint enterprise for the conduct of business for profit. [Treas. Reg. § 301.7701-4(a) (last sentence).]

. . . [I]f an organization that is formed as a trust under local law lacks either associates or a business purpose, it will not be classified as an association for federal tax purposes.

. . . [F]or the beneficiaries of a trust to be considered to be associates, they must display some volitional joint activity directed towards the conduct of business for profit . . . .

. . . [O]ne can distill the following factors to be applied in determining whether the beneficiaries of a trust will be considered to be associates in a joint enterprise for profit: (1) whether the trust relationship came into existence or continues in existence as a result of volitional activity of the beneficiaries; (2) whether the beneficiaries, as beneficiaries, influence the management activities of the trust; and (3) whether the interests of the beneficiaries are freely transferable.

Some custodianships and guardianships typically are ignored for income tax purposes.[4] And entities for which administration improperly has been prolonged also will be disregarded.[5] Assuming, however, that a fiduciary

---

[4] Compare Rev. Rul. 69-300, 1969-1 C.B. 167 (bank required to file fiduciary income tax returns because its status as court-appointed custodian of disputed property was sufficiently like a trust in terms of the bank's powers of administration and management), with Anastasio v. Commissioner, 67 T.C. 814 (1977), Rev. Rul. 56-484, 1956-2 C.B. 23, and Rev. Rul. 59-357, 1959-2 C.B. 212 (custodianships such as under the UGMA and UTMA ignored for Subchapter J purposes, notwithstanding that custodians have extensive discretion with respect to investment and distribution and the minor whose property is being held suffers or benefits from all valuation fluctuations), Rev. Rul. 58-267, 1958-1 C.B. 327 (guardianship for an incompetent was not subject to Subchapter J); cf. Rev. Rul. 64-137, 1964-1 C.B. 487 (beneficiary's taxpayer identification number, not the custodian's, should be furnished to dividend-paying corporation if the stock is recorded in a named person as custodian for a designated beneficiary); Rev. Rul. 66-116, 1966-1 C.B. 198, amplified by Rev. Rul. 68-227, 1968-1 C.B. 381 (consent to S Corporation election must be made by a minor's legal or natural guardian and not by the custodian of a minor's act account because the minor is deemed to own the S stock); Rev. Rul. 71-287, 1971-2 C.B. 317 (because the custodianship beneficiary is considered the owner of stock from the time it is transferred to the custodial account, termination of that account and distribution of the stock to the beneficiary is not considered to be a transfer to a new shareholder).

[5] Treas. Reg. § 1.641(b)-3(a) (administration deemed terminated when all assets have been distributed except a reasonable set aside for unascertained or contingent liabilities and expenses). Compare Carson v. United States, 317 F.2d

entity taxed as a trust or an estate is involved, then the simple and complex trust rules become relevant.

(Footnote Continued)

370 (Ct. Cl. 1963) (administration for 18 years pursuant to local court order that estate remain open to repay debt using estate income rather than selling closely held stock was not unreasonable), and Rev. Rul. 76-23, 1976-1 C.B. 264 (estate administration was not unduly prolonged during a full period of § 6166 deferred payment of FET), with Brown v. United States, 890 F.2d 1329 (5th Cir. 1989) (continuing payment of federal income tax and legacies were insufficient reasons to prolong estate administration), Miller v. Commissioner, 333 F.2d 400 (8th Cir. 1964) (estate should have been closed when litigation was settled 11 years after decedent's death), and Estate of Berger v. Commissioner, 60 T.C.M. (CCH) 1079, 1081 (1990) (normal estate administration was substantially complete more than three years prior to a sale at a gain of property still held by the personal representative; the government denied the estate's § 642(c)(2) charitable set aside deduction for the capital gain generated on that sale because § 642(c)(2) applies only to estates and the government regarded the estate as closed for income tax purposes), in which the Tax Court disregarded an estate, stating:

> all assets had been collected, all taxes, debts, and bequests . . . had been paid, a Federal estate tax return had been filed, and the estate tax paid. The residue of the estate had not been formally distributed . . . but this is not sufficient to keep the estate open for Federal income tax purposes. The remainder interests did not require estate administration . . . but rather any administration necessary was in the nature of trust administration.

See § 5.9 at text accompanying nn.45-46 regarding why the court's conclusion that the estate should be treated as closed for income tax purposes is disturbing.

In Rev. Proc. 83-61, 1983-1 C.B. 78, the government announced that it no longer will rule on the issue whether administration of an estate has been sufficiently prolonged that the estate will not be recognized as a separate tax paying entity. Nevertheless, TAM 9005003 suggested that a constructive receipt theory might cause income not actually distributed to be taxed to an executor who also was the beneficiary of an estate if administration was unduly prolonged, although the government then determined that was not the case in that situation. Accord, TAM 8306003. And PLR 9740009 concluded that an estate was the proper taxpayer to file income tax returns during an eight year period during which no party did any estate administration and therefore incurred interest and penalties for failure to timely file, citing Bowen v. Commissioner, 34 T.C. 222 (1960), aff'd, 295 F.2d 816 (2d Cir. 1961), and Ryan v. Commissioner, 15 T.C. 209 (1950). Quaere whether a different result would have obtained if the estate property had been realty (as to which title would pass under state law automatically at the moment of death), rather than personalty as was the case.

§ 5.2

§5.2.1 Simple Trusts

Simple trusts are the subject of Subpart B (§ §651 and 652) of Subchapter J. This abbreviated version of the rules that govern the income taxation of trusts is applicable only if the trust instrument requires distribution of all income annually and does not provide for charitable distributions or set asides,[6] and then only for years in which the trustee also does not distribute corpus (although corpus distributions may be authorized and may be made in other years).[7]

For purposes of the all important all-income requirement, "income" means "fiduciary accounting income" as determined under local law (such as the local principal and income act) and the governing instrument.[8] This reference to fiduciary accounting income permits reasonable modifications of state law, as illustrated by Treas. Reg. § 1.651(a)-2(a), which specifies that a trust can be a simple trust even if the trust instrument provides that, in determining income required to be distributed currently, the trustee shall maintain a reserve for depreciation or other allowance to keep trust corpus intact.[9]

---

[6] GCM 39306 and TAM 8446007 involved a simple trust from which the income beneficiary assigned a portion of the annual income to charity. A prior PLR determined that the income paid to charity would be includible in the charity's income and not the beneficiary's, and the TAMs concluded that the assignment did not convert the trust to a complex trust (because the trust instrument did not provide for the charity). The trust was denied a § 642(c) charitable set-aside deduction for the same reason, and was not permitted to claim a § 651(a) distributions deduction because simple trusts cannot make charitable distributions. The TAM was modified by PLR 8604080 to not apply retroactively to income already distributed by the trust pursuant to the assignment by the income beneficiary. The net effect apparently was to tax income to the trust that was distributed to charity, when a preferable approach presumably would have been to treat the income as distributed to the income beneficiary as specified in the document and allow that beneficiary to claim an offsetting charitable deduction for income tax purposes, resulting in no income to either the trust or the beneficiary.

[7] § 651(a). Notwithstanding its status as simple in all other years, a trust necessarily will be complex in the year of its termination by virtue of distributing its corpus. Treas. Reg. § 1.651(a)-3.

[8] § 643(b).

[9] See, e.g., Mueller v. Commissioner, 236 F.2d 537 (5th Cir. 1956) (trust-authorized allocations of income to principal properly restored deficit incurred in

Even more important is the authority granted in Treas. Reg. § 1.643(b)-1 to make allocations between income and corpus pursuant to authority granted by local law, either under a specific directive or a more general apportionment rule. These deviations are permitted to the extent the fiduciary's allocations do not "depart fundamentally from traditional principles of income and principal" and instead constitutes "a reasonable apportionment . . . of the total return of the trust for the year, including ordinary and tax exempt income, capital gains, and appreciation."

Examples given of state laws providing such authority are safe harbor provisions that regard "a unitrust amount of no less than 3% and no more than 5% of the FMV of the trust assets, whether determined annually or averaged on a multiple year basis" as the functional equivalent of an all income annually entitlement, and a more general trust law authority "to make adjustments between income and principal to fulfill the trustee's duty of impartiality between the income and remainder beneficiaries." The latter is a reference to discretion such as that granted in Uniform Principal and Income Act § 104(a) to apportion the total investment return of a trust that complies with a prudent investor standard. In addition, an allocation of capital gain to income will be respected if it is pursuant to provisions in the governing instrument and local law, *or* it represents "a reasonable and impartial exercise of discretion . . . (in accordance with power granted to the fiduciary by

---

(Footnote Continued)

prior years when income expenses exceeded current income and corpus was tapped for their payment; as such, income required to be distributed did not include amounts properly allocated to corpus); TAMs 8501011 and 8501084 (same case) (equitable adjustment allocating trust income to corpus to compensate for income taxes paid by corpus on income carried out to it on a "trapping distribution" was proper under state law and thereby reduced fiduciary accounting income for normal distribution purposes). See § 5.8.4 regarding compensatory adjustments, this one commonly referred to as a *Holloway* adjustment after In re Estate of Holloway, 327 N.Y.S.2d 865 (Surr. Ct. 1972). But see Rev. Rul. 90-82, 1990-2 C.B. 44 (simple trust directed mortgage interest and principal payments both to be charged against current trust income, notwithstanding that state law normally would charge the loan principal reduction against corpus; this accounting was regarded as a deemed income to corpus allocation—which required the trust depreciation deduction to be apportioned between income and corpus—and, although it was not at issue, it also would cause the trust to be regarded as complex rather than simple).

§ 5.2.1

applicable local law or by the governing instrument if not prohibited by local law."[10]

This fiduciary accounting income amount may differ from DNI, which is taxable income with several adjustments specified in § 643(a).[11] Because of the existence of deductions that reduce taxable income even if paid from fiduciary accounting corpus, it almost always is the case that DNI will be different than, and often is less than, fiduciary accounting income. DNI also usually will be different than taxable income, although it is harder to predict which will be the larger of taxable income and DNI.[12] In all of this it is helpful to remember that the concept of DNI has only a very limited role in the income taxation of trusts and estates. It serves to define and limit the amount of income—for income tax purposes—that is allocable between the trust or estate and its beneficiaries.[13]

With respect to the last simple trust requirement, the precise rule is that simple trust treatment does not apply if the trust distributes amounts in excess of fiduciary accounting income, with reference to the "amount" of income, not to any particular item that is identified on the trust ledger as an income item. The point is that distributions of assets that are corpus on the trust ledger may be regarded as "income" for Subchapter J purposes if the aggregate amount of distributions for the year do not exceed the dollar amount of fiduciary accounting income for the year, in which case the trust may constitute a simple trust.[14]

---

[10] Treas. Reg. § 1.643(a)-3(b) provides greater detail regarding this apportionment authority. See § 5.3.3 regarding allocation of capital gain to income and the impact on the calculation of DNI.

[11] For example, capital gains that are allocable to corpus for fiduciary accounting purposes ordinarily are excluded from DNI, tax exempt income is included in DNI, and the distributions deduction is ignored in computing the amount of DNI.

[12] See § 5.3.

[13] The mechanism through which DNI performs this limiting function is the distributions deduction in § 651 for simple trusts and its counterpart § 661 for complex trusts. See § § 5.3 and 5.4.1 at text accompanying nn.2, 21.

[14] Note, however, that if corpus is distributed in kind in satisfaction of the trust's obligation to distribute all income annually, Treas. Reg. § § 1.651(a)-2(d) and 1.661(a)-2(f), and Rev. Rul. 67-74, 1967-1 C.B. 194, properly regard the distribution to be a gain or loss realization event, as if the distributed property had been sold and the cash proceeds distributed, which the beneficiary then

§5.2.2 Complex Trusts and Estates

Complex trusts and estates are the subject of Subpart C (§§ 661-664, although § 664 is not relevant to this discussion) of Subchapter J. By definition, these are all those fiduciary entities that do not qualify as simple trusts. Some trusts are complex all the time because their terms do not require distribution of all income annually or because they provide for charity. But some trusts may be simple in one year and complex in another—because their terms call for annual distribution of all income and provide nothing for charity but in some years distributions in excess of income are made, making the trust complex in those years only.

The key difference between the taxation of simple and complex trusts is with respect to income that is accumulated in one year and distributed in another. Probably the most common income item that is not distributed currently is capital gains that, under state principal and income acts, almost always are allocated to corpus and are not "distribut-

---

(Footnote Continued)

used to purchase that property. The result is realization to the trust and a new basis equal to FMV to the beneficiary—in addition to the normal DNI carryout and distributions deduction consequences under §§ 651 and 652.

Quaere whether some indirect benefits provided by a trust are regarded as a distribution at all for these purposes. For example, if a beneficiary owned a home and the trust serviced a mortgage or paid other expenses relative to the property the beneficiary would be treated as having received a distribution. But what if the trust owns the home, makes all the same payments, and merely allows the beneficiary to live rent free in the residence? Is the rental value an indirect distribution that should carry out DNI or, if all income otherwise is being distributed, that might constitute the trust as complex? Ferguson, Freeland, & Ascher, Federal Income Taxation of Estates, Trusts, and Beneficiaries § 7.05[C][4][b] (3d ed. 2011), opine that the law is reasonably clear and that this use of the trust's property is not a distribution at all. Under the current income tax brackets that might be a less desirable result in the sense that it does not allow income to be taxed to the beneficiary at a potentially lower rate, or reduce the beneficiary's net worth that otherwise ultimately will be subject to wealth transfer tax. But it solves a number of problems that a deemed distribution result would generate, not the least of which being a cash flow and liquidity problem if the beneficiary owed income tax on the value of the benefit received. And it is a far better result if the residence is protected from wealth transfer tax (for example, because it is a GST exempt trust) than if the residence was owned by the beneficiary and the trust merely paid the upkeep expense and debt service.

§ 5.2.2

able" until termination of the trust. Otherwise, complex trusts usually are those that permit accumulations of fiduciary accounting income for later distribution, either at or before termination of the trust. In either case, before Congress changed the tax rates, it was with respect to accumulated items of taxable income that trusts and estates presented the advantage of a separate income taxpaying entity. The fiduciary pays tax in the tax year of accumulation on the amount of taxable income in the entity, which reflects the distributions deduction allowed only for income actually distributed or required to be distributed.

Thus, for example, if a trustee may distribute trust income or accumulate it, the trust would be a discretionary accumulation or spray trust and could not be a simple trust in any year, even if all income was distributed currently, because the trust does not require distribution of all income annually. The income would be taxed to the trust beneficiaries to the extent it is distributed to them (or made available by right of withdrawal) [15] and to the trust to the extent it is accumulated. [16]

---

[15] Compare Flato v. Commissioner, 245 F.2d 413 (5th Cir. 1957) (trustee of discretionary trust could exercise distribution discretion by offering to pay income to beneficiary upon request; beneficiary taxed on all income, even if not requested), with Estate of Johnson v. Commissioner, 88 T.C. 225 (1987), in which the decedent's estate was faced with significant contingent liabilities that prevented it from winding up administration and making final distribution. Those liabilities prompted the personal representative to merely make bookkeeping entries on its annual work papers to reflect income "distributions" to various beneficiaries, but no income actually was distributed due to the perceived need to retain funds until all liabilities were settled. The court denied the estate's § 661(a)(2) distributions deduction because the amounts represented as credited to the beneficiaries were not so definitively allocated as to be beyond recall by the estate, nor beyond the reach of creditors of the estate. Quaere whether the same result should have applied in *Flato* notwithstanding that the beneficiaries were entitled to request amounts at their whim. Although the *Johnson* court said that actual physical segregation or payment is not required to support a distributions deduction, and that book entries might be adequate in some cases, it failed to state what would have sufficed in that case.

[16] To the extent repeal of the throwback rules (with respect to most domestic trusts) is not applicable, this accumulated income then is subject to throwback in any future year in which distributions exceed the greater of DNI or fiduciary accounting income (for example, in the year the trust terminates). See the last sentence of § 665(b) and, with respect to what remains of throwback, see § 5.6.

§ 5.2.2

The apparent income tax advantage of accumulating income is very slight because the income tax rates applicable to trusts and estates are the highest rates in the Internal Revenue Code. Little can be gained by the fiduciary's ability to divide income into several pockets, taxing it among various beneficiaries and leaving some to be taxed to the entity at lower brackets than if all income was distributed currently.[17] Because the advantage of the trust or estate's separate taxpayer existence is so small, there are only a few real advantages to be gleaned for income tax purposes, and those are at the beneficiary level.

One advantage is to avoid distributions that might boost a beneficiary into a higher income or wealth transfer tax bracket (or, in the case of a GST exempt trust, subjecting distributed income—after income tax—to wealth transfer tax rather than accumulating it in the exempt trust and avoiding wealth transfer tax entirely). Another is to avoid a phase-out loss of the beneficiary's personal exemption or an increase in the beneficiary's income on which to compute the 2% loss of itemized deductions under § 67 or the 7½% loss of medical expense deductions under § 213.

Against these modest tax advantages should be compared the cost of losing a § 2013 previously taxed property credit.[18] If a trust beneficiary to whom income is payable dies within ten years of the settlor, a § 2013 credit may be available for the value of the beneficiary's income interest,[19] but only if its value can be determined as of the death of the settlor

---

[17] Due to compression of the brackets, the maximum tax saving is roughly $1,000 per trust—it was $1,066 in 2012, but this figure fluctuates annually because the rates are indexed for inflation.

[18] Additional factors to consider with respect to transfers into trust made during the settlor's life are whether the settlor's spouse is one of the beneficiaries to whom discretionary income might be paid, because gift splitting under § 2513 would be unavailable with respect to any interest in the trust from which the spouse might benefit, and unavailability of the gift tax annual exclusion for the value of the income interest. See § 7.1.1.1 regarding the gift tax annual exclusion present interest requirement and discretionary income interests.

[19] See Treas. Reg. § 20.2013-5, which defines the term "property" for purposes of the previously taxed property credit to include "any beneficial interest in property," which the second sentence of Treas. Reg. § 20.2013-4(a) reveals to include an income interest. See also Treas. Reg. § 20.2013-4(a) Example (2), and Rev. Rul. 59-9, 1959-1 C.B. 232 (life estate capable of valuation qualifies for § 2013 credit).

§ 5.2.2

in whose estate the trust corpus was includible.[20] Thus, for example, effective marital deduction planning anticipates a postmortem determination whether to claim less marital deduction in D's estate. A mandatory income nonmarital trust (or preservation of the mandatory income provision in a marital trust made only partially deductible, as with a partial QTIP election) makes sense if the § 2013 credit is one factor being applied in minimizing the aggregate wealth transfer tax burden over both spouses' estates.[21] The value of a beneficiary's right to receive trust income subject to the discretion of another party, such as the trustee, may not be subject to determination with enough precision to support a § 2013 credit.[22]

---

[20] Estate of Edmonds v. Commissioner, 72 T.C. 970 (1979) (3½% valuation tables were in effect when the first decedent died, 6% tables when the subsequent decedent died, and the court upheld use of the 3½% version) confirms that valuation is at the death of the prior decedent based on tables and predictions, rather than at the death of the subsequent decedent based on actual events, notwithstanding that at the time the credit is applied it is possible to know with precision how much income actually was distributed and therefore how much the net worth of the subsequent decedent was increased by this life income interest.

[21] See § 13.2.6, with respect to this marital deduction planning.

[22] See Estate of Pollock v. Commissioner, 77 T.C. 1296, 1304 (1981) (discretionary income trust for S and children; notwithstanding that S received all income for S's overlife, the interest was deemed incapable of valuation because hindsight cannot be employed and value was measurable at D's death: "when viewed as of the date of Mr. Pollock's death, Mrs. Pollock did not have, under the governing instrument, a fixed right to all the distributable income or a determinable portion thereof for the remainder of her life"); TAMs 8717006 (if trust income exceeded S's needs, considering S's other income and means of support, trustees could distribute excess income to D's children; standard referring to S's accustomed manner of living and fact that S had an estate of over $500,000 prompted determination that life estate could not be valued) and 7836009 (no credit for discretionary income interest notwithstanding that decedent was sole beneficiary of the trust). Cf. Holbrook v. United States, 575 F.2d 1288, 1292 (9th Cir. 1978) (life estate could not be valued and § 2013 credit therefore was unavailable because trustees were authorized to invest in unproductive property and "it cannot be said that a decision by the trustees to invest in assets producing little or no income would constitute a remediable abuse of discretion under [local] law"). But see Estate of Lloyd v. United States, 650 F.2d 1196 (Ct. Cl. 1981) (because settlor indicated a primary concern for the welfare of the sole income beneficiary, authority granted to corporate fiduciary to distribute trust

In addition, accumulating income in a trust or an estate to take advantage of the modest annual income tax saving attributable to the entity's separate tax paying existence probably is not worth even the costs incurred in fiduciary fees and separate income tax return preparation expenses. Thus, in the final analysis, it probably is fair to say that the decision whether to make income payable in the fiduciary's discretion or absolutely should be based on other considerations. Such as the §2013 credit or such nontax issues as whether fiduciary investment authority can be exercised to favor growth over income, mandatory income is more than the beneficiary needs or should have, and whether the fiduciary's discretion over income creates psychological angst. It should not be based on any perceived advantage of income tax benefits.

§5.3 DNI

DNI plays a limited but pivotal role in the income taxation of trusts and estates. It serves as a yardstick or measure, placing a limit on the amount of the entity's distributions deduction and on the amount and character of current income that is attributed to the income beneficiaries.[1] Thus, it is an essential aspect in the operation of these depen-

---

(Footnote Continued)

corpus to others if, in the trustee's sole and uncontrolled discretion, it was "necessary or advisable," was not sufficient to preclude valuation of income interest); Estate of Weinstein v. United States, 820 F.2d 201 (6th Cir. 1987) (power to accumulate income otherwise payable to life tenant had to be exercised in light of the primary intent of the settlor to provide for the maintenance of the income beneficiary in accordance with a past style of living, making those powers irrelevant and the §2013 credit capable of evaluation); and TAM 8608002 (life interest was susceptible of valuation so as to qualify for the §2013 credit because trust stated the settlor's intent that the income be expended primarily for the life tenant unless other potential recipients "have real need for any portion of said income," which the government held "constitutes an ascertainable standard which renders the present decedent's life interest susceptible of valuation," referring to Rev. Rul. 67-53, 1967-1 C.B. 265, Rev. Rul. 70-292, 1970-1 C.B. 187, Rev. Rul. 75-550, 1975-1 C.B. 357, and *Estate of Pollock*, in discussing when a life interest is susceptible of valuation for purposes of §2013). See §13.2.5.

[1] **§5.3** Under §§652(a) and 662(a), the amount of income includible to any beneficiary is limited to that beneficiary's pro rata share of the taxable portion of the DNI that was actually, or was deemed to have been, distributed.

dent operations. It also serves as an element in the definitions of UNI and accumulation distributions for throwback purposes, although these have only a very slight impact under current law.[2]

§ 5.3.1 Taxable Income

DNI is based on taxable income of the entity (with several modifications).[3] Occasionally the fundamental question arises whether income belongs for tax purposes to an estate or trust or, in the first instance, to its beneficiaries.[4] For example, if a decedent owned realty at death and specifically devised it, is rental income therefrom estate income or does it belong ab initio to the devisee? Normally the income belongs to the estate if an asset is subject to administration in a decedent's estate.[5] If, on the other hand, state law specifies that title passes directly from the decedent to the devisee, then that income usually is the devisee's and, with it, the tax liability.[6] Nevertheless, income from that portion used is taxable as estate income to the extent the decedent's personal represen-

---

[2] § 665.

[3] § 643(a).

[4] In addition, the issue might be whether the income was earned and belonged to a decedent before death, to be reported on the decedent's final income tax return that will be filed by the decedent's personal representative, or was earned before the decedent died but not paid until thereafter, in which case it belongs to the recipient but is taxable as IRD, subject to a special set of rules. See § 5.10. Similar issues also can apply with respect to losses and other DRD. See, e.g., Estate of Applebaum v. Commissioner, 724 F.2d 375 (3d Cir. 1983) (decedent's share of partnership losses belonged to estate and were not available on decedent's final income tax return).

[5] Rev. Rul. 75-61, 1975-1 C.B. 180.

[6] See Treas. Reg. § 1.661(a)-2(e) (last sentence). Rev. Rul. 68-49, 1968-1 C.B. 304, recognized that ultimate distribution of an asset from an estate will not carry out § 662 income or generate a § 661 distributions deduction if the beneficiary has legal title and receives the income. Prima facie there never will be an estate as a separate income tax paying entity if the beneficiaries never open an estate administration, taking the property without engaging in the formalities needed to prove their entitlement. All income from those assets will be the beneficiaries' from the date of the decedent's death.

tative is entitled to, and does, use any portion of that realty to satisfy claims against or obligations of the estate.[7]

Aside from these entitlement issues, taxable income essentially is the same for a trust or an estate as it is for any individual taxpayer,[8] although it is subject to several modifications.[9] Most common among those deviations from an individual's computation of taxable income is denial of the standard deduction.[10] In addition, a deduction is allowed in lieu of the personal exemption,[11] amounting to $600 annually for an estate, $300 annually for any trust that is required to distribute all its income currently, and $100 annually for all other trusts.[12] By definition,

---

[7] Rev. Rul. 59-375, 1959-2 C.B. 161 (sale of property needed only in part to satisfy estate obligations caused gain to be taxed to the estate only from that portion needed by the estate). Cf. Dauphin Deposit Trust Co. v. McGinnes, 208 F. Supp. 228 (M.D. Pa. 1962) (rejecting government's denial of deduction for expenses of sale by personal representative, applying a state law presumption that sale was for the estate's benefit and not the beneficiaries, as alleged by the government). With respect to deductibility for FET purposes of expenses incurred for the personal benefit of estate beneficiaries, see § 15.5.3.3 n.82 et seq. and accompanying text.

An income tax credit under the § 1341 claim of right doctrine may be available to a beneficiary who receives and reports income and pays tax on it, and then is required to turn over the asset or its income. See Rev. Rul. 77-322, 1977-2 C.B. 314 (applicable even though the taxpayer who improperly included the income and paid the tax was deceased and repayment was made by that taxpayer's estate), and Rev. Rul. 75-339, 1975-2 C.B. 244 (will contest in which devisee prevailed, the government noting that the claim of right doctrine would apply had the devisee been divested of the property in that litigation). And see Estate of Smith v. Commissioner, 108 T.C. 412 (1997), rev'd and rem'd on other grounds, 198 F.3d 515 (5th Cir. 1999) (decedent's estate was entitled to a claim of right deduction for amounts repaid that previous to death were includible in the decedent's income; the § 1341 deduction was regarded as an asset of the estate, however, subject to FET inclusion under § 2033, with valuation determined based on the amount repaid as informed by a postmortem settlement agreement).

[8] § 641(b).

[9] § 642. For a foreign trust see also § 643(a)(6). For an ESBT see also § 641(c)(3)(B).

[10] § 63(c)(6)(D).

[11] See § 151.

[12] § 642(b). It appears that these amounts are not subject to the phase out loss that would apply to a high income individual's personal exemption under

§5.3.1

the $300 deduction applies to all simple trusts, but a complex trust may qualify for the $300 deduction if it requires distribution of all income annually and is complex only because it either provides for charity or distributes corpus during the current year.[13] In this respect and for *most* other purposes, income (when not modified by some other term, such as gross, taxable, or distributable net) means fiduciary accounting income.[14]

A second common deviation from the normal computation of taxable income is attributable to § § 67(e) and 68. The latter provision does not appear to apply at all to taxpayers other than individuals,[15] meaning that its threshold on certain itemized deductions does not apply to fiduciary entities. The former provision specifies that the 2% loss of miscellaneous itemized deductible expenses incurred by individuals will *not* apply with respect to "costs which are paid or incurred in connection with the administration of the estate or trust and would not have been incurred if the property were not held in such trust or estate."

Uncertainty exists with respect to the meaning of § 67(e) in the context of items of deduction that are attributable to expenses that would be incurred even if the property was not held in a trust or estate.[16]

To take the most common example, suppose the grantor of a trust paid for investment advice prior to creation of the trust, but that the trustee of the trust provides investment counsel with respect to trust

---

(Footnote Continued)

§ 151(d)(3), because there is no corresponding provision that appears to import the rules applicable to the personal exemption into its substitute under § 642(b) and no threshold amount is specified for fiduciary entities in § 151(d)(3)(C). Excepted from § 642(b) is any § 642(b)(2)(C) "qualified disability trust"—which is treated as if it was a § 1(c) unmarried individual taxpayer.

[13] Treas. Reg. § 1.642(b)-1.

[14] § 643(b). This term means taxable income for grantor trust purposes under Subpart E. See § 5.11.1 n.17 and accompanying text.

[15] The term "individual," although not specifically defined in the Code, appears to be used in juxtaposition to fiduciary and other legal entities. See § 7701(a)(1) (definition of "person" as an individual or a trust, estate, partnership, corporation, association and such).

[16] See § 4.1.12 n.174 and accompanying text regarding the § 67(e) issue in revocable inter vivos trusts, and § 5.11 n.8 and accompanying text regarding the issue specifically in a grantor trust context.

§ 5.3.1

assets as part of the services it renders. If the trustee does not account or charge separately for this investment function, is the trustee's full fee deductible or should the fiduciary be required to "unbundle" its fees and deduct only 100% of items of expense that would not have been incurred if the property was not held in the trust?

Proposed regulations discussed next below would require such an "unbundling" of fees, which has evoked extensive comment because it would be a difficult administrative chore—given all the functions a fiduciary might perform (including bookkeeping and the exercise of distribution discretion) that arguably the settlor did prior to creation of the trust. Issuance of final regulations has been significantly delayed because a second set of proposed regulations has been issued, and those regulations along with Notices 2011-37,[17] 2010-32,[18] 2008-116,[19] and 2008-32,[20] before the proposed regulations were revised all provide that unbundling is not required for any tax year that began before the proposed regulation ultimately is published in final form. Ultimately, final guidance is expected that will not continue an advantage for professional or institutional fiduciaries, as compared to individuals who contract for a variety of necessary advisors who charge separate identifiable fees for such things as accounting, legal, tax compliance, investment, and valuation services, each that can be subject to § 67 scrutiny.

Knight v. Commissioner,[21] a unanimous Supreme Court decision, makes it clear that fees paid by a trustee to a third party who provided

---

[17] 2011-1 C.B. 785.

[18] 2010-1 C.B. 594.

[19] 2008-2 C.B. 1372.

[20] 2008-1 C.B. 593.

[21] 552 U.S. 181 (2008). *Knight* closed the first chapter of the § 67(e) story, which began with the taxpayer's victory in O'Neill Irrevocable Trust v. Commissioner, 98 T.C. 227, 230 (1992), rev'd, 994 F.2d 302 (6th Cir. 1993), nonacq., and then was followed by government victories in Mellon Bank v. United States, 2000-2 U.S. Tax Cas. (CCH) ¶ 50,642 (Ct. Fed. Cl. 2000), aff'd, 265 F.3d 1275 (Fed. Cir. 2001), Scott v. United States, 186 F. Supp. 2d 664 (E.D. Va. 2002), aff'd, 328 F.2d 132 (4th Cir. 2003), and Rudkin Testamentary Trust v. Commissioner, 467 F.3d 149 (2d Cir. 2006), aff'g 124 T.C. 304 (2005) (a unanimous reviewed opinion), aff'd sub nom. in *Knight* (which was the case affirmed in principle—but not on the proper test—in *Knight*). Each case dealt with fees paid by trustees to independent investment advisors. And each fashioned its own statement of the

investment advice are subject to the 2% loss of deduction rule in § 67(a). This is significant because many fiduciaries charge nearly as much for their investment services alone as they do to serve as a full-fledged fiduciary (a practice that may change in the wake of *Knight* and final regulations that require unbundling). It also may foretell how other deductible expenses will be treated, although the government has been very slow to indicate how it intends to interpret § 67(e).

According to the Supreme Court:

> [T]rust-related administrative expenses are subject to the 2% floor if they constitute expenses commonly incurred by individual taxpayers.

> The question whether a trust-related expense is fully deductible turns on a prediction about what would happen . . . if the property were held by an individual . . . [and] excepts from the 2% floor only those costs that it would be uncommon (or unusual, or unlikely) for . . . [an] individual to incur.

The only item specifically addressed under existing caselaw is investment advisor fees. No opinion yet has treated fiduciary fees as subject to the 2% rule. In addition, *Knight* left dangling the possibility that

> some trust-related investment advisory fees may be fully deductible "if an investment advisor were to impose a special, additional charge applicable only to its fiduciary accounts" . . . such that . . . the incremental cost of expert advice beyond what would normally be required for the ordinary taxpayer would not be subject to the 2% floor.

Presumably the final regulations will address both investment advisor surcharges and fiduciary fees in general.

The first Prop. Treas. Reg. § 1.67-4 articulated a test extracted essentially from the lower court's opinion that was rejected by the Supreme Court in *Knight* (notwithstanding that the underlying decision itself was affirmed). That original position was that only items that are "unique" to fiduciary administration are immune from § 67. The second proposed regulation altered this approach by proposing a new test that more closely mirrors the *Knight* decision, without adding new meaning.

(Footnote Continued)

statutory rule, no doubt to make sense of the double negative in § 67(e) ("would *not* have been incurred if the property were *not* held in trust").

It is significant that the proposed regulation reflects a fundamental fairness issue. A fiduciary could hire outside consultants and incur fees out of its own pocket and then charge a single unbundled fee large enough to cover all its costs. Or the fiduciary could provide all the services it needs from within and again charge a single undifferentiated fee. Or the trustee could hire outside consultants and pay them from the trust directly. The proposed regulation seeks to create a level playing field by requiring an administrative determination of how much of a fiduciary's fee should be allocated to various fiduciary functions—known as "unbundling" the fee—such that § 67 would apply equally in any of these situations.

Thus, the proposed regulation requires what no court has yet mandated, that a fiduciary's commission that includes "both costs that are subject to the 2-percent floor and costs . . . that are not" must be separately stated, using "any reasonable method" to allocate the fee. Potentially the only helpful aspect of the proposed regulation is nonexclusive listings of items that fall on one side or the other of the line.

The first proposed regulation listed items that would be fully deductible as fees for services related to

> fiduciary accountings; judicial or quasi-judicial filings required as part of the administration of the estate or trust; fiduciary income tax and wealth transfer tax returns; the division or distribution of income or corpus to or among beneficiaries; trust or will contest or construction; fiduciary bond premiums; and communications with beneficiaries regarding estate or trust matters.

And falling outside the safe harbor list were fees for services related to

> custody or management of property; advice on investing for total return; gift tax returns; the defense of claims by creditors of the decedent or grantor; and the purchase, sale, maintenance, repair, insurance or management of non-trade or business property.

No similar lists are included in the new proposed regulation, but these prior proposed regulations presumably give a clue regarding the reasonable allocation standard, which did not change. Items that the newly proposed regulation regards as subject to the 2% floor include (1) costs incurred in defense of a claim against the decedent or the estate or trust that are unrelated to the existence, validity, or administration of the estate or trust, (2) carrying costs incurred by an owner of property, such

§ 5.3.1

as condo fees, property taxes, insurance premiums, and maintenance expenses, (3) costs of preparing gift tax returns (but not estate, generation-skipping, or fiduciary income tax returns), and (4) investment fees.

Analyzed under the Supreme Court's test (items that individuals commonly incur) at least some items in these illustrations may be on the wrong list. For example, individuals commonly incur costs to file income tax returns, albeit the particular return filed will differ (a Form 1040 for an individual versus a Form 1041 for a fiduciary entity). So the exception granted for certain income tax returns is a generous application. And Temp. Treas. Reg. § 1.67-1T regards all § 212 expenses for the production or collection of income or for the determination of any tax as subject to the 2% rule when applied to individuals.

The *Knight* test incorporated in Prop. Treas. Reg. § 1.67-4(b)(4)—

> an incremental cost is a special, additional charge added solely because the investment advice is rendered to a trust or estate instead of to an individual, that is attributable to an unusual investment objective or the need for a specialized balancing of the interests of various parties (beyond the usual balancing of the varying interests of current beneficiaries and remaindermen), in each case such that a reasonable comparison with individual investors would be improper

—is so amorphous that the notice issuing the proposed regulation actually asks for comments that will help the government interpret this exception. Note also that Temp. Treas. Reg. § 1.67-1T(a)(1)(ii) states that investment advisory fees are subject to the 2% floor. It effectively was extended to fiduciaries in the form of Prop. Treas. Reg. § 1.67-4, and potentially other items not addressed specifically in a § 67(e) regulation will be applied consistent with that temporary regulation.

Regarding the most important factor under the proposed regulations—unbundling —the only guidance given to guide a fiduciary is that "[a]ny reasonable method may be used to allocate a bundled fee . . . ."

In addition to all of this, the beguiling question for fiduciaries remains whether the government is paying attention to fiduciary income tax returns. Is Form 1041 being audited and, if not, how were the trusts in these cases targeted for litigation? The answer appears to be that investment advisory fees are the one item that the government will

§ 5.3.1

examine on any Form 1041 return, such that a fiduciary that attempts to deduct 100% of these fees may invite an audit.

Knight involved a picayune $4,448 income tax deficiency. Were it just for the 2% floor a fiduciary might wisely apply a cost/benefit analysis and write off that much of the entity's deductions rather than incur the cost involved in an unbundling determination (or risk audit). Before the government's proposed regulation was issued it was not uncommon for fiduciaries to take a blanket position that all fees paid by a fiduciary are *free* from the 2% rule. Now the pendulum may swing in the opposite direction and fiduciaries may choose to assume that none of their fees are free from the 2% rule.

In many cases, however, a potentially much larger AMT consequence will lurk in the background.[22] That liability may preclude fiduciaries from comparing the cost of losing itemized deductions equal to 2% of the trust or estate's adjusted gross income to the cost involved in unbundling its fees. Care will be required to be certain that such ancillary tax consequences have been evaluated closely and that there are no extraordinary or hidden costs of such a decision.

Less common deviations in computing an entity's taxable income include modifications to taxable income relating to the credit for foreign

---

[22] The explanation does *not* turn on the Code provisions, which produce the right result. It is a function of the tax return itself, which misapplies the Code. The law begins with § 56(b)(1)(A)(i), which denies an AMT deduction "for any miscellaneous itemized deduction (as defined in § 67(b)." The deductions defined in § 67(b) include all itemized deductions other than a dozen enumerated exceptions. Fiduciary fees (including investment advisor fees) are not among the listed exceptions, so they constitute miscellaneous itemized deductions as defined in § 67(b), which makes them denied deductions for AMT purposes. Then § 67(e)(1) excludes from the § 67(b) definition any "costs which are paid or incurred in connection with the administration of the estate or trust and which would not have been incurred if the property were not held in such trust or estate." That is the language that raises the unbundling issue, and it means that most fiduciary fees are *not* miscellaneous itemized deductions for purposes of § 67(b). That means that they are not disallowed miscellaneous itemized deductions for purposes of § 56(b)(1)(A)(i), either. Thus seen, there is no AMT issue, to the extent that § 67(e)(1) applies.

§ 5.3.1

taxes,[23] restrictions relating to charitable contributions that permit a current deduction for complex trusts and estates that distribute amounts of gross income for qualified charitable organizations or purposes,[24] and total exclusion of S Corporation income from the DNI of an ESBT and other minor adjustments in computing the net operating loss deduction for businesses operated in any trust or estate.[25]

DNI is essential to the taxation of income between an entity and its beneficiaries. As such it is important to identify which taxpayers are entitled to or saddled with various items (or portions of items) that enter into the computation of taxable income and, therefore, into the determination of DNI. For example, special rules applicable to trusts (but not to estates) govern allocation of deductions for depreciation and depletion, each being apportioned in essentially a two step process.[26]

First, the deduction is allocated to the trust dollar for dollar for any income actually set aside to a reserve established pursuant to local law or the governing instrument. The full deduction will be allocated to the trust by this rule in many states requiring establishment of a depletion reserve because the reserve is set at 27.5% of annual receipts from extraction and the available §613 deduction is only 15% of those receipts.

The second step prorates any excess deduction remaining after this first step (by virtue of a different provision in the governing instrument, in states that do not require such a large reserve for depreciation or depletion, or in estates). The entity and its beneficiaries share that excise on the basis of distributions and accumulations of current income.[27] This

---

[23] See §642(a). The credit for foreign taxes is allocated under §901 among the entity and its beneficiaries, and the credit for political contributions is denied entirely.

[24] See §§642(c), 663(a)(2), 681, and §14.3.6.

[25] See §§641(c)(3)(B) and 642(d), and Treas. Reg. §1.642(d)-1. Excluded from the net operating loss deduction computation is any charitable or distributions deduction, along with both income and deductions that are governed by the grantor trust rules of Subpart E.

[26] §642(e). Under §§167(d) and 611(b)(4), estates do not participate in that portion of the allocation that involves a reserve for depreciation and therefore only the apportionment based on proration of estate income is involved.

[27] Treas. Reg. §§1.167(h)-1(b) (this regulation applies to what now is §167(d)) and 1.611-1(c)(4).

allocation unavoidably fails to maximize use of the deduction if an income beneficiary is a charity or low bracket taxpayer.[28] Allocated deductions may exceed the amount of income allocated to various beneficiaries, but pro ration of the deduction may not be altered to direct a larger portion of the deduction than the pro rata portion of income distributed to any particular beneficiary.[29] Similar principles are adopted for allocation of amortization,[30] and for apportionment of the investment credit.[31]

Finally, in computing taxable income, special rules also disallow deduction of certain items that are claimed as FET deductions, which require an election[32] between claiming certain expenditures as either (1) an income tax deduction on the entity's Form 1041[33] or on a decedent's final income tax return,[34] (2) as a reduction to the selling price in determining gain on the disposition of assets, or (3) as an FET deductible administration expense or loss.[35] Although the objective of this election is to prevent use of the same expenditures to work double duty under both the estate and income taxes, it is common to claim the same amount on Forms 706 and 1041 both and later waive or amend one of

---

[28] Lambert Tree Estate v. Commissioner, 38 T.C. 392 (1962) (allocation of deduction to tax exempt charity).

[29] See § 5.8.3 n.23.

[30] § 642(f).

[31] See § 50(d)(6), referring to § 48(f) as it existed prior to enactment of the Revenue Reconciliation Act of 1990.

[32] § 642(g).

[33] §§ 162, 163, 165, or 212.

[34] § 213. See, e.g., Rev. Rul. 77-357, 1977-2 C.B. 328 (portion of deduction lost on income tax return due to 7.5% threshold cannot be claimed on FET return either; it is deemed to have been utilized on the income tax return if the election otherwise uses the deductions on that return). Payment of these items before the decedent's death would work a double benefit by reducing the estate for FET purposes and generate an income tax deduction. Moreover, compare Rev. Rul. 59-32, 1959-1 C.B. 245 (portion of administration expenses attributable to tax exempt income and thus not deductible for income tax purposes *is* allowable as a § 2053 FET deduction), clarified by Rev. Rul. 63-27, 1963-1 C.B. 57. No authority appears to address whether income tax deductions lost under § 67 can be utilized on an estate's FET return.

[35] §§ 2053 and 2054.

§ 5.3.1

them sometime prior to final audit of the proper return when enough facts are ascertained to know which is preferable. This "double" deduction is permissible only if the amendment or waiver is filed before the income tax statute of limitation expires.[36]

§5.3.2 Adjustments to Determine DNI

DNI is determined by making several adjustments to taxable income. The first is to "add back" the amount of the § 642(b) deduction in lieu of the personal exemption allowed in computing taxable income.[37] By this increase, DNI is larger and, because DNI is a cap on each, (1) a larger distributions deduction is available to the entity for current income distributions and (2) a larger amount is subject to inclusion to beneficiaries of the trust or estate who received distributions. The rationale for this addition is to preclude the beneficiaries from enjoying both their own personal exemption and the entity's deduction in lieu of the personal exemption.

An additional add back is required with respect to § 103 tax exempt interest income, with a similar effect on DNI.[38] The add back serves to permit this form of tax favored income to pass through to the beneficiaries by increasing DNI and thus increasing both the distributions deduction and the amount subject to inclusion at the beneficiary level. If

---

[36] Treas. Reg. § 1.642(g)-1. A proposed amendment to this provision would require the amendment or waiver to be filed at least 180 days before the FET statute of limitation expires, thus permitting the government sufficient time to disallow the deduction on the FET return before allowing the deduction for income tax purposes, or vice versa. In this fashion the government hopes to curb the abuse of filing the waiver or amendment at such a late date that audit of the return on which improperly claimed no longer is feasible. It still is permissible to split the deductions, claiming a portion on each form.

Treas. Reg. § 1.213-1(d)(2) states a slightly different rule with respect to medical expenses paid within one year after the decedent's death and deductible on the decedent's final income tax return, requiring in duplicate a statement that the deductible amount has not been *allowed* and a waiver of the right to claim it as an FET deduction, "filed with or for association with" the income tax return or claim for refund or credit on which it is claimed.

[37] § 643(a)(2).

[38] § 643(a)(5). Notice that this provision does not apply to any other form of tax exempt *income*; it is limited to *interest* made exempt under § 103.

distributed currently, the character pass through rules of the conduit system of taxation[39] permit the beneficiaries to enjoy the special status of interest income items that trigger this adjustment. However, the character of all other items included in DNI also is pro rated.[40] Thus, distributions that generate deductions for the entity are allocated to various items of taxable and tax favored or exempt income.[41] This allocation is imposed to assure proper apportionment of tax favored items to the proper beneficiaries. Otherwise, the government might attempt to allocate deductions to tax exempt income, which essentially wastes the deduction (the income and deductions balancing out) while the taxpayer might attempt to allocate deductibles entirely to taxable income to maximize their utility.

In addition to adding back the deduction in lieu of the personal exemption and tax exempt interest in computing DNI, three items normally considered in the determination of taxable income are ignored for purposes of computing DNI. First ignored[42] is the distributions deduction,[43] which is necessary to avoid a circularity. Because the distributions deduction is limited to the taxable portion of DNI, an unavoidable interrelated computation otherwise would develop if DNI was equal to taxable income after allowance of the distributions deduction.

The second and third items that are ignored involve taxable income that is allocated to corpus and not currently distributed. Thus, for example, ignored are capital gains that are allocated to corpus (either under local law[44] or the terms of the document) and not distributed or set aside for charity, along with capital losses used in computing taxable

---

[39] §§ 652(b) and 662(b). See § 5.4.1 at text accompanying n.3.

[40] §§ 652(b) and 662(b).

[41] Treas. Reg. §§ 1.643(a)-5(b), 1.652(c)-4, 1.661(b)-2 and 1.661(c)-2(d). See § 5.3.4 nn.75-77 and accompanying text.

[42] § 643(a)(1).

[43] See §§ 651(a) and 661(a).

[44] Unless altered by the governing instrument, gains typically are allocated to corpus under state principal and income acts. See Uniform Principal and Income Act (1997 Act) § 103(a)(4), 7A U.L.A. 429 (2006), and Revised Uniform Principal and Income Act (1962 Act) § 3(b)(8), 7A U.L.A. 566 (2006).

§ 5.3.2

income.[45] The effect is to reduce DNI and, correspondingly, to reduce the maximum distributions deduction, thereby causing these gains to be taxed to the entity in years when not distributed to the beneficiaries.[46] Similarly, but applicable only to simple trusts,[47] taxable extraordinary or stock-on-stock dividends that are allocated to corpus under the instrument or local law[48] and not currently distributed also are excluded from

---

[45] § 643(a)(3) and Treas. Reg. § 1.643(a)-3, not applicable, however, with respect to a foreign trust. § 643(a)(6)(C). But cf. Rev. Rul. 74-257, 1974-1 C.B. 153 (deduction for state income tax attributable to capital gains allocable to corpus allowed in determining DNI notwithstanding that income beneficiaries obtained benefit of reduced DNI without corresponding reduction in fiduciary accounting income currently distributed to them).

[46] Distribution of gains to beneficiaries (1) may be dictated by the instrument, (2) may be deemed to occur if corpus distributions regularly equal the amount of sale proceeds realized by the entity and (3) will occur in the year of termination of the trust or estate. However, gains realized by an estate upon sale of realty devised to beneficiaries who take title directly from the decedent under state law are taxable to those beneficiaries, with the estate being treated essentially as an agent in selling the land to facilitate partition. Rev. Rul. 59-375, 1959-2 C.B. 161. For a complete discussion of the gain inclusion in DNI issue, see Pennell, Subchapter J: Evolution or Revolution? 19 U. Miami Inst. Est. Plan. ¶ 903.5 (1985), and § 5.3.3.

[47] Unlike the adjustment for capital gains, which applies to all trusts and estates, this modification applies only to simple trusts. The rationale for this disparity relates to the throwback rules, which (prior to their repeal for most purposes with respect to domestic trusts) were meant to apply if these dividends subsequently are distributed, and the fact that an accumulation distribution cannot be made by a simple trust. See Treas. Reg. § 1.643(a)-4. A similar restriction is unnecessary with respect to capital gains that are accumulated and later distributed because the throwback rules were not meant to apply to capital gains in any entity. See § 5.6 with respect to the accumulation distribution and throwback rules.

[48] See, e.g., Uniform Principal and Income Act (1997 Act) §§ 401(c)(1) (stock-on-stock dividends allocable to principal) and potentially 401(b) or (c) (extraordinary dividends, which appear to be allocable to income unless the trustee chooses to allocate them to principal under the authority of § 104(a)), 7A U.L.A. 489 and 434, respectively (2006), and Revised Uniform Principal and Income Act (1962 Act) §§ 3(b)(4) and 6(b), 7A U.L.A. 566, 572 (2006).

§ 5.3.2

DNI.[49] This also reduces the maximum distributions deduction and causes the tax thereon to fall on the entity.

Finally, § 641(c) establishes an entirely separate share rule with respect to an ESBT. It taxes any S Corporation income to the trust at the highest tax rates under the Code and then, to prevent taxation of any of that income to any beneficiary of the trust, S Corporation income is excluded from DNI of the trust. In addition, the entire distributions deduction and conduit taxation scheme otherwise applicable to simple and complex trusts is disabled for the ESBT.

§ 5.3.3 Capital Gains Allocable to Income

The § 643(a)(3) adjustment for capital gains allocable to corpus is sufficiently problematic that it deserves separate attention.[50] The general notion is that capital gains of an estate or a domestic trust are not

---

[49] § 643(a)(4). See Rev. Rul. 67-117, 1967-1 C.B. 161.

[50] Pursuant to Treas. Reg. § 1.643(a)-3(d), capital losses are reflected in DNI only to the extent they are applied against gains that are included in DNI. The effect is that losses are only partially enjoyed by those beneficiaries who receive DNI. Indeed, losses affect the beneficiary only to the extent, if any, that losses are applied against gains that are includible in DNI. Beneficiaries do not enjoy losses to any greater extent by which losses exceed gains. Agatstein v. Commissioner, 23 T.C.M. (CCH) 62 (1964). Capital loss carryovers may be deducted by beneficiaries under § 642(h), but only in the year the estate or trust terminates. Otherwise, losses are not reflected in DNI. They are "trapped" at the entity level. Note that the same thing should apply for grantor trust purposes, because the "income" that is deemed to be "owned" by a grantor is based on a DNI calculation model. See § 5.11.8 n.181. Yet this rule is hardly understood by taxpayers or their advisors, and it is seldom enforced by the government, either in the context here involved or in the grantor trust arena.

A different but related question was addressed by TAM 9447007, in which a trust computed its DNI for a prior year improperly because it discovered—after filing its return and reporting DNI to the trust's beneficiary—that the trust had a loss carryback that would affect computation of that prior year's DNI. The trust's prior year was open because it had filed Form 872-A, but the beneficiary's prior year was not, and the government held that no relief was available to the beneficiary who reported too much DNI, stating that the liability involved was the beneficiary's, not the trust's, and the beneficiary's statute of limitation under § 6511(d)(2) had expired.

includible in DNI (except in the year of termination of an estate or trust).[51] This exclusion from DNI of capital gains that are not distributed currently is consistent with the repeal in 1976 of the capital gain throwback rule for all but foreign trusts, because exclusion from DNI means that the gains will not be part of UNI and, thus, could not be subject to the accumulation distribution and throwback rules in a future year.[52]

Capital gains *are* includible in the DNI of private domestic trusts,[53] however, to the extent (1) pursuant to a dictate under the terms of the governing instrument *and* applicable local law, *or* (2) pursuant to trustee discretion granted by applicable local law *or* the governing instrument, but only if that discretion is exercised in a reasonable and impartial manner[54] and is not prohibited by applicable local law,[55] or (3) that gain actually is allocated (a) to income,[56] (b) to corpus but it is treated consistently by the fiduciary (on its books and tax returns) as distributed to a beneficiary,[57] or (c) to corpus but it is used to determine the amount

---

[51] Treas. Reg. § 1.643(a)-3(a).

[52] See § 5.6 with regard to UNI, accumulation distributions, and throwback.

[53] Capital gains and losses are included in the computation of DNI if they are paid, permanently set aside, or used for a charitable purpose specified in § 642(c). See § 643(a)(3)(B), Treas. Reg. § 1.643(a)-3(c), and § 5.9. And § 643(a)(6)(C) requires inclusion of gain or loss in the DNI of a foreign trust. See § 5.13.

[54] See Treas. Reg. § 1.643(a)-3(b).

[55] Treas. Reg. § 1.643(a)-3(b).

[56] Treas. Reg. § 1.643(a)-3(b)(1). See also Treas. Reg. § 1.643(a)-3(e) Example 4.

[57] Treas. Reg. § 1.643(a)-3(b)(2). See Treas. Reg. § 1.643(a)-3(e) Example 11 (capital gain allocated to income under a state law ordering rule, for satisfaction of a unitrust distribution elected by the fiduciary under state law discretion in lieu of a mandatory income entitlement); TAM 8728001 (trustees exercised discretion to ascertain income and principal by allocating to income a portion of the gain from a sale of trust corpus; that portion of the gain was includible in DNI) and PLRs 9811037 and 9811036 (regulated investment company ordinary dividend contained some short term capital gain taxable as ordinary income and deemed to be includible in DNI notwithstanding trustee's allocation to trust corpus). Regarding the required consistency see also Treas. Reg. § 1.643(a)-3(e)

§ 5.3.3

that is[58] (or is required to be) distributed to the beneficiary.[59] Otherwise, the inclusion of capital gains and losses in computing taxable income is offset by the § 643(a)(3) adjustment that such gains are not includible in DNI. And losses are netted at the trust against gains (unless the gain is used under (c) to determine the amount that is (or is required to be) distributed to the beneficiary).[60]

The three circumstances involving private domestic trusts in which capital gains are includible in DNI are not as straightforward as they might appear. For example, capital gain normally is allocable to income under the principal and income act of most jurisdictions only to the extent proceeds of any sale or exchange are allocated to income to compensate for a delayed sale of an unproductive or underproductive asset.[61] Otherwise few garden variety trusts and virtually no estates encounter a dictate that capital gains be allocated to income.

(Footnote Continued)

Examples 2, 12, and 13—in each case the government stating that the trustee must follow the same discretionary distribution allocation in future years. That problematic concept (what if the investment climate or the needs of the beneficiaries change, or a successor fiduciary disagrees with a former fiduciary's exercise of this discretion?) is discussed in Sloan, Harris, and Cushing, When Income Isn't "Income"—The Impact of the New Proposed Regulations under Section 643, 94 J. Tax'n 325 (2001).

[58] See Treas. Reg. § 1.643(a)-3(e) Examples 5 and 13.

[59] Treas. Reg. § 1.643(a)-3(b)(3). As noted in Ferguson, Freeland, & Ascher, Federal Income Taxation of Estates, Trusts, and Beneficiaries § 7.06[F] nn.108-115 and accompanying text (3d ed. 2011), it is anomalous to trace capital gains to ascertain whether they were distributed currently to determine whether they are includible in DNI but to reject tracing in the allocation among distributees of the various items includible in DNI. See § 5.4.1 n.4 (6th ed.), regarding that allocation.

[60] Treas. Reg. § 1.643(a)-3(d).

[61] See Uniform Principal and Income Act (1997 Act) § 413, 7A U.L.A. 523 (2006) (which only applies if required for marital deduction qualification purposes and there was no compensating allocation under § 104(a)), and Revised Uniform Principal and Income Act (1962 Act) § 12, 7A U.L.A. 581 (2006), and Rev. Rul. 85-116, 1985-2 C.B. 174, and TAM 8431004.

§ 5.3.3

It is permissible,[62] and it may be attractive,[63] to alter the local law allocation of capital gains and losses to corpus. For example, the authority under state law to invest for a total portfolio return makes it desirable to adjust income or principal accounts to reflect better-than-traditional returns to either income or principal at the expense of worse-than-traditional returns to the other. Thus, during times of high corpus appreciation, investment for capital gain at the expense of ordinary income may result in equitable adjustments of principal to income (to share some of that appreciation with the current beneficiaries), with

---

[62] Crisp v. United States, 95-2 U.S. Tax Cas. (CCH) ¶ 50,493 (Ct. Fed. Cl. 1995), involved a trust that authorized but did not require distributions of income (but never corpus) to the sole current beneficiary for life. Among the trust assets was a limited partner interest in a partnership that was created for the purpose of engaging in "deal arbitrage" (profiting from sudden price fluctuations attendant to investments in the stock of companies that are the target of mergers and acquisitions). The partnership made distributions to the trust of capital gains realized in that trading, the trustee allocated those distributions to the fiduciary income account pursuant to discretion granted under the document and local law, and distributions of trust income to the beneficiary were made that were deemed to carry out the capital gain to the beneficiary. The court found that the state law definition of trust corpus as any "profit resulting from any change in the form of principal" was not descriptive of the receipts involved because the trust's investment was the partnership interest and the distributions reflected trading in assets of the partnership rather than the trust's trading in the assets of the trust. Thus, *Crisp* probably is not persuasive authority in most garden variety trust situations and the opinion made it relatively clear that the profit from normal trading in trust assets would not properly be allocable to income without a specific grant of authority in the document. In that respect, however, see TAM 8728001 (allocation of gain to income in trustee's discretion followed by discretionary distribution of it under the 65 day rule of §663(b)(1) was sufficient to allow inclusion of gain in DNI and then its carry out to the beneficiary).

[63] Given the high tax rate applicable to net income taxed to a fiduciary entity, the incentive may exist in some situations to find ways to increase DNI so that it may be carried out and taxed to beneficiaries who are in lower income tax brackets. Long term capital gain usually is taxed at a fixed rate to any taxpayer, and normal trust distributions of capital gains eventually would deplete the corpus of the trust and disfranchise the remainder beneficiary. As such, a procedure could not be followed by a prudent fiduciary in normal course without specific authority and perhaps additional criteria to guide the fiduciary's exercise of that discretion (such as under a unitrust procedure), along with exculpation to protect the fiduciary from liability to disgruntled remainder beneficiaries.

§5.3.3

concomitant inclusion in DNI of those allocated capital gains. These adjustments minimize significant deviations in the overall enjoyment of trust income and corpus (and may affect gift tax computations that depend upon valuation assumptions that net gains will be allocated to corpus).[64]

Gain or loss also is includible in DNI to the extent the gain is allocated to corpus but actually is distributed to beneficiaries during the current tax year. This would occur if the estate or trust terminated in the year the gain or loss was incurred. The government reflects this termination exception in the case of a partial termination by virtue of an asset being distributed in the trustee's discretion.[65] An entity is "considered terminated [only] if all the assets have been distributed, except for amounts retained to meet unascertained or contingent liabilities and expenses." This is not the normal situation presented on a discretionary distribution (unless separate shares are deemed to exist).[66] It may, however, apply in the case of a scheduled partial termination. And it may occur under an exercise of discretion by which a trustee "intends to follow a regular practice of treating discretionary distributions of principal as being paid first from any net capital gains realized by [the trust] during the year."[67]

---

[64] For example, if a term or life income interest is being valued, the tables presume capital gains are allocable to corpus because historically that was the only way corpus is preserved from erosion or dissipation. Cf. Treas. Reg. §§ 20.7520-3(b)(2)(iii); 25.7520-3(b)(2)(iii).

[65] TAM 8429005.

[66] See § 5.4.3 regarding the separate share rule.

[67] Treas. Reg. § 1.643(a)-3(e) Example 2. See also Treas. Reg. § 1.643(a)-3(e) Example 9 (involving partial termination of a trust on a specified event of a beneficiary reaching a designated birthday).

Several older rulings indicate that capital gains incurred upon a partial termination or incident to distribution of assets in kind are the last items in corpus to be distributed, rather than the first or even a proportionate amount. See TAMs 8606005 and 8429005 (in the latter the distribution carried out a limited amount of gain because the amount remaining in the trust after the distribution was less than the total amount of capital gain allocated to corpus). See also PLRs 8834039 (gain generated on distributions in kind to satisfy unitrust obligation in years in which income was inadequate) and 6404234660A (specifying that "the coincidence of a capital gain which is allocated to corpus and a discretionary distribution of that amount of corpus does not make the gain

§ 5.3.3

Finally, gain and loss are includible in DNI to the extent the net gain is used to determine the amount (required to be) distributed. According to the government, this occurs upon an event *specified* in the document that required the distribution.[68] Under prior regulations it also could occur if there was a practice customarily followed by the fiduciary of distributing net capital gain, such as customary distribution of the exact net proceeds of a sale of estate or trust properties.[69] Under this interpretation, however, net capital gain could not be includible in DNI in the first year of an estate or trust's administration, because there could be no established fiduciary practice of distributing gain (or anything else) in the initial year of that administration.[70] The unstated conclusion appeared to be that the coincidence of distribution of the exact amount of a net capital gain was not itself sufficient to satisfy the condition of a customary distribution pursuant to fiduciary practice. Something more was required.

In that respect, the government has ruled that a fiduciary did not have a practice of distributing net capital gains that would qualify under this exception because, in the nine years of administration of the entity, gains were realized in five but only distributed in three of those five, and "for an act to be carried out pursuant to a practice, . . . the act must be performed in a consistent, repeated fashion."[71] Curious about this conclu-

(Footnote Continued)

includible in DNI"), both responding negatively to the suggestion that realization of gain and distribution at the same time is sufficient to regard the gain as distributed and, therefore, includible in DNI. Treas. Reg. § 1.643(a)-3(e) Example 10 now appears to indicate that the gain is a pro rata portion unless the trustee exercises discretion to determine that the gain is first, last, or any other approach selected by the trustee pursuant to any discretion authorized (and perhaps subject to a consistency requirement, although this is *not* stated in the example as it is elsewhere in the regulations).

[68] Treas. Reg. § 1.643(a)-3(e) Examples 6 and 7 (the specified events being the lapse of a term of years or a beneficiary's designated birthday); Rev. Rul. 68-392, 1968-2 C.B. 284 (distribution of corpus in partial satisfaction of an annual annuity obligation did not qualify); TAM 8506005.

[69] See Treas. Reg. § 1.643(a)-3(d) Example (1) under the former regulations.

[70] See Rev. Rul. 68-392, 1968-2 C.B. 284, and TAM 8324002.

[71] TAM 8506005. See also TAM 8105028 (following a sale of estate assets at a gain, the executor distributed assets in kind with a FMV exceeding the gain recognized on the prior sales, and asserted that the gain therefore was includible

§5.3.3

sion is that the government ignored the fact that net capital gains were distributed consistently in each of the last three years in which gain was incurred. The government appeared to believe that, having once failed to distribute gains, the fiduciary could not thereafter adopt a practice that would qualify under the regulations. That conclusion appears unduly harsh and the government may be backing away from it.[72]

In the past it was a common fiduciary accounting error to allocate net capital gains to income for taxation to the income beneficiaries rather than to the trust, and doing so has been one of the few red flags that the government looked for in its sporadic review of fiduciary income tax returns.[73] It may be that different attention may be devoted to different issues under the current rules for the allocation of capital gain to DNI in the future.

(Footnote Continued)

in DNI, which the government rejected because the executor had not established a practice of taking gains into account in determining the amount of estate distributions, referring to the short duration of the estate).

[72] Compare former Treas. Reg. § 1.643(a)-3(d) Example (1) (last sentence), which read: "However, if the trustee follows a regular practice of distributing the exact net proceeds of the sale of trust property, capital gains will be included in DNI," with current Treas. Reg. § 1.643(a)-3(e) Example 2, which illustrates the first year of a trust and a stated "regular practice" that the trustee "intends to follow . . . of treating discretionary distributions as being first paid from any net capital gains realized by [the trust] during the year." Added, however, to this example is the further statement that: "In future years [the trustee] must treat all discretionary distributions as being made first from any realized capital gains." In PLR 200617004 a court proceeding resulted in a settlement agreement that capital gain henceforth would be excluded from DNI, which was deemed a reasonable allocation subject to the added condition that thereafter the trustees "must consistently follow the practice of excluding all the Trust's capital gains from DNI."

[73] Decades ago the Manhattan District of the Internal Revenue Service produced a list of prime issues for audit under Subchapter J, which revealed this focus. See Melfe, The Manhattan Project, 125 Trusts & Estates 23 (Dec. 1986), which reproduced the entire Manhattan District audit issue list.

§ 5.3.3

§5.3.4 Illustration

The following example illustrates the foregoing adjustments in computing DNI. Assume a simple trust for which receipts and disbursements in the year include:

1. Taxable Dividends, allocable to income	$25,000
2. Taxable Dividends, allocable to corpus	12,000
3. Taxable Interest	15,000
4. Tax Exempt Interest	10,000
5. Long Term Capital Gain	7,000
6. Long Term Capital Loss	(2,000)
7. Fiduciary Fees, charged to income	(5,000)
8. Fiduciary Fees, charged to corpus	(5,000)

Fiduciary Accounting Income reflects the following items:

1. Taxable Dividends	$25,000
3. Taxable Interest	15,000
4. Tax Exempt Interest	10,000
7. Fiduciary Fees	(5,000)
Fiduciary Accounting Income =	**$45,000**

Taxable Income reflects the following items:

1. Taxable Dividends, allocable to income	$25,000
2. Taxable Dividends, allocable to corpus	12,000
3. Taxable Interest	15,000
5. Long Term Capital Gain	7,000
6. Long Term Capital Loss	(2,000)
7. 80%[74] of Fiduciary Fees, charged to income	(4,000)
8. 80% of Fiduciary Fees, charged to corpus	(4,000)
Taxable Income =	**$49,000**

For ease, this taxable income figure is computed before either of the distributions deduction or the deduction in lieu of the personal exemption, with their add back adjustments.[74] The effect is the same as if a long-form computation reflecting those deductions and adjustments was performed.

---

[74] §§ 643(a)(1) and 643(a)(2).

§5.3.4

The remaining adjustments are shown in the determination of DNI, which is computed as:

Taxable Income	$49,000	
Adjusted under:		
§643(a)(3)	(5,000)	(for items 5 & 6)
§643(a)(4)	(12,000)	(for item 2)
§643(a)(5)	8,000	(for 80% of item 4)
Distributable Net Income =	$40,000	

As illustrated, fiduciary accounting income ($45,000), taxable income ($49,000), and DNI ($40,000) all may differ during any given year. Fiduciary accounting income could exceed taxable income if deductible expenses were paid from corpus or due to the deduction in lieu of the personal exemption, but fiduciary accounting income could be less than taxable income if taxable items were allocated to corpus, such as net capital gains or certain dividends. Similarly, taxable income could exceed DNI because the distributions deduction is ignored or because net capital gains or taxable dividends are allocated to corpus and excluded in computing DNI, but taxable income could be less than DNI due to tax exempt interest or the deduction in lieu of the personal exemption, all of which being considered in computing taxable income but not in determining DNI. Finally, there need be no correlation between fiduciary accounting income and DNI.[75] Consequently, using short-cuts that assume a correlation between any of these three concepts in determining the tax treatment of a trust or estate could produce error.

---

[75] For example, DNI could include taxable income that is not includible in fiduciary accounting income (such as the phantom income generated by a discharge of indebtedness attributable to the running of an estate's nonclaim statute). See Miller Trust v. Commissioner, 76 T.C. 191 (1981); Estate of Bankhead v. Commissioner, 60 T.C. 535 (1973).

§5.3.4

§5.4 CONDUIT TAXATION

§5.4.1 In General

The distributions deduction for a simple trust is the amount of income that is required to be distributed currently (even if it is not),[1] but not to exceed the taxable portion of DNI.[2] The effect of the distributions deduction for income tax purposes is "conduit" taxation if a trust qualifies as a simple trust for the year, because no accumulations were made, no corpus was distributed, and no charity is provided for. The trust is entitled to a §651(a) deduction that washes out income of the trust to the

---

[1] **§5.4** This deemed distribution treatment is necessary because a trust that is required to distribute all income annually may not know for accounting purposes how much income it earned in a given year until after that year has ended. Unlike the 65 day rule of §663(b) (which is applicable only with respect to complex trusts and estates and not for simple trusts), there is no provision that permits a trustee of a simple trust to regard a late distribution as if it was made before the end of the year in which the income was earned. In addition, a trust's normal income distribution dates may not correspond with the taxable year end, and there is perceived to be no need to force distributions to conform chronologically to the tax year. See Treas. Reg. §§1.651(a)-1 and 651(a)-2(a).

This provision may result in taxation to the ultimate beneficiary of income that was not timely distributed because there was controversy or uncertainty regarding the proper beneficiary. The entity may pay tax on that income in the year it is earned and accumulated pending distribution, after which the entity is entitled to a refund and the beneficiary is required to report the income as if received in a timely manner. See, e.g., United States v. Higginson, 238 F.2d 439 (1st Cir. 1956); Polt v. Commissioner, 233 F.2d 893(2d Cir. 1956); DeBrabant v. Commissioner, 90 F.2d 433 (2d Cir. 1937); Estate of Bruchmann v. Commissioner, 53 T.C. 403 (1969) (income of a simple trust withheld pending resolution of state law entitlement was taxed to the eventual rightful beneficiary for the years in which it was withheld, even though determination of that entitlement was delayed for over 12 years); Rev. Rul. 62-147, 1962-2 C.B. 151 (suspension of current mandatory distributions pending resolution of a legal dispute did not shift the liability for trust income from the beneficiary to the trust); PLR 9740009 (involving estate income accumulated for eight years due to inaction); but cf. Fidelity Trust Co. v. United States, 253 F.2d 407 (3d Cir. 1958), and Fidelity Trust Co. v. Commissioner, 30 T.C. 278 (1958) (trustee ordered to accumulate income pending resolution of litigation denied charitable deduction because the income was neither distributed nor permanently set aside for charity while the entitlement of the charitable beneficiaries was uncertain).

[2] §651(b) (last sentence).

beneficiaries, who are taxed thereon under § 652(a). In this respect, both the amount and the character of trust income (along with most trust deductions) pass through to the beneficiaries[3] and, unless the document directs otherwise, all tax items in the trust are shared by the beneficiaries pro rata.[4]

To illustrate, if a trust had items of tax exempt interest and two beneficiaries receive distributions equal to 60% and 40% of the total trust income for the year, the tax exempt interest would pass to them for tax purposes in the same 60/40 proportions, even if one beneficiary is in a higher tax bracket than the other and even if the trustee actually flagged and then distributed items of tax exempt interest to the high bracket beneficiary.[5]

> *Illustration*: Trust has $10,000 of income that is taxable and $20,000 of income that is tax exempt for the year, along with an $1,800 fiduciary fee deduction, allocable to the income in the same ⅓ and ⅔ proportions. The trust income is equally distributable between beneficiaries A and B, who are each deemed to receive an amount consisting of the same proportions of taxable and tax exempt income as found in the trust's DNI. Assume DNI in this case is $28,200; each of A and B will receive $4,700 of income that is taxable and $9,400 of income that is tax exempt, in

---

[3] Van Buren v. Commissioner, 89 T.C. 1101 (1987), determined the taxable and tax exempt character of amounts reportable by the beneficiary of a simple trust by reference to the trust's internally generated income *plus* amounts received by the trust in a distribution of corpus from an estate that constituted income to the trust for income tax purposes, notwithstanding that it retained its character as corpus in the trust for fiduciary accounting purposes (a "trapping distribution"; see § 5.8.2 at text accompanying n.17).

[4] § 652(b). Discretion in the trustee in making distributions, or in choosing which assets to distribute to which beneficiaries, will not affect this pro ration. Only if the document specifically directs a non-pro-rata allocation of specific items will the pro rata character rule not apply.

DNI is not tied in any sense to the amount of fiduciary accounting income, and it is fiduciary accounting income that is required to be distributed annually. If distributions for the year exceed the taxable portion of DNI, § 652(a) specifies that each income beneficiary reports a pro rata share of the carry out amount.

[5] See, e.g., Treas. Reg. § 1.651(a)-2(b) (trustee required to pay all income annually—a mandatory spray or "sprinkle" provision—but may allocate it among a class of beneficiaries in trustee's discretion permitting the trustee to determine which beneficiaries have the greatest need or in whose hands the income can be taxed at the lowest rates).

§ 5.4.1

each case with a pro rata portion of the deductible fiduciary fee allocated to each flavor of income.[6]

It might be desirable financially for beneficiary A to receive nothing but income that is tax exempt if A is in a high income tax bracket and it might make little difference to beneficiary B to receive the balance of the tax exempt income and all the income that is taxable if B is in a low bracket.[7] Thus, from an estate planning perspective it might be valuable to allocate different classes of income among multiple income beneficiaries, but this engineering is permissible only to the extent "the terms of the trust specifically allocate different classes of income to different beneficiaries."[8]

An allocation pursuant to discretion granted to the trustee to direct different classes of income to different beneficiaries is not an effective allocation by the terms of the trust. Nor is an allocation pursuant to a provision directing the trustee to pay half the income to A, or $10,000 of income to A to be satisfied first with a specific class of income, to the extent available.[9] Required would be an allocation pursuant to a provision directing the trustee to pay tax exempt income (or a specified portion of

---

[6] See § 652(b) (last sentence regarding the pro ration of deductions), and Treas. Reg. § 1.652(b)-3(b). The same principles apply for complex trusts pursuant to § § 661(b) and 662(b).

Notice that the pro ration of deductions is required so that they may be identified for purposes of § 265, but also note that § 265(a)(1) does *not* disallow *all* expenses allocable to tax exempt *interest* income—it only disallows expenses otherwise deductible under § 212—while § 265(a)(2) only disallows any *interest* expense allocable to tax exempt interest. The result is that deductible expenses allocable to tax exempt *interest* (as opposed to tax exempt income of any other variety) and deductible under any provision other than § § 163 and 212 are not disallowed at either the trust or beneficiary level. See, e.g., Rev. Rul. 61-86, 1961-1 C.B. 41 (state income taxes allocable to tax exempt interest income). Nevertheless, the deductions are identified and linked to the income items to which they are allocable, so that proper application of these rules can occur at the beneficiary level following a carryout distribution.

[7] This particularly would be true if B was a charity (and, therefore, this was a complex trust). The benefit of tax exempt income normally is wasted to the extent it is allocated to a charity that is not taxable in any case. See Treas. Reg. § 1.662(b)-2 with respect to allocations of other items if a charity is involved.

[8] See § § 652(b) and 662(b).

[9] See Treas. Reg. § 1.652(b)-2(b)(2). The complex trust rule in Treas. Reg. § 1.662(b)-1 merely adopts these rules by reference.

it) to A[10] and the balance to B, which provides the trustee only with that limited degree of discretion available through controlling investment of trust corpus in tax exempts.[11]

Although conduit treatment is similar to the beneficiaries receiving trust property directly and earning the income or incurring the deductions themselves, several important differences in the tax results exist. For example, itemized deductions that exceed trust income will not pass out to the beneficiaries except in the year the trust terminates, meaning that they may be wasted in the trust even though they could have been used by a beneficiary.[12] In addition, a trust has its own AMT exemption and computes an AMT DNI, each for special AMT accounting purposes.[13]

---

[10] Treas. Reg. § 1.652(b)-2(b)(3).

[11] Additional specific allocation requirements can apply in complex trusts that provide for charity and as to which the specific character rules in § 664(b) are applicable. See § 5.9.

[12] § 642(h). In addition, because it is not mentioned in § 642(h), any AMT credit available to the entity under § 53 appears to be lost upon termination.

[13] See § 59(c), which provides that the AMT income of an estate or trust and any beneficiary is determined by applying the traditional concepts in Subchapter J "with the adjustments provided in this part." Notwithstanding the reference to "adjustments," the reference to "this part" includes all of § § 53-59 and not just the AMT "adjustments" provision in § 56. Presumably this means that the preferences in § 57 and the losses in § 58 also are meant to be reflected. The intent therefore appears to be that a separate computation of AMT income should be made, as with any individual taxpayer, and then the normal DNI and distributions deduction rules be applied using that as a base. This is confirmed, but with scant additional detail, by the Alternative Minimum Tax—Fiduciaries form, and its concept of Distributable Net AMT Income. The general format is that trust distributions carry out DNI that is includible in the beneficiary's regular taxable income, and distributable net AMT income that is includible in the beneficiary's AMT income. And amounts of either that are not fully carried out to the beneficiary remain to be taxed at the entity level.

Because distributable net AMT income usually will be larger than normal DNI, the situation could occur in which an accumulation distribution by the entity, subject to throwback, carries out distributable net AMT income to the beneficiary. See § 5.6.2, regarding accumulation distributions subject to throwback. However, the AMT Fiduciary Form limits the amount of distributable net AMT income carried out to the amount of the distribution itself, meaning that a distribution of no more than current fiduciary accounting income should preclude an AMT problem to the beneficiary.

§ 5.4.1

The time for reporting income is the beneficiary's tax year in which or with which the entity's tax year ends.[14] Garden variety and charitable split interest trusts (that is, trusts that have private beneficiaries) must report their income and file their returns on a calendar year basis under § 644. This requirement avoids perceived abuses under prior law, which allowed trusts and estates to select any fiscal year that ended on the last day of any month, which (through proper planning) allows extensive deferral of the tax paying obligation on income received by a beneficiary.[15] This selection of tax year continues to apply to estates. But under § 644 a trust's tax year and the beneficiary's tax year both must end on December 31.[16] Thus, in most cases all income of a trust that is distrib-

---

(Footnote Continued)

Although that might cause an AMT problem at the entity level, the § 55(d) exemption and the higher normal income tax rates applicable to fiduciary entities may protect against entity AMT liability. Indeed, a fiduciary probably should attempt to trap sufficient AMT income in the entity to take advantage of its exemption and ability to absorb additional amounts of AMT income without incurring additional tax. The danger to consider in such planning is that some AMT will be incurred by the entity, which would be payable in normal course from fiduciary accounting income, which would reduce the distributions deduction for normal income tax purposes and cause a normal income tax liability, which also would need to be paid from fiduciary accounting income, starting another cycle in a circular whirlpool calculation.

See generally Barnett, No Haruspex Needed to Demystify the Fiduciary Alternative Minimum Tax, 24 U. Miami Inst. Est. Plan. ¶ 500 (1990); Coleman (née Hall), Application of the Alternative Minimum Tax to Estates and Trusts—A Brave New World for Fiduciaries, 22 U. Miami Inst. Est. Plan. ¶ 900 (1988); Barnett, The Transmogrification of Fiduciary Income Tax Practice, 22 U. Miami Inst. Est. Plan. at ¶ ¶ 1518-1520 (1988). See also the explanation of the AMT consequences of § 67(a) in § 5.3.1 n.3.

[14] § § 652(c), 662(c), and Treas. Reg. § § 1.652(c)-1 and 1.662(c)-1.

[15] For example, if an estate with a tax year that ends on January 31 made a February 1 distribution to a taxpayer with a calendar year, the distribution would be estate income for the estate's tax year that ends the next January 31, which would constitute income to the beneficiary for that next calendar year, which would be reported and the tax paid on April 15 of the year following that, some 26½ months after the beneficiary actually received the distribution.

[16] Unless the beneficiary reports on a fiscal year basis (which is very unusual for individuals) or the trust terminates.

§ 5.4.1

uted during the calendar year will be reflected by the beneficiary on a return that is due on the immediately following April 15.[17]

The normal timing rule cannot apply if the beneficiary does not have a tax year in which a trust or an estate's tax year ends (for example, because the beneficiary dies before the end of the entity's year and the beneficiary's last year therefore ends early).[18] Instead, income paid before death of the beneficiary and not yet returned is reported on the deceased beneficiary's return for the year of death, and any income paid after the beneficiary's death is taxable to the beneficiary's estate as IRD.[19]

In the context of an estate with a fiscal year rather than a calendar year, the possibility also exists for a one-time bunching of income in the year the estate terminates. For example, if one estate fiscal year ended on January 31 and the final year of the estate ends prior to December 31, the result would be that the 12 months' income for the year ended in January and the income for the final year all would be taxable to the beneficiary for the calendar year in which the estate terminates.[20]

---

[17] In addition, estimated tax payments reduce the ability of a trust beneficiary to avoid payment of tax for extended periods, even if the tax years of the beneficiary and the trust differ (for example, if the beneficiary is not on a calendar year).

[18] And no additional estimated tax payments would be required because the beneficiary's year ends at death. Treas. Reg. § 1.6153-1(a) (4).

[19] See § 5.10 for a discussion of IRD. Rev. Rul. 59-346, 1959-2 C.B. 165, held that income required to be distributed to an income beneficiary who was on the accrual basis of accounting would be taxable on the beneficiary's final return if it was earned by the trust before the date of death, and that this treatment was not in conflict with § 451(b) (amounts accrued only by reason of death shall not be included in the taxpayer's final income tax return) because it is attributable to the operation of § 652(a) and not by reason of the beneficiary's death. This issue should not occur often, because it is very unusual for an individual (i.e., a taxpayer who might die) to be an accrual basis taxpayer.

[20] See Schimberg v. United States, 365 F.2d 70 (7th Cir. 1966) (involving a trust at a time when trusts also could have fiscal years, and involving death of the beneficiary rather than termination of the entity, but the principle of taxing income received for tax purposes from two different years of the entity would be applicable in the event of entity termination, although it would be relevant today only for an estate that can have a fiscal year end other than December 31).

§ 5.4.1

It does not matter whether a trust is simple or complex to the extent current income is distributed currently. Complex trusts are allowed a distributions deduction under §661(a)(1) that is the same as the deduction under §651(a) for simple trusts, and beneficiaries of complex trusts are subject to the same inclusion,[21] timing,[22] and character[23] rules that apply for simple trusts with respect to amounts distributed currently.[24]

---

[21] See §662(a).

[22] See §662(c), which corresponds with §652(c).

[23] See §662(b), which corresponds with §652(b). There is a difference in the character rules attributable to the tier rules, applicable only to complex trusts with multiple beneficiaries assigned to different tiers by virtue of whether they are mandatory recipients of income or otherwise, and there is a §642(c) charitable distribution or set-aside interplay also to consider. See §§5.4.2, 5.6, and 5.9, respectively, with respect to the tier rules in general, which are most relevant in the context of the accumulation distribution and throwback rules (which have been repealed with respect to most domestic trusts), and with respect to the interplay of the §642(c) charitable distribution or set-aside.

[24] Unlike simple trusts, distributions may be in the fiduciary's discretion, which can be questioned. To the extent a distribution is improper, the distributions deduction and inclusion rules cannot apply. For example, Bohan v. United States, 456 F.2d 851 (8th Cir. 1972), nonacq., Rev. Rul. 72-396, 1972-2 C.B. 312, involved state law that provided that partial distributions prior to payment of all estate debts were conditional and therefore were not deductible by the estate nor includible by the beneficiaries. See also American Nat'l Bank & Trust Co. v. United States, 81-2 U.S. Tax Cas. (CCH) ¶ 9780 (6th Cir. 1981) (distributions to grandchildren were not permissible under trust terms prior to S's death; state court decree authorizing the distributions after the fact was regarded as ineffective to bind the federal government).

State law in Estate of Murphy v. United States, 91-1 U.S. Tax Cas. (CCH) ¶ 50,167 (W.D. Okla. 1991), rev'd sub nom. Buckmaster v. United States, 984 F.2d 379 (10th Cir. 1993), prohibited distributions from an estate without court approval, unless the decedent's will provided otherwise. Because the will was silent and no court order was obtained until after a distribution, the lower court denied the estate's §661(a) deduction for distributions of estate income, which caused this income to be taxed to the estate at its higher income tax rates. On appeal, the court held that the order approving the distributions after the fact was adequate to ratify the fiduciary's action and held that much year end tax planning would be precluded if such retroactive approval was not adequate. Although the court recognized that the fiduciary acts at the risk that a court ultimately will regard the distributions as improper, it held that ultimate approval is adequate to meet the §661(a)(2) "properly paid" requirement to justify the distributions

The only complication created in a complex trust is attributable to accumulations of income that cannot occur in a simple trust and, in a future year, distributions that are deemed to constitute those prior year accumulations. These accumulation distributions are subject to the throwback rule only in foreign trusts (or very rarely with respect to domestic trusts).[25]

A special rule for complex trusts dates back to when the accumulation distribution and throwback rules still were relevant. It is designed to minimize the risk of unintended accumulations, particularly due to problems relating to timing and the administrative need to know the amount of current income before it can be distributed. This "65-day" rule allows the trustee of a complex trust (but not a simple trust) or the executor of an estate (notwithstanding that throwback never was applicable to estates, so the perceived need for this special treatment never existed for estates) to elect to treat distributions properly made or credited within the first 65 days of a new tax year as if they were made or credited on the last day of the prior year.[26] The opportunity therefore

(Footnote Continued)

deduction; Harris v. United States, 370 F.2d 887 (4th Cir. 1966) (notwithstanding appearance that nothing of substance occurred, distributions deduction and beneficiary inclusion regarded as proper because will directed distribution of estate income and authorized estate to borrow back distributed amounts to pay taxes); Wheeling Dollar Savings & Trust Co. v. United States, 526 F. Supp. 1265 (N.D. W. Va. 1981) (statute authorizing distributions one year after decedent's death did not preclude valid transfers within the first year after death). Cf. Annot., Right to partial distribution of estate or distribution of particular assets, prior to final closing, 18 A.L.R.3d 1173 (1968); 31 Am. Jur. 2d Executors and Administrators §§ 1086-1090 (1990).

[25] See § 5.6.

[26] § 663(b)(1). Under Treas. Reg. § 1.663(b)-1(a)(2)(i) the election is limited to the greater of fiduciary accounting income or DNI remaining after all prior distributions attributable to the prior year. Although § 663(b)(1) requires the distribution to be made within 65 days after the entity's tax year ends, the time for making the requisite election (on a timely filed income tax return for that tax year) is prescribed only by Treas. Reg. § 1.663(b)-2(a), not by statute. The Commissioner may not grant an extension of the time to make the distribution, but does have the authority to grant an extension of time to make the election for good cause shown. PLR 8918054 denied a request for a Treas. Reg. § 301.9100-1(a) extension of time to make the § 663(b) election with respect to distributions made within the first 65 days of a new taxable year, because the taxpayer did not demonstrate that the trustees had exercised due diligence and

§ 5.4.1

exists for the trustee of a complex trust to determine the tax situation of discretionary trust beneficiaries and ascertain whether additional distributions for the year just ended would be appropriate. It also allows the personal representative of an estate to consider postmortem income tax planning during estate administration. Because the election is a separate opportunity each year,[27] each fiduciary may do so with respect to each year on the basis of the individual facts and circumstances of the entity and its beneficiaries on a year-to-year basis.[28]

§5.4.2 *Tier Rules*

The "tier" rules are necessary in the taxation of complex trusts because of the ability to accumulate income for later distribution. The term "tier" is not used in the Code or Regulations but refers to the distinction drawn in §§661(a)(1) and 661(a)(2) between amounts of income required to be distributed currently (first tier) and other amounts properly paid, credited, or required to be distributed (second tier). To illustrate the significance of the tier rules, assume a complex trust that has $50,000 of fiduciary accounting income for the year but DNI of only $40,000 (the $10,000 difference being attributable to income tax deductible expenses in computing taxable income that was paid from fiduciary accounting corpus for trust accounting purposes). Assume the trustee is required to distribute all income currently in equal shares to beneficiaries A and B. In addition, assume the trustee makes a discretionary distribution of $50,000 to B. Without the tier rules it would appear that, because A has received $25,000 while B has received $75,000, the $40,000 of DNI should be prorated between them ¾ to B

(Footnote Continued)

therefore had not shown good cause, but PLRs 201115004 200250003, 9215033, 9209025, and 8908005 granted similar requests.

[27] Treas. Reg. § 1.663(b)-1(a)(2)(i)(b).

[28] Because the election is binding on both fiduciary and beneficiary, it should be made with the beneficiary's estimated tax situation in mind. Rev. Rul. 78-158, 1978-1 C.B. 437, held that exceptions to the estimated tax rules then in effect would not be lost by virtue of a 65 day rule election, in a case in which both the trust and the beneficiary were on the same tax year, which ought to be good precedent still. Nevertheless, given the time and changes in the law that have occurred, in some cases the fiduciary might consider whether the election should be accompanied by a §643(g) election to treat the entity's estimated tax as paid by the beneficiary. See §5.7 at nn.16-21 and accompanying text.

and only ¼ to A. But the reality is that, by virtue of the trust terms, A received ½ of the trust's current income, not just ½ of it. Thus, it is proper to tax ½ of the trust's DNI to A and not just ¼ of it.

To accomplish this, the tier rules distinguish A and B's mandatory distributions of income from B's discretionary distribution. Both A and B are first tier beneficiaries of ½ the current income because that is what the trustee was required to distribute to them out of current income.[29] As such, each will be deemed taxable on ½ the DNI in the trust—$20,000 to each. But the full $50,000 discretionary distribution to B is a second tier distribution and (unless there was accumulated UNI in the trust and the trust is subject to throwback) it all would come out tax free.[30] Thus, B would pay tax on $20,000, not the $30,000 that would have been taxed to B without the tier rules.[31] Lacking the tier rules these results would differ and not be as consistent with the reality of the situation.

The technical definitions under the tier rules relate to distributions made by the entity. Under § 661(a)(1), first tier distributions are required current distributions of income (not to exceed DNI). A required distribution that could have been made from corpus (such as an annuity payment or payment of a family allowance) still is a first tier distribution if it actually is made from fiduciary accounting income.[32] Under § 661(a)(2), second tier distributions are all others, whether required or discretionary and whether made from current fiduciary accounting income, from prior years' accumulated income, or from corpus. In the example, A and B are equal first tier beneficiaries because the trustee must distribute all current income to them in equal shares, causing the DNI to be pro rated equally between them.[33] If any DNI remained after satisfaction of all first tier required distributions of current income, the excess similarly would

---

[29] § 662(a)(1).

[30] § 102.

[31] Only to the extent there is UNI and the trust is subject to what remains of the throwback rule would B's distribution be taxable—up to the full $50,000 second tier distribution, if UNI was that great. § § 662(a)(2) and 665(b). Thus, of the total distribution of $90,000 recognized for tax purposes, in rare cases B might include 77.77% in income ($70,000 out of $90,000).

[32] § 661(a)(1) (parenthetical) and Treas. Reg. § 1.661(a)-2(b). See Rev. Rul. 75-124, 1975-1 C.B. 183 (allowance for S treated as first tier distribution notwithstanding classification as a distribution in satisfaction of a debt under local law).

[33] § 662(a)(1) and Treas. Reg. § 1.662(a)-2(b).

§ 5.4.2

be pro rated among any second tier beneficiaries on the basis of their respective second tier distributions.[34] The amount of their second tier distributions in excess of any remaining DNI would be either an accumulation distribution of prior years' UNI to the extent applicable[35] or a tax free distribution of trust corpus.[36]

Finally, any qualified charitable distribution of income from the trust[37] would effectively constitute an "intermediate" tier that may be regarded as falling between the first and second tiers. These distributions to charity essentially exhaust DNI to the full extent of the charitable distribution, after all first tier distributions had been made but before any second tier distributions. Thus, DNI effectively goes to first tier beneficiaries, then to charity, and then to second tier beneficiaries, until exhausted.[38]

To illustrate, assume a trust has $50,000 of fiduciary accounting income, of which $10,000 is tax exempt, and $10,000 of deductible expenses paid from fiduciary accounting corpus. The trust requires a $25,000 distribution to beneficiary A and the trustee makes discretionary distributions of $15,000 to beneficiary B and $10,000 to C, a qualified charity. In the determination of taxable income and then DNI the tax exempt character of a portion of the income must be reflected, as illustrated below:

---

[34] § 662(a)(2)(B) and Treas. Reg. § 1.662(a)-3(c).

[35] Taxable under § 665(b) only to the extent the throwback rule is applicable under § 665(c)(2) because the trust is a foreign trust or a pre-1984 domestic trust that would be subject to the § 643(f) multiple trust rule if it was not chronologically exempt. See § 5.5 with respect to the multiple trust rule.

[36] § 102.

[37] Deductible under § 642(c).

[38] Although the Code contains no actual intermediate tier, the described treatment is attributable to the parenthetical in § 662(a)(1) that is absent from § 662(a)(2). This means that the § 642(c) charitable distribution deduction is considered in determining the amount of taxable income and thus DNI remaining to be carried out to second tier beneficiaries but is ignored in determining the amount of taxable income and thus DNI available to be carried out to first tier beneficiaries. Thus, although DNI is not in fact carried out to charity, the structure of the Code has the same effect as if it was—because DNI is reduced by virtue of the smaller amount of taxable income caused by the § 642(c) deduction, computed after all first tier distributions.

	Taxable	Tax Exempt
Fiduciary Accounting Income =	$40,000	$10,000
Deductible Expenses	(8,000)	(2,000)
§ 642(c) Charitable Deduction	(8,000)	(2,000)[39]
Taxable Income =	24,000	6,000
§ 643(a)(5) Adjustment[40]	6,000	⌐
Distributable Net Income =	30,000	

Although the distributions to A and B total $40,000, they carry out only $30,000 of DNI (retaining the character of the various portions for inclusion by A and B)[41] as illustrated below. The trust may claim a distributions deduction of only $24,000, which is the taxable portion of the DNI. That deduction will offset the trust's entire taxable income, computed after deduction of the $8,000 portion of the charitable distribution that is not deemed to be tax exempt income.

With respect to the beneficiaries, the tier rules produce the following allocation of the $30,000 of DNI:

	Total	Taxable	Tax Exempt
To A (first tier)	25,000	20,000	5,000
To B (second tier)	5,000	4,000	1,000

Of the $50,000 of fiduciary accounting income deemed available for distribution, $10,000 of it effectively went to the charity and generated a deduction that was reflected in computing DNI available for carry out by the second tier distribution to beneficiary B. But that deduction was ignored when computing DNI available for carry out by the first tier distribution to A. As a result, speaking loosely, the $10,000 distribution to the charity effectively carried out $10,000 of DNI to C as an intermediate tier between the first and second tiers, leaving only $5,000 to be carried out to B, who received a total distribution of $15,000. Further, because the total distributions to A and B did not exceed fiduciary accounting

---

[39] See § 643(a) (penultimate sentence) and Treas. Reg. §§ 1.661(c)-2, 1.642(c)-3(b)(1), and 1.642(c)-3)b)(2).

[40] See § 643(a) (penultimate sentence) and Treas. Reg. § 1.643(a)-5(b).

[41] Compare the character rules that would apply if this was a qualified charitable split interest trust under § 664(b).

§ 5.4.2

income in this case, there is no accumulation distribution of any prior year UNI,[42] meaning that the tier rules and the interplay of the charitable intermediate tier result in B receiving $10,000 essentially tax free.

§5.4.3 Separate Share Rule

Applicable to both trusts and estates,[43] the separate share rule provides that substantially independent and separately administered shares of a single trust or of an estate will be treated as separate trusts or estates for DNI allocation. As a result, the calculation of DNI and activity such as accumulations or distributions in one separate share will not affect application of the tier rules or the tax consequences of activity in any other separate share. It does not matter how many beneficiaries there are of any separate share or whether separate books of account are maintained for the various separate shares.[44]

The separate share rule is applicable to the extent a trust or an estate has substantially separate shares in fact—through the format of the trust or will and separate administration. Or if provisions in the document or the governing law generate the result that activity, distributions, and accumulations in one share under administration will not affect the rights of other beneficiaries. For example, separate shares exist if a corpus distribution to one beneficiary is treated as an advancement, so that each beneficiary essentially is being treated as the sole beneficiary of a separate share of the entity.

The regulations apply a standard that separate shares are deemed to exist if beneficiaries (or a class of beneficiaries) have identifiable economic interests that "neither affect nor are affected by the economic interests accruing to another beneficiary or class of beneficiaries."[45]

---

[42] See § 665(b) (last sentence).

[43] See § 663(c).

[44] Treas. Reg. § § 1.663(c)-3(a) and 1.663(c)-3(c). But see Judy Trust for David Quinn v. United States, 87-2 U.S. Tax Cas. (CCH) ¶ 9650 (5th Cir. 1987) (a single group trust cannot be regarded as separate trusts while additional class members might come into the picture; separate trusts cannot be deemed to exist until the class of beneficiaries closes).

[45] Treas. Reg. § 1.663(c)-4(a). Not relied upon in PLR 200550015 (which instead held that three separate trusts had been created), the separate share rule would have been adequate to regard as three separate shares the one trust

§5.4.3

Illustrations listed include a surviving spouse's elective share and any § 645 qualifying trust.[46] The trust could have separate shares within it as well, which will be separate from the estate proper and any of its separate shares.

In addition, a specific bequest is a separate share if it fails to qualify for the § 663(a)(1) exclusion from the DNI carryout rules because it is payable in more than three installments.[47] No mention is made of S's community property share titled in D's name and therefore subject to estate administration. Presumably S's portion of any community property is the quintessential separate share, entitled to its own income but no other DNI carryout.

The separate share rule does not eliminate entirely the potential for inequitable distribution of an estate's income tax burden because a separate share may have multiple beneficiaries whose respective entitlements within that share may not be separate. But situations that do not involve subclasses will benefit from the separate share rule to the extent it precludes much of the potential to impose a disproportionate share of DNI on one beneficiary. In the process, however, postmortem planning also is cabined to the extent distributions were engineered in the past to direct income to some beneficiaries who are better able to absorb it in any given year.

Fortunately (at least for the fiduciary in most cases), the need to make compensatory adjustments in the wake of this form of engineered (or, in some cases, inept) inequity also will wane.[48] In place of the administrative difficulties implicit in making some compensatory adjustments, however, fiduciaries must assume a more invidious administra-

---

(Footnote Continued)

created during the settlor's life but divided at the settlor's death and held for three separate grandchildren (indeed, the trust created vested shares payable to the estates of any who died before full distribution at each grandchild's age 30).

[46] The preamble to the final regulations says even if no election is made.

[47] Note that a § 663(a)(1) qualifying bequest is *not* regarded as a separate share, but only because it is excluded from the §§ 661 and 662 income carryout scheme by virtue of the § 663(a)(1) exception. See § 5.4.4.

[48] See § 5.8.4. Unfortunately, however, Treas. Reg. § 1.663(c)-5 Examples 6 and 9 open new avenues for postmortem engineering with IRD and highlight the potential need for a not yet adjudicated equitable adjustment. See § 5.4.3 n.59 and accompanying text.

§ 5.4.3

tive burden—one that presumably cannot be waived by a provision in a will (as could the need to make compensatory adjustments).

If the government actually enforced these rules an estate administration would take on the look and feel of a fractional marital deduction bequest. In this respect, illustrated overtly[49] and obliquely[50] is the notion that separate but undivided shares would require accounting that allocates income and deductions, and reflects non pro rata distributions, with a "rolling fraction" that changes with every administrative act that alters the respective entitlements of the various separate beneficiaries. To illustrate, if S is entitled to 62% of an estate (after debts, expenses, and taxes) as a marital deduction bequest or an elective share and two children split the other 38%, income and deductions would be prorated between them 62%, 19%, and 19% initially. Thereafter, if a non-lock-step distribution is made to any of the three beneficiaries, the relative proportions would be readjusted. For example, if S received a distribution that reduces the remaining marital entitlement to 60% of the residue and increases the children's respective shares to 20% each, the fraction must be adjusted accordingly.

To make these calculations will require first that the entire estate be revalued to determine the absolute dollar value of each respective share, followed by subtraction of the distribution to reduce the future proportionate distribution entitlement of the particular recipient and increase the proportionate share of all the other beneficiaries. The net result would be calculation of new relative percentages of the balance of the estate for future allocation of income and deductions. Required would be a determination of (1) when the income of the entity was earned, (2) when any capital gain was incurred, (3) when distribution occurs relative to both the income and capital gain generation, and (4) the extent of any valuation changes.

This last matter is highlighted by the preamble to the final regulation, which makes clear that the government intentionally did not provide relief from adjustment, even if the government successfully challenges valuations on audit of an FET return. The only possible relief provided by the regulation is in the form of a loose "reasonable and

---

[49] See Treas. Reg. § 1.663(c)-5 Example 3.
[50] See Treas. Reg. § 1.663(c)-5 Examples 6 and 10.

§5.4.3

equitable" allocation, valuation, and calculation standard[51] that ostensibly provides some flexibility to fiduciaries in making the requisite computations.

It may be that changes in the relative size of various shares of an estate or qualifying trust will occur after filing an income tax return, reflecting valuation changes or the imposition of transfer taxes and other obligations payable from one share only, and perhaps amendment of such a return will not be required. But the math will not often be easy with respect to changes that occur before the end of a tax year, and valuation problems may pose significant administrative costs. Each of these may compel lock step distributions or loans in lieu of interim partial distributions.

One consequence of separate share treatment is that pecuniary formula marital bequests[52] are as administratively cumbersome as fractional marital bequests were in the past (unless pains are taken to avoid any form of interim partial distribution or valuation changes).[53] These complexities were standard operating procedure in revocable inter vivos trusts used as will substitutes, after the settlor's death but before full severance and distribution of marital and nonmarital portions.

A good bit of the devil in the separate share rule is revealed in examples to the regulation that are worthy of elaboration because of gnarly questions they raise but do not answer. To illustrate, one example[54] involves a formula marital bequest and partial non pro rata distribution of some but not all shares under the estate, expressly requiring adjustment of the fraction used in the future to allocate income and deductions to the respective shares. The example contains a statement, however, that "depending on when the distribution is made," it may not be necessary to adjust the fraction for the year of distribution. It gives no detail regarding the intended meaning of that caveat, however.

---

[51] Treas. Reg. § 1.663(c)-2(c).

[52] Treas. Reg. § 1.663(a)-1(b) specifies that formula pecuniary bequests fail to satisfy as § 663(a)(1) specific bequests because the amount typically is not determinable as of the moment of the decedent's death.

[53] See generally Cantrell, Separate Share Regulations Propose Surprising Changes, 138 Trusts & Estates 56 (March 1999).

[54] Treas. Reg. § 1.663(c)-5 Example 3.

§ 5.4.3

Presumably an interim disproportionate distribution made several days before the end of the estate's tax year would not require readjustment of the fraction for the few remaining days of that year, and this might be a useful administrative simplification if the estate terminates during that same year. But surely the fraction must be amended if administration continues into a new year. Perhaps the caveat also suggests that non-lock-step distributions made at different times over a short span and that collectively maintain the proportions of estate shares will not require adjustment of the fraction at all. The caveat does not appear to offer a special dispensation if a deviation from proportionate lock step distributions involves a de minimis dollar amount (such as $1,000 too much to one share or the other) rather than a modest timing disparity, although it is possible (perhaps even probable) that the relevant "reasonable and equitable" standard[55] would apply even in that case.

Another example posits a formula credit shelter pecuniary bequest that is distributable in no more than three installments, making it appear that it is leading to the § 663(a)(1) specific bequest exception.[56] However, a formula bequest that cannot be determined in amount as of the moment of death cannot qualify under § 663(a)(1). Thus, really involved is the added stated fact that the formula bequest "is not entitled to any of the estate's income and does not participate in appreciation or depreciation in estate assets." This is a circumstance in which separate share accounting treatment is easy, "because, under the terms of the will, no estate income is allocated to the bequest . . . [and, therefore,] the DNI for that . . . share is zero."[57] Not clear is whether the two requisites for the caveat to apply must be *expressed* by the document, that there be no income and no fluctuation in value. It ought to be applicable if the nature of the bequest (for example, a true worth pecuniary bequest) freezes the value of the entitlement and state law or the document provides that no income or interest is payable.[58]

---

[55] Treas. Reg. § 1.663(c)-2(c).

[56] Treas. Reg. § 1.663(c)-5 Example 4.

[57] Treas. Reg. § 1.663(c)-4(b), which provides separate share treatment if the double requirements relating to income and valuation fluctuations are met.

[58] It also is curious that Example 4 posits no DNI carryout consequence because no income is allocable to the bequest. The caveat requires both elements to be present—neither an income entitlement nor a valuation fluctuation. Presumably this means that a fractional division of shares that pro rates apprecia-

Additional examples[59] illustrate a special rule that IRD that has been received by an estate (as opposed to the right to receive IRD in the future) is allocable only among those separate shares "that could potentially be funded with these amounts . . . [with the allocation] based on the relative value of each share that could potentially be funded with

---

(Footnote Continued)

tion or depreciation would be subject to income carryout under these regulations even if state law or the governing document provided that the particular share does not benefit from income earned during administration. That statement seems counterintuitive. So does Treas. Reg. § 1.663(c)-5 Example 6, which posits the possibility of an income carryout because DNI contains IRD under Treas. Reg. § 1.663(c)-2(b)(3), as discussed next below, and not because either the appreciation or income entitlement prongs of this rule were triggered.

As explained by an individual who participated in drafting these regulations, the reason why sharing of appreciation or depreciation is relevant (and why this exception is not merely a function of the lack of income entitlement) is because the entitlement involved slices off the top of the estate, more like a debt than a bequest. That does not help explain why a distribution could carry out income in the context of a bequest that cannot share in appreciation or depreciation, or estate income, but that could receive IRD in the fiduciary's discretion.

Treas. Reg. § 1.663(c)-4(b) states that an elective share is a separate share (and not subject to DNI carryout) if state law provides that the spouse is entitled to *neither* income nor appreciation/depreciation during estate administration. Treas. Reg. § 1.663(c)-5 Example 7 is troublesome because it posits an elective share that is not entitled to estate income. Rather, it is entitled to statutory interest on delayed payment. In that case there is no §§ 661 and 662 income tax consequence. Instead, the interest is taxable to the spouse as § 61 income earned, and the estate is denied an interest expense deduction because its payment is personal interest that is nondeductible under § 163(h). It is not clear whether a document could alter this lousy result by dictating that income be paid in lieu of statutory interest (assuming that state law would so permit), and cause the elective share to be regarded as a separate share with §§ 661 and 662 treatment. The preamble to the final regulation discusses elective shares in some length but does not illuminate any of these questions.

A final fact illustrated in Example 4 is capital gain realized on an in-kind distribution of appreciated property in satisfaction of the bequest. The regulation states that no DNI would carry out with the distribution, without making special mention of the issue whether capital gain might be includible in DNI in such a case. This is consistent with the traditional § 643(a)(3) notion that capital gain incurred on funding is not properly includible in DNI. Although that aspect is not specifically noted, that result should not change even if the bequest carried out income.

[59] Treas. Reg. § 1.663(c)-5 Examples 6, 9, and 10.

§ 5.4.3

such amounts."[60] Thus, a document will be respected that apportions IRD among various beneficiaries for income tax purposes.[61] These illustrations reveal that the personal representative controls the tax consequence of the IRD by timing distributions.

For example, if the personal representative makes certain that *no* distributions are made during a year in which IRD is received, then the income tax liability flowing from that income—and presumably any § 691(c) deduction attributable to it as well—will be borne or enjoyed by each separate share of the estate proportionately, because the estate as a whole would be the proper taxpayer with respect to that IRD. Moreover, because the pro ration of IRD is affected by valuation fluctuations, presumably a personal representative can engineer the allocation of IRD tax consequences by timing distributions in concert with valuation changes.[62]

Another example[63] illustrates a bequest that qualifies as a § 663(a)(1) bequest of specific property, which is not a separate share—indeed, it is outside the §§ 661 and 662 income carryout scheme entirely.[64] The example says: "The will . . . directs the executor to distribute *the* X stock and all dividends therefrom to Child A and the residue of the estate to child B." The emphasis is because "the" X stock is not identified and appears to have no antecedent in the regulations, but presumably means *any* X stock in the estate. Notice that a bequest of *any* X stock found in an estate at death—rather than specified shares of X stock—probably is a general bequest under state law, not a specific bequest. Under § 663(a)(1) that fine, technical distinction under wills law appears to be irrelevant with respect to the X stock itself, but the

---

[60] Treas. Reg. § 1.663(c)-2(b)(3).

[61] Allocation of the right to receive IRD has been common in pecuniary marital deduction funding provisions that prohibit the use of that asset to prevent § 691(a)(2) acceleration of the IRD.

[62] All of this may require the personal representative to make an equitable or compensatory adjustment of the same variety as a *Warms* adjustment (in the context of the familiar § 642(g) "swing item" election), as discussed in § 5.8.4. There is, however, no known case calling for such an adjustment, although the equities for one are compelling.

[63] Treas. Reg. § 1.663(c)-5 Example 8.

[64] Treas. Reg. § 1.663(c)-4(a).

§ 5.4.3

example shows that it can be important with respect to an entitlement under state law to income earned postmortem on the X stock.

In most jurisdictions the earnings postmortem from a specific bequest belong to the recipient of that specific bequest, even if the document is silent. A different rule typically applies to a general bequest (which earns interest on a delayed distribution, but is *not* entitled to postmortem earnings on the particular property distributed in satisfaction of the general bequest).[65] This distinction helps to explain why the wills law classification of the bequest can be important, and it also might mean that this example will be applicable in most cases of a specific bequest, even in the absence of a specific document provision directing the income from the specific bequest, such as posited in the example. The regulation finesses this issue by directing that A receive all dividends earned on the X stock. Thus, three things are going on in the example that were relevant to the regulation drafter. First, X stock to A, then dividends from X stock to A, and finally that the estate residue was distributed to B. The example states that "The estate has two separate shares consisting of the income on the X stock bequeathed to A and the residue of the estate bequeathed to B." That is, only the first of the three items—the bequest of X stock to A—is excepted from the separate share regime but the income from that stock *is* another separate share.[66]

Further, the examples[67] contain a bit of a wake up call regarding the rule that a separate share may have more than one beneficiary and the same person may be a beneficiary of more than one separate share.

---

[65] See §3.2.5 with respect to bequests in general and §3.2.5.3 in particular with respect to accessions.

[66] Treating the income from the X stock separately is consistent with Treas. Reg. §1.663(c)-4(a), which says that "[s]eparate shares include, for example, the income on bequeathed property if the recipient of the specific bequest is entitled to such income . . . ." The odd aspect of all this is a statement in the preamble to the final regulations that says: "Under [the §663(c)-4(a)] revised definition [of separate shares], a separate share generally exists only if it includes *both* corpus and the income attributable thereto . . ." (emphasis added), which apparently does not also mean that the two entitlements—the corpus and the income from it—are treated together as a single separate share. The Example concludes that only the income from any X stock dividends is allocable to A.

[67] Treas. Reg. §1.663(c)-5 Example 11, referring to the rule in Treas. Reg. §1.663(c)-4(c).

§5.4.3

Posited is income from an estate payable half to charity and half to three residuary beneficiaries. According to the example, this estate has three separate shares, one for each residuary beneficiary, and each of those separate shares has two beneficiaries—the charity being the other in each of the three shares. Finally, with respect to the charity, separate share treatment is not altered by the fact that payments of income are subject to § 642(c) and are not part of the § § 661 and 662 scheme at all. That result seems inconsistent with the treatment of § 663(a)(1) bequests, which are not part of the § § 661 and 662 scheme either, but in the context posited it is not said to make a difference.

It is well to remember that separate share treatment only regards each share as a separate trust for purposes of computing and allocating DNI (and UNI if throwback is applicable) and for application of the tier rules.[68] The effect might be that less DNI would exist in any separate share than in the undivided entity, and that a larger portion of any second tier distribution would be tax free.[69] "The effect [of the separate share rule] is to prevent a beneficiary from being subjected to tax on a distribution which represents a corpus distribution . . . but which would, except for this provision, be treated as a taxable distribution, since the trust income is being accumulated for another beneficiary to whom it will ultimately be made available."[70]

Finally, consistent with § 663(c) but entirely separate from the normal trust taxation rules, § 641(c) regards S Corporation stock in an ESBT as a separate trust, as to which the income is taxed at the highest

---

[68] But not for other purposes, such as determining under state law whether the tax paid by an estate or trust on income not carried out should be apportioned among the respective income tax separate shares. Separate share treatment also would not alter the excess deduction passthrough rule in § 642(h), which might not permit a termination fee or other deductions to pass out to the beneficiary of a distribution of a separate share that constitutes only a partial termination of a larger trust. The result therefore would be that deductible items that ought to benefit the one beneficiary alone but that exceed the taxable income of that particular share will benefit other beneficiaries of the trust or estate rather than passing out for the exclusive enjoyment of the beneficiary whose share terminated and that generated the deduction. See § 5.8.3 regarding the § 642(h) passthrough rule.

[69] See Treas. Reg. § 1.665(g)-2A(d)(3).

[70] S. Rep. No. 1622, 83d Cong., 2d Sess. 355 (1954).

rates under the Code and the normal distributions deduction, DNI, and conduit passthrough rules are disabled.[71]

§5.4.4 Exclusion of Specific Bequests

Certain distributions of assets in satisfaction of specific bequests[72] do not carry out income—either current DNI or prior years' accumulated income[73]—if the distribution must be made in less than four installments and is not payable only from income.[74] These distributions have no income tax effect at all, either to the trust or estate (which is entitled to no distributions deduction) or to the recipient. Thus, as a general principle, only estate distributions to a residuary beneficiary have the effect of carrying out DNI into the hands of a beneficiary for income tax purposes.[75]

---

[71] Consistent with this treatment is Prop. Treas. Reg. § 1.1361-1(m)(9) Example 1(i), which allows the separate trust ESBT rule to trump otherwise applicable separate share rule treatment of three beneficiaries of a single trust. Presumably this makes sense because the ESBT treatment essentially taxes the S Corporation income to the trust and removes it from DNI, which eliminates the need for separate share treatment. For comparable treatment see § 5.4.1 nn.3, 14, and text accompanying n.21.

[72] Bequest is used here to include gifts, devises, and legacies as well, although there can be some debate whether the provision applies to devises (a testamentary gift of realty) as opposed to any other specific gift. The leading authority on this subject opines that it does apply and that there is no policy reason to suggest otherwise. See Ferguson, Freeland & Ascher, Federal Income Taxation of Estates, Trusts, and Beneficiaries § 7.07[B][1] (3d ed. 2011).

[73] § 663(a)(1). The statutory treatment is that a qualifying distribution "shall not be included as amounts falling within section 661(a) or 662(a)." Although this does not refer to or provide specifically that a qualifying distribution also cannot trigger the accumulation distribution and throwback rules, it has that effect because the definition of an accumulation distribution under § 665(b) is keyed to distribution of an amount specified in § 661(a). Thus, this is a backhanded exception from Subpart D as well as the direct exception from the current distribution rules.

[74] See Harte v. United States, 152 F. Supp. 793 (S.D. N.Y. 1957) (payment from income as required in the settlement of a will contest did not qualify for the exclusion, as it would not if the will itself had required that source for distribution).

[75] And not all residuary distributions necessarily will carry out income. See, e.g., Rev. Rul. 57-214, 1957-1 C.B. 203 (bequest of a specific dollar amount from

For example, assume a will contains three bequests: 100 shares of ATT stock to A, $10,000 to B,[76] and the residue to C.[77] With respect to the residuary bequest to beneficiary C, the common law rule that title passes at death directly to the testator's legatees or heirs (subject to the personal representative's possession for purposes of administration) means that C owns all of the testator's assets, subject to satisfaction of claims, debts, taxes, and those specific and general bequests to A and B that take priority under the will and local law. Thus, in substance it is the residuary beneficiary's assets that are earning income during the period the estate is in administration and the Subchapter J rules work to ensure that estate income is taxed to C or to the estate but not to A or B.

Meanwhile, beneficiary A is deemed under state law to own the ATT stock from the date of the testator's death (subject only to the personal representative's right to possession for purposes of administration) and therefore is entitled to all dividends or other accessions declared and paid on the stock after the testator's death.[78] This income will belong to A for tax and other purposes and will not enter into the Subchapter J regime.[79]

(Footnote Continued)

estate residue qualified for the specific bequest exclusion, notwithstanding the possibility of abatement if the residue was inadequate).

[76] According to S. Rep. No. 1622, 83d Cong., 2d Sess. 354 (1954), the case would be no different if this was a distribution of $10,000 at B's birthday some years in the future.

[77] A stated or implied condition, such as that the beneficiaries must survive the decedent or some other event, will not imperil qualification for the exclusion. Treas. Reg. § 1.663(a)-1(b)(4), using as an example a specific gift to A of $10,000 at each of two birthdays but, if A does not reach those birthdays, to B, as a qualifying gift to A even though it is not certain how much A will receive; unstated but presumably the case is that any amount received by B also will qualify for the exclusion.

[78] See 4 Scott, Fratcher, & Ascher, Scott and Ascher on Trusts § 20.3.1 (5th ed. 2007).

[79] See Treas. Reg. §§ 1.661(b)-1 and 1.662(b)-1. Treatment of the specific legatee as owner of all income earned since the date of death arguably is a better result than applying the normal conduit principles of §§ 661 and 662 to the income earned and distributed, because of timing and character problems that would apply if income was earned in one year but not distributed until a later year, while interim distributions of other assets served to carry out the income earned in the prior year to another beneficiary. See Ferguson, Freeland, &

§ 5.4.4

Beneficiary B has a claim against the estate for $10,000 but does not own specific assets in the estate and no portion of estate income belongs to B for either tax or local law purposes. Distributions in satisfaction of a general bequest of money like this do not carry out estate income,[80] provided that the terms of the instrument make the bequest payable in less than four installments. If payable in more than three installments,[81] however, the rule treats the bequest as if it was an annuity that the testator was attempting to make tax free to the recipient during the period of estate administration, and DNI will be carried out.[82]

(Footnote Continued)

Ascher, Federal Income Taxation of Estates, Trusts, and Beneficiaries § 7.09[B] (3d ed. 2011).

[80] Delayed payment may require that the bequest be augmented with interest or income, in which case that additional amount may be subject to income taxation under the Subchapter J regime as not protected under the specific bequest exclusion. See § 5.4.4 n.85 and accompanying text.

If the bequest is disguised compensation, for example to an employee or advisor for services rendered to the testator before death, normal income tax principles would make the receipt includible and the § 102 exception for bequests inapplicable, but the treatment of any interest paid for delayed payment would not be affected. The difficult issue with respect to these kinds of payments is the initial classification as compensation or a gratuity, as for example when the testator leaves an amount to a companion or caregiver and there are indications that there may have been a promise to do so in exchange for services rendered. See the discussion of Metz v. United States, 91-1 U.S. Tax Cas. (CCH) ¶ 60,071 (10th Cir. 1991), aff'g 89-2 U.S. Tax Cas. (CCH) ¶ 13,822 (D. Kan. 1989), in § 2.1.2 n.17.

[81] Pelowski v. United States, 605 F. Supp. 65 (N.D. Ohio 1985), held that a bequest under a document that did not preclude satisfaction in more than three installments did not qualify for the exclusion, but this should not be taken as indicative that a document must preclude payment in more than three installments to qualify. Treas. Reg. § 1.663(a)-1(c)(1)(iii) specifically provides that bequests under a will "for which no time of payment or crediting is specified, and which are to be paid or credited in the ordinary course of administration of the decedent's estate, are considered as required to be paid or credited in a single installment." And Treas. Reg. § 1.663(a)-1(a) makes reference to gifts that qualify in terms of "the governing instrument must not provide for its payment in more than three installments," which affirms the presumption of qualification if the document is silent.

[82] In re Estate of Dreyfus, N.Y.L.J., May 16, 1963 at 14 (Surr. Ct.), rejected an argument by legatees whose four-part installment bequests did not qualify for the exclusion that they should receive a net amount after income tax equal to the

The treatment of the underlying bequest must be distinguished from the treatment of any income or interest that is paid along with the underlying entitlement. For example, general bequests that earn interest under state law (because distribution is delayed—usually longer than one year after death)[83] are treated as a debt of the estate under current law. Thus, the interest may generate an interest expense deduction to the entity under § 163(d) (to the extent matched by investment income)[84] and will constitute ordinary income to the beneficiary. Arguably

(Footnote Continued)

dollar amount specified in the decedent's will, meaning that the decedent's estate should distribute a sufficient additional amount to compensate them for the income tax incurred on all their distributions. Notwithstanding that the will was executed before adoption of § 663(a)(1), the court determined that the decedent was responsible for knowing the tax law burdens imposed on the beneficiaries and therefore was deemed to have intended the tax result incurred. Mahler v. Commissioner, 52 T.C.M. (CCH) 1552 (1987), rejected a similar argument that, because the will referred to the taxpayer receiving a "fixed" dollar amount every year, the trust should pay the income tax on amounts distributed in payment of that annual annuity.

[83] Uniform Principal and Income Act (1997 Act) § 202, 7A U.L.A. 479 (2006), and Revised Uniform Principal and Income Act (1962 Act) § 5(b)(2), 7A U.L.A. 570 (2006), treat all bequests as carrying a proportionate share of income earned in the estate or trust except pecuniary bequests not in trust, as to which most states grant interest at a statutory rate commencing at a specified date, typically one year after the testator or settlor's death, and regardless of whether income was earned in the entity. This means that pecuniary bequests payable to trusts and all nonpecuniary bequests carry income, if any, calculated from the date of the testator or settlor's death. See also 4 Scott, Fratcher, & Ascher, Scott and Ascher on Trusts § 20.3.2 (5th ed. 2007). A useful summary of state law showing the income sharing or interest payment obligation of outright legacies, legacies in trust, and residuary dispositions is available in Appendix A of Practical Drafting at 3235 (1993), reporting 6 states that call for payment of neither income nor interest on outright legacies and 4 that call for payment of a proportionate share of income, with the 41 remaining jurisdictions calling for interest payable at various rates and from various dates, and reporting 10 states (but not the same 10) that require payment of interest rather than distribution of a proportionate share of income with respect to legacies in trust. Only one state does not call for proportionate sharing of income with respect to residuary bequests.

[84] To the extent the investment interest exception in § 163(h)(2)(B) does not apply, however, the entity will be denied a deduction under the § 163(h)(1) (disallowance of deduction for personal interest). See Schwan v. United States, 264 F. Supp. 2d 887 (D. S.D. 2003) (an estate was denied a § 163(h) deduction because the interest was not on a "debt" as such and there was no showing that

§ 5.4.4

a more appropriate treatment would be a distributions deduction to the estate and carry out of DNI to the legatee.[85] Quaere what the proper treatment would be, however, if S exercised the election against D's estate to take a statutory forced heir share, and then disclaimed any portion of that share in excess of a specified dollar amount. Would this be treated like a bequest that could carry out DNI and, if so, is it a specific bequest that avoids the DNI carryout rules entirely. Or is it like a debt of the estate as to which none of these rules is relevant?[86]

(Footnote Continued)

the interest was incurred so the estate could continue to hold investment property).

[85] Ferguson, Freeland, & Ascher, Federal Income Taxation of Estates, Trusts, and Beneficiaries § 7.09[A] (3d ed. 2011), refers to the law on this issue as "obscure" and there is authority in both directions. Compare United States v. Folckemer, 307 F.2d 171 (5th Cir. 1962) and Rev. Rul. 73-322, 1973-2 C.B. 44 (treating interest as if the legatee was a creditor and denying application of §§ 661 and 662), with Davidson v. United States, 149 F. Supp. 208 (Ct. Cl. 1957) (treating interest payment as an income distribution event, with the vast majority of the interest in that case exceeding the limited income available to be carried out and therefore constituting a tax free distribution of corpus under the court's interpretation; had the result been otherwise the estate would have generated a large interest expense deduction with little income against which to apply it and the beneficiary's entire interest payment would have been taxable income).

As noted in Treas. Reg. §§ 1.663(c)-4(b) and 1.663(c)-5 Example 7 and in TAM 9604002, the difference for income tax purposes is between the estate claiming a § 163 deduction for interest paid and the beneficiary including simple income under § 61, or the estate claiming a § 661 distributions deduction and the beneficiary picking up DNI carried out under § 662. For FET purposes the issue in the TAM was whether a § 2053 deduction was available at all, and the government concluded that it is not, which is a proper result because neither the bequest nor the interest thereon are supported by the requisite full and adequate consideration in money or money's worth.

For income tax purposes the interest income and deduction result is preferred by the government and is problematic for the taxpayer because the entity is likely to be able to deduct only a small portion because of the § 163(h) limitation while the beneficiary will include the full amount. This is a less equitable result than the conduit result generated under §§ 661 and 662, with income in the entity being carried out but any payment in excess of income actually earned being without consequence to both the entity making the payment (usually an estate) and to the beneficiary.

[86] With respect to the inapplicability of the income carryout on a straight elective share distribution, see § 3.4.7 at text accompanying nn.73-76. An exhaustive search, including a computerized legal research session, revealed no law on

To be a qualifying "specific" bequest, the amount must be ascertainable as of inception of the trust or estate. "Formula" amounts, such as common pecuniary or fractional marital deduction provisions that are keyed to a particular tax result in the settlor's taxable estate,[87] do not qualify because they do not produce an amount that is ascertainable at inception of the trust or estate. For the same reason, interest paid on distribution of any specific bequest also is not sufficiently ascertainable to be protected[88] (although the underlying specific bequest should not be disqualified in its own right).

By way of comparison, a bequest of only as many shares of stock in a specified corporation as necessary to constitute a specific dollar value on the date of distribution is regarded by the government as not specific because the identity of the specific property but not the amount (in terms of the number of shares) is not ascertainable at the testator's death.[89] But a bequest of "assets, in cash or in kind or partly in each, the

---

(Footnote Continued)

the issue of an election with a cut-back disclaimer. See Rev. Rul. 90-45, 1990-1 C.B. 175, involving such an election and disclaimer, designed to engineer the appropriate marital deduction for the decedent's estate but with no mention of the income tax consequences of its satisfaction.

[87] See, e.g., § 13.2.7.

[88] Distributions in satisfaction of a pecuniary bequest produced by a formula provision—like the typical optimum marital deduction formula bequest—carry out DNI under Treas. Reg. § 1.663(a)-1(b)(1); the government's position is that these formula bequests are not specific enough as of the decedent's death to qualify under § 663(a)(1) because the formulas adjust during administration to reflect valuation issues and deductions for items such as funeral expenses, debts, and expenses of administration generated after death, as well as the discretion whether to claim many of those deductions for income versus FET purposes.

PLR 9218076 rejected a taxpayer argument that distributions under a settlement agreement involving a decedent's exercise of a power to appoint trust corpus qualified for the exclusion because the amounts distributed were not ascertainable under the trust terms at its inception. Quaere whether the result would have been different under an exercise of a power of appointment that was not challenged. The Ruling did not address the question whether the property law relation back fiction would satisfy the § 663(a)(1) ascertainable-at-inception requirement, and an exhaustive search, including a computerized legal research session, revealed no law on this issue. See Restatement (Second) of Property—Donative Transfers at 4 (1986).

[89] Rev. Rul. 72-295, 1972-1 C.B. 197. Curiously, the government also held that distribution of the stock was not a gain or loss realization event, the critical

selection of which shall be in the absolute discretion of my executor, with a fair market value at the date of distribution equal to [$X] . . ." would be sufficiently specific to qualify for the exclusion.[90] The critical distinction between these is that the former is a gift of an unspecified number of shares of stock (and not a bequest of a specified dollar value to be satisfied only with that stock) whereas the latter is a specific bequest of a determinable dollar amount to be satisfied with property in kind, even if the identity of that property is not specified. Upon a distribution of depreciated stock in satisfaction of the latter bequest, however, the government held that no income was carried out to the beneficiary and the estate was entitled to no distributions deduction. But the distribution was regarded as a sale or exchange in satisfaction of the specific dollar bequest, resulting in realization of loss on the distribution.[91] The beneficiary therefore acquired a basis in the stock equal to its FMV.

This situation differs from the typical pecuniary bequest only in that the amount involved was ascertainable at the testator's death, which frequently is not the case with marital deduction planning because use of a formula bequest prevents the amount from being ascertainable until some time after death. In those more typical pecuniary marital deduction formula bequest cases, distribution is regarded as sufficiently specific to constitute a gain or loss realization event[92] *and* it carries out DNI, resulting in a double detriment for income tax purposes.

§5.5 MULTIPLE TRUST RULE

Notwithstanding that there is little current advantage to accumulating income in a fiduciary entity that is recognized as a separate taxpayer, several additional rules operate either to ignore trusts in certain circumstances or to further minimize the incentive to accumulate income. One

---

(Footnote Continued)

determination apparently being that this was a gift of stock and not a gift of money to be satisfied with stock in the specified corporation. See §5.8.1 n.7 and accompanying text.

[90] Rev. Rul. 86-105, 1986-2 C.B. 83.

[91] See Treas. Reg. §1.661(a)-2(f). The exception to the loss disallowance rule in §267(b)(13) would continue to permit the estate to recognize this loss.

[92] See §5.8.1 n.7 and accompanying text.

§5.5

is a "multiple trust rule" that treats multiple trusts created by substantially the same grantor(s) for substantially the same beneficiaries and with a principal purpose of tax minimization as one trust for income tax purposes.[1] This rule specifies that spouses are treated as one person for purposes of the entire rule, which presumably means either as settlors or as beneficiaries, but the parameters of other aspects of this statutory provision are not known.

There are no regulations and no significant reason to pursue multiple trust planning,[2] and therefore there is no litigation or ruling activity. Thus, it simply is not known what such terms as "substantially" or "tax minimization purpose" mean in practice.[3] It is unlikely that § 643(f) ever will be a viable proscription unless the tax rates are altered in a manner that restores the benefit of creating and maintaining multiple trusts, each with its own progressive tax rates and separate run through the brackets. Indeed, in some cases the multiple trust rule may prove advantageous to taxpayers who remain subject to throwback by collapsing trusts that generate no meaningful tax saving and that pose administrative or

---

[1] **§ 5.5** Established by Treas. Reg. § 1.641(a)-0(c) and ruled invalid in Stephenson Trust Co. v. Commissioner, 81 T.C. 283 (1983), before being codified in 1984 as § 643(f).

[2] Little income tax planning involving trusts is common currently. See Pennell, Income Shifting After TRA'86, 46 N.Y.U. Inst. Fed. Tax'n 50-1 (1988).

[3] Old case law will not help much. See, e.g., Estelle Morris Trusts v. Commissioner, 51 T.C. 20, 44 (1968), aff'd, 427 F.2d 1361 (9th Cir. 1970) (20 separate trusts, identical except for their periods of accumulation and termination; as a matter of law, the court held that "a finding of tax avoidance is simply not enough to invalidate multiple trusts"); Dickinson Testamentary Trust v. Commissioner, 65 T.C.M. (CCH) 1946 (1993) (pre-enactment trusts created by spouses under three separate documents for the same child for life and thereafter for the child's descendants, with division of each of the three trusts into separate shares for the child's three surviving children—for a total of nine separate shares—that were treated for income tax purposes as nine separate tax paying entities; the court rejected the government's effort to treat each of the three original trusts as just one trust for the benefit of the grandchildren as a class, based entirely on the court's reading of the intent of the trust grantors and without application of § 643(f)—which did not control these pre-enactment trusts but that might permit consolidation of the three original trusts or the three separate shares created under each, because they had "substantially the same grantor or grantors and substantially the same primary beneficiary or beneficiaries" (with spouses being treated as one person), provided there was a principal purpose of tax avoidance).

§ 5.5

other problems that can be dodged by affirmative application of this prohibition by taxpayers.[4]

Because the multiple trust rule is not elective on the part of either the government or the taxpayer, consolidation of multiple separate trusts may alter the tax effect of actions taken in those separate trusts and preclude literal conduit treatment to some of them. For example, assume two trusts have equal amounts of income that, if distributed, would be taxed to the beneficiary currently. Instead of making distributions from both trusts, one trust accumulates its income while the other distributes all its income plus an amount of corpus equal to the income accumulated in the first trust. Conduit taxation under § § 661 and 662 recognizing the separate existence of the two trusts would result in the second trust's distributed income being taxed to the beneficiary but the former trust's accumulated income being taxed to the trust. Application of the multiple trust rule would deny recognition of the trusts' separate existence and regard them as one trust that made distributions not exceeding the total aggregated income, resulting in conduit taxation of the combined income to the beneficiary.[5]

If, in this example, the trust investments differed (and, indeed, if the income of one trust was taxable to it as if it was available for distribution when in fact it is not, as might occur if the trust investment was a partnership interest), it might be desirable for the one trust to make all the distributions even though it required a cannibalization of corpus, to preserve untapped the corpus of the other, with the end result being the same as if each trust distributed its own income. As thus illustrated, the multiple trust rule should be considered to be a taxpayer sword as well as a government shield.

---

[4] As revealed by the third trust rule. See § 667(c) and § 5.6.3 nn.43-49 and accompanying text.

[5] Furthermore, if applicable, the discretionary distribution of corpus from the second trust would not run the risk of being taxed as an accumulation distribution subject to throwback.

§ 5.5

§5.6 ACCUMULATION DISTRIBUTIONS AND THROWBACK

Important historically, the accumulation distribution and throwback rules of Subpart D (§§ 665-668) are of slight practical significance since enactment of § 665(c) in 1997. Intended to eliminate the advantages of trust accumulations, today they are nearly meaningless because only marginal income tax benefits from accumulation are available. Nevertheless, there is a concern in some quarters that sufficient savings attributable to trusts may encourage trust accumulation abuses, particularly with respect to foreign trusts or multiple trusts that are chronologically exempt from the § 643(f) multiple trust rule. This may be more likely if multiple beneficiaries could be involved, So, Subpart D remains on the books, notwithstanding the adoption in 1997 of § 665(c), which responded to calls for repeal[1] of throwback with respect to most domestic trusts.

Subpart D is discussed here because it still may apply to some situations. But readers should be aware of its limited application under § 665(c)(2), only to trusts that are or at any time were foreign trusts, or to older domestic trusts that would be subject to the § 643(f) multiple trust rule if the trust was created after March of 1984. The following discussion is totally irrelevant with respect to distributions made in taxable years that began after August 5, 1997, by trusts meeting neither of those tests.

The essential thrust of the accumulation distribution and throwback rules is to tax accumulated income, upon its subsequent distribution, as if it had been distributed to the ultimate recipient in the year it was accumulated (although the mechanics of the rule only roughly approximate nonaccumulation).[2] Because the notion behind this rule is to

---

[1] **§5.6** See, e.g., Ferguson, Freeland, & Ascher, Federal Income Taxation of Estates, Trusts, and Beneficiaries § 9.01[A] (3d ed. 2011).

[2] One notable deviation from this parity paradigm is that, with the exception of tax exempt income, the character of items includible in an accumulation and its subsequent distribution subject to throwback is not preserved. See the parenthetical to § 667(a).

Rev. Rul. 86-76, 1986-1 C.B. 284, confronted the proper income tax treatment of income received during administration of an estate and subsequently distributed to nonresident alien beneficiaries, but the same results would apply to a

preclude abuse, an exception to the accumulation distribution and throwback rules applies to income that was accumulated before the ultimate beneficiary reached the age of 21 (which includes income accumulated before the beneficiary was born),[3] the assumption being that those accumulations were not tax motivated. In addition, because of a questionable presumption that estates are not administered long enough or with tax minimization motives, Subpart D does not apply to estate distributions.[4] Otherwise, because intent is not a relevant inquiry, even trust accumulations that are motivated by concerns such as protection of a profligate or incompetent adult beneficiary are fully subject to these rules—to the extent these rules apply at all.

(Footnote Continued)

complex trust. Although received as interest on a domestic savings account, the income constituted non-U.S. source income in the hands of the beneficiaries by virtue of § 861(a)(1)(A). Thus, if it was distributed in the year received, conduit tax treatment would apply, this character would be preserved, and the income would flow out to the beneficiaries and be totally tax free. However, conduit treatment would be interrupted and the trust would be required to pay tax on the income in the year of accumulation if the entity accumulated the interest in one tax year and distributed it in a subsequent year. Even if there was no accumulation distribution and throwback rules applicable to the entity or its beneficiaries on the subsequent distribution, taxes paid by the entity would reduce the amount distributable and no mechanism refunds the taxes previously paid by the entity, meaning that accumulation essentially would change the character of the income and, correspondingly, its taxation as well.

[3] See the penultimate sentence of § 665(b). No current authority specifies whether income accumulated before the beneficiary reached the age of 21 years is regarded as the first or last item distributed if there also is income accumulated after the beneficiary reached the age of 21 and before the accumulation distribution. The § 666(a) first-in, first-out attribution rule for throwback computation purposes ought to apply for consistency.

The exception is not available in a foreign trust, and it can be lost under the third trust rule in § 667(c). See § 5.6.3 at nn.43-49 and accompanying text. It also may not apply if a distribution is deemed under Treas. Reg. § 1.662(a)-4 to be for the benefit of a person obligated to support the actual distributee. See §§ 5.11.4 nn.75-91 and accompanying text, 7.1.1.10 n.100, 7.1.1.10.1, 7.3.4.2 nn.153-172 and accompanying text, and 12.4.2, with respect to the legal obligation of support issue.

[4] Treas. Reg. § 1.665(a)-0A(d). Notice the absence from these provisions of any reference to an estate, and compare Subpart C in that respect.

§5.6

§5.6.1 UNI

To understand the concepts in Subpart D requires an examination of UNI.[5] It is DNI of the trust (taxable income, with some adjustments)[6] reduced by two amounts: (1) the distributions deduction, for current fiduciary accounting income distributed for the year,[7] and (2) taxes paid by the trust attributable to DNI that was not distributed.[8] Essentially, UNI is the amount of current trust income remaining after all distributions and taxes have been paid. It is the amount that is accumulated and available for subsequent distribution.

In some cases, however, UNI is an unanticipated chimera, generated because the itemized deduction limitation applicable to trusts and estates[9] creates "phantom" DNI that is not—indeed, it cannot be—distributed. It thereby spawns an accumulation distribution and throwback problem, even though the trust distributed all its fiduciary accounting income. The following example illustrates that there may be UNI that can create future accumulation distribution and throwback consequences, even if the entity distributes all current fiduciary accounting income annually and has no taxable income allocable to corpus (and none that represents noncash receipts that would generate tax liability in the entity).[10]

Assume the entity's gross income is $100,000. There are expenses of $10,000 that generate deductions that are subject to the 2% threshold under §67, all of which were paid from income, leaving fiduciary accounting income of $90,000. In this situation, a fiduciary wanting to distribute all income annually would distribute $90,000—that being the income remaining on the fiduciary accounting income ledger after paying all the expenses properly charged to it. The taxable income of the entity, however, would not be reduced to zero, because the 2% loss of the

---

[5] §665(a).

[6] See §5.3 for the definition of DNI.

[7] §665(a)(1).

[8] §665(a)(2).

[9] §67(e).

[10] See §5.3.4 n.76.

§5.6.1

deductions would be $200,[11] meaning that the $10,000 of expenses that were paid would generate a deduction of only $9800. Because the distributions deduction is limited to the $90,000 amount of fiduciary accounting income actually distributed, the trust would end up with $200 of taxable income, on which estimated taxes should be paid—presumably out of income,[12] which would reduce the distributions deduction and that would create UNI.

Similar unexpected UNI problems could arise in any situation in which phantom DNI exists because fiduciary accounting income available for distribution is reduced by expenses (such as interest paid on a loan) that are not deductible (for example, by virtue of § 163(h)). This could leave DNI that is greater than the amount that can be distributed to carry it out to beneficiaries. And, although the AMT rules may be ignored at the present time for estimated tax payment purposes,[13] eventually the AMT DNI rules may create estimated tax problems as well.

Payment of estimated tax out of income in the first example raises additional problems, including the question whether the trust no longer qualifies as a simple trust (it should qualify if the tax is a proper charge to income under state law or the terms of the document) and how the distributions deduction will be altered by the fact that less than $90,000 will be available for distribution after payment of the estimated tax.[14]

---

[11] After allowing a $90,000 distributions deduction, which is reflected in determining adjusted gross income to determine the 2% amount. § 67(e)(2).

[12] With the exception of qualified disability trusts to which a special rule in § 642(b)(2)(C)(i)(II) applies, the § 642(b) deduction in lieu of the personal exemption may avoid the need to pay estimated taxes in some cases. To determine whether this is the case, divide the § 642(b) amount for the trust or estate by 2%. Subtract from that sum the amount of income or gains taxable to corpus. If items not eligible for special treatment under § 67(e)(1) exceed the amount that remains, estimated tax will be a problem—even in a simple trust. Based on the current § 642(b) amounts, if there is no income or gain otherwise taxable to the entity, the amount of the § 67 items in an estate must exceed $30,000 to trigger a problem. This amount is $15,000 annually in a trust that is required to distribute all income annually, and in any other trust this amount is $5,000 annually.

[13] See Notice 87-32, 1987-1 C.B. 477.

[14] An interrelated computation is required. For example, assuming for ease that the deduction in lieu of the personal exemption does not exempt the trust from its need to pay tax on the $200 of taxable income in the prior example and

§ 5.6.1

The way to solve this phantom DNI problem is to pay the otherwise deductible expenses from corpus rather than income in the example, so that there would be a full $100,000 of income available for distribution. But doing so raises a different set of problems, because the distributions deduction would be limited to the amount of DNI,[15] which is determined on the basis of taxable income (subject to the § 643(a) adjustments), which cannot be determined without knowing the amount of the § 67(e) lost deductions, and the § 67(e) amount cannot be determined without knowing the distributions deduction (for purposes of determining adjusted gross income *after* reflecting the distributions deduction).[16]

The bottom line in this example would be that, instead of having $200 of taxable income that would produce phantom UNI, the trust would lose $190 of deductions and DNI of $90,190 would be carried out by the $100,000 distribution. Trust taxable income would be zero, after the distributions deduction,[17] so the effect of this interrelated computa-

(Footnote Continued)

that the trust is in a hypothetical 35% income tax bracket, $70 of tax would be payable and would reduce the $90,000 available for payout, which would reduce the distributions deduction to $89,930 and leave $270 on which to pay tax, which would again increase the tax payment and reduce the distributions deduction, in a circular whirlpool calculation. To determine the amount of tax ultimately payable divide the original taxable income figure by 1 minus the rate of tax (in this case $200 ÷ (1-.35) = $307.69 on which $107.69 in tax is incurred).

[15] § § 651(b) and 661(a) (last clause).

[16] This last problem requires another interrelated computation, illustrated by the following formula, derived from page 22 of the 2010 version of the Form 1041 Instructions in which AMID is allowable miscellaneous itemized deductions:

AGI = GI – § 642(b) Deduction – DNI = ($100,000 – $300 – DNI)
AMID = Deductions – (.02(AGI)) = ($10,000 – (.02($99,700 – DNI)))
DNI = GI – AMID = ($100,000 – AMID)
AMID = $10,000 – (.02($99,700 – ($100,000 – AMID)))
AMID = $10,000 – ($1,994 – ($2,000 – .02AMID))
AMID = $10,000 – (.02AMID + $1,994 – $2,000)
AMID = $10,000 – (.02AMID – $6)
AMID = $10,006 – .02AMID
AMID + .02AMID = $10,006
1.02AMID = $10,006
AMID = $10,006 ÷ 1.02 = $9,810
DNI = $100,000 – $9,810 = $90,190

[17] Because the distributions deduction is the lesser of DNI or fiduciary accounting income, which would be adequate to reduce taxable income to zero.

§ 5.6.1

tion would be on the amount of DNI that the beneficiary would report ($190 more than if § 67(e) had not applied).

§ 5.6.2 Accumulation Distributions

The accumulation distribution and throwback rules require another application of the tier rules as employed in § 662(a).[18] Because first tier beneficiaries receive income that is required to be distributed currently, second tier beneficiaries receive discretionary distributions that constitute current fiduciary accounting income only to the extent any remains after all first tier distributions. Any additional distributions constitute an accumulation distribution and receive favorable corpus distribution status only to the extent there is neither DNI nor UNI remaining.[19]

As defined, an accumulation distribution cannot occur if current first and second tier distributions do not exceed current year fiduciary accounting income.[20] Moreover, accumulation distributions occur only to the extent (1) current second tier discretionary distributions exceed DNI remaining after all first tier mandatory distributions of income for the

---

[18] See § 5.4.2.

[19] § 665(b).

[20] § 665(b) (last sentence).

year,[21] and (2) accumulated UNI exists from prior years.[22] This is the result of a distribution hierarchy by which Subpart D treats distributions as coming first from DNI, then from UNI, and (only after exhaustion of both) finally from corpus. Because first tier beneficiaries receive (by definition) current income, only second tier beneficiaries may receive an accumulation distribution, and then only to the extent DNI has been exhausted and there is any available UNI.

As a necessary consequence of these rules, an accumulation distribution and throwback problem only can apply in a complex trust, because by definition there cannot be a second tier beneficiary in any year that a trust is simple.

---

[21] Because of a glitch in § 665(b) the amount of the accumulation distribution can vary even though the amount distributed and the available UNI does not, depending on the amount of the first tier distribution. To illustrate, assume a trust has $20,000 of fiduciary accounting income and $1,000 of deductible expenses that were paid from corpus for fiduciary accounting purposes, producing $19,000 of DNI.

An accumulation distribution would be deemed to occur if the trust distributes any amount greater than $20,000 for the year. Assume that $20,001 is distributed. In this example, the accumulation distribution subject to throwback could be any amount from $1 to $1,001, depending on the amount of the first tier distributions, because the amount of the accumulation distribution is defined as second tier distributions in excess of DNI remaining after first tier distributions. Thus, if first tier distributions were $20,000 (the amount of fiduciary accounting income), the second tier distribution would be $1 and that amount would exceed DNI ($19,000) remaining after the first tier distribution ($20,000; negative numbers are precluded, so the amount remaining would be deemed to be $0) by only $1.

On the other hand, if the first tier distribution was $19,000, the second tier distribution would be $1,001 and it would exceed DNI ($19,000) remaining after the first tier distribution ($19,000) by $1,001. If the first tier distribution was anything less than $19,000 the accumulation distribution still would be only $1,001. For example, if the first tier was $0, the second tier distribution ($20,001) would exceed DNI ($19,000) remaining after the first tier distribution ($0) by only $1,001.

The disparity in amount illustrated here should not exist, and it would not if the last sentence of § 665(b) read "to the extent" instead of "if" amounts paid do not exceed fiduciary accounting income for the year. Under such a properly drafted provision the accumulation distribution in all these cases would be $1, which would be the right result.

[22] § 666(a) (second sentence) and Treas. Reg. § 1.666(a)-1A(e).

§ 5.6.2

§5.6.3 Throwback

The throwback tax computation applies to second tier accumulation distributions of UNI, meaning discretionary distributions in excess of DNI remaining after all first tier distributions—to the extent prior years' accumulations of UNI remain.[23] That amount is "grossed up" by adding the tax paid by the trust attributable to the accumulation, making the total amount subject to throwback the actual accumulation distribution plus those taxes.[24] The logic behind this gross up rule is to treat the beneficiary as if no accumulation had been made, in which case there would have been no taxes paid by the trust on the accumulation and the larger aggregate amount would have been distributed.

Computation of the throwback tax on an accumulation distribution involves seven basic steps. Notwithstanding widespread assertions that the computation is difficult (which also may have played a role in the repeal of throwback for most trusts), in truth the only difficult aspects of it are reading the Code and figuring out that these *are* the proper steps and then finding the proper records to perform the computation. With the requisite historical information and a guide translated into English, however, the tax is not hard to compute.

- *Allocation to Preceding Taxable Years.* Under §667(b)(1)(A) it is necessary to know the number of years during which UNI was accumulated. Thus, the first step is to determine to what years the accumulation distribution is allocable, based on a first-in, first-out rule.[25] The earliest

---

[23] §665(b).

[24] §§666(b) and 666(c). Notice, however, in the computation that is described below that the first step is performed before this gross up rule is applied.

[25] §666(a). Once a prior year's accumulation has been deemed distributed it is wiped out for purposes of future throwback computations.

Under Treas. Reg. §1.665(e)-1A(b), "[a] taxable year . . . during which the trust was a simple trust for the entire year shall not be considered a 'preceding taxable year' unless during such year the trust received 'outside income' or unless the trustee did not distribute all of the income of the trust that was required to be distributed currently for such year. In such event, the UNI for such year shall not exceed the greater of the 'outside income' or income not distributed during such year." The regulation is wrong to include income required to be but not distributed, because that income would be taxed to the beneficiary under §652 regardless of distribution and should not again be subject to tax by virtue of the accumulation distribution and throwback rules. See Ferguson, Freeland, & Ascher, Federal Income Taxation of Estates, Trusts, and

§5.6.3

accumulation is distributed first, then the next earliest, and so on until enough years' accumulations have been drawn out to total the actual accumulation distribution. For this purpose, it is the actual accumulation distribution *before* application of the gross up rule that is the measure.

• *Gross Up Rule Applied.* After determining the preceding taxable years to which the accumulation distribution is attributable under the first-in, first-out rule, taxes paid by the trust that are attributable to the accumulation distribution are added to the actual accumulation distribution under this second step.[26] The allocation of taxes paid by the trust on UNI for years as to which the entire accumulation is deemed distributed is computed on an average (rather than a marginal) rate basis.[27] So is the pro ration for years as to which only a portion is deemed distributed, all notwithstanding that the accumulations increased the tax incrementally under the progressive rate schedule. Trustees are required to retain all tax returns and all information pertaining to those returns to be able to perform this function.[28] This gross up rule is waived in a third trust that is subject to § 667(c).[29]

• *Average Accumulation Determined.* Having determined the grossed up accumulation distribution and the number of years to which it is allocable, an average accumulation is computed by dividing the grossed up amount of the accumulation distribution as determined in the second step by the number of prior years to which it is attributable as determined in the first step.[30]

• *De Minimis Exclusion.* The average accumulation determined in the third step is fundamental to the throwback tax ultimately payable (a smaller average will result in a lower tax). And that average is reduced if the number of preceding taxable years is increased. As such, there is an incentive to increase the number of preceding years by intentionally distributing only a small amount of income attributable to a prior year. This can be

---

(Footnote Continued)

Beneficiaries § 9.02[D] (3d ed. 2011). Outside income is "amounts that are includible in DNI of the trust for the year but are not 'income' of the trust as that term is defined in § 1.643(b)-1." The most common examples are § 691 IRD that is allocable to corpus, or a trust distribution of corpus to a simple trust that carried out either DNI or UNI from that trust.

In looking to prior years for allocation purposes, years prior to 1969 are ignored and their accumulations are treated as never having occurred. See § 665(e)(1)(B) as written prior to its amendment in 1990.

[26] §§ 666(b) and 666(c).

[27] Treas. Reg. § 1.665(d)-1A(b).

[28] Treas. Reg. § 1.666(d)-1A(a). See § 666(d) for the allocation and gross up rule if adequate records do not exist.

[29] See § 5.6.3. nn.43-49 and accompanying text.

[30] § 667(b)(1)(C).

§ 5.6.3

accomplished by accumulating at least some income in every year of the trust and by planning accumulation distributions to carry out a small amount of income from yet another prior year. To preclude planning like this from distorting the throwback computation, this fourth step determines whether the amount of any accumulation distribution attributable to a prior year[31] is less than 25% of the average accumulation distribution determined in the third step.[32] The year is ignored if the accumulation distribution attributable to any prior year falls below this "de minimis" amount (but the accumulation distribution attributable to it is *not* ignored) and the number of years determined in the first step is reduced. Using that reduced number of years, the third step is reperformed, giving a larger average accumulation.[33]

• *Average Tax Computed.* The fifth step is a compromise. Throwback began as a determination of the exact tax the beneficiary would have incurred if the accumulation had not occurred. The computation caused the accumulation distribution to be "thrown back" to the beneficiary's actual prior year in which the income was accumulated and a recomputation determined the tax that the beneficiary would have paid had the accumulated amount instead been distributed currently. The averaging in the first three steps reveals that the exact method no longer is followed, and the fifth step furthers the approximation by adding the average accumulation to the recipient's *taxable* income for the *mid-three* of his or her previous five years[34] rather than to the beneficiary's *gross* or *adjusted gross* income for the *actual* years of the accumulation.

Excluded for this purpose are the years of the highest and lowest taxable income[35] from among the previous five, and any loss year is treated as having zero income.[36] The five previous years is used to avoid the need to determine the beneficiary's income for the actual years to which the accumulation is attributable, and the high and low income years are excluded and the zero income convention is applied to minimize the risk of distortions due to unusual years.

---

[31] Although it is not established by any authority, it appears that this amount is measured prior to being grossed up.

[32] § 667(b)(3).

[33] Reapplication of this fourth step could cause exclusion of additional years falling below 25% of the new average, which would necessitate even further recomputations. Because the Code and Regulations give no indication that the de minimis exclusion is to be applied more than once, the assumption here is that only one computation is made under this step.

[34] §§ 667(b)(1)(B) and 667(b)(1)(C).

[35] § 667(b)(1)(B).

[36] § 667(b)(2).

§ 5.6.3

Addition of the average accumulation to the beneficiary's *taxable* income for the remaining middle three years prevents the need to work any recomputations based on gross or adjusted gross income. As a result, the throwback computation is only a rough averaged approximation of the beneficiary's tax cost if the income had not been accumulated. This fifth step uses the rate tables for the mid-three prior years to compute the increase that would have occurred in the beneficiary's income tax for each of the mid-three years, caused by adding the average accumulation to taxable income, and no provision appears to preserve the special character of any accumulated income other than tax exempt income.[37]

• *Partial Tax Computed.* The sixth step simply determines an average of the three years' increases from the fifth step[38] and then computes a partial tax by multiplying that average increase in tax by the number of preceding taxable years as determined in the first and fourth steps.[39] The result is the amount of tax attributable to the accumulation distribution.

• *Tax Payable.* The throwback tax computed in the sixth step is not necessarily the amount that will be paid, because either of two credits may be available. One credit applies if any GST or estate tax was imposed on the accumulation amount between the time of accumulation and the time of distribution. The credit for those tax amounts attributable to the accumulation reflects the fact that, had no accumulation been made, those taxes would not have been incurred.[40]

---

[37] See § 667(a) (parenthetical) and cf. Treas. Reg. § 1.667(f)-1A (which was applicable only prior to the 1976 repeal of the capital gains throwback rule).

[38] § 667(b)(1)(D).

[39] § 667(b)(1) (last sentence).

[40] § 667(b)(6). The credit effects a rough justice without recomputing the wealth transfer tax after the income tax is paid. Thus, an income tax credit is given for the wealth transfer tax deemed to be attributable to the income tax on those accumulations that were subject to the wealth transfer tax, rather than giving a refund of the wealth transfer tax incurred improperly. Computation of the credit under §§ 667(b)(6)(A) and 667(b)(6)(C) is based on a formula:

$$\text{credit} = \S667(b) \text{ partial tax} \times$$

$$\frac{\text{accumulation subject to wealth transfer tax}}{\text{total accumulation}} \times \frac{\text{wealth transfer tax attributable to accumulation}}{\text{accumulation subject to wealth transfer tax}}$$

This cumbersome formula nets out to a more manageable:

$$\text{credit} = \text{partial tax} \times \text{wealth transfer tax attributable to accumulation} \div \text{total accumulation}$$

§ 5.6.3

More importantly, in most cases the beneficiary also receives a credit for income taxes already paid by the trust on the accumulation amount.[41] No refund is allowed if the trust already paid taxes in excess of the tax computed under throwback.[42] This is most likely because of the higher tax rates applicable to trusts. It also suggests that the trustee of a discretionary trust that remains subject to throwback should distribute all income currently (unless a good justification exists for the accumulation or unless the tax paid by the trust will be no greater than if current distribution was made to the beneficiary).

Moreover, and probably the only reason why it is important to care about and to plan in anticipation of throwback with respect to any domestic trust, the credit is denied entirely if the distribution is being made by a so-called "third" trust.[43]

Under this third trust rule the focus is on any trusts in excess of two that make accumulation distributions to the same beneficiary that are attributable to the same prior year.[44] Thus, there can be many third trusts if numerous trusts are involved—especially if the multiple trust rule[45] is not applicable (because the trusts were created before March of 1984).[46] The intent of this rule as it now stands is to punish the use of foreign trusts or multiple domestic trusts created by the same settlor for the same beneficiary with a tax avoidance motive that accumulate income for the same beneficiary. The rule punishes trusts that cannot be collapsed because they are chronologically exempt from the § 643(f) multiple trust rule, potentially to prevent reducing the income tax each trust incurs on accumulations.

The third trust rule results in a double tax, once when the trust accumulated the income and again under throwback with no credit. Although the gross up rule does not apply to the extent the third trust

---

[41] § 667(b)(1) (last sentence).

[42] § 666(e).

[43] § 667(c).

[44] Aggregate accumulation distributions of less than $1,000 per trust attributable to a prior year are ignored for purposes of this rule. § 667(c)(2).

[45] See § 5.5.

[46] A trust is not subject to § 643(f) if it was not created by the same settlor for the same beneficiary with a tax avoidance motive, such as three trusts for one beneficiary that were created by separate sets of grandparents and by the beneficiary's parents. Those trusts are excepted from the throwback rule by § 665(c)(2)(B) even if they were created before March of 1984.

§ 5.6.3

rule does[47] (thus reducing the amount of the accumulation distribution subject to tax), both the trust and the beneficiary pay tax on the same income. Even more importantly, the minority exception[48] also is forfeited in any third trust, meaning that accumulations that were made because the beneficiary was a minor are punished the same as accumulations with a tax minimization motive.

Only in partial mitigation of the harshness of this rule, the beneficiary is allowed to select which of several trusts will be regarded as the first two and which as the third trust(s),[49] but this post-accumulation planning is an inadequate alternative to effective coordination of multiple accumulation trusts that avoids application of the third trust rule entirely. Planning might involve having the trusts all distribute their excess income to a single trust that would be the sole income accumulation trust, or by limiting to two the number of trusts that accumulate income in any given year.

The bottom line in an accumulation distribution throwback computation is an approximation of the amount of tax the beneficiary would have paid had accumulation not occurred. Obviously, with all the averaging involved, it is only a rough approximation. Perhaps the only favorable aspects of the throwback tax itself is that it does not apply to more than a very slim percentage of all domestic trusts, and it is computed and imposed with no interest assessed. Any increase in tax between what the trust paid and what the beneficiary ultimately owes is payable after any deferral involved, without penalty or other cost for the delay.[50] This aspect is small comfort in virtually all circumstances, given the fact that usually more tax was paid because of taxation at trust rates instead of the potentially lower rates for the beneficiary.

---

[47] § 667(c)(1).

[48] § 665(b). See § 5.6 n.3 and accompanying text.

[49] § 667(b)(5).

[50] This is not true with respect to a foreign trust, as to which § 667(a)(3) imposes the § 668 interest charge.

§5.7 ESTIMATED TAXES AND COMPLIANCE

An income tax return must be filed by the fiduciary[1] of any estate with gross income for the taxable year of at least $600,[2] by every trust with any positive amount of taxable income (regardless of the amount of its taxable income), by any trust with gross income of at least $600, and by any estate or trust with a nonresident alien beneficiary.[3]

At one time trusts and estates were excepted from the estimated tax payment requirements.[4] Since 1986, however, most trusts are subject to the system of quarterly installment payment of estimated taxes, as are all estates for any tax year ending two or more years after the decedent's death.[5] Estate—substitute funded inter vivos trusts enjoy the same two

------

[1] **§5.7** §6012(b)(4); compare §6012(b)(1), specifying that the *decedent's final* income tax return shall be filed by the decedent's "executor, administrator, or other person charged with the property of such decedent." In some cases the decedent's penultimate return also must be filed, as for example if the decedent died in the new year before April 15 and the prior year's return was not yet due.

[2] For these purposes, it appears that there can be only one estate as a taxable entity and only one return to be filed, presumably requiring consolidation if there are multiple ancillary administrations. See, e.g., Rev. Rul. 64-307, 1964-2 C.B. 163 (decedent left two wills and property subject to administration in two countries but was treated as having only one estate for income tax purposes and it was expected to file a single return). Cf. Rev. Rul. 70-22, 1970-1 C.B. 204, confirming the single-mindedness of the government with respect to multiple estate administrations (in this case involving filings with respect to withholding and other wage related submissions involving employees for ancillary administrations). Curiously, Rev. Rul. 69-658, 1969-2 C.B. 190, recognized that even a testamentary trust is a taxpayer separate from the personal representative of the decedent's will that created that trust, which underscores the suggestion that avoidance of ancillary administration through the use of living trusts may prove desirable for income tax compliance as well as other purposes. See §4.1.6, regarding the use of trusts for ancillary probate avoidance.

[3] See §§6012(a)(3)-6012(a)(5). It may be wise in some cases to file even if a return is not required, to garner any available statute of limitation protection.

[4] §6654. Under Treas. Reg. §1.6153-1(a)(4), no estimated tax need be paid by the fiduciary with respect to D's final year that ended at death, although estimated tax may be required if S will file a joint return with D for that final year—especially if S may receive significant amounts of income (including IRD) by virtue of D's death. See §5.7 n.22.

[5] Note that this rule applicable to estates could pick up a tax year beginning as early as exactly one year and two days after the date of a decedent's death

§5.7

year moratorium if 100% of the trust was treated as a grantor trust[6] prior to the settlor's death and if the residue of the settlor's estate pours over into the trust.

In addition, § 645 permits revocable living trusts to be treated as part of the settlor's estate for all income tax purposes if the executor and trustee both elect that treatment.[7]

The estimated tax[8] requires payment in four installments, each of 25% of the "required annual payment," which means the lesser of 90% of the actual tax for the current year, 90% of the tax for the current year computed on the "expected" income for the year (based on an annualization of income to date),[9] or 100%[10] of the tax for the prior year, if that year was a 12 month year (which often is not the case for the first year of a trust)[11] and a return was filed.

(Footnote Continued)

(meaning the estate's first year is one day in length), and does not guarantee a two calendar year moratorium. In addition, as a pay-back for the two tax year moratorium for estates, former § 6152 was repealed, meaning that estates may not pay their income tax in installments.

[6] See § 5.11.

[7] The election is available to any trust that was subject to § 676 grantor trust treatment during the settlor's life because of a power in the grantor personally, exercisable without the consent of any adverse party (exercisable with the consent of the decedent's spouse is permissible). The trust is treated as a part of the settlor's estate for income tax purposes (although the trust and estate are regarded as separate shares for DNI calculation and carryout purposes) until the later of two years after the settlor's death or six months after final determination of the settlor's FET liability (which in many cases will be six months after the date of any closing letter).

[8] § 6654(d)(1)(A).

[9] § 6654(d)(2), subject to various special exceptions.

[10] This figure is 110% if the adjusted gross income for that prior year was greater than $150,000, in either case with adjusted gross income determined as under § 67(e). § 6654(d)(1)(C).

[11] Notice 87-32, 1987-1 C.B. 477, announced rules for applying the estimated tax rules during a short tax year. Because application of the AMT to trusts and estates still is unclear, Notice 87-32 also provided an exception for failure to consider the effect of this tax on estimated tax liability. The Notice also established due dates for installments during a short tax year, with other pertinent information as illustrated below:

The fiduciary of even a simple trust—or of a complex trust or an estate that intends to distribute all income annually—should not assume that it need not worry about the estimated tax payment rules.[12] Even though it proves to be the case that no tax is due at year end, this may

(Footnote Continued)

Short Year Begins	First Payment Due	Second Payment Due	Third Payment Due	Final Payment Due	Portion of Annual Payment Due
2/1	5/15	7/15	10/15	1/15	1/4 each
3/1	6/15	8/17	11/16	1/15	1/4 each
4/1	7/15	9/15	12/15	1/15	1/4 each
5/1	8/17	10/15	*	1/15	1/3 each
6/1	9/15	11/16	*	1/15	1/3 each
7/1	10/15	*	*	1/15	1/2 each
8/1	11/16	*	*	1/15	1/2 each
9/1	12/15	*	*	1/15	1/2 each
10/1	*	*	*	1/15	Total
11/1	*	*	*	1/15	Total
12/1	*	*	*	1/15	Total

*No installment payment is due

The Notice also established a pro ration approach to annualize income in a short tax year or to convert a prior year's liability to a short current year under the prior year alternative. For example, if the current year will be only 11 months, annualization of income is the alternative being used, and at the end of the second quarter there are 5 months of income, it would be annualized for estimated tax purposes by determining the average income to date (dividing the income to date by 5) and multiplying that average income by the number of months (11) in the short current year. If the current year is a short year and the prior year alternative is used, the tax shown for the prior year would be annualized for current short year estimated tax purposes by multiplying that tax by a fraction, the numerator of which being the number of months in the current short year and the denominator of which being 12.

Notice 88-18, 1988-1 C.B. 486, announced that § 443 annualization rules would be used at year end to compute taxes for the year, which may not produce exactly the same results as Notice 87-32 would produce for quarterly estimated tax payment purposes.

[12] The penalty for failure to comply with § 6654 is interest at the § 6621 rate on the installment deficiencies. Notice 88-15, 1988-1 C.B. 482, provides a procedure to obtain a waiver of penalties for failure to comply with the estimated tax rules. Further, Treas. Reg. § 1.6081-6(d), provides that automatic extension of a trust's return filing deadline (which is for only five months, not the normal six) does not automatically extend the beneficiary's deadline. The beneficiary must independently file for an extension as well.

§ 5.7

not be certain during the middle of the year.[13] Moreover, the example illustrating phantom DNI[14] reveals that there may be a need to pay estimated taxes even if the entity will distribute all fiduciary accounting income annually and has no taxable income allocable to corpus that would generate some tax liability in the entity.[15]

A trustee may treat any portion of the trust's estimated tax payments as a payment made by a beneficiary of the trust.[16] This effectively permits the trustee to move a credit for its estimated tax payments out to the beneficiaries once it is known that the trust has distributed income and will have no liability thereon.[17] A trustee could make this allocation with respect to *all* its estimated tax payments made during the year[18] but, to

---

[13] For purposes of determining the distributions deduction and DNI for a trust or estate for estimated tax purposes, all the books are closed as of the last day of the month two months before the installment is due (for example, the last day of February for the April 15 installment, the last day of May for the July 15 installment, and so on). Some fiduciaries will not know, by the end of that month, the income for the quarter and therefore may not make a distribution that is certain to clean out all that income and avoid the need to make estimated tax payments. The § 651 distributions deduction should protect trusts that are required to distribute all income annually by giving a distributions deduction equal to the income required to be distributed, even if it is not, on a quarter annual basis for estimated tax purposes, but there is no authority establishing this to be the rule.

[14] See § 5.6.1 nn.9-12 and accompanying text.

[15] Excepted from estimated tax under § 6654(e) are taxpayers with less than $1000 of tax liability or those for whom the prior year was 12 months, a return was filed for the prior year, and the taxpayer had a zero tax liability for that prior year (as, for example, may be the case with many trusts due to their distributions deduction). In the paradigm example, however, it may be that none of these safe harbors will be available.

[16] § 643(g).

[17] This provision is applicable to estates in what is expected to be the estate's last tax year. § 643(g)(3). Allocation of any excess estimated tax might avoid the need for the personal representative to seek a refund to recover that amount, although excess estimated tax payments in prior years apparently cannot be allocated and might require a separate refund request.

[18] Conceivably a trustee might consider doing this because an allocation is regarded as an estimated tax payment by the beneficiary, not by the trust. However, the estimated payment is treated as made by the beneficiary on January 15 following the deemed distribution, not when the trust made actual payment, which may be justified by the fact that there would be no facile

avoid incurring a penalty, it should be limited to estimated tax payments that appear to be in excess of the trust's tax burden for the year.[19] The allocation may be in different proportions than income distributions among the various beneficiaries for the year. This means that, if a beneficiary is in estimated tax trouble for the year, presumably the trustee could help bail out the beneficiary by allocating a larger share of the credit for taxes paid to that beneficiary (indeed, the trustee *could* make an allocation to a beneficiary who received no income distributions for the year at all).[20]

Allocations are treated as payments made by the beneficiary on January 15.[21] So they may not completely bail the beneficiary out of

---

(Footnote Continued)

mechanism to determine when the trust's excess payments were made. For purposes of computing interest due on delayed estimated tax payments, however, the trust and the beneficiary both appear to lose the benefit of the trust having made estimated tax payments before January 15.

[19] The election must be made by the trust within 65 days following the close of the trust's tax year and is treated as a distribution to the beneficiary on the last day of the calendar year. Allocation therefore will generate all the income tax consequences of a trust distribution to a beneficiary under the 65 day rule of § 663(b), including a DNI carryout to the beneficiary and a distributions deduction for the trust. This means that an allocation may create a further excess of estimated taxes paid, requiring an interrelated tax computation. Notice, also, that this election is not limited to complex trusts, as would be the case under the 65 day rule of § 663(b).

[20] Among other uncertainties, neither the Code nor the legislative history speak to the state law question whether a trustee's use of fiduciary accounting income to make estimated tax payments is proper (e.g., in a simple trust, is it copacetic to use income that the terms of the trust require the trustee to distribute annually?). In a situation in which tax liability properly falls on the trustee, the most important aspect is that the trustee carefully consider whether state law mandates the use of current fiduciary accounting income or corpus to make the estimated tax payment, based on whether the taxable income items generating estimated tax liability at the trust level were allocable to income or corpus for fiduciary accounting purposes. Under the allocation provision of § 643(g), a trustee should treat estimated tax payments as a distribution from the trust, followed by use by the beneficiary to pay the beneficiary's estimated taxes. Thus, if the trustee is required to distribute a certain amount of income annually, allocation may be one method of satisfying that requirement.

[21] The January 15 presumption in § 643(g)(1)(C)(ii) apparently applies even to an allocation by an estate under § 643(g)(3) with respect to what it anticipates

estimated tax trouble for the prior year. And disproportionate allocations may require an adjustment for any inequity created thereby, if the trustee does not have discretion under the trust to favor some beneficiaries. Nevertheless, a well drafted trust instrument presumably will specify that disproportionate allocations may be made and that no adjustment shall be made to compensate for the effects thereof (or it will specify how an adjustment is to be made), with no liability on the trustee for the effects of any of this.

With respect to compliance, only estates and trusts that have no private beneficiaries (that is, trusts that are tax exempt or wholly charitable—which does not include charitable split interest trusts or pooled income funds), may select a tax year that is not the calendar year (that is, a fiscal year that ends on the last day of any month other than December).[22] Thus, garden variety[23] and charitable split interest trusts are forced to report their income and file their returns on a calendar year basis.[24] This avoids perceived abuses under prior law that took advan-

(Footnote Continued)

will be its last taxable year, notwithstanding that the estate may not be on a calendar year.

[22] § 644. The decedent's last tax year will end early and the estate's first tax year will begin on the date of the decedent's death, meaning that both years are likely to be short years. Under § 6013 the estate may elect to file a joint income tax return with S for D's final year, in which case D's year may end with death but the joint return may cover a full year (assuming S does not also die before the natural end of that year).

According to Treas. Reg. § 20.2053-6(f), if an overpayment is made on a joint income tax return for D's final year, the refund is an asset that is includible in D's gross estate under § 2033 in the amount by which D's contribution toward payment of the joint income tax liability exceeded D's share of the liability as finally determined. See Cherney v. Commissioner, 89-1 U.S. Tax Cas. (CCH) ¶ 13,799 (D. Neb. 1989).

[23] A wholly grantor trust need not file on the calendar year, but the point is irrelevant because a wholly grantor trust essentially is ignored for income tax purposes. See Rev. Rul. 90-55, 1990-2 C.B. 161.

[24] Fiduciaries need to study the penalty and interest provisions that apply to late filing of income tax and information returns, and to the late payment of tax liability. In addition to any interest owed under § 6601 (as determined under § 6621) on a late payment of taxes, § 6651 imposes a penalty for failure to timely file a tax return such as the Form 1041 that is applicable unless there was reasonable cause for the late filing and an absence of willful neglect. Although there would be no penalty or interest to pay under §§ 6601 or 6651 if the trust

§ 5.7

tage of the rule that a beneficiary does not report distributions of trust income until its tax year in which the trust's tax year ended.[25] Unless the beneficiary is the unusual individual taxpayer who reports on a fiscal year basis, the gist of this rule is that the trust's year and the beneficiary's year both will end on December 31. All income of the trust that is distributed during that calendar year will be reported by the beneficiary on a return due April 15 of the immediately following year. In addition, the estimated tax payment obligation reduces the ability of any beneficiary to avoid payment of tax for extended periods, even if the tax years of the beneficiary and the trust differ because the beneficiary is not on a calendar year.

Fiscal year selection still is available for estates,[26] involving a "crystal ball" aspect of administration of estates whereby the personal representative tries to select a tax year that takes into consideration factors such as (1) duration of administration of the estate and the likely conditions at the expected time of termination that will affect the tax situation of the beneficiaries, (2) amounts of income, gains or losses, and deductions of both the estate and the beneficiaries and in which years the best tax results can be obtained, and (3) the relative tax brackets of the estate and its beneficiaries, presently and projected into the future,

---

(Footnote Continued)

incurred no tax (due to distributions during the year) the trust may incur the additional §§ 6721 and 6722 penalties for failure to timely provide a payee statement (the K-1) to a beneficiary, which may be more important than any charges related to filing the Form 1041, given the number of K-1 statements involved in a normal fiduciary's practice.

[25] §§ 652(c) and 662(c). See § 5.4.1 nn.14-17 and accompanying text.

[26] Presumably including a trust as to which a § 645 election was made. During the election period the trust need not file a separate income tax return or have a separate taxpayer identification number and, when the election period ends, the estate is simply deemed to make a distribution to any following trust(s), which has §§ 661 and 662 carryout consequences. During the election period the estate and trust are treated as one for income tax purposes and simply apportion their aggregate income tax liability in a reasonable manner to avoid being deemed to have made a taxable gift otherwise. See generally Notice 2003-33, 2003-1 C.B. 990, and Treas. Reg. § 1.645-1. Probably much more than anyone cares to know about § 645 is described in Jones, Temporary Bliss: An Entity Election for Trusts, 100 Tax Notes 1304 (2003), with a short follow up letter by the author at 102 Tax Notes 1675 (2004).

§ 5.7

again with an eye to when income best would be realized and by which taxpayer(s).

With discretion to choose the estate's tax year, some deferral can be obtained in the early years and timing of distributions and termination of the estate can have an impact on tax consequences in subsequent years. For example, assume that the personal representative was expecting a large amount of income to be received in February of the first year of the estate's existence, and wanted to defer for as long as possible the beneficiary's payment of tax thereon while at the same time making that income available immediately through distribution. The personal representative would select a tax year of February 1 to January 31 to compliment the beneficiary's calendar year.[27] On the other hand, if the personal representative wanted to cause taxation of some or all of that income as early as possible, because the beneficiary's income is expected to rise over time, selection of a short tax year and immediate distribution of the proper amount could cause the income to be included in the beneficiary's calendar year in which the first short year of the estate ends.

Selection of a fiscal, rather than calendar, tax year for an estate often is the best choice, the only question being which of the 11 available alternatives to select. Election of a short first tax year may avoid bunching income in the first return. If death was at the end of a calendar year, a fiscal year may permit receipt of more income in the first year, which could spread estate income into several more equal amounts. Alternatively, if deductions will shortly become available against a large amount of first year income, holding the tax year open to generate those deductions may be advisable. Selection of a short first tax year also may allow an additional $600 deduction in lieu of the personal exemption,[28] although the estate is lost as a taxpaying entity when it terminates. Finally, if the beneficiary is on a calendar year (which almost always is true), selection of a fiscal year will allow deferral in the beneficiary's reporting of estate income distributions.

---

[27] See § 5.4.1 nn. 14-17 and accompanying text.
[28] § 642(b)(1).

§5.8 DISCRETION

The confluence of discretion exercised by a fiduciary and the income taxation of trusts and estates may affect beneficiaries and their tax liabilities in unexpected and potentially inequitable ways. For example, the conduit tax and timing rules make it possible to alter income tax liability (in terms of amount of tax paid, by whom, and when) just by timing distributions (deciding whether and when to distribute or accumulate income). As a consequence, there is more to the exercise of discretion than whether DNI or UNI exists and will be carried out to a particular beneficiary in a certain year. And a raft of fiduciary responsibility concerns must be considered in conjunction with the income tax rules and responsibilities.

§5.8.1 Distributions in Kind

Unless a distribution from a trust or an estate qualifies for the § 663(a)(1) exclusion as a specific bequest,[1] income will be carried out (first DNI, then UNI to the extent the accumulation distribution and throwback rules still apply, to the extent either is available in the year of distribution) regardless of whether the distribution constitutes fiduciary accounting income or corpus and regardless of whether the fiduciary distributes cash or other property in kind.[2] Different appreciated assets of equal FMV may carry out different amounts of income, however, because the amount of income carried out by a distribution of property in kind is limited by § 643(e)(2) to the lesser of the property's FMV or basis. In addition, the basis of depreciated distributed assets in the beneficiary's hands may differ even if the FMV and income carried out are equal.[3]

Thus, for example, the income tax consequences of the distributions will differ if two assets with an equal FMV but lesser (and different bases are distributed to two similarly situated beneficiaries. Moreover, the exercise of a fiduciary's discretion to distribute property in kind entails more than the issue of how much value to give each recipient. Alterna-

---

[1] **§ 5.8** See § 5.4.4.

[2] See §§ 5.4 and 5.6.

[3] § 643(e)(1), which calls for a carryover of basis but also reflects that any gain or loss recognized on a distribution constitutes an adjustment to basis.

§5.8

tively, if the basis of the distributed properties was higher than their FMVs, the income tax consequences of the distributions may be equal but the future income tax attributes of the assets will differ. In either case, the income tax rules may generate different immediate or future income tax costs to each beneficiary, even if their tax brackets are the same. All because different amounts of income may be carried out to the two beneficiaries and any built-in gain or loss represented by the carry-over basis result constitutes a future tax consequence.

Applicable on its face only to noncash[4] second tier distributions[5] (which means that it is limited to discretionary distributions by complex trusts and estates), § 643(e) is not applicable (because it is not needed) to distributions that qualify as specific bequests that are excluded from the DNI carry out rules entirely.[6] Nor does it apply to distributions in kind by simple trusts, or to first tier mandatory distributions from complex trusts, because any property distributed in those situations always will have a basis equal to its FMV. That is because both situations involve distributions of property in kind to satisfy obligations of a trust or an estate, which are gain or loss realization events and result in a basis equal to FMV.[7]

---

[4] Cash is treated differently than property distributed in kind under the terms of this provision, but that difference is not meaningful in practice. The technical tax notion is that cash has no basis, but in actual operation the treatment of cash is as if it has a basis equal to its face amount or FMV. That notion might not be true if transactions involving the purchase and sale of currency are involved, but it is accurate with respect to typical cash dealings.

[5] § 643(e)(2) defines "the amount taken into account under sections 661(a)(2) and 662(a)(2)."

[6] See § 643(e)(4), which reveals that the specific bequest exclusion in § 663(a)(1) trumps all aspects of the DNI carry out rules. See § 5.4.4, regarding the § 663(a)(1) exclusion.

[7] Any distribution of an asset in kind in satisfaction of an obligation of a trust or an estate—in this case the specific bequest or a simple trust or first tier obligation to distribute income—is treated as a sale of the distributed asset for its FMV. Any gain or loss represented by the difference between basis of the asset and its FMV is realized and treated as distribution of the cash received from that sale, which the beneficiary then is deemed to use to acquire the asset in the market, giving it a basis equal to its FMV. See Treas. Reg. §§ 1.651(a)-2(d) and 1.661(a)-2(f) (mandatory income distributions in simple and complex trusts, respectively, satisfied by assets distributed in kind); Rev. Rul. 67-74, 1967-1 C.B. 194 (simple trust distribution of corpus equal in value to income entitlement

Thus, because some property distributed in kind will have a basis equal to its FMV, the summary rule for *all* distributions from estates and either simple or complex trusts can be stated simply that property distributed in kind carries out income to the extent of the lesser of FMV or basis. As a consequence, a trustee exercising discretion to make distributions of assets in kind has the option to cause an immediate income tax consequence (in the form of income carried out equal to the lesser amount) or to leave the beneficiary with a deferred (and potentially avoidable) tax consequence (in the form of a basis that differs from FMV). And the fiduciary can favor different beneficiaries in different ways while giving each cash or assets in kind with equal amounts of FMV.

To illustrate, if a fiduciary has $200 of DNI and distributes two assets, each worth $100 to two different beneficiaries the effect may not be equal carryout of the DNI. Instead, if for example A received Blackacre worth $100 but with an adjusted basis of $90 and B received Greenacre worth $100 but with a basis of only $10, the DNI carried out would be $90 to A and only $10 to B. Beneficiary A likely would believe that beneficiary B received a better result, especially because the gain in either asset might never be realized (and would be taxed at a lower rate than is ordinary income, if it ever was taxable).

In addition, a fiduciary may elect to treat a nonrealization distribution as if it was a sale or exchange, intentionally recognizing gain (but maybe not loss)[8] on the distribution of property in kind.[9] That election

---

(Footnote Continued)

pursuant to agreement with beneficiary); TAM 8447003 (distribution of appreciated stock in satisfaction of beneficiary's right to receive trust income regarded as a realization event because entitlement amount was specific and fixed at the time of distribution, "[t]here [being] no requirement that the specific dollar amount must be determined prior to the date of distribution). See also § 5.8.1 nn.13-15 and accompanying text. As such, these distributions need not be subject to the rule in § 643(e)(2) dealing with distributions of assets with bases that differ from their FMVs.

[8] § 267(b)(6) disallows the recognition of loss for trust-to-beneficiary distributions and § 267(b)(13) disallows recognition of loss for estate-to-beneficiary distributions, with an exception that may not apply if the distribution described is a gain or loss realization event in all cases. See § 5.8.1 n.13.

[9] § 643(e)(3). Unfortunate about the election to incur gain is that it applies to all distributions made during the taxable year, meaning that a desire to generate

§ 5.8.1

would alter the amount of income carried out to the beneficiary by an appreciated asset,[10] and shift the gain from the distributee (who otherwise would receive it in the form of a carryover basis) to the trust or estate (assuming the gain is allocable to corpus).[11] Planning in this respect should consider whether either the entity or the distributee would pay tax in a lower bracket or has available losses to offset against any gain.

The carryover of basis and income carry out limitation of § 643(e) is affected by distributions that otherwise generate a new basis. Gain or loss[12] may be realized by distribution of an asset in kind in satisfaction of the distributee's right to receive cash (for example, Blackacre distributed in payment of a legacy or a debt)[13] or some other asset (for example, Blackacre distributed instead of the subject of a specific be-

---

(Footnote Continued)

gain and alter the income tax consequences to some but not all beneficiaries will require distributions in different tax years or actual realization events. § 643(e)(3)(B).

[10] Because realization of gain by virtue of the election would increase the basis to FMV, allowing that amount of income to carry out rather than just the lower amount of the prerealization basis. The election with respect to a depreciated asset would not alter the amount of income carried out because, in all events, that asset would carry out no more income than its FMV.

[11] See § 5.3.3.

[12] Only distributions in satisfaction of a pecuniary (cash) bequest from an estate (but not a trust) are exempt from the loss disallowance rules in §§ 267(b)(6) and 267(b)(13) and the ordinary income recapture rules in §§ 1239(b)(2) and 1239(b)(3).

[13] Treas. Reg. § 1.661(a)-2(f). See, e.g., Suisman v. Eaton, 15 F. Supp. 113 (D. Conn. 1935) (right to legacy satisfied with stock pursuant to mutual agreement of fiduciary and beneficiary); Kenan v. Commissioner, 114 F.2d 217 (2d Cir. 1940) (same except fiduciary acted pursuant to authority in document); Rev. Rul. 86-105, 1986-2 C.B. 82 (bequest of "assets, in cash or in kind . . . with a fair market value . . . equal to $2,000x" satisfied with depreciated stock, resulting in realization of loss); Rev. Rul. 82-4, 1982-1 C.B. 99 (residue of decedent's estate used to satisfy equalizing bequest under will); Rev. Rul. 56-207, 1956-1 C.B. 325 (in-kind satisfaction of formula marital deduction pecuniary bequest); Rev. Rul. 74-178, 1974-1 C.B. 196 (distribution of stock in satisfaction of creditor's claim).

Rev. Rul. 66-207, 1966-2 C.B. 243, rejected a claim that, because insufficient assets existed to fully satisfy a pecuniary bequest, the distribution of all remaining assets constituted a residuary bequest as to which gain or loss realization would not apply, concluding that the inability to satisfy the full bequest did not

quest of stock, or a non pro rata division of property conveyed in equal fractional shares).[14] In either case the income tax treatment is as if cash or the proper asset was distributed and then used in an exchange for the distributed asset, with gain or loss realization[15] and basis adjustments

---

(Footnote Continued)

alter the nature of the entitlement or the gain and loss consequences of its satisfaction.

[14] Compare Rev. Rul. 69-486, 1969-2 C.B. 159 (unauthorized non-pro-rata division of community property resulted in realization) with TAMs 8145026 (authorized non-pro-rata satisfaction of fractional bequest did not cause realization), 8447003 (distribution of an amount equal to a fraction of trust corpus when beneficiary reached a specified age deemed not a realization event, as if it was a direction to distribute a fraction of the trust, as to which the government has "a longstanding position that a distribution of a portion of principal or residue, whether pro rata or non-pro-rata, valued at the time of the distribution is not a taxable event"), and 9625020 (document and state law authorized non-pro-rata fractional-share distributions, in this case by grandchildren exercising withdrawal rights; representation that adjustments would be made among the shares for any differences in income tax liabilities of the distributions did not indicate what the adjustment would be nor whether they would generate any separate tax consequences).

The 1984 TAM also held that in-kind distributions in satisfaction of beneficiary's right to income from the trust were realization events because the income amount was specific enough at the time of distribution. It seems difficult to distinguish between the specificity in amount in the determination of an income entitlement (which was specific enough to make distribution in satisfaction of it a realization event) and the lack of specificity in the amount of corpus (which was not specific enough to regard distribution as a realization event). It also may be proper to question why fluctuations in value prior to the determination of amount is relevant to the question whether gain or loss is realized once the amount has been established and thereafter the obligation to make that distribution is satisfied with appreciated assets in kind. See also §§ 13.7.3.2.1, 13.7.4.1.1, 13.7.5.1.1, 13.7.8.1.1, and 13.7.9.1.1 regarding gain and loss realization in the most common circumstance most fiduciaries encounter, being the distribution of property in kind in satisfaction of marital deduction formula bequests.

[15] Notice, however, that the treatment generated realization to the distributing entity, not to the beneficiary. The proper treatment would be gain or loss realization to the beneficiary if the beneficiary was in charge of the decision to substitute one asset for another. See Rev. Rul. 68-666 (beneficiary requested personal representative to sell specifically bequeathed property and distribute the proceeds; treated as a distribution of the proper asset and a sale with gain or loss being realized by the distributee).

§ 5.8.1

that may preclude the income limitation in §643(e)(2) from being meaningful.

One way to make realization events such as these harmless (but not to avoid realization entirely) is for the document to specify that assets distributed in satisfaction of a bequest be valued at their basis for income tax purposes, so that the amount realized (value satisfied by distribution) and basis are equal, making any gain or loss realization equal to zero. The advantage of avoiding income tax on the distribution must be measured against the fact that the beneficiary receives property with a basis equal to the amount of the bequest but with a FMV that may be much more or less than that amount.[16]

§5.8.2 Unequal Income Tax Liabilities

A fiduciary may affect income tax consequences by the manner in which distributions are made among various beneficiaries by timing distributions and being mindful of which assets are being distributed and with what effect on basis and income carried out to the beneficiary. For example, assume that a single group trust is created for the benefit of several children of the settlor. Final distribution of the trust will be in equal shares, but interim distributions do not guarantee equality and, therefore, the separate share rules do not regard this as multiple separate trusts. If desirable, the trustee could distribute income or corpus in a manner that allocates the most DNI to the beneficiary in the lowest income tax bracket.

The trustee of this trust could make distributions to one child at the end of a year in which DNI is substantial, causing a good bit of it to be carried out with high basis assets that are distributed. The trustee then could make distributions to a second child at the beginning of the next year when there is little or no DNI to be carried out—or the trustee could make both distributions at the same time, giving the second child low basis assets—in either case with a disproportionate income tax liability.

---

[16] In the context of satisfying marital deduction formula pecuniary bequests this discretion to over- or underfund the entitlement resulted in promulgation of Rev. Proc. 64-19, 1969-1 C.B. 682, which is discussed in the context of marital deduction planning. See §13.7.4.2.1.

A dramatic illustration of this effect is in a group trust with a peel off provision. If DNI may differ in each year of the trust when a child reaches the age for making a distribution, each child who receives a share of the trust will receive a different amount of DNI carried out (to the extent of the aggregate bases of the assets distributed). Even if the FMV of the corpus distributions is equal (which is not likely, unless the fund does not change in value between distributions), the income tax liability to each child is not very likely to be equal.

In a similar vein are so-called trapping distributions, used by estates that make pour over distributions to trusts or when one trust makes distributions to another trust. Distributions of fiduciary accounting principal will be classified and remain as corpus in the recipient trust. DNI of the distributing entity that is carried out to the recipient trust is "trapped" in that trust's corpus. If the distribution had constituted fiduciary accounting income from the distributing entity it would have been allocated to income of the recipient trust. As such, the income carried over would be available for immediate distribution or taxation to the recipient trust's income beneficiary. In this way, the fiduciary accounting classification of amounts distributed has the effect of determining where the DNI will be subjected to tax and at what rates.[17]

---

[17] See United States v. Bank of America Nat'l Trust & Savings Ass'n, 326 F.2d 51 (9th Cir. 1963), and Casco Bank & Trust Co. v. United States, 76-1 U.S. Tax Cas. (CCH) ¶ 9102 (D. Maine 1975) (both involving trapping distributions to trusts with charitable remainder beneficiaries as to which, under the law then in effect, the income carried out was § 642(c) deductible because it did not pass through to the current income beneficiaries and was deemed set aside for charity); Van Buren v. Commissioner, 89 T.C. 1101 (1987) (beneficiary of simple trust could not exclude trapping distribution labeled fiduciary accounting principal that carried out DNI of an estate in an effort to cause trust tax exempt income to represent a larger portion of the trust's DNI taxable to the taxpayer); TAM 7809057.

Note that no portion of the separate share rule regulation appears to address the proper allocation of these trapping distributions (Treas. Reg. § 1.663(c)-2(b)(2) does not apply) because these amounts are not fiduciary accounting income. Treas. Reg. § 1.663(c)-2(b)(3) does not apply, because they are not IRD. And Treas. Reg. § 1.663(c)-2(b)(4) does not apply because they do not enter DNI of the recipient trust because they are allocable to corpus. Nevertheless, a proration presumably is required on the basis of the relative size of the various separate shares.

§ 5.8.2

The course to be taken in handling estate residuary distributions may depend on the relative income tax brackets of the beneficiaries and the extent to which the separate share rules apply. It may be wise to accumulate income in the estate and run administration as long as possible if those beneficiaries are in high tax brackets or have deductions that might be lost under percentage threshold limitation provisions.[18] Delay would take maximum advantage of the estate as a separate tax paying entity or to keep from boosting the beneficiaries' adjusted gross incomes and therefore their thresholds for claiming various deductions.

Alternatively, it might be desirable to make partial distributions if estate income is substantial and would be taxed in higher brackets if retained. Retaining only so much income as will utilize the estate's deduction in lieu of the personal exemption and its income tax brackets would minimize the overall tax bite. Problems may arise, however, if the beneficiaries are in different tax brackets or have other differences in their tax positions, unless the § 663(c) separate share rule for estates is applicable. This requires that the beneficiaries have "substantially separate and independent shares" of the estate that "neither affect nor are affected by the economic interests accruing to another beneficiary or class of beneficiaries."[19]

Thus, for example, assume an estate is left in equal shares to A and B and that this therefore qualifies the estate for separate share treatment. Even if A is in a low income tax bracket (and in need of funds) while B is in a high bracket (with no immediate unmet needs), estate DNI for the year would be apportioned equally between the two shares of the estate. As a result, even if assets with a basis (or FMV, if lower) of $10,000 were distributed to A while assets with a basis (or lower FMV) of only $5,000 were distributed to B, estate DNI would not be apportioned ratably between them ($2/3$ to A and $1/3$ to B). Instead, estate DNI would be split between the two shares and any income not carried out would be taxed to the proper share. Consequently, distributions need not be in lockstep or timed in the same year to equitably apportion the estate's DNI between A and B or their shares. Nevertheless, differing amounts of

---

[18] See, e.g., § § 67 and 213.

[19] H.R. Rep. No. 148, 105th Cong., 1st Sess. 620-621 (1997); Treas. Reg. § 1.663(c)-4(b). See § 5.4.3.

§ 5.8.2

FMV might be distributed (because of differences in the time when distributions are made), with differing DNI carryout consequences to each under § 643(e)(2). Correspondingly different income tax consequences would accrue to the beneficiaries and their respective shares due to the relative tax brackets in which the income might be taxed.

As a caveat with respect to all distributions, if the assets that carry out income are not liquid, the fiduciary also should consider how the beneficiary will pay the income tax on income carried out with in-kind distributions. Cash flow may be as important as the tax burden itself. In most cases early partial distributions usually are useful if a will establishes testamentary trusts or pours over into inter vivos trusts, especially if the trust can spray income among its beneficiaries. Furthermore, the tax liability may differ even though final distributions may be equal in amount in each of these situations (although the separate share rule probably will preclude the need to make any kind of compensating adjustment to equalize the net effect to the various recipients).

§ 5.8.3 Termination Deductions and Carryovers

Ordinarily, deductions allowable to a trust or an estate only benefit income beneficiaries indirectly, by reducing taxable income and, correspondingly, DNI. Deductions that exceed taxable income, however, do not pass out to the beneficiaries—Subchapter J is less than complete conduit taxation—and are wasted unless they constitute a § 172(a) net operating loss or a § 1212(b)(1) capital loss carryover to the entity's next tax year. Nevertheless, the simple trust rules are applied to determine whether all income is required to be distributed currently[20] during the period between the event that caused termination of the entity and the time when distributions and all other events cause the entity to be

---

[20] Treas. Reg. § 1.641(b)-3(c)(1). A facility of payment provision may permit the fiduciary on termination of an entity to place the distribution of a minor or other incapacitated individual in a vested share, to be held and administered by the fiduciary until the beneficiary reaches a certain age or becomes competent. This property is similar in treatment to a guardianship or custodianship for an incompetent, yet it is regarded as a continuation of the trust for income tax purposes. Thus, the fiduciary must file fiduciary income tax returns and apply normal fiduciary income tax principles. See Rev. Rul. 75-61, 1975-1 C.B. 180 (trust property retained under facility of payment provision) and § 5.2 n.4. For a version of facility of payment provision see text accompanying § 13.5.6.1.4 n.58.

§ 5.8.3

regarded as terminated. The entity essentially is ignored, as if it already had been distributed,[21] after termination is deemed to occur.[22]

Deductions that exceed income in the year of final termination[23] pass through to the beneficiaries.[24] Thus, a termination fee or state

---

[21] Treas. Reg. § 1.641(b)-3(d).

[22] As opposed to when termination is ordered. See Westphal v. Commissioner, 37 T.C. 340 (1961) (decree of termination and distribution was issued in one year but actual distribution occurred in the following year; the excess was allowable only for the subsequent year).

[23] But not the entity's § 642(b) deduction in lieu of the personal exemption or any § 642(c) charitable deduction. See § 642(h)(2) (parenthetical) and Treas. Reg. § 1.642(h)-2(a).

O'Bryan v. Commissioner, 75 T.C. 304 (1980), confronted the issue whether there were excess deductions capable of passing through to the beneficiaries in a case that involved some § 642(c) charitable deductions, the § 642(b) deduction, and some other deductions, with the total exceeding the estate's gross income. The taxpayer argued that the §§ 642(b) and 642(c) deductions should be applied against gross income first, allowing the other deductions to constitute the excess, while the government argued the exact opposite order of priority. The court concluded that Congress evinced no concern for preservation of the §§ 642(b) and 642(c) deductions and that they should be ignored entirely, allowing only any excess of the other deductions over the gross income of the estate to pass out to the beneficiaries, essentially adopting the government's theory.

[24] § 642(h). Treas. Reg. § 1.642(h)-3 provides that any beneficiary receiving assets of the entity that generated the deduction or that would abate or suffer any loss attributable to the net operating or capital losses is the proper beneficiary to receive the benefit of the carryover. In a typical estate this would be the residuary beneficiaries and, if there is no residue, any beneficiary whose preresiduary distribution would next abate due to losses in the estate. Similar principles are applied to trusts under Treas. Reg. § 1.642(h)-3(d). Consequently, the remainder beneficiaries, not the income beneficiaries, are entitled to these carryovers, proportionate to their relative interests. Treas. Reg. § 1.642(h)-4; Rev. Rul. 59-392, 1959-2 C.B. 163. Quaere whether this proportionality can be altered by partial distributions prior to the year of termination. This would not be a proper determinant because it would allow allocation of excess deductions to certain favored beneficiaries. In a similar vein, Sletteland v. Commissioner, 43 T.C. 602 (1965), held that the excess deduction passthrough applies only to the actual beneficiary of the estate and not to any assignee of the beneficiary. Furthermore, in a pour over will to a following trust, any carrythrough to the trust is the trust's entitlement, not that of its beneficiaries. Rev. Rul. 57-31, 1957-1 C.B. 201.

§ 5.8.3

income taxes paid in the final year with respect to capital gain, along with any net operating loss or capital loss carryover not previously used by the entity, all pass out as if the entity had not existed for that final year.[25] The character of items distributed is the same for the beneficiaries as it was to the estate or trust.[26] Thus, deductions that would be disallowed to the entity because allocable to tax exempt income similarly are disallowed to the beneficiary[27] and the number of years for carryforward of carryovers is the same as if the entity had not terminated.[28]

Unanswered is the question whether deductions that the entity could claim but that the beneficiary could not are subject to the limitation or lost entirely when they pass out of the entity. For example, fees for administration may be fully deductible by the entity under § 212 but subject to the 2% floor under § 67 if incurred by an individual. In this particular situation § 67(c) appears to indicate that these items should not lose their deductibility by virtue of passing out of the entity. But § 642(h) might be interpreted as if the entity's deductions were original to the beneficiaries, in which case it might be argued that they should be subject to the same limitations as if the entity had not existed and the beneficiary had generated the items in the first instance.

The passive activity loss rules have their greatest significance for trusts and estates in the context of distributions. Although it is clear that these rules are applicable to trusts and estates,[29] only one case has ruled

---

[25] Thus, for example, Rev. Rul. 58-191, 1958-1 C.B. 149, held that § 175 farming expenses that exceeded the § 175(b) limitation (expenses exceeding 25% of gross income cap were not deductible) could not be claimed by the beneficiary any more than they would have been claimed by the trust.

[26] Treas. Reg. § § 1.642(h)-1(b) and 1.642(h)-2, preserving even the tax preference nature of items for purposes of the minimum tax on preference items.

[27] See Whittemore v. United States, 383 F.2d 824 (8th Cir. 1967), rev'g 257 F. Supp. 1008 (E.D. Mo. 1966).

[28] Dorfman v. Commissioner, 294 F.2d 651 (2d Cir. 1968), rev'g 48 T.C. 478 (1967), holding Treas. Reg. § 1.642(h)-1(b) invalid to the extent it reduced the number of carryover years.

[29] See § 469(a)(2)(A) and Temp. Treas. Reg. § § 1.469-1T(b)(2) and (b)(3) (excepting only grantor trusts, presumably only to the extent the trust is treated as a grantor trust and probably only until the trust ceases to be a grantor trust; nothing yet indicates how the conversion of a grantor trust at the grantor's death or otherwise will be treated).

§ 5.8.3

on how to measure active participation in a real estate investment or material participation in a trade or business. It held that the trustee's activities alone were adequate and that activity of any employees and agents of the fiduciary, plus activity of the beneficiary all counts.[30]

Nevertheless, as with individual taxpayers, passive losses cannot be used to offset any income other than passive activity income until there is a taxable disposition of the passive investment.[31] Following disposition

---

[30] Carter Trust v. United States, 256 F. Supp. 2d 536 (N.D. Tex. 2003). See Temp. Treas. Reg. §§ 1.469-5T(g) and -8 (both reserved for future elaboration on the application of the passive activity loss rules to trusts and estates). S. Rep. No. 313, 99th Cong., 2d Sess. 735 (1986), indicates that the fiduciary's activities are the relevant inquiry and the passive versus active determination is meant to be made at the entity level, although the issue is not nearly that easy (which may be indicated by the fact that the regulations have not been drafted in this respect). Nevertheless, relying on the Senate Report and repeating the government's position that *Carter* was wrong to consider employee activity, TAM 200733023 concluded that activities of a "special trustee" did not establish active participation, and PLR 201029014 articulates that "the sole means for a trust to establish material participation is if its fiduciary is involved in the operation of the entity on a regular, continuous, and substantial basis." See generally Ferguson, Freeland, & Ascher, Federal Income Taxation of Estates, Trusts, and Beneficiaries § 8.01 (3d ed. 2011); Schmolka, Passive Activity Losses, Trusts, and Estates: The Regulations (If I Were King), 58 Tax L. Rev. 191 (2005); Lane, Application of Passive Activity and Alternative Minimum Tax Rules to Estates and Trusts, 41 Major Tax Plan. ch. 16 (1989) (arguing that material participation should be tested at the entity level and *again* at the beneficiary level if income passes through so that, if the beneficiary is active, interposition of the fiduciary as owner of the asset will not defeat the proper characterization of income the beneficiary actually receives); Abbin, To Be [Active] or Not to Be [Passive]: That is the Question Confronting Fiduciaries and Beneficiaries Trying to Apply the Passive Activity Loss (PAL) Rules, 23 U. Miami Inst. Est. Plan. ¶¶ 305-306 (1989) (recounting recommendations of the American Institute of Certified Public Accountants and of the American Bar Association, along with predictions of the government's yet to be formulated response).

[31] For example, upon a sale or exchange, presumably including any distribution that is deemed to be a sale or exchange or as to which the fiduciary made the § 643(e)(3) election. See § 5.8.1, regarding the § 643(e)(3) election. In essence the same treatment applies under § 469(g)(2) upon a passive investment owner's death, in the sense that the passive activity losses are converted into nonpassive losses. There is a difference that makes death appear dissimilar under § 469(g)(2) from a taxable disposition in that these losses are lost to the extent of any basis increase under § 1014(b) by virtue of inclusion of the

the losses are offset against any gain from the disposition and then are converted into nonpassive losses[32] that might[33] be utilized by the fiduciary against other income or gains. Excess losses not utilized in either manner are trapped in the entity.[34] Distribution of the passive investment by the entity in a nonrealization transaction preserves the passive activity losses in the sense that the losses are added to the basis of the distributed asset. Although they cannot ever be deducted thereafter, any future realization event will generate a larger loss or a smaller gain due to the basis increase.[35]

§5.8.4 Compensatory (Equitable) Adjustments

On occasion a fiduciary's overriding duty of impartiality to the beneficiaries conflicts with its obligation to preserve corpus by reducing taxes. These conflicts can create a dilemma that must be resolved by taking actions that either are appropriate or unavoidable for tax purposes and then compensating for inequities through various equitable adjustments.

(Footnote Continued)

investment in the decedent's gross estate. The net result is as if death was a realization event and the passive activity losses were used first to offset the gain that the new basis at death rule obviates. See also § 469(i)(4), which preserves some real estate passive activity losses in the context of a decedent's estate.

[32] § 469(g)(1).

[33] Subject to the § 267 related party transaction disallowance rules.

[34] Excess losses are available to beneficiaries only to the extent permitted under § 642(h), on termination of the entity, and § 469(j)(12) appears to trump the passthrough of losses otherwise available at that time. Quaere whether § 469(g)(1)(B) prohibits use by a related party beneficiary, notwithstanding § 267(d), which otherwise permits disallowed losses to be claimed by beneficiaries against future gain.

[35] Under § 469(j)(12) this treatment means that, in an indirect manner, the losses are preserved, subject to disallowance on certain transactions, such as a § 267 related party transaction.

The same result applies when a passive investment is transferred by an individual by gift. See § 469(j)(6) (the words "with respect to which a deduction has not been allowed by reason of subsection (a)" that appear in § 469(j)(6) but do not appear in § 469(j)(12) notwithstanding). A different, pseudo-realization result is imposed by § 469(g)(2) on a passive investment owner's death. § 5.8.3 n.31.

§ 5.8.4

The most frequently encountered of these circumstances involves the § 642(g) election and a corresponding *Warms* adjustment. This situation involves an estate that is subject to payment of FET and has an election whether to use estate expenses as an FET deduction under §§ 2053 and 2054 or to use those expenses (to the extent possible) to reduce estate income taxes.[36] The unavoidable choice is between reducing taxable income that will reduce DNI that should reduce the income tax that income beneficiaries would incur, or reducing FET that would leave more corpus for the remainder beneficiaries.

Unless the income and remainder beneficiaries are the same, the alternative will require that someone be hurt to benefit someone else. This calls for an adjustment, notwithstanding that the fiduciary has no choice about the matter—being required to elect on which return to claim the deduction and probably being required to make the election that produces the greatest tax saving.

More subtle about this election is the consequence in an estate that qualifies for the FET marital deduction. Deduction of the expenses for FET purposes merely reduces the amount of marital bequest needed to eliminate tax in the estate. Followed by a corresponding reduction in the FET incurred on S's subsequent death. Use for income tax purposes, on the other hand, has the consequence of increasing the marital bequest and reducing current income taxes payable by the income beneficiaries.

To illustrate,[37] assume a $6,500,000 gross estate of a decedent who died in 2012, which incurred $50,000 of deductible expenses that are subject to the § 642(g) election, and that the balance of the estate plan is an optimum marital deduction formula bequest to a marital deduction trust of the QTIP variety, with a nonmarital trust of the residue. Because the unified credit in 2012 sheltered $5,120,000 of taxable estate, the effect of claiming the deduction on the two different returns is:

---

[36] See § 5.3.1 at text accompanying nn.32-35.

[37] See § 13.3.6, with respect to the marital deduction aspects of this.

Deduct on Form 706 FET Return		Deduct on Form 1041 Income Tax Return
$6,500,000	Gross Estate	$6,500,000
(50,000)	Deductions	(0)
1,330,000	Marital Bequest	1,380,000
5,120,000	Taxable Estate	5,120,000
5,120,000	Nonmarital Residue	5,070,000

The residue in the right column is $50,000 smaller because the expenses were paid but not deducted, meaning that they are not reflected in the FET calculation. Instead, they reduce income tax.

Obviously, not all beneficiaries will be happy about the results of the election, regardless of how the personal representative chooses, because there is a dollar for dollar shift between the marital and nonmarital shares based on the return on which the deductions are claimed. Moreover, regardless of how the respective remainder beneficiaries come out, S in most cases is the income beneficiary who gains from the income tax deduction, meaning that there is tension between income and remainder beneficiaries as well as between the remainder beneficiaries of the respective portions of the estate. In this context, an adjustment is said to be necessary,[38] although it is not clear how it should be made.[39]

A second common source of inequity relates to more general elections. For example, if a fiduciary sells assets and incurs gain, any selling

---

[38] See, e.g., In re Estate of Warms, 140 N.Y.S.2d 169 (Surr. Ct. 1955); In re Levy's Estate, 167 N.Y.S.2d 16 (Surr. Ct. 1957); Estate of Bixby, 295 P.2d 68 (Cal. Ct. App. 1956); In re Kent's Estate, 23 Fla. Supp. 133 (Palm Beach County 1964); In re Veith's Estate, 26 Fla. Supp. 145 (Dade County 1965).

[39] This uncertainty is particularly acute if the election is made to claim the deductions for income tax purposes, because the formula pecuniary marital bequest must be $1,500,000 in the example to produce the optimum deduction result called for. Reduction of that bequest by a principal to principal allocation to compensate for the effect of the election would diminish the marital deduction and defeat the decedent's intent. Further, if income was used to compensate principal of the nonmarital portion, in this case there is not enough income tax saved ($50,000 of deduction times the income tax rate) to fully compensate for the differential in the respective bequests. Moreover, even if there was, there might be a question whether diversion of income even as required under a state law adjustment requirement might violate the all-income-annually mandate of the QTIP marital trust. It also would cause income tax consequences because the marital and nonmarital shares are separate trusts for income tax purposes.

§ 5.8.4

expenses may be used to reduce the gain (which benefits the remainder beneficiary because corpus ordinarily pays the tax on capital gain) or as a straight income tax deduction (which benefits the income beneficiary). The limited authority in this area splits on the need to make an adjustment, notwithstanding that the benefit or denial of benefit attributable to the election cannot be avoided.[40]

A third source of compensating adjustment concern is "trapping" and non pro rata distributions. Trapping often is an intentional endeavor[41] to cause DNI to be trapped in corpus and taxed to a distributee entity instead of to the income beneficiaries. Non pro rata distributions are less likely to occur because the § 663(c) separate share rule makes it difficult for one beneficiary to receive an early distribution that has the effect of carrying out more DNI than another beneficiary's later but equal distribution. But it can occur in a group trust with a peel off provision[42] or due to distributions of assets with equal FMVs but different bases, causing a different § 643(e)(2) DNI carryout to each.[43] When these situations do occur, however, compensating adjustments have been required to restore the beneficiaries who pay tax to positions of

---

[40] Compare Rice Estate, 8 Pa. D. & C.2d 379 (1956) (calling for an income to principal adjustment), with In re Kent's Estate, 23 Fla. Supp. 133 (1964), and In re Estate of Dick, 218 N.Y.S.2d 185 (1961) (rejecting the suggestion that an adjustment is necessary). Cf. Harris Trust & Savings Bank v. MacLean, 542 N.E.2d 943, 948 (Ill. App. Ct. 1989), and New England Merchants Nat'l Bank v. Converse, 369 N.E.2d 982, 985 (Mass. 1977), in both of which state income taxes paid by corpus on capital gains incurred by trusts was used as a federal income tax deduction. The courts refused to mandate equitable adjustments notwithstanding that trust corpus produced the deduction that benefited the income beneficiaries. *MacLean* stated the belief that "equitable adjustments should be applied only in response to inequities resulting from a trustee's discretionary decisions which favor one beneficiary over another." *Converse* stated that it would not mandate an adjustment program, particularly because the fiduciary had not been doing so from inception and now would be asked to change its practice prospectively. Yet the court did not intend to question those fiduciaries who chose to adjust or to "decide what is to be done . . . if the inequity resulting from the Federal tax laws appears particularly dramatic and significant, as it apparently did in *Rice Estate*. No such case is presented to us."

[41] See § 5.8.2.

[42] See § 5.8.2.

[43] See § 5.8.1.

§ 5.8.4

equality by requiring one beneficiary to compensate the other,[44] as with a principal to principal or an income to principal allocation (which could have DNI consequences).

A fourth source of unavoidable inequity exists if depreciation is available for deduction by a fiduciary entity. Benefited by that deduction would be the income beneficiaries whose income tax is reduced, but paying the price are the beneficiaries of corpus who bear the tax on any gain generated on sale, especially if that gain is subject to recapture and is taxed as ordinary income. Adjustment again is required, by making another income to principal allocation.[45]

Several final sources of inequality still appear to be beyond relief under the limited case law that has developed. The first involves IRD and DRD[46] and the § 691(c) income tax deduction granted to income beneficiaries for FET incurred on items of IRD, even though the income beneficiaries may not have been the beneficiaries who paid the FET. In addition, items of deduction in respect of a decedent reduce income in respect of the same decedent in computing the income tax on the net amount. Again this benefits the income beneficiaries even though they may not have been the ones who paid the expenses that constituted the DRD. In each of these cases the income beneficiaries should compensate the payor of the tax or deductible expense, at least to the extent of the benefit gleaned from avoiding income tax on the amount of the offset

---

[44] In re Estate of Holloway, 323 N.Y.S.2d 534 (1971) (trapping adjustment required), and In re Estate of Cooper, 186 So. 2d 844 (Fla. Dist. Ct. App. 1966) (non-pro-rata division adjustment required). Cf. Harkness v. United States, 469 F.2d 310 (Ct. Cl. 1972) (income tax case, not a state court adjustment action, illustrating the inequity of a fractional division of an estate in which payments of taxes and claims did not carry out income but matching distributions to S to preserve the same income division during administration of the estate did carry out DNI so that, from what should have been an equal division of the estate, a roughly 75-25% split of the income tax liability resulted; one solution would have been to split the estate and cause an equal division of the income tax liability, followed by the nonspousal share paying the taxes and claims from its share, but this was not what the document called for, and the other solution may apply now that Congress has extended the § 663(c) separate share rule to estates, which was not the law when this estate was administered).

[45] See In re Estate of Pross, 396 N.Y.S.2d 309 (Surr. Ct. 1977).

[46] See § 5.10.4 n.64 and accompanying text.

§ 5.8.4

IRD. No problem exists if the equality dictated by the document is pervasive enough to cause the separate share rule to apply.

A second unresolved source of potential adjustment relates to § 643(e),[47] because it is possible for equal distributions of FMV to carry out differing amounts of DNI. Arguably there should be an adjustment if a document calls for equal distributions but the fiduciary causes one recipient to bear a disproportionate share of DNI. In this case the countervailing issue is how to account for any built in capital gain tax liability attributable to the fact that the income tax favored beneficiary received property with a lower basis (which explains why less income was carried out) that will be incurred only at some time in the future and only if that beneficiary ever sells the asset.

A third source of potential adjustment relates to the excess deduction passthrough rule[48] and the absence of the separate share rule[49] for purposes other than the computation of DNI and its carry out to beneficiaries. To illustrate, assume a single trust with separate shares for beneficiaries A and B that distribute when the beneficiary reaches a specified age. Also assume that, in the year A reached that age, taxable income of A's share is less than the termination fee payable from the corpus of A's share. The separate share rule does not apply with respect to allocation of the deduction for this termination fee,[50] and the excess deduction carryout rule will not permit its allocation to A (because this is only a partial termination of the trust), The result is that the deduction will benefit B notwithstanding that A essentially paid for it. No adjustment yet appears to require that B compensate A in this context.

There is virtually no authority regarding the income tax consequences of equitable adjustments. For example, assume a trapping distribution was made from an estate to a trust, followed by a *Holloway* adjustment that allowed trust income in a subsequent year to compensate trust corpus for income taxes that corpus paid attributable to the trapped income. The question is the tax effect of these distributions and adjustments.

---

[47] See § 5.8.1.

[48] § 642(h). See § 5.8.3 nn.23-25 and accompanying text.

[49] § 663(c). See § 5.4.3.

[50] See § 5.4.3 n.68.

TAM 8501011 determined that the trust would not cease to be a simple trust in the year a *Holloway* adjustment was made, notwithstanding allocation of income to corpus rather than current distribution. Applicable state law required the adjustment and, therefore, under Treas. Reg. § 1.651(a)-2, the amount allocated to corpus to work the adjustment was not "income" for purposes of §§ 651 and 661. Instead, income was determined under state law and, by virtue of the adjustment, this taxable income was fiduciary accounting corpus under state law. Thus, the trust did not run afoul of the dictate that all income must be distributed currently to qualify as a simple trust. Moreover, under § 652(a), the trust income beneficiaries would not be required to include the amount of income allocated to corpus in their income for the year (and, presumably, the trust would not have a distributions deduction for the amount of that income either), meaning that the income allocated to corpus would be taxed to the trust.

The TAM did not determine whether the income taxes on income allocated to corpus would be a charge to income or to corpus, but corpus should be entitled to a compensating adjustment "net" of income taxes, sufficient to adjust for the initial inequity of having corpus pay taxes on estate income. This would mean that trust income must compensate corpus and pay income taxes attributable to the adjustment. It should not matter whether the taxes were paid by the income account out of income retained for that purpose or were paid out of the corpus account from amounts transferred to corpus for that use. In either event a circular calculation would be required, because income used to pay taxes would generate no § 651(a) deduction, which would result in higher trust taxes, which would require retention of added income for payment of those taxes, which would result again in a smaller distributions deduction, which would result in higher taxes, ad infinitum. For example, if corpus was to pay income taxes on the adjustment, a formula to determine the amount of the adjustment needed to produce the proper compensation net of tax would be the amount of the adjustment (net of tax) ÷ 1 minus the rate of tax.

As TAM 8501084 illustrates, however, even this formula may not produce exactly the right result. In that situation the government was asked to reconsider its conclusion in TAM 8501011, which it confirmed. In so doing, however, the government noted that the adjustment constituted UNI for purposes of the accumulation distribution and throwback rules. This creates uncertainty regarding the rate of tax in the formula *if* throwback will apply. Because the ultimate distributee's bracket for throwback computation purposes may not be ascertainable until many years in the future. This added wrinkle probably must be ignored if an adjustment is made in the first instance, and in most cases § 665(c)(2) will preclude application of the throwback rule. Assuming these conclusions and extrapolations are correct, one reassuring aspect of these determinations is that they treat state law as controlling in determining the amount of income for the year that is available for distribution (after making the adjustment) and accords the adjustment itself no special income tax treatment.[51]

Two other essential difficulties exist in this area. One is to recognize the inequality and thus the potential need to adjust, and the other is knowing how to adjust. The law on both issues is immature, especially with respect to the second element.[52] A proper adjustment would compensate the injured party for the inequity, but typically the adjustments dictated to date do not purge any additional benefit gained by the other party.[53] Courts appear unsure of how to accomplish the obvious objective. Meaning that estate planners may be well advised to consider

---

[51] With respect to the entire issue of the income tax consequences of equitable adjustments, see Blattmachr, A Primer on the Effects of Equitable Adjustments, 127 Trusts & Estates 21 (June 1985); Blattmachr, The Tax Effects of Equitable Adjustments: An Internal Revenue Code Odyssey, 18 U. Miami Inst. Est. Plan. ¶ 1400 (1984); Boyle, Tax Consequences of Equitable Adjustments, 37 S.C. L. Rev. 583 (1986).

[52] An excellent, comprehensive article on this topic that is essential reading for all estate planners is Dobris, Equitable Adjustments in Postmortem Income Tax Planning: An Unremitting Diet of *Warms*, 65 Iowa L. Rev. 103 (1979), with a sequel in Limits on the Doctrine of Equitable Adjustment in Sophisticated Post-Mortem Tax Planning, 66 Iowa L. Rev. 273 (1981). See also Moore, Conflicting Interests in Postmortem Planning, 9 U. Miami Inst. Est. Plan. ¶ 1900 (1975); Moore, Conflicts in Post-Mortem Planning After the Tax Reform Act, 12 U. Miami Inst. Est. Plan ¶ 600 (1978), Carrico & Bondurant, Equitable Adjustments: A Survey & Analysis of Precedents & Practice, 36 Tax Law. 545 (1983). An updated version of the state law compilation in this article is American College of Trust and Estate Counsel Study 18, Equitable Adjustments (1997).

[53] There always should be a benefit in excess of the detriment suffered by the injured party because, otherwise, the election would have produced no advantage and presumably would have been made the other way.

§ 5.8.4

whether the fiduciary ought to be granted discretion to make the relevant elections or to administer the estate in a manner that produces inequalities, but directed not to make adjustments to compensate for their effects (because it is not clear how to do so,[54] and probably cannot be made clear in advance of some situations). Language such as this would serve the purpose:

> The [fiduciary] shall make such elections under the tax laws as the [fiduciary] deems advisable, without regard to the relative interests of the beneficiaries, and may make distributions from time to time, to one or more but less than all beneficiaries notwithstanding the relative interests of the beneficiaries, and from income or principal of the estate, all in the [fiduciary's] uncontrolled discretion. No adjustment shall be made between principal and income or in the relative interests of the beneficiaries to compensate for the effect of elections under the tax laws or other actions by the [fiduciary].

A second alternative approach would authorize but absolve the fiduciary from the obligation to adjust. This might be problematic because the fiduciary often will be unsure how to exercise the discretion, which also might be deemed to give sufficient latitude to call into question whether some benefits are ascertainable and therefore may be subject to challenge (as, for example, might be the government's argument with respect to a marital deduction formula bequest subject to a *Warms* adjustment in the fiduciary's discretion). And a third alternative would direct the fiduciary not to exercise discretion in administration in a manner that creates the inequity in the first instance. This likely is undesirable because it forecloses too many income tax opportunities.

§5.9 INCOME TAXATION OF CHARITABLE TRUSTS

There are four federal income tax regimes that may apply to trusts that benefit charity:[1]

---

[54] For example, should the fiduciary be directed to obtain the beneficiary's income tax return and attempt to ascertain what their taxes would have been had the fiduciary's election been otherwise, and how should any remaining benefit be allocated after making the beneficiary whole?

[1] §5.9 In addition to the resources cited throughout this material, several detailed, comprehensive, and useful sources on the topic are Breir & Knauer, Charitable Remainder Trusts and Pooled Income Funds, 435-2d Tax Mgmt. (BNA) Estates, Gifts, and Trusts Port. (1995); Breir & Knauer, Charitable

§5.9.1 Wholly Charitable Trusts

Qualified §501 trusts are totally exempt from federal income taxation. Issues that relate to their administration and penalties that may be imposed typically are no concern of estate planners on behalf of donors to such trusts.

§5.9.2 Qualified Remainder ("Split Interest") Trusts

Charitable remainder annuity trusts (CRATs) and charitable remainder unitrusts (CRUTs) provide for a noncharitable beneficiary for a period of time, followed by a remainder to a qualified charity.[2] They too are totally exempt from federal income tax[3] unless tainted with §512 unrelated business taxable income.[4]

Distributions[5] from these trusts to their noncharitable lead beneficiaries carry out income under §664(b) and special character rules

(Footnote Continued)

Income Trusts, 442 Tax Mgmt. (BNA) Estates, Gifts, and Trusts Port. (1993); and the exhaustive policy oriented exegesis in Schmolka, Income Taxation of Charitable Remainder Trusts and Decedents' Estates: Sixty-Six Years of Astigmatism, 40 Tax L. Rev. 1 (1984).

[2] See §14.3.2.

[3] See §664(c) and §14.3.2.1 regarding the qualification of these entities under the highly technical rules of §664.

[4] Prior to 2006 any unrelated business taxable income would taint the entire trust. See Treas. Reg. §1.664-1(c) and Newhall Unitrust v. Commissioner, 104 T.C. 236 (1995). Even a smidgen of unrelated business taxable income made all trust income taxable for the year. Ferguson, Freeland, & Ascher, Federal Income Taxation of Estates, Trusts, and Beneficiaries §9.2.2 n.20 at 7 (2d ed. 1996), suggested that Congress "probably intended to subject only the unrelated business taxable income to taxation." Congress proved them right by amending §664(c)(2)(A) to now impose a 100% excise tax on unrelated business taxable income in a CRT but otherwise not taint the trust's exempt status. See Ferguson, Freeland, & Ascher, Federal Income Taxation of Estates, Trusts, and Beneficiaries §11.02[B] (3d ed. 2011). By Treas. Reg. §1.664-1(c)(1) the excise tax is charged to corpus of the trust and does not generate a deduction; the unreduced income is allocable to the trust tiers like any other income, available to carry out to the trust beneficiaries, apparently with the potential to be taxed as unrelated business taxable income again if a beneficiary is another qualified charitable trust (although that character rule element is not addressed by the regulation).

[5] Like those that govern any mandatory distribution from a noncharitable trust, these tax consequences apply even if required distributions are not timely.

§5.9.2

specify how distributions are treated in the hands of the beneficiary. These character rules apply even in years in which the trust has any unrelated business taxable income[6] and override the normal pro rata allocation rules that govern the balance of Subchapter J.[7]

These "ordering" or character passthrough rules provide that, up to the full amount distributed, a noncharitable beneficiary is regarded as receiving (1) ordinary income of the trust from the pool of undistributed prior years' net ordinary income and then from current year ordinary income, then (2) net short term capital gain (on a cumulative basis) from the pool of undistributed prior years' and then current year net short term capital gain, followed by (3) net long term capital gain (on a cumulative basis) from the pool of undistributed prior years' and then current year net long term capital gain, then (4) "other"[8] income of the prior and current years and, finally, (5) a tax free distribution of corpus. In essence, this is a worst-in, first-out (WIFO) rule.

(Footnote Continued)

See, e.g., Treas. Reg. § 1.664-1(d)(4), which establishes a timing rule that the annuity or unitrust amount is includible in the year in which it is required to be distributed, even if it is not distributed until after the close of that year. If those distributions are made to a beneficiary's estate after the beneficiary's death they are reported as IRD by the beneficiary's estate on its tax return, not on the beneficiary's final income tax return. Treas. Reg. § 1.664-1(d)(4)(iii).

[6] In light of the 2006 amendment to § 664(c)(2)(A), presumably a change will be made to the parenthetical "(whether or not the trust is exempt)" found in Treas. Reg. § 1.664-1(d)(1)(i), referring to trusts that were nonexempt under Treas. Reg. § 1.664-1(c) because of unrelated business taxable income.

[7] The trust is taxed essentially as if it was a complex trust. The § 664 split interest trust rules also trump the grantor trust rules to the extent neither the grantor nor the grantor's spouse is beneficiary of anything more than the lead unitrust or annuity trust interest. Treas. Reg. § 1.664-1(a)(4) provides that retention of the lead interest does not cause the grantor trust rules to apply. However, possession of any other interest or power that would trigger application of the grantor trust rules will cause the trust to fail to qualify as a qualified CRT and allow the grantor trust rules to trump the § 664 allocation rules. See Rev. Rul. 77-285, 1977-2 C.B. 213.

[8] Treas. Reg. § 1.664-1(d)(1)(i)(a)(3) defines other income as any that is excluded under Part III of the income tax provisions, meaning §§ 101-136, and would include such familiar sorts of income as proceeds of life insurance and tax exempt municipal bond interest.

§ 5.9.2

Distributions to a qualified charity from a qualified split interest trust that are made during the term preceding the charitable remainder (and therefore that are very rare) are deemed to be made in the exact reverse order, which preserves the greatest amount of income to be taxed to the noncharitable beneficiary and limits the amount of income distributed to charity that might qualify for a § 642(c) deduction.[9]

In either case, each pool is depleted seriatim by distributions until entirely exhausted before any part of the distribution is deemed to carry out any part of the next pool. Excess deductions and losses do not carry out to the beneficiaries or over to other pools, and losses and deductions within a given pool are netted against only the income or gains in that pool in determining the net amount available in the pool,[10] with a carryover from prior years of items that are not carried out from the prior year.[11] Relatively detailed accounting is required as a result of these and similar rules.

Because of the pool of income and seriatim carryout rules, it is not true that a grantor can create a qualified CRUT or CRAT, retain the lead interest, and transfer appreciated property to the trust to avoid capital gains tax when the trust sells the corpus and reinvests in a diversified portfolio. It is true, however, that the grantor's eventual realization of the trust's capital gain will be deferred until the grantor receives distributions of the lead interest that carry out that gain under these character rules.[12]

---

[9] Treas. Reg. § 1.664-1(e). See § 5.9 n.40 and accompanying text regarding the § 642(c) income tax deduction for amounts paid to charity.

[10] Treas. Reg. § 1.664-1(d)(1)(ii), with the exception in Treas. Reg. § 1.664-1(d)(1)(i)(b) that net long- and short-term gains and losses are offset against each other along the same principles found in § 1212. See Treas. Reg. § 1.664-1(d), Notice 99-17, 1999-1 C.B. 871, and Notice 98-20, 1998-1 C.B. 776, with respect to application of these rules within the context of the various forms of ordinary income and long term capital gain, in each case with some varieties (e.g., qualified dividend income or depreciation recapture long term capital gain) being taxed at more or less favorable rates, and consistently applying the oldest, most expensive, WIFO category-by-category principle applicable throughout this regime, all nicely explained in Teitell, New CRT Capital Gain (Tier Two) Rules Highest Income Tax First Out (HITFO), 24 ACTEC Notes 86 (1998).

[11] Treas. Reg. § 1.664-1(d)(1).

[12] See § 7.1.5.5.

Within the context of these rules, taxpayers have developed a number of strategies designed to accomplish essentially noncharitable objectives, and the government has attempted to minimize or eliminate those. By way of example, PLR 9506015 involved a CRUT provision that changed the lead annual noncharitable payout from the lesser of all income or the designated payment—with a deficiency catch-up provision—to a straight unitrust payment. That change was triggered if the trust disposed of a certain asset. Commonly known as "flip" unitrusts, because the unitrust payment format changes in the trustee's discretion or upon a stated contingency (such as sale of a particular asset), these are referred to by the government as the "combination of methods" approach in its sample CRUT forms (see the listing in § 14.3.2.1 n.50).

These trusts became sufficiently popular and raised issues of such significance to the government that they were the impetus for new regulations[13] that authorize flip unitrusts that change from a net income (with or without deficiency catch-up provision) to a straight unitrust interest (but not vice versa), but only if the conversion is "mandatory"— not subject to the trustee's exercise of discretion.[14] The following conditions must be met: (1) conversion is required upon a specified date or event that is not regarded as discretionary (although the event actually may permit a great deal of control or discretion—such as sale of particular asset contributed to the trust for just that purpose);[15] (2) the conver-

---

[13] Treas. Reg. § 1.664-3(a)(1)(i)(c). Trusts with nonqualifying flip provisions that predate December 10, 1998 (when the regulations became final) may be reformed to meet these requirements, but trusts created after the effective date with a flip provision that does not comply may be reformed only to eliminate the flip provision. The date originally specified in Treas. Reg. § 1.664-3(a)(1)(i)(f)(3) was extended to June 30, 2000 by Notice 99-31. No provision appears to specify the result applicable to trusts created before the effective date that are not reformed.

[14] At least that is the theory, not totally met as Treas. Reg. § 1.664-3(a)(1)(i)(d) and examples in § 1.664-3(a)(1)(i)(e) reveal.

[15] Examples in the regulation include sale of the donor's former personal residence or of an unregistered security or other nonmarketable asset. Unmarketable is defined by reference to Treas. Reg. § 1.664-1(a)(7)(ii). If issues germane to a related party trustee are not a concern, presumably a family member or other amenable trustee can be responsible for making the triggering sale. Other examples are not so susceptible of manipulation, such as a beneficiary's attainment of a specified age, marriage, divorce, death, or birth of a child.

§ 5.9.2

sion—which occurs at the beginning of the next taxable year following the triggering event—is to a fixed percentage unitrust interest with no income exception or deficiency catch-up option; and (3) any prior deficiency amount is forfeited.[16]

The regulations[17] also permit allocation to income of realized capital gain only to the extent the proceeds of any sale exceed the asset's FMV on the date of contribution. This precludes allocation of precontribution capital gain to income, but permits total portfolio return trust investments by which growth or income are both permissible objectives and either can be used to meet the trust's distribution requirements.[18]

In addition, § 2702 precludes a form of aggressive planning by which successive single life unitrust interests would be created in a single trust, with the former being retained by the settlor and consisting of the NIMCRUT variety. The successor would be given to a family member, the anticipation being that the trust would be funded with assets that are invested to produce substantial capital appreciation and little or no current income, meaning that a substantial deficiency catch-up amount would be accumulated. The secondary unitrust beneficiary would become entitled to the deficiency amount following termination of the settlor's unitrust interest, and that amount conveniently would be paid from the proceeds of a sale of corpus of a trust that permits reinvestment of the trust portfolio to produce sufficient income during the second unitrust beneficiary's enjoyment. By ignoring the retained value of the

---

[16] Presumably with no tax consequence to the unitrust beneficiary, although this is not specified in the regulation. Because the prior deficiency amount is extinguished, this requirement squelched the use of flip unitrusts as a method for the lead unitrust beneficiary to use a CRUT as a form of retirement fund—accumulating a huge deficiency tax free prior to the flip that would be paid out at a later time, after the flip, perhaps when the taxpayer was in a lower tax bracket.

[17] Treas. Reg. § 1.664-3(a)(1)(i)(b)(4).

[18] See PLRs 199907013 and 9833008 (allocation of postcontribution capital gain to income is permissible, the 1998 Ruling even allowing reformation of the trust to *add* that authority, based on a representation that it was inadvertently omitted due to scrivener's error). PLRs 9511029 and 9511007 contained lesser of the income or unitrust amount provisions with deficiency catch-up alternatives (sometimes known as a NIMCRUT—a net income CRUT with the income deficiency catch-up option).

donor's lead interest for gift tax purposes[19] the effort sought to avoid wealth transfer taxation on the deficiency amount shifted from the settlor to the secondary beneficiary.

Yet another form of abusive planning was touted at the time as a mechanism to convert a taxpayer's unrealized capital gain with little tax cost. To illustrate, assume D owns stock in Corp. with a basis of virtually zero but a FMV of $10 zillion. D creates a two year CRUT that will pay D an annual annuity equal to 90% of the annual FMV of the trust. For the first year the trust owes D an annuity of $9 zillion but has no cash with which to pay it. If the trust sold the stock[20] to generate sufficient cash the capital gain realized on that sale would constitute the taxpayer's distribution under the ordering rules of § 664(b)(2), so the trustee delays the distribution until shortly into year 2,[21] when the trustee sells the stock and uses the cash proceeds to make the year 1 payment. Under the ordering authority of § 664(b) this distribution is alleged to be a corpus distribution because, during year 1, the trust had no ordinary income, no capital gain, and no other income that could constitute the distribution.

If this was successful, D would receive cash proceeds of $9 zillion from sale of the original stock investment of $10 zillion, totally tax free, whereas if D had sold the stock prior to its contribution to the trust the net wealth remaining after incurring a capital gains tax on the full $10 zillion of proceeds would have been far less than what D has received. As a follow-up but of slight significance to D, in year 2 the trust owes D an annuity of 90% of the FMV of the trust at the beginning of year 2, which is alleged to be only the $1 zillion remaining after the year 1 distribution, and in year 2 the realized capital gain would flavor this minimum distribution to D. Rather than capital gain of almost the full $10 zillion of proceeds (if D had sold the stock personally), D now has capital gain of approximately $0.9 zillion. In the process a very small charitable deduction would be allowed for the value remaining in the trust after the two

---

[19] See Treas. Reg. § 25.2702-1(c)(3).

[20] Using care to avoid the anticipatory assignment of income doctrine applied in Ferguson v. Commissioner, 174 F.3d 997 (9th Cir. 1999) (taxpayer tendered shares before contributing them to a charity).

[21] Relying on Treas. Reg. § 1.664-3(a)(1)(i)(g) (distribution deemed a year 1 distribution notwithstanding that it occurred a reasonable period after the close of year 1).

§5.9.2

unitrust payments, but this is a veritable irrelevancy to the taxpayer, who engaged in the transaction for nothing other than capital gain tax avoidance.

It is no surprise that the government regards the transaction as abusive and only moderately surprising that it acted as quickly as it did to put taxpayers on notice that it will challenge the taxpayer's anticipated results.[22] The government has several theories upon which it might challenge the transaction (prearranged sale by D causes the gain to be taxable to D as if the sale occurred prior to contribution of the stock to the trust, disqualification of the trust as a qualified CRUT because it does not exist exclusively for charitable purposes, or imposition of § 4941 self-dealing transaction penalty) but those are of little moment. The device clearly is abusive, the government is right to challenge it, and no court reviewing the transaction likely would reject the government's challenge on almost any theory.

Nevertheless, leaving nothing to chance the Treasury promulgated regulations[23] providing that annuity trust and unitrust payments that are a fixed percentage (rather than a lesser income amount for the year) may be distributed within a reasonable time after the close of the taxable year, provided that the entire amount distributed is characterized as income to the recipient (of any variety—ordinary income, capital gain, or "other income" under the § 664(b) ordering rules) and not as tax free corpus, except to the extent distribution is a gain or loss realization event and the income generated is allocable to income for tax purposes for the year of distribution, meaning that it is taxed out to the recipient.[24]

---

[22] See Notice 94-78, 1994-2 C.B. 555, highlighting Treas. Reg. § 1.664-1(d)(1)(iii). A summary of the government's response is found in Teitell, IRS Tells Agents: Some NIM-CRUTs Violate Self-dealing Rules, 135 Trusts & Estates 63 (Dec. 1996).

[23] Treas. Reg. § § 1.664-2(a)(1)(i)(a) and 1.664-3(a)(1)(i)(g).

[24] A special rule applies for trusts created before December 10, 1998 if the annuity or unitrust amount is no greater than 15% of the initial FMV of the trust. Because of special administration requirements that apply to income-only uni-trusts, Treas. Reg. § 1.664-3(a)(1)(i)(j) provides a special rule that eliminates these requirements to a NIMCRUT with an income-only distribution.

§5.9.2

A third form of abusive planning was the subject of Notice 2008-99,[25] with consequent disclosure and list maintenance obligations with respect to a form of planning that the government states "has the potential for tax avoidance or evasion, but lacking enough information to determine whether the transaction should be identified specifically as a tax avoidance transaction," the Notice simply "alerts persons involved in these transactions to certain responsibilities that may arise from their involvement." The transaction entails a taxpayer who creates a CRT, retains the lead interest, and transfers an appreciated asset to it. There is no gain or loss realization on this transfer, so the trust takes a carryover of the taxpayer's basis. Then, perhaps as soon as right away, the trust sells the appreciated asset to a third party, perhaps a buyer who previously had negotiated with the taxpayer. Gain is realized on the sale but the trust is § 664(c) income tax exempt so the gain is not recognized by the trust. In ordinary course, the CRT would include the gain in the income tiers that would carry out (in this case under § 664(b)(2) as gain) to the taxpayer as beneficiary of the lead interest, so ultimately the gain would be taxed, albeit with some deferral if it would not all be taxed in the year of the sale but rather as the lead interest is distributed to the beneficiary.

The abuse comes because, before any major portion of the gain can be carried out to the lead beneficiary, the lead interest holder and the charitable remainder beneficiary join forces to sell their respective interests to a third party who will terminate the trust and take the proceeds of the sale of the original corpus. Inside the trust those proceeds have a basis equal to FMV (because the gain on the original asset was realized on the prior sale and the proceeds take a basis equal to the original asset's FMV). The taxpayer's position is that there is no gain on sale of the lead interest as part of this coordinated sale to the third party because the basis disallowance rule in § 1001(e)(1) is not applicable due to the exception in § 1001(e)(3) for sale of all interests in the trust at one time. And, because the trust has a basis equal to the value of the proceeds just received, the taxpayer takes the position that there is no gain on sale of the lead interest either, because the taxpayer's interest is entitled to its pro rata portion of the trust's FMV basis.

---

[25] 2008-2 C.B. 1194. See § 3.6.1 n.10 regarding a related transaction involving commutation of only the lead interest in a CRT.

§ 5.9.2

The taxpayer's hoped-for net result—for the loss of a small charitable component (the value of the remainder interest)—is that the taxpayer has unloaded a highly appreciated asset with no gain recognition. The Notice informs taxpayers that the government intends to study the issue and likely will issue guidance that precludes the perceived abuse. Perhaps by issuing regulations authorized by § 643(a)(7), which grants authority "to prescribe such regulations as may be necessary or appropriate to carry out the purposes of this part [meaning Part I of Subchapter J—being the taxation of estates, trusts, grantors, and beneficiaries], including regulations to prevent avoidance of such purposes."

According to Notice 2008-99 the government is "not concerned about the mere creation and funding of a CRT and/or the trust's reinvestment of the contributed appreciated property" but, instead, it is "concerned about Grantor's claim to an increased basis in the term interest coupled with the termination of the Trust in a single coordinated transaction under section 1001(e) to avoid tax on gain from the sale or other disposition of the Appreciated Assets." One option might be to regard the termination by sale to the third party as an acceleration of the taxpayer's entire interest, with income taxation in the year of that sale. Another might be to alter the basis allocation rule in § 1001(e). Until the government rules, however, it is uncertain how taxpayers should report the transaction—other than to disclose it. The disclosure obligation is stated to apply to transactions entered into after November 1, 2006, and applies to taxpayers and their material advisors who make a tax statement after that date. The Notice itself was dated October 31, 2008.

§ 5.9.3 Nonqualified Estates and Trusts

Distributions from garden-variety trusts and from estates to charity are taxable under the normal Subchapter J income tax rules but may qualify for a § 642(c) deduction[26] for distributions to qualified charities.

---

[26] § 642(c)(1) applies to both trusts and estates. Because of changes made in 1969 by enactment of § 664 with respect to certain trusts, § 642(c)(2) permits a deduction for amounts of gross income permanently set aside for a qualified charitable purpose by any estate but only by trusts created before October 9, 1969. Addition of § 645 in 1997 to provide trusts with the same benefits as estates for a limited period of estate administration may restore some estate/trust equivalence. See H.R. Rep. No. 148, 105th Cong., 1st Sess. 618-619 (1997). In any

These rules supplant the §170 charitable deduction rules otherwise applicable to individuals.[27] One common example of a nonqualified trust that may generate a charitable deduction is a CLT, which provides first for charity for a period of time and then distributes the remainder interest to noncharitable beneficiaries. CLTs are functional opposites of CRTs and are not subject to the special §664 rules for income tax purposes.

Relevant only with respect to estates and complex trusts but not to simple trusts,[28] §642(c)(1) permits an unlimited income tax deduction to the estate or trust for amounts of gross income that are applied under the terms of the governing instrument[29] to a §170(c) qualified charitable

---

(Footnote Continued)

event, in most respects the §642(c)(2) requirements are the same as those under §642(c)(1) and it is not explored separately here.

[27] Subject to a disallowance of the deduction under §681(a) to the extent the trust has unrelated business taxable income. Also subject to the overriding reality, underscored by PLR 200203034, that none of these rules is applicable to the extent the entity is not properly regarded as a trust under Treas. Reg. §§301.7701-1(a)(1) and 301.7701-4(c)(1).

[28] See §642(c) (first parenthetical); by definition under §651(a)(2), a trust cannot be a simple trust if it provides for charity.

[29] Brownstone v. United States, 465 F.3d 525 (2d Cir. 2006), denied a §642(c) deduction for amounts distributed by a trust to the estate of the holder of a general power of appointment that was exercised in favor of the powerholder's estate and, through it, to several charities. The taxpayers should have regarded the distribution as (1) a trust distribution carrying out trust DNI to the estate, followed by (2) an estate distribution to charity generating a §642(c) income tax charitable deduction to the estate. The charitable deduction was denied to the trust because it contained no provision in favor of the charities that received the ultimate distributions, thus violating the §642(c)(1) requirement that the distribution be pursuant to the governing instrument.

The governing-instrument requirement was not met in ILM 200848020, which disregarded a state court order that reformed the beneficiaries of a trust "to ensure that the Trust would meet the regulatory definition of a designated beneficiary" for qualified plan distribution purposes. The reformation was disregarded for purposes of the governing instrument requirement because "there was no conflict with respect to Trust" but, rather, the reformation was obtained merely to affect "the tax benefits that would ensue."

Suggesting that both results may be subject to challenge is PLR 201225004, which involved a trust claiming the §642(c) deduction for income distributed to charity. The issue was satisfaction of the §642(c)(1) requirement that the income be distributed "pursuant to the terms of the governing instrument." The

purpose during the taxable year.[30] If alive, the grantor cannot also claim a § 170 income tax deduction for the value of any income payable to

---

(Footnote Continued)

distribution was directed by a beneficiary's exercise of a nongeneral inter vivos power of appointment, which was deemed to satisfy the "pursuant to" requirement even though the governing instrument did not specify a charitable bequest—it only authorized exercise of the power in favor of charity. The PLR did not explain why that is the correct result, but GCM 34277 (1970) correctly concludes that the holder of a power of appointment acts as an agent for the donor of the power, "so that upon its exercise the property is regarded as passing to the appointee from the donor of the power under the instrument by which it is created rather than from the [powerholder]." As a result, applying the relation-back principle, "the exercised power of appointment is deemed to speak as part of the [donor's estate plan]," which satisfies the "pursuant to the terms of the governing instrument" requirement in § 642(c)(1). Regarding the state law relation-back principle itself see Restatement (Second) of Property—Donative Transfers at 4 (1986). Analgous authority does exist that entails payments to charity pursuant to the settlement of a will contest or other controversy. Curiously, the law on that issue also was slow to develop, although the current position is that these resolutions also relate back and satisfy the governing instrument requirement. See, e.g., GCM 38227 (1979) for a collection of authorities on point and a summary of the conflict that existed prior to reaching the result that applies today.

With respect to the uncertainty that may apply to income entitlement (for example, in the face of a will contest), see cases collected in Ferguson, Freeland, & Ascher, Federal Income Taxation of Estates, Trusts, and Beneficiaries § 6.07 (3d ed. 2011).

[30] Subject to an election to treat a distribution as having been made in the prior taxable year. See § 642(c)(1) (penultimate sentence). PLR 9324033 concluded that § 9100 relief is available if the election required under § 642(c)(1) is not timely made, holding that extension requirements were available because the timing of the election was prescribed only by Treas. Reg. § 1.642(c)-1(b)(2) and not by statute. To the same effect are PLRs 201023015, 200952034, 200939011, and 200418040.

PLRs 9447012, 9447011, and 9446019 elaborated on the mechanism and timing for such a late election. Involved were CLT distributions in years 2 and 3 that § 642(c)(1) would permit to be treated as distributions in years 1 and 2 instead. To be timely, the elections would be required on a year 1 tax return filed before the end of year 2 and a year 2 return filed before the end of year 3, respectively. Posited was a year 1 return that was filed and an election made on it with respect to the year 2 distributions, which was regarded as irrevocable when it no longer was possible to timely file a year 2 return. As to it, § 9100 relief to make a change to the election was unavailable once it was too late to timely file a year 2 income tax return. But the Rulings held that no irrevocability problem was generated and § 9100 relief was available to make a late year 2 return election, as

charity. Instead, § 170(f)(2)(B) precludes an income tax deduction to the grantor unless the trust is a grantor trust for income tax purposes,[31] in which case the trust income would be taxable to the grantor instead of to the trust and, because the trust has no income (it is taxable instead as if owned by the grantor), the trust is denied the deduction.[32]

Unlike the § 170 deduction for individuals who make contributions to charity, § 642(c) has no percentage limitations. Unlike most of Subchapter J and the § 170 income tax deduction, § 642(c) requires a tracing of amounts distributed and limits the deduction to amounts actually paid from gross income of the estate or trust. In that fashion, for example, it precludes claiming an income tax deduction for unrealized appreciation in corpus distributed to charity,[33] which works in its own way to limit the charitable deduction.

(Footnote Continued)

to the year 3 distributions being treated as made in year 2, because no election previously had been made (notwithstanding that a year 3 return had been filed).

Distinguishable from these results because no election was made on the year 1 return is PLR 200344021, in which relief *was* granted to a trust that improperly deducted under § 661 for year 1 and subsequently sought relief to amend and elect under § 642(c)(1) after the time to file a year 2 return had expired. See also PLRs 200517014 and 200517012, in which § 9100 relief was granted to allow an extension of time because amended returns were filed after the date to make the § 642(c)(1) election had passed.

[31] A grantor may cause a CLT to be a grantor trust to accelerate the charitable income tax deduction to the year of creation and pay for it through grantor trust exposure through the term of the charitable interest. See § 14.3.6. But usually any potential wealth transfer tax consequence (as well as the income tax cost without the cash flow) preclude this as an intentional plan. In addition, if grantor trust status terminates early, § 170(f)(2)(B) imposes a recapture tax liability that cannot be avoided even by death. Treas. Reg. §§ 1.170A-6(c)(4), 1.170A-6(c)(5) Example (3). See generally Ferguson, Freeland, & Ascher, Federal Income Taxation of Estates, Trusts, & Beneficiaries § 11.04[B][1] (3d ed. 2011); Westfall, Mair, Buckles, Benson, & Murieko, Estate Planning Law and Taxation ¶ 19.07[1][a] (2009).

[32] § 642(c)(1) (first parenthetical, which specifies that a trust cannot claim the § 642(c) deduction if the income instead qualifies for the § 170 deduction).

[33] See ILM 201042023, involving a trust that authorized distributions of income to charity, pursuant to which the trustee purchased assets using accumulated income from a prior year and distributed those assets when they had appreciated in value. The government held that the charitable deduction must be limited to the trust's basis—the amount of income invested in the asset—rather than FMV, because a holding otherwise would violate two principles. According

Thus, for example, IRD qualifies for the deduction, but the *right to receive* IRD does not.[34] Similarly, neither corpus nor tax exempt income generate a §642(c) deduction when distributed to charity.[35] As a consequence, to avoid the DNI allocation rules[36] that normally would allocate a pro rata share of every type of income in the trust, some drafters specify that distributions to charity follow the WIFO principle, first from ordinary income, then from short-term capital gain, followed by long-term capital gain (that is, to match the §664(b) allocations), to better ensure that amounts distributed to charity will meet the §642(c) gross income requirement.[37]

This strategy is contrary to Treas. Reg. §§1.642(c)-3(b) and 1.643(a)-5(b), which deny this effort to engineer the flavor of income carried out by imposing an "economic effect independent of income tax consequences" requirement and make cross reference to Treas. Reg. §1.651-2(b) for illustrations.[38] As originally addressed in PLRs such as 199917068, 199915058, and 199908002 (and at least a dozen others), occasionally a taxpayer attempts the WIFO strategy to engineer the class of income that is deemed distributed to a charity, by overriding the pro ration dictate of Treas. Reg. §1.642(c)-3(b)(2). According to the govern-

---

(Footnote Continued)

to Ferguson, Freeland, & Ascher, Federal Income Taxation of Estates, Trusts, and Beneficiaries §6.09 (3d ed. 2011); a full FMV deduction would permit the taxpayer to avoid taxation on the appreciation and, because that appreciation would not be income of the trust as a result, it also would allow a deduction for an amount that was not totally attributable to trust income, in violation of §642(c)(1).

[34] Unless distribution of that asset constitutes a §691(a)(2) acceleration event that turns the right into a current income item. Treas. Reg. §1.642(c)-3(a). See §5.10.5.

[35] Treas. Reg. §1.642(c)-3(b). See Goldsby v. Commissioner, 92 T.C.M. (CCH) 52 (2006), in which the taxpayer's attempt to deduct a conservation easement conveyed by a trust was thwarted, among other reasons, because it was not shown that the contribution was made from trust income.

[36] Treas. Reg. §1.643(a)-5(b).

[37] See also §§642(c)(4) and 681(a) for other limitations on the deduction based on the type of income deemed distributed. Consider also §642(e), as discussed in §5.3.1 n.26, as a limitation of the deduction for depletion or depreciation, which might be allocated to the trust because they are wasted to the extent carried to a charitable beneficiary.

[38] As discussed in §5.4.1 nn.8-11.

§5.9.3

ment, such a deviation will be honored only if it specifies a particular subtrust, income producing asset, or perhaps income or principal for fiduciary accounting purposes, but not the kind of ordering found in Treas. Reg. § § 1.664-1(d) and 1.664-1(e), which apply only to CRTs.[39]

Thus, the regulations provide that the effort to specify that taxable income would be carried out to the charity first, followed by capital gains, then tax exempt income, and finally corpus would be valid *only* "to the extent such provision has economic effect independent of income tax consequences." Otherwise every class of amounts available for distribution would be deemed carried out pro rata. No indication was given in the prior PLRs of what economic effect the government anticipated, but Example 2 in Treas. Reg. § 1.642(c)-3(b)(2) illustrates a trust instrument that specifies "that 100 percent of the trust's ordinary income must be distributed currently" to a charity, which would be respected as having economic effect independent of income tax consequences "because the amount to be paid to the charitable organization each year is dependent upon the amount of ordinary income the trust earns within that taxable year." But Example 1 in the same section states that a fixed annuity or unitrust obligation "is not dependent upon the type of income from which it is to be paid" and, therefore, does not vary in amount based on the kinds of income earned. Even if the class of income used to satisfy the annual distribution amount might vary, these trust distribution dictates would not meet the standard.

Application of income for § 642(c) purposes may be performed pursuant to a mandate or discretion granted to the fiduciary, but requires actual use of gross income items under authority of the document or state law and not just arbitrary selection by the fiduciary.[40] In addition,

---

[39] As discussed in § 5.9 at text accompanying notes 8 and 9.

[40] See Old Colony Trust Co. v. Commissioner, 301 U.S. 379 (1937) (authority under document to distribute income is adequate); Crestar Bank v. United States, 47 F. Supp. 2d 670 (E.D. Va. 1999) (rejecting argument that income passes first to charity and therefore satisfies this requirement absent a direction in the document or authority under state law); Frank Trust v. Commissioner, 2 T.C.M. (CCH) 1107 (1943) (distribution of corpus that trustee charged for accounting purposes to income was not deductible); Rev. Rul. 2003-123, 2003-2 C.B. 1200 (a trust that conveyed a conservation easement in corpus directly to charity was denied a charitable deduction under § 661(a)(2) because the only source for a trust to claim a charitable deduction is § 642(c), and was denied a deduction under that provision because it only applies to distributions of trust

certain limitations on the authority under state law or the document to allocate items of fiduciary income must be respected. And an in-kind corpus distribution may constitute a gain or loss realization event, generating capital gain that may constitute gross income and, to that extent, qualify for the § 642(c) deduction.[41]

(Footnote Continued)

income, not corpus); Rev. Rul. 2004-5, 2004-1 C.B. 295 (a trust garnered a charitable deduction for a conservation easement by indirection, because the trust was one of several partners in a partnership that made the charitable contribution and the "trust's deduction for its distributive share of a charitable contribution made by a partnership will not be disallowed under § 642(c)"); Rev. Rul. 71-285, 1971-2 C.B. 248 (document was silent but state law provided that income was distributed first, which was deemed adequate); Rev. Rul. 68-667, 1968-2 C.B. 289 (payment of corpus precluded deduction); PLR 8708033 (authority under state law adequate). Treas. Reg. § 1.642(c)-3(b)(2) establishes a pro ration of income available for distribution that is not necessarily included in gross income (such as tax exempt income) and as to which a deduction therefore would not be allowed. See also Treas. Reg. §§ 1.662(b)-2; 1.662(c)-4 Example (e).

An interesting twist involving discretion over income and principal was decisive in TAM 9714001, which involved a (presumably pre-1969) CRT that granted broad discretion to the trustee to apportion income items such as dividends and capital gain to income or principal, pursuant to which the trustee allocated the proceeds of sale at a profit to corpus and claimed a § 642(c)(2) charitable set aside deduction for that income item. The government denied the deduction because of the fiduciary's broad allocation discretion, stating that the gain may not have been permanently set aside for the charitable remainder beneficiary because the trustee could consume corpus to purchase a bond with a high interest rate that effectively would apportion the gain allocated to corpus to the income beneficiary, thereby denying that corpus to the charity. Citing Rev. Rul. 73-95, 1973-1 C.B. 322, the government stated that "[t]o be permanently set aside, an amount of gross income must be irrevocably apportioned for the charitable purpose pursuant to the terms of the governing instrument" and, in this case, that was not true.

[41] See Rev. Rul. 83-75, 1983-1 C.B. 114; § 8.02(2) of Rev. Proc. 2007-45, 2007-2 C.B. 89, PLRs 200920031 and 9044047; and cf. Treas. Reg. § 1.664-1(d)(5). Under § 643(a)(3)(B) that gain may be includible in DNI and may be carried out by the distribution in which it was realized. Note that the 2009 PLR involved a grantor trust style CLAT (meaning that the grantor obtained a charitable deduction upon creation of the trust and there was no income tax charitable deduction on distributions to charity. See § 14.3.6). In that context the charitable distribution appears similar to a charitable pledge, as to which Rev. Rul. 55-410, 1955-1 C.B. 297, states that no gain or loss is realized on satisfaction with property distributed in kind. The PLR distinguished the two situations on two grounds: (1) a

For example, PLR 8931029 involved a CLT that was to pay a unitrust amount to a charitable organization for 20 years. The trust was funded with stock of a publicly traded company and the unitrust obligation was to be met by distributions of that stock. The government held that a gift tax charitable deduction was allowable with respect to the proposed gift of the stock, equal to the actuarial value of the unitrust interest payable. But the unitrust amount would qualify for the trust's §642(c)(1) income tax deduction only to the extent the amounts were paid out of trust gross income, because the deduction under §642(c)(1) is limited to amounts of gross income paid for a purpose specified in §170(c). PLR 9201029 amended the Ruling to clarify that distribution of stock to satisfy the unitrust obligation would be a gain or loss realization event.

If a document is silent regarding the source of distributions, local law and the apparent intent of the grantor will be scrutinized to determine whether the §642(c)(1) income distribution requirement is met.[42] As is the case with noncharitable beneficiaries,[43] a question can exist under state law whether income from property subject to a specific bequest belongs to the charitable legatee directly (in which case income tax liability is avoided) or to the estate, which ought to qualify for the §642(c) deduction when it is received by the charity.[44] In addition, in some cases the estate will be deemed terminated and any subsequent income deemed that of a following trust, as to which a deduction may not be available.

For example, in Estate of Berger v. Commissioner,[45] normal estate administration was substantially complete more than three years prior to a sale at a gain of property still held by the personal representative. Nevertheless, the estate claimed a §642(c)(2) charitable set aside deduction for the capital gain generated on that sale. The Tax Court agreed

---

(Footnote Continued)

pledge to charity is not a debt but a CLAT charitable beneficiary has a claim against the trust, and (2) a taxpayer who makes a charitable pledge does not obtain a charitable deduction until the pledge is satisfied but the grantor of a grantor trust style CLAT enjoys the deduction in the year of creation.

[42] Rev. Rul. 71-285, 71-2 C.B. 248.

[43] See §5.3.1 nn.4-7 and accompanying text.

[44] See Bowers v. Slocum, 20 F.2d 350 (2d Cir. 1927); Rev. Rul. 57-133, 1957-1 C.B. 200.

[45] 60 T.C.M. (CCH) 1079 (1990).

§5.9.3

with the government's denial of the deduction, noting that all estate assets had been collected, all debts and bequests had been paid, the FET return had been filed, and the FET had been paid. Although the residue of the estate had not been formally distributed, the court held that this was not sufficient to keep the estate open for federal income tax purposes. Because § 642(c)(2) was applicable at that time only to estates, the treatment of the estate as closed for income tax purposes effectively foreclosed the claimed deduction.[46]

The conclusion that the estate should be treated as closed for income tax purposes because the FET return had been filed and all debts, expenses, and taxes had been paid is disturbing. No FET closing letter had been received and, under other facts, distribution of the residue might be premature notwithstanding payment of all estate charges. Perhaps the court's conclusion that the property did not require estate administration—whatever that means—indicates that a case-by-case analysis will apply in the future. The moral of the case, however, is that diligence is necessary to avoid prolonged estate administration that will be ignored for income tax purposes.

§5.9.4 Distributions Deduction

Finally, there is an argument that nonqualified trusts or estates qualify for the § 661(a)(2) distributions deduction to the extent the § 642(c) deduction is not available. If the requirements of § 642(c) are not met, the government's position is that no DNI is carried out and no income tax distributions deduction is allowable to the entity under 661(a)(2) for any other distribution to charity.[47] To date, courts uni-

---

[46] The case probably could have been decided on the ground that the charitable bequest appeared to follow a life estate that did not comply with the charitable split interest trust rules. The result was appropriate if a trust was intended and estate administration was being used to avoid the dictates of § 664.

[47] Treas. Reg. § 1.663(a)-2 (second sentence), which the government contends is a proper interpretation of the rule in § 663(a)(2) that arguably is designed not to limit the charitable deduction to § 642(c) to the exclusion of other provisions but instead only to preclude a *double* deduction for charitable distributions that *are* deductible under § 642(c). See § 5.9 n.48 and accompanying text.

§5.9.4

formly have agreed that § 642(c) is the *only* available source of a deduction for otherwise nonqualified distributions.[48]

Thus, for example, the taxpayer in Crown Income Charitable Fund v. Commissioner[49] was a qualified CLT that distributed amounts to a charity in excess of the specified annual annuity. The government disallowed the trust's income tax deduction for these excess distributions because they were not made pursuant to the terms of the trust for § 642(c)(1) purposes and, because they were charitable in nature, the government argued that they were precluded by § 663(a)(2) from being deducted under § 661 as well.

---

[48] Mott v. United States, 462 F.2d 512, 518 (Ct. Cl. 1972) (case of first impression, involving corpus distributions by an estate to charity, holding that "the Government's position accords with the general intent of Congress in enacting distribution rules and . . . is in accord with what we believe to be an implied Congressional intent to prevent all charitable distributions, whether or not deductible under Section 642(c), from entering into the operation of the distribution rules," citing H.R. Rep. No. 1337, 83d Cong., 2d Sess. 60 (1954) and S. Rep. No. 1622, 83d Cong., 2d Sess. 82 (1954): "to the extent of the trust's current income all distributions are deductible by the estate or trust *and taxable to the beneficiaries*") (emphasis added); Estate of O'Connor v. Commissioner, 69 T.C. 165 (1977) (trust distributions failed the "pursuant to the terms of the governing instrument" requirement under § 642(c) because they were the product of a disclaimer); Pullen v. United States, 80-1 U.S. Tax Cas. (CCH) ¶ 9105 (D. Neb. 1979), aff'd in an unpublished opinion (8th Cir. 1980). And see § 5.9 n.49, dealing with Crown Income Charitable Fund v. United States.

[49] 98 T.C. 327 (1992), aff'd, 8 F.3d 871 (7th Cir. 1993) (the Tax Court's agreement with the government also involved questions of trust interpretation and administration that are important only with respect to trusts that attempt to commute future annuity obligations using current income that exceeds the current annuity obligation, the court specifically noting that it was expressing no opinion whether commutation itself would be acceptable and found only that, in this case, it did not occur; the appellate court stated that the excess income distributions to charity must have worked a commutation because the trustee's action would reduce the remainder improperly if the outstanding charitable entitlement was not reduced by these payments).

§ 5.9.4

A fair reading of § 663(a)(2) is that it exists only to prevent double deductions. Only if a § 642(c) deduction is allowable should the § 661(a)(2) deduction be unavailable.[50] Nevertheless, the regulations

---

[50] See Ferguson, Freeland, & Ascher, Federal Income Taxation of Estates, Trusts, and Beneficiaries § 6.10 (3d ed. 2011), and United States Trust Co. v. United States, 617 F. Supp. 575, 580 (S.D. Miss. 1985), rev'd sub nom., United States Trust Co. v. Internal Revenue Service, 803 F.2d 1363 (5th Cir. 1986) (although distribution by estate to charity did not exceed estate income, it did not qualify under § 642(c) because it was not required to be made from income, the court holding that § 663(a)(2) "is explicit and unambiguous and indicates that Congress intended only to prevent an estate from taking two *income tax* deductions for the same distribution: one under § 642(c) and one under § 661"; the court below nevertheless referred to the income tax deduction as "a loophole" because the same distribution was deductible for FET § 2055 purposes, and the income tax deduction was denied by the court on appeal); TAMs 8810007 and 8603002 (because § 642(c) charitable deductions were not allowable, the § 663(a)(2) restriction also was not applicable and distributions deductions under § 661(a)(2) therefore were permitted). Quaere: if Congress truly thought that § 642(c) should be the sole opportunity to deduct a charitable distribution, would Congress have needed to adopt § 663(a)(2); alternatively, is the government's conclusion in both TAMs wrong?

To the government's suggestion that the § 661 deduction should be disallowed because the estate also deducted the distribution under § 2055 for FET purposes, the district court in *United States Trust* properly noted that § 642(g) appears to be the sole authority limiting "double" deductions for the same items under both the estate and income taxes, and it does not itemize § 2055 as a deduction that is included in the prohibition against double deductions. To illustrate, assume that D's estate is worth $10 million. The estate is directed to distribute $1 million of corpus to charity after D's death, and the estate has $1 million of DNI in the first year after D's death prior to making that distribution. If a deduction was available under § 661(a)(2), the estate's distribution of $1 million from corpus in the first year would cause the $1 million of DNI to be carried out to the charity. If D had been alive and had earned the $1 million of income and made a donation to charity, that $1 million would have qualified for both the income and gift tax charitable deductions and, if death immediately followed, D would have died with a $10 million estate. In *United States Trust*, D's estate received the income tax deduction and the estate also received an *FET* deduction, reducing the size of the estate to $9 million for wealth transfer tax purposes. This difference in result is presumably what the district court saw in *United States Trust* as the "loophole" represented by its decision.

The difference of $1 million between what would have happened if D had made the transfer inter vivos represents income of the estate that D did not earn during life. This $1 million is property of the estate and ultimately its beneficiaries, and it has been given to charity. What the district court in *United States*

specify more broadly that "[a]mounts paid . . . for charitable . . . purposes are deductible . . . *only* as provided in section 642(c)."[51] The net effect in *Crown* was that the charity received an amount of income on which the trust paid income tax, which is inconsistent with congressional policy favoring the deduction of distributions to charity. Moreover, if the distributions had not been made prematurely in that case the same amounts distributed in subsequent years in the form of the lead annuity would have been deductible. Absent some other source of abuse,[52] the time of distribution arguably should not affect deductibility if the charity ultimately receives no less than its guaranteed annuity.[53]

(Footnote Continued)

Trust did, in effect, was give D's estate an FET charitable deduction for that $1 million earned after death, rather than give the estate beneficiaries a gift tax charitable deduction for that amount. However the deductions are parceled out, the final analysis is that there has been $1 million given to charity, generating a $1 million income tax deduction and a $1 million wealth transfer tax deduction. Although the effect of *United States Trust* was to give to D's estate the gift tax charitable deduction that might be seen as properly belonging to the estate beneficiaries, it seems reasonable to suggest that this is not a "doubling" of the deductions; the $1 million gift would have been both wealth transfer tax and income tax deductible by someone.

[51] Treas. Reg. § 1.663(a)-2 (second sentence) (emphasis added), which is unnecessary to preclude abuse. See § 5.9 n.52.

[52] As noted by the *United States Trust* court on appeal, the regulations do not (and in this case neither did the trust instrument) specify whether the interest rate that should be applied to determine the value of the charitable interest for commutation purposes is the rate used to calculate the value of the charitable deduction at creation of the trust or the rate current at the time of commutation. According to the court on appeal, if it is the same rate used upon creation, then the trustee could wait until interest rates have declined and commute the outstanding charitable entitlement, using the higher rate that applied at original creation to distribute to the charity a smaller portion of the trust than currently is needed to generate the specified annuity. If that was the court's concern, then all the government must do to preclude abuse is to promulgate a regulation specifying that commutation should utilize the current rate rather than the original rate. The court on appeal affirmed the Tax Court because the commutation discount rate issue was unsettled, meaning that commutation might be an abuse in the absence of such a rule.

[53] If uncertainty surrounding the appropriate interest rate to determine the commutation amount is eliminated by removing the trustee's incentive to commute in a manner that could diminish the charity's interest, then perhaps the result in another case might differ. But as the law stands currently, it appears

Finally, to illustrate the interplay of the §§ 642(c) and 661(a)(2) deductions and the §§ 662(b) and 664(b) characterization of distributions in the hands of beneficiaries, assume an estate is directed to fund a qualified CRAT and that the estate realizes $20,000 of fiduciary accounting income for the current year, of which $15,000 is taxable dividends and $5,000 is tax exempt interest. During the current year the personal representative of the estate distributes $40,000 in cash to the charitable trust and another $10,000 directly to A, the noncharitable beneficiary of the qualified split interest trust, in satisfaction of income that A is entitled to receive under the terms of the trust. Finally, assume that the estate charges both distributions to fiduciary accounting principal for its accounting purposes, on the grounds that the estate could have funded the trust with the full $50,000 distributed and let the trust distribute the $10,000 to A. The fact that the estate chose to short-cut this by distributing $10,000 directly to A as authorized by the terms of the various documents is deemed not to alter the estate's fiduciary accounting.

In this case, neither the distribution directly to the trust nor that indirectly to the trust by paying the trust's obligation to A is a distribution of estate income and therefore none of the estate distributions meet the requirements of § 642(c). Thus, any deduction available to the estate for income tax purposes would be under § 661(a)(2) as second tier discretionary distributions of corpus, or not at all.[54] As second tier distributions, each would carry out any available DNI, meaning that the charity receives $40,000 of the total $50,000 distributed for the year. If this was regarded as causing 80% of the DNI to be carried out to the charity and 20% of the DNI to be carried out to A, and if those distributions were subject to the § 662(b) character rules, A would enjoy a better result than if the § 664(b) character rules had applied, because A would receive tax exempt income to the extent of 1/4 of the distribution ($5,000

(Footnote Continued)

that a commutation provision may invite denial of the charitable deduction for excess distributions.

[54] Note that the intermediate tier, which distinguishes between § 642(c) deductible distributions of income to charity and mandatory (first tier) distributions of income to noncharitable beneficiaries, does not apply to distributions to charity that do not qualify under § 642(c) and therefore are not deductible under that provision. See § 5.4.2 nn.36-41 and accompanying text, regarding the intermediate tier.

§ 5.9.4

of the $20,000 of DNI was tax exempt) rather than having received all taxable income, then all capital gains, and finally tax exempt income under the special priority rules of § 664(b).

Presumably to avoid that result, the government asserts that a step transaction analysis is appropriate in a case such as this, as if the distribution to A actually had been to the trust, which then made its own distribution to A.[55] The estate still deducts the full amount distributed, but A would be in the same position as if the two step distribution had occurred instead of the single, short-cut distribution actually made.

§ 5.10 IRD

Congress enacted § 691 to address the taxation of income earned by a decedent during life but not paid to the decedent before death. To prevent that income from escaping income tax altogether, one alternative would accelerate it into the decedent's final income tax return. That approach could present onerous cash flow or liquidity consequences to the decedent's estate because it might impose a tax liability before the income was received.[1] A second alternative could regard that income as taxable to the decedent's successor in interest as it is received, along with the recipient's other income, with no special treatment or recognition. That approach would be flawed to the extent the right to receive the income is includible in the decedent's gross estate for FET purposes— and thereby is entitled to a new basis equal to its FMV for FET purposes[2] —because a new basis largely would eliminate any built-in income tax liability. The approach adopted by Congress treats IRD as taxable to the recipient when received,[3] but denies new basis at death with respect to it.[4]

---

[55] See TAM 8810006, holding that both distributions are § 661(a)(2) deductible by the estate as if both distributions had been made to the trust.

[1] **§ 5.10** S. Rep. No. 1622, 83d Cong., 2d Sess. 373 (1954). See generally Ferguson, Freeland, & Ascher, Federal Income Taxation of Estates, Trusts, and Beneficiaries § 3.02 (3d ed. 2011); Keck v. Commissioner, 415 F.2d 531 (6th Cir. 1969).

[2] § 1014(b)(9).

[3] §§ 61(a)(14), 691.

[4] § 1014(c).

§ 5.10

It may be useful in the following discussion to consider several fundamental notions. One is that decedents who reported income on the accrual method usually do not present the problem of an inter vivos entitlement to income that was not realized for income tax purposes and reported on a tax return prior to death. Thus, the concept of IRD essentially is a cash basis deceased taxpayer's concern.

A second notion is that the IRD concept really is important only to the extent a right to receive IRD is includible in the decedent's gross estate for FET purposes. Only in that case does the new basis at death treatment threaten the integrity of the income tax system. Thus, in a perfect world, IRD should be (1) an item that was earned but not returned for income tax purposes before the taxpayer's death[5] (2) of a cash basis taxpayer—or income in respect of a *prior* decedent that is includible in the estate of that prior decedent's successor in interest and that is passing yet again to another successor in interest[6]—and that is (3) subject to FET inclusion in the decedent's gross estate. Although some aberrations in the application of § 691 have crept into the law, in most respects these fundamentals inform the operation of this aspect of the income tax rules that apply to decedents and their estates and beneficiaries.

§ 5.10.1 IRD Defined

Like some other areas of the Internal Revenue Code in which a concept that is fundamental to a taxing regime is not defined, there is no statutory identification of what constitutes IRD. Although there are obvious illustrations of IRD, there is a substantial jurisprudence and uncertainty regarding the parameters of the concept.

---

[5] See Treas. Reg. § 1.691(a)-1(b).

[6] § 691(a)(1) (parenthetical provision, applicable only if the right to receive the income in respect of the prior decedent was received by the successor in interest by reason of the prior decedent's death or by bequest, devise, or inheritance from that prior decedent). Treas. Reg. §§ 1.691(a)-1(c) and -2(b) Example (2). See, e.g., Kitch v. Commissioner, 104 T.C. 1 (1995) (E died shortly before D, who owed alimony to E, the receipt of which by E's estate represented income in respect of D and, in the hands of E's beneficiaries, represented income in respect of a prior decedent notwithstanding the order of deaths of E and then D); PLR 9132021 (IRA received by decedent from a predeceased spouse represented income in respect of that prior decedent).

To make an easy comparison, a decedent's final paycheck—compensation for services rendered by the decedent before death—is IRD when received by the decedent's successor in interest after the decedent's death. The right to receive that payment is an asset owned by the decedent at death and that is includible in the decedent's gross estate for FET purposes. Assuming the decedent was a cash basis taxpayer, all the requisite ingredients for IRD treatment exist.[7]

On the other hand, a wrongful death recovery—which in many cases is at least in part a substitution for the decedent's lost *future* earnings—need not be regarded as IRD. This is understandable in light of two facts. One is that the recovery itself is not includible in the decedent's gross estate for FET purposes,[8] which means that there is no new basis at death that could preclude income taxation of the recovery. As a result, IRD treatment is not required as a means of precluding an untoward income tax benefit. The second reason this treatment makes sense is because, for ordinary income tax purposes, wrongful death recoveries should be excludible from income under § 104(a)(2), as damages received "on account of personal injuries or sickness."[9] This is a little harder to appreciate, given that back or future wages are a prime example of tort recoveries that are includible in income, and these wages are taxable the same as if the injured party had earned them in ordinary course.

Wrongful death recoveries should not be includible in income because wage recoveries are excludible to the extent they are attributable to a physical injury (such as worker's compensation or a similar recovery) and compensate for the inability to work that resulted from the

---

[7] Treas. Reg. § 1.691(a)-2(b) Example (1); Estate of Davis v. Commissioner, 11 T.C.M. (CCH) 814 (1952).

[8] See § 9.0 n.2.

[9] See Commissioner v. Schleier, 515 U.S. 323 (1995); Bagley v. Commissioner, 105 T.C. 396 (1995); and § 104(c) (exclusion must be on account of tort (or tort-like) recovery for damages on account of personal injury or sickness as opposed to recovery for economic harms unrelated to the plaintiff's personal injury or sickness. In addition, the recovery may not constitute punitive damages. Although the income tax exclusion of wrongful death recoveries is not yet clear, § 104(c) would not be necessary (treating certain state law punitive damage recoveries in wrongful death actions as if they were not punitive damages) if wrongful death recoveries could not qualify for the exclusion in the first instance.

§ 5.10.1

personal injury or sickness. In a wrongful death situation one portion of a recovery may be attributable to pain and suffering or medical expense reimbursement—clearly excludible under § 104(a)(2)—and another portion constitutes wages that the decedent could not earn because of the physical injury. Both of these amounts clearly should be excludible for income tax purposes, all notwithstanding that the plaintiff may not be (and may not be acting on behalf of) the individual who suffered the physical injury resulting in death. For purposes of an IRD analysis, this all means that the recovery should not be IRD because it should be excluded from income in all respects.

In defining IRD the proper treatment may not be altogether clear. In a normal compensation case an issue might arise whether a paycheck was delivered to the decedent during life or arrived too late to constitute the decedent's income, but otherwise compensation income is not likely to generate much debate. Alternatively, however, assume that the decedent owned an appreciated asset that was the subject of a sale negotiated by the decedent during life but that did not close until after the decedent's death. If payment for the asset is in the form of an installment note, under which each payment includes some capital gain IRD, § 1014(c) would deny the § 1014(b)(9) basis adjustment at death if the sale is deemed to be complete before the decedent died. All that capital gain would be taxed as the successor in interest receives those payments. If the sale was incomplete when the decedent died, however, then the asset includible in the decedent's gross estate for FET purposes would be the property being sold, not the note, and the estate would be entitled to a new basis equal to the asset's FET FMV. This would eliminate any gain on what would be regarded as a postmortem sale.[10]

---

[10] See Estate of Napolitano v. Commissioner, 63 T.C.M. (CCH) 3092 (1992) (the decedent negotiated a sale of property prior to death that failed to close before death because of housing code violations that were not corrected, the sale instead being completed postmortem after the buyer agreed to take the property subject to the violations in exchange for a reduction in the purchase price; the estate successfully asserted that, because the sale was not complete prior to death, the proceeds could not be IRD and that § 1014(c) did not preclude a basis adjustment for the property at death, eliminating almost $90,000 of gain). Very similar is PLR 200744001 in which the sale did not close on time due to the unexpected discovery of a pipeline traversing the property. Compare § 5.10.1 n.36 and accompanying text.

§ 5.10.1

In the paycheck illustration the decedent's successor in interest will receive essentially the same economic value whether the paycheck is delivered before or after death, and the income tax differences generated by application of § 691 are not likely to be significant.[11] In the sale for a note case the capital gains tax consequence of § 691 treatment could be dramatic. As a result, it is more likely that the issue whether an item represents IRD will arise in a case in which elimination of capital gain is at stake, and these kinds of cases produce more litigation than any other.

The following list illustrates common sources of IRD:

- Compensation income of all varieties, including salary,[12] accounts receivable of professionals (be they doctors or lawyers, engineers or fiduci-

---

(Footnote Continued)

Compare PLR 9829025, in which assets were sold premortem by the decedent's includible grantor trust, and replacement assets were acquired postmortem within the § 1031 nonrecognition period for like-kind exchanges. The government held that the gain on the premortem sale avoided IRD treatment and therefore that the replacement assets qualified for new basis at death (because the trust corpus was includible in the decedent's gross estate). Ignoring the trust because of its grantor trust status meant that the premortem sale was as if the grantor sold the property personally, as discussed in § 5.11.9. Inclusion of the property in the grantor's gross estate solved the new basis at death issue, so the linchpin issue was whether the § 1031 like-kind exchange requirements could be met with the sale and reinvestment straddling the date of the decedent's death. By holding that this exchange did qualify, the government essentially concluded that the gain was not recognizable at all, as opposed to the gain being IRD.

[11] The issue is not likely to be whether income tax is avoidable but only whether to report the income on the decedent's final income tax return or on the estate's first income tax return. Thus, the § 691 issue is not likely to make much difference in the income tax burden. The only true tax difference is attributable to the fact that income tax paid on the decedent's compensation received during life reduces the decedent's estate for FET purposes as a debt that is deductible under § 2053(a)(3). That reduction is unavailable and instead a § 691(c) income tax deduction is available for any FET attributable to inclusion of the paycheck in the gross estate as IRD. See § 5.10.3, regarding the § 691(c) deduction. The FET reduces corpus of the estate while the income tax reduces estate income, and these may pass to different beneficiaries. Thus, the IRD issue may be significant, but less because the overall tax burden will be affected in a meaningful amount and more because it may befall different beneficiaries and at different times.

[12] See § 5.10.1 n.14.

§5.10.1

aries, or professional athletes),[13] and the liquidated payout of fringe benefits such as accrued vacation or sick leave;[14]

- Amounts compensating labor performed by the decedent during life but that are contingent on postmortem events (such as an insurance agent's renewal commissions[15] and bonus or incentive payments);[16]

---

[13] Miller v. United States, 389 F.2d 656 (5th Cir. 1968); Hess v. Commissioner, 271 F.2d 104 (3d Cir. 1959); Estate of Nilssen v. United States, 322 F. Supp. 260 (D. Minn. 1971); Hansberry v. All, 68-1 U.S. Tax Cas. (CCH) ¶ 9185 (N.D. Ill. 1967); Estate of Basch v. Commissioner, 9 T.C. 627 (1947); Estate of Cartwright v. Commissioner, 183 F.3d 1034 (9th Cir. 1999); Rev. Rul. 78-203, 1978-1 C.B. 199; Rev. Rul. 67-242, 1967-2 C.B. 227.

An unusual receivable that constitutes IRD is alimony arrearages. In Kitch v. Commissioner, 104 T.C. 1 (1995), D died owing alimony to E, who had died just weeks earlier. E's estate filed a claim in D's estate and in due course the two estates reached a compromise by which E's estate received assets from D's estate that represented IRD to D. Distribution of these assets was not a DNI carryout event because E was deemed a creditor, not a beneficiary, of D's estate, and distribution by D's estate of the assets in kind in satisfaction of E's claim was deemed a gain or loss realization event. See also Estate of Narischkine v. Commissioner, 14 T.C. 1128 (1950). Cf. Miville v. Commissioner, 29 T.C.M. (CCH) 856 (1970) (because property settlement payments would not have been income to the decedent, they were not IRD to successor in interest).

[14] Rev. Rul. 59-64, 1959-1 C.B. 31 (vacation pay allowance); Rev. Rul. 55-229, 1955-1 C.B. 75 (commuted value of government employee's accrued leave).

[15] Treas. Reg. §§ 1.691(a)-1(b)(3), 1.691(a)-2(b) Example (2); Halliday v. United States, 655 F.2d 68, 72 (5th Cir. 1981), rev'g sub nom. Birmingham Trust Nat'l Bank v. United States, 80-2 U.S. Tax Cas. ¶ 9682 (N.D. Ala. 1980) (although contracts that called for renewal commissions did not mention postmortem benefits, the insurance company's longstanding policy was to pay commissions to the decedent's designated beneficiary; "the district court erred in requiring that the right to income be legally enforceable . . . [if] the evidence shows a substantial certainty that benefits directly related to the decedent's past economic activities will be paid . . . notwithstanding the absence of a legally enforceable obligation"); Wright v. Commissioner, 336 F.2d 121 (2d Cir. 1964); Findlay v. Commissioner, 332 F.2d 620 (2d Cir. 1964); Latendresse v. Commissioner, 243 F.2d 577 (7th Cir. 1957); Estate of Remington v. Commissioner, 9 T.C. 99 (1947); Rev. Rul. 59-162, 1959-2 C.B. 224.

[16] Rollert Residuary Trust v. Commissioner, 80 T.C. 619 (1983), aff'd, 752 F.2d 1128 (6th Cir. 1985) (bonus payments that accrued to the estate of a deceased employee were IRD, notwithstanding that before death the payment was contingent on the employee earning out the bonus; at death the payment became vested and legal enforceability prior to death is not essential, if there was a substantial certainty that the right to the payments would accrue); Jensen v.

§ 5.10.1

- Deferred compensation payments not previously subject to tax,[17] such as under a qualified retirement benefit plan or an IRA,[18] and annuity

---

(Footnote Continued)

United States, 511 F.2d 265 (5th Cir. 1975); Pearson v. United States, 519 F.2d 1279 (4th Cir. 1975); Estate of Bausch v. Commissioner, 186 F.2d 313 (2d Cir. 1951) (IRD notwithstanding lack of enforceability); Estate of O'Daniel v. Commissioner, 10 T.C. 631 (1948), aff'd, 173 F.2d 966 (2d Cir. 1949) (same); Sweeney v. Commissioner, 54 T.C.M. (CCH) 1003 (1987) (gratuitous payments by employers to deceased employees' successors in interest are income and not § 102(a) excludible gifts, particularly if employers with many employees adopt a plan or practice of providing for survivors of deceased employees even though the survivors have no enforceable legal right to the payments); Rev. Rul. 75-79, 1975-1 C.B. 184; Rev. Rul. 68-124, 1968-1 C.B. 44; Rev. Rul. 65-217, 1965-2 C.B. 214.

To the extent these payments are not includible in the gross estate, they need not be regarded as IRD to preclude application of the new basis at death rule, and the § 691(c) deduction would be zero, so it hardly matters whether the IRD designation is applicable. This is an aberrant situation in which the label may apply but it is irrelevant to the accomplishment of the purposes underlying the IRD rule.

A postmortem payment by an employer could constitute a gift, in which case the recipient of that payment would not be required to include it in income. See, e.g., Harper v. United States, 454 F.2d 222 (9th Cir. 1971); Estate of Carter v. Commissioner, 453 F.2d 61 (2d Cir. 1971); Reed v. United States, 177 F. Supp. 205 (W.D. Ky. 1959). Macfarlane v. Commissioner, 19 T.C. 9 (1952).

[17] Estate of Carr v. Commissioner, 37 T.C. 1173 (1962) (commissions were deferred because employer was unable to make payment during decedent's life but the effect was the same as an retirement benefit deferred compensation program); Collins v. United States, 318 F. Supp. 382 (C.D. Cal. 1970); cf. PLR 9352015 (lottery payments that survived the winner's death were treated much the same as retirement benefits that survive a participant in a deferred compensation plan: the payments constituted IRD, they were includible in the winner's gross estate under § 2039, and they constituted § 2056(b)(7)(C) automatic QTIP marital deduction assets because they were payable to a qualifying trust that required distribution to S of the full lottery payment received in any year).

[18] Treas. Reg. § 1.691(a)-2(b) Example (1); Rev. Rul. 92-47, 1992-1 C.B. 198 (postmortem lump sum distribution of IRA constitutes IRD in the amount exceeding the decedent's nondeductible contributions to the account (basis), but not including postmortem appreciation and income (which accretions are taxable under §§ 408(d) and 72 and not as IRD)); Rev. Rul. 73-327, 1973-2 C.B. 214; Rev. Rul. 69-297, 1969-1 C.B. 131 (profit sharing trust distributions postmortem are IRD, including appreciation in employer securities but not the decedent's own contribution to the plan). See § 421 regarding the postmortem income tax treatment of statutory stock options, with § 421(c)(2) allowing a § 691(c) deduc-

payments that survive the decedent's death to the extent they too would have been subject to tax if received by the decedent premortem;[19]

• Partnership liquidating distributions, distributive shares, and accounts receivable representing partnership income generated prior to the decedent's death;[20]

• The decedent's pro rata share of S Corporation income generated prior to the decedent's death;[21]

• Accrued but undistributed income payable by a trust to a deceased beneficiary's estate;[22]

(Footnote Continued)

tion. Treas. Reg. § 1.83-1(d) provides that IRD is generated if an employee dies before § 83 applies. See also Treas. Reg. § 1.691(c)-1(c)(1) (stock options) and §§ 691(d) and 1014(b)(9)(A) (joint and survivor annuities).

[19] Rev. Rul. 2005-30, 2005-1 C.B. 1015; PLR 200041018.

[20] See §§ 691(e) and 753, Quick Trust v. Commissioner, 54 T.C. 1336 (1970), Woodhall v. Commissioner, 28 T.C.M. (CCH) 1438 (1969), and extensive discussions in Acker, Income in Respect of a Decedent, 862-3d Tax Mgmt. (BNA) Estates, Gifts, and Trusts Port. (2010), and Ferguson, Freeland, & Ascher, Federal Income Taxation of Estates, Trusts, and Beneficiaries § 4.02 (3d ed. 2011). IRD treatment can apply even if the decedent received partnership distributions during the year of death and the successor in interest receives little or no cash with which to pay the tax on the partnership income attributed to the successor. Treas. Reg. §§ 1.706-1(c)(3)(v), (vi) Example (4). This result is avoidable if the partnership terminates at the decedent's death, making the partnership year terminate when the decedent's final tax year ends and causing partnership income to be decedent's income, reportable on the decedent's final income tax return.

[21] Providing parity with the result for partnerships and overturning the position established in Rev. Rul. 64-308, 1964-2 C.B. 176, prior to adoption of § 1367(b)(4)(A), IRD treatment applies as if the decedent held each item of income directly rather than owning an interest in the S Corporation. See § 1366(a)(1) regarding items properly includible in the final return of a shareholder who dies before the S Corporation's year ends.

[22] Many well drafted trusts avoid distribution of this item to a deceased income beneficiary's estate with a provision that terminates a life income beneficiary's income entitlement on the last income payment date prior to the beneficiary's death; accrued but undistributed income is directed to the next beneficiary. See, e.g., § 13.6.2.5, regarding marital deduction consequences of calling for distribution of the corpus and undistributed income of a trust at the death of the income beneficiary.

§ 5.10.1

- Postmortem settlement payments under litigation in process before the decedent's death, to the extent the damage recovery is not excluded from income;[23]

- Interest payments attributable to the period prior to the decedent's death on an original issue discount obligation or a United States Treasury or savings bond,[24] to the extent not included in income premortem;

- Rent payments, including crop share rentals, for periods prior to the decedent's death;[25]

---

[23] Estate of Carter v. Commissioner, 298 F.2d 192 (8th Cir. 1962) (decedent's claim to profits that would have accrued if not for antitrust violations); Rev. Rul. 78-292, 1978-2 C.B. 233 (medical expenses deducted by the decedent in a prior year reimbursed in a year after the decedent's death); Rev. Rul. 55-463, 1955-2 C.B. 277 (patent infringement damage action); cf. Krakowski v. Commissioner, 65 T.C.M. (CCH) 2969 (1993) (S received repayment of monies embezzled by a third party from D's campaign contribution fund, which constituted IRD notwithstanding that it subsequently was determined that S was not entitled to retain the funds; the claim of right doctrine applied to require inclusion because, at the time of the embezzler's repayment, it appeared that the law allowed D's successors in interest to retain those funds); PLR 8740042 (employee died before receiving all of a settlement that would have been includible in income had the employee lived).

[24] Treas. Reg. § 1.691(a)-2(b) Example (3); Levin v. United States, 385 F.2d 434 (1st Cir. 1967); Richardson v. United States, 294 F.2d 593 (6th Cir. 1961); Estate of Noel v. Commissioner, 50 T.C. 702 (1968); Rev. Rul. 79-340, 1979-2 C.B. 320; Rev. Rul. 76-153, 1976-1 C.B. 180; Rev. Rul. 58-435, 1958-2 C.B. 370 (the last Ruling involving some interest that represented income in respect of a prior decedent and some that represented income in respect of the current decedent, attributable to accruals that had not been reported as income during the lives of a decedent who inherited bonds with accrued income from a prior decedent, all properly deferred under § 454); TAM 200624065 (installment payment of a property settlement incident to divorce, which was noninterest bearing but contained an annual adjustment to reflect changes in the consumer price index, which the government regarded as an interest component "compensation for the delay in payment of the stated principal amount" that was IRD to the beneficiaries who received payments after the note holder died). See also Rev. Rul. 64-104, 1964-1 C.B. 223 (reissuance of bond distributed in satisfaction of pecuniary legacy treated as a sale or exchange that terminated the income deferral).

[25] Most rentals are paid before the term begins, which is income to the payee at the time of payment without proration, even if the payee dies before expiration of the term. Treas. Reg. § 1.61-8(b). Crop share rentals differ because they are paid upon harvest, at the end of the rent term, and are pro rated for that portion of the growing season during which the decedent was alive. Estate of Davis v. United States, 68-2 U.S. Tax Cas. (CCH) ¶ 9483 (S.D. Ill. 1968); Estate of Davison

§5.10.1

- Royalty payments in connection with works created by the decedent (but not the proceeds from any postmortem licensing agreement or sale of a copyright or patent);[26]

- Dividends payable to the decedent as the shareholder of record on a date that preceded death;[27]

(Footnote Continued)

v. United States, 292 F.2d 937 (Ct. Cl. 1961); Rev. Rul. 64-289, 1964-2 C.B. 173. See also Estate of Rowan v. Commissioner, 54 T.C. 633 (1970) (involving sale of crop shares before death but the proceeds were not received before the decedent's death). Under Treas. Reg. § 1.61-4(a) (last sentence), crop share rentals received in kind do not constitute income until sold, making this an even more likely source of IRD if death occurs anytime after the crop was planted and before it is sold.

Rev. Rul. 64-289, 1964-2 C.B. 173, suggests that the result would differ if the decedent actively and materially participated in production of the crop because, if the crop has not yet been harvested when the decedent dies, it is regarded as part of the property and is entitled to participate in the new basis at death adjustment.

[26] Compare Dorsey v. Commissioner, 49 T.C. 606 (1968) (royalties from sale of patent), and Rev. Rul. 57-544, 1957-2 C.B. 361 (royalties from sale of copyright), holding that payments postmortem constituted IRD, with Rev. Rul. 60-227, 1960-1 C.B. 262 (license permitting manufacturer to use decedent's patent), PLRs 9549023 and 9326043 (fees paid after death under a license to exploit a copyright, as opposed to proceeds from a sale of the copyright itself), and PLR 9043068 (postmortem sale of art created by decedent and as to which there was no negotiation or binding sale agreement concluded prior to the decedent's death), all holding essentially that postmortem royalties are like rent that was earned by and taxable to the successive owners on the basis of the periods covered and activities conducted by the successive owners of the underlying interest. Sale proceeds in excess of a new basis at death are taxable to the new owner to the extent they represent the new owner's negotiation and sale and not the completion of a deal undertaken by the decedent before death. See § 5.10.1 at text accompanying n.10. Presumably the same results would apply to similar income producing assets created by a decedent before death, such as art, music, literature, or intellectual property.

[27] Unlike rent and interest, which are deemed to accrue on a daily basis and that may cover a period that straddles the decedent's date of death and therefore must be prorated, dividends are deemed earned on the date they are paid (or declared, if earlier) and are taxable to the owner of record on that date (or any record date, if later), without proration. Estate of Putnam v. United States, 324 U.S. 393 (1945); Estate of Cooper v. Commissioner, 291 F.2d 831 (4th Cir. 1961); Boyle v. United States, 232 F. Supp. 543 (D. N.J. 1964), rev'd on another ground, 355 F.2d 233 (3d Cir. 1965); Estate of McNary v. Commissioner, 47 T.C. 467 (1967). A different rule is applicable with respect to S Corporation stock, because

• Postmortem installment payments for taxable transfers completed premortem,[28] which is a topic of sufficient controversy to justify elaboration.

Lump sum or installment payments with respect to sales clearly made postmortem are not income of any variety to or in respect of the decedent. Indeed, there may be little or no income or capital gain to tax on a sale closely after the decedent's death if the property being sold was included in the decedent's gross estate and a § 1014(b)(9) basis adjustment was generated.[29] Alternatively, payments under installment receivables with respect to sales clearly completed premortem constitute IRD to the extent the postmortem payments include capital gain or other forms of income realized prior to the decedent's death.[30]

(Footnote Continued)

§ 1377(a)(1) prorates S Corporation taxable income and deductions like interest; unless the § 1377(a)(2) election is made to terminate the corporation's year at the decedent's death, all items are prorated to a decedent for the portion of the year prior to the decedent's death.

[28] Installment obligations are subject to § 691(a)(4), and § 691(a)(3) ensures that payments retain the same character they had in the decedent's hands. See Hedrick v. Commissioner, 63 T.C. 395 (1974); Sun First Nat'l Bank v. United States, 607 F.2d 1347 (Ct. Cl. 1979). Under § 453B(c) death is not an acceleration event unless the obligor is the transferee of the obligation or there is a § 691(a)(5)(A) cancellation of the debt. See, e.g., TAM 8552007 (decedent's will instructed executor to cancel installment obligations includible in decedent's FET gross estate; acceleration transfer occurred upon executor's assent to the cancellation). See also § 5.10.5.

[29] See Treas. Reg. § 1.691(a)-2(b) Example (4), illustrating a buy-sell agreement that clearly contemplated sale after—albeit triggered by—the decedent's death. See also Rev. Rul. 71-265, 1971-1 C.B. 223 (sale under option exercisable only after decedent's demise), and PLR 9325029 (inter vivos grant of option to purchase realty exercisable only after optionor's death was not tantamount to a sale, which prevented postmortem exercise of the option from causing IRD and avoided § 1014(c) disallowance of the new basis at death adjustment).

[30] Treas. Reg. § 1.691(a)-2(b) Example (4) (last sentence); Biewer v. Commissioner, 341 F.2d 394 (6th Cir. 1965), aff'g 41 T.C. 191 (1963) (accounts receivable originating from sales); Poorbaugh v. United States, 423 F.2d 157 (3d Cir. 1970), rev'g 69-1 U.S. Tax Cas. ¶ 9134 (W.D. Pa. 1968) (same); Estate of Bickmeyer v. Commissioner, 84 T.C. 170 (1985) (liquidation proceeds); Coleman v. Commissioner, 87 T.C.M. (CCH) 1367 (2004) (remaining payments to a veterinarian's estate under an anticompetition agreement incident to sale of the decedent's animal hospital). The character of any income is preserved under § 691(a)(3).

§ 5.10.1

For example, if the decedent sold Blackacre in exchange for an installment note payable over many years and died before the last payment, the remaining installment payments made to the decedent's successor in interest would constitute capital gain IRD to the extent each payment would have been capital gain had the decedent still been alive. Any additional interest element in each installment payment would constitute IRD, however, only to the extent the interest component compensated for the use of the deferred sale price for a period prior to the decedent's death.

Although some accounting and similar administrative issues can complicate these situations, neither presents a difficult IRD inquiry. Instead, problems arise when it is not clear whether a sale was complete before the decedent died, making it difficult to know whether the successor in interest acquired a right to receive proceeds from the sale or the asset itself. For example, in Claiborne v. United States,[31] the decedent negotiated a contract for the sale of land, allowed the purchaser to take possession of the property and begin earthwork, received a modest amount of earnest money (described as the total liquidated damages the purchaser would be obliged to pay if the transaction was not consummated), but predeceased the final transfer of title. Nevertheless, holding that the decedent had performed all the necessary substantive acts relative to the sale before dying and thereby generated an enforceable right to payment under the contract, the court determined that the sale was sufficiently complete prior to the decedent's death to regard the postmortem payments as IRD. This triggered the § 1014(c) denial of a new basis in the property and left the income element in each installment payment subject to tax.

On the other hand, however, Estate of Peterson v. Commissioner[32] determined that a sale of cattle negotiated by the decedent premortem but as to which delivery did not occur until after death was not completed by the decedent and therefore postmortem payments under that sale contract were not IRD. Involved was a feedlot operation and fewer than all the livestock were sufficiently developed to be deliverable prior to the decedent's death. The court held that the entire sale was incom-

---

[31] 648 F.2d 448 (6th Cir. 1981), vacating and rem'g 449 F. Supp. 4 (W.D. Ky. 1978).

[32] 667 F.2d 675 (8th Cir. 1981), aff'g 74 T.C. 630 (1980).

§ 5.10.1

plete, notwithstanding a suggestion in a Tax Court concurring opinion that a portion of the proceeds attributable to cattle that were sufficiently mature to be delivered premortem might be regarded as the right to receive IRD if the government argued for severability of the contract. The court on appeal rejected the notion of partial completion and severability as incorrectly emphasizing "the condition or character of the subject matter of the sale instead of the status of the transaction itself at the time of the decedent's death."[33]

In the process, the Tax Court in *Peterson* formulated a four part standard to determine whether a transaction is sufficiently complete prior to a decedent's death to create an enforceable entitlement, of which the proceeds might constitute IRD: (1) there was a legally significant arrangement, such as a contract, regarding the disposition; (2) the decedent performed all the substantive (nonministerial) acts required as a condition of the transaction (such as putting the *Peterson* cattle in a deliverable condition); (3) there were no economically material contingencies that might disrupt the transaction; and (4) the decedent would have been entitled to the proceeds if the decedent had lived.

The key is whether the decedent's successor in interest was entitled to receive the proceeds of the transaction without investing more effort than mere ministerial or nonsubstantive acts, such as physical delivery of the subject of the transaction and collection of the proceeds.[34] If the Tax Court's four conditions are met, then the proceeds constitute IRD to the extent they would have constituted income to the decedent if still alive.

---

[33] 667 F.2d at 679.

[34] See Ferguson, Freeland, & Ascher, Federal Income Taxation of Estates, Trusts, and Beneficiaries § 3.03 (3d ed. 2011), which applies a "working definition" of IRD as "a right or expectancy created almost entirely through the efforts or status of the decedent and that, except for the decedent's death and without further action on his or her part, the decedent would have realized as gross income"; the authors distill four salient characteristics: (1) the item would have been taxable to the decedent because attributable to the decedent's services, sales, or income producing activity, (2) the income did not sufficiently mature to require inclusion before the decedent's death, (3) what passed is a passive right to receive income because the decedent performed all substantial acts needed to generate the right to that income, and (4) the recipient of the right to receive that income acquired it by virtue of the decedent's death and not their own substantial efforts. Ferguson, Freeland, & Ascher, Federal Income Taxation of Estates, Trusts, and Beneficiaries § 3.03 (3d ed. 2011).

§ 5.10.1

The *Peterson* payments were not IRD because the decedent needed to perform significant substantive activities (feeding cattle until they reached a certain age and maturity) before the right to those payments was complete.

A similar case to contrast with *Peterson* is Commissioner v. Linde,[35] in which the decedent delivered a grape harvest to a cooperative that would sell it and remit the proceeds. Although the cooperative had not made the sale and the decedent's entitlement therefore was not yet complete, the decedent had done everything required of the decedent to be entitled to payment of the income and the court appropriately concluded that, once made, the payments represented IRD.[36]

Even with the guidance of the *Peterson* formulation, sales transactions present more uncertainty than cases involving income attributable to a decedent's investments or performance of services. For example, in Estate of Sidles v. Commissioner[37] and Trust Co. v. Ross,[38] the decedents were in charge of sale transactions and fulfilled all of their obligations in transactions that yielded income in respect of those decedents. But Keck v. Commissioner[39] involved a taxpayer who was not in control of a transaction, it was not sufficiently mature to be enforceable, and the court concluded that proceeds of that sale could not be income in

---

[35] 213 F.2d 1 (9th Cir. 1954), rev'g 17 T.C. 584 (1951). See Treas. Reg. § 1.691(a)-2(b) Example (5).

[36] See also Rev. Rul. 78-32, 1978-1 C.B. 198 (contract for sale of realty gave rise to IRD because the decedent had substantially fulfilled all of the substantive prerequisites to consummation of the sale and was unconditionally entitled to the proceeds of the sale at the time of death); PLR 9023012 (decedent entered into a sales contract before death with a 45 day mortgage contingency, during which period the decedent died; notwithstanding that the buyer did not obtain financing within that period, the estate and the buyer agreed to extend the contingency period and ultimately closed the sale without a new contract; the government held that the sale proceeds constituted IRD, citing Rev. Rul. 78-32 and Treas. Reg. § 1.691(a)-1(b)(3) to the effect that IRD can include income as to which the decedent had only a contingent claim at death). Compare § 5.10.1 n.10 and accompanying text.

[37] 65 T.C. 873 (1976).

[38] 262 F. Supp. 900 (N.D. Ga. 1966).

[39] 415 F.2d 531 (6th Cir. 1969), rev'g 49 T.C. 313 (1968).

§ 5.10.1

respect of that decedent.[40] The difference between the cases was probably only the degree of control exercisable by the decedent, as opposed to the actual maturity of the deal and the right to payment when the decedent died. The bottom line is that these types of cases will continue to be fact specific and may turn in part on whether IRD treatment is favorable to the taxpayer, which sometimes is the case.

§5.10.2 Tax Consequences of IRD

Contrary to the notion that income normally is something to be avoided and therefore that IRD also cannot be a good thing, the reality is that sometimes it is preferable to meet the definition of IRD. To the extent the income tax rate applicable with respect to the item in the hands of the decedent's successor in interest is not significantly different than the rate applicable to the decedent or to the decedent's estate, the issue always should be whether the characterization as IRD is better than the next best alternative. In that respect, there are four categories into which an item might fall for income tax purposes:

(1) It is not income to anyone (which may be attributable to the fact that the asset was includible in the decedent's gross estate for FET purposes and is not denied the §1014(b)(9) new basis at death that eliminates any potential postmortem capital gain on premortem appreciation);

(2) It is the decedent's premortem income reportable on the decedent's final income tax return, as to which a §2053(a)(3) FET deduction is allowable for the decedent's unpaid income tax liability on that income. The IRD rules are not relevant and the new basis at death rule probably is not meaningful, because taking the item into the decedent's income gives it a basis equal in most cases to its FMV anyway;

(3) It is IRD, meaning that the §1014(b)(9) new basis at death rule is not applicable[41] but a deduction is allowable under §691(c) for income tax

---

[40] See also PLR 9102018 (decedent owned a partnership interest that owned another partnership interest, and it was the second level partnership that was selling the property; when the decedent died the selling partnership had a contingent contract to sell, but the contingency was beyond the decedent's control, it ultimately was not met, the contract lapsed three weeks after the decedent's death and, although it later was renewed and the sale ultimately closed, the gain on that sale ultimately passing through to the decedent's estate as owner of the first level partnership interest was not regarded as IRD); and see Estate of Napolitano, discussed in §5.10.1 n.10.

[41] §1014(c).

purposes[42] and the character and holding period of the item are the same as if the decedent still was alive to receive it;[43]

(4) It is income of the decedent's successor in interest, making the § 1014(b)(9) new basis rule irrelevant—if it is not the decedent's income it probably is not FET includible[44]—and there is no § 691(c) deduction either, which may be a bigger cost than any difference in income tax rates because the item will be taxed at the recipient's rates whether it is IRD or just the recipient's income.

If an item *is* income, being in category (2) may be preferred because the § 2053(a)(3) deduction for the decedent's outstanding unpaid income tax liability at death likely reduces the taxable amount for both state and federal wealth transfer tax purposes. The § 691(c) deduction does not reflect state death tax so category (3) is not as favorable, even though the deduction is meant to provide equivalent treatment to the § 2053 result for category (2) items.[45]

---

[42] The deduction is a rough justice for the fact that FET is incurred on the full value of the right to receive the IRD, unreduced by the income tax that would have been incurred by the decedent had the income been received during life. Rather than recompute the FET with a deduction when the income tax liability ultimately is determined, § 691(c) allows an income tax deduction for the *federal* (but not for any *state*) GST and estate tax attributable to that item. See § 5.10.3.

[43] § 691(a)(3); Treas. Reg. § 1.691(a)-3. See Lacomble v. United States, 177 F. Supp. 373 (N.D. Cal. 1959) (if pension payments received by deceased participant's surviving spouse were IRD, a portion would have been excluded as deferred compensation for services rendered while the decedent was a nonresident of the United States); Rev. Rul. 82-1, 1982-1 C.B. 26 (because recipient essentially stands in decedent's shoes, § 121 election to exclude gain on sale of decedent's personal residence pursuant to decedent's sale contract was not lost when decedent died); PLR 199901023 (§ 401 qualified plan lump sum payment to CRUT entitled the trust to a § 691(c) deduction—computed with the § 2055 deduction reflected, as illustrated in § 5.10.3—and the net amount retained its character as ordinary income to the trust, carried out to the unitrust beneficiary as first tier income).

[44] It could be that resolution of the IRD question will affect the FET includibility of the item, but it is more likely that the value represented by the right to receive the income will be reflected for FET purposes in one way or another, regardless of the § 691 determination.

[45] This category (2) versus (3) debate essentially describes Eberly v. Commissioner, T.C. Summ. Op. 2006-45 (not citable as precedent). The court found on very unusual facts that it was a category (2) item received by the decedent on the date of death.

If the item clearly is not in category (2) because it clearly is not the *decedent's* income, but it is income to someone, then FET inclusion is not going to generate new basis at death under §1014(b)(9) and IRD treatment in category (3) may be desirable. If the same amount is going to be income to someone, better that it should be IRD and generate the §691(c) deduction[46] than that it be income of the successor and taxable in its full amount, unreduced by the deduction. Thus, in most cases for tax purposes being in a higher category in the foregoing list is preferable to being in a lower category, particularly if the FET inclusion of the asset or the right to receive the income is not affected by the IRD debate and the income tax rates of the respective taxpayers are not significantly different.

A nontax consequence of the determination whether an item is IRD relates to fiduciary accounting, which may regard the right to receive IRD as principal as opposed to normal income earned and collected postmortem and allocable to fiduciary accounting income. This characterization could affect which beneficiary receives the benefit of the item,

---

[46] An alternative to IRD treatment and the §691(c) income tax deduction may be to regard the item as income taxable to the decedent's estate on the decedent's final income tax return that generates an income tax liability that qualifies for an FET §2053(a)(3) deduction as a claim against the decedent's estate. See, e.g., TAM 9232006 (income tax generated postmortem by personal representative's §454 election to incur income tax on decedent's final income tax return was a deductible indebtedness of the estate). The FET deduction is limited to income tax "on income properly includible in an income tax return of the decedent for a period before his death. Taxes on income received after the decedent's death are not deductible." Treas. Reg. §20.2053-6(f). See TAM 200444021 (income tax on right to receive IRD denied as §2053(a)(3) deduction). The §454 election caused taxation of accrued interest in Series HH bonds (and the same situation would exist with Series EE bonds as well) as if it had been received in the year of the decedent's death, reportable on the decedent's final income tax return and qualifying for the §2053 deduction. Excepting for any effect on the marginal tax rates under either the income tax or FET, the choice of approach produces no tax differential at the federal level. The same tax is incurred whether the estate incurs an income tax on the full amount of IRD and then pays an FET on the gross estate as reduced by a §2053 deduction for that income tax, or pays FET on the full amount of IRD and then pays an income tax on an amount that reflects the §691(c) deduction for that FET. If a state death tax is incurred, however, the estate would be better served by receipt inter vivos than by postmortem receipt of the income with a §691(c) deduction, all as illustrated in §5.10.3 n.48.

§5.10.2

and when. And an exception to this preference for IRD may exist if, for example, the character preservation rules mean that the decedent's income is subject to a disadvantageous recapture rule such as § § 1239, 1245, and 1250 that the successor in interest would avoid if it was their income.

§ 5.10.3 Deduction for Wealth Transfer Tax

The linchpin to finding favor in treating an item as IRD is the income tax deduction allowed for federal FET and GST attributable to IRD.[47] If a receipt properly is characterized as income for federal income tax purposes, the fact that it represents IRD may be desirable. The § 691(c) income tax deduction for FET or GST attributable to the right to receive that IRD makes the income less heavily taxed than if this characterization did not apply.

The notion underlying the deduction is that, had the income been received by the decedent during life, any income tax incurred on it would have reduced the decedent's gross estate prior to imposition of these wealth transfer taxes. Congress could allow recomputation of those taxes after the income tax is incurred by the successor in interest. Instead Congress substituted an income tax deduction for the FET or GST attributable to the right to receive the IRD. The computation can result in differences in the aggregate tax being paid[48] (and the income tax payer may reap a deduction attributable to federal GST or estate taxes paid by other beneficiaries), but the general objective is to produce

---

[47] § 691(c). Note that *state* death tax is *not* reflected in this deduction.

[48] For example, assume that the decedent's estate is valued at $4 million, of which $100,000 is IRD, that the estate is in a 35% marginal FET bracket and a 33% income tax bracket. With $35,000 of FET attributable to the IRD, the § 691(c) deduction saves $11,550 of income tax and the income tax on the remaining $65,000 is $21,450. The total tax incurred on the IRD is $35,000 of FET and $21,450 of income tax for a total of $56,450. If the income had been taxed to the decedent before dying at the same 33% income tax rate, only $67,000 of after tax income would remain to inflate the decedent's estate at death and, if the FET marginal rate remained at 35%, the FET attributable to it would be $23,450, for a total tax liability on the IRD of the same $56,450. The only deviation from this equivalence would be if the amounts involved altered the tax bracket in which various computations are performed.

§ 5.10.3

a result that is administratively easier than recomputation of the wealth transfer tax and a refund action.

Added planning is required with respect to the right to receive IRD to maximize the benefit of the § 691(c) deduction,[49] to avoid a § 691(a)(2) acceleration of the income tax liability on a distribution,[50] and to determine the best allocation of the income tax liability among various potential beneficiaries.[51] For example, a specific bequest to charity of a right to receive IRD is preferable to making a bequest of cash or other assets to the charity. To the extent distribution of the right does not accelerate the

---

[49] Under § 691(c)(1)(B), any portion of a right to receive IRD that is paid, credited, or [required] to be distributed [compare Treas. Reg. § 1.691(c)-2(a)(1)—which includes the word "required"—with § 691(c)(1)(B)—which does not] to a trust or estate beneficiary reduces the amount of the IRD of the entity for determining its § 691(c) deduction.

[50] See § 5.10.5.

[51] The normal § 661 distributions deduction and income carryout and character preservation rules preserve the character of the IRD for taxation in the beneficiary's hands when the income represented by that right is received. Thus, the fiduciary may distribute the right to IRD and, by the exercise of discretion, determine to whom that income ultimately will be attributed for income tax purposes. The fiduciary must have discretion to distribute corpus as well as income to accomplish this allocation, however, if state law regards the right to receive IRD as fiduciary accounting corpus.

Treas. Reg. § 1.691(c)-2(a) describes how much of the § 691(c) deduction passes through to the beneficiary. Because IRD is not excluded by § 643(a) in computing the entity's DNI, it will carry out pro rata like any other income item absent a different allocation of various classes of income under specific terms of the governing instrument. The § 691(c) deduction is not considered in computing the entity's DNI to the extent a beneficiary receives that income as part or all of a distribution from the entity and is entitled to the § 691(c) deduction. Treas. Reg. § 1.691(c)-2(a)(2). The § 691(c) deduction is available to the entity, however, to the extent the right to receive IRD is not distributed and the income represented by that right is realized by and taxed to the entity, after which the income loses its character for future throwback purposes, if any will apply. § 667(a); Treas. Reg. § 1.691(c)-2(a)(3).

If there is more than one recipient of the right to receive the IRD, the income tax liability may be fragmented but so too is the § 691(c) deduction, which is pro rated between them. § 691(c)(1)(A); cf. Treas. Reg. § 1.691(c)-1(d) Example (1). If there is more than one recipient due to the fact that the income is in respect of a *prior* decedent, all wealth transfer tax in each prior estate attributable to that item is available. Treas. Reg. §§ 1.691(c)-1(b), -1(d) Example (2).

§5.10.3

income and is not a gain or loss realization event, there will be no income tax consequence to the estate or its other beneficiaries and the charity should be exempt from income tax on the income as it is received.[52]

Similarly, allocation to a marital deduction bequest may be desirable, because inclusion of a right to receive IRD in an FET marital deduction bequest should not affect the amount of the allowable marital deduction[53] and the income tax liability will reduce the amount subject to FET when S subsequently dies. Because some beneficiary must incur the income tax liability, better that it should reduce the amount next subject to FET. And the all-income-annually requirement for § 2056(b)(5) or § 2056(b)(7) marital deduction trust purposes will not be violated, even if controlling local law requires allocation to corpus of the right to receive the IRD.[54] Only the amount of the § 691(c) deduction should be affected by these allocations, as illustrated by the government's relatively artificial method of computing that entitlement.

---

[52] See, e.g., PLR 9634019 (qualified plan proceeds payable to qualified CRUT will not cause taxation to participant and will be income to the private lead beneficiary only as distributed, under the priority rules in § 664(b)(1), and otherwise will not be taxable at the trust level); PLR 9341008 (IRA that designated a private foundation as beneficiary would produce no income to the taxpayer, the taxpayer's estate, or to the beneficiaries of the taxpayer's estate, and would generate income to the foundation only when income was distributed from the account as opposed to when the right to receive the payments was given to the foundation; however, because "a private foundation will not be able to satisfy the requirements" of then Prop. Treas. Reg. § 1.401(a)(9)-1 Q&A D-5 (now Treas. Reg. § 1.401(a)(9)-4 A-1), payments would be required to the private foundation by the IRA within five years after the taxpayer's death, pursuant to § 401(a)(9)(B)(ii)).

[53] The fact that the right to the IRD has a built-in income tax liability does not affect its value for FET marital or charitable deduction purposes. See §§ 13.7.3.2.4 n.80 and 14.1.4 n.71.

[54] Treas. Reg. §§ 20.2056(b)-5(e) and -5(f) adopt the state law principal and income allocation rules as controlling in determining whether S is entitled to the requisite income.

§ 5.10.3

The § 691(c) deduction is determined by reference to the FET imposed on the decedent's estate[55] attributable to the net value[56] of all items of IRD, which is deemed to be "the excess of the estate tax over the estate tax computed without including in the gross estate such net value."[57] Thus, a determination of the excess requires an initial computation with the net value included in the decedent's gross estate and then a recomputation with the net value excluded from the gross estate.

In the context of a bequest of the right to receive the IRD to S or to a marital deduction trust, the government's computation approach is to conclude that the estate would be smaller if there was no IRD. Thus, any marital deduction that is tied to the value of the estate also would be smaller by the *full* amount of any IRD that is allocated to S or to the marital deduction trust, because that income no longer would exist.[58] The result is a taxable estate of the same amount as before the recomputation, with the consequence that no § 691(c) deduction is available— because it is the amount of any tax differential and there is none.

In Estate of Kincaid v. Commissioner[59] the taxpayer asserted that this method of computation was wrong, in that case involving a formula marital deduction bequest equal to 50% of the adjusted gross estate. According to the estate, if there was no IRD, the marital deduction bequest would be 50% of a smaller gross estate, producing a smaller taxable estate and, therefore, a lower tax. The Tax Court agreed with the taxpayer in *Kincaid*, stating first that "there is no guidance in the statute

---

[55] § 691(c)(2)(A); the FET is determined net of allowable credits against the tax. FSA 200011023 clarified that the credit is allowable for FET "imposed," even if the income tax deduction is being claimed before that FET actually is paid, due to the timing of return preparation and deadlines.

[56] § 691(c)(1)(A); "net value" is defined by § 691(c)(2)(B) as the excess of the value for FET purposes of all items of IRD over the value of any § 691(b) DRD, even if the recipient of the IRD is not the same person who incurred the expenses that generated the DRD. Treas. Reg. § 1.691(c)-1(a)(1). See § 5.10.4, regarding DRD. The examples in this segment assume that there is no DRD.

[57] § 691(c)(2)(C).

[58] See Treas. Reg. §§ 1.691(c)-1(a)(2), 1.691(d)-1(e) Example (2); Rev. Rul. 67-242, 1967-2 C.B. 227. Compare Chastain v. Commissioner, 59 T.C. 461 (1972), acq. and nonacq., 1978-2 C.B. 1, 3 (charitable deduction case rejecting government's computation approach), considered in AOD 1978-103.

[59] 85 T.C. 25, 29 (1985).

§ 5.10.3

or the legislative history on the specific point in issue," and then that the taxpayer's method of computation:

> fits more logically into the scheme of the statute . . . [because]
> . . . the IRD produced additional estate tax . . . [and] . . .
> allocation of assets as between marital and nonmarital shares
> should be irrelevant. . . . [L]ogically, it must be concluded that
> the surviving spouse is entitled to some deduction for the excess
> estate tax paid because of the inclusion of the IRD in the estate.
> This conclusion should not be nullified by the happenstance that
> the IRD passed to the marital share rather than the nonmarital
> share.

The issue that remains unresolved following *Kincaid*, however, is the computational effect of post-1981 optimum marital deduction formula provisions. *Kincaid* involved an old-style 50% maximum marital bequest, which produced a different result than would a bequest of the smallest amount needed to reduce FET to the maximum amount that would be offset by the unified credit.[60] This result is not affected by *Kincaid*, making that decision important only in non-optimum but formula marital deduction situations or if any items of IRD must be used to fully satisfy the marital deduction bequest.[61]

§5.10.4 DRD

Analogous to those rules relating to IRD is §691(b), which deals with *deductions* and *credits* in respect of the decedent. Involved are only certain items that would have been the decedent's deductions or credits if still alive[62] and that survive the decedent's death to constitute a

---

[60] See the illustration in §13.7.3.2.5.

[61] See Ferguson, Freeland, & Ascher, Federal Income Taxation of Estates, Trusts, and Beneficiaries §3.07[B][3] (3d ed. 2011).

[62] Itemized under §691(b)(1) are only the §§162 (business expenses), 163 (interest), 164 (taxes), 212 (expenses of producing income or managing or safeguarding income producing property), and 611 (percentage depletion) deductions, and the §27 foreign tax credit. See, e.g., Rev. Rul. 76-498, 1976-2 C.B. 199 (decedent retained trust income for life, so the income was taxable to the decedent under §677(a) and the corpus was includible under §2036(a)(1); trustee commissions and expenses attributable to income producing assets prior to decedent's death were allowed as DRD and could be claimed for both income tax and FET purposes because the §642(g) swing item prohibition is not applicable with respect to DRD).

§5.10.4

reduction in computing or paying the tax on net IRD.[63] These deductible payments would have reduced the decedent's taxable income had the decedent incurred them during life and payment would have reduced the decedent's net worth for FET purposes. Therefore, DRD is excepted from the §642(g) limitation that denies an income tax deduction if an FET deduction is allowed for the same item postmortem.[64]

For postmortem planning purposes, if the §691(c) deduction is available, consideration should be given to taking normal swing items as income tax deductions rather than as FET deductions, to boost the FET attributable to the IRD and correspondingly boost the §691(c) deduction. The swing item election—whether to claim the expenses as an income tax or FET deduction—often produces an inequality that requires an adjustment.[65] The adjustment can be all the more difficult in this context because the §691(c) deduction is affected and because the payor of an item that constitutes DRD may not be the same as the person who receives the IRD and who enjoys the §691(c) deduction. It is made doubly difficult because the deductions paid by one serve to benefit the other by directly reducing the tax paid on the net IRD. This compounded inequity might justify an added equitable adjustment to compensate the payor who produced the DRD by allocating to them the benefit of the tax saving enjoyed by the beneficiary of the IRD. To date, however, there appears to be no authority directing such an additional adjustment.

§5.10.5 Acceleration of Income Tax Liability

Certain transfers of the right to receive IRD cause an acceleration of the income represented by that right.[66] Includible in the transferor's

---

[63] §691(b)(1)(B) allocates the deductions and credit to any person other than the decedent's estate who became subject to the obligation by reason of the decedent's death or their acquisition of property to which the obligation relates. See, e.g., Rev. Rul. 58-69, 1958-1 C.B. 254 (real estate taxes that were a charge against the decedent's real estate prior to death were the estate's §691(b)(1)(A) deduction on its fiduciary income tax return in the year in which the estate paid those taxes, but those taxes paid by the estate on behalf of estate beneficiaries in lieu of paying them the income directly were deductible by the estate under §661).

[64] §642(g) (last sentence).

[65] See §13.3.6.

[66] §691(a)(2).

gross income for the taxable year of the transfer is the greater of the amount of any consideration received for the transfer or the FMV of the right at the time of the transfer.

Some transfers are excepted. For example, in PLR 201116005 a beneficiary's transfer to the beneficiary's self-settled SNT was not an acceleration event because the trust was an income tax grantor trust with respect to that beneficiary, meaning that the transfer was ignored for income tax purposes. In addition, transfers by the decedent's estate to any beneficiary to whom the right was specifically bequeathed or as part of the residue passing to a residuary beneficiary are not acceleration events.[67] Distributions by a trustee in similar circumstances *ought* to be accorded similar treatment, but the law simply is not clear as to whether there is symmetry.[68]

---

[67] Treas. Reg. § 1.691(a)-4(b). Cf. PLRs 200633009, 200618023, 200617020, 200520004, and 200234019 (allocation in satisfaction of pick and choose fraction residuary bequest to charity is not an acceleration event). See § 13.7.9.1.3 n.138. See also PLRs 200845029 (which does not make explicit that the bequest was a fractional entitlement, but it *was* to "a residuary beneficiary"), and 200850004, in which the designated beneficiary of an IRA disclaimed, making the owner's estate the recipient, and the estate obtained a court order "to designate the IRA as the source of [various] charity's (sic) specific shares of [the] Estate," as if the decedent had named the charities originally; the government held that no acceleration would result. It is not clear in the Ruling whether the charities' shares were fractional entitlements.

[68] A terminating distribution by a trust is not an acceleration event. Treas. Reg. § 1.691(a)-4(b)(3). But the § 691(a)(2) exception for estate distributions that do not generate acceleration does not list trust interim transfers. PLR 200023030 is unusual in that it involved the surviving settlor of a joint settlor trust that was the beneficiary of the deceased settlor's IRA and who had the power as trustee to allocate the decedent's IRA to a following trust and from there was deemed to have the power to roll it over to a new IRA of the surviving settlor's own creation. The allocation and ultimate roll over were deemed not to accelerate the income in respect of the deceased settlor because the surviving settlor had grantor trust income tax exposure with respect to both trusts. In a similar vein PLR 200826008 blessed a conservator's allocation of a beneficiary's right to an IRA to an IDGT and held that there was no § 691(a)(2) acceleration because there was no sale or disposition. And PLRs 200826028, 200803002, 200652028, and 200526010 involved pick-and-choose fractional distributions in satisfaction of trust residuary divisions among charities, with no acceleration and no indication that the authors of the Rulings regarded a trust distribution as any different from an estate distribution.

§ 5.10.5

On the other hand, certain distributions are sure to trigger acceleration. For example, distributions in satisfaction of pecuniary bequests are acceleration events,[69] and an estate beneficiary who receives the right to IRD in a nonaccelerating distribution will cause an acceleration by making a gift of the right to a third party.[70]

Of special concern with respect to acceleration is the cancellation or forgiveness of installment obligations held by a decedent and in which capital gain or accumulated unpaid interest constitutes IRD. For example, a will that cancels an installment note causes a § 691(a)(5)(A)(iii) transfer that constitutes a § 691(a)(2) acceleration of any deferred income represented by the note.[71] Indeed, if the cancellation constitutes a § 663(a)(1) specific bequest that precludes any estate DNI from being taxed to the deemed distributee—the obligor on that note—the accelerated income will be includible in estate DNI and be trapped at the estate level, to be taxed to the decedent's estate unless it is carried out by other distributions to other beneficiaries. The right result would be to guarantee that acceleration changes only the timing and not the liability for payment of income tax on income represented by the note.[72] Instead the

---

[69] § 691(a)(2); CCA 200644020 (income represented by the decedent's IRA payable to a trust was accelerated by allocation in partial satisfaction of pecuniary bequests to charities) and PLRs 9507008 and 9315016 (IRD contained in Series E and H bonds recognized in year bonds were distributed in satisfaction of a trust's obligation to pay a pecuniary bequest to a charity). Cf. Estate of Noel v. Commissioner, 50 T.C. 702 (1968) (right to IRD transferred in satisfaction of a debt of the decedent). See § 13.7.3.2.4 with respect to distribution in the context of pecuniary marital deduction funding.

[70] Treas. Reg. § 1.691(a)-4(a) (penultimate sentence).

[71] See, e.g., PLR 9108027.

[72] TAM 9240003 held that a similar cancellation did not produce discharge of indebtedness income to the obligor because the facts showed that the cancellation involved donative intent that qualified it for the gift exception to § 61(a)(12). In discussing the proper value of the notes, which were given in a loan transaction, for inclusion in the decedent's estate, the TAM indicated that the outstanding indebtedness was well in excess of the original principal amount of the debt, presumably indicating that there was unpaid accumulated interest owing when the decedent died. The government did not indicate that this deferred interest was accelerated into the decedent's estate. The unspoken explanation for all of this might be that the obligor was worth only a small fraction of the original amount of the debt and the notes were deemed includible in the decedent's estate at only a discounted value to reflect this lack of credit worthiness.

§ 5.10.5

consequence of acceleration will be to visit unexpected liquidity problems on the fiduciary or inequitable DNI allocation among the beneficiaries.

Instead of a will that cancels a note, assume that the decedent sold property in exchange for SCINs[73] that are extinguished by their own terms on the seller's death. In Rev. Rul. 86-72,[74] such a seller died with two installment payments outstanding and self-cancellation of the installment obligations was treated as a §691(a)(5)(A)(ii) transfer that triggered the §691(a)(2) income acceleration rule. The outstanding gain was recognized by and includible in the gross income of the seller's estate.[75] Similarly, Estate of Frane v. Commissioner[76] involved a SCIN that the Tax Court regarded as subject to §453B(f) upon cancellation, making all deferred gain recognizable under §453B(a) at the decedent's death, reportable on the decedent's final income tax return. The court on appeal affirmed the holding that cancellation was an income taxable event but ruled that inclusion properly was reported by the decedent's estate as an estate income tax liability and not as the decedent's income reportable on the decedent's final income tax return.[77]

---

[73] SCINs are discussed in detail in §6.4.2.

[74] 1986-1 C.B. 253.

[75] See also GCM 39503, which relates to Rev. Rul. 86-72 and stated:

... (1)(A) We believe that when property is transferred in exchange for a transferee's promise to make periodic payments to the transferor until his death, the transaction should be considered a private annuity.

(B) When property is transferred in exchange for a transferee's promise to make periodic payments until a stated monetary amount is reached, or until the transferor's death, whichever occurs first, the transaction should be considered a private annuity, except as stated below.

(C) If the stated monetary amount would be received by the transferor before the expiration of his or her life expectancy (as determined actuarially at the time of the sale agreement), then the transaction will be characterized as an installment sale ....

[76] 98 T.C. 341 (1992) (a 14 to 5 reviewed opinion), aff'd in part and rev'd in part, 998 F.2d 567 (8th Cir. 1993).

[77] The Tax Court previously held that a self-canceling installment note is not includible in the holder's estate for FET purposes because the right to receive payment terminates at the holder's death. See Estate of Moss v. Commissioner, 74 T.C. 1239 (1980), acq. in result only, 1981-1 C.B. 1. See §6.4.2 n.15. That result was not changed by *Frane*.

A Tax Court dissenting opinion in *Frane* is intriguing in several respects. One is its equation of a SCIN to a private annuity, saying that they are not functionally different and should be taxed the same. With an effective single life, no refund, private annuity there would be no gift tax on the original sale, no amount not already paid would be includible in the decedent's estate at death, and no income tax liability would be generated by the decedent's death (indeed, a § 72(a)(3) deduction might be available on the decedent's final income tax return for any unrecovered basis in the annuity). The dissent alluded to an even better analogy for all tax purposes by referring to the holder as "an insurer (or perhaps a gambler)" who accepted the economic risk of death before the total purchase price was paid.

In essence a SCIN may be viewed as a normal installment note with an added premium to cover the contingency of the holder's death before full payment. That premium essentially finances private, decreasing term life insurance that pays when the holder dies. Proceeds equal to the outstanding installments are received and then used immediately by the debtor to pay those outstanding installments. Under this analogy the taxable event occurs as of (or perhaps immediately after) the holder's death, which more accurately implicates § 691(a)(5)(A)(iii) as held by the court on appeal, but any income tax liability is offset because implied payment of the proceeds under this insurance contract analogy should constitute a deduction in respect of the decedent under § 162 as a binding business obligation. For FET purposes the holder's estate has a similar wash because the deemed payment of the outstanding installments is includible but that amount is offset by a § 2053 deduction for the holder's obligation to pay the insurance proceeds.

In each case, if the premium charged for the self-canceling feature was determined properly, it should constitute full and adequate consideration for the obligation and should support both deductions. Moreover, both deductions are permitted under § 642(g) because the obligation to pay is a deduction in respect of the deceased holder. The final result is consistent with the Tax Court dissent in *Frane*, which properly argued that nothing should be taxable for income tax purposes. In the final analysis, however, even if income tax is generated at the decedent's death as held by *Frane*, the SCIN sale may be desirable if the income tax incurred on the accelerated income element is less than the FET cost on

§ 5.10.5

the notes themselves, which escape FET inclusion. In evaluating these tax consequences, however, consideration should be given to the counterbalancing fact that sale during life precludes the new basis at death otherwise generated under § 1014(b)(9). And the premium paid for the self-cancellation feature could increase the decedent's estate over the amount that would exist if the decedent lived to receive all the installments called for by a normal (not self-canceling) obligation.[78]

§ 5.10.6 *Distributions of IRD that Carry Out DNI*

If the right to receive IRD is specifically bequeathed, its distribution should qualify under § 663(a)(1) and not carry out DNI. Otherwise, however, distribution of the right to receive IRD should carry out DNI under the same rules that apply to any other asset. In that respect, however, § 643(e) is relevant because it limits the amount of DNI carried out by a distribution of any property in kind from an estate or trust—presumably including a right to receive IRD—to the lesser of basis or FMV of the distributed asset. Because the basis of most items of IRD is zero,[79] the amount of DNI carried out normally would be zero as well.

If, however, the distribution is an acceleration event under § 691(a)(2), a basis increase in the amount of the income realized by the acceleration should allow application of § 643(e)(2)(A), which would regard the amount of DNI carried out to equal the basis of the distributed item. In such a case, however, it is not clear how or whether to apply two cases decided prior to adoption of § 643(e), both preventing a DNI carryout by distributions of the right to receive IRD.[80] Both cases were correctly decided under the law prior to adoption of § 643(e) because they prevented application of an income tax basis adjustment

---

[78] For an extensive discussion of the SCIN technique and all its ramifications, see Banoff & Hartz, New Tax Court Case Expands Opportunities for Self-Canceling Installment Notes, 76 J. Tax'n 332 (1992), and literature cited therein.

[79] Under § 1014(c), which precludes the new basis at death result normally generated by inclusion of assets in a decedent's gross estate, and because the IRD has not yet been taken into income and therefore has no income tax basis to carry over.

[80] See Rollert Residuary Trust v. Commissioner, 80 T.C. 619 (1983), and Estate of Dean v. Commissioner, 46 T.C.M. (CCH) 184 (1983).

rule[81] that would have made the IRD tax free when received. Because §643(e) eliminated the basis adjustment problem that those cases addressed in the context of IRD, those cases should not prevent a DNI carryout under current law.

Thus, in an accelerating distribution context, the result ought to be an income tax wash to the fiduciary. The DNI carryout should produce (1) a distributions deduction that offsets the income caused by acceleration and (2) income to the recipient who ultimately will receive the IRD tax free due to a new basis in the right to receive the IRD generated by the acceleration. The result of such an income carry out would be simply to accelerate the tax year in which the IRD is taxed but not alter the taxpayer who would be incur the tax liability, which would be appropriate for tax policy reasons.

Stated more broadly, the result in all cases ought to be that an item representing the right to receive IRD should carry out DNI to the same extent as any other asset—the lesser of basis or FMV. Nevertheless, this issue remains in doubt.[82]

§5.11 GRANTOR TRUST RULES

Subchapter J establishes a third category into which trusts may fall. Estates always are taxed as a complex trust and, by virtue of §671, cannot be subject to the following rules. Trusts may be either simple or complex for income tax purposes, and some trusts fluctuate between simple and complex from year to year. However, any trust (whether simple or complex) may be subject in whole or in part to this third category of rules, being Subpart E (§§671 through 679) of Part I of Subchapter J. These are the grantor trust rules. Trusts may be subject to Subpart E only in some years or only to a limited extent[1] but, to the extent the grantor trust rules apply, Subpart E overrides the balance of Subchapter J.

Fundamental to application of the grantor trust rules is possession of prohibited enjoyment or control of trust income or corpus by a grantor

---

[81] Then Treas. Reg. §1.661(a)-2(f)(3).

[82] See Pennell, Subchapter J: Evolution or Revolution? 19 U. Miami Inst. Est. Plan. ¶ 803.2[4] (1985).

[1] **§5.11** See §5.11.8, relating to the portion rules.

§5.11

or someone treated under the §678 pseudo grantor trust rule as if they *were* the grantor. When applicable, the normal principles for imputing ownership of income for federal income tax purposes[2] are supplanted by the grantor trust rules[3] and the applicable portion of the trust is "ignored" for income tax purposes.[4] To the extent this occurs, income, deductions, and credits allocable to that portion of the trust are attributed to the grantor (actual or pseudo), rather than to the trust or its beneficiaries, and retain their character in the grantor's hands,[5] in *most*

---

[2] Such as principles that look to dominion and control. If a trust is not involved, those principles will continue to defeat certain efforts to shift income. See, e.g., Speca v. Commissioner, 630 F.2d 554 (7th Cir. 1980), aff'g 38 T.C.M. (CCH) 544 (1979), Beirne v. Commissioner, 52 T.C. 210 (1969), Duarte v. Commissioner, 44 T.C. 193 (1965); Humphrey v. Commissioner, 28 T.C.M. (CCH) 492 (1969).

[3] §671 (last sentence), although assignment of income and discharge of obligation theories continue to apply under Treas. Reg. §1.671-1(c). For example, a transfer of a property right for a term of years that the donee then applies to an income producing endeavor (such as a lease) typically is effective, but a transfer of property subject to that income producing endeavor typically is not. Compare Commissioner v. Reece, 233 F.2d 30 (1st Cir. 1956), and Heim v. Fitzpatrick, 262 F.2d 887 (2d Cir. 1959) (inventor assigned patent that then was made income producing), with Flacco v. Commissioner, 50 T.C.M. (CCH) 632 (1985) (transfer of installment agreement from sale of farm deemed ineffective to shift income element in each payment), and see Pennell, Income Shifting After TRA'86, 46 N.Y.U. Inst. Fed. Tax'n 50.07[8] (1988), which concludes that uncertainty flowing from diverse results based on facts and circumstances evaluations is best addressed by being

> certain that the term is given before the property is made subject to a lease or otherwise becomes income producing—or be certain that the holder of the term has full power to alter the investment or otherwise to change the income producing character of the asset—in order to better support an argument that the holder of the term interest has legitimate control over a property interest and is not merely acting as a passive recipient of assigned income. "If the transfer is of property, the assignee is usually taxed, but if the transfer is of a mere 'income right,' the transferor remains taxable,"

citing Eustice, Contract Rights, Capital Gain, and Assignment of Income—The Ferrer Case, 20 Tax L. Rev. 1, 34 (1964).

[4] Treating the trust as if it did not exist—ignoring it—is the street-lingo description. But it is not 100% accurate or correct, as revealed in various ways throughout this section.

[5] Treas. Reg. §1.671-2(c); Rev. Rul. 60-370, 1960-2 C.B. 203.

respects as if no trust had been created.[6] Thus, for example, most casual observers believe that a trust loss would be the grantor's deduction,[7] deductions that would be subject to the §67 threshold remain subject to that 2% loss rule,[8] a distribution to charity would be treated as the grantor's contribution, capital gains in the trust would be aggregated with the grantor's capital gains and losses,[9] and the statute of limitation for the trust may be that of the grantor.[10]

---

[6] Treas. Reg. §1.671-2(a). Notice that "losses" are *not* included in the list of items that are attributed to the grantor.

[7] But that is not necessarily correct. See Treas. Reg. §1.671-3(c) and §5.11.8 n.180 and accompanying text.

[8] See Bay v. Commissioner, 76 T.C.M. (CCH) 866 (1998) (taxpayer owned less than a 3% interest in a $200 million grantor trust that apparently operated like a mutual fund and incurred investment management fees, attorney and accountant fees, custodial fees, and other expenses that would be subject to §67 in the hands of any individual taxpayer; in conformity with Temp. Treas. Reg. §§1.67-2T(b)(1) and 1.67-2T(g)(1)(i), the exception to the 2% haircut found in §67(e) for deductible items that are unique to trust administration was deemed not applicable to a grantor trust because of its passthrough nature, making avoidance of §67(a) "not a viable notion" with respect to expenses and other deductions that flow through to the grantor's personal return).

[9] A different rule, adopted in 1976 and repealed in 1997, provided that if appreciated assets contributed to a trust were disposed of by the trust within two years of transfer by the grantor, the tax on that amount of the gain generated before the transfer to the trust would be imposed at the same rate as if the grantor had disposed of the transferred property. Bracket compression in 1986 eventually led Congress to repeal §644 at the same time it eliminated most applications of the accumulation distribution and throwback rules in 1997. Beware, however, transactions that involve contributions *into* trust followed by a sale that was arranged before the asset was transferred. These transactions are not successful at shifting the tax on the gain. Instead the government imposes the income tax on the transferor (which is worse than just imposing the tax at the transferor's income tax rates, because the transferee has the sale proceeds and the transferor has the tax liability). See, e.g., Malkan v. Commissioner, 54 T.C. 1305 (1970); Usher v. Commissioner, 45 T.C. 205 (1965); but compare Edgar v. Commissioner, 56 T.C. 717 (1971) (sufficient period between transfer and sale precluded a finding that the disposition was prearranged).

[10] See FSA 200207007, opining that the trust's statute of limitation did not begin to run until the grantor's return was filed, citing various authorities involving other passthrough entities to the same effect. It was not clear from the opinion why it mattered: the grantor trust presumably would not incur income

The key to application of the grantor trust rules is whether the grantor enjoys trust benefits, has retained so much control, or has left so many "strings" attached to the trust that the grantor should be regarded as the true owner of the trust property for income tax purposes. Accordingly, the grantor trust provisions read like a laundry list of prohibited powers and interests in the trust, any one of which being sufficient to invoke grantor trust treatment.[11]

These rules are consistent with the fundamental income tax principle that tax liability cannot be shifted by anticipatory arrangements that seek to attribute earned income to other taxpayers[12] and that an assignment of income from property (as opposed to an assignment of income from services) equally is improper if the assignor retains ownership of the income producing property.[13] These rules raise questions of what constitutes a relinquishment of both the income from property and ownership of the underlying property itself, sufficient to generate an effective income shift, recognizing that trusts create their own special income shifting problems and opportunities.[14]

(Footnote Continued)

tax on the trust's items and the grantor's own income tax liability would depend on the grantor's own statute of limitation.

[11] Prior to 1986, each was tied to an arbitrary policy that an interest or power would not be considered as prohibited if it could not affect the enjoyment of trust benefits within 10 years after the final transfer of property into the trust. By an amendment to § 673, and indirectly to other provisions of Subpart E, the former 10 year rule was repealed for transfers in trust after March 1, 1986.

[12] See the long line of income tax cases that began with Lucas v. Earl, 281 U.S. 111 (1930), prohibiting gratuitous assignments of earned income. In this context the most likely subjects of failed income shifting are the so-called "constitutional" or "family trusts" that generated significant amounts of litigation in the early to mid 1980s (and that resurface periodically), by which a taxpayer would attempt to assign the right to income from personal services to a trust and make other family members the trust income beneficiaries. See, e.g., United States v. Smith, 814 F.2d 1086 (5th Cir. 1987), aff'g 657 F. Supp. 646 (W.D. La. 1986) (enjoining sale of trust kits and imposing penalties on one of the more egregious marketeers of these gimmicks); Luman v. Commissioner, 79 T.C. 846 (1982); Vercio v. Commissioner, 73 T.C. 1246 (1980).

[13] See, e.g., Helvering v. Horst, 311 U.S. 112 (1940).

[14] Blair v. Commissioner, 300 U.S. 5 (1937) (taxpayer was the income beneficiary of a trust who gratuitously assigned that income interest, which the Court held to be valid because all the taxpayer owned was the right to receive income,

Overall, the grantor trust rules stand for a simple proposition that an assignment of income from property is permissible if the taxpayer relinquishes sufficient control over the income producing property.[15] The difficult question is what constitutes a sufficient relinquishment for these purposes. Most of the grantor trust rules address that question directly or indirectly. For example, the most common powers and interests that will trigger grantor trust treatment under Subpart E include:

(1) a reversion to the grantor or the grantor's spouse, if the value of the reversion exceeds 5% of the value of the trust or portion to which the reversion relates,

(2) certain powers in the grantor or the grantor's spouse to control beneficial enjoyment without the consent of an adverse party (subject to numerous exceptions),

---

(Footnote Continued)

which was relinquished in its entirety), in which the taxpayer never owned the trust corpus and did not create the trust.

[15] In at least one case even total relinquishment will not suffice to shift income. Adopted in 1986 (though advocated in a rudimentary form as early as 1947, in Hearings Before the Committee on Ways & Means, 80th Cong., 1st. Sess., on Proposed Revisions of the Internal Revenue Code (Miscellaneous Recommendations) at 3837 (1947)), the so-called Kiddie Tax of § 1(g) applies to all unearned income of a child who is under the age of 19 (or a full-time student under the age of 24) at the end of the tax year. The child's tax liability on more than a de minimis amount (usually double the amount of the § 63(c)(5)(A) standard deduction, although it could be larger under § 1(g)(4)(A)(ii)(II)) of unearned income is computed as if that income belonged to the child's parents. Special provisions in § 1(g)(5) dictate which parent's tax rates apply if the parents are divorced or legally separated or if the child lives with foster parents, and § 1(g)(1)(A) guarantees that the child's tax cannot be reduced by this provision if the parents' tax rates are less than the child's. But, in normal circumstances, the child is made to pay the income tax on unearned income at the parents' marginal income tax rate, effectively preventing any donor (not just the parents themselves) from transferring income producing property to a young taxpayer in an effort to cause the income from the property to be taxed at the youngster's (hopefully lower) marginal rates.

The arbitrary rules that focus only on the *unearned* income of certain children instead of requiring all members of a single household or nuclear family to file a joint return can be avoided by taxpayers who are well advised—for example, by investing to produce only tax exempt income or by legitimate income deferral with Series EE or HH United States bonds—until the child turns 19 (or ceases being a full-time student under the age of 24).

§ 5.11

(3) administrative powers permitting the grantor or the grantor's spouse to deal at less than arm's length with the trust property,

(4) a power in the grantor or the grantor's spouse to amend or revoke the trust, and

(5) an interest in income that may be used "for the benefit of the grantor," including income that may be paid to the grantor or to the grantor's spouse and income that is actually distributed to a person either the grantor or the grantor's spouse is obliged to support or maintain (for example, a child).

In addition, a final section of Subpart E has the effect of taxing someone other than the grantor as if that person was the grantor, usually if that other person is given a withdrawal right over the trust. In recognition of a leading case in this area, these pseudo grantor trusts often are referred to as "Mallinckrodt" trusts.

§5.11.1 Definitions

Subpart E contains several concepts, terms, and unique definitions that should be assimilated before studying specific provisions and rules. Perhaps the most unfortunate unique definition is of the term "income," which means "fiduciary accounting income" for the balance of Subchapter J[16] but it is said to mean "taxable income" for purposes of Subpart E, reflecting gross income, deductions, losses, credits, and other items that enter into the determination of taxable income for income tax purposes.[17] Further complicating the terminology, "ordinary income" is used to refer to "fiduciary accounting income."[18]

A second frequently encountered concept in Subpart E relates to powers that are exercisable by the grantor, a pseudo grantor, or a

---

[16] § 643(b).

[17] Treas. Reg. § 1.671-2(b) (penultimate sentence). Although the regulation specifies that the definition is applicable for purposes of the Subpart E regulations and not specifically for purposes of the Code itself, this probably is explained by the fact that the regulations cannot alter the Code itself. Nevertheless, the Subpart E regulatory definition is used here as if it was applicable for all purposes.

[18] Treas. Reg. § 1.671-2(b) (last sentence), again ostensibly applicable for purposes only of the regulations.

nonadverse party, without the consent of an "adverse" party.[19] As defined, an adverse party is anyone with a substantial beneficial interest that would be adversely affected by exercise or nonexercise of the power,[20] and a "nonadverse" party is anyone else.[21] For several reasons, however, reliance on those exceptions that rely on an adverse party's consent is not particularly wise. First, because a beneficiary may be adverse only with respect to a portion of a trust.[22] For example, an income beneficiary of a fraction of trust income is not adverse with respect to powers over corpus, income allocable to corpus, or income from the balance of the trust.[23] Second, in addition to direct beneficiaries of a trust,[24] a person who possesses a general power of appointment is deemed to have a beneficial interest in a trust,[25] yet there is no guidance in the statute, regulations, or case law to determine whether a power is

---

[19] See, e.g., §§ 674(a), 675(1), 675(2), 677, and Treas. Reg. § 1.676(a)-1 (for the last of which there is no statutory authority).

[20] § 672(a). Treas. Reg. § 1.677(a)-1(b)(2) (penultimate clause) provides that the grantor's spouse cannot be an adverse party in any trust created after 1969 for purposes of § 677(a), because the spouse's interest constitutes an indirect interest of the grantor. See § 5.11.4 regarding § 677. Conceivably the same is true for all purposes under the grantor trust rules following the 1986 adoption of the spousal unity rule in § 672(e). See Amabile v. Commissioner, 51 T.C.M. (CCH) 963 (1986) and see § 5.11.1 n.36 and accompanying text regarding § 672(e). Quaere, however, whether the spouse would be adverse if, for example, the spouse is entitled to all corpus and accrued income at the grantor's death and has a power during the grantor's life to veto any proposed distributions of income to the grantor.

[21] § 672(b).

[22] In the context of both the income tax and the FET, the notion of adversity with respect to only a portion of a trust is uncertain. Compare PLRs 9030032 (applying § 2041(b)(1)(C)(ii)) and 9016079 (grantor trust rules) (adversity existed with respect to the undivided whole of a trust notwithstanding that the party whose consent was required was entitled to only a fraction of the trust upon termination, because intervening distributions would reduce the entire fund and that would cost the adverse party a certain fraction of every dollar distributed), with Treas. Reg. § 20.2041-3(c)(3) and Laganas v. Commissioner, 281 F.2d 731 (1st Cir. 1960) (grantor trust rules) (adversity deemed to exist only with respect to an aliquot share of the trust based on the consenting party's ultimate entitlement or interest).

[23] Treas. Reg. §§ 1.672(a)-1(b), 1.672(a)-1(c), and 1.672(a)-1(d).

[24] Treas. Reg. § 1.672(a)-1(b).

[25] Treas. Reg. § 1.672(a)-1(a) (penultimate sentence).

§ 5.11.1

"general" as defined at common law (exercisable in favor of the powerholder or the powerholder's estate) or for transfer tax purposes (exercisable in favor of the powerholder, the powerholder's estate, or creditors of either), making the power of appointment rule somewhat unreliable.

In addition, the regulations define a "substantial" beneficial interest as "not insignificant" in relation to total property subject to the power,[26] which leaves a great deal of doubt. For example, the regulations suggest that a contingent income beneficiary may be an adverse party,[27] without discussing the nature or remoteness of the contingency or whether it can be regarded as not insignificant.[28] Thus, it can be uncertain whether a party is adverse with respect to a particular power or portion of a trust, or sufficiently adverse to act as a buffer to insulate against grantor trust treatment.[29] Due to a relative dearth of litigation or other guidance to

---

[26] Treas. Reg. § 1.672(a)-1(a) (last sentence).

[27] Treas. Reg. § 1.672(a)-1(c) (last sentence). But cf. Fulham v. Commissioner, 110 F.2d 916 (1st Cir. 1940) (contingent current income beneficiary not adverse).

[28] See, e.g., Holt v. United States, 669 F. Supp. 751, 752 (W.D. Va. 1987) (the grantor's parents were not sufficiently adverse for purposes of § § 674, 676, and 677 in their role as trustees and contingent remainder beneficiaries if the grantor and the grantor's children were not survived by any grandchild or great grandchild of the grantor; theirs was "an extremely remote contingent interest . . . highly questionable and certainly . . . not . . . a 'substantial interest' that would be adversely affected by exercise of the Trustee's power to distribute income . . . particularly where family members are involved").

[29] See, e.g., Neely v. United States, 775 F.2d 1092 (9th Cir. 1985) (although the grantor and the grantor's spouse were serving as cotrustees with a third party who was adverse, they could act by majority vote and, as a majority of the trustees, the grantor and the spouse had the power to control the trust without the consent of the adverse party and therefore were not protected by this buffer). On the other hand, in PLRs 200731019, 200729025, 200715005, 200647001, 200637025, 200612002, 200502014, 200247013, and 200148028, taxpayers created nongrantor trusts for income tax purposes, settled in domestic asset protection jurisdictions (see § 4.1.4 (6th ed.)) that tax only situs state source income, while the grantor's home state income tax was avoided because the trusts were nonresident and not grantor trusts. All this state income tax minimization was achieved by the settlor retaining a right to receive discretionary distributions of income or principal as approved by a committee that included adverse parties (other current discretionary distributees; retained rights protected the settlor from current wealth transfer tax liability and the government held that no general powers of appointment were created because other powerholders re-

§ 5.11.1

enlarge upon these concepts, it may prove unwise to assume the existence of adequate adversity in planning for administration of trusts in connection with the grantor trust rules.

A third useful concept in Subpart E is the "related or subordinate" party, which is integral to the definition of an "independent trustee"[30] and means a nonadverse party who is subservient to the grantor[31] and who is the grantor's spouse (if living with the grantor), parent, sibling,[32] descendant, or an employee of the grantor or of any corporation in which the grantor is a superior executive or a significant stockholder (in terms of aggregate voting control of the grantor and of the trust).[33] Because both the nonadverse and the subservient aspects of the definition are uncer-

---

(Footnote Continued)

quired adverse party consent to benefit themselves). Notions of reciprocity discussed in § 12.1 were not discussed and may be a weak link in the PLRs.

[30] § 674(c) provides that a trustee is independent and the trustee's powers will not cause § 674(a) grantor trust exposure if not more than half the trustees of a trust are related or subordinate. There is a similar related or subordinate trustee concept in § 675(3) (penultimate sentence), relating to borrowing trust funds. The concept is significant in the context of a trend to create family owned trust companies, as was involved in PLRs 200548035, 200546052 through 200546055, 200531004, and 200523003 and as to which §§ 5.01(14), (15), and (16) of Rev. Proc. 2012-3, 2012-1 C.B. 113, announce that the government no longer will issue guidance, pending a review and likely issuance of guidance on the various wealth transfer tax and income tax consequences of using a private or controlled entity as fiduciary. See Notice 2008-63, 2008-2 C.B. 261, which is labeled as a "proposed" revenue ruling that provides guidance on such questions, as discussed in § 4.1.1.

[31] Subservience is presumed by § 672(c) (last sentence) unless disproven by a preponderance of available evidence, such as proof that the trustee acts contrary to the grantor's wishes. Curiously, a grantor's attorney serving as trustee is not regarded as subservient. See Zand v. Commissioner, 71 T.C.M. (CCH) 1758 (1996), aff'd, 143 F.3d 1393 (11th Cir. 1998); Estate of Goodwyn v. Commissioner, 35 T.C.M. (CCH) 1026 (1976); PLR 200822008.

[32] Including a half-sibling. Rev. Rul. 58-19, 1958-1 C.B. 251.

[33] § 672(c). Neither "executive" nor "significant" voting control is defined. PLRs 9842007 and 9841014 involved five siblings who created 11 separate trusts for their respective children and, together with one other family, created a trust company, which issued stock that these trusts own. In the aggregate no child's trust owned more than 10% of that stock and the government held that the trustee was not related or subordinate. A director of a corporation is not an employee for purposes of this definition. Rev. Rul. 66-160, 1966-1 C.B. 164.

§ 5.11.1

tain, the only certain escape from the related or subordinate definition is by falling entirely outside the defined class of related parties.

A final introductory concept relates to identification of the true grantor of a trust and efforts to obfuscate that grantor's identity, particularly through obvious artifices that are meant to be precluded by the reciprocal trust doctrine that ascertains whether an individual is an ostensible but not a recognizable grantor. An easy example of the identification issue involves trusts created by court order to hold the proceeds of a personal injury claim on behalf of a minor or incapacitated adult. Notwithstanding that the plaintiff on whose behalf the trust was created was incompetent to create the trust, that person is the true party in interest on whose behalf the trust was established and is regarded as the grantor who retained trust benefits.[34]

With respect to the reciprocal trust rule, many older reciprocal trust cases involved spouses,[35] as to whom the spousal unity rule in § 672(e) now will apply.[36] But the doctrine may apply in other situations in which

---

[34] Rev. Rul. 83-25, 1983-1 C.B. 116; PLRs 9831005, 9552039, 9502019, 9502020, 9502024, 9502029, 9502031, and 8449016. Regarding trusts created to hold personal injury damage recoveries see § 4.1.9.

[35] See, e.g., Krause v. Commissioner, 57 T.C. 890 (1972), aff'd, 497 F.2d 1109 (6th Cir. 1974) (spouses created contemporaneous trusts with the other as a permissible distributee and holder of a power to remove the trustee). Today the reciprocal trust doctrine would be unnecessary in *Krause* because each grantor would be taxable pursuant to § 672(e) by virtue of the interests and powers granted to the grantor's spouse. See § 5.11.1 n.36 and accompanying text.

[36] Effective with respect to all of Subpart E, § 672(e) treats all interests and powers of a grantor's spouse as those of the grantor, apparently without regard to who created that interest or power. Thus, § 672(e) would apply even if a trust granted a power of appointment to a third party who exercised it to create the spouse's interest or power, provided that the spouses were not legally separated when the power (as opposed to the trust itself) was created. See § 672(e)(2).

Curiously, § 672(e) does not indicate whether spousal unity ends when the marriage does, § 672(e)(1)(B) making it clear only that marriage when the interest or power was *created* is not required if they subsequently get married. In addition, § 682 overrides the spousal unity rule following a divorce or legal separation, but only to the extent the spouse is *entitled* to *income* from the trust, and not otherwise. Thus, it does not turn off grantor trust status attributable to *powers*—which may inform the choice of method for intentionally making a trust a grantor trust—and it might not apply with respect to discretionary income. Treas. Reg. § 1.682(a)-1(a)(1)(i) would appear to provide that both mandatory

§ 5.11.1

unsuspecting taxpayers may not consider the grantor trust rules. For example, consider the creation of two mirror image trusts, one established by sibling A with sibling B as trustee and the other established by B with A as trustee. To the extent the trusts are found to be "interrelated," they may be regarded as trusts created by A with A as trustee and by B with B as trustee, after which the trustee powers held by the respective grantors as trustee could generate grantor trust treatment.

For this purpose, "interrelation" is not a function of any intent on the part of A and B—it would be deemed to exist under mechanical tests that look to whether the trusts were created at approximately the same time and with substantially identical terms. Key is whether each of A and B are in approximately the same economic position as if the trusts had been created as viewed—as opposed to as actually structured.[37] In a similar vein, if two identical trusts were created by X, one with A as trustee for B and the other with B as trustee for A, the reciprocal trust doctrine may serve to uncross these trusts to regard A as beneficiary of the trust as to which A is trustee and B as beneficiary of the trust as to which B is trustee, with the potential for grantor trust exposure under the pseudo grantor provision in § 678.[38]

(Footnote Continued)

and discretionary income entitlements will suffice—at least to the extent the discretionary income actually is distributed to or for the benefit of the spouse.

As a policy matter (especially to promote a degree of internal consistency), it seems reasonable to argue for application of principles such as those in § 7703(a) (legal separation or divorce is tantamount to not being married) to determine marital status for purposes of § 672(e), and § 7701(a)(17) limits the definition of husband and wife as including a former spouse only for specified purposes. Arguably the failure to include § 672(e) in that list is indicative of an intent that former spouses not be subject to § 672(e). If that was true, however, quaere why Congress made it explicit that §§ 674(c) and 675(3) (last sentences) were applicable only "for periods during which an individual is the spouse of the grantor" but no specific provision otherwise establishes that a § 672(e) problem can be divorced.

[37] See United States v. Estate of Grace, 395 U.S. 316 (1969).

[38] Cf. Flato v. Commissioner, 195 F.2d 580 (5th Cir. 1952), a similar case with a similar result, but not based on the reciprocal trust doctrine. With respect to the reciprocal trust doctrine, its requisites and its limitations, see § 7.3.3 nn.31-43 and accompanying text.

§ 5.11.1

Other efforts to disguise the true grantor or nature of a trust also may be ignored. This is likely if A transferred property to B with the understanding that B would use the property to create a trust for the benefit of A, or granting A powers that otherwise would cause grantor trust exposure if A was the grantor. In either case, A would be regarded as the grantor of the trust for purposes of Subchapter J.[39]

Finally, it is necessary to recognize that any trust may have multiple grantors. For example A and B might created a trust together, or B might add assets to a trust originally created by A.[40] A grantor's liability necessarily ends at death,[41] meaning that the number of grantors can both expand and contract. One common but often overlooked source of multiple grantor treatment is lapse of a withdrawal power. If the property subject to the power remains in trust the donee is regarded as the grantor of the property subject to the power of withdrawal, as if that property had been withdrawn and recontributed to the trust.[42]

§5.11.2 *Reversionary Interests*

As the first grantor trust rule, §673 was a keystone in Subpart E prior to its amendment in 1986.[43] Although it waned in in importance

---

[39] See, e.g., Whiteley v. Commissioner, 120 F.2d 782 (3d Cir. 1941) (husband treated as grantor of a trust created by wife to hold stock husband previously transferred to wife); Balis v. Commissioner, 63 T.C.M. (CCH) 1830 (1992) (wife deemed a joint grantor with respect to property she transferred to husband "several days" before he used it to create a trust along with property of his own).

[40] Treas. Reg. §1.671-3(a)(3) establishes rules for allocation among several individuals as grantors of a single trust. See, e.g., Swanson v. Commissioner, 518 F.2d 59 (8th Cir. 1975) (grantor deemed to own only 91% of trust based on contributions made); Tibbits v. Commissioner, 24 T.C.M. (CCH) 663 (1965) (spouses deemed to be joint grantors of a single trust to which they contributed joint tenancy property that the husband originally acquired and titled in joint name; the effect was to limit to that portion the husband's exposure with respect to income used for the support of their children following their divorce).

[41] See Rev. Rul. 75-267, 1975-1 C.B. 255; cf. §443(a)(2); Treas. Reg. §1.443-1(a)(2).

[42] See §5.11.7 n.156.

[43] For example, each of §§674(b)(2), 676(b), and 677(a) incorporated the same 10 year term of pre-1986 law by simple reference to the period that would not cause exposure under §673. That prior law still applies generally with respect to trusts that were irrevocable before March 2, 1986, and as to which no

with its amendment in 1986, it remains one of the easiest and most straightforward provisions in the grantor trust rules. Disregarded by virtue of § 673 is any portion of a trust as to which the grantor has a reversion of either income or corpus that exceeds 5% in value of the portion that may revert. In addition, because of the spousal unity rule in § 672(e), an interest in the grantor's spouse (not technically a reversion because it is not in the grantor, so this would be a remainder) that met the same requirements also would trigger this provision.

The only exception to this otherwise pervasive rule is if the reversion occurs on the death before age 21 of a "present interest minor lineal descendant beneficiary." With an eye to a § 2503(c) qualified minor's trust but applicable to any qualifying trust, a reversion on the death of the beneficiary before reaching age 21 will not cause grantor trust treatment unless and until the reversion actually occurs. Required is a trust created for the sole present benefit of a lineal descendant of the grantor who is under age 21. The trustee apparently need not be required to distribute certain, identified, or guaranteed amounts of income or corpus, either currently or upon trust termination. Instead, all that is required is that the lineal descendant must possess all present interests that are created in the trust, and there is no guidance in the statute as to what is meant by "present interest."[44] Given the valuation

---

(Footnote Continued)

tainting addition or other transfer was made after March 1, 1986, and provided that a reversion would cause grantor trust exposure only if it would, or might reasonably be expected to, take effect within 10 years of transfer of that portion to the trust. Required for application of § 673 was only a reasonable expectation that the reversion would occur within 10 years. Treas. Reg. § 1.673(a)-1(c).

Specifically excepted from the need to make an actuarial determination was a reversion that would occur only on the death of the income beneficiary; that reversion would not cause grantor trust treatment regardless of the beneficiary's life expectancy. § 673(c) and Treas. Reg. § 1.673(a)-1(b). Any post-1986 extension of an otherwise protected trust should be regarded as a new transfer into trust, as to which the new § 673 rules will apply. In addition to failing to accomplish the income tax objective of deferring grantor trust liability, such an extension also would constitute a gift of a future interest as to which the gift tax annual exclusion would not be available for gift tax purposes. Rev. Rul. 76-179, 1976-1 C.B. 290.

[44] Neither the Committee Reports nor the statute itself indicate whether traditional § 2503 annual exclusion present interest concepts were meant to be imposed. In searching for concepts to explain or illustrate the intended meaning

§ 5.11.2

that would apply to such a reversion (that is, based on the likelihood of the lineal descendant dying before reaching age 21), this exception is unnecessary because the reversion would fall within the 5% valuation exception in virtually all cases.[45] In that respect, this exception merely becomes a "safe harbor" with different (and arguably more certain) requirements.[46]

The portion of a trust that is subject to a reversion that is not excepted from application of § 673 is ignored.[47] Thus, under § 671, all income, deductions, and credits allocable to that portion or flowing from it (including the character, timing, and other tax attributes of those items) would be regarded as those of the grantor, as if no trust had been created.

Most events triggering a reversion are subject to actuarial determination under established rules, the most common of which being death

---

(Footnote Continued)

of "present interest," a reasonable alternative might be to impose requirements similar to those found in §§ 674(b)(6) or 674(b)(7), dealing with interests that are subject to a trustee's powers either "temporarily" or during a beneficiary's incompetence or minority. Although it may be that some present interest must be created and that a single lineal descendant must possess every present interest that is created, some commentators have read § 673(b)(2) to say that only those present interests that are created must be given to only one beneficiary and that there is no mandate requiring that *any* present interest must be created.

[45] The provision might be a mistake—included in an early draft of the statute—that should have been removed but instead was overlooked. Or it might anticipate the rare circumstance in which a trust is created for a minor who is suffering from an incurable physical ailment that is likely to result in death within the year, meaning that the actuarial tables may not be used to value his or her interest in the trust. See Treas. Reg. § 25.7520-3(b)(3).

[46] §§ 674(b)(2), 676(b), and 677(a) continue to refer to a § 673 "event" and should not be overlooked by planners who have drafted in the past under other provisions of Subpart E in reliance on the old 10 year period of § 673. For example, it should be possible to create a § 676 power of revocation that would not cause grantor trust exposure to the extent the power could not affect income earned before the death before reaching age 21 of a present interest minor lineal descendant beneficiary, or after the occurrence of an event that, if it triggered a reversion, would cause the reversion to be valued at creation of the trust at less than 5% of the initial value of the portion that reverts.

[47] See § 5.11.8, regarding the portion rules.

§ 5.11.2

of another person, usually a beneficiary of the trust. In most respects the § 7520 actuarial tables may be used to determine life expectancy and the value of the reversion[48] presumably will be determined in the same manner as under § 2037, which incorporates the same 5% valuation standard. Events that are not subject to actuarial determination would be dangerous to use if avoidance of § 673 is desired, although there are tables of probability of some events (such as the likelihood of remarriage or divorce) upon which an actuary may estimate the probability of some reversion events.[49]

A common source of confusion regarding the § 673 reversion rule relates to items of taxable income (and losses) that are allocated to corpus, either as accumulations made in the trustee's discretion or because allocable thereto under local law.[50] Even if the trust avoids § 673 notwithstanding an otherwise permissible reversion retained by the grantor, those items that are allocated to corpus and that ultimately will return to the grantor are taxable to the grantor under § 677(a)(2),[51] pertaining to income accumulated for future distribution to the grantor.[52] Thus, a trust that is drafted to preclude application of § 673 to the grantor may not be totally protected against grantor trust exposure.[53]

---

[48] See §§ 7.2.2.2 nn.44-45 and 56 and accompanying text, and 7.2.2.2.1, regarding § 7520 and the standards governing when the actuarial tables may not be used.

[49] See Treas. Reg. § 1.673(a)-2(d): "It is immaterial that a reversionary interest in corpus or income is subject to a contingency if the reversionary interest may, taking the contingency into consideration, reasonably be expected to take effect in possession or enjoyment . . . ." Valuation of the grantor's reversion is based on the § 673(c) presumption that all discretion will be exercised in the grantor's favor, presumably meaning all discretion to benefit the grantor plus any discretion of any other variety, with the latter being exercised in whatever manner most would favor the grantor.

[50] For example, capital gains and losses that are allocated to corpus under state law. See § 5.3.3.

[51] See § 5.11.4 nn.71-74.

[52] Treas. Reg. § 1.673(a)-1(a) (last paragraph); Rev. Rul. 75-267, 1975-2 C.B. 254; Rev. Rul. 58-242, 1958-1 C.B. 251. Only income earned and accumulated after a protected § 673 period would avoid this treatment and then only for the period prior to expiration of that period.

[53] Another example of a provision that may avoid § 673 but still cause grantor trust exposure is Rev. Rul. 61-223, 1961-2 C.B. 125, which held that a corporate

§ 5.11.2

In addition to the more traditional reversion of trust corpus, § 673(a) makes reference to a grantor's reservation of a reversion in income, anticipating a trust that would pay income to a third party and then to the grantor, with a remainder to someone other than the grantor after the grantor's secondary income interest terminates. Although § 677(a) would tax the income once the grantor's income interest became possessory, § 673(a) taxes the income to the grantor even before then, by virtue of the income reversion provision.

§5.11.3 *Power to Revoke*

A second straightforward provision puts grantors who retain a § 676(a) power of revocation—allowing reacquisition of trust property in the grantor's discretion—on an even footing with those who retain a § 673 automatic reversion. To maintain this equality between a power to revoke and a reversion, § 676(b) contains an exception that incorporates by reference the § 673 exception[54] for a reversion on the death of a lineal descendant who is the sole present interest beneficiary of a trust and who is under age 21, presumably meaning that a power to revoke that is triggered on such a death will not cause § 676 exposure until that death occurs. To the extent § 676(b) is not applicable, § 676(a) attributes to the grantor those items of income, deductions, and credits of any portion of the trust that is subject to a power to revoke, if the power is exercisable (even if not actually exercised) by the grantor, by the grantor's spouse,[55] or by any nonadverse party, all without the consent of an adverse party.[56]

Powers that will trigger § 676(a) include (1) a direct power to terminate (either expressly retained or existing under state law due to a

---

(Footnote Continued)

trustee's power to distribute income or corpus for the support or maintenance of the grantor's child is not a § 673 reversion, although its exercise may trigger grantor trust exposure under § 677(b). See § 5.11.4 nn.75-80 and accompanying text.

[54] See § 5.11.2. § 676(b) excepts a trust from grantor trust exposure prior to expiration of the § 673 10 year (or earlier death) period. The exception is applicable even if the power is presently vested or exercisable, if the effect of exercise is postponed properly. Treas. Reg. § 1.676(b)-1.

[55] See § 672(e) with respect to post-1986 trusts.

[56] Treas. Reg. § 1.676(a)-1 provides an adverse party exception even though there is no direct authority for it in the statute.

failure to make the trust irrevocable),[57] as well as powers (2) to purchase trust assets for less than a full and adequate consideration,[58] or (3) to invade, withdraw,[59] alter, or amend, in each case if exercisable by, in favor of, or for the benefit of the grantor or the grantor's spouse.[60]

Also sufficient to trigger this provision is a discretionary distribution power in a nonadverse trustee or a nongeneral power of appointment in a nonadverse party to distribute income or corpus to beneficiaries that might include the grantor or the grantor's spouse.[61] To the extent of such a power over corpus this provision dovetails with § 677, which is triggered by a nonadverse trustee's power to distribute *income* to the grantor or to the grantor's spouse in the trustee's discretion. To the extent § 676 is triggered by a power to distribute income to the grantor or to the grantor's spouse, these rules are duplicative with no apparent reason.

§5.11.4 *Direct Beneficial Enjoyment*

Many inter vivos trusts are not created to shift income from the grantor to another taxpayer. In these trusts the grantor's income tax liability is not unexpected—it flows from intentional retention of beneficial enjoyment. A grantor is treated under § 677(a) as owner of any portion of a trust as to which the income, without the consent of an adverse party, either (1) must be paid or (2) in the discretion of the

---

[57] Recall that, contrary to the traditional common law rule, silence makes a trust revocable in situations subject to the UTC and a handful of other states. See § 4.2.2.

[58] And see § 675(1), which would cover this power and more. Quaere whether the overlap is intentional and therefore whether § 676 would not apply to such a power. It should not matter, because § 675(1) clearly would apply.

[59] Quaere whether a demand loan to the trust by any person might rise to this level. See Estate of Musgrove v. United States, 95-2 U.S. Tax Cas. (CCH) ¶ 60,204 (Ct. Fed. Cl. 1995), which made that suggestion for § 2038(a)(1) purposes. See also § 5.11.5 n.95.

[60] With respect to post-1986 trusts. See § 672(e), and see § 5.11.1 n.36 and accompanying text, regarding § 672(e).

[61] Rev. Rul. 57-8, 1957-1 C.B. 204.

grantor, the grantor's spouse,[62] or any nonadverse party, either may be paid currently or may be accumulated for future payment to the grantor, the grantor's spouse,[63] or the indirect benefit of either.

Direct or indirect benefit to the grantor or the grantor's spouse is a broad concept, obviously encompassing direct payments to either plus, for example, authority[64] to pay premiums for insurance on the life of the grantor (or, in post-1969 trusts, on the life of the grantor's spouse as well), which will cause § 677(a)(3) to apply.[65] Although the apparent

---

[62] Although § 677(a) refers to the powerholder as only the grantor or a nonadverse party, see § 672(e), and see § 5.11.1 n.36 and accompanying text regarding § 672(e).

[63] § 677(a) and Treas. Reg. § 1.677(a)-1(b)(2) with respect to trusts created after 1969, even if the spouse is not living with the grantor. Compare §§ 672(c)(1), 672(e)(2), and 674(d), which all require the spouse to be living with the grantor. No such requirement appears in § 677(a). However, if the grantor is separated from the spouse, either of § 71 or § 682 may apply to distributions to the spouse. Generally, § 71 applies to trusts created for the purpose of making alimony payments to the spouse (pursuant to a divorce decree or separation agreement), and § 682 applies to payments from trusts that predated a divorce or legal separation and that discharge the grantor's subsequently incurred obligations to the spouse. In either case, income from a pre-1986 trust payable to the spouse (not as child support) is taxed to the spouse, not to the grantor, under Treas. Reg. § 1.682(a)-1(a)(2) (last sentence). See Zaritsky, Special Trusts and Unique Problems: Grantor Trusts After the Grantor's Death, Alimony Trusts, and Foreign Trusts Versus Domestic Trusts, 37 N.Y.U. Inst. Fed. Tax'n 42.03[2] (1979). With respect to post-1986 trusts that make payments to a spouse who was living with the grantor as of creation of the trust and whether the grantor's exposure changes with a subsequent divorce see § 5.11.1 n.36.

[64] If the trustee is not *precluded* from making distributions to pay premiums for insurance on the grantor or on the spouse's life, but also is not authorized to do so and the trust owns no such insurance, § 677(a)(3) will not apply notwithstanding that income could, in the trustee's discretion, be so used in the future. See Corning v. Commissioner, 104 F.2d 329 (6th Cir. 1939); Iversen v. Commissioner, 3 T.C. 756, 774 (1944); Weil v. Commissioner, 3 T.C. 579 (1944), acq., 1944 C.B. 29; and Moore v. Commissioner, 39 B.T.A. 808 (1939), acq., 1979-2 C.B. 25.

[65] A statutory exception applies if the irrevocable beneficiary designation is a § 170(c) specified charitable purpose. To illustrate, in PLR 199915045 Spouse A created a CRUT, funded with a single premium life insurance policy on Spouse B, and the trust beneficiary was a child. The government held that § 677(a)(3) grantor trust treatment would not apply and therefore qualification under Treas.

§ 5.11.4

theory behind this rule is that the grantor or the grantor's spouse benefits from the insurance being carried, the policies need not be owned by the grantor or the spouse,[66] nor must either be designated as beneficiary.

Meanwhile, payment of premiums for insurance owned by the grantor or the grantor's spouse on the life of someone other than the grantor or the grantor's spouse is not covered under § 677(a)(3). It probably would be covered anyway, under either § 677(a)(1) or 677(a)(2), either as a direct or indirect distribution to the grantor or to the grantor's spouse or an indirect accumulation of income (through any increase in the cash surrender or other value of the policy). Furthermore, payments that discharge a legal or contractual obligation[67] of the

---

(Footnote Continued)

Reg. § 1.664-1(a)(4) was not precluded, notwithstanding that the trust owned insurance on the life of the trust settlor's spouse. The rationale given was that, although the trustee could pay premiums for that insurance, the proceeds were allocable to corpus of the trust, they would not affect the unitrust payments to the child, and therefore the proceeds were deemed to be irrevocably payable for charitable purposes, which entitled the trust to the express parenthetical exception in § 677(a)(3).

[66] For example, assume that the grantor is a party to a buy-sell agreement relating to closely held business stock owned by the grantor and several of the grantor's siblings, under which each sibling established a trust, the income from which being used to pay premiums for insurance that the other siblings own on the grantor's life, all to provide the liquidity to permit each sibling to purchase the stock of a deceased party to the agreement. If the grantor's trust pays the premiums for insurance that each sibling owns on the grantor's life, the proceeds of which will permit the siblings to pay cash to purchase the grantor's stock, that income would be subject to § 677(a)(3) regardless of for whose "benefit" the buy-sell agreement is deemed to exist.

[67] See, e.g., Krause v. Commissioner, 56 T.C. 1242 (1971) (involving a net gift of assets to a trust with imposition of the gift tax liability on the trust constituting the legal obligation being satisfied with trust income and generating grantor trust liability until that liability was fully paid; repayment by the trust borrowing and using future income to service the debt did not cause ongoing grantor trust liability, the logic being that the trust could have sold corpus or come up with the cash in other ways, none of which benefiting the grantor). See also Morgan v. Commissioner, 37 T.C. 981 (1962), aff'd, 316 F.2d 238 (6th Cir. 1963); Estate of Sheaffer v. Commissioner, 25 T.C.M. (CCH) 646 (1966); and the government's losing argument to the contrary in Rev. Rul. 57-564, 1957-2 C.B. 328. And compare Mahoney v. United States, 831 F.2d 641 (6th Cir. 1987), rev'g 628 F.

§ 5.11.4

grantor or of the grantor's spouse are regarded as indirectly beneficial and also may trigger § 677(a).[68]

§5.11.4.1 Accumulated Income

Protected from current grantor trust treatment is a power that permits enjoyment of income earned after a § 673 period.[69] Grantor trust liability with respect to that income does not begin until enjoyment actually begins.[70] *Not* protected by this exception is a power to accumu-

---

(Footnote Continued)

Supp. 273 (S.D. Ohio 1985) (decedent's donor created a trust by net gift transfers and the decedent paid the part-sale consideration by note, the trust providing that income would be used to pay off that note directly as if the income was paid to the decedent and then the decedent directly made the note payments; the decedent reported all the trust income as the decedent's income (including that income paid directly to the donor in satisfaction of the note) and the donor did not report trust income under § 677(a)(1) notwithstanding that the donor had transferred the trust property, because there was no retained income interest notwithstanding the income payments until the note was fully satisfied). Use of trust income to service a debt similarly would constitute such a discharge if the grantor transferred encumbered property and remained personally liable for the debt. See, e.g., Jenn v. United States, 70-1 U.S. Tax Cas. (CCH) ¶ 9264 (S.D. Ind. 1970); Wiles v. Commissioner, 59 T.C. 289 (1972). If the property was transferred subject to the debt the result would be a sale or exchange that might constitute a part-sale, part-gift, in either event with an amount realized equal to the debt, under the principle of Crane v. Commissioner, 331 U.S. 1 (1947), without regard to whether the debt was recourse or nonrecourse or exceeded the FMV of the property. See Commissioner v. Tufts, 461 U.S. 300 (1983); Estate of Levine v. Commissioner, 634 F.2d 12 (2d Cir. 1980); Evangelista v. Commissioner, 629 F.2d 1218 (7th Cir. 1980).

[68] Treas. Reg. §§ 1.677(a)-1(c), which deals with distributions at the direction of the grantor or the grantor's spouse, and 1.677(a)-1(d), which deals with distributions to discharge legal obligations.

[69] § 677(a) (last sentence) and Treas. Reg. § 1.677(a)-1(e), applicable to the extent enjoyment of benefits is deferred in a pre-1986 trust for a 10 year period (or until the earlier death of an income beneficiary other than the grantor or the grantor's spouse), or in a post-1986 trust until the occurrence of a § 673 event (death before age 21 of a present interest lineal descendant beneficiary).

[70] Treas. Reg. § 1.677(a)-1(e) provides that liability begins when current enjoyment becomes possible under the terms of the deferral provision. See, e.g., Rev. Rul. 69-312, 1969-1 C.B. 64 (no current grantor trust exposure from grantor's entitlement to future income earned by trust corpus and by current income that would be accumulated and added to corpus).

late *current* income, even though distribution is postponed for the same § 673 period. Thus, for example, grantor trust exposure *currently* exists if items of trust taxable income are added to corpus, either as accumulations made in the trustee's discretion or because allocable thereto under local law (for example, capital gains), and if there is (a) a reversion to the grantor or a remainder to the grantor's spouse at any time or upon the occurrence of any event, (b) discretion in the trustee to distribute accumulations to the grantor or to the grantor's spouse at any time, present or future, or (c) any power in the grantor or the grantor's spouse to reach those accumulations at any time, present or future.[71]

The most commonly overlooked aspect of § 677(a)(2) liability is with respect to capital gains allocable to fiduciary accounting corpus in trusts with a reversion or other interest that is protected by § 673. Even if no other interest or power would cause grantor trust exposure, gains and losses allocable to corpus that ultimately may pass to the grantor or the grantor's spouse are attributable to the grantor currently because they constitute income accumulated for future distribution to the grantor.[72] This tax exposure may be unsettling if the grantor receives no distributions from the trust with which to pay the tax generated by inclusion of those gains, although the opportunity exists to pay tax on gain that will benefit others without incurring a gift tax liability on that indirect additur to the trust.[73]

With respect to post-1986 trusts, however, the problem is likely to apply only if the grantor created a qualified minor's trust and retained a protected § 673 reversion, and then only if intentional application of the grantor trust rules is not desirable. A simple solution to the grantor trust liability would be to alter the allocations dictated by the local principal

---

[71] Treas. Reg. § 1.677(a)-1(f). See, e.g., Duffy v. United States, 487 F.2d 282 (6th Cir. 1973) (power to amend or revoke after § 673 period generated § 677(a)(2) exposure with respect to currently accumulated income that would become subject to that power when it became exercisable in the future). Even if it otherwise might apply, the throwback rule will not subsequently apply to the extent that accumulated income is taxed currently. Treas. Reg. § 1.665(b)-1A(a)(2).

[72] Treas. Reg. § 1.677(a)-1(g) Example (2).

[73] See § 5.11.9 nn.242-246 and accompanying text, regarding the government's attempt to preclude such indirect tax free gifting to trusts pursuant to the normal operation of the grantor trust rules.

§ 5.11.4.1

and income act by providing in the trust instrument that all items of taxable income be allocated to the income account and paid currently to the minor beneficiary. That solution might cause too much income to be distributable, however, considering the needs of the minor, especially if sales of highly appreciated assets are contemplated. Changing the investment portfolio may ameliorate this concern, but only with respect to future gain.

A second solution would be for the trust to prohibit sale of assets at a gain, either absolutely or unless the grantor consents to the sale,[74] but this suggestion might not be acceptable investment policy.

To deal with the problem of gains being taxable to a grantor who has inadequate assets to pay the tax, the trust also might just authorize withdrawal of sufficient amounts of income or corpus to pay those taxes, or it might direct the trustee to distribute a sufficient amount of income or corpus for that purpose. These solutions would generate §§676 (withdrawal) and 677 (distribution power) exposure and, even if grantor trust exposure was avoidable, distributions likely would carry out DNI to the grantor. Consequently, a withdrawal or distribution amount deemed sufficient to pay the tax on gains generated by the trust presumably would require an additional distribution to pay the tax thereon. Moreover, the trust would fail to meet the requirements of §2503(c) if income was subject to the withdrawal or distribution provision, meaning that the annual exclusion could be unavailable on creation of the trust, if that benefit was being sought.

§5.11.4.2 Support or Maintenance Obligations

A second major exception to §677(a) liability applies if the trustee[75] has discretion to distribute income for the support or maintenance of someone the grantor is obligated to support or maintain. This discretion essentially is a power to benefit the grantor indirectly, and that benefit

---

[74] A veto provision would need to avoid §675(4)(B) if assets in the trust include stock in a business in which the ownership of the grantor and the trust is significant.

[75] In this case the trustee could be the grantor or, presumably, the grantor's spouse, provided that the discretion is exercisable only in a fiduciary capacity. See Treas. Reg. §1.677(b)-1(e).

normally would cause § 677(a) to apply.[76] But trust income is taxable to the grantor under § 677(b) as a result of the power only to the extent income actually is distributed for the support or maintenance of such a dependent.

Again, however, misunderstanding is rife with respect to the scope and application of this exception. For example, the exception does not apply (and therefore § 677(a) is free to apply without restraint) to distributions that are mandatory instead of discretionary,[77] and it does not apply to distributions of corpus.[78] Furthermore, a special rule regards distributions from a trust to be made from income for the year to the fullest extent possible[79] and distributions not out of current trust income may be regarded as accumulation distributions that also may invoke application of § 677(b).[80]

Finally, the parenthetical provision in § 677(b) prevents application of the exception to distributions to the grantor's spouse (even if for support or maintenance of the spouse, notwithstanding the spouse being the grantor's dependent). Further, the statute appears not to apply the exception to distributions for the support or maintenance of someone the grantor's spouse, but not the grantor, must support or maintain.[81]

---

[76] According to Estate of Hamiel v. Commissioner, 253 F.2d 787 (6th Cir. 1958), exposure to § 677(a) would be limited to that amount of income needed for that support or maintenance, meaning that income in excess of the full amount that could be expended in the proper exercise of the trustee's discretion would not be taxable to the grantor; and see Rev. Rul. 56-484, 1956-2 C.B. 23, 24 ("the amount of . . . income includible in the gross income of a person obligated to support or maintain a minor is limited by the extent of his legal obligations under local law").

[77] Treas. Reg. § 1.677(b)-1(f).

[78] All of § 677 is restricted to distributions of income.

[79] Treas. Reg. § 1.677(b)-1(c), meaning that § 677(b) will allow them to be taxed to the grantor to the greatest possible extent.

[80] § 677(b) (last sentence) and Treas. Reg. § 1.677(b)-1(b).

[81] Compare § 677(a) with § 677(b) (the former makes repeated reference to the grantor's spouse for trusts created after 1969 while the latter does not), and compare Treas. Reg. § 1.677(b)-1(a) (last clause of first sentence), which makes reference to a child "whom the grantor *or his spouse* is legally obligated to support" (emphasis added), and Treas. Reg. § 1.677(a)-1(d) (last clause), with Treas. Reg. § 1.677(b)-1(d), which provides that "[t]he exception provided in

§ 5.11.4.2

If the exception is not applicable to distributions for the support or maintenance of someone the grantor's spouse (but not the grantor) is obliged to support or maintain, then the discretion to make such distributions will generate grantor trust liability even if not exercised. It would constitute a power to make distributions indirectly to the grantor's spouse, which would fall within § 677(a)(1). This perverse result is not addressed directly by § 672(e), which dictates that powers and interests of a grantor's spouse shall be deemed to be those of the grantor. The theory of the § 677(b) obligation provision that distributions to dependents are an indirect benefit to the grantor ought to provide that distributions to the spouse's dependents constitute the spouse as having an interest, and that should be treated as a § 672(e) interest of the grantor, causing the protection of § 677(b) to spread across both situations.[82]

A final curiosity under § 677(b) is that its protection applies only to legal, as opposed to contractual, obligations.[83] Thus, distributions for private schooling, music and dance lessons, special camps, and other nonessentials may constitute § 677(a)(1) distributions for a grantor's indirect benefit if the grantor had a contractual obligation to the provider of those items that was discharged by those distributions.[84] Most importantly, § 677(b) does not require that distributions be made that *satisfy* the grantor's legal obligation of support or maintenance. This provision

---

(Footnote Continued)

§ 677(b) relates *solely* to the satisfaction of the *grantor's* legal obligation to support or maintain a beneficiary" (emphasis added).

[82] That result also would be consistent with Congress' intent in 1969 when it amended § 677(a) to add references to the grantor's spouse and again in 1986 when it added § 672(e).

[83] Treas. Reg. § 1.677(b)-1(d); Brooke v. United States, 468 F.2d 1155 (9th Cir. 1972).

[84] See, e.g., Morrill v. United States, 228 F. Supp. 734 (D. Me. 1964). Wyche v. United States, 36 A.F.T.R.2d 5816 (Ct. Cl. 1974), is a very helpful opinion in elucidating the issues involved in these cases. It determined that private school tuition and various other expenses such as for music and dance lessons were not part of a parent's legal obligation under state law, citing Rev. Rul. 56-484, 1956-2 C.B. 23, for the proposition that state law is determinative of that issue. In addition, unlike the taxpayer in *Morrill*, the taxpayer in *Wyche* was not contractually bound to make these various payments, because they were arranged and paid for by the trust in the first instance; no contractual liability ever was assumed by the grantor.

is very carefully worded to apply to distributions for the support or maintenance of someone the grantor is obligated to support or maintain, not to distributions that *discharge* that obligation. Indeed, it recognizes that such distributions probably cannot have the effect of discharging those obligations under most states' laws.[85]

Thus, for example, in Stone v. Commissioner,[86] the issue was whether § 677(b) would tax trust income to the taxpayer as grantor of the trust because it was applied to the support or maintenance of persons the taxpayer was obliged to support or maintain.[87] It was conceded that the taxpayer was obligated to support the beneficiaries and that education was part of a parent's support obligation under state law.[88] Nevertheless, trust income was used to provide private school tuition, and the

---

[85] See Treas. Reg. § 1.662(a)-4. But see Treas. Reg. § 1.677(b)-1(d) (first sentence), which improperly refers to "satisfaction of grantor's legal obligation to support or maintain a beneficiary," and Treas. Reg. § 1.677(a)-1(d), which also improperly refers to the discharge of the grantor's obligation of support. See also §§ 5.11.4 nn.75-91 and accompanying text, 7.1.1.10 n.100, 7.1.1.10.1, 7.3.4.2 nn.153-172 and accompanying text, and 12.4.2, regarding the discharge of obligation theory.

[86] 54 T.C.M. (CCH) 462 (1987), aff'd in an unpublished opinion (9th Cir. 1988).

[87] The taxpayer created a trust with an independent trustee, from whom the taxpayer then immediately borrowed back the corpus, at a 20% rate of interest, which the court determined was adequate. It also held there to be adequate security for the loan, avoiding application of § 675(3) for grantor trust purposes. The government initially attacked the borrow back aspect of the transaction, but abandoned the issue to instead pursue only the § 677(b) question. With respect to the transfer and borrow back issue see § 6.3.3.5.

[88] At that time, supported by Cal. Civ. Code § 196, which was replaced by Cal. Fam. Code § 3900. There are scores of nontax cases decided at the state court level involving the question of a parent's support obligation, determining such issues as whether it includes costs for a college education and continues to postgraduate or professional training, and whether it extends past a child's age of majority. In a tax context, Braun v. Commissioner, 48 T.C.M. (CCH) 210 (1984), held private secondary and post-secondary education to be a parent's legal obligation in New Jersey, based on the grantor's station in life. As recognized in *Stone*, Weiss v. Weiss, 1996 WL 91641 (unpub. S.D. N.Y.), articulated that cases like *Braun* are distinguishable by the fact that they involve support obligations determined in the divorce or separation context and that the finding regarding the level of support of a parent in that context is very different from what a court normally is willing to decree in an intact family. Potentially this means that courts will not establish whether certain expenditures beyond bare necessities are part

§ 5.11.4.2

taxpayer asserted that private schooling is not part of that support obligation. In addressing the issue, the court noted that the issues were framed poorly because § 677(b) deals with amounts distributed for the support or maintenance of someone the taxpayer is legally obliged to support or maintain, but

> [t]he legal obligation required [by § 677(b)] seems to be a general one towards the beneficiary, not a specific obligation to expend particular amounts on particular expenses connected with the person to whom the obligation is owed. However, to the extent an expenditure is found to be a legal obligation, it will surely also be an expenditure for the "support or maintenance of a beneficiary . . . whom the grantor is legally obligated to support."[89]

Thus, the court pursued the issue as briefed by the parties and, based on state law, found that there was an obligation to support a child "in a style and condition consonant with his parent's financial ability and position in society"—considering the parents' earnings and earning capacity.

Most state law support cases arise in the context of divorce or separation, yet the court concluded that those cases are informative regarding the determination involved in § 677(b). It also found that state law cases award support for a child to attend college if the parent is financially able to pay. Therefore, the court focused on the taxpayer's ability to provide private schooling, plus the fact that the parent had been sending the children to private schools for several years before the trust was created, and held:

> Under these circumstances, we conclude that the expenses paid by the trust . . . for the private high school education of petitioners' children are amounts "distributed for the support or maintenance of a beneficiary . . . whom the grantor is legally obligated to support or maintain" under section 677(b).... Consequently, under section 677(a) . . . petitioners are treated as "the owner of [the] portion of [the] trust whose income" has been so distributed.[90]

(Footnote Continued)

of a parent's normal obligation of support in a context that does not involve divorce or separation.

[89] 54 T.C.M. at 465-466 n.6.

[90] 54 T.C.M. at 467.

§ 5.11.4.2

As the opinion reveals, because § 677(b) does not require distributions that "discharge" the obligation of support or maintenance, the court only needed to establish that distributions were for the support or maintenance of someone the grantor was obliged to support or maintain.

This has special significance in drafting because it means that a classic "Upjohn" clause prohibiting distributions that discharge the obligation is not effective to avoid exposure.[91] The protection in cases like *Stone* would be to prohibit distributions for the education involved, which usually is too high a price to pay to avoid § 677(a) liability. Also notable is that an obligation to provide a private high school education does not necessarily indicate that there would be an obligation to provide a college education, nor does *Stone* necessarily imply that any obligation would exist with respect to a differently situated taxpayer.

§5.11.5 *Powers Over Beneficial Enjoyment*

Probably the most cumbersome provision in Subpart E is § 674.[92] It imposes grantor trust liability with respect to any portion of a trust as to which either the grantor, the grantor's spouse (with respect to post-1986 trusts),[93] or a nonadverse party—in each case acting without the consent of an adverse party—has a power to affect beneficial enjoyment of income or corpus. The tax policy justification for this expansive provision is that the power to govern enjoyment of wealth is one of the two significant attributes of wealth (the other being personal enjoyment of the wealth) and ought to be equated with ownership.[94] A direct power over disposition, a power of appointment, or any other power (such as those associated with § § 2036(a)(2) and 2038(a)(1) for FET purposes) that allows alteration of enjoyment, all will trigger application of § 674(a)

---

[91] See Pennell, Income Shifting After TRA'86, 46 N.Y.U. Inst. Fed. Tax'n § 50.07[3] at 50-36 (1988).

[92] See generally Westfall, Trust Grantors and Section 674: Adventures in Income Tax Avoidance, 60 Colum. L. Rev. 326 (1960), and Westfall, Grantors, Trusts, and Beneficiaries Under the Income Tax Provisions of the Internal Revenue Code of 1986, 40 Tax Law. 713 (1987).

[93] See § 672(e), and see § 5.11.1 n.36 and accompanying text, regarding § 672(e).

[94] Commissioner v. Buck, 120 F.2d 775 (2d Cir. 1941).

§5.11.5

even if the grantor cannot in any way benefit or obtain personal enjoyment.[95]

Because of the breadth of §674(a), few trusts would escape grantor trust treatment during the grantor's life if the numerous exceptions to it did not exist. Most of those exceptions are subject to three overriding cautions that must be respected if the plan demands avoidance of grantor trust treatment. If, however, grantor trust treatment is desirable,[96] these exceptions provide opportunities to flunk the grantor trust rules in most instances with no wealth transfer tax exposure to the grantor. In many cases with the ability to "toggle" between grantor trust treatment and normal trust taxation, which provides the most flexibility for ongoing income tax planning involving inter vivos trusts.

The first caution is that a person (either the grantor or anyone else) will be considered to possess powers held by a trustee (and therefore an exception may fail to apply) if the person has a power to remove, substitute, or add trustees and is not prohibited from naming the

---

[95] Treas. Reg. §1.674(a)-1(a). Wysong v. Commissioner, 55 T.C.M. (CCH) 1456 (1988), held that a demand note can cause grantor trust taxation because of what the court regarded as a prohibited §674(a) power to control the disposition of trust corpus, exercisable without the approval or consent of an adverse party. In the course of this opinion it stated, however, that:

> Our holding here does not . . . "create an owner of a trust out of any person who makes a demand loan to a trust." It merely . . . creates an owner of a trust of a *settlor* who makes a demand loan to a trust, and then only to the extent of the demand loan.

55 T.C.M. at 1457 (emphasis in original). This statement seems less than astute to the extent it suggests that grantor trust liability would have been avoided if the beneficiary or any third party had created the trust. In any event (and more relevant here), the court more properly would have treated the demand note as a power of revocation under §676 rather than as a power to govern beneficial enjoyment under §674(a). See §5.11.3 n.59. Without special indications about the propriety of demand loans by persons other than the grantor of the trust, on virtually the same facts and theory the Tax Court cited *Wysong* and reached the same result in Kushner v. Commissioner, 61 T.C.M. (CCH) 1716 (1991), aff'd in an unpublished opinion (4th Cir. 1992). See §6.3.3.5 regarding the tax consequences of an interest free demand note transferred to a trust and for a discussion of the related gift and borrow back transaction.

[96] See §5.11.9 for a discussion of when intentional grantor trust planning is desirable.

§5.11.5

powerholder as a successor trustee.[97] However, attribution of trustee powers will not occur in any year in which no vacancy exists and the powerholder cannot create one.[98] Nor will attribution occur if the powerholder must replace a removed trustee with a comparable trustee (other than the powerholder),[99] such as a corporate replacement to a corporate trustee. Thus, grantor trust exposure might be accomplished by giving the grantor's spouse a power to remove and replace trustees that would permit the spouse to be a successor and that does not require replacements to be comparable to those replaced. This would produce easy grantor trust treatment if the trustee's powers deemed held by the spouse would permit the § 672(e) spousal unity rule to trigger grantor trust treatment without causing untoward wealth transfer tax exposure to the spouse.

The second overriding caution relates to exceptions[100] that are unavailable if any person may add beneficiaries to the trust, except by exercise of a testamentary power of appointment or to account for subsequent births or adoptions.[101] Giving the right party such a power that they subsequently may relinquish, or giving one party the power to

---

[97] Treas. Reg. § 1.674(d)-2(a).

[98] Treas. Reg. § 1.674(d)-2(a) (parenthetical provision).

[99] Treas. Reg. § 1.674(d)-2(a) (last sentence). This provision is not exactly the same as that in Rev. Rul. 79-353, 1979-2 C.B. 325, which was modified by Rev. Rul. 81-51, 1981-1 C.B. 458 (limiting Rev. Rul. 79-353 to prospective application) and then revoked and replaced by Rev. Rul. 95-58, 1995-2 C.B. 191, for estate and gift tax purposes. If the powerholder cannot become successor trustee and without regard to naming comparable successors the government now opines that a "revolving door" power to remove and replace trustees at will does not cause the powerholder to be treated as holding all powers of the trustee if the successor cannot be a related or subordinate party as that term is defined in § 672(c). See § 5.11.1 nn.30-33 and accompanying text. Without that restriction, the power will be analyzed on a facts and circumstances basis and may result in imputed powers or treatment of the powerholder as trustee in cases in which similar treatment would not apply for income tax purposes. See § 7.3.3.

[100] § § 674(b)(5), 674(b)(6), 674(b)(7), 674(c), and 674(d).

[101] Treas. Reg. § 1.674(d)-2(b). There is an adverse party limitation on this exception to the exceptions, referred to in the regulation only in the context of substituting beneficiaries for the powerholder as beneficiary. Adding beneficiaries who would receive a portion of what the powerholder otherwise would receive also should suffice to trigger this adverse party limitation. See § 5.11.1 nn.19-29 regarding the definition of adverse party.

§ 5.11.5

give another party the power to add beneficiaries might be attractive methods to invoke and then retract grantor trust liability.

The third caution relates to exceptions involving the exercise of fiduciary discretion.[102] These exceptions will not apply if the trustee's powers are conclusive or exempt from judicial supervision, as may occur inadvertently under a broadly drawn exoneration or exculpatory provision.[103] Thus, with the proper fiduciary in place, granting or retracting exoneration also might prove an easy method to trigger toggle switch grantor trust liability.

The exceptions in §§ 674(b), 674(c), and 674(d) to the general rule of § 674(a) are grouped below, first according to who may hold a particular power without causing grantor trust liability, and second by the portions of a trust (for example, income or corpus) over which the power may apply. Progressing from the most restrictive class of powerholder to the most expansive, the exceptions to grantor trust exposure for powers over those trust are:

- *Independent trustees* may have any power to accumulate income or to distribute either *income or corpus* to any one,[104] without restraint by any limitation or standard.[105] "Independent" means (1) not the grantor or, for post-1986 trusts, the grantor's spouse[106] and (2) not more than half of the trustees are related or subordinate parties who are subservient to the grantor.[107]

---

102 Treas. Reg. § 1.674(b)-1(b)(5)(i) (penultimate sentence).

103 § 674(b)(5)(A) and, indirectly, § 674(d) due to the parenthetical provision in Treas. Reg. § 1.674(d)-1. Although there is no direct authority for an extension of this caution, it might be prudent for drafters to exercise restraint in drafting exoneration and exculpation provisions for purposes of discretionary actions under §§ 674(b)(8) and 674(c) as well. See, e.g., Bennett v. Commissioner, 79 T.C. 470 (1982) (grantor's misadministration of trust as trustee is not tantamount to a power to affect enjoyment if subject to liability for breach of trust).

104 However, authority to distribute to the grantor or the grantor's spouse would trigger § 676. See § 5.11.3 at text accompanying n.61.

105 § 674(c).

106 § 674(c), which was amended in 1988 to add the last sentence of the flush language, providing that "any reference . . . to the grantor shall be treated as including a reference to" the grantor's spouse as defined in § 672(e)(2), and § 672(e). See § 5.11.1 n.36 and accompanying text regarding § 672(e).

107 As defined in § 672(c). See § 5.11.1 nn.30-33 and accompanying text. Estate of Goodwyn v. Commissioner, 35 T.C.M. (CCH) 1026 (1976), held that indepen-

- *Anyone except the grantor or the grantor's spouse (if living with the grantor), acting as trustee* may have power to distribute *income* to any beneficiary, if the power is limited by a "reasonably definite external standard."[108] This standard may include the terms "education," "support," "maintenance," "health," "to maintain his accustomed standard of living," "reasonable support and comfort," and "to meet an emergency."[109] Drafters familiar with the § 2041(b)(1)(A) ascertainable standard will recognize that the § 674 standard is less restrictive, so drafting to meet the more familiar § 2041 will be adequate for § 674 exception purposes as well.[110]

- *Anyone acting as trustee—including the grantor or the grantor's spouse—*may have the following powers:

Over both income and corpus:

- Unlimited, if exercisable only with the consent of an adverse party.[111]

- To allocate either without limitation among charities.[112]

- To determine the proper allocation of receipts and distributions between income and corpus for fiduciary accounting purposes under the local principal and income act or authority in the document, notwithstanding any incidental effect on the rights of beneficiaries.[113]

Over corpus only:

(Footnote Continued)

dent trustee capitulation to the grantor's exercise of control was not tantamount to a § 674(a) power in the grantor.

[108] § 674(d).

[109] Treas. Reg. § 1.674(d)-1 specifies that the requisite standard is the same as a "reasonably definite standard" as defined at Treas. Reg. § 1.674(b)-1(b)(5)(i), despite the one word (external) difference in their titles.

[110] According to Carpenter Estate v. United States, 80-1 U.S. Tax Cas. (CCH) ¶ 13,339 (W.D. Wis. 1980) (decided under §§ 2036 and 2038), to qualify for an exception from the workings of a distribution provision, the standard must set both a maximum *and a minimum* on distributions that may or shall be made, meaning that distribution must be *required* if the standard is met; otherwise the trustee's discretion to not make a payment that is nevertheless authorized is regarded as too great. Because this case stands alone on that proposition, it may not deserve attention in drafting, although a cautious drafter may want to keep it in mind and pay attention to any future developments to the same effect.

[111] § 674(a).

[112] § 674(b)(4).

[113] § 674(b)(8).

§ 5.11.5

- To make distributions to income beneficiaries without limitation by any standards, provided the distribution is charged against the share of the trust producing that beneficiary's income interest.[114]

- To make distributions (without charging shares) if limited by a "reasonably definite standard."[115]

Over income only:

- To alter enjoyment of income received after the § 673 period,[116] but only until that period ends and the power becomes exercisable.[117]

- To distribute income for the support or maintenance of a beneficiary the grantor is obliged to support or maintain.[118] Because § 677(b) will apply to this power to the extent it is exercised, this dovetail exception permits § 677(b) to operate as the exclusive authority.

- To accumulate income while the beneficiary is under the age of 21 years or is suffering from a legal disability.[119]

- To accumulate income for ultimate distribution (a) to the beneficiary from whom it was withheld, (b) to that beneficiary's estate, (c) as that beneficiary appoints pursuant to a statutory power of appointment[120] (and the document may designate default beneficiaries to take the accumulation to the extent the power is not effectively exercised),[121] (d) in previously specified shares to all current income beneficiaries on

---

[114] § 674(b)(5)(B). It is not necessary that the income beneficiary be a remainder beneficiary; as a consequence, the charging requirement does not refer to advancement treatment of future distributions of any anticipated share of corpus that the beneficiary otherwise ultimately might receive.

[115] § 674(b)(5)(A). For the definition of this standard see § 5.11.5 nn.108-110 and accompanying text.

[116] Applicable in a pre-1986 trust for a 10 year period (or until the earlier death of an income beneficiary other than the grantor or the grantor's spouse), or in a post-1986 trust until the occurrence of a § 673 event (death of a present interest minor lineal descendant beneficiary).

[117] § 674(b)(2) and Treas. Reg. § 1.674(b)-1(b)(2) (last sentence).

[118] § 674(b)(1).

[119] § 674(b)(7).

[120] The statutory power of appointment *must* (not may) be exercisable in favor of anyone except the beneficiary, the beneficiary's estate, or creditors of either, and is the broadest power available without causing § 2041 FET or § 2514 gift tax consequences on exercise, release, or lapse.

[121] § 674(b)(6)(A) (parenthetical provision).

§ 5.11.5

termination of the trust,[122] or (e) to designated default takers[123] if termination and distribution of the trust reasonably may be expected to occur within the beneficiary's life but the beneficiary in fact dies prior to termination.[124]

• *Anyone acting in any capacity* may have a testamentary power to appoint either *income*[125] *or corpus*[126] (not including, however, a power in the grantor or, in post-1986 trusts, in the grantor's spouse[127] to appoint income that was or that could have been specifically accumulated without the consent of an adverse party for purposes of testamentary appointment. Typically subject to this exception to the exception is income allocable to corpus for fiduciary accounting purposes, such as capital gains).

To summarize the essence of § 674, if grantor trust treatment is to be avoided, anyone may have the powers in § 674(b), which grant relatively broad discretion over corpus[128] and income,[129] anyone except the grantor or the grantor's spouse may have the powers in § 674(d) over income if limited by the requisite standard, and § 674(c) independent trustees may have any powers to the extent the trustee is subject to judicial accountability. With the ability in most cases to make a grantor's spouse a trustee without wealth transfer tax exposure it should be relatively easy to keep administration of a trust within the realm of the grantor's influence and tacit supervision without triggering unwanted § 674(a) grantor trust exposure.

§5.11.6 Administrative Powers

Probably the most frequent source of *intentional* grantor trust exposure[130] relates to administrative powers that permit any nonadverse

---

[122] § 674(b)(6)(B).

[123] Other than the grantor or the grantor's estate and, in post-1986 trusts, the grantor's spouse or the spouse's estate.

[124] § 674(b)(6) (penultimate sentence in flush language).

[125] Treas. Reg. § 1.674(b)-1(b)(3).

[126] § 674(b)(3).

[127] See § 672(e) and see § 5.11.1 n.36 and accompanying text, regarding § 672(e).

[128] § § 674(b)(5)(A) and 674(b)(5)(B).

[129] § § 674(b)(6) and 674(b)(7).

[130] See Moore & Pennell, Survey of the Profession II, 30 U. Miami Inst. Est. Plan. ¶ 1501 at question 35 (1996).

§5.11.6

party, including the grantor (or, for post-1986 trusts, the grantor's spouse)[131] to deal with closely held stock or to engage in what amounts in many cases to self-dealing with the trust. If the grantor or the grantor's spouse has a power to amend it, the trust will be treated as if an amendment already had been made. The government's position is that, even if that power would not otherwise suffice to cause § 676 grantor trust exposure, grantor trust exposure exists if the power of amendment would permit the grantor or the grantor's spouse to establish any of the § 675 powers.[132]

Under § 675(1), a grantor is treated as the owner of any portion of a trust as to which the grantor, the grantor's spouse, or a nonadverse party (acting without the consent of an adverse party) may deal with, dispose of, or exchange either income or corpus for less than full and adequate consideration, regardless of whether the grantor may benefit personally from exercise of the power. A nonadverse party with a nongeneral power of appointment could trigger grantor trust treatment if this provision means what it literally appears to say.

Two provisions deal with loans to the grantor or the grantor's spouse from the trust. Under § 675(2) the grantor is treated as the owner of any portion of a trust as to which the grantor or the grantor's spouse has the power to borrow, or a nonadverse party has been given a power to make loans to the grantor or to the spouse, in either case on less than adequate interest or security. It does not apply, however, to any trustee other than the grantor or the grantor's spouse who is authorized by the document generally to make loans to any person, including the grantor or the grantor's spouse, without regard to interest or security. Thus, if the danger is low of a nonadverse party (other than the grantor or the grantor's spouse) acting as trustee making an "improper" loan to a third party, the power to do so may be granted in general and the fact that the grantor and the grantor's spouse are not excluded from the class of potential borrowers will be irrelevant.

Many drafters intentionally trigger this grantor trust rule by providing the trustee with the power to lend to the grantor or to the grantor's

---

[131] See § 672(e) and see § 5.11.1 n.36 and accompanying text, regarding § 672(e).

[132] Treas. Reg. § 1.675-1(a) (penultimate sentence). No authority in the Code supports this provision.

§ 5.11.6

spouse on adequate interest (to avoid any imputed interest under §7872 and any imputed §2036(a)(1) retained enjoyment) but on less than adequate security. By its terms, §675(2) says that it will apply in this circumstance (power to lend on *either* less than adequate interest *or* less than adequate security), but in reality it is nonsense to suggest that interest and security are disjointed, such that one could be adequate but the other not. For example, a zero interest loan can be adequately secured—a pawn shop loan is such. Or an unsecured loan can carry adequate interest—consider junk bonds or credit card debt. So, to have a loan with adequate interest but not adequate security is an oxymoron—if the security is deficient the interest rate must be higher and, if great enough to be "adequate" for that under-secured loan, then the security is not inadequate. Nevertheless, it is common to find intentionally defective grantor trust provisions reading "I retain the right to borrow without giving adequate security so long as such borrowing provides for the payment of adequate interest." The only way this can be meaningful is if "adequate interest" is defined as something less than what the market in general would provide. To wit: "Adequate interest means an interest rate that does not cause the loan to be a below market interest rate loan described in Code §7872(e)(1)." This works because "below market rate" is defined by §7872(e)(1)(A) in terms of the applicable federal rate and not in terms of the true market rate for an unsecured loan.

The power to lend in §675(2) is to be distinguished from an exercise of that power, which §675(3) treats as making the grantor the owner of any portion of the trust that the grantor[133] or the grantor's spouse[134] actually has borrowed and has not completely repaid before the tax year *began* (which necessarily includes amounts borrowed dur-

---

[133] Bennett v. Commissioner, 79 T.C. 470 (1982), held that a loan from the trust to a partnership of which the grantor was a partner is tantamount to loans to the grantor directly, but not if the borrower was a corporation of which the grantor was a shareholder. See also TAM 8802004 regarding loans to partnerships.

[134] Notice that in this case the authority may be either of §672(e) or §675(3) (last sentence) itself, which presumably was added to be certain that this treatment applies because a loan may not constitute either an interest or a power in a trust, as required by §672(e).

§5.11.6

ing the current tax year).[135] It does not apply, however, if the loan was made for an adequate interest and security, by a trustee other than the grantor, the grantor's spouse, or a related or subordinate party. Therefor, an easy and attractive method of triggering grantor trust exposure without wealth transfer tax liability to the grantor is for the grantor's spouse or any other related or subordinated trustee to lend to the grantor or to the grantor's spouse on adequate interest and security, or for any trustee to lend to the grantor's spouse on below market interest or security. The curious aspect of § 675(3) is that it may cause zero income of a trust to be taxed to the grantor if the grantor or the grantor's spouse borrowed the entire trust corpus and paid no interest. It also may produce a wash if interest that is paid or deemed to be paid[136] is an allowable deduction under § 163.[137]

---

[135] See Rev. Rul. 86-82, 1986-1 C.B. 253, holding that the trust is a grantor trust for the entire year in which the loan was outstanding, notwithstanding that the loan was made after the year began and was repaid before it ended. This is because there is no "chronological portion rule" under § 675(3).

[136] See § 7872.

[137] The government argued in Rothstein v. United States, 735 F.2d 704 (2d Cir. 1984) (grantor's installment purchase of trust corpus treated as an indirect loan from the trust for § 675(3) purposes), that the trust was a grantor trust and, by virtue of that characterization, should be ignored for income tax purposes with respect to all transactions with the grantor. This meant that no interest expense deduction would be proper because the grantor cannot pay interest to the grantor (and also meant that the grantor could not receive a new basis in assets purchased from the trust). The court rejected this conclusion on the basis that grantor trust treatment causes income items in the trust to be taxed to the grantor. But it does not go so far as the summary description often used to describe the situation that it is as if the trust did not exist or as if the trust and the grantor were one for income tax purposes. That determination was favorable in *Rothstein*, but it would be uncomfortable in many uses of intentional grantor trusts. Cf. PLR 9525036, which held that loans from a grantor *to* a grantor trust involved neither interest payments nor income to the lender that would be recognized for income tax purposes.

Winter v. United States, 91-2 U.S. Tax Cas. (CCH) ¶ 50,436 (Ct. Cl. 1991), aff'd in an unpublished opinion (Fed. Cir. 1992), held that the imputed gift flowing from an interest free demand loan does not generate an imputed interest expense deduction for the borrower under § 163. Decided without reference to § 7872 (adopted in 1984) because the loans involved were made in 1982, the court relied on Dickman v. Commissioner, 465 U.S. 330 (1984), as establishing the gift tax liability of the loan. Focusing principally on the requirement in § 163

Finally, §675(4) applies only to the extent a nonadverse party (including the grantor or the grantor's spouse) has any power to act in a nonfiduciary capacity, without the consent of a *fiduciary* (which is not necessarily an adverse party), either to vote, invest, or direct either, with respect to securities in any corporation in which the aggregate holdings of the grantor, the grantor's spouse, and the trust are significant,[138] or to reacquire trust corpus by swapping it for property of equivalent value.[139]

(Footnote Continued)

that interest be accrued or paid to be deductible, the court rejected the taxpayer's argument that the *Dickman* interest free loan analysis presupposes imputed payments from the lender to the borrower (the gift element) and back from the borrower to the lender as interest paid. According to the court, "the net economic reality . . . is that the recipient of the loan has received property with tangible value, yet given nothing in exchange" and that

> whatever interest obligation is in theory generated initially is then forgiven by the lender . . . . This court will not . . . recognize as fact what is in reality fiction—the payment of interest by the donee of an interest-free loan. Plaintiff has neither paid nor accrued interest and is not entitled to a deduction under section 163.

91-2 U.S. Tax Cas. at 89,592-89,593. If this conclusion is correct, it might then follow that the lender has no income tax liability flowing from the transaction on the theory that the lender cannot have interest income if no interest has been paid by the borrower. Presumably a different result would be reached on both the income and deduction issues if §7872 was applicable, §7872(a)(1) specifying that "in the case of any below-market loan to which this section applies and which is a gift loan or a demand loan, the forgone interest shall be treated as— (A) transferred from the lender to the borrower, and (B) retransferred by the borrower to the lender as interest."

[138] §§675(4)(A) and 675(4)(B). Quaere whether authority under §2036(b) for FET purposes, such as addressed in Rev. Rul. 81-15, 1981-1 C.B. 457 (power to vote retained voting stock is not tantamount to a prohibited retained voting power with respect to transferred nonvoting stock) will inform decisions under §675(4)(A). See §7.3.4.3.

[139] §675(4)(C). Quaere why this provision makes reference to a power to "*re*acquire" trust corpus if a nonadverse party or the grantor's spouse but not the grantor can trigger its application. PLR 9810019 involved a third party who possessed such a power, which was deemed to raise the factual inquiry whether it was exercised in a nonfiduciary capacity; the "*re*acquire" issue was not even discussed. The government's sample CLT forms, reported in §14.3.6, employ the power to swap assets in a nonadverse party other than the grantor or the grantor's spouse (to create a grantor trust without triggering the self-dealing rules) and presumably, perhaps unintentionally, puts this linguistic concern to rest. Each part of §675(4) is a codification of the prior Clifford regulations, which

§5.11.6

These provisions easily can be avoided by not granting the prohibited powers or by requiring a trustee other than the grantor or the grantor's spouse to consent to any vote, investment, or swap, or requiring the possessor of the power to act in a fiduciary capacity, subject to judicial scrutiny and enforceability. But if grantor trust liability is desirable, allowing anyone to hold any of these powers in a nonfiduciary capacity would suffice.

Among other troublesome aspects of § 675(4), the nonadverse party requirement[140] appears to lack statutory support, the "nonfiduciary capacity" issue is described by the regulations only to mean action that is not in the interests of the beneficiaries,[141] and "significant" holdings is not defined for purposes of §§ 675(4)(A) and 675(4)(B). Most disconcerting of all, the need for some of the § 675 rules in the first instance is not at all apparent.

For example, § 675(3) is of no apparent consequence if there are no items of taxable income in a trust to be taxed to the grantor, by virtue of the grantor having borrowed the full corpus and § 163(d) is applicable to permit an interest expense deduction to match, whether the grantor paid

---

(Footnote Continued)

contained the same glitch as now appears in § 675(4)(C). See Treas. Reg. § 39.22(a)-21(e)(1) (1951) and H.R. Rep. No. 1337, 83d Cong., 2d Sess. A216 (1954), and S. Rep. No. 1622, 83d Cong., 2d Sess. 370 (1954).

The power in this provision to swap trust corpus makes little sense anyway, because essentially it proscribes a power to purchase assets from the trust for their full FMV. *That* notion is what informs the clearly correct holding in Rev. Ruls. 2011-28, 2011-2 C.B. 830, and 2008-22, 2008-1 C.B. 796, that (subject to several caveats that likely never will be raised again) the power will not cause FET inclusion, and the similar result in PLR 200846001 that exercise of the swap power will not constitute a gift to the trust. And the fact that the trust *is* a grantor trust also justifies the PLR's conclusion that an exchange is not a gain or loss realization event. See § 5.11.9 n.246.

140 Treas. Reg. § 1.675-1(b)(4).

141 Treas. Reg. § 1.675-1(b) (flush language), presumes that a trustee acts in a fiduciary capacity "primarily in the interests of the beneficiaries." This provision corresponds with the former Clifford regulation that was the source of § 675, which was adopted without codification of this aspect. See Treas. Reg. § 39.22(a)-21(e)(2) (1951). And see § 5.11.5 n.103 regarding the § 674 regulations with respect to acting in a nonfiduciary capacity if free of judicial scrutiny and enforcement.

interest or was deemed to pay[142] (for example, if the grantor paid adequate interest but invoked application of § 675(3) by virtue of borrowing with inadequate security or because the trustee was related or subordinate).[143] Furthermore, it is not clear why Congress thought the type of power subject to § 675(1) differs from the § 676 power to revoke or, if it is held by a third party, how it is meant to differ from an inter vivos nongeneral power of appointment. And there is no ready explanation for why § 675(4)(C) should apply to a power to purchase assets from the trust for a full and adequate consideration.

Perhaps in light of the nonsense application of the grantor trust rules under these provisions, the government's PLR position for years in the context of § 675 appeared to be designed to chill grantor trust planning that takes advantage of these proscriptions and turn them to the taxpayer's advantage.[144] For example, as early as 1993, the government held that it may refuse to rule on the question whether a trust *is* a grantor trust if warranted by the facts or circumstances presented[145] and declined to determine that an amendment to an inter vivos trust to give the grantor a power to exchange assets of equal value would create § 675(4)(C) grantor trust treatment for income tax purposes.[146] That prohibition appears since to have been lifted. For example, the government will rule that § 675(4)(C) grantor trust liability permits S Corporation qualification of trusts that hold stock in close corporations,[147] which is subject to re-evaluation on a year to year basis, the S Corporation

---

[142] See § 5.11.6 nn.137-138 and accompanying text.

[143] See Rev. Rul. 86-106, 1986-2 C.B. 28 (taxpayer borrowed entire trust corpus on full and adequate interest and security, which the government regarded as an improper effort to shift income to the trust and through it to the trust beneficiaries, notwithstanding that the trust could have loaned the corpus to anyone else for the same interest and accomplished the same purpose). Based on a sham transaction theory, the government denied the taxpayer's interest expense deduction. Consistency should dictate that the trust had no income either (that issue was not addressed), resulting in the same treatment as if §§ 675(3) and 163(d) had applied, notwithstanding that the taxpayer carefully crafted the transaction to avoid application of § 675(3)).

[144] See § 5.11.9 regarding the advantages of intentional grantor trust planning.

[145] Citing § 7 of Rev. Proc. 93-1, 1993-1 C.B. 313, 325. (See § 6.02 of Rev. Proc. 2012-1, 2012-1 C.B. 1).

[146] See PLR 9318019.

[147] See PLR 9335028.

§ 5.11.6

status being subject to annual review whereas normal grantor trust exposure questions are not subject to periodic reinspection.

§5.11.7 *Pseudo Grantor Trusts*

Technically § 678 is not a "grantor trust" provision because it applies only to someone other than the grantor who has (or, under proper circumstances, who has released or modified) certain powers. It is included in Subpart E and it is appropriate to consider it as part of the grantor trust rules, however, because it has the effect of treating that person as the owner of that portion of the trust as to which the power applies. This provision works as if that person was a grantor who transferred property into the trust and retained certain powers or interests.[148]

Under § 678 a person other than the grantor is treated as the owner of that portion of a trust as to which the person has a power to demand or withdraw either income or corpus,[149] although joint powers (even with a nonadverse party) will not cause the powerholder to be treated as owner. This provision applies regardless of whether the power is exercised, provided that the power is exercisable[150] solely by the powerholder.[151] Classic forms of exposure under § 678(a)(1) stem from

---

[148] Sometimes known as demand trusts or *Mallinckrodt* trusts after the seminal case involving this concept, Mallinckrodt v. Nunan, 146 F.2d 1 (8th Cir. 1945) (power in beneficiary to withdraw income deemed the equivalent of ownership and no less substantial than if it was held by the grantor, the court holding that income subject to a beneficiary's unfettered control should be taxable to the beneficiary even if the beneficiary chooses not to withdraw it).

[149] § 678(a)(1). As discussed with respect to the portion rules, it is unclear whether there is a chronological portion rule applicable with respect to § 678 and therefore whether existence of a power for less than an entire year will cause only a fraction of the trust's income tax attributes to be ascribed to the powerholder. See § 5.11.8.

[150] See Treas. Reg. § 1.678(a)-1. The term "exercisable" has the same meaning here as under § 2041. See Trust No. 3 v. Commissioner, 285 F.2d 102 (7th Cir. 1960) (minor with no guardian still subject to § 678 by virtue of power to terminate trust); Rev. Rul. 81-6, 1981-1 C.B. 385 (same); and § 12.3 n.7 and accompanying text.

[151] Treas. Reg. § 1.678(a)-1(b).

five-or-five[152] and Crummey withdrawal rights,[153] granted to qualify for the gift tax annual exclusion of § 2503(b) while avoiding taxable lapses under § 2514(e). Also from inter vivos general powers of appointment, most often found in § 2056(b)(5) marital deduction trusts or trusts for mature family members that permit withdrawal by the beneficiary as an alternative to mandatory termination when the beneficiary reaches a certain age.

Beneficiaries who may exercise a power to withdraw annually an amount not to exceed the greater of $5,000 or 5% of the trust corpus are treated as owners of a portion of the trust under § 678. As such a portion of all income, deductions, and credits of all the trust must be attributed annually to the holder of the power, even if the power is not exercised in a given year and even though the beneficiary may receive no cash distributions from the trust with which to pay the resulting income tax. Moreover, the trustee must maintain accurate records so as to inform the powerholder of those tax consequences and avoid having the trust or some other beneficiary pay their tax. This pseudo grantor trust treatment applies to the *entire* amount subject to the power of withdrawal, not just the amount in excess of the § 2514(e) five-or-five exception. The only escape from this treatment is to the extent the trust's original grantor retains an interest or power that causes overriding grantor trust liability for income tax purposes.[154]

To illustrate the government's position on the proper computation of the income tax consequences of the lapse[155] of a five-or-five withdrawal right, assume that the powerholder is entitled to trust income in future years. Thus, the release generates grantor trust exposure for the duration of the trust that will increase every time a withdrawal power lapses. Because the government will not treat every year's lapse as occurring

---

[152] See, e.g., Rev. Rul. 67-241, 1967-2 C.B. 225.

[153] See, e.g., Rev. Rul. 81-6, 1981-1 C.B. 385.

[154] § 678(b). See § 5.11.7 n.174 and accompanying text.

[155] Although there is an argument that lapse of a power of withdrawal is not tantamount to a release for ongoing § 678(a)(2) purposes, the government has the better side of this debate. See Ferguson, Freeland, & Ascher, Federal Income Taxation of Estates, Trusts, and Beneficiaries § 10.16[B] (3d ed. 2011).

§ 5.11.7

with respect to the same five-or-five portion every year,[156] there is an increase in the portion subject to grantor trust treatment attributable to every new lapse, computed according to a formula:[157]

trust portion not yet owned ÷ total trust corpus × withdrawable amount = increase

Subsequent distributions to the powerholder from the trust are deemed to come proportionately from the owned portion and from the balance of the trust.

Thus, for example, if the taxpayer may withdraw 5% of the trust corpus every year, in the first year of the trust the owned portion would be 100% ÷ 100% × 5% = 5%. The second year increase would be 95% ÷ 100% × 5% = 4.75% and a total of 9.75% would be deemed owned by the powerholder. The third year increase would be 90.25% ÷ 100% × 5% = 4.5125% and a total of 14.2625% would be deemed owned by the powerholder. In the fourth year the increase would be 4.286875% and the owned portion would increase to 18.549375%, and so on. Under this approach, the trust never would become totally owned, no matter how long the withdrawal power existed and lapsed, although the owned portion eventually would approach 100%.

The government's computation is equitable but complicated,[158] and underscores the notion that the lapse of a five-or-five withdrawal power is

---

[156] See PLR 9034004, citing Rev. Rul. 67-241, 1967-2 C.B. 225, for the proposition that the powerholder is treated as the owner of a portion of the trust in the year the power is exercisable. The Ruling also holds that lapse of the withdrawal power is tantamount to a release for purposes of § 678(a)(2). In PLR 9220012 trust beneficiaries persuaded the grantor and trustees to modify a trust to remove powers of withdrawal that subjected the beneficiaries to § 678. This action was not a § 678(d) timely disclaimer, and they continued to be entitled to trust income following the modification. Therefore, the government ruled that the income tax treatment was as if the beneficiaries withdrew the trust corpus and made a recontribution to the trust. Prior to this action these beneficiaries were subject to income tax on the full income and corpus portions of the trust. Following modification they were deemed the owners of only the income portion, so their actions worked an improvement. Given the fact that they were income beneficiaries and would have been taxable on the income portion in any event, the modification served to avoid the income tax on capital gains in the trust.

[157] See Treas. Reg. § 1.671-3(a)(3).

[158] For example, revaluation on an annual basis might be required to adjust the fraction or to compute a new fraction.

§ 5.11.7

not harmless for income tax purposes the way it appears to be under § 2514(e) for most wealth transfer tax purposes. In many cases grantor trust status under § 678 is generated with respect to entire trusts because contributions to the trust do not exceed the beneficiary's withdrawal right. This may produce a favorable result if, for example, pseudo grantor trust status under § 678 allows the trusts to qualify as permissible S Corporation shareholders under § 1361(c)(2)(A)(i),[159] or permits qualification for exclusion of gain on the sale of the beneficiary's principal personal residences held in such a trust.[160]

If the beneficiary already is entitled to all income annually, the added cost of making the trust a pseudo grantor trust with respect to the corpus portion (for example, for capital gain) may be regarded as a small price to pay.[161] Indeed, as with the grantor trust rules themselves, one

---

[159] Notice that one alternative would be for the trust to qualify as an S Corporation shareholder by meeting the QSST rules in § 1361(d)(3). In that case § 1361(d)(1)(A) deems the trust to qualify as a § 1361(c)(2)(A)(i) grantor trust shareholder and § 1361(d)(1)(B) deems the trust to be a pseudo-grantor trust taxable under § 678(a) with respect to only that portion of the trust consisting of the S Corporation stock. The requirements for qualification as a QSST may not be desirable for reasons other than mandatory distribution of all income annually. The taxpayer may prefer to make the trust a pseudo-grantor trust and, by virtue of causing § 678 to apply directly, thereby also qualify as a shareholder under § 1361(c)(2)(A)(i) directly, instead of backing into that treatment through § 1361(d)(3). See § 5.11.9 n.240 and accompanying text.

Treas. Reg. § 1.1361-1(j)(8) restricts the capital gain tax consequence of § 678 treatment, overruling the position previously taken in Rev. Rul. 92-84, 1992-2 C.B. 216, that the income beneficiary must recognize capital gains even if allocated to corpus. A third alternative is the ESBT authorized by § 1361(c)(2)A)(v), with the very different consequence that the trust is taxed on all income regardless of distributions made to the beneficiary; § 641(c) denies a distributions deduction and presumably even intentional qualification as a pseudo-grantor trust under § 678 will not cause income to be taxed to the beneficiary instead of at the trust's rates, which are the highest under the Code.

[160] See § 5.11.9 nn.224-226 and accompanying text.

[161] See, e.g., PLRs 9450014, 9311021, 9232013, and 9226037. The source of the § 678 grantor trust status was lapse of Crummey withdrawal rights with retained rights to income and corpus, producing ongoing grantor trust exposure as if the beneficiaries with the lapsing withdrawal rights were grantors with § 677 retained interests in income. PLR 9321050 apparently was issued on the government's own motion to reverse one of several results stated in PLR 9026036. The issue as to which the government reversed its prior ruling involved a donor who

§ 5.11.7

result of § 678 in general is that planners have the opportunity to cause income taxation to a person other than the recipient of certain income items, presumably with no transfer tax consequences to the pseudo grantor if the power of withdrawal properly is limited for wealth transfer tax power of appointment purposes.[162]

Also reached by § 678(a)(1) is any power to indirectly apply either income or corpus to the person's individual benefit.[163] As this reveals, in most respects taxation under this pseudo grantor trust provision is very similar to traditional grantor trust exposure flowing from a grantor's retention of enjoyment or powers, and it is fitting that two exceptions from other grantor trust rules find application in § 678 as well. The first, although based on very old cases, appears to provide that restrictions on the person's powers, in the form of a limitation such as a "reasonably definite (external) standard," will serve to treat the power as if nonexistent.[164] The same power limitations that would work for income tax

(Footnote Continued)

gave a donee a 30 day Crummey clause power of withdrawal, which the donee allowed to lapse. The only real difference from most Crummey planning was that the donor and donee were spouses and the inter vivos marital deduction was applicable. Other aspects of the Rulings are not relevant to the second Ruling, which reversed only the government's prior holdings on the income tax consequences of the lapse of the withdrawal power.

Originally the position taken was that the donee became the owner of trust income and corpus by virtue of the lapse. Because the donor was treated as the grantor of the trust for income tax purposes due to other powers involved, the donor would be taxed as the owner while alive and the donee only thereafter. See § 678(b) (which may not properly be applicable, because it refers to powers of the donor over only income in the trust and is not determinative with respect to a donor's retained powers over trust corpus). In the revised Ruling the position taken was that the donee does not become the owner of trust income from any part of the trust, either before or after the donor's death. Neither the § 672(e) spousal unity rule nor any other explanation was given for this reversal of position, and any uncertainty about application of the § 678(b) override is not probative because it would apply, if at all, only while the donor is alive.

[162] See § 5.11.9 nn.242-246 and accompanying text, regarding the government's attempts to impute a gift tax consequence to grantor trust treatment.

[163] Treas. Reg. § 1.678(a)-1(b) (first sentence).

[164] United States v. De Bonchamps, 278 F.2d 127 (9th Cir. 1960) (power to consume corpus limited by "needs, maintenance, and comfort"; capital gains in the trust were not taxed to the powerholder); Funk v. Commissioner, 185 F.2d 127 (3d Cir. 1950) ("needs" deemed a sufficient limitation); Smither v. United

§ 5.11.7

purposes under §§ 674(b)(5)(A) and 674(d) or for § 2041(b)(1)(A) FET ascertainable standard purposes will suffice for this purpose.[165]

The second exception is analogous to the § 677(b) exception for a grantor's indirect enjoyment flowing from distributions for the support or maintenance of the grantor's dependents. If the person has a power, as a trustee, to apply income to the support or maintenance of a dependent, grantor trust exposure is limited under § 678(c) to the amount of actual distributions made. Notable about this limitation is that it applies only with respect to the person's power as a fiduciary[166] and only with respect to income distributions.[167] Other aspects of the § 677(b) related limitation also are applicable here,[168] such as regarding certain distributions as accumulation distributions to the person that are subject to throwback[169] and the fact that the provision does not refer to a "discharge" of the person's obligation of support or maintenance.

(Footnote Continued)

States, 108 F. Supp. 772 (S.D. Tex. 1952), aff'd, 205 F.2d 518 (5th Cir. 1953) (power limited by "support, maintenance, comfort, and enjoyment"); May v. Commissioner, 8 T.C. 860 (1947) ("education"). But cf. Koffman v. United States, 193 F. Supp. 946 (E.D. Mich. 1961) (dicta, involving an arrangement the court held was not even a trust, but if it was the language "personal support and maintenance, the reasonableness thereof to be determined by" the powerholder was deemed inadequate).

[165] See Pennell, Estate Planning: Drafting and Tax Considerations in Employing Individual Trustees, 60 N.C. L. Rev. 799, 806-807 (1982), abridged and reprinted in 9 Est. Plan. 264 (1982).

[166] Treas. Reg. § 1.678(c)-1(b); cf. Mesker v. United States, 261 F. Supp. 817 (E.D. Mo. 1966).

[167] Ferguson, Freeland, & Ascher, Federal Income Taxation of Estates, Trusts, and Beneficiaries § 10.16[D] (3d ed. 2011), suggests that this may be a drafting error, and Treas. Reg. § 1.678(a)-1(b) does not appear to respect the distinction between income and corpus for this purpose. That may be attributable to the fact that Treas. Reg. § 1.671-2(b) regards "income" as meaning taxable income, which may encompass items allocable to corpus as well as to fiduciary accounting income.

[168] Treas. Reg. § 1.678(c)-1(a).

[169] See § 5.11.4 n.80 and accompanying text. The government's position in Treas. Reg. § 1.665(b)-1A(d) Example (4) that any distribution from the trust in the future may be an accumulation distribution to the person with the withdrawal right is improper. Being treated as the owner of that portion of the trust, and having paid income tax on it in the year the income was earned, the accumulation distribution rules should not apply at a future date. Their purpose is to

§ 5.11.7

One interesting question, for which no answer appears to exist,[170] is whether a power to distribute income for a dependent's support or maintenance that falls under the protection of the exception for powers limited by a reasonably definite standard is a power described in § 678(a). If it is not a § 678 power because of the limitation, then the limitation in § 678(c) will not apply with respect to it. The better reasoned result is to regard the power as one described in § 678(a) but as to which no tax consequences attach due to the protection afforded by a properly confined standard. Any other result would be perverse, in effect saying that an excepted power under § 678(a) cannot enjoy the protection afforded under § 678(c).

A second part of the pseudo grantor trust rule is applicable under § 678(a)(2) if the person previously released or modified a power over the trust in such a fashion that any of the grantor trust rules would apply if the release or modification had been a transfer by the pseudo grantor of their own property. For example, assume the person has a power to withdraw income from the trust each year, and allows that power to lapse so that income that could have been withdrawn instead is added to corpus. Assume also that the same power to withdraw income will apply in the next year to income generated by the prior year's accumulation. If the prior year's income had been property transferred to the trust by the pseudo grantor, this continuing withdrawal right would cause grantor trust liability under § 677(a)(1) with respect to that portion of the trust represented by the accumulation. Consequently, the continuing withdrawal right will cause the powerholder to be treated as the owner of that same portion of the trust, and multiple lapses over several years can

---

(Footnote Continued)

impose the tax that would have been incurred had the trust never made the accumulation. Because the pseudo grantor trust rules will have imposed just such a tax, no further computation or imputation of tax is necessary. Moreover, because the trust never paid a tax on that accumulation (because of the pseudo grantor trust treatment), there is no provision in the accumulation distribution rules to give the pseudo grantor a credit for the taxes already paid. As such the technical result of application of the accumulation distribution rules could be double taxation, which also is improper. Fortunately, the accumulation distribution and throwback rules no longer are likely to apply to domestic trusts under § 665(c)(2), making this issue academic in most cases.

[170] Cf. Treas. Reg. § 1.678(c)-1(c) (last clause).

§ 5.11.7

cause the beneficiary to be regarded as the owner of an increasing portion of the trust each year.[171]

Two overriding exceptions apply to § 678(a). One is the disclaimer rule of § 678(d), applicable to preclude pre-renunciation[172] income from being taxed to the pseudo grantor if renunciation of a power is made within a reasonable time after learning of it. "Reasonable time" is not defined, although it probably would be construed similarly to the same concept under the gift tax disclaimer rule applicable prior to adoption of § 2518.[173] The other exception is § 678(b), which provides that, with respect to powers over income only,[174] grantor trust liability will pre-empt

---

[171] See PLRs 201038004, 200949012, and 9034004, and see § 5.11.7 at text accompanying nn.156-157 for the computation. Unusual about the 2010 PLR was the government's conclusion that the taxpayer's power to withdraw income constituted a general power of appointment with § 2041 consequences for the year of death *and*, under the second clause of § 2041(a)(2), for all prior year lapse amounts that exceeded the greater of $5,000 or 5% of the prior year's income. See § 12.3.1 regarding application of that second clause.

[172] Ferguson, Freeland, & Ascher, Federal Income Taxation of Estates, Trusts, and Beneficiaries § 10.16[E] (3d ed. 2011), explains that post-renunciation income is not at issue because the power or interest no longer would exist, by virtue of the renunciation. This makes § 678(a)(2) ongoing liability the only issue and only if the pseudo grantor retains *other* interests or powers in the trust.

[173] See, e.g., Jewett v. Commissioner, 455 U.S. 305 (1982), as applied in PLRs 200109041 (timely disclaimer measured from notification of the disclaimant that the interest was deemed to exist), and 200040014 (notwithstanding income distributions to the disclaimant's predeceased spouse, the disclaimant was permitted to claim ignorance of the interest being disclaimed and the reasonable time therefore was deemed to begin to run after that spouse's death). The timing issue is explored in detail in § 7.1.6.2.

[174] Ferguson, Freeland, & Ascher, Federal Income Taxation of Estates, Trusts, and Beneficiaries § 10.16[C] (3d ed. 2011), opine that the limitation to powers over income only makes no sense and that the government treats this provision as if it is a drafting error, causing § 678(b) to apply if the grantor has overlapping income tax exposure from any source, interest and powers alike and with respect to income and corpus alike. See, e.g., PLRs 200606006 and 200603040 (in which the grantor's § 677(a) exposure attributable to the grantor's spouse being a current beneficiary trumped the § 678 pseudo grantor trust liability of the grantor's spouse attributable to the spouse's five-or-five power of withdrawal that, although not clearly specified in the facts of the PLR, presumably allowed withdrawal of corpus and not (just) income), 200730011 (because the grantor's "spouse ha[d] the power to withhold any distribution of principal for

pseudo grantor trust liability under § 678 if the grantor is regarded as the owner of the same portion of the trust, thereby avoiding taxation of the same items of taxable income to two different taxpayers.

§5.11.8 Portion Rules

Grantor trust treatment may not apply with respect to an entire trust. Thus, the Code provides that the grantor (or a § 678 pseudo grantor) is treated as the owner of any "portion" of a trust as to which a requisite power or interest exists. Several different "portions" may be involved, each causing items allocable to that portion to be attributed to the grantor.[175] This raises two issues: (1) What is that portion, and (2) what income, deductions, and credits are allocable to it? The following material illustrates the various portions in the context of interests or powers that generate grantor trust exposure with respect to each.

§5.11.8.1 Entire Trust

A grantor with a § 673 reversion or a § 676 power to revoke the trust in its entirety is treated as the owner of the entire trust. Essentially every item of income, deduction, and credit in the trust is attributed to that deemed owner. Similarly, if the grantor or any nonadverse party is the trustee with unrestricted powers over income and corpus, § 674(a) exposure could apply to the entire trust. For example, an unprotected fiduciary power to distribute corpus among beneficiaries other than the grantor or the grantor's spouse makes the entire trust the appropriate portion and not just the corpus portion (which is the intuitive result and correct as far as it goes) because § 674(a) refers to that "portion of a trust in respect of which the beneficial enjoyment of the corpus or the income therefrom is subject to a power" and a power to distribute corpus will

---

(Footnote Continued)

distribution at a later time to the current income beneficiary . . . [the grantor was] the owner of the entire trust" under § 674, notwithstanding powers of withdrawal in the spouse and beneficiaries; again, no mention was made of the § 678(b) drafting issue regarding powers over income only), and 200840025 (a § 675(2) power in a nonadverse party to lend to the grantor was deemed adequate to trump a § 678 withdrawal power, all with no mention of the portion rules or the breadth of the power to lend).

[175] Treas. Reg. § 1.671-3.

carry with it all income, deductions, and credits generated by that corpus.[176]

In addition, if the grantor is the income beneficiary with § 677(a)(1) exposure and the remainder passes to the grantor's spouse, generating § 677(a)(2) liability as well, the two together (but neither alone) would cause grantor trust exposure with respect to the entire trust. According to one PLR[177] a § 675(2) power to lend also was deemed to create whole trust exposure—which is a bizarre result in light of the proper portion if an actual loan is made.

In this regard a loan that triggers § 675(3) might (but may not) implicate grantor trust treatment as to the entire trust. In Benson v. Commissioner[178] the grantor borrowed an amount equal to all income earned in the trust for a given year. The court stated that the proper inquiry is not what the grantor borrowed but what the borrowing represents in terms of dominion and control over the trust. The court focused on the wording of § 675(3) that the grantor is treated as the owner of that "portion of a trust in respect of which" the grantor borrowed, concluding that this would be the entire trust because the grantor borrowed an amount equal to all income earned by the trust.

In a variation on this result, Bennett v. Commissioner[179] held that a series of loans from income over several years should result in a *fraction* of the trust being regarded as the portion, of which the numerator was the aggregate of those loans still unpaid and the denominator was the aggregate of the income from the years represented by those loans (including the current year). That fraction was deemed to constitute the portion of the entire trust that the outstanding loans represented, and this result differed from that in *Benson* only in that the loans did not consume the entire income for each year and therefore did not make the portion 100% of the entire trust. As such, *Benson* and *Bennett* leave real doubt as to the proper portion, and raise serious issues about whether an

---

[176] Treas. Reg. § 1.671-3(b)(3).

[177] PLR 200840025, with no mention of the portion rules. There appeared to be no limit on the breadth of the trustee's power to make unsecured loans.

[178] 76 T.C. 1040 (1981).

[179] 79 T.C. 470 (1982).

§ 5.11.8.1

actual loan should produce a smaller portion than the mere power to lend, which was implicated in the §675(2) PLR.[180]

§5.11.8.2 Ordinary Income

Meaning fiduciary accounting income,[181] this portion is to be distinguished from the corpus portion, which includes items of taxable income that are allocable to corpus. The ordinary income portion includes those items allocable to the fiduciary accounting income account[182] and is the proper portion if the grantor is subject to §674(a) because of a fiduciary power to distribute ordinary income among beneficiaries with no applicable §674(b) or 674(d) exception.[183] The income portion also is the appropriate result if the grantor possessed a §677(a)(1) income inter-

---

[180] Estate of Holdeen v. Commissioner, 34 T.C.M. (CCH) 129 (1975), preceded both *Benson* and *Bennett* and also differed because the grantor borrowed trust corpus rather than income. The court held that the proper portion was the income attributable to that portion of the corpus. That income might be zero if the loan was interest free and a tracing of income from that actual corpus is dictated. Or it might be a wash if the interest income attributed to the grantor matches a deduction allowable for the interest payments. It would be some other result if the amount of the loan informed a fractional portion of the entire trust and its income from other sources.

Patsey v. United States, 603 F. Supp. 60 (N.D. Cal. 1984), followed all these cases and is distinguishable only in that the grantor borrowed a large chunk of both income and corpus of a trust, making this the case for taxing the largest portion to the grantor. The court imposed grantor trust treatment as in *Benson* on the entire trust because the grantor "evidenced control and dominion over the entire trust," which is hardly the appropriate inquiry. Taken together the loan cases "constitute a highly problematic body of law. They are badly inconsistent among themselves. Taken together, they create horrible distinctions based in part on whether loans come from income or corpus. They also often point in different directions." Ferguson, Freeland, & Ascher, Federal Income Taxation of Estates, Trusts, and Beneficiaries § 10.13[B] (3d ed. 2011).

[181] Treas. Reg. §1.671-2(b).

[182] Treas. Reg. §1.671-3(b)(1).

[183] This is the right answer because "ordinary income" is the way the regulations speak of fiduciary accounting income and Treas. Reg. §1.671-3(c) makes it clear that only the income portion would be attributable to the grantor, notwithstanding that §674(a) refers to that "portion of a trust in respect of which the beneficial enjoyment of the . . . income . . . is subject to a power of disposition" and the fact that this would be the entire trust (producing the income subject to the unprotected power).

est,[184] although it may be possible to argue that a standard limiting § 677(a)(1) distributions to amounts necessary for the grantor's support or maintenance should limit the portion to that amount of corpus needed to generate the income needed for those purposes.[185] If § 677(b) is applicable, the portion similarly is limited to the corpus needed to generate the amount used for the beneficiaries' support and maintenance.

In each of these cases the grantor is deemed to own that portion—along with its income, deductions, and credits—needed to produce the amount of net income needed for the grantor's support or maintenance or distributed to the dependant beneficiaries. In this and other respects involving a determination of the ordinary income portion, the grantor is treated as the current income beneficiary of the portion.[186] By way of example, if taxable income allocable to income is $5,000, taxable income allocable to corpus is $2,000, and deductible expenses total $6,000, the current income beneficiary would be taxed on zero income and the excess deduction of $1,000 would reduce income allocable to corpus. That excess deduction would *not* pass through to the income beneficiary, nor would losses in excess of gains.[187] It thus is assumed here that the same result would apply for grantor trust purposes, meaning that the grantor would not be entitled to deductions in excess of ordinary income in this situation.

Note that this is not the same treatment as if no trust had been created, which is the frequent assumption about the application of the

---

[184] Notwithstanding that § 677(a) refers to the "portion ... whose income ... may be distributed" to the grantor, implying that the entire trust is the proper portion, Treas. Reg. § 1.677(a)-1(g) Example (1) makes clear that only the income portion is implicated by this interest.

[185] See Rev. Rul. 56-484, 1956-2 C.B. 23.

[186] Treas. Reg. § 1.671-3(c).

[187] As in a nongrantor trust, excess deductions and losses do not pass through to the beneficiaries except in the year of termination. § 642(h). See §§ 5.3.3 n.50, 5.4.1 n.12, and 5.8.3. Essentially the calculation of the portion is based on a DNI analogue because the calculation considers items that impact DNI but that do not affect fiduciary accounting income. See Treas. Reg. § 1.677(a)-1(g) Examples (1) and (2).

§ 5.11.8.2

grantor trust rules.[188] Notice also that this message sometimes gets confused. For example, according to the government, each item of income, deduction, and credit of the particular portion should flow through to the grantor's return separately (which is as if there was no trust), such that each item will conspicuously appear on the grantor's return rather than a net amount (zero income, in this case), which would not reveal the various items that comprise the tax attributes of the trust.[189]

§5.11.8.3 Corpus

This portion is all items not reflected in the ordinary income portion, meaning income, deductions, and credits allocable or attributable to corpus (and all income earned thereon after accumulation as a part of corpus).[190] In the prior example, the income allocable to corpus, taxable to the owner of this portion, was $1,000, being the $2,000 of gain allocable to corpus reduced by the $1,000 of excess deductions. A classic example of the applicability of this portion is a trust in which the grantor has a reversion that escapes § 673 but not § 677(a)(2),[191] or a testamentary power to appoint accumulated income that fails the § 674(b)(3) exception.

In a far less common example, the grantor would be treated as the owner of gains allocable to corpus by virtue of a § 677(a)(1) right to all income, *if* the grantor also had a power to allocate receipts between income and corpus.[192] However, a § 674 power over corpus alone could result in the grantor being treated as owner of all income, not just income allocable to corpus, if the power over corpus could affect enjoy-

---

[188] See Edgar v. Commissioner, 56 T.C. 717 (1971); Schmolka, Selected Aspects of the Grantor Trust Rules, 9 U. Miami Inst. Est. Plan. ¶ 1403.2 Example (4) (1975).

[189] See Notice 2000-44, 2000-2 C.B. 255, stating that it is improper for promoters of tax shelters to encourage their customers to invest in the shelter through a grantor trust, such that improper losses spun off by the shelter may be netted against other gains in the grantor trust and only the net amount reported on the investor's return, so as to hide the tax shelter loss.

[190] See Rev. Rul. 66-161, 1966-1 C.B. 164.

[191] Treas. Reg. § 1.671-3(b)(2).

[192] Greenough v. Commissioner, 74 F.2d 25 (1st Cir. 1934).

ment of current income as well.[193] For example, a power to distribute corpus currently (as opposed to a power to distribute corpus only after the occurrence of a §673 event) would affect enjoyment of current income because income would flow with corpus to any distributee.

§5.11.8.4 Fractional Amount of Ordinary Income or Corpus

Fractional portions reflect rights that would cause one of the prior grantor trust portions to apply, limited to less than all of the trust (for example, a §677(a)(1) right to receive half the income from a trust, or a §673 reversion of half the corpus). An interest or power stated in terms of a specific dollar amount of corpus must be converted into a fraction, using the dollar amount as the numerator and the value of the trust as the denominator, valued as of the later to occur of the beginning of the tax year in question or existence of the interest or power.[194]

If the interest or power is computed in reference to a stated dollar amount of income, an added step in determining the numerator is required to identify the portion of trust corpus needed to produce that amount of income and that amount of corpus is used as the numerator.[195] For example, if the grantor retained a §677(a)(1) right to receive $5,000 of income each year, the actuarial tables might specify that (at a current interest rate assumption of 2%) it requires $250,000 of corpus to produce that income, so the numerator would seem to be $250,000, not the $5,000 of income specified. Instead, the regulations dictate that the fraction be determined using the *actual* income rather than income presumed to be generated using the interest assumptions applicable at the time of the calculation.[196] Thus, if the trust produced $25,000 of fiduciary accounting income for the year, the fraction would be a simple one-fifth. This is the appropriate portion with respect to the §678(a)(1) exposure of the holder of a lapsing $5,000 or 5% power of withdrawal, with the larger of the two amounts informing the computation of the numerator of the fraction. Fortunately, in most cases involving such five-or-five powers it is

---

[193] Treas. Reg. § 1.671-3(b)(3).

[194] Treas. Reg. § 1.671-3(a)(3) (antepenultimate sentence).

[195] Treas. Reg. § 1.671-3(c) (penultimate and antepenultimate sentences).

[196] Treas. Reg. § 1.677(a)-1(g) Example (2). Treas. Reg. § 1.671-3(a)(3) specifies that the beginning of the taxable year is the proper time for this calculation.

§5.11.8.4

the 5% amount that is the larger and the added step of converting the dollar amount is avoided.

§5.11.8.5 Specific Asset(s)

In unusual circumstances a grantor has a taxable power over a particular asset, such as a §675(4)(A) power to vote closely held stock transferred to a trust. In those cases the grantor must report the income, deductions, and credits attributable to that asset as if the grantor was its owner, along with a pro rata share of any deductions not specifically identifiable with respect to the asset but properly spread among all trust assets (such as an otherwise unallocated trustee's fee).[197]

§5.11.8.6 Illustration

Assume a trust has the following items of income, gains, losses, and deductions for the current year.

Dividend income	$20,000
Tax exempt income	5,000
Capital gains	16,000
Capital losses	(4,000)
Trustee fees, paid half from income and half from corpus	(3,000)

The ordinary income and the corpus portions would be computed essentially as would be DNI in the trust.

The owner of the corpus portion, for example, would isolate those items of taxable income allocable to corpus and not includible in DNI as a result, and any items of deduction allocable thereto. In this case that would be the $16,000 of capital gains and $4,000 of capital losses, with none of the deductible fees being allocable to the corpus portion regardless of how they are charged for fiduciary accounting purposes.

The income portion would account for all the rest of the items illustrated: $20,000 of dividend income, $5,000 of tax exempt income (which would be included in DNI so that it could carry out to the beneficiary. In this case it would carry out to the grantor owner of the

---

[197] Treas. Reg. § 1.671-3(a)(2).

§5.11.8.6

income portion) and the $3,000 of deductions, some of which might be disallowed at the grantor level under §265 because of the tax exempt income.

If the portion deemed owned was the entire trust, the grantor would simply reflect all these items and, if the portion was of a fractional portion only, that percentage of any of these portions.

§5.11.8.7 Chronological Portion

Rev. Rul. 86-82[198] and Mau v. United States[199] both rejected taxpayer arguments that advocated a *chronological* portion rule that would tax under §675(3) only the income from a portion of a year that a prohibited loan was outstanding, The accepted wisdom appears to be that borrowing for even a day within the year causes all income in the trust for that year to be taxable to the grantor.

This makes §675(3) potentially a perfect "toggle switch" grantor trust rule. If the grantor borrows on the penultimate day of the year and repays the loan on the last day, presumably the grantor becomes entitled to all the trust's income, deductions, and credits for the year in which the loan was outstanding and is able to consider anew in the next year whether to cause grantor trust treatment for that year's trust income tax purposes. This result is not, however, nearly so clear with respect to other aspects of the grantor trust rules, especially including pseudo grantor trust liability under §678 attributable to a power of withdrawal, typically available for only a limited period during each year.

---

[198] 1986-1 C.B. 253 (taxpayer borrowed on June 11 and repaid on November 3 from a trust that reported its income on a calendar year; according to the government, "borrowing of trust corpus or income by a grantor at any time during a taxable year would result in the grantor being taxed on trust income for that entire year" and this result "is not avoided by making repayment before the year closes").

[199] 355 F. Supp. 909 (D. Haw. 1973) (borrowing during the middle of a year triggers §675(3) liability for the entire year because the grantor trust trigger is the loan that was not (and, indeed, could not be) repaid before the *beginning* of the year; repayment cannot occur before the loan is made, which will not occur until after the year begins, meaning that the year of the loan necessarily is a §675(3) grantor trust year if the loan is outstanding at any time during the year).

The government in pseudo grantor trust cases is fond of making a statement that, "until the power [of withdrawal] is exercised, released or allowed to lapse, [the pseudo grantor] will be treated as the owner . . . of that portion . . . that is subject to the power to withdraw."[200] Usually the statement is irrelevant and potentially misleading to the extent it suggests that expiration of the power terminates the pseudo grantor trust liability for the balance of the year. This is because the portion of the trust not withdrawn normally remains in the trust and the powerholder continues to have rights to future income or otherwise that trigger § 678(a)(2) liability. Thus, any suggestion that pseudo grantor trust liability is limited by the period of time the power itself is available essentially is dicta (coming from rulings that are not citable authority).

In a few cases the government further confounds the issue by making reference to "a pro rata share of each item of income, deduction, and credit of the entire trust" being made subject to grantor trust inclusion to the powerholder,[201] without stating whether this pro ration is attributable to application of a chronological portion rule or only makes it clear that a tracing regime does not apply and that the fractional portion represented by a limited power of withdrawal reaches a fractional share of every item of income, deduction, and credit without tracing contributions made to the trust that were subject to the withdrawal power.

At least one PLR makes the additional statement that "calculation of such pro rata share should take into account the length of time during which [the powerholder] has the power to vest in himself the additions of corpus to the trust, as well as the value of these additions relative to the value of the entire trust, measured at the time that . . . power begins."[202] This statement might support an argument in favor of a chronological portion rule based on termination of the power after a certain window of withdrawal opportunity, but it probably only indicates that the pseudo grantor trust liability does not *begin* until the power becomes available, sometime during the trust and powerholder's year. At

---

[200] See, e.g., PLRs 9034004, 8545076, 8517052, and 8142061.

[201] See PLRs 8517052 and 8142061, and cf. PLR 9541029 ("each beneficiary must include . . . those items of income, deduction, and credit . . . attributable to . . . the portion of the trust corpus over which he or she had a right of withdrawal," without any identification of what that portion might be).

[202] PLR 8142061.

§ 5.11.8.7

best, these § 678 authorities leave a great deal of doubt and confusion about the existence of a chronological portion rule, much less its operation.

Finally, two § 677 cases give conflicting answers to the chronological portion question, both involving loans taken out by trusts to satisfy gift tax liabilities imposed on the trusts by the grantor on the transfer of property to the trusts by inter vivos gift. In each case that gift tax liability imposed on the trust constituted a § 677(a)(1) indirect retention of enjoyment of the trust, at least until the liability was discharged. In Estate of Sheaffer v. Commissioner[203] the court rejected the suggestion that grantor trust liability ended in the middle of the year in which the gift tax liability was repaid, stating that "a taxpayer . . . found to be a substantial owner of a portion of a trust . . . is taxable on all the income of such portion during the entire taxable year in issue." Later, in Krause v. Commissioner,[204] the same court stated that *Sheaffer* "does not represent the views of this Court" and held that "where . . . the grantor is divested of all interest in the trust during a taxable year, he is not taxable on the subsequently received income of the trust."

Grantor trust liability cannot arise until there is an interest or power that triggers the requisite provision of the Code, and termination of an interest (for example, because the grantor dies) ordinarily causes expiration of the grantor trust liability. *Krause* may establish an additional limitation on the grantor's exposure under its somewhat unique facts, and may be insufficient authority to support a proposition that a chronological portion rule exists for all purposes under the grantor trust rules (or even under § 677).

In the case of pseudo grantor trust liability under § 678, the issue is even less clear in most cases because of lingering § 678(a)(2) liability with respect to lapsed amounts subject to withdrawal rights and because the power of withdrawal itself often does not become available until late in a calendar year. Typically contributions, made most often to ILITs, are subject to a withdrawal power that is applicable only with respect to the contribution and often in situations in which there is zero income of the trust. Often there are multiple withdrawal rights and in the aggregate

---

[203] 25 T.C.M. (CCH) 646, 652 (1966).

[204] 56 T.C. 1242, 1247-1248 (1971).

§ 5.11.8.7

they constitute the entire trust corpus other than the insurance policy, arguably encompassing all of the income producing property in the trust.

Adding further uncertainty is the fact that in many instances the taxpayer *wants* grantor trust liability for the entire year (even if the triggering interest or power exists for only a smidgen of the year),[205] potentially meaning that the government and perhaps even the courts will have different incentives in addressing this issue in differing situations. The best that can be stated under an expansive reading of current authorities, such as they are, is that the law is in its infancy with respect to a chronological portion notion. In this light, some advisors express the opinion that the taxpayer may take whichever position is best for the taxpayer, making certain to be consistent during the entire period that the issue is relevant.

§5.11.9 Advantages of Grantor Trust Treatment

Grantor trust status results in a trust being treated for most purposes as if it did not exist. To the extent provided under the portion rules, all income, deductions, and credits of the trust are attributed to the deemed owner. Much more importantly, various transactions involving the trust are deemed to be conducted with the deemed owner rather than with the trust. Grantor trust status that causes income to be taxed to the deemed owner without the cash flow represented by receipt of that income usually is not favorable. But sometimes income, deductions, and credits generated by the entity are more useful in the deemed owner's hands, it may be that the deemed owner is in a lower income tax bracket than the trust, and in some cases the deemed owner needs the income generated by the trust to absorb deductions, losses, or credits generated in the deemed owner's individual capacity and that otherwise would be lost. Thus, although disadvantageous in some circumstances, often the result of grantor trust treatment is beneficial, which spawns

---

[205] As, for example, under §675(3), in which the liability intentionally is triggered by a loan taken out and repaid during the year, all in hopes of acquiring toggle switch grantor trust treatment that allows favorable tax consequences for just the one year to flow out to the grantor, or under any number of provisions designed to make the trust qualify for Subchapter S shareholder status under §1361(c)(2)(A) as a grantor trust rather than under §1361(d)(3) as a QSST.

§5.11.9

taxpayer reliance on these rules that historically were designed as a government tool to minimize taxpayer advantage.

To illustrate, in Rothstein v. United States[206] the grantor of a trust purchased assets from the trust, using the grantor's promissory note in payment. The court agreed with the government that the note constituted a §675(3) indirect loan from the trust to the grantor, creating grantor trust status for the trust. Incident to the sale, the grantor claimed a new basis in the acquired assets equal to their purchase price, which the *Rothstein* court allowed over the government's argument that a grantor cannot acquire a new basis in assets purchased from a grantor trust because (1) the entity is treated for income tax purposes as if it was the grantor and (2) it is impossible to purchase assets from yourself.

Essential to the government's vision of the transaction was that the grantor trust status arose "soon enough" to infect the purchase itself.

> It is anomalous to suggest that Congress, in enacting the grantor trust provisions of the Code, intended that the existence of a trust would be ignored for purposes of attribution of income, deduction, and credit, and yet retain its vitality as a separate entity capable of entering into a sales transaction with the grantor.[207]

If the government is right, however, then grantor trust status creates the opportunity to conduct transactions with a trust without worry about income tax sale or exchange treatment. For example, in the most simple application of this principle, PLR 200227022 concluded that transfers between a grantor trust and its grantor and back again of appreciated assets will not be gain or loss recognition events. More refined is PLR 9146025, which involved a 100% owned GRIT. The government ruled that no realization of gain occurred on a distribution of appreciated corpus in kind to the grantor in satisfaction of the trust's obligation to make the retained income payments.[208] Because the trust was ignored for income tax purposes in all its dealings with the grantor, in each case the distributions were regarded as transfers by the grantor to the grantor, which cannot generate a gain.

---

[206] 735 F.2d 704 (2d Cir. 1984), nonacq., Rev. Rul. 85-13, 1985-1 C.B. 184.

[207] Rev. Rul. 85-13, 1985-1 C.B. 184, 185.

[208] Citing Rev. Rul. 85-13, 1985-1 C.B. 184.

§5.11.9

In the same vein, a qualified interest GRUT or GRAT created under § 2702 will not cause realization of gain if the retained annuity or unitrust interest is satisfied by the trustee's distribution of income and appreciated corpus.[209] And PLR 200434012 consistently held that an asset transfer between two wholly grantor owned trusts also is a nonrealization event, because each trust is regarded as the grantor and again a grantor to grantor transfer is not a realization event.[210]

The "street wisdom" regarding grantor trusts is taken from authorities such as these. It regards the trusts as nonexistent or "ignored" for federal income tax purposes. The assumed nuance is that a grantor therefore is treated as owning the assets of the trust. That position is strained when various authorities say that, as a result, transactions involving grantor trusts cannot be recognized as a sale or exchange, which is a stretch, in terms of what the Code and Regulations actually say is the real application of the grantor trust rules.

Every grantor trust rule (§§ 673-677) begins by saying "The grantor shall be treated as the owner of any portion of a trust . . . ." The significance of this is found in § 671:

> Where it is specified . . . that the grantor . . . shall be treated as the owner of any portion of a trust, there shall then be included in computing the taxable income and credits of the grantor . . . those items of income, deductions, and credits against tax of the trust which are attributable to that portion of the trust.

Notice that this does not mention losses, which are considered along with gains only in determining the trust's income. This also does not say that an exchange with a grantor trust is not recognized, *or* that the trust is ignored. Elaborating on this are the regulations, which add only:

> *Treas. Reg. § 1.671-2(a)* . . . . [A] grantor . . . includes in computing his taxable income and credits those items of income, deduction, and credit against tax which are attributable to or included in any portion of a trust of which he is treated as the owner.

---

[209] See PLRs 200001015, 200001013, 9625021, 9519029, 9352017, 9352007, 9351005, and 9239015.

[210] See Rev. Rul. 2007-13, discussed in § 5.11.9 n.234. This often is critically important in ILITs that are making transfers that need to avoid the § 101(a)(2) transfer for value rules.

§ 5.11.9

Treas. Reg. § 1.671-3(a). When a grantor . . . is treated . . . as the owner of any portion of a trust, there are included in computing his tax liability those items of income, deduction, and credit against tax attributable to or included in that portion. For example—

(1) If a grantor . . . is treated as the owner of an entire trust (corpus as well as ordinary income), he takes into account in computing his income tax liability all items of income, deduction, and credit (including capital gains and losses) to which he would have been entitled had the trust not been in existence during the period he is treated as owner.

In a nutshell, then, the tax attributes of a grantor trust are reported by the grantor on the grantor's income tax return, as if the trust's income (which includes net gain in excess of any offsetting losses), deductions, and credits belonged to the grantor. But carefully note that this is the result only if the grantor is treated as the owner of the *entire* trust. It is not necessarily so for other applications under the portion rules.[211]

As a result, the conclusion articulated by various rulings that the trust is "ignored" is not what either the Code or Regulations themselves actually specify. Yet the critically important Rev. Rul. 85-13, the government's nonacquiescence to *Rothstein*, has been interpreted by taxpayers in a vast number of different situations to restate its conclusion by asserting that a grantor trust is treated as if it did not exist. This especially is true involving transfers by a grantor *into* an IDGT, which is the exact opposite of the situation involved in Rev. Rul. 85-13 and *Rothstein*, which involved a transfer by the trust back to the grantor. The articulation itself is based on the government's Ruling position in 1985 (and repeated many times since) that the grantor can have no gain or loss on a transfer involving the grantor trust—that an exchange between the grantor and the trust "is not recognized as a sale" or exchange. It is not a gain or loss realization event.

That result is taxpayer favorable in virtually every context in which taxpayers raise it, but it was disfavorable to the taxpayer in Rev. Rul. 85-13, and in each case it is not quite what the law provides, making it slightly unreliable. Not, presumably, that anyone should worry—the government is consistent, and consistently generous, in this application. But there are aspects of IDGT planning in which taxpayers get over on

---

[211] See § 5.11.8.

§5.11.9

the government in ways that are not as likely to be regarded by the government as benign.

In that regard, TAMs 200011005, 200010011, and 200010010, potentially have a broad significance that exceeds the particular context in which they arose. The basic issue is the proper income tax treatment when IDGT status terminates, or when capital gain property transferred to an IDGT is distributed out of the trust. Unlike the situation in the TAMs, this probably is of greater interest to planners whose clients have experimented with sales to IDGTs, and it also may apply when either a GRAT or a QPRT terminates.[212] The conclusion reached in these TAMs probably indicates just one of several approaches the government might pursue in those cases.

The actual facts of these identical TAMs involved a two year GRAT into which the taxpayer transferred very low basis stock in a family business, retaining a 94.06% annuity interest. To finance the annuity payments, the trust borrowed from another separate trust (and *that* trust borrowed funds from the taxpayer's brother) to provide the aggregate funds needed. For income tax purposes the important fact is that the GRAT incurred debt to finance the annuity payments and apparently encumbered the stock as collateral (with no recourse to the taxpayer; that fact is irrelevant for income tax purposes). After the two year annuity was paid with this borrowed money the GRAT was divided into separate shares, which the TAMs refer to as a "termination and transfer" of the trust asset—the encumbered stock—to those separate share trusts.

That characterization is critical because, under traditional income tax principles, the transfer of an encumbered asset subject to the debt is regarded as a sale, with the amount of the debt constituting an amount realized. That transfer was deemed made by the taxpayer because the original trust was a grantor trust.[213] With a very low basis in the stock, that transfer generated a capital gain, which the government regarded as taxable to the taxpayer, all under the authority of Rev. Rul. 85-13.

---

[212] See § 5.11.8 n.215.

[213] Presumably the grantor trust character did not terminate when the final annuity payment was made. Had it terminated before the division and distribution the termination itself might have generated the same results, under the same authority discussed next.

§ 5.11.9

The effect of the transaction is therefore a gift on creation of the original trust (limited to the 5.94% difference between the FMV of the stock transferred and the retained annuity), no income tax on the annuity payments (because the payor was a grantor trust, and you can't pay income to yourself), and capital gain on the deemed sale of the stock for the amount (essentially) of the annuity (because no part of the loans that financed 100% of that annuity had been repaid). As a part-sale, part-gift transaction, current law permits use of the taxpayer's full basis against the amount realized on that sale portion, meaning that the net result is the same as a straight sale of the nongift portion of the stock, with all the basis in all the stock allowed as an offset in determining that gain.

Some commentators who tout sales to IDGTs posit that the sale aspect and attendant gain or loss would be avoided if payment for the stock had been with borrowed funds but the loan was repaid before grantor trust status terminates. Under the TAMs this appears to be correct, although grantor trust status in the interim would expose the taxpayer to whatever income tax might attend to the trust acquiring the assets to pay down the debt. If, for example, the trust sold the stock to generate those funds, that income tax cost would be at capital gain rates that would be the same to the trust as to the taxpayer.

If the trust was still a grantor trust when that occurred, the tax paid by the grantor presumably would be a desirable result because it would leave fewer assets in the grantor's estate and more wealth in the trust, at no greater transfer tax cost to the taxpayer (another concept with which the government has a problem, as discussed below). If, instead, the funds used to service the debt are ordinary income, the income tax rate could be much higher (particularly if state income tax is involved) and the result would be worse than if the taxpayer had simply liquidated the stock at capital gain rates. A third alternative would apply if the trust used funds transferred to the trust gratuitously, which presumably would entail some other party making a gift to the trust at gift tax rates.[214] Overall, these alternatives indicate that there may be little opportunity for abuse in this particular context.

---

[214] And potentially creating multiple grantor trust status.

§5.11.9

In another context, however, the result witnessed in the TAMs is not so easy to embrace. Assume, for example, that the taxpayer did not retain an annuity and merely sold appreciated assets to the trust, and the trust found a way to finance that purchase without realizing income that would flow out to the grantor. The net reality of these transactions is that, at the end of the day, the grantor has cash and the trust has the grantor's appreciated asset. That looks like a sale (indeed, the TAMs specifically state that the government's analysis of the transaction was not "intended to state or imply that the facts described . . . do not constitute a sale") by the taxpayer of the appreciated assets to the trust. The more appropriate income tax treatment therefore might be to regard the original transfer to the trust as a gain or loss realization event, with recognition of the gain or loss being deferred while the trust is a grantor trust. That is not the position the government has chosen to take, and there is scant authority for that result.

What Rev. Rul. 85-13 and these TAMs show is that the government may regard termination of grantor trust status as a realization event.[215] In a case such as this the gain or loss is determined at that later date—rather than regarding the original transfer to the trust as a realization event with recognition of that realized gain or loss being deferred. If the asset transferred is appreciating, it actually might be preferable to realize the gain or loss at original creation of the trust, rather than later when the defect is cured or the trust terminates. In such a case the govern-

---

[215] See, e.g., Treas. Reg. § 1.1001-2(c) Example (5); Madorin v. Commissioner, 84 T.C. 667 (1985); Rev. Rul. 77-402, 1977-2 C.B. 222. Compare Gans & Blattmachr, No Gain at Death, 149 Trusts & Estates 34 (Feb. 2010), and Blattmachr, Gans, & Jacobson, Income Tax Effects of Termination of Grantor Trust Status by Reason of the Grantor's Death, 97 J. Tax'n 149 (2002), with Cantrell, Gain Is Realized at Death, 149 Trusts & Estates 20 (Feb. 2010), Handler, Beneficiary is treated as an owner of a trust under Internal Revenue Code Section 678, 149 Trusts and Estates 10 (Feb. 2010), and Dunn & Handler, Tax Consequences of Outstanding Trust Liabilities When Grantor Status Terminates, 95 J. Tax'n 49 (2001). See also § 5.11.8 n.187 and accompanying text regarding one circumstance in which the trust is not totally ignored and the grantor is not regarded as outright owner of all items of income, loss, deduction, and credit. But compare § 5.11.8 n.189 and accompanying text regarding another circumstance in which the trust is so totally ignored that each item of income, deduction, and credit is reported separately by the grantor rather than just a net amount of those items that would disguise the tax attributes of various elements of the trust's investment activity.

ment's approach may capture more of that appreciation in the amount realized upon termination of grantor trust status.

Every grantor trust defect eventually will be cured—at the grantor's death, if not sooner—meaning that presumably this consequence cannot (easily?) be avoided. If the transferred assets are not includible in the grantor's gross estate, so no new basis is generated,[216] the deemed transfer at the time of termination would be a gain or loss realization event—potentially to the grantor (reportable on the grantor's final income tax return) or as income in respect of the grantor (as a transaction that was fully performed by the grantor during life but that was not completed until death, in which case the income would be reportable by the grantor's estate on its first income tax return).

To date, however, the government has not pursued such results.[217] Even if it did, perhaps deferral of the income tax on gain until termination of grantor trust status is preferable, although capturing any appreciated FMV as added gain must be offset against the time-value benefit of deferring any of the income tax. If done properly that appreciation will not be includible in the grantor's gross estate for FET purposes, so only the potential income tax consequences of the transaction are at stake. The important aspect of the TAMs, then, is a reminder that planning with IDGTs should consider how, and when, grantor trust status will terminate, and with what income tax consequences then (as well as in

---

[216] Some observers believe that § 1014(b)(9) is not the exclusive new-basis-at-death rule, and that there is property that is "acquired from . . . the decedent" for § 1014(b) purposes but that is not includible in the decedent's gross estate for FET purposes. As articulated in ECC 200937028 this is not the government's understanding, and legislation proposed by the Obama administration during the 111th Congress would make this clear. See, e.g., General Explanations of the Administration's Fiscal Year 2010 Revenue Proposals (the Greenbook), promulgated in 2010.

[217] See, e.g., PLRs 200919027 and 200920032 in which the termination of grantor trust status on the grantor's death did not constitute a gain or loss realization event, as discussed in note 229 infra. In part it distinguished Treas. Reg. § 1.1001-2(c) Example (5), Madorin v. Commissioner, 84 T.C. 667 (1985), and Rev. Rul. 77-402, 1977-2 C.B. 222, by saying "that the rule set forth in these authorities is narrow, insofar as it only affects inter vivos lapses of grantor trust status, not that caused by the death of the owner which is generally not treated as an income tax event."

§ 5.11.9

the interim). As thus seen, therefore, timing issues are implicated by grantor trust planning.

Another illustration of this is found in Rev. Rul. 85-158,[218] in which the grantor was a clearinghouse that created a trust to satisfy financial obligations to customers of the clearinghouse, with § 677(a) grantor trust liability flowing from the trust's discharge of the clearinghouse's legal obligations. The issue was the deductibility of the clearinghouse's transfers to fund the trust. The government ruled that these transfers should be ignored because the trust was a grantor trust. Only when payments were made by the trust to clearinghouse customers would a deduction be allowed.

In Madorin v. Commissioner[219] the trustee of an intentional grantor trust cured the provision that made it so by renouncing the trustee's power to add beneficiaries to the trust. The government successfully treated the trust as if it then for the first time had been created by the grantor, and regarded termination of grantor trust status as a deemed transfer that triggered a recapture of partnership losses previously allowed to the grantor. The trust owned tax shelter investments and the intentional grantor trust was utilized to allow tax benefits to flow to the grantor prior to renouncing the power.

Termination of grantor trust status once the trust's partnership investment "turned the corner" was deemed a tax abuse, which was precluded by the deemed recapture upon the deemed funding.[220] Nevertheless, the government in CCA 200923024 refused to rely on *Madorin* in the converse situation to treat conversion of a nongrantor trust into a grantor trust as a gain realization event, notwithstanding that the particular transaction was recognized as "an abusive transaction," stating that "asserting that the conversion of a nongrantor trust to a grantor trust results in taxable income to the grantor would have an impact on nonabusive situations." Conversion *was* in the opposite direction from the more common termination of IDGT status, but nothing in the CCA

---

[218] 1985-2 C.B. 175.

[219] 84 T.C. 667 (1985).

[220] To the same effect was Rev. Rul. 77-402, 1977-2 C.B. 222 (release of grantor trust generating powers deemed a sale or exchange for an amount realized equal to a partner's share of partnership liabilities immediately before the release).

§ 5.11.9

suggests that the government would treat conversion in either direction as a realization event.

Caution also is in order in cases such as these, however, because nonrealization and other benefits are available only to the extent the trust is owned 100% for grantor trust purposes. Failure to cause the portion rules of §671 to treat the grantor as owner of all parts of the trust might generate a different result. Thus, in creating intentional grantor trusts, careful drafters must consider the portion rules[221] to be certain that the interests or powers retained or otherwise utilized to generate grantor trust exposure produce liability with respect to the appropriate income and corpus portions of the trust. By way of example, a right to receive trust income, triggering §677(a)(1) exposure, does not make the grantor the owner of the corpus portion of the trust.[222] Because capital gain allocable to corpus thus would not be deemed owned by the grantor, this could produce a different result than anticipated.

To illustrate, in PLR 9211026 the taxpayer was grantor of three trusts. Two were treated as grantor trusts with respect to all portions, but the third was a grantor trust only as to the ordinary income portion. Capital gain was realized by the first two trusts in an exchange of the third trust's cash for appreciated property in the first two trusts. Because of the all-portions grantor trust nature of those trusts, this gain was taxable to the grantor, which may have been the grantor's intent (intentionally causing the gain to be taxable to the grantor would preserve more property for the beneficiaries of those two trusts).

Had the third trust been an all-portions grantor trust as well, however, there would have been no realization of gain at all, because a grantor trust cannot engage in a sale or exchange with another grantor trust if the grantor of both trusts is the same. Thus, if realization of gain was the planning objective, the failure to make the third trust an all-portions grantor trust was wise planning. Alternatively, if it was expected that the trusts could swap properties without incurring tax at all, then the

---

[221] See §5.11.8 regarding the portion rules.

[222] See Treas. Reg. §1.677(a)-1(g) Example (1) and see §5.11.8 n.184 and accompanying text.

§5.11.9

plan failed due to inattention to the refinements of the portion rules applicable to grantor trusts.[223]

In a more common context, Rev. Rul. 85-45[224] held that a principal personal residence owned by a marital deduction trust that was treated under § 678 as a pseudo grantor trust was eligible for the § 121 exclusion of gain on the trust's sale of the residence. Because the government treated the trust as nonexistent, the tax result was the same as if S was the deemed owner of the property personally and made the sale. Because it was used as S's principal personal residence, it qualified for the

---

[223] To illuminate that concept better, consider Rev. Rul. 84-14, 1984-1 C.B. 147, in which the grantor of a trust created a short-term trust with a reversion to the grantor, into which the grantor transferred proven oil and gas properties. As directed by the trust, the trustee allocated income of the trust to a depletion reserve in the full amount of the percentage depletion deduction allowable under § 613A for federal income tax purposes. Because the grantor's reversion made the trust a grantor trust under § 677(a)(2) with respect to income allocated to corpus, the grantor was deemed the owner of the depletion reserve. Private Letter Ruling 8307022 involved similar facts, the government holding that, under § 611(b)(3) and Treas. Reg. § 1.611-1(c)(4), the allowable depletion deduction was attributable to the grantor under § 677(a)(2). In each case the ultimate consideration was § 613A(c)(9), which (prior to its repeal) specified that a transfer of proven oil and gas producing properties after 1974 disqualified the percentage depletion deduction. The Rulings held that no transfer was made because a grantor who conveys property to a grantor trust is deemed to have made no transfer at all. Similarly, no transfer would be deemed to occur upon termination of the trust and reversion of the trust corpus to the grantor. See also PLR 8104202.

[224] 1985-1 C.B. 183.

§ 5.11.9

capital gain exclusion.[225] Similarly, Rev. Rul. 66-159[226] applied the same rationale with respect to the § 1034 capital gain deferral provisions (subsequently repealed). The results articulated in both Rulings now are reflected in Treas. Reg. § 1.121-1(c)(3)(i), which regards § § 671-679 grantor trust treatment as the equivalent of the taxpayer's ownership of any residence that is owned by the trust.

Similarly, various cases involving involuntary conversions have ignored the existence of a grantor trust to allow a taxpayer to qualify for § 1033 relief.[227] And PLR 9116009 involved § § 1031 and 6166 in the context of a non-pro-rata trust-terminating distribution between related beneficiaries. Although the trust did not authorize disproportionate distributions, the government held that the termination constituted a § 1031 like kind exchange and did not represent a § 6166 disqualifying distribution.[228] When one of the beneficiaries then contributed distributed amounts to a grantor trust created by that beneficiary, the government concluded that, because a grantor trust "lacks all independent taxpayer identity," this transfer did not trigger the related party disposition rule of § 1031(f) and did not cause loss of the earlier nonrecognition treat-

---

[225] The same issue arose in PLR 9118017 when an irrevocable inter vivos trust sold the personal residence in which the grantor continued to live. In finding grantor trust status the Ruling held that the trustee's power to distribute income or corpus to the grantor was limited by a reasonably definite external standard. Normally this would be a § 674(b)(5)(A) or § 674(d) excluded power for grantor trust purposes, but in this case it was deemed not to be protected because the trustee could act in its absolute discretion, not in a fiduciary capacity. The Ruling also held that the independent trustee exception of § 674(c) was not applicable because the grantor could remove the trustee and name the grantor as a replacement (which might not be a wise retention for wealth transfer tax purposes, so it might be preferable to retain the power to remove the trustee and name the grantor's spouse as replacement). Other situations involving the issue whether § 121 is available if grantor trust treatment is operative include PLRs 200104005, 200018021, 199912026, 9309023, 9026036, 8717010, 8631013, 8549046, 8313025, 8239055, 8221147, 8025027, 8007050, and 8006056.

[226] 1966-1 C.B. 162.

[227] See, e.g., Estate of Gregg v. Commissioner, 69 T.C. 468 (1977); Rev. Rul. 70-376, 1970-2 C.B. 164; Rev. Rul. 88-103, 1988-2 C.B. 304; and PLR 8729023.

[228] Except to the extent one beneficiary gave cash (boot) to another to compensate for distribution of too much property to the payor beneficiary.

§ 5.11.9

ment.[229] Moreover, it also held that the transfer did not constitute a § 6166 accelerating disposition. Each of these results would have been otherwise if the trust ceased to be a grantor trust or on a distribution by the grantor trust to a third party.

Other areas in which a grantor trust may be ignored with favorable tax consequences include:

- borrowing money from or lending it to a trust;

- mortgage and real estate tax payments with respect to trust assets with the §§ 163(h)(3) interest and 164(a)(1) real estate tax deductions still allowable to the grantor;[230]

- the operation of § 1042, involving sales of stock to an ESOP;[231]

- the Series E or EE savings bond interest deferral rules in § 454;[232]

- the transfer of installment obligations that otherwise would cause an acceleration of gain under §§ 453 and 453B;[233]

- avoidance of the § 101(a)(2)(A) income taxation of insurance that was transferred for value because the exception for transfers to the insured under § 101(a)(2)(B) is available;[234]

---

[229] Compare PLRs 200920032 and 200919027, which concluded that § 1031(f) was not triggered, either when the trust of one of three brothers ceased to be a grantor trust at the brother's death, or subsequently when it disposed of that trust's share of a property that the three brothers previously had qualified for § 1031(a) like-kind exchange treatment.

[230] See PLR 9516026.

[231] See PLR 9041027.

[232] As applied in Rev. Rul. 70-248, 1970-2 C.B. 5, Rev. Rul. 64-302, 1964-2 C.B. 170, Rev. Rul. 58-2, 1958-1 C.B. 236, PLR 9009053, and GCM 35599.

[233] See Rev. Rul. 81-98, 1981-1 C.B. 40; Rev. Rul. 76-100, 1976-1 C.B. 123; Rev. Rul. 74-613, 1974-2 C.B. 153; Rev. Rul. 67-167, 1967-1 C.B. 107; Rev. Rul. 67-70, 1967-1 C.B. 106; and PLRs 9149026, 8450031, 8322031, 8319022, 8052089, 8001045, 7943063, 7905079, and 7817119.

[234] As involved in Swanson v. Commissioner, 518 F.2d 59 (8th Cir. 1975), aff'g 33 T.C.M. (CCH) 296 (1974); see also Rev. Rul. 2007-13, 2007-1 C.B. 684, which upgraded and makes reliable a position that was consistent and long standing, as shown in GCM 37228 and PLRs 200636086, 200606027, 200518061, 200514002, 200514001, 200247006, 200228019, 9413045, 9328020, and 9109018. See also § 8.4.1 n.35 and accompanying text.

- qualification for the requirement[235] that the beneficiary of a qualified split interest charitable trust be an individual[236] or that a cooperative apartment corporation's gross income be derived in certain part from tenant-shareholders;[237]

- avoiding § 1041(e) on a transfer of appreciated property with debts exceeding basis;[238]

- avoiding the § 1491 transfer tax with respect to appreciated property transferred to a foreign trust by a United States citizen;[239]

- the permissible Subchapter S Corporation stockholder rules in § 1361(c)(2) and the similar QSST counterpart in § 1361(d);[240]

- and treating distributions from IRAs and qualified plans to a pseudo grantor trust as distributions to the holder of a § 678 withdrawal right—the participant's surviving spouse—which entitles S to elect rollover treatment if those amounts are withdrawn and contributed to a spousal IRA.[241]

Not all grantor trust rulings are favorable, however, even in circumstances in which they should be, in some cases simply because it appears that the government does not like the results these rules produce.[242] The word on the street is that some government officials are

---

[235] Treas. Reg. § 1.664-3(a)(5).

[236] As satisfied in PLR 9202033, which involved a blind trust as beneficiary of payments rather than the grantor directly. See also PLRs 9619042, 9619043, and 9619044.

[237] See Rev. Rul. 71-294, 1971-2 C.B. 167, applying the § 216(b)(1)(D) 80% requirement.

[238] As illustrated in PLR 9230021.

[239] See Rev. Rul. 87-61, 1987-2 C.B. 219.

[240] As illustrated in PLRs 9504021, 9352004, 9337011, 9335028, 9311021, 9232013, 9227037, 9227023, 9227013, and 9226037 (§ 675(4)(C) power to substitute property of equivalent value and § 678 pseudo grantor trust status generated § 1361(c)(2)(A)(i) permissible S Corporation shareholder status), PLRs 200147044 and 9450014 (grantor trust status under § 678 was generated with respect to entire trust because of unlimited power to withdraw trust corpus).

[241] See PLR 9234032 and § 9.3.5.

[242] For example, citing § 7 of Rev. Proc. 93-1, 1993-1 C.B. 313, 325 (updated annually; see, e.g., § 6.02 of Rev. Proc. 2012-1, 2012-1 C.B. 1), for the proposition that the government may refuse to rule if "warranted by the facts or circumstances," PLR 9318019 declined to rule on whether amending a generation-skipping chronologically exempt inter vivos trust to give the grantor a power to exchange assets of equal value would create a § 675(4)(C) grantor trust for income tax purposes, whether it would taint the trust's GST exemption, or whether it would create FET inclusion exposure to the grantor. The government

§ 5.11.9

adverse to planning that takes advantage of the §675(4)(C) power to swap trust assets intentionally to create grantor trust exposure because it permits the grantor to pay the income tax on trust income that otherwise would be taxable to the beneficiaries. This is perceived to be an added benefit that is transferred to those beneficiaries without incurring gift tax liability.

Presumably because there is no authority on which to base a gift tax argument, the government instead is stonewalling the issue. Indeed, in a series of Rulings[243] this aversion to the consequences of grantor trust income taxation resulted in the government conditioning issuance of each Ruling on (or at least on the taxpayers "voluntarily agreeing" to) a requirement that the trusts distribute additional amounts in excess of the retained annuity "to reimburse the grantor for any federal income tax paid by the grantor attributable to any trust income in excess of the

---

(Footnote Continued)

did rule in PLRs 9504021, 9337011, and 9335028 that §675(4)(C) grantor trust liability would permit S Corporation qualification of trusts that would receive stock in close corporations, but in just one week PLRs 9352004 and 9352007 declined to answer the grantor trust question (although they did not refuse to rule, only stating that it was a question of fact) while 9352017 specified that the power to substitute assets would generate grantor trust status. PLR 9407014 also declined to rule on the ground that the issue involved a factual determination. PLRs 9548013, 9525032, 9504024, 9437023, 9437022, 9418024, and 9416009 (in S Corporation qualified shareholder situations and in GRATs or GRITs) took middle of the road positions, saying that the question depends on the facts and circumstances but that, "assuming" exercise of a §675(4)(C) power in a nonfiduciary capacity, the trusts would be regarded as grantor trusts, and PLR 9504024 said that a §678 power in children after the grantor's death would generate S Corporation qualification.

[243] PLRs 9449013, 9449012, 9441031, 9415012, 9413045, 9352007, 9352004, 9351005, and 9345035, all involving GRATs that met the qualified interest requirements under §2702. Assuming the trusts were grantor trusts for income tax purposes, they would not realize capital gain on distributions of corpus in satisfaction of the annuity amount.

§5.11.9

[annuity]."[244] The apparent logic behind these requirements[245] appeared to be that the grantor's payment of income tax on trust income constitutes a form of constructive addition to the trust, which the government wishes to negate.

A series of PLRs attempted to address the question whether these distributions represent the retention of a right to income that would trigger application of an FET inclusion rule. For example, PLR 9413045 held that they were neither §2036(a)(1) triggering, nor was the §675(4)(C) right to swap assets sufficient to trigger application of §§2036, 2038, or 2042 in the subject ILIT.[246] Confirming the noninclusion result from the reimbursement provision with respect to §2038 was Private Letter Ruling 9548013 and with respect to §2036 was PLR 200120021. PLRs 9710006 and 9709001 similarly concluded that mandatory trust distributions to taxing authorities in payment of the grantor's tax liability do not trigger §2036(a)(1) inclusion.

The government ultimately promulgated Rev. Rul. 2004-64[247] in which the government straddled a line between a governing instrument provision that *mandates* distribution to the settlor of a reimbursement amount ("the trustee *shall* distribute") and a provision that merely *authorizes* the trustee in its discretion to distribute a reimbursement amount ("the trustee *may*, in the trustee's discretion").[248] According to the Revenue Ruling, a mandatory distribution provision is adequate to

---

[244] Although it may be necessary for taxpayers to include reimbursement provisions if they want an advance determination that other aspects of a plan accomplish the taxpayer's goals, in PLRs 9402011 and 9352017 the taxpayers did not include such provisions and the Rulings made no mention of it as making any difference in the results sought.

[245] Which are ignored under Treas. Reg. §25.2702-3 in valuing the qualified interest retained by the grantor and therefore do not reduce the gift made in the form of the transferred trust remainder interest.

[246] Curiously, because that power "involves an area that is under extensive study," the government refused to rule on whether the power to swap assets would produce grantor trust treatment in the first instance, citing §5.16 of Rev. Proc. 93-3, 1993-1 C.B. 370, 380 (updated annually); see the discussion of Rev. Ruls. 2011-28 and 2008-22 at note 139).

[247] 2004-2 C.B. 7.

[248] Not surprisingly, PLR 200944002 concluded that a provision *prohibiting* reimbursement also would not cause §2036(a)(1) inclusion to the settlor.

§5.11.9

constitute a § 2036(a)(1) retained "right" that will cause FET inclusion of the trust, and the same would apply if state law mandated the reimbursement rather than the trust terms. In either case it would not matter the extent to which that reimbursement actually was made. But the discretionary provision "alone" will not similarly cause inclusion, regardless of whether (or to the extent) the trustee actually reimburses the settlor, unless it is combined with other facts

> including but not limited to: an understanding or pre-existing arrangement between [the settlor] and the trustee regarding the trustee's exercise of this discretion; a power retained by [the settlor] to remove the trustee and name [the settlor] as successor trustee; or applicable local law subjecting the trust assets to the claims of [the settlor's] creditors . . . .[249]

The Ruling said nothing about FET exposure under either § 2036(a)(2) (retained powers) or § 2038 (retained power to alter, amend, revoke, or terminate) but neither ought to apply. Of the exceptions noted in the extract, the first essentially means that the provision is not truly discretionary, and the second essentially means that the trustee's power would be attributed to the settlor who could at any time become the trustee. Neither exception is surprising and both clearly are the right result. But the third exception harkens to the similarly confused issue of creditor rights and indirect retained enjoyment that has caused extensive confusion under § 2036(a)(1).[250] In the vast majority of American jurisdictions in which a spendthrift provision will not hold the settlor's creditors at bay that third exception may swallow the rule that Rev. Rul. 2004-64 otherwise provides.

As stated in several PLRs,[251] reimbursement "relieves the taxpayer from paying income tax on that part of the trust property that has, in a true economic sense, been given away." The issue itself peaked in PLR 9444033, which stated without citation of authority that, lacking a reimbursement provision, "an additional gift to the remainder [beneficiary] would occur when the grantor paid tax on any income that would otherwise be payable from the corpus of the trust." The Ruling continued

---

[249] See also PLR 200822008 (relying on Rev. Rul. 2004-64 in a discretionary reimbursement case in which the authority was added by reformation and holding that § 2036(a)(1) would not apply at the grantor's death).

[250] See § 7.3.4.2 nn.136-151 and accompanying text.

[251] PLRs 9352007, 9352004, and 9416009.

§ 5.11.9

to provide that, because the taxpayer included a reimbursement provision, "we rule that . . . the income tax paid by the grantor on trust income not paid to the grantor will not constitute an additional gift" by the grantor to the remainder beneficiaries. The suggestion was that failure to reimburse the grantor would constitute a gift to the trust. Curiously, PLR 9543049 modified PLR 9444033. The only change made was that it deleted the paragraph in which these quoted provisions appeared.[252]

Other interesting twists were involved in PLRs 9710006 and 9709001, in which the trustee was required to remit directly to the Internal Revenue Service and its state counterpart the amount by which the grantor's income tax liability was increased by virtue of grantor trust income tax treatment, and PLR 9416009, in which a GRIT granted the trustee "authority" to pay the grantor amounts that the grantor would certify as required to discharge the grantor's income tax liability attributable to trust income not distributed as part of the grantor retained annuity. It may be that the authority to request a distribution was part of the government's attempt to find an imputed gift in these cases, making it easier for the government to assert an ongoing gift if the grantor fails to exercise the requested power.[253] That issue would be avoided with the automatic income tax payment provision in the 1997 Rulings.

All of this, however, is an improper exercise by the government, because planning that subjects a trust to the grantor trust rules for income tax purposes is not abusive and the tax results essentially are the

---

[252] There is no way to know what that modification indicates. It followed receipt by the government of a letter from the American Bar Association Real Property, Probate and Trust Law Section stating that the since deleted statements were not supported by any law and requesting that the statements be removed and not be repeated in future rulings.

[253] If there was a state law right of reimbursement the government's theory might be correct, but lacking such it would need to find a similar entitlement in the document. On the notion that there is no authority supporting a right of reimbursement in any state, see Coleman, The Grantor Trust: Yesterday's Disaster, Today's Delight, Tomorrow's?, 30 U. Miami Inst. Est. Plan. ¶ 806 (1996); Danforth, A Proposal for Integrating the Income and Transfer Taxation of Trusts, 18 Va. Tax Rev. 545, 573 (1999). N.Y. Est. Powers & Trusts Law § 7-1.11 permits but does not require the trustees of a grantor trust to reimburse the grantor for income tax on income attributable to corpus. And Pennsylvania cases alleged to create such a right are distinguished by Coleman.

§ 5.11.9

same as if the grantor retained the income-producing property, paid the income tax on income received by the grantor, and made a gift of the balance. In either case amounts received by the donee are free of income tax and gift tax is incurred only on the amount received by the donee free of income tax.

To illustrate, consider a grantor with $100x of income producing property that generates $5x of income annually, on which $1x of income tax is payable. If one year's income interest is granted to the donee, the grantor trust situation would involve a gift of $5x and the donee would receive a distribution of $5x free of income tax, on which the grantor would pay $1x of income tax. If the grantor retained the $100x and collected the $5x of income and made a gift thereof, the amount subject to gift tax still would be the $5x received by the donee and the grantor still would pay the $1x of income tax. What the government would like is for the grantor to pay gift tax on $5x when the income interest is given to the donee in trust and then for the donee to incur the $1x of income tax, yielding a net benefit to the donee of $4x notwithstanding that the gift tax was paid on $5x of income before income tax.

Regarding the § 675(4)(C) right to swap assets itself, the government did confirm in Rev. Rul. 2008-22[254] that FET inclusion will *not* result under §§ 2036 and 2038 only (and another ruling is expected with respect to § 2042), subject to two caveats.

The first caveat drew on the requirement that a § 675(4)(C) power must be "exercisable in a nonfiduciary capacity . . . without the approval or consent of any person in a fiduciary capacity." The Ruling itself required that "the trustee has a fiduciary obligation (under local law *or the trust instrument*)[255] to ensure the grantor's compliance with the terms of this power by satisfying itself that the properties acquired and substituted by the grantor are in fact of equivalent value." The trust did not require that the fiduciary must consent to or approve of the exchange, yet the Ruling suggests that the trustee had that degree of control.[256]

---

[254] 2008-1 C.B. 796.

[255] Emphasis added because those four words appear in the 'holding' at the end of the Ruling but not in the preamble (first) paragraph of the Ruling.

[256] In addition, the Ruling stated that the grantor could not become the trustee, which is irrelevant to the planning involved because the § 675(4)(C)

The second caveat was that "the substitution power cannot be exercised in a manner that can shift benefits among the trust beneficiaries." If the values of the old and the new properties are the same— that is, if the first caveat is met—the second caveat would be relevant only if a trust directs distribution of particular assets to particular beneficiaries and does not appropriately address issues of ademption by extinction, such that the designated beneficiary is disadvantaged if the specified asset has been replaced with other property.

§5.11.10 Safe and Easy Grantor Trust Planning

Having waded through the foregoing exegesis regarding the various interests and powers that may trigger the grantor trust rules, this final segment discusses safe and easy ways to expose a trust to the grantor or a pseudo grantor trust rules without encountering unwanted wealth transfer tax consequences. The secret is to think in terms of flunking various exceptions to grantor trust liability provisions, with an eye on the estate, GST, and gift tax consequences of a particular interest or power.

By far the most popular defect[257] is one that the government loves to hate and, because it is so easy and safe, upon which the government no longer will rule.[258] The §675(4)(C) power to swap assets essentially authorizes any person not acting in a fiduciary capacity and without the consent of a fiduciary to exchange trust assets for a full and adequate consideration—to purchase trust assets for their FMV—with entire trust portion rule consequences and no wealth transfer tax exposure to the powerholder. Other viable alternatives also might be considered, given the government's antipathy toward §675(4)(C) or the occasional need to generate grantor trust exposure with respect to some other portion of the trust. The following is just a sampler of other less obvious or common approaches, each selected because of their safety from wealth transfer tax consequences to the grantor.

(Footnote Continued)

power of substitution would not serve its intended IDGT purpose if the grantor was acting in a fiduciary capacity.

[257] See Moore & Pennell, Survey of the Profession II, 30 U. Miami Inst. Est. Plan. ¶ 1501 at question 35 (1996).

[258] See §5.11.9 at text accompanying n.242.

§5.11.10

For example, if a married grantor feels confident that the marriage will last, it is relatively easy to trigger grantor trust liability with an interest or power in the grantor's spouse that is only deemed to be an interest or power in the grantor.[259] Like the § 675(4)(C) power to exchange assets, this form of intentional grantor trust exposure will generate no wealth transfer tax consequence to the grantor, although care must be taken to avoid exposing the spouse to unexpected wealth transfer tax. In addition, a fall-back approach would be required if the spouse dies before grantor trust exposure should terminate in the planning context involved. Nevertheless, the simple expedient of reposing powers in the spouse that take advantage of the spousal unity rule in § 672(e) often allows selection of defects that match the portion rule planning required to guarantee the proper degree of grantor trust exposure. With no exposure in most circumstances to the extent the spouse is not an actual grantor of the trust. Thus, for example, giving the spouse the power to distribute income or corpus to third parties—without restriction by a reasonably definite external standard as defined for §§ 674(b)(5)(A) and 674(d)—will permit a grantor to enjoy grantor trust treatment with respect to the income or corpus portions, or both if the power of distribution extends to both.

Alternatively, giving the grantor's spouse the power to remove and replace trustees and allowing the spouse to be a successor trustee would cause the trustee's powers to be attributed to the spouse, with similar results.[260] And a power in the spouse that permits creation of any § 675 power also will cause grantor trust exposure as if the power had been exercised.[261] Thus, actually naming the spouse as trustee or giving the spouse the § 675 powers is not necessary. There should be no untoward wealth transfer tax exposure to the spouse of either of these alternatives if the spouse is not a beneficiary of a particular power, and to the extent a provision prohibits making distributions that would have the effect of discharging the spouse's legal obligations. Furthermore, the spouse can relinquish these powers if at some future date grantor trust exposure is inappropriate. Indeed, at some time after that, if grantor trust treatment again would be appropriate, reinstitution of those powers in the spouse

---

[259] See § 672(e), and see § 5.11.1 n.36.

[260] See § 5.11.5 n.97 and accompanying text.

[261] See § 5.11.6 n.134 and accompanying text.

§ 5.11.10

by a third party acting under a trust provision or a power of appointment also would be effective. With the help of the spouse and a third party in this situation the grantor can have the benefits of toggle switch grantor trust treatment, to turn it on when the grantor wants it, and off otherwise.

Another relatively easy grantor trust trigger without direct involvement of the grantor's spouse involves granting a nonadverse party a nongeneral inter vivos power to create a §676 interest in corpus or a §677(a)(1) income interest, or both for entire trust treatment. Or, consistent with the foregoing, to create almost any other appropriate interest or power in the grantor's spouse. Again, if toggle switch planning is desirable, that appointment could be subject to yet another power that would permit the powerholder to turn off the interest or power and toggle down the grantor's liability.

A relatively unconventional method of creating grantor trust liability, in this case without the help of a spouse or other third party, is for the grantor to borrow the corpus of the trust for less than adequate interest or security, triggering §675(3). Alternatively, if the trustee is the grantor's spouse or any other related or subordinate party, a loan to the grantor or to the grantor's spouse for adequate interest and security still will trigger §675(3) entire trust portion treatment. In either case, when the toggle switch should be turned off in the future the borrower merely returns that corpus before the beginning of the next tax year of the trust. Needed here is the ability to document and execute a loan of assets, so that the trust need not liquidate its corpus and lend cash to the grantor, but this opportunity should be no more complex than borrowing a lawn mower from a next door neighbor—the only difference is that the corpus is likely to be stocks, bonds, realty, and other investment assets.

Equally effective (again without making a trust subject to the grantor trust rules in the first instance) is the ability to trigger §675(1) by giving a nongeneral power of appointment to any nonadverse party, acting without the consent of an adverse party, that allows distributions back to the grantor or to the grantor's spouse. Or give a trusted nonadverse party the power to lend to the grantor's spouse for less than adequate interest or security, causing §675(2) to apply even if no loan is made. Further, §675(4) treatment can be generated with respect to a laser beam portion of the trust by allowing almost anyone other than the

§5.11.10

grantor to vote or invest the subject property without fiduciary constraints.[262] A power to appoint corpus to the grantor may subject the trust to §2036(a)(1) inclusion in the grantor's gross estate at death, so these alternatives may be better crafted with the grantor's spouse as the permissible appointee, unless wealth transfer tax exposure exists anyway (for example, in a GRUT or GRAT during the grantor's term interest).

Finally, reliance on §674 and its various opportunities to tailor the portion of a trust that will be treated as owned by the grantor is a power to add beneficiaries other than to account for births or adoptions,[263] or a simple exoneration of an otherwise independent but nonadverse party as trustee,[264] in each case triggering §674(a) by flunking exceptions that otherwise would exist under §§674(b)(5), 674(b)(8), 674(c), or 674(d). Other, more direct interests or powers in the grantor or in the grantor's spouse, also may accomplish the planning purpose, again with the caution to be mindful of the wealth transfer tax exposure[265] and whether the portion rules allow accomplishment of the desired result.[266]

§5.11.11 Preneed Funeral Trusts

A "preneed funeral" plan is a funeral that is arranged for, and purchased by, the decedent prior to the decedent's death, all pursuant to a contract with a seller that usually is a funeral home. The purchaser selects the desired services, property, and related merchandise and agrees to pay for them in a lump sum or in installments. Most states regulate preneed funeral plans and often the seller is required to deposit a portion of the purchase price into a preneed funeral trust. In 1997 Congress adopted §685 to address the income taxation of these trusts. If its requirements are met and its operation is elected, §685(d) provides

---

[262] See §5.11.6 n.141 and accompanying text.

[263] See §5.11.5 n.101 and accompanying text.

[264] See §5.11.5 nn.102-103 and accompanying text.

[265] For example, a §675(4)(A) power in the grantor almost certainly also would be a §2036(b) inclusion causing retention. In addition, as articulated in §7.2.3.1 n.170, changes in toggle switch grantor trust status may constitute a §2701 transfer if all other requisites for its application are met.

[266] For example, deemed ownership of the income portion would not permit taxation of capital gains recognized in the trust to the grantor, if that would be appropriate.

that each beneficiary's account is treated as a separate trust that is denied the § 642(b) deduction in lieu of the personal exemption and is taxable under the trust income tax rates in § 1(e), rather than as a grantor trust that is taxable to the purchaser. Furthermore, § 685(e) provides that there is no gain or loss if the contract is cancelled and the trust repays monies to the purchaser. To qualify for this tax treatment the aggregate contributions to all plans for a single beneficiary cannot exceed $7,000 (as indexed for inflation), with § 685(c) providing rules requiring aggregation of trusts that are deemed to be related and held for the same beneficiary, to prevent avoidance of the dollar limitation. These plans must be created by contract with the provider of the funeral services or related merchandise and must exist for the sole purpose of making payment on behalf of the designated beneficiary. Curiously, it is the *trustee* that makes the election to be taxed under § 685, not the purchaser or the beneficiary.[267]

If § 685 is not applicable (or is not elected), then the differing character of these preneed funeral trust arrangements (which usually are of one of four types) become relevant and inform how the grantor trust rules apply to each type of plan.[268] In each of the four types of preneed funeral plan the present value of the right to use the deposit to pay for the funeral exceeds 5% of the amount deposited in the trust at its inception. This immediately triggers § 673(a) for grantor trust purposes.

In the first type of plan, the purchaser can cancel the contract at any time. Income earned on the money deposited in the trust is accumulated and, upon performance, the seller receives all the deposited money and the accumulated income. If the purchaser cancels the contract, all the money in the trust, including accumulated income, is returned to the purchaser. In this case, the purchaser is treated as the owner of the trust property under § 676(a) rather than under § 673(a) and the income of the trust is includible in the purchaser's gross income in the year in which it is earned by the trust.

---

[267] See Notice 98-6, 1998-1 C.B. 337, with respect to § 685 and the requirements to make the election.

[268] See Rev. Rul. 87-127, 1987-2 C.B. 156. In all four situations addressed by the Ruling, any money received by the seller is in payment for merchandise or services, includible under § 61 in the seller's gross income.

§ 5.11.11

The second type of trust differs from the first only in that income earned on the money deposited in the trust is paid annually to the seller. In this case the income nevertheless is taxed annually to the purchaser under § 676(a) because of the purchaser's power of revocation and, because the income paid annually to the seller is a payment for merchandise and services, it also is includible in the seller's gross income in the year received or properly accrued, depending upon the seller's method of accounting.

The third type of trust is like the first except a purchaser who cancels the contract is not entitled to receive money from the trust but is entitled only to select a new seller to provide the funeral. In this case, if the purchaser's estate has a legal obligation to pay the purchaser's funeral expenses, the purchaser has a reversion that exceeds 5% in value. Thus, the purchaser is treated as the owner of the entire trust under § 673(a). Similarly, if the married purchaser's spouse has a legal obligation to pay for the funeral, trust income may be used to discharge that legal obligation and the purchaser still is treated as the owner of the trust under § 677(a) because the income is deemed to be distributed to the purchaser's spouse. Conceivably the spouse's indirect interest also could trigger application of § 673(a) through the operation of § 672(e).

The fourth type of trust is like the first except that, if the purchaser cancels the contract, all money deposited in the trust is returned to the purchaser and the accumulated income is paid to the seller. Because the trust corpus can be reclaimed by the purchaser, § 676(a) again imposes grantor trust treatment with respect to income earned by the trust and any income earned by accumulated income that goes to the seller in any event is treated like the income in the third type of trust, taxable to the purchaser either under § 673(a) or, if a spouse is liable under state law for the funeral, under § 677(a). Again, § 673(a) might apply in either case.[269]

[269] PLRs 9123012, 9120024, and 8923018 involved the same sort of preneed funeral trust considered in Situation 3 of Rev. Rul. 87-127, providing that funds deposited with the trustee will be used to pay for the purchaser's funeral. Because the funds will be used to satisfy the obligation of the purchaser's estate to pay for the purchaser's funeral, the Rulings held that these were a sufficient benefit to constitute a reversion under § 673(a). Valued at over 5% of the value of the trust at creation, the reversions generated grantor trust income tax treatment to the purchasers. Similarly, grantor trust liability of the type considered in

It is in the context of these preneed funeral trusts that reporting requirement options for 100% grantor trusts[270] may be significant because of the small size of these trusts and the fact that a single trustee may administer many of them, each with a different purchaser. Under § 685(e) the government is authorized to promulgate simplified reporting requirements for all trusts with a single trustee. Otherwise, the standard compliance obligation of a trustee is to file a Form 1041 with the government that reports the grantor trust status and includes an attachment stating the income (and payor), deductions, and credits of the trust. Alternatively, the trustee may report the same information to the Internal Revenue Service on a Form 1099 and provide a copy to the settlor. A third option allows the trustee to report the name, taxpayer identification number, and address of the settlor to each payor of trust income and a statement of income (and payor), deductions, and credits to the settlor, and then need not provide any form or statement to the government and need not obtain a taxpayer identification number for the trust. In other grantor trust contexts (but typically not relevant in the preneed funeral trust situation), there is no need to send statements to a settlor who is a trustee of the trust, and in every grantor trust case the trustee must furnish taxpayer identification information to each payor of trust income and they must provide information to the trustee (but not to the settlor).

§5.12 DIVORCE TRUSTS

Applicable only with respect to payments to a grantor's spouse or former spouse under a decree of legal separation or divorce,[1] § 682 pre-

---

(Footnote Continued)

Situations 1 and 3 of Rev. Rul. 87-127 were involved in TAM 9140006. PLR 9141040 was deemed to fit into the Situation 2 category.

[270] Treas. Reg. § 1.671-4. In garden variety grantor trusts the authorized alternatives to Form 1041 filing may not be better than the standard compliance regime. See Klinefelter, IRS Issues New Reporting Requirements for Grantor Trusts, 22 ACTEC Notes 171 (1996).

[1] §5.12 § 682(a), limited in application to trusts created after 1984. It is not limited to trusts created as part of a divorce or settlement: it can apply to a predivorce trust that continues to make payments after the divorce or separation. Indeed, § 71 may be the applicable provision if the trust was created specifically as part of a property settlement incident to a divorce or legal separation. See

empts grantor trust income taxation to the grantor[2] and thereby permits taxation of amounts distributed to the spouse or former spouse under the normal distributions deduction and income carryout rules. The spouse or former spouse is regarded as the trust beneficiary[3] notwithstanding notions that the grantor is being relieved of an otherwise personal obligation,[4] and the grantor is denied any § 215 deduction that otherwise might be applicable.[5] However, the grantor remains taxable to the extent payments to the spouse or former spouse are fixed as child support[6] and the payments also may constitute income to the spouse or former spouse to the extent they continue after the grantor's death and are regarded as indirect payments to the spouse or former spouse because they support a child the spouse or former spouse is legally obligated to support.[7]

(Footnote Continued)

Treas. Reg. § 1.682(a)-1(a)(2). The difference could be significant, because § 71 would tax as income the full distribution to the spouse or former spouse, while § 682 would make the grantor trust rules inoperative, and cause the normal trust distribution rules to apply with the spouse or former spouse as the beneficiary, meaning that DNI would be a cap on the amount of income and its character that could be carried out to the spouse or former spouse. For the treatment of trusts created before 1985 see Ferguson, Freeland, & Ascher, Federal Income Taxation of Estates, Trusts, and Beneficiaries § 7.10[A] (3d ed. 2011).

[2] Either under § 677(a)(1), by virtue of § 672(e), or due to any other retained interest or power that would cause the grantor to be treated as the owner of any portion of the trust.

[3] § 682(b), subject to the normal trust distributions deduction and income carryout rules, such as the DNI limitation. See Treas. Reg. § 1.682(a)-1(a)(2).

[4] See Treas. Reg. § 1.662(a)-4, which otherwise might be applicable even if grantor trust exposure was not relevant.

[5] § 215(d).

[6] § 682(a) (second sentence). See § 677(b) and Treas. Reg. § 1.662(a)-4.

[7] See Treas. Reg. § 1.662(a)-4, dealing with distributions that are for the indirect benefit of someone other than the actual distributee.

§5.13 FOREIGN TRUSTS AND STATE INCOME TAXATION

Nonresident aliens are not subject to United States income tax, either as grantors or as beneficiaries of foreign trusts or estates.[1] Thus, only of concern here are grantors or beneficiaries who are "United States persons," meaning citizens or residents of the United States[2] who suffer special disadvantageous tax consequences by virtue of approximately half a dozen rules unique to the income taxation of foreign trusts and estates.

By definition,[3] the income of a foreign estate is not includible in gross income if it is from sources outside the United States that are not connected with the conduct of a trade or business within the United States[4] and the estate is a nonresident alien.[5] The nonresident alien determination requires a balancing of factors such as the place of the estate's administration, the situs of the estate, and the nationality and residence of the personal representative and beneficiaries.[6]

---

[1] **§5.13** See §871.

[2] §7701(a)(30).

[3] §7701(a)(31).

[4] §872(a).

[5] See §871 and Treas. Reg. §1.871-1(a).

[6] Location of the assets and, even more importantly, the situs of their administration appear to be the most significant factors. See, e.g., Rev. Rul. 81-112, 1981-1 C.B. 598 (foreign estate: administration and assets were abroad; the decedent was a United States citizen and the estate assets were includible in the decedent's gross estate for FET purposes); Rev. Rul. 64-307, 1964-2 C.B. 163 (United States estate: decedent was a United States citizen and domiciliary, who had a foreign as well as a United States will; most assets were abroad but the government noted that an estate is a single entity for income tax purposes and that it has only one characterization with respect to all its income from all sources, which is not necessarily determined by the situs of either administration); Rev. Rul. 62-154, 1962-2 C.B. 148 (ancillary estate administration in United States and domiciliary administration abroad; without resolution of the question the government noted that the same factors would apply to estate classification as to a trust). Cf. Maximov v. United States, 373 U.S. 49 (1963) (United States trust: United States trustee; foreign beneficiaries); B. W. Jones Trust v. Commissioner, 46 B.T.A. 531 (1942), aff'd, 132 F.2d 914 (4th Cir. 1943) (United States trust: corpus was domestic corporation stock that was located and traded in the United States where one of several cotrustees was situated; settlor, beneficiaries, and a

This determination is necessarily sensitive to a facts and circumstances analysis, making it difficult to predict whether an estate with ties to multiple jurisdictions properly is regarded as a foreign estate.[7] By contrast, since 1996 it is relatively easy to determine whether a trust is a foreign trust for United States taxation purposes. Under §§ 7701(a)(30)(E) and 7701(a)(31)(B), a foreign trust is any trust that is not a United States person, which requires that the trust be subject to the primary supervision of a United States court and that all its substantial decisions are controlled by United States trustees.

§5.13.1 Grantor Trust Consequences

The most important deviation from the familiar rules applicable to domestic trusts and estates is § 679, a special grantor trust provision treating the transferor of property to a foreign trust as the owner of the income of that foreign trust if the trust has at least one United States citizen or resident beneficiary.[8] Effectively overriding any other provision for the taxation of trust income, § 679 is triggered by the actual or deemed existence of a proper beneficiary of a foreign trust to which a United States transferor has contributed. By the expansive rule of § 679(c)(1), a trust is deemed to have a United States beneficiary if any

---

(Footnote Continued)

majority of the cotrustees were abroad); Treas. Reg. § 1.643(a)-6(b) Example (1) (foreign trust: foreign trustee; United States grantor and beneficiary); Rev. Rul. 73-521, 1973-2 C.B. 209 (United States trust: United States trustee; grantor and beneficiaries were abroad and corpus was foreign corporation securities); Rev. Rul. 70-242, 1970-1 C.B. 89 (United States pension trust: trustee and trust assets were in the United States); Rev. Rul. 87-61, 1987-2 C.B. 219 (foreign trust: foreign trustee and foreign assets; United States grantor and beneficiaries); Rev. Rul. 60-181, 1960-1 C.B. 257 (United States trust: trustee and assets were in the United States; foreign grantor and beneficiaries).

[7] See Zaritsky & Rosen, U.S. Taxation of Foreign Estates, Trusts and Beneficiaries, 854-3d Tax Mgmt. (BNA) Estates, Gifts, and Trusts Port. A-5 et seq. (2008), for an exhaustive exegesis of the various elements contained in the definition of a foreign estate. The seventh Revenue Procedure issued each year contains information regarding areas in which Rulings or determination letters ordinarily will not be issued. See, e.g., Rev. Proc. 2012-7, 2012-1 C.B. 232, § 4.01(28) of which providing that the government will not rule on whether an estate is treated as a nonresident alien for federal income tax purposes.

[8] The § 679(c)(1)(A) reference is to a United States person, which is defined in § 7701(a)(30)(A) as a United States citizen or resident.

part of the income or principal may be accumulated for or paid to or for the benefit of a United States citizen or resident, including upon termination of the trust during the taxable year or pursuant to exercise of any power of appointment.[9] In addition, under § 679(c)(2), attribution rules may treat a foreign corporation, partnership, trust, or estate as a United States beneficiary if United States beneficiaries own sufficient stock in the corporation, are partners of the partnership, or are beneficiaries of the trust or estate.

Moreover, § 679 will be triggered for future income tax purposes if a foreign trust acquires a United States beneficiary some time after its creation (for example, by marriage, birth, or immigration of a trust beneficiary) and the grantor will be taxed under § 679(b) in that year upon all previous UNI in the transferred portion of the trust. In addition, a trust that formerly was a United States trust may become a foreign trust by a mere change of trustee.[10] Or a deemed expatriation may cause a trust to become a § 679 grantor trust (if the trust has any United States beneficiary and the grantor is alive) and the § 679(a)(5) deemed transfer rule may trigger the § 684 capital gains tax on unrealized capital appreciation in trust assets. That result might be avoided if the trust was a grantor trust before its deemed expatriation, under the authority of § 684(b) and Rev. Rul. 87-61, although a deemed transfer that allows the § 684 capital gain tax to apply may occur at a future time under § 684(c) when grantor trust status eventually terminates.[11]

A trust also may lose its status as a qualified S Corporation shareholder, causing loss of S Corporation status under § 1361(c)(2)(A)(i). All sorts of reporting requirements (and the penalties that accompany a failure to comply) may become operative,[12] and United States payors of income to the trust may become subject to § 1441 withholding at the

---

[9] See Treas. Reg. § 1.679-2(a)(1); Staff of the Joint Comm. on Tax'n, 94th Cong., 2d Sess., General Explanation of the Tax Reform Act of 1976 at 222 (Comm. Print 1976).

[10] See §§ 7701(a)(31) and 7701(a)(30)(E). See Treas. Reg. § 301.7701-7(f) and Notice 96-65, 1996-2 C.B. 232, regarding domestic trusts created before August 20, 1996 that were not grantor trusts and that were United States persons before these changes were made and that elected to continue to be treated as a United States person notwithstanding § 7701(a)(30)(E).

[11] See § 5.13.1 n.22.

[12] See § 5.13.2 n.48.

§5.13.1

source.[13] It remains to be seen whether the deemed expatriation is sufficient to trigger Treas. Reg. § 1.671-4 (b) (6) (ii) to deny alternative income tax reporting if the trust already was a grantor trust (the issue being whether either the assets or the situs of the trust would be deemed to be located outside the United States).

In 1996 Congress made it more difficult for an inbound foreign trust to be treated as a grantor trust, the income of which would be taxable to a foreign person rather than to its United States beneficiary. By adding § 672 (f) and amending § 672 (c) (the related or subordinate party rule) as they apply to foreign trusts, Congress specified that only two forms of garden-variety estate planning foreign trust will be treated as grantor trusts.[14] One is trusts that are revocable without consent, or with the consent of a related or subordinate party who is subservient to the foreign grantor. Subservience is presumed by the change to § 672 (c). As to those trusts § 676 normally would apply. The other is trusts that distribute income or principal only to the grantor or the grantor's spouse during the grantor's life, as to which § 677 would apply. Also added was § 672 (f) (5) to deny foreign grantor trust status to the extent a trust was created in a step transaction by which a United States beneficiary gratuitously transferred property directly or indirectly to a foreign person who created the trust.[15] Corresponding changes in § 679 treat the United States beneficiary as the owner of that portion of the trust.

If applicable because (1) a United States person (2) made a transfer (3) to a foreign trust (4) with at least one United States person as beneficiary, § 679 applies to any portion[16] of the trust that was transferred

---

13 See Treas. Reg. § 1.1441-1 (c) (2).

14 See Treas. Reg. § § 1.672 (f)-3 (a) (1), 1.672 (f)-3 (b) (1).

15 See Treas. Reg. § § 1.671-2 (e) and 1.672 (f)-3.

16 There is no chronological portion rule under Treas. Reg. § 1.679-2 (c) (2), which establishes that the trust is a grantor trust for the entire year if on any day during the year the trust has a U.S. beneficiary. But it is not clear how the portion rules apply if less than 100% of the trust is involved. Consistent with Subchapter J in general would be a pro ration based on the values of the trust and of the grantor's contribution when made (or later when the trust is first subjected to § 679), thereby avoiding a tracing procedure that would require revaluation of contributed property. Cf. Treas. Reg. § 1.679-1 (b).

directly or indirectly[17] by the United States citizen or resident prior to death. Transfers made by reason of a transferor's death are excepted,[18] and § 679 ceases to apply when a transferor dies.[19]

Another exception applies if the transfer was a sale or exchange for consideration at least equal to the FMV of the transferred property, presumably causing immediate realization of the full gain or loss in transferred assets.[20] In the absence of incurring such gain, however, § 684 as enacted in 1997 (in lieu of former § 1491) may apply, causing a gain or loss realization as if a transfer to a foreign trust (or a trust becoming a foreign trust because it no longer meets the definition as a United States person) was a sale or exchange with an amount realized equal to the FMV of the trust corpus.[21] An exception to this treatment applies under § 684(b) if the trust is a § 671 grantor trust but, in that case, a transfer may be deemed to occur when the trust ceases to be a grantor trust, which will occur at the grantor's death, if not sooner.[22]

---

[17] See Treas. Reg. §§ 1.679-3(a) and 1.679-3(c). Treas. Reg. § 1.679-3(e) and Staff of the Joint Comm. on Tax'n, 94th Cong., 2d Sess., General Explanation of the Tax Reform Act of 1976 at 221 (Comm. Print 1976), refer to such indirect transfers as having a foreign trust borrow funds, the repayment of which is guaranteed by a United States person, or a loan itself by the United States person to the trust. Further, § 672(f) defeats the artifice of the trust beneficiary having gratuitously transferred property to a foreign person who created the trust for the beneficiary. Other indirect transfers or the creation of a trust by a controlled entity or person also will not succeed. See, e.g., § 679(a)(3).

[18] § 679(a)(2)(A). Cf. Treas. Reg. § 1.679-2(a)(2)(iii) Example 5.

[19] See Treas. Reg. § 1.673(f)-3(b)(4) Example 2; Staff of the Joint Comm. on Tax'n, 94th Cong., 2d Sess., General Explanation of the Tax Reform Act of 1976 at 221 (Comm. Print 1976).

[20] § 679(a)(2)(B).

[21] Treas. Reg. § 1.684-1.

[22] Treas. Reg. §§ 1.684-2(e), 1.684-2(e)(2) Example 2. Cf. Rev. Rul. 87-61, 1987-2 C.B. 219 (applicable with respect to now repealed § 1491, holding that the income tax under that rule was deferred until the trust lost grantor trust status). Rev. Rul. 87-61 involved a citizen of the United States who established a trust under the laws of a foreign country by executing a trust document and transferring appreciated property to the trustee (a bank incorporated, and having its only place of business, in the foreign country). As a result of the transfer, the trustee acquired legal title to the appreciated property; that property became located in the foreign country, of which the beneficiaries were citizens and residents. The settlor retained certain powers that had the effect of causing the settlor to be

§ 5.13.1

§5.13.2 Special Rules for Estates and Nongrantor Trusts

Several additional special rules affect the tax consequences of a foreign estate or any portion of a foreign trust as to which the grantor is not taxable as owner under §679 (for example, because of death,[23] because transfer to the trust was for full and adequate consideration,[24] or

---

(Footnote Continued)

treated as the §671 owner of the trust property. Thus, the transfer of appreciated property to the foreign trust was not a transfer subject to the tax imposed by §1491 because the settlor was treated as the owner of the entire trust within the meaning of §671. The §1491 tax was imposed at the time the settlor ceased to be the owner of the trust, at which time the settlor had to comply with the reporting requirements of §1491 and the related regulations; §1491 was repealed in 1997, when the capital gain provision in §684 was enacted, but the same result ought to apply with respect to loss of the §684(b) exception. See §684(c). According to the Ruling:

> The holding of this ruling would be the same if the settlor, rather than being treated as the owner of the entire trust, were treated as owning only the portion of the trust represented by the transferred property. See Section 1.671-3(a)(2) of the regulations. In addition, the holding of this ruling would be the same if the settlor ceased to be treated as the owner of the trust due to the expiration or lapse of powers. Further, the holding would be the same if the settlor was treated as the owner of the trust because of powers exercisable by a party other than the settlor, and the settlor's ownership of the trust ceased due to the release or renunciation of those powers by that other party, or by the expiration or lapse of the powers.

Treas. Reg. §1.684-2(d)(1) also has a portion rule. Any §1014 new basis attributable to FET inclusion of the trust corpus at the grantor's death may be deemed to occur for tax purposes before any §684 liability can attach, and may thereby eliminate any gain or loss in most cases. Treas. Reg. §1.684-3(c).

[23] §679(a)(2)(A).

[24] §679(a)(2)(B).

because of the effective date[25] of § 679).[26] First, a credit is allowed[27] for taxes paid by the estate or trust to a foreign country.[28]

Second, DNI of the estate or trust is computed differently than in a domestic estate or trust,[29] the most important difference being inclusion in DNI of all net capital gains of the estate or trust (without benefit of any deduction for long term capital gains),[30] even if those gains are allocated to corpus. This treatment differs from the taxation of domestic trusts and estates because § 643(a)(3) excludes from DNI any capital gains that are allocable to corpus. The effect of this deviation is felt under the accumulation distribution and throwback rules, which continue to apply under

---

[25] Trusts created and transfers made before May 22, 1974, are not subject to § 679 and therefore are governed by the normal grantor trust and other trust income tax rules.

[26] Treas. Reg. § 1.643(h)-1(a)(1), with timing consequences noted in Treas. Reg. § 1.643(h)-1(c).

[27] § 642(a).

[28] See § 901. Alternatively, those taxes may be taken as a deduction. See §§ 164(a)(1) and 164(a)(3); Treas. Reg. §§ 1.164-1 and 1.164-2(d); Rev. Rul. 70-429, 1970-2 C.B. 49 (also holding that § 265 does not preclude the § 164 deduction even to the extent the estate or trust paid foreign taxes attributable to income that is exempt from United States tax).

TAM 9413005 involved a United States estate of a United States citizen administered in the United States by a United States bank, which was taxable in the United States on its undistributed income notwithstanding that its German beneficiaries also were taxed on the same income because, under German law, the estate was not recognized as a separate income tax paying entity and the estate income was deemed to be theirs for German income tax purposes. No § 661 distributions deduction was available to preclude United States income taxation of the estate income because no distributions were made, and there was no foreign tax credit available in the United States for the German income tax imposed on the beneficiaries because the taxpayer in the United States was the estate and the beneficiaries were the taxpayers in Germany. The resulting double taxation of the same income was deemed a problem subject to correction only by Germany under the treaty between the United States and Germany.

[29] Deviations from the normal computation of DNI are itemized in § 643(a)(6) and also include (1) a provision directing inclusion of net foreign source income (as reduced by deductions allocable thereto) and (2) an exception to application of the foreign treaty exempt income rules of § 894.

[30] The deduction permitted before repeal of § 1202 specifically was denied, except in the case of accumulation distributions of pre-1976 taxable year UNI, as to which the deduction still is permitted under § 643(a)(6)(D).

§ 5.13.2

§ 665 (c) (2) (A) to foreign trusts (but not foreign estates, which are not subject to Subpart D) notwithstanding repeal of throwback in 1997 for most domestic trusts. This deviation is important in a foreign trust because the inclusion of gain increases DNI, which increases UNI under § 665 (a) for future accumulation distribution computation purposes (to the extent those gains are allocated to corpus rather than currently paid out, which normally is the case).

Although capital gains distributed currently by either a foreign or a domestic trust retain their character as capital gain,[31] capital gain allocated to corpus may lose its special character if subsequently carried out to a beneficiary by an accumulation distribution. The special character of the gain is preserved in an accumulation distribution to a nonresident alien,[32] but all other distributions are subject to a rule[33] that denies a character pass through on any accumulation distribution except of tax exempt income. This is contrary to the consequence in a domestic trust, in which capital gain allocated to corpus was not thereafter carried out to beneficiaries by accumulation distributions, even when throwback still applied to domestic trusts (because the gain was not includible in DNI and, therefore, was not included in UNI either). Exclusion of gain from DNI in a domestic trust means that gains normally are taxed to the domestic trust. In a foreign trust, however, because the gain loses its character if subsequently carried out to the beneficiary, inclusion of the gain in DNI means that it can be taxed to a beneficiary without favorable capital gain treatment.[34] Consequently, foreign trusts with United States beneficiaries pose disfavorable capital gain possibilities.

Third, § 643 (i) regards loans of cash or marketable securities as distributions if the trust is a foreign trust and the borrower is a United States person who is the grantor, any beneficiary of the trust, or any

---

[31] See §§ 652(b) and 662(b).

[32] § 667(e).

[33] § 667(a) (parenthetical provision in the first sentence).

[34] See Staff of the Joint Comm. on Tax'n, 94th Cong., 2d Sess., General Explanation of the Tax Reform Act of 1976 at 225 (Comm. Print 1976).

§ 5.13.2

person related to either as defined in §267 (with a special modification to §267(c)(4) to include spouses of the listed family members).[35]

To exacerbate this treatment of foreign trusts (but, again, not foreign estates), two added deviations deny both the minority exception[36] and the pre-1969 exception to the accumulation distribution and throwback rules.[37] More negatively affecting the beneficiaries of a foreign trust is a nondeductible[38] interest[39] excise assessed on the throwback tax computed on accumulation distributions.[40] The interest charge is computed at the §6621 underpayment of tax rate[41] and is determined on the basis of an average number of years to which the accumulation distribution is attributable under §668(a)(5), which imposes a pro rata carryout mechanism rather than the first-in-first-out rule in §666.[42] For computation purposes, determining the number of years each accumulation was deferred involves counting the full year in which the income was accumulated but not the year of distribution.[43] For example, year 3 to year 10 is seven years, even if the accumulation was late in year 3 and the distribution was early in year 10.[44] The added interest charge is

---

[35] See Notice 97-34, 1997-1 C.B. 422, with respect to §643(i) and the definition of "beneficiary" to include any person who reasonably could be anticipated to possibly benefit directly or indirectly at any time under the trust.

[36] See §665(b) (parenthetical provision in penultimate sentence).

[37] See §665(e)(1).

[38] §668(c).

[39] Interest is not compounded. Staff of the Joint Comm. on Tax'n, 94th Cong., 2d Sess., General Explanation of the Tax Reform Act of 1976 at 224 (Comm. Print 1976).

[40] §667(a)(3). Rev. Rul. 91-6, 1991-1 C.B. 89, involved a foreign trust that accumulated income while it was a foreign trust but distributed it only after changing its situs to become a domestic trust; the government held that it was subject to the §668 interest rule based on the situs of the trust for the year to which the accumulation distribution was attributed under §666, notwithstanding distribution of the accumulation only after becoming a domestic trust.

[41] Under §668(a)(6) it is computed at a 6% simple interest rate for pre-1996 years.

[42] §668(a)(3).

[43] §668(a)(3)(B)(ii).

[44] Some modest relief may be available by virtue of the introduction to the de minimis rule of §667(b)(3) (reading "for purposes of paragraph (1)"), by which it appears that the computation of the average under §668(a) does not exclude de

§5.13.2

limited only to an amount that, when added to taxes otherwise generated on the accumulation distribution, may be no greater than the beneficiary's actual receipts from the trust in the year of distribution.[45]

In computing the throwback tax to be imposed on the recipient of an accumulation distribution, foreign taxes[46] imposed on the trust in the year of, and attributable to, the accumulation are applied differently than are other similar taxes.[47] And special returns and reporting requirements are imposed with respect to foreign trusts.[48] Overall, given all of the

(Footnote Continued)

minimis years. If this is correct, a trustee could intentionally make minor accumulations to increase both the numerator and denominator, which could have the effect of reducing the average number of accumulation years determined under the computation. For example, in the computation illustrated, an accumulation in the year just prior to the year of an expected accumulation distribution would increase the numerator and the denominator, reducing the average, potentially reducing the total excise imposed. Unfortunately, partial years count as full years in assessing interest. Thus, if an accumulation was made late in year one and distribution was made early in year two, the accumulation would be assessed a full year's interest, and the same apparently would apply if the de minimis gimmick did not result in a full year's reduction. See Staff of the Joint Comm. on Tax'n, 94th Cong., 2d Sess., General Explanation of the Tax Reform Act of 1976 at 224 (Comm. Print 1976).

[45] § 668(b).

[46] Determined under § 665(d)(2).

[47] Unlike the normal application of taxes paid against the final amount of throwback tax computed under § 667, the credit for foreign taxes is applied under § 667(d)(1)(A) against the increase in taxes prior to determination of the average increase in those taxes. Moreover, § 667(d)(1)(B) grants the beneficiary an option to apply the taxes as a deduction in lieu of the credit in computing the beneficiary's taxable income. For a detailed explanation of the operation of § 667(d), see Zaritsky & Rosen, U.S. Taxation of Foreign Trusts, Estates, and Beneficiaries, 854-3d Tax Mgmt. (BNA) Estates, Gifts, and Trusts Port. A-80 to A-83 (2008).

[48] See Zaritsky & Rosen, U.S. Taxation of Foreign Trusts, Estates, and Beneficiaries, 854-3d Tax Mgmt. (BNA) Estates, Gifts, and Trusts Port. A-91et seq. (2008). With respect to reporting requirements, see §§ 6048(a) (requiring a responsible party to file notice of reportable events, such as creation of or transfers of property to a foreign trust, termination of grantor trust status on the death of a citizen or resident grantor of the foreign trust, or inclusion of any portion of the foreign trust in the estate of a citizen or resident decedent), 6048(b) (United States owners of foreign trusts are responsible for ensuring that trustees comply with trust reporting requirements), 6048(c) (United States

special rules applicable only to foreign trusts, it is highly questionable whether any significant income tax advantages flow from a United States person's creation of a foreign trust for a United States beneficiary.

§ 5.13.3 State Income Taxation of Trusts and Estates

Almost every state imposes its own income tax,[49] and most states that tax income recognize trusts and estates as separate taxpayers under principles that sometimes only vaguely resemble the federal income tax regime in Subchapter J.[50] Just as the issue can arise at the federal level whether a trust or estate is subject to income taxation in the United States or a foreign jurisdiction, the question at the state level is whether a trust or estate is subject to income taxation under the laws of more than one state. Unfortunately, the nature of the various state income taxes is such that many trusts and estates are exposed to income taxation on at least a portion of their income in multiple jurisdictions.

The issue at the state law level is whether a particular state has enough of a connection to a trust or estate to impose an income tax with respect to the entity's undistributed income. One or more of at least six different factors may constitute a sufficient nexus to permit a state's income tax to apply to a trust or an estate: locus of the trust or estate's (1) creation or (2) administration, (3) situs of trust or estate corpus (which might differ from the locus of the entity's administration), and domicile of (4) the settlor or decedent, (5) the fiduciary (which might

---

(Footnote Continued)

beneficiaries of foreign trusts are required to report distributions), and 6677 (imposing penalties that can reach as high as 35% of the gross reportable amount—as opposed to the § 684 capital gains tax on "just" the unrealized appreciation in trust corpus—plus additional penalties that may reach as high as $10,000 for every 30 day period of delay in excess of 90 days after the government notifies the taxpayer of the failure to comply). Also included among the special returns required are Forms 926, 3520, and 3520A (relating to settlors of and transferors to foreign trusts), Form 1040NR (nonresident alien income tax return), and the § 6039C reports required by the Foreign Investment in Real Property Tax Act of 1980.

[49] Data may be found at taxpolicycenter.org/taxfacts/displayafact.cfm?Docid=406.

[50] See Nenno, Proposed New York Fiduciary Income Tax Changes: Let My Trustees Go!, 35 Estates, Gifts & Trusts J. 147 (2010), for a state-by-state summary of the income taxation of trusts.

§ 5.13.3

differ from the situs of entity assets or the locus of its administration, although the latter is not common), and (6) the beneficiaries.[51] Because there may be trust or estate assets, administration, and beneficiaries sprinkled among multiple jurisdictions, a number of states may claim the right to tax some or all of the entity's income, although entity administration, assets, and fiduciary domicile provide the strongest anchors to justify state income taxation of the entity.[52] In addition, the beneficiaries may be subject at the individual level to the same form of taxation of distributions as they encounter at the federal level.

Because there is such a wide diversity in potential sources of taxation, there is no substitute for careful investigation into the tax statutes of the various states that may attempt to reach the income of a particular entity, with an eye toward whether multiple answers are raised by questions such as:

- Applying the various factors at the time of taxation, which states enjoy a sufficient nexus—in terms of current benefits and protections provided by that jurisdiction—to justify imposing that state's tax on entity income? For example, the location of the trust's creation is not likely to be a sufficient contact to justify taxation in a subsequent year unless some other connection to that state exists.[53]

---

[51] See Chase Manhattan Bank, v. Gavin, 733 A.2d 782 (Conn. 1999); John S. Swift, Jr. Trusts v. Director of Revenue, 727 S.W.2d 880 (Mo. 1987), cited in and distinguished by Westfall v. Director of Revenue, 812 S.W.2d 513 (Mo. 1991), and 804 S.W.2d 27 (Mo. Ct. App. 1991), confirming that more than just items (1) and (4) must exist, but in Westfall item (3) was met because a portion of the trust corpus was Missouri realty. Westfall paid no income tax to any other jurisdiction, and the court rejected the contention that only income earned from the trust's Missouri assets could be taxed in Missouri.

[52] See generally Schoenblum, 2013 Multistate Guide to Estate Planning, Table 12 (2012); Fogel, What Have You Done For Me Lately? Constitutional Limitations on State Taxation of Trusts, 32 U. Richmond L. Rev. 165 (1998); Gutierrez, The State Income Taxation of Multi-Jurisdictional Trusts, 36 U. Miami Inst. Est. Plan. ¶ 1300 (2002); Gutierrez, Oops! The State Income Taxation of Multi-Jurisdictional Trusts, 25 U. Miami Inst. Est. Plan. ¶ 1200 (1991), and American College of Trust and Estate Counsel Study 6, State Income Taxation of Trusts with Multi-State Connections (2001).

[53] Contra, District of Columbia v. Chase Manhattan Bank, 689 A.2d 539 (D.C. Ct. App. 1997) (although the trustee, trust assets, and trust beneficiaries all were located elsewhere, the District constitutionally could tax all the net income of a testamentary trust because the testator's domicile in the District at death gave a sufficient nexus through District court continuing supervisory authority-jurisdic-

- What actions might the fiduciary consider to minimize the income tax in one or more jurisdiction—such as a change in situs for administration,[54] a change in the nature or scope of administration, addition or deletion of cofiduciaries to alter the locus of that administration, or even alteration of the entity's investments to preclude taxation based on the source of income?

- If more than one state imposes its income tax, are there credits provided by those overlapping jurisdictions that minimize double taxation of the same income?

- Is there an entity level distributions deduction under the state income tax that precludes double taxation of the entity and its beneficiary to the extent income has been distributed?

- Are other taxes applicable, such as business and profit or intangible and personal property taxes?

Because the situs of entity assets, the locus of the entity's administration, and the domicile of the fiduciary all are the same in the vast majority of garden variety trusts and estates—particularly if the assets are not realty and only a single fiduciary is acting—the scope of exposure to income taxation in multiple jurisdictions can be minimized. Often only the domicile of the beneficiaries is likely to be beyond the fiduciary's control. Because most state income taxes look to the beneficiaries only to impose an income tax on amounts distributed to the beneficiary and, in turn, do not tax the entity on amounts distributed, double taxation is less likely to be a source of concern based on beneficiary domicile.

(Footnote Continued)

tion-over the trust; double taxation was not involved because District law granted the trust a distributions deduction and a credit for any income tax paid to any other state). Nenno, Proposed New York Fiduciary Income Tax Changes: Let My Trustees Go!, 35 Estates, Gifts & Trusts J. 147 (2010), argues that an inter vivos trust—as to which there is no probate court jurisdiction—may not be subjected to income taxation based solely on the settlor's domicile.

[54] See, e.g., the rulings cited in § 5.11.1 n.29 relating to taxpayer action to shift the state income tax liability of self-settled trusts.

§ 5.13.3

Inter Vivos Transfers

§6.0 INTRODUCTION

Prior chapters addressed transfers that become irrevocable at death, including intestacy, wills, trusts, and other will substitutes. We also saw that revocable inter vivos trusts may serve important lifetime purposes as well, such as to provide asset management and protection against incapacity or against various claimants at death. This chapter considers *irrevocable* inter vivos transfers that achieve family and business planning objectives and often accomplish two primary tax objectives. One is to shift future income and appreciation to the recipient of the inter vivos transfer. The other is to avoid or minimize wealth transfer tax by subjecting wealth to the cheaper gift tax instead of the more expensive FET.

The most immediate costs of irrevocable inter vivos transfers are imposition of wealth transfer tax prior to death and loss of the new basis at death adjustment that often eliminates unrealized appreciation in assets and thereby avoids capital gain income tax on that appreciation. Deferral of the wealth transfer tax is almost never an economically intuitive rationale for waiting until death to make taxable transfers, and the new basis at death rule may diminish but it does not eliminate the economic advantages of inter vivos transfers.

Nevertheless, many of the following concepts are too difficult to apply or to persuade clients to embrace. Thus, this chapter may have little value except to the extent it describes low- or no-tax inter vivos transfers.

§6.1 BASIS

Basis is the income tax concept that determines appreciation or depreciation in the value of an asset. The difference between any amount realized on a taxable transfer and the basis of the transferred asset measures the gain or loss that may be recognized for income taxation in the year of the transfer.[1] Property transferred by gift inter vivos retains its basis in the hands of the donee, meaning that any appreciation generated in the hands of the donor is preserved and may be realized by the donee and subjected to the capital gains income tax in the future.[2]

---

[1] **§6.1** See § 1012.

[2] See § 1015(a). The carryover basis of property acquired by inter vivos gift may be increased to reflect any gift tax incurred on the transfer. If the gift was made after 1976 this increase in basis is limited to that *portion* of the gift tax that is attributable to appreciation in the asset. See § 1015(d)(6). This basis increase is available even if a sale occurs after the gift but before the gift tax is paid. Treas. Reg. § 1.1015-5(a)(1)(i) ("the basis of the property is increased as of the date of the gift regardless of the date of payment of the gift tax"). Regardless of the date of the gift, basis never is increased above FMV at the time of the gift. See

On the other hand, under current law[3] most property includible in a decedent's gross estate for FET purposes receives a new basis at death equal to the includible FMV of the asset.[4] Sometimes inaccurately known

---

(Footnote Continued)

§ 1015(d)(1)(A) (parenthetical). A similar basis increase is available under § 2654(a) for that portion of any GST incurred on a transfer that is attributable to appreciation. The § 1015 basis adjustment is computed first, and then the § 2654(a) adjustment is made to the basis as so determined.

Closely related to carryover of basis is tacking of holding periods following a gift, which is provided under § 1223(2) if the basis in the hands of the taxpayer is the same "in whole or in part" as that of the taxpayer's transferor. Carryover basis under § 1015(a) is the same as basis in the hands of the transferor, *increased* by any § 1015(d) gift tax attributable to appreciation in the gifted asset. Under § 1015(d)(4) an increase in basis under § 1015(d) is regarded as an adjustment under § 1016(a) to the § 1016(b) substituted basis, which reveals that the § 1223(2) holding period rule properly applies notwithstanding that the taxpayer's basis is the transferor's basis with an adjustment rather than an exact carryover of basis. The basis is "in part" determined by reference to the transferor's basis. See Citizen's Nat'l Bank v. United States, 417 F.2d 675 (5th Cir. 1969) (tacking of holding periods applied notwithstanding part-sale, part-gift transfer in which the Treas. Reg. § 1.1015-4(a) basis—the greater of cost or carryover—was cost, the court referring to the language of § 1015(b), which provides that the basis in the event of a sale to a trust is the transferor's basis increased by any gain recognized on the transfer, which means that basis to the taxpayer is substituted basis with adjustments and tacking should apply). Contra, TAM 7752001 (net gift treated as a part-sale, part-gift in which basis was deemed not to be a carryover and tacking was held not to apply).

[3] A concept included in many legislative proposals to reform the income tax was adopted as § 1023 in 1976 but repealed in 1979, and applied by election to decedents who died in 2010. See § 1022. Essentially it imposes at death the same rule found in § 1015 for inter vivos gifts. The transferor's basis carries over to the beneficiary, which preserves for later recognition any unrealized appreciation or depreciation in the transferred asset. See § 6.1 n.2 and accompanying text.

[4] The includible value may be determined under § 2031 (value at the date of death), § 2032 (alternate value, determined in most cases on the earlier to occur of six months after the decedent's death or a disposition from the decedent's estate), or § 2032A (special use value for certain property used in farming or by closely held corporations). By estoppel, federal estate tax value reported on a decedent's estate tax return generally is accepted as the asset's basis unless there is a permissible dispute regarding that value. See, e.g., Shook v. United States, 713 F.2d 662 (11th Cir. 1983) (dicta identifying criteria for deviation from the value reported on the decedent's federal estate tax return). See also §§ 5.11.9 n.216 and 15.3 n.14.

as the "step-*up* in basis" rule because it eliminates any unrealized capital gain in appreciated assets held at death, the new-basis-at-death rule also can have a step-*down* in basis consequence if the FMV of includible property is less than the owner's premortem basis.[5] Even assuming that appreciation is the case, however, the new-basis-at-death rule does not inform a strategy of holding property until death to avoid capital gain income tax on the appreciation. Instead, the advantages of giving and paying wealth transfer tax inter vivos outweigh in all cases but one the new-basis-at-death opportunity to eliminate capital gain.

§6.2 THE ECONOMICS OF PREPAYING WEALTH TRANSFER TAX

The following discussion is premised on the law in 2012 and does not attempt to predict changes to the highest marginal tax rate or the basic exclusion amount, both of which are moving targets that Congress may alter. As a result, this digression is more useful as a learning tool than as a way to model predictable results for particular situations. It is presented with the realization that uncertainty about the stability of wealth transfer tax will prevent most clients from making taxable inter vivos transfers.

Most taxpayers with wealth appreciate that many reasons exist *not* to make gifts during life. Leading the list are loss of control over the transferred funds, lack of liquidity to pay any resulting gift tax, and a fear that the remaining wealth will be inadequate to support the donor for

---

[5] That loss of basis cannot be precluded by an inter vivos transfer subject to the carryover of basis rule of §1015(a) because basis for property transferred inter vivos is the lesser of the donor's basis or the asset's FMV for gift tax purposes, meaning that losses cannot be shifted from one owner to the next. For example, if Blackacre has a FMV value of $1x and an adjusted basis for income tax purposes of $5x, there is an unrealized loss of the $4x difference. Basis to a donee of an inter vivos gift or to the recipient of the asset at the owner's death would be the $1x FMV of the asset, and the $4x of loss for income tax purposes would be unavailable to either taxpayer. An inter vivos sale that realizes the loss would be the owner's only means of taking advantage of the loss for income tax purposes, but a sale may be out of the question for other reasons and it may not produce a recognizable loss (for example, if the sale is to a related party or constitutes a "wash" sale by which the property is replaced within a 60 day period). See, e.g., §§267 and 1091.

§6.2

life. Another reason commonly given for not incurring wealth transfer tax earlier than necessary (for example, by making a completed taxable gift) is debunked by the following discussion. That "time-value-of-money" notion is that a taxpayer who defers wealth transfer tax can use the tax dollars that ultimately will be paid to the government and, over a sufficient time, earn more on the use of those dollars than any increase in tax attributable to deferral. That notion is wrong.

§ 6.2.1 *The Tax Exclusive Gift Tax Computation Outweighs New Basis at Death*

One difference between the FET and gift tax (it also exists under the GST as between direct skips and taxable distributions or terminations) is the tax base against which the tax is computed. The gift tax (and the GST on direct skips) is computed "tax exclusive," which means that the tax is computed only on the value received by the donee. The dollars used to pay the gift tax (or the direct skip GST) are not themselves subject to the tax.[1] The FET (and the GST on taxable distributions and terminations) are computed "tax inclusive," meaning that the dollars used to pay the tax are subject to the tax.

For example, under the FET, the decedent's taxable estate includes some wealth that passes to the government in the form of taxes paid on the entire estate. The FET is computed on the entire taxable estate, not

---

[1] **§ 6.2** If the donor dies within three years of a gift the gift tax dollars are subject to wealth transfer tax under the "gross up rule" of § 2035(b). The wealth transfer tax incurred is an estate tax, not an additional gift tax. There is no counterpart to § 2035(b) for GST purposes, although § 2515 provides that a donor's payment of the GST is an additional gift for gift tax purposes.

In Estate of Jameson v. Commissioner, 77 T.C.M. (CCH) 1383 (1999), vac'd and rem'd on other grounds, 267 F.3d 366 (5th Cir. 2001), the taxpayer unsuccessfully asserted that this difference between the estate and gift tax—imposition of the estate tax on the dollars used to pay the estate tax, as illustrated directly by the gross up rule—is an unconstitutional imposition directly on the wealth represented by those tax dollars, rather than the required tax on the transfer of that wealth, as discussed in § 6.2.3 n.30. The court disagreed because the tax was on the termination of the decedent's ownership of that wealth, which was the requisite "transfer" for constitutional purposes, regardless of the destination of those dollars—as a bequest to the decedent's beneficiaries or as taxes paid to the government. See Pennell, Wealth Transfer Taxation: Transfer Defined, 128 Tax Notes 615 (2010).

just on the residue that remains to pass to beneficiaries after payment of the FET. (The GST taxable distribution and taxable termination rules work in the same manner.) This means that gifts (and direct skips) always are less expensive than taxing the same wealth at death (or under the GST taxable distribution or termination rules), because of the different method of computing the excise.

To illustrate, assume a taxpayer is willing to part with $1 million during life rather than holding it until death. Between the gift tax incurred and the actual gift made, the taxpayer is willing to suffer a diminution in net worth of $1 million. The gift tax in this case is computed on that portion of the $1 million that passes to the donee, after reserving the dollars needed to pay the tax on that gift. Although this creates a circular computation (the amount of the gift is not known until the amount of the tax is computed, and the tax cannot be determined until the amount of the gift is known), an algebraic formula is available to solve the math, in our hypothetical being:

$$\text{taxable transfer} = \$1 \text{ million} \div 1 + \text{rate of tax}$$

In this case, if the tax rate is (let's assume for ease of illustration) 50%, the taxable transfer would be $666,666, the gift tax at 50% on that amount would be $333,333 (computed without subtracting any available credits), and the total of the tax paid and the amount given to the donee would equal the $1 million the taxpayer is willing to relinquish.

Computed as a percentage of the $1 million that would have existed in the estate at death if no gift was made, the $333,333 gift tax rate is an effective 33.33%, compared to the 50% rate that would apply for FET purposes on the same wealth at death. The $1 million would incur an FET of $500,000. Notwithstanding that the nominal tax rate is the same in both cases, the difference in tax is one-third, attributable purely to the different base against which the tax is applied (and this differential is the same regardless of the amount of any available credits).

If the taxpayer's marginal tax bracket rises in a progressive wealth transfer tax system, the disparity in effective tax rate also grows. For example, at a 55% rate, the gift tax in this $1 million example would be $354,839 on a gift of $645,161 (again ignoring credits), for an effective gift tax rate of 35.48%, which compares to the $550,000 of FET that would be incurred on the same $1 million at death. By way of comparison, in this highest marginal rate example, the gift tax is only about 64% of the FET or, more meaningfully, there is about a 36% saving at that higher marginal rate by incurring the tax exclusive gift tax rather than the tax inclusive FET. These relative percentages will change with the size of any available credits and the maximum tax rate.[2] For example, in the current 35% flat tax environment the effective maximum gift tax rate is 25.9%.

Any inter vivos gift tax saving should be discounted by any income tax that might be incurred on appreciation in the gifted asset, because that appreciation would escape the income tax if the property was held until death and qualified for the §1014(b)(9) new-basis-at-death adjustment.[3] Even if the income tax adjusted basis in the $1 million of transferred property was zero, and then only to the extent the transferred property was subjected to a realization event (such as a postmortem sale, which is unlikely in many cases because the gifted asset is stock in a family business, the family farm, or other legacy assets the family intends to retain) the long-term *capital gains* income tax is not likely to exceed the wealth transfer tax saving attributable to the tax exclusive computation of the gift tax.

Put another way, retaining property until death to obtain a new basis at death is no reason to defer wealth transfer tax, forsaking the benefits of the tax exclusive gift tax computation. Instead, a new-basis strategy would make sense only if the income tax rate is higher than the percentage saving attributable to the difference in the effective wealth transfer tax rates under the two different systems of computation. That

---

[2] As discussed at §7.2.2.7 n.117 and accompanying text, in a transaction such as a QPRT the real advantage is the tax exclusive calculation, meaning that an outright gift of the entire asset with no retained enjoyment or interest (instead of a gift of just the remainder interest in the QPRT transaction) is preferable because it increases the amount of the gift, which increases the amount of the gift tax incurred, which increases the tax exclusive calculation benefit derived. Although it seems counterintuitive to incur more tax inter vivos, the benefit of doing so is the real lesson of this discussion.

[3] It also would be offset by any income tax that the donor would incur in generating liquidity to pay any gift tax incurred, versus waiting until death and using new basis assets to provide cash with which to pay tax at little or no income tax cost. Often the liquidity equation is difficult to quantify, so the focus here is on only the income taxation of the gifted property itself.

can occur, but only if the wealth transfer tax effective rate differential is sufficiently low and the income tax will be computed without favorable long-term capital gain treatment. If the wealth transfer tax rate is low because the client has very little wealth, a discussion such as this is not very meaningful, because the taxpayer is not likely to consider gifts in any event. There simply is not enough wealth to afford taxable inter vivos transfers subject to the gift tax. If, however, the property that would be the subject of the gift would not generate long-term capital gain treatment, a little number crunching quickly will reveal whether the gift tax advantage will outweigh the potential income tax detriment if the donee ultimately realizes the appreciation on the asset.

§6.2.2 *The Time-Value-of-Money Myth*

The time-value-of-money notion is that deferral of wealth transfer tax is beneficial because, during the interim, the taxpayer may invest and enjoy the use of money destined to go to the government in the form of taxes. Assume for illustration purposes that the estate and gift taxes are computed in the same manner, so that the tax exclusive advantage of gifting does not skew the example. Thus, assume that the taxpayer has $2 million that can be transferred (by transfer and the tax payment thereon) inter vivos or at death, and that whatever amount that exists during life (that is, after payment of any gift tax incurred inter vivos or before a taxable transfer at death) will earn income or produce capital appreciation over a sufficient period of time that the wealth will double prior to the donor's death.[4] Finally, because we will illustrate it below, assume here that the gift tax unified credit has been consumed by prior gifts.

If the time-value of money notion is correct, any favorable difference in wealth transfer tax attributable to gifting would be offset by the benefits of investing the dollars that eventually will be paid to the government during the period of any deferral in tax payment. So, assume

---

[4] Rather than engage in speculation whether the taxpayer will live x years and earn income (after income tax) at y% and generate capital appreciation (after capital gains tax) at z%, this assumption merely eliminates guess work and suspect illustrations by assuming that the combination of relevant factors is adequate to produce the stated result of doubling the available wealth.

the taxpayer could transfer the $2 million inter vivos by gift, or make no gift and instead hold it until death, and that the tax rate is 35%:

Gift		No Gift
$20,000,000	initial wealth	$20,000,000
1,481,481	gift	0
518,518	gift tax (before credits)	0
0	unified credit[5]	0
518,518	gift tax paid	0
18,000,000	wealth remaining to invest	20,000,000
×2	growth	×2
36,000,000	wealth taxable at taxpayer's death	40,000,000
1,481,481	amount of taxable gift in tax base	0
12,600,000	FET after all credits	14,000,000
23,400,000	estate remaining after FET	26,000,000
2,962,962	gifted property (plus its growth)	0
$26,362,962	family wealth remaining	$26,000,000

If the time-value notion was correct, the deferral result in the No Gift column should exceed the result in the Gift column, but that does not happen. In the example the difference in result ($362,962) is the 35% tax on the $518,518 of gift tax that would have doubled in the taxpayer's estate during the interim, which appreciation is avoided. When that differential is backed out of the example the results are the same because (1) the time-value notion is wrong, and (2) the assumed 35% rate of tax was the same. If a progressive tax rate was applicable and the FET in the no-gift column is greater because the taxable estate is larger, then a difference would result. In that case the no-gift column would be even worse because the FET would be greater.

---

[5] Rather than predict any future changes in the unified credit, this example assumes use of the inter vivos unified credit on prior transfers. The principle being illustrated will not change unless the gift or the estate are entirely tax-free because the unified credit will shelter the full transfer. New conclusions will need to be drawn in that case. For example, if the inter vivos transfer imposes no gift tax cost, then any delay in making the transfer—if appreciation is assumed—must produce a worse result if an estate tax would apply. This is because, if no inter vivos transfer was made, estate tax would be incurred at death on appreciation generated during the deferral period, which would be a net loss to the taxpayer. The point is that static assumptions need to be reconsidered and tested against the tax environment.

Another factor to consider is capital gain on growth in the gifted assets in the gift column. That growth escapes tax in the no-gift column because it is eliminated by FET inclusion and the new basis at death adjustment. The gift still would be preferable if there is a progressive wealth tax rate structure but sale is not likely. Otherwise, this illustration shows that the time-value notion is not correct but without consideration of the income tax imponderable.

A second illustration is more realistic, using the same assumptions except a gift that does not require payment of gift tax inter vivos (instead relying just on the unified credit, which for this illustration shelters a gift of $5,120,000). Now the results are more favorable for the taxpayer who makes the inter vivos transfer:

Gift		*No Gift*
$20,000,000	initial wealth	$20,000,000
5,120,000	gift	0
1,772,800	gift tax (before credits)	0
1,772,800	unified credit	1,772,800
0	gift tax paid	0
14,880,000	wealth remaining to invest	20,000,000
×2	growth	×2
29,760,000	wealth taxable at taxpayer's death	40,000,000
5,120,000	amount of taxable gift in tax base	0
10,416,000	FET after all credits	12,208,000
19,344,000	estate remaining after FET	27,792,000
10,240,000	gifted property (plus its growth)	0
$29,584,000	family wealth remaining	$27,792,000

The $1,792,000 difference in the gift column equals a 35% tax on $5,120,000 of appreciation that is avoided by taxing the property inter vivos rather than at death.

To the question whether there simply was not enough growth in these illustrations to offset the gift tax advantage, the answer is that (1) in a flat tax environment it does not matter, and (2) in a progressive tax situation the greater the growth, the greater the advantage to an inter vivos transfer. To illustrate, run an example that assumes that all the wealth triples (rather than just doubles, as first illustrated) and recompute the respective tax saving. Counter to the time-value-of-money notion

§6.2.2

that the wealth transfer tax saving will be recovered and deferral will be preferable, over a longer deferral period in which the taxpayer earns more appreciation, the disparity in net worth *increases* rather than shrinks. This is simply because the time-value-of-money notion is exactly wrong in the wealth transfer tax context. The sooner the wealth transfer tax is paid, the better the wealth transfer tax result.

The only exception to this result applies due to a failure to generate a new basis by subjecting the transferred asset to the FET, which can result in an income tax that offsets any wealth transfer tax saving. This will occur, however, only if the growth is appreciation that is subject to income tax that is not eliminated by the § 1014(b)(9) new-basis-at-death rule, and only if the income tax is incurred because there is a realization event (such as a sale). The point of the illustrations is only to reveal that the time-value-of-money explanation for favoring deferral of wealth transfer tax simply is not correct. As a consequence, unless there are other (nontax) reasons to favor deferral, inter vivos transfers that trigger the gift tax and avoid a subsequent FET—prepayment as it were—are preferable to the FET at death.[6]

§6.2.3 *Other Reasons to Favor Inter Vivos Transfers*

The tax exclusive method of computing the gift tax is one of several demonstrable reasons to favor an early and complete transfer of wealth, even if it incurs a gift tax. Another reason to favor inter vivos transfers is the § 2503(b) gift tax annual exclusion and the § 2503(e) ed/med exclusion, which make it possible to transfer some wealth during life entirely tax free.[7] A corollary is split annual exclusion gifts and gifts to use or to shelter a spouse's unified credit. Yet another is the ability to shift future income and appreciation from the transferred property to the new owner for income tax purposes, and in the process to avoid a future wealth transfer tax to the transferor on the income or the appreciation.

---

[6] For a more detailed discussion see Pennell & Williamson, The Economics of Prepaying Wealth Transfer Tax, 136 Trusts & Estates 49-60 (June 1997), 40-51 (July 1997), and 52-56 (Aug. 1997), the July issue being most relevant to the gifting illustration.

[7] See § 7.1.1.1 with respect to the annual exclusion, and § 7.1.1.11 with respect to the ed/med exclusion.

Saving income tax is a function of the spread between the marginal brackets applicable to the transferor and the transferee, which in many cases is not significant. The opportunity to shift appreciation should be weighed against the different potential for consumption by the transferor or the transferee in ways that show no value for subsequent wealth transfer tax purposes (as well as the ability of the transferor to consume other retained wealth and even further reduce the amount subject to wealth transfer tax).

In addition, shifting appreciation makes no sense when the wealth transfer tax is a flat tax (which it became in 2006 when the maximum rate dropped to 46% and the applicable exclusion amount (now called the basic exclusion amount) rose to $2.0 million). No saving is available other than the dollars saved by the tax exclusive feature of the gift tax. To illustrate, compare owning an asset worth $100x that is expected to double in value. If a 35% tax is imposed, leaving $65x that will double to $310x, the taxpayer is in no better position than if the $100x was held, it doubles to $200x, and 35% of that is paid in tax, leaving the same $130x. So, depending on the law at any given time—and what Congress might do in the future—shifting appreciation might pay no dividend. On the other hand, it is not likely to be harmful.

A related but slightly different opportunity remains even if the wealth transfer tax remains flat. The "Half Hot Example" in §13.2.3 illustrates the benefit of paying tax early with assets that will not grow in value. This opportunity is most likely available to a taxpayer who is using cash or the unified credit to pay any gift tax. The concept is that the unified credit will shelter all of the tax on $5,120,000 of value transferred by gift in 2012 but that same credit would offset only half the tax on the includible value if no transfer was made and the property doubled in value before the taxpayer died. This concept is not about freezing the value of the transferred property for wealth transfer tax purposes. It is about paying the tax with dollars that are frozen in value. This opportunity does not disappear even if the wealth transfer tax is a flat tax.

A further example of the advantage of inter vivos transfers is to shift ownership to set up valuation discounts at death. A good example is conversion of joint tenancy between spouses into tenancy-in-common ownership that will generate a fractional interest discount in the estate of each spouse. This requires only that the two halves of that property not

§6.2.3

be aggregated in S's estate, in the manner unsuccessfully sought by the government in the *Bonner* line of cases, all as discussed in § 10.5.4.

A final advantage relates to a major and, notwithstanding the following statement, apparently intentional distinction in the law between the method for valuing gifts and that for valuing property at death:

> Congress intended to largely eliminate the disparity between gift tax and estate tax, and to unify them into a fully integrated system by "elimina[ting] ways by which estate planners can reduce the estate and gift tax burden through special patterns of transferring their property."[8]

The tax exclusive computation of the gift tax and the gift tax annual and ed/med exclusions confirm that this statement is not totally accurate. But these differences all pale in comparison to another longstanding failure to unify the transfer tax system and remove an unexpected (and inappropriate) benefit available only to taxpayers who can afford (and are willing) to make gifts. This benefit is not affected by recent and promised changes in the law. To appreciate the magnitude of this requires only an understanding of the significant and fundamental difference in valuation as between the FET and gift tax, as illustrated by several TAMs.

For example, TAM 9432001 reached a result that is correct for FET purposes and that was favorable to the taxpayer involved, but in a fact situation that is contrary to the norm. The decedent in that situation owned 48% of the stock of a family corporation. The decedent's legatee was the 52% shareholder and the question was whether the decedent's stock was entitled to a minority interest valuation reduction for FET purposes. In that respect the same issue would have existed if the legatee had owned anything more than 2% of the stock and, indeed, the issue might have been more interesting if the decedent's transfer had given the legatee control that the legatee did not enjoy previously. Notwithstanding that the legatee would hold the 48% interest as part of a control block, the government held that the decedent's stock should be valued without reference to the number of legatees or the stock they

---

[8] Estate of Murphy v. Commissioner, 60 T.C.M. (CCH) 645, 664 (1990), quoting H.R. Rep. No. 1380 (1976), 76-3 C.B. 735, 741.

already held.[9] Thus, the legatee's post-gift control of the business was irrelevant.

In a more normal situation the decedent controls an entity and divides that ownership among a group of legatees, no one of whom receiving a controlling interest. The amount includible for FET purposes is the decedent's controlling interest, not the minority interests received by each legatee. According to *Ahmanson Foundation v. United States*:[10]

> The estate tax is a tax . . . on the privilege of passing on property, not a tax on the privilege of receiving property.
>
> . . . . There is nothing in the statutes or in the case law that suggests that valuation of the gross estate should take into account that the assets will come to rest in several hands rather than one.
>
> To take into account for valuation purposes the fact that the testator's unitary holding has become divided in the hands of two or more beneficiaries, would invite abuse.

And *Estate of Chenoweth v. Commissioner*[11] instructs that:

> the estate tax is laid only on that which passes at death, not . . . what the legatee receives after death. Since the tax is laid upon the decedent's estate as a whole, and not upon the property which is received by the various legatees, the valuation of decedent's assets, at least for purposes of computing his gross taxable estate under section 2031, can usually be made without reference to the destination of those assets.

The point here is that the result may differ for gift tax purposes, despite the following gift tax regulation:[12]

---

[9] Citing Estate of Lee v. Commissioner, 69 T.C. 860 (1978), nonacq., 1980-2 C.B. 2, withdrawn and acq., Rev. Rul. 93-12, 1993-1 C.B. 202, and Estate of Zaiger v. Commissioner, 64 T.C. 927 (1975), acq., 1976-1 C.B. 1.

[10] 674 F.2d 761, 768 (9th Cir. 1981) (division of voting and nonvoting stock held at decedent's death, with the nonvoting stock passing to charity).

[11] 88 T.C. 1577, 1582 (1987) (outright bequest to S for marital deduction purposes of 51% of the stock in a family corporation, the remaining 49% going to D's daughter by a former marriage).

[12] Treas. Reg. §25.2511-2(a). See McCord v. Commissioner, 120 T.C. 358 (2003), rev'd on other grounds, 461 F.3d 614 (5th Cir. 2006) (stating that the gift tax is imposed on the value of what the donor transfers, not on what the donee receives), citing Shepherd v. Commissioner, 115 T.C. 376, 385 (2000), and Robinette v. Helvering, 318 U.S. 184, 186 (1943), but not the regulation. Indeed, very few cases have so much as *cited* this regulation, much less applied it. A

§6.2.3

> The gift tax is not imposed upon the receipt of the property by the donee, nor is it necessarily determined by the measure of enrichment resulting to the donee from the transfer. . . . On the contrary, the tax . . . is an excise upon [the] act of making the transfer, is measured by the value of the property passing from the donor, and attaches regardless of the fact that the identity of the donee may not then be known or ascertainable.

On its face, this regulation is consistent with both the FET valuation regime and the British gift tax valuation regime,[13] under each of which it does not matter how property is distributed by a decedent or a donor.

Particularly notable about the government's statement in TAM 9432001 that the number of donees is irrelevant for FET purposes is that the result is otherwise for gift tax purposes. Rev. Rul. 93-12[14] involved a

---

(Footnote Continued)

computer search produced the following list, and many of the cited cases refer to the regulation with respect to dominion and control or timing of a completed gift, rather than ascertainability of the donee or the measure of the gift involved: Okerlund v. United States, 365 F.3d 1044 (Fed. Cir. 2004); Stinson Estate v. United States, 214 F.3d 846 (7th Cir. 2000); Estate of Davenport v. Commissioner, 184 F.3d 1176 (10th Cir. 1999); Becker v. United States, 751 F. Supp. 827 (D. Neb. 1990), Pierre v. Commissioner, 133 T.C. 24 (2009), Holman v. Commissioner, 131 T.C. 170 (2008); Estate of Bongard v. Commissioner, 124 T.C. 95 (2005); Estate of Jones v. Commissioner, 116 T.C. 121 (2001), Estate of Strangi v. Commissioner, 115 T.C. 478 (2000), rev'd on other grounds, 293 F.3d 279 (5th Cir. 2002); Ripley v. Commissioner, 105 T.C. 358 (1995); Estate of DiMarco v. Commissioner, 87 T.C. 653 (1986), Northern Trust Co. v. Commissioner, 87 T.C. 349 (1986), Ward v. Commissioner, 87 T.C. 78 (1986), Estate of Goelet v. Commissioner, 51 T.C. 352 (1968), Goldstein v. Commissioner, 37 T.C. 897 (1962), Gross v. Commissioner, 96 T.C.M. (CCH) 187 (2008); Huber v. Commissioner, 91 T.C.M. (CCH) 1132 (2006); Koblick v. Commissioner, 91 T.C.M. (CCH) 959 (2006); Senda v. Commissioner, 88 T.C.M. (CCH) 8 (2004); Estate of True v. Commissioner, 82 T.C.M. (CCH) 27 (2001); Ripley v. Commissioner, 105 T.C. 358 (1995), rev'd on other grounds, 103 F.3d 332 (4th Cir. 1996); DePaoli v. Commissioner, 66 T.C.M. (CCH) 1493 (1993), LeFrak v. Commissioner, 66 T.C.M. (CCH) 1297 (1993), Estate of Vak v. Commissioner, 62 T.C.M. (CCH) 942 (1991), Estate of Whitt v. Commissioner, 46 T.C.M. (CCH) 118 (1983), Cullman v. Commissioner, 42 T.C.M. (CCH) 1691 (1981), Buckley v. Commissioner, 42 T.C.M. (CCH) 1592 (1981). In addition, there have been a handful of government rulings that refer to the regulation, but all in the context of dominion and control rather than ascertainability of the donee.

[13] See § 6.2.3 n.29 and accompanying text.

[14] 1993-1 C.B. 202.

donor who transferred 100% of the stock in a corporation in five equal inter vivos gifts during one year. The Ruling stated that a minority interest valuation adjustment would not be denied to any of those five separate gifts on account of the donees being related family members, and did not even mention the issue of consistency with the FET or whether some other theory—such as the apparent thrust of the gift tax regulation—nevertheless would preclude valuation as five separate minority interest gifts.

Although Rev. Rul. 93-12 did not state that a reduction would be allowed, nor did it indicate what the government's opinion might be if the donor made five equal gifts spread over five years, either to the same or to different donees, TAMs 9449001 and 9436005 subsequently addressed several valuation questions raised by Rev. Rul. 93-12 in the context of donors who owned 100% of the stock of family businesses. In the earlier TAM the donor proposed to transfer 5% to the donor's spouse and 30% to each of three children, and the government agreed to value each gift separately with both minority interest and lack of marketability adjustments.[15] The later TAM involved equal gifts to 11 children and the government again agreed to value each donee's gift separately,[16] stating the rules as follows:

> Although the estate tax and the gift tax are generally construed in pari materia, there are some material differences in the administration of the two taxes. . . .
>
> Unlike the estate tax where the tax is imposed on an aggregation of all the decedent's assets, the gift tax is imposed on the property passing from the donor to each donee and it is the value of that property passing from the donor to the donee that is the basis for measuring the tax. Thus, where a donor makes simulta-

---

[15] The TAM did reduce a claimed 25% minority interest and lack of marketability adjustment for each gift because each of the 30% blocks carried a swing vote opportunity that required a slight valuation increase, reflecting the fact that each recipient had the ability to combine with any other recipient to generate effective control. See Pennell, Valuation Discord: An Exegesis of Wealth Transfer Tax Valuation Theory and Practice, 30 U. Miami Inst. Est. Plan. ¶ 905.2 (1996) and § 15.3.1 n.55 and accompanying text for a more complete discussion of the very limited authorities on the swing vote issue.

[16] In this case with only a passing reference to swing vote considerations, which is understandable, because it would require five other children to combine with any one to exert absolute control, making any valuation increase de minimis at best.

§ 6.2.3

neous gifts of property to multiple donees, the gift tax is imposed on the value of each separate gift. Accordingly, the value of property that is the subject of multiple simultaneous gifts may be different from the value of that same property if that property were included in the donor's gross estate at his death . . . .

. . . [C]ourts have consistently held that, where a donor makes gifts of multiple shares of the same security to different donees at the same time, each gift is to be valued separately.

Presumably reference was made to multiple *simultaneous* gifts because that was the case in the TAM and not because somehow that is required.

Significant about these TAMs was the government's conclusion that, for gift tax purposes, value is determined by the gift each donee receives rather than by the donor's disposition of control, measured by the aggregate transfers made inter vivos or the diminution in the donor's net worth.[17]

---

[17] See, e.g., Estate of Bosca v. Commissioner, 76 T.C.M. (CCH) 62 (1998) (showing the schizophrenia of the gift tax, regarding a gift as made because what transferor gave up—voting stock—was worth more than what the transferor received—nonvoting stock—which reflects a diminution in value notion to establish that a gift was made, but valuing the gifts made as two separate transfers because two separate shareholders of the business benefited from the exchange), citing two very early cases on the issue: Phipps v. Commissioner, 43 B.T.A. 1010, 1022 (1940) (13 separate gifts of stock cannot be aggregated for blockage adjustment purposes, stating that "[t]he property to be valued . . . is the property constituting the gift. Here there were 13 gifts"), and Whittemore v. Fitzpatrick, 127 F. Supp. 710, 714 (D. Conn. 1954) (involving a gift of 200 shares to each of three sons from a total of 820, of which the taxpayer owned all; apparently the corporation was a personal investment operation that owned nonliquid assets and the court described the case as one of first impression, holding that the valuation should be of each 200 share gift separately, rather than as a single gift of 600 shares total):

[T]here is inherent in the problem an underlying question as to whether the plaintiff . . . made three gifts or only one. As to this, there can be no question that, as tested by the law governing inter vivos gifts, although . . . there was only one transfer which comprised 600 shares [to a trust for the three sons], there were three gifts: certainly each of the three sons received a gift. . . . I find nothing in the federal tax law which requires that . . . the transaction . . . must be treated as one creating a single gift.

[F]or purposes of computing the tax the "sum of the net gifts" for the taxable year . . . shall be aggregated. It is significant that this . . . says

This gift tax concept has been recognized historically[18] and fundamentally is unlike the FET, which does not consider whether a decedent disposes of property in a single bequest or divides the property between numerous legatees. Although it is not universally accepted,[19] it is well

(Footnote Continued)

nothing about the valuation of the gifts: . . . the aggregation is pertinent only to the "computation of tax" under the statutory scheme.

Other cases denying aggregation for purpose of determining a blockage adjustment include Standish v. Commissioner, 8 T.C. 1204 (1947), Clause v. Commissioner, 5 T.C. 647 (1945), aff'd, 154 F.2d 655 (3d Cir. 1946), and Avery v. Commissioner, 3 T.C. 963 (1944). But see Helvering v. Kimberly, 97 F.2d 433 (4th Cir. 1938), which allowed aggregation. Cf. income tax cases depending on the same principle: Minahan v. Commissioner, 88 T.C. 492 (1987) (rejecting aggregation for purposes of assessing a control premium for valuation of stock sold to multiple separate trusts), and Adair v. Commissioner, 54 T.C.M. (CCH) 705 (1987) (involving imputed interest under § 483), citing Treas. Reg. § 25.2512-2(e) generally for the proposition that "each one of several gifts made on the same day [must] be valued on the basis of each separate gift," and citing Calder v. Commissioner, 85 T.C. 713 (1985), and Rushton v. Commissioner, 60 T.C. 272 (1973), aff'd, 498 F.2d 88 (5th Cir. 1974) (denying blockage discount based on an aggregation of all gifts made by the taxpayer in that year). Although Ward v. Commissioner, 87 T.C. 78, 108 (1986), stated that, "[l]ike the estate tax, the gift tax is imposed upon the act of transfer and is measured by the value of the property passing from the donor, and not on the value of the property in the hands of a particular recipient," it did so only for purposes of valuing what left the donor's control and passed to each respective individual donee and not for purposes of valuing the aggregate of what the donor transferred. See generally Fellows & Painter, Valuing Close Corporations for Federal Wealth Transfer Taxes: A Statutory Solution to the Disappearing Wealth Syndrome, 30 Stan. L. Rev. 895 (1978).

[18] Also notwithstanding statements like those in LeFrak v. Commissioner, 66 T.C.M. (CCH) 1297 (1993), that "the gift tax is imposed on what the donor transferred, not what the donee received." The issue in *LeFrak* was whether the donor gave realty, which the donees then contributed to a partnership, or created the partnership first and gave partnership interests. The court held that the former was the case and determined the value of the gifted property accordingly, before creation of the partnership.

[19] See, e.g., Driver v. United States, 76-2 U.S. Tax Cas. (CCH) ¶ 13,155 at 85,699 (W.D. Wis. 1976) (gifts of stock to multiple beneficiaries on December 31 and then January 2 combined to deny minority discount; donor was left with a small minority interest):

We deal here with an effort to convert a transfer of a majority interest into one of a minority interest by effecting it in two installments two days apart.

§ 6.2.3

illustrated by Estate of Jones v. Commissioner,[20] in which one gift of an 83% interest in a partnership was made to a single donee and the aggregate discount (for lack of marketability) allowed was a mere 8%, but separate 17% interests in a second partnership given to each of four donees were granted the same 8% lack of marketability discount and an added 40% lack of control discount, reflecting what each separate donee received rather than what the donor conveyed in the aggregate.

Worthy of consideration in this respect is Estate of Frank v. Commissioner,[21] TAMs 9550002 and 9140002, and Estate of Murphy v. Commissioner.[22] The decedent in *Frank* was the settlor of a revocable inter vivos trust that owned just over 50% of the stock of a family corporation. Two days before D's death D's child, acting under the authority of a

---

(Footnote Continued)

> The cases are legion which hold that the substance not the form of a transaction controls for tax purposes and the niceties of conveyancing or the form of a contract will not serve to hide the substance and practical significance of the actual transaction.

Citing Gregory v. Helvering, 293 U.S. 465 (1938), Helvering v. Halleck, 309 U.S. 106 (1940), and Commissioner v. Estate of Church, 335 U.S. 632 (1949), with no apparent recognition that combining the gifts to the various donees (as well as combining each donee's gifts on December 31 and January 2) was extraordinary under the gift tax. *Driver* was soundly criticized in Estate of Bright v. United States, 658 F.2d 999 (5th Cir. 1981) (en banc). See also Griffin v. United States, 42 F. Supp. 2d 700 (W.D. Tex. 1998), discussed in §7.1.3 n.148, denying a similar effort to produce minority interest discounts using a transfer to the donor's spouse followed by separate gifts by each spouse (in lieu of split gifts or transfers in each of two different tax years).

A more compelling decision contrary to the traditional gift tax regime is Cullman v. Commissioner, 42 T.C.M. (CCH) 1691, 1695 (1981) (the taxpayer transferred recreational realty to a trust that provided for "trust certificates" evidencing division of the beneficial interest into six shares, only one of which the taxpayer retained; the court denied 50% valuation reductions claimed on each of the five gifts attributable to restrictions on disposition of the certificates and their lack of marketability), one of the few cases that cite Treas. Reg. §25.2511-2(a) for this concept. Citing Robinette v. Helvering, 318 U.S. 184 (1943), the court held that the taxpayer "made a gift of the entire property that she transferred to the trust reduced by her retained interest" as if she made a single gift. Nevertheless, five annual exclusions were allowed.

[20] 116 T.C. 121 (2001).

[21] 69 T.C.M. (CCH) 2255 (1995).

[22] 60 T.C.M. (CCH) 645 (1990).

durable power of attorney, withdrew enough stock from the trust to reduce the amount includible in D's gross estate to 32% of the stock in the corporation. That stock was given to S, who died 15 days after D, without receiving any more stock under D's estate plan. This gift[23] raised S's stock ownership to just two shares less than D's and, by virtue of this death bed planning, both estates were entitled to minority interest valuation adjustments.

Most notable about the Tax Court's opinion was its statement that the motive for the death bed transfer was irrelevant to the question of inclusion in D's gross estate, making the government's substance over form argument of no avail. The net result was a 30% lack of marketability valuation reduction for both D and S's 32% interests and an additional 20% minority interest valuation adjustment on the remaining 70% of the value, or a total 45% overall reduction of the value of each block of the stock includible in their respective estates.

In *Murphy* the court denied a minority interest valuation adjustment for a 49.65% interest remaining in S's estate at death, following a gift made 18 days before death of 1.76% of the stock for the apparent purpose[24] of producing a minority interest valuation adjustment. *Murphy* is troubling because its conclusion essentially ignored the inter vivos transfer, in large part because of the taxpayer's motive, which is reminiscent of the repealed contemplation of death rule under old §2035(a). Nevertheless, the court made a number of very compelling points bottomed on a finding that "[t]he only intended purpose was to make decedent's control of the corporation appear to disappear, to obtain a minority discount," and that this "fragmentation . . . did not substantially affect [the decedent's] interest in the corporation."

As a result, the *Murphy* court found the inter vivos transfer by the decedent ineffective for FET purposes, stating simply that the court believed that any future sale of the stock would entail a coordinated transfer of the decedent's remaining shares with those transferred at the end of life, so as to maximize the value of it all. The opinion stated that

---

[23] Presumably the gift qualified for the §2523 gift tax marital deduction, which would explain why the government did not challenge the value of the stock for gift tax purposes.

[24] Revealed by a less than subtle communication from the decedent's tax advisor that apparently was not protected by an attorney-client privilege.

§6.2.3

unification of the estate and gift taxes in 1976 indicated a "congressional intent that all property be subject to relatively uniform transfer taxes, which may be undermined if owners of control may pass it to their relatives by using transactions structured to avoid transfer taxation of the control premium."[25] Although this may be correct in theory, it is not what Congress did, nor has the gift tax ever been structured to preclude that result.

The gift tax exists primarily to backstop the FET.[26] If taxpayers could transfer property tax free during life, only individuals who could not afford—or were not advised by competent counsel—to make gifts during life would pay an FET. As first enacted, the gift tax was not very effective, because it taxed gifts separately, on an annual basis, and gifts in one year did not impact the taxation of gifts in a subsequent year. Thus, the tax easily was minimized by making a series of smaller gifts spread over several years even if they resulted in a shift of a controlling interest.[27]

As revised in 1932, that aspect of the gift tax was cured. Under § 2502 gifts are taxable cumulatively under the progressive rate system, with the taxation of the next gift dependent on the aggregate of gifts previously made.[28] This eliminated the ability to plan seriatim lifetime gifts that minimized the impact of progressivity, but it did nothing to

---

[25] 60 T.C.M. at 664.

[26] 1939-1 C.B. (Part 2) 462.

[27] 1939-1 C.B. (Part 2) 477.

[28] To compute the gift tax under § 2502(a) on any present gift the current transfer is added to the amount of all taxable gifts made both before and after unification in 1976, the gift tax is computed on the total amount, the amount of tax incurred on all prior taxable gifts is subtracted, and the difference is the amount owing on the current gift. Thus, pre-1977 gifts are part of the computation of the incremental tax on a post-1976 gift. However, only lifetime gifts after 1976 are considered in determining the marginal estate tax bracket in the unified rate schedule under § 2001(b). Pre-1977 taxable gifts are not aggregated with the post-1976 taxable gifts and the taxable estate to determine the tax computed on the total under the unified *estate* tax computation regime, and only the tax on the post-1976 gifts is subtracted to leave the incremental estate tax on the taxable estate at death. See TAM 9642001, which properly concluded that pre-1977 taxable gifts are considered for purposes of determining the *tax* on the post-1976 taxable *gifts*, notwithstanding that the pre-1977 gifts are not considered otherwise in determining the estate tax liability. See § 1.2.8.

eliminate the opportunity sought in *Murphy*, of making a small current transfer at a deeply reduced value to reflect its minority status, and in the process leave a minority interest to be subject to tax in the estate of the donor, again with a minority interest valuation adjustment. The legislative correction to this extant opportunity would be to impose the gift tax on any diminution in a taxpayer's net worth, rather than to tax the value of each respective transfer. But that is not how the gift tax works.

When Congress addressed the lack of effective progressivity in 1932, and when it unified the estate and gift taxes in 1976, it could have adopted such an alternative, to apply a progressive tax on the cumulative diminutions in a transferor's net worth, as determined on an annual basis.[29] Either of the current system or the diminution-in-net-worth approach would be consistent with the need for a gift tax that is not easily avoided by seriatim annual gifts, but only the diminution approach effectively would protect the integrity of the total wealth transfer tax system by precluding the valuation opportunity the taxpayer sought to exploit in *Murphy*.

It may be the case that Congress, in subtle and not so subtle ways, wants to *preserve* a system that provides benefits that only taxpayers with enough wealth to make inter vivos transfers can and do exploit. Moreover, a change to the diminution-in-net-worth approach might be thought inconsistent with the mandate that any tax must be imposed on the *transfer* of wealth as opposed to taxing the wealth itself (which would violate the United States Constitution).[30] For example, if the *Murphy* gift

---

[29] Such a system would resemble the British Capital Transfer Tax. Under § 3 of the Inheritance Tax Act of 1984, taxing Transfers of Value, the Capital Transfer Tax is imposed on all taxable transfers, which are defined as any "disposition made by a person (the transferor) as a result of which the value of [the transferor's] estate immediately after the disposition is less than it would be but for the disposition; and the amount by which it is less is the value transferred by the transfer." Under a mechanism that refers to a potentially exempt transfer, the British tax does not cut as deeply as the United States gift tax because survival of a gift by three (and then by seven) years results in a reduction (and then an elimination) of the tax itself, but that would not be an essential aspect of the British approach for emulation in the United States.

[30] See the fourth clause of § 9 of art. I of the United States Constitution, which provides that: "No Capitation, or other direct, Tax shall be laid, unless in Proportion to the Census or Enumeration herein before directed to be taken." See United States v. Land, 303 F.2d 170, 172 (5th Cir. 1962), citing Treas. Reg.

of a sliver of stock was valued at the difference between the taxpayer's net worth with control and then without control of the business, the concern might be that the donee receives a much smaller amount of wealth than the diminution-in-net-worth approach would subject to tax, which would belie the existence of a transfer of that differential.[31] For our purposes the issue is academic because the gift tax and FET differ, and that difference significantly favors the gift tax in cases in which fractional or minority interest discounts are available.[32]

§6.3 INCOME SHIFTING

Within the life span of some current estate planners the income tax rates in America were as high as 77%. Income shifting then was vastly more beneficial than today, when maximum rates are essentially half of what they were not so long ago (although income shifting might return to some prominence if tax rate differentials expand). Even if rates do increase, however, many techniques employed in the past will not succeed because of changes in the income taxation of trusts and their beneficiaries,[1] and due to the Kiddie tax, discussed below. With those caveats, it may be worthwhile to consider the inter vivos transfer opportunity to shift future income from property—including by the most expedient mechanism, which is an outright gift of income producing property.

(Footnote Continued)

§ 20.2033-1(a) (which explains that the estate tax "is an excise tax on the transfer of property at death and is not a tax on the property transferred") and stating the "imperative that the tax be imposed on the transfer of property in order to avoid the constitutional prohibition against unapportioned direct taxes." The concept of a "transfer" of wealth is only sparsely defined, as explored in Pennell, Wealth Transfer Taxation: Transfer Defined, 128 Tax Notes 615 (2010).

[31] For a further elaboration on these issues see Pennell, Valuation Discord: An Exegesis of Wealth Transfer Tax Valuation Theory and Practice, 30 U. Miami Inst. Est. Plan. ¶ 900 (1996).

[32] With respect to certain disadvantages of making inter vivos transfers, mostly attributable to Congress' failure to properly unify the transfer taxes in 1976, see § 1.3.3 n.35 and accompanying text.

[1] §6.3 See Chapter 5.

§6.3.1 *Hazards of Income Shifting*

The issue under the current compressed income tax rates is whether income shifting is worthwhile. In making any calculation for income shifting comparison purposes, the standard deduction and personal exemption(s) available to the potential beneficiary are important items to consider, particularly because someone who may be claimed as a dependent on another taxpayer's return is denied the use of their own personal exemption[2] and their standard deduction is limited.[3] On the other hand, some potential beneficiaries are the elderly who may qualify for several standard deductions by virtue of being over age 65 or being blind.[4]

In some cases it may be wise to accumulate income in a trust to avoid distributions that would prevent a supporting taxpayer from claiming the beneficiary as a dependent. Trust accumulation also may be wise if distributions would increase the beneficiary's adjusted gross income and thereby affect the amount of itemized deductions lost under the percentage threshold of §67 or medical expense deductions lost under the percentage floor of §213. Similarly, income of the trust may have AMT or passive activity consequences to the beneficiary that can be deferred or avoided entirely by virtue of accumulation.

In many cases, however, the accumulation of income in a trust for these reasons, or to take advantage of the de minimis maximum annual saving of the entity's run through the brackets, may be imprudent, considering fiduciary fees, other costs of administration, and Form 1041 preparation costs. In some cases the ability to shield a beneficiary by accumulating income may make continued use of multiple trusts *appear* attractive, but without great care this could be a mistake.[5]

---

[2] See §151(d)(2).

[3] See §63(c)(5).

[4] §63(c)(3).

[5] Maintaining multiple trusts to accumulate income is hazardous if the throwback rule may apply, due to the potential application of §667(c). Throwback was repealed in 1997 for all but foreign trusts or any domestic trust that once was a foreign trust or that was created before March of 1984 and would be subject to the §643(f) multiple trust rule were they not chronologically exempt. With respect to these trusts only, the §667(c) accumulation distribution and throwback "third trust" rule is a seldom recognized draconian counterpart to the

§6.3.2 *Kiddie Tax*

An additional concern in this arena arises because the so-called Kiddie tax seeks to prevent taxpayers from shifting unearned income to children for taxation in their lower income tax brackets.[6] To accomplish this anti-shifting objective, the tax imposed under §1(g) essentially treats a portion of the family as a single economic unit for tax computation purposes. Thus, although spouses may file income tax separate returns, the Kiddie tax effectively requires certain (and not just minor or dependent) children and their parents to aggregate their income to determine the rate of tax on each affected child's unearned income.[7]

(Footnote Continued)

multiple trust rule of §643(f), with devastatingly unexpected results because the essential effect of its operation is double taxation. The gross-up rules of §§665(d) and 666(b) and (c) are avoided, but the §667(b) credit for taxes paid by the trust is disallowed, meaning that taxes are paid by the trust on accumulated income in the year of accumulation and again by the beneficiary on the accumulation distribution in the year of distribution. In addition, the §665(b) minority exception to the throwback rules is lost. Even more invidious is the fact that, unlike §643(f), the third trust rule applies regardless of the grantor(s) or trustee(s) of the multiple trusts involved, even if no tax avoidance motive existed in the creation or administration of the subject trusts, and even if the trusts are not at all similar. See §5.6.3 nn.47-48 and accompanying text.

[6] See the explanation of the Kiddie tax in Treasury Decision 8158, which promulgated Temp. Treas. Reg. §1.1(i)-1T in question and answer format.

[7] Carlton v. United States, 789 F. Supp. 746 (N.D. Miss. 1991), involved a minor taxpayer's challenge to the Kiddie tax, claiming that it is an unconstitutional violation of equal protection of the laws as an impermissible discrimination on the basis of age. Involved was the unearned income from funds received by the taxpayer as damages in a personal injury lawsuit, taxed at the highest marginal bracket applicable to the taxpayer's parents. According to the court, the imposition of the parents' tax rate on this taxpayer's income was similar to the imposition of higher tax rates on married individuals, based solely on their marital status, and did not run afoul of the real constitutional prohibition, established in Hoeper v. Tax Commissioner, 284 U.S. 206 (1931), against measuring the income (rather than the tax rate) of one taxpayer by the income or property of another taxpayer. Citing Mapes v. United States, 576 F.2d 896, 902 (Ct. Cl. 1978), and Barter v. United States, 550 F.2d 1239, 1240 (7th Cir. 1977), the court held that perfect equality and absolute logical consistency among taxpayers under the Internal Revenue Code is not a constitutional mandate and dismissed the suit on a motion for summary judgment by the government.

The Kiddie tax is imposed on the "net unearned income" of a child who has at least one living parent and is under age 19 (24 for full-time students) at the end of the child's tax year.[8] A child who is subject to §1(g) is required to pay a tax on this "net unearned income" as if (broadly speaking) the income belonged to the child's parents, unless the child's tax computed without §1(g) would be higher than the tax computed under the Kiddie tax regime.[9] This means that two computations are required by every taxpaying child, to determine the method that produces the higher tax. Indeed, in those situations in which a taxpaying child has sufficient AMT income, the Kiddie AMT of §59(j) will require two additional computations to determine which of the Kiddie AMT and the normal AMT produces the higher tax.[10]

"Unearned income" is all income that is not §911(d)(2) earned income,[11] essentially meaning any income other than personal service compensation income. The Kiddie tax is applicable to all unearned income, regardless of source and regardless of when earned, if it happens to be includible in the child's income for a current tax year, regardless of the fact that some may have accrued in years prior to adoption of §1(g).[12] Fortunately, tax exempt income is not subject to the

---

[8] See §1(g)(2)(A)(ii)(I), which relies on definitions in §§152(c)(3) and 152(f)(2). Statements made at the time the Kiddie tax was proposed indicated that the age (then 14, raised to 18 after 2005 and to 19 (or in some cases 24) in 2007) originally was chosen because it was the age under the Fair Labor Standards Act at which employment for certain purposes is first permitted. The legislative history of the Act does not preserve this (or any other reason) as the rationale for the age chosen, if it was in fact the logic followed, and it certainly does not inform the matter any longer, given the changes Congress made in 2005 and 2007.

[9] §1(g)(1)(A).

[10] Added in 1987, §59(j) mirrors §1(g) in terms of its requisites and mechanism. Especially because of its (hopefully) limited application, it is not considered separately here. However, it should not be overlooked that the Kiddie tax system may require that a child make four separate tax computations.

[11] §1(g)(4)(A)(i). Excepted by §1(g)(4)(C) is income from §642(b)(2)(C)(ii) qualified disability trusts.

[12] For example, if a trust was still subject to throwback and made an accumulation distribution to a child under the applicable age (and the distribution failed to qualify for the minority exception to the throwback rule), that trust distribution would be subject to the Kiddie tax even if the accumulation years to which it is attributed were all prior to adoption of §1(g) in 1986. The minority exception to

§6.3.2

Kiddie tax because it is not includible in gross income in the first instance. Furthermore, income that is generated currently but that is properly deferred until a tax year that ends when the child is over the age specified also will escape this imposition. The most important point to recognize is simply that the Kiddie tax applies on an annual basis regardless of the source or date of the child's acquisition of the income.

Two amounts reduce a child's unearned adjusted gross income in determining "net unearned income," which is the amount subject to the § 1(g) tax, computed at the parent's rates. The first reduction, referred to as the "standard deduction amount,"[13] is a defined amount that is not necessarily the amount of the child's standard deduction.[14] Also allowed as a reduction in determining net unearned income for application of the Kiddie tax is the "general offset amount."[15] This amount is the greater of the § 63(c)(5)(A) "standard deduction amount" or, if the child itemizes deductions, the amount of the child's itemized deductions that are directly attributable to the child's unearned adjusted gross income.[16]

If net unearned income proves to be greater than the child's total taxable income (computed without any of this complexity), then net unearned income is limited to the taxable income figure.[17] For example, if the child had $10,000 of unearned income, earned income of $100, and itemized deductions of $1,200 (all attributable to the earned income), the

(Footnote Continued)

throwback is contained in § 665(b). Loss of the minority exception could occur because the trust was a "third" trust, as defined in § 667(c). See § 5.6.3 nn.47-48 and accompanying text.

[13] See § 1(g)(4)(A)(ii)(I).

[14] The child's standard deduction is the amount of the child's earned income (not to exceed the normal § 63(c)(2)(C) standard deduction for an unmarried taxpayer) if a child has earned income for the year in excess of the § 63(c)(5)(A) standard deduction amount. This will not, however, change the "standard deduction amount" for Kiddie tax purposes. Even more unlikely, if the child has itemized deductions in excess of the child's standard deduction, the child will likely itemize and not use the standard deduction at all. This too will not change the Kiddie tax "standard deduction amount."

[15] § 1(g)(4)(A)(ii)(II).

[16] Thus, this "general offset amount" should not be confused with the "standard deduction amount," even though both may be determined by reference to the child's § 63(c)(5)(A) standard deduction amount.

[17] § 1(g)(4)(B).

child's taxable income would be $8,900 ($10,100 less $1,200). Even if the child's net unearned income computed under the Kiddie tax would be larger, in this unusual situation net unearned income would be limited to $8,900, being the amount of the child's taxable income.

Computation of the Kiddie tax at the appropriate parent's rates is a simple three-step process. The mechanism is to add the net unearned income figure to the appropriate parent's bottom line taxable income.[18] Using this new taxable income figure, the parent's taxes are then recomputed. The excess (if any) of this recomputed tax over the parent's actual taxes (without the net unearned income) is the amount of the parent's tax attributable to the net unearned income.[19] That increase in the parent's tax, attributable to the net unearned income, is the amount that must be paid by the child on the net unearned income. This tax is *not* paid by the parent unless the § 1(g)(7) election is made to treat the child's income as the parent's and all the technical rules of that provision are met.

The child computes the remaining tax liability on any balance of the child's taxable income (i.e., the child's total taxable income, reduced by the net unearned income amount that was taxed at the parent's rates).[20] In this process, the parent's own computation for payment of the parent's own income taxes is unaffected. Thus, the net unearned income figure will not alter the parent's charitable deduction limitation, percentage floor for miscellaneous itemized deductions, medical expense deduction, casualty loss deduction, or otherwise. The converse also appears to be true. The tax character of the parent's income, deductions, and credits will not infect or alter the taxation of the child's other income.[21]

---

[18] § 1(g)(3)(A)(i).

[19] § 1(g)(3)(A)(ii).

[20] § 1(g)(1)(B)(i). Two computations are required by the child because, if the tax the child would pay on the net unearned income at the child's own rates would be higher (for example, because the parent was in a loss year, or had significant carryover deductions), then the higher tax computed entirely at the child's rates will apply. § 1(g)(1)(A). And the same is true for the Kiddie AMT.

[21] The last sentence of § 1(g)(3)(A) provides that the character of the child's income will not affect the deductions and credits of the parent, but it is silent on whether the character of the parent's income will carry over when the *child's* tax is computed at the parent's rates. Thus, on the face of the statute, the parent's income tax posture could affect the Kiddie tax computation (but presumably not

If the parent's income is later adjusted (for example, on audit), the child's tax on the net unearned income also will be subject to adjustment.[22] Further, if there is more than one child with net unearned income for taxation at the same parent's marginal rates, all such income is aggregated, the aggregate increase is computed, and that aggregate increase is pro rated among the children on the basis of each child's net unearned income.[23] In each case, audit of any of these family member's returns will affect all the minor children's returns, and recomputation of a child's income could introduce a raft of difficult problems involving statutes of limitation (and extensions thereof), notice requirements, settlement procedures, and so forth. Moreover, according to the government, audit of one family member's return could create an underpayment by a child, with a corresponding interest expense liability.[24]

If the child's parents do not file a joint return because the parents are divorced or legally separated, then the parent with custody of the

---

(Footnote Continued)

the tax on the child's other income). For example, if the parent had capital losses and the child had capital gains, or the parent had passive activity losses and the child had passive activity income (or vice versa, in either case), the statute does not preclude netting these items in computing the taxes the parent would have paid had the net unearned income been the parent's own income for the year. Similarly, it would seem that the parent's AMT posture could affect the computation of any Kiddie AMT liability of the child, attributable to the child's net unearned income. Nevertheless, Temp. Treas. Reg. § 1.1(i)-1T Question & Answer 21 states that "a child's net unearned income is not taken into account in computing *any* deduction or credit for purposes of determining . . . the child's allocable parental tax" (emphasis added).

With respect to an accumulation distribution that is not protected by the minority exception from what little remains of the throwback rule, the parent's tax presumably would be computed under Subpart D as if the parent, not the child, had been the beneficiary of the trust during the year of accumulation, and that amount then would be used as the § 1(g) amount that the child must pay. Any other interrelation of the Kiddie tax with Subchapter J will need elucidation, and the Temporary Kiddie tax Regulations state that further guidance will be provided only in the form of future rulings or regulations, of which there have been none.

[22] See Temp. Treas. Reg. § 1.1(i)-1T Question & Answer 17.

[23] § 1(g)(3)(B); Temp. Treas. Reg. § 1.1(i)-1T Question & Answer 5.

[24] See Temp. Treas. Reg. § 1.1(i)-1T Question & Answer 19; no penalties would be imposed.

child is the one whose rates are used.[25] This may be the rule even if the parents have a §152(e)(2) agreement allocating the child's dependency deduction to the noncustodial parent.[26] There is no answer to the question of whose rates are used in the case of divorced or separated parents with joint custody. If the child's parents do not file a joint return but they are not divorced or legally separated, then the parent with the higher marginal bracket is the one whose rates are used.[27]

Planning suggestions for avoiding the Kiddie tax include using Series EE, deep discount, or zero coupon bonds that mature after the child's tax year that would end when the child is beyond the reach of the Kiddie tax, investing in low income growth stock that can be held for sale at a gain after that time, use of a §2503(c) qualified minor's trust that can accumulate income until after the Kiddie tax no longer applies (remembering, however, that trust distribution at age 21 may occur within the window of Kiddie tax application for certain full-time students), or employment of the child (for example, in a family business) so that the child's wages will be earned income that is not subject to the Kiddie tax.

§6.3.3 *Evaluating Alternative Income Shifting Devices*

With these overriding concerns in mind, the special challenge to successful income shifting is to find devices that generate sufficient savings under the current rate regime to make the transactional and other costs worthwhile. Determining whether income shifting is worth considering is as difficult as planning how to do it, because it involves so many variables, including whether:

- the Kiddie tax will apply to thwart any income shifting effort;

- the transaction costs, compliance costs, administration costs, and wealth transfer tax costs of the device used will consume any income shifting advantages;

---

[25] §1(g)(5)(A).

[26] Temp. Treas. Reg. §1.1(i)-1T Question & Answer 12 deals with this issue by providing that the taxable income "of the custodial parent (within the meaning of section 152(e))" shall be used. §152(e) establishes a "deemed support" rule, meaning that the regulation is not helpful unless §152(e) is regarded as also establishing a "deemed custody" rule for purposes of the Kiddie tax.

[27] §1(g)(5)(B).

§6.3.3

- the maximum income tax saving at the current time justifies the device in terms of the effect of the device to lock the parties into a plan through a period of any additional changes that may diminish or destroy the benefits sought;

- there are ancillary benefits to be generated by the device used, such as to shift appreciation in property for wealth transfer tax purposes at the same time income is being shifted; and

- the device, even if generally effective, will run afoul of some special tax rule[28] in a particular situation.

The following discussion is not an exhaustive summary of potential income shifting techniques. Instead, listed below are only methods that all are within the reasonable reach of clients with average amounts of wealth, requiring no large investment and no particularly complex or convoluted transactions. Several have the redeeming grace of ancillary benefits in the form of wealth transfers that make the modest income shifting seem more attractive.

§6.3.3.1 Employment

One easy technique is to employ children or other dependents in hopes of shifting enough earned income to ease the financing of a child's education, support an active but dependent parent, or fund other costly activities. There is nothing new about this traditionally viable income shifting alternative, §73 specifically protects a child's personal services earned income from taxation at a parent's rates, and the Kiddie tax does not apply to earned income. Nevertheless, there are elusive limits to what may be paid as reasonable (deductible)[29] compensation, and any social security tax payments that are required under §3111[30] would increase the cost of such a program.

---

[28] Such as the §667(c) third trust rule or the §677(b) imputed or indirect beneficiary rules. See §§5.6.3 nn.47-48 and accompanying text and 5.11.4 nn.75-91 and accompanying text, respectively.

[29] Rev. Rul. 73-393, 1973-2 C.B. 33, permits the deduction for reasonable wages paid to a child "even though the child uses the wages for part of [the child's] support" that otherwise is the parent's obligation.

[30] Employment of a child under age 18 will qualify for the §3121(b)(3)(A) exception, but domestic service employment not in the course of a trade or business of a child under age 21 or of a parent or other dependent is not likely to qualify for the §3121(b)(3)(B) exception.

§6.3.3.1

§6.3.3.2 Leasebacks and Family Partnerships

Two traditional devices that also have continued vitality are the classic leaseback and family partnership. The use of a trust to hold the subject property in a leaseback or to hold partnership interests in a family partnership must be assessed, and application of the Kiddie tax must be considered. Nevertheless, both devices shift income if traditional cautions are observed.[31]

§6.3.3.3 Qualified Minors' Trusts

Qualified §2503(c) minors' trusts that will accumulate income during minority may be effective to avoid the Kiddie tax and can be used to earn income at the trust's tax rates, assuming that distribution of corpus and accumulated income at the beneficiary's age 21 (or the risk of withdrawal under a rollover-if-not-withdrawn provision) is acceptable, and the grantor trust rules are avoided. The most important hurdle is that no income be taxed to the trust's grantor under the support obligation provisions of §677(b).[32] This is not as easy to accomplish as many

---

[31] As the watershed case involving leaseback transactions, Mathews v. Commissioner, 61 T.C. 12 (1973), rev'd, 520 F.2d 323 (5th Cir. 1975), established the standards for determining whether payments under a lease from a trust to the former owner of the property or a corporation owned by the former owner are deductible business expenses under §162(a)(3): (1) the transferor must not retain substantially the same control over the property that existed before the transfer (use of an independent trustee or cotrustee will meet this requirement); (2) the leaseback normally should be in writing and must require payment of a reasonable rent; and (3) the leaseback (as distinguished from the original transfer) must have a bona fide business purpose. See also Frank Lyon Co. v. United States, 435 U.S. 561 (1978) (different circumstances but leaseback arrangement respected); May v. Commissioner, 723 F.2d 1434 (9th Cir. 1984) (taxpayer victory notwithstanding that transferor was cotrustee and there was no written lease); Rosenfeld v. Commissioner, 706 F.2d 1277 (2d Cir. 1983); Brooke v. United States, 468 F.2d 1155, 1158 (9th Cir. 1972) (transferor conveyed office property outright to children, was appointed their guardian and leased the property back), the court stating that "non-tax motives . . . are abundant and grounded in economic reality. The taxpayer desired to provide for the health and education of his children . . . ; withdraw his assets from the threat of malpractice suits . . . and diminish the ethical conflict arising from the ownership of a medical practice with an adjoining pharmacy"; Quinlivan v. Commissioner, 599 F.2d 269 (8th Cir. 1979); Lerner v. Commissioner, 71 T.C. 290 (1978).

[32] See §5.11.4 nn.75-91 and accompanying text.

drafters assume, because § 677(b) does *not* require that distributions be made that *satisfy* or *discharge* a grantor's obligation of support.[33]

Instead, § 677(b) taxes the grantor to the extent income is distributed for the support or maintenance of anyone the grantor is obliged to support or maintain—even if those distributions do not serve to satisfy or discharge the obligation. Thus, a so-called "Upjohn clause"[34]—prohibiting distributions that have the effect of discharging anyone's legal obligation of support or maintenance—is not sufficient to prevent taxation of distributed income to the grantor under § 677(b). To avoid this inclusion, distributions for the support or maintenance of the beneficiary must be forbidden (as they would be in a SNT, but typically not otherwise). And, although § 677(b) *is* easy to avoid (if the grantor is willing to prohibit the trustee from making distributions for the support or maintenance of anyone the grantor is obligated to support or maintain), this may be too high a price to pay because of the flexibility it denies to the trustee.[35]

---

[33] Although Treas. Reg. § 1.677(b)-1(d) makes reference to "the satisfaction of the grantor's legal obligation to support or maintain a beneficiary," a careful reading of this provision reveals that it does not address § 677(b) liability at all and that this statement is both irrelevant to § 677(b) and is inconsistent with §§ 1.677(b)-1(a), -1(b) and 1.662(a)-4. The careful practitioner is cautioned not to be mislead by statements to the contrary by commentators not well acquainted with this little understood provision. See §§ 5.11.4 nn.75-91 and accompanying text, 7.1.1.10 n.100, 7.1.1.10.1, and 7.3.4.2 nn.153-172 and accompanying text with respect to § 677(b) and the discharge of obligation theory.

[34] So named after the case of Upjohn v. United States, 72-2 U.S. Tax Cas. (CCH) ¶ 12,888 (W.D. Mich. 1972) (clause prohibiting distributions that discharge grantor's obligations did not constitute a "substantial restriction" for purposes of § 2503(c)). Today Upjohn provisions also may prohibit any distribution that would decrease a beneficiary's entitlement to public benefits.

Treas. Reg. § 25.2503-4(b)(1) specifies that there must be "no substantial restrictions under the terms of the trust instrument on the exercise of [the trustee's § 2503(c)(1) mandated] discretion" to make distributions of income or corpus to the beneficiary prior to reaching age 21. It is unlikely that a third-party SNT also could qualify as a qualified minor's trust, although there appears to be no authority on point. Nor is there authority on the question whether such a limitation might be regarded as a "substantial restriction." Thus, it probably is wise not to include this added restriction in a trust that is meant to qualify as a § 2503(c) qualified minor's trust.

[35] It also may constitute a substantial restriction that would disqualify a trust that otherwise would meet the § 2503(c) qualified minor's trust requirements.

If the trust was created for income shifting, and not because the income is needed for the support or maintenance of the beneficiary, the trust can authorize distributions with the notion that distributions for the beneficiary's support or maintenance will not actually be made unless something unusual occurs. Therefore, income in the trust will not be taxable to the grantor under §677(b). This should be acceptable if the grantor lives in a state in which higher education is not part of the legal obligation of support, or if the grantor is not a parent with a legal support obligation. Furthermore, this planning implies an understanding that trust income distributed for education may be taxed to the grantor in states in which higher education *is* part of a grantor's legal obligation. It may be possible to minimize the impact of this by engineering investment in those years to minimize the income yield or to produce tax exempt income, but this consequence often cannot be avoided entirely.

Without creating §673 grantor trust liability a §2503(c) trust's grantor may retain a reversion on the beneficiary's death before age 21, if the minor beneficiary is a lineal descendant.[36] However, because of the wealth transfer tax consequences of a retained reversion,[37] it is not recommended that this be done unless there is no other viable contingent beneficiary if the trust becomes distributable because of the beneficiary's untimely death. For the same reason, it is not recommended that a taxpayer engage in planning that permits a trust reversion to qualify for the §673(a) 5% reversion exception. The wealth transfer tax cost probably is not worth the effort.

---

[36] See §673(b) and §5.11.2 nn.45-46 and accompanying text.

[37] Inclusion could result to the grantor under §2037 if, at the grantor's death, the value of the retained reversion exceeded 5% of the value of the trust itself and some other beneficiary was named to take the property if the grantor dies before the reversion became possessory. Moreover, full inclusion will result under §2033 if the reversion becomes possessory before the grantor's death, meaning that the grantor will have paid gift tax on creation of the trust (presumably the amount of the gift would be nearly 100% of the value of the trust) and then paid estate tax on the value of the property received back from the trust, with no §2001(b) purge of the prior gift from the estate tax computation base (because the gift was of the income interest transferred and the estate tax inclusion is of the value of the reversion received after that income interest terminated).

§6.3.3.3

§6.3.3.4 IDGTs

Much traditional income shifting planning is directed at shifting income to a minor, such as a child or grandchild, but many potential consumers of income shifting advice also need to find ways to reduce the cost to support an elderly dependent, such as a parent. One manner to accomplish this is to create a trust, income to parent for life, remainder to the transferor's children. Income from this trust would be regarded as the parent's income for income tax purposes, which may allow it to be taxed at a lower income tax bracket than if the income was received by the transferor and transferred after tax to the parent.[38]

Care is required, however, because causing this income to belong to the parent may create problems in qualification for certain governmental benefits[39] or in determining the standard deduction and personal exemption of the transferor who may claim the parent as a dependent. Therefore, special caution should be exercised to ascertain the effect of the income shift on the level of support being provided by the transferor directly and whether the transferor could lose the added personal exemption otherwise available under §151(c)(1)(A) for supporting the parent. It also is wise to consider how many standard deductions are available to the parent under §63(c)(3) (for aged or blind taxpayers) and whether they will be regained under §63(c)(5) if the parent no longer is a dependent of the transferor.

Transferors who wish to avoid the potential problems created by such a trust may find a form of IDGT planning appropriate.[40] For example, a transferor's child who has funds (perhaps representing gifts from the transferor) could place the property in trust to pay income to the transferor's parent (grandparent of transferor's child), with a reversion to the child as grantor on the death of the transferor's parent. This

---

[38] Subject again to §677(b), which is not limited to the obligation to support or maintain children. See §5.11.4 nn.75-91 and accompanying text. In some states a child may have an obligation to support an otherwise destitute parent. See Moskowitz, Adult Children and Indigent Parents: Intergenerational Responsibilities in International Perspective, 86 Marq. L. Rev. 401, 421-429 (2002). Therefore, it is possible that §677(b) would apply to prevent taxation to the parent to the extent the income instead is taxable to the grantor.

[39] See generally §4.4.

[40] See §5.11.2.

reversion would create grantor trust treatment to the child under § 673 if the reversion is valued in excess of 5% of the value of the trust, making trust income taxable to the child, not to the transferor's parent. In such a case, the transferor effectively would be providing (through the gift to the child) the means to support the transferor's parent (with funds that belong to the child for wealth transfer tax purposes), taxing the income therefrom as the child's income rather than either the transferor's income or, more important, as income of the transferor's parent.

Even if the income tax bracket of the child is no lower than the income tax bracket of the transferor, this transaction would work wealth shifting objectives without giving the parent property that might avoid the loss of governmental benefits that otherwise are available to the parent.

In addition, this would avoid giving the parent income that could affect the ability of the transferor to claim the parent as a dependent and, although probably not a concern in most cases in which a parent needs assistance, this approach also would avoid any wealth transfer taxation when the transferor's parent dies.

§ 6.3.3.5 *Crown* Loans

Demand loans at below-market-rate interest (*Crown* loans)[41] may make sense for an asset-rich lender (such as a retired parent) whose income tax bracket is no higher than a cash-poor borrower (such as a highly compensated but financially strapped child with large monetary obligations) who the lender wishes to benefit.[42] In such a transaction, the

---

[41] So named after Crown v. Commissioner, 585 F.2d 234 (7th Cir. 1978), aff'g 67 T.C. 1060 (1977), which remained viable until the decision in Dickman v. Commissioner, 465 U.S. 330 (1984), and the eventual adoption of § 7872.

[42] Note that, if the loan is for a term certain, the *Crown* loan approach may not work as intended because the timing aspects of § 7872 may not correlate as intended with any allowable interest expense deduction under § 163. If the loan is for a term the § 7872 interest received by the lender and the gift made by the lender fall into the year of the loan (based on the term of the loan), but the borrower's § 163 interest expense deduction is allowed, if at all, only in each year in which interest is deemed to have been paid (and a determination is made on the deductibility of the deemed payment in that year).

lender is deemed to make a gift to the borrower[43] in the amount of market interest that is forgone (thereby potentially incurring a gift tax liability),[44] and is deemed to receive imputed interest from the borrower (which may result in an income tax liability to the lender).[45] One

[43] Although not the subject of this section, care must be exercised that the loan itself not be regarded as a gift. See § 6.4.2.

[44] In the context of a sale for installment payments, foregone market-rate interest can produce a gift even if there is no imputed interest under § 483 for income tax purposes. See, e.g., GCM 39566 (conveyance of a farm in exchange for a note having a face amount less than the value of the farm and bearing interest below the prevailing rate, concluding that there was a taxable gift under § 2501 because the note bore interest at only the test rate under § 483 rather than the higher prevailing AFR); Krabbenhoft v. Commissioner, 94 T.C. 887 (1990) (a reviewed opinion), aff'd, 939 F.2d 529 (8th Cir. 1991) (sale on installments with interest pegged at the § 483(e)(1) 6% rate to avoid unstated interest being imputed for income tax purposes; because an 11% interest rate would have been more appropriate (given the fact that the prime rate was over 20% and first mortgages and Treasury obligations carried interest of over 13% at the time) the notes (discounted to present value) were worth less than the property transferred and part-sale, part-gift treatment therefore applied, the court holding that § 483 is not applicable for all purposes under all parts of the Code and, specifically, was irrelevant to a determination of the present value of a gift for gift tax purposes; § 483 is limited to a determination for all tax purposes whether a payment is properly treated as interest or principal, but this characterization does not affect whether the aggregate of those payments is full and adequate compensation for the property transferred to avoid a gift on the transaction); Schusterman v. United States, 94-1 U.S. Tax Cas. (CCH) ¶ 60,161 (N.D. Okla. 1994), aff'd, 63 F.3d 986 (10th Cir. 1995); Lundquist v. United States, 99-1 U.S. Tax Cas. (CCH) ¶ 60,336 (N.D. N.Y. 1999); Frazee v. Commissioner, 98 T.C. 554 (1992); Estate of True v. Commissioner, 82 T.C.M. (CCH) 27 (2001); but see Ballard v. Commissioner, 854 F.2d 185 (7th Cir. 1988), rev'g 53 T.C.M. (CCH) 323 (1987) (purchase price paid in annual installments with simple interest at 6%, although the contract was executed when the interest charged by banks was 20%); the court on appeal held that § 483 is applicable for gift tax purposes, stating:

> We conclude that § 483 meant what it clearly said, that it applied for purposes of Title 26 which includes both income and gift tax provisions. Mrs. Ballard properly relied on the "safe harbor" rate of interest provided in § 483 when she filed her 1981 gift tax return. Consequently, the Commissioner's assessment of gift taxes was improper.

854 F.2d at 189.

[45] § 7872. Rev. Rul. 86-17, 1986-1 C.B. 377, describes generally the computation of the forgone interest in the case of certain below-market-interest loans, which

§ 6.3.3.5

planning attraction underlying the *Crown* loan approach is the lender's ability to pay this income tax liability without an additional gift taxable transfer to the borrower, as illustrated next.

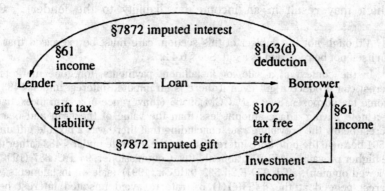

In a traditional *Crown* loan, the borrower should qualify to deduct the deemed payment of interest to the lender to the extent the borrower has investment income attributable to the loan,[46] allowing the borrower to shelter income earned by investment of the borrowed funds. The

(Footnote Continued)

is treated as transferred from the lender to the borrower and then returned by the borrower to the lender as interest.

[46] § 163(d). Winter v. United States, 91-2 U.S. Tax Cas. (CCH) ¶ 50,436 (Ct. Cl. 1991), aff'd in an unpublished opinion (Fed. Cir. 1992), held that the imputed gift flowing from an interest free demand loan does not generate an imputed interest expense deduction for the borrower under § 163. Decided without reference to § 7872 (adopted in 1984) because the loans involved were made in 1982, the court relied on Dickman v. Commissioner, 465 U.S. 330 (1984), as establishing the gift tax liability of the loan. Focusing principally on the requirement in § 163 that interest be accrued or paid to be deductible, the court rejected the taxpayer's argument that the *Dickman* interest free loan analysis presupposes imputed payments from the lender to the borrower (the gift element) and back from the borrower to the lender as interest paid. According to the court, "the net economic reality . . . is that the recipient of the loan has received property with tangible value, yet given nothing in exchange" and that

> whatever interest obligation is in theory generated initially is then forgiven by the lender. . . .
>
> . . . This court will not recognize as fact what is in reality fiction—the payment of interest by the donee of an interest-free loan. Plaintiff has neither paid nor accrued interest and is not entitled to a deduction under section 163.

§ 6.3.3.5

lender has income from the imputed interest payment, effectively resulting in the lender paying the tax incurred on income that essentially was earned "tax-free" by the borrower.[47]

This is not, however, as "unique" or appealing a result as some might suggest, nor is it as abusive as the government might allege, because similar results are available if the lender simply invests the loan fund, earns the income therefrom and gives that pre-tax income to the borrower, paying the income tax on that income from other assets. In this event, the borrower winds up with the same cash flow, again without paying income tax thereon. If the lender and the borrower are in the same income tax bracket (or the lender is in a lower bracket), either transaction would be effective to give a benefit to the borrower—at an identical gift tax cost in each case.

The *Crown* loan transaction *can* be the better of the two alternatives *if* the borrower earns more on investment of the borrowed funds than could the lender (and more than the § 7872 AFR). In such a case, a larger effective gift of the use of the money occurs than is taken into consideration under § 7872.[48] Another advantage of the *Crown* loan approach is that it allows the borrower to invest the loaned amount, which

---

(Footnote Continued)

91-2 U.S. Tax Cas. at 89,592-89,593. If this conclusion is correct, then it should follow that the lender has no income tax liability flowing from the transaction. If no interest has been paid by the borrower, the lender cannot have interest income. Presumably a different result would be reached on both the income and deduction issues if § 7872 were applicable, § 7872(a)(1) specifying that "in the case of any below-market loan to which this section applies and which is a gift loan or a demand loan, the forgone interest shall be treated as—(A) transferred from the lender to the borrower, and (B) retransferred by the borrower to the lender as interest."

[47] If the borrower earns less on the invested fund than § 7872 imputes to the lender, the *Crown* loan imposes a cost on the lender that is not matched by the borrower's deduction, making this a less desirable form of planning.

[48] There would be no income tax advantage to the interest earned in excess of the § 7872 applicable rate because the excess would be taxed to the borrower with no § 163 interest expense deduction to wash that extra income. A relief provision for loans not in excess of $100,000 limits § 7872 imputed interest to the lender to the amount of investment income earned by the borrower. § 7872(d)(1). If the borrower can earn *more* than the amount imputed to the lender, however, the situation presented here is even more favorable than if the § 7872(d)(1) relief provision was applicable.

§ 6.3.3.5

may be wise for psychological reasons or because the lender is either unwilling or unable to invest as wisely as the borrower. It also allows the borrower to invest for capital appreciation that will not inflate the lender's net worth.

Furthermore, a "safe harbor" provision permits de minimis interest free loans with no income tax consequences. By § 7872(c)(2), a gift loan that does not exceed $10,000 on any given day is excepted from § 7872 treatment, provided the borrowed funds are not used to acquire income producing property. This could be a modest means of assisting the borrower in acquiring a home or other property for personal use, or to fund educational, health, or other needs. This is, however, only an indirect method of shifting income, in the sense that the lender is forsaking investment income from the loan fund while the borrower is avoiding the need to borrow funds in a commercial transaction that would incur an interest expense.

In a sense, the transaction described above—in which the lender (Parent) is in a lower income tax bracket than the borrower (Child)—is a "reverse" *Crown* loan, the exact opposite of the traditional situation in which interest-free demand loans were common before adoption of § 7872. A more dramatic example of the "reverse" loan approach may succeed in circumstances that are more familiar. Here, however, the use of trusts, the Kiddie tax, and limits on the deduction of interest should be considered carefully. Under this format, a low income tax bracket lender, such as Child, loans property at below market rates to a high bracket borrower, such as Parent. By operation of § 7872, the hope is to shift the income tax incidence to the lender (the low bracket taxpayer) even though the borrower (the high bracket taxpayer) invests the loan proceeds and enjoys the cash flow generated thereby.[49]

---

[49] See, e.g., Estate of Flandreau v. Commissioner, 63 T.C.M. (CCH) 2512 (1992), aff'd, 994 F.2d 91 (2d Cir. 1993) (decedent made gifts to children and their spouses and contemporaneously borrowed the funds back interest free in what the court regarded as a single integrated transaction; because the notes were not sooner repaid, the estate claimed a § 2053(a)(3) deduction for claims against the estate in the amount of these notes, which the court rejected based on a § 2053(c)(1)(A) lack of consideration, stating that the transaction evidenced an improper effort to retain enjoyment and control of transferred property while seeking to remove it from the estate for federal estate tax purposes).

§ 6.3.3.5

Like a traditional *Crown* loan, this transaction puts the investment income in the hands of the borrower (Parent) with income tax liability at the lender's (Child) level. And the transaction may be more attractive than a traditional plan because this approach does not shift wealth. It merely produces income for the high bracket borrower at an income tax cost computed at the lender's lower brackets. That is, Parent gets to enjoy the investment income, but at an income tax cost computed at Child's rates. This is income shifting without loss of the income earned, which is probably far more attractive to many clients than the wealth shifting attribute of the more traditional *Crown* loan.

This approach requires that Child, as the low bracket lender, have some assets with which to make the loan and pay the tax on the imputed income, and may cause the Kiddie tax to apply and defeat the deal if the lender is a child who is still under the age of 19 (or 24 if a full-time student). Gifts from grandparents might work as a successful source of the loan fund (although state law must be consulted to judge whether the lender has power under local law to make a loan to the borrower). This form of planning may put added pressure on GST direct skip transfers from grandparents and much greater emphasis should be placed on these forms of gifting[50] with the annual exclusion and ed/med expense exceptions to the GST direct skip rules.[51]

In addition, the government may be able to collapse sham transactions—which is what the government is likely to argue if the source of the loan proceeds was a prior gift (even an old and cold one) from the borrower to the lender. For example, in Rev. Rul. 86-106,[52] the taxpayer created a then-effective short-term trust with a reversion (today a trust with no reversion would be used) for minor children, contributed cash to the trust and proceeded to borrow the corpus back within 15 days thereafter pursuant to an oral agreement with the trustee. The note provided for payment of adequate interest, the loan was adequately

---

[50] It is conceivable that the government would argue that a grandparent to grandchild gift with loan back to parent should be treated as a grandparent to parent gift by collapsing the transaction. That treatment should fail if the transaction is properly documented for gift tax purposes at the grandparent level and for both income and gift tax purposes at the grandchild level.

[51] See §§ 2611(b)(2), 2612(c)(1) and 2642(c)(1).

[52] 1986-2 C.B. 28.

§6.3.3.5

secured, and the trustee was neither related nor subordinate. Therefore, §675(3) was avoided, meaning that grantor trust exposure was not generated by the transaction.

The Ruling produced pseudo §675(3) results by denying an interest expense deduction to the grantor[53]—meaning that investment income received on the borrowed funds would not be offset with an interest expense deduction, causing taxation to the grantor.[54] According to the Ruling:[55]

> For interest to be deductible, the payments must arise from genuine indebtedness. . . . In this instance . . . the parties have failed to create a genuine debtor-creditor relationship . . . . The trust was merely a conduit for [the taxpayer] to lend money to himself because of the prearrangement with the trustee to have the corpus returned in the form of a loan. The trust and loan serve no purpose except to create a circular flow of money designed to create a tax deduction for gifts to [the children] in the amount of the purported interest. This transaction is not a loan in substance. Under the facts in the present situation, the note is a gratuitous promise to make a series of gifts in the future. Because a genuine debtor-creditor relationship was not created, [the taxpayer] may not deduct the annual payments to the trust.

The Ruling did not state, but it should be the result, that treating the payment of interest as a gift to deny the taxpayer's interest expense deduction means there could be no imputed income to the trust and no gift upon creation. Instead, if the payment of interest is treated as a series of gifts, the taxpayer should be able to apply the gift tax annual exclusion against those gifts. The bottom line, however, (assuming this

---

[53] In Karlin v. Commissioner, 54 T.C.M. (CCH) 1381 (1987), in addition to preventing the interest expense deduction, the government successfully imposed a §6653 negligence penalty, but only because the taxpayer was unable to sustain the burden of proving that there had been a bona fide gift to children in a prior year and then a bona fide loan back to the taxpayer in the years in question.

[54] In a leaseback related situation the government might be tempted to deny a rental expense deduction on similar grounds—that there was no bona fide leasehold transaction. See §6.3.3.2.

[55] 1986-2 C.B. at 28-29 (citations omitted).

§6.3.3.5

consistent treatment) is that no income would be shifted by the transaction.[56]

Although involving a different series of steps, Wilken v. Commissioner,[57] Strimling v. Commissioner,[58] and TAM 8709001 each concluded that taxpayers failed to create bona fide debts to trusts, with consistent results. Only slightly different, Rev. Rul. 87-69[59] involved a parental gift outright to a child who immediately loaned the funds back to the parent, again with denial of an interest expense deduction to the parent and, instead, treatment of each purported loan interest payment as one in a series of gifts. Of them all, Rev. Rul. 86-106 is the most troubling because it is premised on authorities[60] that involved payment of less than adequate interest, making them fundamentally distinguishable, and the TAM went out of its way to also find the trust involved was a grantor trust, on grounds that were spurious.[61]

---

[56] This is the same result that would apply under §675(3), raising a strong presumption that the result reached is wrong. That is, it should not be proper to conclude that avoidance of the specific grantor trust rule properly results in the same consequences as if the grantor trust rule had applied.

[57] 53 T.C.M. (CCH) 965 (1987) (taxpayer borrowed from a bank to create a trust from which taxpayer then borrowed the full corpus to repay the bank).

[58] 734 F.2d 1377 (9th Cir. 1984), aff'g 46 T.C.M. (CCH) 211 (1983) (taxpayer created a trust with $10 cash and a "note" payable by the taxpayer to the trust that was regarded as unenforceable because supported by no consideration; the government was upheld in denying deductibility of the interest paid, with the ultimate effect being that alleged interest payments were regarded as gifts in the year paid, with no income shifting effect).

[59] 1987-2 C.B. 46.

[60] The government relied primarily on Perrett v. Commissioner, 74 T.C. 111 (1980) (taxpayer loaned monies to a trust at 3% interest, then immediately borrowed them back at 6%), and Rev. Rul. 82-94, 1982-1 C.B. 31 (interest-free loan to child with borrow-back at interest).

[61] The TAM stated, without appreciating the difference between retaining a power and merely acting with the consent of a trustee who is in breach of the terms of the trust:

Although the terms of the trust agreement provide that the trust is not subject to modification or amendment, one month after the trust was established it was, in fact amended by . . . the grantors . . . . Therefore, from the inception of the trust, [the grantors] have possessed the power to affect the beneficial enjoyment of the . . . trust, and this power . . . is not within one of the enumerated exceptions of section 674(b), (c) or (d).

§6.3.3.5

More importantly, both Revenue Rulings are wrong on policy grounds. The donee (trust or child, respectively) could have loaned the gifted dollars to any borrower other than the taxpayer for the same interest and security. And there would have been no question about the donee having received income that would be taxable to the donee (or the trust's beneficiaries). Similarly, payment of the same interest would have been deductible if the donor had borrowed money from any lender other than the donee. There was no abuse in these situations, other than the fact that the taxpayer in each was using a then effective Clifford trust or a completed gift to the child to accomplish a permissible form of income shifting.[62]

(Footnote Continued)

> Accordingly, [the grantors] are treated as the owners of . . . the trust pursuant to section 674.
>
> Further, [the grantors] are treated as the owners of the entire trust under section 675 of the Code. The circumstances attendant on the operation of the trust from its inception is such that administrative control has been exercised primarily for the benefit of the grantors, as evidenced by the fact that the trustee has not adjusted interest rates pursuant to the terms of the mortgage note. Also, although the trust agreement provides that no person shall have the power to deal with the corpus of the trust for less than an adequate consideration of money's worth, the trustee did allow the trust's mortgage lien to be subordinated to another lien so that [the grantors] could obtain another loan. [The grantors] gave no consideration to the trustee for agreeing to the subordination. Consequently, [the grantors] had the power, without the consent of any adverse party, to deal with the corpus of the trust for less than an adequate consideration in money or money's worth. Therefore, pursuant to section 675(1) of the Code and section 1.671-3(b)(3) of the regulations, [the grantors] are treated as the owners of the entire trust.
>
> Because [the grantors] are treated as the owners of the entire trust they are considered to be the owners of the mortgage note for federal income tax purposes. Rev. Rul. 85-13. . . . Accordingly, no deduction is allowed to [the grantors] under section 163 of the Code for interest payments made on their own note.

[62] In *Wilken* and *Strimling*, however, it is easy to see that no legitimate transfers occurred, because no wealth existed either before the transaction or after the shuffle of documents, leaving the purported donors owing money to the ostensible donees with what the *Wilken* court characterized as an unenforceable promise to repay notes at some time in the future. Although not significantly different, it is important that the Revenue Rulings involved a true transfer of

§6.3.3.5

A prudent counselor should advise a client who is in a position to make the transfer of funds in a case like these not to borrow back from the trust. To the extent that advice is not taken, then any loan back to the transferor should be at an interest rate that does not *exceed* the §7872 interest rate. Otherwise too high a payment may constitute a disguised gift that would generate an additional gift tax and denial of any otherwise available §163(d) interest expense deduction.[63] Similar cautions probably need not be exercised if the grantor and the borrower are not the same person, although conservative advisors will regard the grantor's spouse as being the grantor for these purposes, in light of §672(e).

An interesting juxtaposition is posed to all of these developments by Kuga v. United States.[64] The taxpayer purchased a townhouse in July, using in part monies the taxpayer borrowed at market rates from the taxpayer's parents. The parents moved into the townhouse in August and began paying rent to the taxpayer, who took deductions for depreciation and for interest paid to the parents. The government attempted to disallow those deductions under §280A on the ground that the rent being paid was not a fair rent (due to the taxpayer's "offsetting return" of interest on the loan) and that the parents' use of the townhouse therefore constituted a personal family use. The government also alleged that the loan and lease were sham transactions and should be disregarded. The court rejected both arguments, finding that the loan and the lease were independent, legitimate transactions, giving some solace to planners involved in leaseback transactions. The loanback should be treated no differently.

A final consideration in the context of below-market-interest loans is that the interplay of §7872 and the normal Subchapter J income distribu-

---

(Footnote Continued)

wealth that did exist and that the donee was not required to lend back to the donor to allow the transaction to work.

[63] Cf. Barton v. Commissioner, 38 T.C.M. (CCH) 933 (1979) (loan from stepfather to stepson at 60% interest), holding that the parties entered into a bona fide loan arrangement and the interest payment was deductible. Quaere the result had the loan been from the child to the parent.

[64] 87-2 U.S. Tax Cas. (CCH) ¶ 9449 (E.D. Va. 1987).

§6.3.3.5

tion rules may cause these transactions not to work if a trust for the benefit of a lender-child is employed, as illustrated below.[65]

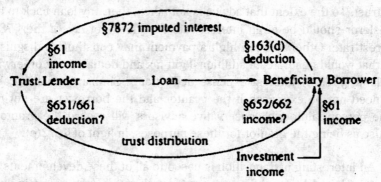

In this case, if the lender is a trust, presumably the borrower is a beneficiary of the trust (because the trustee probably needs specific authority to make such a loan—to avoid breach of fiduciary duty problems—which authority probably raises the borrower to the status of a beneficiary).

If the illustrated treatment is correct, then the imputed interest to the trust as lender should be regarded like any other income that is includible in DNI that can be carried out to whomever is regarded as receiving trust distributions. The question arises whether the trust is entitled to a distributions deduction with respect to the imputed amount deemed transferred to the borrower. If no interest payments actually are

---

[65] To analyze the §7872 consequences of a below-market-interest loan made by a trust to an individual, the following discussion assumes that §7872 applies to a below-market-rate loan from a trust to a third party, notwithstanding that this assumption is in some doubt because a trust loan does not fit easily into any of the three principal categories of §7872 loans: gift loans (because only natural persons—who would be subject to the estate tax at death—can make gifts under the gift tax, Treas. Reg. §25.2501-1(a)(1), and, although the income tax treatment of a gift is not necessarily the same as the gift tax treatment of a gift, it seems likely that this is not a gift loan for purposes of §7872), an employer to employee loan, and a corporation to shareholder loan. Nevertheless, the §7872(c)(1)(D) (tax avoidance loans) or §7872(c)(1)(E) (other below-market-interest loans as provided in regulations) categories may apply. For purposes of this discussion, the grantor trust rules of §675(3) are ignored, and the assumption is that the borrower is not the grantor (although the §7872 results should not be affected by the identity of the borrower).

§6.3.3.5

received and there is no other income in the trust, it is difficult to see how there could be a distribution as to which § 652 or § 662 would impute income to the distributee or as to which § 651 or § 661 would give the trust a distributions deduction. If this is a simple trust, however, it might be argued that income of the trust (including imputed income) is taxable to the beneficiaries, even if not distributed.

More importantly, in either a simple or a complex trust, the reduced interest loan effectively makes the borrower a beneficiary of the trust, which ought to cause the imputed distribution to constitute a § 651 or § 661 distribution with § 652 or § 662 income carryout consequences to the borrower. Indeed, if the borrower is deemed to be a beneficiary by virtue of the below-market-interest loan, it might be argued that the borrower and any other beneficiaries should share the trust's DNI the same as any other beneficiaries would share income under the rules of Subchapter J.

The proper treatment of this transaction under Subchapter J, in conjunction with § 7872, thus appears to involve a three step analysis. First, the trust as lender should receive income equal to the imputed interest, which is includible in DNI. Second, the loan should make the borrower a de facto beneficiary of the trust.[66] As a trust beneficiary, the imputed distribution under § 7872 should constitute a distribution to the borrower for purposes of §§ 651 and 652 or §§ 661 and 662, carrying DNI out to the borrower and giving the trust a distributions deduction equal to its imputed interest income.

---

[66] Presumably the document authorizes such loans and the borrower should be treated as a beneficiary for tax purposes whether specifically identified as a beneficiary under the trust document or only made a permissible borrower under a general power to make such loans. If below-market-interest loans are not authorized under the terms of the trust (specifically identifying a particular permissible borrower or class of permissible borrowers), presumably such a loan is improper as a diversion of trust income to nonbeneficiaries or as a failure to make corpus productive of a reasonable amount of income. See 3 Scott, Fratcher, & Ascher, Scott and Ascher on Trusts § 17.13 (5th ed. 2007); 4 Scott, Fratcher, & Ascher, Scott and Ascher on Trusts § 24.31 (5th ed. 2007). In such a case, the trustee could be regarded as the lender in its personal capacity because the loan otherwise is a breach of trust, or the beneficiaries of the trust could be regarded as the lender by virtue of having authorized the loan. In either case the tax consequences should be determined under § 7872 with either the trustee or each beneficiary regarded as the lender in their individual capacities.

§ 6.3.3.5

Finally, independent of Subchapter J, the borrower should receive a §163(d) investment interest expense deduction, which should balance the income under §652 or §662 from the imputed distribution and any income earned from its investment of the borrowed funds. The net result is as if the trust as lender invested the borrowed money, received income, and made a distribution of the earned amount to the borrower, with a DNI carryout and ultimate taxation to the borrower.

The transaction as described becomes slightly more complicated if distributions are made to another beneficiary during the year. Notwithstanding the existence of the borrower and the loan, if the trust is a simple trust all other income presumably would be taxed to the beneficiary and the results above involving the borrower would be unaffected. If, however, the trust is a complex trust (because it is not required to distribute all income annually or because it makes distributions in excess of current income), then the tier rules[67] must be considered. By the mandatory nature of the deemed income distribution to the borrower, it would be appropriate to regard the borrower as a first tier beneficiary. If the other beneficiary is a second tier beneficiary, then that other beneficiary should bear no portion of the tax on the imputed income in this situation because that imputed income should be carried out first to the borrower as a first tier beneficiary. This seems particularly appropriate because otherwise the beneficiary would indirectly pay tax on income the borrower "received" by virtue of the reduced interest loan.

If, however, the other beneficiary also is a first tier beneficiary, then DNI should be carried out to each of the borrower and the other beneficiary in the full amount of their distributions, whether imputed or actual, and the results to the borrower should remain the same. Only in the event that the borrower and the other beneficiary are treated as equals (that is, as first tier beneficiaries or as beneficiaries of a simple trust) and DNI is less than the aggregate actual and imputed distributions of income would the end result be affected. In such a case DNI should be prorated between the two, meaning that the borrower would benefit from those deductions or adjustments in the trust that caused DNI to be less than the total actual and imputed income available for distribution. Although this may seem inappropriate, it is thought to be

---

[67] See §5.4.2.

§6.3.3.5

proper because the borrower essentially is in the position of a named beneficiary, and it is difficult to view the other beneficiaries as somehow more entitled to the benefit of those items that reduce DNI below the amount of income actually distributed.

Notable about this suggested treatment of a reduced interest loan from a trust is that it produces a result that is exactly the opposite of a gift loan between individuals. Income coming into the trust is carried right back out to the borrower, causing a tax wash to the trust as the lender and income to the borrower as a beneficiary. This would defeat the reverse-*Crown* loan objective but accomplish the result reached in the original *Crown* loan, which is to shift income to the borrower. If the lender was not a trust, it would have imputed income under § 7872 with no distributions deduction to wash that income out, and the borrower would have an interest expense deduction with no DNI inclusion to balance against that benefit.

Although it might impress some that this difference in result indicates that the analysis here is improper, it seems realistic to view such a loan differently when made in the context of a trust because the loan truly constitutes the borrower as a trust beneficiary like any others who receive beneficial enjoyment from the trust. In any event, if the analysis is correct, it alters the economics of below-market-interest loans involving a trust, as compared to those made directly by a grantor to a beneficiary.

It is unlikely that a UTMA or UGMA account could be used if a low-bracket lender is a minor (who is nevertheless no longer subject to the Kiddie tax), because state law would not authorize below-market-interest loans from such an account.[68] Thus, a guardian of the property of the minor presumably would be necessary and, even in such a case, the guardian might be reluctant to make such a loan due to the obviously disadvantageous nature of the transaction to the minor. As a consequence, this form of planning may be available only if the child as lender

---

[68] Although § 13 of the UTMA authorizes the custodian to act in the same manner that unmarried adult owners may act with respect to their own property, the comment to that provision makes it clear that this authority is subject to the prudent person rule in § 12 of the Act, which presumably would preclude any non-income producing investment that also generates no growth.

is of legal age to either make the loan or consent to it being made by a fiduciary acting on the child's behalf. Below-market-interest loans from trusts that shift the income tax liability to the borrower may be worth considering in their own right, however, given the high income tax brackets in which trusts are taxed, although a distribution of trust income to the beneficiary should effect the same result in most cases.

§6.3.3.6 Shifting Opportunities

A form of "gifting" and income shifting effected by "shifting opportunities" requires less wealth in the form of property in the hands of a low bracket taxpayer. To illustrate, Parent informs Child of a certain-to-succeed business opportunity that Child pursues and earns a profit that Parent otherwise would have generated. This form of transaction is not subject to the gift tax (which applies only to transfers of "property," not to sharing knowledge or services)[69] and effectively produces wealth that is income taxable to Child rather than to Parent.

The difficult problems that arises from such a deal are whether Parent may (or even should) make gifts or loans to Child, to be used by Child to invest in the opportunity, or the tax consequences if Parent instead guarantees a loan taken by Child for these purposes. The direct Parent to Child gift or loan raises the possibility that the government would argue that a step or sham transaction has occurred, or that Parent acquired the opportunity and later gave it to Child. With respect to a guarantee, significant gift or discharge of indebtedness income considerations would arise if Parent is never called upon to make good on the guarantee. Giving the guarantee alone may be totally tax free—because Parent's net worth has not been diminished or transferred. At most it should be treated as a gift only of the value of the guarantee—presumably what Child would pay an independent third party to obtain the guarantee (which could be quite expensive in some circumstances).

Similarly, a donor who owns an option that is transferable (for example, an ISO that is transferable within a limited group of potential donees, such as lineal descendants) may transfer the option at its present gift tax value, effectively allowing the transferee to seize any

---

[69] § 2501(a)(1). See Caron, Taxing Opportunity, 14 Va. Tax Rev. 347 (1994).

future growth in the property that is the subject of the option. These types of options, typically ISOs issued by a corporate employer, are a common retirement benefit that present a popular gifting opportunity because of the perception that the gift tax value at the time the option is assigned is much less than the value of the stock that may be acquired by exercise of the option. PLRs 9722022, 9725032, and 9737015 all involved stock options that permitted the holder to acquire stock at a specified striking price that was less than FMV at the time the option was exercised. They addressed several important issues, although not all in any one of the PLRs.

For example, if there is no § 421(b) disqualifying disposition prior to satisfaction of the holding period requirements, the first and third PLRs articulated the government's position that income accrues to the transferor when the option is exercised by the transferee. The amount equals the difference between the FMV of the stock acquired by exercise and the striking price. That is a traditional application of the income tax valuation and timing elements common to stock options, and the only news is the notion that this income is not shifted by the transfer of the option. The third PLR added a statement that this income is not wages subject to withholding if the option is exercised after the transferor's death. It did not state whether the income is IRD of the transferor for income tax purposes, but that would be the right result.[70] The first and second PLRs also established that the gift is taxable at the time the option is assigned, not when it is exercised, but declined to rule on the value of the option for gift tax purposes.[71]

---

[70] See Treas. Reg. § § 1.83-1(d) and 1.421-6(d)(5)(iii) and cf. § § 1.421-8(c)(2) and 1.691(c)-1(c) (the latter establishing different rules with respect to § 423 statutory stock purchase plans, which are necessitated by the otherwise applicable IRD rules). And see § 5.10.1 n.18.

[71] The third PLR involved different facts that entailed a charitable intent and retention of some controls that made the assignments incomplete for gift tax purposes and subject to estate tax if the transferor died before exercise. The first and second PLRs established that the potential expiration of the options on the transferor's termination of employment is not a sufficient retention of control in the transferor to cause exposure to estate tax, nor to make the transfer an incomplete gift. See Rev. Rul. 84-130, 1984-2 C.B. 194 (group term life insurance not subject to § 2042 inclusion merely because employee could terminate the

§6.3.3.7 Products With Internal Tax Free Build-Up

Single premium and other tax deferred insurance (such as universal life) and annuity products may be effective devices for shifting (or at least deferring) income. Especially if a purchase today for a pay-out in the future is attractive because the internal tax-free build-up in value is at a competitive rate. Some policies acquired early in a child's life and paid for subsequently can provide classic policy loans that fund higher education when the child reaches college age, with potentially better results than a §529 plan.

§6.3.3.8 Legal Term of Years

A beguiling opportunity is presented by a legal term of years, a legal life estate, or other limited legal ownership of property. These forms of property ownership are not trusts, so they are not subject to the rules of Subchapter J, meaning that it may be possible to reproduce the effects of short term trusts without grantor trust liability. According to Treas. Reg. §301.7701-4(a):

> . . . an arrangement will be treated as a trust under the Internal Revenue Code if it can be shown that the purpose of the arrangement is to vest in trustees responsibility for the protection and conservation of property for beneficiaries who cannot share in the discharge of this responsibility . . . .

The converse of this is that an arrangement will not be treated as a trust if this bifurcation of legal and beneficial interests is not generated, allowing a grantor to transfer a legal term of years to an intended donee who is in a lower income tax bracket and effectively shift income to that donee without concern over the grantor trust rules. To succeed, however, the transferee must have all the rights of an owner of a legal term (which differ from those of a trust beneficiary), the arrangement should not resemble a trust in terms of responsibility denied to the donee and

---

(Footnote Continued)

coverage by quitting work). With respect to the timing of a completed gift of stock options and proper valuation see §7.1.7 nn.338-340.

§6.3.3.7

vested in another who resembles a trustee,[72] and § 2702 gift tax consequences should be considered.[73]

There is uncertainty about this conclusion, because the law has not been clarified since the following was written:[74]

> This raises the question of how the courts should treat a donor who gives away a life estate in Blackacre but retains the reversion. The answer should be that if the donor does not in fact retain any control over the property except that which he normally would have as a reversioner, then he has divided his interest just as though he had given the donee in fee a physical portion of Blackacre. But where he retains other substantial rights with respect to the entire property, whether as controls, use rights or other indicia of ownership, income from the property should be taxed to him.

> Under just what circumstances it will be found a person has retained such control over property from which income arises as to be taxable thereon cannot be predicted with certainty. It has been noted that the Supreme Court has specifically left the line to be drawn by future decisions; but in drawing this line, the courts are not left entirely without guidance or direction. There are special statutory sections dealing with the redirection of income through trust devices, and it would seem proper that the standards applicable to trust devices should be taken as guides in the cases involving devices other than trusts. The principal distinction between the two is that in the trust arrangement a transferor may seek to maintain control of the property by placing control of the corpus in a third person who is subject to his will. This avenue is not open to the person who transfers property directly to a donee but nevertheless seeks to retain control of it. But if the transfer is made under such circumstances—familiar or other—that the donor as a practical matter

---

[72] A term of years should be treated as different from a below-market-interest loan *if* the rights of the holder of the term interest are different from the rights of a borrower. If this is not true, under state law or because of the parties' agreement, it might be possible for the government to argue that § 7872 applies to the legal term of years transaction.

[73] Because § 2702(c)(1) regards this as a trust equivalent for gift tax purposes, § 2702(a)(1) would apply if the trustee is a family member, and the transferor retains an interest in the trust. The resolution is to cause the term of years interest to be a § 2702(b) qualified interest rather than a straight income interest, or to retain no interest.

[74] Rice, Judicial Trends in Gratuitous Assignments to Avoid Federal Income Taxes, 64 Yale L.J. 991, 1015-1016 (1955) (citations omitted).

may be expected to dominate the donee, this should obviously be a factor in determining whether the donor should be taxed on income arising from the corpus.

If Subchapter J is avoided with respect to such a transaction, the other major income tax concern with this transaction is the assignment of income doctrine. The limited available authority appears to hold that the assignor will continue to be taxed under the assignment of income rules if the transaction is viewed as only the transfer of an income right and not the transfer of an underlying property interest that can be held or invested by the transferee in the transferee's legitimate independent judgment.[75]

Perhaps the best advice in this essentially uncharted arena is to be certain that the term is given before the property is made subject to a lease or otherwise becomes income producing. Or be certain that the holder of the term has full power to alter the investment or otherwise to change the income producing character of the asset. Either approach will better support an argument that the holder of the term interest has legitimate control over a property interest and is not merely acting as a passive recipient of assigned income. "If the transfer is of property, the

---

[75] See, e.g., Commissioner v. Sunnen, 333 U.S. 591 (1948) (assignment of royalties rather than of the underlying producing properties); Galt v. Commissioner, 216 F.2d 41, 48 (7th Cir. 1954) (assignment of rents rather than of lease or of underlying property), distinguishing Hawaiian Trust Co. v. Kanne, 172 F.2d 74 (9th Cir. 1949), and Farkas v. Commissioner, 170 F.2d 201 (5th Cir. 1948), on the grounds that:

> In both of those cases there was an assignment not only of income but an interest in the property from which the income was produced. . . . [H]ere there was no assignment of the property which produced the income or in the lease . . . ;

and see Rev. Rul. 55-38, 1955-1 C.B. 389 (adopting a ten year period as the dividing line between a valid assignment, by analogy to then § 673). But see Mercer v. Commissioner, 7 T.C. 834 (1946), and Rev. Rul. 61-102, 1961-1 C.B. 245, both involving the proper income taxation of capital gains following sale by a life tenant, in each case assuming that the life tenant was responsible for ordinary income from the property in his or her personal capacity but applying a trust-like rule to impose the gains tax on that portion of those proceeds that was deemed to be held by the life tenant as a fiduciary for the remainder beneficiary.

§ 6.3.3.8

assignee is usually taxed, but if the transfer is of a mere 'income right,' the transferor remains taxable."[76]

If this analysis is reliable, the most significant concern is potential application of the assignment of income rules and any gift tax consequence attributable to application of § 2702 for gift tax valuation purposes.

§ 6.3.3.9 Tenancy at Will

Assume that Child has located the perfect residential property, but cannot afford to buy it because the debt service would be too great or the required down payment is too high. So Parent acquires the property and immediately transfers it to a QPRT. Or, using the Child's limited available capital, Child and Parent make a split purchase of the property, with Parent acquiring a term interest that meets the QPRT requirements and Child acquiring the remainder. Then assume that Parent allows Child to enjoy Parent's term interest on a year to year tenancy-at-will. If the rent charged to Child is less than a fair market rental, it appears that Parent is making a gift to Child in the amount of the difference. That gift presumably occurs in each year that the tenancy is not terminated, measured by the value of that year's fair rental value in excess of what Child paid. It ought to qualify as a present interest for purposes of the gift tax annual exclusion,[77] which (in many cases) may preclude the need to file a gift tax return to reveal the transaction.

More importantly, there appears to be no income tax concept similar to § 7872 dealing with the rent-free (or rent-reduced) use of property, as opposed to the interest-free ("rent-free") or below-market-interest use of money—which is what a *Crown* loan is all about.[78] If these

---

[76] Eustice, Contract Rights, Capital Gain, and Assignment of Income—the Ferrer Case, 20 Tax L. Rev. 1, 34 (1964).

[77] Indeed, the gift probably is being made to Child and Child's family, meaning that multiple annual exclusions may be available. If, however, Child is obligated under state law to provide housing for the family, it may be that the gift is entirely to Child (or perhaps to Child and Child's spouse, if any) due to the indirect benefit represented by this deemed transfer to the family.

[78] Until adoption of § 7872, the below-market-interest use of money was not an income taxable event, and it took an act of Congress to change that result. There is no similar act of Congress to establish an income tax consequence to the

conclusions are correct, then this is an effective shift of "income" in the form of rents that Child has avoided paying or debt service that Child has not incurred. It is a transfer that need not be reported on an income tax return, and it is a transfer that is not dependent on the income tax brackets of Child. Thus, there is no "limit" on the amount of this income that can be transferred before running through Child's brackets, making this a particularly attractive way of doing such a purchase with both wealth transfer and income shifting attributes.[79]

§6.3.3.10 Net Gifts

Net gifting may be attractive (requiring the donee to pay the gift tax, which normally is imposed on the donor), using income from gifted property to pay the donor's gift tax obligation that is assumed by the donee. This transaction will cause §677(a)(1) grantor trust treatment if the gift is to a trust and the trust is directed to use income to pay the

---

(Footnote Continued)

analogous reduced-rent use of property. What little authority there is supports this conclusion (except in the context of a corporation owning a residence and allowing a shareholder to reside therein, with dividend treatment). More closely related to the present situation is a trust holding a residence and allowing a beneficiary to reside in it, with no DNI carryout as if the use of the residence was tantamount to an income distribution. Cf. Commissioner v. Plant, 76 F.2d 8 (2d Cir. 1935); Carson v. United States, 317 F.2d 370 (Ct. Cl. 1963); DuPont Testamentary Trust v. Commissioner, 62 T.C. 36 (1974), aff'd in part and rem'd in part, 514 F.2d 917 (5th Cir. 1975), on remand, 66 T.C. 761 (1976), aff'd, 574 F.2d 1332 (5th Cir. 1978) (all involving the more limited question whether a trust or estate's payment of expenses to maintain such property should be treated as income to the beneficiary residing in it; none except *DuPont* suggested that the actual residence was income to the beneficiary, and *DuPont* resolved the case on other grounds); Prince Trust v. Commissioner, 35 T.C. 974 (1961) (trust-owned residence was not income producing because beneficiary lived in it rent free), and see §5.2.1 n.14.

[79] Allowing Child to live rent-free in the home constitutes a §280A(d)(3) "use" by Parent for income tax purposes, meaning that the deductibility of items like amortization, depreciation, property taxes, and interest on a mortgage are the same as with any other residential property that Parent owns and personally uses. In that respect, the transaction is not all that a taxpayer may want. Amounts spent by the trustee on such personal-use residential realty would not qualify as §212 expenses incurred in connection with property held for the production of income, but most of those expenses would not be deductible even if the beneficiary had received the property outright.

§6.3.3.10

tax.[80] However, a transfer to a trust, with the net gift obligation being imposed on the trust's beneficiary personally, ought to avoid § 677(a)(1), even if trust income, paid to the beneficiary, is thereafter used by the beneficiary to pay the assumed gift tax liability.[81] Although net gifts generate part-sale, part-gift treatment for income tax purposes,[82] this treatment will be harmless for income tax purposes if the gift tax (the amount realized) is less than the donor's basis. Meanwhile, net gift treatment reduces the value of the gift for wealth transfer tax purposes while making it possible for a liquidity- or cash-poor donor to shift value and obtain other gifting advantages.

§6.4 ADDITIONAL INCOME TAX CONSIDERATIONS

Inter vivos trusts that are "defective" for income tax purposes normally are irrevocable and, therefore, transfers to them may constitute completed gifts for gift tax purposes (but, if everything is done properly, they will not be includible in the transferor's gross estate at death).[1] Consideration whether new basis at death is a worthy objective may militate against the transfer of appreciated assets inter vivos. With these considerations in mind, two alternatives that seem to raise the greatest income tax concerns are annuities (including the private or family annuity, and GRATs or GRUTs), and installment sales (including traditional sales and sales for death-terminating or SCINs).

§6.4.1 *Private Annuities*

An irrevocable inter vivos transfer of property can be an expensive form of planning for gift tax purposes if the property owner retains no interest and therefore incurs a gift tax on the full value of the transferred

---

[80] Krause v. Commissioner, 56 T.C. 1242 (1971). See §§ 5.11.4 n.67 and 7.3.4.1 n.89.

[81] See, e.g., Mahoney v. United States, 628 F. Supp. 273 (S.D. Ohio 1985)), rev'd on other grounds, 831 F.2d 641 (7th Cir. 1987). See §7.3.4.1 n.90 and accompanying text.

[82] Diedrich v. Commissioner, 457 U.S. 191 (1982).

[1] **§6.4** This planning tightrope between the income tax and wealth transfer taxes can be navigated in most situations with careful consideration of the grantor trust rules and the string provisions of the wealth transfer taxes. See §§ 5.11.10, 6.3.3.4, and 7.3.3 respectively.

property. Moreover, an irrevocable inter vivos transfer of property can be an even *more* expensive proposition for FET purposes if the property owner retains personal economic enjoyment of the transferred property for life to guarantee the transferor's future financial security. This potential for FET inclusion of the transferred property at death under § 2036(a)(1) or § 2039 may be avoided if the property owner purchases a single life annuity instead, but a commercial annuity backed by the financial security of the issuer means that the property used to purchase the annuity is permanently removed from the family. So the annuity of choice for many property owners is a noncommercial, nongratuitous irrevocable inter vivos transfer of the property to a trust or a family member, subject to the transferee's agreement to pay the transferor an annuity—whether for life or for a defined term.[2]

In either case the annuity is a promise that lacks financial security to the transferor if the transferee becomes insolvent. Historically the absence of financial security was the hallmark of the private annuity and the linchpin of one of its prime advantages, because an exchange of appreciated property for a commercial annuity triggers immediate recognition of all appreciation realized on the exchange. Preferable to most transferors was deferred payment of the income tax on any realized gain through a private annuity transfer, which was treated differently because the annuity was not secured or otherwise collateralized.[3]

---

[2] The term annuity alternative essentially is the GRAT or GRUT transaction that is subject to § 2702, as addressed in § 7.2.2.2.

[3] See 212 Corp. v. Commissioner, 70 T.C. 788 (1978); Estate of Bell v. Commissioner, 60 T.C. 469 (1973); Rev. Rul. 62-136, 1962-2 C.B. 12; GCM 39503 (1986). The gain or loss and periodic income taxable to the transferor who exchanged property for the private annuity was reportable under the annuity income rules of § 72, *not* under the installment reporting rules of § 453, although they might appear to apply. See S. Rep. No. 1000, 96th Cong., 2d Sess. 12 n.12, and H.R. Rep. No. 1042, 96th Cong., 2d Sess. 10 n.12 (1980); 1980-2 C.B. 506 n.12. Those § 72 rules determined the portion of each annual payment that is ordinary income, capital gain, and a tax-free recovery of basis. To ascertain the income taxation of each portion it was necessary to determine the transferor's § 72(c)(1) "investment in the contract" and the transferor's adjusted basis prior to the transfer. Gain or loss on the transfer was measured by the difference between the transferor's amount realized and adjusted basis prior to the exchange. Rev. Rul. 69-74, 1969-1 C.B. 43, which will be obsolete upon final adoption of Treas. Reg. §§ 1.72-6(e) and 1.1001-1(j), which deny open transaction treatment to

Today, by virtue of a pending change that has a proposed effective date that already has passed, the difference between commercial and private annuities has changed. The effect of each is as if the taxpayer sold the appreciated property and used the cash proceeds to purchase the annuity. This causes an immediate realization of gain or loss and gives a basis (investment in the contract) equal to FMV[4] at the time of the transaction. Any realized loss may not be recognizable under the related party transfer rules of §267, in which case the loss could be recognized by the transferee on a future transfer of the property at a gain, but otherwise the loss would be lost.[5] In addition, if the amount realized is less than the FMV of the asset transferred, the transfer may constitute a part-sale, part-gift transaction in which the income tax consequences are as just described and the transferor's gift tax liability

---

(Footnote Continued)

private annuities, essentially by regarding the taxpayer as selling property for cash and then investing in a commercial annuity.

When made final these changes will apply retroactively, so the window for such planning essentially already is closed. The amount realized was determined under the wealth transfer tax annuity valuation tables based on the life expectancy factor for a measuring life of the transferor's age multiplied by the amount of the annuity. The reference in GCM 39503 (1986) was to Treas. Reg. §20.2031-10 and Rev. Rul. 80-80, 1980-1 C.B. 194, which have been superseded by Treas. Reg. §25.7520-3(b)(3). Now life expectancy must be determined using the standard mortality tables unless the transferor is terminally ill when the transaction is completed. See §7.2 n.7. McGrath, Private Annuity Trusts—The Numbers Don't Support the Hype, 109 Tax Notes 93 (2005), is a comprehensive critique of one popular form of private annuity transaction.

See §6.4.1 nn.3-10 and accompanying text for an exegesis of the prior treatment (which may continue to be applicable, but only if proposed regulations do not become final as anticipated).

[4] *Private* annuities may be valued differently because commercial annuity issuers are regulated, they price their products to make a profit, and they suffer from the self-selection of purchasers who expect to live *longer* than the mortality tables predict (meaning that the transferor receives the benefit of the annuity gamble). Private annuity transactions are more attractive to families in which death of the annuitant is expected *earlier* than the mortality tables predict (meaning that the transferee would receive the benefit of the annuity gamble).

[5] The loss also may not be deductible if the property transferred in exchange for the annuity is a personal use asset as to which losses never are deductible, as opposed to an investment asset. See, e.g., Rev. Rul. 71-492, 1971-2 C.B. 127 (involving a principal personal residence).

§6.4.1

is determined on the value of the transferred property in excess of the amount realized.[6] The proposed regulations essentially deny any different treatment to private annuities than applies to commercial annuities, and thus accelerate the time for reporting gain or loss on a private annuity transaction.

For income tax purposes each annuity payment received is deemed to consist in part of basis recovery as determined under an exclusion ratio calculation that regards basis to be recovered pro rata over the expected life of the annuity. Any amount received in excess of those pro rata amounts (and all amounts received after recovery of the full amount of basis) is ordinary income, essentially representing interest on the deferred payment of the annuity as the consideration for the original transfer (and, after full recovery of basis, as income representing the benefit of the transferor's annuity gamble (in this case, attributable to being longer lived than the tables predicted)).[7]

To illustrate, assume that the transferor's life expectancy is 20 years, basis in the transferred asset is $100,000, and the value of the annuity for

---

[6] A bargain sale to charity differs, as illustrated in Treas. Reg. § 1.1011-2(c) Example (8), because basis is allocated to the purchase and gift parts pro rata under § 1011(b), rather than the part-sale, part-gift result that allows the taxpayer to allocate all of the basis against the purchase portion.

[7] See GCM 39503 (1986), elaborating in detail on the deferred, ratable recognition of the various income taxable elements.

Although a portion of the annuity may be taxable to the annuitant as ordinary income as if it was interest paid on a loan, the transferee's payment of that amount is not regarded as interest and may not be deducted for income tax purposes, because the payor is regarded as making a capital investment and not as financing an installment purchase obligation. Bell v. Commissioner, 76 T.C. 232, 237 (1981), aff'd, 668 F.2d 448 (8th Cir. 1982) (each annuity payment constitutes part of the purchase price of the property, a capital expenditure, and no part thereof is deductible as interest on indebtedness under § 163); Dix v. Commissioner, 46 T.C. 796 (1966), aff'd, 392 F.2d 313, 318 (4th Cir. 1968) ("[t]he parties . . . contemplated a sale, not an indebtedness"); Garvey Inc. v. United States, 726 F.2d 1569 (Fed. Cir. 1984); GCM 39503 (1986) (also stating that the imputed interest rules of §§ 483 and 1274 do not apply to private annuities); PLR 8102029. Accord, Perkins v. United States, 701 F.2d 771 (9th Cir. 1983) (private annuity payments are nondeductible capital expenditures that preclude a deductible loss if the annuitant lives longer than predicted in the mortality tables and, as a result, is paid more than the calculated value of the annuity as provided in the annuity agreement).

§6.4.1

amount realized purposes is $1 million. Under the proposed regulations capital gain would be realized on the exchange, so $900,000 of gain is subject to recognition in the year the asset is exchanged for the annuity, and basis in the annuity is $1 million. In each payment year the annuity amount received will consist of $50,000 of basis recovery ($1 million basis ÷ 20). Any annual annuity payment in excess of this $50,000 per annum figure will constitute § 72(a) ordinary income. After the annuity is paid for 20 years (if the transferor lives longer than their predicted life expectancy) the payments will be ordinary income in their entirety because, after 20 years, the full basis will be recovered. If the transferor dies before receiving all 20 expected payments, however, the transferor's income tax return for the year of death will reflect a deduction for the amount of unrecovered basis[8] and the sale price will be regarded as adjusted downward, meaning that the transferee will be regarded as having paid a smaller amount for the property, resulting in a downward basis adjustment for the transferee.[9]

For gift tax purposes a gift is made to the extent the value of any transferred property exceeds the value of a private annuity received in exchange,[10] and it is unlikely in the family context that the business

---

[8] § 72(b)(3).

[9] See Rev. Rul. 55-119, 1955-1 C.B. 352, and Rev. Rul. 72-81, 1972-1 C.B. 98. Basis to the transferee who is paying the annuity is determined in three different ways, depending on when basis is being determined. While the annuitant is alive basis is the present value of the prospective payments under the annuity agreement, which is equal to the amount realized to the transferor. If payments under the annuity exceed that amount because the annuitant outlives the life expectancy used to determine the amount realized, then basis increases with each additional payment, as made. Once the annuitant dies the transferee's basis becomes the total amount paid to the annuitant. Even if the annuitant must include some value in their gross estate under § 2039 (for example, because the annuity has a survivorship feature), neither the surviving annuitant nor the transferee who is paying the annuity is entitled to a new basis at the transferor's death. § 1014(b)(9)(A). The surviving annuitant would, however, be entitled to any § 691(d) deduction attributable to the income element of the survivor annuity to the extent it is includible under § 72.

[10] See §§ 7.2.2.1 and 7.2.2.9, expressing uncertainty whether § 2702 applies to a straight private annuity or installment payment, and with respect to application of § 2702 in determining the value of this gift, and for the unique gift tax requirements generated by § 2702 with respect to GRATs and GRUTs.

transaction exception[11] would apply. Furthermore, a transferor who purchases a sole and survivor or a joint and survivor annuity makes a gift to the other annuitant measured by the value of the property transferred reduced only by the value of the transferor's annuity interest. If the other annuitant is the transferor's spouse, however, a gift tax marital deduction is applicable unless the transferor opts out of automatic QTIP treatment.[12] For FET purposes, the value of any survivorship annuity attributable to any portion of the purchase price contributed by the transferor is includible in the transferor's gross estate at death under § 2039.[13] If the surviving annuitant is the decedent's spouse, however, the same value should qualify for the FET marital deduction if nothing passes to any other person upon termination of the spouse's survivorship interest.[14]

---

[11] Treas. Reg. § 25.2512-8 (transfer in ordinary course of business that is bona fide, at arm's length, and free of donative intent is regarded as made for full and adequate consideration and therefore not subject to gift tax). But see Ellis Sarasota Bank & Trust Co. v. United States, 77-2 U.S. Tax Cas. (CCH) ¶ 13,204 (M.D. Fla. 1977) (parents' transfers to children in exchange for private annuity; jury determined that there was no donative intent, that it was arbitrary and unreasonable for the government to use valuation tables that did not reflect current mortality experience and the difference between males and females, and that the annuities were substantially equal in value to the property exchanged for them, resulting in no gift for gift tax purposes).

Rev. Rul. 77-454, 1977-2 C.B. 351, involved valuation of a settlor's retained annuity in an irrevocable trust, valued under the tables at exactly the FMV of the property transferred to the trust. The government declared that the annuity could not equal the value of the transferred property and therefore assessed a gift tax, because (1) the table was based on the assumption that payments could be made until the annuitant's age of 109 years, (2) the trust was only sufficient to make payments for slightly longer than 18 years, and (3) the 51 year old settlor reserved an annual payment until death or until the fund was exhausted, whichever occurred first. That result is adopted in Treas. Reg. §§ 1.7520-3(b)(2)(i), 20.7520-3(b)(2)(i), and 25.7520-3(b)(2)(i), and was rejected in Estate of Shapiro v. Commissioner, 66 T.C.M. (CCH) 1067 (1993). See §§ 7.2.2.2 nn.56-57 and accompanying text and 7.2.2.2.1, for an extensive discussion.

[12] See § 2523(f)(6).

[13] See, e.g., Estate of Bell v. United States, 80-2 U.S. Tax Cas. (CCH) ¶ 13,356 (E.D. Wash. 1980) (private joint and survivor annuity acquired with community property deemed owned by D and S in equal shares and therefore only half the value of the annuity measured by S's life expectancy was includible in D's gross estate).

[14] § 2056(b)(7)(C). See § 13.5.6.7.

§ 6.4.1

§6.4.2 SCINs

"Death terminating" or "self-canceling" installment notes are installment sales to a family member or other object of the transferor's bounty that may be a viable alternative to a private annuity transaction. Under each, payments end at the transferor's death, with no FET inclusion in a proper case[15] under the SCIN situation because the notes simply expire by their own terms when the transferor dies.

That FET result is not a given, as illustrated by Estate of Musgrove v. United States,[16] which involved a transfer in exchange for an interest free, unsecured, self-canceling demand note made 18 days before the lender's death. This exchange did not avoid FET inclusion of the principal amount of the debt.[17] The loan amount was less than the repayment obligation, but the court concluded as a matter of fact that this difference was not a negotiated premium for the forgiveness feature. Instead, it was attributable to the fact that the loan was documented before the amount of the borrower's tax liability was finally determined and the amount

---

[15] See Estate of Moss v. Commissioner, 74 T.C. 1239 (1980), acq. in result only, 1981-1 C.B. 2 (decedent sold closely held stock at arm's length to individual employees who were not natural objects of the decedent's bounty, taking in exchange installment notes for a term less than the decedent's life expectancy; inclusion did not result notwithstanding the decedent's unexpected death within two years of the sale and the fact that the notes terminated by their own terms, because the parties stipulated that the sale was bona fide and for adequate and full consideration, and the cancellation provision was part of the negotiated agreement for which separate consideration was paid); Estate of Costanza v. Commissioner, 320 F.3d 595 (6th Cir. 2003), rev'g and rem'g 81 T.C.M. (CCH) 1693 (2001) (gift tax liability on a purported sale made proximate to death to a child who failed to make some installment payments, made others late, and back dated certain documents, all resulting in the Tax Court performing a part-sale, part-gift analysis for §2001 estate tax calculation purposes; on appeal the taxpayer's death within five months was regarded as irrelevant because the life expectancy for an individual the taxpayer's age was between five and 14 years and the note was for 11 years); compare Estate of Mitchell v. Commissioner, 43 T.C.M. (CCH) 1034 (1982) (gift tax liability on transfer of property to children two weeks before the decedent's impending and diagnosed death in exchange for a private annuity that the court held was not a bona fide sale because the children never intended to pay the decedent any significant amount).

[16] 95-2 U.S. Tax Cas. (CCH) ¶ 60,204 (Ct. Fed. Cl. 1995).

[17] See §6.5.2 n.37 for a discussion of the facts leading the court to hold that a bona fide loan transaction did not exist for wealth transfer tax purposes.

designated in the note was chosen to safely exceed the amount that actually would be needed. The note simply was not revised when the actual disbursement was made because it did not matter, the borrower being the lender's sole beneficiary at death and the parties never expected any payments to be made.

Worse facts than *Musgrove* hardly could be involved, and the court correctly held that the mere designation of the transfer of funds as a debt could not preclude FET inclusion of the debt amount. That being the case, the source of inclusion is unimportant to this topic, and the significance of the case is that it recognized and distinguished the leading taxpayer victory (*Moss*) rather than refusing to follow it.

According to the court, *Moss* was very different in that the loan was made at arm's length to borrowers who were not natural objects of the lender's bounty. The government stipulated that the sale price represented by the loan was full and adequate consideration for a bona fide sale of the lender's business. And, perhaps most important, the parties also stipulated that the term of the loan did not exceed the lender's life expectancy. In *Musgrove* there was no term (and almost any term selected would have been in excess of the very seriously ill lender's life expectancy). Also different about *Moss* was that there was a clearly negotiated and denominated premium for the self-canceling feature, which also clearly was not the case in *Musgrove*.

If constructed properly, the difference between a private annuity and a SCIN may be analyzed on a purely economic and income tax basis.[18] The SCIN approach may result in more wealth that is subject to inclusion in the estate of the transferor—particularly if death does not precede the term of the notes—because the death-termination or self-cancellation feature must be supported by added consideration, usually paid in the form of a premium added to the normal amortization of the installment note amount. Thus, a transferor may collect more under a SCIN approach than if the notes were not self-canceling, and potentially more even than if the transfer was for a private annuity. Nevertheless, a longer life than the actuarial tables predict will cause the holder of a lifetime annuity to receive more payments than anticipated and also cause an increase in the transferor's gross estate (in either case, to the

---

[18] See the comparison of SCINs to private annuities in GCM 39503, and see § 6.4.3 for a summary comparison in chart form.

§ 6.4.2

extent those payments have not been consumed in ways that have no value at death). The installment notes will not cause this form of excess inclusion, because the notes have a set duration that does not extend just because the transferor outlives the term of the notes.

The happy result in either case is that both approaches avoid a taxable gift inter vivos. The installment note may be more desirable than the private annuity because any gain on the original exchange is recognized as installments are paid. The private annuity regulations provide that all the gain is recognized immediately. In addition, the installment note approach will entail payment of interest by the recipient of the underlying property that may be deductible under § 163, although the consequence to the transferor will not differ from that in a private annuity.

A third difference between annuities and installment notes may arise if the recipient of the transferred property is a related party[19] who disposes of the property within two years. In that case there will be an acceleration of the amount realized to the transferor who received installment notes, requiring all unrecognized gain to be reported by the transferor in the year of the transferee's disposition.[20] That still may allow a greater deferral than in a private annuity transaction.

However, cancellation of the note by the transferor's will, or it becoming unenforceable by its own terms, is treated as a disposition of the installment obligation for income tax purposes, resulting in gain or loss to the transferor.[21] If this occurs at the transferor's death, there is some uncertainty about the proper taxpayer to report the income and pay the tax generated by this treatment. On the other hand the note need not be made to terminate. If there will be no FET at the transferor's

---

[19] See § 453(f)(1).

[20] See § 453(e). The § 453(e)(2) two year limitation does not apply if the transfer was of marketable securities, in which case acceleration may occur if the transferee's disposition occurs while any outstanding installment note remains unpaid.

[21] The cancellation is regarded under § 453B(f) as a transaction other than a sale or exchange for purposes of § 453B(a)(2) and the FMV of the obligation is treated as no less than the face amount of the notes, resulting in an acceleration of the unrecognized gain in those notes.

§ 6.4.2

death the note can simply be repaid by the borrower out of assets of the lender's estate otherwise inherited by the borrower.

To illustrate the income tax issue created by cancellation, PLR 9108027 held that a will that cancelled an installment note caused a § 691(a)(5)(A)(iii) transfer that constituted a § 691(a)(2) acceleration to the transferor's estate of any deferred income represented by the notes that were cancelled. It also held that cancellation constituted a § 663(a)(1) specific bequest that precluded any estate income from being taxed to the transferee who made that deemed transfer. Thus, the accelerated income was taxable to the decedent's estate, which is the right result because it guarantees that acceleration will change only the timing and not the liability for payment of the tax on income represented by the note.

TAM 9240003 further clarified the situation by holding that a similar cancellation did not produce discharge of indebtedness income to the transferee because the facts showed that the cancellation involved donative intent that qualified it for the gift exception to § 61(a)(12).[22] Most cases arising in an estate planning context probably will involve similar donative intent.

Unlike the facts involved and results reached in these two pronouncements, that cancellation of the installment note *by the transferor's will* constituted income to the transferor's estate, Estate of Frane v. Commissioner[23] involved a self-canceling note that ceased to exist *by its*

---

[22] The notes were given in a loan transaction. In discussing the proper value of the notes for inclusion in the decedent's gross estate, the TAM also indicated that the outstanding indebtedness was well in excess of the original principal amount of the debt, presumably indicating that there was unpaid accumulated interest owing when the decedent died. The government did not indicate whether this deferred interest was accelerated into the decedent's estate. The unspoken explanation for this might relate to the fact that the transferee was worth only a small fraction of the original amount of the debt and the notes were deemed includible in the transferor's estate at only that discounted amount. If that reduced inclusion amount was less than the outstanding original principal balance of the debt, perhaps the TAM reflects that there was no recognition of the unpaid interest owed on the notes for both estate and income tax purposes.

[23] 98 T.C. 341 (1992) (a 14-to-5 reviewed opinion), aff'd in part and rev'd in part, 998 F.2d 567 (8th Cir. 1993). See the discussion of *Frane* in § 5.10.5.

§ 6.4.2

own terms when the transferor died.[24] Based on that distinction, the Tax Court rejected the government's argument that § 691(a)(5) was applicable and instead concluded that the cancellation was subject to § 453B(f). All deferred gain was recognized under § 453B(a) at the transferor's death, as under the government's approach, but the court held that it was reportable on the transferor's final income tax return rather than as IRD reportable on the first income tax return of the transferor's estate. When the court on appeal affirmed the holding that cancellation was an income taxable event, it ruled consistently with the government's original position that inclusion properly is under § 691(a)(5)(A)(iii) and that the income properly is reported by the decedent's estate, not on the decedent's final income tax return as held by the Tax Court.[25]

---

[24] The effect of a SCIN provision is testamentary, in the sense that it confers a benefit on the buyer if the seller dies before complete payment of the installments, but it is not a testamentary disposition that is ineffective because the contract is not executed with the formalities required of a will. See In re Estate of Lundgren, 98 N.W.2d 839 (Iowa 1959) (contract for sale of realty under which title was to be conveyed on seller's death and seller received all income from the property prior thereto); McGrath v. McGrath, 220 A.2d 760 (N.H. 1966) (as a contractual arrangement, it was not invalid just because it accomplished in part what could have been accomplished by a will); In re Estate of Verbeek, 467 P.2d 178 (Wash. Ct. App. 1970) (same). But cf. Lauritsen v. Wallace, 67 So. 3d 285 (Fla. Dist. Ct. App. 2011), holding that a will provision forgiving a regular note (not a SCIN) was tantamount to a testamentary bequest and, as such, it had to abate because debts of the estate would be unpaid if the note was not collected; the court distinguished a SCIN on the basis that, at death, there is nothing left upon which to collect in a SCIN.

[25] The Tax Court assumed its answer by characterizing the note as an installment obligation under which all unpaid amounts owed to the holder are "cancelled and extinguished as if paid," because the purchase agreement that yielded the notes in question stated that the notes "shall be deemed cancelled and extinguished as though paid" upon the holder's death, which the court regarded as precisely the transaction contemplated by the express provisions of § 453B(f). Although the court on appeal disagreed with the characterization for § 453B purposes, it agreed that the cancellation was a transfer for § 691(a)(2) purposes.

A dissent in the Tax Court rejoined that, if the note had been worded differently (for example, if it had stated that the purchase price depends on how long the transferor lives and, if the transferor dies before any scheduled potential payment, no obligation to make further payments arises), "the majority would be hard pressed persuasively to argue that the obligations to make payments subsequent to [the] decedent's death (1) were not contingent, (2) arose, and (3)

None of this altered the favorable conclusion that a SCIN is not includible in the transferor's gross estate for FET purposes.[26] That conclusion was not challenged by the debate in *Frane* whether for income tax purposes cancellation at the decedent's death should be treated as a transfer by the decedent's estate that triggers the § 691(a)(2) income acceleration rule, or a satisfaction at other than its face value or a distribution, transmittal, sale, or other disposition for purposes of accelerating any deferred gain inherent in the note under § 453B(a). Thus, for FET purposes, both the private annuity and the SCIN cause the payments to cease at death and no part of the underlying annuity or note obligation to be includible. And properly done neither entails a taxable inter vivos gift either.

A dissent to the Tax Court's opinion in *Frane* is intriguing in several respects. One is its equation of a SCIN to a private annuity, saying that they are not functionally different and should be taxed the same.[27] With an effective single life, no refund, private annuity there would be no gift

_____

(Footnote Continued)

were thereafter canceled." 98 T.C. at 361. The Tax Court majority's answer to the suggestion that the note was a contingent obligation was to refer to the definition in Temp. Treas. Reg. § 15A.453-1(c)(1) of a "contingent payment sale" as one "in which the aggregate selling price cannot be determined by the close of the taxable year in which such sale . . . occurs" and held that *Frane* did not meet that definition, the note instead treating the specified purchase price as fully paid. And the court on appeal merely compared the wording in § 691(a)(5) ("any cancellation of such an obligation") with the wording in the purchase agreement itself.

The Tax Court also ruled that the term "cancelled" in § 453B(f) "must include any cessation of an obligation to pay that would otherwise continue to exist," as supported by the legislative history to § 453B(f). 98 T.C. at 350. In this respect, the Tax Court's statement that "Congress intended that when income is deferred under the installment method, a cancellation of the obligation cannot prevent the remaining unreported income from being recognized," assumed the answer to the underlying question whether the sale price was larger than the actual payments made (two installments out of 20 in this case). On this the appellate opinion essentially was in accord because the result of its decision was to give the transferees a basis equal to the full amount they were obligated to pay under the notes without cancellation.

[26] See § 6.4.2 n.14.

[27] This comparison could be relevant when evaluating the effect of the original issue discount rules and whether the exception for annuities in § 1275(a)(1)(B)(i) is applicable. See Treas. Reg. § 1.1275-1(j).

§ 6.4.2

tax on the original transfer, no amount not already paid would be includible in the transferor's gross estate at death, and no income tax liability would be generated by the transferor's death (indeed, a § 72 (a) (3) deduction might be available on the transferor's final income tax return for any unrecovered basis in the annuity).

An even better analogy for *all* tax purposes was *alluded* to by the dissent, which referred to the transferor as "an insurer (or perhaps a gambler)" who accepted the economic risk of death before the total purchase price was paid. In essence, a SCIN may be viewed as a normal installment note with an added premium to cover the contingency of the transferor's death before full payment. That premium essentially finances private, decreasing, term life insurance that pays when the transferor dies. The analogue is that proceeds equal to the outstanding installments are paid by the transferor to the transferee and then used immediately by the transferee to pay those outstanding installments to the transferor.

Under this analogy the taxable event occurs as of (or perhaps immediately after) the transferor's death, which more accurately implicates § 691 (a) (5) (A) (iii) as held by the *Frane* court on appeal, but any income tax liability is offset because implied payment of the proceeds under this insurance contract analogy should constitute DRD (under § 162 as a binding business obligation). For FET purposes the transferor's estate has a similar wash because the deemed payment of the outstanding installments is includible but that amount is offset by a § 2053 (a) (3) deduction for the transferor's obligation to pay the insurance proceeds.

In each case, if the premium charged for the death-terminating feature was determined properly, it should constitute full and adequate consideration for the insurance obligation and should support both deductions. Moreover, both deductions are permitted under the last sentence of § 642 (g) because the obligation to pay is a § 691 (b) DRD of the transferor. The final result is consistent with the exclusion for FET purposes, with a no gift result inter vivos, and with the Tax Court dissent in *Frane* that properly argued (as determined on appeal) that nothing should be taxable for income tax purposes.

In the final analysis, as held by *Frane*, the SCIN sale may be desirable even if income tax is generated at the transferor's death, if the income tax incurred on the income element is less than the FET cost would be if the notes survived death and were includible in the transferor's estate. Sale during life loses the new basis at death otherwise generated under § 1014, however, and the premium paid for the death-terminating feature could increase the transferor's estate over the amount that would exist if the transferor lived to receive all the installments called for by the obligation.[28] So there is some gamble represented in this transaction, as well as in a simple annuity situation.

§ 6.4.3 *Comparison of Various Techniques*

As a means of evaluating the advantages and consequences of the private annuity and SCIN, the following chart illustrates various attributes discussed herein and not, along with the results involving two other closely related techniques not addressed here at all.[29]

If an early death is anticipated, the private annuity may be preferable because the payments made will be the lowest among the alternatives. A SCIN also would be better than a normal installment sale, but a GRAT or GRUT would be a § 2036(a)(1) disaster if death occurred within the term and the FET still is in operation. If a prolonged life is expected, a normal installment sale or a GRAT or a GRUT for a term the transferor is expected to outlive would be preferable because the SCIN inflates the transferor's estate by the amount of the premium for the cancellation feature, and the private annuity inflates the estate by payments made for life long after normal installments would have terminated. In any of these cases, sale to an IDGT will avoid capital gains treatment on the original transfer[30] but the income tax avoided on the original transfer may be

---

[28] For an extensive discussion of the SCIN transaction and all its ramifications, see Banoff & Hartz, New Tax Court Case Expands Opportunities for Self-Canceling Installment Notes, 76 J. Tax'n 332 (1992), and literature cited therein.

[29] GRATs and GRUTs are discussed in more detail in the context of § 2702. See § 7.2.2.2.

[30] See § 5.11.9 at text accompanying nn.208-209. Mulligan, Sale to an Intentionally Defective Irrevocable Trust for a Balloon Note—An End Run Around Chapter 14, 32 U. Miami Inst. Est. Plan. ¶ 1500 (1998), advocates such a sale as preferable to a GRAT or a GRUT because future appreciation in the transferred asset is shifted to the trust and the note received is frozen in value, all without compliance with the requisites of § 2702, and death within the term of the note causes inclusion of only the value of the note for estate tax purposes (a value that

accelerated when the trust ceases to be a grantor trust (presumably no later than death of the transferor),[31] leaving only the question whether the income tax properly is reported on the transferor's final income tax return or on the first income tax return of the transferor's estate.[32] That consequence should be no different than in a SCIN context in which all remaining income tax would be accelerated.

(Footnote Continued)

may be zero if it is a SCIN). Shifting appreciation disappears as an advantage in a flat tax world or if the estate tax is repealed, so avoiding an inter vivos gift and minimizing income tax costs may be more important objectives.

[31] See §5.11.9 at text accompanying nn.219-220.

[32] See §6.5.2 at text accompanying nn.23-25 regarding the realization issue in the context of the SCIN. The issue appears to be the same.

§6.4.3

	Private Annuity	GRAT/GRUT	Death-Terminating Installment Sale (SCIN)	Normal Installment Sale
Valuation Method?	Gift tax tables	Gift tax tables	FMV plus cancellation premium	FMV
Consistent Annual Payments Required?	Yes	Yes	No	No
Payments Continue If Seller Dies Before Life Expectancy?	No	Depends on Document	No	Continue for full term of installment notes
FET Inclusion If Transferor Dies Before Term?	None	Yes: §2036(a)(1)	No, but cancellation premium increases transferor's estate	Balance of unpaid installment notes, if any
FET Inclusion If Transferor Dies After Term?	None	None	No, but cancellation premium increases transferor's estate	None
Gain on Transfer?	Immediate if secured; deferred if not	No realization if IDGT is used	Immediate realization; reported in installments	Immediate realization; reported in installments
Transferor's Treatment of "Excess" Income?	All ordinary income after life expectancy exceeded	Payments stop at term, which should not exceed life expectancy	Payments end at term, which should not exceed life expectancy	Payments stop at term, without regard to life expectancy
Transferee's Treatment of "Interest"?	No deduction	No deduction	§163 deduction possible	§163 deduction possible
Potential for §483 Interest to be Imputed to Transferor?	§483(f)(5) exclusion	§483(f)(5) exclusion	Yes	Yes
§453(e) Related Party Disposition Issue?	Not applicable	Not applicable	Yes	Yes
Income Tax at Death?	None	None	*Frane*: acceleration of gain as §691 income	Gain as §691 income without acceleration
Transferee's Basis?	Payments made	Carryover	FMV	FMV
New Basis Postmortem?	No inclusion so no §1014	To the extent §2036 includible	*Frane*: acceleration yields basis adjustment	§1014(c) to the extent payments are IRD

§6.4.3

§6.5 SELECTED INTER VIVOS TRANSFER APPROACHES

Transfers in trust or other property management and protective nonprobate vehicles predominate in sophisticated estate planning,[1] but there are many circumstances in which outright transfers are appropriate. An inter vivos transfer not in trust must comply with proper formalities. Realty transactions usually involve a professional advisor such as an attorney because of the need to draft a deed. But many inter vivos transfers fail because of ignorance of or too casual adherence to the formalities required to accomplish a valid transfer by gift.

Among those property law requirements to make an effective inter vivos gift of property, there must be a present,[2] voluntary, and complete[3]

---

[1] **§6.5** Many of the more sophisticated and tax sensitive planning techniques involving inter vivos property transfers are considered elsewhere in this material, as appropriate with respect to the particular wealth transfer tax objective and exposure they present. For an excellent practical summary comparison of various timely techniques, see Abbin, [S]he Loves Me, [S]he Loves Me Not—Responding To Succession Planning Needs Through A Three Dimensional Analysis Of Considerations To Be Applied In Selecting From The Cafeteria Of Techniques, 31 U. Miami Inst. Est. Plan. ¶ 1300 (1997).

[2] See Dalton v. Commissioner, 32 T.C.M. (CCH) 782 (1973) (income tax charitable deduction denied to taxpayer who telephoned the charity on December 31 to announce a desire to contribute land and on the same evening typed a letter that said "I hereby give" the interest, subject however to an option to buy it back within three years and to a retained right to use and control the property until it was sold; the letter described how the proceeds should be distributed when the land was sold and was notarized and placed in a mailbox before midnight; it was regarded as consistent with an intent to make a gift of future sale proceeds and not with an intent to make a present gift, and it therefore was not a completed gift that would support a current deduction for income tax purposes).

[3] See Estate of Whitt v. Commissioner, 46 T.C.M. (CCH) 118, 127 (1983): "to be a completed gift of real property [the taxpayer] must prove that there was a conveyance sufficient to vest legal title in the donee and also that the donor relinquished dominion and control of the subject matter of the gift by delivery to the donee." In Estate of Whitt v. Commissioner, 751 F.2d 1548 (11th Cir. 1985), the parcels of land (with respect to which deeds properly were executed and recorded prior to the decedent's death) were not includible in the decedent's gross estate under §2033 because recording is prima facie evidence of delivery that was not rebutted by evidence that the deeds were never delivered to the

act with the intent to make a gratuitous transfer, accompanied by delivery to and acceptance of the property by the transferee.[4] In addition to the subjective intent required, the objective capacity to *form* the requisite intent also must exist.[5] With respect to the requisite delivery with the

(Footnote Continued)

donee. Inclusion under another provision, such as § 2036, may occur if the transferor retains rights in the transferred property other than by deed, sufficient to constitute an implied retention of a life estate. See § 7.3.4.1.

[4] Restatement (Third) of Property (Wills and Other Donative Transfers (2003) formulates these requirements as:

§ 6.2: The transfer of personal property, necessary to perfect a gift may be made:

(1) by delivering the property to the donee or

(2) by inter vivos donative document

§ 6.3: The transfer of land, necessary to perfect a gift, must be evidenced in a writing that is executed in compliance with the formalities required by the applicable statute of frauds.

Implicit within these statements are certain core requirements, such as a writing, adequate identification of the donee, identification of the specified property, and of the specified interest therein. Chebatoris v. Moyer, 757 N.W.2d 212, 215, 216, 217 (Neb. 2008), held that a revocable inter vivos trust had been funded with realty that was listed on an Appendix to the trust, notwithstanding there was no formal deed or other conveyance, stating that under state law "[a] conveyance of land may occur in a document that is not formally drafted as a deed," that "any writing may be effective as a legal conveyance if it names the grantor and grantee, contains words of grant, describes the land, and is delivered," and that "it is not necessary to transfer legal title to the trustee when the settlor is the sole trustee . . . ." The fact that the trust agreement was not filed with the register of deeds before the trust settlor's death was deemed to be irrelevant. A gift of land is not complete until it is accepted, but acceptance by the donee is presumed, subject to a disclaimer.

[5] Because the presumption favors capacity, the burden of proof normally is on the party challenging the gift, but that presumption and the burden of proof may shift to the transferee if a confidential relation existed with the transferor. See, e.g., Beinlich v. Campbell, 567 So. 2d 852 (Ala. 1990) (decedent's friends and beneficiaries found to be in confidential relation; burden of proof shifted to them); Fogel v. Swann, 523 So. 2d 1227 (Fla. Ct. App. 1988) (confidential relation existed with brother-in-law who acted as transferor's attorney and with whom transferor lived, with respect to gifts to the attorney's spouse who was the transferor's sibling); In re Estate of DeJernette, 677 N.E.2d 1024 (Ill. App. Ct. 1997) (durable power of attorney holder required to return property placed in joint tenancy shortly before decedent's death); Lemp v. Hauptmann, 525 N.E.2d 203 (Ill. App. Ct. 1988) (burden of proof on child who benefited self under

§ 6.5

intent to make a gift, conveyance of a deed of gift in which the property is described is a more demonstrable and therefore more reliable technique than mere delivery of the property itself, even with respect to a gift of tangible personal property, because it avoids challenges regarding the intent of the donor to make a gift.

A number of unintended consequences may apply if a transferor's intended inter vivos gift fails. One is that income generated by the asset will continue to be taxable to the frustrated transferor[6] and the value of the subject of the intended gift will be includible in the transferor's gross estate at death for FET purposes.[7] Some gifts fail because the transferor was not mentally competent on the date the gift was attempted, again

(Footnote Continued)

durable power of attorney); In re Estate of Clements, 505 N.E.2d 7 (Ill. App. Ct. 1987) (testimony of decedent's doctors sufficient to overcome presumption of capacity); Crider v. Crider, 635 N.E.2d 204 (Ind. Ct. App. 1994) (similar); In re Estate of Baessler, 561 N.W.2d 88 (Iowa Ct. App. 1997) (daughter with whom 106 year old transferor lived could not rebut presumption); Logan v. Logan, 937 P.2d 967 (Kan. Ct. App. 1997) (similar); Madden v. Rhodes, 626 So. 2d 608 (Miss. 1993) (decedent's nurse unable to overcome presumption); Greenlee v. Mitchell, 607 So. 2d 97 (Miss. 1992) (deed overturned over 40 years after delivery to son who was in confidential relation); Estate of McRae, 522 So. 2d 731 (Miss. 1988) (burden of proof imposed on doctor whose children were transferees); Pascale v. Pascale, 549 A.2d 782 (N.J. 1988) (notwithstanding confidential relation with transferee, determination made that transferor understood the consequences of the gift but miscalculated the transferor's ability to control the transferee); In re Estate of Carano, 868 P.2d 699 (Okla. 1994) (gift to charity; confidential relation triggered application of rule even though the infecting relation was not between the transferor and the transferee); Lewis v. Estate of Lewis, 725 P.2d 644 (Wash. Ct. App. 1986) (no confidential relation with child with whom transferor lived).

[6] See, e.g., Lang v. Commissioner, 20 T.C.M. (CCH) 666 (1961) (transfers deemed ineffective because the deed was neither recorded nor delivered; income from the property remained taxable to the transferor).

[7] See, e.g., Kirkpatrick v. Sanders, 261 F.2d 480 (4th Cir. 1958) (deed gifting realty not recorded within two years was void under controlling law and the value of the property was includible in the transferor's gross estate); Estate of Devline v. Commissioner, 78 T.C.M. (CCH) 948 (1999) (gifts authorized by court order were never made and the order itself was not tantamount to actual gifts, so funds eventually transferred postmortem were includible in the decedent's gross estate); Estate of Baldwin v. Commissioner, 18 T.C.M. (CCH) 902 (1959) (recorded deed of realty named decedent's child as grantee but neither the deed nor possession and control of the property was delivered to the child; the value of the realty was includible in the decedent's gross estate).

resulting in the value of the property being includible in the transferor's gross estate.[8] The government may raise the question of the transferor's capacity to make the gift in a tax case.[9] In addition, creditors and beneficiaries of the transferor's estate also may benefit from invalidating an inter vivos transfer, causing the property to pass through the transferor's probate estate. This might even be beneficial for federal tax purposes if, for example, the estate is too small to incur wealth transfer tax and the §1014(b)(9) new basis at death rule would be advantageous in eliminating a large capital gain that is carried over to a transferee under §1015 on an inter vivos gift.[10]

§6.5.1 *Time and Manner of Transfer*

There are myriad forms of gratuitous inter vivos transfers, not all being obvious or intentional gifts. The gift tax requires a voluntary and complete transfer (for less than full and adequate consideration in money or money's worth), but not one with a "donative intent." Thus, it is possible for taxpayers to incur unanticipated and unintended gift tax liability. In addition, some transfers involve subterfuges meant to disguise the true gratuitous nature of the property disposition. Seldom will these succeed in moving wealth free of the transfer taxes, especially if they are not disclosed properly.[11]

---

[8] See, e.g., Estate of Thompson v. Commissioner, 18 T.C.M. (CCH) 801 (1959).

[9] Clark v. United States, 209 F. Supp. 895 (D. Colo. 1962) (the court assumed that the government properly could raise the matter but the testimony established that the transferor had the requisite capacity).

[10] See, e.g., Klee v. United States, 59-1 U.S. Tax Cas. (CCH) ¶ 9375 (D. Kan. 1959) (heirs of an intestate decedent who transferred real property to them by unqualified quitclaim deed subsequently conveyed the land and asserted that the property acquired a new basis on the decedent's death because the decedent conveyed title to them under an oral trust that ended on the decedent's death, causing the property to pass through the decedent's estate; under local law an oral trust of realty was voidable, not void, but unassailable only by a third party, which allowed the heirs to acquire the land by descent and, with it, a new basis.

[11] See §6501(c)(9), with respect to the failure to disclose taxable transfers, imposing unlimited statute of limitation exposure with respect to the transferor.

Some transfers are in a form that reduces the gift tax cost involved. Good illustrations of this include net gifts,[12] seriatim annual gifts of fractional interests in property,[13] or annual forgiveness of indebtedness (to the extent these gifts are not accelerated into a prior year and denied annual exclusion treatment).[14] Moreover, the appropriate form of transfer may be an outright transfer or in trust, including an IDGT for income tax minimization.[15] In addition, estate planners always must keep one eye on state law to be certain that delivery and other requirements for an effective transfer[16] have been met.

To illustrate, under state law the ownership of bearer bonds is transferable merely by delivery of the bonds themselves to the intended transferee. In Estate of Kincade v. Commissioner,[17] D acquired bonds through a brokerage house, some through an account in D's name, some through an account in the name of S, and some through an account in the names of D and S together. All the bonds were delivered to D and placed in a safety deposit box to which S did not have access. Some of the bearer bonds were in an envelope in the safety deposit box on which was written S's name.

A lower state court determined that the bonds bought through the brokerage account in S's name were property of S and that those bought under the joint account passed to S by right of survivorship. Nevertheless, the Tax Court concluded that the highest state court would hold that no completed gift was made because of a lack of delivery. Consequently, no effective inter vivos transfer occurred, the bonds were included in D's gross estate at death, and no FET marital deduction was available because D also did not provide a testamentary transfer of the bonds to S.

---

[12] See § 6.3.3.10.

[13] See § 6.2.3.

[14] See § 6.5.2.

[15] Regarding the use of IDGTs for indirect gifting (of the benefit of tax free income), and for a myriad of other benefits such as continuing to qualify for special capital gains treatment under § 121, to avoid disqualification of an S corporation, or to avoid the income tax transfer for value problem under § 101, see § § 5.11.9 and 6.3.3.4.

[16] See § 6.5 at text accompanying nn.2-5.

[17] 69 T.C. 247 (1977).

State law also is an important concern if it is desirable to give undivided interests in property over several years rather than to give the entire property in one year. Seriatim transfers of present interests permit the use of multiple annual exclusions for gift tax purposes and fractional interest gifts permit valuation reductions or the transfer may produce more favorable income tax charitable deductions. A transferor may have a state law right to reform a deed if the transferor intended to give the transferee an undivided interest in property each year for several years but the deed of gift initially delivered gives the transferee the entire interest in the property. But reformation will alter the gift tax consequences of the original transfer only if a court in a tax controversy so holds.

Thus, for example, the transferor's gift of real property to a charity in Dodge v. Commissioner[18] originally conveyed the transferor's entire interest, notwithstanding an alleged intent to convey only 20% of the title in each of five years. Upon petition for reformation of the original deed, the state court concluded that the transferor had a right to revoke 80% of the original transfer because of the mistake, and the Tax Court then held that no completed taxable gift of that portion occurred in the year of the original conveyance. Thus, for tax purposes, reformation was permitted notwithstanding that the charitable deduction was more valuable to the transferor if spread over a period of years than if all of it was taken in the year of the erroneous conveyance.[19]

Similarly, the taxpayer in Touche v. Commissioner[20] desired to transfer undivided interests over a period of time that would not involve a gift tax but the attorney who drew the deeds erroneously transferred undivided interests that were twice as large as the transferor intended. The court concluded that, under controlling local law, the transferor could have revoked the deeds to the extent they were erroneous and, to that extent, that there was no completed gift for gift tax purposes.

---

[18] 27 T.C.M. (CCH) 1170 (1968).

[19] A companion case involving the transferor's spouse was litigated as a refund suit. Dodge v. United States, 292 F. Supp. 573 (S.D. Fla. 1968), aff'd, 413 F.2d 1239 (5th Cir. 1969).

[20] 58 T.C. 565 (1972).

§6.5.1

Berger v. United States[21] involved a plaintiff who sought public service employment and, under the mistaken belief that possible conflicts of interest required creation of a "blind" irrevocable trust, proceeded to convey property in a manner that would generate a gift tax. A gift tax return was filed but later amended contending that no taxable gift occurred, because the taxpayer did not obtain the job. A lower court decreed that the irrevocable trust would be regarded as revocable, but the government claimed a gift tax nevertheless. Under local law a gratuitous transfer into trust could be revoked if made as a result of the transferor's unilateral mistake of fact or law and, because that was the situation, the transfer was regarded as incomplete until the transferor relinquished the state law right of revocation. The federal court therefore held in favor of the taxpayer for gift tax purposes, concluding that the integrity and efficacy of the federal gift tax system was not threatened. In large part this was because, before the taxpayer may obtain ultimate tax relief from the mistake, the taxpayer must perfect a state right to reform the transfer, present evidence to a state court to meet the requisite state law standard of proof, not be guilty of laches under state law, and then satisfy the federal court that the state court properly applied its own state law.

In some circumstances the form or timing of a transfer is important because the transferor does not want to part with enjoyment or control of property prior to death. In some cases a transferor wants to make an inter vivos transfer of property that will be effective at death to prevent the property from passing through the transferor's probate estate, but that will not result in a loss of enjoyment or control over the property until death. Any probate avoidance device may be employed, including trusts, annuities, joint ownership with survivorship rights, Totten trusts, POD or TOD accounts, and future interests, all depending on the circumstances, the nature of the property, and any ancillary objectives to be accomplished. In each case, however, the transfer may not be complete for gift tax purposes and, even more important, the transferred

---

[21] 487 F. Supp. 49 (W.D. Pa. 1980). See also Neal v. United States, 98-2 U.S. Tax Cas. (CCH) ¶ 60,318 (W.D. Pa. 1998), aff'd, 151 F.3d 1201 (3d Cir. 1999) (subject to gift tax, taxpayer relinquished an interest in the wake of Congress' adoption of § 2036(c), which subsequently was repealed *nunc pro tunc;* the court allowed a refund of the gift tax paid on the basis that the relinquishment was a mistake that was reformed under state law), discussed in § 7.2.2 n.37.

property almost certainly will be includible in the transferor's gross estate at death.[22] So, depending on the transferor's objectives with respect to taxation, intentional or unintentional retention may be problematic and should be analyzed carefully and fully, keeping in mind that the advantages explored in this chapter on inter vivos transfers almost always require completed irrevocable gifts.

In most cases the nature of any transferred property and the income and wealth transfer tax objectives dictate that a no-strings-attached gift be made, and this may be wise for nontax reasons as well. For example, tangible personal property—even income producing personal property—does not readily lend itself to trust ownership[23] (nor to most other forms of bifurcated ownership designed to permit continued enjoyment or control until death) unless it is contemplated that the property will be sold and the proceeds invested and administered in the trust. Similarly, residential real estate (whether it will be occupied by the transferor or a different beneficiary) normally is not placed in trust (except, perhaps, in a GST exempt dynasty trust)[24] because the taxpayer that owns the property is the trust and not an individual who can use the property as a personal residence. Thus, unless the trust qualifies as a grantor trust for income tax purposes, income tax benefits such as the exclusion from gain on the sale of a principal personal residence likely will be unavailable.[25]

On the other hand, land that will be managed to produce income may be just as adaptable to a trust as income producing personal property, although its management may entail a different form of exper-

---

[22] See § 7.3.4.

[23] See, e.g., Edinburg v. Edinburg, 492 N.E.2d 1164 (Mass. Ct. App. 1986) (sixteen art works deemed trust assets by virtue of physical markings, documents, and sworn testimony in a divorce action).

[24] See generally § 11.4.5.5.

[25] See § § 5.11.9 nn.224-225 and accompanying text and 6.3.3.9 n.78. Alternatively, however, a beneficiary's rent free use of residential realty held in trust is not an income taxable benefit. Compare ownership of income producing assets that generate cash that is distributed to the beneficiary to use to pay rent or a mortgage. This tax free use does not require a trust, however, because living in your own home does not generate imputed income equal to the rental value of the home (notwithstanding periodic calls for tax reform that would generate that result). See § 6.3.3.9 n.78.

§ 6.5.1

tise (such as farm or ranch management) than does the management of a securities portfolio. As an alternative to using a trust, however, land also lends itself more readily than does personal property to division into legal present and future interests (although historically bifurcation of title without the benefit of a trust has proven to be troublesome).[26] Moreover, care must be exercised with respect to realty because the interest retained by the settlor of a trust, which may be regarded as personalty rather than realty, may affect its taxation for state tax purposes.[27]

The point is that many varied tax and nontax considerations must be weighed when analyzing the time or form of inter vivos transfer to employ. Not the least of these should be the ability of the transferee to manage the gifted property, particularly if the property needs expert management and especially if a trust is an appropriate vehicle to provide management that is separated from beneficial enjoyment.

§6.5.2 *Cancellation of Indebtedness*

A taxpayer who wants to make a completed transfer of cash or other property to a transferee without incurring an immediate gift tax may attempt to leverage the gift tax annual exclusion by loaning the cash or selling the property in exchange for an installment note and then canceling a portion of the debt equal to the gift tax annual exclusion in each subsequent year until the notes have been extinguished. Without care, however, the gift and income tax consequences of this approach may be worse than if the taxpayer had conveyed a fractional portion of the

---

[26] See § 4.1.2.

[27] See, e.g., Indiana Department of State Revenue v. Estate of Puschel, 582 N.E.2d 923 (Ind. Tax Ct. 1991) (Indiana decedent established revocable inter vivos trust of Florida realty; Indiana Department of Revenue successfully argued that the decedent therefore died with a beneficial interest in intangible personal property that was subject to Indiana inheritance tax, notwithstanding the estate's argument that the Florida realty did not lose its character by being held in trust and was exempt from Indiana tax because it was located outside the taxing jurisdiction; the Florida tax consequences of the asset held at death were not involved).

property or a dollop of the cash in each year,[28] forsaking the opportunity to freeze the value of transferred property and shift future income from it in an immediate transfer.

For income tax purposes, a sale for an installment note generates gain or loss that is reportable in installments under §453,[29] but the annual forgiveness constitutes a §453B disposition that causes the deferred income tax liability to be recognized by the taxpayer. Furthermore, the forgiveness is a §61(a)(12) discharge of indebtedness that generates income to the transferee.[30] The transferee's income tax liability is avoidable if forgiveness of the debt is deemed to be supported by the transferor's donative intent, making the discharge a gift that may qualify for the gift tax annual exclusion. The hazard with a gift characterization is that the government will successfully recharacterize the *initial* transfer as a gift rather than a loan or a sale, thereby accelerating into the initial year all of the taxpayer's gift tax liability, thereby defeating the objective of leveraging the annual exclusion.

Treatment as an immediate gift rather than a loan may be based on the lack of any demonstrable intent to collect on the debt, as illustrated in Miller v. Commissioner,[31] in which most of the indicia of a bona fide

---

[28] See Rev. Rul. 83-180, 1983-1 C.B. 169 (permitting annual exclusion for gifts of specified acres of land over three years, in each case based on the amount of the available exclusion and the value of the land per acre).

[29] Subject to the §453(e) acceleration rule if the transferee is a §453(f)(1) related party who disposes of the transferred property within two years.

[30] See, e.g., Stackhouse v. United States, 71-1 U.S. Tax Cas. (CCH) ¶9128 (W.D. Tex. 1970), rev'd and rem'd, 441 F.2d 465 (5th Cir. 1971) (cancellation of a partnership debt to which §§752 and 731(a) were applicable to cause income from cancellation of the debt to be taxed as capital gain); Miller Trust v. Commissioner, 76 T.C. 191 (1981) (D was indebted to a corporation, the stock of which was owned by D and S; discharge of indebtedness income resulted to the estate when the corporation failed to file a timely claim against D's estate, thus barring collection of the debt); Dosek v. Commissioner, 30 T.C.M. (CCH) 688 (1971).

[31] 71 T.C.M. (CCH) 1674 (1996), aff'd in an unpublished opinion (9th Cir. 1997). See also Rev. Rul. 77-299, 1977-2 C.B. 343 (sale of nonincome producing land for interest free notes payable annually in the amount of the gift tax annual exclusion and accompanied by a letter from the seller announcing the intent to forgive one note each year, which occurred, the taxpayer obviously contemplating cancellation to take advantage of the gift tax annual exclusion); citing Deal v.

loan were lacking. According to the *Miller* court, nine facts and circumstances may be considered in determining whether there is a real expectation of repayment and a bona fide intent to enforce a debt, as opposed to making a completed gift upon the original transfer of funds, including: (1) a promissory note or other evidence of indebtedness, (2) interest charged, (3) security or collateral, (4) a fixed maturity date, (5) a demand for repayment, (6) actual repayment, (7) a transferee with the ability to repay, (8) records that reflect the transfer as a loan, and (9) federal tax reporting of the transfer that is consistent with a loan.

As applied to the *Miller* facts, there was a notation on each check constituting a transfer of funds that the transaction was a loan and the transferees signed notes reflecting that the alleged loans were repayable in one balloon payment three years later or on any earlier demand, but the loans were unsecured, they were interest free, and only one payment ($15,000 out of $200,000 transferred) was made. The remaining amounts were forgiven in annual amounts that never exceeded the gift tax annual exclusion for split gifts by the transferor and the transferor's spouse (although no gift tax returns making the split gift election were filed for most of the years in question[32] and, in those years in which returns *were* filed, the gifts reported did not match the forgiveness amounts stated in the transferor's letters of forgiveness).

Working from a presumption that transfers within a family are gifts in the year of the original transfer, the *Miller* court found that the taxpayer failed to carry the burden of proving that they instead were loans, in this case meaning in the year of the original transfer, meaning that the annual exclusion did not shelter these transfers. Among the most damning factors were (1) inadequate and inconsistent documenta-

---

(Footnote Continued)

Commissioner, 29 T.C. 730 (1958), Estate of Reynolds v. Commissioner, 55 T.C. 172 (1970), DeGoldschmidt-Rothschild v. Commissioner, 9 T.C. 325 (1947), aff'd, 168 F.2d 975 (2d Cir. 1948), accelerating the gift to the year of the initial transfer and denial of seriatim annual exclusions, and PLR 200603002 (raised on the government's own motion "for purposes of sound tax administration" involving a transfer of life insurance policies in exchange for a note that was canceled several months later in a new year, prior to any payments being made). But see Haygood v. Commissioner, 42 T.C. 936 (1964), nonacq., Rev. Rul. 77-299, and Estate of Kelley v. Commissioner, 63 T.C. 321 (1974).

[32] See § 7.1.3 n.138 and accompanying text.

tion, (2) a lack of commercially reasonable terms (such as charging interest and obtaining adequate security or collateral), (3) a failure to establish the kinds of facts that a commercial lender would rely upon before making bona fide loans, such as evidence of the transferee's ability to repay, and (4) improper tax return documentation of the transaction reflecting the treatment asserted by the taxpayer.

Similar factors were cited in Hunt v. Commissioner,[33] the Tax Court stressing a number of factors that should be considered in determining whether a transfer is a bona fide loan or merely a gift in disguise: (1) was there a note or other evidence of the debt, (2) was there a written loan

---

[33] 57 T.C.M. (CCH) 919 (1989). The primary issue in *Hunt* was whether forgiveness of loans entitled the lender to a bad debt deduction, all flowing from a failed effort by the lender and several children to corner the silver market. The taxpayer and these children undertook massive buying programs that eventually turned sour and, as their margin buying accounts were called, the taxpayer made loans to the children to attempt to keep them solvent. When the market got away from them, the taxpayer demanded repayment of the debts and deducted the loans as bad debt losses when the children could not perform.

In challenging the deduction the government alleged that the loans were gifts when made and that discharge of the debts constituted income to the children. According to the Tax Court, transfers made to the taxpayer's children were loans prior to a date when the court deemed the taxpayer was aware that the children were hopelessly insolvent. Thereafter transfers to the children were deemed to be gifts. As a result of this holding, the taxpayer was allowed to deduct over $97 million in bad debts and, to the extent the children were insolvent even after the taxpayer forgave those debts (only one child came out of the red, to the tune of just $32,000), no § 108 income to the children was imputed either.

To the government's argument that the loans were gifts because they were not made at arm's length, the court responded that intra family loans are subject to closer scrutiny but that these passed muster. The fact that the terms of the loans were more favorable than could be obtained in the market in general was not sufficient to negate the bona fides of these transactions and, because the taxpayer charged interest at the prevailing prime rate, these loans did not produce the imputed gift tax consequence of below-market-interest loans under § 7872. See also Goldstein v. Commissioner, 40 T.C.M. (CCH) 752 (1980) (bad debt deduction allowed when loans to trusts for lender's children could not be repaid).

A further potential gift tax issue is illustrated by Estate of Lang v. Commissioner, 613 F.2d 770 (9th Cir. 1980), and Rev. Rul. 81-264, 1981-2 C.B. 185 (failure to call for repayment of a demand loan to a child was deemed a gift when the statute of limitation for enforcement of the loan expired under state law).

§ 6.5.2

agreement, (3) did the parties' records reflect the transfer as a loan, (4) was interest charged, (5) was there a fixed repayment schedule, (6) was there any security or collateral for the debt, (7) was the alleged borrower solvent when the loan was made, (8) was any demand for repayment ever made, and (9) did the borrower actually repay any part of the loan?

The *Hunt* court rejected the government's request that several additional factors be considered, which the government gleaned from cases involving the question whether contributions to a corporation are debt or equity: (1) what was the source of the debtor's payments of principal and interest, (2) what was the status of the loans relative to debt owed to other creditors, (3) what was the borrower's ability to borrow from other lenders, (4) did the borrower make payments on time, and (5) what was the lender's risk in making the loans?

Similar consequences may apply to a straight loan of cash, without a sale.[34] If there is no gift when the loan is made, then a gift occurs when the loan later is forgiven, equal to the principal amount forgiven and any interest accrued to the date of forgiveness.

Unanticipated FET inclusion of the transferred property may add further consequences to an alleged loan or sale that is deemed to be an immediate inter vivos gift. To illustrate, Estate of Maxwell v. Commissioner[35] recharacterized an attempted sale of a personal residence to the decedent's only child with a lease back to the decedent as a transfer with a retained life estate that was not a bona fide sale for full and adequate consideration in money or money's worth for purposes of avoiding FET inclusion under § 2036(a)(1).[36] Because the decedent died during the

---

[34] See Vinikoor v. Commissioner, 75 T.C.M. (CCH) 2185 (1998) (there was no bona fide debt because there was no repayment nor any demand for repayment (nor was repayment ever likely), interest was not at market rates and also was not paid, the alleged notes had no fixed maturity dates or collateral, and there was no discernable business rationale for the loans); Rev. Rul. 81-264, 1981-2 C.B. 185 (a note will not be considered valuable consideration and the taxpayer will be deemed to have made a gift at the time of the loan to the full extent of the loan if the loan was part of a prearranged plan in which the taxpayer intended to forgive or not to collect on the note).

[35] 98 T.C. 594 (1992), aff'd, 3 F.3d 521 (2d Cir. 1993).

[36] See § 7.3.4.1 nn.115-123 and accompanying text. Intent may speak to the bona fides of a sale in some cases but in *Maxwell* the decedent made too many mistakes to substantiate a legitimate sale argument. For example, the sale price

term of the lease and no evidence indicated that the decedent (who had cancer and was 82 years old when the property was sold) reasonably could expect to outlive that leasehold, the court found an "express or implied understanding" that possession was retained for life, causing inclusion of the full date-of-death value of the property in the decedent's gross estate. Moreover, the court determined that the transfer was not a bona fide sale because the parties never intended that the note be repaid, based on the fact that it was forgiven in annual increments equal to the annual exclusions of the transferor and the transferor's spouse. The balance was forgiven under the decedent's will, which was executed two days after the original transaction. The note was deemed to have no value from the outset, and therefore it did not represent full and adequate consideration in money or money's worth to avoid § 2036(a)(1) inclusion because the parties never intended that the child would pay the note.[37]

(Footnote Continued)

for the residence was $30,000 less than the appraised value of the property, the decedent taking a note from the child and treating $20,000 of the deficiency as annual exclusion gifts to the child and the child's spouse. Perhaps the remaining $10,000 deficiency was meant to be covered by a cash down payment, but there was no evidence of an actual payment. This alone would cause § 2036(a)(1) to apply because there is no exception of sales for less than full and adequate consideration. Moreover, each year after the transfer the note was reduced by $20,000 (again purportedly tax free under the gift tax annual exclusion), and the child only paid interest on the note, in an amount roughly equal to the rent paid by the decedent to the child for the right to continue living in the residence, all causing the court to conclude that the parties' economic situation did not change meaningfully under the transaction.

[37] To the same estate tax inclusion effect, based on the lack of a bona fide note as consideration, see Estate of Musgrove v. United States, 95-2 U.S. Tax Cas. (CCH) ¶ 60,204 (Ct. Fed. Cl. 1995) (interest free, unsecured, death-terminating demand note made 18 days before the lender's death, which the court held to be not effective to preclude estate tax inclusion of the principal amount of the debt), in which the decedent was seriously ill when the loan was made, the borrower was the decedent's only heir and the sole beneficiary of the decedent's estate, and the borrower had no funds with which to repay the debt because the borrowed funds were used to pay a pre-existing tax liability. The note itself made it clear that there was no legitimate expectation of repayment. There was no payment schedule, no interest obligation, and the face of the note indicated that it would be forgiven if the lender died before repayment. Citing Deal v. Commissioner, 29 T.C. 730 (1958), and Rev. Ruls. 81-286, 1981-2 C.B. 185, and 77-299,

§ 6.5.3 *Capital Contributions and Gifts of Stock*

In addition to recharacterizing loan and sale transactions as immediate gifts (or as nonevents with FET inclusion results), taxpayers must worry about unexpected gifts in the context of contributions to the capital of a corporation or partnership. For example, the taxpayer in Hollingsworth v. Commissioner[38] contributed property to a closely held corporation in exchange for a promissory note. The court determined that the value of the property was greater than the value of the promissory note, which was regarded as a gift to the corporation. Because the decedent was one of six equal shareholders, the total gift was five-sixths of the differential in value, as to which no gift tax annual exclusions were available because a gift to a corporation is treated as a future interest gift to the shareholders.[39]

Similarly, the taxpayer in PLR 9114023 proposed to make transfers of corporate stock to unrelated key employees that other shareholders of the corporation were not going to match. The government held[40] that the transfers would be treated as capital contributions to the corporation that would constitute indirect gifts to the other shareholders. The taxpayer would have been in a better position by making simple gifts to those key employees out of affection or other nonbusiness related motives because, presumably, the gift tax annual exclusion would apply. As pro-

---

(Footnote Continued)

1977-2 C.B. 343, the court held that the note was not consideration for the loan because the decedent never intended to collect on the debt by demanding repayment. That statement is troubling because, if it was true, the loan should have been taxed as a gift when made rather than an includible asset at death. Nevertheless, citing Buckwalter v. Commissioner, 46 T.C. 805 (1966), in which the note was not self-canceling but the parties agreed that it would be forgiven if the lender died before repayment, the court concluded that the lender held an interest in the note that was includible under § 2033 notwithstanding the forgiveness. In addition, the court held that the demand feature of the loan was tantamount to a § 2038(a)(1) power to revoke the transfer, which on its own is a dangerous and unprecedented conclusion in the demand loan arena. See §§ 5.10.5, 5.11.3 n.59, and 7.3.1 respectively.

[38] 86 T.C. 91 (1986).

[39] See § 7.1.1.1 n.26 and accompanying text.

[40] Citing Rev. Rul. 80-196, 1980-2 C.B. 32.

posed, all the taxpayer would gain from the transfers was a basis increase for the value of the deemed capital contribution.[41]

Transfers of voting stock should not be made with retained voting control if FET inclusion is to be avoided. But it is permissible to retain voting control through retention of voting stock following a transfer of nonvoting stock.[42] In addition, caution should be exercised in making transfers of stock (or other assets) so as not to cause retained assets to be insufficient to satisfy the requirements for dividend-free stock redemption under §303, deferred FET payment under §6166, and special use valuation under §2032A. Conversely, an inter vivos transfer may be desirable to ensure qualification under those rules—subject to the §2035(c)(1) and (c)(2) restrictions on the ability to engineer qualification through gifts made within three years of death.[43] Inter vivos transfers of life insurance policies on the donor's life also may be especially important in achieving this objective. Moreover, in choosing among assets, loss of §1014 new basis at death with respect to transferred assets may dictate that higher basis assets should be transferred inter vivos and lower basis assets (like stock in a family business) be retained for new basis at death purposes, all other factors being equal.

---

[41] See also PLR 7935115, which concluded that a gift of closely-held stock by a shareholder to the closely-held corporation was a taxable gift to the other shareholders (who were the donor's children). The value of the gift was the difference between the value of the transferor's interest in the corporation prior to the transfer and the value of that interest after the transfer.

[42] See §7.3.4.3.

[43] See §§ 15.2.2, 15.3.3, and 15.8.3.

§6.5.3

7

Wealth Transfer Taxation of Inter Vivos Transfers

§7.0 INTRODUCTION

Prior chapters discussed the advantages of inter vivos transfers and the comparative estate planning attributes of employing inter vivos transfers or wills. This chapter addresses various wealth transfer tax consequences of inter vivos transfers, particularly to the extent those transfers are made without gift tax or GST or to the extent FET at the transferor's death will not be avoided.

The gift tax definition of a gift is difficult to cobble together because there is no single articulation of it that currently exists in the Code or Regulations. By collecting requirements from a number of sources, however, the present definition of a gift for wealth transfer tax purposes[1]

---

[1] **§7.0** The familiar income tax definition of a gift is found in Commissioner v. Duberstein, 363 U.S. 278 (1960) ("a gift proceeds from a 'detached and disinterested generosity' . . . 'out of affection, respect, admiration, charity or like impulses'"). It is *not* the proper definition for wealth transfer tax purposes. Indeed, there are cases in which a gift for gift tax purposes was a sale or income for income tax purposes, showing the inconsistent treatment attributable to the two different definitions. See, e.g., TAM 7921017:

the definition of a gift for gift tax purposes is not dependent upon donative intent or the common law concept of a gift. The definition is based upon whether consideration in money's worth is received by the transferor when the property is transferred. This definition is substantially different from the one applied to the income tax concept of a gift, namely, whether

the transfer is primarily motivated by the donative intent of the transferor; Fared-Es-Sultaneh v. Commissioner, 160 F.2d 812 (2d Cir. 1947) (sale to transferee for income tax basis determination purposes was a gift for the transferor's gift tax purposes); Getty v. Commissioner, 91 T.C. 160 (1988), rev'd, 913 F.2d 1486 (9th Cir. 1990) (lump sum settlement paid to a child of the decedent by the residuary beneficiary of the decedent's estate, against whom the child had brought suit, was taxable income under §102(b) because it replaced taxable income the child would have received from the decedent; reversal was based on a determination that the Tax Court's factual determination about the nature of the payment was in error).

Counterintuitive as it may seem, the transferee has income in the year of receipt that cannot be excluded under §102(a) if the alleged gift is not effective because the donor is incompetent and the transfer was unauthorized. This is because the transfer was not a valid gift. Zips v. Commissioner, 38 T.C. 620 (1962); Eaton v. Commissioner, 36 T.C.M. (CCH) 354 (1977); Bader v. Commissioner, 32 T.C.M. (CCH) 813 (1973). As discussed in §3.10.4.3, the transfer is voidable (not void) and, if returned, may create a claim of right action, allowing a deduction or a credit against tax as authorized under §1341.

can be stated as "a voluntary and complete transfer of property by an individual for less than full and adequate consideration in money or money's worth."[2] For purposes of this discussion the gift tax definition of a gift is the premier focus because the only inter vivos transfer that is subject to immediate GST is a direct skip and the definition of a direct skip requires that the transfer be "subject to" the gift tax.[3] Furthermore, there is no need for a definition of a gift for FET purposes separate from that for gift tax purposes.

Considered first in this analysis are transfers that are "subject to" the gift tax but that may not incur a tax payment obligation. This may occur for a variety of reasons, such as the transfer is not yet complete and therefore not yet ripe for taxation or the transfer qualifies for an exclusion from the tax. Next is a discussion of gifts that are subject to taxation presently, along with valuation aspects that often are the most significant issues and that may present the most attractive reasons to engage in inter vivos planning.

This discussion of the gift tax is followed by a summary of FET rules that may cause the subject matter of an inter vivos transfer to be included in the transferor's gross estate for FET purposes. This may occur notwithstanding completed gift treatment during the transferor's life, and an illustration shows how the tax law avoids inappropriate double taxation in such a case while it negates some (but not all) of the expected advantages of inter vivos transfers. A final segment addresses ancillary concepts, such as compliance issues and statute of limitation considerations that flow from them.

Before undertaking that journey, however, one additional introductory notion deserves mention. The prospect of making inter vivos transfers based on tax consequences that are known and reliable under the current law to accomplish desirable long-term results is troubled by the fact that change is the only constant in this area of the tax law. If a taxpayer engages in a transaction based on the current state of the law,

---

[2] See § 2512(b) and Treas. Reg. §§ 25.0-1(b); 25.2501-1(a)(1); 25.2511-2(b). The full and adequate consideration element is really a subset of the valuation regime.

[3] § 2612(c)(1). As the discussion at § 7.1.1.8 reveals, a gift may be subject to gift tax and therefore constitute a direct skip even if the annual exclusion precludes gift tax liability for the gift.

one consideration must be whether Congress will change the rules in a manner that negates the taxpayer's reliance.

A long and somewhat checkered jurisprudence on the question whether retroactive changes are constitutional came to a head with the United States Supreme Court decision in United States v. Carlton,[4] in which the Court essentially concluded that Congress may impose retroactive tax law changes with constitutional impunity. The constitutionality issue arose in a case in which there was no prior notice that a change might be made, no overall net gain from the tax law changes made by the particular Act, and detrimental reliance on prior law with respect to a transaction that occurred prior to adoption of the new legislation. This probably was the very best situation for finding a retroactive legislative change to be invalid, yet the Supreme Court held that retroactive tax legislation is not invalid. In the process it may have guaranteed "that all retroactive tax laws will henceforth be valid."[5]

Carlton involved a decedent's estate that engaged in a transaction that the government criticized[6] and then Congress eventually negated by retroactively imposing a requirement that did not exist when the decedent's estate engaged in the transaction. By stipulation, the parties agreed the estate would not have engaged in the deal had the law been what it later became. It also was agreed that the estate suffered a financial loss of over $631,000 in generating what would have been a $2.5 million tax saving based on the law in effect when the deal was executed. The sole issue was the constitutionality of the change that retroactively negated this benefit but left the estate with the financial detriment. The Court held that the results of the legislation were not so harsh or oppressive as to constitute a denial of due process of law.

The lower court in *Carlton* rejected "the notion of a per se rule that tax statutes can *always* be retroactively applied so long as they do not enact a 'wholly new' tax."[7] Summarizing over 70 years of case law, that court concluded that "two circumstances emerge as of paramount importance in determining whether the retroactive application of a tax is

---

[4] 512 U.S. 26 (1994), rev'g 972 F.2d 1051 (9th Cir. 1992).

[5] 512 U.S. at 40 (Scalia, concurring).

[6] See Notice 87-13, 1987-1 C.B. 432.

[7] 972 F.2d at 1056 (emphasis in original).

§7.0

unduly harsh and oppressive":[8] (1) did the taxpayer have actual or constructive notice that the law would be amended retroactively, and (2) did the taxpayer reasonably and detrimentally rely on the prelegislative law. Because there was detrimental reliance and no notice, the lower court held that the change was invalid as applied retroactively.

In the process, the court stressed that the legislation that created the tax opportunity seized by the estate was not a last minute endeavor that might have contained an error or oversight that allowed a result not intended by Congress. This opportunity was the result of a long deliberated change with a clear policy that favored the type of transaction involved. The court also found[9] that the estate was not even close to being in the same position it would have been in had the law not changed. Although its tax was no greater than if there had been no transaction, the estate incurred costs and suffered real losses in the transaction itself. Nevertheless, on appeal the Supreme Court concluded that each of these elements was insufficient to render the retroactivity of the change unconstitutional.

The Supreme Court's opinion in *Carlton* should lay the issue of constitutional retroactivity to rest and, although the retroactive application of tax law changes is a serious and troublesome issue, it seems unlikely that Congress will be deemed to have overstepped the broad latitude granted to it in *Carlton*. According to the Court's opinion, joined in or concurred with by all nine Justices, due process is not violated by retroactive tax legislation that is "justified by a rational legislative purpose," with the same standard applied to retroactive economic legislation in general being applied to retroactive tax legislation, making the sole inquiry whether Congress has acted in an arbitrary and irrational manner.[10]

---

[8] 972 F.2d at 1059.

[9] Distinguishing United States v. Hemme, 476 U.S. 558 (1986), rev'g 85-2 U.S. Tax Cas. (CCH) ¶ 13,619 (S.D. Ill. 1985) (§ 2010(c) reduced the decedent's unified credit on account of gifts made before enactment of that credit, which the taxpayer argued was arbitrary and capricious, rendering the change unconstitutional under the Due Process Clause of the Fifth Amendment; the district court agreed, notwithstanding the court's recognition that the taxpayer may have acted in full knowledge of the pending legislative change when the gifts were made).

[10] 512 U.S. at 30.

The Court stated in *Carlton* that Congress' purposes (correction of a mistake) and the modest period of retroactivity (about 14 months from final enactment of the amendment, but less than 3 months from enactment of the original legislation to notification that a change would be made) were adequate to support Congress' retroactive action. And the Court held that the taxpayer's detrimental reliance and lack of notice were not dispositive. "Tax legislation is not a promise, and a taxpayer has no vested right in the Internal Revenue Code."[11]

One concurring opinion suggested that a "wholly new tax" cannot be imposed retroactively and that a period of retroactivity of longer than "the year preceding the legislative session in which the law was enacted" would raise serious constitutional questions.[12] Nevertheless, it seems unlikely that Congress will be deemed to have overstepped its bounds even in such a case in the tax arena.[13] As paraphrased by a second concurring opinion, "[t]o pass constitutional muster the retroactive aspects of the statute need only be 'rationally related to a legitimate purpose.' Revenue raising is certainly a legitimate legislative purpose, and any law that retroactively adds a tax, removes a deduction, or increases a rate rationally furthers that goal."[14]

Perhaps in a "good for the goose, good for the gander" sense in light of all this, Neal v. United States[15] held that the federal tax consequences of a prior transfer could be reversed upon a determination that

---

[11] 512 U.S. at 33.

[12] 512 U.S. at 38 (O'Connor, concurring).

[13] See Quarty v. United States, 170 F.3d 961 (9th Cir. 1999), NationsBank v. United States, 269 F.3d 1332 (Fed. Cir. 2001), US Bank v. United States, 74 F. Supp. 2d 934 (D. Neb. 1999), and Kane v. United States, 942 F. Supp. 233 (E.D. Pa. 1996), aff'd without opinion, 118 F.3d 1576 (3d Cir. 1997) (decedents all died after the maximum tax rate dropped to 50%, after which Congress constitutionally restored the 55% rate retroactive to before each decedent's death); National Taxpayers Union, Inc. v. United States, 68 F.3d 1428 (D.C. Cir. 1995), aff'g 862 F. Supp. 531 (D. D.C. 1994) (dismissing constitutional challenge). See also Oberhand v. Director, Div. of Tax'n, 907 A.2d 428 (N.J. Super. Ct. App. Div. 2006) (retroactive amendment to the New Jersey FET to replace revenue lost due to the increased federal applicable exclusion amount was constitutional, relying heavily on *Carlton*).

[14] 512 U.S. at 40 (Scalia, concurring).

[15] 151 F.3d 1201 (3d Cir. 1999), aff'g 98-2 U.S. Tax Cas. (CCH) ¶ 60,318 (W.D. Pa. 1998).

§7.0

the transfer was made on the basis of a mistake and could be rescinded or reformed under state law. The (alleged) "mistake" was in not knowing that Congress would repeal §2036(c) subsequent to the taxpayer's transfer—and how *could* such a thing as a retroactive tax law change be known? Following a state court action allowing rescission of the transaction, the court permitted recovery of $420,000 of gift tax paid.

Most interesting about the court's decision was its statement relative to the effect of the retroactive legislation. Speaking of the *nunc pro tunc* (as if it never happened) nature of the retroactive revocation, the court said that "if a taxpayer may be made by Congress to pay taxes on events that were not taxable . . . when they occurred, . . . the government may be made to refund taxes paid on previously taxable events that have become non-taxable, pursuant to Congress' explicit, retroactive repeal, *nunc pro tunc*, of the taxing legislation."[16] In this respect, if retroactive wealth transfer tax law changes are constitutional, perhaps taxpayers have a right to retrace their steps to undo taxable transfers and obtain a refund of any taxes paid. None of this, however, is likely to increase a taxpayer's feeling of security in any transaction executed earlier than otherwise might be required.

§7.1 TRANSFERS THAT AVOID PAYMENT OF WEALTH TRANSFER TAX

A gift tax may not be payable even if a transfer meets the definition of a taxable gift for federal gift tax purposes. Transfers that do not incur a tax payment are discussed first because frequently they are the most appealing forms of inter vivos planning.

§7.1.1 Exclusions and Exceptions

The "business transaction" exception protects a transfer from gift taxation notwithstanding that it was a voluntary transfer for less than full and adequate consideration, if it was not meant to be gratuitous. Instead, the transfer merely represents a bad business bargain. Thus, a transfer that is "a sale, exchange, or other transfer of property made in the ordinary course of business (a transaction which is bona fide, at arm's

---

[16] 98-2 U.S. Tax Cas. at 75,648.

length, and free from any donative intent), [is] considered as made for an adequate and full consideration in money or money's worth" and therefore does not constitute a taxable gift.[1]

By way of example, a purchaser of a used car who pays too much does not make a gift of the amount paid in excess of the FMV of the automobile, unless the seller is a natural object of the buyer's bounty and the excess payment is motivated by donative intent in a less than arm's length transaction.[2] This subjective test is the only place in the gift tax in which motive or intent is relevant to an evaluation of whether a gift was made. Otherwise any shortfall from full and adequate consideration is the gift. The existence of a family relation between the parties normally is an indication that the exception cannot apply, although it will not necessarily defeat qualification for the exception.[3]

---

[1] §7.1 Treas. Reg. § 25.2512-8.

[2] See, e.g., Kincaid v. United States, 682 F.2d 1220, 1226 (5th Cir. 1982) (parent and children organized a corporation; parents made a gift to the other shareholders to the extent the value of stock the parent received was less than the value of property contributed to the corporation and that gift was taxable because it was not in the ordinary course of business: "There may indeed have been business reasons for transferring the land to the corporation in exchange for stock, but there was no business purpose, only a donative one, for [the taxpayer] to accept less value in return than [the taxpayer] gave up"); Harwood v. Commissioner, 82 T.C. 239 (1984), aff'd in an unpublished opinion, 786 F.2d 1174 (9th Cir. 1986) (transfer from a parent to children of an interest in a family partnership, structured totally by the family accountant, with no arm's length bargaining, in exchange for the children's promissory note was regarded as not in the ordinary course of business); Estate of Slutsky v. Commissioner, 46 T.C.M. (CCH) 1423, 1432 (1983) (real estate lease and purchase option agreement between parent and children was a gift for gift tax purposes "inferred from the inadequacy of consideration, regardless of the transferor's subjective intent, [not] negated by the arms length nature of the transaction, [because the] transactions . . . were between closely related parties, and as such . . . subject to rigid scrutiny"); TAM 8821005 (transfer to a family partnership was not in the ordinary course of business, as revealed by the close family relationships involved, the absence of arm's length negotiations, the transfer of a fee interest in realty in exchange for a low yield minority interest subject to termination before the donor's death).

[3] See, e.g., Estate of Noland v. Commissioner, 47 T.C.M. (CCH) 1640 (1984) (parent's transfer to child in settlement of bona fide family property dispute lacked donative intent and constituted an arm's length transaction that was

§7.1.1

A second exception that seldom is relevant to estate planning situations applies the same deemed consideration result to property transfers incident to a divorce.[4] Along with the income tax rule that intraspousal transfers are ignored, § 1041 applies the gift tax carryover basis rule (notwithstanding that the gift tax exception applies), meaning that for all tax purposes inter vivos intraspousal transfers are totally tax neutral.

In this respect, Revenue Ruling 79-118[5] reviewed the gift tax consequences in several divorce situations. For example, a transfer in exchange for relinquishment of the transferee's support rights is a transfer for consideration in money or money's worth that may constitute a gift, but only to the extent the transfer exceeds the value of those support rights.[6] In addition, although relinquishment of marital rights other than

---

(Footnote Continued)

deemed to be for full and adequate consideration and therefore exempt from gift taxation).

[4] See § 2516, along with § § 2043(b)(2) and 2053(e), which provide an FET deduction for § 2516 qualified property settlement obligations outstanding at death.

[5] 1979-1 C.B. 315 (separation agreement called for payment of $10x per month in exchange for relinquishment of all rights of support, and a divorce decree incorporated the agreement; when the payor voluntarily increased the monthly payments, that increase—but not the $10x base amount—constituted a gift and, because the increase was not supported by consideration and therefore was not enforceable, the gift occurred when each additional payment was made).

[6] Cf. Rev. Rul. 79-363, 1979-2 C.B. 345 (in a divorce settlement transaction the transferor created a trust of $600,000 under which the transferee received a life annuity worth $300,000, with a remainder to an adult child; the transferee specifically relinquished all support rights—valued at $200,000—and all other marital rights—valued at $400,000—as to which § 2516 was applicable and the Ruling concluded that the transferor therefore was protected from gift tax liability to the full extent of the $300,000 life annuity (rather than just $200,000 of it); although release of the support rights was consideration in money or money's worth, the transferee did not bargain for the remainder interest in the adult child in exchange for that release, so that portion of the transfer was a gift by the transferor; if the transferee's release had been given in return for that remainder interest, then the transferee would have made the same gift to the adult child). The wrinkle added by PLR 201116006 in a similar situation was that the gift on creation, also made by the transferor, of the remainder interest to their descendants would be subject to § 2702 if it occurred today. The PLR also confirmed that the transferee spouse had no estate tax inclusion at death. Had the spouses simply divided their property and had the transferee created the same trust with

§ 7.1.1

support does not constitute consideration in money or money's worth, a transfer pursuant to a divorce decree is not a voluntary transfer. Therefore, a decree-mandated transfer also is not a taxable gift.[7] Finally, compliance with the requirements of § 2516 prevents a gift tax from being incurred if the transfer is made pursuant to a property settlement agreement and the divorce occurs within one year before or two years after execution of the agreement.[8]

In addition, certain inter vivos transfers are excluded entirely from the gift tax calculation. These transfers constitute otherwise taxable gifts but they qualify for either the § 2503(b) annual exclusion or the § 2503(e) ed/med exclusion. As such, they do not exhaust any of the donor's unified credit and do not increase the tax base upon which the progressive tax rate is determined for subsequent taxable transfers.

§ 7.1.1.1 Annual Exclusion

For example, the transferor may give up to $14,000 (in 2013, reflecting an inflation index amount)[9] per donee, per year, to as many separate individual donees as the transferor chooses, all tax free, but only if a transfer constitutes a "present interest" in property. The regulations reflect the § 2503(b) parenthetical exclusion from the annual exclusion

---

(Footnote Continued)

the same remainder to their descendants the transferee would have incurred all the gift and estate tax consequences, which reveals that spouses may negotiate in a property settlement which of them will incur the wealth transfer tax consequences of whatever remains for their descendants.

[7] See Harris v. Commissioner, 340 U.S. 106 (1950).

[8] An interesting application of these various principle is found in PLR 201029002, in which divorcing spouses were the sole and then survivor beneficiaries of a two-life CRUT. The court severed that annuity and created two separate CRUTs, one for each spouse, which constituted a gift from the one spouse who previously was the sole annuitant to the other whose survivor benefit was upgraded. That severance also materially altered their entitlements for income tax purposes and was regarded as a gain or loss realization event. But then the PLR concluded that § 1041 would provide nonrecognition of the income tax consequences, and the *Harris* principle precluded gift tax consequences because—although the requirements of § 2516 were not met—the severance was pursuant to a divorce court's order and therefore was not voluntary, which meant that it could not constitute a transfer subject to gift tax.

[9] § 2503(b)(2).

for gifts of "future interests in property" and refer to a present interest as "[a]n unrestricted right to the immediate use, possession, or enjoyment of property or the income from property (such as a life estate or term certain)."[10] A future interest is a legal term that includes "reversions, remainders, and other interests or estates, whether vested or contingent, . . . limited to commence in use, possession, or enjoyment at some future date or time."[11]

In some rare cases a future interest transfer will qualify. For example, in Clark v. Commissioner[12] and Revenue Ruling 78-168[13] income was payable to a named beneficiary for life and the remainder beneficiary gratuitously transferred half of the remainder to that income beneficiary, which merged under controlling local law with the life estate in that half and therefore was deemed to constitute a present interest for annual exclusion purposes. "If, however, [the] . . . life interest was required to remain in trust until its termination[], then the transfer of the remainder would have been a transfer of a future interest."[14]

---

[10] Treas. Reg. § 2503-3(b).

[11] Treas. Reg. § 25.2503-3(a). Compare Rev. Rul. 78-272, 1978-2 C.B. 247, in which the settlor of a trust for a life income beneficiary conveyed a retained reversion to the income beneficiary but, according to the Ruling, did not intend the trust to terminate by merger of the life estate and the reversion; thus, the beneficiary's present enjoyment was not increased by the transfer and the gift of the reversion did not qualify as a transfer of a present interest for annual exclusion purposes.

Cf. Rev. Rul. 76-179, 1976-1 C.B. 290 (extension of qualifying present income interest for an additional term is a separate gift of a future interest that could not be aggregated with the lead interest to qualify for the annual exclusion). With respect to aggregation of interests for present interest qualification see § 7.1.1.9 n.95 and accompanying text. And see Estate of Grossinger v. Commissioner, 723 F.2d 1057 (2d Cir. 1983), which reveals that not every interest that will commence only in the future is disqualified. However, the facts involved were unusual: the gift was of an annuity following a life estate in an individual whose death was imminent (and who in fact died the next day); the court held that the outstanding life estate should be disregarded in determining whether the annuity was a present interest because doing otherwise would be a "ludicrous" exaltation of form over substance.

[12] 65 T.C. 126 (1975).

[13] 1978-1 C.B. 298.

[14] 1978-1 C.B. at 298.

Examples of interests that appear to qualify as present interests but that may not be excluded from the gift tax under § 2503(b) are interests that do not guarantee to any particular beneficiary any specific entitlement or enjoyment,[15] typically due to trustee discretion.[16] For instance,

---

[15] See, e.g., Massey v. United States, 82-1 U.S. Tax Cas. (CCH) ¶ 13,460 (E.D. Va. 1982) (interest in a three year escrow deposit was a future interest because it was subject to forfeiture; although the interest could be sold by the donee, it was not regarded as sufficiently marketable to constitute a present interest); Blasdel v. Commissioner, 58 T.C. 1014 (1972) (fractional share beneficial interests in trust given to various family members were future interests because no distribution of income or corpus could be made unless all the beneficiaries unanimously agreed that a distribution should be made or a majority of the beneficiaries and a majority of the Board of Directors of a named bank so agreed); Ritland v. Commissioner, 51 T.C.M. (CCH) 1458 (1986) (income and principal could be distributed only by unanimous consent of the trustees, who were the three beneficiaries; notwithstanding that each beneficiary was given a general testamentary power to appoint one-third of the trust, the unanimous consent requirement and absence of a present power of appointment precluded present interest annual exclusion treatment); Estate of Kolker v. Commissioner, 80 T.C. 1082 (1983) (direction to pay amount equal to annual exclusion to each grandchild who was alive on the annual anniversary of the settlor's birth was not a present interest in any grandchild because the contingency of death meant that no beneficiary had a right to any entitlement); Estate of McClure v. United States, 608 F.2d 478 (Ct. Cl. 1979) (Florida land trust interests subject to control of the donors, who retained a majority interest under the land trust that controlled whether current benefits were available); PLR 8433024 (income and principal were not available for distribution on written demand of the income beneficiary until six months after creation). And cf. Estate of Babbitt v. Commissioner, 87 T.C. 1270 (1986) (FET case that turned on application of the gift tax annual exclusion; donees who were unable to partition property were without present enjoyment of any part of the property).

Compare PLR 8906026 (present interests for annual exclusion purposes deemed to exist with respect to the transfer of property to a trust, followed by a gift to eight donees of fractional interests in the trust, because the trustee was required to distribute all trust income to the current beneficiaries, a majority of the trust beneficiaries could terminate the trust and, on termination, principal was distributable to the beneficiaries in proportion to their interests).

[16] TAM 8219002 (trust required the trustee to distribute all income each year, but the trustee had discretion to determine which beneficiaries would receive that income); citing Rev. Rul. 55-303, 1955-1 C.B. 471 (trustee's discretion when to distribute funds was a barrier to any beneficiary's present enjoyment, and the trustee's discretion as to which beneficiary would receive funds made it impossible to say that any one beneficiary ever would receive income from the trust);

§ 7.1.1.1

Treas. Reg. § 25.2503-3(c) Example (3) posits a trustee that must distribute all trust income annually but has discretion to distribute that income among a class of beneficiaries, no one of whom is entitled to receive any distribution during any given year. The regulation concludes that no beneficiary of that trust has an interest that can be presently ascertained. Therefore, no annual exclusions are available with respect to transfers to that trust.

Further, two companion Revenue Rulings posit situations in which only a portion of a beneficiary's interest qualifies for the annual exclusion. In the first of those Rulings trust income was payable in equal shares to beneficiaries A and B, whose interests would be reduced to one-third of the income each if beneficiary C dropped out of school. Because that act was entirely within C's unfettered control, A and B's present interests were ascertainable only to the extent of their right to one-third of the income.[17] In the second Ruling the trust income also was payable in equal shares between two income beneficiaries, with the survivor to receive all the income after the death of the first of them to die. In this case each beneficiary's separate equal income entitlement was regarded as a present interest but the additional income interest of the survivor was regarded as a future interest because it was not ascertainable which beneficiary would be the survivor.[18]

Similarly with respect to partial qualification for the annual exclusion, an income interest alone may constitute a present interest and the value of that entitlement alone may qualify for the annual exclusion if income from the trust or other transfer is payable to a designated beneficiary and that income entitlement can be valued.[19] This is true

---

(Footnote Continued)

TAM 7905088 (broad trustee discretion whether to pay income was not rectified by a saving clause limiting trustee powers so as not to disqualify the transfer under the present interest rule); PLR 7830145 (guarantee of 5% of the annual income for five years qualified for the annual exclusion but sprinkle provision distribution of additional annual income among a group did not qualify because no one beneficiary was guaranteed to receive any of that additional distribution).

[17] Rev. Rul. 75-415, 1975-2 C.B. 374.

[18] Rev. Rul. 75-506, 1975-2 C.B. 375.

[19] Calder v. Commissioner, 85 T.C. 713 (1985) (there must be an income flow to the donee in an ascertainable amount to qualify for the annual exclusion; although the trusts were authorized to sell—and had engaged in sales of—

even if other elements of the trust or other transfer do not qualify. Such an income interest may qualify notwithstanding a spendthrift provision prohibiting the beneficiary from alienating, assigning, or otherwise anticipating the income,[20] even if the trustee has the power to distribute principal to the income beneficiary.[21] But a trustee power to divert income producing principal to a third party will preclude qualification of an income interest.[22] And interests that entitle the beneficiary to present enjoyment of an identifiable portion of the income of a trust or other transfer will not qualify if the assets are such that there is no guarantee that any present income will be generated.[23]

(Footnote Continued)

artwork and invest the proceeds in income producing assets, the court regarded the possibility of sale as too tentative, making the value of the income flow too uncertain to qualify for the exclusion); Rev. Rul. 77-358, 1977-2 C.B. 342 (losses incurred on trust investments were chargeable to trust income, making it impossible to ascertain the value of the income interest and precluding qualification for the annual exclusion). But see Swetland v. Commissioner, 37 T.C.M. (CCH) 249 (1978) (authority to allocate receipts between income and principal did not prevent annual exclusion valuation of a life income interest because controlling local fiduciary law principles would constrain exercise of the power).

[20] See Quatman v. Commissioner, 54 T.C. 339 (1970); Hutchinson v. Commissioner, 47 T.C. 680 (1967); Charles v. Hassett, 43 F. Supp. 432 (D. Mass. 1942).

[21] Treas. Reg. § 25.2503-3(b).

[22] Funkhouser's Trusts v. Commissioner, 275 F.2d 245 (4th Cir. 1960) (trustee power to distribute principal to income beneficiary's descendants).

[23] Fondren v. Commissioner, 324 U.S. 18, 20-21 (1945), held: "to qualify as a present interest, such a gift must confer on the donee . . . a substantial present economic benefit by reason of use, possession, or enjoyment of either the property itself or income from the property." Notwithstanding that it is an old requirement, cases for decades have denied the annual exclusion if, for example, transferred property does not produce income and cannot be converted into either personal use or income producing property. There must be an ascertainable income flow or other present enjoyment. See, e.g., Maryland Nat'l Bank v. United States, 609 F.2d 1078 (4th Cir. 1979), aff'g sub nom. Willis v. United States, 450 F. Supp. 52 (D. Md. 1978) (annual exclusion denied for trust income interests because the trust property had a history of not producing income and the trustees were authorized to retain unproductive property and could not reinvest sale proceeds for more than three years); Berzon v. Commissioner, 534 F.2d 528 (2d Cir. 1976) (taxpayer with burden to establish the value of an income interest could not use the actuarial tables to do so because restrictions in the trust precluded sale of nonproductive investments or reinvestment in income producing assets); Phillips v. Commissioner, 12 T.C. 216 (1949) (gift of the right

§7.1.1.1

Hackl v. Commissioner[24] is a fine illustration of the present enjoyment requisite not involving a trust, holding that transferred interests in

---

(Footnote Continued)

to income from non-income-producing property, such as a life insurance policy held in trust, is a gift of a future interest); McManus v. Commissioner, 40 T.C.M. (CCH) 866, 868 (1980) (transfer in trust of unproductive woodland; the trust was terminable when all the property was sold but until then the beneficiaries had only future interests: "At the time of making the gifts, any sale and subsequent distribution of the proceeds to the donees was a mere future possibility"); Rev. Rul. 76-360, 1976-2 C.B. 298 (stock transferred was subject to a restriction preventing any retransfer for two years and no dividends had been or were likely to be declared); Rev. Rul. 69-344, 1969-1 C.B. 225 (trustee investment powers authorized retention of nonproductive property and acquisition of life insurance and payment of premiums); TAM 9751003 (FLP limited partner interests did not qualify for the annual exclusion because a provision in the partnership agreement permitted the general partner to retain income "for any reason whatsoever" and the limited partners' inability to withdraw from the partnership, liquidate it, or transfer their interests meant that there was no guarantee of any substantial present economic enjoyment of the transferred interests); TAM 8320007 (annual exclusion denied for transfers in trust of nonproductive nonvoting common stock).

But see Rosen v. Commissioner, 397 F.2d 245 (4th Cir. 1968), nonacq., 1969-1 C.B. 225 (although the trust was invested in stock that had never paid a dividend, the trustee had unrestricted ability to sell and reinvest the proceeds); TAM 9346003 (outright gifts of stock in a family farming operation that had no history of paying dividends; the government nevertheless allowed the annual exclusion because there were no restrictions on conversion of the stock); TAM 8121003 (voting stock subject to a right of first refusal in the event of any proposed sale did not preclude present interest treatment because it did not prevent a shareholder from transferring shares; it did, however, affect the value of the gifts).

[24] 118 T.C. 279 (2002), aff'd, 335 F.3d 664 (7th Cir. 2003). There is some question whether the Tax Court properly characterized the agreement involved—whether transfer truly was precluded or whether it merely made a transferee an assignee (which is not an unusual provision in FLPs or LLCs). The Tax Court stated that the agreement barred alienation "for all practical purposes" because the transfers permitted in violation of the restriction, resulting in a transferee being merely an assignee, meant that conveyance as a means to generate substantial economic benefit was a chimera. On appeal the court stated that

restrictions on the transferability of the shares meant that they were essentially without immediate value to the donees. Granted, [the] operating agreement did address the possibility that a shareholder might violate the agreement and sell his or her shares without the manager's approval.

an LLC did not afford a substantial current economic benefit. Indeed, because the asset involved was not likely to produce any income for quite some time, it was critically important that the court found that the operating agreement foreclosed the donees' ability to presently access any substantial economic or financial benefit. This was because the agreement also foreclosed any transfer of the gifted units to third parties and therefore barred alienation as a means of reaching any present economic value. Therefore, the court disallowed split gift annual exclusions for transfers of deeply discounted LLC interests. Having created an entity with restrictions designed to generate significant wealth transfer tax valuation discounts, the taxpayers precluded the more immediate benefit of gift tax free, annual exclusion transfer of the operating entity units.

The court of appeals rejected taxpayer protests "that [the *Hackl* entity] is set up like any other limited liability corporation and that its restrictions on the alienability of its shares are common in closely held companies." Said the court, "While that may be true, the fact that other companies operate this way does not mean that shares in such companies should automatically be considered present interests for purposes of the gift tax exclusion." This has spawned denial of the annual exclusion in other cases, as if the present enjoyment issue was the sole element of the *Hackl* disallowance. Instead, the key was the confluence of no present return *and* the courts' conclusion that the donees were unable to convert to more productive assets.[25]

(Footnote Continued)

> But, as the Tax Court found, the possibility that a shareholder might violate the operating agreement and sell his or her shares to a transferee who would then not have any membership or voting rights can hardly be called a substantial economic benefit.

This appears to miss the point. If the donee could convert the interests into cash or invest the proceeds in other income producing property the question more properly would appear to be just a valuation dispute. That is not how either court viewed the issue, however, and the courts' finding on these aspects was predictive of the result in other circumstances. See the next note.

[25] To the same effect, involving gifts of interests in discount entities as to which restrictions on transfer were the intended source of valuation adjustments, the government correctly denied the gift tax annual exclusion for failure to meet the present interest requirement. See Fisher v. United States, 2010-2 U.S. Tax Cas. (CCH) ¶ 60,588 (S.D. Ind. 2010) (involving an LLC that primarily held

A further example of transfers that cannot qualify for the annual exclusion because they are not present interests would be a transfer for less than full and adequate consideration in money or money's worth to an entity. These transfers may constitute gifts of a future interest if the real parties in interest are individuals (such as partners in a partnership or shareholders in a corporation) who cannot immediately benefit from the transfer. For example, in Hollingsworth v. Commissioner[26] the tax-

---

(Footnote Continued)

undeveloped land on the shore of Lake Michigan), and Price v. Commissioner, T.C. Memo. 2010-2 (2010) (involving interests in an FLP that owned closely held business stock and commercial real estate). The *Price* FLP prevented any partner from withdrawing, it restricted assignments or transfers to third parties of partnership interests, and it allowed the general partner to control the distribution of profits or income. Similarly, the *Fisher* LLC restricted transfers and subjected all distributions to the discretion of a general manager. The *Fisher* LLC contained a right of first refusal if an owner attempted a transfer to a third party. But it was deemed inadequate to salvage the annual exclusion (notwithstanding speculation by some observers that such a right would suffice) because "it is impossible for [the donees] to presently realize a substantial economic benefit." A put right is different but it is uncertain whether that would alter the result, *Price* saying that the present interest requirement would be subverted "[i]f the possibility of a donor's agreeing to buy back a gift sufficed to establish a present interest in the donee." A gift of cash that the donee would use to purchase the discount entity interest would avoid this annual exclusion issue if the step transaction doctrine did not apply and if the donor was willing to incur any income tax on the sale. Or the donor could simply make a taxable gift and take advantage of annual exclusion gifting with other assets transferred during the year.

[26] 86 T.C. 91 (1986). See also Chanin v. United States, 393 F.2d 972 (Ct. Cl. 1968) (rejecting the contention that each donee received a present interest because the stock value increase could be realized immediately, noting that the donee of every future interest receives something of value that usually could be sold); and cf. Heringer v. Commissioner, 235 F.2d 149 (9th Cir. 1956) (if property transferred to a closely held corporation was a gift to the shareholders—a question the court did not resolve—it would be a gift of a future interest of 60% of the value of the transferred property because the donor owned 40% of the stock and a donor cannot make a gift to the donor); Stinson Estate v. United States, 2000-1 U.S. Tax Cas. (CCH) ¶ 60,377 (7th Cir. 2000) (forgiveness of corporate debt was an indirect gift in the amount of the debt and not the increase in the per share value of the stock of the shareholders, and it is not a present interest); Estate of Lauder v. Commissioner, 68 T.C.M. (CCH) 985 (1994) (the indirect gift to shareholders of a closely held corporation qualified in part for the marital deduction because one of those shareholders was S, and D's stock was pur-

payer contributed property to a closely held corporation for a note that the court determined was worth less than the value of the transferred property. That gift to the corporation was taxable as a gift to the five equal shareholders of the corporation other than the taxpayer and no annual exclusion was allowed.

As articulated by Revenue Ruling 71-443,[27] the logic for denial of the annual exclusion in such cases is that:

> Shareholders of [a] corporation do not have any present or immediate right to use, possess, or enjoy the donated property or the income from the property. This they can do only upon liquidation of the corporation or declaration of dividends, the first of which usually requires approval by the owners of a majority of the stock, and both of which usually require approval by a majority of the corporation's directors.

The same concept is illustrated by PLR 9114023, in which the taxpayer proposed to make transfers of corporate stock to unrelated key employees as to which other shareholders would not make matching contributions. Those transfers would be capital contributions to the corporation that would constitute indirect gifts to those other shareholders.[28] As such the taxpayer would have been in a better position by making simple gifts to the employees out of affection or other nonbusiness motives because, presumably, then the annual exclusion would apply.

In comparison to these contributions to corporations that constitute gifts, however, consider PLRs 9323020 and 9104024, which involved contributions to clubs that were regarded as gifts to the other club members. Unlike the corporate situations, however, these gifts qualified for the annual exclusion because the members were deemed to enjoy

---

(Footnote Continued)

chased by the corporation at a below market price under a buy-sell agreement). But see Estate of Anderson v. Commissioner, 56 T.C.M. (CCH) 553 (1988) (contribution of stock to newly formed company was not a gift because the decedent received stock that was approximately equal in value to the contributed stock).

[27] 1971-2 C.B. 337, 338.

[28] See Rev. Rul. 80-196, 1980-2 C.B. 32. The converse principle is illustrated by PLR 8038193, in which a religious organization made a contribution of property back to its original donor's family, which was treated as a pro rata present interest transfer by each member of the organization that would qualify for the annual exclusion.

§7.1.1.1

immediate benefits from the contributions.[29] Similarly, in Wooley v. United States,[30] the taxpayer made contributions to a child's capital contribution account in a family partnership. The government argued that these transfers did not qualify for the annual exclusion, which the court determined to be a case of first impression in the context of contributions to a partnership. The court allowed annual exclusion treatment based on an analogy to Crummey v. Commissioner[31] and any partner's ability under the Uniform Partnership Act to withdraw the capital account without restriction (unless the partnership agreement provides otherwise).[32]

§7.1.1.2 Crummey Withdrawal Power

Often the present interest requirement is satisfied by granting a beneficiary an immediate, albeit limited, power to obtain possession of transferred property, typically through exercise of a withdrawal power (referred to as a Crummey clause power).[33] This technique is so contro-

---

[29] However, because club membership expired at death in the 1993 Ruling, each annual exclusion had to be computed on the basis of the life expectancy of each member. See also PLRs 200608011, 200533004, and 9818042, holding that the gift is to the club itself, as to which the annual exclusion is available under the exception found in Treas. Reg. § 25.2511-1(h)(1), generating what appeared to be a single exclusion (not an exclusion for each member of the club).

[30] 736 F. Supp. 1506 (S.D. Ind. 1990).

[31] 397 F.2d 82 (9th Cir. 1968). See § 7.1.1.2.

[32] To illustrate compare TAM 9751003, in which the government ruled that transferred FLP interests did not qualify for the annual exclusion because a provision in the partnership agreement permitted the general partner to retain income "for any reason whatsoever" and the partners were unable to withdraw from the partnership, liquidate it, or transfer their interests, meaning that there was no guarantee of any substantial present economic enjoyment of the interests transferred, with TAMs 199944003 and 9131006, and PLRs 199905010, and 9415007, in which discretionary partnership income interests were deemed to be no more restricted than under state law in general and constituted present interests, because the general partner's powers were subject to a higher fiduciary obligation and therefore were not the equivalent of a trustee's discretion to withhold trust income.

[33] So named after the decision in Crummey v. Commissioner, 397 F.2d 82 (9th Cir. 1968), which concluded that the power of withdrawal constituted a transfer as immediately available to the powerholder and therefore qualified as a present interest for annual exclusion purposes.

versial that the third Revenue Procedure promulgated each year contains updated information regarding subjects or issues upon which advance rulings, determination letters, and memoranda will not be issued,[34] and one issue that has been on that list since 1981[35] is whether a transfer of property to a trust is a gift of a present interest if the trust beneficiaries have the power to withdraw, on demand, any transfers to the trust (which is what a Crummey power authorizes).

A spate of Rulings and a series of cases[36] reveal the government's antipathy to this planning, and periodic proposals for law reform would negate this planning opportunity,[37] all of which *confirms* that the Crummey power can be a very useful device. Thus, notwithstanding the government's dislike for its use, and the potential for its repeal or alteration in the future, the Crummey power is one of the most used and useful planning devices in the current arsenal of most estate planners.

A Crummey power of withdrawal authorizes one or more beneficiaries to withdraw property transferred to a trust that otherwise does not grant enjoyment that would satisfy the annual exclusion present interest requirements. The donor's contributions to the trust constitute gifts of a present interest to the powerholder to the extent of this power of withdrawal. As a result, those contributions are not precluded from qualifying for the annual exclusion by the present interest requirement or the future interest prohibition.

Most often the power of withdrawal lapses if it is not exercised within a certain time period. Because the lapse is a potentially taxable event to the powerholder under § 2514, the most common form of this planning either limits the power itself or the amount as to which the lapse occurs to the greater of 5% of the value of the trust or $5,000, so as

---

[34] See, e.g., § 4.01(49) of Rev. Proc. 2012-3, 2012-1 C.B. 113.

[35] See Rev. Proc. 81-37, 1981-2 C.B. 555.

[36] See § 7.1.1.4.

[37] For example, compare § 2642(c), which for GST annual exclusion integration purposes requires only that a trust beneficiary have an identifiable interest that is vested for tax purposes (meaning that it will cause inclusion in the beneficiary's estate, such as through the grant of a nonlapsing general power of appointment), with a proposal by the Clinton administration in 1998 to require that any gift must be made outright to the beneficiary to qualify for the annual exclusion and another in 1999 to adopt the § 2642(c) rule for gift tax purposes.

§ 7.1.1.2

to fit within the exceptions and avoid gift tax liability to the donee under §§ 2514(e) and 2041(b)(2).[38] If no withdrawal is made and the power lapses, these provisions specify that the lapse is not treated as a gift by the powerholder and, when the powerholder dies, the lapsed property is not includible in the powerholder's gross estate for FET purposes.[39] Only any amount subject to a nonlapsed power of withdrawal still available at the date of death would be subject to FET under § 2041(a)(2).[40] Although there is no authority to establish that the planning proposition works, some drafters limit the availability of the power of withdrawal to one day annually, in hopes that the powerholder's death on any other date will avoid even this exposure.[41]

In almost all cases it is the design that the powerholder will not exercise the power to withdraw in the absence of a real need for the wealth. Thus, it is expected that the full contribution will remain subject to trust terms that do not otherwise satisfy the present interest requirement. Nevertheless, the ability to withdraw, even for only a limited term and even if not exercised, is regarded as adequate to qualify for the annual exclusion.[42]

---

[38] See §§ 12.3.2.5. See also PLR 9804047, in which the lapse amount exceeded the 5% limit and constituted a taxable gift, as to which the powerholder's ongoing beneficial interests were ignored under § 2702 (discussed in § 7.2.2) because the remainder beneficiaries were family members of the powerholder.

[39] Even if the powerholder enjoyed ongoing income or other rights in the lapsed property. See the second clause of § 2041(a)(2), as discussed in § 12.3.1.

[40] See, e.g., Estate of Kurz v. Commissioner, 101 T.C. 44 (1993), Estate of Dietz v. Commissioner, 72 T.C.M. (CCH) 1058 (1996), and PLR 8949088 (5% includible in gross estate attributable to power of withdrawal not yet exercised or lapsed at the moment of death).

[41] Oddly, those who do this often make that date the last day of the calendar year, even though New Year's Eve (and the wee hours of New Year's Day) probably rank near the top of any list of high mortality dates. A better date would have a predictably low mortality, which would exclude Memorial Day, Fourth of July, Labor Day, Thanksgiving and the end-of-year holiday weekends when traffic and other fatalities are common, and birthdays, anniversaries, or other times when caution may be cast to the wind. There does not appear to be a list of which days have the lowest mortality, but available statistics show that July and August are the lowest mortality months. One pundit suggests the day when the nation goes onto daylight saving time—because it is only 23 hours in length!

[42] But see Jacobson v. United States, 78-2 U.S. Tax Cas. (CCH) ¶ 13,256 (D. Neb. 1978) (trust that otherwise created no present interests provided that each

This treatment applies even if the powerholder with the withdrawal right is a minor, unable under local law to exercise the power, provided that there is no impediment to appointment of a legal guardian who could exercise the power of withdrawal on the minor's behalf.[43] This is such a well accepted estate planning principle that the government in no way challenges the initial proposition any longer. That the government accepts the withdrawal power as creating a present interest does not, however, prevent the government from challenging qualification for the annual exclusion in the Crummey power context.

(Footnote Continued)

beneficiary could exercise an inter vivos power to appoint the beneficiary's share to the beneficiary's children, which did not generate present interest treatment, because the power could not be exercised in the beneficiary's own favor).

[43] Crummey v. Commissioner, 397 F.2d 82 (9th Cir. 1968), which rejected Stifel v. Commissioner, 197 F.2d 107 (2d Cir. 1952) (a guardian must exist before the minor's power may generate present interest treatment) and embraced Kieckhefer v. Commissioner, 189 F.2d 118 (7th Cir. 1951), and Perkins v. Commissioner, 27 T.C. 601 (1956), which stressed a "right to enjoy" test in determining whether a present interest was created:

> We decline to follow a strict reading of the *Stifel* case in our situation because we feel that the solution suggested by that case is inconsistent and unfair. It becomes arbitrary for the I.R.S. to step in and decide who is likely to make an effective demand. Under the circumstances suggested in our case, it is doubtful that any demands will be made against the trust— yet the Commissioner always allowed the exclusion as to adult beneficiaries. There is nothing to indicate that it is any more likely that [an adult beneficiary] will demand funds than that any other beneficiary will do so. The only distinction is that it might be easier for him to make such a demand. Since we conclude that the demand can be made by the others, it follows that the exclusion should also apply to them. . . . [T]he broader *Kieckhefer* rule . . . seems less arbitrary and establishes a clear standard.
>
> We conclude that the result under the *Perkins* or "right to enjoy" tests is preferable in our case.

397 F.2d at 88. Rev. Rul. 73-405, 1973-2 C.B. 321, adopts the *Crummey* result if there is no impediment under controlling local law to the appointment of a guardian.

§7.1.1.2

§7.1.1.3 Notice and Timing

Until the government promulgated Revenue Ruling 81-7[44] there was little assurance that a powerholder would either know about the power to withdraw or have a sufficient opportunity to exercise the power with respect to contributions made late in the year in which withdrawal was permitted. The subject trust in the Ruling gave an adult beneficiary a noncumulative power of withdrawal that lapsed at year end, which was two days after the trust was established. Moreover, the beneficiary was not informed of the withdrawal right with regard to the initial contribution to the trust before that right lapsed. The Ruling concluded that the beneficiary's power to withdraw did not create a present interest with respect to the initial contribution to the trust, because the timing and lack of notice made it illusory.

Subsequently, Revenue Ruling 83-108[45] distinguished Revenue Ruling 81-7 because, although the trust again was established on December 29, the powerholder's right of withdrawal did not lapse until 45 days after written notice was given to the powerholder. In addition, the trustee was required to give the powerholder written notice of the withdrawal right within 10 days of any transfer to the trust that was subject to that power. This Ruling concluded that the beneficiary received a present interest in transfers to the trust that were subject to the right of withdrawal. Therefore, contributions qualified for the annual exclusion.

The Ruling further held that exercise or lapse of the withdrawal power in a different calendar year than the year in which the trust was created or a transfer was made was irrelevant for annual exclusion purposes.[46] Indeed, it explained that the length of time between the date of creation of the trust and the end of the calendar year was significant in Revenue Ruling 81-7 only because the withdrawal right in that case

---

[44] 1981-1 C.B. 474. See also TAM 7946007, involving virtually identical facts and the same conclusion.

[45] 1983-2 C.B. 167.

[46] See also PLR 8806003 (transfers to a trust for minor beneficiaries recognized for present interest annual exclusion treatment regardless of the calendar year in which the beneficiaries' withdrawal rights would terminate, if notice must be given promptly after a transfer to the trust was received and there was no impediment to appointment of a guardian to exercise the withdrawal right under local law).

§7.1.1.3

lapsed at the end of the calendar year. Thus, if an adequate notice and time for withdrawal exist, the Ruling announced that the annual exclusion will be available in the year of transfer, allowing the transferor to wait until literally the last minute before deciding to make an annual exclusion transfer to the trust. Subsequent pronouncements reveal that 30 days is an ample window within which to exercise a withdrawal right before its lapse[47] and at least one notable case allowed the exclusion with a 15 day power of withdrawal.[48]

Caution must be exercised to ensure that several years' withdrawal rights do not inadvertently lapse in a single year in amounts causing unexpected §2514(e) consequences to the powerholder. In addition, with respect to withdrawal rights in a transferor's spouse, a window of more than 60 days should be avoided if GST exemption allocation might be important.[49] For planning purposes, and to guarantee that the annual

---

[47] See, e.g., PLRs 200123034, 200011054, 199912016, 8004172, and 8003033. Cf. PLRs 201042004 and 200917015, both involving modification of trusts to limit powers of withdrawal to a one month entitlement. The 2010 PLR stated expressly that FET would result only if the powerholder died during that one month and dealt with a raft of other issues, *not* including the annual exclusion aspect. The 2009 PLR expressly stated that "after the modification, each beneficiary will have the same interest in the Trust assets as he or she had before the modification," which should mean that a one-month power is "as good as" a year-long power. The government's no-ruling policy regarding Crummey powers may explain why the immediate annual exclusion question was not addressed, but it is likely that the parties discussed that aspect and would not have proceeded with the modifications, nor would the PLRs have blessed them, had this been a problem, all of which likely was considered during the ruling application and grant process.

[48] Estate of Cristofani v. Commissioner, 97 T.C. 74 (1991), acq. in result only, 1992-1 C.B. 1, a reviewed opinion with no dissent. The time period issue was not central to the government's challenge to the exclusion and the result therefore probably is not relied upon by careful planners. On the other hand, PLR 200520009 involved a reduction to 15 days (the Ruling does not say from what, although it does say the modification is to "reduce the likelihood that 5 percent of Trust assets would be treated as an asset of [a child, includible] for estate tax purposes") and the government ruled that "each beneficiary will have the same interest in Trust assets as each beneficiary had before the modification" for §2601 GST purposes.

[49] See the ETIP rule and Treas. Reg. §26.2632-1(c)(2)(ii)(B), as discussed in §11.4.5.5.3 n.200 and accompanying text, with respect to the spousal unity rule and its exception.

§7.1.1.3

exclusion opportunity is not lost for any year, normally it is preferable to take advantage of annual exclusion giving early in a new year rather than waiting until the final moment.

Another interesting question is whether notice of each year's withdrawal right must be given. Many donors and trustees fail to actually notify the Crummey powerholders of their entitlement as annual transfers to a trust are made or, at a minimum, they are unable to prove that the notice was given. All sorts of practices are employed to minimize the administrative hassle of giving notice on a periodic basis. One approach blessed in PLRs 8133070 and 8121069 is to give one notice to the powerholder that annual contributions will be made and that withdrawal powers will be available with respect to those transfers, with the notion being that the notice is an ongoing information until the powerholder is informed otherwise. Another is waiver by the powerholder of the right to receive future notices.[50]

In TAM 9532001 the government opined that:

> Without the current notice that a gift is being transferred, it is not possible for a donee to have the real and immediate benefit of the gift. The immediate use, possession, or enjoyment of property is clearly restricted if the donee does not know of its existence. Accordingly, a donee must have current notice of any gift in order for that gift to be a transfer of a present interest.

Without present interest status the contribution will not qualify for the annual exclusion, resulting in gift tax and frustrating the donor's most fundamental purpose. Although the TAM involved an unusual fact (pursuant to the trust itself, the withdrawal right existed only if the donor gave notice of the right to the trustee, which was not done after the first year's contribution to the trust), this did not appear to inform the

---

[50] See, e.g., Blattmachr & Slade, Life Insurance Trusts: How to Avoid Estate and GST Taxes, 22 Est. Plan. 259, 262 (1995), which recommended as "the better practice" that the right to receive notice of contributions subject to a withdrawal power (but not the right to withdraw itself) be waived, to relieve the trustee or the donor of the sometimes onerous and often forgotten (or conveniently "overlooked") obligation to communicate with the beneficiary regarding contributions and the corresponding withdrawal rights. According to Blattmachr and Slade, "[s]uch a waiver would direct the trustee to refrain from sending notices of withdrawal rights until . . . the beneficiary demands that the . . . notices be reinstated. This direction to the trustee by the beneficiary should provide adequate proof that the power of withdrawal is not illusory."

government's position and, notwithstanding those PLRs dating from more than three decades ago, today a different result should not be expected in the more generic Crummey withdrawal right situation in which the power of withdrawal automatically exists as to every contribution made to the trust.

On the other hand, a number of authorities hold that the annual exclusion is available if actual notice existed, even if no formal notice was sent to the powerholder. For example, notice would exist if the powerholder also was a trustee of a trust granting the right of withdrawal or the donor also was the legal guardian of the powerholder.[51] Nevertheless, the better practice probably leaves nothing to chance in this important planning arena and seeks to have written confirmation from each powerholder that actual notice was timely given with respect to each withdrawal power that the powerholder allows to lapse (the exercised powers being rare but also obvious and not an abuse in the government's eyes).

In this respect it also is critical to remember that § 2514(e) is a safe harbor only if a power lapses by its own terms and *not* if the powerholder *releases* the power. Thus, it is not wise for the powerholder to acknowledge receipt of the notice and state an affirmative intent to not exercise the withdrawal power. Instead the powerholder should let the power lapse on its own terms due to a failure to exercise the power.

---

[51] Estate of Holland v. Commissioner, 73 T.C.M. (CCH) 3236 (1997) (court refused to disallow the annual exclusion notwithstanding that notice of withdrawal powers never was given, because testimony indicated that adult beneficiaries knew of the powers on their own behalf and that the trustees also were guardians of the minor beneficiaries); PLR 8022048 ("in your dual capacity as donor and natural guardian, you possess actual knowledge of the legal right to withdraw trust property you have contributed"); PLR 9030005 (no actual notice need be given to a minor powerholder if the minor's parent is trustee of the trust granting the power, is another beneficiary of the trust, and is the child's natural guardian; as beneficiary the parent would receive notice both personally and on behalf of the minor and, although the Ruling did not so hold, it ought to be the case that being a trustee *or* a beneficiary as well as the guardian should suffice because in either capacity the parent is aware of the minor's withdrawal right with respect to any contribution made to the trust).

§ 7.1.1.3

§7.1.1.4 Contingent Beneficiaries

A reality that makes the government crazy is that no one expects the powerholder to exercise the withdrawal right, and seldom is that expectation defeated—and certainly not more than once. Indeed, often the desire is to make a transfer that exceeds the amount of a single gift tax annual exclusion but nevertheless avoid gift tax to the donor and to beneficiaries to whom withdrawal rights are given (which requires that the lapse of these Crummey rights not exceed the §2514(e) five-or-five limitation in any given year). To accomplish this, donors sometimes grant withdrawal rights to many more individuals than the primary beneficiaries of an intended transfer.

For example, it is not uncommon to grant powers to withdraw the greater of $5,000 or 5% of the value of the trust to every descendant of the donor, and their spouses, all with the expectation that none of these beneficiaries (primary or otherwise) will exercise their rights of withdrawal. In the pejorative, these rights in nonprimary beneficiaries are regarded as "dummy Crummey" rights because neither the powerholders nor the donor really regard them as a legitimate entitlement. They are a device to shelter a large transfer with annual exclusions.

Because the government understands this use of Crummey powers and regards the dummy Crummey technique as an abuse, it has attempted through a series of TAMs and a string of cases to deny the effect of Crummey powers of withdrawal in certain individuals that it regards as not having legitimate interests in the subject property. For example, in TAM 8727003 trusts were created for the primary benefit of two children of the settlor. In addition to granting each child a power of withdrawal over contributions made to the trust created for his or her benefit, each child's spouse, descendants, and their spouses also were granted powers of withdrawal, each with respect to a fraction of every contribution. Proper notice and timing provisions were included, and some of the beneficiaries actually exercised their withdrawal rights. Unfortunately, adding to the appearance that the Crummey withdrawal rights in beneficiaries other than the children were bogus was the fact that the trustee followed up each exercise of a withdrawal right with a letter asking the beneficiary to revoke the withdrawal election, which each did.

The TAM held that only the children, as the "primary" beneficiaries of the trusts, had legitimate withdrawal rights that would be respected for annual exclusion purposes. The government noted that "there are demand rights in beneficiaries who have either no other interests in the trust or only remote contingent interests in the remainder." Thus, according to the TAM:

> the question is whether each of the trust beneficiaries had a sufficient interest in the property for the annual exclusion to apply to it. If so, then the taxpayers will have been able to parlay transfers of property in trust that, in fact, were for the benefit of their two children into as many as eighteen annual exclusions.

Moreover, in distinguishing prior cases involving similar facts,[52] the TAM opined that the donors in the instant case could not have achieved the same result through separate trusts (because there was deemed to be no intent to actually bestow a benefit on the holders of withdrawal rights other than the two children). Thus, according to the TAM, the only complete disposition the donors could have made using separate trusts would have been for the benefit of "the primary beneficiaries" (the children). The government concluded that "[i]t was never intended that the limited rights conferred on the other . . . beneficiaries . . . be exercised."

The TAM was unusual because some of the powerholders actually attempted to make withdrawals and were informed that the powers were not meant to be exercised, upon which they retracted their withdrawal requests. Yet the absence of this fact did not distinguish other power of withdrawal situations and the government continued to reject withdrawal rights in individuals not regarded as legitimate powerholders.[53]

The government correctly concludes that drafters assume that the withdrawal rights will not be exercised especially in ILITs (in which the annual contributions being sheltered by the annual exclusion through the use of Crummey withdrawal rights will be used by the trustee to pay insurance policy premiums).[54] Nevertheless, intent is not a relevant

---

[52] See, e.g., Helvering v. Hutchins, 312 U.S. 393 (1941).

[53] See TAMs 9141008 and 9045002.

[54] See, e.g., PLR 8813019, in which, with the exception of a Crummey clause power of withdrawal, the beneficiary was entitled to no other benefits of the trust until reaching age 60, after which the trustee could distribute income or principal to or for the benefit of the beneficiary in the trustee's exclusive discretion. Only

§7.1.1.4

factor in qualifying for the §2503(b) annual exclusion through the mechanism of a present interest generated by granting a power of withdrawal. And the Tax Court has not embraced the government's objection, notwithstanding that most attorneys who draft Crummey clause withdrawal rights concede that they create a fictional present interest (because the likelihood of an actual withdrawal is slight).

Thus, for example, Estate of Cristofani v. Commissioner[55] held that the government's challenge in a situation that functionally was identical to TAM 9045002 was meritless because *Crummey* does not require trust beneficiaries to receive vested present or remainder interests in either trust corpus or income to qualify for the annual exclusion:

> As discussed in *Crummey*, the likelihood that the beneficiary will actually receive present enjoyment of the property is not the test for determining whether a present interest was received. Rather, we must examine the ability of the beneficiaries, in a legal sense, to exercise their right to withdraw trust corpus, and the trustee's right to legally resist a beneficiary's demand for payment. . . . Based upon the language of the trust instrument and stipulations of the parties, we believe that each grandchild possessed the legal right to withdraw trust corpus and that the trustees would be unable to legally resist a grandchild's withdrawal demand. We note that there was no agreement or understanding between decedent, the trustees, and the beneficiaries that the grandchildren would not exercise their withdrawal rights following a contribution to the . . . trust.[56]

The court could not have more directly rejected the government's notion that intent is relevant for §2503(b) annual exclusion purposes.

Nevertheless, the government announced in AOD 1996-010 that it "will deny the exclusions for *Crummey* powers, regardless of the power holder's other interests in the trust, where the . . . facts indicate that the substance of the transfers was merely to obtain annual exclusions and that no bona fide gift of a present interest was intended."

(Footnote Continued)

after the beneficiary reached age 70 was there any guarantee that the beneficiary would receive any benefit from the trust ($1,000 per month).

[55] 97 T.C. 74 (1991), acq. in result only, 1992-1 C.B. 1, a reviewed opinion with no dissent.

[56] 94 T.C. at 83.

Almost simultaneously TAM 9628004 became public, dealing with the same issue. Several trusts were involved, one of which did not require the trustee to give notice that Crummey withdrawal rights existed or that additions had been made to the trust. The powerholders were remote descendants and spouses of descendants, and contributions into the trust in some years were made so late that it practically was impossible to make a withdrawal. Together those facts would have justified denial of the annual exclusion under the authority of Revenue Ruling 81-7,[57] at least for some of the years involved, but the government used the TAM to announce that:

> where nominal beneficiaries enjoy only discretionary income interests, remote contingent rights to the remainder, or no rights whatsoever in the income or remainder, their nonexercise [of withdrawal rights] indicates that there was some kind of prearranged understanding with the donor that these rights were not meant to be exercised or that their exercise would result in undesirable consequences, or both.

Based on those facts and the reality that "[n]one of the rights were ever exercised, even by those who had no other interests in the trusts," the government denied annual exclusions for those withdrawal rights, stating that:

> we conclude that as part of a prearranged understanding, all of the beneficiaries knew that their rights were paper rights only, or that exercising them would result in unfavorable consequences. There is no other logical reason why these individuals would choose not to withdraw $10,000 [the then annual exclusion amount] a year as a gift which would not be includible in their income or subject the Donor to the gift tax.

At the same time, however, the TAM stated that:

> The Service generally does not contest annual gift tax exclusions for Crummey powers held by current income beneficiaries and persons with vested remainder interests. These individuals have current or long term economic interests in the trust and in the value of the corpus. It is understandable that in weighing these interests, they decide not to exercise their withdrawal rights.

The logical expectation, therefore, is that the government will challenge the annual exclusion on a selective basis in only the most egregious cases that it hopes even the Tax Court can agree are over the edge.

---

[57] See § 7.1.1.3.

§7.1.1.4

TAM 9731004 involved a trust in which a child was the primary beneficiary but over a dozen more powers of withdrawal were denied as present interests because none of these other powerholders were in line to take property in the trust. The government stated that "where the transaction is designed to conform to the statute but the normal consequences which flow from such transaction do not occur and were never intended to occur, the formal appearance of the transaction cannot prevail over what is, in substance, a tax avoidance scheme." That TAM confirmed that "vested" as used by the government in referring to a child in this case did not mean "vested" in a true future interest sense because the child would not take if not alive when distribution was triggered. Perhaps "vested subject to divestment" is what the government has in mind (although it is unlikely that this was how the trust was drafted), or perhaps just that no other beneficiary has an interest that would supersede their interest.

It still remains to be seen, however, what the parameters of such a selection might be. For half a dozen years the latest evidence on that score was Estate of Kohlsaat v. Commissioner,[58] in which the Tax Court followed *Cristofani* in rejecting the government's denial of 16 annual exclusions for withdrawal powers in contingent remainder beneficiaries. The facts as stated do not indicate the nature of the primary beneficiary interests (although they appeared to be life estates with nongeneral powers of appointment), so it is not possible to glean from the opinion exactly how contingent the remainder beneficial interests were. Presumably that uncertainty indicates that the distinction between primary and contingent remainder beneficial interests was not relevant to the Tax Court.

The *Kohlsaat* opinion did note that timely notices were given to the beneficiaries, who had 30 days within which to exercise their withdrawal powers. In addition, the court pointedly concluded that there was no evidence of any understandings that these beneficiaries would not exercise their powers of withdrawal, and noted that credible reasons were offered at trial as to why various beneficiaries did not exercise their rights (although none of those reasons were recounted by the opinion). Perhaps most useful, therefore, was the court's statement that "[t]he fact that none of the beneficiaries exercised their rights . . . does not imply

---

[58] 73 T.C.M. (CCH) 2732 (1997).

. . . that the beneficiaries had agreed . . . not to do so, and we refuse to infer any understanding."[59] The court also noted that there was no evidence to support the government's contention that the remainder beneficiaries believed they would be penalized for exercising their withdrawal rights.[60]

This issue was quiet for over half a decade but resurfaced in TAM 200341002, which involved unexercised dummy Crummey powers granted to charities, among others. Although the authority is sparse, Treas. Reg. § 25.2502-1(d) Examples 3(ii) and 4(iii), along with PLR 8552053 all confirm that gifts to charity qualify *first* for the annual exclusion and only any excess taxable gift amount needs to qualify under § 2522 for the gift tax charitable deduction. The government disallowed the annual exclusion for the Crummey powers in charity in large part due to flaws in the notices given, which confirms that otherwise the exclusion would be available.

In light of these developments, then, perhaps it is most telling that proper notices were given in *Kohlsaat* and an ample window of opportunity to withdraw was provided. Quaere whether any of these cases would be different in the government's mind if Crummey withdrawal right holders exercised the power on occasion. On the other hand, the Tax Court does not appear to care whether powers to withdraw are exercised, so long as there is no objective evidence of an agreement not to.

Another potential soft spot against which the government may exert pressure in Crummey withdrawal right cases is the practical ability to satisfy all demands to withdraw that might be asserted at one time. For example, in Revenue Ruling 80-261,[61] each of five beneficiaries had the right to withdraw $4,000 from a trust with a corpus of only $13,000,

---

[59] 73 T.C.M. at 2734.

[60] See also Estate of Holland v. Commissioner, 73 T.C.M. (CCH) 3236 (1997), in which the court refused to disallow the annual exclusion notwithstanding that notice of withdrawal powers never was given, because testimony indicated that adult beneficiaries knew of the powers on their own behalf and that the trustees also were guardians of the minor beneficiaries. Indeed, despite an agreement to use trust corpus not withdrawn to purchase a certificate of deposit, the court held that there was no evidence of any agreement with the donees not to withdraw contributions made to the trust or otherwise to limit their ability to make withdrawals.

[61] 1980-2 C.B. 279.

§ 7.1.1.4

meaning that withdrawal demands could not all be satisfied. The government therefore limited present interest treatment to the pro rata amount each powerholder would receive if all made a demand to withdraw. If that amount was the full amount contributed to the trust the result likely would be acceptable to the transferor. But in many Crummey withdrawal power cases the trust is an ILIT and the contributed amount is intended to be used to pay insurance premiums.

If the timing of contribution, payment of premium, and lapse of the withdrawal powers is not coordinated, the amount available to satisfy withdrawal powers when they lapse will be less than the contribution. In such a case the annual exclusion will not protect against gift tax on the total contribution. Several PLRs reveal that an effective remedy may exist if the beneficiaries with Crummey withdrawal rights may be satisfied by distributions of cash or the policies of insurance that are financed by the contribution.[62] Better, however, would be to have a cash cushion sufficient to satisfy any demand for withdrawal, for example by delaying payment of premiums until the withdrawal rights all lapse for that year.

§7.1.1.5 Other Forms of Artifice

On occasion taxpayers have engaged in other thinly disguised artifices designed to increase the number of annual exclusions available in any given year. One recurring theme involves family members, business partners, or other close and reliable associates who employ reciprocal transfers. To illustrate, siblings A and B each made annual exclusion gifts to their own children and to their sibling's children (their nieces and nephews). Thus, sibling A gave $28,000 (in 2013) to each of A's two children and $28,000 to each of B's three children, and B gave $28,000 to each of B's three children and $28,000 to each of A's two children.

---

[62] Annual exclusions were permitted in the context of ILITs in PLRs 8134135 (trust was funded with permanent and group term policies; the trustee was required to maintain sufficient liquid assets to pay any beneficiary exercising a withdrawal power); 8021058 (trust was funded with group term policy; any trust asset, including the policy, could be used to satisfy a withdrawal demand); and 8103074 (trust was funded with an initial contribution of $1,000 and an assignment of a group term policy; although the policy itself was not subject to withdrawal, the initial contribution was regarded as giving the trustee a resource to honor demand rights).

Each sibling's spouse split each gift and together, A and B and their spouses all claimed five annual exclusions for gifts to the five children of A and B. Predictably, the government's conclusion is that the "reciprocal trust doctrine"[63] properly applies to regard each sibling as making $56,000 gifts to each of their own children (which, even split with their spouses, exceed the annual exclusion limits for the year) and none to the sibling's children.

Curiously enough, a technical historical application of the reciprocal trust doctrine would require an uncrossing of these interrelated transfers only to the extent of mutual value (that is, to the extent of two children of each sibling). With respect to the fifth child, sibling A would be deemed to make a gift either to sibling B or to that "excess" child of sibling B, unmatched by any gift by sibling B to children of A. That "excess" amount should not be subject to uncrossing under the reciprocal trust doctrine. If, however, A's gift to that fifth child was in exchange for gifts made by sibling B to sibling A and then A turned around and made the added gift to B's child, this form of prearrangement also would not succeed.

In the overall picture, the substance of the reciprocal trust doctrine and its application clearly is correct, although it is questionable whether the government was correct when it asserted that the doctrine "does not require that the transferred amounts be exactly equal. In the present case, although the transfers are not exactly equal, they were interrelated and there has been a general matching or equality of transfers over the . . . years during which the transfers were made."[64]

---

[63] See § 7.3.2.

[64] TAM 8717003. See Schultz v. United States, 493 F.2d 1225 (4th Cir. 1974); Furst v. Commissioner, 21 T.C.M. (CCH) 1169 (1962) (both involving siblings and equal gifts). In Estate of Schuler v. Commissioner, 282 F.3d 575 (8th Cir. 2002) (siblings rearranged ownership of two companies to allow each sibling's children to control one company, using reciprocal transfers in late December and again in early January seeking to accomplish the cross transfers without gift tax under the annual exclusion), following Sather v. Commissioner, 251 F.3d 1168 (8th Cir. 2001) (three of four siblings who were married with children all made cross gifts to the children of the other siblings), the respective taxpayers were denied the annual exclusion for amounts exceeding $20,000 per child of each donor (reflecting that the siblings' spouses split all the gifts). A fourth *Sather* sibling who was childless was allowed annual exclusions for gifts to all of that sibling's nieces and nephews. Most interesting was that the *Sather* siblings were

§ 7.1.1.5

A variation on this theme entailed business partners A, B, and C, who each created a trust for the benefit of their respective children, with each giving the beneficiary a Crummey power of withdrawal and each giving the other two partners a withdrawal power as well. The government allowed the annual exclusion with respect to each partner's own child, but not with respect to each partner's withdrawal powers. As a result, because the reciprocal withdrawal rights represented gifts to each other partner matched by the same gifts from each other partner, the respective transfers among the partners netted out. The effect was that no partner was deemed to make a gift to any other partner and the amounts not subject to withdrawal by a child were taxable gifts to the trusts that did not otherwise qualify as present interests for annual exclusion purposes.[65]

A final obvious artifice involved a donor who attempted to manufacture additional gifting opportunities for annual exclusion purposes by giving stock to 29 individuals (many subordinates or employees of the donor), all in amounts sheltered by the annual exclusion. All but two of these donees immediately endorsing the stock they received in blank. Those shares subsequently were reissued in the names of various members of the donor's family. According to the court,[66] the 27 purported donees ignorantly believed they were merely participating in stock transfers or they intentionally agreed before receiving the stock that they would endorse the certificates in furtherance of the donor's scheme. Either way, the court agreed with the government's characterization of the transaction as tax fraud and upheld its imposition of a fraud

---

(Footnote Continued)

advised by a C.P.A. and therefore were protected from the § 6662 accuracy related negligence penalty. The Tax Court was reversed in holding that their spouses, who never consulted with that C.P.A., therefore could not have reasonably relied on the advice of an expert advisor and were liable for those penalties. The court on appeal held that those spouses "indirectly" relied on that advice.

[65] Rev. Rul. 85-24, 1985-1 C.B. 329.

[66] Heyen v. United States, 945 F.2d 359 (10th Cir. 1991), followed in Estate of Bies v. Commissioner, 80 T.C.M. (CCH) 628 (2000) (annual exclusion gifts to sons were matched with identical gifts to their wives, who immediately transferred that property to their husbands, all pursuant to a single integrated transaction coordinated by the same attorney who represented the family business and were regarded as an ineffective artifice to double the annual exclusion gifts to the sons).

§ 7.1.1.5

penalty. Obviously, then, as powerful as the annual exclusion is, a more legitimate mechanism is needed to take maximum advantage of it.

§7.1.1.6 Hanging Powers

The "hanging" power is a more effective method of maximizing the annual exclusion opportunity presented by the use of Crummey withdrawal powers without exceeding the §2514(e) five-or-five safe harbor for tax free lapse of these powers. With a proper formulation, contributions may be made excludible in whole by a properly engineered collection of withdrawal rights, without resorting to techniques that are likely to be challenged by the government.

The problem is that the per donee annual exclusion is greater than the amount as to which any donee may have a withdrawal power that lapses with no gift tax or subsequent FET liability.[67] This is because lapse of a withdrawal power is harmless to the powerholder only to the extent protected by the $5,000 or 5% exception of §2514(e), and the annual exclusion is over twice the $5,000 dollar amount (which frequently is the applicable limitation because the trust is unfunded, making the 5% alternative a cipher). Thus, to take maximum advantage of the full annual exclusion without causing any gift tax exposure to the beneficiary if the power of withdrawal lapses (which is expected), many planners permit contributions in excess of the five-or-five exception and rely on a nonlapsing power of withdrawal to preclude immediate wealth transfer taxation to the powerholder.

Although there are a number of ways to draft this provision, the format involved in TAM 8901004 illustrates that some are better than others. It provided that:

> if upon the termination of any power of withdrawal the person holding the power will be deemed to have made a taxable gift for federal gift tax purposes, then such power of withdrawal will not lapse, but will continue to exist ["hang"] with respect to the amount that would have been a taxable gift and will terminate as soon as such termination will not result in a taxable gift.

---

[67] See §2041(b)(2) with respect to the FET liability attributable to lapsed inter vivos general powers of appointment, such as a withdrawal right. And see Whitty, Crummey Trust Computations, 9 Prob. & Prop. 35 (Jan./Feb. 1995), for a mechanism and spreadsheet to calculate the exposure amount attributable to lapsing withdrawal powers.

§7.1.1.6

The government regarded the hanging powers as discouraging efforts to tax the lapse of the power because a hanging power limitation applies only to the extent the amount subject to withdrawal is in excess of the amount that could lapse tax free. That is, the amount subject to withdrawal would be cut back to a nontaxable amount if a taxable lapse otherwise would occur. Thus, the government characterized these hanging power provisions as conditions subsequent limiting the withdrawal powers and, as such, "not valid as tending to discourage enforcement of federal gift tax provisions by either defeating the gift or rendering examination of the return ineffective."[68]

In juxtaposition to this TAM is Revenue Ruling 83-180,[69] in which the donor over a period of years gave a specified number of acres of land so that, at the end of the gifting program, all the land had been given to the donee. The number of acres given each year had a value equal to the available annual exclusion at the time of each annual gift, and the Ruling held that the annual exclusion was available with respect to each annual gift.

If the government is correct in each of these pronouncements, then a cut back style hanging power provision is invalid and the power of withdrawal would extend to the entire contribution. This would make lapse of the power a taxable gift by the powerholder in the year the power lapsed, taxable to the extent that full amount exceeds the five-or-five limitation. The donor still would qualify for the annual exclusion, but the powerholder would incur gift tax liability. That result is consistent with cases involving conditions subsequent but it can be circumvented by granting a lapsing withdrawal power that is defined in the first instance like the gift in Revenue Ruling 83-180—equal to only the amount that can lapse tax free in any given year. That is, the government's interpretation should be avoidable with a formula lapsing power of withdrawal,[70] rather than a blanket power over the entire contribution

---

[68] Relying on Commissioner v. Procter, 142 F.2d 824 (4th Cir. 1944); Rev. Rul. 86-41, 1986-1 C.B. 300; Rev. Rul. 65-144, 1965-1 C.B. 442. See § 15.3.1.2.4 n.139.

[69] 1983-2 C.B. 169.

[70] See the discussion of formula provisions in § 7.2.1.1.

§7.1.1.6

with a cut back condition subsequent.[71] As to the balance, the power would not lapse at all.

As an alternative, the power could lapse with respect to the entire amount but the beneficiary would retain a testamentary power to appoint the amount that exceeds the five-or-five limitation. That testamentary power would make the lapse an incomplete transfer that avoids gift taxation, but instead there would be FET at the powerholder's death. In whatever format it is used, this hanging power can lapse in subsequent years to the extent those subsequent lapses are tax free under §2514(e). The hope is that all of the hanging power can lapse out before the beneficiary dies. Curiously, there appears to be no authority testing the underlying premises or effect of this planning, notwithstanding use of such hanging powers for many years.

§7.1.1.7 Multiple Powers

Also notable in designing a beneficiary's hanging power of withdrawal for Crummey power purposes is a clearly correct interpretation of §2514(e). Revenue Ruling 85-88[72] considered application of the five-or-five exception in the context of withdrawal rights in multiple trusts or multiple withdrawal rights in a single trust. For example, a person might possess two separate $5,000 or 5% withdrawal powers created by the same donor in two separate trusts, or two such powers created by contributions to the same trust by two separate donors.

In each case a taxable gift will result if the beneficiary allows the multiple withdrawal rights to lapse in a single year,[73] unless an appropri-

---

[71] PLR 8022048 illustrates the need for the formula to define an ascertainable amount at the time of the lapse. Involved was an irrevocable trust with a noncumulative annual power to withdraw the lesser of all amounts added to the trust in any calendar year or an amount that was dependent on whether married donors elected to split gifts to the trust under §2513. Gift splitting does not become effective until the due date for filing the gift tax return, which was after the lapse would occur. As a result, at the time of lapse the amount subject to withdrawal was not ascertainable, which precluded present interest qualification to the extent based on that aspect of the formula.

[72] 1985-2 C.B. 201.

[73] The Ruling held that multiple withdrawal rights in a single trust do not permit multiple tax free lapses. Apparently the government was prepared to rule favorably to the taxpayer with respect to multiple withdrawal rights in separate

§7.1.1.7

ate hanging power or testamentary power is applicable. This is because the Ruling appropriately limits the number of $5,000 withdrawal rights that can be made available to any one beneficiary to one. The Ruling did not need to restrict application of the 5% lapse rule under § 2514(e) because the 5% test properly is based on the value of total trust assets subject to the withdrawal right at the time of lapse. Thus, if the donee has multiple withdrawal rights in a single trust, the 5% test is based on "the maximum amount subject to the donee's withdrawal power *on the date of lapse of any such power* during the calendar year."[74] As regards multiple withdrawal rights in separate trusts (regardless of their settlors), the 5% test is applied by *aggregating* the amount subject to the power in each trust, determined in the same manner.[75]

As an example that informs the need to be cognizant of how many trusts (created by the same or different donors) grant the same beneficiary five-or-five withdrawal rights, the Ruling assumed withdrawal rights in each of two trusts, one of $300,000 and one of $400,000, and determined that the 5% test would be applied against the aggregate value of $700,000. Thus, the 5% exception under § 2514(e) would be $35,000 for the year. If this implies that multiple trusts could be drafted to direct satisfaction of such a withdrawal right all from one trust rather than pro rata from each, the Ruling may permit a greater degree of flexibility in granting Crummey withdrawal rights.

For example, it would be desirable if the Ruling authorizes withdrawal from a single trust with certain liquid assets (or certain assets that are undesirable to the powerholder, depending on the objectives of the donor), based on the aggregate value of the several trusts, not all of the trusts lending well to actual exercise of the withdrawal right. But to date there is no confirmation of such an opportunity. With multiple trusts

---

(Footnote Continued)

trusts but effectively was reversed by the Treasury Department in GCM 39371 and ultimately ruled that multiple withdrawal rights in separate trusts also do not generate multiple tax free lapse opportunities.

[74] 1985-2 C.B. at 202 (emphasis added).

[75] In giving examples, the government first assumed a trust worth $300,000 at the time of one lapse during the year and worth $400,000 at the time of a later lapse, concluding that the 5% test would be applied against $400,000. Presumably the same result would apply even if the trust was $400,000 earlier in the year and only $300,000 at the time of the later lapse, but this was not stated.

§ 7.1.1.7

created by separate donors the much greater concern needs to be whether multiple $5,000 powers will exceed any permissible 5% figure. If so, then the additional question is whether any hanging power provision is drafted properly with respect to multiple trust powers, to prevent a taxable lapse by the powerholder.

§7.1.1.8 Generation-Skipping Transfer Tax

Another tax consequence to the powerholder relates to the GST. One is illustrated by TAM 8901004. Because grandchildren of the trusts' settlor were given Crummey withdrawal rights, the government ruled that they possessed present interests in a generation-skipping trust. By virtue thereof, the amount subject to withdrawal by grandchildren ("skip persons" under the GST)[76] constituted a direct skip for GST purposes. Moreover, these contributions did not qualify for inclusion-ratio-of-zero treatment under §2642(c) because separate shares were not created for each beneficiary.[77]

Notwithstanding that they generated no gift tax because they qualified for the annual exclusion, these contributions were "transfer[s] subject to a tax imposed by chapter . . . 12" as required by §2612(c)(1), meaning that they incurred an immediate GST. This result illustrates that an immediate GST on the full amount subject to a skip person's power of withdrawal is payable by the transferor when the contribution is made to a trust that does not comply with the §2642(c) requirements, which may be unexpected.

The other GST consequence of the lapsing power is that the grandchild becomes the transferor of the trust for subsequent GST purposes to the extent the lapse is taxable under Chapter 12. New

---

[76] See §11.4.1.1.

[77] See §11.4.1.3. Cf. PLR 200229032, in which a similar failure to properly tax vest annual exclusion transfers in trust caused the trust to fail to qualify for zero inclusion ratio treatment, requiring allocation of the taxpayer's GST exemption, which an accountant wrongly concluded was unnecessary, resulting in the need for this request (which was granted) for an extension of time to make a late exemption allocation.

§7.1.1.8

transferor treatment is denied, however, to the extent the lapse is tax free under the five-or-five provisions of § 2514(e).[78]

§7.1.1.9 Pseudo Grantor Trust Status

The GST new-transferor treatment is mirrored and enlarged upon for § 678 income tax purposes. It provides that a beneficiary who allows a Crummey power of withdrawal to lapse becomes a grantor of the full lapsed amount in the trust for income tax purposes. This treatment applies to the entire lapse amount, not just the amount in excess of the § 2514(e) five-or-five exception, and is avoided only to the extent the trust's original settlor retains an interest or power that causes overriding grantor trust liability for income tax purposes.

PLR 9034004 illustrates the government's position on the proper computation of the income tax consequences of the lapse of a five-or-five withdrawal right. Because the powerholder is treated as the owner of a portion of the trust in the year the power is exercisable, the Ruling held that lapse of the withdrawal power is tantamount to a release for purposes of § 678(a)(2).[79] If the powerholder is entitled to trust income in future years, this release generates grantor trust exposure for the duration of the trust, and it grows every time a withdrawal power lapses.[80] The government's computation underscores the notion that the lapse of a five-or-five withdrawal power is not harmless for income tax purposes the way it appears to be under § 2514(e) for most wealth transfer tax purposes.[81]

§7.1.1.10 Qualified Minors' Trusts

Some transfers, typically in trust, that otherwise do not meet the annual exclusion present interest requirements[82] nevertheless qualify for

---

[78] See Treas. Reg. §§ 26.2601-1(b)(1)(v)(A) (penultimate sentence) and 26.2652-1(a)(5) Example 5.

[79] Citing Rev. Rul. 67-241, 1967-2 C.B. 225.

[80] See § 5.11.7.

[81] Remember that a power that has not yet lapsed in the year of death will cause inclusion of the amount subject to that available power at death. See § 7.1.1.2 n.40 and accompanying text.

[82] See § 7.1.1.1.

the annual exclusion because of a special exception for "qualified minors' trusts" in § 2503(c). This available tool is important because annual gifts to minors that take advantage of the annual gift tax exclusion may be a significant component of any comprehensive estate plan. And the dollar amounts involved may exceed the amount the donor (or the donee's parents) would want the minor to control at a tender age.

The subject matter of an annual exclusion gift may be transferred directly to a minor and qualify for the annual exclusion notwithstanding that the minor does not have legal capacity to deal with the transferred property and even if no legal guardian has been appointed.[83] Even though legal incapacity has certain implicit protections against loss or mismanagement by the minor, Congress recognized that the inherent disadvantages of transferring property outright to a minor make this an undesirable mechanism to take advantage of the annual exclusion.

So Congress enacted § 2503(c), which deems that a transfer creates a present interest in a minor beneficiary if the principal[84] and income of the gifted property may[85] be expended by or for the benefit of the beneficiary before the beneficiary attains age 21. In addition, any

---

[83] See Snyder v. United States, 134 F. Supp. 319 (W.D. N.C. 1955) (stock given to a minor's guardian was a present interest gift and the annual exclusion was available because there was no delay in the enjoyment of the stock under state law concerning guardians; title vested in the minor absolutely and the guardian was no barrier to present enjoyment); Rev. Rul. 54-400, 1954-2 C.B. 319 (stock given to a minor and issued in the minor's name is a present interest gift even though no legal guardian exists for the minor, unless use or enjoyment of the property is limited or restricted by the terms of the donor's conveyance; any disability implicit under state law is irrelevant in determining whether a minor has immediate enjoyment of the property or its income for federal gift tax purposes).

[84] Ross v. United States, 226 F. Supp. 333 (S.D. Tex. 1963), rev'd, 348 F.2d 577 (5th Cir. 1965), held that discretion to distribute only income during the beneficiary's minority is inadequate; the trustee's discretion must extend to corpus as well. The reversal was based on a finding that the trustee had all the powers of a guardian under state law, which included authority to distribute corpus for maintenance or education if parents of the beneficiary could not provide adequate support, which was sufficient.

[85] As originally passed by the House of Representatives, § 2503(c) required that the income "will" be expended by or for the benefit of the minor prior to attaining age 21. The Senate amended this by changing "will" to "may." S. Rep. No. 1622, 83d Cong., 2d Sess. 479 (1954).

§7.1.1.10

unexpended principal and accumulated income must be subject to the beneficiary's control when the beneficiary attains age 21[86] or must be distributed to the beneficiary's estate[87] or as the beneficiary may appoint under a general power of appointment if the beneficiary dies before then.[88]

In many cases the §2503(c)(2)(B) power of appointment is the preferable alternative. This will be true if the settlor of an inter vivos §2503(c) trust for the minor is a potential heir of the beneficiary. In such a case, trust property that is payable to the beneficiary's estate if the beneficiary dies before reaching age 21 may pass back to the settlor. Although this potential reacquisition is not a retained reversion that would trigger §2037 inclusion in the settlor's gross estate if the settlor

---

(Footnote Continued)

Unlike the annual exclusion present interest requirement discussed in §7.1.1.1, there is no §2503(c) requirement that the trust property be income producing. See De Concini v. Wood, 60-1 U.S. Tax Cas. (CCH) ¶ 11,938 (D. Ariz. 1960) (interest in unimproved vacant land transferred to qualifying §2503(c) trust); TAM 8320007. PLR 8936032 held that gifts of stock in trust would be complete for gift tax purposes and qualify under §2503(c) as present interests eligible for the annual exclusion even though the trust income would be added to principal, because the trustee had discretion to pay trust corpus to the beneficiary without considering other financial resources of the beneficiary and the beneficiary would receive the balance of the trust at age 21. Any part of the trust not paid to the beneficiary would be distributable as the beneficiary appointed by will and, in default of effective exercise, to the beneficiary's descendants.

[86] Rev. Rul. 73-287, 1973-2 C.B. 321, held that distribution at age 18 (which is common under many states' UGMA or UTMA statutes) was permissible because §2503(c) establishes the maximum restriction that may attach to a gift and still qualify as a present interest for annual exclusion purposes.

[87] Messing v. Commissioner, 48 T.C. 502 (1967), held that distribution to the beneficiary's surviving descendants and, if none, to the beneficiary's estate was not adequate and, lacking a power of appointment, qualification under §2503(c) was precluded. Similarly, Ross v. Commissioner, 71 T.C. 897 (1979), aff'd, 652 F.2d 1365 (9th Cir. 1981), concluded that distribution to the beneficiary's "heirs at law" was not a qualified substitute for distribution to the beneficiary's estate.

[88] Rev. Rul. 67-384, 1967-2 C.B. 348, denied the annual exclusion for a transfer into a trust for the benefit of a child still in gestation because an unborn child cannot possess a power of appointment and does not have an estate.

dies first,[89] the settlor typically does not want to receive by inheritance any of the property the settlor was seeking to remove from the settlor's estate through annual exclusion gifts.

Because the beneficiary cannot make a will in most states until reaching a certain age, this possible inheritance is not avoidable if the trust provides for payment to the beneficiary's estate and the beneficiary dies before reaching that age. For this reason, it typically is preferable to provide that the trust property will pass as the beneficiary appoints pursuant to a general inter vivos or testamentary power of appointment[90] and, to the extent there is no effective exercise of that power, to designated default beneficiaries other than the settlor. This trust will qualify under § 2503(c) notwithstanding that the beneficiary also may be unable due to age to exercise the power of appointment (and, thus, that the property will pass to designated default beneficiaries).[91]

Notice that a beneficiary who dies before age 21 need not exercise the power of appointment, nor must the property pass to the beneficiary's estate in default of exercise. Treas. Reg. § 25.2503-4(b)(3) clearly permits an alternate disposition in default of exercise. It also appears that, state law permitting, the beneficiary's personal representative may disclaim that power of appointment and thereby prevent any § 2041 inclusion in the beneficiary's estate attributable to the trust. This avoidance of pay-back inclusion is possible because § 2518(b)(2)(B) permits

---

[89] It also likely is the case that any reversion would be worth less than the 5% threshold of § 2037(a)(2) due to the relative ages of the settlor and the beneficiary.

[90] Under Treas. Reg. § 25.2503-4(b) the general power may be exercisable by deed or by will or by either. To limit the possibility of inadvertent exercise if exercise is permitted by inter vivos document it may be advisable to require its execution with all the formalities of a will.

[91] Treas. Reg. § 25.2503-4(b) requires that there be no substantial restrictions on exercise of the power by the beneficiary but provides that restrictions under controlling local law that preclude the beneficiary from exercising the power do not prevent the power from satisfying this requirement. See also Rev. Rul. 75-351, 1975-1 C.B. 368 (existence of the general power and not its exercisability is the requisite) and § 12.3. However, Gall v. United States, 521 F.2d 878 (5th Cir. 1975), involved a trust instrument creating the power that imposed a restriction that was more strict than state law; the court concluded that the power of appointment requirement of § 2503(c) was not satisfied.

§ 7.1.1.10

the beneficiary 9 months after reaching age 21 in which to disclaim, regardless of any acceptance of benefits prior to reaching age 21.

At first blush it would appear that such a disclaimer would be an abuse of the qualified minor's trust requisite power or payment to the beneficiary's estate, to cause inclusion of the property that qualified for the annual exclusion. But consider that a beneficiary who receives property outright that qualifies for the § 2503(b) annual exclusion also may disclaim many years later (but within the requisite window of 9 months after reaching age 21). There thus appears to be no impropriety in planning that allows the donor to benefit from the annual exclusion *without* there being the requisite pay-back inclusion in the donee's estate. Consider also in this respect Treas. Reg. § 25.2518-2(d)(4) Examples (3), (9), and (11), all of which involve qualified disclaimers of gifts that clearly could qualify for the annual exclusion. Further, all this seems to be available notwithstanding that the recipient who ultimately benefits from the disclaimer also may have received an annual exclusion gift from the same donor for the same year in which the original transfer to the ultimate disclaimant was made.

If only an income interest or other less than fee simple interest in such a trust is given to the minor, that lesser interest alone may qualify for the § 2503(c) annual exclusion.[92] For example, the settlor in Konner v. Commissioner[93] established a trust to pay income to a § 2503(c) trust for a ten year period (or earlier termination of the § 2503(c) trust). The

---

[92] Herr v. Commissioner, 35 T.C. 732 (1961), aff'd, 303 F.2d 780 (3d Cir. 1962), acq., 1968-2 C.B. 2 (trust income held for the benefit of a minor, to be paid currently or accumulated and paid when the minor attained age 21 or died prior thereto, constituted a § 2503(c) present interest equal to the value of the income interest for the number of years the beneficiary was under that age), followed in Commissioner v. Thebaut, 361 F.2d 428 (5th Cir. 1966), and Rollman v. United States, 342 F.2d 62 (Ct. Cl. 1965), held that provisions regarding trust income during the beneficiary's minority may be separated from the balance of a trust and alone qualify under § 2503(c) as a present interest; Rev. Rul. 68-670, 1968-2 C.B. 413 (right to receive trust income alone may be the corpus of a § 2503(c) trust). Cf. PLR 7910042 (income interest in trust did not qualify because income earned while the beneficiary was under age 21 could be accumulated in the trustee's discretion, not to be distributed until the beneficiary attained age 26; if that income had been distributable at age 21 or the beneficiary's prior death the pre-21 income interest alone would have qualified).

[93] 35 T.C. 727 (1961), acq. 1968-2 C.B. 2.

court recognized that the ten year trust income interest could be the corpus of a valid §2503(c) trust and qualify as a present interest gift for annual exclusion purposes. Similarly, PLR 8119025 concluded that a one-third slice of the donor's life estate in an irrevocable trust was a qualifying gift of a present interest.[94]

A different result was reached in Estate of Levine v. Commissioner.[95] The taxpayer attempted to bootstrap §2503(c) qualification of a limited income interest that met the §2503(c) requirements with a future right to receive trust income beginning at the beneficiary's age 21. The intent was to regard the two interests together as one continuous income entitlement, the aggregate value of which could qualify as a present interest for annual exclusion purposes. The government successfully contended that the future interest income entitlement after the beneficiary's age 21 could not be tacked onto the §2503(c) qualified interest to give it present interest status. Therefore, the two interests were evaluated on their own. According to the court, the §2503(c) salvation of a pre-21 interest that otherwise would not qualify cannot also redeem a future interest that could not qualify on its own and that is not within the scope of §2503(c).

In other cases it may be desirable to establish a trust that requires the trustee to pay trust income to a minor beneficiary for life, perhaps granting the trustee discretion to distribute trust corpus to the beneficiary, but reserving the remainder after the minor's death for other designated beneficiaries. The life estate in such a trust, also standing alone, qualifies just the value of that temporal interest for the annual exclusion. This will reduce the value of the taxable transfer of corpus to the trust and, if the value of that income interest is sufficient, it alone may fully utilize the donor's allowable annual exclusion with respect to that beneficiary for that year. Only the value of the remainder—as a future interest—would not qualify for the annual exclusion.

---

[94] That interest would be valued today by multiplying the FMV of the donor's share in the trust corpus by a life estate factor based on the donor's life expectancy and reflecting the §7520 monthly revision of the interest assumption tied to the annual mid-term AFR established under §1274, all then divided by three.

[95] 526 F.2d 717 (2d Cir. 1975), rev'g 63 T.C. 136 (1974).

§7.1.1.10

One advantage of this kind of approach is that it avoids the possible undesirable result of subjecting the trust property to the control of the beneficiary at what might be an immature age 21, which is a requisite of the §2503(c) trust. As an alternative, however, it is permissible to provide the beneficiary with a limited window of opportunity to withdraw the trust corpus upon reaching age 21 and, to the extent the power of withdrawal is not exercised, to provide after the time window has closed that the trust will continue until a later date.[96] As with a lapsed Crummey power of withdrawal, the trust will be regarded as the beneficiary's property for income and wealth transfer tax purposes following the lapse of such a power.[97]

In lieu of drafting and administering separate trusts for minor beneficiaries (or a single trust with separate shares), a settlor may wish to take advantage of the fact that every American jurisdiction has enacted custodianship legislation, usually modeled after the UTMA (or its

---

[96] See Rev. Rul. 74-43, 1974-1 C.B. 285, 286:

> a gift to a minor in trust, with provision that the beneficiary has, upon reaching age 21, either (1) a continuing right to compel immediate distribution of the trust corpus by giving written notice to the trustee, or to permit the trust to continue by its own terms, or (2) a right during a limited period to compel immediate distribution of the trust corpus by giving written notice to the trustee which if not exercised will permit the trust to continue by its own terms, will not be considered to be the gift of a future interest as the gift satisfies the requirements of section 2503(c) of the Code, and the exclusion provided for in section 2503(b) is allowable.

See also PLRs 8507017 (60 day withdrawal period; extension until age 30), 8334071 (90 day withdrawal period; extension until age 30), 8039023 (extension until age 30), and 7805037 (60 day withdrawal period; extension until age 25). Parameters such as those informing the validity of Crummey withdrawal powers probably are adequate. See §7.1.1.3.

[97] See §§7.1.1.6-7.1.1.9 (6th ed.). Note, however, that the trust will not be subject to §2041(a)(2) FET inclusion when the beneficiary dies to the extent lapse of the power is protected by §2514(e) from being a gift taxable event. As a result, the trust to that extent also will fail to qualify for §2642(c) inclusion-ratio-of-zero treatment for GST purposes. See §2642(c)(2)(B), which requires inclusion in the beneficiary's estate. As a result, gift tax annual exclusion treatment may prevent gift taxation on creation, but the trust will be exposed to potential GST and the §2632 automatic allocation of exemption rules also may apply to that extent. Cf. PLR 200633015.

§7.1.1.10

predecessor UGMA).[98] These custodianship arrangements qualify under § 2503(c)[99] and permit a donor to transfer property to a custodian for the benefit of a minor, usually to be retained until the custodianship terminates, typically at the beneficiary's age 18 or 21 (or the minor's death), at which time the property is distributable to the minor (or to the minor's estate).

Custodianships offer a convenient and inexpensive mechanism for making gifts to minors that qualify under § 2503(c) and, until termination, protect against the hazards of an outright transfer. Nevertheless, certain cautions must be exercised. For example, the statutory provisions governing the account cannot be changed. Thus, a distribution to the beneficiary's estate and potential distribution back to the donor cannot be prevented. More importantly, the government asserts that the value of custodianship property is includible in donor's gross estate under § 2038 if the donor dies while serving as the custodian, because the donor's powers are deemed to be retained powers over the gifted property.[100] Unfortunately, this FET exposure cannot easily be avoided

---

[98] 8C U.L.A. 1 (2001), and 8A U.L.A. 297 (2003), respectively. See also the Uniform Custodial Trust Act, 7A Part I U.L.A. 103 (2002), which allows property to be placed under the control of a custodial trustee. It specifically refers to the property of adults, both mentally competent and incompetent, but presumably could be used in lieu of an account under the UTMA or the earlier UGMA (after which it was modeled). A custodial trustee takes control of and collects, holds, manages, invests, and reinvests custodial trust property and has all the rights and powers over custodial trust property that an adult owner has over individually owned property, exercisable in a fiduciary capacity.

[99] Rev. Rul. 59-357, 1959-2 C.B. 212, 213, amplified by Rev. Rul. 74-556, 1974-2 C.B. 300 (comparing the UGMA and the Model Gifts of Securities to Minors Act and concluding that a gift qualifying for § 2503(c) is made on creation of the account and not "by reason of a subsequent resignation of the custodian or termination of the custodianship" under either Act); Rev. Rul. 56-86, 1956-1 C.B. 449. There has been no Revenue Ruling confirming that UTMA revisions of the Uniform Act paradigm did not alter these results, but that appears to be a reliable conclusion. See PLR 8806063, which concluded that transfers pursuant to the Massachusetts version of the UTMA, Mass. Gen. L. ch. 201A, qualify as § 2503(c) transfers.

[100] Treas. Reg. § 20.2038-1(a); Rev. Rul. 59-357, 1959-2 C.B. 212; Rev. Rul. 57-366, 1957-2 C.B. 618, based on Lober v. United States, 346 U.S. 335 (1953) (trust assets includible in donor trustee's gross estate under predecessor to § 2038 because of the power to accelerate termination of the account through

by a donor who wants to maintain control over the gift. For example, the reciprocal transfers doctrine prevents avoidance of this exposure by merely employing reciprocal transfers by which one parent acts as fiduciary of accounts created by the other and vice versa.[101]

§ 7.1.1.10.1 Obligation of Support Issues

Similarly, the government has asserted § 2036(a)(1) indirect retained beneficial ownership and § 2041(a)(2) general power of appoint-

---

(Footnote Continued)

distributions to the beneficiaries). The government was successful in Stuit v. Commissioner, 54 T.C. 580 (1970), aff'd, 452 F.2d 190 (7th Cir. 1971) (rejecting contention that the power to pay for the "benefit" of a child imposed a standard on the donor as custodian that negated any § 2038 power, because the word "benefit" did not impose a standard that would negate a § 2038 power). Cf. Estate of Chrysler v. Commissioner, 44 T.C. 55 (1965), rev'd on other grounds, 361 F.2d 508 (2d Cir. 1966) (also basing inclusion on § 2036 because of the right in the donor to use the income to discharge a legal obligation to support the beneficiary; the court on appeal determined that the funds placed in the custodianship account were the beneficiary's property as a matter of state law and, based thereon, that the custodian was not the transferor, making §§ 2036 and 2038 inapplicable); Rev. Rul. 74-556, 1974-2 C.B. 300 (successor custodian for minor donee under a UGMA account was the donor's spouse who split under § 2513 the donor's transfers to the account; because the consenting spouse did not own or transfer any account assets, no part of their value was subject to § 2038 inclusion in the spouse's estate).

[101] See Exchange Bank & Trust Co. v. United States, 82-1 U.S. Tax Cas. (CCH) ¶ 13,444 (Ct. Cl. 1981), aff'd, 694 F.2d 1261 (Fed. Cir. 1982), in which spouses each transferred assets under custodianships for their children. To the extent the husband was the donor the wife was named as custodian, and to the extent the wife was the donor the husband was named as custodian. The husband died while several of the children were under age 21, and the court held that assets held by the husband as custodian, which were transferred by his wife, were includible in the husband's gross estate as they would have been if he had been the transferor, under an application of the reciprocal trust doctrine discussed in § 7.3.2: "The fact that the focus in this case is upon crossed custodianship rather than crossed trusts offers no basis for denying the application of the reciprocal trust doctrine." 82-1 U.S. Tax Cas. at 84,232. The court on appeal concluded "that the reciprocal trust doctrine should be applied to uncross the custodianships because the transfers were interrelated, and because the arrangements left the donors in the same economic positions as they would have been in had they retained the property as custodians under the Florida Gifts to Minors Act." 694 F.2d at 1269.

ment inclusion with respect to any donor or any third party acting as trustee or custodian over assets held for their own dependents. In each case the government's theory is that the donor or the fiduciary is the indirect beneficiary of funds that may be used to support or maintain a person the donor or the fiduciary is legally obligated to support or maintain.[102] This discharge of obligation of support theory is significantly misunderstood and not supportable under the law of most states.

In most cases under the law of most states, a trust or custodial account created for a dependent child may *not* be used to discharge or satisfy the legal obligation of the child's parent to support or maintain the child.[103] For example, in Sutliff v. Sutliff,[104] a father and his parents established UGMA accounts for each of the father's four children. After his divorce, the father used the funds in those accounts to make about 75% of his child support payments, and his ex-wife sued, alleging misuse of the children's funds. Notwithstanding UGMA § 5, which was applicable and specifies that a custodian may use custodial property to support, maintain, educate, and benefit the account beneficiary, the court held that the Act does not permit custodial funds to be diverted to discharge a parent's support obligation if the parent has sufficient funds to provide that support.

According to the court, if the father had been allowed to make the child support payments from these accounts, the expenditures "would benefit the father, not the children. When he can reasonably do so, the father is obliged to provide support for his minor children regardless of the UGMA property."[105]

The father also used custodial funds to pay college expenses of a 20-year-old child. The court determined that the obligation of a parent to pay for college expenses is not absolute and that independent resources of the child, including custodial funds, may be considered in establishing

---

[102] See Treas. Reg. § § 20.2036-1(b) (2), 20.2041-1(c) (1).

[103] Indeed, UTC § 814 is a statutory Upjohn clause, enacted to preclude unintended tax consequences flowing from the government's discharge of obligation theory, and does not preclude intended distributions for a beneficiary's support. See In re Margolis Revocable Trust, 765 N.W.2d 919 (Minn. Ct. App. 2009).

[104] 528 A.2d 1318 (Pa. 1986), aff'g 489 A.2d 764 (Pa. Super. 1985).

[105] 528 A.2d 1323-1324.

§ 7.1.1.10.1

the level of support required of the father and the amount that should be provided from the child's own resources. That holding, however, negates the government's discharge theory in the other direction, by finding that no such obligation existed.[106]

Similarly, in Weiss v. Weiss[107] a son sued his adoptive father to recover funds that the father had placed in a UGMA account for the son. As custodian of those accounts, the father used the funds to pay for a variety of the son's expenses, including summer camps, sports activities, vacations, and college expenses, although the father had sufficient resources of his own to pay for those activities. The court held that the father was permitted to use the account funds for these purposes because these expenses were not a part of the father's legal obligation to support the son. More importantly, however, the court explicitly stated that, if these expenses *had* been the father's obligation, the use of the account funds would not have been a discharge of his obligation—it would have been a theft—showing clearly that the discharge of obligation theory is wrong on the state law level.[108]

If a case involves custodial accounts rather than trust funds, the issue is slightly confused by provisions in most state statutes providing that the custodian can use the accounts for the child's support and maintenance "with or without regard" to the child's other sources of support. However, state courts that have considered the issue have

---

[106] With respect to the state law question whether a parent has an obligation to pay for higher education, see Annot., Postsecondary education as within nondivorced parent's child-support obligation, 42 A.L.R.4th 819 (1985), and Annot., Responsibility of noncustodial divorced parent to pay for, or contribute to, costs of child's college education, 99 A.L.R.3d 322 (1980).

[107] 1996 WL 91641 (unpub. S.D. N.Y.).

[108] Erdmann v. Erdmann, 226 N.W.2d 439, 442-443 (Wis. 1975), involved a similar fact pattern, the court stating: "Where the parent, who has resources of his own sufficient to maintain his children, is also guardian of their estate, his obligation to support them out of his own means is not changed thereby. In such cases recourse on the ward's estate is not permitted." See also Cohen v. Cohen, 609 A.2d 57, 60 (N.J. Super. 1992) (parent, as donor and custodian of UGMA account, required to repay amounts used to pay for school tuition and other expenses deemed to be related to the support of the child who was the donee of the account, stating that "a parent cannot properly use assets of a UGMA account to defray the parent's legal obligations to a child if the parent is financially able to support the child").

consistently held that this provision is intended to give the trustee discretion to provide for the child as necessary, even in cases in which, for example, a parent is able but unwilling to provide support. But nothing in the statute is intended to relieve a parent's obligation to support the child.

To illustrate, in Gold v. Gold[109] a husband in a divorce proceeding filed for discovery of the money in trusts and UGMA accounts that the wife held for their children, on the grounds that the wife would be able to use that money to pay her portion of the children's support, making the amount in the accounts relevant in setting child support. The court denied the request because the mother would not be permitted to invade the children's accounts to pay for their support as long as she was able to provide that support through her own funds:

> True, under the trust instrument she may have discretion to apply the trust funds for the benefit of the children without regard to other sources of income or support. Similarly, Estates, Powers and Trusts Law § 7-4.3(b) authorizes a custodian to pay for the infant's support and maintenance from funds held under the Uniform Gifts to Minors Act. But as trustee and custodian, plaintiff is a fiduciary with the duty to account to her children for the use of their funds. She may not use the children's money for her own benefit. She is barred from using the children's money for their support, since by reducing her child care obligations, she would receive an indirect financial advantage.[110]

In the context presented, this inability to use assets held for the benefit of a minor should mean that § 2036(a)(1) indirect enjoyment should not be deemed to exist and that acting as trustee or custodian of such a trust or account should not cause § 2041 discharge of obligation general power of appointment exposure. In either case, this is because distributions from the account may not have the effect of satisfying the parent's legal obligation of support.

This should be true regardless of whether the trust or UTMA or UGMA account statute governing a child's funds allows the custodian to spend the funds for the child's support. Indeed, fiduciary duties prevent

---

[109] 409 N.Y.S.2d 114 (1978).

[110] 409 N.Y.S.2d at 116. Regarding the use of a child's own monies, see also 59 Am. Jur. 2d Parent & Child (1964), and Annot. Child's ownership of or right to income or property as affecting parent's duty to support, or as grounds for reimbursing parent for expenditures in that regard, 121 A.L.R. 176 (1939).

§ 7.1.1.10.1

a parent who is the custodian from using the funds to supplant rather than to supplement the parent's support obligation, and a trust (but not a custodianship account established pursuant to statute, because its terms may not be altered) may be drafted to preclude distributions that would benefit the donor indirectly.[111]

More importantly, the theory upon which the government's discharge theory rests is wrong, and the trust or custodianship assets should not be included in the parent's gross estate.[112] Nevertheless, naming a parent as fiduciary in these cases may be begging for a controversy that it would be better to avoid, although a provision precluding the use of assets in a way that may discharge a support obligation is wise drafting to guard against either § 2036 or § 2041 exposure.[113]

The discharge of obligation issue for wealth transfer tax purposes is all the more interesting in light of the income tax treatment of these trusts and accounts. For example, it is clear that the income generated by property held under a custodial arrangement is taxable to the beneficiary, because the custodianship is ignored for income tax purposes and

---

[111] See § 7.1.1.10.2.

[112] The government understands and accepts this analysis. See FSA 199930026 (absent application of an exception, authority to distribute funds to a dependent is not sufficient to cause § 2041 general power of appointment inclusion to the powerholding fiduciary). One of two exceptions to the general rule is a trust created for the express purpose of supplanting the legal obligation of support, as illustrated by In re Estate of Wallens, 816 N.Y.S.2d 793 (Sup. Ct. 2006) (funds in a testamentary trust created by a grandfather could be used by the beneficiary's father to pay for support and secondary school and college tuition expenses because it was deemed to have been created for the express purpose of providing for support and education). See also Guardianship of K.S., 100 Cal. Rptr. 3d 78 (Ct. App. 2009), finding that a trust for a minor "was specifically created by the minor's mother for the 'health, maintenance, education, travel, and welfare, and general welfare' of the minor" and, therefore, the minor's father could use trust funds (along with his own monies) for the minor's support. For an exegesis in the context of § 2041 exposure to a parent acting as custodian of an account for a minor child, see Pennell, Custodians, Incompetents, Trustees and Others: Taxable Powers of Appointment?, 15 U. Miami Inst. Est. Plan. ¶ 1602.3 (1981).

[113] And, because state law does not usually regard distributions as a discharge or satisfaction, normally such a provision will not preclude any desired distribution. See Pennell & Fleming, Avoiding the Discharge of Obligation Theory, 12 Prob. & Prop. 49-54 (Sept./Oct. 1998).

the account corpus is treated as the beneficiary's own property.[114] According to the income tax regulations, this result is defeated only to the extent that income is used for the support or maintenance of someone the donor is obligated to support or maintain. This provision carefully avoids use of the terms "discharge" or "satisfaction" in conjunction with the obligation.[115]

---

[114] See § 5.2 n.4 and accompanying text.

[115] In the income tax context, the discharge of an obligation is required before income will be taxed to a person who is obligated, and the regulations recognize that it would be unusual for a discharge to occur. Treas. Reg. § 1.662(a)-4 states that:

> The term "legal obligation" includes a legal obligation to support another person if, and only if, the obligation is not affected by the adequacy of the dependent's own resources. For example, a parent has a "legal obligation" within the meaning of the preceding sentence to support his minor child if under local law property or income from property owned by the child cannot be used for his support so long as his parent is able to support him. On the other hand, if under local law a mother may use the resources of a child for the child's support in lieu of supporting him herself, no obligation of support exists within the meaning of this paragraph, whether or not income is actually used for support.

This is consistent with the grantor trust rules, under which a "discharge" of obligation is not required before income is attributable to the settlor, presumably because such a requirement would be greater than Congress wanted to impose before causing trust income to be taxable to the trust's settlor. For example, in § 677(b), the Code refers to income being taxable to the trust's settlor if it was "distributed for the support or maintenance of a beneficiary . . . whom the grantor is legally obligated to support or maintain," and the concept of a discharge or satisfaction of that obligation is not presented. It is only in Treas. Reg. §§ 1.677(a)-1(d), Reg. § 1.677(b)-1(d) (first sentence), and 1.678(a)-1(b) that the "discharge" or "satisfaction" concepts are introduced and with an apparent lack of appreciation for the distinction here discussed or for the fact that the discharge theory is not properly applicable under the law of most states. See §§ 5.11.4 n.85 and 5.11.7 nn.166-169 and accompanying text.

Rev. Rul. 56-484, 1956-2 C.B. 23, involved the taxation of income from stock transferred under a custodianship act. Under state law that followed the majority rule a parent was obliged to support and maintain minor children without resort to their separate estates. If a gift expressly provided that the gifted property could be used for the support of the minor child, however, that property could be so applied without regard to the parent's ability to support the child. Under these circumstances, the Ruling concluded that the income was taxable to the person who was obligated to support the minor, regardless of the identity of the donor or of the custodian, to the extent income was used in discharge of that legal

§ 7.1.1.10.1

More curious is that this income tax position is more informative of the GST situation under § 2652(c)(3)[116] than is the FET position. That GST provision disregards an obligated individual in determining trust beneficiaries unless the trust mandates the use of trust income or corpus to supplant that individual's legal obligations, which seldom would be the case. The discretion to use trust income or corpus for the support or maintenance of a trust beneficiary to whom another person is obligated is not sufficient to make the obligated individual a beneficiary of the trust. Furthermore, it does not give that person an interest for purposes of determining the application of the GST or whether the inclusion-ratio-of-zero rule in § 2642(c) is lost because the sole beneficiary requirement in § 2642(c)(2)(A) is not met.

§ 7.1.1.10.2 Substantial Restriction Prohibition

The addition of language to a § 2503(c) trust prohibiting distributions that might be deemed to discharge or satisfy any person's legal obligation to support or maintain a minor beneficiary may raise the issue whether the trust fails the requirement that there be no substantial restriction on the provision of benefits[117] in a § 2503(c) account for the

---

(Footnote Continued)

obligation of support. To the extent the income was *not* used to discharge that legal obligation of support, however, it was taxable to the child. That result is consistent with the grantor trust rules in §§ 674(b)(1), (b)(5), and (b)(7)(B) that collectively preclude income taxation to the grantor in the absence of a § 677(b) distribution for the support or maintenance of someone the grantor is obliged to support or maintain.

Cf. Friedman v. Commissioner, 27 T.C.M. (CCH) 714 (1968) (income of stock held by a parent as custodian for a minor child was taxed to the parent because it was used by the parent to satisfy personal obligations, including obligations to support the child; the court indicated that actions of a parent may refute any gift, in which case the income would be taxable to the parent because no gift was made).

116 "The fact that income or corpus of [a] trust may be used to satisfy an obligation of support arising under State law shall be disregarded in determining whether a person has an interest in [a] trust if—such use is discretionary, or such use is pursuant to the provisions of any State law substantially equivalent to the Uniform Gifts to Minors Act."

117 Rev. Rul. 67-270, 1967-2 C.B. 349 (trustee's discretion to use principal and income for the donee's "support, care, education, comfort and welfare" was not

minor beneficiary.[118] Such a prohibition, sometimes referred to as an "Upjohn" clause,[119] has been found not to constitute an impermissible restriction:

> The "restriction" . . . does not in any way impair, but, rather insulates the minor beneficiaries' present interest in the trust contributions. The trustee is empowered to distribute all or any part of these funds for any purpose and toward any end not already provided by law.[120]

The government suggested that the restriction might be substantial if the settlors were not financially able to fulfill their legal obligations to the beneficiary. The court rejected this notion because the settlors' financial condition made this possibility remote and because, under state law, the settlors' legal obligation would decline with any diminution in their financial resources, which would release the trustee from the restriction against expending funds for the beneficiary.

(Footnote Continued)

subject to substantial restriction), defined "benefit" for §2503(c) purposes in a somewhat tautological manner:

If, in addition to provisions for a minor's health or education, a trust instrument provides that the trust property may be expended during the donee's minority for purposes which have no objective limitations (i.e., "welfare," "happiness," and "convenience") and which provisions when read as a whole approximate the scope of the term "benefit," . . . the transfer is deemed to meet the requirements of section 2503(c) that the property be expendable for the minor's "benefit."

[118] Treas. Reg. §25.2503-4(b)(1).

[119] So named after Upjohn v. United States, 72-2 U.S. Tax Cas. (CCH) ¶ 12,888 at 86,077 (W.D. Mich. 1972) (provision that "no income or principal shall be paid, distributed or applied for support or maintenance which the settlors or either of them are legally obligated to provide a beneficiary, nor to defray any legal obligation of the settlors or either of them" did not preclude §2503(c) qualification). Today Upjohn provisions also may prohibit any distribution that would decrease a beneficiary's entitlement to public benefits. It probably is wise not to include this added restriction in a trust that is meant to qualify as a §2503(c) qualified minor's trust, because there must be no substantial restriction on the trustee's discretion to make distributions of income or corpus to the beneficiary prior to reaching age 21, and because it is unlikely that a SNT also could qualify as a qualified minor's trust (there appears to be no authority on point, nor is there authority on the question whether such a limitation might be regarded as a "substantial restriction").

[120] 72-2 U.S. Tax Cas. (CCH) at 86,078.

§7.1.1.10.2

Although not articulated by the court, if state law provides that a parent's legal obligation is not discharged or satisfied by trust distributions, then no distribution made by the trust would run afoul of the prohibition. In that respect, the proscription on the trustee is meaningful only in that it blocks the government's improper discharge of obligation argument and does not hang tie the fiduciary or violate the substantial restriction prohibition.

Most authorities have held that the substantial restriction standard means that the fiduciary has less authority to make distributions than does a guardian under state law.[121] For example, the government regards a requirement that the trustee consider "other resources available to the beneficiary and other payments made to . . . or for [the beneficiary's] benefit" as improper[122] if it is greater than that imposed under state law on a guardian. Because the same situation might be presented if local law required the trustee to consider the beneficiary's other resources

---

[121] See, e.g., Illinois Nat'l Bank v. United States, 756 F. Supp. 1117 (C.D. Ill. 1991) (stating that the issue involves an evaluation of the trustee's power to make distributions rather than the likelihood of its exercise, and focusing on the highlighted restriction on the trustee's authority, the court concluded that distributions for educational purposes and "in the event of an accident, illness or disability affecting the beneficiary, *or in the event of the* death or *disability of* either or both *of the beneficiary's parents* for the care, support, health and education of the beneficiary" constituted a substantial restriction that precluded § 2503(c) annual exclusion treatment); Faber v. United States, 439 F.2d 1189 (6th Cir. 1971) (income distribution authority limited "to provide for accident, illness or other emergency affecting the beneficiary" was substantially restricted because it did not include authority to make distributions for such items as education, general support, or maintenance); Ross v. United States, 348 F.2d 577 (5th Cir. 1965) (authority to distribute corpus for maintenance or education if beneficiary's parents could not provide adequate support was not more limited than state law guardian's power and therefore was not substantially restricted); Heidrich v. Commissioner, 55 T.C. 746 (1971) (distributions for "education, comfort, and support" was not too limited); Pettus v. Commissioner, 54 T.C. 112 (1970) (unlimited income discretion qualified the value of an income interest but restriction on corpus distributions to amounts "needed because of illness, infirmity, or disability" was too restrictive); Williams v. United States, 378 F.2d 693 (Ct. Cl. 1967) (power not more limited than that of a state law guardian).

[122] Rev. Rul. 69-345, 1969-1 C.B. 226 (trustee authorized to expend trust property for the "care, support, education, and welfare" of the beneficiary but subject to the restriction regarding other resources).

unless there is a contrary manifestation of intent in the document, cautious drafters might specifically provide that the beneficiary's other resources shall not be taken into account by the trustee in deciding whether to make distributions, but this undesirable restriction on the trustee's discretion should not be necessary.

§7.1.1.11 Ed/Med Exclusion

In addition to the §2503(b) annual exclusion, §2503(e) allows an unlimited exclusion for amounts properly paid for the education or medical expenses of any person.[123] Qualified transfers include amounts paid for tuition of full or part time students but not for ancillary expenses such as room and board, books, and fees.[124] Medical expenses are more broadly defined to include costs for "diagnosis, cure, mitigation, treatment or prevention of disease, or for the purpose of affecting any structure or function of the body or for transportation primarily for and essential to medical care."[125] Not covered, however, are amounts paid for expenses that are reimbursed by insurance, but amounts paid *for* medical insurance for any individual *is* within the exclusion.

Both the education and medical payments must be made directly to the education or medical service provider. Payments that reimburse the donee do *not* qualify.[126] For example, a deposit in a student's checking account to cover a check from the student to the University for tuition will not qualify. The donor must pay that amount directly to the University Bursar.

Regarding medical expenses, Revenue Ruling 82-98[127] discusses the requirements of §2503(e)(2)(B) in the context of an adult child who was

---

[123] Also as in §2503(b), payments meeting the §2503(e) requirements may be shielded from GST by §2642(c)(3)(B) if its requirements are met. See §11.4.1.3.

[124] Treas. Reg. §25.2503-6(a)(2).

[125] Treas. Reg. §25.2503-6(a)(3).

[126] §2503(e)(2); Treas. Reg. §25.2503-6(c) Examples (2) and (4). Note, however, that Lang v. Commissioner, 100 T.C.M. (CCH) 603 (2010), held that payment directly to the medical provider is tantamount to an indirect gift to the donee, followed by the donee's payment of those medical expenses, qualifying the donee for the §213 medical expense deduction for income tax purposes.

[127] 1982-1 C.B. 141.

§7.1.1.11

injured in an automobile accident and whose various medical expenses were paid by checks payable directly to the physician and the hospital. These medical and hospital expenses were of the type described in §213(e) and were not reimbursable by insurance or otherwise, making these payments qualified. But payments made during the child's medical disability to cover the child's home mortgage payments were taxable gifts that otherwise could qualify for the annual exclusion or that would incur a gift tax. Further, any medical expenses that were paid by the child and for which the donor reimbursed the child also would be subject to gift tax.

In a similar vein, Revenue Ruling 82-143[128] held that a tuition payment made directly to a §170(b)(1)(A)(ii) foreign educational institution was exempt from gift tax under §2503(e). But the Regulations[129] establish that a transfer to a trust for the ultimate payment of tuition charges to an educational organization are not qualified tuition payments that would be excluded from the gift tax under §2503(e), because the qualifying transfer must be directly to a qualifying educational organization as required.

In a similar context, however, PLR 200602002 and TAM 199941013 authorized payments to an educational institution that essentially constituted nonrefundable prepayment of tuition that might be incurred in the future. The students currently were enrolled but had no guarantee of continued enrollment, nor any assurance that tuition would not increase (in which case added monies would be needed to cover any deficiency in the fund set aside). Because the school was the payee and not a trust, the government determined that these prepayments were within the letter of the law and permitted total exclusion of the one time transfers.

Donors who do not want to transfer funds directly to an educational institution but who are considering a gift designed to further the education of a donee may wish to consult §§529 and 530, which provide income tax exemptions for qualified state tuition programs.[130] For gift tax

---

[128] 1982-2 C.B. 221.

[129] Treas. Reg. §25.2503-6(c) Example (2).

[130] PLR 8825027 ruled on the tax consequences of a State of Michigan college tuition annuity program. For a one time payment, the Michigan Education Trust established by the state contracted to pay four years' tuition at an in state public

purposes, §§ 529(c)(2), 529(c)(4), and 529(c)(5) provide that contributions to these programs are completed gifts for gift tax purposes, with present interest § 2503(b) gift tax and § 2642(c) GST annual exclusion (but not § 2503(e) and 2642(c)(3)(B) ed/med exclusion) qualification. There also is a special five year ratable carry forward provision if the contribution exceeds the donor's annual exclusion limitation for the year of contribution. In exchange for immediate gift tax exclusion for the donor, however, there is an FET inclusion to the donor under § 529(c)(4)(C) for any outstanding carry forward amount if death occurs within the five year carry forward period.

Distributions from the plan may be used for § 529(e)(3)(A) qualified higher education expenses, which are more than just tuition and fees (such as for room, board, books, and other required expenses) and they are not gifts to the beneficiary (nor is a change of beneficiary taxable unless a younger beneficiary is substituted for GST purposes). In essence, then, these trusts provide a convenient form of investment with

---

(Footnote Continued)

or private college for an irrevocably designated beneficiary. On certain designated conditions, the trust instead would make a cash refund (less an administrative fee) to another designated beneficiary. Under an alternative plan, the refund would show growth determined under an index based on increases in college tuition and was available if the designated beneficiary went to school out-of-state. The Ruling determined that there was no current income tax consequence when the contract was signed and that there was a basis equal to the contributor's investment in the contract that would be recovered over the four years that tuition was paid from the trust or over the period during which any refund was paid. Payments from the trust in excess of basis would constitute income to the designated beneficiary in the year paid, so income was shifted and deferred, but then bunched into the short period during which payments were made by the trust. In addition, because the trust could benefit nonpublic interests (the designated beneficiaries), it was denied a charitable exemption, meaning that income earned by the trust was taxable as earned. This denial of exempt trust status was upheld in Michigan v. United States, 802 F. Supp. 120 (W.D. Mich. 1992), but then reversed and remanded, 40 F.3d 817 (6th Cir. 1994).

In the wake of that treatment, § 529 now provides that the trust is exempt from federal income taxation other than with respect to any § 511 unrelated business taxable income. And distributions (including in-kind benefits such as tuition free attendance that is not a § 117 scholarship) are income tax free to the designated beneficiary (as well as to the contributor).

§ 7.1.1.11

no income tax to the designated beneficiary and automatic qualification for the § 2503(b) gift tax annual exclusion.

Other options include gift to minor act accounts, § 530 Coverdell Education Savings Accounts (a form of tax benefited saving account with much smaller contribution limitations but similar permitted uses and taxation), and prepaid tuition plans.[131]

§ 7.1.2 Unified Credit

Any gift tax incurred on a taxable gift that exceeds the annual exclusion or does not qualify for the annual or ed/med expense exclusions may be offset by the unified credit and therefore may not actually be payable. The unified credit is not elective and cannot be reserved for future use. Instead, it is automatic and offsets the tax on the first taxable

---

[131] For another potential income tax opportunity, see § 135, which permits the payment of qualified higher education expenses with United States savings bonds without recognition of any unrealized income in the bond. Unlike § 529, there is a graduated reduction in the amount of income that may be excluded under § 135 as adjusted gross income of the taxpayer exceeds $72,850 for single filers or $109,250 for a joint return (adjusted for inflation in 2012; see Rev. Proc. 2011-52 2011-2 C.B. 701). The exclusion is fully phased out (again using 2012 inflation indexed figures) for singles with adjusted gross income exceeding $87,850 and joint filers with $139,250, and is not available at all to married taxpayers filing separate returns. See §§ 135(b)(2) and 135(d)(3). Only bonds issued after 1989 qualify, and only tuition and fees of the taxpayer, the taxpayer's spouse, or any dependent of the taxpayer may be paid in this manner.

These and other income tax benefits are discussed in more detail by Bart, Section 529 College Savings Accounts: More Than a Decade Without Final Rules, 42 U. Miami Inst. Est. Plan. ¶ 900 (2008); Bart, Education Planning and Gifts to Minors (2004 ed.); and Melone, Tax-Favored Strategies for Funding a Child's Higher Education, 27 Est. Plan. 21 (2000). See also Whitty & Such, Qualified State Tuition Programs Under IRC 529: One of the Best Ways to Save for College, 140 Trusts & Estates 44, 48 (Dec. 2001), with a fine comparison chart of various tax consequences and restrictions of alternative techniques, including § 529 accounts, education IRAs, prepaid tuition programs, annual exclusion and qualified minors trusts, custodial accounts, and the ed/med exclusion. See also An Introduction to 529 Plans, http://www.sec.gov/investor/pubs/intro529.htm, and find a link to state specific § 529 plans by touring the National Association of State Treasurers website: http://www.collegesavings.org/index.aspx.

transfers made[132] by citizens and residents of the United States,[133] up to

---

[132] See, e.g., Reilly v. United States, 88-1 U.S. Tax Cas. (CCH) ¶ 13,752 (S.D. Ind. 1987) (married taxpayers made split gifts of stock, reporting no tax as due because of their gift tax annual exclusions; the government revalued the gifted property and, based thereon, asserted that a taxable gift was made that exhausted part of the taxpayers' unified credits); Rev. Rul. 79-398, 1979-2 C.B. 338 (unified credit must be used first with respect to inter vivos transfers).

Inter vivos use of the credit is not necessarily the result of this rule, however, if the unified credit has been used already for FET purposes. For example, in TAM 8743001, the taxpayer sold property for what the government ultimately determined was less than full and adequate consideration in money or money's worth, thereby constituting a part-sale, part-gift transaction. No gift tax return was filed, however, and no gift tax was paid, because the taxpayer thought the sale was for full and adequate consideration. At death this transfer was not subject to FET inclusion in the taxpayer's gross estate because no interest or power was retained, and the government did not challenge the inter vivos transfer until after the FET statute of limitation had run. At that time the taxpayer's estate had filed an FET return, claimed the full unified credit with respect to the FET liability, received a closing letter, and made its distributions. The government determined first that no statute of limitation would preclude its assessment of a gift tax liability (because no gift tax return had been filed) and then concluded that the unified credit was no help to the taxpayer because it had been consumed previously in the FET calculation. Transferee liability therefore was assessed against the recipient of the inter vivos transfer.

Similarly, PLR 200934023 and TAM 199930002 involved two inter vivos transfers, the first of which was never reported and the unified credit was used on the second, as to which the statute of limitation ran. The 2009 case involved a request to allocate GST exemption that had not been allocated because the first year gift was never reported. The 1999 case raised the issue on audit of the transferor's FET return, when it was discovered that the first transfer was made but not reported. In each case the government opined that the taxpayers could not assert that any gift tax on the first transfers would be covered by the unified credit. Instead, the duty of consistency applied because the taxpayers used their credits on the second transfers, essentially representing that there had been no prior gifts and that the credit was fully available, which they could not later contradict by alleging that the credit was available to offset any tax on the first transfer.

[133] Unlike §2102(b), which simply limits the unified credit at death with respect to nonresidents who are not citizens, §2505(a) does not allow the credit at all with respect to United States taxable inter vivos gifts made by nonresidents who are not citizens.

§7.1.2

the applicable exclusion amount.[134] To the extent it is not used during life, the unified credit remains available at death.[135] There is no need to use it to avoid losing it. But because the unified credit is a fixed entitlement, the most benefit is garnered the sooner the unified credit is used to transfer property that is expected to appreciate in value in the future.[136]

It likely is of slight significance today but note that the unified credit is reduced if gifts were made after September 8, 1976 and before 1977 that utilized the former $30,000 gift tax specific exemption. There is no affirmative planning that may be done to affect this reduction because it depends entirely on facts that already occurred.[137]

---

[134] Congress has amended this entitlement on numerous occasions. For example, in 1997 the unified credit was $192,800, which was the wealth transfer tax on the first $600,000 of taxable transfers. After 1997 the credit was defined as the tax on the applicable exclusion amount, which was increased in stages so that, after 2010, the first $5 million of taxable transfers was rendered nontaxable by the unified credit (and the term "applicable" exclusion amount was changed to "basic" exclusion amount). The exclusion is indexed for inflation after 2011. So, for example, it rose to $5,120,000 in 2012.

[135] Actually, due to the FET calculation method in § 2001(b), the full unified credit is available at death notwithstanding use during life, but inter vivos taxable transfers for which no gift tax was paid have the effect of consuming it first at death, meaning that effectively all that remains at death is any portion not absorbed by taxable inter vivos transfers.

[136] See § 6.2. For example, if property is worth $1 million today and could be transferred entirely tax free under the taxpayer's available unified credit, and if the asset is expected to double in value before the taxpayer's death, the taxpayer could eliminate the payment of any FET on all the value of the asset and all of its growth by a present transfer but only a fraction of its total value if it still is held at death. Alternatively, however, it seldom makes sense to transfer an asset early that is expected to decline in value. For a strategy to cause inclusion at death of property transferred inter vivos if in fact the value has declined, see McCaffrey, Some Tips on Tax Tuning Gifts, 137 Trusts & Estates 87, 90 (Aug. 1998), reprinted and expanded upon in McCaffrey, Tax Tuning the Estate Plan by Formula, 33 U. Miami Inst. Est. Plan. ¶ 403.5 (1999).

[137] Under §§ 2010(b) and 2505(b), the unified credit is reduced for estate and gift tax purposes by an amount equal to 20% of the aggregate specific exemption allowed with respect to gifts made during that portion of 1976. United States v. Hemme, 476 U.S. 558 (1986), held that the reduction was applicable even though the donor died within three years of the transfer and the gifts were includible under the former § 2035(a) three year rule, notwithstanding double taxation and

§7.1.3 *Gift-Splitting*

Married United States citizen or resident taxpayers may essentially double the benefit of the unified credit, GST exemption, or gift tax exclusions available to either of them alone. Authorized by § 2513 is a gift made by one of them that is treated as split equally between them and made half by each, just by executing the § 2513(b) consent.[138]

(Footnote Continued)

constitutional arguments under the Due Process Clause of the Fifth Amendment. See also Renick v. United States, 687 F.2d 371 (Ct. Cl. 1982); Estate of Gawne v. Commissioner, 80 T.C. 478 (1983) (reduction also applied to a decedent who was the nondonor consenting spouse to a § 2513 split gift made during the 1976 period); Allgood v. Commissioner, 52 T.C.M. (CCH) 575 (1986). The Supreme Court stated that, even if no benefit had flowed from it, the exemption could be regarded as "allowed," noting that the taxpayer benefited from avoiding the payment of gift taxes during life by virtue of the claimed exemption and the taxpayer had notice of the change in 1976 when making the transfers in question. In addition, even with the application of the § 2010(b) reduction in the unified credit, the taxpayer in *Hemme* was required to pay less tax overall by virtue of all the changes made in 1976, meaning that any effect of the 1976 Act on the taxpayer hardly could qualify as sufficiently oppressive to transgress the Due Process clause. Finally, without saying that it did constitute double taxation, the Court noted that even if the taxpayer was incurring double taxation on the same transfer, this result clearly was contemplated by Congress and, having expressed this as its intent, it also was not unconstitutional.

[138] The consent must be on the original gift tax return filed—even if it is late— and cannot be made on an amended return. McLean v. United States, 79-1 U.S. Tax Cas. (CCH) ¶ 13,293 (N.D. Cal. 1979); Rev. Rul. 80-224, 1980-2 C.B. 281 (failure to consent on the first return filed precludes a subsequent election, even if the failure was due to oversight or a lack of knowledge of the law); TAM 8843005 (both the donor and the consenting spouse died after making a gift but before filing a gift tax return reporting the gift made while each spouse was alive; the donor's estate filed a gift tax return after both spouses' death without reporting the gift in question, and the TAM concluded that no gift splitting election could be made on another return reporting that gift, and stated that this would be true if a gift tax return had been filed by either spouse for the year of the gift). In addition, the consent may not be made after a notice of deficiency for the taxable period has been sent to either spouse. § 2513(b)(2)(B). Nor may the consent normally be made on behalf of the consenting spouse. Rev. Rul. 78-27, 1978-1 C.B. 387 (donor spouse signed consenting spouse's name to the consent as a convenience, not under circumstances specified by Treas. Reg. § 25.6019-1(d) involving illness, absence, or nonresidence; the return was valid, the consent was not, and a subsequent amended return signed by the consenting spouse could not correct the situation).

§7.1.3

Thus, for example, if a donor has substantial wealth but the donor's spouse has little, one way to take advantage of the spouse's tax benefits would be for the donor to make a taxable gift and the spouse to consent to it for gift-splitting purposes. In this manner the donor can transfer double the amount of the transfers either could make alone and generate effectively the same result as if the donor made a gift to the spouse tax free under the § 2523 marital deduction and then each spouse made their own transfers to take advantage of their own benefits. Alternatively, § 2010(c)(2)(B) DSUEA portability of the unused exclusion amount allows the spouse to leave any remaining exclusion to the donor, to be used later, and if the donor died first a marital deduction bequest could soak up the spouse's exclusion amount on a subsequent taxable event. Gift splitting still might be useful if the spouses truly wish to move maximum wealth to a third party while both still are alive, but it may wane in importance as a method to avoid wasting the less wealthy spouse's exclusion amount.

The advantage of gift splitting is that it does not give control to the donor's spouse or subject the gifted property to creditors of the donor's spouse. In many cases, however, an outright gift to the spouse followed by separate gifts by each may be preferable because the gift splitting option is an all-or-nothing endeavor. The spouses must make the § 2513 election with respect to all gifts made by either of them during any part of the taxable period, and cannot elect split gift treatment for only

(Footnote Continued)

In Drybrough v. United States, 208 F. Supp. 279 (W.D. Ky. 1962), the consenting spouse elected to split the donor spouse's gifts without knowing that they exceeded the annual exclusion, and innocently failed to file a gift tax return that was required, incurring the § 6651(a) failure to file 25% penalty because reliance on the donor spouse was not reasonable cause for not filing. See also True v. United States, 354 F.2d 323 (Ct. Cl. 1965) (consenting spouse's consent on the donor spouse's return was not tantamount to filing a gift tax return that would toll the statute of limitation; the government disallowed the annual exclusion for split gifts and could not assert a deficiency against the donor spouse but could against the consenting spouse); CCA 200205027 involved a gift splitting transfer that the donor spouse sufficiently undervalued to constitute fraud, about which the consenting spouse knew nothing and as to which the government decided not to impute liability, nor to extend the innocent spouse's statute of limitation exposure. No mention was made of whether § 2513(d) joint and several liability for the gift tax would extend to liability for any penalties assessed to the donor spouse.

§ 7.1.3

selected gifts during the taxable period.[139] Indeed, as illustrated by TAM 200147021, gift splitting is effective even with respect to inadvertent or unintended gifts, in that case involving taxable transfers as to which the donor spouse paid the GST, which constituted an additional gift under § 2515 that was deemed made in the year of the original gift and therefore was deemed split by the original gift splitting election.

If split gift treatment is elected, the only gifts that would be excepted are any gifts made during the taxable period while the spouses were not married to each other. For example, either the gifts were made before the spouses married during that period, or S made them after D died during that period.[140] Also excepted are any gifts made while one spouse was not a citizen or resident of the United States.[141] Furthermore, gift splitting would not be available at all if either spouse is married to a different individual at year end, even if they were married to each other at the time of the gift.[142]

----

[139] § 2513(a)(2); Treas. Reg. § 25.2513-1(b)(5); Nordstrom v. United States, 97-1 U.S. Tax Cas. (CCH) ¶ 60,255 (N.D. Iowa 1997).

[140] Treas. Reg. § 25.2513-2(c) authorizes a decedent's executor to split gifts made by either spouse before the decedent's death, which may be desirable if, for example, § 2010(c)(2)(B) DSUEA portability is not viable and the decedent's unified credit and annual or ed/med exclusion gifting opportunities for the year of death otherwise would be wasted. In some cases S will be the executor with this authority. See, e.g., Rev. Rul. 67-55, 1967-1 C.B. 278 (D's estate did not require administration, no personal representative therefore was appointed, and S was regarded by default as D's executor for §§ 2513 and 6019 purposes). Any gift tax liability with respect to the gift is joint and several, meaning that either spouse may pay all the tax. If D was the donor spouse, payment of this tax would be deductible under § 2053 but would trigger application of the § 2035(b) gross up rule, producing an FET wash. However, any gift tax paid by a deceased consenting spouse's estate is not deductible under § 2053 and the gross up rule still will apply. See § 15.1 n.11.

A gift splitting consent was rejected in Rev. Rul. 73-207, 1973-1 C.B. 409, with respect to spouse owned insurance that was payable to a third party beneficiary because both spouses must be alive when a split gift is made and the gift occurred at the exact moment when the insured spouse died and the marital relation ceased to exist.

[141] See § 2513(a)(1), requiring each spouse to be a United States citizen or resident at the time of the gift.

[142] A person is a § 2513(a)(1) spouse for gift splitting purposes only if married at the time of the gift and not remarried to a third party during the balance of the

In addition, gift splitting is available only with respect to gifts to donees other than the consenting spouse. Thus, a different approach is required if any portion of a gift benefits the consenting spouse and the value of that interest is not ascertainable and therefore cannot be evaluated separately or severed.[143] For example, if a donor wishes to establish an inter vivos trust to provide income and principal in the discretion of a disinterested trustee among a group consisting of the consenting spouse and the donor's descendants, no part of that gift could be split by the spouses unless the portion for the donor's spouse could be valued separately from the other interests given.[144]

(Footnote Continued)

taxable period. Traditional notions regarding the validity of a marriage are relevant in this respect. See, e.g., Rev. Rul. 67-442, 1967-2 C.B. 65 (government will not normally challenge the validity of a marriage on its own accord and normally will respect a state court decree regarding the validity of a marriage or divorce), and § 13.4.2.2.2.

143 For example, PLR 8044080 held that annual exclusion gifts to a trust with Crummey withdrawal powers in the consenting spouse and others may be split with respect to all but the spouse's portion of that gift. Thus, withdrawal powers in all but the spouse could equal the combined amount of the donor and consenting spouses' unused annual exclusions for gifts to those beneficiaries, and the spouse's withdrawal power could equal the donor's unused annual exclusion for gifts to the spouse alone.

144 For example, the trust in Falk v. Commissioner, 24 T.C.M. (CCH) 86 (1965), authorized the trustees to distribute income to the consenting spouse as they deemed "appropriate under all the facts and circumstances" and to distribute principal "to provide for the proper care, comfort, support, maintenance and general welfare" of the consenting spouse, considering the standard of living of the consenting spouse during the donor's life and other funds known by the trustees to be available to the consenting spouse from all other sources, including the donor. The court held the invasion power was sufficiently ascertainable to determine the likelihood of exercise and concluded that the possibility of invasion while the donor was alive was so remote as to be negligible and thereafter the spouse's financial position was such that distributions of income but not principal might be necessary. Gift splitting therefore was allowed for the value of a remainder interest following a life income interest in the consenting spouse. In PLR 200551009, however, invasion authority after the taxpayer's death for the benefit of children and the taxpayer's spouse was not susceptible to valuation, which precluded gift splitting for any interest in the children only during the taxpayer's life, because it was impossible to sever the interests before and after the taxpayer's death.

In such a case a separate marital deduction trust for the donor's spouse and another separate trust for the descendants (as to which the spouse could make the gift-splitting election) might be a more appropriate technique. A similar separation might be required if the donor spouse wanted the consenting spouse to have control over the gifted property in the form of a power of appointment.[145]

Another more significant reason to avoid gift splitting and rely on the alternative of a marital deduction transfer and separate gifts relates to the seriously flawed operation of §§ 2001(e), 2035(a), and 2513. If there is gift splitting and the donor spouse dies within three years, if it is applicable the automatic three-year return rule in § 2035(a) brings both halves of the gift back into the donor spouse's gross estate. If the consenting spouse used any unified credit on that gift, it essentially is restored to the consenting spouse for future FET purposes because the consenting spouse's § 2001(b)(1)(B) adjusted taxable gifts base is purged under the operation of § 2001(e). In addition, § 2001(d) gives the donor spouse's estate a § 2001(b)(2) credit for any gift tax actually paid by the consenting spouse (and § 2001(e) denies the consenting spouse the same credit for future FET purposes), all as if the donor spouse made the entire gift and paid all the gift tax.[146]

---

[145] The express language of § 2513(a)(1) denies gift splitting if the consenting spouse has a general power to appoint the gifted property. Apparently a nongeneral power in either spouse will not preclude gift splitting, although the power might cause the gift attributable to the powerholder to be incomplete. The gift may not be incomplete if the power is contingent or is limited by a standard such that § 2036 or § 2038 would not apply at the powerholder's death. See § 7.3.3 nn.54-58 and accompanying text.

[146] See, e.g., TAM 8747001, in which spouses D and S owned property as a tenancy by the entirety that they transferred by gift and split under § 2513. When D died half of the gift was includible in D's gross estate (under then applicable § 2035) but when S died there was no FET inclusion. The half that was includible in D's gross estate was purged from S's adjusted taxable gifts under § 2001(e), meaning that S was deemed to have made a gift of only S's half of the entireties property during life. Proper application of the purge and credit mechanism in § 2001(b) meant that D's half was treated as transferred at death as if D never made a transfer during life. In effect, the result was as if D and S partitioned the property and each made their own separate transfers of their respective halves, S during life and D at death.

§ 7.1.3

Unfortunately, the operation of § 2001(e) is flawed because the consenting spouse's § 2001(b)(1)(B) adjusted taxable gifts base is *not* purged under § 2001(e) if the split gifted property is includible in the donor spouse's gross estate under any FET provision other than § 2035(a). Moreover, it is not purged under any circumstances for the consenting spouse's future *gift* tax purposes. The latter flaw means that the consenting spouse is in an improperly inflated gift tax marginal bracket for future gift tax purposes if the split gift is included in the donor's gross estate. And the former flaw means that the source of the donor spouse's FET inclusion is critical.

For example, if spouses make a split gift transfer to a trust in which the donor spouse retains an interest, a power, or an incident of ownership that triggers FET inclusion under § 2036, § 2038, or § 2042, the effect is to tax 100% of the value of the transferred property in the estate of the donor spouse by virtue of that inclusion plus 50% in the gift tax base of the consenting spouse as a gift that § 2001(e) does not purge. Under § 2001(d) the donor spouse still gets a credit for any gift tax actually paid by the consenting spouse and under § 2001(e) the consenting spouse does not lose that credit if inclusion in the donor's gross estate is not under § 2035(a). But the consenting spouse is left in an improperly inflated marginal bracket for both estate and gift tax purposes.[147]

Finally, a donor spouse's advisor should consider conflict of interest and adequate representation issues when advising the consenting spouse regarding gift splitting. It may be that the § 2513 consent is harmless or desirable in a given situation, but consider whether the same advice would be given by the consenting spouse's advisor if the donor was represented by someone else. For example, if the marriage was not the first for either and the consenting spouse had natural objects of the bounty who differ from those of the donor spouse, would a competent advisor for just the consenting spouse suggest that the donor spouse compensate the consenting spouse for the use of the consenting

---

[147] Moreover, the operation of the § 2701(e)(6) adjustment in the context of a split gift that triggers either of § 2701 or § 2702 also fails to avoid this problem, meaning that much greater than 100% taxation of a single transfer is a distinct possibility that ought to discourage spouses from taking advantage of § 2513 gift splitting in any transfer that may be subject to the anti-freeze rules of § § 2701 and 2702. See § § 7.2.2 and 7.2.3.

spouse's unified credit or GST exemption, which are one-time benefits that cannot be replaced after they are used? Annual exclusion gifts to objects of just the donor's bounty would be different, because the consenting spouse loses nothing by agreeing to split gifts that the consenting spouse otherwise would not make to those individuals. But use of the consenting spouse's unified credit or GST exemption to shelter gifts to the donor's beneficiaries denies the opportunity to use those benefits for transfers to the consenting spouse's own beneficiaries.

Those tax benefits may not be worth much to a consenting spouse who has little wealth currently, but people inherit, win the lottery, accumulate earnings, and find other ways to acquire wealth. Against that possibility, a separate advisor for the consenting spouse might suggest that the donor should compensate the consenting spouse for the use of the consenting spouse's nonrenewable entitlements. The challenging issue is knowing what they are worth. For example, should the unified credit be measured in terms of the actual tax offset by a gift taxed at the bottom estate or gift tax brackets, or should the cost to the consenting spouse of splitting a gift be measured by the cost of increasing the consenting spouse's tax base, measured by the tax that might be incurred at the top marginal brackets that might apply to wealth transfers by the consenting spouse during life or at death? How should the likelihood of acquiring sufficient wealth to take advantage of these tax benefits be factored into the equation? And would a demand for compensation cause such a rift between the donor and consenting spouses that the possibility should not be broached? Also note that § 2010(c)(2)(B) DSUEA portability of the consenting spouse's unused exclusion may be a viable alternative and that it may raise similar issues.

These ethical and practical concerns, along with the technical flaws in the operation of the gift splitting provision in the context of transfers that are brought back into the donor's gross estate at death, ought to give pause to advisors who are planning with spouses who make inter vivos transfers. Annual exclusion split gifts are relatively easy and potentially harmless. Other gifts raise more significant concerns. Unfortunately, it is not known whether a separate marital deduction transfer to the spouse, followed by separate gifts by both spouses, will be respected by the government as a viable alternative to gift splitting. As a consequence, if the latter alternative is considered safer or more desirable, it

§7.1.3

should be pursued with some caution, the dollar amounts should not be identical to a split gift alternative, and some time might be inserted between the marital deduction transfer and the spouse's separate gift. Independence should be guaranteed, and even the appearance of an implied understanding or coerced planning should be avoided.[148] Finally, portability should be considered as a better alternative.

§7.1.4 Inter Vivos Marital Deduction

The unlimited inter vivos marital deduction provides a welcome opportunity for spouses to engage in asset reallocations for tax minimization or any other purpose. Planners should be cautious regarding planning in lieu of gift splitting,[149] however, to avoid a marital deduction gift made by a donor spouse to what otherwise would be a consenting spouse, who the government alleges by prearrangement thereafter made a gift to objects of the donor spouse's bounty. The concern is that the government will treat the gift as a transfer of all the property by the donor spouse to those objects directly, as to which neither the marital deduction nor gift splitting would apply.

In addition, planning close to the end of a donee spouse's life should beware of inadvertent application of §1014(e),[150] which would deny a new basis at death to any appreciated property transferred to a dying spouse who directly or indirectly transfers the property back to the donor spouse. Otherwise, inter vivos interspousal property transfers are virtually ignored for income and wealth transfer tax purposes by virtue of

---

[148] See Griffin v. United States, 42 F. Supp. 2d 700 (W.D. Tex. 1998) (donor who owned 100% of the stock in a family corporation gave 45% to spouse and claimed a gift tax marital deduction; within one month spouse transferred that same stock to a newly created trust for their child and five days after that transfer the donor conveyed another 45% to the same trust, retaining a mere 10% of the original 100% interest), in which donor and spouse each reported separate gifts to a trust that were valued with minority interest discounts, which the court rejected because the collective transfers were a sham; "the only purpose" for making the transfer through the spouse was to generate a minority interest discount. As such, the donor was treated as having made the 90% transfer personally to the trust. No mention was made whether any other aspect of the separate gifts would be respected.

[149] See §7.1.3.

[150] See §1.6.3 n.7.

the unlimited lifetime marital deduction in § 2523 and the nearly unlimited lifetime income tax free interspousal transfer rule in § 1041. They also likely are not necessary if § 2010(c)(2)(B) portability of a dying spouse's unused exclusion amount is viable. Spouses are a single economic unit for virtually all tax purposes, the one notable exception being § 1014 new basis at the death of a decedent whose property is not subject to estate due to the unlimited marital deduction but it nevertheless receives a new basis.

One notable exception to spousal unity treatment is if the donee spouse is not a citizen or resident of the United States, in which case the special rules in §§ 1041(d) and 2523(i) may deny tax free status for either income or wealth transfer tax purposes. A useful gift tax alternative is provided in § 2523(i)(2), however, authorizing a $143,000 (in 2013, reflecting the inflation index amount) annual exclusion for transfers to the noncitizen spouse.[151]

One form of inter vivos planning may be particularly attractive to spouses with significant but disparate wealth. Assume, for example, that spouses D and S seek estate planning and that the initial interview discloses that S has more wealth than the amount that can pass free of tax under the basic exclusion amount of the unified credit and, more importantly, that D has little independent wealth. Moreover, based on age, lifestyle, and physical characteristics, it seems pretty obvious that D is likely to die first. In such a case one very obvious planning suggestion would be to rely on § 2010(c)(2)(B) portability of D's unused exclusion amount to S. A better alternative would be to encourage S to give D enough wealth to shelter D's tax benefits in a nonmarital trust for S if in fact D does die first. This might include an amount equal to D's unused basic exclusion amount[152] and GST exemption and, if the FET imposes a truly progressive rate of tax, giving D enough wealth to run through the less than maximum FET brackets in D's gross estate.

In a typical situation S might balk at this advice until it is made clear that an inter vivos QTIP trust[153] may be employed to protect the wealth

---

[151] See § 13.5.7.1 n.304 and accompanying text.

[152] Indeed, D might be a surviving spouse who has an even larger applicable exclusion amount because of a § 2010(c)(2)(B) DSUEA from D's predeceased former spouse.

[153] See § 13.5.6.5.

§ 7.1.4

against predators who might attempt to reach those assets in D's hands. For example, a not unlikely scenario would entail D as the less wealthy spouse because of a failed business venture, with creditor problems that linger. The spendthrift nature of the inter vivos QTIP trust for D's benefit, created by S, can provide protection against claims that might be respected if the property was transferred to D outright. Other reasons (such as denial of control) also might recommend use of the inter vivos trust for D. With sufficient protection, S might be willing to engage in this form of inter vivos planning designed to shelter D's tax benefits. But a stumbling block might be S's desire to continue to enjoy the income from the trust property after D's death, if events turn out as this planning anticipates.

The planning issue is whether S may retain a secondary life estate following the marital deduction mandated income interest in D for the balance of D's life.[154] Under § 2523 (f) (5) (A), a donor spouse may retain a secondary life estate in an inter vivos trust created for the benefit of a donee spouse and the trust property will not be includible in the donor's gross estate (under § 2036 (a) (1) or any other FET inclusion section), nor will a subsequent transfer of the retained secondary life estate by the donor spouse generate any gift tax consequences. Although § 2523 (f) (5) (B) appears to disallow this useful protection "after the donee spouse [D] is treated as having transferred [the trust] property under section 2519, or such property is includible in the donee spouse's gross estate under section 2044," the government has interpreted this provision to negate what it appears to say.

According to Treas. Reg. § 25.2523 (f)-1 (f) Example 11, S's retained secondary life estate will *not* cause estate or gift tax exposure to S as the donor spouse even if S survives D or D makes an inter vivos assignment of trust income that triggers the application of § 2519. Instead, § 2044 inclusion to D effectively cleanses the trust, meaning that S's retained secondary income interest will not cause either § 2036 or § 2038 inclusion when S subsequently dies.

This conclusion ignores the seemingly clear statement of the law found in § 2523 (f) (5) (B) and Treas. Reg. § § 25.2523 (f)-1 (d) (1), that the donor spouse is not protected by § 2044 inclusion to the donee spouse,

---

154 See § 13.5 for all the detailed marital deduction qualification rules.

and Example 11 does not explain why § 2523 (f) (5) (B) does not apply. It instead simply ignores § 2523 (f) (5) (B) to state the simple and favorable conclusion that the donor's retained interest will not cause inclusion to the donor who dies second.

That result is not likely to be challenged by taxpayers, and the government is bound by the Regulations. Thus, although it appears to be a wrong result under the statute, PLR 9731009 adhered to it, specifying that if D dies first and makes no QTIP election, S's retained secondary life estate will not cause inclusion in S's gross estate. It also stated that D would be the GST transferor of that trust, unless a reverse QTIP election was made by S when the trust was created or a QTIP election was made in D's estate.[155]

As a result, it is relatively easy for a donor spouse to shift wealth to a donee spouse by inter vivos transfer with the only potential risk being that, if they divorce, the income interest for the balance of the donee spouse's life will be lost to the donor spouse. Depending on state law, that income interest may count in the divorce property settlement action and offset any obligation that otherwise might be imposed on the donor spouse anyway.

§ 7.1.5 *Inter Vivos Charitable Deduction*

Like the § 2523 unlimited lifetime marital deduction, § 2522 offers an unlimited gift tax charitable deduction for qualifying transfers that are made inter vivos. In addition, § 2501 (a) (5) allows a gift tax political contribution exclusion.[156] Like gifts in general, a § 2522 deductible inter vivos charitable gift can be more valuable than one made at death, for many of the same reasons.

Most obvious are those reasons that apply if the transfer has both taxable and deductible components, in which case shifting income and growth out of the donor's estate, paying any gift tax attributable to the transfer to avoid paying FET on the gift tax dollars themselves, and generating valuation opportunities all can be important. And the exclu-

---

[155] Further, even if a QTIP election is made by D, the regulation specifies that inclusion to S will be under § 2044 rather than § 2036, which probably matters for § § 2207A versus 2207B right of reimbursement purposes.

[156] Applicable to transfers to a § 527 (e) (1) political organization.

sion under § 2501(a)(5) for inter vivos transfers to a political organization is preferable to a testamentary transfer to the same organization because there is no FET exclusion or deduction available for political contributions.

An additional reason to favor accelerating charitable transfers into lifetime planning even in cases involving a 100% deductible charitable gift[157] involves an advantage that is unique to inter vivos charitable planning. The § 170 income tax charitable deduction[158] has no counterpart for other gift planning and is not available at death (nor is it matched if a § 642(c) charitable set-aside deduction is generated for the donor's estate at death). This deduction generates an income tax saving attributable to the inter vivos charitable gift, which can finance other planning that also may be attractive.

For example, a donor may choose to transfer the income tax dollars saved with an inter vivos charitable contribution to a donee who will use the money to purchase life insurance on the donor's life (or other investments) to compensate for the dollars contributed to charity. To the extent this replacement wealth is excluded from the donor's gross estate at death, the transaction has many of the advantages of inter vivos giving in general, financed by the tax saving produced by the income tax deduction.

Just as gifts made inter vivos are more attractive for wealth transfer tax purposes than those at death, this income tax advantage makes the inter vivos charitable gift a better plan *if* the donor was going to make the charitable transfer in all events. The income tax deduction also recommends planning that relies on the FET marital deduction if D fails to provide for charity inter vivos, by leaving property to S who then will make charitable transfers that D otherwise would have made under a will. A gift by S inter vivos clearly is preferable to D's testamentary bequest because of the § 170 income tax deduction. In addition, using the marital deduction in this manner could preserve D's unified credit for § 2010(c)(2)(B) portability to S, meaning that all of D's wealth could be available to S for § 170 charitable deduction purposes.

---

[157] As to which a charitable deduction at death is as effective as a charitable deduction inter vivos, regardless of the size of the transferred property.

[158] See § 7.1.5.1.

§ 7.1.5

An additional reason to favor a charitable gift inter vivos may be to qualify an estate for benefits under §§ 6166 and 303 if it appears that the qualification percentages may not be met. By making a gift inter vivos that reduces the gross estate at death, §§ 2035(c)(1) and 2035(c)(2) may apply to defeat the plan if the donor dies within three years of the transfer. But a charitable pledge inter vivos in lieu of a charitable bequest at death will generate a § 2053(a)(3) deduction for the pledge that will reduce the amount against which the percentage qualification is tested and may result in qualification.[159]

It also is undeniable that inter vivos charitable giving provides psychic benefits to the donor that are not available at death. To take the extreme example, a donor who contributes enough wealth to name a building (and who can afford to do so currently) may take immeasurable pleasure from *living* to see the day.

Notwithstanding occasional claims to the contrary, it is not likely the case that any charitable planning technique will fully replace the wealth contributed to charity or that an inter vivos or testamentary plan can be undertaken without cost to the donor or the donor's family.[160] Nevertheless, if charitable giving is a part of the donor's estate planning

---

[159] The deduction itself is not questionable, as revealed by § 2053(c)(1)(A), and §§ 303(c)(2)(A) and 6166(b)(6) both speak in terms of a percentage of the gross estate as reduced by allowable § 2053 deductions. The issue is whether the pledge is a transfer that would trigger application of §§ 2035(c)(1) and 2035(c)(2).

[160] See, e.g., Hoisington, The Truth About Charitable Remainder Trusts (*How to Separate the Help from the Hype*), 45 Tax Law. 293, 315 (1992), concluding that an insurance funded "asset replacement" plan to compensate a donor's family for the loss of trust corpus to charity in a CRT only makes sense in terms of the potential economic loss of a premature death of the private lead beneficiary. This is the insurable risk—the beneficiary dying before any increased payments attributable to the annuity itself compensate for payment of the remainder to charity—because the plan itself is not viable economically otherwise and would not be undertaken unless the donor was independently charitably motivated. And in that case the premise in the text is not involved.

In addition, according to Hoisington, an insurance funded asset replacement plan only makes sense if the insurance is cheaper than the economic loss that might occur, which easily could not be the case. Further, in a CRT, the insurance should be a declining amount because the longer the lead interest is paid back to the donor the less the economic loss of premature death will be. Finally, in many cases a CRT with a term of years versus a life estate lead interest makes better

§ 7.1.5

objectives, inter vivos execution of that portion of the plan can produce more favorable results than testamentary charitable transfers. So one lesson to learn from the following discussion is to compare inter vivos versus testamentary charitable planning for clients who are charitably inclined—as a preferable method to accomplish their charitable intentions.

An ancillary lesson to consider is to be wary of claims that charitable planning techniques can *increase* a client's net worth that will remain available to the client's ultimate beneficiaries. Inter vivos charitable giving may generate a smaller *reduction* in net worth, but it is not likely to prove beneficial in pure economic terms in comparison to no charitable giving whatsoever.

To illustrate just one popular technique, using the income tax saving from a CRT to purchase life insurance to replace the wealth that ultimately passes to charity,[161] frequently the flaw in the proposal is that the income tax deduction is available only for a limited number of years but the premium payment obligation extends for the donor's lifetime. Or the plan is dependent upon techniques that the donor could employ without the charitable component, such as using inter vivos annual exclusion gifts to fund an ILIT, and therefore the plan's success is not a function of the charitable element at all.

Further, in some cases the saving illustrated is a function of the donor dying prematurely, which often produces a tax saving when life insurance is involved. Betting on a premature death is not likely to be a successful strategy unless the taxpayer is better at predicting death than the insurer's actuary and medical examiner.[162] In this respect, planners

---

(Footnote Continued)

sense because it eliminates the risk of early termination of the private lead interest.

[161] Hoisington, The Truth About Charitable Remainder Trusts (*How to Separate the Help from the Hype*), 45 Tax Law. 293 (1992), is a very useful article illustrating the economics and the method needed to analyze a proposed "asset replacement" plan involving charitable planning.

[162] For a revealing case see Smallegan v. Kooistra, 2007 WL 840123 (unpub. Mich. Ct. App.), in which an asset replacement plan was recommended, the taxpayer created and funded a CRUT, but was denied the requisite insurance coverage (presumably because the insurers' medical examiners *were* better at

also should be wary of unrealistic investment projections, as well as unrealistic life expectancy predictions.

§ 7.1.5.1 Income Tax Charitable Deduction

Unlike the wealth transfer tax charitable deductions in § § 2055 and 2522, the income tax deduction is not unlimited in all cases, although there is a five year carry forward provision for that portion of any charitable gift that exceeds the deduction limitations in the year of contribution.[163] There are two sets of rules to consider with respect to the income tax deduction for qualified charitable transfers.

The first set of rules establishes what portion of the value of gifted property is deductible. If the donee is a public charity, gifts of cash and gifts of any property (other than intellectual property and tangible personal property, the use of which is unrelated to the function of the recipient charity) held long term for capital gain purposes may be deducted in virtually all common estate planning cases up to the full FMV of the property.[164]

In some cases it may be wise economically to sell an appreciated asset, incur capital gain at the donor's capital gains tax rate, and give those proceeds to produce a charitable deduction at the donor's marginal income tax rate for the full amount of the proceeds. In either case, the deduction for encumbered property cannot exceed the donor's equity in the asset, as if it was sold and only the proceeds were given to charity. Indeed, the transfer of an encumbered asset is treated as a sale for the amount of the debt that encumbers the asset, with bargain sale to charity consequences.[165]

(Footnote Continued)

predicting mortality), and the taxpayer's diminished and disappointed family beneficiaries sued the planner for malpractice (without success).

[163] § 170(b)(1)(B). See § 14.1.

[164] See § 170(e)(1), which does not reduce the deduction for these assets. Under this same provision, gifts (other than § 170(e)(5) "qualified appreciated stock") to a private foundation, and gifts of certain property not held long term for capital gain purposes, such as intellectual property or tangible personal property, the use of which is unrelated to the function of the recipient charity, may be deducted only to the extent of the lesser of their FMV or basis.

[165] See § 14.1.4 nn.67-70 and accompanying text for a discussion of the bargain sale to charity rules.

The second set of rules limits the deduction that may be taken in any year for the aggregate of the donor's transfers to a percentage of the donor's "contribution base."[166] In most cases the aggregate income tax charitable deduction for the year may not exceed 50% of the donor's contribution base.[167] The aggregate deduction for contributions of appreciated long term capital gain property to a public charity cannot exceed 30% of the contribution base, or 20% in the case of contributions to a private foundation.[168] In a funny kind of trade off for the smaller deduction allowable under the first set of rules (limiting the deduction to basis instead of FMV), the aggregate deduction for contributions of appreciated property not held long term (and intellectual property or tangible personal property, the use of which is unrelated to the function of the recipient charity) cannot exceed 50% of the contribution base, or 30% in the case of contributions to a private foundation.[169]

Pass through private foundations are treated as public charities for purposes of these rules, and there is an election applicable to gifts of appreciated long term property (including intellectual property and tangible personal property, the use of which is related to the function of the recipient charity) that permits deduction of only an amount equal to basis but with a limitation of 50% of the contribution base.[170] That election is applicable to all deductions for the year, including any carryovers from prior years and, once made, is irrevocable.

In many cases it may be preferable to carry any deduction exceeding the 30% limitation forward rather than making the election to reduce the amount deductible to increase the limitation percentage. Indeed, in some cases it might be preferable to sell the asset and incur the capital gain represented by the appreciation in exchange for being able to donate the proceeds without limitation on the deduction.[171]

---

166 Essentially adjusted gross income, as defined in § 170(b)(1)(G) to exclude net operating loss carrybacks.

167 § 170(b)(1)(A).

168 §§ 170(b)(1)(C)(i) and 170(b)(1)(D)(i). Consult the table in § 14.1.2.

169 See § 170(b)(1)(C)(i) and Treas. Reg. § 1.170A-8.

170 §§ 170(b)(1)(C)(iii) and § 170(e)(1)(B). See Treas. Reg. § 1.170A-8(d)(2).

171 See Teitell, Charitable Giving Tax Strategies: Windfalls and Pitfalls, 27 U. Miami Inst. Est. Plan. ¶ 1100.3D (1993).

These contribution deduction limitations are equally applicable to gifts *to* and gifts *for the benefit of* charity.[172]

§ 7.1.5.2 Conservation Easements

One notable exception to the suggestion that it is not common to benefit economically by charitable planning is the charitable conservation easement. Motivated by a Congressional policy to reduce the pressure to develop or sell open spaces to help finance the payment of FET, § 2031(c) establishes an exclusion of value from a decedent's gross estate that reduces the amount subject to FET. The provision applies to the extent a qualified conservation easement is donated to a § 170(h)(3) qualified organization, irrevocably and perpetually restricting the ability of the owner of property includible in the gross estate to develop that property for commercial purposes other than farming.[173]

Although the underlying asset is includible in the gross estate, the estate is entitled to an exclusion—a tax benefit like a deduction—that reduces the FET liability. In addition, the § 2031(c)(1)(A) definition of the exclusion reveals that it is in addition to any FET § 2055(f) deduction (or, if granted inter vivos, the § 2031 valuation reduction) for the same qualified contribution of the easement.[174] Because this estate tax exclusion cannot be combined with a § 170(h) income tax deduction if the

---

[172] See Treas. Reg. § 1.170A-8(a)(2).

[173] Public access need not be a condition of the grant of the easement. Treas. Reg. § 1.170A-14(d).

[174] Usually the deduction is measured by the difference between the value of the land before and after granting the easement. Treas. Reg. § 1.170A-14(h)(3). Theoretically the value should be based on sales of comparable easements, but often there are none to be found, and that evidence is not essential. See Symington v. Commissioner, 87 T.C. 892 (1986); Higgins v. Commissioner, 58 T.C.M. (CCH) 1536 (1990); Fannon v. Commissioner, 56 T.C.M. (CCH) 1587 (1989); Stotler v. Commissioner, 53 T.C.M. (CCH) 973 (1987); Rev. Rul. 76-376, 1976-2 C.B. 53 (all involving inter vivos transfers). This deduction generally is limited by the 30% ceiling under § 170(b)(1)(C). Although no cases or rulings have been found to date, the same valuation approach ought to apply for § 2055(f) purposes. See generally Lindstrom, Income Tax Aspects of Conservation Easements, 5 Wyo. L. Rev. 1 (2005).

§ 7.1.5.2

beneficiaries are the donors of the easement,[175] generating the income tax deduction for the donor during life usually is the better approach. And, most importantly for this discussion, taken together at current maximum tax rates, the aggregate tax saving can exceed two-thirds of the value of the easement involved.[176]

The interest that generates this exclusion is a "qualified conservation easement,"[177] which is tied to the income tax definition of a qualified conservation contribution.[178] In essence, this involves preservation of land areas for outdoor recreation or education, protection of natural habitat, or preservation of open space for scenic enjoyment or pursuant to federal, state, or local conservation policies that will "yield a significant public benefit."[179] As originally enacted the subject property also had to meet certain location requirements that were repealed in 2001.[180]

An estate that meets these requirements may elect to exclude the lesser of $500,000 under § 2031(c)(3) or basically 40% of the net value of the underlying property *after* reflecting the effect of the easement on the FMV of the property. De minimis easements generate no FET benefit, however.[181] Therefore, it may be wise to obtain a ballpark estimate of the value of dedicating in perpetuity the development rights of the property

---

[175] Under the authority of § 2031(c)(8)(A)(iii) the exclusion can be a matter of postmortem estate planning, but an election is forced by § 2031(c)(9) between the §§ 170(h) and 2031(c) benefits. PLR 200143011 held that respective tenants in common may claim the § 2055(f) FET deduction for some undivided interests and the § 170(h) deduction for others.

[176] In addition, the benefits at the state and local tax level may include income tax credits and property tax reductions due to the value-reducing consequence of the easement. See Airey, Conservation Easements in Private Practice, 44 Real Prop., Trust, & Est. J. 745 (2010).

[177] § 2031(c)(8)(B). See the Uniform Conservation Easement Act § 1(1), 12 U.L.A. 165 (2008), for the typical state law definition.

[178] Meaning a perpetual restriction on use with a § 170(h)(4) conservation purpose (other than a § 170(h)(4)(A)(iv) "preservation of an historically important land area or a certified historic structure"). § 170(h)(1).

[179] Whatever that means. See § 170(h)(4)(A)(iii).

[180] See § 14.3.5 nn.131-132 and accompanying text.

[181] The 40% exclusion is subject to a reduction under § 2031(c)(2) to the extent the value of the easement does not exceed 30% of the value of the

before spending any significant amount of time evaluating qualification for this exclusion. The exclusion may be worthless (or next to it) if the location of the realty makes this value minimal. A simple illustration shows the net cost of a contribution of the easement.

Assume the unrestricted FMV of the underlying qualified property is $1,000,000, there is no purchase money debt or retained development rights, and the easement would reduce the appraised value of the property by $300,000. If the § 2055(f) deduction for that easement would be the same $300,000, then the value of the property for computing the 40% exclusion limitation would be $700,000 and the exclusion itself would be $280,000. Between the § 2055(f) deduction of $300,000 and the § 2031(c) exclusion of $280,000, the amount remaining subject to FET is only $420,000 and the FET saving at a 35% assumed rate would be $203,000 (as compared to 35% of $1 million of FMV). This is not nearly equal to the $300,000 value of the easement (this almost one-third gap between FMV lost and taxes saved compares to when the easement opportunity originally was enacted and a 55% tax rate saving was actually more—$319,000—than the FMV reduction).

If the decedent contributed the easement prior to death and generated a § 170(h) income tax charitable deduction, the income tax saving would increase the value of the gross estate. But even after FET on that income the donor's family again would be financially better off, and the added wealth could be put to work to generate yet additional wealth for the donor's family. The inter vivos contribution would reduce the includible value of the property (much the same as if the § 2055(f) deduction was available at death), and the exclusion under § 2031(c) still would apply, making the inter vivos contribution preferable due to the § 170(h) deduction.

It may be that planning to take advantage of § 2031(c) is a valuable entitlement if the property is such that no one in the decedent's family would likely want to change its current use by development or sell it at a

---

(Footnote Continued)

underlying property—determined in a *different* manner, discussed in § 14.3.5 n.139.

§ 7.1.5.2

capital gain,[182] assuming the location of the property informs a meaningful value and qualification for the exclusion. As with any kind of charitable planning, however, careful calculations and evaluation are required before reaching that conclusion.

§7.1.5.3 CLTs

In a CLT plan a temporal interest—not an income interest but similar to it[183] —is paid from a trust to a qualified charity for a designated period of time, either a term of years or the life of one or more designated individuals.[184] At the end of that "lead" interest the trust corpus is held in further trust for or distributed to the noncharitable objects of the donor's bounty. Thus, for example, a trust could be created to benefit one or more charities for X years, remainder to the donor's living descendants. The charitable deduction is allowable for the value of the temporal interest and reduces the gift tax cost of making the ultimate transfer to the remainder beneficiaries, in the process shifting future appreciation tax free because the remainder interest is valued as a percentage of the gift tax value of the trust corpus when the trust is created. If desirable, the lead charitable beneficiary could be the donor's private foundation or a donor advised fund in a community foundation, providing greater continuing control over the use of those funds without delaying the time of the completed gift.

Meanwhile, if established by an inter vivos trust that is made income taxable to the donor under the grantor trust rules, the trust also generates an immediate § 170 income tax charitable deduction for the donor in the year of creation, which may be wise if it reduces income tax in a year in which the donor is in a high income tax bracket. Although

---

182 Basis of the property subject to the easement is affected by the exclusion and the easement itself. See Treas. Reg. §§ 1.170A-14(h)(3)(iii) and -14(h)(4) Examples 11 and 12 and § 14.3.5 nn.145-148 and accompanying text.

183 Explained in greater detail in § 14.3.6, the lead interest must be an annuity (a guaranteed dollar amount, often but not necessarily based on a percentage of the initial FMV of the trust corpus) or a "unitrust" interest (a fixed percentage of the fluctuating annual FMV of the trust).

184 The lead interest need not constitute any minimum or maximum period or value. See § 14.3.6 n.154.

future income will be taxable to the donor for the balance of the charitable term interest, this may be wise economically if the donor's future income tax brackets will be lower or if the trust is funded with tax exempt bonds that will produce no future income tax, notwithstanding the grantor trust rules. If this grantor trust income tax treatment is not desirable, however, the immediate income tax deduction can be forgone by making the trust subject to income taxation annually under the traditional income tax rules applicable to trusts, with no taxation to the donor and a trust § 642(c) income tax deduction for annual payments of income made to the charity.[185]

Perhaps most importantly, the donor's charitable objectives can be accomplished while retaining trust corpus for the objects of the donor's ultimate bounty. Thus, for example, the trust corpus could be a control stock interest in a family business, with dividends adequate to support the CLT payments to the charity (or sale of some stock from corpus to the business to support those payments). The donor might transfer enough stock to the CLT to reduce the amount of stock taxable at the donor's death to a minority interest for valuation purposes, while preserving control of the business in the family by naming a friendly trustee of the CLT (or, if very carefully done, naming the donor personally as trustee) and not otherwise marketing the trust's interest in the family business stock that ultimately will return to the remainder beneficiaries.

Like all charitable planning, this technique is not without detriments. The CLT diverts or suspends the noncharitable enjoyment of trust corpus during the charitable term interest, the remainder interest is a gift of a future interest for which the gift tax annual exclusion is not available, there is no new basis attributable to inclusion in the donor's gross estate, and the remainder beneficiaries must wait until the charitable term expires before acquiring their beneficial interest.

However, even this has a silver lining because, if done properly so that the trust corpus will not be includible in the donor's gross estate at death, the transfer is not subject to the GST ETIP rule.[186] This means

---

[185] This charitable deduction is not collared by the percentage of gross income limitations normally applicable to individual taxpayers.

[186] § 2642(f).

§7.1.5.3

that GST exemption may be allocated to the remainder interest at the time of the trust's creation. Special rules are applicable[187] if the trust is a CLAT, and these rules make it nearly impossible to create a totally exempt trust. But if the trust is a CLUT the exemption may be allocated using the discounted present value of the remainder interest and produce a totally exempt transfer.[188] In this manner, if the remainder is a GST taxable transfer, the donor may be able to leverage the exemption in a way that few other transfers permit.

Indeed, in terms of leverage, if the trust corpus outperforms the income assumption in the valuation tables by generating more income than the tables anticipate, the excess production will inure to the benefit of the remainder beneficiaries tax free.[189] And if the charitable term is measured by the life of an individual who dies sooner than the valuation tables predict, the remainder interest will be payable sooner than anticipated and again will be worth more to the remainder beneficiaries than the valuation tables make subject to gift taxation.[190]

---

[187] § 2642(e).

[188] The difference in these approaches reflects that CLATs maximize the amount passing to the noncharitable remainder beneficiaries better than CLUTs do.

[189] For example, if the tables predict that the trust will generate 5% annual income and the CLT unitrust payment is 6% of the annual FMV, the tables assume that all the income and a 1% slice of corpus will be distributed to the charity annually. If the trust actually produces 6% income or more during the year, there will be no cannibalization of corpus and the remainder will be worth more when the charitable term interest ends than the tables anticipate. Thus viewed, the lower the income rate assumed in the valuation tables at the time of creation, the more value—a larger percentage—of the trust corpus will be assigned to the lead interest and the less value will be attributed to the remainder interest that is taxable for gift tax purposes. CLTs are exceedingly attractive in times of both depressed asset values and low interest rates, because the remainder that is subjected to gift tax is valued significantly lower than the anticipated value that will remain at the end of the charitable lead term, if asset values recover or if income rates rise in the interim.

[190] Provided that the § 7520 valuation tables are applicable because the measuring life was not suffering from a terminal illness such that there was a greater than 50% likelihood of dying within one year of creation. See Treas. Reg. § 25.7520-3(b)(3). And subject to the so-called "ghoul rule" of Rev. Rul. 85-49, 1985-1 C.B. 330, precluding the use of measuring lives other than the donor, the

§ 7.1.5.3

§7.1.5.4 Charitable Gift Annuities

A more simplified approach to charitable giving involves the purchase of an annuity from a charitable organization that represents the charity's general, unsecured promise to pay the designated annuitant a guaranteed annual amount. Most charities base their annuity payments on tables employing uniform rates published by the nonprofit American Council on Gift Annuities, which discourages donors from "shopping" and charities from "competing" based on relative rates rather than the merits of the charitable purpose. Regardless of how they are set, charitable gift annuity rates are not meant to be commercially competitive, because the charity is receiving a benefit from the transaction (often from 40% to 60% of the value of the transferred property). That charitable benefit constitutes the gift and income tax deductible element in the transaction and is determined by subtracting the value of the annuity from the value of the property transferred to the charity.[191]

To the extent of the annuity itself, however, the transfer of property to the charity is a purchase and sale transaction with potential capital gain consequences to the transferor. These two elements—the charitable gift and the purchase—cause the transaction to be taxed as a part-sale, part-gift transaction that, in the charitable arena, is subject to the bargain sale to charity rules.[192] For income tax purposes, these rules may produce a gain on the sale portion measured by the difference between the value of the annuity received and the transferor's allocated basis in

(Footnote Continued)

donor's spouse, or a lineal ancestor (or that ancestor's spouse) of every remainder beneficiary (not counting any individual whose likelihood of taking is less than 15%, based on the §7520 mortality table factors).

[191] To qualify for charitable gift annuity treatment the value of the annuity must be less than 90% of the value of the property transferred, meaning that the charitable gift must exceed 10% of the value of the property transferred. See §§501(m)(5)(B) and 514(c)(5)(A). The value of the annuity is determined under Treas. Reg. §§25.2512-5 and 25.7520-2. See also Rev. Ruls. 72-438, 1972-2 C.B. 38, and 84-162, 1984-2 C.B. 200. Generally the value of the deduction will be greater if the annuity is deferred so that payments begin at a later date, because the charity has the use of the transferor's money for a longer period before having to pay anything back. But see note 183.1 regarding flexible gift annuities with delayed starting dates that adjust the amount of the annuity to always produce the same size charitable deduction.

[192] Treas. Reg. §§1.170A-1(d); 1.170A-4(c)(2); 1.1011-2(a)(4); 1.1011-2(b).

§7.1.5.4

the sale portion.[193] The balance of the income tax consequences relate to the annuity payments themselves, which follow the § 72 rules.[194]

A charitable gift annuity is a useful alternative that is easier to create and administer than a CRT (discussed next). The documentation is simple. The relative cost of the transaction should be lower. The annuity payments are fixed at inception, so there is no ongoing revaluation required (as in a CRUT, but not a CRAT). Installment reporting of gain as a portion of each annuity payment received may be preferable to selling an asset and reinvesting the proceeds for a higher income yield. (But note that a CRT also offers favorable capital gain consequences— indeed, any gain in a CRT transaction is not taxable to the transferor at all except under the tier rules as payments carry out gain (to the extent ordinary income is insufficient), as discussed below.)

---

[193] § 1011(b); Treas. Reg. § 1.1011-2; Rev. Rul. 72-436, 1976-2 C.B. 643. In a gift annuity transaction involving the sale of appreciated property in exchange for the annuity a number of steps are required. The first is simple pro ration of the donor's basis between the gift portion and the sale portion. Then, with respect to the sale portion only, that percentage of the donor's basis is subtracted from the discounted present value of the annuity (which is the amount realized) to determine gain on the transaction. Treas. Reg. § 1.1011-2(c) Example (8). That gain then may be taxable in installments over the life of the annuity if the annuity is nonassignable and the donor (or the donor and the designated survivor annuitant(s)) are the only annuitants. Treas. Reg. § 1.1011-2(a)(4). Gain not taxable because the annuity terminates on the transferor's premature death is not recognized. Treas. Reg. § 1.1011-2(a)(4)(iii)(a). The theory is that the amount realized on the sale portion is reduced due to termination of the annuity before the life expectancy used in valuing the annuity.

[194] The amount of the property transferred, reduced by the amount of the charitable deduction, is the amount deemed invested in the annuity and determines the portion of every payment over the expected life of the annuitant that is excluded (the exclusion portion) as a tax free recovery of basis in the annuity. Amounts received in excess of that basis recovery are fully taxable under § 72(b)(2). Thus, if the annuitant lives longer than the life expectancy used to determine the recovery of basis, the full amount of any payments received after full recovery of that basis is taxable. If, however, the annuitant dies earlier than full recovery of the entire basis, the unrecovered balance is deductible on the annuitant's final income tax return. See § 72(b)(3). Within the exclusion portion may be some element that constitutes capital gain deferred and reportable in installments, as discussed in § 7.1.5.4 n.193.

Either transaction may increase cash flow to the lead annuitant or beneficiary, relative to the income flowing from the assets used to fund the annuity. The charitable gift annuity must be for the life of the annuitant(s), which diminishes flexibility but may be more palatable to the annuitant(s) than a CRT, which can be for life or for a term of years. In years in which the AFR is high, the charitable gift annuity may produce larger payments than a comparable CRT, although the charitable deduction in the CRT may be greater in such a case. The point is that a donor needs to run the numbers to compare the options.

The charitable gift annuity can be deferred, which can boost the charitable deduction and permit its use for income tax saving immediately even though the annuity doesn't begin until some future date (for example, retirement).[195] Deferral is not possible in a CRT except by using an income only option and engineering the trust investments to produce no income, also as discussed next.

§7.1.5.5 Inter Vivos CRTs

One of the primary reasons cited for creation of an inter vivos CRT—other than to provide a benefit for the charity—is to provide an opportunity to liquidate investments without gain or loss, reinvest the proceeds (unreduced by income tax) and any income tax saved by generating the §170 deduction,[196] and produce a subsequent cash flow that is sufficiently better than before the reinvestment to make up for the

---

[195] See, e.g., PLR 200742010, in which the government blessed "two special kinds of deferred gift annuities, known as flexible gift annuities" that essentially allowed the donor to select when to begin receiving the annuity payments. The charitable deduction and value of the annuity itself would not change, however, because the annuity rate was adjustable, to produce the same charitable deduction, based on the donor's age when the payments began. Thus, by delaying the starting date a donor would increase the amount of each annuity payment, itself a desirable option if the donor can forsake payments and, by deferral, generate a higher annual return once payments begin (much like deferring the start of Social Security by delaying retirement).

[196] Caution is required with respect to the type of corpus used to fund the trust. As illustrated in PLR 9452026, §170(a)(3) defers any charitable deduction if the trust corpus is tangible personal property until the interest of the transferor and any other close family members terminates (as, for example, when the trust sells it, which would then cause the property to be regarded as an unrelated use asset, the deduction for which is limited to basis under §170(e)(1)(B)(i)(I)).

§7.1.5.5

gift of the charitable remainder. The fact that the trust is a qualified CRT means that the capital gain realized on reinvestment is not taxable at the trust level.[197] It also will not be taxable to the transferor *if* creation of the trust, the transfer of property to it, and then the sale of trust corpus and reinvestment of the proceeds is not one integrated transaction and there is no binding obligation on the trust to make a sale that was prearranged by the transferor.[198] Therefore, the gain will be taxable only to the extent it is carried out under the tier rules and taxed in that fashion to the beneficiary as part of the lead interest.[199]

---

[197] § 664(c).

[198] An express or implied obligation on the charity will prevent avoidance of the tax, however. See Ferguson v. Commissioner, 174 F.3d 997 (9th Cir. 1999); Jones v. United States, 531 F.2d 1343 (6th Cir. 1976); Kinsey v. Commissioner, 477 F.2d 1058 (2d Cir. 1973); Hudspeth v. United States, 471 F.2d 275 (8th Cir. 1972); Palmer v. Commissioner, 62 T.C. 684 (1974), acq., Rev. Rul. 78-197, 1978-1 C.B. 83; Rev. Rul. 74-562, 1974-2 C.B. 28; Rev. Rul. 67-178, 1967-1 C.B. 64; Rev. Rul. 60-370, 1960-2 C.B. 203. A step transaction analysis may yield the same result. Blake v. Commissioner, 697 F.2d 473 (2d Cir. 1982).

Beware of prenegotiated sales to a third party, which similarly will fail to shift the gain to the trust. Cf. Martin v. Machiz, 251 F. Supp. 381 (D. Md. 1966). Teitell, Charitable Giving Strategies: Windfalls and Pitfalls, 27 U. Miami Inst. Est. Plan. ¶ 1100.7 (1993). Also pay special attention to Notice 2008-99, 2008-2 C.B. 1194, as discussed in § 5.9 n.10.14 and accompanying text (6th ed.), announcing a transaction of interest involving sale of the contributed asset followed almost immediately by termination of the trust through commutation by sale of both lead and remainder interests to a third party.

If, however, there is no evidence of any prior understanding, agreement, or obligation, the form of the transaction will be respected. See Grove v. Commissioner, 490 F.2d 241 (2d Cir. 1973); Carrington v. Commissioner, 476 F.2d 704 (5th Cir. 1973); Crosby v. United States, 73-1 U.S. Tax Cas. (CCH) ¶ 9399 (S.D. Miss. 1973); Wekesser v. Commissioner, 35 T.C.M. (CCH) 936 (1976); PLRs 9452026 and 9452020. And cf. Commissioner v. Brown, 380 U.S. 563 (1965) (capital gain result respected following a transfer to charity in exchange for the charity's note, which was payable from rent earned from leasing the purchased assets).

[199] See § 664(b) and Treas. Reg. § 1.664-1(d), as elaborated upon in § 5.9 nn.8-25 and accompanying text. In order of priority, annual distributions are deemed to constitute income to the beneficiary to the fullest possible extent under an oldest, most expensive "worst in, first out" regime that treats distributions as (1) ordinary income of the trust from the pool of undistributed prior years' net ordinary income and then from current year ordinary income, then (2) net short term capital gain (on a cumulative basis) from the pool of undistributed

Because the tier rules look to income from prior years until it all has been exhausted or the lead interest terminates, these rules may serve only as a capital gain deferral device rather than as a capital gain avoidance opportunity.[200] Thus, although it often is assumed that the gain is eliminated altogether (because the trust itself is nontaxable), these characterizations of CRT planning are exaggerated.

Even if taxation of any gain to the transferor is avoided, however, the transferor cannot be better off for the transaction unless the increase in cash flow, discounted to present value, exceeds the value of the charitable remainder, also discounted to present value. For that to be the case, in almost every situation the charitable deduction must produce a sizeable income tax saving that can be used to endow a portion of the new increased income flow, *and* one of three things also usually must be the case:

> (1) The property contributed to the trust is so substantially appreciated that the transferor's own sale during life would produce a significant capital gain tax that would reduce the income generating capital by a huge amount;[201]

(Footnote Continued)

prior years' and then current year net short term capital gain, followed by (3) net long term capital gain (on a cumulative basis) from the pool of undistributed prior years' and then current year net long term capital gain, then (4) "other" income of the prior and current years and, finally, (5) a tax free distribution of corpus. See also Notice 99-17, 1999-1 C.B. 871, and Notice 98-20, 1998-1 C.B. 776, with respect to the three tier capital gain priority carryout rules.

[200] See Hoisington, The Truth About Charitable Remainder Trusts (*How to Separate the Help from the Hype*), 45 Tax Law. 293, 294-295 (1992). These trusts can be gain shifting devices to the extent the transferor is not the lead private beneficiary, which entails gift tax consequences that must be factored into the equation. The lead interest may qualify for the annual exclusion under Treas. Reg. § 25.2503-3(b), and for the marital deduction under § 2523(g) but, in the latter case, shifting the gain to a spouse is not likely to produce a major income tax benefit unless the spouses do not file jointly. See PLRs 200813006 and 200813023, validating CRUT provisions that permitted allocation of a portion (75% and 50%, respectively) of the lead unitrust amount among either the settlor(s) (spouses in the first case), or any qualified § 170(c) charitable recipient. The exercise of this authority could accomplish an assignment of gain in the tiers to charity.

[201] See Hoisington, The Truth About Charitable Remainder Trusts (*How to Separate the Help from the Hype*), 45 Tax Law. 293, 307 (1992).

§ 7.1.5.5

(2) The transferor is so young that the increased cash flow will continue for a significant period of time; or

(3) The transferor could not afford to hold those appreciated assets until death to obtain a new basis equal to FMV, presumably because the transferor could not live on the income flow from the current investments until death.[202]

In cases in which a charitable intent exists, greater all around benefits may be available under an alternative plan by which the transferor takes a portion of the available wealth to purchase a commercial annuity, and gives the balance outright to charity. And if no freestanding charitable intent exists it often will be economically preferable to incur the capital gains tax and reinvest the balance or hold the property until death (perhaps by borrowing against the equity if necessary to finance the transferor's lifestyle in the interim).

A different advantage sometimes touted for inter vivos CRT planning is as a substitute for a qualified retirement plan. The notion is that a CRUT would be employed with both the net income and income deficiency makeup features.[203] Taken together these would permit (1) investment in highly appreciating assets that produce little or no income, generating an increase in the value of the trust corpus during the years prior to when the transferor wishes to begin receiving distributions, followed by (2) a nontaxable liquidation and reinvestment of the proceeds in assets that produce a significant income flow, (3) that then can be used during the retirement years to make the requisite unitrust payments for those years and make up for income deficiencies from the prior years. If the unitrust beneficiary's income tax bracket drops during retirement, the hope is that the tax saved by deferring income in this manner, coupled with tax free growth and then reinvestment by the trust, will produce an increased unitrust payment (based on a higher corpus value when payments begin) and make up for the eventual gift of the trust remainder to charity.

---

[202] In addition, it is important to avoid unnecessary taxes at the trust level, as would occur if the asset contributed was stock in a family corporation that the corporation redeemed from the trust, constituting a prohibited act of self dealing. §§ 4941, 4947(a)(2). See § 4941(d)(2)(f) for an exception if the corporation pays FMV to redeem all the outstanding stock of that class held by the trust and any other shareholder.

[203] See §§ 664(d)(3)(A) and 664(d)(3)(B) and § 14.3.2.

§7.1.5.5

An economic model will reveal that this CRT technique is meritorious (lacking an independent charitable intent) only if the lead unitrust payments will be made for a sufficient number of years at a sufficiently increased rate to compensate for the gift of the remainder payable to charity.[204] This assumption often is made but usually it is not the predictable result.[205]

In each of these situations the planner must perform a present value analysis that is based on assumptions regarding income yield, life expectancy, and tax rates. This makes an informed prediction impossible without running the numbers and yielding a good deal of uncertainty. Nevertheless, it is a relatively safe prediction that none of these plans is likely to be economically attractive in the vast majority of cases absent a legitimate charitable motivation on the client's part.[206]

---

[204] And no untoward penalties or taxes are incurred, as could occur if the asset transferred to the trust is encumbered, generating potential unrelated business taxable income and self-dealing issues, as discussed in Woodburn, Handling Charitable Gifts of Debt-Encumbered Property, 21 Est. Plan. 287 (1994).

[205] Cf. Shumaker & Riley, Strategies for Transferring Retirement Plan Death Benefits to Charity, 19 ACTEC Notes 162 at note 27 and accompanying text (1993), showing illustrations in a comparable situation revealing that the income and life expectancy assumptions must be quite high before the anticipated benefit is produced.

[206] Any effort to increase the lead interest to better engineer the economics runs the risk of not qualifying as a § 664(d) CRT because the remainder interest is valued at less than 10% of the initial FMV of the trust corpus. See §§ 664(d)(1)(D) and 664(d)(2)(D), as discussed in § 14.3.2 n.38 and accompanying text (6th ed.)). It also could disqualify the gift tax charitable deduction under the Treas. Reg. § 25.2522(c)-3(b) standard that the charitable remainder is "so remote as to be negligible," measured by a 5% probability of exhaustion test evaluated in terms of the remainder being at risk due to the inter vivos payout. Cf. Rev. Rul. 77-374, 1977-2 C.B. 329; Rev. Rul. 70-452, 1970-2 C.B. 199. The lower the AFR, the higher the probability of this occurring (because the trust is assumed to be making a lower amount of income to finance the lead private beneficiary's interest). It is a good gamble that this problem may arise if the annuity percentage exceeds the AFR, particularly with a younger beneficiary.

§ 7.1.5.5

§ 7.1.5.6 Gifts of Insurance to Charity

An owner of insurance may transfer the policy to a charity or a charitable split interest trust in most jurisdictions[207] as an alternative to merely naming the charity as the beneficiary of a policy of life insurance. A gift of the policy may be preferable to naming the charity as beneficiary of the proceeds because, otherwise, income and gift tax deductions are available[208] only if the owner is not the insured and the policy matures while the owner is still alive (a gift occurs when the proceeds are payable to the charity as beneficiary instead of to the owner). Future gift and income tax deductions may be available for on-going premium payments if the charity or a charitable trust is the owner of the policy, although valuation difficulties and limitations on the deduction[209] may make it more palatable to make a direct contribution to the charity of cash that the charity then can use to pay the premium. Added cautions relate to the transfer of policies subject to outstanding policy loans, which will constitute a bargain sale to charity[210] and may trigger application of the undesirable transfer for value rules.[211]

---

[207] The government will not recognize the gift of a policy unless local law provides that the charity has a valid insurable interest in the insured. See PLR 9110016, later revoked by PLR 9147040, in which the government reflected an amendment to state law clarifying the charity's insurable interest in the transferor of a policy.

[208] § 170(f)(3). Cf. PLR 8030043.

[209] The deduction with respect to an insurance policy cannot exceed the transferor's basis in the policy. § 170(e)(1)(A). Consider whether the basis determination rules in CCA 200504001 should apply (premium paid reduced by the cost of insurance protection already provided and by amounts previously received under the contract but not included in gross income). See Treas. Reg. § 25.2512-6(a) for rules relating to the valuation of insurance policies for gift tax purposes, with differing rules for policies as to which further premiums are due, for policies as to which no further premiums are due, and for policies on the life of an individual who has become uninsurable.

[210] Treas. Reg. § 1.1011-2(a)(3). Cf. Rev. Rul. 2009-13, 2009-1 C.B. 1029 (income tax consequences of a sale of a life insurance policy).

[211] See § 101(a)(2), which may not be a problem because the charity is tax exempt but may create ordinary income that will carry out to the lead interest beneficiaries under § 664(b) if the trust is a split interest charitable trust.

§7.1.5.7 Economics of Charitable Transfers

As the foregoing discussion suggests, it is nearly impossible in most cases to formulate a charitable giving plan that generates a net increase in a family's wealth. Notwithstanding claims made to the contrary by some individuals who market insurance and other plans that rely on a charitable component, charitable planning will not normally generate more economic value than if no charitable element was involved. Careful analysis of a proposal that suggests otherwise will *almost* without exception reveal that doing better by doing good is not realistic—particularly when aspects of the proposal that are not unique to charitable planning are divorced from the illustration. For example, anyone can make use of an irrevocable insurance trust or annual exclusion gifts to reduce their taxable estate at death. To avoid comparing apples to giraffes any charitable plan that makes use of either technique should be compared with a similar noncharitable plan that makes use of the same generic opportunities.

Nevertheless, a charitable plan may entail little diminution in the wealth remaining for a client's family *and* in the process provide a significant benefit to an intended charity. In many cases clients who have pre-existing charitable intentions may be pleased to engage in planning that does not affect their family's ultimate wealth by any significant amount while it satisfies their charitable inclinations. They can do well by doing good.

For example, when Jacqueline Kennedy Onassis died in 1994 the news media reported that her estate plan included a $100 million CLT with a 24 year term and a remainder that would pass to grandchildren. Calculations based on information and supposition, all produced by the appropriately well regarded charitable planner Conrad Teitell, estimate a 96.8% charitable deduction, leaving a taxable estate of only 3.2% of the value of the fund. Projections of the wealth that would be available after the 24 year term and all GST was paid further estimated that $96 million would remain for Mrs. Onassis' ultimate beneficiaries.[212] An aggregate

---

[212] Using Teitell's rough numbers, the calculation was:

- $100 million CLT paying $8 million annually to charity for 24 years.

- $96.8 million charitable deduction based on 6.4% AFR.

loss of just 4% of the original fund might be regarded as a tiny price to pay for the charitable benefit bestowed by this plan.

But these results might be compared to the results that could have been obtained if the plan had not employed the charitable element at all. In that case the FET at Mrs. Onassis' death would have consumed roughly $55 million, leaving only $45 million, which makes the $96 million result generated look pretty attractive at first blush. But if that $45 million had been sequestered in an accumulation trust that made the grandchildren wait for the same 24 years, and that trust was able to generate an aggregate growth consisting of the same income and appreciation yield assumed by Teitell over the same period, it would compound to approximately $443 million and generate a GST at termination of roughly $243 million, netting $200 million for the remainder beneficiaries. That's a huge difference in result.

This illustration is not very accurate because it does not factor into the equation income tax on the income or capital gain generated in the noncharitable accumulation trust over the 24 year period, but we don't know how those taxes were reflected in the Teitell calculations either. It would take a crystal ball to know for sure what capital gain rate to use and whether the income earned by the trust would be taxable or exempt. Because the income and gain accumulated in the CLT would have been exempt during the deferral period, however, it would be appropriate to subtract a certain factor for income taxes, and even at a 40% assumed combined annual income tax rate (reducing the assumed accumulation rate to 6% annually instead of 10%), trust accumulations still would have yielded approximately $382 million after 24 years. After a 55% GST (the rate then in effect, which would have informed their projections), the net amount for the family still would have been $172 million.

Somewhere between those two numbers is probably a good estimate of what the remainder beneficiaries would have received had charity not been involved but all other facts had been the same. Either

(Footnote Continued)

- $214 million value after 24 years, assuming 8% income yield and 2% appreciation.

- $118 million GST taxable termination tax.

- $96 million remaining wealth for the grandchildren.

way the numbers are estimated, the remainder beneficiaries would have been far better off had the charitable lead interest not been employed.

The difference, however, is that the estate plan generated $8 million per year for 24 years for charity, a total of $192 million before the benefits of compounding or any income and appreciation is calculated on that amount in the hands of the charity. Overall the plan generated at least a $192 million charitable benefit at a "cost" to the remainder beneficiaries of somewhere between $76 and $104 million (using very rough numbers).

In the final analysis the remainder beneficiaries would receive virtually the same amount that existed at Mrs. Onassis' death. Depending on how all the involved parties view the situation, the charitable element in this plan "cost" the family between $4 million (the original $100 million less the remaining $96 million to the beneficiaries when all is said and done) and $104 million ($200 million that the remainder beneficiaries might have received, less the $96 million they will receive), or it produced a net benefit of between $88 million ($192 million to charity less a cost to the family of $104 million) and $188 million ($192 million to charity less a family loss of just $4 million).

Although this illustration draws on a well known testamentary plan rather than inter vivos charitable giving, the caution it produces is the same. A charitable giving component to any plan may yield a huge benefit or a substantial cost, depending on how a family defines its views. Historically inter vivos planning almost always generated a better result than testamentary planning, regardless of how the final consequences were defined.

§7.1.5.8 Comparisons of Alternate Charitable Plans

It is nearly impossible to fairly and accurately compare alternative wealth distribution plans without making assumptions or begging certain unanswerable questions. In a vacuum it is even more difficult to develop hard and fast rules about which plans are preferable to others. Indeed, it is reasonably difficult just to marshal all the factors that might be relevant in any comparison. But among all the elements that might be implicated, a couple of lists can be generated that planners might consider when creating their own spreadsheet analyses. One of these lists is the various commonplace alternative types of planning that a client might consider. The other is the various costs and benefits that may visit the client or the client's family in the process.

On that first list of alternative types of planning, the questions that might be asked include: whether to do anything during life or wait until death; whether to make a transfer outright or through a split interest trust (and which type of split interest trust is preferable—lead or remainder, annuity or unitrust); and whether to sell assets and reinvest the proceeds to produce a better return, purchase a charitable annuity, or transfer the assets in kind and allow the recipient to make any investment conversions.

On the second list of costs and benefits the questions that may be relevant include:

1. Will any wealth transfer tax be incurred inter vivos?

2. Will generating the liquidity to pay that wealth transfer tax incur any capital gain tax?

3. How much will investment returns be diminished by these wealth transfer and capital gain tax costs?

4. Will an income tax charitable deduction be generated and, if so, subject to what limitations?

5. How much will after tax investment returns be improved by any tax saving attributable to an income tax charitable deduction?

6. Will there be an improvement in investment performance generated by the underlying property or its reinvestment, to whose benefit, and at what income tax cost?

7. Who will enjoy the investment return—both income and appreciation—generated by the underlying property after any inter vivos planning but before the client's death, and with what income and wealth transfer tax costs?

8. Will capital gain before or after any inter vivos planning be eliminated by a new basis at the client's death?

There may be other factors to consider as well, and some assumptions almost certainly will be required regarding income yield, life expectancy, and tax rates before concrete estimates can be modeled based on these factors.

§7.1.5.8

§7.1.6 Disclaimers

Another form of inter vivos rearrangement of property as to which no wealth transfer tax is incurred is a qualified disclaimer (or a renunciation, as it may be known for state law purposes). If the technical requirements of §2518 are met, the effect for purposes of the entire wealth transfer tax Subtitle (which includes the FET, gift tax, GST, and the special valuation rules of Chapter 14) is "as if the interest had never been transferred" to the disclaimant.

Fortunately, there are numerous opportunities that may be capitalized upon by making a qualified disclaimer. Unfortunately, there are almost as many ways to fail to accomplish a qualified disclaimer. So, although this discussion may prove helpful and the opportunities should not be overlooked or squandered, affirmative advance planning seldom should depend on disclaimers. It may work out, and options often present themselves, but this discussion does not proceed on the notion that this is more than reactive planning.

The lack of reliability of disclaimer planning is a function of a number of factors. The most common limitation is sometimes labeled greed but probably is more accurately described as fear. People who renounce property must feel comfortable with the notion that there will be enough other wealth to support them for the balance of their lives. This need not be a problem if S is the disclaimant, if D's plan anticipated the disclaimer and directs that the disclaimed property falls into a nonmarital trust that provides a continuing benefit to S, as authorized under §2518(b)(4)(A).[213] But for anyone else the cost of a qualified disclaimer is loss of any enjoyment of the disclaimed interest.[214]

A second and related issue is that a qualified disclaimer cannot be made after acceptance of the interest or any of its benefits,[215] meaning that inadvertent or even unintentional enjoyment can disqualify an otherwise intentional disclaimer. A third factor is timing: In many cases in

---

[213] Indeed, as authorized by Treas. Reg. §25.2518-2(e)(5) Example (7), some planners might include a $5,000 or 5% withdrawal power in the nonmarital trust just to make it more palatable and less "costly" to S to disclaim from an outright or in-trust marital bequest.

[214] See §§2518(b)(3) and (b)(4)(B), as discussed at §7.1.6.3.

[215] §§2518(b)(3) and (b)(4)(B).

which disclaimers would be a wise and tax free method of inter vivos property transfer it already is too late. For example, the potential disclaimant is incompetent to renounce enjoyment or already is deceased,[216] or the nine month limitation on making a qualified disclaimer has elapsed before the plan can be recommended and implemented.[217]

Before delving into the technical requirements for a qualified disclaimer, first consider the types of circumstances in which renunciation might be effective wealth transfer tax planning. The most common is the least strategic. The disclaimant simply has more wealth than necessary and would prefer that the alternate taker of a disposition that otherwise goes to the disclaimant should receive the disclaimed property instead.

For example, assume Parent died leaving property to Child, who has done very well (through employment, marriage, winning the lottery, or whatever). If Child would prefer that Grandchild receive the wealth instead, Child's qualified disclaimer could effect a transfer to Grandchild in lieu of Child's taxable gift (of Child's own wealth or of Parent's wealth that Child moved along but not in a qualified manner). Alternatively, Child may be terminally ill and, although not possessing a great deal of wealth, also aware that not much additional wealth will be required for the short balance of Child's life. An even more dramatic illustration would entail Child as the decedent whose estate passed by intestacy to Parent, who died within the permissible disclaimer period. Wise postmortem planning would consider whether FET would be reduced if Parent (or Parent's personal representative) disclaimed the wealth.[218]

---

[216] On the issue whether a personal representative may disclaim on behalf of a ward see § 7.1.6.6.

[217] See § 2518(b)(2) and § 7.1.6.2.

[218] See Sims v. Hall, 592 S.E.2d 315 (S.C. 2003), in which the personal representative's attorney was found liable for malpractice for failing to advise the personal representative of the opportunity to disclaim in just such a case. Note that the personal representative was the ultimate beneficiary of both Child and Parent's estates, so the disclaimer would not have altered the ultimate destination of the property. Also note that death in rapid succession and inclusion of the same wealth in both Child and Parent's estates would spawn a § 2013 previously taxed property credit, which (along with the unified credits available in the two estates) might make the double inclusion harmless for tax purposes. Still the court was correct to conclude that responsible planners would recommend an evaluation of whether there was any potential benefit of disclaimer.

§ 7.1.6

In either case the disclaimer by Child could trigger a GST as a direct skip, and that might be a second good reason to consider a disclaimer. If Parent had not planned for the use of Parent's GST exemption, Child might realize that Parent's unused GST exemption is not portable and disclaim to take advantage of that benefit by causing a direct skip to Grandchild that will utilize Parent's exemption.[219] This could avoid GST at the same time the disclaimer also avoids the gift tax that would apply if Child received the property and waited too long to give it away, or FET if Child received the property and held it until death.

For GST planning of a more strategic variety, Child also might make a disclaimer that causes the wealth to pass into a trust that could be made GST exempt and held for multiple generations, making even better use of that exemption. This opportunity would not be available, however, unless Parent's own plan established the trust and provided that property not passing to Child would pass into that entity.[220]

Other forms of GST planning also are available through the use of disclaimers. For example, property left in trust for S might be made to qualify for a reverse QTIP election that would allow the use of D's GST exemption that otherwise would be wasted. If, for example, the mechanism used by D was an outright disposition to S, or a trust with a general power of appointment, disclaimer of the bequest or of the power to appoint could result in a secondary disposition in a trust providing S with

---

[219] See, e.g., PLR 9822014 (nieces and spouses disclaimed a formula amount equal to the exemption to permit direct skips tax free to the nieces' descendants).

[220] Although not stated in the opinion, Offner v. United States, 2008-1 U.S. Tax Cas. (CCH) ¶ 60,556 (W.D. Pa. 2008), appears to have been an effort by children to send additional property to the decedent's irrevocable inter vivos grandchildren's trust, that was funded by the decedent's residuary estate, and perhaps was meant to be made GST exempt. The disclaimers failed because the decedent's will provided that a predeceased child's share would pass to the child's descendants (an antilapse form of disposition found in most well-drafted documents) and those descendants needed to disclaim their interest under this provision so that the gifts to the children would lapse and fall into the residue. An interesting question is whether the government would have respected a disclaimer by those descendants if the disclaimed property would thereby fund a trust for their benefit. See § 7.1.6.3 (6th ed.). Showcasing the perils of disclaimer planning, a formula gift by the decedent might have been a better way to fund the irrevocable trust in the largest amount that could be made exempt from the GST.

§ 7.1.6

the right to all income annually and eligible for the § 2056(b)(7) QTIP election, with the concomitant opportunity to make the § 2652(a)(3) reverse QTIP election too.

Furthermore, a timely disclaimer again might be wise if a transfer happened to originate in a chronologically exempt trust and could be made to skip generations tax free with a renunciation by a higher generation beneficiary. Alternatively, if property is slated for a GST and disclaimer might cause it to remain at a higher generation instead, some situations might justify deferral of tax by precluding or delaying the generation-skipping transfer.[221]

GST planning with disclaimers actually gets pretty far afield from traditional disclaimer planning that is employed for transfer tax minimization purposes, the more likely of which being planning in the context of the marital deduction. One likely use of disclaimers—indeed probably the most common single use—is to qualify a trust for the marital deduction by eliminating interests (such as a discretionary income or principal entitlement in someone other than S[222] or a nongeneral inter vivos power in S to appoint from a QTIP trust) that otherwise would preclude marital deduction entitlement.[223] Another frequent use is to adjust the size of the deduction.

In some cases it may be wise for S to selectively disclaim certain high growth assets to shelter their future appreciation from inclusion in

---

[221] See § 11.4.14, illustrating that, normally, deferral of the GST is not economically the wise choice, but numerous other factors might inform an intelligent decision to the contrary.

[222] Cf. TAM 9228004 (decedent's testamentary trust did not qualify for the FET marital deduction; rather than employing disclaimers, the beneficiaries executed an agreement not to probate the will, allowing the property to pass by intestacy, and then all of the descendants disclaimed all but a specified dollar amount of the property—presumably the nondisclaimed amount was meant to shelter the decedent's unified credit—causing the balance to pass outright to S and qualify for the marital deduction; regarding the agreement not to probate the will as tantamount to a § 2518(c)(3) transfer of property to the persons who would take in the event of a qualified disclaimer, as discussed in § 7.1.6.5, the government held that these actions constituted a qualified disclaimer). See also § 7.1.6.5 regarding multiple level disclaimers that accomplish the same results.

[223] See § 13.4.2.3.1 with respect to disclaimers for marital deduction passing requirement purposes, and § 13.5.2.2 nn.31-32 and accompanying text with respect to purifying a defective income interest.

S's estate. A more viable alternative may be available if S obtains those assets through exercise of an inter vivos power of appointment or by distributions by the trustee and then makes a gift of them instead, intentionally incurring gift tax in S's brackets rather than additional FET in D's brackets. Another counterintuitive but similarly preferable alternative would be an intentionally *non* qualified disclaimer by S, generating gift tax the same as if S had a more affirmative control over disposition of the property.[224]

To illustrate several of these consequences, in some cases too little property passes to S to make optimum use of the marital deduction, with nonspousal takers disclaiming to cause more property to pass to S. This is "expensive" postmortem planning for those disclaimants because they must relinquish all interests in the property during S's overlife. Fortunately, this problem was more prevalent shortly after the increase in 1981 from a limited to an unlimited marital deduction, and not much postmortem planning currently is required to take maximum advantage of the marital deduction.[225]

---

[224] For a discussion of the economics of these alternatives see § 6.2.

[225] For a sample of transition date disclaimers designed to increase the amount passing to S, see Estate of Boyd v. Commissioner, 819 F.2d 170 (7th Cir. 1987) (beneficiary of life insurance on D's life renounced the benefit of D's waiver of the § 2206 right of reimbursement against the taxpayer for the FET attributable to inclusion of the insurance, with the effect of leaving the statutory apportionment obligation on the taxpayer and preserving more of the residue, which passed to S and was deemed to come directly from D, not from the taxpayer, so as to qualify for the marital deduction); TAM 8435056 and PLR 8309030 (S disclaimed certain powers of appointment and withdrawal or other interests, to permit QTIP election and qualify for the marital deduction); TAM 9301005 (remainder beneficiaries disclaimed remainder interests to pass a fee simple interest to S for marital deduction purposes); TAM 8639002 (disclaimer by children to optimize marital deduction) and PLRs 9148018 and 8906036 (disclaimer by children to permit balance of trusts to comply as QTIP trusts). A number of cases highlight a particularly inventive form of this planning by which S renounces any entitlement under D's estate plan in favor of a statutory elective share under state law, and then tailors the amount of marital deduction with a disclaimer of any portion of that share that exceeds the amount desired. See, e.g., Rev. Rul. 90-45, 1990-1 C.B. 175, and PLR 8817061, as discussed in § 13.4.2.3 n.36.

§ 7.1.6

Alternatively, these days it is more likely that too much property passes to S or otherwise qualifies for the marital deduction,[226] leaving some of D's unified credit unconsumed. This failure to optimize a bequest may spawn a disclaimer by S that will subject more property to tax in D's estate and utilize D's unified credit, precluding taxation of that property when S ultimately disposes of it. With the adoption of § 2518(b)(4)(A), allowing S to remain a beneficiary of disclaimed property, this form of postmortem planning is not nearly so difficult. Nevertheless, because of the problems associated with making a qualified disclaimer in general,[227] and with the availability of § 2010(c)(2)(B) portability of the unused exclusion amount, even this form of postmortem engineering probably is not wise as an affirmative planning anticipation as opposed to a rear guard defense or safety net technique.

Better yet, S could delay making a disclaimer just long enough to avoid qualification under the nine month rule.[228] This might be wise planning if D's unified credit has been sheltered but the marital deduction still is too great, provided that S can afford to incur gift taxes (and otherwise is likely to incur FET at death) that will further reduce S's estate and save additional wealth transfer tax. As a consequence, the marital deduction will be allowed in D's estate and gift tax will be incurred by S, which often produces the most favorable tax results over both estates assuming S is likely to be subject to the FET at death.[229]

A third form of transfer tax planning that is similar to qualification for the marital deduction is to generate a charitable deduction. By way of example, if the transferor created a split interest entitlement that does not satisfy the special requirements of § 664, the noncharitable beneficiary might disclaim all rights, title, and interest in the disposition to allow

---

[226] See, e.g., § 10.5.3 regarding disclaimer of the "accretive" share of jointly owned property that passes to S by operation of law and that may overqualify the marital deduction.

[227] The list of problem areas potentially includes acceptance of benefits, the need to renounce certain powers in a nonmarital trust to which disclaimed property passes, timing issues, and the possibility that S may die before a disclaimer is made and state law may not permit postmortem disclaimer on behalf of S.

[228] See § 7.1.6.2.

[229] See § 6.2.

the charitable portion to qualify for the deduction.[230] In other cases a partial disclaimer may make it possible for the balance of the trust to qualify for reformation under § 2055(e)(3)[231] or simply to cause more property to pass to a qualified charity.

This was the case in PLR 200127007, in which the government held that S's waiver of the § 2207A right of reimbursement was an interest in property that the remainder beneficiaries of a QTIP trust were permitted to disclaim. The effect was to increase a charitable bequest of S's residuary estate that otherwise would have been reduced to pay the taxes caused by FET inclusion of the QTIP trust under § 2044.

In some instances the plan may anticipate that property a private beneficiary does not care to receive should pass to charity in the alternative and generate a deduction for the original transferor as opposed to the transferee accepting the asset and making their own deductible transfer.[232]

Further tax planning may entail income tax minimization through the redirection of property transfers that carry income tax liability.[233]

---

[230] See, e.g., PLR 8146038 (spouse disclaimed right to occupy apartment otherwise left to charity). But see TAM 8106013 (disclaimant's quitclaim of life estate to charitable remainder beneficiary did not generate charitable deduction because there was another remainder beneficiary to whom an interest should have passed, so the effort was regarded as an acceptance and gift instead of a qualified disclaimer). See also § 14.3.7.1 regarding disclaimers to qualify for the charitable deduction in general.

[231] See, e.g., TAM 9123023 and PLRs 9716019, 9633004, 9529042, 9527040, and 9341003.

[232] See, e.g., PLRs 199903019 (requiring disclaimant also to renounce powers as trustee of a trust to which the property would pass for the benefit of charity, to preclude the disclaimant from having any control over the disclaimed portion) and 9113004 (art collection bequeathed to child with any work disclaimed by the child passing directly to charity).

[233] The income tax aspects of qualified disclaimer planning are unclear because § 2518 speaks only of the Subtitle in which the wealth transfer taxes appear. See Marcus v. Commissioner, 22 T.C. 824 (1954) (income is taxable to disclaimant until date of disclaimer, presumably even if the disclaimant is not entitled to retain that income because it passes with the underlying property by virtue of the disclaimer), and Rev. Rul. 64-64, 1964-1 C.B. 221 (disclaimant is not taxable on any income earned after the disclaimer date). Disclaimers are respected for purposes of §§ 691, 402, and 408 income taxation of retirement

§ 7.1.6

One simple example is the IRD aspects of qualified retirement plan distributions that may be less onerous in the hands of some lower income beneficiaries or deferrable for a longer period if S qualifies for a rollover to S's own IRA.[234]

Another example might be to prevent the return of property subject to § 1014(e), transferred to a decedent and bequeathed back to the original donor within the prohibited one year of the transfer, all with an eye to obtaining a new basis at the death of the transferee decedent.[235] And disclaimers might be employed to fractionalize the ownership of property to generate discounts that otherwise would not be available.[236]

Two other aspects of disclaimer planning are considered on occasion, both raising more concern about legitimacy and efficacy. One is to preclude attachment of federal tax liens and the other is to defeat the disclaimant's creditors.[237] For those in need of care, disclaimers gener-

---

(Footnote Continued)

benefits. See § 9.4 n.7. And proposals occasionally are made to amend the Code to clarify for income tax purposes that the same consequences of § 2518 qualified disclaimer planning for wealth transfer tax purposes apply.

[234] See, e.g., PLRs 200532060 and 9820010 (designated beneficiary of IRA disclaimed, causing beneficiary designation to fail and the account to be distributable to the decedent's estate, which passed to S and, because S was personal representative of the estate, also permitted S to make a qualified rollover election to S's own IRA; the unbelievable aspect of the 2005 Ruling is that the designated beneficiary was D's *former* spouse). See § 9.3.5 regarding the spousal rollover election in general.

[235] Cf. PLR 8628030 (income tax element not discussed).

[236] Fractional interest and minority interest discounts for valuation purposes are discussed in § 15.3.1.

[237] Drye v. United States, 528 U.S. 49 (1999), aff'g sub nom. Drye Family 1995 Trust v. United States, 152 F.3d 892 (8th Cir. 1998), held that state law cannot preclude attachment of a federal lien when a taxpayer's decedent dies and cannot be defeated by the taxpayer's subsequent disclaimer, even if timely and effective for state and federal wealth transfer tax purposes. According to the Court, state law determined the taxpayer's rights or interests in the disclaimed property but federal law determined whether those rights or interests were "property" as to which the tax lien could attach. Adopting the view that the absence of any recognition of disclaimers in the federal lien provisions—in contrast to their acceptance as controlling in the wealth transfer tax provisions of the Code—is indicative that disclaimer is not sufficient to exempt inherited property from the reach of the lien provisions. Furthermore, the Court regarded the taxpayer's

§ 7.1.6

ally are regarded as disqualifying dispositions for Medicaid planning purposes, so the opportunity to produce an affirmative benefit may be precluded, although a disclaimer of property that drops into a SNT may be viable planning.[238] In addition, dodging or delaying creditor claims in the private sector may be facilitated by some disclaimers.

(Footnote Continued)

right to either accept or disclaim the property as a sufficient "right to property" to which the federal lien could attach.

[238] See § 4.4 n.10 and accompanying text regarding the (d)(4)(C) form of self-settled SNT, which might be a useful alternative for a disclaimant notwithstanding its limitations. The self-settled classification is not a traditional vision regarding disclaimed property because the donor whose property is being disclaimed normally would create the receptacle trust, but the disclaimer is treated as a disqualifying disposition, meaning that it essentially is being regarded as an acceptance of the disclaimed property followed by the disclaimant's personal transfer. Compare In re Estate of Kirk, 591 N.W.2d 630 (Iowa 1999), and Neilsen v. Cass County Social Services Board, 395 N.W.2d 157 (N.D. 1986) (efficacy of disclaimers upheld against the defendant's determination that it was a transfer that would disqualify the disclaimant's right to receive medical benefits) with Hoesly v. State, 498 N.W.2d 571 (Neb. 1993) (surviving joint tenant's renunciation was an act with the intent and purpose to become eligible for public assistance that was forbidden by state law), which distinguished *Neilsen* because the state law regarding transfers that would disqualify was narrowly drafted and the disclaimer authority relation back principle was extensive. *Kirk* permitted disclaimer of joint tenancy property only to the extent of the accretive share caused by the decedent's death.

In re Estate of Heater, 640 N.E.2d 654 (Ill. App. Ct. 1994) (renunciation effected by the personal representative of a decedent who inherited property from a predeceased sibling and died shortly thereafter), added an interesting wrinkle. Although the court specifically denied special status to the state public assistance authority (which was seeking reimbursement for assistance previously provided), the court nevertheless refused to grant a requisite order to authorize the personal representative to disclaim, notwithstanding that the decedent validly could have disclaimed during life and could have provided the authority by will for the personal representative validly to renounce after the decedent's death. Finding, however, that specific authority did not exist in the decedent's will and holding the personal representative unequivocally to the standards of a fiduciary representing all parties interested in the decedent's estate, the court found that the attempted renunciation could not be authorized by the court, stating that it would be improper to allow an action that would render the estate insolvent and deprive any creditor of payment. Cf. the Medicaid spend down authorization by In re Keri, 853 A.2d 909 (N.J. 2004), overcoming many similar objections.

§ 7.1.6

In that respect, the Supreme Court has stated that one "important consequence of treating a disclaimer as an *ab initio* defeasance is that the disclaimant's creditors are barred from reaching the disclaimed property."[239] That statement was dicta, however, because the case did not involve a creditor rights question. State law goes both ways on the issue.[240] Fortunately, regardless of the proper state law result on this

---

[239] See United States v. Irvine, 511 U.S. 224, 239-240 (1994).

[240] See, e.g., Fla. Stat. Ann. § 739.402(2)(d); Mass. Gen. L. ch. 191A, § 8(2); Minn. Stat. § 524.2-1106(b)(4); Stein v. Brown, 480 N.E.2d 1121 (Ohio 1985), and Pennington v. Bigham, 512 So. 2d 1344 (Ala. 1987) (disclaimers were invalid as fraudulent conveyances made with intent to defraud creditors within the meaning of the Uniform Fraudulent Conveyance Act); Tompkins State Bank v. Niles, 537 N.E.2d 274 (Ill. 1989) (the disclaimer statute was superior as against an after acquired title statute and, because the disclaimer related back to the decedent's death, the disclaimant never acquired title to which the creditor's claim could attach); In re Estate of Martin, 666 N.E.2d 411 (Ind. Ct. App. 1996); Baltrusaitis v. Cook, 435 N.W.2d 417 (Mich. Ct. App. 1988); Essen v. Gilmore, 607 N.W.2d 829 (Neb. 2000); Trew v. Trew, 558 N.W.2d 314 (Neb. Ct. App. 1996), rev'd and rem'd on jurisdictional grounds, 567 N.W.2d 284 (Neb. 1997); In re Estate of Opatz, 554 N.W.2d 813 (N.D. 1996); Dyer v. Eckols, 808 S.W.2d 531 (Tex. Ct. App. 1991); and Abbott v. Willey, 479 S.E.2d 528 (Va. 1997) (all similar, allowing disclaimers to defeat creditors); In re Atchison, 101 Bankr. 556 (Bankr. S.D. Ill. 1989), aff'd, 925 F.2d 209 (7th Cir. 1991), followed by In re Simpson, 36 F.3d 450 (5th Cir. 1994) (a bankruptcy debtor's disclaimer was not a prohibited "transfer" because, under state law, a disclaimer relates back to the date of the decedent's death with the effect that the disclaimed property passes as if the debtor was deceased). If the debtor's bankruptcy petition was filed before the disclaimer, In re Watson, 65 Bankr. 9 (Bankr. C.D. Ill. 1986), may apply (bankruptcy trustee permitted to set aside disclaimer involving life insurance notwithstanding that the debtor had no knowledge of the insurance policy when the bankruptcy petition was filed). But in the factually similar case of National City Bank v. Oldham, 537 N.E.2d 1193 (Ind. Ct. App. 1989), the court permitted a debtor to disclaim an inheritance over eight months after filing a bankruptcy petition, based on the relation back theory, which also was used to support a disclaimer in frustration of creditors in Estate of Goldammer, 405 N.W.2d 693 (Wis. Ct. App. 1987).

Badouh v. Hale, 22 S.W.3d 392 (Tex. 2000), concluded that a pledge of an expectancy (as collateral for a debt owed to an attorney) prior to the benefactor's death was an acceptance of benefits from the property that precluded an effective disclaimer by the beneficiary after the expectancy matured, turning the relation back notion on its head. See generally Parker, Can Debtors Disclaim Inheritances to the Detriment of Their Creditors?, 25 Loy. U. Chi. L.J. 31 (1993), predominantly involving bankruptcy law aspects of the issue. And see Citizens State Bank v. Kaiser, 750 P.2d 422 (Kan. Ct. App. 1988), involving an attempted

issue, the tax law provides that a disclaimer still qualifies for wealth transfer tax purposes unless it is totally invalid or it is voided by creditors. Being voidable is not an impediment to its wealth transfer tax efficacy otherwise.[241]

A useful set of guidelines regarding state law on the creditor rights issue is provided by the Uniform Fraudulent Transfer Act.[242] Under this Act certain transfers made with the intent to hinder, delay, or defraud creditors are deemed fraudulent and therefore reversible.[243] Under § 4(b) of the Act various badges of fraud are specified, several of which might apply in the context of a beneficiary who makes a disclaimer: before the transfer was made the debtor had been sued or was threatened with a suit, the transfer was of substantially all of the debtor's remaining assets, the debtor was or became insolvent shortly after the transfer was made, and the transfer occurred shortly before or after a substantial debt was incurred. Some states by statute preclude disclaimers with the intent or effect of defeating creditor claims.[244] The predictability of successful disclaimer planning is probably pretty good under any state's law if these criteria are avoided.

(Footnote Continued)

disclaimer of joint bank accounts by the surviving joint owner, filed after a final judgment was entered against the disclaimant, and Niklason v. Ramsey, 353 S.E.2d 783 (Va. 1987), in which the disclaimant's participation in a will contest was deemed an exercise of dominion over the decedent's estate that precluded a subsequent disclaimer designed to thwart the disclaimant's creditors.

The one-off creditor-related issue raised by In re Bowman Trust, 804 N.W.2d 361 (Minn. Ct. App. 2011), was whether a valid spendthrift provision would preclude a trust beneficiary's disclaimer. That question was made more interesting because the disclaimer was not qualified, because it was tardy. The court nevertheless held that a spendthrift provision does *not* preclude disclaimer, meaning that an affirmative assignment of a beneficiary's interest would be precluded but not rejection of it, followed by its enjoyment by the trust's successor beneficiaries.

[241] Treas. Reg. § 25.2518-1(c)(2).

[242] 7A Part II U.L.A. 2 (2006).

[243] In addition, it may be an ethical violation for an attorney to counsel a client engaged in fraudulent activities. Model Rules of Professional Conduct Rule 1.2(d): "A lawyer shall not counsel a client to engage, or assist a client, in conduct that the lawyers knows is . . . fraudulent."

[244] See, e.g., state statutes cited in Dyer v. Eckols, 808 S.W.2d 531 (Tex. Ct. App. 1991).

§ 7.1.6

§7.1.6.1 Federal Transfer Tax Requirements

Most of the statutory requirements for a qualified disclaimer are straightforward:

- The disclaimer must be irrevocable[245] and unqualified;[246]

---

[245] Very little case law exists on the question whether a disclaimer is irrevocable under state law. In TAMs 8228011 and 8239002 state law allowed revocation of any disclaimer upon a showing of reasonable cause within three months of the disclaimer and the government ruled that the disclaimers would fail if that three month period did not expire within the federal nine month period to make a qualified disclaimer. According to Carvalho v. Estate of Carvalho, 978 A.2d 455 (Vt. 2009), only a handful of cases have considered whether or when a disclaimer may be revoked for state property law purposes (including under the Uniform Disclaimer of Property Interests Act) and held that disclaimers are absolute and irrevocable, regardless of mistake of fact or law (separately or working together). But then it provided instructions for the lower court on remand to treat disclaimers as "similar to the execution or alteration of a will," and directed a determination whether there was undue influence, coercion, or incompetence sufficient to find that the disclaimer, in effect, never was effective or binding on the disclaimant. Breakiron v. Gudonis, 2010-2 U.S. Tax Cas. (CCH) ¶ 60,597 (D. Mass. 2010), held that a disclaimer was *not* irrevocable in that case, even for federal gift tax purposes. It involved two ten-year QPRTs that terminated in favor of the plaintiff and a sibling, who the plaintiff wanted to take both remainder interests and was advised that a disclaimer would accomplish that disposition without gift tax liability. That advice was wrong because the nine months disclaimer period began upon creation of the QPRTs and, based on this error, the plaintiff sought to rescind the disclaimers to avoid gift tax. The court held that Massachusetts law permits a written instrument to be reformed or rescinded in equity on the grounds of mistake if there is "full, clear, and decisive proof" of the mistake, which is a different standard from what *Carvalho* announced.

[246] State law or the facts of the disclaimer may preclude qualification. See, e.g., Maddox v. United States, 81-1 U.S. Tax Cas. ¶ 13,391 (N.D. Ohio 1981) (the disclaimer was not effective under local law and therefore failed for federal wealth transfer tax purposes, notwithstanding that it would have been effective otherwise); TAMs 9743002 (involving pre-§ 2518 law but the same requirement that a qualified disclaimer must comply with state law, in that case finding that the disclaimer was not valid until filed with the probate court as required by local law) and 7947008 (involving an attempt to disclaim on behalf of minors, which could be done only by a guardian ad litem and only with probate court approval, neither of which occurred); Estate of Griffin, 812 P.2d 1256 (Mont. 1991) (a revocation of a disclaimer was delivered before compliance with the state law requirement to file the disclaimer itself; failure to file precluded the disclaimer from being effective and the revocation negated any intent to disclaim).

- In writing;[247]

- Delivered to the transferor, or the transferor's legal representative, or whoever else holds legal title to the property being renounced;

- Within nine months after the last taxable transfer with respect to the interest (or nine months after the disclaimant reaches age 21, if later);

- Without acceptance of any benefits from or enjoyment of the property during that nine month period;

- The disclaimed property must constitute an undivided interest or portion;

- The disclaimed property must pass without improper direction by the disclaimant;

- The disclaimed property must pass to someone other than the disclaimant or the transferor's surviving spouse.[248]

Of these, the timing, acceptance of benefits, portion, and direction requirements generate the most difficulty, and are the focus of more extensive discussion.

---

[247] See, e.g., Estate of Chamberlain v. Commissioner, 77 T.C.M. (CCH) 2080 (1999), in which an alleged intent to disclaim failed because there was no signed writing that constituted the requisite act; the court refused all proffered extrinsic evidence and ancillary documents that purported to reveal the intent, and rejected a "horseshoes" or substantial compliance argument that "close is good enough."

[248] § 2518(b)(4)(A) specifically permits the disclaimed property to benefit S, meaning that S may make a qualified disclaimer of property that will pass into a trust for the benefit of S. Indeed, S may even retain some control over that property. For example, although S may not retain a power to appoint the disclaimed property that passes into that trust, S may be trustee with fiduciary discretion to make distribution of that property. The power will not disqualify the disclaimer if it is limited by an ascertainable standard. See Treas. Reg. §§ 25.2518-2(e)(1) and 25.2518-2(e)(5) Examples (4), (5), and (12). If that receptacle trust is drafted so that inclusion otherwise will not occur when S dies, the opportunity provided is to guarantee enjoyment for S's overlife without wealth transfer tax inclusion, as is common in the typical nonmarital trust context. The consequent and fully intended circumstance in which this opportunity is used is when too much property is left to S, typically overqualifying for the marital deduction and leaving less than enough wealth to shelter D's unified credit, as illustrated in § 13.1.1. Another solution to the problem of an unused exclusion amount would be to take advantage of § 2010(c)(2)(B) portability.

§ 7.1.6.1

§7.1.6.2 Timing

With respect to disclaimers of interests created before 1977, the time within which to disclaim was a function of case law that was not uniform prior to adoption of §2518. The pre-§2518 case law became more clear with the Supreme Court decision in Jewett v. Commissioner[249] and today the timing requirement for disclaimers of interests created before §2518 became effective in 1977 is not very controversial. Nevertheless, the standard is subjective. The disclaimer must be made within a "reasonable" time after knowledge of the existence of the transfer.[250] If a future interest is involved, Keinath v. Commissioner[251] held that the reasonable time began from the date the remainder interest no longer was subject to divestment (which may be the time it becomes possessory but may occur earlier). Subsequently, *Jewett* made it clear that knowledge of the interest being disclaimed (applying a "should have known" reasonableness standard) is the key.[252]

---

[249] 455 U.S. 305 (1982), aff'g 638 F.2d 92 (9th Cir. 1980), aff'g 70 T.C. 430 (1978).

[250] Treas. Reg. §25.2511-1(c)(2). In various respects the government has interpreted this subjective standard in the same manner as the requirements that apply under §2518. See, e.g., §7.1.6.3 n.255 regarding the acceptance of benefits requirements with respect to disclaimers by minors of interests created prior to 1977. Today a similar issue continues to apply the "reasonable" time standard under §678(d), as discussed in §5.11.7 at text accompanying n.173.

[251] 480 F.2d 57 (8th Cir. 1973).

[252] Accord, Poinier v. Commissioner, 86 T.C. 478 (1986), aff'd, 858 F.2d 917 (3d Cir. 1988) (remainder beneficiary disclaimed within one week after preceding life estate ended, but the remainder was created some 34 years earlier and the disclaimer was deemed untimely); Griswold v. Commissioner, 81 T.C. 141 (1983), aff'd, 812 F.2d 712 (2d Cir. 1987), and Hallenbeck v. Commissioner, 46 T.C.M. (CCH) 1204 (1983) (contingent remainder beneficiaries in each case became aware of their contingent interests under a trust 17 years prior to their renunciations, which were not timely).

PLRs 201004006, 201001007, 200953010, 200516004, 9515034, and 9413026 involved disclaimers of interests created in pre-1977 trusts and the question of timeliness under the *Jewett* reasonable time standard. The government ruled that the disclaimant could disclaim for up to nine months after reaching the age of majority, which was age 18 in each situation in which that information was disclosed, stating that the disclaimer period is delayed while the disclaimant is "under a legal disability." The interesting unanswered question is whether a reasonable time would extend to age 21, as under §2518(b)(2)(B), even if 18 is

Some lingering uncertainty of the law relating to pre-1977 transfers was resolved by two cases involving siblings who disclaimed their respective trust interests shortly after they vested in possession. This vesting occurred over three years before the Supreme Court's *Jewett* opinion that a timely disclaimer must be measured from the transfer creating the interest and not from vesting in possession. Because the taxpayers failed to argue that *Jewett* should apply only prospectively, however, the courts in both cases held that the *Jewett* rule could apply, which the Supreme Court confirmed.[253]

That raised the more troubling issue whether a disclaimer could be taxable if the transfer that created the disclaimed interests occurred before the gift tax was enacted. On this issue both courts originally held that, for purposes of measuring a reasonable time within which to disclaim, a taxable transfer occurs even if the transaction was not subject to the gift tax because the transfer predated adoption of the gift tax. Thus, the period within which the taxpayer could make a timely disclaimer was held to begin in 1917, when the subject trust was created, even though the taxpayers did not learn of the trust for over a decade and the gift tax was not first validly enacted until 1932. According to the Court:

> the timeliness determination in this case would be the same whether the reasonable time was calculated from . . . first knowledge of the interest (1931) or from the enactment of the federal gift tax statute (1932) . . . . [The taxpayer's] delay for at least 47 years after the clock began running, until she reached age 68, could not possibly be thought reasonable.[254]

The Court did not specifically hold that the period for disclaiming began in 1917. It did state, however, that Congress is not prohibited from taxing interests transferred after enactment of the gift tax merely because the

---

(Footnote Continued)

the age of majority. See §7.1.6.3 n.273 and accompanying text. It did in PLR 9801036 in a jurisdiction in which the age of majority was 21. If it does not in a state in which majority is age 18, then the *Jewett* rule would produce a more restrictive time within which to disclaim, which is contrary to most expectations.

[253] Irvine v. United States, 511 U.S. 224 (1994), rev'g 981 F.2d 991 (8th Cir. 1992), en banc, rev'g 936 F.2d 343 (8th Cir. 1991), and Ordway v. United States, 908 F.2d 890 (11th Cir. 1990).

[254] 511 U.S. at 235.

§7.1.6.2

state law relation back doctrine treats the transfer occasioned by disclaimer as having occurred when the original transfer was made.

With respect to disclaimers of interests created after 1976, the time within which to disclaim usually runs from the last taxable transfer[255] (unless the disclaimant is under age 21). Presumably because the Supreme Court did not expressly hold that the period began to run in 1917, however, the government amended the § 2518 regulations to remove the words "taxable transfer" in various locations and replaced them with "transfer creating the interest" in describing when the period for making a qualified disclaimer begins.[256] At the heart of the change is the notion that some transfers that start the period to run are not taxable, the examples given being a transfer of foreign situs property by a nonresident alien, which would not be subject to United States taxation at all,

---

[255] A notable exception to this rule is QTIP that qualifies for the marital deduction under § 2056(b)(7) and is includible in S's gross estate under § 2044, but as to which Treas. Reg. § 25.2518-2(c)(3)(i) provides that the nine month period begins to run at creation of the trust and not S's death, notwithstanding inclusion in S's gross estate. PLR 8607013 addressed the nine month period allowed for a disclaimer with respect to contingent beneficial interests in permissible appointees under a QTIP marital trust in which S had a nongeneral testamentary power of appointment. Consistent with the final regulations, the Ruling held that the period began to run at the settlor's death, even with respect to disclaimer of the contingent beneficial interests that would take in default of exercise of the nongeneral power.

If a general power had been granted—including a withdrawal power in S exercisable inter vivos—presumably the takers in default of exercise would have nine months after exercise or lapse of the power within which to disclaim. See Treas. Reg. § 25.2518-2(c)(3), which would apply the same rule even if the general power of appointment is not taxable because it predated 1942 and was not exercised. See note 241 and accompanying text.

A similar disparity under the same regulation applies with respect to property that is the subject of a completed gift inter vivos but that is includible in the transferor's gross estate at death, as to which the position taken is that the nine month period begins to run with the *first* taxable transfer—the gift—rather than the last—inclusion at death. In that respect, the statement in text regarding the last taxable transfer should be taken to refer to taxable transfers by different transferors, except in the § 2044 situation.

[256] The preamble to the proposed regulations indicated that the essence of the amendment was to conform the regulations to the rule as it exists in accordance with the Supreme Court's decision.

and the nontaxable lapse or release of a pre-1942 general power of appointment.[257]

Notwithstanding these machinations, for purposes of current disclaimer planning the time within which to disclaim can be thought of as beginning at the last taxable event. For example, the holder of a §2041

---

[257] PLRs 9447021 and 9245011 involved disclaimers of default interests in trusts that followed nontaxable (pre-1942) general powers of appointment and predated the change to the regulation. In the 1994 Ruling the general power was cut back to a nongeneral power in 1943 and it was not exercised at the powerholder's death. In the 1992 Ruling the general power was released in the same integrated transaction as the disclaimer. In each situation relying on Treas. Reg. §25.2518-2(c)(3)(i) as it existed at the time, the government held that disclaimer of the default interests was timely as measured from lapse or release of the pre-1942 power, rather than from original creation of the trusts, in each case notwithstanding that the pre-1942 powers did not cause estate or gift tax consequences.

Given the fact that the cutback or release of these pre-1942 general powers was not taxable, it may seem curious that the government did not regard the pre-1942 general powers as nongeneral powers for disclaimer purposes (because they were not taxable), with the same §2518 timing requirement that would apply to nongeneral powers (the nine month disclaimer period would begin to run upon creation of the power or, perhaps, the 1943 cutback to a nongeneral power in the 1994 Ruling). After all, the interests disclaimed were created at inception of the trusts and were subject to divestment only by exercise of these nontaxable powers. Yet the final regulation as amended specifies that, if the power is general, the lack of tax consequence to the exercise, lapse, or release is irrelevant and a new nine month period begins from the exercise, lapse, or release. Consistent with this result are PLRs 200825037, 200225015, 199942010, 9842060 (with no discussion or explanation), and 9818053 (which appears to involve facts that predated the amendment to the final regulation and held that the time for a default beneficiary to disclaim their interest was within nine months after a nontaxable release of a pre-1942 general power of appointment)

The government held in the 1994 Ruling that "[the disclaimant's] interest in the trust was created on [the powerholder's] death notwithstanding that a transfer tax will not be imposed at [the powerholder's] death" and, under this fiction, the disclaimer was timely. Again, in the 1992 Ruling the release started the nine month clock for disclaimer of the following interest. Compliance with the dictates of §2518 is more difficult than dealing with the broad pre-1977 law governing the timeliness of disclaimers. If the government believes that the more difficult standards under §2518 were met, then it should be the case, prima facie, that the requirements of pre-1977 disclaimer law also were met.

For the GST chronological exemption aspects of these results, see §11.4.16.3.

§7.1.6.2

general power of appointment must disclaim the power within nine months after creation of the power (or when the trust granting the power became irrevocable),[258] but the persons to whom the appointive assets pass by reason of exercise or lapse of the power have nine months after the exercise or lapse of the power, because either exercise or lapse is the last taxable event.[259] In the case of a nongeneral power of appointment, however, the powerholder, permissible appointees, and takers in default of exercise all must disclaim within nine months after creation of the power (or when the trust granting the power became irrevocable) because neither exercise nor lapse of the power normally is taxable.

In many cases involving nongeneral powers, therefore, particularly a statutory power or one that is broadly exercisable, permissible appointees cannot possibly be identified and therefore will not be in a position to timely disclaim (although most conceivable appointees might be identified and they could disclaim within the statutory nine month period after creation of the power). Similarly, in many cases the takers in default of exercise may not be identifiable until the powerholder's death (for example, because those default takers are descendants alive at that time or they are the powerholder's heirs at law determined when the powerholder dies—which may not be when the power lapses or is exercised). This too likely will be too late (although the likely default takers might be identifiable earlier and they might be able to make a knowledgeable and timely disclaimer).[260]

---

[258] See Treas. Reg. § 25.2518-2(c)(3)(i).

[259] Treas. Reg. § 25.2518-2(c)(3). Even if no tax is incurred.

[260] But cf. Estate of Fleming v. Commissioner, 58 T.C.M. (CCH) 1034 (1989), aff'd, 92-2 U.S. Tax Cas. (CCH) ¶ 60,113 (7th Cir. 1992), which involved a disclaimer that was filed more than nine months after the decedent transferor died but within nine months after the decedent's will was probated. In holding that the disclaimer must be made within nine months of the decedent's death to be timely, reference was made to Treas. Reg. § 25.2518-2(c)(3), which provides that "with respect to transfers made by a decedent at death or transfers which become irrevocable at death, a taxable transfer occurs upon the date of the decedent's death." The court appeared to recognize that, under some circumstances, it may not be ascertainable at the time the decedent dies whether the transfer creates an interest in the person disclaiming; in such case the nine month period for a disclaimer may not begin to run until it is determined that an interest is created in that person. And Fitzgerald v. United States, 94-1 U.S. Tax Cas. (CCH) ¶ 60,152 (W.D. La. 1993), aff'd in an unpublished opinion (5th Cir.

§7.1.6.3 Acceptance of Benefits

A disclaimer is disqualified by the acceptance of benefits or enjoyment from the interest being disclaimed. The regulations regard an "acceptance [as] manifested by an affirmative act which is consistent with ownership of the interest, includ[ing] using the property . . . ; accepting dividends, interest, or rents . . . ; and directing others to act with respect to the property . . . ."[261]

In this respect, separate interests or portions in property are discussed in §7.1.6.4 and are considered separately, which makes the notion of severability important. Indeed, some interests that seem to be undivided may be treated as divisible for disclaimer purposes.[262] The most important illustration is jointly held property, such as joint tenancy with the right of survivorship and tenancies by the entireties.[263] For example, a surviving joint tenant's continued occupancy in a joint tenancy residence after renouncing the accretive share may not taint an

---

(Footnote Continued)

1994), held that an extension for filing the decedent's FET return does not extend the qualified disclaimer deadline, because the nine month limitation is not tied to filing an FET return.

[261] Treas. Reg. §25.2518-2(d)(1). In PLR 200832018 the acceptance was authorizing a broker to reinvest proceeds from a joint brokerage account.

[262] In PLR 9036028, the decedent's trust directed distributions of income and authorized distributions of principal and, although no income was distributed, some modest principal distributions were made before the taxpayer executed an otherwise qualified disclaimer of a fraction of the trust. Notwithstanding this acceptance of benefits from the trust, the Ruling treated the disclaimer as qualified, stating that "the amounts previously distributed to Taxpayer, even if characterized as income distributions, are sufficiently small so as to be supported by that portion of the income generated by the nondisclaimed portion of the Trust." The effect was to allow distributions to be regarded as coming from that portion that was not disclaimed. See also PLRs 200503024 and 9218015 (qualified disclaimers of the accretive share of joint tenancy brokerage accounts; payments made from the joint accounts to reduce the taxpayer's credit card obligations or to support investment decisions did not disqualify the disclaimers because they were well below the amount of the taxpayer's half of the account); PLR 8637113 (S may disclaim an undivided fractional interest in a marital deduction trust if, during the period prior to the disclaimer, income from the trust is carefully segregated between the disclaimed and nondisclaimed portions and only income attributable to the latter is paid to S).

[263] As to which a separate discussion is warranted, in §10.5.3.

otherwise qualified disclaimer (although some cases of multiple owner-ship may require payment of fair market rental for the portion not owned by the disclaimant).[264]

On the issue of acceptance of benefits, Revenue Ruling 2005-36[265] involved a decedent's IRA. Three months after the decedent died that IRA made the RMD for the year of the decedent's death. The designated beneficiary accepted that amount, and the postmortem income attributa-ble to it, but disclaimed the balance of the IRA and any postmortem income on that disclaimed balance. Without saying so in quite so many words, the Ruling essentially treated the accepted minimum distribution amount and its income as if it had been paid prior to the decedent's death and therefore was separable from the balance of the IRA and the income earned on that balance. Thus, acceptance of the minimum distribution and its income was no impediment to a qualified disclaimer of the balance.

The significance of this is the government's recognition that the minimum distribution requirements may force a beneficiary to accept a payment prior to expiration of the § 2518 qualified disclaimer nine month period, and that the clash in these rules should not preclude an other-wise qualified disclaimer. The Ruling also establishes that timely dis-claimer prior to September 30 of the year following the year of the decedent's death precluded the disclaimant from being regarded as a designated beneficiary for future years.[266]

Acceptance of benefits need not be direct. Acceptance of any consid-eration in exchange for a disclaimer is deemed to run afoul of the prohibition in § 2518(b)(3) with respect to the entire interest disclaimed, not just some portion from which the acceptance can be identified.[267] But

---

[264] See Treas. Reg. § 25.2518-2(d)(4) Example (8) with respect to community property and the severance of D and S's shares, reaching the same result. See also PLR 8124118 (S's payment of fair rental value with respect to D's half interest), and PLRs 9135044, 9135043, and 8512022 (no rental required because of the joint owner's right to occupy the entire undivided property).

[265] 2005-1 C.B. 1368.

[266] See § 9.3.3 n.29 and accompanying text.

[267] Treas. Reg. § 25.2518-2(d)(1). See, e.g., PLR 8225096 (split interest trust for the benefit of A and charitable organizations that did not qualify under § 2055(e); to generate the charitable deduction A proposed to execute a disclaimer in consideration for which A would receive payments from charitable organizations

acceptance of enjoyment or benefits must be an individual entitlement,[268] in the sense that acting in a fiduciary capacity with respect to disclaimed property will not constitute a disqualifying enjoyment unless the fiduciary has discretion to act in an unrestricted manner.[269]

(Footnote Continued)

interested in the trust, which the government held would preclude a qualified disclaimer and prevent a charitable deduction).

[268] Estate of Selby v. United States, 726 F.2d 643 (10th Cir. 1984), concluded that activity in a fiduciary capacity by a beneficiary and the beneficiary's personal representative *was* adequate to constitute an acceptance of benefits and preclude a qualified disclaimer. D bequeathed everything to S who also was D's personal representative. When S died five months later their child was appointed personal representative of both estates and in that capacity ultimately concluded that disclaimer was best. Notwithstanding that the child obtained a state court decree to permit the disclaimer, the court held that the actions taken by S and then the child precluded qualified disclaimer treatment.

[269] Treas. Reg. §§ 25.2518-2(d)(2), Reg. § 25.2518-2(e)(1). See, e.g., TAM 8015014, in which spouses had mutual wills under which S would take all the property of D, with alternative gifts to their children. The spouses died within nine months of each other and two children, as executors under each will, disclaimed part of S's interest in D's estate. Although these children received the disclaimed property by virtue of the disclaimer, their role as fiduciaries did not constitute an acceptance of benefits or an improper direction of the disclaimed assets. To the same effect see PLR 8326110, involving a child acting as fiduciary for S and who was the ultimate beneficiary of the disclaimer. PLRs 8439008, 8437016, 8429085, and 7922018 confirm that merely acting as a fiduciary is not an acceptance of benefits nor a disqualification if the fiduciary's powers are limited by an ascertainable standard or also are renounced.

In PLR 8922082, the taxpayer was beneficiary and a cotrustee of a trust and manager of a group of apartment properties that were used to fund the trust. The taxpayer's disclaimer of a specific pecuniary amount out of the trust, coupled with the taxpayer's resignation as trustee, was regarded as a qualified disclaimer, and continued management of the apartment properties for compensation did not constitute an acceptance of benefits if the compensation was bona fide, determined on an arm's length basis solely for services rendered, and not based on the value or profitability of the properties. The disclaimer would be qualified even if the taxpayer continued to serve as trustee with power to make distributions, provided that any discretion as trustee was limited by an ascertainable standard. Moreover, as trustee, compensation based on income generated or value of the trust corpus would not be unusual and would not preclude a qualified disclaimer. Thus, the statement regarding compensation might be premised on the difference between a fiduciary and a mere manager of property, but no such distinction was noted, nor were the regulations relating to fiduciaries cited or

Thus, to illustrate, PLR 8509092 involved a decedent's will that provided that any amount disclaimed by the decedent's child would go into trusts for grandchildren. The child, as trustee for each trust, was required to distribute income for the beneficiaries' reasonable support, health, maintenance, and education, but was precluded from making distributions in fulfillment of any support obligation to the beneficiary (unless no other funds were available to fulfill that obligation). The trustee could distribute the trust principal to a beneficiary who had attained age 21, which power the child proposed to irrevocably release. This qualified the original disclaimer because the child's fiduciary powers were limited by an ascertainable standard.

Similarly, in PLR 8906036 D created a trust for S and five children, with all six to act as cotrustees to pay income to S for life and principal for S's "reasonable comfort, including the cost of support and education of our children." The remainder was distributable in equal shares to the children, who disclaimed the right to receive distributions during S's overlife. The government held this to be a qualified disclaimer because the trustees' powers were limited by an ascertainable standard. The children did not need to disclaim their remainder interests, which were regarded as separable interests.

With respect to the extent of discretion that may be retained, however, consider a series of rulings involving ongoing control over property disclaimed into charitable foundations, as to which the disclaimant had some control. For example, PLR 9008011 involved disclaimed property that would pass to a charitable foundation with the disclaimant as trustee with the power to apply foundation assets for charitable purposes in any manner and amount the disclaimant determined. The Ruling held the proposed disclaimer was qualified, but only if the disclaimant's spouse and children were substituted as trustees of the foundation in lieu of the disclaimant. Similarly, PLRs 9235033, 9235022, and

---

(Footnote Continued)

discussed. The position taken in the Ruling may be indefensible, therefore, but it nevertheless creates a trap for anyone who might extrapolate from the existing regulations to determine the proper result with respect to a management arrangement.

9141017 required the foundation to segregate disclaimed property to a separate fund, as to which the disclaimant would have no control.[270]

PLRs 201032002, 200802010, 200649023, 200149015, 199944038, 9320008, and 9317039 authorized disclaimers because the by-laws of recipient foundations were amended to preclude the disclaimants from being able to control the disclaimed funds or the people who could control those amounts. And Private Letter Rulings 199929027, 9350032, and 9319022 conditioned their determination that disclaimers were qualified on the disclaimants' resignations as trustees or members of the grants committees of private foundations and otherwise taking themselves out of any position to determine the disposition of disclaimed property or the sale proceeds of disclaimed property passing to the foundations. Curiously, a different situation existed in PLRs 200518012 and 9532027, in which the government determined that disclaimers were qualified and made charitable deductions available to the estates from which the disclaimed property passed, because the taxpayers disclaimed into donor advised funds as to which the taxpayers could make recommendations but over which the taxpayer had no binding control or right to make directions.

The situation in PLR 8702024 is distinguishable from activity in a fiduciary capacity. The decedent named the taxpayer as beneficiary of insurance on the decedent's life. The insurer sent claim forms to the taxpayer, which the taxpayer completed and returned to the insurer. Pursuant to the returned forms, the insurer established an account for the taxpayer against which the taxpayer could make withdrawals. Before making any withdrawal, however, the taxpayer attempted to disclaim half of the account balance, which the government rejected as an ineffective attempt to make a qualified disclaimer. According to the government, completion and submission of the claim forms was an affirmative act consistent with ownership of the proceeds, an acceptance of benefits that disqualified the subsequent disclaimer.[271] But in PLR 9507017 S had title

---

[270] Citing Treas. Reg. § 25.2518-2(d)(2) regarding control as a fiduciary over disclaimed property.

[271] Under Treas. Reg. § 25.2518-2(d)(2). Similarly, in PLR 9214022, the government described the disclaimant's activity as granting "permission" to sell some stock and reinvest the proceeds but in fact it involved a custodial joint brokerage account; the disclaimant effectively directed the activity, which was deemed an adequate exercise of control to preclude a qualified disclaimer of that portion of

§7.1.6.3

to D's share of their community property reissued in S's name and later disclaimed it without otherwise accepting benefits from the property and the government held that this was a qualified disclaimer.[272]

An additional exception exists with respect to the §2518(b)(2)(B) timing provision for minors. According to Treas. Reg. §25.2518-2(d)(3), acceptance of benefits while the disclaimant is under age 21 is not a disqualification, although caution must be exercised to avoid acceptance of benefits during the permitted nine month period in which to disclaim after turning age 21.[273] Other illustrations found in the Regulations and various cases and rulings include:

- Payment of property taxes or utilities with respect to disclaimed property is not a disqualifying acceptance of benefits.[274]

(Footnote Continued)

the account. See Treas. Reg. §25.2518-2(d)(4) Example (4), specifying that directing a sale or selling is an acceptance.

[272] Citing Treas. Reg. §25.2518-2(d)(1) ("merely taking delivery of an instrument of title, without more, does not constitute acceptance") for the proposition that title alone is not relevant without some additional affirmative act of acceptance. See also PLRs 199932042 (surviving joint tenant of a revocable brokerage account timely disclaimed but, prior to disclaimer, the brokerage firm distributed income that was deposited to a joint account originally created with the decedent and moved the assets from the joint account into an account in the survivor's sole name, all of which the survivor subsequently reversed by transferring half the postmortem income and half the account assets into a separate account in the name of the decedent's estate; on the representation that no benefits were enjoyed in the interim, the government found disclaimer of that half to be qualified), 200832018 (establishment of new brokerage accounts following the decedent's death was not the acceptance of benefits that disqualified portions of this disclaimer), and PLR200003023 (to the same effect involving disclaimer of the accretive share of a joint settlor trust, jointly owned Treasury Direct Accounts, and several bank accounts; disclaimer was qualified notwithstanding some postmortem payments were commingled in the joint accounts and subsequently extracted).

[273] See Treas. Reg. §25.2518-2(d)(4) Examples (9) and (11) with respect to the exception, and Example (10) with respect to the danger period after turning 21 but before disclaimer. See PLRs 201004006, 201001007, 200953010, and 200516004, confirming that the same exception for an acceptance of benefits prior to the age of majority (stated as age 18 in each case except the 2009 PLR) applies for pre-1977 trusts as well.

[274] Treas. Reg. §25.2518-2(d)(4) Example (3); PLRs 9135043, 8143022, and 8140025 (the latter two involving the same situation).

- Execution of a will that exercises a testamentary power of appointment is not an acceptance of benefits if the power of appointment is disclaimed before the powerholder dies, but dying with the power exercised by the powerholder's will would disqualify the attempted disclaimer.[275]

- Payment by D's estate of S's expenses until a timely renunciation of all interest in D's estate is an acceptance of benefits, even if S ultimately repays all amounts distributed or paid.[276]

---

[275] Treas. Reg. § 25.2518-2(d)(4) Example (7). E.g., Estate of Engelman v. Commissioner, 121 T.C. 54 (2003), held that S's exercise of a general power of appointment in a marital deduction trust precluded qualified disclaimer by S's personal representative, who attempted postmortem estate planning when S died less than 10 weeks after D. Exercise of the power by a document executed five weeks after D's death was deemed an acceptance of benefits that precluded the personal representative's argument that disclaimer related back to D's date of death. Similarly, in TAM 8142008 D's will gave S a general testamentary power of appointment that S's will exercised to the extent of directing payment of taxes out of the appointive assets. S's executor within nine months after D's death undertook to disclaim S's interest under D's will, including the power of appointment, which was effective under controlling local law. The government nevertheless held that S's exercise of the power constituted an acceptance and the disclaimer therefore was ineffective. Quaere, however, whether the proper result would be to equate this exercise of the power with retention of the § 2207 right of reimbursement and, by virtue of a qualified disclaimer of the power, there being no tax and therefore no reimbursement amount.

[276] See TAM 8405003. Quaere whether a loan during the disclaimer period would produce a different result, and whether a state family allowance provision would permit payment of only the state mandated amount and not constitute acceptance of benefits from the entire estate under an analogue that S is a creditor and not a beneficiary or that the interest accepted is limited and should not disqualify the disclaimer with respect to the entire estate. See PLR 9244012 (S was deemed to have accepted the benefit of income from property subsequently disclaimed because that income was paid to D's estate and the estate used it to pay a joint income tax liability of D and S; S paid the estate an amount equal to S's share of that tax liability, with interest at a market rate) in which the government held that borrowing constitutes an acceptance of benefits (use of the income) from disclaimed property, which precludes a qualified disclaimer of a *portion* of the property measured by a fraction of which the numerator is the loan amount and the denominator is the total income paid by that property. If the estate received income from other sources, quaere why the denominator should not be the total income available to the estate to pay the tax liability, and indeed it may be possible to argue that this other income was used first, with no disqualification consequence to that extent. See § 7.1.6.4 n.305 and accompanying text.

§ 7.1.6.3

- Although activity in a partnership or corporate fiduciary capacity may be distinguishable from activities in a trust or estate fiduciary capacity, a disqualifying acceptance of benefits may be found if control of the partnership or corporation in a fiduciary capacity (for example, as a general partner or controlling shareholder or director) is exercised to the individual benefit of the disclaimant.[277]

- Pledging disclaimed property as collateral for a loan is a disqualifying acceptance of benefits.[278]

An especially effective form of postmortem planning was involved in Revenue Ruling 90-45,[279] relating to disclaimers of a portion of S's statutory forced heir share. In each of two situations presented, S elected

---

[277] TAM 9123003 determined that a qualified disclaimer of inherited partnership interests was precluded by the disclaimant's exercise of control over the partnership and initiation of a major recapitalization of the partnership. The disclaimant received those interests from a deceased sibling, who was general partner and named the disclaimant as personal representative and residuary beneficiary. In the fiduciary capacity as personal representative the disclaimant exercised the estate's partnership votes to elect the disclaimant personally as general partner to succeed the decedent and to convert the decedent's general partnership interests into limited partnership interests (and convert the disclaimant's own limited partnership interests into general partnership interests). Notwithstanding Treas. Reg. § 25.2518-2(d)(2), which permits a disclaimant to act in a fiduciary capacity with respect to disclaimed interests without prejudicing an otherwise qualified disclaimer, the government held that the disclaimant's actions constituted an acceptance of the partnership interests. Moreover, because the partnership recapitalization reduced the value of the estate's partnership interests, the TAM concluded that the disclaimant must have been acting in the capacity as a beneficiary of the estate rather than as personal representative. Thus, the regulations' exception for activities in a fiduciary capacity was deemed unavailable. Presumably the same conclusion would obtain in any situation in which the value of a decedent's interest is diminished by actions initiated by a disclaimant, provided that it is necessary for the disclaimant to vote the decedent's interests to effect the action. If, however, the disclaimant was able to effect these changes without the decedent's votes, then the disclaimant's actions should not affect an otherwise qualified disclaimer.

[278] Treas. Reg. § 25.2518-2(d)(4) Example (5), cited in Badouh v. Hale, 22 S.W.3d 392 (Tex. 2000), which concluded that a pledge of an expectancy prior to the benefactor's death was an acceptance of benefits from the property that precluded an effective disclaimer by the beneficiary after the expectancy matured. The Regulation example only anticipates a postmortem pledge, prior to the attempted disclaimer.

[279] 1990-1 C.B. 175.

§7.1.6.3

against D's will in favor of a statutory share of the estate and then disclaimed a portion of that share. In each case the Ruling held that election of the statutory share was not a §2518(b)(3) acceptance that would preclude a qualified disclaimer of any portion of it. Instead, it was deemed to "effectuate or perfect" S's right under state law to receive that portion of D's estate, as if D bequeathed that share to S or died intestate and S had inherited it.[280] The Ruling positions are internally consistent and follow the position in PLR 8817061, which allowed S to elect a statutory share and then disclaim all of it in excess of a specified dollar amount, stating:

> neither the mere taking delivery of an instrument of title nor the immediate vesting of title to the property in the disclaimant upon the decedent's death constitutes acceptance of the property that will preclude a qualified disclaimer. In those situations, there is no positive action on the part of the disclaimant that would constitute acceptance.
>
> Although [S's] interest in [D's] estate is vested by operation of law, in order for [S] to claim the statutory interest, [S] must take the affirmative step of filing an election. However, the filing of an election to take a statutory share of an estate is the exercise of a right to take delivery of title to the property interest and does not constitute acceptance of the property which would preclude the making of a qualified disclaimer. Therefore, the filing of an election . . . to take [a] statutory share of [D's] estate does not constitute acceptance by [S] of any interest in [D's estate] that would preclude . . . a qualified disclaimer of part or all of [the] statutory share. . . .
>
> Provided all other requirements are satisfied, the Service will permit a qualified disclaimer to be made in the form of . . . a "reverse pecuniary amount." Such a disclaimer may take the form of a disclaimer of the entire property interest less a specific pecuniary amount.

---

[280] A second question was when must a timely disclaimer be made following election of the statutory share. In the first situation the disclaimer was made within nine months after the decedent's death; it was timely. In the second situation the disclaimer was made more than nine months after the decedent's death but within nine months of the election to take the statutory share; it was untimely because the statutory entitlement relates back to the date of the decedent's death for all purposes, including measuring the time for a qualified disclaimer under §2518(b)(2).

§7.1.6.3

The pecuniary amount could be described by a formula calling for the smallest amount that will reduce taxes to the lowest possible amount, meaning that, in this case, S was able to perform postmortem planning to create an optimum marital bequest in an estate that failed to properly plan for the marital deduction.[281]

A more serious concern is illustrated by PLR 9427030, which posited that S and descendants all would engage in disclaimers that would cause more property to pass to S under intestacy and maximize qualification for the state estate tax marital deduction. To accomplish this planning the descendants had to relinquish their rights in D's nonmarital trust and then as intestate takers. At the same time as these disclaimers, the Ruling posits that, subject to "no agreement or understanding, express or implied, between [S] and the children or grandchildren (or their guardians)," S would create an inter vivos revocable trust and a pour over will that would provide for dispositions after S's death under terms "similar to those taking effect . . . under [D's] . . . trust." The net effect was that the monies received by S would end up in essentially the same form of trust that would have benefited the disclaimants under D's original estate plan.

According to the Ruling, neither the increase in the total wealth generated by reducing state estate tax as a result of these disclaimers, nor S's corresponding estate planning actions, would constitute an acceptance of benefits by the descendants in consideration of their disclaimers that would disqualify their otherwise qualified disclaimers. Because there were no enforceable agreements that would require S to leave the inter vivos trust intact for the descendants' benefit, this conclusion appears to be legally sound, although in practical application it seems reasonably clear that the entire package was a coordinated set of actions, none of which would have been undertaken without the others. In that sense, then, the Ruling is a generous application of the § 2518(b)(3) acceptance of benefits disqualification rule.

---

[281] Cf. TAM 8432032 (disclaimer by S of the largest fractional share of S's interest in a trust that might be disclaimed without causing an FET to be payable by D's estate—with a QTIP election as to the remaining portion of S's interest in the trust—was a qualified disclaimer). See § 13.1.1 regarding optimum marital deduction planning.

In light of this conclusion, then, the government's argument and the original decision in Estate of Monroe v. Commissioner[282] was somewhat unexpected because the Tax Court ultimately concluded that the results were sufficiently clear that a negligent underpayment of tax penalty should be imposed under §6662. D made bequests to 29 different legatees, all of whom disclaimed upon S's request. S received what they disclaimed and, within one month thereafter, S made "gifts" to each of the 29 legatees in the same or larger amounts than the legatees disclaimed.

The government argued and the Tax Court concluded[283] that the bequests were disclaimed in exchange for the express or implied consideration of S's gifts in return, the court relying on testimony of various legatees that the clear but unstated understanding was that disclaimers would be rewarded and failure to disclaim would be punished by S.[284] With the exception of only one legatee who decided to disclaim even before being contacted by S (and who allegedly accepted S's gift only to avoid giving offense), every other disclaimer was disregarded and the property passing to S by virtue of those disclaimers therefore was deemed by the Tax Court not to qualify for the FET marital deduction in D's estate.

On appeal the court concluded that the Tax Court's factual findings were premised on an incorrect legal standard and therefore could be reviewed and, ultimately, its holding could be reversed. The court on appeal determined that the Tax Court was wrong to regard receipt of the gifts as indicative of an implied promise that would constitute consideration and disqualify the disclaimers. Stating that the Tax Court's determination required a "subjective interpretation" that would undermine the purpose behind original adoption of §2518, which was to provide a uniform federal standard to judge qualification, the court on appeal stated that "actual consideration" is required to disqualify the disclaimer

---

[282] 104 T.C. 352 (1995), rev'd and rem'd, 124 F.3d 699 (5th Cir. 1997).

[283] Citing Treas. Reg. §25.2518-2(d)(1).

[284] S's motives might have been to use the gift tax annual exclusion and minimize GST by making inter vivos direct skip gifts rather than allowing D's estate to incur the higher direct skip tax at death, but S's attorney alleged that the sole object was merely to maximize the marital deduction to avoid incurring FET in D's estate.

§7.1.6.3

and a "mere expectation" of some future benefit would not suffice. According to the dissent, the majority opinion therefore requires a finding of consideration that is mutually and explicitly negotiated and more tangible than a mere promise.

§7.1.6.4 Specific Interest or Portion

Treas. Reg. §25.2518-3 provides that only certain partial disclaimers will be respected, and distinguishes between gifts outright and in trust. The former are easier to understand, requiring that only separable interests created by the transferor may be disclaimed, including an undivided fractional or percentage of a separable interest. Thus, for example, if a transferor bequeathed Blackacre and Greenacre to the disclaimant, either property may be disclaimed in a qualified disclaimer and the other accepted, as can a vertical slice (such as an undivided 25% interest) of either or of both properties.

On the other hand, a temporal or horizontal slice may not be disclaimed—such as rejection of a remainder interest in a gift of a fee simple absolute while retaining a life estate[285] or rejecting a few years out

---

[285] See Treas. Reg. §25.2518-3(b), upheld against challenge of invalidity in Walshire v. United States, 288 F.3d 342 (8th Cir. 2002). The converse also could not be validly disclaimed; see PLR 8908068 (fee cannot be disclaimed down to a remainder interest only). The effect of a horizontal disclaimer may not be so obvious. For example, in PLR 8617065, specific bequests were made to the testator's children and the residue was given to a QTIP marital deduction trust with a remainder to the two children, who attempted to disclaim a portion of the specific bequests, which fell into the residue in which they retained the remainder interest. Although the residuary trust remainder interest would be deemed to pass to the children from S, under §2044(c) for estate and GST purposes, for purposes of §2518 it was deemed retained by the children and precluded a qualified disclaimer.

Nor is every temporal disclaimer clear cut. For example, in TAM 9140004, D left a personal residence to two children, subject to S's right to occupy the residence. Failure to actually occupy the residence, or S's remarriage, would terminate this overriding use and the children would be entitled to immediate possession. In an effort to qualify S's interest for QTIP marital deduction treatment, the children and their descendants disclaimed all interests in the residence during S's overlife. Without discussing whether an effective disclaimer would have yielded a qualifiable interest (which is doubtful, unless failure to personally occupy the residence would permit S to rent it and keep the proceeds), the government ruled that the disclaimers were not qualified because

of a life estate or longer term of years.[286] Confusing this is the result if the fee was separated into nonmergeable interests by the transferor, in which case some but not all of those interests could be rejected in a qualified disclaimer. The example given in the regulations is a life estate to A, then a life estate to B, followed by a remainder to A (or A's estate). A could disclaim either the life estate or the remainder in this case.[287] For these purposes, a power of appointment is regarded as a separate disclaimable interest in property, meaning that the beneficiary of a life estate or a remainder, in either case coupled with a power of appointment, could validly disclaim the power and retain either other interest separately.[288]

This last illustration anticipates the more interesting situation, because powers of appointment are so seldom created outside trusts and separate portions for disclaimer purposes are more challenging in the context of transfers in trust. Under the regulations, separate assets held in a trust (much less separate interests in trust assets) cannot be the subject of a qualified disclaimer unless the disclaimed asset falls outside

---

(Footnote Continued)

they represented an impermissible effort to disclaim temporal interests not separately created by D and not in trust, in violation of Treas. Reg. § 25.2518-3(a)(1)(i).

Notwithstanding that the charitable deduction regulations treated lead and remainder interests as separable (thus allowing a charitable deduction for the lead interest alone), Estate of Christiansen v. Commissioner, 130 T.C. 1 (2008), held that a disclaimer was not qualified to the extent the disclaimed property passed to a CLT of which the disclaimant was the remainder beneficiary, holding that the remainder was not separable for qualified disclaimer purposes *and* that the disclaimer rules trumped the charitable deduction rules. The court also rejected the efficacy of a saving clause that purported to do whatever was "necessary to make the disclaimer . . . qualified" because it was neither a promise to be performed within the requisite time nor was it an unqualified and specific identification of the property being disclaimed.

[286] Treas. Reg. § 25.2518-3(a)(1)(i).

[287] Treas. Reg. § 25.2518-3(a)(1)(i), but not if B's interest was nominal and created solely to prevent the merger. Treas. Reg. § 25.2518-3(a)(1)(iv).

[288] Treas. Reg. § 25.2518-3(a)(1)(ii); cf. Treas. Reg. § 25.2518-3(d) Examples (9) and (21), the latter involving a trust and the former involving an ongoing power to make discretionary distributions of corpus from a trust, which may be retained notwithstanding disclaimer of the power of appointment, provided that the distribution power is limited by an ascertainable standard.

§ 7.1.6.4

the trust for ultimate disposition.[289] Moreover, to disclaim a separate interest in the trust requires that all such interests be disclaimed.

For example, a disclaimer of income must apply to the disclaimant's income interest in the entire trust (or in any separately created portion of the trust) or a properly defined fractional or percentile portion of the trust as defined by the disclaimer.[290] And the disclaimant cannot thereafter retain or enjoy any other income interest in the trust (or that separately defined and disclaimed portion). All because, lacking separate portions created by a transferor or properly defined by the disclaimant, the regulations preclude a disclaimer that converts what would be a fee interest by rejecting an income interest and retaining the remainder, or vice versa.[291]

Nevertheless, PLR 7913082 held that a life income beneficiary who also was remainder beneficiary under a trust established by exercise of a general power of appointment could disclaim the remainder interest but retain the income entitlement. The rationale was that the disclaimant's interests were created separately under the trust rather than by the attempted disclaimer.[292] Similarly, PLR 8309030 allowed S, who was entitled to an income interest under a trust, to disclaim a beneficial interest that granted the trustee discretion to distribute principal to S, and a nongeneral power of appointment. Meanwhile, S retained the income interest, thereby generating a QTIP trust for marital deduction

---

[289] Treas. Reg. § 25.2518-3(a)(2). See Treas. Reg. § 25.2518-3(d) Example (6) (disclaimer of all interests in stock held by a trust, with the disclaimed stock falling out of the trust and passing to the remainder beneficiary).

[290] PLR 8951041 involved a trust created by separate transfers from the disclaimant's parents. Notwithstanding that it remained in the trust, the disclaimant was permitted to disclaim property added to the trust by just one of the parents because the trust terms treated that property as a separate portion, meeting the requirements of Treas. Reg. § 25.2518-3(a)(2).

[291] Treas. Reg. §§ 25.2518-3(a)(2) and 25.2518-3(b).

[292] See Treas. Reg. §§ 25.2518-3(a)(1)(i) and 25.2518-3(d) Example (8). The Ruling should have addressed whether a merger of the life estate and remainder would occur under state law, preventing a qualified disclaimer of either interest separately. That was not an issue in PLR 200029048, which also permitted an income beneficiary to disclaim a fractional portion of a remainder interest in principal.

§7.1.6.4

qualification purposes.[293] PLR 9827010 permitted an annuitant to disclaim only a consumer price index adjustment provision but retain rights otherwise under the annuity. And several authorities allow disclaimer of a present interest in trust while retaining a future interest in the same trust.[294]

Along the same line, PLR 8321057 involved a trust paying income to a beneficiary for life, with a power of withdrawal in that beneficiary and a power in the trustee to pay principal for the beneficiary's health and maintenance. The government concluded that the beneficiary's principal entitlements were a single interest and that the beneficiary could not make a qualified disclaimer of just the power of withdrawal.[295]

It appears that the result under the regulations *might* differ, the power of withdrawal and the right to receive principal distributions apparently being regarded as separate interests under some circumstances.[296] This position seems to be reflected in PLR 9236018, which

---

[293] Accord, PLRs 9526019 and 9526018 (trust beneficiary with discretionary income and principal entitlement disclaimed inter vivos and testamentary nongeneral powers of appointment), 9104041 (income beneficiary disclaimed withdrawal power), and 8435056 (trust beneficiary with a life estate, inter vivos and testamentary powers of appointment, and a right to withdraw annually on a noncumulative basis the greater of $5,000 or 5% of the principal disclaimed the powers but not the life estate, and also retained powers as trustee and a power to select a successor cotrustee that did not constitute a retention of an interest in the trust because they were subject to fiduciary standards).

[294] In TAM 8546007, D's children made a qualified disclaimer to permit qualification of D's nonmarital trust for the marital deduction as a QTIP trust, by renouncing their right to receive discretionary distributions of principal during S's overlife. Although the children also were remainder beneficiaries of the trust, and they did not disclaim their remainder interests, disclaimer of their right to receive discretionary distributions was qualified because S's intervening interest prevented merger of their respective interests. To the same effect are PLRs 199949023, 8706066, 8637044, and 8501033. Compare the similar facts but involving an outright gift of property, producing the opposite result, in PLR 8617065, discussed in § 7.1.6.2 n. 258.

[295] See also PLR 8337071 (all income interests considered separately from all beneficial interests in principal; either could be disclaimed without disclaiming the other).

[296] Compare Treas. Reg. § 25.2518-3(d) Examples (8), (10) and (11). And cf. TAM 9610005 (beneficiary's right to receive principal distributions in trustee's discretion was separate from beneficiary's potential receipt of corpus as part of

deemed a disclaimer of a general power of appointment over a fractional portion of a trust to be qualified, with the disclaimant retaining the power over the balance of the trust (along with an income interest in the entire trust). The power of appointment was recognized as a separate asset that may be disclaimed in whole or in fractional part[297] and without the need to disclaim other interests in the trust.[298]

Disclaimers with respect to powers of appointment raise other interesting issues. For example, in addition to disclaimer of a power by the powerholder, TAM 8443005 recognized that a power of appointment may be eliminated by a qualified disclaimer executed by the objects of the power. Quaere whether all must act or whether disclaimer by a selected group of permissible objects might cause a partial disclaimer—for example, in the nature of a cut-back of a general power to a nongeneral power.

That topic is controversial and confused, TAM 8146020 holding that a powerholder's attempt to eliminate some objects of a power was not a qualified disclaimer (for purposes of qualifying for special use valuation under § 2032A) because it was not a disclaimer of the powerholder's entire interest nor of an undivided portion of that entire interest in the property. But Goudy v. United States[299] held two things of interest in the context of the intersection of § § 2041 and 2518. The first was relatively straightforward. The court concluded that a holder of a general power of appointment who makes a qualified disclaimer with respect to the power

---

(Footnote Continued)

unitrust interest distribution if current income was inadequate to fully satisfy that entitlement); PLR 9436041 and TAM 8523010 (disclaimers by trust beneficiaries of rights to receive discretionary payments of principal while beneficiaries retained rights to receive discretionary payments of income regarded as qualified notwithstanding that state law did not consider partial disclaimer of this type).

[297] Citing Treas. Reg. § 25.2518-3(a)(1)(iii).

[298] Unusual but not explained in sufficient detail to know whether it was essential to the holding was that the disclaimant also declined to serve as trustee of the trust, which may indicate that the trustee's powers to control principal were too extensive.

Following the disclaimer the trust sought to treat the fractional portion as to which the general power was disclaimed as a separate trust for GST purposes, presumably to generate a zero inclusion ratio with respect to it, which the Ruling held was not permissible. See § 11.4.8.

[299] 86-2 U.S. Tax Cas. (CCH) ¶ 13,690 (D. Or. 1986).

§7.1.6.4

is not considered to have released the power for purposes of applying the second clause of §2041(a)(2). Thus, the disclaimer was deemed to be tantamount to never having possessed the power. PLR 9104041 similarly allowed a taxpayer to disclaim a general power of appointment in the form of a power to withdraw trust corpus, again with no gift tax liability.

On the second issue in *Goudy*, the court held that it is possible to execute an effective disclaimer to cut back a general power of appointment to a nongeneral power. Involving pre-1976 law, the court permitted that cut back on the basis of Treas. Reg. §20.2041-3(d)(6), which permitted such an alteration if it was effective under local law. A similar result probably would be challenged by the government today under Treas. Reg. §§25.2518-3(a)(1)(iii) and 25.2518-3(d) Example (9).

Those authorities might be subject to challenge because the result sought does not represent a danger to the federal fisc if an effective disclaimer is deemed to relate back to the time the power was created. In that case any tax benefit that is granted in trade for creation of the power (such as the marital deduction under §2056(b)(5)) appropriately can be withheld. Nevertheless, unless a taxpayer successfully litigates the validity of the cited regulations, it appears that a cut back disclaimer of a power of appointment will not be effective.

Specifically with respect to the severable property requirement, Treas. Reg. §25.2518-3(a)(1)(ii) provides that severable property is that which can be divided into separate parts, each with its own existence completely independent of other property interests after the disclaimer. And an undivided portion must be a fraction or percentage of each and every substantial interest or right in the property and "must extend over the entire term of the disclaimant's interest."

With respect to cash bequests, PLRs 8708069 and 8113061 reveal that disclaimers of amounts in excess of a specific dollar amount or an amount determined by formula (in the earlier Ruling that amount was what the disclaimant owed the decedent) may qualify as a severable portion of a residuary bequest. More traditionally, PLR 8409089 held that disclaimers of all interests in a decedent's estate in excess of a specified dollar amount may be a qualified disclaimer. And, approached from the other direction, TAMs 8549001 and 8015014 regarded as qualified two

§7.1.6.4

disclaimers of specific dollar amounts from larger funds. But care in drafting the disclaimer is required.

For example, TAM 8240012 held that a residuary beneficiary's attempt to disclaim "all my right, title and interest in $195,000 of the residuary estate" would not be a qualified disclaimer because the assets in the residuary gift that the beneficiary wished to disclaim were not an identified or a severable portion. The TAM stated: "A qualified disclaimer can be made with respect to part of an interest in property if the part disclaimed is severable from the part accepted. Severable property is property that can be separated from property to which it is joined and that maintains a complete and independent existence after severance." A disclaimer of $195,000 from a larger cash legacy would not be prevented by this holding, nor would a disclaimer of a fraction of the residuary estate of which the numerator was $195,000 and the denominator was the value of the residuary estate. It may be that the pecuniary amount disclaimed in the Ruling would be authorized by the regulations as finally promulgated,[300] but care may be more wise than controversy to establish that proposition.

With respect to other assets, PLR 8130127 concluded that a disclaimer of so much of a devise of realty as necessary for the estate to pay the expenses of estate administration also was a severable portion from the interest not disclaimed and qualified. Consistent with the regulations,[301] PLR 8510023 also recognized as valid the disclaimer by a legatee of all but a specified number of corporate shares. The residuary beneficiary also disclaimed all of the residuary gift except a specific number of corporate shares that were in the residue. With respect to that disclaimer, the government noted that "a residuary legatee's interest . . . is regarded as an interest in severable property; therefore, a residuary

---

[300] Treas. Reg. § 25.2518-3(c). See PLR 9733006 (qualified disclaimer of that formula amount of the estate that would generate $X of tax in the decedent's estate); TAM 8515005 (qualified disclaimer by executor of deceased beneficiary did not identify the particular assets disclaimed but referred to the amount disclaimed as $A, which was what the will creating the beneficiary's interest provided by formula as the amount the beneficiary should receive; the TAM held that the disclaimer was qualified despite the failure to identify the particular assets disclaimed); TAM 8549001 (qualified disclaimer of a portion of a decedent's residuary estate equal to a specific pecuniary amount).

[301] See Treas. Reg. §§ 25.2518-3(a)(1)(ii), 25.2518-3(d) Example (1).

legatee may make a qualified disclaimer with respect to specific estate assets that may become residuary items."

Similarly, PLR 8406014 permitted a residuary beneficiary to make a qualified disclaimer of specific items of property that *might* end up in the residue, made when it was uncertain exactly what items would constitute the residuary estate. It also recognized that a residuary beneficiary may make a qualified disclaimer of a fractional share of the residue determined after taking into account the value of the specific property disclaimed, defined as a formula and based on asset values as finally determined for FET purposes. Also involving formula disclaimer planning, Estate of Christiansen v. Commissioner[302] allowed rejection of a fraction of an estate of which the numerator was the FMV of the estate in excess of a specific dollar amount.

In the context of disclaiming a pecuniary amount of noncash assets, the regulations[303] specify that the disclaimer must be defined in terms of a the FMV of those assets on the disclaimer date or must comply with the fairly representative allocation of valuation changes that are familiar requisites in marital deduction funding and GST exemption allocation regimes.[304] Furthermore, income produced by the disclaimed portion must not be accepted, with the allocation of income from a portion accepted and the portion disclaimed being determined on the basis of a fraction using the total income earned prior to the disclaimer.[305] All things considered, even disclaimer of a pecuniary amount may be most

---

[302] 130 T.C. 1 (2008) (a unanimous Tax Court reviewed opinion rejecting government arguments that such formula planning is invalid as against public policy (as discussed in § 7.2.1.1 n.15).

[303] Treas. Reg. § 25.2518-3(c), relied on in an unusual context involving a minimum required distribution and the income attributable to it, as distinct from the balance of an IRA that was disclaimed, all as discussed in § 7.1.6.3 at text accompanying n.265.

[304] See Rev. Proc. 64-19, 1964-1 C.B. 682, relating to the marital deduction, and §§ 11.4.3.2, 11.4.5.5.4, and 11.4.8 relating to GST exemption allocation and severance of trusts.

[305] See the illustrations in Treas. Reg. § 25.2518-3(d) Examples (17), (18), and (19), and PLR 200832018, involving a joint brokerage account from which the disclaimant accepted some benefits that precluded a simple rejection of the accretive share alone; both fractional and dollar amount disclaimers were required, along with income generated by each portion.

§ 7.1.6.4

efficient as a fraction of the entire fund of which the pecuniary amount (determined as a specified dollar amount or by formula) is the numerator and the denominator is the value of the total fund from which the disclaimed assets or amount is to be taken.

§7.1.6.5 Pass Without Direction

A fundamental concept in the disclaimer context is that failure to meet the §2518 requirements means that the disclaimer is a gift with federal wealth transfer tax consequences. Rather than presenting an opportunity to move wealth *without* tax, sometimes it is just as effective to make a nonqualified disclaimer as it would be to merely accept the property and make a taxable transfer (whether subject only to the gift tax or also to the GST and possibly raising FET liability). In some cases it may be *more* desirable for a transferee to simply accept the property and make a subsequent transfer, because it allows the transferee to direct where the property will pass. But if state law causes the property to pass where the transferee would want it to go anyway, then a disclaimer— qualified or otherwise—may be preferable. Because avoiding wealth transfer taxation at the transferee level is only one of several concerns (such as avoiding creditor claims or Medicaid asset spend down concerns).[306]

As illustrated with respect to marital deduction planning,[307] avoiding tax at the disclaimant level is not desirable—the gift tax being preferable to an FET in either spouse's estate. So if a direct gift by S is not possible under the terms of a marital deduction trust, a nonqualified disclaimer might be. In addition, a qualified disclaimer might result in a more expensive GST as the property passes from the original transferor to the ultimate taker, rather than a gift tax as it passes from the disclaimant to the ultimate taker.

That being the case, one key problem is if state law does not permit the disclaimer, or does not produce the desired result. One traditional illustration of this phenomenon is the historical inability to disclaim intestate realty under the common law.[308] Most states have rectified the

---

306 See §4.4.

307 See §6.2.

308 See Hardenbergh v. Commissioner, 198 F.2d 63 (8th Cir. 1952).

issue by legislation[309] that overcomes the common law property notion that the title to intestate realty must be owned at all times by some living person—in this case the intestate taker—who became the owner immediately upon the intestate decedent's death, regardless of the intestate taker's unwillingness to accept the property. To preclude a gap in title under this vision, an attempted disclaimer was instead regarded as a second transfer, after the title vested in the disclaimant. State laws that employ the relation back fiction treat the disclaimant as predeceasing the transferor and the title as passing to the next taker as of the date of the intestate decedent's death, thus avoiding this issue, but state law must authorize that treatment and the disclaimer requirements of state law must be met.

More importantly, the disclaimant must be certain how the property will pass as a result of an effective qualified disclaimer. That is, if the disclaimant is treated as predeceased, how will that cause the title to pass, and is that the anticipated result? One important aspect of this issue is application of state law antilapse statutes,[310] which may send the disclaimed property in a direction other than intended and produce results unlike those anticipated. For example, TAM 8926001 involved an individual who died intestate, leaving a spouse and four adult children as heirs at law, each entitled to 20% of the intestate estate under state law. Each child executed a qualified disclaimer of a portion of their share, which a lower state court wrongly held would pass to S (which was the intent, because increasing the marital deduction was the ultimate goal). Because the disclaimed property actually passed as though the disclaimants predeceased D, three grandchildren should have received the

---

[309] See, e.g., the Uniform Disclaimer of Property Interests Acts (1999 and 1978), Uniform Disclaimer of Transfers by Will, Intestacy, or Appointment Act, and the Uniform Disclaimer of Transfers Under Nontestamentary Instruments Act, 8A U.L.A. 159, 191, 209, and 211 (2003), respectively. Hirsch, The Uniform Disclaimer of Property Interests Act: Opportunities and Pitfalls, 28 Est. Plan. 571 (2001), is a succinct summary that includes helpful references.

[310] See §3.2.5.4 regarding application of antilapse statutes. A survivorship provision in a document that dictates where property should pass if a named beneficiary does not survive to take it also appropriately might dictate where the property should pass in the event of a disclaimer, if the antilapse result is not the preferred result. Note that it might be that the two dispositions should differ—if the named taker actually predeceases or is only deemed to have predeceased by virtue of disclaimer.

§7.1.6.5

disclaimed property and no marital deduction was available with respect to what the grandchildren should have received.[311]

A more favorable result may apply, however, under state law or the terms of any applicable document. For example, under similar facts involving a testate residuary gift to S and others, TAM 8347001 concluded that the will should be construed to pass the entire residue to the surviving residuary taker (S) to the exclusion of any representatives of the deemed predeceased disclaimants, resulting in an increased marital deduction as intended. So careful inspection of the applicable rules relating to transfer of the disclaimed property is necessary before undertaking a disclaimer.

A second aspect of this passing requisite is the frequent need for multiple disclaimers by a single disclaimant. PLR 8831032 is illustrative. Involved was a disclaimer of property bequeathed outright under a preresiduary bequest. As a result of that disclaimer the property became part of a residuary disposition that also benefited the disclaimant, who therefore also disclaimed all interests in the decedent's residuary estate, which ultimately caused the property to pass to another and provided qualified disclaimer treatment. But the disclaimants in Estate of Tatum v. United States[312] and in TAM 9417002 each failed to make such a two step disclaimer and the disclaimed bequest under a will was deemed to come

---

311 Quite similar is TAM 7947008, again involving S and four children, with the children disclaiming on their own behalf and then, because their interests did drop down to their descendants, they purported to disclaim on behalf of their children as well, which was not effective under state law. Cf. Richey v. Hurst, 798 So. 2d 841 (Fla. Dist. Ct. App. 2001) (S's disclaimer of a marital deduction trust did not cause acceleration of the trust's remainder to four nieces but instead caused the trust not to be created at all, because the marital gift was conditioned on S surviving D, which caused that trust corpus to pass to just three of those four nieces as the only beneficiaries of the residue of D's estate). Cf. Offner v. United States, 2008-1 U.S. Tax Cas. (CCH) ¶ 60,556 (W.D. Pa. 2008), in which disclaimer of a specific bequest failed to pass property pursuant to the decedent's residuary clause because an alternative bequest operating in essentially the same manner as an antilapse statute was applicable instead.

312 2010 WL 3942738 (S.D. Miss. 2010), rev'd, 436 Fed. Appx. 320 (unpub. 5th Cir. 2011).

back to the disclaimant under intestacy[313] as a result of the first disclaimer.[314] As a consequence, a gift was made when the disclaimed property was distributed as if the first level disclaimer was effective to cause the alternative beneficiaries to take the disclaimed property. That result would have been avoided if the disclaimant had made the second step disclaimer or if the document had provided that, upon disclaimer, the disclaimed property would pass to the alternate beneficiaries.

Most commonly encountered in this respect is a will or trust that does not benefit S as fully as desired to eliminate FET in D's estate. Frequently this prompts a disclaimer by beneficiaries other than S, which generates an intestacy with respect to the disclaimed property. The first disclaimer therefore must be followed by another disclaimer by all intestate takers other than S to cause the disclaimed property to pass exclusively to S, and thereby qualify for the marital deduction.[315] Closely related was PLR 200846003, in which children disclaimed interests in an IRA, causing the IRA to be payable to a trust for S, which was distributable at S's death to the children, who did not disclaim that entitlement. The disclaimer thus was not qualified and the IRA was deemed to pass to S by gift from the children, not from D, which precluded marital deduction qualification.

With respect to the state law qualification of a disclaimer, the rule often misstated is found only in the regulation applicable to interests created before 1982.[316] It specifies only that a qualified disclaimer requires that the action be effective "under applicable local law to divest

---

[313] See also Treas. Reg. § 25.2518-2(e)(3), with respect to acquiring by intestacy what was disclaimed under a document.

[314] The document provided that alternative beneficiaries would take only if the disclaimant predeceased the testator and state law did not create a presumption of being predeceased as a result of disclaimer. In *Tatum*, the controversy turned in part on whether a state law change that altered this situation was applicable, the lower court holding that it was not and the court on appeal reversed, based on the intent of the disclaimant's benefactor.

[315] See § 7.1.6 nn.222-225 and accompanying text regarding qualification for the marital deduction through disclaimer.

[316] Treas. Reg. § 25.2518-1(c)(1)(i). The regulatory provision addressing disclaimers of interests created after 1981 is "reserved" at Treas. Reg. § 25.2518-1(c)(1)(ii) for future promulgation.

§ 7.1.6.5

ownership of the disclaimed property in the disclaimant and to vest it in another." Congress enacted § 2518(c)(3) in 1981[317] to specify that a disclaimer is qualified for federal wealth transfer tax purposes if it otherwise *would* be effective under federal law absent an affirmative transfer that conveys the disclaimed property to those takers who would receive the property if the disclaimer was effective under state law.

That is, Congress recognized that some disclaimers may be effective without more under federal law but may require additional action or perhaps even an affirmative transfer to accomplish this result under state law. Not wishing to penalize disclaimants living in different states, Congress permits a disclaimant to perfect an otherwise valid federal disclaimer by directing the result that would apply if the disclaimer was effective under state law. This transfer technically violates the § 2518(b)(4) "pass without direction" requirement for a qualified federal disclaimer. Nevertheless, Congress effectively followed the example set in TAM 7951034, in which the disclaimer specified where the disclaimed interest should pass but, under controlling local law, that interest would have passed in the same direction and in the same proportions without specification. The government merely ignored the direction and regarded the disclaimer as qualified. As a consequence, flaws in state law or a disclaimer's compliance with state law might be overcome in producing a qualified disclaimer under federal law.[318]

---

[317] Effective "for transfers creating an interest in the person disclaiming" made after 1981.

[318] Treas. Reg. § 25.2518-1(c)(1)(i) clarifies that, even if the requirements of local law are not met, a qualified disclaimer under § 2518 could be made if, under applicable local law, the interest is transferred, as a result of attempting the disclaimer, to another person without any direction on the part of the disclaimant. Because this regulation is applicable only with respect to interests created before § 2518(c)(3) was enacted to address disclaimers with respect to transfers made before 1982, it leaves open the issue that was raised by In re Estate of Lee, 589 N.Y.S.2d 753 (Surr. Ct. 1992). The taxpayer, as beneficiary of a 1991 decedent's estate, complied with the federal requirements for a qualified disclaimer but did not accomplish one requisite under state law within the federal time limit. In an effort to generate an effective disclaimer under state law within the time required by federal law, the taxpayer sought an order that this final step was effective retroactively. The court refused the retroactive application because it determined that § 2518(c)(3)(B) would apply. In *Lee* the court found that the federal requirements were met because subsequent completion of the state

§ 7.1.6.6 Disclaimer Authority

Yet another issue that reveals the fragility of disclaimers as an affirmative planning device is whether a fiduciary (such as a personal representative, guardian, or conservator for a living incompetent or a decedent's executor or administrator) may make a disclaimer on behalf of the ward or decedent. By way of example, TAM 8701001 considered the application of a court appointed guardian of minor grandchildren to obtain court approval of a disclaimer on behalf of the minors with respect to a decedent's property. Coupled with disclaimers by adult children of the decedent, these disclaimers were approved in recognition of the intent to increase the marital deduction available to the decedent's estate. On the question whether these disclaimers were effective under § 2518 if a minor grandchild might, upon attaining majority, set aside the disclaimer, the government stated that the "mere fact that local law may allow [the minor grandchildren] to set aside the disclaimer under certain circumstances, when in the interest of equity, is not in itself fatal to the validity of the disclaimer."

Similarly, PLRs 8749041 and 8326110 involved personal representatives who would receive disclaimed property if they, acting in their fiduciary capacities, made disclaimers on behalf of the wards or decedents they represented. Nevertheless, the government determined that the disclaimer would be qualified for federal wealth transfer tax purposes if, under local law, the fiduciary may properly disclaim notwithstanding the conflict of interest, all despite the fact that the fiduciary would personally benefit from the disclaimer. According to both Rulings, the personal representative acting in a fiduciary capacity was different from

---

(Footnote Continued)

requirements was effective to cause the property to be transferred to the appropriate takers, which the court interpreted to mean that no retroactive application of the final step was necessary and that the disclaimer was effective under § 2518 anyway. That determination is not binding for federal tax purposes but the state court's determination that the disclaimer was effective for state law purposes should be binding for purposes of determining whether § 2518(c)(3)(B) was met and the disclaimer therefore was effective for federal purposes. Although not cited, Treas. Reg. § 25.2518-1(c)(3) Example (1) appears to be on point in its holding that a timely disclaimer under federal law that was untimely under state law but otherwise effective to cause the disclaimed property to pass to the next rightful takers is a qualified disclaimer for § 2518 purposes.

the person who would benefit personally, so there was no acceptance of benefits that would disqualify the disclaimers.[319] Deciding a similar issue in PLR 8337071, the government also ruled that S could make a qualified disclaimer notwithstanding continued activity involving administration of the property disclaimed in S's capacity as personal representative of D's estate.

On the other hand, the government has been known to challenge a court order authorizing a disclaimer on behalf of minors, on the grounds that the state court applied the wrong standard or was not the highest court of the state and therefore its determination that the disclaimer was in the best interests of the minors was in error and not binding on the federal government.[320] In addition, in any fiduciary situation, care is required to be certain that the authority exists to disclaim.

For example, TAM 8522003 involved an attempt to disclaim property otherwise passing to a decedent's estate from a prior decedent. The disclaimer was made by the person who later became the executor of the disclaiming decedent's estate, but who had not attained that status when the disclaimer was filed. According to the government, "[i]n order for previous acts of an executrix that were carried out prior to her appointment to be validated upon her appointment such acts must be beneficial in nature to the estate and within the scope of the executor's authority." Here the disclaimer was not beneficial to the estate (and usually that will be the case—the disclaimer is for the benefit of those who receive the disclaimed property and enjoy the wealth transfer tax saving attributable to the disclaimer). Instead, it was an act solely beneficial to the disclaimant. Thus, the government concluded that it was not a valid act and, correspondingly, also not a qualified disclaimer.

In addition, state law may simply not grant the authority to disclaim to a personal representative acting on behalf of an incompetent or

---

[319] See § 7.1.6.3 regarding the prohibition on accepting benefits from disclaimed property.

[320] See, e.g., Estate of Goree v. Commissioner, 68 T.C.M. (CCH) 123 (1994), nonacq., AOD 1996-001, 1996-1 C.B. 1. And see TAM 7947008 in which disclaimers on behalf of minor grandchildren would require probate court approval and, "[even] then, there is some question as to whether the minor [grand]children, upon reaching majority, could attack the settlement," indicating that the probate court approval may not be binding or effective.

decedent.[321] To illustrate, Estate of Allen v. Commissioner[322] involved spouses who died within seven months of each other. The issue was whether S's estate made an effective disclaimer of property bequeathed by D. The personal representative of S's estate, who was unable to execute the disclaimer on time because out of state and unable to return due to inclement weather, authorized the estate's attorney to execute and file the disclaimer, which was done in a timely manner. The court noted that neither § 2518 nor its regulations address the issue of who may disclaim an interest in an estate for FET purposes. The court determined that the controlling state law did not require an authorization for someone to act as agent for another to be in writing, concluding that the attorney was authorized to act for the personal representative in executing the disclaimer.

More important was the issue whether a personal representative may disclaim at all, which the court found according to a state statute patterned after the Uniform Disclaimer of Transfer by Will, Intestacy or Appointment Act. In a similar vein, PLR 9015017 concluded that a trust beneficiary's grant of a power of attorney with the specific power to disclaim on behalf of the beneficiary was a permissible form of delegation and that the attorney in fact therefore made an effective disclaimer.

---

[321] See, e.g., the pre-1990 version of UPC § 2-801, as discussed in § 13.4.4.2 n.117, which did not permit disclaimer if the transferee already had died. See also Detroit Bank & Trust Co. v. Internal Revenue Service, 80-2 U.S. Tax Cas. (CCH) ¶ 13,382 (E.D. Mich. 1980) (the individual beneficiary died slightly less than one month after the settlor of a unitrust as to which the beneficiary's personal representative tried to exercise a disclaimer, for which the court found no state law authority). In addition, many state laws would require a showing that the disclaimer is in the best interests of the ward or the decedent, which a court may conclude but that probably seldom is the case. To illustrate the lengths to which a state court may go to permit postmortem disclaimer planning to minimize federal wealth transfer taxes, see In re Estate of Kravis, 584 N.Y.S.2d 274 (Surr. Ct. 1992), which allowed a decedent's personal representative to disclaim an interest in trust to minimize FET. Notwithstanding that the disclaimer came before the decedent would have reached age 21 and therefore was timely under § 2518(b)(2)(B), there was no age 21 exception to the state law period for a timely disclaimer. The court nevertheless allowed the disclaimer for state law purposes because the decedent's untimely death was regarded as reasonable cause to deviate from the dictates of state law.

[322] 56 T.C.M. (CCH) 1494 (1989).

§ 7.1.6.6

Similarly, PLR 8911028 involved a contingent remainder in trust, payable to the settlor's siblings who survived the settlor, or their surviving issue per stirpes. One of the settlor's sisters died shortly after the settlor and the sister's executor proposed to disclaim her interest, so that it would pass directly to the sister's children, not through the sister's estate. The Ruling held that the disclaimer would be qualified if received within nine months of the settlor's death, again with the presumption that the fiduciary had this power. But in McClintock v. Scahill[323] a revocable trust instructed the trustees to distribute trust assets to a grandchildren's trust, the trustee of which disclaimed the distribution to save FET. The government questioned that trustee's authority to disclaim under state law.

Noting that state law permits a trust to disclaim but does not specify whether the trustee or beneficiaries of the trust must disclaim on behalf of the trust, the court concluded that, "[g]iven the broad powers of the trustee there is no indication either in the trust instrument or the statutory framework that the disclaimer power should not be exercised by the trustee." The court opined that its decision would not adversely affect the beneficiaries of a trust because the trustee's fiduciary status requires any decision to disclaim to be made in good faith with the best interests of the trust beneficiaries in mind. There was no claim that the trustee's disclaimer was improvident and the court held the disclaimer by the trustee was valid. So, disclaimer by a fiduciary on behalf of a decedent or a ward may be viable if the authority exists and any conflict of interest is absolved because the fiduciary acted fairly and impartially.

On the other hand, unlike the situation in which a fiduciary is acting on behalf of an individual and making a qualified disclaimer as their personal representative, sometimes a fiduciary attempts to disclaim fiduciary powers in an effort to rectify a drafting glitch, frequently in search of qualification for some tax benefit[324] and less often to avoid an unattrac-

---

[323] 530 N.E.2d 164, 166 (Mass. 1988).

[324] See authorities cited in § § 13.5.2.2 nn.31-32 and accompanying text, involving the marital deduction. Notable among them are Cleaveland v. United States, 88-1 U.S. Tax Cas. (CCH) ¶ 13,766 (C.D. Ill. 1988), Estate of Bennett v. Commissioner, 100 T.C. 42 (1993), Rev. Rul. 90-110, 1990-1 C.B. 209, and TAMs 8729002, 8605004, and 8527009. Compare § 14.3.7.1 with respect to charitable deduction qualification.

tive tax consequence to the trustee personally.[325] In these cases the predictability of success is much lower. Still, the effort may be worthwhile because, if effective, the fiduciary's action may rectify the situation without requiring beneficiaries to renounce more interests in the property than necessary just to overcome the drafting flaw.[326]

For example, notwithstanding a state statute purporting to give the fiduciary the power to renounce such powers, PLR 8409024 held that a trustee could not disclaim a contingent discretionary power to withhold income from S as the life income beneficiary. The government reached this conclusion because the trustee had no beneficial ownership interest in the power and the disclaimer would have deprived the remainder beneficiaries of their property interest in income that otherwise might be accumulated if the trustee exercised the discretion to withhold income. Thus, the disclaimer was regarded as a potential breach of the trustee's duty of impartiality.

In a similar vein, TAM 8549004 considered whether a corporate trustee of a decedent's residuary trust could disclaim the residue passing to the trust and thereby cause it to pass as intestate property. The TAM held that the corporate trustee had no authority to renounce property otherwise receivable by the trust because "the corporate fiduciary's function is to gather the trust assets, invest and preserve them, and pay income and principal according to the decedent's directions in the will . . . . [A]ny action by the corporate fiduciary to defeat the trust would be in derogation of its duties imposed by the trust."

And, finally, In re Estate of Morgan[327] denied the efficacy of a personal representative's disclaimer on behalf of a decedent because the

---

[325] See, e.g., PLR 9521032, in which a beneficiary acting as trustee was allowed to disclaim powers that would cause inappropriate FET inclusion to the individual; although the disclaimer would not negate the power for a successor trustee, it would effectively preclude this particular trustee from possessing the offending power. See also TAM 8618067 and PLRs 8815038 and 8810080, in which disclaimers by beneficiaries were effective to accomplish what a disclaimer by the trustee alone would not accomplish.

[326] See § 7.1.6.4 regarding specific separate portions and giving up future interests along with present interests, even though only a present interest is the flaw.

[327] 411 N.E.2d 213 (Ill. 1980) (under state law that authorized disclaimer by a decedent's personal representative, with leave of court).

§ 7.1.6.6

court concluded that, notwithstanding a tax benefit gleaned by that act, the decedent would not have favored the property passing as it would in the wake of that disclaimer.

§7.1.7 Incomplete Gifts

There is a final manner in which inter vivos transfers can avoid gift taxation, although almost without exception it is a deferral and not a true avoidance of tax. Because deferral of taxation typically is not advantageous from an economic perspective,[328] this final mechanism is not normally recommended unless unusual circumstances exist.

For example, financing the payment of gift tax may be problematic until liquidity needs have been resolved. Or deferral by making a gift incomplete and therefore not yet ripe for imposition of gift tax may be desirable if the value of the property involved is likely to decline in the future, making it more appropriate to subject the lower value to tax in the future than the current higher value to immediate taxation.

More unusual yet would be a transfer—such as an engagement ring or property subject to a prenuptial agreement—that is regarded by state law or the terms of transfer as conditional because contingent upon future events (in these cases, marriage) and therefore not final until a later time when more attractive results are available—for example, the gift tax marital deduction that flows from completion of the gift upon marriage.

Another situation that might beg for deferral is if there is an expectation of a higher basis being generated without adverse tax consequence. An example might involve a principal personal residence that might, upon an expected sale, generate less than the maximum capital gain that is avoidable under §121, followed by a gift of the proceeds with no built in capital gain tax liability.

Before beginning on a short discussion of when a gift is complete or incomplete for wealth transfer tax purposes, it is important to underscore a notion that is counterintuitive but well known and accepted by initiates of the intersecting worlds of wealth transfer and income taxation. There is no pari materia between the estate, gift, and income tax rules that may

---

[328] See §6.2.

apply.[329] Although reality almost always is consistent with the logic that an inter vivos transfer will not avoid both gift and FET, there is no other seemingly logical interplay among these taxes that is predictable. For example, an inter vivos transfer may be regarded as complete and taxable for gift tax purposes and yet trigger FET inclusion at death.[330] And the income from transferred property either can or will not be taxable to the transferor, without regard to whether the transfer was complete or incomplete for wealth transfer tax purposes.[331] So it is imperative to analyze each element in the taxation of inter vivos transfers separately, without relying on the consequence known under another arm of the tax law and extrapolating to a predictable result. Often it is not that easy.

A transfer may be incomplete for gift tax purposes for a variety of reasons, most relating to retained powers over transferred property that

---

[329] Statements to the contrary in Estate of Sanford v. Commissioner, 308 U.S. 39 (1939) (Congress did not intend the gift tax test for completeness to differ from that for FET purposes), notwithstanding. See Smith v. Shaughnessy, 318 U.S. 176, 178-179 (1943): "As we said [in *Sanford*], the gift and estate tax laws are closely related [but] . . . the taxes are not 'always mutually exclusive,' and . . . Congress plainly pointed out that 'some' of the 'total gifts subject to gift taxes . . . may be included for estate tax purposes. . . .' H.R. Rep. No. 708, 72d Cong. 1st Sess. 45."

[330] Subject to the purge and credit rules of §§ 2001(b) (flush language) and 2001(b)(2). See § 7.3. A good illustration of this phenomena is contained in the discussion in § 7.1.7.1 relating to creditor rights and whether a gift that is complete during life can be includible at death in a spendthrift trust for the trust settlor's own benefit.

[331] For example, § 2035(a) could apply to cause FET inclusion of property transferred by completed gift inter vivos, with no grantor trust income tax exposure during the balance of the transferor's life. It is less likely that another FET string provision could apply at death, however, without grantor trust income tax exposure following the gift. Regarding transfers that are completed gifts with no FET exposure at death, but as to which the grantor trust rules still tax the income to the transferor, consider the many grantor trust provisions that are triggered by an interest or power in the transferor's spouse, as discussed throughout § 5.11. And see Talge v. United States, 229 F. Supp. 836 (W.D. Mo. 1964) (trust settlor taxable on trust income but gift on creation of the trust was complete for wealth transfer tax purposes and not at higher values as distributions were made from the trust in the future).

§ 7.1.7

are exercisable without the consent of an adverse party.[332] It also may be attributable to retained enjoyment of some but less than all of the transferred property (which may result in a transfer that is either entirely incomplete or complete in part—such as a gift of the remainder following a retained life estate—and incomplete in part—such as the income interest that is shared by the transferor and other named beneficiaries, all entitled to receive income in the trustee's discretion).

Usually retained powers are intentional and obvious—as with a transfer into a trust as to which the transferor has retained the power of revocation or appointment.[333] Sometimes retained powers are less obvi-

---

[332] See Treas. Reg. § § 25.2511-2(b) through 25.2511-2(e) for illustrations of powers retained by a transferor that will cause a transfer to be incomplete. For example, a gift is not complete to the extent the transferor has a power to affect the beneficial interests under the trust, even if it is exercisable only in conjunction with a trustee or other nonadverse party. Treas. Reg. § 25.2511-2(e); Camp v. Commissioner, 195 F.2d 999 (1st Cir. 1952); Latta v. Commissioner, 212 F.2d 164 (3d Cir. 1954); Rev. Rul. 58-395, 1958-2 C.B. 398; PLR 8637043 (power just to veto trustee distributions and allocation of principal and income between beneficiaries made transfer incomplete for gift tax purposes; consequently, distributions of income and principal were taxable as completed gifts when made rather than on trust creation).

[333] Some transactions are regarded as a present gift that is complete notwithstanding retention of a testamentary power of appointment, if the power is contingent on events over which the transferor has no control. See, e.g., TAM 8546001 and PLRs 9112007, 9105030, 8905045, 8849067, and 8815005 (all involving pre-§ 2072 GRITs). Otherwise, an all events testamentary power of appointment typically will make a transfer incomplete. See Treas. Reg. § 25.2511-2(b). However, ILM 201208026 reveals a potential trap in the incomplete gift regulation. The taxpayer relied on a retained testamentary power to make transfers into the trust incomplete for gift tax purposes but the taxpayer did not retain a right to trust enjoyment until death. The ILM held that the value of rights in the trust that were not subject to change by exercise of the testamentary power was a completed gift on creation. The testamentary power only precluded the transfer from being a competed gift of the remainder interest in the trust. (The ILM also regarded the *testamentary* power as a "retained interest" that was ignored for gift taxation, due to § 2702, meaning that the value of the gift was the full fair market value of the property transferred into the trust.)

Note that Treas. Reg. § 25.2511-2(b) thus contains a gap in the government's treatment of the competed gift issue. It provides that:

if a donor transfers property to another in trust to pay the income to the donor or accumulate it in the discretion of the trustee, and the donor retains a testamentary power to appoint the remainder among his descend-

§7.1.7

ous—as with a gift causa mortis, which is incomplete for gift tax purposes because it automatically is revoked if the transferor survives the apprehended peril.[334] As a middle ground, there may be transfers in which powers are implied—as for example if the transferor allegedly did not intend to make a legitimate transfer but only engaged in the transaction to deceive creditors or a spouse in a divorce action,[335] or had an oral

---

(Footnote Continued)

> ants, no portion of the transfer is a completed gift. On the other hand, if the donor had not retained the testamentary power of appointment, but instead provided that the remainder should go to X or his heirs, the entire transfer would be a completed gift.

The gap exists if a transfer is made with retained testamentary power but *without* retained personal enjoyment. The ILM states that the power alone does not make the entire transfer incomplete. To make a transfer that is not yet a completed gift while avoiding grantor trust income taxation to the donor, the donor may retain a § 674(b)(5)(A) nonfiduciary power to distribute corpus among other trust beneficiaries, limited by a "reasonably definite standard." See § 5.11.5 n.115 and accompanying text. The result will be total avoidance of completed gift treatment on creation and avoidance of defective grantor trust taxation of trust income.

[334] Rev. Rul. 74-365, 1974-2 C.B. 324. See § 1.3.1 n.6.

[335] See, e.g., Estate of Saunders v. Commissioner, 58 T.C.M. (CCH) 282 (1989) (involved was whether property transferred to the transferor's parent to keep it away from the transferor's spouse and children was includible in the parent's gross estate at death, but the more immediate question for this discussion was whether the transferor made a gift to the parent on the original transfer, as to which the opinion reveals quite a struggle in deciding the case; because the parent never lived on the property or leased it to anyone, instead allowing the transferor to continue to reside there, the parent's estate contended that it was held in constructive trust for the transferor, but the court concluded that the parent had full title, that the purpose of the transfer would not have been achieved if a constructive trust had been created, and focused on the fact that no evidence was introduced regarding who paid insurance premiums or paid and claimed the income tax deduction for property taxes, which the court presumed to mean that the parent made those payments and all of which indicated that the parent was the true owner of the property); Warner v. Commissioner, 49 T.C.M. (CCH) 5 (1984) (to keep property from being reached in a divorce action the transferor's parent established a trust using property that originated with the transferor; notwithstanding the express terms of the trust the oral agreement with the trustee was that the transferor would have complete control of the trust, which the court held to mean that the transferor did not make a completed gift to the parent for gift tax purposes).

§ 7.1.7

understanding that differed from the terms of the transfer.[336] Other reasons may relate to a failure to comply with state law requirements for making an effective transfer of property[337] or, often more important, questions of the timing of an effective gift.

For example, timing is key to the proper value or effect of an inter vivos transfer. An excellent illustration of the valuation aspect relates to gifts of options, as when a corporation compensates an employee with a transferable option to purchase stock of the employer corporation in the future at a designated striking price.[338] The value of an option may be higher if the option period is shorter (which reduces the volatility of the

[336] See, e.g., Publicker v. Miles, 55-1 U.S. Tax Cas. (CCH) ¶ 11.531 (E.D. Pa. 1955) (transferor reserved a right to alter or revoke a trust only with the consent of a beneficiary who therefore was an adverse party, making the transfer a completed gift based on the express terms of the trust, but there was ample evidence that the transferor and the beneficiary had an oral understanding regarding the retained powers that caused the court to hold that the gift was incomplete, which result is correct if the oral understanding was enforceable by the transferor if the beneficiary declined to consent to the transferor's wishes).

[337] See § 6.5 regarding delivery requirements. But consider Wells Fargo Bank New Mexico v. United States, 319 F.3d 1222 (10th Cir. 2003), rejecting a notion that state law donative intent was lacking and therefore precluded an effective inter vivos gift for federal transfer tax purposes, the taxpayer attempting to overcome failure to timely make an inter vivos QTIP election by alleging that the QTIP trust was includible in the taxpayer's estate at death and the election to qualify for the marital deduction therefore could be made then.

[338] See, e.g., Rev. Proc. 98-34, 1998-1 C.B. 983, and Rev. Rul. 98-21, 1998-1 C.B. 975 (proper time and method for wealth transfer tax valuation of nonstatutory compensatory stock options that are not publicly traded but the *stock* available by exercise is, the Procedure itemizing six valuation factors that are similar to those established by the Financial Accounting Standards Board Statement of Financial Accounting Standards No. 123 on Stock-Based Compensation (FAS 123), including the trading price of the underlying stock on the valuation date, the exercise price under the option, the expected life of the option, the expected price volatility of the underlying stock, the expected dividends on the underlying stock, and the risk-free interest rate for the remaining term of the option); and see Rev. Rul. 80-186, 1980-2 C.B. 280 (option to purchase realty, the FMV on the date the option was given of the property that may be acquired by exercise of the option being a function of striking price, length of the option period, and volatility of the market for the option property). Additional discounts, such as for lack of marketability for the option, are appropriate only to the extent the listed factors do not subsume the same elements that would inform traditional valuation adjustments.

underlying stock price), and the later in time the gift is deemed to be completed (if the value of the stock relative to the striking price has been rising). This means that there is an inherent incentive for the government to delay completion of the gift and to artificially shorten the option period. In either case value therefore may be a function of when the gift of an option is regarded as complete. Thus, the government's position is that the gift cannot be complete while the option is unenforceable, as for example if the option is contingent until the employee performs services for a certain period of time.[339] However, the fact that the employer may alter or terminate the agreement or the employee may forfeit the option by quitting employment is not regarded as making the transfer of an option an incomplete gift.[340]

A transferor also must be certain to perform an effective act of inter vivos transfer. It is not adequate to have the intent to make a transfer if not supported by timely inter vivos action.[341] In the context of stock transfers, for example, the completion of an inter vivos gift is a function of complying with the regulations. A gift is effective on the first to occur

---

[339] Rev. Rul. 98-21, 1998-1 C.B. 975 (option that was not exercisable until the transferor performed additional services was transferred before those services were performed but the option was not deemed to be enforceable until those prerequisite services were performed, making the gift complete at that later time and requiring valuation at that later time as well, unreduced by the prior contingency of potential nonperformance, and altering every valuation factor except the option price itself).

[340] See, e.g., Rev. Rul. 98-21, 1998-1 C.B. 975, and PLR 9514017 (gift of an option to purchase employer stock was complete upon transfer without regard to whether employer might alter the agreement or the transferor might terminate the option by quitting employment), citing Estate of Smead v. Commissioner, 78 T.C. 43 (1982) (ability to terminate employment-provided group term life insurance by quitting employment is not an incident of ownership for § 2042(2) purposes, nor would it attract FET inclusion under § 2038(a)(1) or cause a gift of the insurance to be incomplete).

[341] See, e.g., Naylor v. Unites States, 81-2 U.S. Tax Cas. (CCH) ¶ 13,416 (S.D. Tex. 1979) (decedent periodically cancelled notes and filed tax returns to report those gifts but died before doing so for the last two calendar years of life; according to the court, the decedent undoubtedly would have verified the intent to cancel the balance due on additional notes by filing appropriate gift tax returns but, not having completed the formalities for completing those gifts the mere intent to cancel the notes was inadequate to preclude inclusion of the remaining notes in the decedent's gross estate).

of delivery to the transferee of an endorsed stock certificate or reregistration of the stock on the books of the corporation's transfer agent.[342] A

---

[342] Treas. Reg. § 25.2511-2(h); see Rev. Rul. 54-135, 1954-1 C.B. 205 (transferor instructed broker to transfer stock and at the same time informed the transferee of the gift, but the transfer was not effective until recorded on the corporation's books); Rev. Rul. 54-554, 1954-2 C.B. 317 (gift of stock is complete on the date the transferor endorses the stock certificate and delivers it to transferee); Richardson v. Commissioner, 49 T.C.M. (CCH) 67 (1984) (gift of stock to charity was completed in the year in which the stock certificates were delivered to the transferee); cf., Estate of Novetzke v. Commissioner, 55 T.C.M. (CCH) 1116 (1988) (gift of bonds physically delivered to a transferee occurred at the time of delivery, not when they were endorsed by the transferee, because the transferee had an enforceable right to have any requisite endorsement supplied); Phillips v. Plastridge, 179 A. 157 (Vt. 1935) (completed gift during transferor's life notwithstanding that the transferor, who had stock issued in the name of a child, failed to deliver the new stock certificates before death).

But see Autin v. Commissioner, 102 T.C. 760 (1994), rev'd, 97-1 U.S. Tax Cas. (CCH) ¶ 60,265 (5th Cir. 1997) (taxpayer retained title to stock notwithstanding purported transfer to child pursuant to a practice in Louisiana known as a counterletter; on appeal the court found that the taxpayer's "simulation"—under civil law, "a collusive effort consisting of a visible act that is artificial"—in the form of purporting to retain title and representing to the world that the taxpayer was the true stockholder, was not fraudulent and that the counterletter bestowed real rights on the child at the time it was executed, long before title to the stock formally was transferred, making the gift taxable at the date of the counterletter and not thereafter); and Keller v. United States, 2009-2 U.S. Tax Cas. (CCH) ¶ 60,579 (S.D. Tex. 2009), which was a taxpayer victory involving seriously incomplete planning that sought to transfer a $300 million pool of cash, certificates of deposit, and bonds. The taxpayer signed a partnership agreement in her capacity as both general and limited partner, acting individually and as trustee of two trusts, but there was no funding of the partnership prior to death (no partnership document even indicated the required or anticipated contributions), and a seed money deposit check for the corporate general partner was unsigned when the decedent died. The facts were such that, when the decedent died, "those who had been working in the formation of the Partnership essentially stood down, ceasing all activity with respect to the Partnership, the corporate general partner, and the transfer of assets. At this time, no assets had been formally transferred to the Partnership . . . ." A year after death the team of advisors "resumed their efforts with respect to formally establishing" the partnership, and the court concluded that "[d]espite the fact [the decedent] passed away before certain formalities were observed, the Court finds it clear that, at the time of her death, she intended" certain assets to be partnership assets and certain transactions to be executed.

§7.1.7

gift of realty may require recordation of the deed.[343] And gifts by check now are regarded by the government as complete on the *earlier* of the date on which the donor relinquishes all power to change the disposition (e.g., by giving a cashier's check or a form of check that cannot be the subject of a stop payment order) or the date when the donee cashes the check, deposits it, presents it for payment, or otherwise negotiates it. Negotiation, not payment, completes the gift, *if* (1) the check is paid when first presented, (2) the donor is still alive when the check is paid, (3) the donor intended to make a gift, (4) delivery of the check was

(Footnote Continued)

The *Keller* court concluded under Texas law that the agreement was enforceable. The critical issue was proving that there was an agreement among the partners. According to the court's conclusion of law, "well-established principles of Texas law provide that the intent of an owner to make an asset partnership property will cause the asset to be property of the partnership." Even though the partnership did nothing for the hiatus year and the decedent was the only party involved in the creation of the family partnership, the court found that a valid partnership existed because "[the decedent], as trustee of [the two contributing trusts], and as the initial sole owner of the general partner, represented all of the partners, and therefore her intent was the intent of all the partners at the time of the Partnership's formation."

[343] Estate of Whitt v. Commissioner, 751 F.2d 1548 (11th Cir. 1985) (gift of realty not complete until recordation because a bona fide purchaser of land is protected against an unrecorded deed of which the purchaser has no knowledge); TAM 9513001 (taxpayer—who purported to sell property retained title for approximately eight years and collected all income and government subsidies, lived on the property, and paid taxes and other obligations with respect to the property—did not effectively transfer the property until possession and title were relinquished; values at that time controlled for gift tax purposes and alleged loan forgiveness in the interim was ineffective to reduce purported purchase money loans on the ostensible sale when the transfer purportedly occurred); TAM 8901004 (deeds in the hands of the transferor's attorney were subject to recall by the transferor because the attorney was the transferor's agent and gifts of these parcels were not completed until they passed to the control of the transferee).

But see Chebatoris v. Moyer, 757 N.W.2d 212, 215, 216, 217 (Neb. 2008) (a revocable inter vivos trust was deemed funded with realty listed on an Appendix to the trust, with no formal deed or other conveyance, stating that under state law "[a] conveyance of land may occur in a document that is not formally drafted as a deed," that "any writing may be effective as a legal conveyance if it names the grantor and grantee, contains words of grant, describes the land, and is delivered," and that "it is not necessary to transfer legal title to the trustee when the settlor is the sole trustee . . . ."; that the trust agreement was not filed with the register of deeds until after the trust settlor's death was deemed irrelevant).

§7.1.7

unconditional, and (5) the check was cashed, deposited, presented for payment, or otherwise negotiated in the same calendar year in which completed gift treatment is sought and within a reasonable time after issuance of the check.[344]

Often a transferor's retention of interests in transferred property causes an inter vivos transfer to be incomplete for gift tax purposes.[345] But a transfer in trust with a retained interest may nevertheless be subject to gift tax if the trustee is merely authorized to distribute income or principal to the transferor in the trustee's sole and broad discretion,[346] if it *also* is the case that the transferor's creditors cannot reach the trust in satisfaction of any unpaid claims against the transferor. A number of related propositions may be true in such a case. One is that the transferor's transfer into the trust is a completed gift for gift tax purposes (whereas if these conditions are not met the transferor's retained interest will preclude completed gift treatment, at least with respect to some

---

[344] Rev. Rul. 96-56, 1996-2 C.B. 161; see also Estate of Metzger v. Commissioner, 38 F.3d 118 (4th Cir. 1994), articulating slightly different standards upon which the Ruling is based. Rosano v. United States, 245 F.3d 212 (2d Cir. 2001) (gifts by checks written before death but not presented for payment until after death were ineffective); Estate of Newman v. Commissioner, 111 T.C. 81 (1998), aff'd per curiam, 99-2 U.S. Tax Cas. (CCH) ¶ 60,358 (D.C. Cir. 1999), applied these standards and found that gifts made by a child (under a power of attorney that may not have been durable, or as joint owner of the checking account) failed to remove the gifted property from the decedent's estate because the decedent died before payment of the checks.

[345] See, e.g., Estate of Vander Weele v. Commissioner, 27 T.C. 340 (1956) (trustees authorized to pay settlor such amounts of income and principal as desirable for the settlor's comfortable well being and enjoyment); Rev. Rul. 62-13, 1962-1 C.B. 180 (trustee had very broad discretionary power over income and principal distributions to the settlor).

[346] Trustee discretion never can be so broad as to be unenforceable under state law, notwithstanding what the document says, because a fiduciary cannot be completely absolved of fiduciary duties. The intent of such provisions (as it is here also) is to preclude any assertion that the beneficiary has greater rights than those meant to be granted by the trust. See, e.g., the discussion of SNTs in § 4.4. For purposes of this discussion, "sole" implies that no one (such as a trust protector) other than the trustee is authorized to exercise discretion and "broad" implies that any standard by which the trustee is guided is sufficiently broad that the transferor's "entitlement" is too nebulous to quantify.

portion of the trust).[347] A second is that, absent creditor rights to reach the trust, there will be no §2038(a)(1) risk of inclusion of the trust property in the estate of the transferor at death. And a third is that §2036(a)(1) inclusion of the trust property in the estate of the transferor at death also may be avoided.

§7.1.7.1 Creditor Rights and Incomplete Gifts

This topic is interesting because at least 20% of the states have made it possible—in varying degrees—to create a self-settled trust for the benefit of the settlor and prevent creditors from reaching the trust corpus. Statutes in these states deviate from the common law relating to spendthrift trust provisions,[348] because they purport to permit creditor protection with respect to interests created in *any* beneficiary, including the settlor of a trust.[349]

---

[347] See Rev. Rul. 77-378, 1977-2 C.B. 347 (broad powers given to trustee, allegedly in its absolute and uncontrolled discretion, to invade trust income and principal for the grantor's benefit, all deemed insufficient to render the gift incomplete if the grantor's interest in the trust is unenforceable and creditors may not reach the trust assets); Rev. Rul. 54-538, 1954-2 C.B. 316 (gift on trust creation may be complete to the extent the standard for distributions is ascertainable and the amount required annually can be established and valued as an annuity, resulting in any amount of the trust in excess of that retained entitlement being regarded as a completed gift); TAM 8752064 (transfer in trust under which transferor reserved the right to income for life and the trustees were directed to distribute principal in whatever amounts deemed proper for the transferor's comfort, maintenance, and support in the transferor's accustomed style of living; the power of invasion was deemed limited by an ascertainable standard—notwithstanding the term "comfort," which would not be ascertainable for §2041 purposes, as noted in §12.3.2.4 n.58 and accompanying text—so there was a completed gift only to the extent the value of the trust exceeded the value of what the transferor reserved). See also Estate of Gramm v. Commissioner, 17 T.C. 1063 (1951) (entire transfer regarded as an incomplete gift because the trust was so modest that complete invasion of corpus for the settlor's benefit was probable).

[348] See §4.1.4 n.52 and accompanying text.

[349] Each statute contains similar (but not identical) exceptions to their expansive application of spendthrift protection to the settlor if (1) the transfer into the trust violates the Uniform Fraudulent Transfers Act limitation on fraudulent transfers, (2) the trust is revocable by the settlor (in Alaska "without the consent of a person who has a substantial [adverse] beneficial interest"), (3) the settlor retained a *mandatory* income or principal distribution interest, or (4) the settlor

These statutes are intriguing because limited jurisprudence suggests that a transfer into such a trust constitutes a completed gift, notwithstanding retained enjoyment, if creditors cannot reach the trust corpus. The allure of this opportunity is if there is no subsequent FET inclusion at death. The taxpayer would garner benefits attributable to incurring the gift tax upon a transfer of property into a trust, while retaining enjoyment (in the trustee's discretion) for the balance of the settlor's life, all with no FET cost.[350]

The suggestion of this tax objective should warn that it is not to be expected, because it certainly is not the intent of existing law to permit accelerated and complete wealth transfer tax, coupled with retained enjoyment. Moreover, the most important question is *not* whether the gift on creation of such a trust is complete. The easy answer to that insignificant question is that the government is happy to take the taxpayer's money earlier rather than later. If the taxpayer is willing to report a completed gift on creation, the government is not likely to object. The essential question is whether payment of gift tax on creation also means that the transfer is sufficiently complete to avoid FET inclusion at death. It is that second and essential proposition that is not adequately answered.[351]

Estate of German v. United States[352] may be the most commonly cited decision on this issue. It was a suit for refund of FET, apparently (but not expressly noted) paid because the government asserted that §§ 2036 and 2038 required inclusion of trust property at the settlor's death. Involved was a discretionary income and principal trust, requiring

---
(Footnote Continued)

was in arrears in making child support payments or is indebted for alimony, defrauded creditors by representing trust assets as personal property, is liable to a tort judgment creditor, and so on. In addition, under various alternatives, creditors who seek to reach trust assets under one of these exceptions must do so within a specified period after the transfer in trust. In some cases these provisions require that some assets are deposited in the state and that they be administered by a resident individual or corporate fiduciary.

[350] See generally § 7.3.4 regarding the FET inclusion of property transferred during life with retained enjoyment until death.

[351] See § 7.3.4.2 and particularly the discussion of Rev. Rul. 2004-64, 2004-2 C.B. 7, with respect to that issue and whether the government's position has changed.

[352] 85-1 U.S. Tax Cas. (CCH) ¶ 13,610 (Ct. Cl. 1985).

the consent of an adverse party (the remainder beneficiary) for distributions to the settlor. No gift was reported on creation and the FET return likewise did not include the property transferred to the trust. The government failed to establish whether creditors could reach the settlor's interest and the estate ultimately conceded that it owed gift tax on creation. Thus, the reported decision—which only denied the government's motion for summary judgment—was not a determination on the FET merits.[353] The court's discussion was of the easy gift tax completed transfer aspect and the issue of state law.[354]

Two additional cases, Outwin v. Commissioner[355] and Paolozzi v. Commissioner,[356] also frequently are referenced. In *Outwin* the trustee had discretion to distribute income or principal to the settlor, with the approval of an adverse party (the settlor's spouse, who was a secondary beneficiary). Finding that state law allowed creditors to reach the trust property, the court concluded that the transfer into trust was not a completed gift for gift tax purposes. *Paolozzi* also involved the gift tax and also held that retention of discretionary income was adequate to prevent a completed gift because, under local law, creditors had full recourse to the full trust income and, "[t]herefore, petitioner . . . can at any time realize all of the economic benefit of the income accruing to the trust during her lifetime by the simple expedient of borrowing money or otherwise becoming indebted, and then relegating the creditor to the trust income for reimbursement."[357]

Several other cases showcase the seeming inconsistency of the government asserting completed gift status during life and FET inclusion at death. For example, in Estate of Wells v. Commissioner[358] the

---

[353] The summary judgment determination did put the matter to rest for the parties, who presumably settled thereafter. There is no record of the resolution of the controversy after the government's motion for summary judgment was denied.

[354] Under similar facts TAMs 199917001 and 8350004 concluded that no gift tax was payable on creation and § 2038 inclusion should apply at death, presumably revealing how the government would prefer such a case to be resolved if only one tax—gift or estate—can be imposed.

[355] 76 T.C. 153 (1981).

[356] 23 T.C. 182 (1954).

[357] 23 T.C. at 186.

[358] 42 T.C.M. (CCH) 1305 (1981).

§ 7.1.7.1

decedent created a discretionary income and principal trust and filed a gift tax return, using the former gift tax lifetime exemption to shelter creation of the trust from gift tax.

Similarly, Estate of Skinner v. United States[359] highlights the lack of parity between the gift tax and FET, here in which the government asserted during the taxpayer's life that creation of the trust was a completed gift of the full value of the trust corpus because the retained life enjoyment was not susceptible to accurate determination, and then successfully included the full value of the trust at death.[360] That result negates the suggestion that making a completed inter vivos gift is inconsistent with FET inclusion.

Estate of Uhl v. Commissioner[361] also espoused the frequently stated but essentially bankrupt notion that the estate and gift tax results should be applied consistently (in pari materia).[362] The court concluded that there should be no FET inclusion in *Uhl* because the settlor incurred gift tax on creation of a trust,[363] and only by indirection did the court reveal that there was a discretionary income interest in that gift-taxed portion of the trust.

Among the government's pronouncements on this issue, Revenue Ruling 76-103[364] is most directly relevant to the gift tax completeness question on creation of a discretionary income trust. It properly held that the existence of creditor rights prevented a completed gift. Consistent with it PLR 9837007 concluded that an Alaskan trust with creditor protection and discretionary income or principal distribution authority constituted a completed gift on creation.

An additional PLR entailed special facts that may have influenced the result articulated. PLR 9332006 involved a discretionary entitlement and the absence of creditor rights. It concluded that creation was a

---

359 316 F.2d 517 (3d Cir. 1963).

360 With the appropriate §2001(b)(2) credit for the gift tax previously collected, and purge from the adjusted taxable gifts base under the flush language of §2001(b).

361 241 F.2d 867 (7th Cir. 1957).

362 See text accompanying §7.1.7 n.330.

363 With respect to that portion of the corpus that was not producing a retained $100 per month annuity payable to the settlor.

364 1976-1 C.B. 293. See also PLR 8040039.

completed gift and may have been informed by the government's desire to impose wealth transfer tax immediately because the facts involved offshore trusts and the government may have felt that there was a good risk that it would not be able to collect FET at the settlor's death.[365]

§7.1.7.2 Timing for Completion

Many gifts made by individuals inter vivos also are incomplete by virtue of the fact that the transferor was unaware that a gift was made. Those unanticipated gifts often occur by indirection. In addition, some gifts are not meant to be effective immediately—these future interests or future gifts also may be incomplete. These categories of gifts are discussed here because they provide good illustrations of when a gift may be deemed to occur and when it becomes complete for gift tax purposes.

For example, a right of first refusal or buy-sell agreement may generate inter vivos gift consequences by virtue of a *failure* to exercise rights to acquire property for less than full and adequate consideration in money or money's worth. In these cases execution of the agreement is not the gift. Instead, it is allowing the right to expire when presented, with completion occurring when the right lapses. To illustrate, in PLR 9117035 two individuals (A and B) had a right of first refusal buy-sell agreement exercisable during their respective lifetimes, as well as at death. B agreed not to exercise the purchase right under the buy-sell agreement if A transferred stock with a FMV of almost $600,000 to an ESOP, notwithstanding that B could have acquired A's stock for just under $150,000. The government held that B's failure to exercise this right was tantamount to a gift at that time by B to A of the almost $450,000 differential.

The Ruling made special note of the fact that B could afford to exercise the right, including by borrowing to finance the purchase if

---

[365] That FET noninclusion result may be bolstered by Rev. Rul. 2004-64, 2004-2 C.B. 7, as discussed in §7.3.4.2. In a similar vein, see PLR 8037116, which involved a nonresident alien who created a trust with totally discretionary income and principal distribution authority in a trustee who was deemed not subject to creditor rights. It did not address the gift tax issue but concluded that FET inclusion was not applicable at death.

necessary.[366] TAM 9315005 also found an imputed gift because the donor could control a family corporation and could have caused the corporation to redeem the stock of a deceased shareholder at a bargain price. The donor instead allowed the deceased shareholder's estate to transfer a portion of that stock to the donor's child, which was deemed a gift by the donor to the child equal to the benefit the corporation would have generated by the bargain purchase, multiplied by the donor's percentage ownership of the corporation.

In both of these cases it is notable that the gifts did not occur when the agreements were executed. TAMs 8612001 and 8140016 confirm that no completed gift is made at the time of execution of a cross-purchase buy-sell agreement, notwithstanding that the purchase price is less than FMV.[367]

In a different vein, sometimes a gift occurs when a loan is made (because enforcement never is intended)[368] or from time to time under § 7872 (due to below market interest rates).[369] But in other cases a gift occurs due to inaction—for example, by allowing the statute of limitation to run and thereby preclude enforcement of a loan, as was the case involving an uncalled demand loan in Estate of Lang v. Commissioner.[370] In a related but slightly less obvious sense the same gift of forgone income may occur in a case like that presented by TAM 8403010, in which dividends were omitted on preferred stock and paid to common shareholders instead. Because the preferred shareholder was legally entitled to dividends, the TAM held that the failure to insist on payment of those dividends was a gift to the owners of the common stock. Presumably that gift occurred when the right to object to the failure to pay expired or, if the owner of the preferred stock owned a control interest, when the dividend payment was made—as if the dividend had

---

[366] See also PLR 8839059, discussed in § 12.0 n.17 and accompanying text, which held that lapse of a similar power was a § 2514 taxable event as the lapse of a general power of appointment.

[367] Although the later TAM suggested that the government would assert a gift tax liability under an enforceable agreement if the facts were such that any consideration received by either party by virtue of execution of the agreement did not equal the value given thereby, which probably would not be the case.

[368] See § 6.5.2.

[369] See § 6.3.3.5.

[370] 613 F.2d 770 (9th Cir. 1980).

§ 7.1.7.2

been paid to the controlling shareholder and then given to the common shareholders.

Again just slightly removed from that gift was the situation in Snyder v. Commissioner,[371] in which the taxpayer's personal holding company was authorized to issue three classes of stock: Class A preferred, Class B preferred, and common. In a classic estate freeze, the taxpayer transferred common stock to an irrevocable inter vivos trust for great-grandchildren and retained Class A preferred stock. No Class B preferred stock was issued but it could be obtained by conversion of the Class A preferred. The only difference between those classes of preferred stock relevant to the case was that Class A preferred was entitled to a *non* cumulative annual dividend and the Class B preferred was entitled to a *cumulative* dividend of the same amount. The corporation actually paid lower dividends on the Class A preferred than it would have paid on the Class B preferred, and the court accepted the government's theory that this difference constituted a gift attributable to the taxpayer's failure to exercise the conversion privilege. That gift was deemed to equal the amount by which the common stock increased in value and was deemed to occur when the taxpayer no longer could obtain those dividends through conversion.

As articulated in TAM 9301001, which involved very similar facts, the taxpayer made continuing gifts by failing to exercise control over the corporation or to convert the preferred stock to benefit from any appreciation in the value of the corporation attributable to the failure to pay higher dividends. The measure of that gift was determined to be "the difference between the annual dividend that [the corporation] was capable of paying for the preferred shares (up to a rate commensurate with prevailing market rates for preferred shares) and the . . . annual dividend that was actually paid."[372]

---

[371] 93 T.C. 529 (1989).

[372] See also TAM 8029001 (settlor of short term trust could control flow of dividends to it and was deemed to make a completed gift each time dividends were declared and became payable to third party beneficiaries out of the short term trust). In TAM 8726005 the taxpayer gave common stock to children and retained preferred stock. Subsequently the taxpayer agreed that no dividends would be declared on the preferred stock until certain installment loans were repaid. Drawing an analogy to interest free loans, the government opined that this was a gift to the holders of the common stock who acquired the increase in

§ 7.1.7.2

Quaere whether these cases can be distinguished from the case in TAM 8723007, in which the taxpayer possessed voting control of a corporation through ownership of noncumulative preferred stock. Notwithstanding the existence of legitimate reasons for failing to declare a dividend on the preferred stock, the TAM held that this failure constituted a gift to the other shareholders of the corporation who benefited thereby, saying that the needs of the corporation that were met by the accumulation of earnings could have been met in a number of ways. Such as by paying the dividend to the taxpayer and having the taxpayer loan that amount back to the corporation, or by the corporation declaring the dividend but giving the taxpayer a note therefor, or otherwise by not paying the dividend and having it constitute an obligation of the corporation. Given the effect each of these alternatives might have on the corporation's ability to borrow, service its other debt, attract other investors, and so forth, it seems questionable whether the TAM was on firm ground.

The Tax Court rejected the government's theory in Hutchens Non-Marital Trust v. Commissioner,[373] stating that the corporation had legitimate business reasons to withhold dividends, such as the need to provide for future corporate liquidity, the threat of successful product liability litigation, a general business downturn that might make borrowing difficult or expensive, and the need to provide for future research and development expenses. In the process the court distinguished *Snyder* because a right to convert the decedent's noncumulative preferred stock to a cumulative preferred stock in *Hutchens* was not absolute, as it was in *Snyder*. The court held this to be significant because the directors had fiduciary obligations to other shareholders in the exercise of their discretion whether to convert that preferred stock. These obligations were adequate to reject the government's assertion that control over the corporation translated into a gift when that control was not asserted.

(Footnote Continued)

the value of the corporation attributable to any accumulation of earnings. The TAM did not determine the value of that gift (whether it was the amount of earnings that would have been paid as dividends, or the market value increase in the common stock, if different and determinable), nor when it occurred. See also § 7.2.3.1 n.156 regarding cases in which inaction in a corporate recapitalization setting resulted in imputed gifts and gift tax liability.

[373] 66 T.C.M. (CCH) 1599 (1993).

§ 7.1.7.2

More forceful than *Hutchens* in rejecting the government's imputed gift theory from the nonpayment of dividends was Daniels v. Commissioner.[374] Again the alleged gift was imputed from the fact that the taxpayers' controlled corporation was not paying a 16% noncumulative preferred stock dividend on shares the taxpayers retained, following a preferred stock recapitalization and gift of the common stock to the taxpayers' children. Citing *Hutchens*, however, the Tax Court again rejected the government's argument because it failed to establish that the corporation abused its discretion or lacked a rational business purpose for not paying dividends.[375] According to the Tax Court, the issue is not whether the corporation could afford to pay dividends but rather whether it had a valid business reason not to do so.[376] A different result might have applied if the preferred stock was convertible into common stock and therefore the failure to declare dividends coupled with the failure to convert constituted an indirect gift to the common stockholders, as in *Snyder*. That apparently was not the case in *Daniels*.

For purposes of this discussion, however, one very interesting but irresolvable question is whether the day-to-day changing circumstances of a business would expose a taxpayer to a gift tax concern, and whether any gift of that nature would be deemed complete. With annual exclusion and other opportunities, it may be that gift tax would not be incurred on many of these imputed gifts, but timing is an essential issue with respect to those questions too.

Further in reliance on *Snyder*, as much or more like the buy-sell cases and conversion right cases,[377] TAM 9420001 held that an imputed gift occurred when the taxpayer allowed children to convert nonvoting preferred stock to common stock in a corporation that the taxpayer controlled. The corporation had sufficient liquidity to exercise a right to

---

[374] 68 T.C.M. (CCH) 1310 (1994).

[375] Noting in the process that the government never asserted an excess accumulated earnings tax liability and that its own appraiser conceded that the corporation's declaration of dividends would have hampered its growth and would have saddled the corporation with debt to finance operations that would have limited its future earnings and dividend paying capability.

[376] The court granted summary judgment on this issue because the government produced no facts to rebut the taxpayer's demonstration that the business purpose test was met.

[377] See text accompanying § 7.1.7.2 n.366.

§ 7.1.7.2

redeem the children's preferred stock at a price well below the FMV of the common stock they received by virtue of conversion. Thus, the deemed gift was measured by the differential between the redemption price and the FMV of the stock the children received on conversion.

Finally, again considering inaction to be the cause of a gift, in TAM 8610011 the decedent, as the 100% shareholder of a corporation, caused a recapitalization by which the decedent relinquished all common stock in the corporation and retained only preferred shares that carried voting rights until death. Two adult children each owned 200 shares of common stock after the recapitalization and, in the year the decedent died, the corporation issued one share of common stock that was purchased by the decedent, providing the "swing" vote among the common shareholders. One month before the decedent's death the corporation purchased the 200 shares of common stock owned by one of the decedent's children. Because of the decedent's swing vote with respect to the common stock, the decedent could have prevented the purchase of the 200 shares by the corporation and was deemed to make a gift because that purchase destroyed the swing vote with respect to the common stock. Therefore, the transaction was regarded as a transfer by the decedent of an interest in property, represented by the loss of the swing vote, completed at the time of the corporation's purchase.

Yet another set of issues arise in the context of timing gifts. There was a raft of PLRs that are representative of situations in which the taxpayer created a GRIT and reserved the power to alter trust investments or to compel the trustee to make corpus productive.[378] As a consequence of those powers, the government determined that the current yield on trust investments would not be considered in establishing the value of the gift of the remainder interest upon creation of the trust. Instead, the normal valuation tables would be applied for that purpose.[379] Initially those Rulings seemed favorable because, under the applicable facts, the term income interest retained by each trust's settlor

---

[378] See, e.g., PLRs 9052031, 9052011, 9049033, 9045047, 9035029, 9035022, 9035017, 9021035, 9015024, 8945006, 8911040, 8905046, 8905045, 8844008, 8823030, 8823029, 8806082, 8805029, and 8606082.

[379] See TAM 9004002 with respect to use of the valuation tables in general to value the gift in a pre-§ 2702 GRIT transfer.

§ 7.1.7.2

would be significantly overvalued, reducing substantially the value of the remainder for gift tax purposes in the year of the trust's creation.

The Rulings continued to state, however, that if the settlor failed to exercise in any future year the right to provide "a return on the income interest that is within the standard of State law," this failure to exercise the power to compel the trustee to produce more income would make the retained income interest worth less. That would correspondingly increase the value of the remainder interest, constituting a gift to the remainder beneficiaries at that time.[380] Thus, additional gifts could be imputed in any year in which investment performance was deficient, based on an assumed rate of return that would change from month to month.[381]

---

[380] See also PLR 9112007 and cf. PLR 8642028 (gift tax valuation of a remainder interest in a GRIT that authorized the trustee to retain the original trust corpus, without challenge by any beneficiary, notwithstanding that it was producing a below market dividend; the government stated that the transfer would have been incomplete for gift tax purposes if the donor had retained the power to compel the trustee to convert the corpus and invest at a more reasonable rate but, because the settlor relinquished the state law right as income beneficiary to compel the trustee to make the trust more fairly productive, the value of the remainder interest was to be determined according to the actual and expected dividend yield, not according to the tables' assumed income yield). Treas. Reg. § 25.7520-3(b)(2)(ii)(A) is to the same effect.

[381] It appears that the government would apply the assumed rate of return from time to time to determine whether a gift was made in that year. Moreover, although some vague standard under local law would be used to determine *whether* an adequate return was produced and, therefore, whether a gift was made, the federal rates then would be used to determine the *amount* of that gift. Although this may not be inconsistent, it certainly produces unusual results. It would seem logical instead to value any periodic gifts of income using the same actuarial assumptions applied at creation of the trust. For example, a gift of 3% annually should be imputed if the tables at creation assumed a 9% income flow over the term certain and income earned actually is only 6%. Thus, the discounted value of all income received by the settlor plus all gifts at and after creation of the trust would equal the value of the trust at its creation. As the Rulings have concluded, however, if the assumed rates of return rise, then instead of needing to produce a rate equal to or better than that assumed in the tables at the time the trust was created, the trust would need to produce a greater amount of income annually to avoid a deemed gift. The gift of the remainder and any deemed gift, added to any income received by the settlor, all properly discounted to values at creation of the trust, would thereby exceed 100%

§7.1.7.2

Those gifts would be the value of a remainder interest in the income not paid, presumably based on the number of years left to run in the term, and would be future interests, not qualifying for the annual exclusion. Worse, to determine the amount of the gift, it would be necessary to revalue the trust corpus periodically (to apply the relevant percentage return assumption), and any appreciation in the trust would create an increasing liability unless income kept pace with that growth. GRITs are a thing of the past,[382] so the point of these illustrations is that ostensibly similar results could be advocated in any case in which income yield was below whatever might be the requisite standard or entitlement of the income beneficiary.[383]

A related form of inadvertent gift is illustrated by a series of cases beginning with Revenue Ruling 84-105,[384] which involved S's gift tax liability. D created a marital deduction trust that was to receive a pecuniary bequest of $200x. D's estate was allowed a deduction for the full $200x even though the estate funded the bequest only to the extent of $160x. The executor's final account revealed the underfunding of $40x but was approved without objection by S, and no appeal was filed to contest that accounting. Finding that S could have recovered the deficiency by a timely filed action, the Ruling concluded that the marital deduction was not subject to reduction. Instead, S was regarded as if the bequest had been fully funded, followed by a gift of the differential by S.

Further, because S made no qualified disclaimer of the excess $40x, the gift was subject to gift tax and, for timing purposes, it was deemed effective on the date the order approving the executor's account became

(Footnote Continued)

of the initial value of the trust. Conversely, if interest rates were to decline below the assumed rate in the valuation tables at creation, the aggregate transfers would total less than 100% of the value of the trust. Either result appears to be wrong because a portion of the value of the trust might escape gift tax entirely or be taxed twice.

[382] See § 2702, discussed in § 7.2.2.

[383] O'Reilly v. Commissioner, 973 F.2d 1403 (8th Cir. 1992), rev'g 95 T.C. 646 (1990), presented a similar question that, although mooted by adoption of § 2702 in the particular transaction involved, could have continuing wealth transfer tax significance because it again made uncertain what the income beneficiary's interest was worth and left unresolved questions such as whether a gift is made if actual yield is lower than that assume for original valuation.

[384] 1984-2 C.B. 197.

§ 7.1.7.2

final. In Bergeron v. Commissioner,[385] similar facts led to the same conclusion, the difference being that the gift was deemed to be complete only when the ability to appeal the probate order expired.[386] *Bergeron* and the Ruling raise the specter of gift tax liability in any situation in which assets are not revalued for distribution in satisfaction of any bequest.[387] This may encourage some taxpayers to file a gift tax return to report the funding of marital deduction trusts, disclosing all relevant facts and stating that no gift has occurred, all in hopes of making the gift tax statute of limitation run on the event and potentially foreclosing a taxable gift allegation by the government in the future.[388]

Some transactions are not yet a gift, or they are a gift of only a portion of property and the balance will be a gift in the future, in each case as opposed to being a present gift that is incomplete. For example,

---

[385] 52 T.C.M. (CCH) 1177 (1986).

[386] The amount of the gift also was deemed to be less. It was only the value of the remainder interest in the underfunded amount following a life estate in S, because the underfunded amount effectively increased the value of a nonmarital trust, in which S enjoyed a life estate.

[387] See also Nelson v. United States, 89-2 U.S. Tax Cas. (CCH) ¶ 13,823 (D. N.D. 1989) (S made a gift to D's nieces and nephews because S allowed 50% of D's estate to be paid to those individuals under D's will; state law entitled S to 100% of D's estate because D's will, executed before their marriage, failed to provide for S and because, under the facts, S's intestate share was the entire estate). Cf. TAM 8535004, which is similar to *Bergeron* and Rev. Rul. 84-105, although it involved the value of property subject to a lapsed § 2041 general power of appointment. Lapse occurred prior to full funding of a trust, and the issue was whether § 2041 should require inclusion of only the actual value of the trust or the value to which the trust was entitled after full funding. Reasoning that the taxpayer could have compelled full funding, the TAM concluded that lapse must be measured by the full funded value, even though that was not the amount available to the taxpayer at the time of the lapse. And see § 7.2.3.1 n.156 regarding cases in which inaction in a corporate recapitalization setting resulted in imputed gifts and gift tax liability.

[388] See Treas. Reg. § 301.6501(c)-1(f)(3) and § 7.2.4.5 n.322 and accompanying text with respect to obtaining closure for gift tax purposes. This provision only applies for valuation controversies and only if disclosure is provided to adequately apprise the government of all relevant issues, so it may not be an effective foreclosure of the kind of issue that arises in a marital deduction funding situation. The difficult issue is whether filing the return will do more harm than good.

§ 7.1.7.2

Alexander v. United States[389] involved a gift of property subject to a mortgage as to which the donors remained personally liable. The government attempted to subject to gift tax the full FMV of the encumbered property, which the court rejected because there was no enforceable promise to make future mortgage payments as they came due. Instead, the current gift was regarded as just the equity in the property and each future mortgage payment would constitute a separate gift in the future when payment was made.

Subsequently the government ruled that a transfer of a legally enforceable promissory note may be a completed gift under § 2511 when the promise is binding and determinable in value, rather than when each promised payment actually is made, provided that the note is binding and enforceable[390] (which could be a challenge, considering that the transfer *is* a gift because it was made for less than full and adequate consideration in money or money's worth).[391] Similarly, a gift of future profits may be deemed to occur only as the profits are generated in the future if the transaction producing those profits is terminable at will.[392]

---

[389] 640 F.2d 1250 (Ct. Cl. 1981).

[390] Rev. Rul. 84-25, 1984-1 C.B. 191; Rev. Rul. 79-384, 1979-2 C.B. 344 (parent's promise to pay a child $10,000 upon graduation from college was enforced by a court order when the parent refused to pay following the child's performance by graduating; because graduation was not full and adequate consideration in money or money's worth the enforced payment was a gift for gift tax purposes, made when the promise became enforceable upon the graduation and not later when the court order was issued or even later when the payment eventually was made); Rev. Rul. 69-347, 1969-2 C.B. 227 (transfers pursuant to prenuptial agreement deemed a gift when the agreement became enforceable upon marriage of the parties, and not as each payment was made), cited in Estate of Grossinger v. Commissioner, 44 T.C.M. (CCH) 443 (1982). Enforceability of a debt or note is a state law issue. See, e.g., Strimling v. Commissioner, 734 F.2d 1377 (9th Cir. 1984), and Brown v. Commissioner, 25 T.C. 920 (1956), denying income tax interest expense deductions because the debts involved were not regarded as valid and enforceable.

[391] Rev. Rul. 84-25 also held that no FET deduction is available under § 2053(a)(3) to the extent the note remains unpaid at the promisor's death, because deductions founded on a promise or agreement are deductible under § 2053(c)(1) only to the extent the obligation was contracted bona fide and for an adequate and full consideration in money or money's worth. See § 15.4.2.

[392] See Rev. Rul. 81-54, 1981-1 C.B. 476 (shareholders of two separate corporations gave all the stock of one to irrevocable trusts, then arranged for the other

Finally, it pays to stand back and consider the government's most glaring loss on the incomplete gift issue, because it reveals some of the weakness in its application on some occasions as well as a few principles of overriding significance. In Estate of DiMarco v. Commissioner[393] the government asserted that gift tax liability was incurred when the decedent was employed. But that gift was regarded as incomplete until the decedent's death, with respect to the full value of a survivor's death benefit that became payable by virtue of the decedent's death. The benefit involved was an employee plan to which the decedent had made no contributions, had made no beneficiary designation, and over which the decedent had no powers of any type. The benefit was fixed by the terms of the plan and was totally contingent on the plan being in effect at death and there being named takers under the plan who survived the decedent. The government argued that the decedent made a gift of this benefit by accepting employment (presumably, if the plan had been adopted thereafter, the relevant date would have been the later adoption of the plan) but that the gift was incapable of valuation prior to death because the benefit was tied to factors that would not be known until the date of death.

The taxpayer rejoined that there was no gift at all, based on the fact that no transfer was made, no control ever existed, no power was exercised over the benefit, and the arrangement was totally involuntary on the part of the decedent. The court agreed, rejecting the government's argument and stating:

> [We] reject any suggestion . . . that transfers of property are incomplete for gift tax purposes simply because "no realistic value can be placed" on the property . . . or that transfers of property become complete for gift tax purposes only when the value of the transferred property can be easily ascertained. . . .
>
> . . . We also agree . . . that decedent never made a taxable gift of any property interest in the survivors income benefit because we find no act by decedent that qualifies as an act of "transfer" of an interest in property. His participation in the Plan

---

(Footnote Continued)

corporation to engage in a terminable-at-will arrangement that would generate profits from future dealings between the two corporations, flowing to the trusts).

[393] 87 T.C. 653 (1986), acq., 1990-2 C.B. 1. See also Rev. Rul. 92-68, 1992-2 C.B. 257, retracting Rev. Rul. 81-31, 1981-1 C.B. 475.

§7.1.7.2

was involuntary [and] he had no power [over the Plan or the benefit]. . . .

. . . None of the cases cited . . . hold that, without more, the simple act of going to work for an employer that has an automatic, non-elective, company-wide survivors income benefit plan . . . constitutes a "transfer" of an interest in the benefit for either estate or gift tax purposes. . . . While we agree . . . that a taxable event may occur without a volitional act by the donor . . . we do not believe that a taxable event can occur for gift tax purposes unless there is first . . . an act of transfer by the donor; and there can be no act of transfer unless the act is voluntary and the transferor has some awareness that he is in fact making a transfer of property. . . .

. . . Moreover, we question whether decedent ever owned a property interest in the survivors income benefit that he was capable of transferring during his lifetime. He had no voice in selecting the beneficiaries . . . and no ability to affect or determine the benefits. . . . Most importantly, [the employer] had the power and the right to modify the Plan. . . . Under these circumstances . . . decedent never acquired fixed and enforceable property rights in the survivors income benefit that he was capable of transferring during his lifetime.[394]

The government did not assert FET liability in *DiMarco*. Its theory was that there was a taxable gift and, therefore, nothing remained for FET inclusion.

In such a death-benefit-only situation it seems undeniable that wealth is being generated and left to survivors that is attributable to the

---

[394] 87 T.C. at 660-664. Further, to the government's argument that the benefit must be a taxable gift because "it is not taxable under section 2039," the court stated "[w]e . . . express no view . . . as to whether the survivors income benefit is taxable under sec. 2039," 87 T.C. at 665 n.11, presumably leaving open the door for this theory of FET inclusion. As discussed in §7.3.3 n.54, FET inclusion of a similar plan benefit was mandated in Estate of Levin v. Commissioner, 90 T.C. 723 (1988), but the inclusion was found under §2038(a)(1).

See also Carpenter v. United States, 85-1 U.S. Tax Cas. (CCH) ¶ 13,612 (Ct. Cl. 1985), which dealt with a valuation issue not resolved in Carpenter v. United States, 84-1 U.S. Tax Cas. (CCH) ¶ 13,565 (Ct. Cl. 1984), which held that the taxpayer had made a gift of a remainder interest notwithstanding the *taxpayer's* contention that the gift was not complete because it was not susceptible to valuation until certain contingent interests of the donor were resolved. Consistent with *DiMarco*, the court rejected this position and valued the gift as of the date it was made. Any contingent interests that could not be valued were simply disregarded.

§7.1.7.2

decedent's efforts. Failure to tax this wealth represents a significant estate planning opportunity. Alternatively, however, in a case involving no hidden control or other indications of impropriety, the decedent has neither enjoyment nor control of this wealth, making it difficult to conjure a theory of taxation that makes appropriate its inclusion in the employee-decedent's estate. In at least some plans, it also is notable that, during the employee's life, it always is possible that there may never be a benefit paid (because of contingencies in the plan—like leaving the employment prior to death or unilateral termination of the plan by the employer). As far as the government is concerned it is no answer that the wealth usually will be taxable upon the death of the designated recipient, if not sooner disposed of or consumed in ways that have no lasting value at death. Nevertheless, at least in this one situation, that may be the best result the government can achieve.

§7.1.8 State Gift Tax

The very few states that impose a gift tax[395] frequently piggyback on the federal gift tax return, meaning that inter vivos transfers that avoid federal gift tax also often avoid state gift tax as well. Generalizations regarding state law on this score are not wise, however, so the full gift tax cost of making inter vivos transfers cannot be ascertained without examining local law to determine whether there is a state gift tax.[396]

---

[395] See § 1.1 n.5 for a listing.

[396] For which there is no § 164(a) income tax deduction, although federal and state gift taxes owed by a decedent at death are § 2053(a)(3) deductible as a debt. See §7.3 n.2. Other taxes, such as income tax on income received after the decedent's death, property taxes not accrued before death, or estate, succession, legacy, or inheritance taxes of any flavor are nondeductible for FET purposes. § 2053(c)(1)(B). See § 15.4.2. Rev. Rul. 71-355, 1971-2 C.B. 334, held that state gift tax on property subject to state death tax is not deductible under §2053 if the state treats that tax as an advance payment of the state death tax, and Rev. Rul. 75-63, 1975-1 C.B. 294, held that state gift tax was includible in the decedent' gross estate for FET purposes if it was includible in the state estate tax computation under the state counterpart of the § 2035(b) gross up rule. Otherwise, according to the government, the effect would be to give the decedent's estate an improper deduction for the state inheritance tax. Both Rulings were followed in First Nat'l Bank and Trust Co. v. United States, 787 F.2d 1393 (10th Cir. 1986) (no deduction as a claim against the decedent's estate for state gift tax paid on a transfer later included in the state death tax base), but both Rulings were

§7.2 TAXATION OF COMPLETED GIFTS

Notwithstanding the attraction of nontaxable inter vivos transfers, a discussion regarding the economics of prepaying wealth transfer tax[1] reveals that incurring gift tax on a completed, taxable, inter vivos transfer is preferable to holding wealth and incurring an FET instead.

Perhaps the first thing to recognize is the almost too obvious point that it is essential to know what is the subject of the gift. It may be that the typical gift is an outright transfer of property easily identified, with valuation based on accepted principles and easily determined. For example, a transfer of a fixed number of shares of publicly traded securities would be easy to evaluate. Only slightly more difficult would be a gift about which there might be some valuation uncertainty, such as a used automobile, but as to which the principles at work are equally simple, the donee is clear, and the gift tax consequences are unremarkable. Some inter vivos transfers in the estate planning context are this direct and easy, but the ones for which costly advice is employed likely create more uncertainty.

For example, a transaction may not look exactly like a gift—because there is a sale element—but the amount paid is less than full and adequate consideration in money or money's worth. If the bargain element is not just a bad deal among parties dealing at arm's length and without donative intent,[2] then a part-sale, part-gift transfer probably occurred and this would create its own special consequences. These would include valuation of the gift element (the FMV of the transferred

---

(Footnote Continued)

rejected in Estate of Lang v. Commissioner, 64 T.C. 404 (1975), aff'd, 613 F.2d 770 (9th Cir. 1980), Horton v. United States, 79-2 U.S. Tax Cas. ¶ 13,316 (M.D. N.C. 1979), and Estate of Gamble v. Commissioner, 69 T.C. 942 (1978). Rev. Rul. 81-302, 1981-2 C.B. 170, subsequently revoked Rev. Rul. 75-63 in light of *Gamble* ("payment of a state gift tax before death, which is subsequently credited against the state inheritance tax, does not create an asset includible in the decedent's gross estate") and revoked Rev. Rul. 71-335 in light of *Lang* ("state gift tax paid after death remains a gift tax and is, therefore, deductible" under §2053(a)(3)).

[1] §7.2 See §6.2.

[2] See the business transaction exception discussed in §7.1.1.

property, in excess of the consideration received),[3] capital gain or loss on the sale portion (based on the amount realized in excess of the transferor's full basis in the property transferred), and basis to the transferee (being the greater of the transferee's cost or the transferor's carryover basis, not to exceed FMV for purposes of determining loss).[4]

Harder yet would be a transfer of a temporal interest in property. This would not be a vertically sliced fractional portion, such as half ownership as a tenant in common in that used car, in which case fractional or minority interest discount valuation questions might arise[5] but otherwise the issues would be no more complicated. Instead, it would be a horizontally sliced interest like a life estate or term of years (or the remainder following either), raising yet again more challenging questions of valuation and the proper gift taxation of the transfer.[6]

To illustrate, the regulations provide that standard valuation tables for split interests may not be used to value temporal interests if they may produce unreasonable results because the individual who is a measuring life is known to be terminally ill. "Terminally ill" is defined to mean suffering from an incurable illness or other deteriorating physical condition that would substantially reduce the individual's life expectancy.[7] The same regulations provide in this regard that an individual is "considered terminally ill" if there is at least a 50% probability that the individual will die within one year. If, however, the individual survives for 18 months or longer, then the person "shall be presumed to have not been terminally ill . . . unless the contrary is proved by clear and convincing evidence." Thus, the valuation of temporal interests will generate difficult factual issues in some circumstances.

Finally, perhaps hardest of all (because it may not be clear that transfer tax consequences are involved at all), a disguised or indirect gift may be involved in a property transfer or transaction, requiring that the gift itself be identified before the nature of that transfer and the relevant valuation rules can be applied. By way of example, a demand loan to a

---

[3] See, e.g., Heim v. Commissioner, 52 T.C.M. (CCH) 1272 (1987), and the discussion in § 7.0.

[4] See § 6.4.1 n.6 and accompanying text.

[5] See § 7.2.4.2.

[6] See § 7.2.2 dealing with § 2702.

[7] See Treas. Reg. § § 1.7520-3 (b) (3), 20.7520-3 (b) (3) (i), 25.7520-3 (b) (3).

§ 7.2

child for less than a market rate of interest[8] or a transfer subject to a price adjustment provision that the government regards as invalid[9] might involve taxable gifts that were not obvious or intended. To properly plan for these transactions requires first that the gift transfer be identified, and then the other valuation and related gift tax issues be addressed and resolved.

§ 7.2.1 *Strategic Gifting Illustrations*

With this in mind, TAM 9504004 illustrates a number of these gift tax factors. The decedent died within six months after being diagnosed with cancer. Within the last month of the decedent's life and following several unsuccessful therapies and one serious hospitalization, the decedent sold half and redeemed half of a 60% controlling shareholder interest, leaving the decedent with no interest and putting one child in control of the corporation. Each half of the decedent's interest was valued with a minority discount and the private annuity paid by the child for the sale portion was computed on the basis of the decedent's life expectancy determined under the mortality tables rather than on the basis of the decedent's actual life expectancy in light of the cancer.

Only one payment was received before the decedent's death, representing 1.3% of the total purchase price. The redemption portion of the transaction was in exchange for cash and notes issued by the corporation, and those were transferred by the decedent to a CLUT that paid a unitrust interest to a charity for a term measured by the decedent's life, again based on mortality assumptions and not the decedent's actual terminal condition. Total payments made to the charity were 0.8% of the value claimed for §2522 charitable deduction purposes and the value of the gift of the remainder interest reported by the decedent was 34.3% of the total value of the property transferred notwithstanding that the remainder beneficiaries acquired the property one month later.

In this context the government held that the standard mortality tables were not properly employed to value the various annuities, unitrust interests, or remainders for gift tax purposes. Moreover, by regarding the sale and redemption as a single coordinated transaction, the

---

[8] See § 6.3.3.5 dealing with § 7872.

[9] See § 7.2.1 n.16 dealing with so-called King clauses.

TAM deemed the decedent to have transferred a 60% interest and not two discounted 30% minority interests, thereby disallowing the claimed minority discounts.[10] The whole package of transactions was "aggressive" and if the decedent had lived long enough for the §7520 mortality assumptions to bind the government, then less substantial wealth transfer tax saving would have resulted than the parties anticipated.

Far more dramatic results actually were obtained in Estate of McLendon v. Commissioner,[11] the litigated case that a comparison of the facts reveals almost without question was the situation involved in TAM 9133001. For ease of explanation, and because it illustrates several aspects of the gifting analysis and the government's positions, the TAM is discussed here in some detail, along with the courts' conclusions in *McLendon*. Several aspects of each stand out.

§7.2.1.1 Formula Adjustment Provisions

A saving clause provision was included in the transaction specifying that the purchase price would be adjusted in response to any valuation agreement reached with the government or any determination of value rendered in a final decision of the Tax Court. The TAM characterized the saving clause as making the transfer "void" as to that part of the property transferred that was subject to gift tax.[12] The TAM held that the business

---

[10] See also TAM 8906002 (sale of stock by controlling shareholder to another corporation controlled by that shareholder's children, the government describing the factors to consider in determining whether the transaction involved a gift and whether a death terminating provision and the risk premium for a note should be considered in determining whether the sale constituted a transfer in an ordinary business transaction). See §6.4.2 regarding SCINs.

[11] 66 T.C.M. (CCH) 946 (1993), rev'd and rem'd in an unpublished opinion, 96-1 U.S. Tax Cas. (CCH) ¶ 60,220 (5th Cir. 1995), on remand, 72 T.C.M. (CCH) 42 (1996), rev'd, 135 F.2d 1017 (5th Cir. 1998) (Tax Court's finding that a partnership interest was transferred rather than an assignee interest in the partnership was deemed improper, and an essential conclusion regarding use of the decedent's mortality as determined under the tables was "ambiguous and ambivalent" and therefore required clarification that, once given, was reversed to hold that the tables must be used).

[12] Citing Commissioner v. Procter, 142 F.2d 824 (4th Cir. 1944), and Rev. Rul. 86-41, 1986-1 C.B. 300, in the process mischaracterizing the provision and failing to distinguish King v. United States, 545 F.2d 700 (7th Cir. 1976), or explain why it was not the better analogy.

transaction exception to the gift tax[13] could not apply because it is reliant on the absence of donative intent underlying the transaction.[14] And the structure of the transaction was deemed to be donative, the TAM stating that, "had the annuity agreement been executed between the decedent and a third party who was not a family member, the estate would have most likely taken action to set the transfer aside . . . ." Indeed, the government's position was that the price adjustment clause indicated that the transaction was not a bona fide arm's length business arrangement because the parties were willing to pay whatever the government or the Tax Court established as the proper value of the underlying assets.

The Tax Court essentially agreed with the government that the adjustment provision was invalid, stating that the taxpayer was "an astute and sophisticated businessman [who] would not have entered into a similar arrangement with an unrelated third party."[15] Consequently, the

---

13 Treas. Reg. § 25.2512-8, discussed in § 7.1.1.

14 Citing Harwood v. Commissioner, 82 T.C. 239 (1984).

15 66 T.C.M. at 969, stating that this case did not present an arm's length transaction free of donative intent.

In TAM 9309001, the provision (used in a transfer that would be subject to § 2701 today) at issue specified: "If the value . . . is determined to be different than [assumed], pursuant to any agreed settlement . . . or any final determination of bona fide disputes by a court of competent jurisdiction, then the finally agreed or determined value shall control . . . , it being intended that the value of this gift be [$X]." According to the TAM, this provision "was designed to permit the Donor to avoid paying gift tax on a valuable property interest by taking advantage of the proverbial 'audit lottery,'" because the gift element would be adjusted away if the government audited the gift tax return and any unreported gift value would escape tax if the government did not audit the return. The government also held that, although it may be reasonable that a final sale price in a transaction between unrelated parties might be subject to adjustment (based for example on an appraisal that was not completed at the time of closing), it would not be reasonable to find an adjustment provision that would operate a long time in the future after extended litigation is resolved. Therefore, the TAM held that the adjustment provision was invalid "[b]ecause it is apparent that the valuation contingency imposed by the Donor would only arise if the Internal Revenue Service were to dispute the value for gift tax purposes." This may be the first occurrence in which the government used the "audit lottery" rationale as its justification. Note that increased FET exclusion amounts mean that fewer estates are taxable and fewer FET returns therefore are selected for audit, which allows the government to select more gift tax returns for audit.

provision was deemed to lack bona fides and the court concluded that the adjustment provision should be ignored. Nevertheless, provisions of this ilk are not necessarily or even predictably invalid, as more recent litigation reveals.

The price adjustment provision involved in the TAM sometimes is known as a King clause after King v. United States,[16] which held that a provision designed to establish full and adequate consideration based on the government's determination of value is not invalid. The antithesis is a so-called Procter provision, which was regarded by Commissioner v. Procter[17] as a condition subsequent on a gift transfer that must be ignored for public policy reasons. To illustrate the difference, consider the planning involved in FSA 200122011. The provision was designed to dissuade the government from challenging the valuation of an inter vivos transfer. Basically it specified that any increase in the value of difficult to value assets (in that case interests in an FLP) would constitute a gift to charity, such that any increase in value would be matched with a charitable contribution deduction. That would produce a wash to the government and prevent it from benefiting from the valuation challenge in the first instance. For just that reason the government regarded that price adjustment provision as invalid, asserting that it contravenes the public policy pronounced in *Procter*.

McCord v. Commissioner[18] may be the same case as the FSA. In a footnote 47 in a very lengthy and controversial decision the Tax Court dodged the issue by misconstruing the provision itself, and the court on appeal dodged the issue entirely, saying that the government did not pursue it in its arguments, all leaving concern and doubt lingering about this form of planning.

TAM 200245053 similarly regarded a provision as invalid because the government perceived it to be an effort to discourage litigation. That clause was a good bit different, however, and involved a multi-tier transaction with a gift of a 0.1% interest in an FLP, a sale of a 98.9% interest in the same partnership, and a formula provision designed to negate any gift in the sale transaction. The formula keyed off the gift tax

---

[16] 545 F.2d 700 (7th Cir. 1976).

[17] 142 F.2d 824 (4th Cir. 1944).

[18] 120 T.C. 358 (2003), rev'd on other grounds, 461 F.3d 614 (5th Cir. 2006).

§7.2.1.1

value established from the sliver interest gift, the apparent purpose being to negate a *Procter* challenge by giving the government a potential tax to collect if valuation litigation was successful (albeit any gift tax would pale relative to the vastly more valuable sale transaction). The government regarded the formula sale provision as flawed and distinguished *King*[19] because it was an arm's length transfer in the ordinary course of business whereas the taxpayer in the TAM was trustee of two trusts that engaged in the transfers and the partnership itself bespoke an effort to depress values rather than to obtain a fair price from a disinterested outsider.

The TAM distinguished other forms of formula adjustment provisions that are valid because they are not manipulative, unlike the subject provision, citing marital deduction formula bequests that are keyed to values that cannot be known at the time of drafting and that serve a "legitimate" planning purpose, suggesting that formula provisions influenced by the type of mala fides found in a *Procter* type clause or the subject provision should fail. Such a distinction might be meritorious, but TAM 200337012 threw notions of bona fides into confusion in holding that a benign provision that merely specified that the taxpayer "desires to transfer as a gift . . . that fraction of [taxpayer's] Limited Partnership Interest in Partnership which has a FMV on the date hereof of [$X]" was invalid. It is not readily apparent how this provision operates any differently than the implicit understanding that a customer will return the incorrect amount if a store clerk delivers too much change to that customer, all according to the implied terms of any common sale transaction. If a provision such as this is not good, it is hard to imagine a formula provision that is acceptable. As it turns out, this TAM may have been the situation involved in Petter v. Commissioner[20] and, as noted below, the court did not regard it as improper.

More important than *Petter*, and predicting that result, the Tax Court in Estate of Christiansen v. Commissioner[21] approved the provi-

---

[19] Relying on *Procter*, Ward v. Commissioner, 87 T.C. 78 (1986), and Rev. Rul. 86-41, 1986-1 C.B. 300.

[20] 93 T.C.M. (CCH) 534 (2009), aff'd, 653 F.3d 1012 (9th Cir. 2011).

[21] 130 T.C. 1 (2008), aff'd, 586 F.3d 1061 (8th Cir. 2009) (a unanimous reviewed opinion involving a formula disclaimer that passed to charity any added value flowing from a successful government valuation challenge).

sion over the same *Procter* objection as the government raised in opposition to the formula gift provision in *McCord*, stating:

> We do recognize that the incentive to the IRS to audit returns affected by such disclaimer language will marginally decrease if we allow the increased deduction for property passing to the foundation. Lurking behind the Commissioner's argument is the intimation that this will increase the probability that people . . . will lowball the value of an estate to cheat charities. There's no doubt that this is possible. But . . . executors and administrators of estates are fiduciaries, and owe a duty to settle and distribute an estate according to the terms of the will . . . [and] the state attorney general has authority to enforce these fiduciary duties. . . . We therefore hold that allowing an increase in the charitable deduction to reflect the increase in the value of the estate's property going to the Foundation violates no public policy and should be allowed.

Notwithstanding the suggestion that the government's concern is the incentive to cheat charities, the Tax Court acknowledged earlier in the majority opinion that the real issue is a lowball FET valuation. In cases that do not involve a charitable component it is possible that the lack of state Attorney General involvement could persuade the court to rule otherwise, although the same fiduciary duties would exist regardless of the ultimate beneficiary of the disclaimer.

Following *Christiansen* it was no surprise that *Petter* carefully distinguished an invalid *Procter* type of saving provision (one that "tries to take property back" if the government asserts a gift tax liability), from the formula provision in *Petter* that "gives away a fixed set of rights with uncertain value," defined by a formula that refers to an ascertainable amount. Indeed, the *Petter* gift was quite similar to a formula credit shelter pecuniary bequest, with a residuary marital. The taxpayer's gift (to trusts for children) was of "the number of Units [in an FLP] that equals . . . the [maximum] dollar amount that can pass free of federal gift tax by reason of [the taxpayer's] applicable exclusion amount." The balance of the FLP units were given to charity.

The challenged provision required the trusts to remit to the charity any excess "if the value of the Units . . . is finally determined for federal gift tax purposes to exceed the amount" described in the formula gift of the applicable exclusion amount, and the charity likewise was required to return units to the trusts if a valuation error favored the charity. The

§7.2.1.1

Petter formula provision was a bona fide effort to effect a legitimate division of a hard-to-value asset between recipients—which happened to include charities. The Tax Court specifically found that the charities "conducted arm's-length negotiations, retained their own counsel, and won changes to the transfer documents to protect their interests," leaving the court "confident that this gift was made in good faith"—the opposite of the mala fides in *Procter*—and that "we find that this gift is not as susceptible to abuse as the Commissioner would have us believe." Channeling *Christiansen*, the Tax Court also concluded that "[w]e simply don't share the Commissioner's fear, in gifts structured like this one, that taxpayers are using charities just to avoid tax. We certainly don't find that these kinds of formulas would cause severe and immediate frustration of the public policy in favor of promoting tax audits."

There is a distinction between "adjustment clauses" that alter a gift or purchase price retroactively, and "definition clauses" that work simultaneously with a transfer to establish the amount involved in a transfer ab initio. Arguably only the former should be subject to invalidation arguments under the condition subsequent analysis of *Procter*.[22] *Christiansen* and *Petter* fall on the "definition" side of that distinction and, not in so few words, support that analysis. Such that, today, it seems relatively predictable that a properly crafted formula adjustment provision will pass muster in the Tax Court.[23]

---

[22] See McCaffrey, Tax Tuning the Estate Plan by Formula, 33 U. Miami Inst. Est. Plan. ¶ 400 (1999); McCaffrey, Formulaic Planning to Reduce Transfer Tax Risks, 45 U. Miami Inst. Est. Plan. ¶ 700 (2011).

[23] As confirmation see Hendrix v. Commissioner, 101 T.C.M. (CCH) 1642 (2011) (valid defined value formula clause divided closely held stock between trusts for descendants and a donor advised fund; it involved arm's length negotiation and did not contravene public policy); and Wandry v. Commissioner, 103 T.C.M. (CCH) 1472 (2012) (inter vivos formula gifts defined by the gift tax annual exclusion and the gift tax applicable exclusion amount). According to the *Wandry* court, the "only gifts . . . that [the taxpayers] ever intended to give were of dollar amounts equal to the Federal gift tax exclusions." And, as such, the court determined that nothing about the formula provision would undo the gift. Meaning that the formula provision was not an invalid effort to take back any part of the gifts that were made. The court cited and followed *Christiansen* and *Petter*, made reference to *McCord*, but did not cite or refer to *Hendrix*.

An important distinction between *Wandry* and all of these other cases is that *Wandry* did not have a charitable component. Language in *Petter* caused some observers to wonder whether the charitable element made the difference in

§7.2.1.2 Reliance on Mortality Assumptions

The other controversial aspect of these cases involved taxpayer reliance on mortality assumptions. For example, the taxpayer in *McLendon* sold a remainder interest in various assets that otherwise would have been §2033 includible in the decedent's gross estate at death, including the decedent's general partnership interests in various family enterprises and "the decedent's rights in" the business' pension plan. Valuation for purposes of this transaction was pursuant to the regulation mortality tables that, at the time, presumed that a person the decedent's age would live another 15 years.[24] The transaction was designed to fully capitalize on valuation presumptions based on the decedent's actuarial life expectancy, and the purchase price for this remainder interest sale was payable as an annuity for the decedent's life, also determined using the government's mortality assumptions notwithstanding the decedent's diagnosed terminal illness, which actually resulted in death within seven months.

The TAM stated that:

> The actuarial tables . . . take into account that the health of a particular person may be somewhat better or worse than the health of an "average" person of the same age. But it has been a longstanding position of the Service that, because the actuarial tables are compiled from statistical data of the general population, the tables were never intended to apply to a case in which the measuring life is an individual who is afflicted with an advanced stage of an incurable disease.[25] For example, if, on the valuation date, an individual was afflicted with a fatal and incur-

---

(Footnote Continued)

result. *Wandry* confirmed that it does not: "In Estate of Petter we cited Congress' overall policy of encouraging gifts to charitable organizations. This factor contributed to our conclusion, but it was not determinative." And, further, "In Estate of Petter . . . we held that there is no well established public policy against formula clauses."

Only a rare taxpayer will pay tax and sue for a refund in district court or the Federal Claims Court, rather than relying on defined valuation formula clause precedent in the Tax Court. As a result, notwithstanding that *Hendrix* and *Wandry* are only Tax Court Memorandum decisions, it seems reasonably reliable to plan in accordance with the conclusions reached in all of these cases.

[24] Applicable at the time was Treas. Reg. §25.2512-5, which since has been replaced with the regulations in Treas. Reg. §25.7520-3.

[25] Rev. Rul. 66-307, 1966-2 C.B. 429.

§7.2.1.2

able disease, and it was apparent that the individual's life expectancy was one year or less, the impending date of the individual's predictable and imminent death would be at considerable variance from the life expectancy factors provided by the valuation tables. In such a case, departure from the valuation tables would be required. Thus, based on the facts and circumstances of the particular case, where, because an individual's death is (1) imminent within a year, and (2) predictable, the actual facts of the individual's condition on the valuation date are so exceptional that departure from the actuarial tables is required, and the present worth of the particular life estate, remainder, or annuity, as the case may be, is determined by the individual's actual life expectancy on the valuation date.[26]

The government thus determined that the mortality assumptions in the tables could not be used. As a consequence, the remainder interest was valued much higher and the annuity much lower than the tables assumed, and the consideration paid for the transfer was deemed to be less than full and adequate, resulting in a gift.

The TAM focused extensively on the apparent intent of the parties, particularly in view of the decedent's diagnosis, prognosis, and actual date of death. According to facts detailed at length, the buyers of the remainder interests regarded the transaction as "a gift in lieu of an inheritance" and, probably more importantly, lacked the resources to make the annuity payments if the decedent did not die. For example, having purchased only a remainder interest, they were not able to rely on the purchased asset to provide the cash flow to meet their obligations.

This focus on the parties' apparent intent should have been relevant only with respect to the business transaction exception. Otherwise, under the gift tax donative intent is not required to constitute a transfer as a gift. Instead, unless that exception for transfers in the ordinary course of business lacking in donative intent is applicable, the only requirement for gift tax purposes is a transfer for less than full and adequate consideration in money or money's worth.

---

[26] Rev. Rul. 80-80, 1980-1 C.B. 194; Continental Illinois Nat'l Bank and Trust Co. v. United States, 504 F.2d 586 (11th Cir. 1974); Miami Beach First Nat'l Bank v. United States, 443 F.2d 116 (5th Cir. 1971); Estate of Fabric v. Commissioner, 83 T.C. 932 (1984); Estate of Jennings v. Commissioner, 10 T.C. 323 (1948) (holding that the use of established mortality tables must give way to proven facts when, in view of the condition of an individual, the individual's actual life expectancy, on the valuation date, was not greater than one year).

§7.2.1.2

On appeal the taxpayer ultimately prevailed, the court finding that the taxpayer's reliance on the mortality tables was justified and that the government could not deviate from its own published criteria for application of them. The transaction involved in *McLendon* predated the adoption of §2036(c) and its replacement Chapter 14 and, as discussed next, the *McLendon* transaction no longer would be viable for affirmative planning, given the effect of §2702 on the sale of a remainder interest transaction. That the transaction was abusive is easy to recognize from the facts involved.

The need for §2702 as remedial legislation is illustrated by the results the taxpayer obtained in *McLendon*. Whether the government successfully could have repelled such results in other litigation with the type of analysis applied in the TAM is unclear, and may never be known. Congress made inquiries into intent and other subjective factors irrelevant with its adoption of §2702. With promulgation of the §7520 regulations[27] the government took further steps to eliminate the abuse in the *McLendon* split interest transaction that depended on life expectancy. Nevertheless, notwithstanding all these changes, planning opportunities remain viable, to the extent the mortality tables are applicable under the new standards, also as discussed next.

As one easy example, the mortality assumptions are based on unisex factors, which overstate the life expectancy of men and understate the life expectancy of women. This means that an interest measured by the life of a man is overvalued (men die on average earlier than do women, and younger than the blended unisex tables predict, meaning that the interest measured by a man's life actually will run for a shorter time than the tables predict) and for the same reason a remainder interest following an interest measured by the life of a woman is overvalued under the tables. Understanding just those glitches in the tables can allow planning that takes advantage of the fundamental inaccuracies in the tables.

§7.2.1.3 Reliance on Income Projections

Before turning to that topic, however, one last illustration shows why §2702 was necessary to address inaccuracies in the evaluation of

---

[27] See §7.2.1 n.29.

income entitlements. Although O'Reilly v. Commissioner[28] also was mooted by adoption of §2702, the issues involved have continuing wealth transfer tax significance and illustrate the merits of §2702. The taxpayers created several GRITs to which they transferred stock in a family corporation that historically paid dividends of less than 0.2% of FMV. At issue was whether either the retained income interest or the transferred remainder interest could be valued using the §2512 valuation tables—which assumed (at the time of the gifts involved) a 10% annual income yield (the tables produced a value for the income interest of just over $100,000, but the amount of income actually paid was $1,800).

The position adopted by the §7520 regulations[29] regarding under-productive property was designed to overcome the result reached by the Tax Court in *O'Reilly*. It held that the valuation tables must be used notwithstanding the yield, noting that, to hold otherwise "would be opening up Pandora's box in that we could have to decide, in every case, where the line should be drawn in terms of the dividend potential of stock for the purpose of determining whether the actuarial tables should be used."[30]

In support of its holding, the court noted that *O'Reilly* was distinguishable from cases like Calder v. Commissioner,[31] in which the Tax Court refused to rely on the valuation tables because the gifted property was non-income-producing and there was no assurance it would be sold and the proceeds reinvested in income producing property. In *Calder* the issue was whether the gift tax annual exclusion was available for the gift of a present interest. In *O'Reilly* the issue was only whether the tables or some other method should be used to value the gifted interest.

The Tax Court also took notice in *O'Reilly* of the fact that "there are a substantial number of publicly held corporations whose dividends represent less than a 1-percent yield."[32] It also stated that the valuation

---

[28] 973 F.2d 1403 (8th Cir. 1992), rev'g 95 T.C. 646 (1990).

[29] Treas. Reg. §25.7520-3(b)(2)(ii)(A), effective after 1989. The preamble to the proposed §7520 regulations contained information that may help determine which interest rate and regulation provision is applicable for valuation purposes, depending on the date of the transaction. See §7.2.1 n.29.

[30] 95 T.C. at 652-653.

[31] 85 T.C. 713 (1985). See §7.1.1.1 n.19.

[32] 95 T.C. at 653.

tables incorporate a market rate of return based on fixed obligations, such as Treasury bills, and that "a comparison of yield on these two types of securities is like mixing apples and pears."[33]

In reversing on appeal, the court first confirmed that it is only in unusual cases that deviation from the tables is justifiable, but then embraced the principle that:

> whenever use of the tables would produce a substantially unrealistic and unreasonable result, and a more reasonable and realistic means of determining value is available, the statute requires, and decades of case law confirm, that the tables may not be used by either the Commissioner or the taxpayer.[34]

Finding that the tables would produce such a deviant result and that the history of dividends paid on the stock was adequate to allow its use as an alternative, the court remanded to the Tax Court for a redetermination of value based on that evidence. It also ruled that (1) the taxpayer was entitled to rely on the tables for valuation in the first instance and (2) the government bore the "considerable burden" of proving that the tables produced an improper result. In the process the appellate court rejected the government's assertion that, if the tables produce an unreasonable value, the only alternative must be to value the retained income interest at zero.

The precise result advanced by the Commissioner (and rejected) in *O'Reilly* was enacted as § 2702. A gift of 100% of the value of the underlying property transferred to the GRIT, as if the retained income interest was valueless. The court's overall conclusion is significant nevertheless, holding that the valuation tables may not be used simply because they facilitate simplified administration of the tax laws. Instead, they must be used only if they do not produce unreasonable and unrealistic results such as those produced in *O'Reilly*.[35]

---

[33] 95 T.C. at 653.

[34] 973 F.2d at 1408.

[35] Similarly, TAM 9232002 involved a pre-§ 2702 GRIT that also no longer would be viable planning today but illustrated a valuation principle of enduring importance in a total portfolio investment performance and principal and income environment that permits (and may even command) adjustments between fiduciary accounting income and principal of the variety discussed in § 5.3.3. The issue was the proper valuation of the donor's retained income interest for computing the gift tax on property transferred to the trust. Because the trust instrument

§ 7.2.1.3

As with any discussion of the legal aspects that inform inter vivos planning strategies, change is inevitable and a myriad of factors influence proper recommendations. There are so many factors to consider, ranging from the nature of the assets involved and their income or growth potential, the risk tolerance of the transferor, the need or demand to exert continuing control over the transferees or the transferred assets, the presence of charitable motivations, the mortality and income yield assumptions that apply and their reality in terms of the actors and assets involved, and the income and wealth transfer tax landscape and consequences of various alternatives, as well as the potential for change in those laws.

Few recommendations in this forum are reliable for an extended period of time, but cited in the margin is a wonderfully complete (albeit necessarily complex) matrix of decisional criteria that may help readers analyze alternatives and that some might regard as necessary reading in the process of evaluating strategic opportunities.[36]

§ 7.2.2 Special Valuation of Temporal Interest Transfers

Adopted in 1990,[37] § 2702 is a special valuation rule that applies to determine whether a gift has been made and its value. It involves

---

(Footnote Continued)

authorized a deviation from the state principal and income act, the government held that normal valuation approaches that presume compliance with state principal and income principles could not be applied. Reasonable and reasonably consistent deviations will be permitted under the regulations defining income for fiduciary income tax purposes and should be respected as well for valuation and other purposes. See, e.g., Treas. Reg. § 20.2056(b)-5(f) as discussed in the context of marital deduction qualification in § § 13.5.2.1, 13.6.2.1.

36 Abbin, [S]he Loves Me, [S]he Loves Me Not—Responding To Succession Planning Needs Through A Three Dimensional Analysis Of Considerations To Be Applied In Selecting From The Cafeteria Of Techniques, 31 U. Miami Inst. Est. Plan. ¶ 1300 (1997).

37 Effective with respect to transfers made after October 8, 1990. Revenue Reconciliation Act of 1990 § 11602(e). With respect to effective dates in general, consider PLR 200502035, extending the safe harbor of the effective date to the proceeds, investments, and reinvestments of a trust created prior to October 8, 1990, and TAM 9408005, in which the transferor released a reversion in several trusts in response to the government's Notice 89-99, promulgated under

retained and transferred interests in trusts or trust equivalents for the benefit of family members,[38] such as the income interest in a GRIT with a child as remainder beneficiary. The perceived abuse in this arena is the form of misvaluation in *McLendon* made possible under the valuation tables that apply to temporal interests.[39] To combat that this rule specifies that the value of any retained temporal interest (like a life estate or term of years) that is not a "qualified interest" is zero for gift tax purposes. Thus, gifts of trust interests are deemed to carry all the value of the trust corpus at original transfer of the remainder interest (and, presumably, at any subsequent transfer of less than all of the retained interest).[40]

§ 7.2.2.1 Trust Equivalents

A "trust equivalents" rule specifies that § 2702 applies to the transfer of any interest in property with respect to which there is one or more term interests, because these are equivalent to a transfer of an interest in a trust.[41] One easy example would be a transfer of property with a reserved legal life estate. Another is an insurance policy beneficiary designation under which the designated beneficiary opts to leave the

(Footnote Continued)

§ 2036(c), causing a gift and incurring a gift tax; when § 2036(c) was repealed retroactively the taxpayer requested restoration of the status quo by refund of the gift tax incurred, which the government refused because Congress did not provide that form of relief. In Neal v. United States, 151 F.3d 1201 (W.D. Pa. 1998), the court permitted that recovery, on the grounds that, "if a taxpayer may be required to pay retroactively enacted taxes on events that were not taxable . . . when they occurred, . . . the government must refund taxes paid on events that became nontaxable when Congress retroactively repealed § 2036(c)."

[38] The term "family member" is defined in § 2704(c)(2) and incorporated by reference by § 2702(e). It includes an individual's spouse, lineal ancestors and descendants of the individual and the spouse, siblings of the individual (but not the spouse's siblings), and spouses of all these individuals (other than any other spouse of the individual's spouse).

[39] See § 7.2.1 n.23 and accompanying text.

[40] § 2702(a)(2). Under this rule, a qualified interest GRIT with a retained reversion or general power of appointment if the transferor dies before the term expires would be permissible, but the reversion or general power of appointment would not be considered in determining the value of the gift made upon creation of the trust.

[41] § 2702(c)(1).

§ 7.2.2.1

proceeds on deposit with the insurer with terms that mirror those of a life estate in trust and remainder to a third party. It also is possible that this rule could be applied to a transfer of property in exchange for a private annuity.[42]

On the other hand, there is no definitive guidance on whether the transfer of realty subject to an outstanding lease in favor of the transferor, or a transfer into a joint tenancy or tenancy in common, is subject to §2702. But it seems relatively clear that these transactions were not meant to be covered by the zero valuation rule. For example, a lease and the rental expense thereunder are not ignored under Treas. Reg. §25.2702-4(b) in determining the value of transferred property if the lease is for full and adequate consideration. PLR 9638016 also held that §2702 does not apply to a corporate redemption in which the corporation retained the rental payments but transferred to shareholders the reversion following certain ground leases. It cited legislative history and stated that §2702 need not apply because the shareholders would have substantially identical interests before and after the proposed redemption.[43]

§7.2.2.2 Qualified Interest Exception

The §2702 zero valuation rule does not apply if the interest retained by the transferor is a "qualified interest."[44] The logic behind this exception lies in the defects in the §7520 split interest valuation regime, which the qualified interest rules in §2702 effectively negate.

---

[42] PLR 9151045 involved deferred payment to a withdrawing partner of the consideration specified under a buy-sell agreement, which the government stated was "best ... characterized as a private annuity or a similar form of debt rather than an interest in the entity." It then concluded that §2701 would not apply, because neither the taxpayer nor any applicable family member retained any other interest in the entity after withdrawal. Presumably this indicates that the private annuity itself is not a sufficient retained interest in an entity to trigger the application of §2701 and it should not be regarded as a temporal interest in a larger entity for §2702 purposes either.

[43] Cf. PLR 8943079 (owner of operating facility leased to a corporation at arm's length for FMV did not retain a prohibited §2036(c) interest in the corporation's income).

[44] §2702(a)(2). Instead, normal §7520 valuation is applicable.

For example, the value of a straight term interest under §7520 is dependent upon interest rate and mortality assumptions that typically overvalue straight income interests and undervalue the remainder interests that follow them. This occurs because the §7520 interest rate assumption is 120% of the AFR, which seldom (if ever) is attainable by a trust because of prudent fiduciary investment confines. Moreover, §7520 valuation relies on mortality assumptions based on the general population and these transactions typically are engaged in by taxpayers who believe—based on a diagnosis, family history, or just general feelings regarding their physical well-being—that they will "beat the odds" by dying earlier than the tables predict. Further, if the measuring life is a male the unisex mortality assumptions also overstate life expectancy. As a result of these glitches, any retained interest that is based on a mortality component (such as a private annuity) tends to be overvalued and a gift of the following interest is undervalued and therefore subjected to less tax than it should be.

Because it is the remainder interest that is transferred in a GRIT and related transactions, straight §7520 valuation typically produces disadvantageous results to the government in these transactions. So the qualified interest exception imposes requirements that are designed to minimize these misvaluations.

The key to understanding the qualified interest requirements is to recognize that they were modeled after the noncharitable interest in a §664 qualified CRT. Those requirements were created to better assure proper valuation for charitable deduction purposes of the remainder interest in a split interest trust. In this case the requirements assure more accurate valuation of the gifted remainder interest in a typical split interest transfer.

Thus, qualified interests are defined as (1) annuity interests that guarantee distribution of a fixed amount annually, or (2) unitrust interests that guarantee distribution of a fixed percentage of the annually determined FMV of the trust, payable annually. In addition, a qualified interest can be (3) a noncontingent remainder interest following either of the annuity or unitrust qualified interests.[45] Within these boundaries, valuation is more precise (as it is under §664 for charitable deduction

---

[45] §2702(b). It is not altogether clear why this third element was added to the Code, other than to recognize that, if the lead interests are not susceptible to

purposes), because it reflects the fixed absolute annuity or percentage unitrust distribution.

No provision is made to reflect the potential for delayed payments, and no regime is established for payments that are not made, because these payments *must* be made. This mandatory payment requirement makes a commutation power in a qualified interest trust impermissible.[46] It also explains why TAM 9604005 concluded that payment by issuing notes is not permissible. Involved was an annuity that purportedly was paid by the trust distributing cash that was received from the annuitant (actually involving an intermediary that the TAM ignored) pursuant to interest free loans (that would become interest bearing only if the trust ceased to be a grantor trust) in exchange for notes calling for balloon payments in the future. The TAM characterized this approach as constituting deferred payments in violation of the annual payment requirement.[47]

In addition to the fundamental annuity or unitrust interest requirement, there are a slew of additional technical drafting requirements.[48] For example, in both annuity and unitrusts, income in excess of the annual distribution amounts may be paid to or for the benefit of the transferor[49] (or to any other applicable family member retaining the qualified interest), but this interest is ignored for valuation purposes under § 2702. Moreover, no other beneficiary may receive an interest in

---

(Footnote Continued)

valuation abuses, then neither is the remainder, and a transferor of the remainder ought to be able to rely on the same valuation regime.

Although planning involving these retained reversionary interests is allowable, it is unlikely that taxpayers will find this planning attractive, because the taxpayer reacquires the trust corpus at its (presumably) appreciated value at the end of the transferred term. Because lead interests in such trusts must comply with the fixed annuity or percentage unitrust rules, a reverse freeze using this alternative also should not work.

[46] See Treas. Reg. § 25.2702-3(d)(5).

[47] Treas. Reg. § 25.2702-3(b)(1). It also regarded the interest free nature of each note as constituting an economic benefit to the trust remainder beneficiaries that constituted an additional contribution to the trust in violation of Treas. Reg. § 25.2702-3(b)(4). See § 7.2.2.2.3 with respect to payment of annuities with financial instruments such as notes.

[48] Imposed under Treas. Reg. § 25.2702-3.

[49] See, e.g., PLR 9519029.

§7.2.2.2

the trust during the term. Then, by virtue of this, the government in numerous PLRs in the mid-1990s required that these trusts mandate distribution of an additional amount in excess of the retained annuity "to reimburse the grantor for any federal income tax paid by the grantor attributable to any trust income in excess of the [annuity]." These additional payments are ignored in valuing the retained qualified interest (and therefore do not reduce the gift made in the form of the transferred trust remainder interest), all to preclude the grantor's payment of income tax on trust income from constituting a form of constructive addition to the trust that bestows an indirect untaxed increase in the value of the remainder.[50]

Furthermore, unlike a CRUT, the requirements under § 2702 do not permit distribution to be limited to just all income earned for the year. Also, in both annuity and unitrusts, the governing instrument must (1) prohibit commutation of the retained interest, (2) contain provisions relating to the computation of the guaranteed payment in a short tax year, and (3) if the guaranteed payment is expressed as a fraction or percentage of the initial FMV of the trust, contain a provision adjusting the guaranteed amount if the initial FMV is determined incorrectly. Further, (4) annuity trusts must prohibit additions to the trust, (5) remainder interest trusts must prohibit payments of income in excess of the guaranteed payment amount, and (6) "each remainder interest must be . . . payable to the beneficiary or the beneficiary's estate in all events."

A fixed payment equal to the greater of $X or a percentage of the trust FMV is permissible and recognized for valuation purposes to the extent of the *greater* of the two payments,[51] and a payment that increases at no more than 20% annually is permitted.[52] But an annual payment limited to the *lesser* of the fixed percentage or a specified dollar amount

---

[50] See § 5.11.9 nn.242-245 and accompanying text. PLR 200846001 confirmed that neither the existence nor the exercise of a power to substitute assets will disqualify a grantor's retained interest trust.

[51] See Treas. Reg. § 25.2702-3(d) and examples contained in Treas. Reg. § 25.2702-3(e).

[52] The authority for which is found in Treas. Reg. §§ 25.2702-3(b)(1)(ii)(A), 25.2702-3(c)(1)(ii). Calculation of the value of a graduated annuity is illustrated in Treas. Reg. §§ 20.2036-1(c)(2)(ii) and 20.2036-1(c)(2)(iii) Example 7.

§7.2.2.2

(or all the trust income) is impermissible.[53] Term interests for the *shorter* of the life of the term interest holder or a specified period are permitted, but those for the *longer* of those periods are forbidden.[54]

Illustrating several of these principles and requirements was the GRAT in PLR 9351005, in which a 15 year grantor retained annuity was supplemented annually (as was the case in PLR 9345035) with an amount equal to any increase in the grantor's income tax attributable to the trust being a § 675(4)(C) grantor trust. In addition, the annuity would terminate early on the death of the grantor. The government held that the trust met the requirements of § 2702 and the annuity could be subtracted from the value of the property transferred to the trust to determine the amount of the gift on creation. But the Ruling also held that the supplemental amount could not be factored into the determination of the value of that annuity because only the minimum amount guaranteed to be paid annually qualifies for computation purposes.

Collectively, these various rules are meant to preclude beating the government on income yield because the annuity or unitrust amount must be paid regardless of the actual yield in the entity. And mortality assumptions are not a source of abuse under the qualified interest regime because § 2036(a)(1) inclusion at the transferor's death will apply if the grantor does not outlive the term annuity or unitrust.[55] Thus, the

---

[53] Treas. Reg. § 25.2702-3(d)(1).

[54] Treas. Reg. § 25.2702-3(d)(4).

[55] See Rev. Rul. 76-273, 1976-2 C.B. 268, Rev. Rul. 82-105, 1982-1 C.B. 133, and PLR 9448018 regarding inclusion upon the death of a beneficiary of an annuity or unitrust interest for a term.

Treas. Reg. § 20.2036-1(c)(2)(ii) gives an algebraic formula for determining the portion of a trust that is § 2036(a) includible in the estate of a grantor of a trust paying the annuity. It is the annual annuity divided by the § 7520 assumed rate of return in effect when the decedent died (or on the alternate valuation date, if § 2032 is elected). So, if a retained annuity payment is $100,000 annually from a trust of $2 million and the applicable § 7520 rate is 6%, the amount includible is $1,666,666—that being the amount of the trust, producing income at 6%, that is needed to generate an annual payment of $100,000. As the regulation states, "the portion of the trust's corpus includible in D's gross estate bears the same ratio to the entire corpus as D's income interest in the trust bears to the entire income interest in the trust." Here "income interest" means the annuity amount and the entire income interest is a function of the § 7520 assumed rate of return. So, at 6% the $2 million trust is deemed to generate $120,000 annually, of

transferor's premature death is irrelevant, because no value escapes wealth transfer taxation. In addition, life expectancy is irrelevant to the valuation of a term of years.

Other more subtle consequences are generated by the qualified interest requirements and they typically favor the government. For example, the §7520 interest assumption (120% of the annual midterm AFR interest) usually is far greater than the typical trust can produce. If the assumed rate is lower than the retained annuity rate the valuation rules anticipate that trust corpus will be invaded to satisfy the annuity or unitrust payments. That invasion would reduce the amount passing to the remainder beneficiaries, and lowers the value of the gift of that remainder interest. If the trust is expected to produce more income than the rate assumes, then that invasion is not likely, excess income is expected to be accumulated, the remainder is deemed to be worth more,

---

(Footnote Continued)

which the decedent receives $100,000 or 83.33%, generating inclusion of just $1,666,666 of the total $2 million.

The regulation illustrates a term annuity that the decedent did not outlive and shows that the amount includible is not the discounted present value of the balance of that annuity. This is because the annuity is not includible. Rather, like a trust in which enjoyment did not end before death, the amount includible is the value of the trust portion in which enjoyment was retained—making the value of the remaining term of the retained enjoyment irrelevant.

Many trusts continue to pay the annuity to the grantor's estate if death occurs before expiration of the term. A few trusts may revert to the grantor's estate, reflecting a desire to have the trust corpus available to pay FET (and perhaps to govern disposition of the wealth if the tax objective of creating the trust is defeated by that premature death). With §2036 inclusion the §2207B right of reimbursement is available, which guarantees access to the trust for tax payment purposes, making the reversion unnecessary (and harmful if the reversion returns more than the portion that otherwise would be §2036 includible). Also note that §2036 inclusion means that §2035(a) three-year-rule exposure also exists if, for example, the annuitant seeks to transfer or relinquish the inclusion-generating interest in anticipation of an impending death. (Further, note that basis adjustment issues attendant to partial inclusion also are not explained or illustrated by the regulation.)

All of this §2036(a) application raises the question why anything should be includible in the gross estate of a taxpayer who created a no-refund, single life annuity, such that no entitlement continues past death. On the issue of the full and adequate consideration exception in this context see §§7.2.2.2.1 and 9.2 n.9 and accompanying text.

§7.2.2.2

and the valuation rules work to the taxpayer's disadvantage. Put another way, if the assumed rate (remember, 120% of the federal annual midterm rate) is higher than the trust actually can generate, the rules impose more tax on a higher assumed value of the remainder than is proper.

This misvaluation of the remainder does not apply in a GRUT because interest rate assumptions are irrelevant for unitrust valuation.[56] But GRUTs are not favored in most planning for other reasons—most notably because the unitrust amount paid to the transferor grows as the trust grows in value (and, thus, less value is shifted to the remainder beneficiary) and because trust corpus must be revalued annually.

The valuation rules ignore the possibility of corpus valuation fluctuations due to appreciation or depreciation, or due to invasions. They assume the trust corpus is frozen in value (or that it grows due to accumulations), notwithstanding that it actually may decline in value due to invasion. Thus, for gift tax purposes, a transferred remainder interest may be smaller than the valuation rules assume, and more gift tax may be imposed on creation of the trust than is appropriate. But the transferred remainder interest also might prove to be larger than the valuation rules assume, in which case the gift tax is a bargain. Thus, selection of a term the transferor will outlive, a rate the trust can afford to pay, and assets that will grow without incurring gift tax all are fundamental to the economics and ultimate success of this planning.

§ 7.2.2.2.1 Zero Gift GRATs

On occasion the government asserts in the valuation process that a retained qualified interest is worth less than the tables appear to indicate and, therefore, that a gift of a remainder interest following that retained annuity interest is worth more than expected for gift tax purposes.

---

[56] In recognition of this and notwithstanding the clear rule in § 2702(a)(2)(B) that "[t]he value of any . . . qualified interest shall be determined under section 7520," Treas. Reg. § 25.2702-2(b)(2) specifies that the value of a qualified unitrust interest is determined as if it was a § 664 CRUT interest and specifically limits valuation of qualified interests under § 7520 to the qualified annuity and remainder interests. This deviation reflects the fact that the unitrust tables under § 664 do not rely directly on the § 7520 interest rate valuation approach that is utilized for qualified annuity and remainder trusts.

An annuity that is designed to equal 100% of the value of property transferred to a trust that will pay the annuity may be deemed to be worth less, based on an assumption that the annuity may end prematurely.[57] To illustrate, the taxpayer in PLR 9239015 proposed to create a two year GRAT that would terminate before the two year term expired if the settlor did not survive that entire period. The annuity amount was selected to produce a retained interest valued at 99.171% of the property transferred and a gift of only the balance. In the course of the Ruling the government stated that the annuity amount would exhaust the corpus of the trust prior to expiration of the term, because the payout amount for the term produced a value under the tables of 100% or more.

As a result, "the value of the retained annuity interest [would be] the present value of the right to receive the payments [only] until the fund exhausts or until the prior death of the annuitant, rather than the value computed from the actuarial tables based on the stated term of the trust." An annuity for this shorter term is worth less than the tables otherwise would indicate for the term indicated in the agreement. Therefore, a larger gift of the remainder would be made. Thus, because the fund might be exhausted or the annuitant might die prematurely, the Ruling held that a taxpayer cannot engineer an annuity to produce a retained interest value of exactly 100% of the value of the property transferred and a remainder valued for gift tax purposes at zero.

The Ruling explained that, "[if] the annuity amount will exhaust the funds of the trust precisely at the termination of the trust, the value of the retained interest cannot equal the amount transferred to the trust because of the possibility that the grantor may die before the expiration of the term of the trust." In essence, the government's position is that there must be some value to a remainder interest and, therefore, a gift of some amount.

It may be possible to successfully challenge the government's position, but it also may be prudent to structure transactions on the assump-

---

[57] Based on Rev. Rul. 77-454, 77-1 C.B. 351. A computer search revealed that the government's position had not been litigated prior to 1993 and has been addressed only in an oblique manner that did not cite Rev. Rul. 77-454.

§ 7.2.2.2.1

tion that the government's position is correct[58] and to recognize that the remainder interest in a GRAT or a GRUT may have a greater gift tax value than a simple determination under the actuarial tables may assume. Difficult problems will arise in reporting the value of such a gift, absent a request for a ruling on a proposed transaction.[59] That will make it difficult to know with precision the amount of unified credit used on a particular transfer or remaining at death. And the possibility for a valuation challenge many years after making a transfer exists due to the government's position on the effect of the gift tax statute of limitation in § 2504(c) if no gift tax return is filed, adequately disclosing the transaction.[60] All this may speak in favor of planning that is not dependent on precise determinations, through the use of formula provisions.[61]

The opinion in Estate of Shapiro v. Commissioner[62] should be considered before conceding the government's position. The government raised the issue of valuation of a life annuity for § 2013 purposes and argued unsuccessfully in *Shapiro* that the valuation tables could not be used because, if the annuitant lived to age 109 (the greatest attained age recognized in the tables), the trust paying the annuity would be exhausted prior thereto. According to the Tax Court, the potential for invasions of corpus to make the annuity payments and eventual exhaustion of the trust is not grounds for converting the valuation from a straight life annuity to an annuity for a lesser term certain that would produce a lower valuation, stating:

---

58 The government's position also may be helpful if Congress amends § 2702 to require that there be a gift of some amount in every GRAT. See the discussion of this notion later in this section.

59 And a ruling may not issue. See § 4.01(53) of Rev. Proc. 2012-3, 2012-1 C.B. 113 (updated annually), in which the government states that ruling letters ordinarily will not issue if the annuity payable annually exceeds 50% of the initial FMV of the trust or the remainder interest following the annuity is less than 10% of the initial FMV of the trust. For an excellent rejoinder to the government's arguments against zero-gift GRATs, see Lee, Zero-Out GRATs and GRUTs—Can Still More Be Done, 115 Tax Notes 637 (2007).

60 See § 7.2.4.5.

61 Like those routinely used to create marital deduction or credit shelter bequests and in the creation or severance of trusts for allocation of the GST exemption. See §§ 11.4.5.5, 13.2.7, and 13.7.1.

62 66 T.C.M. (CCH) 1067 (1993).

the mere risk of corpus depletion does not restrict the duration of decedent's interest . . . to a "term certain" for valuation purposes. . . .

Taking [the government's] argument to its theoretical conclusions, *any trust* created with corpus funds equivalent to the present value of a lifetime annuity obligation . . . would have insufficient funds to sustain the annual payments should the annuitant live beyond his or her average life expectancy. In this regard, [the government's] argument contravenes the fundamental purposes and presumptions underlying the actuarial tables.[63]

Promulgated after its loss in *Shapiro*, the government's §7520 regulations indicate that the standard valuation tables will not be used for valuing life estates, terms of years, annuities, and other temporal interests if "the use of standard actuarial tables would produce unreasonable results." As applied in the case of an annuity, the regulations adopt the position directly rejected by the Tax Court in *Shapiro*, stating that:

an annuity payable from a trust or other limited fund . . . is not considered payable for the entire defined period if, considering the applicable section 7520 interest rate, the annuity is expected to exhaust the fund before the last possible payment is made in full. For this purpose, it must be assumed that it is possible for each measuring life to survive until age 110.[64]

As illustrated by an example in the regulations,[65] this means that an annuity payable from a fund that could self-exhaust (because the annuity exceeds the §7520 interest rate and, therefore, the tables must assume that corpus will be invaded to make the annual payment) essentially is treated as a term annuity rather than a life annuity, with the term being 110 years less the starting age of the annuitant. The result is that an annuity that ends upon the annuitant's death before reaching age 110 may be misvalued. As illustrated by an example, this position is not applicable "if the amount of the annuity payment (expressed as a percentage of the initial corpus) is less than or equal to the applicable section 7520 interest rate at the date of the transfer . . . " which may make it harmless in some situations. But in the case of payments from trusts created after the 2008 economic meltdown, when the §7520 rate

---

[63] 66 T.C.M. at 1074 (emphasis in original).

[64] Treas. Reg. §§ 1.7520-3(b)(2)(i), 20.7520-3(b)(2)(i), and 25.7520-3(b)(2)(i).

[65] Treas. Reg. § 25.7520-3(b)(2)(i) Example 5.

§7.2.2.2.1

was very low, the government's position is very significant. And it may need to be litigated to test its validity under the holding in *Shapiro*.

These trusts may be effective for value shifting purposes notwithstanding the government's position if significant growth is expected and annuity (or unitrust) payments can be made without a net decline in the value of trust corpus.

Imagine for discussion purposes that a zero gift GRAT or GRUT *can* be created. How should the adequate and full consideration exception to § 2036(a) apply in such a situation? The government addressed this question in the preamble to final Treas. Reg. § 20.2036-1(c)(2) by comparing a GRAT or a GRUT to the creation of a trust with retention of the entire income interest, stating that:[66]

> the full and adequate consideration exception ... does not apply [because] [t]here is a significant difference between the bona fide sale of property to a third party in exchange for an annuity, and the retention of an annuity interest in property transferred to a third party. In a bona fide sale, there is a negotiation and agreement between two parties, each of whom is the owner of a property interest before the sale; each uses his or her own property to provide consideration to the other party in exchange for the property interest to be received from the other in the sale. When the transferor retains an annuity or similar interest in the transferred property (as in the case of a GRAT or GRUT), the transferor is not selling the transferred property to a third party in exchange for an annuity because there is no other owner of property negotiating or engaging in a sale transaction with the transferor. The transferor, instead, is transferring the property subject to a retained possession and enjoyment of, or right to, the income from the property.

These statements are not correct—particularly to the extent the GRAT or GRUT payments exceeded the income that would have been generated before death. Indeed, the government is being completely disingenuous to the extent it would compare a short term GRAT or GRUT to a transfer with a retained income interest for life. For example, the annuity or unitrust payments in a two year GRAT or GRUT would exceed 50% of the value of the trust on creation,[67] making this look totally

---

[66] T.D. 9414, 2008-2 C.B. 454.

[67] See § 7.2.2.2.1 n.59. These are precisely the situations the government loathes, to the point that it will not grant PLRs regarding them.

different from the traditional § 2036 transfer with retained income interest.

Even if the adequate and full consideration exception to § 2036 does not apply (which is not a concession that taxpayers should make), the result in these regulations is improper for another reason. Inclusion of the annuity amounts already received premortem, plus the value of the right to receive any remaining annuity payments that will be made to the estate postmortem, along with the underlying corpus of the GRAT or GRUT itself, is a form of double inclusion as to which the § 2043 consideration offset rule should apply. In these cases, § 2043 should purge the estate of the consideration received on creation of the trust (precisely because the adequate and full consideration exception to § 2036(a) does not apply), yet there is no mention of § 2043 in the regulations or their preamble. This element is illustrated below.

Before turning to these matters, however, consider the *potential* implications of what the government is suggesting in the extract above. It is not uncommon for taxpayers to create IDGTs and then to transfer highly appreciated assets to those entities, usually in exchange for a note (perhaps a SCIN, but not necessarily) or, as most relevant here, for an annuity or unitrust entitlement. Because a grantor trust is involved, the taxpayer claims that the transfer is not a sale for income tax gain or loss realization purposes. And as a transfer in exchange for consideration, the taxpayer also claims that the transaction is not a gift for wealth transfer tax purposes. Is it really possible to craft a transaction that is neither a gift nor a sale? What *is* that? By its grantor trust promulgations[68] the government appears to accede to the notion that there is no income tax realization event in this sale-to-IDGT transaction. It hardly matters whether that position is correct.[69]

Instead, *if* the preamble to these § 2036 regulations is predictive, *perhaps* the government is staking out a position that the transfer to any self-settled trust cannot be a transfer for consideration. In the immediate context this would mean that the adequate and full consideration exception to § 2036 inclusion at death is inapplicable. It is just conjecture, but it

---

[68] See Rev. Rul. 85-13, 1985-1 C.B. 184, recently confirmed in Rev. Rul. 2007-13, 2007-1 C.B. 684.

[69] A notion discussed in § 5.11.9 n.216 et seq. and accompanying text, because it is unlikely that the government will reverse itself on this income tax issue.

§ 7.2.2.2.1

would appear that the same position *might* be applicable to disregard consideration in the sale-to-IDGT context. This would mean that the transfer does not avoid gift tax, because the note, annuity, or unitrust interest used to pay for the alleged sale is not consideration for wealth transfer tax purpose.

As illustrated below, this too is wrong minded. But the overall strategy is what matters, and it appears that the government is forsaking income tax gain or loss realization on the transfer, which is not a major concession if the gain remains locked into the basis of the transferred asset and may be realized on any subsequent sale or exchange by the trust. Meanwhile, is the government asserting wealth transfer tax— presumably gift tax on the initial transaction and potentially FET inclusion at the transferor's death? This would be favorable to the government, because the wealth transfer tax rates typically are higher. *If* this prediction of the government's strategy is accurate, the preamble to these regulations could be the precursor of a major crack down on a transaction that taxpayers have employed for years.

To examine the significance of this in the immediate GRAT or GRUT context, consider a taxpayer who transfers $3 million in cash to a trust in exchange for a 10 year annuity payable at $374,000 per year, and that the AFR at the time of creation is 4.2%. If we round the numbers for illustration purposes only, let's assume that the value of the annuity is equal to the $3 million transferred in exchange for it. Assume death in year eight, after the taxpayer received $2,992,000 in annuity payments. If the trust assets had not grown whatsoever, the balance of the trust would be $8,000 (having paid out $374,000 annually for eight years). Most observers would assume that, together, the two amounts would generate $3 million of inclusion—the $2,992,000 under § 2033 (to the extent that money had not been consumed by the taxpayer with no value at death) and the $8,000 under § 2036 (as the balance of the trust)—and that the result appropriately would mimic the inclusion had there been no transfer inter vivos (cash worth $3 million at death). This example is unrealistic, because it assumes that there has been no change through investment, appreciation, depreciation, or consumption of the $3 million transferred.

The example also is wrong under § 2036, which requires inclusion of the value of the property transferred inter vivos with retained enjoy-

§ 7.2.2.2.1

ment until death, and that means inclusion of $3 million of cash, not the $8,000 that remains of it at death. If you don't believe this notion, consider an analogous transaction, in which the taxpayer transfers gold bullion worth $3 million with the same retained enjoyment until death, and the trustee thereafter financed payment of the annuity by borrowing against the bullion as collateral. At death § 2036 reaches the value of the bullion transferred by the taxpayer and does not consider the debt that was incurred by the trustee to make the annuity payments.[70]

The correct result under the Code would be inclusion under § 2036 of the FET value of the $3 million of cash (or the gold bullion transferred), and then another $2,992,000 under § 2033, which is inappropriate, because it generates a form of double inclusion—once as if the transaction never was done (include the $3 million of cash, or the bullion) and again as if it was done (include the $2,992,000)—a result that the § 2043 consideration offset rule ameliorates. The Code calls for a subtraction from the gross estate of the $2,992,000 received as consideration for the transfer that § 2036 is ignoring. (Indeed, if the annuity would continue for the balance of the 10 year term, also includible would be the right to the last two annual payments of $374,000 each, and the consideration offset would be allowed for the very same amount.)

It may seem silly to include and then subtract, but the Code operates in this way because the amounts includible at death and the consideration received may not be as easy to trace and identify, or value, as in this simplistic example. Saying here that § 2036 includes only the remaining value of $8,000 in the trust is a shorthand application of the two steps that actually are required—include the $3 million value transferred and then subtract the $2,992,000 consideration received. But as values change and as consideration received is consumed or reinvested in ways that make tracing difficult—that is to say, in a realistic illustration—it is likely that the numbers illustrated here will not produce an identical result, making the shorthand approach shown here and illustrated in the regulations misleading.

Note also that the § 2043 consideration offset rule should apply notwithstanding the government's bona fide sale position in the pream-

---

[70] This rule may differ in a trust involving investment and reinvestment, making tracing impossible. See Estate of Kroger v. Commissioner, 145 F.2d 901 (6th Cir. 1944). But that is not this illustration.

§ 7.2.2.2.1

ble. That is, some observers may wonder whether neither the adequate and full consideration exception to § 2036 *nor* the § 2043 consideration offset rule can apply if there is no bona fide sale. In that regard, consider the language of § 2043: it applies "if any one of the transfers, trusts, interests, rights, or powers enumerated and described in sections 2035 to 2038 . . . is made, created, exercised, or relinquished for a consideration in money or money's worth, but is not a bona fide sale for an adequate and full consideration in money or money's worth." That describes this situation. By the government's own admission, this is not a bona fide sale for adequate consideration. Thus, § 2043 must apply.

This is not to concede the government's position, nor to even suggest that this illustration involves an exchange that is neither a bona fide sale nor a transfer for consideration. Indeed, the whole position here is identical to a transfer for the exact same annuity done with a commercial annuity issuer or a third party's trust, as to which the government appears to think that the result would be totally different. It is difficult to perceive that the taxpayer receives anything different in any of those three transfers, based on the different identity of the payor of the annuity. And that informs the conclusion here that the government is wrong to deny the § 2036 adequate and full consideration exception. It also explains why the government wants Congress to amend § 2702 to require that there be some minimal gift in any GRAT—precluding a zero gift GRAT precludes reliance on the full-and-adequate consideration exception to § 2036.

Illustrations like this get dicey if the asset transferred is property that changes in value, or if the payments received by the taxpayer are spent in ways that have no value at death, making tracing and valuation convoluted. Yet the principles remain the same—even though their application may be occluded. Run an illustration, for example, in which the $3 million transferred is the stock in a closely held business that explodes in value before the taxpayer dies, or it is Blackacre that the trustee swaps for Greenacre, which the trustee thereafter uses as collateral to borrow the cash to make annual annuity payments. Notice that the logistics of these inclusion and offset provisions get complicated (and there still would be no § 2053 deduction for the trust's debt, because the debt is not the taxpayer's obligation). Unfortunately, there is virtually no authority illustrating these kinds of transactions, because taxpayers historically did not make transfers to which § 2036 might apply, in exchange for consideration paid in return to which § 2043 might apply. Note also that these transactions are nothing like a traditional transfer into a revocable trust with a retained right to income, as alleged by the preamble.

Also remember that taxpayers have long asserted that these transactions are not sales or exchanges—for income tax purposes—based on their objective of avoiding capital gain on the initial transfer of appreciated property into the trust, and later on the trust's use of appreciated property in payment of SCINs or the annual annuity or unitrust in a GRAT or GRUT transaction. In a sense, the government would be simply turning the IDGT notion back on the taxpayer—saying that there is no sale and therefore that the bona fide sale exception to § 2036 cannot apply.

Never mind that this confuses income and wealth transfer tax notions of sale or exchange treatment, or that the same annuity, acquired in exchange for a transfer into a trust that a third party created, would be regarded by the government as a candidate for bona fide sale treatment. (Indeed, it would appear that a qualifying GRAT or GRUT transfer could be made in conjunction with a third party trust, but taxpayers likely would not favor such a transaction because it is very hard to generate defective grantor trust nonrealization treatment in a third party trust context.)

§ 7.2.2.2.2 Terms for Life or a Specified Period

Walton v. Commissioner[71] held that (then) Treas. Reg. § 25.2702-3(d)(3) (now -3(d)(4)), as illustrated in Treas. Reg. § 25.2702-3(e) Example 5, was "an invalid and unreasonable interpretation" of § 2702. As a result of the "historical unity between a taxpayer and the taxpayer's estate," the court held that designating the taxpayer's estate as the alternative payee in the event of the taxpayer's death before expiration of a term annuity was permissible and the full value of that annuity would be considered in determining the value of the gift of the

---

[71] 115 T.C. 589, 603-604 (2000), acq., Notice 2003-72, 2003-2 C.B. 964 (a unanimous reviewed opinion involving a taxpayer who created two "substantially identical" two year GRATs with the annuity payable to the settlor's estate if death occurred before the term annuity ended).

following remainder. "Congress meant to allow individuals to retain qualified annuity interests for a specified term of years, and . . . the proper method for doing so is to make the balance of any payments due after the grantor's death payable to the grantor's estate." In the wake of this loss the government revised that example to permit the entire term interest to qualify. The simple change made by addition of a new Treas. Reg. § 25.2702-2 (a) (5) was to regard a person and that person's estate as a single qualified recipient. And a revised Example 5 illustrates that change.

In addition, in a new Example 8 the regulation provides that a following annuity in S can be a qualified spousal interest and will be considered in valuing the remainder following both. If S's interest is for a fixed term or until S's prior death. But, by Example 9, the government states that an annuity payable to S (rather than to the grantor's estate) for only the remaining term of the grantor's primary annuity (if the grantor dies within the term) *cannot* qualify because there is no way to know, at inception of the trust, when S's annuity will begin and therefore how long it will last.[72] The way to address this, then, is to make an annuity payable to the grantor's estate if the grantor dies early, and make that annuity payable to S by the grantor's estate.[73]

§ 7.2.2.2.3 Payment with Notes

Another hot button issue for the government was illustrated by TAM 9717008, which involved an annuity that would continue to S if D died during the annuity term, and some payments that were made with

---

[72] See Schott v. Commissioner, 319 F.3d 1203 (9th Cir. 2003); Estate of Focardi v. Commissioner, 91 T.C.M. (CCH) 936 (2006) (explaining that the problem with recognizing the value of the spousal annuity component was because it "is dependent on when the grantor dies and, in particular, on how much of the term remains at the grantor's death" and also stating that "[t]he possibility of . . . an abuse is present where, as here, it is not certain at the outset of the trusts that payments will ever be made under a survivorship annuity," although the court did not explain why that matters if, between the grantor and the spouse, the full annuity will be paid).

[73] See McCaffrey, Plaine, & Schneider, The Aftermath of *Walton*: The Rehabilitation of the Fixed-Term, Zeroed-Out GRAT, 95 J. Tax'n 325 (2001), regarding ancillary planning implications of *Walton*, and see § 13.5.6.7 regarding transfer of the remaining annuity term interest from the estate to S and qualification for the marital deduction.

notes. The GRAT was for two years only, paying 54.8% of the initial value of the trust annually. Of the over $24 million annuity, almost $11 million was satisfied in the first year with a note that was repaid at termination of the GRAT in the next year. When all payments back to D were tallied, only approximately 57% of the original corpus was returned in the form of the annuity. The remainder beneficiaries received the over $20 million of remaining corpus, meaning that the property transferred into the GRAT had grown pretty substantially during the short two year period. The gift reported on creation of the GRAT was $121,000 (the value of the remainder). To make the government all the more anxious, S did a mirror image GRAT at the same time, using identical corpus, the same term, the same secondary annuity interest, the same valuation, and so on. The government concluded that neither annuity satisfied the requirements of § 2702 and therefore each was worth $0 in determining the amount of the gifts made on creation of the GRATs.[74]

---

[74] Citing Treas. Reg. § § 25.2702-3(e) Examples 5 and 6 (which the government has done before) and 25.2702-2(d)(1) Examples 6 and 7 (which was not clear or explained), the government also denied all value to the secondary annuity interest in the respective spouses of the donors. Examples 5 and 6 subsequently were amended in the wake of *Walton*, as discussed in § 7.2.2.2.2. Also consider § 7.3.2 regarding the reciprocal trust doctrine as it may apply in the context of "parallel" or "mirror image" GRATs created by spouses, each with a short term retained annuity for the grantor followed by a much longer term annuity for the grantor's spouse, which is regarded by some as a more desirable form of § 2702 planning because it limits the retained term exposure to § 2036 of an early death of the respective grantors.

Cook v. Commissioner, 115 T.C. 15 (2000), aff'd, 269 F.3d 854 (7th Cir. 2001), involved spouses who created GRATs subject to § 2702, with S to receive the balance of D's grantor annuity if D died during the annuity term. Based on Treas. Reg. § 25.2702-3(e) Examples 5 and 6 (prior to subsequent post-*Walton* amendments, which are not relevant here), the Tax Court held that only the value of each annuity for the respective grantor's life or the specified term, whichever ended first, would be respected as a reduction from the full FMV of the trusts for gift tax valuation purposes. Walton v. Commissioner, 115 T.C. 589 (2000), acq., Notice 2003-72, 2003-2 C.B. 964, concluded in its final footnote that, although the court declared Example 5 to be invalid, its decision in *Cook* would not change and the government's post-*Walton* revision of Example 5 would not alter that reality. See n.57.3. To the same effect see Schott v. Commissioner, 81 T.C.M. 1600 (2001), rev'd, 319 F.3d 1203 (9th Cir. 2003) (involving a two life GRAT, payable to S if death occurred within the term), which concluded that S's secondary annuity (which was revocable by the grantor) would be ignored under

§ 7.2.2.2.3

The TAM took exception to use of the notes to pay a portion of the annuity in the first year, regarding it as a method to delay distribution of corpus in satisfaction of the annuity obligation and thereby trap more of the extraordinary appreciation in the trust corpus for ultimate distribution to the remainder beneficiaries. The government stated that this was a loan transaction and not an annuity payment and, on that basis, failed to qualify under § 2702. The TAM held that "the annuity interests created . . . do not satisfy the § 2702 requirements that the annuity be *paid* (1) in a stated dollar amount, and (2) not less frequently than annually. Therefore, the annuity interests . . . do not meet the requirements for a qualified interest, and the interests are valued at zero."[75] Even with that result, however, it is notable that the donors transferred all the appreciation during the trust term free of gift tax. So, although the gift on creation was larger than expected, the plan still had significant merit.

This form of transaction led to the issuance of Treas. Reg. §§ 25.2702-3(b)(1)(i), 25.2702-3(c)(1)(i), and 25.2702-3(d)(5) (now -3(d)(6)), in 1999, which are premised on the absolute position stated in the preamble to the proposed regulations that use of debt instruments or other financial arrangements (such as options) does not constitute payment of the requisite annuity or unitrust amount. This wrong-minded position is based on the government's notion expressed in the TAM that

---

(Footnote Continued)

§ 2702 for valuation of the grantor's gift upon creation of the trust. Thus, only a 15 year or single life annuity interest was regarded as retained in determining the value of the remainder following that transfer. According to the Tax Court, under then Treas. Reg. § 25.2702-2(a)(5) (now -2(a)(6) due to post-*Walton* revisions), "retention of a power to revoke a qualified annuity interest . . . of the transferor's spouse is treated as the retention of a qualified annuity interest" by the grantor, but S's secondary annuity was not a qualified annuity interest. More recently, see also TAM 200230003 (reciprocal, mirror image, laddered, and graduated GRATs created by spouses for each of them for life or the specified term with a secondary annuity to S or S's estate and, if the spouse did not survive the grantor, giving the original grantor a general power to appoint with default in the reminder to the grantor's estate; the government still rejected the secondary spousal annuity because it was contingent on surviving the grantor and was not for the lesser of life or the term of years but, instead, for the full term regardless of death). Notwithstanding the acquiescence to *Walton* and reversal of *Schott* the government did not revise the regulations regarding these two-spouse GRATs.

[75] Emphasis in original; citations omitted. See § 7.2.2.2 n.47 and accompanying text regarding delayed payment and the use of notes.

qualified interests must be payable annually, by a specified date each year, and that issuance of a note or similar instrument is not tantamount to payment. "A note is merely a promise to pay in the future. Delaying payment by the use of a note . . . alters the true value of the transferor's retained interest, contrary to Congressional intent . . . ."

That conclusion is wrong to the extent of the FMV of the note or other instrument issued, provided that the grantor could sell or otherwise market the trust's instrument and immediately realize cash. Nevertheless, the regulations provide that a trust cannot qualify as a GRAT or GRUT unless it prohibits the trustee from making payment in such a manner.

The preamble to the proposed regulations also stated that the government "will apply the step transaction doctrine where more than one step is used to achieve similar results." The final regulations preamble moderated this only to the extent it provided that a trustee may borrow from an unrelated party to make a payment, but still provided that step transaction treatment would apply if the trustee borrowed cash from the grantor to repay that third party loan, or if the third party lender required the grantor to make a deposit with the lender in an amount equal to the trust's loan. Although it thus does not expressly preclude the use of borrowed cash to make annuity payments, borrowing from a third party to make a cash payment is impossible to distinguish from borrowing from the grantor by issuing a note directly in payment of the annual obligation. Nevertheless, the step transaction statement presumably could prohibit a trust from selling trust assets to a third party on installment payments and distributing the notes received in satisfaction of the annual payment.

Apparently it would be permissible to pledge appreciating assets in the trust as collateral for a market interest loan from a bank or other third party lender and use the borrowed cash to make annual payments. Neither form of making payment is abusive and the regulations appear to be an inappropriate overreaction to the extent consistent application of the position articulated would preclude any form of payment that entails debt or similar instruments. Further, application of the step transaction doctrine would require some form of tracing of the proceeds of any kind of borrowing, which in many cases would be unrealistic. It is odd, perhaps, that the regulations did not just preclude GRATs and GRUTs

§7.2.2.2.3

from being in debt or otherwise having outstanding obligations that might be satisfied against trust assets and the fact that they did not go to those lengths may indicate that the step transaction statement is just saber rattling.

§7.2.2.2.4 *Traditional GRIT Strategy*

The garden-variety or common law GRIT no longer is viable unless the remainder beneficiary is not a family member, as defined in §2704(c)(2), or the settlor is willing to incur a gift tax on 100% of the value of transferred property at the time of creation (in hopes of avoiding wealth transfer taxation on an appreciated value at a later time).[76] Whether the alternative qualified interest GRUT or GRAT is worth implementing depends on appreciation potential in the corpus, the expected income yield relative to the forced payment specified, and whether the transferor is likely to outlive the retained term. In addition, shifting appreciation is not meaningful unless the wealth transfer tax imposes progressive rates, which means that an estate freeze is of no value whenever the highest marginal rate has dropped and the applicable exclusion amount has risen to a point at which the excise essentially is a flat tax.

For example, if a taxpayer has an asset worth $100x that is expected to double in value, and the taxpayer has consumed the applicable exclusion amount and therefore will pay gift tax on an inter vivos transfer of that asset (at, say, a 35% maximum rate), it won't matter if the taxpayer gives the asset and pays a $35x tax, leaving $65x net of tax to double in value to $130x, or holds the $100x asset, allows it to double in value to $200x, and then incurs the same 35% tax of $70x, leaving $130x after tax.[77] Other factors may inform making the gift (such as removing the gift tax dollars from the taxpayer's gross estate at death more than three years later), but shifting appreciation is not one of them.

---

[76] Presumably deemed gift problems attributable to a trust holding non-income-producing property can be avoided if the trust authorizes retention of such property and gift taxation on creation as a consequence thereof is irrelevant because, in a nonqualified interest GRUT or GRAT, 100% of the trust corpus is taxable as a gift at creation anyway. See TAM 8723007 and PLRs 8932083, 8932082, 8905045, 8844008, 8805029, and 8642028.

[77] See §7.2.3 at text following n.149.

§7.2.2.2.4

A qualified interest GRUT or GRAT may be a qualified S Corporation shareholder,[78] so planning involving these trusts is not necessarily precluded even for owners of closely held businesses. The decision whether to utilize this device will require careful calculations and realistic projections. In many cases an outright gift or a § 2701 qualified payment freeze will be superior, especially because they will avoid the potential for § 2036(a) inclusion if the transferor fails to outlive the term interest in the GRUT or GRAT.

§ 7.2.2.3 Incomplete Transfer Exception

Not all retained temporal interests are subject to the § 2702 retained interest valuation rule. For example, incomplete transfers, as to which the gift tax is not yet applicable and, therefore, as to which § § 2036(a)(2) and 2038(a)(1) would apply at the transferor's death, are not subject to § 2702.[79] The rationale for this rule is *not* because FET inclusion precludes a tax free shift of future appreciation and makes inter vivos valuation irrelevant (if that was true all GRITs would be exempt until the term expired). Instead, this exception simply recognizes that a gift tax valuation rule cannot apply before the gift tax applies, which requires a completed and therefore taxable gift.

---

[78] One hundred percent grantor trust status is available with a § 673 reversion or under § 675(4)(C), among other sections. See § 5.11. For example, PLR 9152034 illustrated the proper computation of the value of a 12% annuity for eight years in a GRAT and concluded that the trust was a grantor trust because the grantor retained a reversion in the trust if death occurred within the eight year term and the value of that reversion exceeded 5% of the value of the trust. Based on this conclusion, the Ruling then held that the trust was a qualified shareholder of S Corporation stock. To the same effect see PLR 8945006, involving 100% grantor trust status under § § 673(a) and 677(a)(1).

[79] I.R.C. § 2702(a)(3). The § 2702(a)(3)(A)(i) exception "to the extent [a] transfer is an incomplete transfer" is deemed to apply only to a transfer "no portion of which would be treated as a completed gift" under Chapter 12; it is available, however, to the extent a transfer "is wholly incomplete as to an undivided fractional share of the property transferred (without regard to any consideration received by the transferor) . . . ." See Treas. Reg. § § 25.2702-1(c)(1), 25.2702-2(d)(1) Examples 4-5. § 2702(a)(3)(B) specifies that an incomplete transfer means "any transfer which would not be treated as a gift whether or not consideration was received for such transfer," which is not necessarily inconsistent with this regulatory position.

§7.2.2.4 Disclaimer and Nongeneral Power Exceptions

The government provided by regulation[80] that, although "an assignment of an interest in an existing trust" would be subject to §2702, a qualified §2518 disclaimer is not. As illustrated by PLR 200530002, however, a nonqualified disclaimer will be treated the same as a transfer that is fully subject to §2702. Involved in that case was a pre-1977 trust with chronologically exempt generation-skipping provisions and a tardy renunciation of 20% of the taxpayer's remainder interest. Because the disclaimant retained an income interest, the government regarded this renunciation as a transfer that was subject to §2702, as to which the income interest therefore would be deemed to have no value and the remainder disclaimed was therefore a gift of 100% of the value of that 20% portion of the trust.

The same regulation also provides that the exercise, release, or lapse of a nongeneral power of appointment is not a transfer in trust, which means that §2702 cannot apply. Presumably this permits a beneficiary to appoint an interest in trust that the beneficiary could not have given away, had it been transferred to the beneficiary outright, and to exercise a nongeneral power to create interests that could not be created by the beneficiary with the beneficiary's own property.

If these are accurate interpretations, powers of appointment may be a significant planning tool to allow powerholders to engage in planning that neither the donor nor the powerholder could have employed with their own assets. The availability of this planning appears to be confirmed by a statement in the regulations[81] that a retained interest (subject to §2702) is only one that was "held by the same individual both before and after the transfer." If state property law concepts are respected, the holder of a power of appointment is only an agent acting on behalf of the donor and not an owner of the appointive property itself, meaning that §2702 cannot apply.

---

[80] Treas. Reg. §25.2702-2(a)(2)(ii), which is similar to the same rule in Treas. Reg. §25.2701-1(b)(3)(ii).

[81] Treas. Reg. §25.2702-2(a)(3).

§7.2.2.5 Spousal Exception

The creation of a trust for the benefit of a spouse for life, remainder to a child, in which the settlor retains no interest, is not subject to §2702 (notwithstanding that the spouse is an applicable family member), because the spouse did not hold an interest in the trust both before and after its creation.[82] Furthermore, election of QTIP treatment does not alter this result because, (1) if the settlor did not elect the marital deduction, a gift tax was incurred on the full value of the property transferred to the trust at its creation (meaning no valuation abuse occurs), and (2) if the settlor did elect marital deduction treatment a tax on the full value of the trust corpus will be incurred when the spouse's interest in the trust terminates, again meaning there is no valuation abuse.[83] The intriguing issue that this exception raises is whether allocation of split interests to marital and nonmarital trusts (for example, allocation of a life estate or term of years to a marital deduction trust and a remainder to a nonmarital trust) is permissible without triggering §2702 because there is no transfer or retention by the spouse that meets the requisites for application of that section. There is no direct answer to this question in either the Code or regulations, but the following analysis may be helpful.

A "joint purchase" rule in §2702(c)(2) appears to be the only relevant authority. It applies if more than one *family member acquires* property in split interest format (for example, a life estate and a remainder interest). It is notable that, although the title of this provision uses the word "purchases," the body of the provision uses the word "acquires." Although it does not appear to have been Congress' intent, this difference in language might allow §2702 to reach acquisitions by purchase or any other method. This probably is the weakest link in this analysis, however, because it seems clear that §2702(c)(2) was not meant to apply if, for example, two family members receive property by gift or devise from a third party in the form of a life estate and remainder. The situation involved here—funding marital and nonmarital trusts after an individual's death—seems to be analogous even if the decision to fund using temporal interests is made by the decedent's personal representative (rather than by the decedent in the form of a specific devise). And

---

[82] See Treas. Reg. §25.2702-2(d)(1) Example 3.

[83] Treas. Reg. §25.2702-2(d)(1) Example 3.

that personal representative might be either the spouse or the remainder beneficiary.

Assume, however, just for the sake of argument, that "acquires" does encompass the form of acquisition involved in a split interest funding. The issue then arises whether family members are involved if it is marital and nonmarital trusts that actually acquire title to property. In this respect, § 2702(e) is relevant, incorporating by reference § 2704(c)(2) for the definition of "member of the family." Although a trust is not a family member under § 2702(c)(2), an attribution rule[84] may apply for purposes of all of § 2704(c), although this is not expressly stated. That attribution rule[85] appears to apply with respect to a marital deduction trust of any variety authorized under § 2056. So it seems fair to assume that split interest funding involving trusts could be regarded as split interest ownership by the trust beneficiaries, rather than by the trusts or their trustees, for purposes of § 2702.

Now the question returns to the relevance of the regulation[86] that prompted this digression. Can it be that D's transfer of property to an irrevocable marital deduction trust for the benefit of S is not subject to § 2702 but that a personal representative's decision to allocate a temporal split interest to such a trust is? The regulation states that S did not hold an interest in the property both before and after the transfer into trust and, therefore, that § 2702 cannot apply. The crux is that the regulations[87] define the "retained" requirement for purposes of § 2702(a)(1) to mean that an interest was held by the same individual both before and after the subject transfer. In this case, the result of § 2702(c)(4) joint purchase treatment, if applicable, would be that S (by attribution through the marital deduction trust) would be treated as having acquired the entire property and then made a transfer of the remainder interest to the nonmarital trust. This analysis is applicable, however, only if split interest funding is regarded as an "acquisition" for § 2702(c)(4) purposes.[88]

---

[84] § 2704(c)(3).

[85] Which is an incorporation by reference of the entity attribution rule in § 2701(e)(3).

[86] Treas. Reg. § 25.2702-2(d)(1) Example 3.

[87] Treas. Reg. § 25.2702-2(a)(3).

[88] Another question may be appropriate: if §§ 2701 and 2702 are in pari materia, in the sense that each is designed to preclude valuation abuses through

An overriding policy oriented question is whether there is any reason to suggest that § 2702 was meant to apply to bifurcated enjoyment of this nature. No indication appears in the direct provisions of the Code or the regulations, although the ability to engage in split interest funding would represent an opportunity to engage in postmortem estate planning during S's overlife, which may encourage the government and ultimately the courts to conclude that this provision must be applicable. And yet the regulations[89] seem to indicate that the converse is true.

There should be no question about the validity of funding a marital deduction trust with a naked life estate, provided that S's beneficial interest in that trust is not a nondeductible terminable interest for purposes of § 2056(b).[90] As an investment, a naked life estate is like any other asset that might be owned by a marital deduction trust. If the document authorizes the trustee to invest in wasting assets (the life estate) for the marital trust and in non-income-producing assets (the remainder interest) for the nonmarital trust, then this form of investment should not be problematic for marital deduction purposes, any more than it would if the marital and nonmarital trusts took cash and purchased split interests belong after the marital deduction was allowed. And if S is likely to die sooner than the government's valuation tables predict, all of this planning translates into estate freezing for S's overlife.

(Footnote Continued)

freezing transactions that bifurcate ownership interests, would it be proper to apply § 2702 in a situation in which § 2701 does not apply? In this respect, § 2701(a)(1) is relevant, it speaking of a transfer of an interest to a member of a decedent's family with an applicable retained interest held by the transferor or an applicable family member. If entity attribution applies here to treat the beneficiaries of marital and nonmarital trusts as holding the interests transferred to those trusts, it may be possible for the government to argue that § 2701 applies to freeze-funding of marital and nonmarital trusts. And because S could be defined as both a family member (as beneficiary of the nonmarital trust) and an applicable family member (as beneficiary of the marital deduction trust), it seems possible that § 2701 could apply to freeze-funding as well. Perhaps the most difficult aspect of this analysis is figuring out who has made a gift to whom, if S is a (perhaps the only current) beneficiary of both trusts in which S has only a life estate.

[89] Treas. Reg. § 25.2702-2(d)(1) Example 3.

[90] See § 13.7.13.

§ 7.2.2.5

§7.2.2.6 Tangible Property Exception

Also excluded from the reach of §2702 are terminable interests in tangible property (not a defined term)[91] if the failure to exercise rights under the term interest would not have a substantial effect on the value of a remainder interest in that property.[92] By way of example, the failure to exercise a retained right to enjoy collectibles or jewelry for a retained term would not likely alter the value of the collectibles or jewelry itself.[93] The same also might be true of the right to use unimproved realty (such as range or timber lands) for a defined term if holding the property for enjoyment during that term will not alter substantially the value of the property and, therefore, nonexercise of the enjoyment right will not substantially affect the value of the remainder. Curiously, if this tangible property exception is met, the value of a retained term interest in the tangible property is not based on the Treasury tables but, instead, is determined as the amount an unrelated third party would pay to purchase the term interest, presumably considering the illiquidity and, typically, non-income-producing nature of the interest.

The value of a term interest in tangible property that is not ignored under §2702 is said by §2702(c)(4)(B) to be the amount "for which such interest could be sold to an unrelated third party." The regulations[94] adopt a more traditional notion that the value of the term interest is what a willing buyer would pay a willing seller, each having reasonable

---

[91] This rule is not limited to tangible *personal* property, the Senate Finance Committee Report at 67 specifically referring to undeveloped realty. That same report says it would not apply to depletable property, however. Curiously, depreciable property was not mentioned. In any event, the tangible property exception is made available under Treas. Reg. §25.2702-2(c)(2)(i)(A) only for property that is *neither* depreciable nor depletable, although a de minimis exception is granted in Treas. Reg. §25.2702-2(c)(2)(ii) for appurtenant depreciable property that has a FMV not exceeding 5% of the FMV of the entire property. The example given in the general explanation is a fence surrounding rangeland that was the subject of a split interest trust.

[92] §2702(c)(4).

[93] See, e.g., PLR 8951065 (transfer of art to trust that reserved to settlor any income from the art—which never had been offered for sale or rent—and rent free possession of the collection; the trustees had the power to lend the art to museums or galleries and to sell it).

[94] Treas. Reg. §25.2702-2(c)(1).

knowledge of the relevant facts and neither being under any compulsion to buy or sell. Stating that "little weight is accorded appraisals,"[95] this value probably is best established by comparable sales or rentals of similar property held for a similar duration. Unfortunately, comparables may be impossible to garner for many types of term interests in tangible property, and the use of the § 7520 tables to value such an interest specifically is denied.[96] This will prevent the type of result reached in TAM 9313005, in which the § 7520 tables were used to value the retained three year term interest in non-income-producing artworks and reduced the value of a gift of the remainder to almost half the FMV of the art.

Conversion of tangible property into property that otherwise would not qualify under this exception is treated as a transfer that triggers application of § 2702 at that time unless the proceeds are converted into a qualified GRAT.[97] Moreover, an addition or improvement that affects the nature of the property to such an extent that the property would not be treated as meeting the tangible property exception will be regarded as a conversion for this purpose.[98]

§ 7.2.2.7 Personal Residence Exception

Finally, a term interest in a trust that holds property used as a personal residence by the term interest holder is not subject to the § 2702 special valuation rule.[99] This personal residence GRIT exception is interpreted in regulations that establish "personal residence trust" and "qualified personal residence trust" (QPRT) provisions.[100] These regulations:

---

[95] Treas. Reg. § 25.2702-2(c)(3).

[96] Treas. Reg. § 25.2702-2(c)(3).

[97] Treas. Reg. § 25.2702-2(c)(4).

[98] Treas. Reg. § 25.2702-2(c)(5).

[99] § 2702(a)(3)(A)(ii).

[100] Treas. Reg. § 25.2702-5. In addition, Rev. Proc. 2003-42, 2003-2 C.B. 993, provides sample QPRT declaration of trust forms. With this promulgation the government also established that rulings generally will not be issued on whether a trust otherwise will qualify (unless the subject of a ruling request is a provision other than those contained in the Procedure). As is true for all government sample forms, users need to be aware that the provisions authorized are not always the most favorable to taxpayers, and options otherwise permissible are not always illustrated. By way of example, the sample provided does not illustrate

- Permit the transfer of cash to a trust in that amount needed to pay (within a six month period) either trust expenses (including mortgage payments) or for improvements that will be made.

- Permit retention of proceeds from a sale or from casualty insurance for up to two years if the trustee intends to purchase another personal residence (sale is not a cessation of use as a personal residence if the proceeds are used within two years to purchase a replacement personal residence).

- Require the trust instrument to preclude commutation of the term interest holder's entitlement (commutation being an express prohibition in a QPRT and—based on statements made by Treasury officials informally—an inadvertently omitted but intended prohibition in personal residence trusts too; whether this will be reflected by ruling or announcement is uncertain but prudence probably dictates that a commutation provision not be included in either form of trust).

- If the property ceases to be the term interest holder's personal residence (and no replacement is intended), require termination of the trust or conversion of the trust into a GRAT.[101]

- Preclude any distribution of assets to persons other than the term interest holder.

- Define a personal residence to include the term interest holder's principal residence and one other. The regulations (1) permit the term interest holder to use the property as a principal place of business, (2) permit rental of the residence during a portion of a year in which it is not occupied by the term interest holder, including (in the context of a vacation home) for most of the year if the term interest holder occupies it for a sufficient term to constitute it as the owner's residence under § 280A(d)(1), and (3) permit family members to use the property rent free if such use does not preclude § 280A treatment.[102]

(Footnote Continued)

a reversion to the settlor's estate if death occurs within the retained term, notwithstanding that a reversion in the case of a § 2036(a)(1) inclusion (death within the term) is harmless, it will reduce the value of the gift made on creation, and it will permit the settlor's estate to use the property to qualify for the marital deduction if, for example, S survives the settlor. It also addresses the § 2207B reimbursement issue discussed in the tax payment material at § 3.3.5.

[101] Treas. Reg. § § 25.2702-5(c)(7)(i) and 25.2702-5(d) Example 5 clarify that residence is not deemed to terminate if the term interest holder ceases to reside in the home because of ill health that forces a move to a nursing home, unless the property no longer is held available for the exclusive enjoyment of the term interest holder and his or her spouse and dependents.

[102] Shared enjoyment may, however, constitute a gift, as to which the annual exclusion ought to apply.

§ 7.2.2.7

- Preclude rental of any portion of the property, such as a commercial lodging[103] on a routine basis that belies use primarily as a personal residence.

- Permit inclusion of "appurtenant structures used for residential purposes and adjacent land not in excess of that which is reasonably appropriate for residential purposes" but preclude the transfer of personal property (such as furnishings) to the trust.[104] Illustrated[105] is a farm with various structures used for farming. Although the farm did not qualify as a personal residence, presumably the farmhouse alone, and a bit of land around it, could have qualified.[106]

- Permit acquisition of a personal residence by way of split interest purchase by family members without application of § 2702 if a QPRT is used as the mechanism.[107]

A very controversial 1997 amendment added a requirement[108] that the governing instrument must prohibit any direct or indirect transfer of the

---

[103] Treas. Reg. § 25.2702-5(c)(2)(iii) uses the example of a hotel or a bed and breakfast establishment.

[104] Treas. Reg. § 25.2702-5(b)(2)(ii).

[105] Treas. Reg. § 25.2702-5(d) Example 3.

[106] Indeed, PLR 9717017 permitted division of farm property that separated the personal residence and eight acres of surrounding land that became a QPRT, notwithstanding that the minimum zoning acreage requirement was three acres; in partial justification for this result was that eight acres was too small to subdivide in the future. And PLR 9739024 involved a 40 acre parcel on which a barn and several pens were located, along with a manager's house, all used in a commercial horse breeding operation on another parcel but permitted to be part of a QPRT based on representations that the manager spent half-time working on the residential property and the barn and pens would no longer be used in the commercial activity.

[107] PLR 9841017. See Schwartz, IRS Approves Split-Purchase Qualified Personal Residence Trust, 13 Prob. & Prop. 55 (Mar./Apr. 1999), and Blattmachr, Split Purchase Trusts vs. Qualified Personal Residence Trusts, 138 Trusts & Estates 56 (Feb. 1999). See also § 6.3.3.9. This position is odd in light of reports that the government believes that the Treas. Reg. § 25.2702-5(c)(7)(i) exclusive possession of property requirement precludes the use of concurrent ownership property, such as a tenant in common interest. See Hartog & McCall, QPRTs for Co-Tenancy Interests—Do They Work?, 6 California Trusts & Estates Quarterly 4 (Fall 2000). The authors surmise that the same impediment could prevent laddered trusts that own slivers of the property for varying lengths of time, although perhaps the use of grantor trusts would cause the government to ignore the trusts for purposes of the exclusive possession requirement.

[108] See Treas. Reg. §§ 25.2702-5(b)(1) and 25.2702-5(c)(9).

§ 7.2.2.7

residence for consideration either to the term interest holder or to the holder's spouse, either during the original term of the trust or thereafter while the trust remains a grantor trust for income tax purposes. The intent of this prohibition is to preclude repurchase of the residence by the term interest holder or the holder's spouse without capital gain realization, intentionally to cause inclusion of the residence in the estate of either the holder or the spouse to generate a new basis at death, meanwhile allowing the purchase proceeds to pass from the trust to the remainder beneficiaries while the purchaser remains in possession of the residence after the term expires.[109]

Valuation of the gifted remainder interest in such a transaction should be based on the normal tables used to value temporal interests, which will make these transfers more useful if the property is expected to appreciate in value.[110] The prospect for long-term appreciation is a

---

[109] The regulation does not, however, preclude the term interest holder's spouse from being the ultimate remainder beneficiary of the trust at expiration of the retained term interest (either by a premature death or by natural expiration of the retained interest), because the abusive objective perceived by the government cannot be accomplished by a gratuitous distribution that leaves no proceeds in the trust for other remainder beneficiaries. Thus, the regulations permit a terminating distribution of the remainder in the personal residence to the spouse, either under the original terms of the trust or pursuant to any exercise of a retained power of appointment by the term interest holder.

Nor did § 2702 preclude planning such as in PLRs 201131006, 201129017, 201039001, 201024012, 201019912, 201019007, 201029006, 201014044, 200935005, 200935004, 200920003, 200904023, 200904022, 200901019, 200848008, 200848007, 200848003, 200816025, and 200814011, in each of which a parent originally created a QPRT and survived the term, and thereafter wished to remain in possession. The parents could rent the dwelling back from the remainder beneficiaries—children in each case—or the remainder beneficiaries could transfer the dwelling to a new trust or exercise a power of appointment over the trust (created in some cases by a judicial modification) to provide a short term (such as one year) interest in the parent (motivated, perhaps, by the parent's inability or unwillingness to continue paying rent).

[110] Because the property is valued for its personal use, the failure to produce income equal to the assumed rate of return employed by § 7520 should not be relevant. Nevertheless, the transferor might include a provision in the document that transfers the remainder and retains the term interest, requiring sale of the property and reinvestment of the proceeds in a reasonable income producing asset if the term interest holder insists. See Treas. Reg. § 25.7520-3(b)(2)(ii)(A), discussed in § 7.2.1 n.29.

§ 7.2.2.7

pretty good gamble whenever residential real estate is depressed in value, although it may not be for a short-term GRIT.

A great many of the PLRs to date under the QPRT exception relate to factual questions regarding personal residence qualification itself. A few principles or trends have developed, and so far the government has been generous in its interpretation and application of this provision. To illustrate the issues:

• PLR 9609015 allowed a 4000 square foot property to qualify as primarily held for residential purposes notwithstanding that 500 square feet of it constituted "a separate rental unit that is rented on an unfurnished basis to unrelated third parties," because the taxpayer provided no substantial services and the rental use was secondary to use as the taxpayer's personal residence. PLR 9816003 permitted rental of a guest house to an unrelated third party because it was located on a single parcel with the main house and could not be divided due to local zoning and water use restrictions. And PLR 199916030 permitted rental of a caretaker's residence and distribution of the rent as income to the grantor as beneficiary of the QPRT. PLR 200751022 similarly allowed rental of a caretaker's residence, without mention of how the rental income would be enjoyed.

• PLR 9741004 permitted QPRT creation of two lots used as one property notwithstanding that there were two separate rental units in the personal residence itself, finding that the rental use was secondary to the primary use as a personal residence.

• PLR 200039031 permitted partition of a single parcel held as tenants by the entirety into a tenancy in common, followed by each spouse putting their half into a QPRT. PLRs 200825004 and 200822011 both involved property held by spouses as tenants in common, the difference being that only one of them transferred their interest into a QPRT.

• PLRs 9448035, 9433016, and 9151046 held that the proprietary lease and shares of stock in a cooperative housing corporation may constitute a personal residence for § 2702(a)(3)(A) purposes if the property otherwise meets the personal residence requirements of § 1034 or § 280A(d)(1).[111]

---

[111] Since repealed. See § 121(d)(4), applicable with respect to stock in a cooperative and qualified for the exclusion from capital gain on sale of a qualifying principal residence. PLRs 199925027 and 9447036 involved an unusual but still acceptable application of this principle; because the cooperatives would not allow transfer of the shares to the trust, the grantors remained the owner of record as nominees of the trusts and transferred all beneficial interests in the property and the shares to the trusts, which the government held to be acceptable.

§ 7.2.2.7

- PLR 9544018 involved shareholdings in a landholding corporation, not a traditional cooperative, but still permitted qualification.

- PLRs 9433016 and 9425028 state that a QPRT may be accompanied by a separate agreement obligating the remainder beneficiaries to sell or rent the property to the settlor at FMV or rent, without altering the trust's qualification for the exemption from the application of §2702. PLR Rulings 9829002, 9714025, 9626041, and 9448035 went one step further and held that such a leaseback at the end of the term would not constitute a §2036(a)(1) retained interest because it was required to be at a FMV rental.

- PLR 9343034 refused to rule whether adjacent land to the tract on which the principal residence was located would qualify if it was transferred to an otherwise QPRT. Local zoning law required that each parcel consist of a certain minimum acreage and the tract on which the house was located alone did not conform to that requirement. PLR 9328040 did rule that a guest house adjoining the main home on a 1.65 acre parcel used as a vacation property qualified as one personal residence for purposes of the Treas. Reg. §25.2702-5(c)(2)(ii) definition of appurtenant structures in a QPRT.[112] Similarly, PLR 9503025 held that a lot owned by the taxpayer located across the street from a vacation home would qualify as appurtenant to the primary residence because it guaranteed a view of and access to a bay on that side of the road, it had been owned for 30 years along with the residence, and the taxpayer had forgone forever the opportunity to build on or develop that property. According to the government, "distinct parcels of land can, in appropriate circumstances, constitute adjacent land as that term is used in the regulations."

- PLRs 9645010 and 9544018 involved 16.6 acres and 18 acres, respectively, on which single homes were developed and that otherwise mostly was floodplain, wetlands, swampland, and streams. The government concluded in each case that they qualified in their totality as a residence because each property was comparable in size to other properties in the area and had been used for many years consistent with its zoning as a single homesite. This "comparability" test seems to be a touchstone in later Rulings. Using that standard, all the following favorable Rulings were issued:

  — PLR 9739010 involved three parcels of land, totaling four acres on which stood a main house and a guest house, with the balance being unimproved land.

  — PLR 9701046 held that five contiguous lots that contained only a single residence could be treated as one property not in excess of that amount of land reasonably appropriate for residential purposes.

---

[112] The government noted that the guest house was used by friends and family members and was not rented to outsiders and, therefore, was not incompatible with use of the vacation home as a personal residence.

§7.2.2.7

— PLR 9442019 held that a 10 acre parcel of land qualified as a single property notwithstanding that, on a development map, it consisted of three lots and the residence was located on only one of them, which constituted approximately 70% of the total land. The other two lots had no separate roads, the well for all of the property was located on one of those two lots, the single 10 acre parcel had been used as a single residence for over 20 years, and it appeared as a single parcel on the tax map.

— PLR 9529035 involved three separate parcels shown on the tax assessor's map as a single tax lot that also had been used for over 20 years as a single residence. There were no additional buildings that were not integral to the residential use and the property was not farmed.

— PLR 9829026 involved five parcels, four of which were entirely woodlands but all five of which constituting just one parcel on the tax map, three acres of which representing the residential development.

— PLRs 9735012 and 9735011 permitted a 75% interest in two parcels used as a single residence to be a QPRT property, in part because the resulting property would be smaller than the other residential properties in the area.

— PLR 9725010 entailed subdivision of property resulting in a single parcel on the tax map that could not be further subdivided and that included a main house, a pool house, a horse barn, and a greenhouse.

— PLR 9714025 involved three parcels and a main house, a guest house, caretaker's residence, carriage house, pool building, and storage barn.

— PLR 9729024 involved a split of property carving out of a larger parcel the residence, guest house, caretaker's residence, garage, and pool to create the minimum sized estate allowed by a restrictive covenant.

• In terms of the number and quality of appurtenant structures permitted:

— PLR 9730013 granted QPRT status to property that consisted of a main house, a guest house, caretaker's residence, detached garage, barn, storage buildings, and an indoor riding barn.

— PLRs 9718007 and 9705017 permitted vacation properties that consisted of a main house, separate guest facilities, and in the later PLR a caretaker's house (occupied by the caretaker), and "other appurtenant structures."

§7.2.2.7

— PLR 9722009 permitted a property that included the main house, a guest cottage, swimming pool and pool house, caretaker's apartment, and a horse barn.

— PLR 9750048 qualified a house, pool house, guest house and garage that in toto constituted a smaller acreage than required by local ordinance.

It is wise to remember that §2702 is not the only arrow in the government's quiver. For example, the transaction in TAM 9206006 occurred prior to the effective date of §2702,[113] so the government addressed the case instead under §2036(a)(1), employing a theory that the transaction constituted a transfer of property with a retained life estate. The decedent acquired a life estate in a condominium and the primary remainder beneficiary of the decedent's estate acquired the remainder interest.[114] The government focused on the fact that most of the remainder beneficiary's consideration was borrowed (at a market rate of interest) from a trust that this beneficiary would inherit at the decedent's death. With a balloon repayment provision keyed to the decedent's life expectancy, the government ignored the borrowed funds, stating that the borrowed portion of the purchase price "was provided exclusively by the Decedent." No authority was cited for this treatment, which supported the government's conclusion that over 97% of the purchase price was paid by the decedent. With lifetime enjoyment of the purchased property, the government held that 97% of the FET value of the property was includible in the decedent's gross estate under §2036(a)(1) because the purchase involved a transfer with a retained life estate.[115]

---

[113] Although presumably it would have avoided application of §2702 because it involved a joint purchase of a personal residence condominium.

[114] There was a dispute over the proper actuarial factor to value the respective interests, because a down payment was made several years before closing on the purchase of the unit, and the actuarial factor for valuation of each interest changed in the interim, but this aspect of the TAM was not determinative.

[115] Gradow v. United States, 87-1 U.S. Tax Cas. (CCH) ¶ 13,711 (Ct. Cl. 1987), aff'd, 897 F.2d 516 (Fed. Cir. 1990) (involving sale of a remainder interest for less than full and adequate consideration), and Gordon v. Commissioner, 85 T.C. 209 (1985) (involving the income tax consequences of a joint purchase of property), were mentioned but the government did not rely on their holdings in concluding that inclusion was required. Although it is unclear from the TAM, it seems likely that the government would have concluded under *Gradow* that full and adequate

Under a proper application of §2036(a)(1), however, the result should have been inclusion of 100% of the FET value of the property, with a §2043 consideration offset for the value of any legitimate independent consideration furnished by the remainder beneficiary at the time of purchase. It may be that, because the decedent died approximately seven months after the date of purchase, the values involved had not changed enough to be a matter of concern to the government, making the inclusion of just 97% of the value of the property a sufficient victory for the government. Under the QPRT exception, however, a subterfuge like that employed in the TAM would not be necessary, although outliving the retained term interest would be necessary to avoid §2036(a)(1) inclusion at death.[116]

That reality and one other reveal that the QPRT is not the most wealth transfer tax effective form of planning involving a personal residence. Rather, it is preferable if the transferor makes a completed gift of the entire fee simple interest in the property and, if continued residence is desired, pays rent to the new owner to lease the premises. Basis is the same carryover as in the QPRT alternative, future appreciation in value still is shifted, the FET inclusion potential of dying during the term interest is avoided, and a greater wealth transfer tax saving is generated by the mere expedient of incurring gift tax during life on the full fee simple interest rather than on just the remainder interest that is transferred.[117]

(Footnote Continued)

consideration to avoid §2036(a)(1) inclusion should be measured against the full value of the property, rather than the value of the interest purchased by the remainder beneficiary, which would require FET inclusion even if the remainder beneficiary provided independent funds in an amount that properly reflected the value of the interest purchased. See, e.g., Estate of Magnin v. Commissioner, 71 T.C.M. (CCH) 1856 (1996), rev'd and rem'd, 184 F.3d 1074 (CCH) ¶ 60,347 (9th Cir. 1999), on remand, 81 T.C.M. (CCH) 1126 (2001) (government argument originally confirmed notwithstanding its holding that, even under the taxpayer's argument in *Gradow*, the consideration received was not full and adequate).

[116] See §7.3.1 and Estate of D'Ambrosio v. Commissioner, 105 T.C. 252 (1995), rev'd on other grounds, 101 F.3d 309 (3d Cir. 1996), for a discussion of the full and adequate consideration exception to the application of §2036(a)(1).

[117] As discussed in §6.2.1, the more wealth transfer tax that is incurred under the tax exclusive gift tax than under the tax inclusive FET, the lower the overall burden, regardless of the bankrupt time value of money notion. That this is true

§7.2.2.7

§7.2.2.8 Sales of Remainders and Joint Purchases

Nontrust property as to which term interests exist is subject to §2702 as if a trust was involved,[118] and §2702 specifically is applicable to joint purchase transactions involving family members.[119] Joint purchases may involve a single transaction or a series of related transactions by which the taxpayer acquires a term interest and a family member acquires the balance of the fee. This rule will apply to either form of transfer. Thus, for example, if Parent and Child purchase property with Parent acquiring a term interest and Child the remainder, Parent will be deemed to have acquired the full fee and transferred the remainder interest to Child in exchange for the amount Child paid to acquire the remainder interest. Normally the result is a gift of the full FMV, less the value of Child's consideration furnished, although the deemed gift may be limited to the total amount paid less Child's consideration furnished if Parent acquired the property for less than its FMV.[120] Curiously, the regulations do not address the possibility that Child's consideration may have been acquired from Parent.

The related transaction involving sale of a remainder interest is not specifically mentioned by §2702, but the regulations[121] illustrate such a transaction and treat §2702 as being applicable. Thus, even if the remainder is transferred for consideration equal to its FMV, the transfer will be treated as a gift for gift tax purposes and the full and adequate consideration exception to §2036 will not apply unless the consideration furnished is equal to the full FMV of the remainder at termination of the retained term interest, which is not likely.[122]

(Footnote Continued)

in this context is ably illustrated by comparing a QPRT to an outright inter vivos transfer of the entire property, all subject to gift tax. See Melcher & Rosenbloom, How Well Do QPRTs Really Work, 77 Taxes 27 (Feb. 1999).

118 §2702(c)(1).

119 §2702(c)(2).

120 Treas. Reg. §25.2702-4(d) Example 4.

121 Treas. Reg. §25.2702-4(d) Example 2.

122 Although Gradow v. United States, 897 F.2d 516 (Fed. Cir. 1990) (involving sale of a remainder interest, effectively precluding application of the full and adequate consideration exception for estate and gift taxation), is wrongly decided, Congress clearly meant to codify its results in §2702 to preclude gaming with temporal interests that abuse the valuation tables using split interests of all

§7.2.2.9 Uncertain Scope of §2702

It is not certain that a private annuity or a sale in exchange for a SCIN[123] is enough like a retained interest in transferred property that §2702(c)(1) should apply. Nevertheless, the annuity or installment payments could be structured to meet the qualified interest exception requirements.[124] Similarly, §2702 may apply if the holder of a retained interest (such as a life estate or a term interest in a trust that is chronologically exempt from application of §2702) transfers a portion of that interest (such as half the income, all income in excess of a certain amount, or all income after a term of years carved out of the life estate). Moreover, §2702 will apply to creation of a short-term trust in which income is transferred to a third party by a transferor who retains a reversion, unless the retained reversionary interest is noncontingent and follows a qualified annuity or unitrust interest.[125] The §2702(a)(3)(A)(i) exception for "incomplete" transfers should be inapplicable in such a case because the gift of the lead interest is subject to gift taxation, notwithstanding that the original transfer is "incomplete" in the sense

---

(Footnote Continued)

types, including sales of remainder interests, split purchases, and most grantor retained interest trusts. For a critique of *Gradow*, see Estate of D'Ambrosio v. Commissioner, 101 F.3d 309 (3d Cir. 1996), rev'g 105 T.C. 252 (1995), and Pennell, Sale of Remainder Interest Triggers Section 2036(a)(1) Inclusion, 13 Prob. Notes 188-192 (1987). *Gradow* was followed in Estate of Magnin v. Commissioner, 71 T.C.M. (CCH) 1856 (1996), rev'd and rem'd, 184 F.3d 1074 (9th Cir. 1999), on remand, 81 T.C.M. (CCH) 1126 (2001), in a mindless decision in Pittman v. United States, 878 F. Supp. 833 (E.D. N.C. 1994), and again it was followed in Wheeler v. United States, 77 A.F.T.R.2d (P-H) 1405 (W.D. Tex. 1996), because facts indicated a disguised gift, and in Parker v. United States, 894 F. Supp. 445 (N.D. Ga. 1995), aff'd without opinion (11th Cir. 1995), because the taxpayer failed in its burden of proof, the court in *Parker* stating without specification that it had "some reservations about the correctness of *Gradow*." The facts also indicated that the consideration allegedly received in *Parker* may have belonged to the taxpayer and therefore would not be consideration at all.

[123] SCINs are not subject to FET at the seller's death if the self-canceling feature is supported by an appropriate premium. See §6.4.2.

[124] See, e.g., PLR 9253031 (private annuity arrangement was deemed subject to §2702 but the annuity payments met the qualified interest exception under §2702(b)(1)). And see PLRs 9535026 and 9436006 (simple sales for straight installment notes were not subject to §2702).

[125] §§2702(a)(1) and 2702(b)(3).

§7.2.2.9

that FET inclusion will occur because of the retained reversion. FET inclusion should be irrelevant to application of the incomplete transfer exception because it is hard to conjure a case in which the entire transfer would be regarded as complete but a reversionary interest or interests in or powers over the trust are retained.

Finally, a CRUT may be subject to §2702 if a net income with deficiency catch-up provision is employed in a trust in which the donor or any applicable family member enjoys the first lead interest and then a secondary unitrust interest is created in another private individual before the remainder passes to charity.[126] The notion is that the donor may structure the situation such that the lead unitrust interest pays little or nothing because income during the lead interest is artificially low by virtue of trust investment in growth assets versus current income producing assets. This will cause the deficiency account to build up, followed by the donor or other family member's interest ending and the secondary interest becoming entitled to the income deficiency when the trustee subsequently alters the trust investments to begin to produce substantial income.

In such a case the perceived abuse is that the secondary interest holder would receive far more wealth than the tables would predict and more than the amount on which the gift tax otherwise would be imposed. In such a case the primary lead interest is ignored in valuing the gift made to the other private individual beneficiary, unless that secondary gift qualifies for the marital deduction. The charitable remainder interest will not be affected, however, and the donor's gift would be that portion of the FMV that does not qualify for the charitable deduction in creation of the trust, unreduced by any interest retained by the donor.

§7.2.2.10 Adjustment to Avoid Double Taxation

It is hard to determine why retention of a reversion should trigger application of §2702, because there is no estate freeze abuse. For example, if a transferor creates a trust to pay for the support of an elderly relative for life, reversion to the transferor, there is no freeze potential even if the trust principal appreciates and the term interest is not in

---

126 Treas. Reg. §25.2702-1(c)(3). This provision does not apply, however, to a fixed percentage unitrust (without the net income limitation) or to any annuity trust.

qualified interest format. Guaranteed exposure to § 2033 or § 2037 inclusion of the reversion in the transferor's gross estate should preclude application of § 2702.

If, however, § 2702 requires 100% of the value of trust property to be taxed at creation of the trust (assuming the qualified interest rules were not met and the transfer was complete), subsequent FET inclusion will constitute double taxation unless an adjustment provided in the regulations works properly. Moreover, if creation of the trust was by a split gift, the failure of § 2001(e) to apply[127] means that the consenting spouse's prior taxable gifts will not be purged, which also will result in inappropriate double taxation. In each of these cases, the need for adjustment is clear. It therefore is curious that Congress did not mandate that the Treasury Department provide an adjustment. Perhaps even more curiously, however, the government did so anyway.[128]

A reduction of a transferor's prior adjusted taxable gifts for future wealth transfer tax computation purposes may be required if a prior transfer was subject to § 2702. A reduction ought to be provided if the § 2702 retained interest is sold or otherwise is not includible in the transferor's gross estate at death because it terminates naturally (for example, the transferor retained a term interest that expired before the transferor expired). In each of these cases double taxation will result unless the prior gift is purged, because the proceeds of the sale or the earnings generated and paid to the transferor as owner of the retained interest will be taxable at the transferor's death. In such cases § 2702 clearly results in double taxation.

To illustrate, if the transferor retained an income interest in trust for 10 years that was not a qualified interest under § 2702, all the income earned and paid to the transferor under that interest would increase the transferor's net worth for subsequent taxation. Without an adjustment that reflects this economic reality, double taxation will result because the value of that income interest was ignored in valuing the transferred interest for gift tax purposes.

---

[127] See § 7.3.6 nn.241-244 and accompanying text.

[128] Treas. Reg. § 25.2702-6, which is like the analogous but mandated adjustment provisions in Treas. Reg. § 25.2701-5.

§ 7.2.2.10

The adjustment[129] that applies is improper because it is restricted to the lesser of "(i) [t]he increase in the individual's taxable gifts resulting from the interest being valued [under §2702] at the time of the initial transfer," and "(ii) [t]he increase in the individual's taxable gifts (or gross estate) resulting from the subsequent transfer of the interest." That is, the adjustment is the smaller of the value of the retained interest when the original transfer triggered §2702 and when the retained interest is transferred. Thus, the regulation effectively imposes transfer tax on the higher of those two values.

This limitation precludes taxpayers from overvaluing retained trust interests to reduce the value of transferred interests. But this limitation is problematic in the context of §2702 because most retained trust interests that are subject to §2702 are subject to a legitimate decline in value due to the mere passage of time (such as a retained temporal interest), regardless of any abuse in the valuation process. Thus, the limitation invariably and inappropriately will allow some value to be taxed twice.

To further illustrate, assume that the transferor retained a life income interest with an actual FMV of $40,000 that was ignored under §2702 in valuing a transfer into trust. One year later the transferor relinquished that income interest when it was worth $30,000. The regulations[130] conclude that the adjustment is limited to $20,000, being the lesser value of the original $40,000 and the later value of $30,000 as reduced by the annual exclusion available to the transferor with respect to relinquishment of the income interest. The annual exclusion adjustment is appropriate because that value will not be subject to double tax. The subsequent gift of that amount passes tax free. But the limitation issue arises because the retained income interest had declined in value when it subsequently was transferred, presumably (at least in large part) because a year's worth of income had been paid to the transferor, who was a year older when the subsequent transfer was made. Unless that income was consumed in a manner that reflects no increase in the transferor's net worth, the value of that year's income will be taxable when the transferor subsequently disposes of it (now that it is separate from the retained life estate). Because the adjustment is limited to the

---

129 Treas. Reg. §25.2702-6(b)(1).
130 Treas. Reg. §25.2702-6(c) Example 1.

§7.2.2.10

lesser value of the retained interest, the $10,000 value differential was subject to tax when the trust was created and will be subject to tax again when the transferor disposes of that increased net worth.

To work properly in this situation, the limitation should reflect reductions in the value of the retained interest that reflect value that will be subject to double taxation. As opposed to those that merely reflect the passage of time (which is a familiar concept under § 2032(a)(3)). Without such a refinement, § 2702 improperly punishes taxpayers for engaging in transactions that trigger § 2702.

§ 7.2.2.10.1 Gift Splitting

A gift splitting provision specifies that any adjustment that reduces the value of prior § 2702 gifts may be split equally between the transferor and a consenting spouse, if the transferor so elects when a subsequent split gift transfer is made of the previously retained interest.[131] Regardless of how that subsequent transfer of the retained interest occurs, the regulation requires the adjustment splitting decision to be signified by an attachment to the consenting spouse's Form 709 gift tax return reporting the spouse's share of the split gift, which seems a little odd. Why shouldn't this be on the *transferor's* Form 706 FET or Form 709 gift tax return? It is likely that an inexperienced personal representative or inter vivos gift advisor to the transferor will overlook the election to assign a portion of the adjustment under this proposed procedure.

In addition, the § 2702 regulations need to, but do not, elaborate on the interplay of the split gift assignment with § 2001(d) (which gives the transferor a credit against FET for any gift tax paid by the consenting spouse on a split gift that subsequently is includible in the transferor's gross estate at death) and the operation of § 2001(e) (which applies only if the transferred interest is includible in the transferor's gross estate under § 2035(a)). That the original transfer was a split gift is irrelevant under this provision, so these subjects arise only with respect to a subsequent transfer that is split.[132]

---

[131] Treas. Reg. § 25.2702-6(a)(3).

[132] See, e.g., Treas. Reg. § 25.2702-6(c) Example 5 (if § 2001(e) also purges the tax base of the consenting spouse in the limited circumstance that the subsequently transferred interest is included in the transferor's gross estate under

§ 7.2.2.10.2 *Miscellaneous Problems*

The regulations treat a transferor's retention of a power to direct the distribution of income among third parties as an interest for § 2702 purposes.[133] As a result, they treat § 2702 as applicable upon creation of the trust because this power is not a qualified interest, and further conclude that the transfer of income on an annual basis is not a transfer of the retained interest that would permit an adjustment against double taxation.[134] The net result is that § 2702 taxes the value of the transfer into trust as if an easy-to-complete rule was applicable (100% of the value of the transferred property being subjected to gift tax, notwithstanding that the gift of the income interest is subject to the retained power), but no adjustment is provided against gift tax incurred as income is paid in each year. This is improper if there is a taxable gift each year as income is distributed. Indeed, it would appear that income could not be distributed unless the transferor exercised the power, because the example does not specify that income could be accumulated.

An adjustment is permitted if the retained power is relinquished,[135] although the regulations do not indicate how the adjustment limitation would be applied, other than the statement that "the increase in taxable gifts resulting from the transfer of the retained interest" would constitute one of the two limitation amounts. These results are all the more unsettling because they do not indicate how to value that gift, and there is no explanation of the more likely subsequent taxable event of the transferor's death with § § 2036(a)(2) and 2038(a)(1) generating inclusion of the value of the entire trust in the transferor's gross estate because of the retained power.

The § 2702(a)(1) valuation rule also applies to any trust interest retained by "any applicable family member" of a transferor who created

---

(Footnote Continued)

§ 2035(a), a "double" adjustment is precluded by the limitation imposed on the Treas. Reg. § 25.2702-6 adjustment).

[133] Treas. Reg. § 25.2702-6(c) Examples 6 and 7.

[134] Notwithstanding a statement in Treas. Reg. § 25.2702-6 Example 7 alluding to "the increase in taxable gifts resulting from the exercise of the same retained right," suggesting that transfer tax is generated only by an affirmative exercise of that retained power.

[135] Treas. Reg. § 25.2702-6 Example 7.

or transferred an interest in a trust. Thus, §2702 would apply if a transferor and an applicable family member owned property and the transferor alone transferred an interest in the transferor's portion, meaning that the applicable family member's interest would be ignored in valuing the interest transferred unless it was a qualified interest. The regulations appear to deny an adjustment in this situation,[136] which is inappropriate.

In addition, if Parent gave a remainder interest to Child and incurred gift tax on 100% of the trust property because Parent's retained interest was not a qualified interest, and if Child thereafter gave that remainder interest to Grandchild, it appears that no rule prevents an inappropriate double taxation of 100% of the value of the trust to Child. For GST purposes, the §2702 value will not govern if Parent gives the remainder to Grandchild directly, incurring a GST, and §2642(f) would preclude allocation of exemption to the remainder interest until Parent's §2036(a)(1) exposure attributable to the retained income interest terminated.

As an extreme example of the inappropriate double taxation that could occur, assume that Parent (P), Child (C), and Grandchild (GC) jointly purchased property from an unrelated third party. P purchased a term interest, C purchased a life estate measured by C's life following P's term interest, and GC purchased the remainder. Because members of the same family have purchased interests in this property, §2702(c) is applicable, making P a deemed transferor to C and to GC, in each case for consideration equal to the amounts each paid. If P's term interest is not a qualified interest, its value will be deemed to be zero and gifts to both C and GC will result. In addition, C will be deemed to have purchased the entire property and sold interests in it to both P and GC for the amount of the consideration they paid. If C's interest is not in qualified form, it too would be treated as having a zero value, resulting in gifts by C to P and to GC. Perhaps some form of net gift[137] treatment would work in this situation, but the gifts made by each of P and C should not double up and will require an appropriate adjustment, which is not provided in the regulation.

---

[136] See Treas. Reg. §25.2702-6(a)(1) (parenthetical).

[137] See §§7.2.5 n.341 and 7.3.6 n.237 and accompanying text.

§7.2.2.10.2

§7.2.3 *Special Valuation of Certain Business Interest Transfers*

A second special rule exists in Chapter 14 of the Code,[138] again determining whether a transfer has occurred and its gift tax value when a form of "estate freeze" transaction occurs in the context of planning that involves corporate and partnership interests. This provision reflects the congressional determination that certain "bells and whistles" that can be built into stock or partnership interests may be designed to increase artificially the value of interests in a corporation or a partnership that are retained when other interests are given away. In that manner, these special provisions are used to reduce or distort the gift tax consequences of the transfer.

To preclude such planning, §2701(a)(1) applies a special valuation regime that ignores certain liquidation, put, call, and conversion rights, and noncumulative dividend rights, all for purposes of determining the value of any corporate or partnership interests that are retained by a transferor. This treatment correspondingly affects the value of related corporate or partnership interests that are transferred by the transferor. The net result is to diminish the value of what is retained and correspondingly increase the value of the transferred interests, under a "subtraction" method of determining the value of a transfer. This approach looks to the value of the entire entity (or the transferor's interest in it) and subtracts only the value of what the transferor retains, regarding the balance as the value of the gift.

Technically, the rule in §2701(a)(3)(A) specifies that, in the context of transfers between family members,[139] the value of an "applicable retained interest" that is not a "qualified payment" is zero for purposes of determining the gift tax consequences of a transfer. If this provision applies, other interests in the corporation or partnership are deemed to represent all of the value of the entity for wealth transfer tax purposes.[140] Thus, if a taxpayer transfers an interest in the entity, the result is a gift

---

[138] Applicable to transfers made after October 8, 1990.

[139] Defined in §2701(e)(1) to mean lineal descendants of the transferor, with the added aspect that spouses are treated as one, so spouses of descendants, descendants of the transferor's spouse (and their spouses), and the transferor's spouse also are included.

[140] §2701(a)(3).

subject to tax as if the transferor did not retain the applicable retained interest.

To illustrate, if Parent (P) owned all the noncumulative preferred and common stock in Family Corp. and transferred all of that common stock to Child (C), the value of the gift would be computed as if the preferred stock owned by P (which is an applicable retained interest) had no value.[141] In effect, P would be taxed on a gift of 100% of the value of Family Corp. to C, notwithstanding P's retention of the preferred stock.

To make this example a little more interesting, consider § 2701(a)(1)(B), which specifies that interests retained by an "applicable family member"[142] of a transferor also are subject to § 2701 in valuing a gift. Thus, if C later gives the common stock received from P to C's child (GC), and if at that time P still holds the preferred stock, C also would be deemed to make a gift of 100% of the value of Family Corp., notwithstanding that C owned no other interest in the corporation and engaged in no estate planning activities that might be regarded as strategic.

---

[141] This statement is oversimplified because, as defined, any value attributable to voting power of the preferred stock would not be ignored even if all other rights of the stock fell within the § 2701(b)(1) definition of an applicable retained interest. See Treas. Reg. § 25.2701-1(e) Example 2, in which preferred stock is deemed to have a zero value. Although no indication is given whether the stock in that example is voting preferred stock, the regulation states that only the preferred dividend right is valued at zero and all "other rights in the preferred stock are valued as if [the] dividend right does not exist but otherwise without regard to section 2701." See, e.g., Estate of Simplot v. Commissioner, 112 T.C. 130 (1999), rev'd and rem'd, 249 F.3d. 1191 (9th Cir. 2001) (the Tax Court held for valuation purposes that a slight premium should be accorded to voting stock because it would give the buyer "a seat at the table" in the inner circle with the other decision makers and might at some future date acquire swing vote potential; over a strong dissent the court on appeal concluded that voting and nonvoting stock should be valued the same). Because the stock in this illustration is noncumulative it would not be a qualified payment as defined in § 2701(c)(3) unless an election was made under § 2701(c)(3)(C) to be treated as a qualified payment. See § § 7.2.3.3 and 7.2.3.3.2, respectively.

[142] This term is defined in § 2701(e)(2) to mean ancestors of the transferor, with the added aspect that spouses are treated as one, so spouses of ancestors, ancestors of the transferor's spouse (and their spouses), and the transferor's spouse also are included.

§ 7.2.3

There is double taxation here, because P and C both incur gift tax on the value of an interest that P still owns and that probably will be subject to tax a third time when P ultimately transfers the preferred stock (such as at P's death). To address this fact, §2701(e)(6) directs the Secretary of the Treasury to promulgate regulations that make adjustments "to reflect the increase in the amount of any prior taxable gift made by the transferor" pursuant to these rules. For example, if P was to give the retained preferred stock to either C or GC, one possible implementation of this mandate would be to presume the preferred stock to be worthless for future wealth transfer tax purposes—the full value of what P originally owned already having been taxed (in this case twice).

Instead, the regulations[143] adopt a different interpretation of §2701(e)(6) that treats P's subsequent gift of the preferred stock as another taxable gift. To avoid double taxation (because the value of that stock was subject to tax when P earlier transferred the common stock to C), this approach reduces P's adjusted taxable gifts base to regard the prior gift as limited to the true FMV of P's common stock. With a proper purge of the deemed gift of P's preferred stock and a credit for any gift tax paid by P on that deemed gift, subsequent taxation of P's actual gift of the preferred stock should not be unfair. But this solution does nothing about the fact that C paid tax on the value of P's preferred stock as well, and no subsequent gift by C necessarily will trigger an opportunity to adjust for this impropriety (for example, if C transfers it after P's death).

The proper end result would be to tax no more than 100% of the value of the entity as ownership in the form of junior and senior equity interests (common and preferred stock) is transferred by P and again on the correct value of the common stock when it is transferred by C. This is not exactly what the mandated regulation provides. It comes close with respect to P, but not with respect to C because, in this case, the prior taxable gift that is inconsistent with 100% taxation when C gives the common stock to GC was made by P, not by C. The regulation does not reflect that both P and C have been assessed a gift tax that ignores the value of P's preferred stock.[144]

---

143 Treas. Reg. §25.2701-5.

144 The explanation offered for this deficiency when these regulations originally were proposed was "[b]ecause the transferor [C] will often acquire an

In the foregoing examples, if P had owned only 60% of the preferred and common stock in Family Corp. and transferred all of the common stock P owned to C, § 2701 would treat P as making a gift of the full value of what P owned—P's 60% controlling interest in the corporation— notwithstanding P's retention of the preferred stock. A control stock premium would be applied in valuing that 60% interest.[145] If, however, P transferred only one-sixth of P's common stock (10% of the total common stock in the corporation) to C, P's preferred stock still would be ignored in its entirety in valuing P's gift, P would be treated as giving C an amount equal to one-sixth of the total value owned by P, and a minority discount would be applied to the sliver actually transferred, after determining that one-sixth amount.[146] In this case, that amount would not be

---

(Footnote Continued)

applicable retained interest initially held by an applicable family member [P] and because of the administrative complexity inherent in allowing assignability [of an adjustment] . . . ." The final regulations did not correct this defect. The original statement was not persuasive; no assignment of an adjustment is needed to make C whole in this example. Instead, P should pay tax on the value of the preferred stock when P transfers it, and *both* C and P should receive an adjustment, not share or assign one between them. The only issue of complexity is when and by how much C's prior taxable gifts should be adjusted to reflect this ultimate taxation to P. Nevertheless, the preamble to the final regulations stated that, after careful consideration, "the IRS and the Treasury have determined that . . . the administrative complexity involved in tracking the adjustment would far outweigh the additional benefit that would be gained therefrom." This is improper and should be challenged.

[145] Disregarding any value attributable to the voting power of P's preferred stock, the statute properly is read by the government as ignoring the value of P's preferred stock but not the value attributable to the remaining 40% of the preferred stock held by shareholders who are not applicable family members and as to whom § 2701(e)(3) attribution does not apply. P's gift of 60% of the common stock is valued accordingly. Thus, if Family Corp. was worth $10 million and P's 60% controlling interest in it was worth $7.2 million, the gift would be $7.2 million computed under the four step computation method adopted in Treas. Reg. § 25.2701-3(b).

[146] Again disregarding any value attributable to the voting power of P's preferred stock, Step 4 in the computation under Treas. Reg. § 25.2701-3(b)(4)(ii) calls for a reduction to the pro rata portion of the value determined ($1.2 million in the example in note 127) by the straight allocation directed in Step 3 of that computation "if the value of the transferred interest (determined without regard to section 2701) would be determined after application of a minority or similar discount with respect to the transferred interest."

§ 7.2.3

just 10% of the total value of the corporation, adjusted to reflect the minority discount, because the starting point of the computation under the government's interpretation is the value held by P prior to the gift, which includes a control premium.[147]

The general explanation that accompanied the proposed Chapter 14 regulations specifically stated that "sections 2701 and 2702 determine gift tax consequences at the time a transfer is made [but] they do not change the value of the transferred property for other tax purposes. Thus, in general, [they] do not apply for purposes of the generation-skipping transfer tax." The preamble to the final Chapter 14 regulations confirmed this position by stating that "the final regulations reject the argument that section 2701 determines the value of the transferred property" for any other purpose. Thus, a §2701 zero valuation of P's preferred stock presumably would not apply for GST purposes if P made a direct skip transfer of the common stock to GC, or placed it in a trust for the benefit of C for life, remainder to GC.[148]

Otherwise, if it was the case that a transfer has a value of zero, one difficult issue would be whether P could avoid allocation of any part of P's GST exemption to the transfer and still guarantee that it would be exempt for GST purposes when otherwise taxable distributions or terminations later occur.[149] That simply would not be the right result, and the government's interpretation precludes it.

---

[147] See TAM 8907002. The computation methodology established by the regulations is discussed and illustrated in more detail in §7.2.3.5.

[148] Although §2642(b) relies on gift tax or FET values for purposes of allocating the GST exemption, the taxable amount and valuation rules in §§2622 through 2624 establish no such linkage, and §2701 does not dictate universal application for all wealth transfer tax purposes. Although §2623 provides that the taxable amount in a direct skip is the "value of the property received by the transferee," this is designed to produce the tax exclusive character of the direct skip tax and not to establish a valuation rule for GST purposes, so it does not speak to whether §2701 is applicable for all wealth transfer tax purposes. Thus, the government was not precluded from taking the position that the deemed valuation rule of §2701 does not apply for GST purposes.

[149] Also unanswered are the consequences if C subsequently gives the common stock to GC, again triggering the application of §2701 because P is an applicable family member and continues to hold the applicable retained interest. The regulations could have applied §2701(e)(6) to purge P's adjusted taxable gifts base of the original gift or to prevent a second tax from being imposed on

Thus, if P gives common stock to GC and retains preferred stock, P will incur gift tax on 100% of the value of the entity due to § 2701 but will incur GST only on the actual FMV of the transferred common stock. A subsequent transfer of the preferred stock to C, or to GC, or to C followed by a second transfer to GC, should trigger the § 2701(e)(6) adjustment rules to avoid gift tax or FET on that same value again, but it ought to be subject to GST without regard to § 2701 or the prior gift tax incurred. If this is correct, strategic estate planning through the senior and junior equity interest approach remains available for GST purposes even though it is not for gift tax or FET. The benefit of any GST opportunity is diminished, however, because the GST is imposed at a flat rate, and any benefit disappears entirely if growth assets are used to pay the tax.

To illustrate, if Family Corp. is worth $100x today and is expected to double in value before the next taxable event, incurring a 35% GST immediately and paying it with corporate value would leave $65x that would grow to $130x. Incurring the same 35% tax at the next taxable event on $200x would leave the same $130x. Only if the immediate tax could be paid with assets that would not grow at the same rate would this result be improved. Mystifying about all this is that, if § 2701 does not apply for GST purposes, then no special § 2701(e)(6) adjustment is needed for GST purposes, making the reference in § 2701(e)(6) to Chapter 13 a puzzle. Nothing in the regulations addresses this quandary, and questions about the ultimate operation of a § 2701(e)(6) adjustment and the interplay with the GST are incapable of being answered on the basis of information now available.

§ 7.2.3.1 Technical Requirements

Section 2701(a) only applies if there is a transfer of a nonmarketable junior equity interest in a corporation or partnership[150] to or for the

(Footnote Continued)

the same value when C makes this transfer. The drafters of Treas. Reg. § 25.2701-5 chose not to address the issue, the preamble to the regulation citing unspecified administrative complexity as the justification. See § 7.2.3 n.144.

[150] No definition is given of a corporation or partnership, although the familiar definitions in §§ 7701(a)(2) and 7701(a)(3) should suffice. Some pressure may be put on the use of trusts in lieu of associations taxed as corporations if § 2701 can be avoided in such a facile manner, but efforts of this nature will likely

benefit of a family member. Moreover, it does not apply if the transferor holds and transfers any part of only one class of interest (ignoring differences in nonlapsing voting power or partnership management rights and limits on liability),[151] if the transferor retains only marketable interests,[152] or if the transferor retains only distribution rights that constitute "qualified payments."[153] These requirements and exceptions are the heart of the statute's application.

A nonmarketable interest is one for which quotations are not readily available on an established securities market.[154] The term "family" is used in several contexts in Chapter 14 and is defined differently in several places. For purposes of § 2701(a)(1), which deals with transferees, the term includes the transferor's spouse, lineal decedents of the transferor or of the transferor's spouse, and spouses of those lineal descendants.[155] This is the most narrow definition of "family" found in Chapter 14. The term "transfer" includes recapitalizations, redemptions, capital contributions, and similar transactions[156] or changes in an entity's

---

(Footnote Continued)

generate attacks of the type in Bedell v. Commissioner, 86 T.C. 1207 (1986), seeking to tax a trust as a corporation. Such treatment may not be required, however, if the rules in § 2702 are adequate to combat that abuse.

[151] §§ 2701(a)(2)(B) and 2701(a)(2)(C).

[152] § 2701(a)(2)(A).

[153] §§ 2701(c)(1)(B) and 2701(c)(3).

[154] § 2701(a)(2)(A).

[155] § 2701(e)(1).

[156] A number of authorities have concluded that a gift can be made in the context of a change in corporate capital structure. See, e.g., Estate of Maggos v. Commissioner, 79 T.C.M. (CCH) 1861 (2000), rem'd in unpublished opinion, 2002-1 U.S. Tax Cas. (CCH) ¶ 60,433 (9th Cir. 2002) to evaluate a valuation issue, but otherwise aff'd (redemption of stock worth $4.9 million in exchange for $3 million deemed a gift of the difference to a child who became the sole shareholder by virtue of the redemption); Estate of Bosca v. Commissioner, 76 T.C.M. (CCH) 62 (1998) (exchange of voting common stock for nonvoting common stock was a gift to children who owned the remaining voting common stock); Furman v. Commissioner, 75 T.C.M. (CCH) 2206 (1998) (redemption of common stock in exchange for preferred was a gift to other shareholders of common stock); Estate of Trenchard v. Commissioner, 69 T.C.M. (CCH) 2164 (1995) (gift attributable to government's application of a 40% lack of marketability discount with respect to stock received in an exchange). But see Estate of Anderson v. Commissioner, 56 T.C.M. (CCH) 553 (1988) (no gift attributable to contribution

capital structure[157] if the taxpayer or an "applicable family member" receives or otherwise holds thereafter an "applicable retained interest."[158]

With respect to capital structure transactions, it remains to be seen whether creation of a new business, or a § 355 spin off or split up, will trigger § 2701. PLR 8936083 may be helpful in this respect. It evaluated a complicated § 355 corporate consolidation and distribution that effectively put the stock of several divisions or subsidiaries in the hands of various employees and shareholders. After concluding that the transactions generated no income tax, the Ruling addressed the consequences of the proposed distributions under the since repealed § 2036(c) anti-freeze provision. The important § 2036(c) question was whether a § 355 division of an existing corporation, followed by a transfer of all of the stock, both preferred and common, of one of the resulting corporations, avoided the application of § 2036(c). The Ruling indicated that such a transfer was copacetic if it was a sale for full and adequate consideration.

More interesting was the question whether a taxpayer could effect a § 355 division and gratuitously transfer all rights in one of the resulting corporations. The Ruling gave some pause if the division allocates appreciating assets into one of those divisions.

> Where separate entities are utilized to engage in common or interrelated activities, section 2036(c) may be applicable to the entire enterprise as well as to the separate, isolated activities. For example, where an enterprise is separated into an operating entity and an entity designed to hold appreciating assets, an individual may not avoid the application of section 2036(c) by limiting his holdings to the operating entity.

But what if the transaction merely separates identifiable divisions of a corporation, and the more profitable or growth division is transferred? For example, if Parent owns Furniture Co. with one store in a declining downtown region and another in an affluent suburb, could the operation be divided into two separate entities, followed by a gift to Child of all the stock in the suburban store entity? The regulations under § 355 indicate

(Footnote Continued)

of common stock in exchange for preferred stock because the values were approximately equal).

[157] § 2701(e)(5).

[158] § 2701(b).

§ 7.2.3.1

the types of entity divisions that would be income tax free and that might succeed for estate planning purposes.

A transfer is not deemed to occur if the pre- and post-transaction interests of the taxpayer and the applicable family members are substantially the same as before the transaction.[159]

The regulations[160] specify that "section 2701 applies to a transfer that would not otherwise be a gift under Chapter 12 because it was a transfer for full and adequate consideration." For example, it applies to transactions that are treated as transfers for purposes of triggering § 2701, including those § 2701(e)(5) deemed transfers (capital contributions, redemptions, recapitalizations, or other changes in the capital structure of the entity)—a capital structure transaction—if an applicable retained interest is received or retained in conjunction with it.[161]

A "capital structure transaction" is a transfer if the transferor or an applicable family member (1) thereby receives an applicable retained interest, or (2) held an applicable retained interest before the transaction and, in exchange for the surrender of a subordinate equity interest, receives property other than an applicable retained interest as a result of the transaction, or (3) surrenders a nonsubordinate equity interest, causing the FMV of any applicable retained interest already held to increase.[162] Specifically mentioned are contributions to a start up entity[163]

---

159 PLR 9451051 addressed the effect of a capital restructuring transaction that involved a conversion of debt into Class A preferred stock. The issue was whether Class A and Class B common stock should be treated as different from the Class A preferred stock for purposes of the substantially identical interest rule. The government held that the Class A preferred was substantially the same as the Class B common stock because the dividend right on the Class A preferred was the same as the dividend right on the Class B common stock, and because the nonlapsing and nondiscretionary liquidation preference of the Class A preferred stock was only $10 per share. Therefore, the Ruling held that § 2701 would not apply to the conversion as if it was a capital contribution. And see PLR 9848006, treating convertible preferred as a junior equity interest.

160 Treas. Reg. § 25.2701-1(b)(1).

161 Treas. Reg. § 25.2701-1(b)(2).

162 Treas. Reg. § 25.2701-1(b)(2)(i)(B).

163 Treas. Reg. § 25.2701-1(b)(2)(i)(A).

§ 7.2.3.1

and termination of any interest attributed to the transferor, such as from an entity (another corporation, a partnership, a trust, or the like).[164]

Specifically excluded are three items not anticipated by the statute:[165]

* A capital structure transaction, if the transferor, each applicable family member, and each member of the transferor's family holds substantially the same interest after the transaction as that individual held before the transaction.[166] For this purpose, common stock with non-lapsing voting rights and nonvoting common stock are interests that are substantially the same.[167]

* A shift of rights occurring upon the execution of a §2518 qualified disclaimer.

* A shift of rights occurring upon the release, exercise, or lapse of a power of appointment other than a general power of appointment described in §2514, except to the extent the release, exercise, or lapse otherwise would be a transfer under Chapter 12.

For purposes of determining who retains an interest that will trigger §2701, an "*applicable* family member" includes the taxpayer's spouse, ancestors of the taxpayer or of the taxpayer's spouse, and spouses of those ancestors.[168] And transfers by a partnership, corporation, trust, or other similar entity are attributed to the partners, shareholders, beneficiaries, settlors, or other appropriate individuals who are deemed to hold the entity's interests.[169] Under this entity attribution rule:

---

[164] See §2701(e)(3) and Treas. Reg. §25.2701-6.

[165] Treas. Reg. §25.2701-1(b)(3).

[166] See, e.g., PLRs 199947034 (multiclass stock corporation being converted to an LLC and all classes of stock being replaced with units of the same structure and rights will qualify for this exception) and 9427023 (a partnership in which each partner contributed capital proportionate to the partner's prior ownership interest in the partnership met this exception).

[167] See Treas. Reg. §25.2701-1(b)(3)(i) and PLR 200026011. Similar perhaps are PLRs 199952012 and 199927002, which held that the transfer of options is not the same as a transfer of stock and that the transferee does not hold an equity interest, such that §2701 cannot apply. To the extent the options are exercisable to acquire stock of the same class, "substantially the same interest" treatment ought to apply.

[168] §2701(e)(2).

[169] §2701(e)(3).

§7.2.3.1

- Interests held by a corporation are attributed to shareholders in proportion to the FMV of their ownership of the corporation.

- Interests held in a partnership are attributed on the basis of the FMV of the higher of the partner's interest in profits or capital.

- Interests in trust are attributed to a beneficiary to the extent the beneficiary could receive a distribution of the equity interest or the income or proceeds therefrom in the maximum exercise of the trustee's discretion.

- Trust interests are attributed to the trust's settlor to the extent the trust is deemed owned by the settlor under the grantor trust rules.[170]

Because these rules could cause attribution to more than one person, or cause multiple levels of attribution,[171] ordering rules are imposed to determine which individual should be the "recipient" of attributed amounts,[172] and an interest that is attributed to an individual in more than one capacity is treated as held only once—in the capacity that results in the largest amount being attributed.[173]

Assuming they are correct, the positions stated in PLR 9321046 reveal how convoluted these rules may become. Involved was the multiple attribution rule applicable to stock held in a trust.[174] The situation involved a family held corporation, the stock being owned 47% by the taxpayer, 50% by a nonmarital trust created by the taxpayer's predeceased spouse, and 3% by their descendants. The Ruling addressed the consequences if the corporation was recapitalized so that its existing common stock was replaced with both common and preferred stock. A recapitalization is not a transfer for §2701 purposes if all stockholders in the transferor's family hold substantially the same interest after the

---

[170] To illustrate, PLR 9253018 involved a sale of common stock to an ESOP in which a family member of the seller had an interest and held that this constituted a transfer subject to §2701. Because the underlying facts in the Ruling were not clear it is difficult to ascertain the conclusion reached, but it appears that the value of the transferred common stock for gift tax purposes was greater than the FMV consideration paid for it. Treas. Reg. §25.2701-6(a)(4)(ii)(C). If all the other requisites for §2701 application are met it may be that changes in toggle switch grantor trust status (discussed in §5.11) will constitute a transfer under Treas. Reg. §25.2701-1(b)(2)(i)(C)(1).

[171] As, for example, if attribution is to a trust and then from the trust to its beneficiaries.

[172] Treas. Reg. §25.2701-6(a)(5).

[173] Treas. Reg. §25.2701-6(a)(1).

[174] Treas. Reg. §25.2701-6(a)(5).

transaction as before,[175] and in this case each stockholder would end up with the same percentages of both common and preferred stock as they previously held of common stock alone. As a result, at first blush it appeared that the recapitalization would not trigger § 2701.

Then the question arose about how to regard the stock held in the trust, which the attribution rules require to be treated as held by its beneficiaries. That alone would not be a problem, because the relative interests of the beneficiaries would not change in the trust. Upon closer inspection, however, the Ruling stated that different attribution occurs with respect to preferred stock (an applicable retained interest) than with respect to common stock (a subordinate equity interest) under the disparate rules applied by the regulations.[176] Because of this disparity, the Ruling concluded that the taxpayer and the descendants would not be deemed to hold substantially the same interest before and after the recapitalization, which meant that the recapitalization alone would trigger § 2701 even though nothing occurred other than issuance of new stock certificates to represent the same percentage ownership of the corporation.

Because of this deemed transfer, the Ruling held that the § 2701 valuation rules must be employed to determine the value of what the taxpayer and the descendants were deemed to own before and after the recapitalization, all reflecting deemed ownership under the attribution rules, with a potentially substantial gift tax liability notwithstanding that no transfers of any kind actually occurred. If the Ruling is correct, it also could mean that a postmortem recapitalization by an estate in anticipation of using preferred and common stock to fund, respectively, a marital and a nonmarital trust to accomplish a freeze during S's overlife could result in gift tax liability. This could be the result even before an allocation is made and even though that liability would not apply if the estate made the same allocations of preferred and common stock that was held by D at death. That result does not appear to be correct, and the actual Ruling position may not be either.

---

[175] Treas. Reg. § 25.2701-1(b)(3)(i).

[176] See Treas. Reg. §§ 25.2701-6(a)(5)(i) and 25.2701-6(a)(5)(ii).

§ 7.2.3.1

§7.2.3.2 Applicable Retained Interests

The primary objective of §2701 is to deny value to certain "applicable retained interests." In determining the value of transferred interests, it ignores the value otherwise attributable to interests such as most liquidation, put, call, and conversion rights.[177] But other interests in the entity—distribution rights that include the right to stock dividends or partnership distributions—are disregarded as applicable retained interests only if, immediately before the transfer, the transferor and applicable family members held control of the entity.[178] This requirement is not imposed with respect to liquidation, put, call, and conversion rights. Excepted from the rule that disregards their value are rights that must be exercised at a specified time and in a specific amount,[179] or rights to convert into a fixed number or percentage of the same class of interest transferred, if the right is nonlapsing and is adjusted to reflect stock splits, accumulated unpaid dividends, and similar changes to the capital structure that should not affect the shareholders' relative ownership interests.[180]

The regulations further refine these concepts in some cases by employing terms that are not found in the statute. There are "qualified payment rights,"[181] "distribution rights" (which include qualified payment rights),[182] and "extraordinary payment rights," which include any retained "put, call, or conversion right, any right to compel liquidation, or any similar right, the exercise or nonexercise of which affects the value of the transferred interest."[183] A "mandatory payment right" is a right to

---

177 §2701(b)(1)(B), to the extent not excepted under §2701(c)(2)(B) or (C).

178 §2701(b)(1)(A), with attribution under §2701(e)(3). Control is relevant only with respect to distribution rights; liquidation, put, call, and conversion rights are subject to this rule even if the transferor's family does not control the entity.

179 §2701(c)(2)(B).

180 §2701(c)(2)(C). See, e.g., PLRs 9417024 and 9241014. Many conversion features fail to adjust as required and will be treated mistakenly as excluded from §2701 by inattention to this requisite.

181 Treas. Reg. §25.2701-2(b)(6).

182 Treas. Reg. §25.2701-2(b)(3).

183 Treas. Reg. §25.2701-2(b)(2). PLR 9848006 involved certain "tag along" (certain shareholders were entitled to participate if others exercised put options) and "drag along" (institutional investors who chose to sell could require certain

receive payments that are fixed as to both time and amount (for example, a preferred stock redemption right), including a right to receive a specific amount on death.[184] But "liquidation participation rights" (just what the name implies) generally are deemed not to exist if the transferor, members of the transferor's family, or applicable family members have the ability to compel liquidation.[185] Finally, "nonlapsing conversion rights" entitle the owner to convert an equity interest into a fixed number or percentage of shares of the same class as the transferred interest, and all of these are defined as neither extraordinary payment rights nor distribution rights.[186] This means that they are not ignored, their value is deemed to exist for gift tax purposes, and their retention reduces the value of any gift of other interests in the entity.

A "distribution right" that will be ignored as a retained interest is defined as a right to receive corporate or partnership distributions with respect to stock or partnership interests that are not "junior equity." This is logical because the special valuation rule is not necessary if junior equity is retained rather than transferred—junior equity participates in future growth and therefore does not constitute a strategic estate planning instrument.[187] In addition, § 2701 does not apply if the applicable retained interest is of the same class as the transferred interest (or is proportionally the same as the transferred interest when differences in

---

(Footnote Continued)

shareholders also to sell) and rights of first refusal, all of which the government held to be not extraordinary payment rights because they did not affect the value of transferred junior equity interests.

[184] Treas. Reg. § 25.2701-2(b)(4)(i). See, e.g., PLR 9848006 (preferred stock redemption rights).

[185] Treas. Reg. § 25.2701-2(b)(4)(ii).

[186] Treas. Reg. § 25.2701-2(b)(4)(iv).

[187] See § 2701(c)(1). "Junior equity" is defined in § 2701(a)(4)(B)(i) as any common stock and the most junior partnership interest. Liquidation, put, call, and conversion rights are not distribution rights because they are separately defined as applicable retained interests and are specially valued in their own right under § 2701(b)(1)(B). And § 707(c) rights to receive guaranteed partnership fixed payments are excluded from the zero valuation rule because these payments are outside the normal partnership distribution regime.

§ 7.2.3.2

nonlapsing[188] voting rights or, in a partnership, in management rights and limited liability are ignored).[189] Thus, the §2701 valuation rule does not apply to distribution rights (1) in a corporation with only one class of stock, (2) to a one tier partnership, or (3) to a multiclass corporation or multitiered partnership if the transferor held only one class of stock or tier of partnership interest.[190]

The regulations contain a statement that "any right to receive distributions with respect to an interest that is of the same class as, or a class that is subordinate to, the transferred interest" is not a distribution right.[191] This appears to be the regulatory embodiment of the §2701(c)(1)(B)(i) rule that "a right to distributions with respect to any interest which is junior to the rights of the transferred interest" is not a

---

188 According to the Staff of the House Ways and Means Comm., 101st Cong., 2d Sess., Conference Committee Report No. 964, Statement of the Managers (1990) at 151:

Except as provided in Treasury regulations, a right that lapses by reason of Federal or State law generally would be treated as nonlapsing under this exception. The conferees intend, however, that Treasury regulations may give zero value to rights which lapse by reason of Federal or State law that effectively transfer wealth that would not pass in the absence of a specific agreement. Such regulations could, for example, give zero value to a management right that lapses by reason of the death of a partner under the Uniform Partnership Act as adopted in a State if the decedent had waived in the partnership agreement the right to be redeemed at fair market value under that Act.

And see §2704, discussed in §7.2.4.4.

189 §§2701(a)(2)(B) and (C).

190 See, e.g., PLRs 9414013, 9414012, and 9229028, also stating that the exception for proportional partnership interests is denied if the transferor, or an applicable family member, can alter the transferee's liability as a partner. §2701(a)(2) (flush language). PLR 9415007 held that the Treas. Reg. §25.2701-1(c)(3) same class requirement was deemed met in a limited partnership setting in which the transferor was a general partner who transferred limited partnership interests, because rights in the retained and the transferred interests were the same except for nonlapsing differences in management and liability limitations, which do not affect the one class of stock definition. But TAM 199933002 concluded that limited and general partnership interests in that case did not qualify under the same class or proportional interests exceptions because capital transaction distributions would be made to the limited partners first, followed by the general partners, rather than pro rata to each.

191 Treas. Reg. §25.2701-2(b)(3)(i).

distribution right. An applicable retained interest is described as any equity interest with respect to which there is either an extraordinary payment right or a distribution right.[192] The result is to exclude rights with respect to junior equity from the class of retained interests that are valued at zero under § 2701.

Because § 2701(a)(2)(B) excepts retained interests that are of the same class as the transferred interest, and § 2701(a)(2)(C) excepts retained interests that are "proportionally the same as the transferred interest," either provision might apply with respect to a multiclass entity in which the transferor owns interests in several classes and transfers the same proportionate share of each holding. For example, § 2701 should not apply if the transferor owned 80% of the preferred stock of X Corp. and 50% of the common stock of X Corp. and transferred to a family member one-fifth of each holding (16% of the total preferred stock and 10% of the total common stock in X Corp.). In this respect, the regulations refer to transfers of a "vertical slice" of interests in an entity that effect "a proportionate reduction in each class of interest held by the transferor and all applicable family members in the aggregate." Thus,

> section 2701 does not apply if P owns 50 percent of each class of equity interest in a corporation and transfers a portion of each class to P's child in a manner that reduces each interest held by P *and* any applicable family members, *in the aggregate*, by 10 percent *even if the transfer does not proportionately reduce P's interest in each class.*[193]

Apparently this means that, of P's 50% ownership of each class, something other than 10% of some classes could be transferred and the proportionate transfer exception could apply.

For example, assume P owned 50% of Class A common, 50% of Class B common, and 50% of the preferred stock, and that applicable family members own another 10% of Class A common, 20% of Class B common, and 40% of the preferred stock. Apparently the proportionate transfer rule will apply if P transfers an amount of Class A common that reduces the aggregate 60% ownership interest by 10%, and transfers an amount of Class B common that reduces that aggregate 70% ownership interest by 10%, and transfers an amount of preferred stock that reduces that

---

[192] Treas. Reg. § 25.2701-2(b)(1).

[193] Treas. Reg. § 25.2701-1(c)(4) (emphasis added).

§ 7.2.3.2

aggregate 90% ownership by 10%, even though P's transfers are not proportionately the same slice of the stock interests owned solely by P.

The Secretary of the Treasury is authorized by § 2701(e)(7) to promulgate regulations treating a retained interest as two or more separate interests to facilitate qualification for the one class of interest exception, as illustrated by the Conference Committee Report:[194]

> *Example 3.* Mother owns all the stock in a corporation. One class is entitled to the first $100 in dividends each year plus half the dividends paid in excess of $100 that year; the second class is entitled to one half of the dividends paid above $100. The preferred right under the first class is cumulative. Mother retains the first class and gives the second class to Child. Under the conference agreement, Treasury regulations may treat an instrument of the first class as two instruments under the provision: one, an instrument bearing a preferred right to dividends of $100; the other, an instrument bearing the right to half the annual dividends in excess of $100, which would fall within the exception for retained interests of the same class as the transferred interest.

Because control is required with respect to distribution rights, "control" is defined to mean (1) 50% of the vote or value of a corporation's stock, (2) 50% of the capital or profit interests in any partnership or, (3) any general partnership interest, if the partnership is a limited partnership interest.[195] Again, an attribution rule imputes ownership from entities such as corporations, partnerships, and trusts to shareholders, partners, beneficiaries, and settlors.[196]

---

[194] Staff of the House Ways and Means Comm., 101st Cong., 2d Sess., Conference Committee Report No. 964, Statement of the Managers (1990) at 154.

[195] § 2701(b)(2); Treas. Reg. § 25.2701-2(b)(5)(ii)(A). For this purpose, § 25.2701-2(b)(5)(ii)(B) provides that "[e]quity interests that carry no right to vote other than on liquidation, merger, or a similar event are not considered to have voting rights," and contingent rights are ignored unless the holder has control over the contingency.

[196] § 2701(e)(3). In this context only, "applicable family member" includes the transferor's spouse, ancestors of the transferor or of the transferor's spouse, and spouses of such ancestors, under § 2701(e)(2). It also includes, by attribution, lineal descendants of the parents of the transferor or of the transferor's spouse. § 2701(b)(2)(C). For purposes of determining whether an entity is a controlled entity, Treas. Reg. § 25.2701-2(b)(5) limits the attribution to an individual to only those interests held by the transferor, applicable family members, and the lineal

§7.2.3.3 Qualified Payments Exception

If all the threshold requirements for §2701 to apply are met, there is yet another way to avoid its application to a gift of a junior equity interest, because §2701 does not apply to a retained distribution right that "consists of a right to receive a qualified payment."[197] Such as a periodic cumulative preferred dividend (or similar partnership distribution) payable at a fixed rate or tied to a specific market interest rate.[198] As to these, the special valuation rule is not imposed and normal valuation principles will be applied.

Valuation of the retained interest for purposes of valuing the transferred interest reflects the rate of return specified in the qualified payment and gives "due regard to the corporation's net worth, prospective earning power, and dividend-paying capacity."[199] As to these interests, the Code reflects a degree of assurance that the payments will be made, and this reduces the risk than an untaxed imputed valuation increase to the transferee attributable to undervalued dividends will occur. That is, the transferee does not stand to get richer because the transferor does not receive dividends or other retained enjoyment. Thus, the Code permits a portion of the value of the entity to be assigned to these qualified payment applicable retained interests held by the trans-

---

(Footnote Continued)

descendants of the parents of the individual and of the individual's spouse. This alters the Code as drafted if it means that attribution will not impute a holding to a family member that then would be counted for purposes of determining control under this test. Excluded, for example, would be attribution from descendants and siblings of an ancestor's spouse to the ancestor and then to the transferor. Caution is required, however, because multiple attribution will apply under §2701(e)(3) from an entity to an individual and from that individual to others. See Treas. Reg. §25.2701-6(a)(1).

[197] §2701(c)(3). According to PLR 200114004, a qualified payment may be prepaid but not entirely commuted, without running afoul of Treas. Reg. §25.2701-2(b)(6)(i)(B). The prepayment term was not stated but the Ruling posited that the document precluded prepayment by more than a certain term.

[198] §2701(c)(3). According to PLR 200114004, a qualified payment may be prepaid but not entirely commuted, without running afoul of Treas. Reg. §25.2701-2(b)(6)(i)(B). The prepayment term was not stated but the Ruling posited that the document precluded prepayment by more than a certain term.

[199] As illustrated in Treas. Reg. §25.2701-2(d) Example 5.

§7.2.3.3

feror, and to that extent the transferred interest is worth less and incurs less gift tax liability.

A qualified payment that can be reduced or eliminated because it is subject to a liquidation, put, call, or conversion right will be valued, however, as if each right was exercised in the manner that produces the lowest value for the entire bundle of rights held by the transferor.[200] As illustrated by the Conference Committee Report:[201]

> *Example 1.* Father retains cumulative preferred stock in a transaction to which [§ 2701] applies. The cumulative dividend is $100 per year and the stock may be redeemed at any time after two years for $1,000. . . . [T]he value of the cumulative preferred stock is the lesser of (1) the present value of two years of $100 dividends plus the present value of the redemption for $1,000 in year two, or (2) the present value of $100 paid every year in perpetuity. If the present values are substantially identical, the stock receives such value.

The regulations posit an illustration in which a transferor has an immediate right to put retained preferred stock to the corporation for $900,000 and a qualified payment right valued at $1 million, resulting in a value being placed on the preferred stock of the lesser amount, reflecting a valuation assumption that exercise of the put right will occur immediately.[202] As so limited, however, the value attributed to a qualified payment reduces the value of any transferred interest for gift tax purposes, which usually is desirable to the transferor.

§ 7.2.3.3.1 *Unpaid distributions*

Fundamental to ascertaining the proper gift tax value of a retained qualified payment right is that the specified payments must be made. If they are not, § 2701(d) dictates that, on future taxable events, the value of the applicable retained interest is deemed to include the value of unpaid qualified payments.[203] This "suspense account" value is deter-

---

[200] § 2701(a)(3). See also Treas. Reg. § 25.2701-2(a)(3).

[201] Staff of the House Ways and Means Comm., 101st Cong., 2d Sess., Conference Committee Report No. 964, Statement of the Managers (1990) at 153.

[202] Treas. Reg. § 25.2701-2(a)(5).

[203] It is not clear whether this deemed increase in value will apply for GST purposes other than for exemption allocation under § 2642(b). See § 7.2.3 n.148.

mined under a compounding approach that assumes the qualified payment was distributed when due and then invested by the transferor at an annually compounding yield equal to the discount rate originally used to value the stream of qualified payments that constitute the applicable retained interest.[204]

Consistent with the rationale for §2701—to prevent strategic estate planning but not legitimate transfers—the suspense account increase in value under this unpaid dividend rule cannot exceed the transferor's share of the increase in value of all equity interests that are junior to the applicable retained interest, accruing since the subject transfer.[205] To determine the transferor's maximum unpaid dividend suspense account value, the transferor is deemed to own only a proportionate share of the appreciation in the junior equity interest(s), reflecting the fraction of the class of applicable retained interest owned by the transferor.[206] This is sensible because it is only to the extent of appreciation in the value of junior interests that any strategic planning shift of value has occurred, and only that amount should be subject to wealth transfer tax recapture under this unpaid dividend rule.

For this purpose, amounts paid in redemption of subordinate equity interests are treated as appreciation,[207] the notion being that amounts paid to redeem junior equity interests are growth that this rule was meant to tax. Furthermore, if an individual owns applicable retained interests in more than one class of the entity, the percentage of the entity's growth that constitutes the appreciation limitation is the greater ownership percentage.[208]

Moreover, a four year grace period is granted within which to make cumulative preferred dividend payments before invoking the unpaid dividend rule.[209] No provision specifies whether partial payments can be

---

[204] § 2701(d)(2).

[205] § 2701(d)(2)(B).

[206] § 2701(d)(2)(B). To determine the transferor's maximum unpaid dividend suspense account value, the transferor is deemed to own only a proportionate share of the appreciation in the junior equity interest(s), reflecting the fraction of the class of applicable retained interest owned by the transferor.

[207] Treas. Reg. § 25.2701-4(c)(6)(i)(A)(2).

[208] Treas. Reg. § 25.2701-4(c)(6)(iii).

[209] § 2701(d)(2)(C).

§7.2.3.3.1

made at any time within the four year catch-up period, nor does the Code dictate how payments are to be applied against accumulated deficiencies from several years. However, arrearage payments are deemed to satisfy the oldest unpaid qualified payment,[210] which might cause a payment to be regarded as made too late to fall within the four year grace period. And the Code provides no relief from the imposition of tax on an arrearage if the transferor dies or transfers the retained interest within the four year grace period.[211] Thus, the Code taxes the suspense account value as if the deficiency will not be caught up and there is no procedure to file a refund claim if later it is.

Taxable events that will trigger taxation of this suspense account value include death of the transferor, disposition of the applicable re-tained interest,[212] termination of the interest, or an election by the taxpayer.[213] The rule in § 2701(d)(3)(A)(iii) that permits a taxpayer to treat a dividend payment coming after expiration of the four year grace period as a taxable gift (to incur tax immediately on the payment rather than have it increase the annually compounding suspense account), cannot be used in conjunction with the § 2701(d)(2)(B) appreciation limitation. The election to immediately incur tax will result in the full

---

[210] Treas. Reg. § 25.2701-4(c)(4).

[211] If the donee on either event is the transferor's spouse and the transfer qualifies for the gift tax annual exclusion or the marital deduction, § 2701(d)(3)(B) allows a carryover to the spouse of the suspense account value and thus acts like a marital deduction provision, deferring tax on the suspense account until a taxable event occurs involving the surviving spouse. Treas. Reg. § 25.2701-4(b)(3)(ii)(B) provides guidance in determining whether S is the do-nee if the stock is or will be used to satisfy a marital deduction bequest or if S will purchase the interest from D's estate.

[212] §§ 2701(d)(3) and (d)(5). Under Treas. Reg. § 25.2701-4(b)(2), a transfer during the transferor's life to a trust that would be includible in the transferor's gross estate for FET purposes will not trigger the deemed gift rule.

[213] The mechanics for making a § 2701(d)(3)(A)(iii) election to treat a late payment coming after expiration of the grace period as a taxable event are established by Treas. Reg. § 25.2701-4(d)(3). Expected is a statement on a timely filed gift tax return for the year in which the payment was received. If made on a return that is not timely filed for that year, the payment is deemed received on the first day of the month immediately preceding the month in which the return was filed (or, if this late filed election is made after the interest holder's death, on the date of death, if later) rather than on the date it actually was received, which will affect the computation of the compounding cumulative dividend arrearage.

distribution being subjected to tax even if there is little or no actual appreciation in the value of the junior equity interests of the entity.[214] This position will preclude a taxpayer from manipulating the timing of late payments (and elections with respect to them) to minimize tax by tracking periodic market value fluctuations. Moreover, a taxpayer who makes this election is treated as making it with respect to every late qualified payment previously made as to which the immediate tax election could have been made but was not.[215]

The statute does not specify who will pay the tax on the occurrence of any of these events. Because there is no federal reimbursement provision dealing with this question, presumably any applicable state law will control. In most cases, any FET attributable to this suspense account value most appropriately would be apportioned to the recipient of the transferred interest because the tax attributable to the suspense account value is invoked by treating the transferred interest as worth more than otherwise it would be. It might be argued, however, that the entity is holding the unpaid dividends generating this suspense account value and liability, and that the entity therefore ought to pay the increased taxes attributable to it. The problem with this approach is that the entity may be unable to pay the tax for the same reasons it is unable to pay the distributions that are in arrears.

Moreover, it is possible that the transferor does not own the applicable retained interest (instead, it may be held by an applicable family member) and that any § 2701(d) tax invoked by the transferor's death will relate to an asset not includible in the transferor's estate. Although § 2701(d)(1)(A) deems the transferor's estate to increase by virtue of the suspense account value, there would be no actual transfer of the applicable retained interest and, thus, under the tax apportionment rules of most states, no one to whom the tax would be attributable. In such a case, it might be the actual owner of the interest—the applicable family member—to whom the tax should be apportioned.

The specter of this apportionment occurring raises the issue whether this tax is unconstitutional, imposed as it is with no transfer of the applicable retained interest and no transferee. To be valid, the tax

---

[214] Treas. Reg. § 25.2701-4(d)(2).
[215] Treas. Reg. § 25.2701-4(d)(1).

§ 7.2.3.3.1

under Chapters 11 through 14 must be a wealth *transfer* tax, not a direct (unapportioned) tax on property.[216] Adding to the complexity of this rule is the fact that a gift tax apportionment regime is not likely to exist under state law if the taxable event is an inter vivos transfer of the applicable retained interest or a §2701(d)(3)(A)(iii) election by the holder of the interest. Nor is it clear that this rule applies at all for GST purposes or, if it does, who is the donor or transferee.

The transferor will face double taxation if the §2701(d) taxable event is sale of the applicable retained interest and the buyer pays consideration that reflects the probability that the accumulated preferred dividend will be paid. One tax will be imposed on the full suspense account value as a deemed gift triggered by disposition of the applicable retained interest. The other tax is imposed on the consideration paid in contemplation of the suspense account payments being made. No §2701(e)(6) offset or credit is provided in these circumstances, nor is it clear how to determine whether any consideration received from a transfer is attributable to accumulated dividends that the buyer expects to be paid in the future.

If the accumulation ultimately is paid, double taxation should permit a refund of any tax imposed that is attributable to the suspense account value.[217] Moreover, there also would be an improper double inclusion problem at death if the §2033 value of the applicable retained interest itself reflects the cumulative unpaid dividend. Treas. Reg. §25.2701-4(c)(1)(ii)(C) precludes this double taxation of the suspense account value, once under §2701(d)(1) and again as a part of the value of the underlying stock interest (because the dividend payment accrued but unpaid is a cumulative right that increases the value of the stock to which it adheres). It effectively provides for a reduction of the suspense account value for amounts includible in the gift tax or FET base without regard to §2701(d).

---

[216] See §6.2.3 n.30 and accompanying text.

[217] Treas. Reg. §25.2701-5. These problems would be exacerbated if the transferor's spouse agreed under §2513 to split any gift that triggered taxation of the suspense account value (assuming gift splitting is permitted with respect to such a deemed transfer; it should be automatic if other gifts for the year are split by the spouses). See §7.1.3.

§7.2.3.3.1

Although there are no basis provisions anywhere in Chapter 14, a § 1015 basis adjustment should be permitted (presumably to the holder of the transferred interest, because that person is deemed to have received added value attributable to the overdue dividends) for the gift tax attributable to the suspense account value. In addition, § 1014 should apply with respect to that value if a deemed transfer occurs at the transferor's death. In this respect, however, § 1014(c) may apply if the taxable event is death of the transferor and the suspense account is treated as IRD for income tax purposes.[218]

In explaining the unpaid dividend rule, the Conference Committee Report provides the following helpful, albeit flawed, illustration:[219]

> *Example 5.* A corporation has four classes of stock. Class A is entitled to the first $10 of dividends each year; Class B is entitled to the second $10 of dividends each year; Class C is entitled to the third $10 of dividends each year; and Class D is entitled to all dividends in excess of those paid to Classes A, B, and C. Classes A, B, and C all have cumulative rights to dividends. In a transaction to which [§ 2701] applies, Father gives Daughter stock in classes A and C while retaining stock in class B. Class D is owned by an unrelated party. Dividends are not paid on the Class C [*sic*—this should be Class B] stock. The cap on future amounts subject to transfer tax equals the excess of the fair market value of stock in Classes C and D at the date of Father's death over such value at the date of the gift multiplied by a fraction equal to the percentage of Class B stock held by Father.

In applying the unpaid dividend rule the taxable event will be ignored and the spouse will be treated as the transferor for future application of these rules[220] if a transfer is not taxable as a gift because it qualifies for the gift tax annual exclusion or the marital deduction, or constitutes a

---

[218] See § 5.10.2.

[219] Staff of the House Ways and Means Comm., 101st Cong., 2d Sess., Conference Committee Report No. 964, Statement of the Managers (1990) at 155.

[220] § 2701(d)(3)(B). Apparently consideration paid by the transferor's spouse will not alter future operation of this suspense account rule and does not alter the immediate income tax consequences of the transfer to the spouse because, under § 1041, gain is not realized on that transfer. Thus, the only potential benefit attributable to the spouse making a payment for the transferred interest is a higher basis if cost is greater than carryover basis under the part-sale, part-gift transaction rules of Treas. Reg. § 1.1015-4(a). See § 6.1 n.2.

§ 7.2.3.3.1

sale for full and adequate consideration to the transferor's spouse. Again this raises difficult unanswerable questions regarding payment of the tax and the appropriate § 2701(e)(6) adjustments.[221]

§ 7.2.3.3.2 Qualified payment elections

Two irrevocable elections are provided by § 2701(c)(3)(C), one to waive qualified payment treatment to preclude application of the suspense account compounding rule, and the other to treat any distribution right as a qualified payment to the extent not inconsistent with the underlying legal instrument generating that right. A requirement added by the regulations to the § 2701(c)(3)(C)(ii) election into qualified payment status is that the payments elected are permissible under the legal instrument and "are consistent with the legal right of the entity to make the payment."[222] In addition, the regulation specifies that the value of a qualified payment, following an election in, cannot exceed the FMV of that right determined without regard to the election.

Little detail is given as to how this can be accomplished as a practical matter,[223] but the Conference Committee Report provides the following illustrations:[224]

---

[221] Treas. Reg. § 25.2701-4(b)(3)(ii)(B) provides rules to determine whether the transfer qualifies for this marital deduction exception to the taxable event rule if allocation of the qualified payment to S is discretionary, particularly if it does not occur before the transferor's FET return is filed.

[222] Treas. Reg. § 25.2701-2(c)(2)(ii).

[223] The mechanism for making § 2701(c)(3)(C) elections into or out of qualified payment treatment is established by Treas. Reg. § 25.2701-2(c)(5). Required is a statement containing specified information and attachment to the gift tax return filed by the transferor to report the transfer. Unlike § 2701(c)(3)(C)(i), which distinguishes between interests held by the transferor and those held by an applicable family member (creating a presumption *in favor of* qualified payment treatment unless the *transferor* elects out but a presumption *against* qualified payment treatment unless the *applicable family member* elects in), § 2701(c)(3)(C)(ii) does not distinguish the two holders and appears to indicate that a transferor may make the election even if the applicable retained interest is held by another applicable family member.

[224] Staff of the House Ways and Means Comm., 101st Cong., 2d Sess., Conference Committee Report No. 964, Statement of the Managers (1990) at 154-155.

§ 7.2.3.3.2

Example 2. Father and Daughter are partners in a partnership to which Father contributes an existing business. Father is entitled to 80 percent of the net cash receipts of the partnership until he receives $1 million, after which time he and Daughter both receive 50 percent of the partnership's cash flow. Father's liquidation preference equals $1 million. [T]he retained right to $1 million is valued at zero, unless Father elects to treat it as a right to receive qualified payments in the amounts, and at the times, specified in the election. If Father elects such treatment, amounts not paid at the times specified in the election become subject to the compounding rules.

Example 4. ... Treasury regulations may treat Father's retained interest as consisting of two interests: (1) a distribution right to $1 million and (2) a 50 percent partnership interest. Father could elect to treat the first interest as a right to receive qualified payments at specified amounts and times; the second interest would fall within the exception for retained interests of the same class as the transferred interest.

Partial elections may be exercised "with respect to a consistent portion of each payment right in the class as to which the election has been made,"[225] which apparently indicates that different retained interests may be the subject of separate inconsistent elections. An election out of qualified payment treatment may be made to treat *all* rights held by the transferor *of the same class* as rights that are not qualified payment rights but a partial election is permitted if "exercised with respect to a consistent portion of each payment right in the class as to which the election has been made."[226] More guidance will be required before the operation of this partial election option is clear.

An election out of the qualified payment rules may be desirable for a number of reasons. One is to avoid the complexity of the suspense account rules in § 2701(d). Another is because the compounding rule is likely to subject far more value to tax than if qualified payment treatment did not apply and the gift tax was incurred on the original transfer. This gift tax would be computed tax exclusive, and it would be incurred without any suspense account value and at the value of the applicable retained interest at the time of the gift rather than at a potentially greater value when the applicable retained interest later is transferred.

---

[225] Treas. Reg. § 25.2701-2(c)(2).

[226] Treas. Reg. § 25.2701-2(c)(1) (emphasis added).

§ 7.2.3.3.2

Electing into qualified payment treatment has the advantage of deferring any gift tax on the value of the applicable retained interest until its subsequent transfer. This tax deferral—usually irresistibly attractive to taxpayers—may be a siren song that should be avoided.[227] It also will be far cheaper, once subjected to a qualified payment regime, to pay a dividend in a timely manner than to pass on it (perhaps in the misguided effort to increase the value of the transferred interest) at the cost of suspense account taxation. Finally, as compared to qualified payment distributions, interest payments on corporate debt also would be more desirable, which may generate interest in preferred debt recapitalizations and raise the stakes of the debt/equity debate common to other corners of the tax world.

§7.2.3.4 Minimum Capitalization Requirement

One final qualified payment requirement for transfer valuation purposes is that the aggregate junior equity interests in the entity (common stock or comparable partnership interests) must represent at least 10% of the total value of the entity and a transferred junior equity interest must be worth at least a pro rata share of that total value. Which is to say that valuation of a retained interest, even reflecting its qualified payments entitlement, cannot exceed 90% of the value of the entity.[228] For this purpose, the entity is deemed to be worth 100% of the value of all equity interests in the entity plus the amount of any debt owed to the transferor or to applicable family members (the transferor's spouse, ancestors of the transferor or of the transferor's spouse, and spouses of these ancestors). The effect of this rule is to preclude assignment of too much value to applicable retained interests in an effort to undervalue junior equity interests that are transferred to family members.

For purposes of computing this 10% of equity and debt requirement, guarantees and qualified deferred compensation obligations are not debt, nor is debt "incurred with respect to the current conduct of [a] trade or business."[229] The regulations refer to amounts payable for "current services" as an example of such business debt and also note that a lease of property is not debt if the lease payments are current and represent full

---

[227] See § 6.2.

[228] § 2701(a)(4)(A).

[229] Treas. Reg. § 25.2701-3(c)(3).

and adequate consideration for use of the property, reflecting "a good faith effort . . . to determine the fair rental value" of the property. But arrearages with respect to a lease are regarded as debt.[230]

§ 7.2.3.5 Computation of Value

The § 2701 method of determining the value of a transferred interest is described as a four step "subtraction" computation.[231] The first step requires a determination of "the FMV of all family-held equity interests in the entity . . . determined by assuming that the interests are held by one individual, using a consistent set of assumptions."[232]

The second computation step reduces this full value of the family held equity interests in the entity by[233]

- the FMV of any family held senior equity interests that are not applicable retained interests[234] and by the FMV of any family held equity interests that are not held by the transferor, members of the transferor's family, or applicable family members of the transferor and that are of the same or any subordinate class to the interest transferred.

- It is further reduced by the family-interest-percentage-adjusted[235] § 2701 value of all applicable retained interests held by the transferor or applicable family members.

- Finally, if an interest retained by the transferor or an applicable family member is a qualified payment, its value is subtracted in this step.

The "family-interest-percentage" adjustment[236] in the second computation step is dictated if a family owns a greater percentage of senior equity interests than of junior interests.[237] For example, assume a transferor owned 100% of the preferred stock in a corporation and only 40% of the common stock, with the remaining 60% of the common stock owned by

---

[230] Treas. Reg. § 25.2701-3(c)(3)(ii).

[231] Treas. Reg. § 25.2701-3(b). For an illustration, see TAM 9447004.

[232] Treas. Reg. § 25.2701-3(b)(1)(i).

[233] Treas. Reg. § 25.2701-3(b)(2).

[234] As that concept is defined in § 2701(b) and Treas. Reg. § 25.2701-2(b).

[235] Treas. Reg. § 25.2701-3(b)(5), described next.

[236] Treas. Reg. § 25.2701-3(b)(5).

[237] "If the percentage of any class of applicable retained interest held by the transferor and by applicable family members . . . exceeds . . . the highest ownership percentage (determined on the basis of relative fair market values) of family-held interests" in subordinate equity interests.

§ 7.2.3.5

nonfamily members. In such a case any failure to pay dividends on nonqualified payment preferred stock would inure only 40% to the benefit of any family member donees of the common stock owned by the transferor. Thus, the family-interest-percentage adjustment permits valuation of the remaining 60% of the preferred stock as if it was held by a nonfamily member. Its actual FMV (rather than its § 2701 deemed zero value) would be reflected in the second step reductions.[238]

The family-interest-percentage adjustment in this illustration would begin by determining the "family-interest percentage," which is the highest ownership percentage held by the transferor and other applicable family members in any single class of equity interest that is subordinate to the interest transferred (or the highest ownership percentage in *all* classes of equity interests that are subordinate). In this case, the family interest percentage is the 40% common stock interest because no applicable family member owned any part of the remaining 60% of the common stock.

The percentage of any class of senior equity interest held by the family (60% in this example) that exceeds this family interest percentage thus "is treated as a family held interest that is not held by the transferor or an applicable family member." This means that its value is determined as a "pro rata share of the FMV of all family-held equity interests of the same class (determined . . . as if all family-held senior equity interests were held by one individual)."[239] This speaks to whether minority discounts or control premiums are to be reflected in this determination.

Under the third computation step the remaining value is allocated pro rata, beginning with the most senior equity interests, among the remaining equity interests held by the transferor, applicable family

---

[238] Treas. Reg. § 25.2701-3(b)(2)(i)(A). Technically, the Treas. Reg. § 25.2701-3(b)(5) adjustment specifies that the interest held in excess of the family interest percentage is "treated as a family-held interest that is not held by the transferor or an applicable family member," which qualifies as a reduction in Step 2 as the "fair market value of all family-held senior equity interests (other than applicable retained interests held by the transferor or applicable family members)."

[239] Treas. Reg. § 25.2701-3(b)(5)(i)(A).

§ 7.2.3.5

members, and members of the transferor's family, all as if no special valuation adjustments were required under §2701.[240]

Finally, in the last step the amount allocated to the transferred interest in the third step is reduced by minority or "similar" discounts, by any §2702 retained-term-interest valuation adjustment that might be relevant if the gift triggers that provision, and by any consideration received by the transferor.[241] This final value then constitutes the gift tax value under §2701 of the transferred interest.

§7.2.3.6 Summary of the Rule and Examples of Its Application

The cumulative effect of §2701 in a typical preferred stock recapitalization is to assign a value to any preferred interest retained by senior family members only if it complies with the qualified payment requirements (or some other exception to §2701 applies). Otherwise, the value of any applicable retained interest is deemed to be zero in determining the value of common stock transferred to family members. (Similar results apply to comparable partnership transactions.) In many cases these transferred interests will be deemed for gift tax purposes to carry 100% of the value of the entity owned by the transferor.

This "easy-to-complete" valuation and taxation rule accelerates the wealth transfer tax liability attributable to the transferor's interest and guarantees that no portion of the entity's value slips into a crack between gift tax and FET. Recapitalizations are respected under this regime but taxpayers are put to a choice whether to incur tax at the time of the transfer or to guarantee through the qualified payment structure that the applicable retained interest will have an ascertainable value that is subject to tax at a later taxable event.

An applicable retained interest that is deemed to have zero value for gift tax purposes under this special valuation rule should not generate double taxation for subsequent FET purposes. But the appropriate ad-

---

[240] Treas. Reg. §25.2701-3(b)(3).

[241] Treas. Reg. §25.2701-3(b)(4). See PLR 9848006, holding that minority interest, lack of marketability, and other discounts should be reflected in the first step of the calculation and could not be duplicated in this fourth step.

§7.2.3.6

justment regulations fail to completely accomplish that objective.[242] As the following examples illustrate, these adjustment regulations are a key element to the proper functioning of these rules and, because the regulations do not operate properly, sometimes this regime will produce inappropriate results.

In each of the following illustrations, assume that a freeze transaction occurred and that the transferor retained an applicable retained interest that was *not* (and was not elected to be treated as) a qualified payment. The initial transfer constituted a gift of 100% of the value of the transferor's interest because the applicable retained interest was deemed to have zero value, and the possibility of double taxation posed by § 2701 arises when the transferor subsequently transfers the applicable retained interest.

Subsequent Transfer of the Applicable Retained Interest: Following a preferred stock recapitalization involving a gift of a junior equity interest (e.g., common stock), a subsequent taxable transfer of the applicable retained interest (e.g., the preferred stock) will trigger a § 2701(e)(6) adjustment. Consistent treatment for all wealth transfer tax purposes should provide that the applicable retained interest is worth only the § 2701(d) value, if any, attributable to suspense account accumulated unpaid dividends, meaning that a second tax of the underlying retained interest would not occur.

Instead, the regulatory mechanism[243] taxes the subsequent transfer at its actual FMV, determined at the time of the subsequent taxable transaction, plus any suspense account value, as if the value of the applicable retained interest was not subjected to gift tax previously. The regulation then reduces the transferor's adjusted taxable gifts for wealth transfer tax computation purposes by the lesser of (1) the § 2701 generated increase in the gift tax value of the initial transfer, and (2) the federal wealth transfer tax value of the underlying retained interest (but not any § 2701(d) suspense account value).

Similar to the purge that is directed under § 2001(b) if an interest includible at death (for example, under §§ 2035-2038 or § 2042) was

---

[242] See Treas. Reg. § 25.2701-5, discussed in § 7.2.3.

[243] Treas. Reg. § 25.2701-5(b).

§ 7.2.3.6

subject to gift tax because transferred during life,[244] this mechanism is designed to prevent the subsequent transfer from incurring double taxation. Because the transferor also receives a credit for any gift taxes already paid, the net effect should be to impose a tax only on any deemed (suspense account) or actual increase in value between the original and subsequent transfers. To work properly, however, this reduction approach requires that the actual value of the applicable retained interest be determined at the time of the original transfer (perhaps based on hindsight) and that it be determined again when the subsequent taxable transfer occurs. Moreover, it ought not be limited to the *lesser* value of the §2701(d) retained interest at the later transfer.

Sale of Junior Equity: If common stock is sold to a family member rather than given away in a preferred stock recapitalization, the only difference in result would be part-sale, part-gift treatment with respect to the consideration paid. The applicable retained interest still would be deemed to have zero value if no exception to §2701 was applicable, and the transferred interest still would be deemed to carry 100% of the value of the transferor's interest in the entity, making it unlikely that the consideration paid for the common stock would be adequate to avoid gift tax liability on the transaction.[245]

Gift of Applicable Retained Interest to Spouse: An adjustment is allowed if the applicable retained interest is transferred to an applicable family member[246] so that it is not includible in the transferor's gross

---

[244] See §7.3.

[245] See Treas. Reg. §25.2701-3(b)(4)(iv).

[246] A transfer of the applicable retained interest normally would be a taxable event if the applicable retained interest meets the qualified payment requirements, causing the transferor to incur tax under §2701(d)(3) on the suspense account value of any qualified payment arrearages. But §2701(d)(3)(B) precludes that deemed taxable event if the transfer qualifies for the gift tax annual exclusion or the marital deduction and, instead, specifies that the spouse acquires the applicable retained interest with a carryover liability as if the spouse was the transferor. Treas. Reg. §25.2701-4(b)(3) establishes rules by which it is determined whether a pecuniary marital bequest will be satisfied with the applicable retained interest and thus qualifies for the §2701(d)(3)(B) exception.

§7.2.3.6

estate at death.[247] This result is as if the transferor gave it away immediately before death, and the adjustment is not lost in such a case.[248]

Split Gift Freeze Transaction: If the transferor's spouse consents to split the gift in a freeze transaction and the applicable retained interest is not a qualified payment, then when the applicable retained interest subsequently is transferred the § 2701(e)(6) regulations should dictate three adjustments. First, the transferor's prior taxable gifts should be reduced under § § 2001(b) and 2502 to prevent the inter vivos deemed transfer of the value of the applicable retained interest from being taxed to the transferor twice. Second, under § 2001(d), the transferor should receive a credit for any gift tax paid by the transferor's consenting spouse.

Third, § 2001(e) ought to reduce the consenting spouse's prior taxable gifts by the value of the applicable retained interest for the consenting spouse's future gift tax and FET purposes, but it is inadequate to accomplish that result.[249] As a consequence, no part of the consenting spouse's unified credit consumed on the split gift will be restored. Although the adjustment regulation could have solved this problem, it capitulated to § 2001(e) instead. The real culprit in the split gift situation is the inadequate reach of § 2001(e),[250] and that problem has been recognized since its adoption in 1976, with no previous corrective action. Thus, split gifts that invoke § 2701 are a very poor planning device.

New Business or Split Purchase: Either § 2701(e)(5) (dealing with contributions to capital)[251] or § 2702(c)(2) (dealing with split purchases)[252] may be applicable if a client and another family member

---

247 Treas. Reg. § 25.2701-5(c)(3)(ii).

248 Quaere whether the government chose this premortem valuation technique because it understood that for gift tax purposes a lower value likely would apply. See § 6.2.

249 § 2001(e) only applies if the interest is includible in the transferor's gross estate under § 2035. This structural flaw should be corrected by Congress and probably cannot be cured by regulation (although taxpayers would not challenge a regulation that was improperly favorable in this context).

250 See § 7.1.3 n.146 and accompanying text and § 7.3.6 at text following n.244.

251 As noted in Treas. Reg. § 25.2701-1(b)(2)(i)(A).

252 Treas. Reg. § 25.2702-4(c).

§ 7.2.3.6

combine their assets to form a new business or to jointly purchase an existing business. The unanswered question is, if the applicable retained interest is to have a value other than zero, must the qualified payment requirements of §2701 or the qualified interest requirements of §2702 be met? Although these transactions are relatively similar, these rules differ significantly. Without the use of a trust and temporal interests, it would appear that §2702 is not the appropriate provision, although a purchase of term interests presumably would trigger §2702(c)(1).

Negative Freeze: In a negative freeze the value of the transferred interest declines rather than appreciates after the original transfer. The §2701(e)(6) double taxation adjustment is limited to the lesser of (1) the value of the deemed gift when the original transfer occurred and (2) the value of the applicable retained interest on the subsequent taxable transfer that triggers the adjustment.[253] This means that the regulation precludes a refund of tax paid on the basis of a higher value assigned to the transferred interest when the transaction was effected.

These regulations ought to prevent double taxation of the value of the applicable retained interest by purging the full amount of the prior taxable gift of the transferor who retained the applicable retained interest. If the applicable retained interest declined in value, inevitably the transferred interest and the underlying business entity declined in value as well. In that case no freeze occurred and none of the value of the applicable retained interest needed to be taxed at the original transfer. Thus, a §2701(e)(6) adjustment should allow taxation of the applicable retained interest at its now reduced FMV, purge the full previously taxed gift tax value of the applicable retained interest, and give a credit for any gift tax previously paid. Those results effectively would tax the applicable retained interest at the lower subsequent value, which is the right result.

Unfortunately, that is not the result selected by the regulation. The preamble to the final regulation explained that this result is attributable to the government's fear that "a reduction in the value of the entity may occur as the result of indirect (hard to detect) transfers to younger generations." Quaere whether the proper response to this subsequent transfer tax compliance issue would be to disallow the proper adjustment in all cases of diminished value, including those that involve no abusive

---

[253] Treas. Reg. §27.2701-5(b).

§7.2.3.6

transfers after the initial transfer. The net consequences is that a tax-payer may want to "undo" a prior transfer, such as by arguing that a string provision (§§ 2036-2038) is applicable, to include the transferred interest at death and trigger the purge and credit mechanisms in § 2001(b).[254]

Disposition of the Entity: In a "short freeze" the donee of a junior equity interest and the holder of an applicable retained interest sell the business, or their interests in it, to a third party. The applicable retained interest has zero value under § 2701 for gift tax purposes, but that characterization does not apply for income tax purposes. Thus, the transferor might be deemed to have made a gift of the applicable retained interest, and then a sale of the applicable retained interest also might occur, which is inconsistent. The § 2701(e)(6) adjustment is meant to apply "if there is any subsequent transfer . . . of any applicable retained interest," which should include a subsequent sale as well as a wealth transfer taxable event.

To accommodate this interpretation, the prior adjusted taxable gift of the applicable retained interest is adjusted whether the applicable retained interest is included in the transferor's gross estate, is gifted during life, or is sold and the consideration received is subject to subsequent taxation,[255] all of which are proper results. Improper about this mechanism is that the consideration received is valued as of the sale or exchange, not at death, and no interest is paid on the amount of tax prepaid under this regime.[256] The consideration received instead should be recognized at its actual subsequent FMV.

---

[254] See § 7.3.

[255] Treas. Reg. §§ 25.2701-5(a)(2) and 25.2701-5(c)(3)(i).

[256] Valuation of the consideration received at the time of the exchange is consistent with § 2043, but both provisions are improper. Moreover, Treas. Reg. § 25.2701-5(c)(3)(iii) values any like kind replacement property for adjustment purposes at its FET value, which is the proper result but is inconsistent with the result in § 25.2701-5(c)(3)(i). Inconsistent gift and income tax treatment of an applicable retained interest might permit the transferor to claim the same type of relief available under the concept of equitable recoupment, which would allow application of the gift tax previously paid against the subsequent income tax even if the limitation period for challenging the § 2701 valuation had expired. See, e.g., United States v. Dalm, 494 U.S. 596 (1990), rev'g 867 F.2d 305 (6th Cir. 1989),

Reverse Freeze: The § 2701(c)(1)(B)(i) exception from the definition of applicable retained interest for junior equity interests should preclude application of § 2701 to a transaction in which the transferor retains the growth interest and transfers the frozen interest. With sufficiently large dividend payments on the preferred interest, it may be possible to prevent growth in the junior equity and shift value to the frozen interest holder, all without application of § 2701.

Preferred Debt Recapitalization: § 2701 applies only to applicable retained interests, which do not include debt. Thus, debt issued in a recapitalization in lieu of preferred frozen *equitable* interests ought to be reflected in valuing the entity for purposes of determining the value of transferred growth interests. It would be preferable to a qualified payment because the interest on debt would be deductible by the entity. It will, however, affect the § 2701(a)(4) minimum capitalization requirement. Even if the debt involved is disguised equity that could meet the definition of an applicable retained interest, it may meet the definition of a qualified payment, in which case its value would not be ignored.

Sale of an interest in an entity for a note, and perhaps also for an annuity, also should not be subject to the valuation rules of § 2701 for the same reasons.[257] Nor should retained interests in the form of compensation (salary or deferred payments) or lease payments be subject to § 2701, even if each entitles the payee to a percentage of the profits of the entity as part of the negotiated payments.[258] Quaere whether a different result would be argued on the more fundamental debt versus equity issue.

Pro Rata Gift Freeze: A transaction in which the transferor makes a gift or sells a portion of the only ownership interest held will qualify for the § 2701(a)(2)(B) exception for one class of equity.[259] This transfer of a *portion* of all future appreciation is an easy and effective way to freeze a

---

(Footnote Continued)

rev'g 89-1 U.S. Tax Cas. (CCH) ¶ 13,807 (W.D. Mich. 1987), discussed at § 3.3.23. Success under such a theory does not seem likely, however.

[257] See PLRs 9535026 and 9436006.

[258] Treas. Reg. § 25.2701-3(c)(3) designates what counts as debt for purposes of the minimum value rule, and deferred compensation and lease payments not in arrears specifically are excluded.

[259] See Treas. Reg. § 25.2701-1(c)(3).

§ 7.2.3.6

portion of the value of the entity without dealing with the complexities of §2701. The same should be true with respect to a transfer of nonvoting stock or a partnership interest that qualifies for the §2701(a)(2)(C) exception while the transferor retains voting interests of the same class or tier.

In either case, discounts for lack of marketability and for minority interests were not affected by §2701. Similarly, any transaction that does not alter the existing ownership percentages of the existing owners of the entity will not trigger §2701.[260] And a gift of a proportionate share of several classes of an enterprise (if, for example, the transferor owns both common and preferred interests and gives the same percentage of the transferor's holding of each) is permissible because there is no freeze abuse in such a transaction.[261]

No Retained Interest Generation-Skipping Freeze: A transferor may give all frozen interests to children and all growth interests to grandchildren, in which case §2701 should not apply (because the transferor retains no interest in the entity). This generation-skipping freeze should continue to work under §2701, although §2701 will apply if a grandchild subsequently transfers a growth interest to a family member while a lineal ancestor (the child) continues to hold the frozen interest.[262]

Split Interest Funding: The definition of family in §2702(e) refers to §2704(c)(2), which incorporates the entity attribution rule of §2701(e)(3). As a result funding a marital and nonmarital trust with frozen and growth interests, respectively, may not escape the joint purchase rules of §2702(a)(1).[263] Although funding is not itself a gift, and §2701 is a gift valuation provision, the entity attribution and joint purchase rules might deem a gift to occur for these purposes.

If this is correct, postmortem freezes through split interest funding or funding with frozen (to the marital) and growth (to the nonmarital) interests will not succeed. To the extent it is predictive of result, how-

---

[260] See, e.g., PLR 9309018 (involving a reverse stock split). See the exception found in Treas. Reg. §25.2701-1(b)(3)(i).

[261] Treas. Reg. §25.2701-1(c)(4). See, e.g., PLR 9226063, replaced by PLR 9248026.

[262] §2701(a)(1)(B).

[263] See §7.2.2.8.

ever, the regulations indicate that freeze funding will not implicate §2701.[264] A best case scenario for this favorable result would be if S is not the personal representative doing the funding and the junior and senior equity interest were includible in D's estate, so no postmortem recapitalization or other deemed capital structure transaction is required to put freeze funding into motion.

§7.2.4 Additional Gift Tax Valuation Concepts

Other valuation concepts may affect the gift taxation of inter vivos transfers in ways that are taxpayer favorable. In some cases these are not distinct from the valuation that would apply for FET purposes. Thus, this discussion does not necessarily inform inter vivos transfers instead of testamentary dispositions.

§7.2.4.1 Blockage Discounts

A taxpayer may own and transfer such a large quantity of a particular asset that the market for that asset would be depressed by an immediate sale of the entire holding. This depressive effect in the willing-buyer, willing-seller valuation context leads to a "blockage" discount and is best illustrated by Calder v. Commissioner,[265] a gift tax case involving artwork that previously was included in the estate of the donor's deceased husband, artist Alexander Calder. The donor made transfers of over 1,000 gouaches (opaque watercolor paintings) to four separate trusts. In valuing the transfer for gift tax purposes, the donor used the value of the gouaches established for FET purposes in the decedent's estate, reflecting a 60% discount for blockage because the art market could not readily absorb a sale of the number of these watercolors involved.[266]

The government wished to increase the gift tax value of these transfers. It argued that the total number of gouaches transferred to the

---

[264] Treas. Reg. §25.2702-2(d)(1) Example 3.

[265] 85 T.C. 713 (1985).

[266] Dribble-out sales of the remaining works left by a deceased artist is the preferred method to preserve the market value of the artist's entire portfolio, which all may increase in value upon the artist's death because (presumably) there will be no more works created by that artist.

four trusts could not be aggregated for purposes of determining blockage, notwithstanding the fact that the total transfers collectively would depress the market if all the gouaches were sold at one time. The Tax Court agreed with this proposition, citing the government's regulatory position[267] that the value of each gift must be determined separately.

The government attempted to ascertain the value of each gouache, and thereby the value of each of the gifts, using a figure that it estimated as the total number of sales that the market could absorb in a given year, without prorating that total sales figure across the separate gifts made. The Tax Court took exception with this, holding that the market could absorb only a certain number in a given year, whether from a single trust or from several, and that it was improper to value each of the gifts as if *each* trust could sell the *total* number received in a given year.

The end result was a value suspiciously similar to that determined by the government as the FET value of the total number of gouaches in the decedent's estate, giving the impression that the blockage issue with respect to each *separate* gift was a chimera. Whether the same result would obtain in another situation, however, remains subject to the court's admonition that blockage is a question of fact to be decided under the special circumstances of each case.

Similarly to *Calder*, the sole issue in Estate of O'Keeffe v. Commissioner[268] was the appropriate blockage discount for the approximately 400 works of art created and owned by the decedent at death (rather than for gift tax purposes, but the same principles inform both determinations). The court rejected as a matter of law the government's expert witness valuation because it excluded from the blockage consideration all works bequeathed to museums or otherwise unavailable for sale (the government's theory being that they would not be sold, much less all at once), stating that valuation must assume that the entire collection is marketed at the same time.

The court also rejected as unsupported by reason or authority the approach of one expert for the estate who assumed sale of the entire collection at one time to a single purchaser (a syndicate of investors) that would sell the collection piecemeal over a substantial period of time.

---

[267] Treas. Reg. § 25.2512-2(e).

[268] 63 T.C.M. (CCH) 2699 (1992).

Eventually the court determined that the collection should be bifurcated into a group that could be sold in a relatively short time and another that would require substantial effort over an extended period.[269]

Blockage discounts can be applied to other types of assets—most commonly collectibles, some types of real estate,[270] or other assets for which there is a relatively thin market[271]—but on occasion can be relevant with respect to even a small percentage of the stock of a publicly traded corporation, if the evidence supports the notion that sale of that holding all at once would move the market.[272]

§7.2.4.2 Fractional Interests

A simple and relatively noncontroversial method to reduce values for wealth transfer tax purposes is to create a fractional interest in property that is not easily severed. For example, splitting a 1000 share holding of IBM stock is easy and no fractional interest discount would be generated by a gift of 50% of that interest. But undivided tenancy in common[273] ownership of Blackacre usually is far different. As a conse-

---

[269] The court accepted the estate's opinion with respect to one of these groups, the government's opinion with respect to the other, and concluded that, "for want of a more reliable breakdown," half the value of the collection would fall into each category. It then applied a discount of 75% to one group, 25% to the other, and determined the value of the entire collection at 50% of the agreed FMV of the collection before any discounts.

[270] See, e.g., Estate of Auker v. Commissioner, 75 T.C.M. (CCH) 2321 (1998) (stating that the court will use the term "market absorption" discount when it refers to blockage as applied to assets other than stock, in this case involving apartment complexes; the court also stated that property owned by an entity that is not slated for liquidation would not qualify for such a discount in valuing the entity).

[271] Although the blockage adjustment was not involved in the case, an excellent illustration is provided in Hunt v. Commissioner, 57 T.C.M. (CCH) 919 (1989) (failed attempt to corner the silver market yielded disastrous results when the taxpayers liquidated their substantial holdings to repay loans incurred in the endeavor). See also Estate of Sturgis v. Commissioner, 54 T.C.M. (CCH) 221 (1987) (timberland).

[272] See generally Moore, "Blockage" Redux: The Challenge Posed by Blockage, 131 Trusts & Estates 35 (Feb. 1992).

[273] See §7.2.4.2 n.287 and accompanying text to illustrate that joint tenancy with right of survivorship is *not* the right approach because co-ownership disap-

quence, with select assets the amount a willing buyer would pay a willing seller for an undivided fractional interest is less—in many cases substantially less—than a pro rata portion of the FMV of an undivided property interest. Thus, especially in anticipation of FET liability at death, a transfer inter vivos that bifurcates ownership title in certain assets can be a particularly effective gifting technique.

Mooneyham v. Commissioner[274] is an excellent illustration. The court granted a 15% fractional interest discount in establishing the proper gift tax valuation of a half interest in the taxpayer's interest in development realty that was transferred to the taxpayer's sibling (and, presumably, a similar discount would apply for the retained half if still owned when the taxpayer died).[275] The court sharply rejected the government's argument that the availability of a discount should depend on the relationship of the donor and donee and adopted instead a hypothetical unrelated willing-buyer, willing-seller approach.[276] Apparently no argument was advanced by the government that the donor's transfer of the undivided interest that generated the fractional interest reduction in value constituted an additional gift, much like the transfer of a controlling shareholder's control premium may occur when a sliver interest gift

---

(Footnote Continued)

pears at death (assuming just two co-owners) and this valuation option is lost. And see § 10.5.4 in general with respect to discounts for fractional interests.

[274] 61 T.C.M. (CCH) 2445 (1991).

[275] The court cited favorable precedent in Propstra v. United States, 680 F.2d 1248 (9th Cir. 1982) (15% discount); Estate of Campanari v. Commissioner, 5 T.C. 488 (1945) (12.5% discount); Estate of Henry v. Commissioner, 4 T.C. 423 (1944) (10% discount); Stewart v. Commissioner, 31 B.T.A. 201 (1934) (15% discount); and Estate of Youle v. Commissioner, 56 T.C.M. (CCH) 1594 (1989) (12.5% discount). See also Estate of Wildman v. Commissioner, 58 T.C.M. (CCH) 1006 (1989) (15% fractional interest discount aggregated with other adjustments to constitute a total 40% discount for a 20% undivided interest). Cf. Estate of Babbitt v. Commissioner, 87 T.C. 1270 (1986) (distinguishing cases in which an undivided fractional interest in realty was worth less than a proportionate share of the FMV of the whole).

[276] Citing Propstra v. United States, 680 F.2d 1248 (9th Cir. 1982); Estate of Bright v. United States, 658 F.2d 999 (5th Cir. 1981); and Minahan v. Commissioner, 88 T.C. 492 (1987).

§ 7.2.4.2

is made,[277] although such an argument would be hard to maintain because that value was not directed at the donee of the ostensible gift.[278]

Citing the gift tax valuation decision in *Mooneyham*, the Tax Court in Estate of Pillsbury v. Commissioner[279] similarly concluded that a hypothetical willing-buyer, willing-seller analysis should apply to value fractional interests in real estate. The government resisted that discount because 100% of the value of the property was owned by two trusts with the same trustee and the taxable portion (flowing out of a marital deduction trust at the death of S) passed to a nonmarital trust that owned the other portion of the property, meaning that the property could be sold as an undivided entirety. The court specifically stated that ownership of the remainder interest and the ultimate disposition of the fractional interest was irrelevant, instead noting that the government's unity of ownership notion is inconsistent with a willing-buyer analysis of the amount that would be paid to purchase only the taxable portion of the property.[280]

Subsequently, and presumably reflecting its losses in *Mooneyham* and *Pillsbury*, the government issued TAM 9336002, in which it took a new position that did not challenge the discount itself. Instead, that

---

[277] TAM 8907002 involved a gift of a sufficient percentage of a donor's stockholding that the donor's prior control interest was reduced to a minority position; the government held that the control premium relinquished by that transfer was taxable as a gift in addition to the value that a willing buyer would have paid for the sliver of stock actually transferred.

[278] In theory value is transferred in the sense that the donor no longer has it. See Pennell, Wealth Transfer Taxation: Transfer Defined, 128 Tax Notes 615 (2010); Pennell, Valuation Discord: An Exegesis of Wealth Transfer Tax Valuation Theory and Practice, 30 U. Miami Inst. Est. Plan. ¶ 903.5 (1996) (using the example of division of the world's largest diamond into niblets, causing the next largest diamond to increase in value). That is not how even the government views the situation, however. See CCA 201020009.

[279] 64 T.C.M. (CCH) 284 (1992) (15% discount allowed from the pro rata portion of the total property's FMV).

[280] Cf. § 13.7.3.1.1 n.25 and accompanying text discussing aggregation of fractional interests in property includible in S's gross estate, one part owned by a QTIP marital deduction trust and another part owned by S outright or by a revocable inter vivos trust of S's creation that is includible in S's gross estate under a provision like § 2036 or § 2038. The reason for aggregation is to deny fractional interest discounts to each portion that is includible.

§ 7.2.4.2

position was that the discount should be *limited*, to "the petitioner's share of the estimated cost of a partition of the property,"[281] based on the theory that partition would be the most efficient means to generate the most economic benefit from property owned by multiple parties. But in Estate of Cervin v. Commissioner[282] the Tax Court rejected the very similar position advocated by the government that the estate's fractional interest discount should be limited to 5% *plus* half the cost to partition the property. Instead, the court granted a 20% discount to an undivided 50% fractional interest that was includible in the decedent's gross estate and passed to the owner of the other 50% interest.

Note that the typical fractional interest discount case involves realty. Ludwick v. Commissioner[283] involved a 50% undivided tenant in common interest in a dwelling and limited the discount to 17% (roughly half of what the taxpayer claimed) considering only factors such as the cost to partition, the time it would take to sell, operating costs, and rates of return and appreciation expected during that time. The taxpayer was unable to produce comparable sale figures. Stone v. United States[284] also involved a 50% undivided (probably community property) interest, in that case in art,[285] as to which the estate's expert presented no data regarding sales of undivided interests and the court correspondingly allowed no meaningful discount. It did say that "the costs of a court-ordered partition must be considered" and that "some discount is appropriate to allow for the uncertainties involved in waiting to sell the collection until after a hypothetical partition action is resolved." This was odd, given the court's other conclusion, that a hypothetical seller would not partition the art and then sell an interest. Instead, there would be a sale of the undivided

---

281 Citing Estate of Fittl v. Commissioner, 804 F.2d 1332 (7th Cir. 1986).

282 68 T.C.M. (CCH) 1115 (1994) (the facts revealed that the property was such that partition would destroy its value because of issues relating to access, presence of a creek dividing the property, the number of acres needed to run a profitable agricultural operation, soil conditions in various locations, and the like).

283 99 T.C.M. (CCH) 1424 (2010).

284 2007-1 U.S. Tax Cas. (CCH) ¶ 60,540 (N.D. Cal.); 2007-2 U.S. Tax Cas. (CCH) ¶ 60,545 (N.D. Cal.) (granting a 5% discount because the government conceded as much "in a spirit of compromise").

285 Fractional interests in tangible personal property also raise interesting charitable deduction issues under § 170(o), as noted in § 14.3.1 n.18.

work, followed by partition of the proceeds. At bottom *Ludwick* and *Stone* both may only confirm the need to produce proof to support a discount.

Several other cautions in this arena also may be relevant. One is illustrated by Estate of Casey v. Commissioner,[286] which denied a fractional interest adjustment to a beneficial interest in a liquidating trust (although it did grant a 15% discount that it refused to label, reflecting the anticipated delay in realization of proceeds from the sale of trust property). The fractional interest discount likely will not be available if the ownership interest (in this case the trust corpus) is not a fractional interest, nor is it likely to be applied to a beneficial interest (such as the interest of one of several trust beneficiaries).

A second caution is highlighted by TAM 9146002 in which a taxpayer purported to sell a 5% fractional interest in a personal residence (at 66% of the pro rata FMV of that interest) and then leased it back, reporting on the taxpayer's FET return the 95% interest remaining with a 43% discount that the government rejected on the grounds that the sale and leaseback was not legitimate.

Finally, Estate of Young v. Commissioner[287] concluded that, once death occurs (at least in the two person joint tenancy situation), the co-ownership aspects of joint tenancy disappear and, with it, any impediments to sale that might justify a discount for fractional interests. Notable was the court's final footnote, in which it recognized that in a normal case of qualified joint tenancy between spouses the amount includible and the amount of the marital deduction should produce an FET wash, meaning that income tax basis is the only issue at stake in most

---

[286] 71 T.C.M. (CCH) 2599 (1996) (trust was to liquidate a personal residence and distribute its proceeds among multiple beneficiaries).

[287] 110 T.C. 297 (1998), followed by Estate of Fratini v. Commissioner, 76 T.C.M. (CCH) 342 (1998). *Young* involved a noncitizen S and a joint tenancy exclusively between D and S that could not qualify for the §2040(b) qualified joint tenancy 50% inclusion rule by virtue of §2056(d)(1)(B). The government apparently did not recognize this until the eve of trial, however, so to avoid unfairness it conceded that the amount includible under the default rule in §2040(a) should be only half the value of the property, as if S provided half the consideration for acquisition of the property. With that concession, the case essentially was the same as if the jointly owned property was 50% includible under §2040(b), and the court made no distinction based on the source of the fractional amount includible.

§7.2.4.2

situations. It was clear that the court realized that the consequence of its holding will be a higher basis in the traditional § 2040(b) qualified joint tenancy situation.

§ 7.2.4.3 Nonmarketable and Minority Interest Discounts

Valuation of the same asset may differ for gift tax purposes as opposed to for FET purposes,[288] almost without exception favoring inter vivos transfers that involve minority interests. This is best described by the fact that each gift made inter vivos is valued separately, not as the diminution in the donor's net worth nor as the increase in the donee's net worth either, but essentially as the gifted interest travels between the donor and the donee.[289] For example, consider the illustration of the world's largest diamond, being gifted in undivided fractional interests inter vivos. If that diamond was held until death and given in equal shares to the same donees the value for FET purposes would be the undivided diamond owned at death, regardless of the destination of the shares and the number of beneficiaries. But if that diamond was transferred to multiple donees inter vivos the value of the gift would be the value of each separate niblet, multiplied by the number of donees. And the product of that valuation would be lower than the value of the undivided whole.

Care is required in applying these principles, however, and it is easiest to consider the valuation question as if the gifted property was in neither the donor nor the donee's hands. For example, in Citizens Bank & Trust Co. v. Commissioner[290] four taxpayers collectively owned 100% of the voting and nonvoting stock of a corporation. They each created

---

[288] See the discussion in § 6.2.3.

[289] Notwithstanding the holding in Rev. Rul. 67-230, 1967-2 C.B. 352, that the value of a gift for gift tax purposes is not determined by the measure of enrichment of the donee but, rather, by the value of the property passing from the donor. In that case the gift was in trust and trustee fees would diminish the amount the donees would receive, which the government held could not be considered. Cf. Rev. Rul. 81-230, 1981-2 C.B. 186, which held that a gift of property that had been valued under § 2032A was not reduced in value by the amount of recapture tax the donee might incur under § 2032A(c). See the comparable issues listed in § 15.3.3.3 n.298.

[290] 839 F.2d 1249 (7th Cir. 1988).

irrevocable trusts that would run for the full period of the Rule, to which three of them transferred their nonvoting stock and all four transferred their voting stock. For valuation purposes, each then alleged that the nonvoting stock was entitled to a 90% discount to reflect the fact that any purchaser from any one trust would acquire no vote and, therefore, could not acquire control of the corporation. Moreover, it was argued that valuation should reflect the reality that a purchaser would realize that acquiring voting stock from the other trusts was unlikely (because the perpetuities term trusts indicated a desire to control the corporations for as long as possible).[291] The government instead granted only a normal discount for lack of marketability and asserted that the irrevocable nature and term of the trusts should be disregarded.

In essence, the court agreed with the government's valuation without regard to the terms of the trusts, holding that restrictions imposed in an instrument of transfer are to be ignored for valuation purposes. But as illustrated in TAMs 9449001 and 9436005,[292] if a donor transfers a control block of stock (to use an easy example) in several noncontrolling interests by gift, the government will value each gift separately, each with a minority interest (and usually also a lack of marketability) discount. As these principles reveal, there are differences in the valuation of property for gift tax and FET purposes that taxpayers may exploit for estate planning purposes.

These valuation issues can be of great significance. Assume, for example, that the taxpayer owned 51% of the stock in a closely held corporation and that two children owned equal amounts of the remaining

---

[291] The court recognized that the existence of some of the trusts could have an effect on the value of any other owner's transfer of stock, if all the trusts were not created at once, but declined to consider such an effect in this case because all the trusts were created as part of a single "package" transaction conducted by all the owners at essentially the same time. Estate of Davis v. Commissioner, 110 T.C. 530 (1998), embraced the similar notion that other family members would not go along with an outside, hypothetical, willing-buyer and that this fact should be reflected in the valuation of transferred property. As discussed in § 15.3.1.3, Congress added § 2704 in 1990 to deny the consideration of restrictions imposed on the transferability of property for wealth transfer tax valuation purposes. If applicable, presumably it would preclude the argument advanced by the taxpayers in *Citizens Bank*.

[292] As discussed in § 6.2.3.

§ 7.2.4.3

stock. If the taxpayer gave 1% of the stock to each of those children, the issue would be whether the collective value of those gifts is (1) two times 1% of the total value of the corporation, (2) a discount from that amount because each child receives a minority interest, (3) an amount equal to 2/51 of the value of the taxpayer's 51% controlling interest, or (4) an even greater premium amount because, by virtue of the gifts, the taxpayer relinquishes the control element represented by the 51% interest. It appears that the government recognizes that (2) is correct, notwithstanding that a gift tax that truly served to backstop the FET would impose a tax on (4). Given the difference between these values and the tax they would generate, the inter vivos transfer in this type of situation is vastly preferable.

§7.2.4.4 Concerns under §§2703 and 2704

Both §§2703 and 2704 are significant for FET[293] and gift tax valuations. For example, in a transaction that the government properly regarded as a gift because it was not supported by full and adequate consideration and did not fall within the business transaction exception,[294] the taxpayer in TAM 9352001[295] essentially gave control of a newly created corporation and gave a preference to the corporate earnings in the form of a transfer of the only voting stock in the corporation and an excessively generous employee compensation agreement. The net result was a gift that would be valued under §2704(a) because the transfer of all voting stock effected a loss of the state law ability to liquidate the corporation unilaterally.[296] Because the taxpayer did not lose the right to liquidate the corporation entirely (it was only restricted by the gift of voting common stock), the proper amount of the gift was deemed to be the difference between the value of the taxpayer's ownership prior to and after the transfer and execution of the compensation

---

[293] They are discussed in much greater detail in the FET context. See §§15.3.1.2 and 15.3.1.3, respectively.

[294] See Treas. Reg. §25.2512-8 and §7.1.1.

[295] The taxpayer acted through a child, who possessed a durable power of attorney.

[296] Because the employee compensation agreement was a priority claim on the corporate earnings, it was treated as a priority interest like preferred stock. The taxpayer's retained nonvoting stock was treated as a subordinate interest, thereby meeting the requirements of Treas. Reg. §25.2704-1(c)(1).

agreement, rather than just the value of the voting common stock and the right to receive guaranteed payments under the employee compensation agreement.

With respect to the application of § 2703, in a series of TAMs[297] the government addressed valuation issues raised by fact situations that typically involve transfers to an FLP followed by transfers of partnership interests. Of several theories advanced by the government in these TAMs, one is based on § 2703(a)(2), which provides that restrictions on the sale or use of transferred property will be disregarded for all wealth transfer tax valuation purposes. In this alternative the government asserts that "the series of transactions (the creation and funding of the partnership, and the transfer of the partnership interests) is properly characterized as one integrated [inter vivos] transaction" as to the whole of which § 2703(a)(2) is applicable.[298]

In each of these cases the decedent transferred marketable securities or land in exchange for partnership interests that carried certain restrictions on what the decedent could do with respect to the transferred property—the partnership assets. If § 2703(a)(2) is applicable those restrictions would be ignored in valuing the partnership interests received in the first transfer. Thus, unless other discounts would account for some reduction in value, the partnership interests received in exchange for the transferred assets would be worth essentially the same amount as the value of the property transferred. To the extent the partnership interests remain in the decedent's estate at death, this result would deny discounts for inclusion purposes except to the extent the partnership interests are discountable for reasons that do not relate to restrictions under state law or the terms of the partnership agreement

---

[297] TAMs 9842003, 9736004, 9735003, 9730004, 9725002, 9723009, and 9719006.

[298] It may be that the government collapsed the two steps involved in most of these transfers into a single transaction because it is unsure of how § 2703(a)(2) is meant to apply to the creation and funding of the partnership, and the § 2703(a)(2) reference to "any restriction on the right to sell or use *such property*" is not entirely clear. But the government's theory would apply even if the two steps of the transaction were looked at separately, which may be important to a proper interpretation of § 2703.

§ 7.2.4.4

(that is, for reasons other than those that §2703(a)(2) would ignore for valuation purposes).[299]

Regarding the second step in the integrated transaction (the decedent's transfer of partnership interests), the transfer would be regarded as an inter vivos gift to the extent those transfers are for less than full and adequate consideration—determined without regard to the restrictions on sale or use that are ignored by §2703(a)(2).[300] In each TAM the government asserted that §2703(a)(2) would apply even assuming the transaction steps are not collapsed, correctly noting that those elements of the partnership agreements that reduce value should be ignored, including that the limited partners had no liquidation or withdrawal rights, could not bring an action for partition, and could not terminate the partnership.

There is a safe harbor exception in §2703(b) to the application of §2703(a), which the government discussed and rejected in these cases. Under it, §2703(a) will not apply to the extent the taxpayer can establish that the transaction was (1) a bona fide business arrangement, (2) comparable to similar transactions, and (3) not a device to transfer value to family members for less than full and adequate consideration in money or money's worth. The government did not address comparability in these cases—probably because it was aware that the plain vanilla

---

[299] That possibility would require the government to allege that the transfer of assets in exchange for the partnership interests constituted a gift for gift tax purposes, which raises an issue the government articulated in TAM 9842003 that the initial transfer into the partnership may constitute a gift. This appears to be the thrust of an argument first articulated by the government in FSA 200143004 that "property" for §2703(a)(2) purposes means the assets transferred into the entity, subject to the restrictions of the agreement establishing the entity.

[300] It may be that the government does not like that result because the transferred interests in the partnerships would be entitled to some discount for minority interest—even without considering any valuation discounts that are attributable to restrictions on sale or use that are ignored by §2703(a)(2)—so the TAMs' allegations that the two steps (the transfer of property to the partnership and then the transfer of partnership interests) in reality are only one transaction may be based on its effort to preclude any gift tax discount at all. That portion of the TAMs is questionable.

terms of the FLPs resembled other similar transactions.[301] It also gave short shrift to the device element, stating in full only that:

> Even assuming arguendo that there was some legitimate business purpose for these transactions, the facts evidence that the transaction, including the formation of the limited partnership, was contrived primarily (if not exclusively) for the purpose of artificially reducing the value of the decedent's gross estate in order to reduce the estate tax liability. Accordingly, the partnership arrangement was a device to transfer property to members of the decedent's family for less than adequate consideration.

This unfortunate lack of detail is telling in that the device test under § 2703(b)(2) is the most uncertain, and the TAMs provide no guidance on how the government might assess the issue or the elements of proof that it might accept in making the case that a transaction is not a device.

Case law similarly is devoid of meaningful assistance on that score. Perhaps it is in light of the dearth of authority that the government chose to hang its hat on the bona fide transaction peg of § 2703(b)(1), asserting first that intra-family transactions are subject to special scrutiny and are presumed not to be at arm's length, and then more specifically concluding that:

> The transaction in this case can hardly be classified as a bona fide, arm's length, business arrangement. The children, acting in their representative capacities, were essentially dealing with themselves on behalf of the trusts, and the decedent. Rather than attempting to maximize the value of the trusts, the parties structured this transaction to achieve the opposite result. . . . It is inconceivable that the decedent would have accepted, if dealing at arm's length, a partnership interest purportedly worth only a fraction of the value of the assets she transferred. This is especially the case given the state of her health, because it was impossible for her to ever recoup this immediate loss. Further, it is inconceivable that the decedent (or her representatives) would transfer all her liquid assets to a partnership, in exchange for the limited interest that terminated her control over the assets and their income stream, if the other partners had not been family members.

---

[301] Proving comparability may be difficult, in terms of locating a data set or expert testimony. One source suggested by Burns, Ratliff, & Rowe, Valuing Limited Partnership Interests, 149 Trusts & Estates 33 (Oct. 2010), is Securities and Exchange Commission filings of publicly available partnership agreements.

§ 7.2.4.4

The later TAMs make note of various business reasons that might support the transaction and say that they do not establish the requisite bona fides of the business *arrangement,* which is what the statute requires. Indeed, one TAM suggested that all the reasons proffered related to the decedent's family and not to the decedent, which presumably ought to be the focus to justify the decedent's participation in these transactions. And notice that the last sentence quoted more appropriately might be directed to the device element. Nevertheless, the point is that the §2703(b) safe harbor was deemed to provide no refuge for the taxpayers in these cases.

Not applicable in every TAM but applied in several is another government alternative argument, based on §2704(b) and the fact that each partnership had terms that were more restrictive than state law.[302] That is a factual hickey that many partnerships avoid with proper selection of the applicable law.

One final aspect of the TAMs is interesting. The government recognized that some discount may be available in failed FLP transactions, as if the assets contributed to the entity were held by the decedent outright at death. As phrased by the first TAM, "attempting to cover the decedent's assets with a partnership wrapper" may not create or increase any available discounts, but it also should not remove discounts that otherwise would apply. In an all-marketable-assets partnership this would be of no use, but presumably some fractional interest discount would be available if partnership assets were held outright and a sliver interest was given away or includible in the decedent's gross estate at death.

In the context of all these pronouncements, the FLP issue finally was joined in court proceedings that have resulted in opinions in Kerr v. Commissioner,[303] holding that §2704(b) was not applicable because the provisions in the *Kerr* partnership agreement were no more restrictive than state law otherwise would impose,[304] and in Church v. United

---

302 See also TAM 9804001.

303 113 T.C. 449 (1999), aff'd, 292 F.3d 490 (5th Cir. 2002) (on the different ground that the family alone could not remove the restrictions imposed, and not because those restrictions were no more restrictive than state law, which was the finding below).

304 In the process the court rejected a government argument that restrictions on disposition of partnership interests or withdrawal by a partner from the

States.[305] Among the arguments made by the government in *Church*, the court summarily rejected a §§ 2036-2038 argument that the parties expressly or impliedly agreed that the decedent would continue to enjoy the partnership property and its income. More immediately significant, the court accepted as true that the partnership agreement met the § 2703(b) safe harbor requirements (a bona fide business arrangement, comparable to similar arrangements, and not a device to transfer value for less than full and adequate consideration to natural objects of the decedent's bounty). The court did not, however, explain what the device test means, nor what facts supported these conclusions.

It seems clear that the government presented the § 2703 argument that restrictions on assets transferred to the partnership, imposed by the partnership agreement, should be ignored in valuing the partnership interest received by the taxpayer on formation of the partnership. According to the *Church* court, however, § 2703 does not support that application because the property owned and subject to valuation at death was the partnership interest itself, not the assets transferred to the partnership, and there were no restrictions on transfer of the partnership interest that Congress meant to reach with § 2703. Without authority to cite, the opinion nevertheless held as a matter of law that "no case . . . and nothing in the legislative history, or the regulations adopted by the IRS itself, convince this Court [that] . . . restrictions . . . on the sale or assignment of a partnership interest . . . are [the type] Congress intended to reach in passing" § 2703, which the court said was intended to deal only with buy-sell agreements and options that artificially reduce value.

(Footnote Continued)

partnership were relevant under § 2704(b), finding that these were not limitations on the ability of the entity to liquidate, as required by § 2704(b)(2)(A). The court also decided that it need not address the taxpayer's contention that the interests transferred to charity demonstrated that the family did not have the requisite unilateral ability to lift the restrictions on liquidation, within the meaning of § 2704(b)(2)(B)(ii).

[305] 2000-1 U.S. Tax Cas. (CCH) ¶ 60,369 (W.D. Tex. 2000) (an opinion that is only marginally useful because it is merely a string of numbered paragraphs of fact and law conclusions that are terse, conclusory, and lacking in legal analysis).

§ 7.2.4.4

In juxtaposition to *Church* is Holman v. Commissioner,[306] in which the government succeed in using § 2703 to disregard a call provision in a partnership agreement and prevented a valuation discount. The opinion focused primarily on three provisions, the last being the right to purchase partnership units following an impermissible assignment. This issue differed from that asserted with mixed success in Smith v. United States[307] that § 2703 disregards restrictions on a taxpayer's ability to deal with the assets transferred into an FLP. *Smith* resulted in a trial on value, in which a jury granted a larger refund than the taxpayer sought. *Holman* is more like *Church*, which held that § 2703 does *not* disregard restrictions in a partnership agreement on the transfer of partnership units themselves. Note the different applications (and success) of § 2703 in these cases.[308]

The Magistrate in *Smith* determined that § 2703 disregards partnership agreement provisions that hinder dealing with the underlying assets (common stock of an operating company in that case) of the partnership, based on legislative history to § 2703, which establishes that the restrictive provisions in the partnership agreement are "precisely the type of restriction to which § 2703 was intended to apply." Senate Finance Comm. Rep. 3209 (1990) specifies that:

> the value of property for transfer tax purposes is determined without regard to . . . any restriction on the right to sell or use

---

306 130 T.C. 170 (2008), aff'd, 601 F.3d 763 (8th Cir. 2010) (dealing with a single issue of marketable stock; on the major gift involved the taxpayer obtained a 22.4% discount from net asset value for gift tax valuation of transfers of limited partner units in a family partnership that the court held to have no business plan, no employees, only the one asset, no income, prepared no annual statements, and never filed a federal income tax return).

307 2004-2 U.S. Tax Cas. (CCH) ¶ 60,488 (W.D. Pa. 2004) (a Magistrate's recommendation to the District Judge hearing the case), and 2004-2 U.S. Tax Cas. (CCH) ¶ 60,490 (W.D. Pa. 2004) (the District Judge's order accepting that recommendation).

308 *Holman* was followed in Fisher v. United States, 2010-2 U.S. Tax Cas. (CCH) ¶ 50,601 (S.D. Ind. 2010) (involving undeveloped property on Lake Michigan as to which there was no evidence that the taxpayers had any investment strategy, nor did they seek to improve the commercial value of the property or acquire added investment properties and therefore they failed to satisfy the safe harbor requirement that there be a bona fide business for § 2703(b)(1) purposes).

> such property, unless the . . . restriction meets three require-
> ments. These requirements apply to any restriction, however
> created. For example, they apply to restrictions implicit in the
> capital structure of the partnership or contained in a partnership
> agreement . . . .

That committee report is reflected in Treas. Reg. § 25.2703-1(a)(3), which states that a right or restriction that may be subject to § 2703 could be contained "in a partnership agreement, articles of incorporation, corporate bylaws, a shareholders' agreement, or any other agreement." And this application is not limited to FET.

The Tax Court in *Holman* relied primarily on traditional buy-sell agreement jurisprudence in holding that (1) the provisions involved were "not part of a bona fide business arrangement" because "the partnership carried on little activity other than holding shares of . . . stock" and that, although a "restrictive agreement need not directly involve an actively managed business," there must be some "bona fide business purposes" involved. Here "educating [the donees] as to wealth management" and "asset preservation" in the context of discouraging the donees from dissipating the wealth were recognized reasons for the partnership proper but they did not relate to protecting some legitimate business purpose. Which meant that these partnership provisions failed to pass muster under § 2703(b)(1). Moreover, (2) they constituted a device "to discourage the [donees] from dissipating the wealth," so they flunked under the "not a device to transfer property" test of § 2703(b)(2). The § 2703(b)(3) requirement that restrictions be "comparable to similar arrangements entered into by persons in an arms' length transaction" was discussed but the court determined that its holdings under (b)(1) and (b)(2) meant that "we need not (and do not) decide" the (b)(3) comparability question.

Interesting about all of this is the message that the § 2703(b) safe harbor only applies to business related rights/restrictions, while § 2703(a) denies recognition to restrictions in any context, for any wealth transfer tax ("for purposes of this subtitle" meaning the FET, gift, and GST, in chapters 11, 12, and 13, of Subtitle B of Title 26).

In light of the government's inconsistent success in these cases, it pays to consider other recent pronouncements seeking to impose transfer tax on the voluntary diminution in value that taxpayers allege to occur on creation of FLPs. FSA 199950014 and TAM 9842003 articulate

§ 7.2.4.4

some refinements that indicated that the government was honing its litigation strategy and arguments. Among the more interesting is an assertion in the TAM that there was a gift on creation of a partnership because the taxpayer did not receive the full value of what the taxpayer transferred, in the sense that a 99% partnership interest received was restricted in ways that reduced its value and that differential, along with the 1% interest owned by other partners, constituted a gift on creation of the partnership that would represent most (but not necessarily all) of the claimed discount in value.[309] The FSA addressed the same issue merely by stating that the transferors did not receive back a pro rata interest representing their pro rata contribution to the entity, to the extent they receive limited partner interests.

Also in juxtaposition to these results, the government lost a gift on creation assertion in *Holman*, that the two steps of funding the partnership and then giving partnership units to donees six days later should be collapsed and treated as a single gift of the underlying assets to the donees. The court had little trouble rejecting both an indirect gift and a step transaction theory because the proper steps were taken in the proper order (creation of the partnership, then the transfer of assets to it, followed by transfers of partnership units) and because the ultimate gifts were not made on the same day assets were transferred to the partnership.[310] Although the time delay was a mere six days, the court determined that "a real economic risk of a change in value of the partnership" existed due to "the nature of the [transferred] stock as a heavily traded, relatively volatile common stock. We might view the impact of a 6-day hiatus differently in the case of another type of investment; e.g., a preferred stock or a long-term government bond." The court noted that the government "apparently concedes that a 2-month separation is sufficient to give independent significance to the funding of the partnership and a subsequent gift."

---

[309] Curiously, on the gift on creation issue, the TAM and FSA both state that the 1% general partners do not make a gift because any diminution in the value of what they receive in exchange for what they transfer is exempt under the business transaction exception: they enter into the deal to acquire the added value coming from the decedent as limited partner.

[310] Distinguishing Senda v. Commissioner, 88 T.C.M. (CCH) 8 (2004), aff'd, 433 F.3d 1044 (8th Cir. 2005). See § 7.3.4.1.

§7.2.4.4

The government asserted, and similarly lost, the same gift on creation argument in Gross v. Commissioner,[311] which also involved publicly traded securities, a short delay (11 days—and the same caveat in a footnote that a different result might obtain in a different situation), but more difficult facts in the sense that it was not clear when the partnership was created under state law, due to the taxpayer's failure to satisfy all state law requirements to establish the partnership. Relying on the notion that conduct may indict the creation of the partnership, the court ruled in the taxpayer's favor and then, relying on the taxpayer's "uncontradicted" expert testimony, accepted the discounts claimed. Which is to say that the government did not invest in an expert's opinion on the valuation issue.

The government yet again asserted the gift on creation argument in Linton v. United States,[312] which relied principally on otherwise avoidable mistakes made by the taxpayer's advisors in the sequencing of a transaction (or at least their proof of that sequence). It was not proven when trusts and an LLC were created or when the gifts were made to those trusts. The government argued that property was transferred indirectly to the trusts and then contributions were made by the taxpayers and the trusts to the entity, which was created after these transfers. That argument allowed for imposition of gift tax without discounts attributable to restrictions in the entity structure. The court distinguished cases such as *Gross* on the ground that the taxpayer in those taxpayer victories created a clear sequence of events that established the entity first, funded the entity second, and then (after an appropriate delay) made gifts of entity interests.

Heckerman v. United States[313] underscores that procedure is critical. The facts reveal a transfer of mutual funds on the very same day as gifts were made of partnership units,[314] as to which the government

---

[311] 96 T.C.M. (CCH) 187 (2008) (decided by the same judge as *Holman*, with substantial reliance on that earlier opinion).

[312] 638 F. Supp. 2d 1277 (W.D. Wash. 2009), rev'd and rem'd, 630 F.3d 1211 (9th Cir. 2011).

[313] 2009-2 U.S. Tax Cas. (CCH) ¶ 60,578 (W.D. Wash. 2009) (decided by a different judge on the same court as decided *Linton*).

[314] A transfer of realty into the partnership two weeks prior to the gift of partnership units was not challenged by the government.

§7.2.4.4

made the same successful attack as in *Linton*. In *Heckerman* it simply was not clear whether proper adjustments were made to the partners' capital contribution accounts, nor whether it would matter, the court quoting from Senda v. Commissioner[315] that "even if the taxpayers' contributions . . . had been properly reflected in their capital accounts before the gifting, 'this formal extra step does not matter' because, under the step transaction doctrine, 'formally distinct steps are considered as an integrated whole' [and] . . . 'liability is based on a realistic view of the entire transaction'." In this regard, the critical element of *Heckerman* was its embrace of the step transaction doctrine, which built off the court's holding in *Linton*, which subsequently was reversed on this score. Which leaves all of this unresolved.

§ 7.2.4.5 Statute of Limitation for Revaluation

Even before unification of the estate and gift taxes in 1976, the amount of gifts made in a prior year was subject to adjustment for the purpose of computing the gift tax for a current year, even though the statutory period within which an additional gift tax might be assessed for

---

[315] 88 T.C.M. (CCH) 8 (2004), which was a gift tax case and not really in the same category as these FET decisions. A partnership was involved, the interests in which ostensibly were transferred to trusts for the taxpayers' children, but no trust agreements existed and those trusts never filed income tax returns. The government stipulated that the partnerships were valid for state law purposes and agreed to discounts of a relatively generous amount, if discounts were available at all. But the Tax Court simply found that the alleged contribution of assets to the partnerships followed by gifts of partnership interests to the trusts for the children were in reality just indirect gifts of the underlying assets directly to the children, to be valued on the basis of the value of those assets proper, and not the alleged value of the partnership interests ostensibly transferred.

As an aside, the *Senda* opinion stated that gifts should be measured by what the donor relinquished rather than by what the donees received. This is a major determination in its own right, the court citing Treas. Reg. § 25.2511-2(a), which is seldom even mentioned in cases of this nature, but this was not the court's primary holding and thus it was unimportant in *Senda*. Judge Goeke merely referenced the rule in Huber v. Commissioner, 91 T.C.M. (CCH) 1132 (2006), but he relied upon it in Koblick v. Commissioner, 91 T.C.M. (CCH) 959 (2006), to reduce a lack of control discount and thereby increase the value of a tax-payer's part-sale, part-gift transfer of a 45% stock interest to a charity as part of a prearranged transfer of 100% ownership involving simultaneous transfers by two other shareholders. For a full citation of similar authority, see § 6.2.3 n.12.

§ 7.2.4.5

the prior year had expired.[316] The result was that it was impossible to be certain what gift tax would be payable on gifts in the current year if the subject of gifts made in prior years was property that might be revalued at a greater amount than reported in the prior gift tax return. This uncertainty made it unwise in some cases to proceed with what otherwise would have been desirable inter vivos transfers.

Congress corrected this gift tax revaluation problem in 1954 by enacting § 2504(c), which eliminated in some cases the significance of a change in the value placed on prior gifts in calculating the tax on current gifts. The value of a gift made in a prior year was not subject to adjustment if a tax was assessed or paid for the prior year and the time had expired within which an additional gift tax could be assessed on the transfer.[317] But § 2504(c) did not prevent an adjustment if no tax was assessed or paid for the prior year.[318]

Furthermore, after unification of the estate and gift taxes in 1976, a problem arose because adjusted taxable gifts made after 1976 are reflected in the FET computation and § 2504(c) only provided closure for future gift tax calculations.[319] As a result, the government successfully

---

[316] See S. Rep. No. 1622, 82d Cong., 2d Sess. 479 (1954).

[317] As noted below, the requirement that a gift tax was assessed or paid for the preceding calendar period no longer exists. Thus, the significance of Rev. Rul. 79-398, 1979-2 C.B. 338, that use of the unified credit with respect to taxable gifts made after 1976 is mandatory before a gift tax may be paid is largely eliminated. See, e.g., Rev. Rul. 84-11, 1984-1 C.B. 201 (use of unified credit to eliminate the actual payment of a gift tax did not mean that a tax was assessed or paid for purposes of § 2504(c), leaving those gifts open to revaluation, a result that was perverse because it permitted revaluation of the gifts for which most taxpayers would not be inclined to keep records).

[318] Now Treas. Reg. § § 20.2001-1(b) and 25.2504-2(a) preclude reconsideration of any issues that may impact on the taxation of prior gifts. Once the limitation period has expired the government will not challenge any aspect of the adequately disclosed gift except to the extent that a completed gift otherwise may be subject to FET inclusion (such as under the string rules of § § 2036-2038). Compare the results under prior law, reported in § 7.2.4.5 n.283 (6th ed.).

[319] In Daniels v. Commissioner, 68 T.C.M. (CCH) 1310 (1994), the government was rebuffed in its effort to assert a gift tax notwithstanding § 2504(c). Because the government failed to assess a deficiency within the normal § 6501(a) three year statute of limitation period for revaluing gifts for which a return was filed, it asserted a novel argument that contradicted its own Treas. Reg. § 301.6501(e)-1(b)(2), that the differential between the value reported by the

§ 7.2.4.5

revalued adjusted taxable gifts in FET proceedings even after those gifts were protected from revaluation by § 2504(c) for future gift tax purposes.

In 1997 Congress cured this disparity by enacting § 2001(f) to extend the § 2504(c) gift tax statute of limitation to the FET.[320] Now, reflecting technical changes made in 1998,[321] if a gift is disclosed in a gift

---

(Footnote Continued)

taxpayers and the value as determined by the government was a separate gift that was substantial and unreported and thus allowed the government to assess a deficiency under the six year § 6501(e)(2) limitation for substantial unreported gifts. The Tax Court properly and summarily rejected this argument.

[320] The 1997 legislation also amended § 6501(c)(9) to provide that the government may assess a gift tax at any time if a gift should have been returned but it was not, or if the transfer was not disclosed in a manner adequate to apprise the government of the nature of the transfer. See, e.g., Small v. Commissioner, 56 T.C.M. (CCH) 1189 (1989), which previously held that the § 6501(a) statute of limitation was not tolled in a case in which the donor's estate could not prove that the donor filed a return. The government prepared a proposed return based on the value of the asset at the time of the gift and assessed a gift tax based on that proposed return, all after the donor's death.

In re Tax Liabilities of John Does, 2012-1 U.S. Tax Cas. (CCH) ¶ 50,104 (E.D. Cal. 2011), granted the government a "John Doe" summons against the California State Board of Equalization, seeking information that may reveal intra-family transfers of real property that were not properly returned for gift tax purposes. Its petition revealed that the government is using state tax records to identify taxpayers who have made transfers without filing the requisite gift tax returns. A statement disclosed "that between 60% and 90% of taxpayers that transfer real property for little or no consideration to family members fail to file a Form 709. . . . ." Also revealed is that the government already had obtained voluntary disclosure of property transfer information from authorities in Connecticut, Florida, Hawaii, Nebraska, New Hampshire, New Jersey, New York, North Carolina, Ohio, Pennsylvania, Tennessee, Texas, Virginia, Washington, and Wisconsin. The requested summons in California was to provide protection to authorities because of their concern about violating state disclosure restrictions. With the grant of its summons, the government now may have an open road to gather information to pursue nonfilers in every state.

[321] § 2001(f) was amended to specifically require closure under § 6501, which applies if a "return" is required to be filed "(without regard to section 2503(b))." This means that (even though no return is required because the gift qualifies for the annual exclusion), a return filed for an annual exclusion gift can start the gift tax statute of limitation. The upshot is that returns filed to generate closure for FET calculation purposes are effective for both gift tax and FET purposes, even with respect to gifts covered by the gift tax annual exclusion and therefore not required to be reported in the first instance.

§ 7.2.4.5

tax return that is "adequate to apprise the Secretary of the nature" of the gift,[322] under § 6501(c)(9) the value of the gift for both gift tax and FET calculation purposes is the value as finally determined[323] for gift tax purposes. Thus, if the time within which to assess gift tax expires under the § 6501(c)(9) gift tax statute of limitation, the government is bound by the value of the asset and cannot revalue it for either tax calculation purpose.

Notable is that this closure is applicable to more than just valuation questions. There is statute of limitation protection that precludes any future investigation and litigation of an issue of qualification for the marital deduction, charitable deduction, or annual exclusion if the adequate disclosure standard is met. Disclosure designed to trigger the running of the statute of limitation may be appropriate if an issue is whether a marital or charitable bequest was funded in the proper amount and that question turns on the value of assets allocated, or if the question is whether creation of an FLP was a gift because the value of interests transferred into the partnership was greater than the partnership interests received, or whether the taxpayer made gifts of difficult to value assets that were worth more than the annual exclusion.

---

[322] Treas. Reg. § 301.6501(c)-1(f)(2) describes adequate disclosure "to apprise the Service of the nature of the gift and the basis for the value reported" by requiring a description of the relationship of the parties, a "detailed" description of the method used to determine the FMV, including any relevant financial data and any discounts claimed. The regulation specifically requires disclosure regarding the value of 100% of an entity or interest determined without discounts and then the pro rata portion of the entity or interest subject to the transfer. Nested entities or pyramiding discounts must be revealed with the appropriate information at each level for each entity or asset held. In addition, disclosure must articulate any restrictions on the transferred property considered in the valuation and a "statement describing any position taken that is contrary to any proposed, temporary or final Treasury regulation or revenue rulings published at the time of the transfer."

[323] Changes made in 1998 further specified in § 2001(f)(2) (and added a cross reference in § 2504(c) to that specification) that "final determination" of value means any of (1) the taxpayer's uncontested value as stated on the return, (2) a court's determination if the value is litigated, (3) a negotiated value if the Secretary of the Treasury contests the value and the taxpayer settles with the government, or (4) the Secretary's determination of value, but only if the value is not reported on a return and the taxpayer does not timely contest the Secretary's determination.

§ 7.2.4.5

When evaluating disclosure it pays to consider whether information ultimately will be produced in litigation (should things come to that), meaning that it may be wise to produce relevant documents in hopes of garnering statute of limitation protection. Congress altered the § 7491 burden of proof rule in 1997, which effectively only shifted the burden of persuasion. The government must produce some reasonable determination upon which an asserted deficiency relies, which the taxpayer must rebut with evidence that is credible enough that a reasonable person *could* believe it (*not* the more rigorous "more likely true than not" standard of prior law), which then shifts the burden to produce evidence back to the government for rebuttal. The burden of persuasion is on the government, however, in the sense that a 50-50 equipoise of evidence results in a taxpayer victory. Thus, the taxpayer still carries the burden of production—most notably of documents and proof of valuation. But once the taxpayer has met its obligation to produce credible evidence to support its position, the government then must counter with evidence of its own or risk losing the case under the burden of persuasion. Reflecting the modesty of this change is Tax Court Interim Rule 142, which describes the shift in the burden of going forward with the proof once the taxpayer has provided credible evidence to support the taxpayer's position.

However, the position stated in Interim Rule 217 is that the taxpayer continues to bear the burden of production and of persuasion with respect to § 7477—Tax Court declaratory judgments regarding valuation—which Congress added in 1997 to provide an opportunity for taxpayers to secure a gift tax valuation determination in cases in which a lifetime transfer did not generate a gift tax liability (usually because the gift tax did not exceed the available unified credit). The lack of tax liability meant that, even if the government adjusted the taxpayer's reported valuation, the taxpayer could not pay the tax and sue for a refund, nor would the government assess a deficiency that would allow the taxpayer to challenge the adjustment by a petition to the Tax Court. The result was that, before adoption of § 7477, the government could adjust values, which would affect the adjusted taxable gifts base for calculation of future gift tax and ultimately for FET liability, but preclude a resolution of the valuation question until long after the facts had become old and cold. The addition of § 7477 allows taxpayers to seek

§ 7.2.4.5

declaratory judgments on valuation questions, notwithstanding that no gift tax is due.

Treas. Reg. § 301.7477-1 provides guidance on the declaratory judgment procedure. Relevant only if the government chooses "to put the transfer into controversy," the government will issue a "Preliminary Determination Letter," to which the taxpayer may respond. Essential to the declaratory judgment process is that the taxpayer must exhaust all administrative remedies within the Internal Revenue Service—which means that the taxpayer may not avoid an Appeals office consideration by going straight to court. Indeed, the regulation provides that the taxpayer must participate in any Appeals office consideration offered by the government, even if the case is in docketed status before the Tax Court after filing a petition for a declaratory judgment.

As Example 3 in the regulation posits, if the statute of limitation is about to expire, the taxpayer declines the government's request to extend the limitation period, and the government determines that there is no time for an Appeals consideration, a Notice of Determination of Value Letter 3569 will issue to the taxpayer, which the taxpayer then may challenge by a petition to the Tax Court. In essence, the regulation provides that then the government may require the Appeals conference that it did not have time to conduct before the taxpayer filed, and the taxpayer must fully comply in that Appeals consideration—essentially as if the statute had been extended as originally requested.

In addition, the taxpayer must "participate[] fully in the Appeals consideration process, including, without limitation, timely submitting all information related to the transfer that is requested by the IRS in connection with the Appeals consideration." Which compliance sometimes is the reason a taxpayer refuses to go to Appeals and wishes to force the government to start the litigation process directly. That option is foreclosed by this procedure if the taxpayer wants a Tax Court declaratory judgment determination.

None of this is likely to be relevant unless the taxpayer tolls the gift tax statute of limitation by making the requisite adequate disclosure of a valuation position taken on a gift tax return, forcing the government to make a determination now or lose the ability to contest valuation after the limitation period has expired. Without concern for the gift tax statute of limitation, the government may intentionally choose not to challenge a

§ 7.2.4.5

lifetime valuation, instead preferring to wait until later when hindsight reveals that a transferred asset has appreciated significantly in value, "suggesting" that the taxpayer's gift tax valuation was too low. More importantly, if the taxpayer never starts the statute of limitation to run, and therefore the government never makes an adjustment, then the taxpayer cannot force the declaratory judgment procedure by asking for a Tax Court determination. On the other hand, if the statute is running, a refusal to extend the statute will not be regarded as a failure by the taxpayer to exhaust all administrative remedies, which means that the government cannot knock the taxpayer out of the §7477 process by asking for an extension.

It is well to remember than none of these changes is relevant unless the taxpayer has met the significant administrative proceeding requirement of producing all information reasonably requested by the government in discovery, the case has gone to court, and the taxpayer falls under a $7 million net worth threshold.[324] Clarified by technical correction in 1998 was that this net worth threshold does not apply to estates *or* to revocable inter vivos trusts that make the §645 election, but only during the period of that election.

The §6501(c)(9) statute of limitation *never* prevents a gift tax assessment based on a revaluation if the taxpayer failed to properly disclose the gift, although an amended return may be filed to begin the adequate disclosure statute of limitation running.[325] The resulting lack of §2504(c) or §2001(f) protection for gifts not properly reported (or for

---

324 See §7491(a)(2)(C), which refers to §7430(c)(4)(A)(ii), which refers to 28 U.S.C. §2412(d)(2)(B), which contains the $7 million threshold.

325 See Rev. Proc. 2000-34, 2000-2 C.B. 186, which addressed the situation in which a gift tax return was filed but did not satisfy the adequate disclosure requirements (either because the gift was not reported on that return or the information provided was not adequate). This pronouncement reasonably provides that an amendment to the original return may be filed. If prominently labeled on the top of the first page "Amended Form 709 for gift(s) made in [year]—In accordance with Rev. Proc. 2000-34, 2000-34 I.R.B. 186" the amendment will put the government on notice and the adequate disclosure protection will begin to run with the amended return as if the statute of limitation for the gift began to run with the amendment. *Not* covered by this Procedure is the situation in which *no* return was timely filed, the rationale being that no permission or special rules are required to file a late return that will start the statute with adequate disclosure at that time. Also excluded from the amended return

transfers made under prior law) permits the government to redetermine the value or taxability of a prior gift, the proper gift tax thereon, the amount of unified credit exhausted thereby, and the effect on the determination of the donor's subsequent gift and FET, all at any time in the future, regardless of how old and cold the facts and basis for determination of these questions may have become in the interim.

For example, if the taxpayer fails to properly report a taxable gift made during life, §2001(f) does not preclude the kind of revaluation results in Estate of Smith v. Commissioner,[326] in which the government increased the value of the gift to compute the taxpayer's adjusted taxable gifts, not to assess a gift tax on that gift but only to determine the taxpayer's FET. The §2001(b)(2) credit against the tentative tax for gift taxes paid is not for the tax *actually* paid on the value originally reported but "the aggregate amount of tax which *would have been payable* under [the gift tax] with respect to gifts made by the decedent . . . if {the rates . . . in effect at the decedent's death . . . } had been applicable at the time of such gifts."[327] Thus, the credit also was recomputed based on revaluation of the gift. The effect of higher valuation was only to begin taxing the estate at a higher level in the FET rate tables.[328]

(Footnote Continued)

Procedure is any gift tax return that was false or a willful evasion, for which no subsequent protection may be had through the filing of an amendment.

[326] 94 T.C. 872 (1990), acq., 1990-2 C.B. 1, a reviewed opinion with nine judges concurring and eight dissenting.

[327] §2001(b)(2) (emphasis added), with the {language} now appearing in §2001(g), to which current §2001(b)(2) refers. That language originally appeared in §2001(b)(2) and was moved and expanded upon in 2010 to clarify (but not to alter) Congress' intent.

[328] See also Estate of Lenheim v. Commissioner, 60 T.C.M. (CCH) 356 (1990), (same); and Stalcup v. United States, 91-2 U.S. Tax Cas. (CCH) ¶ 60,086 (W.D. Okla. 1991) (same), and see Estate of Prince v. Commissioner, 61 T.C.M. (CCH) 2594 (1991), aff'd sub nom., Levin v. Commissioner, 986 F.2d 91 (4th Cir. 1993) (§2001(b)(2) adjustment for gift tax paid was denied for the amount of gift tax that would have been payable if gifts had been taxed properly inter vivos because no gift tax would have been payable—the taxpayer's unified credit would have covered that liability; the effect was to improperly consume the unified credit at death as if the gift tax assessment was not time barred); TAM 9141008 (same). If it applies, §2001(f) essentially codifies Boatman's First Nat'l Bank v. United States, 705 F. Supp. 1407 (W.D. Mo. 1988) (decedent died after the §2504(c) gift tax limitation period had run; government's attempt to revalue the gift in comput-

§7.2.4.5

It is important to note that the § 2001(b)(2) credit is not for the tax actually paid on the value originally reported but, instead, the tax that would have been paid on the amount of the gift as revalued by the government at the decedent's death. The effect for FET purposes is to eliminate all but one problem posed by the government's attempts at revaluation. Revaluation does not generate an increase in tax on the prior gift because a larger credit would be generated at the same time. Instead, revaluation only has the potential to push the estate into a higher marginal bracket for computing the FET (and that matters only to the extent progressivity in the rates is applicable). If the gift tax statute of limitation is still open the government may assess an added impost. Otherwise, if only FET liability is involved but the § 6501(c)(9) statute of limitation does not bar the government's inquiry, then § 2001(b)(2) determines the credit against FET for the amount of gift tax that would have been payable based on the government's assessment, not just for the gift tax actually paid.[329]

An illustration by the dissent in *Smith* showed that the application of § 2001(b)(2) does not solve an inequity that favors larger estates that already are taxable in the highest marginal bracket before revaluation of a prior gift. Revaluation of a prior gift generates a higher gift tax credit under § 2001(b)(2) in both large and small estates alike, but revaluation of a prior gift only increases total taxes if it boosts the marginal bracket in which the estate is taxed.[330] Any revaluation at death would make no difference at all if the highest marginal bracket already was reached by taxable inter vivos gifts made by the taxpayer, because the increase in tax would be matched by the same increase in the § 2001(b)(2) credit. So

---

(Footnote Continued)

ing FET was rejected because it indirectly would be imposing an additional tax on the gift in violation of the spirit of § 2504(c) if the government could increase the gift in determining the tentative FET and then reduce that tax by only the gift tax paid on the lower previously reported gift tax value; the court did not consider the § 2001(b)(2) credit issue properly resolved in *Smith, Lenheim*, and *Stalcup*).

[329] The government acquiesced to this point in AOD 1990-032.

[330] Although the dissent's example showed a smaller tax attributable to a larger valuation increase, the same tax would be payable if the taxpayer made all transfers at death or some during life and some at death, and does not speak to whether § 2504(c) should provide protection against valuation disputes long after a gift was complete.

§ 7.2.4.5

smaller taxable estates are hurt by revaluation and nontaxable ones or large estates are not.

Another impropriety is illustrated by Estate of Prince v. Commissioner,[331] which denied a §2001(b)(2) adjustment for the amount of gift tax that would have been payable if the gifts involved had been taxed inter vivos. This was because no gift tax would have been payable—the taxpayer's unified credit would have covered that liability. The effect of the court's holding was to consume the estate's unified credit at death as if the gift tax assessment was not time barred. In that respect the court's conclusion was improper. A §2001(b)(2) adjustment should be available even if the taxpayer did not exhaust the unified credit during life and regardless of whether gift tax actually was paid—or should have been paid—on the transfer.

To better illustrate this principle, consider an inter vivos transfer in 2011 that was valued at $4,000,000 for gift tax purposes. The tax at 35% was less than the full unified credit, so no payment actually was made. Assume this taxpayer then died with an estate of $2 million. Computing the FET with the adjusted taxable gift valued at $4,000,000 would produce a payment obligation at death of $2,080,800 before applying any credits. Now assume the government at death successfully revalued the gift at $5,000,000 so that the FET computation was on a tentative tax base of $7 million and the taxpayer owed $2,430,800 before applying the available credits. Allowing the unified credit, but not the §2001(b)(2) adjustment, the taxpayer would pay $350,000 more tax due to revaluation of the lifetime gift (reflecting the additional $1,000,000 assessed at a 35% marginal FET bracket).

Changing the facts, assume the lifetime transfer was reported at $6 million and was revalued at death at $7 million. Lifetime taxes would have consumed the available unified credit and at death the §2001(b)(2) credit for gift tax that *would have* been payable on the gift produces a larger credit to match the larger value and no more tax actually will be paid at death. The difference between this and the first example is that §2001(b)(2) applied in this example because, during life, the taxpayer exhausted the unified credit.

---

[331] 61 T.C.M. (CCH) 2594 (1991), aff'd sub nom., Levin v. Commissioner, 986 F.2d 91 (4th Cir. 1993).

§7.2.4.5

The two illustrations should produce the same increase in tax if the added $1,000,000 is taxed in the same marginal bracket in both cases (as it was, in this example, because the tax system presently imposes a flat tax). A difference in the respective tax rates might apply under different circumstances (if the increase in value pushes the estate into a higher marginal bracket) but that is the only difference that ought to apply in this example. And that difference is overshadowed by the *Prince* court's denial of the §2001(b)(2) adjustment in the first example. The disparity in *Prince* is improper, because the §2001(b)(2) adjustment to reflect the tax that would be payable on the revalued gift should be available in either case. The proper computation would ignore the unified credit in determining the increase in tax attributable to revaluation of the inter vivos transfer, whether the gift tax on the originally valued gift or the revalued gift, on both or on neither, was greater than the unified credit available with respect thereto.

One consequence of these holdings and legislation is that taxpayers must be *more* vigilant in maintaining adequate records upon which they may rely in future challenges, especially for future gift tax purposes with respect to gifts they otherwise would not think they needed to disclose, due to the annual exclusion, the marital deduction or charitable deduction, or the unified credit. Taxpayer vigilance in these cases must be greater than with respect to gifts on which a gift tax actually is assessed and paid. This problem is the exact converse of most taxpayers' expectations. Nevertheless, the 1997 legislation reflects a policy that the limitation period ought to run to protect the taxpayer from stale challenges in cases in which a gift tax return is filed, putting the government on notice and providing it with an opportunity to challenge the facts revealed therein.

§7.2.5 Liability to Pay Gift Tax

The federal gift tax cost is the primary liability of the donor[332] but may shift to the donee by agreement with the donor as a condition of the

---

[332] Under §2502(c) the gift tax cost incurred on a taxable transfer "shall be paid by the donor."

gift[333] or by virtue of transferee liability[334] enforceable by the government through a lien that exists for ten years from the date of the gift (or until the tax is sooner paid).[335] This transferee liability has a longer statute of limitation against the transferee than against the transferor and the government need not assert the tax liability first against the transferor as a prerequisite to assessment against the transferees.[336] Indeed, there is no § 6324(b) requirement that the limitation period for assessment of a

---

[333] See, e.g., Estate of Morgan v. Commissioner, 316 F.2d 238 (6th Cir. 1963); Estate of Sheaffer v. Commissioner, 313 F.2d 738 (8th Cir. 1963). Cf. § 6.3.3.10 at text accompanying n.82 and the income tax cases involving net gifts, such as Diedrich v. Commissioner, 457 U.S. 191 (1982); Owen v. Commissioner, 652 F.2d 1271 (6th Cir. 1981); Evangelista v. Commissioner, 629 F.2d 1218 (7th Cir. 1980); and authorities cited in each.

[334] Although § 2502(c) imposes primary gift tax liability on the donor, § 6901(a)(1)(A)(iii) imposes transferee liability on the donees for any unpaid gift tax the donor does not pay.

[335] § 6324(b). See, e.g., Tilton v. Commissioner, 88 T.C. 590 (1987) (donee-transferees liable for unpaid gift tax attributable to transfers from their parents to the extent of the value of the transfers; also considered was a gift to a family corporation and the possible liability of the shareholders for the gift tax as donee-transferees).

United States v. MacIntyre, 2012-1 U.S. Tax Cas. (CCH) ¶ 60,642 (S.D. Tex. 2012), involved unpaid gift tax liability with respect to stock held in a trust. The question was whether the trust, or its income or remainder beneficiary (both deceased before the question arose), should pay that gift tax, which the court stated was a question of first impression. The court imposed the liability on the income beneficiary, which was error because timely payment from corpus would have amortized that cost (a reduced corpus would have produced less income, and the corpus remaining at termination of the trust also would have been less, reflecting the appropriate amortization against the value of both interests), and because the state law Principal and Income Act also likely dictated that this transfer tax be paid from corpus, not income. See, e.g., Uniform Principal and Income Act § 502(a)(6) ("A trustee shall make the following disbursements from principal: . . . estate, inheritance, and other transfer taxes, including penalties, apportioned to the trust").

[336] In O'Neal v. Commissioner, 102 T.C. 666 (1994), having failed to assert liability against the transferor within the § 6501(a) statute of limitation period, the government brought a § 6324(b) transferee liability action against the transferees within the § 6901(c) one year period after the limitation period for assessment against the transferor expired, the court holding that § 6501 does not protect the transferees at all. Accord, United States v. Estate of Davenport, 159 F. Supp. 2d 1330 (N.D. Okla. 2001), rev'd in part but aff'd sub nom. on this issue, U.S. v.

§ 7.2.5

gift tax against the transferor has not expired, nor does it appear to matter that, at least in theory, there cannot be a transferee liability unless it has been determined that a tax is owing and unpaid.

Rather, it is immaterial that the reason for the transferor not having paid the tax when due is that no deficiency has been determined before the limitation period expired. And the § 2504(c) gift tax statute of limitation is no bar—even if a gift tax return adequately disclosing the gift was filed—because § 2504(c) only restricts the time within which the government may revalue a gift for purposes of determining the gift tax liability itself. The net result is that some transferees can be forced to litigate questions that the transferor created and that the government could not contest as against transferor, which can place the government at a distinct advantage by proceeding against parties less able to validate the transferor's tax positions.[337]

This bifurcated system has led to some confusion, even on the part of the government. To illustrate, the decedent whose estate was involved in PLR 9339010 made substantial gifts and paid over $1.8 million in gift tax within three years of death, triggering application of the § 2035(b) gross up rule. Inclusion of the gift tax in the decedent's gross estate produced an FET that substantially exceed the amount of the decedent's

---

(Footnote Continued)

Botefuhr, 309 F.3d 1263 (10th Cir. 2002); Sather v. Commissioner, 78 T.C.M. (CCH) 456 (1999).

Additional litigation in the *Davenport/Botefuhr* saga includes (but is not limited to) United States v. Davenport, 327 F. Supp. 2d 725 (S.D. Tex. 2004), which involved the taxpayer and several cousins, each of whom received stock by gift from the same transferor. The transfer to the taxpayer was by sale for installment notes that the transferor later forgave. The transfer to another cousin was by pure gift. The sale and forgiveness were deemed adequately revealed to the government by the transferor's income tax returns, which caused the statute of limitation to run on any gift tax liability relating to the taxpayer's transaction. But no gift tax return was filed on the pure gift until many years later, so gift tax liability attributable to it was not barred. Moreover, the taxpayer had transferee liability for *any* gift tax incurred on any gift made in the same year as the transfer to the taxpayer. Thus, although the taxpayer was not responsible for any gift tax attributable to the taxpayer's sale and forgiveness transaction, the taxpayer *was* liable for gift tax attributable to the cousin's pure gift.

[337] For example, the period for gift tax records retained by the transferor is permanent under Treas. Reg. § 25.6001-1, but the transferees may have no such records and may not be privy to those held by the transferor.

probate estate available for payment of that liability. The government opined that "under State law, the federal estate taxes are to be apportioned" among the donees of the gifts.[338] The Ruling did not establish the donee's responsibility to pay the tax as either a gift tax or FET transferee liability under § 6324, notwithstanding that § 2035(c)(1)(C) indicates that it could.[339] Thus, the lien exists even though it is not accurate to consider the donees as receiving the property that produced the FET (because the federal government received the gift tax upon which the FET was incurred).

Curiously, however, the Ruling did not depend on this analysis. Of the limited sources for payment of the gross up rule FET, it is equitable that the donees who received the gifted assets should pay the tax generated by the property they received, as presumably they would if the decedent had died with that property includible in the gross estate and left it to the donees at death. Without that result in this situation the tax would remain unpaid, and it hardly seems proper that a decedent

---

[338] The Ruling cited no authority for this result, which made it impossible to verify the government's conclusion; a computer assisted search as well as discussions with several commentators who have extensive knowledge in this area were unsuccessful in determining that any state had a tax apportionment rule that is on point. Today § 102(1)(C) of the Uniform Estate Tax Apportionment Act would apply (and is contrary to the result dictated by the Ruling) but the amendment that produces that result was not promulgated until a decade after the Ruling.

[339] The tax is not a gift tax imposed by Chapter 12 as required for application of §6324(b) gift tax transferee liability. But FET transferee liability under §6324(a)(2) is applicable to any beneficiary, who receives, or has on the date of the decedent's death, property included in the gross estate under §§2034 to 2042, inclusive, to the extent of the value, at the time of the decedent's death, of such property. And §2035(c)(1)(C) provides that the gifted property is deemed includible in the gross estate for this purpose. See Armstrong v. Commissioner, 114 T.C. 94 (2000) (imposing §6324(a)(2) liability on the transferees of the gifted property, applying the provision now in §2035(c)(1)(C) under the number by which it was identified prior to 1997 revisions), and Estate of Armstrong v. Commissioner, 119 T.C. 220 (2002) (also denying the transferee's argument that their gross up tax liability constitutes §2043 consideration furnished to qualify for the offset, the court holding that the gross up rule merely requires the gross estate to be increased, rather than describe a "transfer" as to which a full and adequate consideration exception could apply or the consideration offset rule in default).

§7.2.5

should be able to make gifts shortly before death that, coupled with the gift tax itself, would diminish the decedent's estate to the point that the gross up rule FET could not be paid and therefore would be avoided entirely.

An interesting question is whether the decedent in this type of situation could impose the gross up rule FET liability on the donees as a form of net gift, applicable as a condition on the gift itself if the decedent dies within three years of the gift. If so, quaere whether this conditional liability would reduce the value of the gifted property for gift tax computation purposes, thereby also reducing the gross up rule FET. Ripley v. Commissioner[340] held that a transferee's potential § 6324(b) liability does not affect the gift tax value of a gift because that value is determined under a willing-buyer, willing-seller analysis and a willing buyer for full and adequate consideration in money or money's worth would take free and clear of the lien, which instead would attach to the proceeds of sale in the hands of the donee. Because the transferee liability therefore does not encumber the gifted property, it was deemed not to affect the value of that property for gift tax purposes.

In the context of PLR 9339010, a useful analogy might be to a decedent who made no transfers and instead died with all the gifted property, which passes to the same beneficiaries at the decedent's death. Any tax liability incurred in that case would reduce the amount received by the donees but would not reduce the value of the decedent's gross

---

[340] 105 T.C. 358 (1995), rev'd on other grounds, 103 F.3d 332 (4th Cir. 1996), followed in Estate of Armstrong v. United States, 277 F.3d 490 (4th Cir. 2002) (also relevant was the court's finding that the transferees' liability was speculative and a net gift agreement by which they assumed the transferor's gift tax liability was "illusory," as revealed by postmortem facts), which itself was cited in McCord v. Commissioner, 120 T.C. 358 (2003), rev'd, 461 F.3d 614 (5th Cir. 2006) (the Tax Court stated, among other things, that the agreement was consideration to the beneficiaries of the decedent's estate and not to the decedent, but the court on appeal held that the amount of this tax payment obligation properly was considered and reasonably susceptible of calculation, and therefore ought to be reflected in valuing any gift involved), and FSA 200122011, which also rejected a discount in the context of a similar donees' agreement to assume transferee liability. See also the comparable issue of built in income tax liability in valuing items of IRD, as discussed in the context of marital deduction funding in § 13.7.3.2.4 n.80, and special use valuation recapture tax liability in Rev. Rul. 81-230, discussed in § 15.3.3.3 n.298 and accompanying text.

estate for FET computation purposes. It seems unlikely that a court would accept a different effective result if the decedent made the transfers as death bed gifts, given the fact that the gross up rule is designed to eliminate any advantage of planning to pay gift tax on transfers made in contemplation of death.

On the other hand, in a true net gift in which the donee is obligated to pay the gift tax as a condition of the gift, the value of the gift is the amount of the gift minus the gift tax.[341] Were this not true, a net gift would result in a gift tax being imposed on that portion of the gift that the donee used to pay the gift tax, whereas when the donor pays the gift tax there is no tax on the money used to pay the gift tax.

An important element to remember is the government's position[342] that, even if the gift tax liability is shifted to the transferee, the transferor's unified credit must be exhausted before any gift tax may be paid by either the transferor or the transferee. Also recall that payment of the gift tax by the transferee constitutes the transaction a part-sale, part-gift

---

[341] See Rev. Rul. 71-232, 1971-1 C.B. 275, for the formula to calculate the value of the gift when the donee is required to pay the gift tax. Rev. Rul. 75-72, 1975-1 C.B. 310, restated Rev. Rul. 71-232 with an expansion of Example 2, which relates to valuation of a gift subject to the condition that the donee pay the gift tax. The gift is considered as made half by the donor and half by the donor's spouse, each of whom may be in a different gift tax bracket by reason of one or both spouses having made prior taxable gifts. Rev. Rul. 76-49, 1976-1 C.B. 297, adds a state gift tax for a donor who previously made taxable gifts but the donor's spouse did not. Two more computations are found in Rev. Rul. 76-104, 1976-1 C.B. 301, and Rev. Rul. 76-105, 1976-1 C.B. 304. Rev. Rul. 80-111, 1980-1 C.B. 208, computed the value of the gift when the state gift tax cost is imposed on the donee as a condition of the gift, holding that the state gift tax paid by the donee reduces the value of the gift for federal gift tax purposes but only to the extent the donor would have been liable for payment of that tax. The state gift tax involved was a liability of the donor and donee jointly (one who pays all the tax is entitled to contribution from the other for half the tax) so the agreement by the donee to pay all the tax only reduced the value of the gift by an amount equal to half the state gift tax.

[342] Rev. Rul. 79-398, 1979-2 C.B. 338; PLR 7842068. Rev. Rul. 81-223, 1981-2 C.B. 189, illustrated the calculation involving use of the transferor's unified credit as the actual amount transferred, reduced by an annual exclusion and the gift tax liability payable by the transferee, and that payment reflected a gift tax computed under the tables on the taxable gift, reduced by the transferor's then available unified credit.

§7.2.5

transfer by which the gifted property is deemed sold to the transferee for an amount realized equal to the gift tax obligation imposed on the transferee, which may generate capital gain to the transferor.[343] Nevertheless, even with any resulting capital gain realized if the gift tax liability is greater than the donor's basis in the transferred property, the part-sale, part-gift result still is favorable due to the part-sale, part-gift basis rules, which allow the transferor to apply his or her full basis against the deemed amount realized net gift payment.

Had the transferor instead sold a portion of the property to finance the gift tax payment, only a corresponding portion of the donor's basis would be available to offset gain on that sale. In addition, the net gift produces no income tax problem if the transferor's basis is greater than the gift tax cost. In such a situation the net gift can be attractive to some transferors who are transferring property that is not marketable or liquid, if the transferor has no cash with which to pay the gift tax but the transferee does. Gifting is possible for the client with the same overall wealth transfer tax costs in such a situation as if a normal gift was made.

This reality is further illustrated by a series of transferee liability cases. In Estate of O'Neal v. United States,[344] after the transferees were obliged to pay the transferor's gift tax[345] they successfully asserted a right of reimbursement against the transferor, who subsequently had died (not within the §2035(b) gross up rule three year period, however). The estate claimed a §2053(a)(3) deduction because the transferees collected from the transferor's estate, essentially as a debt asserted against the decedent. The lower court allowed that deduction, holding that the transferor's estate would have been smaller if the government had sued the transferor for the gift tax liability in a timely manner and collected, or if the transferees had prosecuted their reimbursement claim before the transferor died. Payment by the transferees followed by reimbursement under state law and a deduction for FET purposes produced essentially the same result. On remand the appellate court

---

[343] In addition, payment of the gift tax by a trust as transferee may generate grantor trust consequences. In both respects see §6.3.3.10 at text accompanying nn.80-82.

[344] 81 F. Supp. 2d 1205 (N.D. Ala. 1999), aff'd, vac'd, and rem'd, 258 F.3d 1265 (11th Cir. 2001).

[345] For the original transferee liability case see n.336.

commanded the lower court to determine the date of death value of that liability without considering postmortem events.[346]

The gift tax paid by the transferee will be taken into account in computing the FET of the transferor if the transferee pays the gift tax and the transferor dies within three years after the gift, all as if the transferor had paid the gift tax personally.[347] Sachs v. Commissioner[348] involved such a net gift transaction within three years of the transferor's death and raised the added complication of a §2513 split net gift. The government required §2035(b) gross up rule inclusion in the donor's gross estate of *all* the gift tax paid by the transferees, even though the

---

[346] Estate of O'Neal v. United States, 228 F. Supp. 2d 1290 (N.D. Ala. 2002), held on remand that the §2053(a)(3) deduction for the value of the claim at the decedent's death should not consider postmortem developments. The government's gift tax claim was in excess of $16.0 million in gift tax, interest, and penalties. The taxpayer's experts valued the claim at $5.8 million in consideration of the hazards of litigation. The estate was valued at only $5.3 million, so the deduction on that basis eliminated all FET value and the taxpayer won a full refund. The government did not put on any evidence, perhaps because, to win, it needed to persuade the court that its $16.0 million assessment was way too high for §2053 purposes. In the estate of that decedent's predeceased spouse the same District Court ultimately held that at the earlier death there were no facts that would support a deduction for any claim and granted the government's motion for summary judgment. Basically the court held that no §2053(a)(3) deduction is available for a *potential* claim by donees for reimbursement of gift tax that those donees might be liable to pay as transferee liability, because at the decedent's death there was no gift tax litigation yet and therefore no claim. Estate of O'Neal v. United States, 291 F. Supp. 2d 1253 (N.D. Ala. 2003). A similar rejection of such a built in liability for gift tax valuation is found in *McCord* but, as noted in §7.2.5 n.340, that holding at the Tax Court level was reversed on appeal. Most notable is that the issue in *McCord* was the proper valuation discount attributable to this obligation, but in *O'Neal* the issue was deduction under §2053(a)(3) for the amount as a claim against the estate. As discussed in §15.5.2.2 (6th ed.), the issue now is addressed by Treas. Reg. §§20.2053-1(d)(2), which essentially denies any deduction for claims that are not actually paid. It would be inconsistent to reflect such a liability for valuation purposes that would not be reflected for §2053(a)(3) deduction purposes.

[347] §2001(d); Rev. Rul. 74-363, 1974-2 C.B. 290. See §7.3.6 n.238 and accompanying text.

[348] 856 F.2d 1158 (8th Cir. 1988), aff'g in part and rev'g in part 88 T.C. 769 (1987).

§7.2.5

decedent's spouse split the gift. According to the Court of Appeals for the Eighth Circuit:

> If Mrs. Sachs had paid the gift tax on her half of the split gift from assets separate from her husband's estate, [the estate tax gross up rule] would not include that payment in [Mr. Sachs'] gross estate. In this case, however, the payment of the gift tax was made entirely from the proceeds of the donated stock, all of which would have been included in [Mr. Sachs'] estate absent the gift. The assets which were used to pay the gift tax would have been part of the gross estate if the gift had never been made, and so the entire amount of the gift tax was properly included under [the gross up rule].[349]

Estate of Morgens v. Commissioner[350] was similar to *Sachs*, involving a QTIP marital deduction trust, as to which S triggered § 2519 gift tax liability by assigning the income interest. The gift tax generated was subject to the § 2207A QTIP right of reimbursement, which essentially apportions the gift tax liability to the QTIP trust. Because all of this occurs inter vivos, the result is a net gift—the transfer essentially is the § 2519 value, reduced by the § 2207A reimbursement amount.[351] *Morgens* followed *Sachs*, as if S had withdrawn the amount of the gift tax from the QTIP trust, made a gift of the balance, and paid the tax directly.[352] This result is beneficial to the extent the net gift calculation subjects a smaller amount to gift tax—the tax is less than if S had made the § 2519 transfer and paid the tax out of other funds—but it is not as favorable as would be total exclusion of the gift tax amount. As decided, death within three years of the event causes the gift tax dollars to be subjected to § 2035(b) FET inclusion in S's estate at death.

---

[349] 856 F.2d at 1165.

[350] 133 T.C. 402 (2009), aff'd, 678 F.3d 769 (9th Cir. 2012).

[351] See Treas. Reg. § 25.2519-1(c)(4) (which was promulgated after this taxpayer's death).

[352] Two issues make that analogy shaky. First, because a "normal" case precludes the spouse from doing what the court analogized, because a typical QTIP would not permit the spouse to make a withdrawal of the amount of the gift tax to hold back to pay the tax. (Indeed, state law also may provide that a spendthrift provision would preclude the initial assignment of income.) Second, because the § 2519 gift is of only the value of the remainder interest in the QTIP trust.

§ 7.2.5

In the typical net gift, § 2035(a) proper would not cause inclusion of the value of the transferred property in the transferor's gross estate. Only the gift tax paid (or deemed paid) by the transferor would be subject to inclusion under the § 2035(b) gross up rule. Thus, the court's logic is suspect, and it seems more reasonable to view a split net gift as if the transferee paid the gift tax liability of the transferor spouse on half the gift and the gift tax liability of the consenting spouse on the other half of the gift, with § 2035(b) liability for either spouse being limited to the gift tax that spouse was deemed to have paid through the transferee.[353]

---

[353] For example, PLR 9214027, also involving a split gift, held that § 2035(b) will not apply if the transferor spouse dies within three years of the gift, if the consenting spouse paid all the gift tax. If the consenting spouse dies within three years of the gift, however, all tax paid by the consenting spouse would be subject to the gross up rule in the consenting spouse's gross estate. In a related situation involving a split gift in close proximity to death, the decedent transferred funds to the decedent's spouse, who wrote a check in the same amount to fund a trust for the decedent's children. The decedent and the spouse elected to split that gift for § 2513 gift tax purposes. Ostensibly, then, the decedent was the consenting spouse. When the gift tax on that transfer was coming due, the decedent again transferred the full amount of the gift tax on both halves of that split gift to the spouse who wrote a single check to pay all the gift tax on both halves of the split gift. The decedent's spouse otherwise had insufficient funds to make either the gifts or to pay the gift tax. On these facts, the government concluded in TAM 9729005 that the gross up rule would apply to require inclusion in the decedent's gross estate of the full gift tax paid by the spouse within three years of the decedent's death. The theory was that the decedent transferred the funds to the spouse with the understanding that the spouse would use the money to make the gifts and then to pay their gift tax liabilities. Quaere, however, legislative history of § 2035(b), which makes it clear that any gift tax paid by a consenting spouse on the consenting spouse's share of any gifts made by the decedent and split by the spouse is not includible under the gross up rule. H.R. Rep. No. 1380, 94th Cong., 2d Sess. 14 (1976), 1976-3 C.B. 735, 748. Should only half the gift tax be returned to the decedent's gross estate, leaving excluded the spouse's payment of half the tax on the half that the consenting spouse was deemed to have given by virtue of the gift splitting election? By all appearances this was the case litigated in the government's favor in Brown v. United States, 329 F.3d 664 (9th Cir. 2003). The government's litigation position was that the decedent paid all the gift tax on the split gifts and that the spouse effectively made none of the gifts and paid none of the tax. See §§ 7.3.6 n.232 and 13.4.2.3.3 n.59.

§7.2.5

§7.3 ESTATE TAXATION OF INTER VIVOS TRANSFERS

Some inter vivos transfers fail to preclude inclusion of the transferred property in the transferor's gross estate at death. Typically this occurs because the decedent retained prohibited "strings" in the form of personal enjoyment of the transferred property or powers over enjoyment of it. If this occurs, one or more of the so-called string provisions in §§ 2035 through 2038 may apply to cause inclusion in the transferor's gross estate of the FET value of the property transferred inter vivos.

Inappropriate double taxation must be avoided if FET inclusion is required with respect to a transfer that was subject to the gift tax when made after 1976. The unified transfer tax mechanism in § 2001 provides a "purge and credit" mechanism that is meant to restore the taxpayer to the situation as it would have existed if the inter vivos transfer had never been made. The gift is subtracted (purged) from the § 2001(b)(1)(B) adjusted taxable gifts component of the tax computation by virtue of the flush language in § 2001(b). This is appropriate because inclusion of the transferred property causes it to be part of the § 2001(b)(1)(A) taxable estate instead. Failure to purge the gift would cause it to be taxed twice, once during life and again at death.[1]

Meanwhile, the credit in § 2001(b)(2) for gift tax payable reflects any gift tax actually incurred with respect to the transfer, even if it was not yet paid prior to death.[2] This gift tax effectively counts as a prepayment against the FET at death.

---

[1] **§7.3** It is the failure of the purge-and-credit mechanism to operate properly in the context of § 2513 split gifts that constitutes § 2001(e) as flawed, as discussed in §§ 7.1.3 in general and § 7.2.2.10 with respect to § 2702.

[2] Indeed, if the gift tax was incurred so close to death that it has not yet been paid by the decedent, it is a § 2053(a)(3) deductible claim against the estate that is not disallowed by the § 2053(c)(1)(B) prohibition on deduction of transfer taxes incurred at death. Treas. Reg. § 20.2053-6(d). Cf. Estate of Elkins v. United States, 457 F. Supp. 870 (S.D. Tex. 1978) (taxpayer borrowed to pay gift tax and was allowed to deduct the value of the outstanding loan).

To illustrate the propriety of allowing the § 2053(a)(3) deduction for the unpaid gift tax, consider a decedent who, within very close proximity of death, made a gift of $20,000,000 out of an estate of $100 million, incurring a gift tax payable of $5,250,000 and leaving a gross estate of the remaining $74,750,000. For tax computation purposes, the $5,250,000 of gift tax would be brought back

Among other more immediate advantages of unification of the gift tax and FET, this purge and credit mechanism makes it virtually unnecessary to rely on the doctrine of equitable recoupment in cases in which recovery of an inter vivos gift tax overpayment is barred by the statute of limitation and an FET is owed because the transfer was ineffective for FET purposes.[3] Instead, in most cases[4] the gift tax overpayment need not

(Footnote Continued)

into the gross estate computation under the gross up rule of § 2035(b). See § 7.3.7. With the $20,000,000 gift reflected in the FET computation as an adjusted taxable gift, the result is the same as if the decedent made no transfers at all.

To change the illustration to reflect the point in the text, assume that the decedent did not pay the gift tax prior to dying and that a § 2053(a)(3) deduction is available for the outstanding liability. That deduction is allowable to the extent the gift tax liability actually is paid by the decedent's estate, and to that extent § 2035(b) will apply even if the gift tax is not paid until after the decedent's death. The result is that the decedent dies with $80,000,000 (after making the inter vivos gift but before paying the $5,250,000 of tax), the § 2053(a)(3) deduction reduces that amount to $74,750,000, and the § 2035(b) gross up rule restores the $5,250,000 of gift tax paid to yield the same $80,000,000 amount for tax computation purposes. With the same adjusted taxable gifts, the decedent's computation is exactly the same as with the prior example.

If the decedent had made no gifts at all, or if inclusion of the transferred assets causes the FET calculation to be the same as if there had been no inter vivos transfers, the same $100 million of value would be taxable for FET purposes rather than in part under the gift tax. A disparity is created only if the decedent's $20,000,000 gift is made more than three years prior to death, in which case § 2035(b) will not apply regardless of when the gift tax is paid by the decedent or the decedent's estate, and that disparity should have no effect on the availability of the § 2053(a)(3) deduction if the gift tax is an outstanding obligation at death.

[3] This is not universally true, as illustrated in FSA 200118002 (improper reporting of a pre-1977 gift when calculating post-1976 gifts affected the gift tax that was paid inter vivos but did not alter the gift tax payable calculation for offset against the taxpayer's ultimate FET liability, and there was no equitable recoupment opportunity to correct for the error). But see, e.g., TAM 8215011 (recovery of gift tax improperly paid for 1976 was barred by statute of limitation and gift, deemed made in 1977, was deemed includible in the taxpayer's gross estate at death; gift tax allowed as offset against FET liability); TAM 7921012 (gift tax was paid on a gift by an incompetent that was brought back into the incompetent's estate at death; statute of limitation barred refund of gift tax but not its use to reduce the FET deficiency).

[4] Examples of when the concept of equitable recoupment may still be required include the interplay of income and wealth transfer tax producing inconsistent

be offset against the FET deficiency—the unified tax system does this automatically by removing the gift from the tax base and giving a credit for the gift tax paid.

The net result of inclusion at death of the subject of an inter vivos transfer is threefold. First, the taxpayer loses the use of any gift tax dollars paid if gift tax was paid inter vivos (which often is not the case, because the gift qualified under the annual exclusion or the gift tax did not exceed the available unified credit). This loss simply reflects that the credit mechanism does not pay interest or otherwise compensate for the fact that property taxable at death was subjected to gift tax during the taxpayer's life. Second, however, inclusion normally results in application of the new basis at death rule in § 1014(b)(9). If the asset has gone up in value since the taxpayer acquired it, this normally results in an increase in basis that may eliminate a capital gain tax and thereby constitutes an offsetting benefit to the taxpayer's beneficiaries.

Finally, and the real significance in most cases, the asset is taxed at its FET value rather than what normally was a lower federal gift tax value, usually resulting in an increase in wealth transfer tax. Although it is not necessarily the case that property transferred inter vivos goes up in value, usually it is the taxpayer's objective to make an inter vivos transfer that incurs tax at a lower value than if nothing was done during life.[5] The string provisions are premised on the need to negate the valuation reduction of inter vivos planning in those cases in which they apply.[6] Were it not for the opportunity to make inter vivos transfers that reduce the taxpayer's wealth transfer tax liability, the unified transfer tax

---

(Footnote Continued)

positions flowing from the same transaction. See § 3.3.23 and recall that the doctrine is applicable to both taxpayers and the government alike. In this last respect, see § 3.3.23 n.311 and accompanying text and TAM 8441003 (government reduced estate's timely claim for refund of overpaid FET by amount of barred income tax deficiency).

[5] See § 6.2.3 regarding the types of valuation reduction techniques that inter vivos planning makes available.

[6] In some cases FET inclusion negates the tax benefit of an inter vivos transfer that qualified for the annual exclusion. And if death occurs within three years of the gift the application of the gross up rule in § 2035(b) negates the tax exclusive benefit of gifting inter vivos. See § 7.3.7. But the benefit, for example, of either the marital or charitable deductions on an inter vivos transfer usually is not lost when the string provisions apply at death, because the included property usually

system would make it irrelevant whether the tax was incurred inter vivos or at death.

If both the estate and gift taxes are in effect and the tax rates are progressive it will be desirable to plan inter vivos transfers so that the string provisions are not applicable at the taxpayer's death. The following material is directed at the question for planning purposes: How much power over or enjoyment of transferred property may a taxpayer retain and avoid FET inclusion under the string provisions at death?

Of the four provisions that may trigger inclusion of an inter vivos transfer at death, §2036(a)(1) deals with retained enjoyment of the transferred property, §§2036(a)(2) and 2038(a)(1) are triggered by retained powers over the transferred property, §2037 deals with the exceptionally rare retention of a reversion that meets its requirements, and §2035 deals with the relatively unlikely application of what little remains of the rule that is triggered by death within three years of a transfer. As a consequence, it is §§2036 and 2038 that command the greatest attention in the planning process and, of those, retained personal enjoyment or a power of revocation are more likely to be intentional, whereas retained powers of any other variety more commonly are indirect and unexpected.

§7.3.1 Full and Adequate Consideration Exception

There is a common requisite of each of these provisions. Each provision excepts from its reach a bona fide sale for adequate and full consideration in money or money's worth, which means that the inter vivos transfer must have been a gift.[7] The purge and credit rule in §2001(a) is of major practical significance to avoid double taxation, precisely because these FET inclusion rules do not apply if the inter vivos transfer was supported by consideration and therefore was not subject to the gift tax.[8]

(Footnote Continued)

can qualify for the deduction again in the decedent's estate. Thus, primarily it is valuation differences that justify the FET inclusion rules.

[7] See §§2035(d), 2036(a) (parenthetical), 2037(a) (parenthetical), and 2038(a)(1) (parenthetical).

[8] See §7.3.

§7.3.1

The full and adequate consideration exception has been a troubled concept and its poorly defined parameters make it the hottest issue in the application of § 2036(a)(1) to defeat FLPs, all as explored in § 7.3.4.1. In addition, with the existence of § 2702,[9] it is not often likely to be a viable planning option to sell an interest in property as to which enjoyment (but not necessarily a power) is retained.[10] For example, § 2702(c)(2) will apply if family members purchase property in temporal interests, one buying either a life estate, a term of years, or a remainder and another buying the balance.[11] And § 2702(a) will apply if one family member merely sells a temporal interest to another for the full FMV of that interest.[12]

---

[9] See § 7.2.2.

[10] With respect to the sale of remainder interest transaction prior to adoption of § 2702 see Gradow v. United States, 897 F.2d 516 (Fed. Cir. 1990), and its progeny, as discussed in § 3.6.2.

[11] Although it could be the case that a younger generation family member supplies independent consideration, most split purchase transactions involve consideration furnished by the older generation. Although these transactions might be viewed as a gift of the funds that will be used by the younger generation family member, with each thereafter independently purchasing their interests separately, the courts have held that a § 2036(a)(1) transfer is a more accurate vision of the facts presented. For example, in Estate of Shafer v. Commissioner, 80 T.C. 1145 (1983), the decedent supplied all the consideration for the purchase of property transferred into the names of the decedent and the decedent's spouse as life tenants, with the remainder being conveyed by the seller directly to the decedent's children; § 2036(a)(1) was applied as if the decedent purchased the fee and transferred the property with a retained life estate. Cf. Gordon v. Commissioner, 85 T.C. 309 (1985) (income tax case involving amortization of an alleged purchase of an income interest in property; the taxpayer created trusts for children that jointly acquired municipal bonds with the taxpayer in a split purchase by which the taxpayer acquired the income interest and the trusts acquired the remainder, which the court held to be part of an integrated transaction by which the taxpayer acquired the entire fee interest in the bonds rather than just the income interest); Kornfeld v. Commissioner, 72 T.C.M. (CCH) 1062 (1996) (taxpayer provided the exact amount used by daughters and a secretary to purchase remainder and secondary income interests in tax exempt bonds in which the taxpayer bought a life estate; the court held that the taxpayer effectively purchased the full fee and gratuitously transferred the remainder and secondary income interests, again making an amortization deduction unavailable).

[12] See § 7.2.1 regarding the valuation of those temporal interests in the absence of § 2702, and § 7.2.2 regarding their valuation if § 2702 is applicable.

In either case, the §2702 treatment is as a transfer of 100% of the value of the underlying property, as if any interest the seller retains was worthless, resulting in a gift or the need for consideration equal to the full FMV of the entire property and not just the value of the temporal interest acquired by the purchaser. Thus, a transaction like that in TAM 8145012 (parent sold remainder interest to child for the actuarial value of the remainder alone, preventing inclusion of the value of the property in the parent's gross estate) would not be viable today unless the relation of the transferor to the transferee falls outside the definition of family under §§ 2702(e) and 2704(c)(2),[13] the structure of the transaction is such that it avoids the application of § 2702,[14] or for some reason it makes sense to pay more for the transferred temporal interest than its actuarial FMV (which is unlikely, because it would constitute a gift by the individual who overpaid).

Given the discounts that may be generated with merely fractional interests in property, however, some planning like that involved in TAM

---

[13] Cf. Richard Hansen Land, Inc. v. Commissioner, 65 T.C.M. (CCH) 2869 (1993) (pre-§ 2702 income tax case allowing amortization for cost of term interest in farmland purchased by a corporation, distinguishing similar cases because the remainder was purchased by a shareholder-employee using funds that were received from the corporation as wages paid and reported as income by the shareholder-employee).

[14] For example, the transactions in TAM 9206006 and Estate of Kitchin v. Commissioner, 53 T.C.M. (CCH) 1275 (1975), occurred prior to the effective date of § 2702 but presumably could have avoided application of that provision under § 2702(a)(3)(A)(ii) because each involved a personal residence. The government applied § 2036(a)(1) in the TAM because the decedent acquired a life estate and the primary remainder beneficiary of her estate acquired the remainder interest by borrowing (at a market rate of interest) from the same trust that the beneficiary would inherit at the decedent's death. With a balloon repayment provision keyed to the decedent's life expectancy, the government ignored the loan, stating that the borrowed portion of the purchase price "was provided exclusively by the Decedent." In *Kitchin* the decedent sold a one-third interest in the personal residence to a child and child-in-law, who owned the remaining two-thirds interest in the property and, as consideration for the sale, gave the decedent the right to live with them in the home until death. Thus, the decedent effectively sold a remainder interest in the one-third interest for a life estate in the two-thirds interest. The court concluded that the value of the two interests was "approximately" the same, sufficient to constitute full and adequate consideration to avoid § 2036(a)(1) inclusion. See also PLR 9841017 involving a split interest purchase of a personal residence in QPRT format.

§7.3.1

9146002 may still be viable and is not reached by § 2702. The decedent in that case was the settlor of a revocable inter vivos trust that held the decedent's personal residence. Within three years of the decedent's death the trust sold a 5% fractional interest in that residence to a trust for the decedent's children for an amount determined using a one-third minority interest discount. The selling trust immediately rented that 5% interest so that the decedent could remain in sole possession of the residence until death. The decedent's FET return reported only the selling trust's 95% ownership interest in the residence as includible and, presumably because a willing buyer would not pay FMV for less than 100% ownership of the residence, valued that interest with a discount of approximately 43%. In the TAM, the government determined that the sale should be disregarded for FET purposes and the residence included at 100% of its actual FMV, citing § § 2035, 2036, and 2038 as authority under two different theories.

Under the first theory the TAM stated that the sale within three years of the decedent's death constituted a transfer that would trigger § 2035(a) (then § 2035(d)(2)) and the last clause of § 2038(a)(1) (relating to the relinquishment of a power to revoke within three years of death). The theory was that the sale generating the claimed 43% discount in the 95% retained interest constituted a breach of fiduciary duty by the trustee of the selling trust. The government determined that the decedent's acquiescence constituted a release of the decedent's rights over that portion of the trust for purposes of § § 2035 and 2038.

Under the second theory, the government asserted that no one would sell a 5% ownership interest in a personal residence unless there was a prior leaseback arrangement permitting uninterrupted exclusive enjoyment and that this agreement therefore constituted a transfer with a retained interest subject to § 2036(a)(1). In so holding, the TAM rejected the contrary authority of Estate of Barlow v. Commissioner,[15] based on the fact that *Barlow* involved a sale of 100% of the subject property, and the leaseback was for business purposes (the property was farmland) rather than personal use. The Memorandum also stated that § 2036 was implicated because the lease term, with a renewal right, was for a period that exceeded the decedent's life expectancy.

---

[15] 55 T.C. 666 (1971).

Both theories are a stretch in search of a way to prevent a transaction that abused the valuation rules. Assuming that the claimed discounts reflect the reality of a willing-buyer, willing-seller valuation, it seems clear that the overall transaction was designed solely to generate a tax free transfer of a substantial portion of the overall value of the residence. In that light, the real issue was whether the sale for two-thirds of the nondiscounted FMV of a 5% interest was for full and adequate consideration. If it was not, gift tax on the transfer would be the proper result. *Barlow* should not be limited to a sale of 100% of the property, a business transaction requirement should not apply to the leaseback, the leaseback term should be irrelevant if its terms reflect an arm's length negotiation, and the rent paid was full and adequate.

In addition, certain assets do not constitute consideration for wealth transfer tax purposes, the most notable being marital property rights in a transaction that does not meet the requirements of §§ 2516 and 2043.[16] Another easy example would be funds ostensibly provided by the transferee but that effectively originated with the transferor or that otherwise are regarded by the tax law as belonging to the transferor already.[17] And a third example may be certain notes, the bona fides of which are subject to challenge.

A good illustration is Estate of Musgrove v. United States,[18] which involved an interest free, unsecured, self-canceling demand note made 18 days before the lender's death, which the court held to be not effective to preclude FET inclusion of the principal amount of the debt in

---

[16] See, e.g., Estate of Graegin v. Commissioner, 56 T.C.M. (CCH) 387 (1988) (pursuant to a prenuptial agreement that was not incident to a § 2516 divorce, decedent created a revocable inter vivos trust with a retained secondary life estate that caused § 2036(a)(1) FET inclusion; a § 2043 consideration offset was denied because decedent's spouse only surrendered marital property rights, not support rights, which do not constitute consideration in money or money's worth), and § 7.1.1 nn.4-6 and accompanying text.

[17] See, e.g., Estate of Marshall v. Commissioner, 51 T.C. 696 (1969) (decedent transferred stock worth $375,000 in exchange for a life estate in a trust created by the transferee, which was deemed to be includible as if the decedent had created the trust with the stock originally transferred and retained the life estate). See also the authorities discussed in notes 11 and 14, and the *Olsten* case discussed in § 13.6.2.2 at text accompanying note 48 et seq.

[18] 95-2 U.S. Tax Cas. (CCH) ¶ 60,204 (Ct. Fed. Cl. 1995). See also Estate of Maxwell v. Commissioner, discussed at text accompanying § 7.3.4.1 n.125.

§ 7.3.1

the lender's estate. The decedent was seriously ill when the loan was made, the borrower was the decedent's only heir and the sole beneficiary of the decedent's estate, who had no funds with which to repay the debt (the borrowed funds were used to pay a pre-existing tax liability). The note on its face made it clear that there was no legitimate expectation of repayment. There was no repayment schedule, no interest obligation, and the face of the note declared that it would be forgiven if the lender died before repayment. The court held that the note was not consideration for the loan because the decedent never intended to collect on the debt by demanding repayment.[19]

§ 7.3.2 *Identifying the Proper Transferor(s)*

Each of the rules addressed in this segment is a function of transfers by an individual who retains certain strings. As a consequence, it is essential to identify the proper party as the transferor. Sometimes this is a problem because of commingling of property, because of lapses of rights of withdrawal over property, because the gift tax identity of a transferor may differ from the FET identity,[20] and occasionally because of intentional efforts to obfuscate the identify of the proper transferor.

To illustrate, it is easy to imagine multiple transferors to a single trust, sometimes as a function of the intentional creation of joint settlor

---

[19] Citing Deal v. Commissioner, 29 T.C. 730 (1958), Rev. Rul. 81-286, 1981-2 C.B. 177, and Rev. Rul. 77-299, 1977-2 C.B. 343. See § 6.5.2 n.31 and accompanying text. This holding is troubling because, if it was true that repayment was never anticipated, the loan should have been taxed as a gift when made rather than as an includible asset at death. Nevertheless, citing Buckwalter v. Commissioner, 46 T.C. 805 (1966), in which the note was not self-canceling but the parties agreed that it would be forgiven if the lender died before repayment, the court held that the lender held an interest in the note that was includible under § 2033 notwithstanding the forgiveness. The court also held that the demand feature of the loan was tantamount to a § 2038(a)(1) power to revoke the transfer, which on its own is a dangerous and unprecedented conclusion in the demand loan arena.

[20] See, e.g., Rev. Rul. 54-246, 1954-1 C.B. 179 (in a § 2513 split gift the consenting spouse's election is treated as a gift only for gift tax purposes—and today for the subsequent FET calculations that depend on the amount of inter vivos gifts and gift tax paid, according to TAM 8515001—but not for FET purposes, making the actual transferor the only taxpayer subject to the string provisions at death). See § 7.1.3 with respect to gift splitting in general.

trusts and sometimes by inadvertence. In a community property jurisdiction it is common for spouses to create a joint settlor trust of their community property, with identification of each spouse's contribution and an aliquot share of the trust usually being relatively easy to determine because of the typical equal ownership of the community property transferred to the trust. Issues of tracing and exposure to the string provisions become much more difficult to address if spouses contribute separate property to a joint settlor trust (either in conjunction with community property or as the only property contributed to the joint trust).[21]

Inadvertent commingling also occurs in some cases because, for example, spouses have a plan that combines their wealth after S dies and property that belongs to S is added to a trust created by D for administration purposes during S's overlife. This probably is not a major concern if the receptacle is a marital deduction trust that will be includible in S's gross estate anyway and as to which all income is being taxed to S.[22] But the identification of respective contributions becomes critical if that addition is made by inadvertence to a nonmarital trust that is not meant to be includible when S dies, because only the contributed portion of that otherwise nontaxable trust is includible.[23]

Similar issues could arise with respect to a trust created for a child or, worse, in a GST exempt trust that could continue for multiple generations. This especially is true because multiple transferors and additions can play havoc with the exempt status and the generation assignment of trust beneficiaries.[24] In this respect an inadvertent addition could be as simple as failing to exercise a taxable power of withdrawal,

---

[21] See, e.g., Estate of Hoffman v. Commissioner, 78 T.C. 1069 (1982) (S's property inadvertently allocated to testamentary trust created by D to hold D's share of their community property); and §§ 3.7 and 4.1.14 addressing joint settlor trusts.

[22] Although it might create multiple grantor problems for income tax capital gains tax purposes. With respect to multiple grantors for income tax purposes see § 5.11.1.

[23] Valuation issues exist with respect to a multiple transferor trust, whether to apply a tracing rule or establish a percentage of the trust that is attributable to each transferor, all as discussed in § 7.3.7 n.246.

[24] See § 11.4.16 with respect to the GST and additions to otherwise exempt trusts.

§ 7.3.2

with lapse being a deemed contribution to the trust of the amount that could have been withdrawn,[25] or failure to assert rights to income that otherwise remains in the trust.[26]

---

[25] See Horner v. United States, 485 F.2d 596 (Ct. Cl. 1973) (S had power to withdraw income that, to the extent not requested, was accumulated and added to principal, as to which S had the same ongoing right to withdraw income generated by that accumulated income; had that accumulated income been S's own property transferred with a retained right to the income for life, § 2036(a)(1) would require inclusion of it at S's death and, as a consequence, the second clause of § 2041(a)(2) was applicable with respect to it instead—the court inappropriately applied § 2036(a)(1), but the result is the same and the error was harmless in this context). See Estate of Halpern v. Commissioner, 70 T.C.M. (CCH) 229 (1995) (rejecting government's argument that §§ 2036 and 2038 could require inclusion of marital deduction trust property in S's gross estate, stating that S's power over the trust would trigger § 2041 inclusion or no inclusion at all), and Treas. Reg. § 20.2041-1(b)(2), as discussed in § 12.3.2.2 n.23 and accompanying text with respect to the distinction between §§ 2036 and 2038 as opposed to § 2041 inclusion in the estate of a decedent other than the settlor of a trust.

[26] See Estate of Miller v. Commissioner, 58 T.C. 699, 715 (1972) (income beneficiary consented to an account that showed income that should have been distributed but instead was added to principal, constituting a transfer of property from which the beneficiary was entitled to income in the future, making the value of that accumulation includible based on a "percentage of the total value of the trust as of the alternate valuation date as the dollar amount of income [added to principal] ... bears to the value of those assets as of the date of the approval of the final accounting [to which the income beneficiary consented]"); TAM 8208010 (on sale of underproductive property the controlling local law required a portion of the proceeds to be allocated to the income beneficiary as delayed income; a § 2036(a)(1) transfer was deemed made when the income beneficiary did not assert the right to this amount); and cf. Rev. Rul. 90-82, 1990-2 C.B. 44 (contrary to state law a trust directed payment of mortgage interest and principal from current trust income, resulting in a deemed income to principal allocation in the amount of the principal amortization on that mortgage, requiring apportionment of a depreciation deduction between the income beneficiaries and the trust; § 2036(a)(1) liability was not involved), and see contra Estate of Tull v. United States, 74-2 U.S. Tax Cas. (CCH) ¶ 13,010 (E.D. Mich. 1971) (income beneficiary did not object to fiduciary account showing expenses of administration charged to estate income). The government also might argue that any failure to demand that corpus be invested to produce a reasonable rate of income is a gift from the income beneficiary to the remainder beneficiaries. See PLRs 8905045, 8844008, 8805029, and 8642028 (in the context of GRITs, now subject to § 2702, as discussed in § 7.2.2.

§ 7.3.2

Confusion with respect to the proper identity of the transferor also can be a function of rearrangements that alter the original disposition of property, such as by disclaimer,[27] by settlement of a bona fide controversy,[28] by exercise of a surviving spouse's elective share,[29] or other rejection of a decedent's estate plan followed by establishment of an alternative disposition.[30]

---

[27] See § 7.1.6 regarding disclaimers being treated as if the disclaimant predeceased the transfer and the original transferor created the default disposition.

[28] See, e.g., Centerre Trust Co. v. United States, 676 F. Supp. 928 (E.D. Mo. 1988) (litigation was settled by distributing property to trusts in which life interests were given to the litigants; when a life beneficiary died the court concluded that the agreement constituted a bona fide compromise and therefore did not constitute a transfer to the trust by the decedent for § 2036 purposes); Estate of Prochet v. United States, 76-1 U.S. Tax Cas. (CCH) ¶ 13,131 (D. R.I. 1976) (decedent regarded as settlor of a trust with a retained life estate in stocks titled in the name of the decedent's predeceased spouse for convenience but not ownership purposes and as to which a court proceeding resulted in a transfer into the trust); TAMs 9811006 and 9506004, and PLR 9437034 (§ § 2036 and 2038, respectively, would apply at the death of minors who were deemed to be the settlors of SNTs created for their benefit as part of tort litigation settlements); and cases cited in each of these authorities.

[29] Rev. Rul. 90-45, 1990-1 C.B. 175 (S elected against D's will in favor of a statutory share of the estate and then disclaimed a portion of that share; the Ruling held that the election was not a § 2518(b)(3) acceptance that would preclude a qualified disclaimer of any portion of it but instead was deemed to "effectuate or perfect" S's rights under state law to receive that portion of D's estate as if D bequeathed that share to S or died intestate and S inherited it); PLR 8817061 (similar; allowed S to elect a statutory share and then disclaim all of it in excess of a specified dollar amount). See § § 3.4.7 n.63 and 7.1.6.3 nn.279-281 and accompanying text.

[30] National Bank of Commerce v. Clauson, 226 F.2d 446 (1st Cir. 1955) (S and other estate beneficiaries agreed to terminate D's testamentary trust and created a new trust giving S a life estate in the entire estate, with § 2036(a)(1) inclusion based on the amount S would have received upon renunciation of D's will and election to receive a one-third statutory share outright, placed in an irrevocable inter vivos trust with the same right to income for life; the result was fairly costly given that the only difference between the rejected testamentary trust and the new trust was the possibility that S might receive principal distributions in the trustee's discretion); but see Rev. Rul. 70-84, 1970-1 C.B. 188 (decedent obtained a court order authorizing receipt of insurance proceeds in a lump sum that the decedent then placed in a trust for the decedent for life; the government held that the decedent was not the settlor of the trust established with the insurance

§ 7.3.2

More importantly, confusion as to the proper transferor may result from intentional efforts to obfuscate the proper treatment of the trust through the use of reciprocal trusts. In the classic illustration, siblings or spouses each create mirror image trusts in which the other settlor is granted interests or powers that would cause inclusion under § 2036 or § 2038 if the beneficiary or powerholder had been the settlor.[31] In these cases the reciprocal trust doctrine uncrosses the trusts at the settlor level, treating the beneficiary or powerholder as the settlor of the trust in which their interests or powers are granted.

According to the doctrine as established in Estate of Grace v. United States,[32] asking whether the decedent established the trust as consideration for the trust of which the decedent was beneficiary places "too much emphasis on the subjective intent of the parties in creating the trusts and for that reason hinders proper application of the federal estate tax laws."[33] Instead, the reciprocal trust doctrine does not depend on finding a quid pro quo. It also is not necessary to prove the existence of any tax avoidance motive. "Rather . . . application of the reciprocal trust doctrine requires only that the trusts be interrelated, and that the arrangement, to the extent of mutual value, leaves the settlors in approximately the same economic position as they would have been in had they created trusts naming themselves as life beneficiaries."[34]

Presumably the doctrine may not be used to require inclusion of both trusts in either settlor's gross estate, one based on the facts as they

(Footnote Continued)

proceeds, regarding the decedent as a conduit with no power to vary from the stipulated court order).

[31] Other applications of the reciprocal trust doctrine are discussed with respect to the annual exclusion, in § 7.1.1.5, and in the § 2041 context in § 12.1 nn.14-17 and accompanying text.

[32] 395 U.S. 316 (1969) (spouses); for other classic illustrations see Lehman v. Commissioner, 109 F.2d 99 (2d Cir. 1940) (siblings); TAM 8019041.

[33] 395 U.S. at 322.

[34] 395 U.S. at 324. "To the extent of mutual value" is illustrated by Rev. Rul. 74-533, 1974-2 C.B. 293, and Rev. Rul. 57-422, 1957-2 C.B. 617: assume that reciprocal trusts are created, one of $400,000 and the other of $300,000; all the FMV of the smaller trust and 75% of the value of the larger would be subject to uncrossing, regardless of their relative sizes when the taxable event ultimately occurs that causes the reciprocal trust doctrine to be relevant.

§ 7.3.2

exist and the other under the reciprocal trust doctrine, although this does not appear to have been tested. Estate of Guenzel v. Commissioner[35] came close, involving spouses who established irrevocable trusts that named each other as initial income beneficiary and reserved a secondary life estate for S. When D died the reciprocal trust doctrine was used to include under § 2036(a)(1) the trust created by S, as if D had created it and reserved that life estate. Thereafter S relinquished the life estate in the trust created by D but retained the secondary life estate in the trust that actually was created by S (but that was treated under the doctrine as created by D).

When S died § 2036(a)(1) again was used to include the trust actually created by S, without application of the reciprocal trust doctrine. The court held that it was no defense that the value of this same trust earlier had been included in D's gross estate on the fiction created by the reciprocal trust doctrine.[36] The other trust also was not includible, but only by virtue of S's relinquishment of the life estate in it.

One problem with the reciprocal trust doctrine is that its parameters are ill defined. Thus, for example, Estate of Levy v. Commissioner[37] denied application of the doctrine because the trusts differed in one respect. One granted a nongeneral inter vivos statutory power of appointment that the other did not, preventing the trusts from putting the two settlors in approximately the same economic position.[38] More recently, Estate of Green v. United States[39] rejected application of the reciprocal

---

[35] 28 T.C. 59 (1957).

[36] And see Rev. Rul. 74-533, 1974-2 C.B. 293, discussed in note 34, on the issue of the gift tax and FET unification consequences of uncrossing; it involved preunification law but, to the extent the doctrine applied (100% of the smaller trust and 75% of the larger trust in that case), treated the spouses as if H created the trust and paid the tax that W in fact created and paid, and vice versa. It is not yet known whether the same consistent fiction would be applied under §§ 2001 and 2010 for unified transfer tax calculation purposes today.

[37] 46 T.C.M. (CCH) 910 (1983) (spouses).

[38] The government conceded that the power prevented the trusts from being interrelated if the power was valid. 46 T.C.M. at 912. Further, citing *Levy*, PLR 200426008 held that trusts created by spouses were sufficiently different to avoid the reciprocal trust doctrine, including disparate distribution provisions and nongeneral inter vivos and testamentary powers to withdraw or appoint.

[39] 68 F.3d 151 (6th Cir. 1995).

§ 7.3.2

trust doctrine in a case involving grandparents who created separate identical trusts, one for each of their two grandchildren, his with her as trustee for the benefit of one grandchild and hers with him as trustee for the benefit of the other grandchild. Because neither settlor could benefit personally, the court rejected application of the doctrine to uncross the trusts and cause him to be regarded as trustee of the trust he created and her as trustee of the trust she created, followed by application of §§ 2036(a)(2) and 2038(a)(1) by virtue of their respective retained powers over beneficial enjoyment of trust benefits by the respective grandchildren.[40]

According to the court, the reciprocal trust doctrine requires that the settlor be in "the same economic position" as if no crossing occurred on creation of the trusts and that, if there is *no* economic enjoyment of trust benefits by the settlors, there can be no economic position upon which the doctrine can apply.[41] The court also concluded that the government cannot apply the reciprocal trust doctrine with respect to retained *powers* because the "core mandate" of *Grace* is retained *economic* benefit.

The dissent in *Green* argued that the settlors did maintain "the same economic position" as if the trusts had not been crossed, because their powers constituted as much of an economic benefit as would retained personal enjoyment.[42] In that respect the dissent makes a good point that

---

[40] See also PLR 9804012, in which sisters created trusts for their respective children, with their brother as cotrustee with a corporate fiduciary. When the brother resigned one sister became cotrustee of the trust for the other's children, and vice versa. The government held that the reciprocal trust doctrine would not apply because there was no intent on creation to cross the trusts or these powers.

[41] The opinion specifically cited Estate of Bischoff v. Commissioner, 69 T.C. 32 (1977) (essentially the same facts), which held otherwise, and stated that it is the sole opinion in the government's favor and that it has been rejected by every circuit that had considered application of the doctrine as it might apply to powers instead of interests. That claim is regarded as "curious" by Marty-Nelson, Taxing Reciprocal Trusts: Charting a Doctrine's Fall from *Grace*, 75 N.C. L. Rev. 1781, 1798 (1997), which opines that no circuit court has *explicitly* rejected *Bischoff*.

[42] It also maintained that the retained economic enjoyment that the majority regarded as the "core mandate" of *Grace* was merely the operative fact of that case and not an immutable requirement for application of the doctrine, to which

it makes little sense to regard the reciprocal trust doctrine as applicable for purposes of § 2036(a)(1), which deals with retained enjoyment, and not for purposes of its counterpart § 2036(a)(2), which deals with retained control over another beneficiary's enjoyment, given the fact that the Code addresses each as two peas from the same pod. The dissent also is compelling in the sense that, once personal needs are satisfied, the next most important benefit of wealth is the control it gives over others and the personal enjoyment that flows from that power. Distinguishing consumptive enjoyment from control seems difficult to justify, particularly because Congress chooses to predicate inclusion under § 2036 on the retention of either.

Nevertheless, for estate planning purposes, *Levy* and *Green* appear to make it possible to dodge application of the reciprocal trust doctrine with easy drafting that includes (or perhaps just alters the permissible appointees of) a nongeneral power of appointment in one of two related trusts, or that does not retain personal enjoyment at all.[43]

§ 7.3.3 Retained Powers

Several aspects that are common and fundamental to the operation of the string provisions applicable to retained powers are not relevant to the string provisions relating to retained enjoyment, reversions, or transfers within three years of death.

One is that the mere existence of a power is adequate to trigger inclusion, regardless of any practical impediments or costs that might

---

(Footnote Continued)

the majority retorted with an ad hominem attack that the dissent "totally misconstrues and reflects a misunderstanding of the concept and elements of the reciprocal trust doctrine generally and its limited application as dictated by the Supreme Court in *Grace*" and then distinguished every retained power case as *also* involving retained enjoyment.

[43] Or perhaps by merely altering sufficiently when the trusts are created so that they are not created at "approximately" the same time, which was another ill defined aspect of the *Grace* determination of what constitutes interrelated trusts. In *Grace* they were created 15 days apart; there is no reliable indication of what timing differential would suffice.

inhibit exercise of the power, be they contractual,[44] temporal,[45] mental, or physical.[46] Another is that, absent an indication to the contrary, the power is not exhausted by its prior exercise,[47] although relinquishment or termination of the power may be possible,[48] with potential gift tax consequences if the original transfer is made complete thereby.

In addition, a power merely to alter the size of a beneficiary's share[49] or to affect the timing of a beneficiary's enjoyment is adequate to trigger

---

[44] See, e.g., Kurz v. United States, 156 F. Supp. 99 (S.D. N.Y. 1957) (marital settlement agreement precluded revocation without consent; power nevertheless triggered inclusion, notwithstanding that exercise might have generated breach of contract damages).

[45] See, e.g., Marshall v. United States, 338 F. Supp. 1321 (D. Md. 1971) (power exercisable only by will).

[46] The now well accepted proposition is that the mental or physical inability to exercise a power is irrelevant and that the existence of the power alone is critical to application of the FET inclusion rules. See, e.g., Estate of Gilchrist v. Commissioner and Estate of Reid v. Commissioner, 630 F.2d 340 (5th Cir. 1980) (consolidated cases involving §§ 2041 and 2038, respectively); Armata v. United States, 494 F.2d 1371 (Ct. Cl. 1974), Round v. Commissioner, 332 F.2d 590 (1st Cir. 1964); Hurd v. Commissioner, 160 F.2d 610 (1st Cir. 1947), and the analogous issue under § 2041 discussed in § 12.3 n.7 and accompanying text, the only important issue being whether the document dispossesses the power upon the powerholder's incapacity to exercise it.

[47] Cf. Rhode Island Hospital Trust Co. v. Commissioner, 219 F.2d 923 (1st Cir. 1955) (trust originally was revocable and subject to alteration and amendment; the settlor executed an instrument modifying the trust, stating that the trust as amended was irrevocable, and paid a gift tax after making the modification, but the court nevertheless held that the modification only expressly eliminated the power to revoke and did not exhaust the power to alter or amend). A completed gift for gift tax purposes may result if exercise of the power causes its lapse or termination, in which case any gift tax paid and the trust property itself may escape FET, but only if three years elapse after termination of the power. See § 7.3.7 with respect to application of the three year rule in this context.

[48] Estate of Ware v. Commissioner, 480 F.2d 444 (7th Cir. 1973), rev'g 55 T.C. 69 (1970) (power as trustee to pay or accumulate income, with no express authority to resign; state law was deemed to permit resignation or termination of the settlor's personal exercise of the power, even without permission of a proper court, express authority in the trust, or consent of all beneficiaries).

[49] See, e.g., Rifkind v. United States, 84-2 U.S. Tax Cas. (CCH) ¶ 13,577 (Ct. Fed. Cl. 1984) (CLT paying all income during decedent's life to a foundation of which the decedent was a director, with control over the ultimate recipients of the income, causing inclusion of trust corpus in the decedent's estate under

the retained power provisions, even if the identity of the beneficiary cannot be altered.[50] And jointly held powers (even if held with an adverse party)[51] and the power to simply veto some other party's exercise of a power[52] are regarded as tantamount to solo direct powers to act affirmatively, all adequate to trigger the retained power inclusion provisions.

(Footnote Continued)

§ 2036(a)(2); that the decedent was limited to qualified charities in the selection of permissible distributees from the foundation was irrelevant); Crile v. United States, 76-2 U.S. Tax Cas. (CCH) ¶ 13,161 at 85,717 (Ct. Cl. 1976) ("[t]he retained power to vary shares among named beneficiaries and the included power to eliminate a named beneficiary [are] sufficient powers to include the trust property in the donor's estate"). Even without express language like that found in § 674 excepting the power to add beneficiaries only by birth or adoption, the same result is held to apply under § § 2036 and 2038. Thus, neither provision is triggered by the ability to alter enjoyment solely by birth or adoption, provided that the terms of the transfer establish the right of children already born and those after born or adopted. Rev. Rul. 80-255, 1980-2 C.B. 272, 273 ("[a]lthough [the] act of bearing or adopting children will automatically result in adding the child as beneficiary to the trust, such result is merely a collateral consequence of the bearing or adopting of children").

[50] See, e.g., O'Malley v. United States, 383 U.S. 627 (1966) (power to pay or accumulate income caused inclusion of both corpus and accumulated income); Round v. Commissioner, 332 F.2d 590 (1st Cir. 1964) (power to accumulate income); Industrial Trust Co. v. Commissioner, 165 F.2d 142 (1st Cir. 1947) (spray provision among designated beneficiaries is adequate); Estate of Alexander v. Commissioner, 81 T.C. 757 (1983) (power to accumulate trust income alone is adequate to restrict beneficial enjoyment and cause inclusion); and cases cited in each authority.

[51] Treas. Reg. § § 20.2036-1(b)(3)(i), 20.2038-1(a) (flush language) unless Treas. Reg. § 20.2038-1(d) is applicable because the transfer predated June 2, 1924. In that respect, Rev. Rul. 78-16, 1978-1 C.B. 289, held that an adverse party consent requirement failed to preclude inclusion because it was added by amendment of the trust after 1924.

[52] See Estate of Gebbie v. Commissioner, 13 T.C.M. (CCH) 136 (1954), which regarded as a joint power a requirement that the transferor must consent to the trustee's action, but see Estate of Graham v. Commissioner, 46 T.C. 415 (1966), which rejected § 2038 inclusion because a requirement that the transferor be consulted about changes did not allow the transferor to initiate or preclude any action. Rev. Rul. 70-513, 1970-2 C.B. 194, holds to the contrary, stating that, although the power to veto or consent to action is different from a power to initiate action, "there is little practical difference between the two" when the power is held by the trust settlor. Without enforceability of the trust under state law the settlor essentially has no power or rights in an irrevocable inter vivos

However, an express power must exist, not just de facto trustee abdication to the transferor's wishes[53] (although indirect powers may suffice if, for example, the transferor controls an entity and the entity possesses the power).[54]

Furthermore, the ability to exercise discretion is essential: a definite external standard will protect against inclusion, and administrative or ministerial powers are harmless.[55] Although these exceptions are neither statutory nor regulatory, they are a reasonably well established product

(Footnote Continued)

trust, making the statement and holding of questionable validity. See 4 Scott, Fratcher, & Ascher, Scott and Ascher on Trusts § 24.4.1 (5th ed. 2007).

[53] See Estate of Goodwyn v. Commissioner, 32 T.C.M. (CCH) 740, 754 (1973) (decedent in effect controlled the trusts and made all the decisions even after resignation as trustee, the successor trustees effectively acting as the decedent's surrogates; nevertheless, de facto control with no express authority or agreement was inadequate to require inclusion: "[t]he right or power upon which the tax is predicated must thus be a legal right reserved in the trust instrument, or at least by some form of agreement between the trustees and the settlor").

[54] Compare Estate of Levin v. Commissioner, 90 T.C. 723 (1988) (transfer of postmortem annuity payable by a corporation controlled by the decedent was includible in the decedent's gross estate under § 2038 because the decedent controlled the corporation through stock ownership, procured the annuity through services to the corporation, transferred the annuity by virtue of continued employment and control over the corporation, and could have terminated the annuity by terminating work, divorcing the designated beneficiary, or by directly agreeing to terminate the plan), with DiMarco v. Commissioner, 87 T.C. 653 (1986), acq., 1990-2 C.B. 1 (decedent did not possess any powers over the corporation), and Estate of Tully v. United States, 528 F.2d 1401 (Ct. Cl. 1976) and TAM 8701003 (no inclusion in circumstances similar to *Levin*).

[55] See, e.g., Winchell v. United States, 180 F. Supp. 710 (S.D. Cal. 1960) (power to amend administrative provisions was inadequate to cause inclusion); Estate of Budd v. Commissioner, 49 T.C. 468, 476 (1968) (administrative powers to determine income and principal "were hardly broad enough to be regarded as enabling the decedent to designate who would enjoy the trust property or income therefrom, or to alter, amend or revoke the trust"); PLR 200919008 (power derived only from state statute and that only affected administrative provisions such as a trustee or trust protector's liability, payment of compensation and expenses, disclosure of health information, and investment provisions); TAM 8606002 (power to apportion gains and losses, charges, credits, and income between income and principal, thereby affecting the interests of the primary and remainder beneficiaries, was deemed inadequate to constitute a power that was sufficiently broad to cause inclusion under either § 2036(a)(2) or § 2038(a)(1)).

§ 7.3.3

of case law and rulings,[56] many relatively old. In essence, standards that would qualify as ascertainable under Treas. Reg. § 20.2041-1(c)(2) will more than fit within the parameters established by these authorities.[57]

Thus, for example, terms such as education, maintenance or support, and varying terms relative to health or medical care will suffice to collar a fiduciary's discretion and preclude §§ 2036(a)(2) and 2038(a)(1) inclusion.[58] Curiously, even broader standards than those permitted

---

[56] For a smattering of rulings see, e.g., Rev. Rul. 73-143, 1973-1 C.B. 407 (of two trusts of which the transferor was trustee, one limited the power to distribute principal to the beneficiary's "special needs for support and education" and the second was limited to only the beneficiary's "special needs"; only the second was subject to § 2038(a)(1) because not limited by a nondiscretionary power circumscribed by the ascertainable standard of support and education); TAM 8606002 (retained power to direct distributions for the "emergency needs" of the primary beneficiary), which held that the power was not properly limited to avoid §§ 2036(a)(2) and 2038(a)(1) and is consistent with similar holdings under more stringent standards, but appropriately limited powers under the § 2041 ascertainable standard definition were involved in PLRs 9118009, 9113010, 9049041, and 8922062. Approval in the TAM of a power to terminate the trust if necessary "to avoid an anticipated disaster to or destruction of the property of the trust or a material impairment thereof" is interesting because it might indicate that such a power normally would be ignored, regardless of by whom held (except, perhaps, if termination would result in distribution to the powerholder), which makes inclusion as a safety valve type of provision less risky.

[57] Ascertainable standards are discussed in the context of § 2041 at § 12.3.2.4. With respect to the issue in the context of §§ 2036 and 2038 and the historical development of this exception and the terms that have been involved in various older cases, see generally Pennell, Estate Planning: Drafting and Tax Considerations in Employing Individual Trustees, 60 N.C. L. Rev. 799, 802-810 (1982), abridged and reprinted in 9 Est. Plan. 264, 264-267 (1982). There is one possible exception to the notion that an ascertainable standard in the § 2041 context will suffice under §§ 2036 and 2038, found in the form of Carpenter Estate v. United States, 80-1 U.S. Tax Cas. (CCH) ¶ 13,339 (W.D. Wis. 1980) (although a power to accumulate or distribute income controlled by an ascertainable external standard would preclude inclusion, the court considered the powers in the trustee as not governed by a standard because they did not *require* distribution even when the standards were satisfied), the only case from among all the jurisprudence involving standards governing distributions that suggests that both a *minimum* and a maximum limitation on a trustee's discretion is required.

[58] See, e.g., United States v. Powell, 307 F.2d 821 (10th Cir. 1962) (maintenance or support); Estate of Ford v. Commissioner, 53 T.C. 114 (1969) (maintenance or support, health); Estate of Budd v. Commissioner, 49 T.C. 468 (1968)

§ 7.3.3

under §2041 also have been blessed, including emergency, welfare, comfort (standing alone), and happiness.[59]

In addition, a transferor's power to remove a trustee and designate the transferor as a successor trustee (or cotrustee)[60] will cause attribution of the trustee's powers to the transferor, even if not actually acting as trustee at death.[61] However, the power to remove and replace trustees (sometimes referred to as a revolving door power) will not cause the transferor to be regarded as holding the trustee's powers if the succes-

---

(Footnote Continued)

(education, maintenance or support, medical); Estate of Pardee v. Commissioner, 49 T.C. 140 (1967), acq., 1973-2 C.B. 3 (education, maintenance, medical); Estate of Kasch v. Commissioner, 30 T.C. 102 (1958), acq., 1958-2 C.B. 6 (health); Estate of Weir v. Commissioner, 17 T.C. 409 (1951) (education, maintenance or support).

[59] See, e.g., United States v. Powell, 307 F.2d 821 (10th Cir. 1962 (comfort, happiness); Estate of Budd v. Commissioner, 49 T.C. 468 (1968) ("in the event of sickness, accident, misfortune or other emergency"); Estate of Pardee v. Commissioner, 49 T.C. 140 (1967), acq., 1973-2 C.B. 3 ("education, maintenance, medical expenses, or other needs occasioned by emergency"); Estate of Ford v. Commissioner, 53 T.C. 114 (1969) (welfare, happiness); PLR 199903025 (welfare, education, maintenance in health and reasonable comfort).

[60] See Durst v. United States, 409 F. Supp. 1046 (W.D. Pa. 1976), aff'd, 559 F.2d 910 (3d Cir. 1977), for accord on the proposition that powers held as a cotrustee are as powerful for inclusion as those held alone.

[61] Treas. Reg. §§ 20.2036-1(b)(3) (last sentence), 20.2038-1(a)(3) (second sentence). See Rev. Rul. 73-142, 1973-1 C.B. 405 (state court determined that power permitted a single exercise and, having done so, that the transferor no longer possessed the power at death; although that determination would not bind the government if rendered postmortem, it was binding on the parties premortem and precluded inclusion in the transferor's estate). If neither the power to remove and replace trustees nor state law specifies otherwise, the power may be presumed to permit the powerholder to name the powerholder as a successor trustee. See Estate of Alexander v. Commissioner, 81 T.C. 757, 766 (1983) (inclusion based on conclusion that, notwithstanding decedent had been and resigned as trustee, the decedent could have become trustee again and there was "no convincing indication in either the [trust] or any of the documents by which the decedent appointed successor trustees or co-trustees that the decedent was at any time precluded from once again serving as a trustee"); Estate of Edmonds v. Commissioner, 72 T.C. 970 (1979) (use of gender neutral terminology and original appointment of corporate trustee did not inform conclusion that only corporate successors could be named).

sor trustee cannot be—and cannot be related or subordinate to—the transferor.[62]

The Tax Court once stated in an analogous income tax case with a revolving door power that "[s]ince an uncooperative trustee could be summarily replaced, [the taxpayers] could effectively deplete, appoint, or cash out the trust assets . . . ,"[63] and in the context of a power to remove trustees and replace them with anyone, including the powerholder as successor, again stated that the powerholder "for all practical purposes, can control the actions of the trustee by removing any uncooperative trustee and appointing one who will act as [the powerholder] directs."[64]

Nevertheless, in Estate of Wall v. Commissioner[65] the Tax Court addressed the question directly in the FET context and held that the government's revolving door power argument was neither cogent nor supported by authority, and concluded forcefully that the government was wrong in its fundamental premise that a trustee who is subject to removal and replacement will do the powerholder's bidding. Instead, the Tax Court held that established fiduciary law principles would be violated if a trustee merely acquiesced by doing something the powerholder requested that the trustee otherwise would not do. Absent some form of prearrangement or understanding between the powerholder and the

---

[62] Rev. Rul. 79-353, 1979-2 C.B. 325, would have required inclusion regardless of the successor's identity, but Estate of Beckwith v. Commissioner, 55 T.C. 242 (1970), acq. 1971-1 C.B. 1, held otherwise and the government eventually modified Rev. Rul. 79-353 by Rev. Rul. 81-51, 1981-1 C.B. 458, to make it prospective only and then revoked Rev. Rul. 79-353 by Rev. Rul. 95-58, 1995-2 C.B. 191, citing its losses in Estate of Wall v. Commissioner, 101 T.C. 300 (1993), and Estate of Vak v. Commissioner, 62 T.C.M. (CCH) 942 (1991), rev'd, 973 F.2d 1409 (8th Cir. 1992) (irrevocable inter vivos trust as to which the decedent retained a power to remove and replace trustees but neither the decedent nor any related or subordinated party could be named as a successor trustee; on appeal the court held that the government "overstated" its case when it contended that the decedent had the power to replace the trustee with individuals who would do as the decedent directed).

[63] Stern v. Commissioner, 64 T.C.M. (CCH) 1, 3 (1992), on remand from 747 F.2d 555 (9th Cir. 1984), rev'g 77 T.C. 614 (1981).

[64] Estate of Wilson v. Commissioner, 64 T.C.M. (CCH) 576, 582 (1992).

[65] 101 T.C. 300 (1993).

§ 7.3.3

trustee, the court held that the government's fundamental assumption underlying the revolving door power theory could not be supported.

According to Revenue Ruling 95-58,[66] which is the government's current position on this issue, the revolving door power to replace individual or corporate trustees at will is not adequate to regard the powerholder as possessing the trustee's control over trust distributions, provided that any individual or corporate successor is "not related or subordinate to the [powerholder] (within the meaning of §672(c))."[67] Informal comments by government officials at the 1995 American Bar Association Annual Meeting indicated that this is a safe harbor ruling and that other cases may not be litigated even if not within the "not related or subordinate" confine.

The same government officials as appeared at the 1995 Annual Meeting would not comment upon whether a power to remove the trustee alone would constitute sufficient control over the trustee to regard the powerholder as possessing the trustee's discretionary control,[68] but a joint revolving door power may insulate either individual powerholder while they both are acting.[69] A joint power may not be exercisable after the death of one holder,[70] meaning the protection may

---

[66] 1995-2 C.B. 191.

[67] See §5.11.1 at nn.30-33 and accompanying text for a discussion of "related or subordinate" under §672(c). In PLR 9607008 a 1966 trust was reformed to provide that no replacement trustee could be related or subordinate and the government issued a favorable ruling that §2041 exposure to a beneficiary who was the powerholder would be prevented. A similar result surely would apply under §§2036 and 2038 if the transferor was the powerholder.

[68] But cf. PLR 9809032, which held that a settlor's retained power to set trustee compensation, which provided the ability to "encourage the trustee to resign," was not adequate to attribute trustee powers to the settlor.

[69] PLR 9524023 (analogous §2041 application of the revolving door power issue involving a revolving door power that could be exercised only by unanimous vote of all of the adult members of a particular family line, holding that it would not cause any beneficiary in possession of the power to be treated as possessing the trustees' powers).

[70] James v. United States, 448 F. Supp. 177 (D. Neb. 1978) (three grantors of irrevocable trust with joint right to remove the trustee and appoint themselves; when one died the court determined that a power coupled with a beneficial interest might survive but jointly held powers not coupled with an interest

not be lost (although the power itself may be lost) when one coholder dies. Ironically, a power that does not permit removal of a trustee but that does allow replacement may not be as useful a tool to control a trustee (if it is useful at all) but a power to name replacements that includes the opportunity to name the powerholder individually as successor trustee is not as safe as the power to remove. It may avoid § 2038 inclusion, but it will not avoid § 2036.[71]

It should be safe to allow the transferor to designate a successor in the office of trustee if the transferor is not the trustee, cannot remove the trustee, and cannot be appointed to fill any vacancy in the office of trustee. This should be true regardless of what powers are given to the trustee by the trust instrument, provided that the successor cannot be related or subordinate to the powerholder.[72] And if even this minor qualification on the revolving door or replacement power is not accept-

---

(Footnote Continued)

generally are not exercisable by survivors, absent some indication otherwise). See also Estate of Webster v. Commissioner, 65 T.C. 968 (1976) (trust revocable only with consent of two children was not includible because the decedent survived three of the decedent's four children), Rev. Rul. 79-177, 1979-1 C.B. 298 (inclusion avoided because, under state law, death of one holder of joint power terminated the power), and cf. Restatement (Second) of Trusts § 194 (1959) and Restatement (Third) of Trusts § 39 (2003) (relating to multiple trustees, the current formulation being that two trustees must act in concert but more than two may act by majority).

[71] Compare Treas. Reg. § 20.2038-1(b), discussed at § 7.3.3 n.81 and accompanying text (§ 2038 does not reach contingent powers if the contingency—here a vacancy—does not exist at death) with Treas. Reg. § 20.2036-1(b)(3), discussed at § 7.3.3 n.82 and accompanying text (§ 2036 does reach contingent powers even if the contingency has not been met). Accord, First Nat'l Bank v. United States, 81-2 U.S. Tax Cas. (CCH) ¶ 13,422 (D. S.C. 1981); Estate of Farrel v. United States, 553 F.2d 637 (Ct. Cl. 1977); Rev. Rul. 73-21, 1973-1 C.B. 405 (all involving decedent's power to name a successor trustee, including the decedent personally, upon a vacancy in trustee).

[72] Accord, Rev. Rul. 77-182, 1977-1 C.B. 273 (power to appoint a successor corporate trustee if the original corporate trustee resigned or was removed by judicial process), modified by Rev. Rul. 95-58, 1995-2 C.B. 191 (power to appoint *an individual or* a corporate successor trustee will not be deemed a retention of the trustee's discretionary control over trust income, but only if the successor "was not related or subordinate to the decedent (within the meaning of § 672(c))").

§ 7.3.3

able, appropriate, or desirable, advisors may want to consider defusing any trust that contains an otherwise problematic power in the manner provided in PLRs 9303018 and 9328015, which involved revolving door powers in trust beneficiaries to remove and replace any disinterested trustee.

Court orders were obtained in those situations to modify the revolving door provisions to clarify the settlor's intent that they be exercisable only for "cause" and, in the process, preclude application of Revenue Ruling 95-58 under § 2041. As defined by those proposed court orders, a list of 13 items would constitute sufficient cause. The PLRs confirmed that the government's revolving door position will not apply to a power that is "sufficiently restricted" and found that the proposed court orders would confirm the settlor's intent that the powerholders never held and would not be releasing general powers of appointment by virtue of the trusts and their modifications.

The same attorneys obtained both PLRs on behalf of the same clients (involving different trusts), and the government blessed the same verbiage to incorporate in each court order. Thus, the approach approved seems likely to be the safe way to address this issue in modifying any existing trust. The definitions of cause provided in both PLRs appear to be an appropriate way to draft either a court ordered "clarification" of an existing trust or any new provision being inserted into documents being drafted currently.

Because the ability to remove and replace trustees is valuable and appropriate, especially when using an individual trustee who has no fiduciary track record or experience, the government's approved definition of cause is reproduced in its entirety.[73]

---

[73] Both Rulings involved trusts with multiple trustees but, excepting the wording of the parenthetical in item 10, this did not appear to be an essential aspect of either Ruling. Given the lack of specificity in such standards as "mismanagement," "abuse," "inattention," or "unreasonable compensation" authorized by the government, this definition ought to be adequate to provide sufficient latitude in most trusts to remove a trustee whose performance or personal prejudices make continued service undesirable.

Removal of a trustee for cause shall mean any one of the following:

    1. The legal incapacity of a trustee.

    2. The willful or negligent mismanagement by the trustee of the trust's assets.

    3. The abuse or abandonment of, or inattention to, the trust by the trustee.

    4. A federal or state charge against the trustee involving the commission of a felony or serious misdemeanor.

    5. An act of stealing, dishonesty, fraud, embezzlement, moral turpitude, or moral degeneration by the trustee.

    6. The use of narcotics or excessive use of alcohol by the trustee.

    7. The poor health of the trustee such that the trustee is physically, mentally, or emotionally unable to devote sufficient time to administer the trust.

    8. The failure by the trustee to comply with a written fee agreement or other written agreement in the operation of the trust.

    9. The failure of a corporate trustee to appoint a senior officer with at least five years of experience in the administration of trusts to handle the trust account.

    10. Changes by a corporate trustee in the account officer responsible for handling the trust account more frequently than every five years (unless such change is made at the request of or with the acquiescence of the other trustee).

    11. The relocation by a trustee away from the location where the trust operates so as to interfere with the administration of the trust.

    12. A demand from the trustee for unreasonable compensation for such trustee's services.

    13. Any other reason for which a [state] court of competent jurisdiction would remove a trustee.

The listing of items that constitute cause illustrates that the government is being flexible in terms of the types of concerns it has about the misuse of revolving door powers to gain effective control over the administration and distribution of a trust.

In the rare case in which §§ 2036(a)(2) and 2038(a)(1) do not operate in tandem, they may cause inclusion of different amounts in the transferor's gross estate. Thus, it can be useful to know that there are a number of differences between the reach of these two retained power provisions. For example, § 2036(a)(2) requires inclusion of the same amount that would be includible if the transferor retained personal enjoyment of trust income until death, which typically is the full value of

§7.3.3

the corpus producing that income. But § 2038(a)(1) only causes inclusion of the value of the interest that is subject to the transferor's power, which could be just the value of the income beneficiary's interest or just the value of a remainder interest.[74]

Considering that difference in the amount includible, it is appropriate that the differences between the operation of these provisions almost always make it harder to trigger inclusion under § 2036(a)(2). To illustrate, § 2038(a)(1) is applicable if the power was created by the transferor and held at death (or treated as held at death), regardless in most cases of whether that power was retained or subsequently *acquired* by the transferor, but § 2036(a)(2) requires that the power was *retained* by the transferor.[75] An example of a power created but not retained by the transferor, who subsequently acquired the power before dying and therefore was subject to § 2038(a)(1) at death, would be a trust of which the transferor was not named as a trustee but who became a successor trustee by virtue of some other party's action, in which capacity the

---

[74] This difference is not discernable by comparing the wording of § 2036(a) ("the value of all property to the extent of any interest therein of which the decedent has . . . made a transfer . . . under which he has retained") with § 2038(a)(1) ("the value of all property . . . to the extent of any interest therein of which the decedent has . . . made a transfer . . . where the enjoyment thereof was subject"). But see, e.g., Walter v. United States, 341 F.2d 182 (6th Cir. 1965), and Rev. Rul. 70-513, 1970-2 C.B. 194 (in each case, transferor's power to distribute corpus to the current income beneficiary did not alter enjoyment of the income, because that beneficiary already possessed the right to income; the power thus amounted to control over only the remainder interest, and the discounted present value of only that interest was subject to § 2038(a)(1) inclusion).

[75] Compare § 2038(a)(1) (third parenthetical) with § 2036(a)(2); the same restriction on application of § 2036(a)(2) exists under § 2038(a)(2) with respect to transfers made before June 23, 1936. See Treas. Reg. § 20.2038-1(c). Cf. Estate of Skifter v. United States, 468 F.2d 699 (2d Cir. 1972) (rule that decedent must have created the power even if it was not retained stated in a § 2042 case, looking at the issue by analogy); Estate of Reed v. United States, 75-1 U.S. Tax Cas. (CCH) ¶ 13,073 (M.D. Fla. 1975) (power acquired by original transferor who conveyed property unqualifiedly to transferee who later established a trust under which the transferor was trustee with various powers; § 2038(a)(1) applies if the power was created under the terms of the original transfer but not if it was created by a third party thereafter).

transferor possessed at death § 2038(a)(1) powers created in the original trust instrument.[76]

This distinction in the retention requirement makes implied understandings or arrangements important under § 2036(a)(2) but not under § 2038(a)(1). As a result, the § 2036 regulations[77] treat the transferor as having retained a power if there was an express or implied understanding at the time of the original transfer that the power later would be conferred on the transferor, although this is not a very well defined provision. For example, in Estate of Giselman v. Commissioner,[78] the transferor retained a right to rent trust property and, after the trust terminated, the transferor's wholly owned corporation continued to occupy that property, yet the court held that § 2036 inclusion was avoided because it does not apply to arrangements permitting the transferor to enjoy the benefits of transferred property that were not contemplated before the transfer was complete.[79] Nevertheless, the government has

---

[76] Rev. Rul. 70-348, 1970-2 C.B. 193. For an expansive application of this principle see TAM 8038021 (transferor established a trust that gave the trustee the power to distribute corpus and a second trust was established under which a closely held corporation controlled by the transferor was the trustee and held a power to terminate the second trust; the first trust property was made subject to the terms of the second trust and there was a general family understanding that the transferor should continue to control the trust property for life, resulting in inclusion under § 2038(a)(1), the government holding that "[w]hether the power . . . should be regarded as 'retained' from the time of the transfer or as merely 'acquired' at some time after the initial transfer, the property is nevertheless includible under section 2038").

[77] See Treas. Reg. § 20.2036-1(a) (last sentence).

[78] 55 T.C.M. (CCH) 1654 (1988).

[79] To simplify the facts in TAM 9128005, assume that Donor and Donee jointly owned Blackacre. Subsequently, and all on the same day, Donor transferred Greenacre (which was owned by Donor alone) into tenancy in common with Donee, in exchange for Donee's transfer to Donor of Donee's interest in Blackacre. Also on that same day Donee executed a will giving Donor a life estate in Donee's share of Greenacre, which Donor had just transferred to Donee. When Donee died 15 months later, Donee's estate reported half the value of Greenacre on its FET return and, when Donor subsequently died, Donor's estate reported only the other half thereof on its FET return. The question presented was whether the full value of Donee's half of Greenacre, having been transferred to Donee by Donor and then bequeathed back to Donor for life only, was includible in Donor's estate under § 2036(a)(1) as a transfer by Donor during life with an

§ 7.3.3

been known to rely on the implied understanding theory, sometimes even in lieu of better supported theories for inclusion.

To illustrate (in the context of § 2036(a)(1) rather than § 2036(a)(2), but the principle is the same), in PLR 9141027 the taxpayer proposed to create an inter vivos trust for the taxpayer's spouse and children that granted the spouse a nongeneral testamentary power of appointment, which the spouse proposed to exercise in favor of a trust created by the spouse for the benefit of the taxpayer. The government concluded that the taxpayer retained a § 2036 interest in the transferred property because there was "an implied agreement" that the transferred property would be settled by the spouse for the taxpayer's enjoyment, resulting in a retained interest subject to § 2036(a)(1).[80]

A second difference between these provisions is that § 2038(a)(1) can be triggered with a negative power that merely permits the transferor to *prevent* enjoyment by someone, whereas § 2036(a)(2) requires an affirmative power to *designate* who will enjoy trust benefits.

Furthermore, as is true under its counterpart § 2036(a)(1), § 2036(a)(2) only applies to powers over the enjoyment of income or the possession of non-income-producing principal of a trust. It does not apply

---

(Footnote Continued)

indirectly retained life estate. The TAM held that no interrelated transaction or implied retention of the life estate could be imputed to Donor, because Donee had full rights to half of Greenacre following the conveyance into tenancy in common and prior to death, and because Donee's conveyance of the life estate back to Donor did not occur until Donee's death over 15 months later. This precluded § 2036(a)(1) inclusion in Donor's estate of that half. A different result might have applied if Donee had created the same trust of that half of Greenacre on the day (or closely thereafter) Donor transferred it to Donee.

[80] All by virtue of Treas. Reg. § 20.2036-1(a). If state law adhered to the "relation back" doctrine regarding interests created by exercise of a nongeneral power of appointment (the holder of a nongeneral power is regarded as the agent of the donor of the power), then creation of the taxpayer's interest by the spouse's exercise of the nongeneral power probably should have been regarded as a directly retained interest by the taxpayer. In such a case, interests created by exercise of the power should be treated as created ab initio by the donor, not by the powerholder. See 1 Scott, Fratcher, & Ascher, Scott and Ascher on Trusts § 3.1.2 (5th ed. 2006). Thus, if state law followed that general principle, the government's implied agreement theory would have been unnecessary to create § 2036(a) inclusion.

to the enjoyment of income producing corpus. Moreover, §2036(a)(2) requires retention of the power for one of the three §2036(a)(1) periods: (a) for life, (b) for a period that does not end before death, or (c) for a period that is not ascertainable without reference to the transferor's death. Neither aspect has a counterpart under §2038(a)(1), which can apply if the power is simply held at death and may affect the enjoyment of either income or corpus alone.

There is only one difference between these power provisions that makes it easier for the government to apply §2036(a)(2). This difference is the protection afforded against inclusion under §2038(a)(1) if the power is subject to an unmet contingency or condition that was beyond the transferor's control at death.[81] In that case §2036(a)(2) may apply even if the power is not exercisable at death because of an unmet contingency or condition.[82] This difference can be exploited in any situation in which FET inclusion of an inter vivos transfer might be desirable, for example because the new basis at death benefit of inclusion exceeds any increased wealth transfer tax cost. A formula contingent §2038(a)(1) power can be included in a document of transfer, triggered only upon that contingency being met.[83]

§7.3.4 Retained Enjoyment

An inter vivos transfer may be subject to §2036(a)(1) inclusion at death because the transferor retained enjoyment or possession of the transferred property for life or for a period that did not end before

---

[81] Treas. Reg. §20.2038-1(b) (penultimate sentence). See Estate of Farrel v. United States, 77-1 U.S. Tax Cas. (CCH) ¶ 13,185 (Ct. Cl. 1977). A contingent or conditional power is distinguishable from a §2038(b) power that "takes effect only on the expiration of a stated period after the exercise of the power" or the situation in Rev. Rul. 68-538, 1968-2 C.B. 406, in which the retained power to amend or revoke was exercisable after a specified future date that the settlor predeceased, the government holding that inclusion was required but at a discounted value to reflect the delay, which is not exactly within the literal meaning of §2038(b).

[82] Treas. Reg. §20.2036-1(b)(3)(iii).

[83] See McCaffrey, Some Tips on Tax Tuning Gifts, 137 Trusts & Estates 87, 90 (Aug. 1998), reprinted and expanded upon in McCaffrey, Tax Tuning the Estate Plan by Formula, 33 U. Miami Inst. Est. Plan. ¶ 403.5 (1999).

death.[84] The traditional funded revocable inter vivos trust created for asset management or probate avoidance purposes usually is subject to inclusion under this provision because the transferor intentionally retains a life estate, and most cases of § 2036(a)(1) inclusion are entirely anticipated and inclusion is appropriate.

Indeed, most of the transfers that are subject to § 2036(a)(1) did not involve payment of a gift tax because the transfer was incomplete for gift tax purposes. The transferor also retained a power to revoke that makes both §§ 2036(a)(1) and 2038(a)(1) applicable at death, either of the two provisions together requiring inclusion of (but no more than) 100% of the value of the property. In these cases the transfer is not a gift at all, which makes both the full and adequate consideration exception and the § 2001(b) purge and credit rules that avoid improper double taxation at death irrelevant.

Not every inter vivos transfer that is subject to § 2036(a)(1) is anticipated, however, and on some occasions the retained enjoyment or possession of transferred property is less than intuitive. Certainly it is easy to anticipate the application of § 2036(a)(1) to a retained right to receive income, rents, dividends, or other income from transferred assets,[85] and the same is almost as obvious with respect to retained use

---

[84] There actually are three periods for which § 2036(a)(1) inclusion may apply, the third being for a period that is not ascertainable without reference to the transferor's death. The first two periods are not uncommon, applying to a straight life estate or a term of years that the transferor does not survive. The third is quite unusual in normal planning and is included in the statute to prevent creation of an interest that technically avoids the first two periods referenced under the statute but is the functional equivalent of a life estate, such as income for a period ending one day before death.

[85] See, e.g., Estate of Cooper v. Commissioner, 74 T.C. 1373 (1980) (transfer to a trust of coupon bonds from which the transferor detached and retained the interest coupons, the federal gift tax return reporting the bonds less the value of the retained coupons, which alone were included in the decedent's gross estate for FET purposes; the court rejected the contention that the coupons and the bonds were separable and held that the decedent made a transfer with income retained and that the full value of the bonds and the coupons was includible under § 2036(a)(1)); Estate of Nicol v. Commissioner, 56 T.C. 179 (1971) (transfer with reserved right to crop share rent); Rev. Rul. 78-26, 1978-1 C.B. 286 (gift of woodlands with retained timber rights); TAM 7746004 (transfer with reserved timber and mineral rights, stating that a factual determination is required be-

or enjoyment of tangible assets, such as the right to drive an automobile, view transferred artwork, or occupy a personal residence. Other sources of retention that will cause inclusion are not so intuitive and there are questions that may affect application of § 2036(a)(1) to even some of the more obvious situations. Those are the subject of most of the discussion below.

§ 7.3.4.1 Possession or Enjoyment of Transferred Property

One step removed from direct retention of an income interest in transferred property was the enjoyment the government perceived in PLR 8504011. According to its theory, the taxpayer indirectly retained a life estate in *common* stock that was transferred as part of a corporate freeze transaction, because the taxpayer allegedly was entitled to too large an income preference with respect to retained *preferred* stock. The government asserted that the preferred stock entitlement essentially amounted to a right to all income attributable to the preferred stock plus a portion of the income properly attributable to the transferred common stock. The Tax Court rejected this contention in Estate of Boykin v. Commissioner,[86] although the court failed to indicate that the theory could not apply in a proper case. Instead, it said only that, in the subject transaction, the income entitlement of the retained preferred stock was not excessive.

On the other hand, it is possible that, even if there never was a transfer with a retained interest, the decedent will be treated as if there was. If, for example, the decedent furnished the consideration for the purchase of property and directed that the title be transferred by the seller to the decedent for life and the remainder to others, the decedent made an indirect transfer of the property and retained a life estate.[87] Less

---

(Footnote Continued)

cause "a reservation of mineral interest [may] not provide for the rights or interest requiring includibility" under § 2036(a)(1)).

[86] 53 T.C.M. (CCH) 345 (1987).

[87] See, e.g., Estate of Shafer v. Commissioner, 80 T.C. 1145 (1983), aff'd, 749 F.2d 1216, 1222 (6th Cir. 1984) (case of first impression, the court stating that: "If . . . this case fell outside of Section 2036(a), a buyer of land could avoid [inclusion] simply by directing the grantor to make out the deed in a particular

obviously correct would be the case of a joint or split purchase of property, with the decedent buying only a life estate or term of years and the remainder beneficiary purchasing the remainder with consideration furnished either by the decedent or from independent funds. It was sufficiently unclear whether § 2036(a)(1) would apply to such a case that § 2702(c)(2) specifically addresses this form of transaction.[88]

Retention also may result from imposing the transferor's obligations on the transferee. For example, a transferor who transfers property by net gift and directs that income from the transferred assets be used to pay the gift tax obligation may suffer § 2036(a)(1) inclusion if the obligation remains outstanding when the transferor dies.[89]

Mahoney v. United States[90] was one step removed but illustrates the point. The decedent's father created a trust to which transfers were made by net gift, resulting in part-sale, part-gift treatment.[91] The decedent paid the part-sale consideration with a note, and the trust provided that income would be used to pay off the note, as if that income was paid to the decedent and then the decedent made the payments. The court held that the part-sale portion was tantamount to the decedent making a contribution to the trust with a retained § 2036(a)(1) life estate. Because that portion represented 11% of the total trust corpus, the same percentage of the trust as valued at the decedent's death was includible in the decedent's gross estate. The court regarded the transaction as the decedent's contribution with a retained interest, notwithstanding the fact

---

(Footnote Continued)

manner. Such a result would permit the technicalities and diversities of property law to thwart the purposes of federal estate tax law").

[88] See § 7.2.2.

[89] Cf. Krause v. Commissioner, 56 T.C. 1242 (1971) (income tax grantor trust case). But see PLR 199922062 (irrevocable trust with direction to pay income tax liability incurred by taxpayer on creation or operation of the trust deemed not a § 2036(a) interest or power "[b]ecause the distributions on Taxpayer's behalf represent tax payments allocable to the trust [and] not . . . the retention of the right to income . . .").

[90] 831 F.2d 641 (6th Cir. 1987), rev'g 628 F. Supp. 273 (S.D. Ohio 1985).

[91] See § 6.3.3.10.

that the decedent's father established the trust and arranged for the part-sale and the note entirely without the decedent's participation.[92]

As *Mahoney* also illustrates, if the transferor retains the right to only a portion of the income from the transferred property, or the right to all the income from or possession of only a portion of the transferred property, then only the portion of the trust property needed to produce that income (or the portion from which the income or possession is retained) is includible under § 2036(a)(1).[93] The difficult issue can be how to compute that portion.

For example, in Estate of Tomec v. Commissioner[94] a trust provided that $2500 of income should be paid each year to each of the settlor's four children, with only the balance of the income payable to the settlor for life. If a child died there was a possibility that the income payable to the settlor would increase, but the court concluded that the value of the portion of the trust corpus includible in the settlor's gross estate would be computed by reducing the value of the total trust by the amount needed to produce $10,000 at the applicable interest rate (today that rate would be determined under § 7520).[95] The fact that the settlor's income might increase was disregarded. Unlike this one example, however,

---

[92] Notably, during life the decedent reported all the trust income, including that paid directly to the decedent's father in satisfaction of the note, while the father did not report trust income under § 677(a)(1) as the trust grantor until the note was exhausted. Thus, the wealth transfer tax result was consistent with the parties' own income tax treatment during the decedent's life—although a coincidence of income and wealth transfer tax rules is not necessary. See § 5.11.10 regarding the lack of pari materia. Presumably a different result would have been generated if the trust had been saddled with the net gift obligation rather than the decedent, but the result would have been taxation of trust income to the father under § 677(a)(1) until that liability was satisfied and § 2036(a)(1) exposure to the father if he died before satisfaction of that debt.

[93] See the valuation principle in Rev. Rul. 79-109, 1979-1 C.B. 297 (right to possess a house for part of the year; value for inclusion based on whether the property had seasonal fluctuations in the rental value that might vary the pro ration from a straight percentage of the annual rental value to a seasonally weighted pro ration).

[94] 40 T.C. 134 (1963), acq. 1964-2 C.B. 7.

[95] See, e.g., the inclusion valuation rules in Treas. Reg. § 20.2036-1(c) that apply if a GRAT transferor dies before the retained annuity interest terminates, as discussed in § 7.2.2 n.46.

§ 7.3.4.1

valuation uncertainties probably work against the taxpayer in the majority of cases.[96]

An additional uncertainty can exist if there was no express retention of enjoyment or possession, but the transferor nevertheless enjoyed the transferred property or its proceeds after the transfer. For example, FET inclusion was appropriate in Estate of McNichol v. Commissioner,[97] in which the taxpayer deeded income producing real estate without reservation of an interest but continued to receive and report for income tax purposes all rents from the property until death.

On occasion possession or enjoyment of transferred property with no retained entitlement is not sufficient to require inclusion, but those cases are not common. To illustrate, in Goethe v. United States[98] the court determined that the taxpayer did not inappropriately retain possession or enjoyment of transferred property, notwithstanding the taxpayer's continued collection of the income from that property, because the income was an appropriate payment for services rendered by the taxpayer.[99] More common are cases like Estate of Wedum v. Commissioner,[100] in which the decedent established irrevocable inter vivos trusts

---

[96] See § 14.3.2.2 n.70 and accompanying text for the amount includible in a charitable split interest trust in which the settlor retained an annuity or unitrust amount; quaere whether the same amount would be includible if a settlor dies during a retained qualified interest under § 2702, as discussed in § 7.2.2.2.

[97] 29 T.C. 1179 (1958), aff'd, 265 F.2d 667 (3d Cir. 1959).

[98] 56-1 U.S. Tax Cas. (CCH) ¶ 11,609 (S.D. Fla. 1956).

[99] See also TAM 8821005, which involved a decedent who transferred real estate inter vivos to a family partnership as a capital contribution. Under the partnership agreement the decedent was entitled to net cash receipts attributable to the rental of capital assets, which was tantamount to a retained right to the income from the transferred property. If the transfer was donative, then the property would be includible in the decedent's gross estate under § 2036(a)(1), an issue the TAM left for ultimate determination by the District Director.

[100] 51 T.C.M. (CCH) 1225, 1231 (1986). Estate of Wedum v. Commissioner, 57 T.C.M. (CCH) 219 (1989), subsequently determined that the trust property was includible and further addressed an ancillary issue:

> Decedent transferred his property into trust but violated his fiduciary duties as trustee by using the trust property as his own. Each beneficiary had a personal claim against him at his death for the amount of the converted assets .... To allow a deduction to the estate for the amount of the property legally belonging to the trust beneficiaries but enjoyed by

with no retained beneficial interest but there was evidence that trust assets were retained in an account over which the decedent had sole signatory authority. The court agreed that a retention of possession or enjoyment of property may be inferred from circumstances surrounding a transfer and the way in which the transferred property is used. There may be an informal agreement by which the decedent was to retain possession or enjoyment of the assets and "[t]he existence of such an agreement or understanding would be sufficient to cause the value of the property to be includible in [the] decedent's gross estate under section 2036(a)(1)."

§ 7.3.4.1.1 *Failure to Respect Entity*

The government has enjoyed some § 2036(a)(1) success in areas of abuse involving entities such as FLPs or LLCs created to generate valuation discounts for gift tax and FET purposes, if the taxpayer fails to respect the underlying entity. In these cases the government and the courts may not respect an entity that the client did not respect. In a long and growing line of cases the government has scored victories under § 2036(a)(1) by causing inclusion of property transferred by the decedent into a discount entity FLP because the decedent's history of dealing with the entity and the properties transferred belied a complete relinquishment for transfer tax purposes.[101]

Frequent bad facts include that a decedent • of advanced age or poor health • transferred virtually all of the decedent's assets to the entity, • lack of contributions by other purported partners, • the decedent "standing on all sides of the transaction" and the transaction not being conducted in a way in which unrelated parties to a business

---

(Footnote Continued)

[the] decedent as his own would emasculate section 2036. We believe section 2053(c) specifically forecloses deductibility of the beneficiaries' claims because the beneficiaries provided no consideration in money or money's worth for the assets in the trusts . . . .

57 T.C.M. at 227 (footnotes omitted). It might have been more accurate to say that § 2036(a)(1) retention of the enjoyment or possession meant the decedent was entitled to the property and the beneficiaries therefore had no cause of action.

[101] See the exegesis of cases cited in Casner & Pennell, Estate Planning § 7.3.4.1 (6th ed.).

§ 7.3.4.1.1

transaction would deal with each other, • drafting glitches, • mangled dates and backdating, • delays in funding, • commingling of personal funds, • backwashing of funds or postmortem payment of the taxpayer's debts, administration expenses, and taxes, • the lack of appraisals supporting values asserted, • discounting the value of interests in the entity relative to the value of the property contributed, • mistakes in partner contributions, distributions, and capital accounts, • faulty compliance, • use of the entity's checking account as a personal account, • personal receipt of rental income from transferred property, • living rent-free in a personal residence that was transferred to the entity, • the taxpayer's financial dependence on distributions from the entity, and other indicators of • a lack of any meaningful change in the taxpayer's relation to the assets allegedly transferred. In some cases • failure to change investment strategies was critical, because an alleged reason for the entity was to permit forms of otherwise unavailable investments. In others the • lack of separate representation or negotiation among the partners also was an important factor.

A second category of discount entity cases involves taxpayers who dot every I and cross every T but still are precluded from using the entity to generate valuation discounts. The government successfully applies §2036(a) to ignore the entity and value the underlying assets as if they were not held in the entity. Estate of Bongard v. Commissioner[102] essentially established the test that informs the vast majority of these cases going forward. The basic concept is that §2036 will not apply if the full-and-adequate consideration exception is met. Here is what *Bongard* said about that:

> In the context of family limited partnerships, the bona fide sale for adequate and full consideration exception is met where the record establishes the existence of a legitimate and significant nontax reason for creating the family limited partnership, and the transferors received partnership interests proportionate to the value of the property transferred. The objective evidence must indicate that the nontax reason was a significant factor that

---

[102] 124 T.C. 95 (2005) (a 13-to-4 reviewed opinion favoring the government, with ten judges signing the majority opinion, one judge concurring in the majority result without opinion, two judges concurring in that result with a separate opinion, and two dissenting opinions representing the views of four judges; only Judge Cohen was not accounted for on any opinion).

motivated the partnership's creation. A significant purposes must be an actual motivation, not a theoretical justification.

By contrast, the bona fide sale exception is not applicable where the facts fail to establish that the transaction was motivated by a legitimate and significant nontax purpose. A list of factors that support such a finding includes the taxpayer standing on both sides of the transaction; the taxpayer's financial dependence on distributions from the partnership; the partners' commingling of partnership funds with their own; and the taxpayer's actual failure to transfer the property to the partnership.

Notice that *business* reasons were not required—only "nontax" purposes ("significant and legitimate" being the only adjectives used) but elsewhere *Bongard* referenced both business and nontax purposes when evaluating whether the entity met the full and adequate consideration exception.[103]

An additional factor that receives less attention is revealed by Tax Court Judge Nims, who rejected the full and adequate consideration exception in Estate of Harper v. Commissioner,[104] saying that it requires "a bona fide sale, meaning an arm's-length transaction," as well as full and adequate consideration. The court held that creation "falls short of meeting the bona fide sale requirement" because the decedent controlled all aspects of the creation and operation of the entity.

---

[103] Other cases have alluded to a business purpose element. Indeed, Judge Laro's concurring opinion in *Bongard* said the full and adequate consideration exception would be met if the transfer was "an ordinary commercial transaction . . . made with a business purpose or, in other words, a 'useful nontax purpose . . . '." In Estate of Rosen v. Commissioner, 91 T.C.M. (CCH) 1220 (2006), Judge Laro stated the test in this manner: "We must find that the reason was an important one that actually motivated the formation of the partnership from a business point of view." On appeal in Estate of Bigelow v. Commissioner, 503 F.3d 955 (9th Cir. 2007), the court morphed the test slightly again thusly: "The crux of the bona fide transfer inquiry is whether the taxpayer can demonstrate that the transfer had 'legitimate and significant non-tax reasons)." But then in deciding the case against the taxpayer the court's conclusion was that the Tax Court was correct in finding "the inter vivos transfer . . . was not executed for any legitimate, significant non-tax related business purpose based on objective criteria that would have informed the partners . . . if they had been operating at arm's length." In Estate of Rector v. Commissioner, 94 T.C.M. (CCH) 567 (2007), Judge Laro said it thus: "good faith requires that the transfer be made for a legitimate and significant nontax business purpose."

[104] 83 T.C.M. (CCH) 1641 (2002).

§ 7.3.4.1.1

> It would be an oxymoron to say that one can engage in an arm's-length transaction with oneself, and we simply are unable to find any other independent party involved in the creation of [the partnership].... Without any change whatsoever in the underlying pool of assets or prospect for profit, as, for example, where others make contributions of property or services in the interest of true joint ownership or enterprise, there exists nothing but a circuitous "recycling" of value. We are satisfied that such instances of pure recycling do not rise to the level of a payment of consideration.

Bongard cited this "recycling of value" notion with approval, saying that all the decedent did was change the form but not the substance of the property ownership and relied on *Harper* to find that the transfer therefore failed the bona fide sale exception.

Tax Court Judge Jacobs in Estate of Thompson v. Commissioner[105] raised a different impediment to the taxpayer's reliance on the full and adequate consideration exception, notwithstanding that it appears to improperly conflate the Treas. Reg. § 25.2512-8 *business transaction exception* to the gift tax itself (no transfer for less than full and adequate consideration in money or money's worth is a gift if it is an arm's length business transaction free of donative intent) with the *full and adequate consideration exception* to § 2036(a). "[W]here a transaction involves only the genre of value 'recycling' and does not appear to be motivated primarily by legitimate business concerns, no transfer for consideration within the meaning of [§ 2036(a)] has taken place." The full and adequate consideration exception was rejected because none of the individual partners was involved in the conduct of an active business, they did not actually pool assets in a business enterprise with the decedent, there was no substantial change in investment strategy or activity, the partners did not conduct the partnerships in a businesslike manner, and the partnership did not engage in transactions with anyone outside the family or for business purposes.

The gift tax business transaction exception does not require a business, nor does the full and adequate consideration exception to § 2036(a). Rather, the former is about a "sale, exchange, or other transfer of property made in the ordinary course of business (a transaction which is bona fide, at arm's length, and free from any donative intent)" and

---

[105] 84 T.C.M. (CCH) 374 (2002), aff'd, 382 F.3d 367 (3d Cir. 2004).

there are plenty of intrafamily transactions that are not at arm's length and are not bona fide business transactions that still qualify for the full and adequate consideration exception to § 2036(a)(1). A sale in exchange for a private annuity or a sale to a IDGT are obvious examples. *Bongard* said that an arm's length transaction is one between two parties conducted *as if* they were strangers. This test does not require unrelated parties. Rather, the record simply must show that unrelated parties would have agreed to the same terms and conditions, negotiating at arm's length.

As this short exegesis reveals, the jurisprudence on this score involving discount entities is confused. Courts struggle in each case with the full and adequate consideration exception. *Thompson* said "[w]here . . . the . . . partnership does not operate legitimate business . . . there is no transfer for consideration" for these purposes. It is not clear why a business purpose informs a transfer for consideration, which would exist if two taxpayers merely swapped Blackacre for Greenacre of equal values. All of which generates a dizzy headache because these cases have so many either wrong or (at a minimum) inconsistent statements within them. Yet a few clear conclusions can be stated.

For example, one cogent message is that entities must be created and managed properly. Another is that the full and adequate consideration exception is focused on a diminution in net worth determination. To wit: if Blackacre and Greenacre are of equal value, and two parties choose to exchange them, there is no reason for the wealth transfer tax to apply in any respect—neither gift tax inter vivos nor FET string provisions at death—because neither taxpayer has caused a reduction in their net worth by virtue of their exchange. This would be true even if, for whatever reason, one party allowed the other to retain the right to control the enjoyment of both assets. That retained control might actually increase the controlling transferor's net worth, but this transfer with retained control is of no concern to the wealth transfer tax. It is only when an inter vivos transfer *diminishes* the transferor's net worth that the gift tax or any of the estate tax string provision rules is needed to protect the fisc. Thus, retained enjoyment or control in a full and adequate consideration transfer is irrelevant, and the critical inquiry is whether the transfer reduced the transferor's net worth.

§7.3.4.1.1

In commercially reasonable transactions, the government is not seeking to cause an innocent business start-up to be regarded as a gift just because contributions into the business are worth more than equity interests taken in exchange, especially when those interests are valued under a traditional willing-buyer, willing-seller test. In a typical start up business transaction an individual transfers cash or other assets in exchange for restricted business interests, based on financial considerations other than the mere ability to sell the new interest for the same amount that was contributed to the entity. The notion that taxpayers transfer assets into start up business entities in exchange for interests that are objectively worth less than what they transfer is explained by the "intrinsic" value of the investment to the transferor, based on expectations for business success. One way to explain why this transfer or exchange is not subject to transfer taxation is to apply the business transaction exception to test whether the transfer was bona fide, at arm's length, and free of donative intent. That, however, is different from saying that a business exchange entails full and adequate consideration. In fact, the test being applied in the discount entity cases is an invention by courts that were in need of a theory upon which to deny abusive valuation discounts. Theoretically the whole concept is flawed.

The concept that appears to be developing entails refinement of the particular "test" being applied, in terms of what the courts are looking for and the types of facts or factors that might establish the kind of legitimate, significant, business, nontax, or other kind of distinction between legitimate planning and inappropriate tax minimization. No one yet can do more than guess at what might suffice, especially because the myriad factors involved in these cases is a different mix in each. This is a facts and circumstances test—a subjective analysis (notwithstanding statements to the contrary in several opinions)[106]—and there is yet no way to

---

106 See, e.g., Estate of Strangi v. Commissioner, 85 T.C.M. (CCH) 1331 (2003) (Strangi II):

> [A] sale is bona fide if, as an objective matter, it serves a "substantial business [or] other non-tax" purpose. . . . Congress has foreclosed the possibility of determining the purpose of a given transaction based on findings as to the subjective motive of the transferor. Instead, the proper inquiry is whether the transfer in question was objectively likely to serve a substantial non-tax purpose. Thus, the finder of fact is charged with

establish a checklist or "best reasons" kind of summary of the things that will succeed.

Indeed, it may be the folly of seeking bright lines to ask "what business purposes will suffice," because at the end of the day courts appear to be opening the taxpayer's file and flipping through all the pages to see if the propriety of the planning is plainly apparent or whether the reasons propounded merely attempt to mask an abuse. It ought to be clear to an objective observer that the entity used was the right plan under the circumstances—a judge, for example, should be able to peruse the file and say "oh, sure, I understand why this approach made sense," without regard to any tax motives or saving that might *also* flow. Trying to cobble together a check list of possible successful motives is likely to be perceived as just sprinkling cologne on illegitimate planning. Indeed, trying to dress up what otherwise would be legitimate planning to make sure it will pass muster may actually hurt a taxpayer, by burying a perfectly legitimate case under layers of cosmetics that sully rather than improve the appearance of the situation.

Thus said, there is no uniformity in the approach that the courts are following. There is a clear trend, but Judge Halpern in his dissent to *Bongard* concluded that "the majority has strayed from the traditional interpretation of the bona fide sale exception by incorporating . . . an inappropriate motive test ('a legitimate and significant nontax reason'), and by concluding that a partnership interest proportionate' to the value of the property transferred constitutes adequate and full consideration in money or money's worth," which confirms that courts struggle to preclude abuse while employing traditional precedent without creating inappropriate consequences to legitimate businesses.

The critical component in all this mess is the bona fides of a legitimate entity, rather than a "wrapper" designed to do nothing other than fabricate valuation discounts generally. The courts are savvy about the distinction between what *Bongard* called "the true nontax reasons for [an] entity's formation [and] those that merely clothe transfer tax saving motives. Legitimate nontax purposes are often inextricably interwoven with testamentary objectives." *Rosen* said it thus: "The reason must be an

---

(Footnote Continued)

   making an objective determination as to what, if any, non-tax business purposes the transfer was reasonably likely to serve at its inception.

§7.3.4.1.1

actual motivation, not a theoretical justification, for a limited partnership's formation." What that means remains to be established, but several taxpayer victories reveal situations in which the government probably never should have sought to make a case, because the realities as finally uncovered are so unlike the manipulations found in more common abuse cases.

By way of example, in the *Stone* consolidated cases[107] involving the estates of spouses who died within less than 17 months of each other, the evidence disclosed FLPs created primarily to resolve protracted squabbling by the couple's children, and not to gin up valuation discounts.

The taxpayers' children battled with such severity that relations between the family business and both customers and suppliers became strained and potentially imperiled. One plan to resolve their controversy was proposed but cratered. Two years later the parents hired a lawyer who held a dozen different meetings and prepared five rounds of partnership drafts that circulated among the children and each of their separate independent counselors, who generated numerous changes in the agreements.

Each child became the sole second-generation partner with the decedents in separate partnerships that divvied up particular assets in which each child had a particular interest. A fifth partnership essentially held the family crown jewel asset. Not all of the decedents' assets went into these five partnerships. Accountants worked with the decedents' attorney to calculate (using different income yield and life expectancy factors) the amount of wealth the decedents needed to retain to maintain their accustomed life styles. The court specifically found that the *Stone* taxpayers intentionally and carefully estimated their needs and retained adequate independent assets.

The court held that transfers into the partnerships were made for adequate and full consideration in money or money's worth, which quashed every part of the government's case. The court also concluded that these were bona fide agreements reached at arm's length, with each party to the transactions being separately represented.

---

[107] 86 T.C.M. (CCH) 551 (2003).

The court also found that the taxpayers did more than "change the form in which [they] held [the] beneficial interest in the contributed property" and that the five partnerships "had economic substance and operated as joint enterprises for profit," such that each child was an active participant with respect to management of the respective assets that each child cared about. It also held that there was a legitimate pooling of assets with a joint enterprise expectation and profit motive.

Estate of Murphy v. United States[108] may be the most reasonable taxpayer victory in all the cases decided to date. The Murphy family had a history dating back to 1937 of pooling resources, using partnerships to own and operate active businesses, with multiple generations of family members actively involved in managing entities. The plan was designed to insulate family business assets from the fallout consequences of the dysfunction of two black sheep children, who engaged in misadventures, detrimental behavior, and conflict with their two successful siblings. Crafted over a long time period, the taxpayer retained over 50% of his wealth outside the partnership, did not commingle personal wealth with partnership assets, was in good health, and lived an active retirement lifestyle for half a decade after creation of the partnership.

The two successful children were involved in the planning (and one was independently represented), and they made legitimate contributions (not of acquired consideration) to the partnership, which operated several active businesses, bought and sold assets, hired and managed employees, prepared and disseminated financial statements, had bi-monthly partner meetings, filed tax returns, maintained bank accounts, and exhibited all the earmarks of a real, actively managed business. This

---

[108] 2009-2 U.S. Tax Cas. (CCH) ¶ 60,583 (W.D. Ark. 2009).

Similar is Estate of Kelly v. Commissioner, 103 T.C.M. (CCH) 1393 (2012), in which limited liability entities were formed to manage primary assets (27 parcels of real estate) that posed inherent risks of liability (including two active rock quarries), partnerships formed by court order (the decedent was suffering from Alzheimer's dementia), by children who determined to share the decedent's estate equally notwithstanding provisions in the decedent's will that would have caused inequities among them due to valuation fluctuations since that will was executed; over $1 million of liquid property was held outside of the partnerships, the children met regularly and kept minutes of their meetings as managers of the corporate general partner and worked over 60 hours per week in actively managing the family businesses.

§7.3.4.1.1

was not a wrapper inside which the family placed its dwelling and passive portfolio investments. The court found legitimate and significant nontax purposes for creation of the partnership to (1) pool assets for centralized management,[109] (2) more easily transition management to responsible members of the next generation, (3) make transfers to and educate donees about wealth management and preservation, and (4) protect against black sheep family-member misadventures and profligacy.

Estate of Schutt v. Commissioner[110] thrice reminded readers of "the unique circumstances of this case," probably signaling that the decision therefore is not predictive of the result to expect in other cases. Among the salient facts was that the decedent had a 30 year relationship with the planning attorney, the significant nontax purpose involved was a buy-and-hold investment philosophy supported by a 20 year documented record of intent (and one that likely is the opposite of what good investment advisors would recommend today but that the decedent strenuously wanted to force on family legacy assets that he did not have the power to control). The planning involved an independent third party (a corporate trustee) that was not under the decedent's control, that was separately represented, and that very carefully evaluated its potential for liability from engaging in the transaction, which itself took over 13 months to structure and accomplish, with numerous conferences, memoranda, drafts, and indemnifications from living beneficiaries of the three affected family trusts. Funding of the discount entity was timely and proper, all the appropriate forms were correctly completed, and distributions following creation were carefully monitored, periodic, timely, and made pro rata. There was no commingling of assets or personal use by contributors, and the decedent withheld approximately $30 million of his own wealth to avoid the need to invade the entity for his support.

Tax aspects did not predominate in either the taxpayer's focus or selection of the mechanism employed, and the fact that the portfolio was untraded following creation was appropriate only because the objective

---

[109] A similar result was reached in Estate of Shurtz v. Commissioner, 99 T.C.M. (CCH) 1096 (2010), in which at least 14 family members owned undivided timber interests that made their active management (planting, thinning, pest control, road management, harvest, and reforestation) more difficult.

[110] 89 T.C.M. (CCH) 1353 (2005).

§7.3.4.1.1

of the planning was the decedent's desire to impose dead hand restraints on future family generations. This lack of trading activity often scuttles other cases, and the notion that the decedent was motivated to accomplish real control over property that was not his to govern is a distinction that likely differentiates *Schutt* from most situations.

Like *Schutt*, Estate of Black v. Commissioner[111] involved publicly traded stock and the taxpayer's buy-and-hold investment strategy. According to the court, the FLP "did not conduct an active trade or business" and the court acknowledged "that a family limited partnership that does not conduct an active trade or business may nonetheless be formed for a legitimate and significant nontax reason." The company was not widely owned, however,[112] and the business itself was an active operating company in which the taxpayer had been a principal for over 60 years, which made his buy-and-hold philosophy different in significance than in many cases. The partnership also owned commercial realty that was used in an active insurance agency that the family operated and that also was owned by the partnership. Thus, notwithstanding the court's statement that an active trade or business is not critical, this was not a generic passive-investment portfolio situation. The partnership was not end-of-life scramble planning, and concerns about a child's marriage (which ended in divorce after the decedent's death) and about two adult grandchildren constituted legitimate and significant nontax reasons for the partnership. In addition, the buy-and-hold investment philosophy was proven wise by a valuation increase from about $80 million to nearly $320 million.

Estate of Mirowski v. Commissioner[113] involved creation of an LLC when the taxpayer was only 73 and not expected to die. The planning process began years earlier and followed a proposal that was introduced to the taxpayer over 15 months before she died. It involved documents prepared in draft form over a year before her death, which she shared with her primary beneficiaries, who waited to decide whether to embrace the plan until an annual family meeting that was scheduled for nearly a year later (in the month prior to the decedent's death).This

---

[111] 133 T.C. 15 (2009).

[112] The taxpayer's family owned nearly 14% of the stock and the founder's family owned over 76%.

[113] 95 T.C.M. (CCH) 1277 (2008).

§ 7.3.4.1.1

chronology was a strong indicator that no one expected the decedent to die so quickly. It also underscored the court's determination that one significant reason for the entity itself was to involve the decedent's family in a collective endeavor. The decedent retained more than enough personal assets to meet her living expenses and expected significant income distributions from the LLC (which was receiving substantial revenue from a patent license agreement).

The court said that "potential tax benefits were not the most significant factor" and, without saying as much, confirms that the "legitimate and significant nontax reasons" standard is subjective, a smell test, not an objective or a legal standard, meaning that there is less predictability in determining whether a particular circumstance will resonate with or satisfy a court. In essence, there is no "bright line test"—the unique facts and circumstances of every case are critical, which places great significance on trial preparation, credibility of witnesses, telltales that bespeak true motives and bona fides as opposed to make-believe and make-weight reasons dummied up for popular consumption. Markers and the aroma that emanates from a matter will better explain cases than any specific rationale, rule, or standard. The reasons indicating that the test was met in one case may not suffice in another case. The bottom line is that this is not an objective standard or test, with a defined or even a definable meaning. The only predictably successful cases are those with an active trade or business—not just a basket full of alleged nontax reasons for the entity—and a legitimate profit motive that is enhanced by the chosen entity. Shy of those kinds of bona fides, it is anyone's guess what will come of such planning. Finally, note that the most recent government challenges to discount entity planning have been under § 2703, in which a business purpose test clearly applies.[114]

§ 7.3.4.1.2 *Personal Use Assets*

The most common circumstance in which a § 2036(a)(1) implied retention is found involves transfers of personal use assets, most frequently a personal residence. In this respect, not much different from

---

[114] See § 15.3.1.2.2.

the easy case in which possession is an expressly retained right[115] are those in which there is no expressed retention but the decedent nevertheless remained in exclusive possession until death.[116] In these cases the implied agreement to retain possession is a difficult presumption for the taxpayer to disprove.[117] On occasion, however, continued exclusive

---

[115] See, e.g., National Bank of Commerce v. Henslee, 179 F. Supp. 346 (M.D. Tenn. 1959) (family residence transferred to trust with retained right to remain in possession).

[116] Estate of Adler v. Commissioner, 101 T.C.M. (CCH) 1118 (2011) (the taxpayer retained exclusive use of transferred property for life, paid all of the taxes and expenses for upkeep, and did not pay rent); Estate of Rapelje v. Commissioner, 73 T.C. 82, 88 (1979) (not quite exclusive possession, the court stating that "with the exception of the change in the record title the gift of the property did not effect any substantial changes in the relationship of the parties to the residence. Thus, we find that there was an implied understanding between the parties arising contemporaneously with the transfer whereby the decedent was allowed to retain possession or enjoyment of the residence for a period which did not in fact end before his death"); Estate of Honigman v. Commissioner, 66 T.C. 1080 (1976); Estate of Hendry v. Commissioner, 62 T.C. 861 (1974); Estate of Kerdolff v. Commissioner, 57 T.C. 643 (1972); Estate of Linderme v. Commissioner, 52 T.C. 305 (1969); Estate of Trotter v. Commissioner, 82 T.C.M. (CCH) 633 (2001); Estate of Bianchi v. Commissioner, 44 T.C.M. (CCH) 422 (1982); Estate of Stubblefield v. Commissioner, 42 T.C.M. 342 (1981) (along with issues related to transfer of farmland with retained use for 13 years without rent and for 5 more with rent, decedent constructed a residence on land owned by a child that never was owned by the decedent and then resided in that residence until death, with the treatment being as a gift of the residence to the child with a retained life estate); Rev. Rul. 70-155, 1970-1 C.B. 189, 189 (transfer to child and child's spouse with an understanding that the transferor was going to live in the house until death; "The retained interest need not be stated in the instrument of transfer, nor need it be a legally enforceable right. An understanding or agreement, expressed or implied, as to the donor's retained use of the transferred property is sufficient"); TAM 7837003 (transfer of land to a corporation with continued use by transferor, who owned 56% of the stock; the other 44% was sold to decedent's descendants and, if for full and adequate consideration, was not subject to §2036(a)(1) inclusion, as if the property had been sold directly with the same retained life estate).

[117] Estate of Whitt v. Commissioner, 751 F.2d 1548 (11th Cir. 1985); Estate of Garner v. Commissioner, 44 T.C.M. (CCH) 903, 907 (1982) ("The burden of proof is on [the taxpayer] to establish that an implied agreement or understanding did not in fact exist. The burden is especially difficult in a case such as this where all objective evidence implies a pre-arrangement. Further, as we have

§7.3.4.1.2

residence will not result in inclusion, but the circumstances are not ordinary.

For example, in Estate of Powell v. Commissioner[118] the decedent had made several annual exclusion gifts of tenancy in common fractional interests in a personal residence to children and their spouses but still owned 40% of the residence at death. The decedent continued to live in the residence until shortly before death when it was necessary to move to an extended care facility. The decedent (and a revocable trust created by the decedent) paid the real estate taxes and all of the expense for maintenance and upkeep of the residence, and the donees never lived there. The court nevertheless found that the decedent did not retain an interest in the gifted portion and that there was no agreement regarding continued enjoyment that would cause § 2036(a)(1) inclusion. Instead, the decedent's continued possession of the entire property was not inconsistent with the rights of a tenant in common and differed from cases in which enjoyment of a gifted asset (such as a consumable) by one tenant in common precludes enjoyment by others.

By comparison, the taxpayer in Estate of Tehan v. Commissioner[119] attempted unsuccessfully to make such an argument following several years of similar fractional interest annual exclusion gifts. One critical distinction was that, by the time of death, the decedent had conveyed 100% ownership and had no remaining concurrent tenancy entitlement.

A third situation that raises more difficulty is the decedent making a transfer and continuing to reside in the property, but not alone. The difficult issue arises if the decedent continues to reside with a transferee who resided in the property when the transfer was made[120] or who

---

(Footnote Continued)

recognized, the task of disproving the existence of an agreement or understanding between family members is a heavy one.").

[118] 63 T.C.M. (CCH) 3192 (1992).

[119] 89 T.C.M. (CCH) 1374 (2005).

[120] See Estate of Callahan v. Commissioner, 42 T.C.M. (CCH) 362 (1981) (inclusion in the estate of a decedent who transferred a residence to a trust, retaining an undivided one-third interest in the trust property and remaining in possession of it); Rev. Rul. 78-409, 1978-2 C.B. 234 (inclusion notwithstanding transferee paid for upkeep of the property).

§ 7.3.4.1.2

moves into the property and allows the decedent to remain.[121] Most cases require inclusion, but this is not a universal result[122] and will not likely invoke inclusion if the transferee is the transferor's spouse, continued occupancy being regarded as a natural concomitant of marriage to the new property owner.[123] Nor is inclusion appropriate if retention of possession or enjoyment is for full and adequate consideration in the form of market rent.[124] But careful attention to the bona fides of the arrangement and rent paid is essential.

---

[121] In some of these cases the child is a caregiver who moves in with a parent, who transferred the dwelling as compensation for the child's agreement to allow the parent to remain in the home until death, rather than move to a nursing home or an extended care facility. The full and adequate consideration exception may apply based on the value of the child's care giving services.

[122] See Estate of Spruill v. Commissioner, 88 T.C. 1197 (1987) (decedent and decedent's spouse moved in with a child to whom they deeded a homesite and with whom they lived until the decedent died; no agreement or understanding, express or implied, was deemed to exist between the decedent and the child with respect to continued occupancy of the homesite); Estate of Roemer v. Commissioner, 46 T.C.M. (CCH) 1176 (1983) (parent and child resided together in a house owned by parent, which had been conveyed to a child; the court found no implied agreement and that the actions of both parties were consistent with a true transfer of ownership and continued occupancy with a family relative, rather than an implied retention pursuant to an agreement or understanding); City Nat'l Bank v. United States, 78-1 U.S. Tax Cas. (CCH) ¶ 13,219 (D. Conn. 1977); Diehl v. United States, 68-1 U.S. Tax Cas. (CCH) ¶ 12,506 (W.D. Tenn. 1967).

[123] Union Planters Nat'l Bank v. United States, 361 F.2d 662 (6th Cir. 1966); Estate of Binkley v. United States, 358 F.2d 639 (3d Cir. 1966); Estate of Gutchess v. Commissioner, 46 T.C. 554 (1966); Rev. Rul. 70-155, 1970-1 C.B. 189, 189 (if the transferor and transferee are spouses the continued co-occupancy of the residence by the transferor "does not of itself support an inference of an agreement or understanding as to retained possession or enjoyment by the donor").

[124] Estate of Barlow v. Commissioner, 55 T.C. 666, 671 (1971), acq., 1972-2 C.B. 1 (gift of land to children who immediately leased it back for a reasonable rent; there was "no evidence whatever of a contemporaneous agreement, oral or written, express or implied, qualifying in any way the terms of the deed and lease"). In Estate of Riese v. Commissioner, 101 T.C.M. (CCH) 1269 (2011), the taxpayer's estate avoided § 2036(a)(1) inclusion even through the taxpayer remained in exclusive possession of a transferred residence and the parties never agreed upon a fair market rental, no lease was signed, and the remainder beneficiaries did not begin to pay property taxes, liability insurance premiums, or costs of upkeep and maintenance. Yet the court held that the parties intended

§ 7.3.4.1.2

For example, in *Tehan* the parties also agreed at the outset that the decedent would retain sole and exclusive possession and would not pay rent but would be responsible for all carrying charges, such as mortgage payments and condominium homeowner assessments, real estate taxes, insurance premiums for the property, and all maintenance and repair costs. Rather than seeking to determine the rental value of the ownership interests already transferred and paying fair market rent for that portion, along with a pro rata share of the carrying charges and other periodic expenses of the retained portion, the parties' agreement made it undeniably clear to the court that the decedent retained § 2036(a)(1) possession and enjoyment.

Another example is Estate of Maxwell v. Commissioner,[125] which recharacterized an attempted sale of a personal residence to the dece-

---

(Footnote Continued)

that the taxpayer would pay rent and that there was no implied or explicit retention of enjoyment.

[125] 98 T.C. 594 (1992), aff'd, 3 F.3d 591 (2d Cir. 1993). See Disbrow v. Commissioner, 91 T.C.M. (CCH) 794 (2006), for another illustration that the existence of a lease will not necessarily salvage such a situation. The taxpayer transferred the residence into a partnership, then transferred by gift all interests in the partnership, but continued to reside in the residence until death. Although the taxpayer executed a lease and paid rent, the stated rent was less than half the fair rental value and the taxpayer paid most expenses, taxes, and other carrying charges related to the dwelling without regard to the true arm's length rental value of the property. In addition, the partnership, as landlord, failed to treat the taxpayer as it would an arm's length tenant, agreeing to accept rental payments late and in lesser amounts than the lease required. Testimony from partners (children and their spouses) made clear that the lease was a subterfuge and the court had no trouble finding the implied retention that triggered § 2036(a)(1) inclusion.

See also Estate of Stewart v. Commissioner, 617 F.3d 148 (2d Cir. 2010), vac'g and rem'g 92 T.C.M. 357 (2006), in which the decedent transferred a 49% interest in her dwelling to her son, who co-occupied the home with the decedent both before and after the transfer. The top three stories of the building were leased to a third party, the taxpayer and her son owned a second rental property, and the receipt of rents and payment of costs from the two properties did not mirror their respective ownership interests. The Tax Court agreed with the government's inclusion of the 49% interest in the dwelling as a transfer with retained enjoyment. The court on appeal affirmed the finding that an implied agreement existed but did not agree that 100% of the 49% interest transferred would be subject to § 2036(a)(1) inclusion. On remand, the Tax Court was

dent's only child with a lease back to the decedent as a transfer with a retained life estate that was not a bona fide sale for full and adequate consideration in money or money's worth. Nor was it a legitimate rental for purposes of avoiding § 2036(a)(1) inclusion. The decedent died during the term of the lease and no evidence indicated that the decedent (who had cancer and was 82 years old when the property was sold) reasonably could expect to outlive that term. Thus, the court found an express or implied understanding that possession was retained for life, causing inclusion of the full date of death FMV of the property in the decedent's gross estate. The determination of intent was unnecessary, because § 2036(a)(1) was triggered by the decedent being in possession or enjoyment of the property, which did not end before death. Although intent may speak to the bona fides of a sale, in this case the decedent made too many mistakes to substantiate a legitimate sale argument.

Among the *Maxwell* mistakes were that the sale price for the residence was $30,000 less than the appraised value of the property, the decedent taking a note from the child and treating $20,000 of the deficiency as annual exclusion gifts to the child and the child's spouse. Although the remaining $10,000 deficiency may have been meant to be covered by a cash down payment or the amount a broker would have received on a brokered sale, there was no evidence of any actual payment, nor was a broker involved. This alone would cause § 2036(a)(1) inclusion because there is no exception for sales for consideration that is less than full and adequate. Moreover, each year after the transfer the child's note was reduced by $20,000 (again, purportedly tax free under the gift tax annual exclusion). The child only paid interest on the note, and that only in an amount roughly equal to the rent paid by the decedent to the child for the right to continue living in the residence. All these facts caused the court to conclude that the parties' economic situation did not change meaningfully under the transaction and that the parties never intended that the child would pay the note. As a result, the note was deemed to have no value from the outset, and it therefore did

---

(Footnote Continued)

instructed to "make the factual determinations necessary to determine the amount of the net income from [the son's] 49% interest enjoyed by Decedent. Then the Tax Court can calculate the 'corresponding proportion' of 'the value of the entire property,' and include it in the Decedent's gross estate" under § 2036(a)(1).

§ 7.3.4.1.2

not represent full and adequate consideration in money or money's worth to avoid §2036(a)(1) inclusion.

Finally, of a different ilk than the personal use asset cases but involving the same principle was Estate of Abraham v. Commissioner,[126] which originally appeared to be a garden-variety discount entity case but, on appeal, was revealed to be a classic situation in which the taxpayer made inter vivos transfers (in this case the not-so-common second-step transfer of interests received upon creation of the entity) to children who, by their own testimony, had agreed that income from the transferred interests would be used for the decedent's exclusive benefit to the fullest extent needed. Direct testimony made clear that nothing was meant to change prior to the decedent's death. Very few specific facts were given in the *Abraham* opinion below, that testimony apparently being persuasive to the Tax Court about the §2036(a)(1) implied retention of enjoyment.

§7.3.4.2 Discretionary, Expectant, or Unanticipated Interests

Retention of enjoyment or possession of transferred property may be implied, inadvertent, or unintentional, and it may be revealed by the circumstances or conduct of the parties.[127] But §2036(a)(1) may apply even if the transferor has done everything possible to divest ownership and enjoyment of transferred property, if what the transferor does possess or retain rises to the level of a right or entitlement. The notion of an affirmative retention and an enforceable entitlement is addressed most directly in a context that is not commonplace but the principle established may have a broader application.

Involved is the law in some community property jurisdictions that income from the separate property of one spouse is the community property of both spouses. The potential for application of §2036(a)(1) is triggered by a transfer from one spouse to the other of income producing property that constitutes the donee spouse's separate property but the income from which is shared by the donor and donee spouses as community property.

---

[126] 87 T.C.M. (CCH) 975 (2004), aff'd, 408 F.3d 26 (1st Cir. 2005).

[127] See §7.3.4.1.

§7.3.4.2

The government's original position was that the income from this separate property "may be placed under the donee-spouse's exclusive control and may be exempted from liabilities created by the donor-spouse, but the ownership interest of the donor-spouse in that income cannot be eliminated." Therefore, the government asserted that the gifted property was includible in the donor spouse's gross estate under §2036(a)(1).[128] Ultimately that position was rejected, the courts holding that

> the interest of the donor spouse in the income produced by the property transferred to the donee spouse is neither 'retained' within the meaning of [§2036(a)(1)], nor arisen 'under' the transfers concerned. . . . [Rather, it] is so limited, contingent, and expectant that it does not amount to a 'right to income' . . . . [Therefore,] we have sought to lay the Government's position to rest, once and for all.[129]

Eventually the government retreated from this position.[130]

Outside this community property context, however, the notion that a transferor must possess or retain more than an inchoate interest—it must approach a right or entitlement and not be a mere expectancy—is a difficult concept to embrace, and its parameters have defied description

---

[128] Rev. Rul. 75-504, 1975-2 C.B. 363, 364.

[129] Estate of Wyly v. Commissioner, 610 F.2d 1282, 1290, 1295 (5th Cir. 1980) (a consolidated case reversing lower court decisions in Estate of Wyly and Estate of Castleberry v. Commissioner, 68 T.C. 682 (1977), and affirming the lower court in Frankel v. United States, an unreported district court decision granting partial summary judgment to the taxpayer). See also Commissioner v. Estate of Hinds, 180 F.2d 930, 932 (5th Cir. 1950) ("whether the income be regarded as separate property of the [donee] or as community income from the [donee's] separate property, the taxpayer retained neither 'the possession or enjoyment of, or the right to the income from,' the property so as to make applicable" the predecessor to §2036(a)(1)); Estate of Deobald v. United States, 444 F. Supp. 374, 383 (E.D. La. 1977) ("to carry the government's legal contentions to their logical conclusion . . . would . . . be declaring that a husband and wife . . . living under a community property regime could never make a bona fide transfer to each other where the grantor absolutely, unequivocally, and irrevocably parts with all of his title, possession, and enjoyment of income-bearing community or separate property . . . even where the [donor] has done everything unilaterally possible to make a complete gift . . ."); Pearson v. Campbell, 62-2 U.S. Tax Cas. (CCH) ¶ 12,120 (N.D. Tex. 1962).

[130] Rev. Rul. 81-221, 1981-2 C.B. 178; TAM 8111018.

§7.3.4.2

in several other contexts. For example, a much more difficult setting in which this issue arises involves a transferor's intentionally retained discretionary interest in a trust that, albeit enforceable, is not ascertainable or quantifiable.[131]

Before reading the following summary of prior authority, review the description of Revenue Ruling 2004-64 in §5.11.9 n.245. The critical element of that Ruling (issued in the context of a IDGT income tax reimbursement provision) is the government distinction between a mandatory entitlement and authority in the trustee to make discretionary distributions. The Ruling held that the discretionary interest does not rise to the level of the entitlement needed to trigger §2036(a)(1) inclusion, but there are three caveats in the Ruling. One applies if the settlor may remove the trustee and become the successor, which effectively means the settlor may possess the trustee's powers at any time. A second exists if there was any understanding or agreement relating to the trustee's exercise of the discretion, which is tantamount to saying the "discretion" is something more, like an entitlement.

The third is important to this discussion because it relates to the ability of the settlor's creditors to reach the trust corpus under normal spendthrift trust rules, which (as the following discussion reveals) is a surrogate for saying the settlor has a sufficient indirect interest in the trust for §2036(a)(1) to apply. Subject to this third caveat, however, the Ruling provides that the settlor's opportunity to receive distributions in the trustee's legitimate independent discretion is benign for §2036(a)(1) purposes. Judge in reading the following material whether this Ruling breaks new ground, establishes a position already well established by prior authority, or is an irrelevancy. Also note that nothing in that Ruling spoke to §§2036(a)(2) or 2038(a)(1) inclusion.

---

[131] See, e.g., PLR 7838042, which held that the release of all interests in a trust by a beneficiary to whom discretionary income could be paid in the trustee's absolute discretion had no value for gift tax purposes, stating that normally such a release of rights would be a taxable event but, "in this case, the putative donor's rights are too speculative in nature to be valued. It cannot be said that she has transferred anything of value. Therefore she can release her rights in the trust without making a taxable gift." Although the beneficiary was not the grantor, it nevertheless may be proper to argue that these rights have no quantifiable value in any situation.

Relevant to the caveat in Revenue Ruling 2004-64 (and potentially the reason why that caveat swallows the otherwise favorable rule that the government may have announced) is the reality that a settlor's interest in a self-settled trust is subject to creditor claims in most American jurisdictions.[132] This makes it easy to conclude that the trust property should be regarded as if it still belonged to the settlor for wealth transfer tax purposes and should be includible in the settlor's gross estate at death. The best explanation for this result is that the settlor may indirectly enjoy trust assets by running up debt that would be satisfied by creditors being paid from the trust. A more precise articulation of the rationale for inclusion attributable to creditor rights, however, is that the ability to relegate creditors to trust assets is a § 2038(a)(1) power to indirectly revoke the trust, and not that it is an indirect § 2036(a)(1) right to enjoy trust income.

Contrary to the majority approach regarding self-settled spendthrift trusts, a number of states by statute grant creditor protection with respect to interests created in any trust beneficiary, *including the settlor*.[133] These statutes are intriguing in the context of the string provisions and, more specifically, § 2036(a)(1) because they raise the question whether the inability of a settlor's creditors to reach a retained discretionary trust interest means that the settlor did not retain sufficient enjoyment to avoid a completed inter vivos gift upon creation of the trust[134] or, more immediate to this discussion, to cause § 2036(a)(1) inclusion at death.

This is the proposition that Revenue Ruling 2004-64 appears to reflect. Under it, if the settlor incurs gift taxation upon creation and avoids FET at death, the result is to freeze the value of appreciating property by incurring the wealth transfer tax upon the lower gift tax value at the time of creation while retaining enjoyment in the trustee's discretion for the balance of the settlor's life. In historical context even the suggestion that this estate freeze might be the right result appears too good to be true, but case law historically has looked only to the rights of creditors in applying the string provisions.

---

[132] See § 4.1.4.

[133] See § 4.1.4 n.52 and accompanying text.

[134] See § 7.1.7.1.

§7.3.4.2

In this respect, the creditor entitlement test has been an easy answer to the degree of enjoyment question in those states that follow the majority rule that creditors may reach a settlor's retained discretionary interest. But prior to Revenue Ruling 2004-64 there was no direct answer to the question of how much enjoyment may be retained in the form of the ability to receive discretionary distributions without triggering § 2036(a)(1).

Furthermore, the creditors' rights approach is an inadequate surrogate for a more precise articulation of the degree of enjoyment that must be retained before § 2036(a)(1) is triggered.[135] Quaere whether it is anomalous for a settlor to retain the same degree of personal enjoyment in two different but identical trusts and have different § 2036(a)(1) inclusion results based on the applicable state law relating to creditor rights. Is it legitimate to regard the ability to incur debt and then relegate creditors to a judgment against a discretionary trust as adequate to trigger § 2036(a)(1)? Application of § 2036(a)(1) should turn on a consistent answer to the fundamental question of how much of a retained interest is sufficient to trigger § 2036(a)(1). Unless the creditor rights issue alone is enough in its own right, the answer to that question has not adequately been provided by case law or rulings prior to Revenue Ruling 2004-64, and may not yet be reliable.

Because this issue is bound to come to the courts, and because many misconceptions exist and misstatements have been made about

---

135 PLR 8829030 reveals the major difference between § § 2036(a)(1) and 2038(a)(1). The Ruling properly states that, absent creditor rights in the discretionary trust under state law, § 2038(a)(1) cannot apply unless there is an expressly retained power to alter, amend, revoke, or terminate the trust. Then it states that "we decline to rule whether [the settlors], with respect to property which they transferred to [the trust], retained interests therein which would necessitate the inclusion of the values in their respective gross estates pursuant to section 2036 . . . ." The important point is that § § 2036 and 2038 are separate on this issue, with § 2038 being the proper source of inclusion with respect to a creditor's right to reach the trust in satisfaction of a decedent's debts—which constitutes the settlor's indirect power to revoke the trust—and § 2036 being the proper section to address the naked discretionary income interest—which has nothing to do with creditor rights. To the extent courts talk about creditor rights in the context of § 2036 enjoyment they are using the easy surrogate of "creditor rights" for the more difficult issue of "what is sufficient enjoyment to trigger inclusion" in the context of a totally discretionary income interest.

existing authorities, a relatively detailed summary is provided here, illustrating that there is a less than reliable answer to the question. In large part this is because the courts have avoided the difficult inquiry of determining how much direct enjoyment ought to be adequate. In some cases the answer also has been clouded by a need to reach certain results to prevent total avoidance of the wealth transfer tax.[136] This issue may yet take more time to resolve, and there may be even more fits and starts as various authorities analyze the question.

For example, regarded by many as a critical authority, Estate of German v. United States[137] was a suit for refund of FET, apparently (but not expressly noted) assessed based on the government's conclusion that §§ 2036 and 2038 required inclusion of the value of property in a trust at the settlor's death. Involved was a discretionary income and principal trust,[138] as to which no gift was reported on creation, nor did the FET return include the property transferred to the trust. The government failed to establish whether creditors could reach the settlor's

---

[136] See, e.g., PLR 9332006. The result of this Ruling (completed gifts) probably was informed by the government's desire to impose wealth transfer tax immediately because offshore trusts were involved and the government may have felt there was a good risk that it would not be able to collect FET at death. Involved were facts that included discretionary entitlement and the absence of creditor rights. The Ruling concluded that "interests . . . transferred to the Trust by either Settlor will not be included in that Settlor's gross estate under sections 2036, 2037, or 2038, since under the facts presented, the Trustee's discretion to make distributions to a Settlor is not a retained interest or power for purposes of those sections. See Rev. Rul. 76-103." That conclusion was improper for a number of reasons. Rev. Rul. 76-103, 1976-1 C.B. 293, discussed in § 7.3.4.2 n.143, did not conclude that § 2036 would not apply, and its statement regarding § 2038 was dicta. Moreover, it did not deal with the lack of creditor rights nor whether a discretionary entitlement without creditor exposure would suffice to cause § 2036(a)(1) inclusion.

Similarly, PLR 8037116 involved a nonresident alien who created a trust deemed not subject to creditor rights with totally discretionary income and principal distribution authority in the trustee. It concluded that § 2036(a)(1) was not applicable. It relied, however, on *Uhl* and *Herzog*, discussed in notes 151 and 141, respectively, and the accompanying text, both of which are suspect today.

[137] 85-1 U.S. Tax Cas. (CCH) ¶ 13,610 (Ct. Cl. 1985).

[138] Distributions required the consent of an adverse party (a remainder beneficiary), but that consent alone would not preclude application of the string provisions. See § 7.3.3 n.51 and accompanying text.

§ 7.3.4.2

interest, the estate conceded that it owed gift tax on creation, and there is no record of any resolution of the substance of the controversy because this decision resulted only in denial of the government's motion for summary judgment and not a determination on the merits. There was no discussion of the §§ 2036 and 2038 inclusion issue. The court's discussion was of the gift tax completed transfer issue and the question of state law. As a result, *German* is not authority on the immediate question, notwithstanding that it probably is the leading case cited on the question.

Estate of Paxton v. Commissioner[139] was an abuse case involving a family/constitutional trust[140] created by the decedent inter vivos, as to which no gift tax was paid on creation nor was the corpus included for FET purposes. The court found that § 2036(a)(1) was applicable for two reasons. There was an express or implied understanding that the settlor would receive income or principal upon request, and the settlor retained an interest that creditors could reach,[141] which the court concluded to be sufficient to trigger § 2036(a)(1) inclusion. Several notable glitches in the case include the fact that § 2036(a)(1) would not apply with respect to a retained right to distributions of corpus,[142] so the opinion is not especially reassuring with respect to its analysis and application of the law, and the case should have been argued under § 2038(a)(1) with respect to the retained right to indirectly terminate the trust by relegating creditors to it for payment.[143] Most importantly, the case does not establish the

---

[139] 86 T.C. 785 (1986).

[140] See § 5.11 n.12.

[141] The court noted that Herzog v. Commissioner, 116 F.2d 591 (2d Cir. 1941), which held that New York creditors could not reach a trust of this nature, had changed by the time of this case, meaning that *Herzog* and cases relying on it may no longer be reliable precedent.

[142] See § 7.3.4.2 n.165.

[143] This point is supported but not clearly resolved by earlier authorities. See, e.g., Outwin v. Commissioner, 76 T.C. 153 (1981), which was a gift tax case in which the trustee had discretion to distribute income or principal to the settlor, again with the § 2036(a)(1) irrelevant approval of an adverse party (the settlor's spouse, who was a secondary beneficiary). The court concluded that the transfer into trust was not a completed gift for gift tax purposes because state law allowed creditors to reach the trust property. Because it is not an FET case, footnote 5 of the opinion is pure dicta but it does state that "[a]lthough the transfers in trust in these cases are not subject to gift tax, the settlor's ability to secure the economic

§ 7.3.4.2

contrary proposition, that if creditors could *not* reach the trust there would be no inclusion under either § 2036 or § 2038.

Estate of Wells v. Commissioner,[144] which also frequently is cited, never addressed the creditor rights issue. The decedent created a discretionary income and principal trust and filed a gift tax return.[145] The government probably lost the case by arguing that there was sufficient retained enjoyment for § 2036(a)(1) purposes merely because the decedent in fact received all the income for life. The court rejected that proposition, noting that the government did not assert that the decedent had a "right to the income" from the property but instead that § 2036(a)(1) was implicated simply by receipt of all the trust income.

On just this proposition the government was successful in Lee v. United States,[146] in which there was no evidence of an agreement but the

---

(Footnote Continued)

benefit of the trust assets by borrowing and relegating creditors to those assets for repayment may well trigger inclusion of the property in the settlor's gross estate under § § 2036(a)(1) or 2038(a)(1)."

Paolozzi v. Commissioner, 23 T.C. 182 (1954), also involved the gift tax and held that retention of discretionary income was adequate to prevent a completed gift because, under applicable local law, creditors had full recourse to the full trust income. As a consequence, the transferor was indirectly able to realize economic benefits from the trust by becoming indebted and relegating creditors to the trust for reimbursement. In most cases that possibility should be regarded as a disguised power to revoke the trust, which should be taxable under § 2038(a)(1). *Paolozzi* was unusual in that creditors only could reach trust income, which left only § 2036(a)(1) as an appropriate FET inclusion authority.

Rev. Rul. 76-103, 1976-1 C.B. 293, addressed only the gift tax consequences on creation of a discretionary income trust, and it properly held that the existence of creditor rights prevented a completed gift. In dicta it stated what should be the proper § 2038(a)(1) inclusion result if the grantor dies before the gift becomes complete, due to the indirect power to terminate the trust by relegating creditors to the trust for payment.

TAM 8213004 also confirms that § 2038(a)(1) is the proper section to address creditor rights and inclusion, finding that the absence of creditor rights under applicable local law precluded § 2038 inclusion. It did not address the § 2036(a)(1) issue and the conclusion reached was that a gift tax was owing on creation.

[144] 42 T.C.M. (CCH) 1305 (1981).

[145] Using her then $30,000 lifetime exemption to preclude creation of the trust from incurring gift tax.

[146] 86-1 U.S. Tax Cas. (CCH) ¶ 13,649 (W.D. Ky. 1985).

§ 7.3.4.2

court concluded that no agreement must be found, the decedent having in fact received all the income. But the *Wells* court rejected this proposition, correctly noting that enjoyment must be retained pursuant to an agreement or understanding, express or implied, entered into contemporaneously with the transfer of property to the trust, even if that agreement was not legally enforceable.[147] The court found the proof lacking on this element. The opinion therefore might be authority for the proposition that, absent creditor rights, § 2036(a)(1) will not cause inclusion in a discretionary income trust situation, but that was not the litigated issue and *Wells* does not answer the precise § 2036(a)(1) question.

Estate of Skinner v. United States[148] comes closer to answering the question, finding inclusion based on the decedent's expressly retained right to receive income in the trustee's discretion for the decedent's comfortable support and maintenance. The trial court was unwilling to conclude that the mere fact that income was paid to the settlor was a retention of enjoyment, but also concluded that there need not be a legally enforceable right to trust income. In affirming on appeal the court simply concluded that the trial court was not clearly erroneous in finding that there was an understanding that the trustee's discretion would be exercised exclusively in favor of the settlor for life. Nothing in *Skinner*

---

147 Compare Lettice v. United States, 237 F. Supp. 123, 123 (S.D. Cal. 1964), which involved the settlor of a trust that required the payment of $300 per month out of income "and in addition thereto the Trustees shall, in their absolute discretion use all or any part of the remaining income to provide suitable support, maintenance, comfort and enjoyment for Settlor." The government claimed that the word "enjoyment" meant that the trustee had to distribute any amount the settlor requested. The court concluded that, under controlling local law, a beneficiary does not have the right to demand anything if payments are to be made in the absolute discretion of the trustee, even though a standard is elaborated for the trustee. Thus, only that portion of the trust property that was needed to provide $300 per month was includible in the settlor's gross estate. In Estate of Green v. Commissioner, 64 T.C. 1049 (1975), however, authority to make distributions for the settlor's "happiness" was deemed to mean that the trustees had to pay the decedent whatever amount the settlor claimed was needed for happiness, and concluded that there was an understanding that the settlor would receive trust income, resulting in inclusion. With respect to the "absolute discretion" issue in *Lettice* see the statement of the majority rule that is contrary to the court's holding, as discussed in § 7.1.7.

148 316 F.2d 517 (3d Cir. 1963), decided under § 811(c)(1)(B)(i) of the 1939 Code.

supports the proposition that also was not resolved in *Wells*, that discretionary income is insufficient to require inclusion.

There was a lack of parity between the gift tax and FET in *Skinner*, the government asserting that creation of the trust was a completed gift of the full value of the trust corpus because the retained life enjoyment was not susceptible of accurate determination, and then successfully including the full value at death (with the appropriate § 2001(b) purge and credit for the gift tax previously collected). The result negates the suggestion that making a completed inter vivos gift is inconsistent with FET inclusion.

Yet Estate of Uhl v. Commissioner[149] curiously accepted the notion that the estate and gift tax results should be consistent. Having paid gift tax on creation with respect to that portion of the corpus that was not producing a retained $100 per month annuity payable to the settlor, the court concluded that there should be no FET inclusion of that portion.[150] Moreover, it made the palpably improper statement that the rights of creditors would not inform the decedent's FET liability because that right, if it existed, was the *creditors'* right and not that of the grantor. The court did conclude, however, that any portion of the trust over which the settlor had no control other than in the uncontrolled discretion in the trustee was not subject to retained enjoyment inclusion.[151] That is the § 2036(a)(1) issue and the result disfavors the government.

A third context in which the concept of an enforceable or ascertainable retained interest defies description or quantification involves a notion found throughout the regulations and that is virtually always wrong. If a trust requires that income be used for the support or maintenance of someone the settlor is legally obligated to support or maintain, the

---

[149] 241 F.2d 867 (7th Cir. 1957), also involving the precursor of § 2036(a)(1).

[150] Only by indirection did the court reveal that there was a discretionary income interest in that gift-taxed portion of the trust, and the court made reference to a failure on the government's part to prove the rights of creditors under state law.

[151] Given its vintage, the improper equation of the gift tax and FET treatment, and the notable glitch regarding creditor rights not equating with the decedent's enjoyment, *Uhl* may be regarded as slim precedent for the question whether a naked discretionary entitlement is adequate to cause § 2036(a)(1) inclusion at death.

§ 7.3.4.2

regulations[152] regard the settlor as having retained a § 2036(a)(1) right to that income.[153] If, however, the trust authorizes but does not require that income be distributed, then the sparse existing authority appears to recognize the reality of the prior discussion and—given that it is unclear whether *direct* enjoyment in a trustee's discretion is adequate to trigger § 2036(a)(1) inclusion—concludes that the settlor has not retained a sufficient *indirect* right to trust income for § 2036(a)(1) purposes.[154]

---

152 Treas. Reg. § 20.2036-1(b)(2).

153 See Commissioner v. Dwight's Estate, 205 F.2d 298 (2d Cir. 1953) (inclusion under § 811(c)(1)(B) of the 1939 Code, being the predecessor to § 2036(a)(1)); First Nat'l Bank v. United States, 211 F. Supp. 403 (M.D. Ala. 1962) (entire net income of a trust for the settlor's spouse was paid for "support and comfort" and then used to pay household and personal living expenses, which the court determined to discharge the settlor's legal obligation and therefore constituted the equivalent of § 2036(a)(1) reservation of the income); Estate of Gokey v. Commissioner, 72 T.C. 721, 722 (1979) (trust direction to use so much of the income "for the support, care, welfare, and education of the beneficiary," with "payments from such net income to be made to such beneficiary or in such manner as the trustee deems to be in the best interest of the beneficiary" was construed as a mandate to use trust income for the beneficiary's support with discretion only as to the manner of making the payment; the beneficiary was a child the settlor was obligated to support and the value of the trust was includible in the settlor's gross estate under § 2036(a)(1)).

154 See, e.g., Estate of Chrysler v. Commissioner, 44 T.C. 55 (1965), rev'd on other grounds, 361 F.2d 508 (2d Cir. 1966) (trustees could but never did apply trust income for the maintenance, education, or support of the settlor's minor child, with no inclusion because the power to apply the income rested in others than the settlor and there was no requirement that the income be used); cf. Colonial-American Nat'l Bank v. United States, 243 F.2d 312 (4th Cir. 1957) (trust for settlor's incompetent spouse required trustees to pay net income but income the spouse did not use was added to corpus, effectively making the trust a discretionary income trust and, because the settlor continued to pay for the spouse's support, trust income was used for support only once—to pay one hospital bill; the court held that the decedent's purpose was to provide for the spouse after the settlor's death and, therefore, the trust was not includible); and Ellis v. Commissioner, 51 T.C. 182 (1968) (for gift tax purposes the settlor of a trust granting the trustee discretion to distribute trust income for the "care, comfort and support" of the settlor's spouse made a completed gift on creation).

The issue in Estate of Richards v. Commissioner, 24 T.C.M. (CCH) 1436, 1437, 1439 (1965), was whether the trust gave the trustees discretion to use income to discharge the settlor's legal obligation to support the beneficiary or required the trustees to so use it. The trust provided that the trustees "shall pay

All of this reflects one of the most misunderstood elements of the wealth transfer tax. This is the theory found in § § 2036 and 2041[155] that a person who is obliged to support a beneficiary is indirectly benefited by trust distributions to that beneficiary. This "discharge of obligation" theory was involved in Estate of Sullivan v. Commissioner,[156] which is a disturbing case that addresses or dances around a number of very troubling wealth transfer tax issues and, therefore, well illustrates the concept and its flaws.[157]

Involved was a trust created by the decedent at the end of the year in which the decedent married for the second time. The opinion did not state whether the trust might have been the product of a prenuptial agreement, but it was irrevocable, the decedent was named as a co-trustee, and the facts indicate that the decedent alone controlled admin-

---

(Footnote Continued)

. . . for . . . maintenance and support the net income from my trust estate at such times as they in their sole discretion shall determine" and the court held the trust was includible in the settlor's gross estate under § 2036(a)(1) because "the only discretion given to the trustees was as to the time payments were to be made. There was no discretion as to the purpose for which payments were or were not to be made. Under these particular circumstances we think a court would have compelled the trustees to provide for the [beneficiary's] maintenance and support out of trust income." The fact that the property transferred to the trust produced no income did not alter the result.

A different result may apply if the settlor is the trustee with the discretion. Estate of McTighe v. Commissioner, 36 T.C.M. (CCH) 1655, 1660, 1661 (1977) (settlor had the power to remove the trustee and appoint the settlor and, as trustee, would have enjoyed the power to apply current or accumulated trust income "for the support, maintenance or education" of a child who, at the settlor's death, was over age 18; the court held that the settlor retained the "enjoyment of, or the right to the income from," the trust property within the meaning of § 2036(a)(1) and that the settlor's legal obligation to support the 18-year-old child had not ended before the settlor's death). See § 7.1.1.10.1 with respect to the obligation of support.

[155] See § 7.1.1.10.1.

[156] 66 T.C.M. (CCH) 1329 (1993).

[157] *Sullivan* is significant notwithstanding that the taxpayer avoided 80% of the assessed deficiency, and its holdings are sufficiently disturbing that its non-precedential status as a Memorandum opinion may be a blessing to other taxpayers.

§7.3.4.2

istration of the trust until death.[158] The trust did not qualify for the marital deduction because it denied the spouse control and predated enactment of the QTIP trust provisions.[159]

The government argued that the trust was includible in the decedent's gross estate under § 2036(a)(1) under the discharge of obligation theory because trust income and principal were payable to the decedent's spouse. The court stated that "[t]he trust income would be considered as retained by the decedent under section 2036 if it could be applied toward discharging decedent's legal obligation to support [a] spouse."[160] There was no evaluation or challenge to the underlying assumption that, under state law, a spousal support obligation can be discharged by trust distributions of the type involved in *Sullivan*. In that respect alone the opinion is troublesome because the law in most states specifies that trust distributions do *not* have the effect of discharging a legal obligation of support, although no taxpayer ever has litigated the propriety of the discharge theory on that ground.[161]

---

[158] *Sullivan* was without question the subject of TAM 9122005, which suggested that the decedent's status as cotrustee was significant in creating § 2036(a)(1) exposure, relying on Estate of McTighe v. Commissioner, 36 T.C.M. (CCH) 1655 (1977) (trust for children; decedent could name self as trustee and was treated as holding the trustee's powers), and Estate of Pardee v. Commissioner, 49 T.C. 140 (1967) (decedent was trustee for children). The court did not address this element of the government's argument in *Sullivan* because the indirect benefit attributable to the discharge theory was adequate to reach its result; the decedent's retained power as trustee to govern distribution of trust property was unnecessary.

[159] See § 2056(b)(7). There was no indication whether the trust qualified for or actually was elected for QTIP treatment after the decedent's death. Presumably the transfer into trust was a completed lifetime gift, although no mention was made of the estate's entitlement to a § 2012 credit, and the gift tax treatment is irrelevant to the proper FET result.

[160] 66 T.C.M. at 1332.

[161] See Pennell & Fleming, Avoiding the Discharge of Obligation Theory, 12 Prob. & Prop. 49-54 (Sept.-Oct. 1998); Pennell, Custodians, Incompetents, Trustees and Others: Taxable Powers of Appointment?, 15 U. Miami Inst. Est. Plan. ¶ 1602.3 (1981); § 7.1.1.10.1 (addressing the issue in the context of UGMA or UTMA accounts). The government understands and accepts this analysis. See FSA 199930026 (absent application of an exception, authority to distribute funds to a dependent is not sufficient to cause § 2041 general power of appointment inclusion to the powerholding fiduciary).

§ 7.3.4.2

Curiously, the court held that the spouse's mandatory income entitlement would not trigger § 2036(a)(1) inclusion because the trust was not designed to discharge or relieve the decedent of the support obligation, notwithstanding that nowhere in the Regulations is there any indication that intent plays a role in the discharge theory. And although intent can be controlling under state law, no reliance on the state law aspects of the discharge theory was involved in *Sullivan* either. Nevertheless, the income entitlement was irrelevant to the court, which stated that: "A grantor is not deemed to have retained a right to trust income where, as here, it is payable to a [spouse] or child without any restriction that it be used for the beneficiary's support or applied toward the discharge of a legal obligation of the grantor."[162]

In that respect the opinion could be helpful to taxpayers because it presumably means that mandatory use of income rather than distributions for some purpose that might entail a discharge of the support obligation is immune from the government's discharge theory. In light of the court's next described holding, regarding the discretionary use of trust corpus as triggering the discharge of obligation theory, the court's determination regarding the effect of the income entitlement almost certainly is wrong if the balance of the court's opinion is right. And note that it is nearly the exact opposite of the holding in Revenue Ruling 2004-64, which regards the mandatory use of income to be the critical inclusion generating entitlement.

Notwithstanding the foregoing, the *Sullivan* court found that § 2036(a)(1) was triggered by the authority lodged in the trustee to make discretionary *principal* distributions to the spouse. Curious about this result is that the court's inclusion result was not based on § 2036(a)(2), which is the provision that normally applies with respect to retained powers. It was not based on the fact that the decedent, as trustee, retained control over enjoyment of the property. That aspect of the case is a muddle and it is not clear whether the same result would apply if the decedent was not trustee, the court stating that inclusion is mandated "where it is clear from the trust document that the trust property is to be applied to discharge a support obligation," and then that "[i]nclusion is *also* warranted when trust income may be applied at the settlor's discretion to discharge a legal obligation by virtue of the settlor's power as

---

[162] 66 T.C.M. at 1333.

§ 7.3.4.2

trustee."[163] Notice also that income distributed in the trustee's discretion is what Revenue Ruling 2004-64 sanctioned as immune to § 2036(a)(1) (subject to the creditor rights caveat).

Another troubling aspect of *Sullivan* revolves around the inclusion authority relied upon by the government and the court alike. Congress intended that powers retained by a transferor would trigger inclusion, if at all, under §§ 2036(a)(2) and 2038(a)(1). In this case, had the government relied upon those provisions it would not have prevailed because the decedent's powers as trustee were circumscribed by a definite external standard, which protects against inclusion under both §§ 2036(a)(2) and 2038(a)(1) in the same manner that an ascertainable standard insulates against § 2041 general power of appointment exposure.[164] In addition, control over *income producing* corpus does not trigger § 2036(a)(2). Only powers over income or over the enjoyment or possession of *non-income-producing* corpus are subject to § 2036(a)(2).[165] That limitation is sensible in light of the traditional application of § 2036(a)(1), which is meant to reach a taxpayer's retained enjoyment of transferred property, either through receipt of the income produced by that property or through the possession or other enjoyment of non-income-producing property. § 2036(a)(2) is designed to impose FET if the decedent did not retain enjoyment personally but did retain control over someone else's enjoyment.

Thus, the taxpayer argued that this § 2036(a)(2) limitation should apply equally for § 2036(a)(1) purposes, and that argument would preclude § 2036 inclusion entirely if the income interest alone was not adequate on its own to trigger inclusion. The court rejected this alleged symmetry argument in concluding that § 2036(a)(1) was triggered because, through trust distributions for the support of the spouse as

---

[163] 66 T.C.M. at 1333 (emphasis added). Notice that, in the first quoted phrase, the court referred to trust *property* while, in the second, it referred to trust *income*, creating even more confusion and the impression that the court really did not clearly understand what it was holding, or why. The court also referred in both quotations to "discharge" of the support obligation without ever addressing the fundamental state law question whether that would be the result.

[164] See § 7.3.3.

[165] Treas. Reg. § 20.2036-1(b)(3).

beneficiary, the decedent indirectly retained personal enjoyment from the trust.[166]

Having found that inclusion was warranted, the court then turned to the question of the proper amount subject to FET. The court did not agree with the government's predictable argument that the full value of the trust was includible, holding instead that only that amount of corpus needed to produce the income required to support the decedent's spouse was includible.[167] The court's computation of the support amount showed that the spouse had annual expenses that would leave a "net obligation" of support of about $20,000 annually after considering *only* the spouse's "fixed sources of income" (social security and a pension).[168] The net result was the court's conclusion that it would take 20% of the trust corpus to generate the $20,000 of income needed annually,[169] and that was the amount that was deemed includible. Thus, the taxpayer effectively reduced a $1 million deficiency (the size of the trust) to 20% of that amount.[170]

Most applications of the discharge theory reach the wrong result because they disregard state law limitations on the discharge of obliga-

---

[166] The court did not articulate a reason for rejecting the taxpayer's symmetry argument but it is fair to note that no provision corresponding to Treas. Reg. § 20.2036-1(b)(3) limits application of § 2036(a)(1) to entitlements to income or the enjoyment or possession of *only* non-income-producing corpus. In that respect the Code or Regulations probably are flawed.

[167] Abnormal about this holding is that the income distribution provision did not trigger the § 2036(a)(1) inclusion.

[168] The trust required the trustees to consider the spouse's "needs and the other sources of financial assistance, if any, which may be or may become available for" the spouse's support. Even if this did not anticipate the trust income, which was guaranteed to the spouse in all events, the spouse still had outside sources of income more than twice the amount of the spouse's needs.

[169] Based on the court's use of the 10% income tables in Treas. Reg. § 20.2031-7 (no explanation being given for that choice).

[170] This would be a very favorable conclusion *if* § 2036 is applicable in its own right and the marital deduction is not available to offset the inclusion. To the extent, however, a trust qualifies for QTIP marital deduction treatment (the *Sullivan* trust was created in 1967 but the terms might nevertheless qualify), inclusion is harmless for FET purposes and beneficial for income tax purposes if the basis adjustment at death eliminated unrealized gain in the trust assets, making the limitation on inclusion potentially not a good result.

§7.3.4.2

tion theory.[171] Although not universally true, the law in the vast majority of American jurisdictions is that distributions from a trust do not discharge a legal obligation of support unless either of two conditions exists. One is the unlikely event that the trust was created for the specific purpose of supplanting the legal obligation of someone to support the beneficiary.[172] The other is that the person obliged to support the beneficiary financially is unable to do so.[173] The discharge theory should not apply if neither exception is applicable under the facts of a case because, under state law, distributions from the trust would not have the effect of reducing or discharging the decedent's legal obligation of support.[174]

[171] Indeed, UTC §814 is a statutory Upjohn clause, enacted to preclude unintended tax consequences flowing from the government's discharge of obligation theory, and does not preclude intended distributions for a beneficiary's support. See In re Margolis Revocable Trust, 765 N.W.2d 919 (Minn. Ct. App. 2009).

[172] The exception for a trust created for the express purpose of supplanting the legal obligation of support is illustrated by In re Estate of Wallens, 816 N.Y.S.2d 793 (Sup. Ct. 2006) (funds in a testamentary trust created by a grandfather could be used by the beneficiary's father to pay for support and secondary school and college tuition expenses because it was deemed to have been created for the express purpose of providing for support and education). See also Guardianship of K.S., 100 Cal. Rptr. 3d 78 (Ct. App. 2009), finding that a trust for a minor "was specifically created by the minor's mother for the 'health, maintenance, education, travel, and welfare, and general welfare' of the minor" and, therefore, the minor's father could use trust funds (along with his own monies) for the minor's support.

[173] Pennell & Fleming, Avoiding the Discharge of Obligation Theory, 12 Probate & Property 49, 54 (Sept.-Oct. 1998), includes a comprehensive list of state decisions on point. FSA 199930026 accepted that, absent the presence of one of these exceptions, the government had no inclusion case under §2041.

[174] See Fisher v. United States, 93-1 U.S. Tax Cas. (CCH) ¶ 60,132 (Ct. Fed. Cl. 1993) (parent had no duty to support emancipated but disabled adult child; thus, payments for support were a taxable gift). The *Sullivan* estate argued that the trust required the trustee to consider other resources of the spouse, which should preclude §2036(a)(1) inclusion because, under the actual facts involved, the spouse had adequate assets to preclude the need for trust distributions. The government responded that it is the existence of the right to use trust property and not its actual exercise that is significant. Both parties missed the point that the discharge theory should not apply in any case if the decedent could afford to satisfy the support obligation without assistance from the trust, meaning that distributions from the trust would not discharge the state law obligation.

§7.3.4.2

A case like *Sullivan* would be harmless if it involved an inter vivos QTIP trust and the marital deduction is claimed at the decedent's death by making the requisite election.[175] In such an inter vivos marital trust situation, no provision should be added to the trust prohibiting income distributions that would have the effect of discharging the settlor's legal obligation to support the beneficiary because that restriction (sometimes referred to as an Upjohn clause)[176] would disqualify the trust for QTIP marital deduction purposes.

Because the mandatory income entitlement was not the source of the problem in *Sullivan*, no provision restricting income distributions presumably would be needed. An Upjohn prohibition on the distribution of *corpus* that might discharge the obligation of support would not be a problem for marital deduction qualification. Such a provision should be considered in any trust, made applicable to both income and principal distributions from a trust for any beneficiary other than a spouse to whom the settlor owes a duty of support and for whom the trust was created. So for prospective drafting purposes, the use of such a limitation is desirable to negate the government's §2036(a)(1) inclusion argument entirely.

§7.3.4.3 Right to Vote Transferred Stock

United States v. Byrum[177] rejected the government's contention that the settlor of a trust retained a §2036(a)(2) right to designate the persons who would enjoy the income from stock transferred to that trust flowing from the settlor's retention of voting control over the corporation. After noting various restraints on directors of a corporation and on a majority shareholder in regard to paying or withholding dividends, the court concluded that there was no merit in the government's contention that control, subject to those constraints, was tantamount to a §2036(a)(2) right to designate the persons who may enjoy trust income. Based on *Byrum*, an alleged "fiduciary duty" defense asserted by some as an important aspect of that controversy. Dutiful readers must read the *Byrum* decision, and judge the various interpretations and make an

---

[175] See §2056(b)(7)(B)(i)(III).

[176] See §§6.3.3.3 n.34, 7.1.1.10.2.

[177] 408 U.S. 125 (1972).

§7.3.4.3

informed determination, and factor into the equation the hazards of litigation and a client's tolerance for risk.

Asserted by these observers and litigants is that certain fiduciary duties should preclude application of §2036(a). Longstanding jurisprudence in this area provides a "reasonably definite external standard" exception to §2036(a). Cases establish it as a counterpart to the §2041 ascertainable standard exception, and the alleged fiduciary duty exception is just a subset of that much broader judicial standard. As such, that may not add anything to the §2036 landscape.[178]

That notion aside, it is not clear that *Byrum* created any additional defense to §2036(a). It is completely opaque about whether the Supreme Court thought that the (1) the taxpayer never had a "right" that would attract §2036(a) exposure, or (2) the taxpayer had a "right" that was subject to a "duty" of some sort that precluded it from being subject to §2036(a). Traditional tax jurisprudence would say that rules for inclusion are interpreted broadly and exceptions to those rules are applied restrictively, which may suggest that it would be better for taxpayers to avoid being swept into the inclusion rule in the first instance than being able to except out of it once it applies. *Byrum* leaves a disquieting feeling that the Supreme Court, exercising judicial restraint or caution, did nothing more than find that the facts of that particular case did not support the government's theory for inclusion.

The conclusions below reflect a reading of *Byrum* as saying that the taxpayer never had the kind of "right" to which §2036(a) applies, and that the Court therefore did not create any fiduciary duty *defense* or *exception* to the application of §2036(a). That interpretation is informed in part by the notion that, if there is such a defense, the court and subsequent jurisprudence have not yielded much of a clue what it entails. In four decades no case has really elaborated on it under §2036(a), and it would be difficult to establish anything that resembles the parameters of this safe harbor or exception. *Byrum* has been cited numerous times for the proposition that a fiduciary duty collars a majority shareholder in activities that impact minority shareholders, but virtually all of those cases are in the corporate governance arena, not in the tax world. As will be revealed in course, the dissent in *Byrum*, later

---

[178] See in this regard footnote 6 in *Byrum* and §7.3.3 nn.55-59 and accompanying text.

commentators, and a few "lesser" authorities than the Supreme Court, all have *assumed* or *alleged* that the *Byrum* majority recognized such a defense for § 2036(a) purposes, and there has been a lot of ink spilled on the issue with little definitive guidance.

The first item of note is how the majority explicitly rejected the notion that it was creating a fiduciary duty defense. Here is the Court's footnote 25, in its entirety. The reference to United States v. O'Malley[179] is significant because the taxpayer in *O'Malley* was acting as trustee of a traditional trust and the question in *Byrum* was whether the decedent's alleged control was sufficiently distinguishable. It is notable that the later cases discussed below, and virtually all the commentators, never even recognize that the Court said the following:

> In purporting to summarize the basis of our distinction of *O'Malley*, the dissenting opinion states: "Now the majority would have us accept the incompatible position that a settlor seeking tax exemption may keep the power of income allocation by rendering the trust dependent on an income flow he controls because the general fiduciary obligations of a director are sufficient to eliminate the power to designate within the meaning of § 2036(a)(2)." This statement, which assumes the critical and ultimate conclusion, incorrectly states the position of the Court. We do not hold that a settlor "may keep the power of income allocation" in the way Mr. Justice White sets out; we hold, for the reasons stated in this opinion, that this settlor did not retain the power to allocate income within the meaning of the statute.

This pretty plainly says that the taxpayer never had a power or "right" that would attract § 2036(a) inclusion, and not that he had such a right but was spared because it was properly constrained. That distinction is important, in the sense that *Byrum* talks about fiduciary duty but essentially held that the taxpayer never had the kind of right that is reached by the Code, as opposed to having such a right and being excepted from FET because of this alleged fiduciary duty exception.

Basing an evaluation on a mere footnote is not very satisfying, so what appears next below is the totality of what a complete reading of *Byrum* reveals on this entire issue. To set the stage, the trustee in *Byrum* (not the taxpayer) "was authorized in its 'absolute and sole discretion' to pay the income and principle." Which is to say that the reasonably definite external standard exception that otherwise might provide protec-

---

[179] 383 U.S. 627 (1966).

§ 7.3.4.3

tion was not applicable in *Byrum*.[180] Instead, the government's theory of the case, as articulated by the Court, was this:

> The Commissioner determined that the stock transferred into the trust should be included in Byrum's gross estate because of the rights reserved by him in the trust agreement. It was asserted that his right to vote the transferred shares and to veto any sale thereof by the trustee, together with the ownership of other shares, enabled Byrum to retain the "enjoyment of . . . the property," and also allowed him to determine the flow of income to the trust and thereby "designate the persons who shall . . . enjoy . . . the income."[181]
>
> . . . . Byrum was in a position to select the corporate directors. He could retain this position by not selling the shares he owned and by vetoing any sale by the trustee of the transferred shares. These rights, it is said, gave him control over corporate dividend policy. By increasing, decreasing, or stopping dividends completely, it is argued that Byrum could "regulate the flow of income to the trust" and thereby shift or defer the beneficial enjoyment of trust income between the present beneficiaries and the remaindermen.[182]

Said the dissent, "by instructing the directors he elected in the controlled corporation that he thought dividends should or should not be declared Byrum was able to open or close the spigot through which income flowed to the trust's life tenants."[183] According to the Court, these powers were not adequate to generate § 2036(a) inclusion, citing several lower court decisions and stating[184] that:

> The dissenting opinion attempts to distinguish the cases, holding that a settlor-trustee's retained powers of management do not bring adverse estate-tax consequences, on the ground that management of trust assets is not the same as the powers retained by Byrum because a settlor-trustee is bound by a fiduciary duty to treat the life tenant beneficiaries and remaindermen as the trust specifies. But the argument that in the reserved-power-of-man-

---

[180] It also was the case (but by all accounts also not relevant) that the settlor could remove the trustee and replace it with another corporate trustee. *Byrum* predated the now discredited Rev. Rul. 79-353 "revolving door power" theory of imputing trustee powers, and that fact also did not implicate § 2036 inclusion in *Byrum*. See § 7.3.3 nn.60-73 and accompanying text.

[181] 408 U.S. at 131.

[182] 408 U.S. at 132.

[183] 408 U.S. at 152.

[184] In the majority's footnote 7, 408 U.S. at 135.

§ 7.3.4.3

agement cases there was "a judicially enforceable strict standard capable of invocation by the trust beneficiaries by reference to the terms of the trust agreement," ignores the fact that trust agreements may and often do provide for the widest investment discretion.

This reference to a "fiduciary duty" did not constitute any defense. Rather, the primary holding of the case is the following:

> It must be conceded that Byrum reserved no such "right" in the trust instrument or otherwise. The term "right," certainly when used in a tax statute, must be given its normal and customary meaning. It connotes an ascertainable and legally enforceable power, such as that involved in *O'Malley* [in which the taxpayer was a trustee.]. Here the right ascribed to Byrum was the power to use his majority position and influence over the corporate directors to "regulate the flow of dividends" to the trust. That "right" was neither ascertainable nor legally enforceable and hence was not a right in any normal sense of that term.[185]

>   ... [T]he corporate trustee alone, not Byrum, had the right to pay out or withhold income and thereby to designate who among the beneficiaries enjoyed such income. Whatever power Byrum may have possessed with respect to the flow of income into the trust was derived not from an enforceable legal right specified in the trust instrument, but from the fact that he could elect a majority of the directors of the three corporations. The power to elect the directors conferred no legal right to command them to pay or not to pay dividends. A majority shareholder has a fiduciary duty not to misuse his power by promoting his personal interests at the expense of corporate interests. Moreover, the directors also have a fiduciary duty to promote the interests of the corporation. However great Byrum's influence may have been with the corporate directors, their responsibilities were to all stockholders and were enforceable according to legal standards entirely unrelated to the needs of the trust or to Byrum's desires with respect thereto.[186]

>   The government seeks to equate the de facto position of a controlling stockholder with the legally enforceable "right" specified by the statute. Retention of corporate control (through the right to vote the shares) is said to be "tantamount to the power to accumulate income" in the trust which resulted in estate-tax consequences in *O'Malley*. The Government goes on to assert that "through exercise of that retained power, [Byrum] could increase or decrease corporate dividends ... and thereby shift

---

[185] 408 U.S. at 136-137.

[186] 408 U.S. at 137-138.

§7.3.4.3